PSYCHOLOGY
AN INTRODUCTION SIXTH EDITION

PSYCHOLOGY
AN INTRODUCTION SIXTH EDITION

JEROME KAGAN
Harvard University

JULIUS SEGAL

Harcourt Brace Jovanovich, Publishers
San Diego   New York   Chicago   Austin   Washington, D.C.
London   Sydney   Tokyo   Toronto

Copyright © 1988, 1984, 1980, 1976, 1972, 1968 by Harcourt Brace Jovanovich, Inc.

All rights reserved. No part of this publication may be reproduced or transmitted in any form or by any means, electronic or mechanical, including photocopy, recording, or any information storage and retrieval system, without permission in writing from the publisher.

Requests for permission to make copies of any part of the work should be mailed to: Permissions, Harcourt Brace Jovanovich, Publishers, Orlando, Florida 32887.

ISBN: 0-15-572639-0
Library of Congress Catalog Card Number: 87-81138

Printed in the United States of America

Copyrights and Acknowledgments and Illustration Credits appear on pages 651–84, which constitute a continuation of the copyright page.

PREFACE

This Sixth Edition of *Psychology: An Introduction*, the product of a new collaboration, appears exactly two decades after the first edition of the textbook was published. Like the child grown to adulthood, the book is characterized by both continuity and change. As in the past, the enduring themes of psychology—the classic theories, ground-breaking experiments, landmark clinical approaches—continue to be presented with what one reviewer described as "brevity, clarity, rigor, and relevance." But these continuing threads are combined with a plethora of new developments that define the science of psychology today. As one measure of our effort to encompass contemporary work in the field, this edition contains over 450 new references—or 43 percent of all the references cited in the book.

In selecting which new material to include in a thoroughly updated edition, we constantly asked ourselves whether a particular item was likely to reflect a substantial development or instead was likely to prove ephemeral. Helped by the comments of reviewers of each chapter, we applied other important criteria as well: Is this really essential to students? Is this a topic that can be explained adequately within our limitations of space? Is it sound and scientific or is it mere "pop psychology"? Does the discussion encompass today's thinking among specialists in the field? Is it accurate? The results of our efforts are manifest in additions and changes found throughout the book.

To begin with, two chapters—on psychotherapy and on adult development—appear for the first time in this edition.

In the past, the subject of psychotherapy was treated in a chapter along with that of personality. But the range of treatments has increased so dramatically in recent years that a separate chapter is now devoted to the subject (Chapter 13). This addition allows more detailed coverage of techniques of behavior therapy, group approaches, and biological therapies—including recent efforts to assess the benefits and the hazards of drug and electroconvulsive treatments. New materials also presented on community mental health approaches, among them crisis intervention programs and self-help groups and the role of public and family attitudes in the recovery from mental disorders.

Expanded interest in development along the entire life span dictated the addition of a new chapter on adult development (Chapter 15). Now paired with a companion chapter on development from conception through the childhood years, the addition allows expanded coverage of the adolescent period, including such topics as the role of bodily changes in adolescent behavior and the world of sex during the teenage years. It also permits more detailed discussion than was possible in the past of some of the major challenges of adult life: the pursuit of a career, sex-role conflicts, the experience of love and the responsibilities of marriage and parenthood, and the adaptations of middle age. Coverage of the increasingly important topic of aging includes the latest evidence regarding the intellectual and emotional capacities of older people, as well as material describing how elderly individuals deal with bereavement and with the reality of their own approaching death.

In this edition, the order in which the topics are presented has been rearranged—now moving more logically from the biological, to the intrapersonal, to the social domains of psychology. The material provided in previous editions as supplements has either been incorporated into relevant chapters or eliminated. Indeed virtually every chapter has undergone substantial revision in order to achieve enhanced balance and clarity and to take account of new developments. To cite some major examples:

- The introduction to the world of psychology in Chapter 1 has been revised and expanded to acquaint the student with areas of the science in a manner that anticipates later substantive chapters of the text. In addition, a separate section now introduces three major issues that will surface throughout the book: the roles of biological nature and psychological nurture, the contrasting themes of continuity versus change, and the importance of context in human behavior. Also new in this edition is material emphasizing the importance of the adherence by psychologists to ethical standards—especially by protecting the confidentiality and rights of research subjects and by exerting care in the use of animals for research.

- The discussion of brain and behavior in Chapter 2 was prepared with an awareness of the great importance of the topic to psychology, but with a recognition as well that a catalogue-like presentation of brain structures begins to read like pure physiology—inviting the danger of putting off students who expect something quite different from the course. The chapter is carefully organized, therefore, around the essential *functions* performed by the brain rather than around the nomenclature of brain anatomy. Included in this edition is new evidence concerning the specialization of the brain hemispheres and the importance of various neurotransmitters for normal brain functioning and behavior. Through fresh and clearly explained studies of brain biochemistry, the chapter lays a solid groundwork for discussions later in the book of such important topics as the biological basis of memory problems (Chapter 6) and mental disorders (Chapter 12), drug treatment of these disorders (Chapter 13), and the relationship between brain growth and the flowering of intellectual capacities (Chapter 14).

- In the discussion of learning found in Chapter 5, traditional topics have been made more relevant with the addition of compelling applied material. Included in this edition, for example, are data describing how such disparate phenomena as the body's immune system and sexual responsivity can be influenced by conditioning.

- In Chapter 6, on memory, we have added material describing the role of neurotransmitters in normal memory processes as well as in pathological states such as Alzheimer's disease, the nature of amnesia, and cognitive and emotional factors that interfere with memory.

- The discussion of intelligence in Chapter 8 now includes material making clearer the distinctions between an individual's overall intellectual ability and hierarchy of individual abilities. Also newly introduced are major contemporary views concerning the components of intelligence and the roles of genetics and experience in the manifestation of specific intellectual capacities.

- To allow room for additions to the text, the topics of emotions, drives, and motives are now treated together in Chapter 9—but without slighting important content. Indeed much new research appears in this chapter on a variety of topics: the role of facial expressions in emotion; the differential activity of the brain hemispheres in sharply contrasting emotions; the regulation of emotional behavior; the role of intestinal hormones, the liver, brain activity, and environmental cues in the experience of the hunger drive; the genetic component in obesity; the biological and psychological dynamics of obesity; the nature of sleep and the sex drive; and the role of parents in shaping the expression of the achievement motive. Emphasized throughout is the importance of both biological and cognitive factors in the experience of emotions and drives.

- The discussion of stress and coping found in Chapter 11 has been reorganized to include the subjects of frustration and conflict. Included as well is new material on the role of stress in the development of both physical and psychological disorders; the impact of personal and situational factors—including attributional style and social supports—that can affect the impact of stress; the role of attitudes and emotions in healing; characteristics of stress-resistant individuals; the nature of Type-A behavior and its role in heart disease; and the impact of stress on the functioning of the body's immune system.
- Chapter 12, on abnormal psychology, has been expanded with fresh data on the incidence, prevalence, and cost of mental disorders; the environmental and biological antecedents of various psychopathological conditions such as schizophrenia, depression, anxiety disorders, and alcoholism; and new theories and studies of the addiction process.
- The discussion of early development in Chapter 14 has been enriched with the addition of new evidence of factors affecting prenatal development and the importance of events surrounding the birth process; the surprising range of reflexes and perceptual capacities of newborns; early temperamental characteristics and how they may influence later development; the sources of resilience in children; the impact on children of life events such as bereavement and divorce; and the process of sex typing during the preschool and early school years and how it affects cognitive style.

This edition contains an expanded number of boxed inserts, now titled "Psychology in Everyday Life," which are intended to help the student understand how psychological findings apply to the real world and how they can be used to help solve real-life problems. Despite their practical flavor, the boxes were written to convey salient content. The student will find in them discussions of topics as varied and compelling as the scientific basis of health psychology, recent applications of brain grafting techniques, the use of mnemonic devices to enhance memory, the application of behavior control techniques in weight reduction programs, the hazards of drugs used for sleep, the role of the patient's attitudes in the healing process, the uses of hypnotherapy, and correlates of adolescent suicide.

One of the chapter supplements included in earlier editions, "How to Study This Book," is retained in this edition as Appendix A. This practical guide, using material from Chapter 1 as examples, continues to present the study method referred to as SQ3R: survey, question, read, recite, and review. The *Study Guide* that accompanies the book has been restructured and rewritten once again to facilitate the use of the SQ3R method.

Despite the incorporation of a wealth of new material, the book continues to be compact enough to be useful to students who will have no further exposure to psychology, but at the same time sufficiently detailed to provide necessary preparation for students who go on to advanced courses.

The freshness of the content and organization of this edition is matched by its dramatic redesign, featuring the liberal use of color and the introduction of a wealth of new illustrations and photographs. The overall result is in many ways a brand-new book—honest to the traditions of the past, but cognizant of the new directions and the best of contemporary thinking that mark the field.

Jerome Kagan

Julius Segal

Acknowledgements

Classroom consultants

The following people, who have been teaching the introductory course, have provided us with many helpful suggestions in this and in past editions:

Leonore Loeb Adler, The College of Staten Island, CUNY
Mary J. Allen, California State College
J. R. Arneson, South Dakota School of Mines & Technology
Heesoon Aust, Centralia College
Vergie Lee Behrens, Scottsdale Community College
Otto A. Berliner, SUNY, Alfred State College
James Bickley, Pasadena City College
Jack Blakemore, Monterey Peninsula College
Sue Bowen, Cleveland State Community College
James Brandt, Minot State College
Myron Brender, Kingsborough Community College, CUNY
Thomas Brothen, University of Minnesota
Dean Brysen, South Dakota School of Mines & Technology
Patrick Butler, San Jose City College
Roland Calhoun, Humboldt State University
Susie C. Campbell, Davidson County Community College
W. John Cannon, Columbia Union College
Michael Ceddia, Massachusetts Bay Community College
Carol E. Chandler, McHenry County College
Garvin Chastain, Boise State University
William Coggan, Massasoit Community College
David Stewart-Cohen, California State College
Francis B. Colavita, University of Pittsburgh
Betty T. Conover, Miami-Dade Community College
Alice M. Crichlow, Massasoit Community College
Anne Louise Dailey, Community College of Allegheny County
Anne G. English, University of Toledo
Elliot E. Entin, Ohio University
Paul E. Finn, Saint Anselm's College
Bess Fleckman, Miami-Dade Community College, North Campus
B. L. Garrett, DePauw University
Robert Gibson, Centralia College
Jon Gosser, Delta College
Mary Hamilton, Highline Community College
Judith Roes Hammerle, Adrian College
Gordon Hammerle, Adrian College
James M. Hammond, Columbia Union College
Francis J. Hanrahan, Hudson Valley Community College
W. Bruce Haslam, Weber State College
Roy K. Heintz, California State University, Long Beach
Judy Hensley, Otero Junior College
Faunie Hewlett, Cleveland State Community College
Annette Hiedemann, West Virginia Wesleyan College
Robert R. Higgins, Oakland Community College
John E. Hoffman, East Los Angeles College
Richard D. Honey, Transylvania University
Philip Howard, Enterprise State Junior College
Michael Hughmanick, West Valley College

Morton Isaacs, Rochester Institute of Technology
Charles W. Johnson, University of Evansville
James L. Johnston, Madison Area Technical College
Richard Kellogg, SUNY, Agricultural & Technical College
Kenneth A. Koenigshofer, Chaffey College
Charlton R. Lee, Cypress College
Edward E. Leech, Cleveland State Community College
Tim Lehmann, Valencia Community College
Diane Leroi, College of San Mateo
Harold List, Massachusetts Bay Community College
Cameron Marshman, Rio Hondo College
William A. Marzano, Illinois Valley Community College
Ann B. McNeer, Polk Community College
Douglas Miller, Miami University
Donald H. Millikan, San Diego Mesa College
Elizabeth Morelli, Henry Ford Community College
C. Thomas Musgrave, Weber State College
Dennis L. Nagi, Hudson Valley Community College
Edward F. O'Day, San Diego State University
Dan E. Perkins, Richland College
F. A. Perry, Jr., Erie Community College
David W. Prull, Community College of the Finger Lakes
David L. Quinby, Youngstown State University
Bob Rainey, Florida Junior College
Robert L. Ramlet, Elgin Community College
Mary Renfer, Mt. View College
Sue H. Rhodamer, Cleveland State Community College
O. L. Riner, Gulf Coast Community College
Carol Roberts, San Diego Mesa College
John C. Roehr, Hudson Valley Community College
Steve Rosengarten, Middlesex County College
Frank M. Rosenkrans, III, Eastern Washington University
Joel Rosevelt, Golden West College
Douglas A. Ross, Indiana University of Pennsylvania
Alva Sachs, College of San Mateo
Ganus Scarborough Jr., Jefferson State Junior College
Gary Schaumberg, Cerritos College
Jerome Seidman, Montclair State College
Michael B. Sewall, Mohawk Valley Community College
Ruth B. Shapiro, John Jay College
Jack P. Shilkret, Ann Arundel Community College
Charlotte Simon, Montgomery College
Lora S. Simon, Holyoke Community College
Ronold E. Siry, University of Cincinnati
David Skinner, Valencia Community College
Joseph L. Slosser, Chemeketa Community College
Leo V. Soriano, Winona State University
Donovan Swanson, El Camino College
Givens L. Thornton, Clarion State College
Jerome D. Tietz, Santa Barbara City College
William K. Trinkaus, South Connecticut State College
Luis Vazquez, Cleveland State College
Jerry L. Vogt, Stanford University School of Medicine
Albert C. Widhalm, Kankakee Community College
Michael Witmer, Skagit Valley College
Sherman Yen, Essex Community College

Reviewers

We have also had the benefit of advice from scholars who provided us with critiques of individual chapters. Some of the following reviewed the Fifth Edition chapters and provided us with suggestions for additional new materials. Some reviewed preliminary drafts of the new chapters, and some did both. The authors, of course, take full responsibility for any defects that may nonetheless appear.

Robert Adamson, Florida Atlantic University
Tom R. Alley, Clemson University
Hal R. Arkes, Ohio University
Harry H. Avis, Sierra College
Frank M. Bagrash, California State University, Fullerton
Lawrence W. Barsalou, Georgia Institute of Technology
Brian R. Bate, Cuyahoga City College
Ellen Beck, Sinclair Community College
Elizabeth Blanchard, San Juaquin Delta College
Samuel S. Bottosto
James A. Briley, Jefferson State College
Maurice Cadwalder, San Jacinto College
Charles S. Carver, University of Miami
Donna M. Casperson, Harrisburg Area Community College
Parnell W. Cephus, Jefferson State Junior College
Betty D. Clayton, Hinds Junior College
Ruth A. Cline, Los Angeles Valley College
Nancy Cobb, California State University, Los Angeles
Margaret Condon,
John R. Dill
Thomas K. Eckle, Modesto Junior College
Monroe Friedman, Eastern Michigan University
Sandra Anderson Garcia
E. Scott Geller, Virginia Polytechnic Institute & State University
B. Gordon Gibb, California State University, Chico
Howard H. Goldman, University of Maryland
John A. Greaves, Jefferson State Junior College
Susan Green, University of Oregon
J. Tyra Harris, Jefferson State Junior College
John H. Harvey, University of Iowa
Richard H. Haude, University of Akron
D. Lamar Jacks, Santa Fe Community College

Charles W. Johnson, University of Evansville
Eileen Kaufman, Union County College
Kenneth B. LeSure, Cuyahoga Community College
Bert D. Levine, Pan American University
John C. Liebeskind, University of California, Los Angeles
R. Martin Lobdell, Pierce College
Gregory Lockhead, Duke University
Ross J. Loomis, Colorado State University
Scott A. Miller, University of Florida
Henry O. Patterson, Pennsylvania State University
Marion Perlmutter, University of Michigan
Gail B. Peterson, University of Minnesota, Twin Cities
Linda C. Petty, Hampton University
Gregory Pezzetti, Rancho Santiago College
J. Randall Price, Richland College
Barbara Robinson, Portland Community College
Joan A. Royce, Riverside Community College
William McKinley Runyan, University of California, Berkeley
Robert Rutherford, Jefferson Community College
Donald H. Ryujin, DePauw University
Alan Schultz, Prince George's Community College
Francis R. Smith, Frederick Community College
William P. Smotherman, Oregon State University
Hans H. Strupp, Vanderbilt University
Benjamin Wallace, Cleveland State University
Charles R. Walsmith, Bellevue Community College
Arnold Bond Woodruff, Northern Illinois University
David Wilder, Rutgers—The State University of New Jersey
Richard Jed Wyatt, National Institute of Mental Health

Besides the consultants and reviewers, we are indebted to Kareen Gholl for her valuable help in various capacities throughout the preparation of this edition. We are also grateful to Dolly Gattozzi, Jeris Miller, and Anne H. Rosenfeld for their considerable contributions. Finally we wish to express our thanks for the skillful efforts of the Harcourt Brace Jovanovich staff—our manuscript editor, Robert Watrous; production editor, Karen Baicker; art editor, Susan Holtz; designer, Martha Gilman; and production manager, Lesley Lenox.

CONTENTS

PART 1
THE WORLD OF PSYCHOLOGY　　　1

CHAPTER 1　THE AIMS AND METHODS OF PSYCHOLOGY　　3

Psychology's Goals and Interests　　5
How Psychologists Study Human Behavior　　11
The Ultimate Method: Experimentation　　17
Psychology Yesterday, Today, and Tomorrow　　21
Three Major Issues in Modern Psychology　　29
Ethical Standards of Psychologists　　33
Summary　　35

PART 2
BIOLOGICAL BASES OF BEHAVIOR　　　39

CHAPTER 2　BRAIN, BODY, AND BEHAVIOR　　41

The Privileged Brain and Its Powerful Connections　　42
The Brain in Action: 1. Sensing the World and Responding to It　　46
The Brain in Action: 2. Thinking, Planning, and Remembering　　52
The Brain in Action: 3. Producing Emotions and Keeping Our Bodies in Tune　　57
The Brain's Communications Network　　64
Summary　　73

CHAPTER 3　SENSATION: HOW WE GATHER INFORMATION　　79

How the Senses Work　　81
Light Waves and Vision　　84
The Special Wonders of Color Vision　　91
Hearing: Turning Sound Waves into Sounds　　98
Taste, Smell, Touch—and the Two Forgotten Senses　　107
Summary　　114

CHAPTER 4　PERCEPTION: MAKING SENSE OUT OF OUR SENSATIONS　　119

How Perception Enables Us to Survive　　120
Our Perceptual Specialties: Selection and Attention　　126
How We Organize Our Perceptions　　132
Interpretation: Discovering the Meaning of Our Perceptions　　141
Summary　　145

PART 3
THE POWERS OF THE HUMAN INTELLECT 149

CHAPTER 5 PRINCIPLES OF LEARNING 151

Classical Conditioning 152
Operant Conditioning 162
Operant Escape, Punishment, and Learned Helplessness 172
The Cognitive View of Learning 178
Summary 184

CHAPTER 6 HOW WE REMEMBER AND WHY WE FORGET 189

The Range of Human Memory 191
Why Do We Forget? 196
Encoding and Transfer 204
The Encoding Process and Learning 209
Some Strategies for Encoding 213
Summary 220

CHAPTER 7 LANGUAGE AND THOUGHT 225

The Role, Structure, and Rules of Language 227
How We Produce and Understand Messages 229
The Remarkable Feat of Learning Language 231
Concepts: Words That Do Double Duty 239
How We Think and Solve Problems 246
Summary 255

CHAPTER 8 INTELLIGENCE: ITS MEANING AND MEASUREMENT 259

The Nature of Intelligence: Some Different Views 261
Intelligence Tests: What Can They Actually Tell Us? 270
IQ and the Issue of Heredity versus Environment 282
The Science of Testing Mental Abilities 290
Summary 293

PART 4
EXPLAINING INDIVIDUAL BEHAVIOR AND PERSONALITY 297

CHAPTER 9 EMOTIONS, DRIVES, AND MOTIVES 299

The Role of the Body in Emotions 301
The Brain: Key to Emotional Behavior 310
Individual Differences in Emotion and Their Expression 314

xiii

How Drives Affect Behavior: Hunger
   and Thirst   317
Sleep: The Other Third of Our
   Lives   324
The Power of the Sex Drive—and
   Other Drives   327
The Nature of Human Motivation   331
Other Motives That Shapes Who
   We Are   338
How Motives Influence Behavior   340
Summary   344

CHAPTER 10   PERSONALITY AND ITS MEASUREMENT   349

Theories of Personality   350
The Psychoanalytic Theory of
   Sigmund Freud   352
Dissenting Disciples: Other Schools
   of Psychoanalytic Theory   356
Humanistic Theories of Personality   364
Personality from the Behavioral
   Point of View   367
Type and Trait Theories   370
Measuring Personality   378
Summary   381

PART 5
PERSONAL ADJUSTMENT AND MENTAL HEALTH   385

CHAPTER 11   COPING WITH LIFE'S ANXIETIES AND STRESS   387

How Anxiety Affects Behavior   389
Stress and Its Repercussions in the
   Body and Mind   399
Successful Coping and Mental
   Health   411
Defense Mechanisms and Other
   Problematic Forms of Coping   416
Summary   422

CHAPTER 12   ABNORMAL PERSONALITY AND BEHAVIOR   427

The Nature and Scope of Abnormal
   Behavior   428
The Roots and Varieties of Abnormal
   Behavior   431
Schizophrenia: Rare but Devastating   435
Affective Disorders: Disturbances of
   Mood   438
Anxiety Disorders   441
Personality Disorders: More Disturbing
   than Disturbed   446
Substance Abuse: The Perilous
   Pleasures of Alcohol and
   Drugs   450
Summary   459

CHAPTER 13   PSYCHOTHERAPY AND OTHER TREATMENT APPROACHES   463

Dynamic Therapy   465
Humanistic Theory   468
Behavior Therapy   470

Therapy in Groups	477	Summary	490
Biological Therapies	480		
Community Mental Health	484		
Attitudes toward People Who Need Psychological Help: How They Can Hurt or Heal	487		

PART 6
HOW WE DEVELOP AND RELATE TO SOCIETY 493

CHAPTER 14 THE WORLD OF CHILDHOOD 495

Life's Overture: From Conception to Birth	496
Newborn Babies: Similar but Different	502
The Development of Body and Mind	510
The Flowering Personality: Birth to Eighteen Months	515
Learning Life's Social Requirements: Eighteen Months Through Three Years	520
The Preschool Years: Four and Five	523
The Influence of Teachers and Peers: Six to Ten	527
Summary	531

CHAPTER 15 ADOLESCENCE, ADULT LIFE, AND OLD AGE 535

Adolescence: Joy or Misery?	536
Development in Adulthood	544
Growing Old: The Challenges and the Triumphs	554
The Psychology of Dying	559
Summary	564

CHAPTER 16 SOCIAL PSYCHOLOGY: HOW WE RELATE TO EACH OTHER 569

Learning Society's Ways—and Conforming to Them	570
How We Acquire—and Sometimes Change—Our Attitudes Toward Life	580
Trying to Figure Out Why People Behave as They Do: Attribution Theories	586
Forming Social Relationships: How We Become Attracted to One Another	591
Aggression and Altruism	597
Summary	601

Appendix A: How to Study This Book (and Others)	605
Appendix B: Statistical Methods	611
Glossary	633
References	651
Name Index	685
Subject Index	693

PART 1

THE WORLD OF PSYCHOLOGY

CHAPTER

1

THE AIMS AND METHODS OF PSYCHOLOGY

PSYCHOLOGY'S GOALS AND INTERESTS   5

Psychology defined
The objectives of psychology
"Basic" and "applied" psychology
The practice of clinical and counseling psychology

HOW PSYCHOLOGISTS STUDY HUMAN BEHAVIOR   11

Observation
Interviews and case histories
Questionnaires and opinion surveys
Tests of psychological traits and behavior
Physiological measures
Measurements, individual differences, and the normal curve
The method of correlation

THE ULTIMATE METHOD: EXPERIMENTATION   17

Independent and dependent variables
Experimental and control groups
Single-blind and double-blind experiments

PSYCHOLOGY YESTERDAY, TODAY, AND TOMORROW   21

William James, "mental life," and the era of introspection
John Watson, conditioned reflexes, and the behavioristic revolution
B. F. Skinner and the behaviorist era
The Gestalt school of thought
The rise of the cognitive school
Cognitive psychology and our "mental models of reality"
The humanistic school
Sigmund Freud and psychoanalysis
The new vistas of psychobiology

THREE MAJOR ISSUES IN MODERN PSYCHOLOGY   29

Biological nature or psychological nurture?
Continuity or change?
Context: does who you are depend on where you are?

ETHICAL STANDARDS OF PSYCHOLOGISTS   33

Protecting the confidentiality and rights of subjects
Care in the use of animals for research

SUMMARY   35

IMPORTANT TERMS   37

RECOMMENDED READINGS   38

As you start this course you are embarking on an exciting journey into the mysteries and marvels of human existence. The pathway leads through territory that fascinated our ancestors throughout written history—and probably long before that—but remained uncharted until very recently. Now it has been opened up for exploration by the science of psychology, much as outer space has been made accessible by modern scientists who have created spacecraft that can fly to the moon.

Our concern here is the vast and varied realm of human behavior—the workings of the body and brain, the ways in which we humans resemble and differ from one another, our physical actions, and our thoughts, emotions, dreams, aspirations, loves, hates, worries, and joys. The goal we seek is an answer to these fundamental questions: Why do we act as we do, for better or for worse? What are the forces that shape our lives? Or, to put this in the simplest and most personal terms, what makes us tick?

More than any other subject you are ever likely to study, psychology is about you. Here you are just starting to read this book. Strangely, you are very much like all people all over the world, yet there is no one exactly like you. You are a unique individual with your own special abilities and weaknesses, your own personality, your own likes and dislikes, your own feelings of joy or depression or fear.

Were you born the way you are or did you get that way (and if so, how)? Are you the master of your fate or a helpless pawn of your environment? Can you change if you want to?

What about humanity in general? Are we humans just another form of animal life, closely related to the beasts of the jungle and especially to the apes? Or do we possess some special quality that separates us from all other living creatures? What accounts for the differences within the human species? Why are some people so quick to learn, others so slow? Why are some people generally cheerful, others generally glum; some aggressive, others passive; some withdrawn, others friendly? Why do some people appear to be perfectly "normal" while others behave in ways that are labeled strange, or even "crazy"?

Psychologists search for the characteristics humans share in common—but also those that make each of us unique.

Psychologists do not pretend to have all the answers, for human behavior is so complex that it may forever defy full scientific analysis. But they do have some of the answers and clues to many others, and they are making new discoveries all the time. When you finish this course you will know more about the human experience than anybody in the world did little over a century ago, when the science of psychology opened its first laboratory.*

PSYCHOLOGY'S GOALS AND INTERESTS

In the last half century, the number of psychologists in the United States has grown by leaps and bounds. As shown in Figure 1-1, psychologists have received an increasing proportion of the total number of doctorate degrees awarded by American universities (American Psychological Association, 1985). Over 100,000 individuals are engaged in one form of psychological endeavor or other, and over 60,000 are members of the field's professional organization, the American Psychological Association (Stapp, Tucker, and VandenBos, 1985).

The number of books and magazine articles built around psychological themes has also grown. And so has the number of people who pride themselves on being "good psychologists" who can see through all the camouflage to the very core of human nature—their own as well as other people's. Oddly enough, the very popularity of psychology is

---

*Before reading this chapter further, and to ensure that you get the most out of your study time, you may want to turn to pages 605–10 and read Appendix A: "How to Study This Book (and Others)."

Figure 1-1 Increase in psychology Ph.D.'s

The bars show that the percentage of all doctoral degrees awarded in the United States to psychologists has increased steadily in the past four decades—from 4 percent in 1945 to over 10 percent in 1984. This is in contrast to a decline in the percentage of Ph.D.'s awarded in the physical and mathematical sciences.

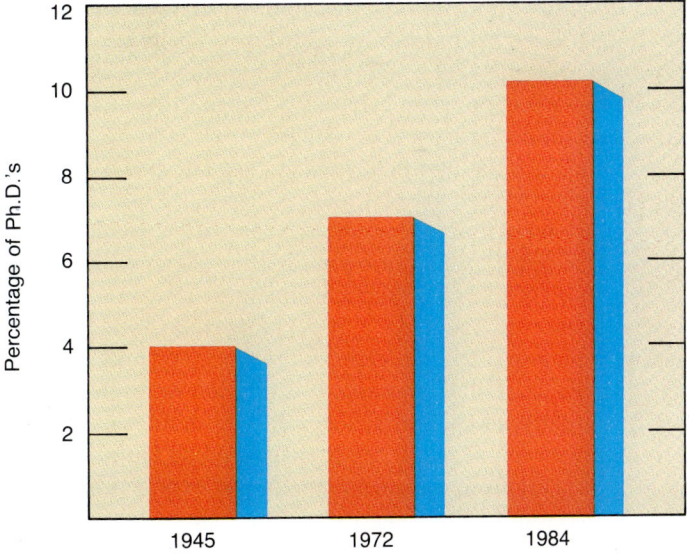

something of a handicap to the student who embarks on an introductory course. The fact of the matter is that the science of psychology is quite different from what people who have never seriously studied it usually believe it to be. Its methods are different. The topics in which it is interested cover a much wider range than is generally thought. And, as you will find throughout this book, many of its findings have been almost the exact opposite of what people have generally taken for granted about human nature.

Psychology Defined

A definition of psychology takes only a few brief words: It is *the systematic study of behavior and the factors that influence behavior.* Yet that simple statement covers a range of subject matter so vast that, like the universe itself, its boundaries defy imagination.

Just the single word *behavior* means many things. Our physical actions begin each morning when we wake, yawn, stretch, dress, and eat breakfast, and do not end until we go back to bed and fall asleep—after a long day in which we walk, talk, study, work, play, and sometimes laugh or cry. Inside ourselves is another world of activity. We think, learn, remember, and forget. We feel hunger and thirst—and such emotions as anger, fear, joy, and sadness. We have stirrings of desire for accomplishment and success, friendship, and sometimes revenge. We worry over our problems and seek ways to cope with them.

The *factors that influence behavior* are also many and varied. The most important is the human brain, but the brain itself is immensely complex—made up of 10 billion nerve cells, of scores of different kinds performing different functions, that are intricately connected and interconnected and constantly exchanging messages coded into little jolts of electricity and chemical activity. The brain would be useless without the help it gets from other parts of the body. It would not know anything about the environment without the specialized nerve cells of the sense organs, sensitive to light, sound, smell, taste, and pressure. It would not even know hunger or thirst without signals provided by the bloodstream and some of the visceral organs. It would not produce emotions without the aid of various chemicals released by the human glands.

To understand behavior, psychology must study all these many relationships between the brain and the rest of the body. It must also ponder the workings of heredity—and the extent to which our conduct is governed by traits and tendencies handed down to us from the countless generations of forebears from whom we are descended. At the same time it must examine the influence of environment, including the many ways we learn from our experiences, remember them, and apply them. In particular it must look at the way the actions of other people affect our own behavior—which turns out to be much more significant and far-reaching than we might ever suspect.

Our definition includes the words *systematic study* because psychology uses the rigorous and highly disciplined methods of science. It does not rely on some mysterious and supernatural explanation for human behavior, as our early ancestors presumably did. It is not content to describe behavior as some philosopher of the past, however brilliant, may have imagined it to be. Psychology is skeptical and demands proof. It is based on controlled experiments and on observations made with the greatest possible precision and objectivity (meaning freedom from personal prejudices or preconceived notions).

Without taking the scientific approach, it is difficult to reach valid conclusions about human behavior. The nonscientist is almost bound to commit numerous mistakes of observation and interpretation and to make judgments based on faulty or insufficient evidence. All of us tend to generalize from our own feelings and experiences—though what we see in ourselves is not necessarily characteristic of people in general. (Psychology has established conclusively that there is a wide range of individual differences in almost all human traits.) Or we generalize from the actions and opinions of the people we know, which again are not necessarily universal. (Psychology has shown that we tend to surround ourselves with people whose opinions, interests, and tastes are similar to our own.)

The Objectives of Psychology

In the study of behavior and the factors that influence it, psychology has two goals: (1) *to understand behavior* and (2) *to predict behavior.* Indeed, understanding and predicting are the goals of all sciences. Chemists, for example, have sought from the beginning to understand why wood burns and gold does not—and to predict what will happen when a chemical substance is subjected to flame or combined with another chemical in a test tube. Psychologists seek, among other things, to understand why individuals behave as they do in a classroom or in social situations—and to predict what would happen if certain changes were made in the school or social environment.

Most scientists seek not only to understand and predict events but to control them as well. Chemists want to be able to control the substances they deal with so that they can produce new chemicals to serve useful new purposes, such as the various synthetics now used in clothing and automobiles. To a certain extent, psychologists also look for ways to control human behavior. This is especially true of those who devote their careers to helping people overcome mental and emotional problems. They want to control the behavior of the people who consult them by trying to relieve an unreasonable fear of going out in public, an inability to establish satisfactory sexual relationships, or alcohol addiction.

But dealing with humans is far different from mixing chemicals in a test tube. The possibility of controlling human behavior raises thorny questions of moral and social policy. Therefore psychologists have mixed feelings about whether control of behavior should or should not be considered a third goal of the science. Some psychologists have argued that human behavior is always under some kind of control—by the ways in which parents rear their children, the school systems, the rewards and punishments provided in the business world, and the nation's laws—and that it would be better to have the control exercised in a scientific fashion by scientists dedicated to improving the human condition (Skinner, 1971). Most psychologists, however, shun the awful responsibility—and the dangers of abuse—inherent in efforts to manipulate human behavior.

"Basic" and "Applied" Psychology

Some psychologists, as pictured in Figure 1-2, are concerned only with *basic science*—that is, knowledge for the sake of knowledge. Their chief activities are teaching and research. Some of their investigations are scarcely distinguishable from the work of their colleagues in the older sciences like physics or physiology. *Experimental psychologists* are interested in the way forms of energy affect our sense organs and therefore the way we perceive the world, as well as in such basic processes as learning, memory, and motivation. *Physiological psychologists* seek information about the structure and functioning of the body and brain, and they examine chemical substances that influence our nervous systems and emotions. They, as well as many other psychologists, are interested in lower organisms as well as people—*organism* meaning any living creature. Among psychologists interested in basic research are also *developmental psychologists*, who study how individuals grow and change throughout their existence; and *personality* and *social psychologists*, who study how people differ in their enduring inner characteristics and traits, and how they influence and are influenced by others. Some basic psychologists, of course, deal directly with all the many forms that behavior takes and cannot, therefore, be pigeonholed very easily into one subspecialty.

Other psychologists, also pictured in Figure 1-2, are concerned not so much with basic science, or the discovery of knowledge, as with *applied science*, or using knowledge to help

Figure 1-2 Basic and applied psychologists at work

Pictured here are psychologists working in the two diverse fields of psychology—basic research (top) and applied (bottom).

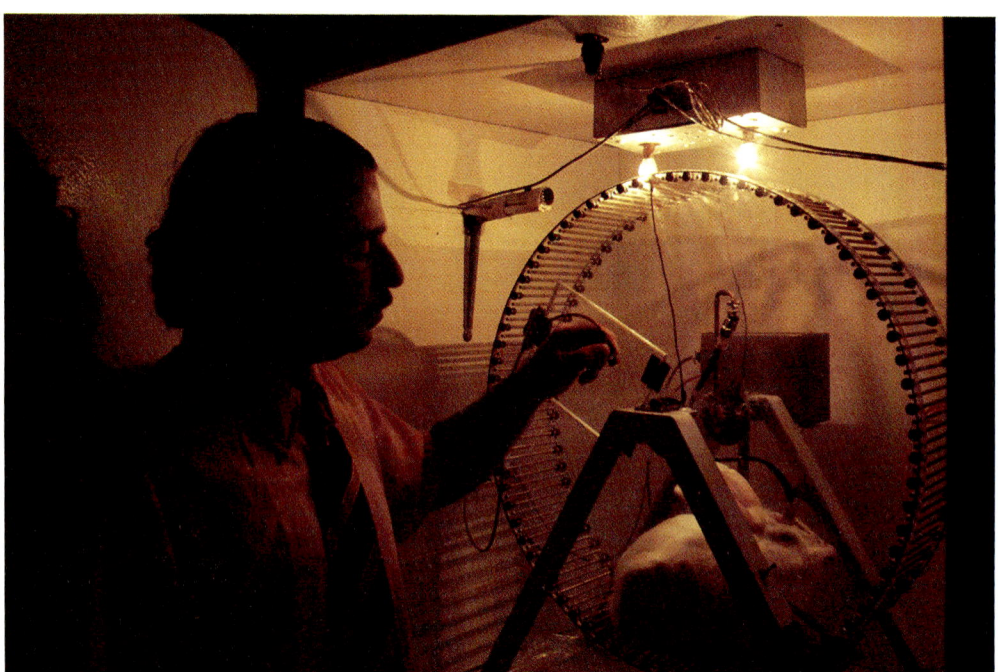

8 Chapter 1 The Aims and Methods of Psychology

society carry on its everyday tasks, tackle its problems, and improve the quality of life. *School psychologists* test pupils, analyze learning problems, and evaluate teaching methods, the curriculum, textbooks, and educational films. *Industrial psychologists* help select and train workers and improve working conditions, employee morale, and staff cooperation.

Environmental psychologists are especially concerned with ecological problems like smog, water pollution, crowding, and noise—and with helping our industrial society maintain an environment that preserves the balance of nature and enables humanity and other organisms to continue to thrive. *Community psychologists*, sometimes called specialists in *community mental health*, are concerned with the social environment and the way schools and other institutions might better serve individual human needs. And *health psychologists* deal with the ways we can improve health by altering our behavior.

The line between basic science and its applications is, of course, by no means a rigid one. Indeed many of the findings from basic psychological research have found important uses—for example, in the education of young children who have learning difficulties and in the treatment of various forms of abnormal behavior (Silver and Segal, 1984).

The Practice of Clinical and Counseling Psychology

Most applied psychologists, the largest group of all psychologists in the United States, are in the fields of *clinical* or *counseling psychology*. They use the findings of science to help people solve the various problems in society that trouble people from time to time—everything from deciding on a suitable line of work, to dealing with marital or sexual maladjustments, to overcoming crippling depression and anxieties. Of all professionally trained psychologists in the nation, about half are in this particular arena of psychology (American Psychological Association, 1985).

Clinical psychology is the diagnosis and treatment of psychological disorders—all of the traits and behaviors that are thought of as abnormal, described in Chapter 12. Clinical psychologists sometimes work with individuals, sometimes with groups. They use the

A clinical psychologist (gesturing with her hands) leads a group therapy session.

Figure 1-3   The birthplace of psychotherapy

It was in this room, on this couch, that psychoanalysis began. The photograph was made in the office of Sigmund Freud about 1895.

technique called *psychotherapy*—or treatment through discussing problems, trying to get at the root of them, and modifying attitudes, emotional responses, and behavior.

Psychotherapy began with Sigmund Freud, an Austrian physician and neurologist, who asked his troubled patients to lie on a couch (see Figure 1-3) and talk about themselves, their experiences, and what was troubling them, simply letting their thoughts roam in any direction. By analyzing the patients' flow of ideas as described in Chapter 13, Freud tried to discover the origin of the problems and eventually lead his patients to understand and overcome them.

Psychotherapy was originally the sole province of specialists who, like Freud, were physicians with advanced training in *psychoanalysis*, as Freud's method is called. The first psychologists who entered the field also used Freud's technique, and many of today's clinical psychologists continue to be influenced to some degree by Freudian theory. But others have developed different methods of approaching the special problems of the individuals they are trying to help. There are now far more clinical psychologists than psychoanalysts in the United States, using a wide array of psychotherapy techniques as described in Chapter 13. (Unlike psychiatrists, who have an M.D. degree, clinical psychologists do not assess the physical roots of an individual's psychological problems, nor do they prescribe drugs or use other medical therapies also described in Chapter 13.)

In general, *counseling psychology* usually involves helping those with milder problems of social and emotional adjustment. Some provide assistance to people who need guidance on such temporary problems as difficulties in school or choice of a vocation. In their search for the best solution, counselors often administer tests that have been developed by psy-

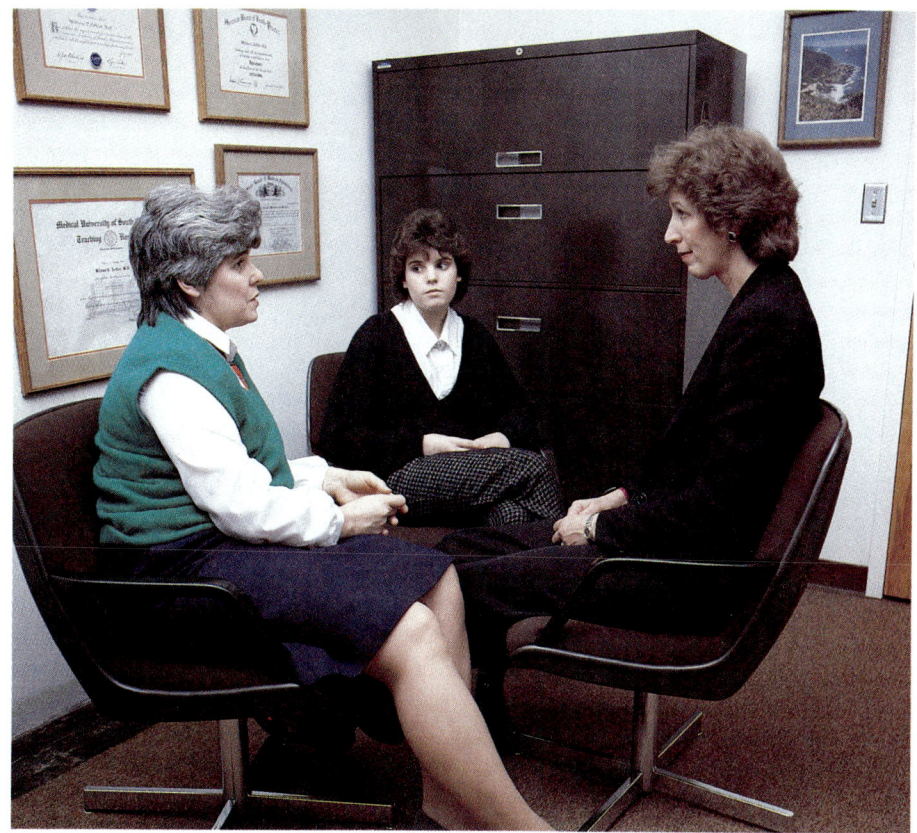

A counseling psychologist works to improve mother-daughter communications.

chology for everything from general intelligence to aptitude for specific tasks. One of psychology's most important findings, as you will see in Chapter 8, is that people are usually very good at doing some things but only mediocre to poor at others—and one secret of success, in both school and jobs, is to take advantage of your own particular strengths. Psychological counselors attempt to discover and encourage these strengths.

Some counselors specialize in helping married couples overcome difficulties in their relationships—often caused not so much by deep-seated emotional problems as by poor communication or stressful circumstances. Like clinical psychologists, these marriage counselors sometimes work with individual couples, sometimes with groups.

HOW PSYCHOLOGISTS STUDY HUMAN BEHAVIOR

In any science, the methods of investigation depend largely on the subject matter. Chemistry, dealing with substances that can be seen, felt, tasted, and manipulated, uses direct methods. The chemist can put two substances together in a test tube, see what happens, and measure and anlayze the result. Astronomy has to use more indirect methods. It cannot in any way manipulate the stars and planets. It must be content to observe them through telescopes or through the eyes of cameras and television equipment sent on spacecraft to Venus and Mars.

Because behavior takes such a wide variety of forms, psychologists have had to improvise. No single method can be applied to all the activities that interest the science. Therefore psychologists have had to adopt a number of different ways of studying their subject matter—and they are constantly seeking new ways. The most prominent methods of study now in use are described in the following pages.

Observation

In many cases, psychologists do what astronomers do—that is, observe events pertinent to the science, such as the actual behavior of people in various kinds of social situations. To what extent, for example, is the way we behave toward other people dictated by how wealthy or important we think they are? One clue was found in a study in which psychologists observed how motorists behaved toward another driver who was slow to start and held up traffic when the light changed from red to green. If the offending driver was in an old rattletrap, it was found that the motorist behind was quick to honk in protest. If the slowmoving driver was in a shiny new luxury car, other motorists were much more patient (Doob and Gross, 1968).

In a sense all humans continually use the technique of observation. Everybody observes the behavior of other people and draws some conclusions from their actions. If we note that a woman student rarely speaks up in class and blushes easily in social situations, we conclude that she is shy, and we treat her accordingly. (We may try to put her at ease, or, if we feel so inclined, we may enjoy embarrassing her and making her squirm.) Psychologists make their observations in a more disciplined fashion. They try to describe behavior objectively and exactly, and they are loath to jump to conclusions about the motives behind it.

In studying behavior through observation, psychologists usually try to remain aloof from what is going on in order to avoid influencing events in any way. They practice what is called *naturalistic observation*, in which they try to be as inconspicuous and anonymous as possible, lest their very presence affect the behavior they are studying. Sometimes they even arrange to be unseen, as illustrated in Figure 1-4. Some of our most valuable knowledge about the behavior of infants and the way they develop has come from observers who used this method. The famous Masters and Johnson findings on sexual response were obtained in part in this manner.

At other times, psychologists engage in *participant observation*. They take an active part in a social situation—sometimes deliberately playacting to see how other people behave toward someone who seems unusually withdrawn or hostile. Or they may participate in an encounter group to study their own as well as other people's reactions.

Interviews and Case Histories

Another way to discover how people behave and feel is to ask them—and therefore psychologists often use the *interview method*, questioning subjects in depth about their life experiences. A special application of the interview method is the *case history*, in which many years of a person's life are reconstructed to show how various behavior patterns have developed. Case histories are particularly useful in revealing the origins of abnormal behavior. Some forms of psychotherapy rely on building up a long and detailed case history as an aid to understanding and correcting the client's problems.

Questionnaires and Opinion Surveys

Closely related to the interview is the *questionnaire*, which is especially useful in gathering information quickly from large numbers of people. A questionnaire is a set of written questions that can be answered easily, usually with a check mark. To produce accurate results, a questionnaire must be worded with extreme care. The creation of a reliable

Figure 1-4 Invisible observers study child behavior

Unseen behind a one-way mirror, investigators use the method of naturalistic observation to study a child at play. To the observers outside the room, the wall panel looks like a sheet of clear glass. To the child inside, it looks like a mirror.

questionnaire is a fine art, for the slightest change in the way the questions are worded may completely distort the results.

Questionnaires and interviews are sometimes challenged on the ground that people may not respond truthfully. But experienced investigators have many ways of spotting people who are lying or exaggerating. Perhaps interviews and questionnaires do not always reveal the complete truth. When carefully planned and conducted, however, they can be extremely useful.

Questionnaires and interviews find a special use in the study of public opinion, in which psychologists are also active. Scientific methods of choosing a sample of people to poll, and analyzing the results, have made it possible to show how all the people in the United States are divided on any controversial issue, within a few percentage points of possible error, by questioning a mere 1,500 or so.

Public opinion surveys are a valuable contribution to the democratic process because they provide an accurate picture of how citizens actually feel about such issues as taxation, defense expenditures, foreign policy, abortion, and laws regulating sexual conduct and the use of drugs. Before such information was available, there was no accurate way to gauge public opinion—and often small but vociferous minorities were able to convince politicians that they represented the majority view by waging intense publicity campaigns. Now many

After casting her ballot, a voter responds to a network survey of voter opinions.

congressional and other political leaders base their votes on the will of the majority (which is often unorganized and silent) as expressed in the polls.

Some well-known, though less important, uses of public opinion surveys include predictions of election results and the Nielsen ratings of the popularity of television shows. Business firms use surveys to measure public response to new products and to sales and advertising campaigns.

Tests of Psychological Traits and Behavior

Among the oldest tools of psychology are the *tests* it has developed for many human characteristics, abilities, and achievements. You have probably taken a number of such tests—for example, the Scholastic Aptitude Tests, or SAT, which is a form of intelligence test, or examinations that showed your elementary and high school teachers how your progress in reading or mathematics compared with the national average. When applying for a job you may be asked to take tests that psychologists have devised for measuring ability at specific tasks, ranging from clerical work to being an astronaut. If you have occasion to visit a clinical psychologist, you may be tested for various personality traits.

The construction of truly scientific tests—which actually measure what they are supposed to measure and do so accurately and consistently—is much more difficult than is commonly supposed. Many of the so-called psychological tests in newspapers and magazines, which claim to tell you how happy, self-fulfilled, or neurotic you are, or how good you are likely to be as a husband, wife, or parent, have no value at all. They are simply parlor games dreamed up out of thin air by some nonpsychologist, and any score you may make on them, good or bad, is not to be taken seriously. Even psychology's best tests have weaknesses despite all the scientific knowledge and effort that have gone into creating them. But they also have their uses, and the search goes on constantly for new and better versions.

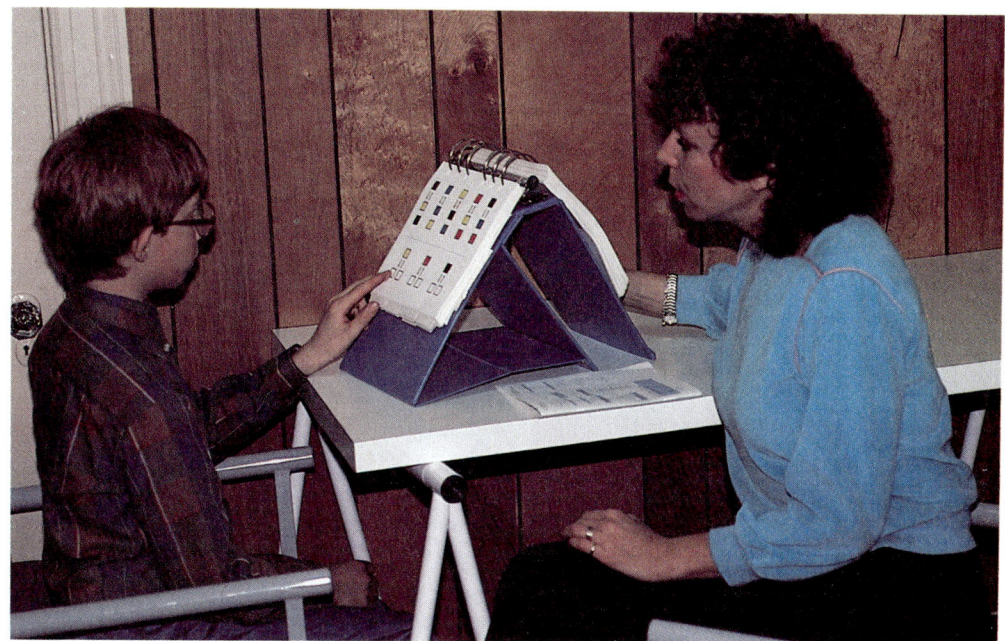
The test will help tell the psychologist about the child's ability and achievement levels.

Physiological Measures

Besides trying to develop tests for psychological traits, psychologists are also interested in the *measurement* of any physiological characteristics that may have a bearing on behavior. They have found, for example, that feelings of hunger are not necessarily caused by activity of the stomach, as popularly believed, but by measurable changes in the composition of the bloodstream. They have also shown that the body may respond at times with changes in hormones that are related to anxiety, although the individual reports feeling no emotion.

Researchers have measured the size and activity of the glands that influence emotions, and the way the arousal of emotions produce changes in the heart rate, blood pressure, and breathing. They have measured muscle tension and brain wave activity in states of stress and relaxation. In identifying some of the chemicals, produced in nerve endings, that transmit nervous impulses, they have found how irregularities in these chemicals play a part in mood and abnormal behavior. They have also measured electrical and chemical changes in the brain and body while individuals are experiencing unusual states of consciousness—such as those produced by sleep, hypnosis, meditation, and the use of drugs such as marijuana, LSD, PCP, or cocaine.

Measurements, Individual Differences, and the Normal Curve

Psychology's tests and measurements have been particularly helpful in adding to our knowledge of *individual differences*. They have shown that every person is indeed unique and that all kinds of physical and psychological traits, from height and muscular strength to intelligence and emotional sensitivity, vary over a wide range from small to large, low to high, and weak to strong.

In studying what tests and measurements show about individual differences, the science relies heavily on mathematical techniques known as *psychological statistics*, which are described in Appendix B to the book. One of the most important findings has been the discovery that almost all human traits, from height and weight to intelligence, fall into a similar pattern. In height, for example, the measurements for adult American men range all the way from around 3 feet to around 8 feet. But most cluster around the average, which is now about 5 feet 9 inches, and the number found at each point in the range goes down steadily with each inch up or down from the average. Note the graph in Figure 1-5, which shows how IQs as measured by intelligence tests range from below 40 to above 160—but with the majority falling close to the average of 100, and only a very few at the extreme low or high levels.

The graph line in Figure 1-5 is so typical of the results generally found in all tests and measurements that it is known as the *normal curve of distribution*. The message of the curve is that in almost all measurable traits, physical and psychological, most people are average or close to it, some are a fair distance above or below, and a few are very far above or below. Those who are about average have a lot of company. Those who are far removed from the average—in intelligence the geniuses and the mentally retarded, in height the seven-footers and the four-footers—are rare.

The curve of normal distribution helps explain a great deal about behavior, including the general similarities displayed by most people and the wide deviations shown by a few others. The curve applies to performance in school. (Most students have to do an average amount of struggling; some can make A's without turning a hair; some cannot handle the work at all.) It applies to musical talent, athletic skill, and interest or lack of interest in sex—as well as to the intensity of emotional arousal and the strength of motives for achievement, power, and friendship. These and many other individual differences are the reason you cannot generalize about humanity as a whole from your own traits—especially on a matter in which you happen to fall at an unusually low or high point on the curve.

The Method of Correlation

One question that has interested psychologists almost from the beginning of the science is: Do children resemble their parents in intelligence? This is a question that has many implications for study of the part played in human behavior by heredity and environment—which, as you will see a little later, is one of the basic issues in psychology. How would you try to go about answering it?

A person totally untrained in the methods of science might jump to conclusions based on personal experience: "No, obviously not. My neighbors the Smiths are both smart people—they went to college and have good jobs—but their two kids are having a terrible time in school." Or, "Certainly. My neighbors the Joneses are geniuses and their two daughters are the smartest kids in their school."

A more sophisticated approach would be to look at a much larger sample of children and parents than provided by just the Smiths or the Joneses—and give both generations intelligence tests rather than to rely on personal impressions of how smart they seemed to be. This would be a good start toward a scientific answer. But the results would be difficult to interpret, because the tests would show all kinds of contradictions. One mother and father, both with IQs of 120, turn out to have an only child whose IQ is also 120—but another couple with the same IQ has an only child with an IQ of 90. One mother at 95 and father at 85 have an only child with an IQ of 90—but a similar couple has a child at 125. Even in the same family the tests would sometimes show three children with IQs as far apart as 85, 115, and 135. Without some method of analyzing and interpreting the test results, any scientific answer to the question would still be elusive.

Figure 1-5 Individual differences in IQ

The graph was obtained by testing the IQs of a large number of people in the United States. Note how many people scored right around the average of 100. (A total of 46.5 percent showed IQs between 90 and 109.) Note also how the number falls off rapidly from the midpoint to the lower and upper extremes. Fewer than 1 percent of all people showed IQs under 60 and only 1.33 percent were at 140 or over (Terman and Merrill, 1937).

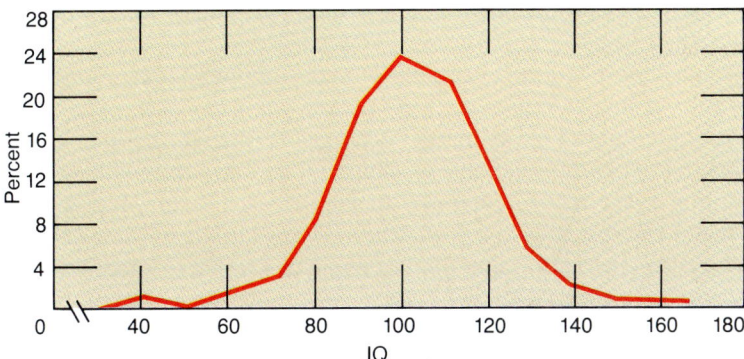

In this type of situation, psychologists apply another statistical tool called *correlation*. This is a mathematical method used to examine two different measurements (such as the IQs of parents and the IQs of their children)—and to determine, from what would otherwise seem hopelessly jumbled numbers, what relationship if any actually exists between the two. The method, which is explained in the appendix on statistics, boils down the figures into a *coefficient of correlation* ranging from 0.00 (no relationship at all) to 1.00 (a one-to-one or absolutely perfect relationship). In the case of parents and children, the coefficient of correlation between IQs has generally been found to indicate a fairly high, though by no means perfect, relationship.

You will find many correlations mentioned throughout the book, but one word of caution is in order. Correlations reveal the existence and extent of relationships, but they do not necessarily indicate cause and effect. Unless they are carefully interpreted, correlations can be misleading. There is a high correlation between the number of permanent teeth in children and their ability to answer increasingly difficult questions on intelligence tests. But this does not mean that having more teeth causes increased mental ability. The correlation is high because increasing age accounts for both the new teeth and the mental development.

THE ULTIMATE METHOD: EXPERIMENTATION

One other method of investigation is so important and productive that it deserves a separate section of the chapter. This is the *experiment*—in which the psychologist makes a careful and rigidly controlled examination of cause and effect. The experimenter sets up one set of conditions and determines what kind of behavior takes place under those conditions. Then the conditions are changed and the effect of the changes, if any, is measured.

Independent and Dependent Variables

Every psychological experiment is an attempt to discover whether behavior—in any of its many forms—changes when conditions change. Both the possible behavior change and the change in conditions are called *variables*. The change in conditions is set up and controlled by the experimenter. Note the example illustrated in Figure 1-6, in which the change in conditions is the fact that the experimenter or an assistant deliberately sits down right next to a person seated on a park bench. Since the change is manipulated by the experimenter and in no way dependent on anything the subject does or does not do, it is called the *independent variable*.

The behavior that occurs in response to the independent variable—in this case the fact that the subject almost immediately got up and went away—is called the *dependent variable*. In all experiments, the experimenter arranges to change the independent variable, then measures the dependent variable as exhibited by a group of subjects. The results for the bench-sitting subjects are illustrated in Figure 1-7. The graph shows that changing the independent variable caused a pronounced change in the behavior of a significant number of the subjects—indicating that many people like to have "elbow room" and get uncomfortable when crowded.

The bench-sitting study is a good example of the way psychological experiments can be conducted outside the confines of a laboratory—often, as in this case, with the help of the technique of observation. Such experiments, which are becoming increasingly common because they offer a direct approach to "the problems and insights that a study of the everyday world provides," frequently produce findings that go far beyond those obtained under laboratory conditions where all the influential factors in a real-life situation cannot be duplicated—or that may even be at odds with laboratory results (Baddeley, 1981).

Experimental and Control Groups

It is important to note that the graph in Figure 1-7 has two lines—one for the bench-sitters who were joined by the "stranger," the other for bench-sitters who were left alone. This is because the findings would not mean much if only the first of these two groups had been observed. True, many of these bench-sitters moved away, often very quickly. But how many of them were planning to leave anyway and would have walked off even if no one had joined them?

The problem was solved by observing the second group and timing how long they remained on the bench. Thus there were (1) an *experimental group* for whom the independent variable was the intrusion by the stranger, and (2) a *control group* who were left alone. The wide difference in behavior between the experimental group and the control group became a clear indication of the effect of the independent variable.

In the bench-sitting experiment the subjects in both groups had to be selected by chance, since they were unknown to the experimenter and were not even aware they were taking part in a psychological study. In most experiments, however, the experimental and control subjects are chosen with great care. Note, for example, Figure 1-8, showing the results of an experiment that demonstrated the value of recitation as a study technique. The results would have been meaningless if the experimental group, which used recitation, had been made up entirely of good students and the control group of poor students. Instead the experimenter had to make sure that the two groups were evenly matched. In experiments on learning, the subjects have to be approximately equal in such matters as average age, years of school completed, grades, and IQ, and they have to study for the same amount of time and under similar conditions. Often it is also important to match the experimental and control groups for sex, race, and social background. Only in this way can

Figure 1-6 An experiment in crowding produces a two-minute drama

At top, a man who is about to become the subject of the experiment sits alone on a park bench, enjoying his newspaper. Middle, an experimenter sits down beside him. Bottom, the man with the newspaper has left. The photos reconstruct what happened frequently in a study of how much "elbow room" people prefer and the effects of crowding, the full results of which are illustrated in Figure 1-7.

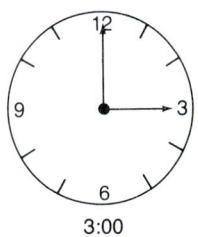
3:00

3:01

3:02

The Ultimate Method: Experimentation

Figure 1-7 How the unwanted experimenter drove the bench-sitters away

In the study illustrated in Figure 1-6, it turned out that 40 percent of people sitting alone on a park bench left within 3 minutes after the experimenter or an assistant sat down beside them. By the end of 15 minutes, 60 percent had moved on. Their departures were clearly prompted by the unwanted "stranger"—because almost all similar bench-sitters observed at the same time, but left alone, remained for at least 5 minutes and 70 percent were still there after 15 minutes (after Sommers, 1969).

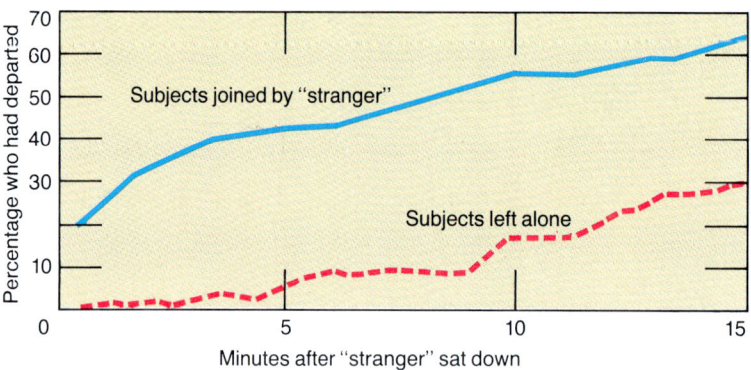

experimenters make sure that the independent variable they are trying to study (in Figure 1-8, the use of recitation) is the only one that could have produced the change in the dependent variable (in Figure 1-8, the number of syllables remembered).

Single-blind and Double-blind Experiments

In an experiment on the effects of marijuana on driving ability, psychologists would divide their subjects into an experimental group that was under the influence of the drug and a control group that was not. But a further precaution would be necessary—for the subjects' performance might be affected by their knowledge that they had taken the drug and their expectations of how it might affect them. To avoid this possibility, it would be important to keep the subjects from knowing whether they had received the drug. This could be done by giving half the subjects an injection of the drug's active ingredient, THC, and the other half an injection of a salt solution that would have no effect, without telling them which was which. This method, in which subjects cannot know whether they belong to the experimental group or the control group, is called the *single-blind technique*.

There is the further danger that the experimenter's own ratings of the subjects' performance might be affected by knowing which of them had taken the drug and which had not. To make the experiment foolproof, the drug or salt solution would have to be injected by a third party, so that even the experimenter would have no way of knowing which subjects had received which kind of injection. This method, in which neither the subject nor the experimenter knows who is in the experimental group and who is in the control group, is called the *double-blind technique*. It is particularly valuable in studying the effects of drugs, including the tranquilizers and antidepressants used to treat mental disturbances. It is also used in any other experiment in which knowledge of the conditions might affect the judgment of the experimenter as well as the performance of the subjects.

Figure 1-8 Experimental group (recitation) versus control group (no recitation)

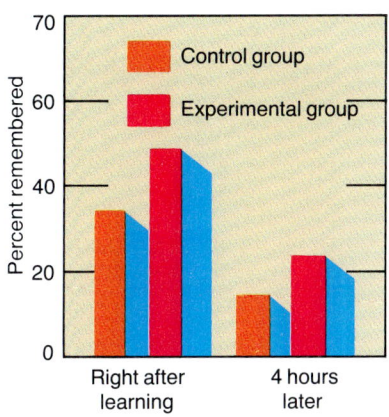

In an experiment on the effectiveness of recitation, both groups spent the same amount of time studying a list of nonsense syllables (like KOV, TUS, and PIM). But the experimental group devoted 20 percent of the time to reciting the syllables, while the control group did no reciting at all. As the bars show, the experimental group demonstrated significantly greater memory for the list, both immediately after the study period and several hours later (Gates, 1917). For the precautions that had to be taken in selecting the two groups, see the text.

As developed and refined over the years, and with the checks provided by such methods as the use of a control group and the double-blind technique, the experiment is psychology's most powerful tool.

PSYCHOLOGY YESTERDAY, TODAY, AND TOMORROW

The psychological experiment—and psychology itself—has come a long way since the science began. At the start, the idea of taking a scientific approach to the study of behavior required a radical shift in human thinking and the invention of brand-new techniques of study.

The year the science was founded is usually put at 1879, when Wilhelm Wundt opened the first psychological laboratory at Germany's University of Leipzig. Wundt had studied to be a physician, then, instead of practicing medicine, taught as a professor of physiology. But he soon lost interest, because he was much more concerned with human consciousness than with the workings of the body. His experiments, in retrospect, seem rather trivial. For example, he and his students spent hours in the laboratory listening to the click of a metronome—sometimes set fast and sometimes set slow, sounding only a few times or many—and analyzed their conscious reactions. They decided that a rapid series of clicks produced excitement and a slow series made them relaxed, and that they had slight feelings of tension before each click and of relief afterward.

Wundt was the most popular professor at his university, and no classroom was big enough to hold all the students who wanted to hear his lectures. A few years later, similar acclaim came to Sir Francis Galton, one of the first British psychologists. Galton, who was interested in individual differences, invented numerous devices to test such traits as hearing, sense of smell, color vision, and ability to judge weights. At one time he set up his equipment at an International Health Exhibition in London—and people flocked in to be his subjects, gladly paying an entrance fee for the privilege. Even in those early years, when psychology was just taking a few tentative steps into the vast realm of human behavior, it captured the public's imagination.

Wilhelm Wundt (1832–1920)

William James, "Mental Life," and the Era of Introspection

Like Wundt, most of the pioneers concentrated on an attempt to discover the nature, origins, and significance of conscious experiences. Their chief method of investigation was *introspection*, or looking inward. They tried to analyze the processes that went on inside their minds, asked their subjects to do the same, and recorded their findings, as objectively as possible, for comparison with other observers.

The most prominent of the early American psychologists was William James, who came to the science from an unusual background. Like Wundt, he studied medicine but never practiced. Indeed he had a difficult time finding his true vocation. At one time he wanted to be an artist, then a chemist, and once he joined a zoological expedition to Brazil. In his late twenties he suffered a mental breakdown and went through a prolonged depression in which he seriously thought of committing suicide. But he recovered—largely, he believed, through what he called "an achievement of the will"—and went on to become a Harvard professor and prolific writer on psychology and philosophy.

James had no doubt about the mission of the new science. A textbook he wrote began with the words: "Psychology is the study of mental life." The distinguishing feature of this mental life, he felt, was that human beings constantly seek certain end results and must constantly choose among various methods of achieving them. In one passage he wrote:

> I would . . . if I could, be both handsome and fat and well-dressed, and make a million a year, be a wit, a *bon vivant*, and a lady-killer, as well as a philosopher, a philanthropist, statesman, warrior, and African explorer, as well as a "tone poet" and saint. But the thing is simply impossible. The millionaire's work would run counter to the saint's; the *bon vivant* and the philanthropist would trip each other up; the philosopher and the lady-killer could not well keep house in the same tenement of clay. Such different characters may conceivably at the outset of life be possible. But to make any of them actual, the rest must more or less be suppressed. . . . This is as strong an example as there is of selective industry of the mind (James, 1890).

John B. Watson (1878–1958)

As those words indicate, James was interested in the broad pattern of human strivings—the cradle-to-grave progress of human beings as thinking organisms who adopt certain goals and ambitions, including spiritual ones, and struggle in various ways to attain the goals or become reconciled to failure.

John Watson, Conditioned Reflexes, and the Behavioristic Revolution

Was William James perhaps more philosopher than psychologist? Was introspection really scientific or just another form of mere speculation about the human condition? These questions raised some nagging doubts as the years went on, and in 1913 another American, John Watson, revolutionized psychology by breaking completely with the school of introspection and founding the movement called *behaviorism*.

Watson declared that "mental life" is something that cannot be seen or measured and thus cannot be studied scientifically. Instead of trying to examine any such vague thing as "mental life" or consciousness, he concluded, psychologists should concentrate on actions that are plainly visible. In other words, he wanted the science to study what people *do*, not what they think.

Watson did not believe in anything like "free will," or the ability to control our own destiny. Instead he believed that everything we do is predetermined by our past experiences. He considered all human behavior to be a series of actions in which a *stimulus*, that is, an event in the environment, produces a *response*, that is, an observable muscular movement or some physiological reaction, such as increased heart rate or glandular secretion, that can also be observed and measured with the proper instruments. (For example, shining a bright light into the eye is a stimulus that causes an immediate response in which the pupil of the eye contracts.) Watson believed that through the establishment of *conditioned reflexes*, a type of learning discussed in Chapter 5, almost any kind of stimulus can be made to produce almost any kind of response. He once said that he could take any dozen babies at birth and, by conditioning them in various ways, turn them into anything he wished—doctor, lawyer, beggar, or thief.

Even the existence of a human mind was doubted by Watson. He conceded that human beings had thoughts, but he believed that these were simply a form of talking to oneself, by making tiny movements of the vocal cords. He also conceded that people have what they call feelings, but he believed that these were only some form of conditioned response to a stimulus in the environment.

B. F. Skinner and the Behaviorist Era

For many decades behaviorism was the dominant force in psychology. Watson was succeeded as leader of the movement by B. F. Skinner, who has been chiefly interested in the learning process and has revised and expanded Watson's ideas. He has made many important contributions to our knowledge of how patterns of rewards and punishments produce and modify connections between many kinds of stimuli and responses and thus help control the organism's behavior—often in the most complex ways.

Skinner's best-known book is *Beyond Freedom and Dignity,* published in 1971. In it he argues that people possess neither of the two attributes mentioned in his title. To Skinner, people are not responsible for their conduct, neither to blame for their failures nor deserving of credit for their achievements. They are simply the creatures of their environment. Their behavior depends on the kinds of learning to which they have been subjected, particularly which of their actions have been rewarded. A "social engineer" aware of all the principles of learning could mold people into any form desired, whether for good or for evil.

The behaviorists in general, in their efforts to avoid introspective speculation and confine their investigations to forms of behavior that can be seen and measured, have tended to experiment with lower animals. Skinner built his principles of learning on the behavior of rats and pigeons. Other behaviorists have worked with various animals to explore such matters as motives, aggression, cooperation, conflicts, and even abnormal behavior. The thrust of the science was to find universal laws that applied to all organisms, rather than just to some unique and perhaps imaginary mental quality, spiritual superiority, or "achievement of the will" possessed by human beings.

The great contribution of the behaviorists has been to pull psychology back from the danger of becoming a mere branch of philosophic speculation, relying solely on an inward examination of a mental life that nobody but its possessor can see or examine. The behaviorists, with their search for simple, universal, and observable knowledge, pushed psychology into more disciplined channels—and to the realization that a science must be objective and based on controlled experiments and measurements of behavior.

On the other hand, behaviorism was always controversial. Many psychologists rejected the idea that human beings are like mere pieces of machinery that automatically perform in a certain way whenever a certain button is pushed. In particular, they disagreed with Skinner's belief that we have no real freedom of choice or responsibility for our own actions. We do seem, as William James pointed out, to make choices. We have complicated thoughts, feelings, emotions, and attitudes that are difficult to explain through a simple push-button theory.

The Gestalt School of Thought

One movement of considerable historic importance in the opposition to behaviorism was *Gestalt psychology,* which originated in Germany at about the same time Watson's ideas were becoming influential in the United States. The movement took its name from a German word that has no exact English equivalent. *Gestalt* is roughly translated as "pattern" or "configuration," but it means something more than that. The Gestalt school believed that in studying any psychological phenomenon, from a perceptual process to the human personality, it is essential to look at events considered *as a whole*. Indeed the Gestalt theories have often been summarized as maintaining that "the whole is greater than the sum of its parts."

On the matter of perception, for example, note Figure 1-9. If you look at the panel marked *a* in the upper left-hand corner, you see merely four miscellaneous lines. If asked to describe them, you might call them just "an arrangement of lines," or "four sticks," or "four sticks with spaces between them." These lines, however, can be put together in various other ways. In *b* they become clearly and unmistakably a square, and in *c* a pennant or a flag on a golf course. In *d* they strike the eye immediately as a letter in the English alphabet, and in *e* they become a word. Or they can be seen as a Roman numeral (*f*), the number 4 (*g*), or even 77 (*h*). When you see these configurations, you no longer even think about the four basic parts from which they are constructed.

The Gestalt psychologists stressed not only the whole rather than the parts but also the importance of the entire situation, or context, in which the "whole" is found. A demonstration is shown in Figure 1-10. Note how your interpretation of the man pointed to by the arrows is dictated by the rest of what you see in the drawings. Though the Gestalt movement is no longer active, many of its ideas survive in today's emerging view of mental activity and human behavior in general as a pattern and a unity.

The Rise of the Cognitive School

In a sense the opposite directions taken by the behaviorists and the introspectionists were like the efforts of a gunner who first aims too far to the left, next too far to the right—and

Figure 1-9   Some Gestalts that are far greater than the sum of their parts

The four little lines in a *make no sense at all. But note how many significant forms they can take when rearranged into patterns, or Gestalts, as described in the text. You can probably create some other meaningful patterns from the same four-line raw materials.*

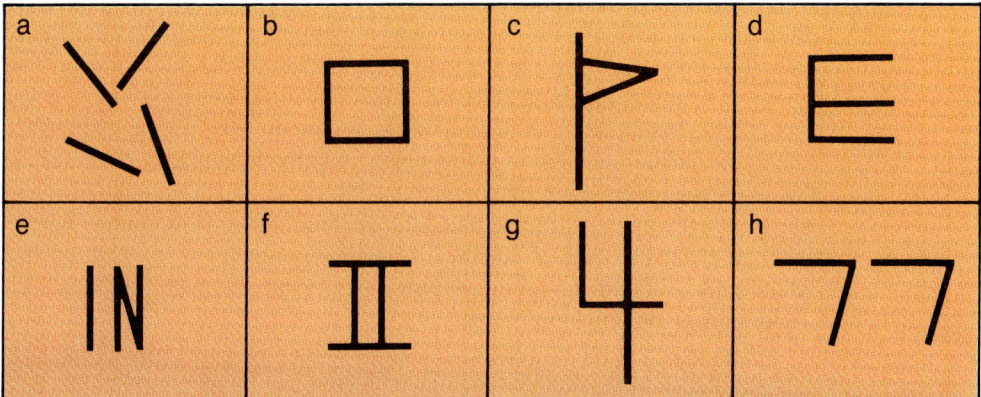

Figure 1-10   How the context, or surrounding, influences the Gestalt

What do you see in the left-hand drawing when you look where the arrow points? Certainly you do not say to yourself: "I see a head, a body, two arms, and two legs—and therefore I see a person." Instead, as the Gestalt psychologists emphasized, you take in the whole pattern and see the person without any effort at all. Moreover the drawing illustrates another Gestalt principle—the fact that the uniform, taxi, and hotel make you immediately aware that the person is a doorman. In the right-hand drawing, the same man in a different context becomes a military officer.

then, with the target bracketed, scores a direct hit. Both schools of thought were somewhat wide of the mark, yet both were essential to the growth of psychology into its present form. Many aspects of "mental life" have now been drawn back into the field of study, and psychologists in recent years have been busy exploring the human use of language, thinking, and memory, as well as human emotions, motives, and social relationships. Yet at the same time, thanks to the influence of Watson and Skinner, the study has become much more disciplined and systematic, relying on observations of actual behavior rather than mere speculation.

The trend today is toward what is called *cognitive psychology*—"cognitive" referring to all the ways in which we learn about our environment, store the knowledge in memory, think about it, and use it to act intelligently in new situations. These various forms of mental activity are often referred to as *information processing*, a term borrowed from computer science. They begin with what in a computer would be called the inputs—the raw data about the environment that we gather through our sense organs as they respond to light and sound waves, the mechanical forces of pressure and heat, and the chemical forces that cause sensations of taste and smell. Our brain then tries to make sense out of all this jumble of stimuli, comparing it to previous information and interpreting its significance (through the process of perception as described in Chapter 4). The information, thus transformed into meaningful patterns, is then stored in memory, where it is associated with other information to which it bears some relationship. We call on the information whenever we need it—as a computer would tap its memory bank—to help us think, understand, and solve problems.

Cognitive Psychology and Our "Mental Models of Reality"

The cognitive psychologists reject the behaviorist proposal that people are mere passive creatures of the environment, responding unthinkingly to the world's stimuli. Instead they view the human organism as "an active seeker of knowledge and processor of information," from which it actively builds "mental representations of the world" (Klatzky, 1980). These *mental models of reality* are a core idea in cognitive psychology. Kenneth Craik, one of the founders of the school, has said that our mental picture of the world, plus our knowledge of our own possible actions, enables us to "try out various alternatives, conclude which is the best of them, react to future situations before they arise, use the knowledge of past events in dealing with the future, and in every way react in a much fuller, safer, and a more competent manner" (Craik, 1952).

To put this another way, the cognitive psychologists think of the human mind as a sort of mental executive that organizes the world's stimuli into perceptual patterns (for example, perceiving a girl or a boy rather than a collection of arms, legs, and body), makes comparisons, and processes the information it receives into new forms and categories. It discovers meanings and uses its stored knowledge to find new principles that aid in constructive thinking, making judgments, and deciding on appropriate behavior. These ideas have influenced most of today's psychologists in one way or another, in all the branches of the science from the study of the senses to psychotherapy.

The Humanistic School

Psychology has of course taken many other directions, as would be expected in a science embracing such a wide field of inquiry. One of today's prominent movements is *humanistic psychology*, which also stems in part from the Gestalt school. Like the Gestalt psychologists, the humanists prefer to view the human personality as a pattern and an entity. To try to study human behavior by breaking it down into fragments, such as individual responses to individual stimuli, is regarded as futile and indeed a display of "disrespect" for the unique quality of the human spirit (Matson, 1971).

Humanistic psychologists take the view that we human beings are totally different from other organisms. We are distinguished by the fact that we have values and goals and seek to express ourselves, grow, fulfill ourselves, and find peace and happiness. Our thoughts and aspirations, which Watson considered inappropriate for study, appear to the humanistic psychologists to be the most important aspects of behavior.

The humanists take a broad and very hopeful view of the true quality of human nature, its accomplishments, and its potentialities. They believe that human beings are strongly motivated to realize their possibilities for creativity, dignity, and self-worth. The techniques of psychotherapy used by humanistic psychologists are built around the assumption that people will always grow in a constructive way if their environment permits them to do so.

The humanistic psychologists are in some ways more oriented toward philosophy, literature, and religion than toward the investigative methods of the sciences. Many humanistic psychologists have been associated with efforts to expand consciousness and achieve unity of mind and body through encounter groups, sensitivity training, and other kinds of mental and physical "reaching out."

Sigmund Freud and Psychoanalysis

Sigmund Freud, as mentioned earlier, was not a psychologist but a physician, yet he had a profound influence on many aspects of psychological thinking. Beginning his career in the 1880s in Vienna, he turned his attention to psychological processes as a result of his experience with patients who were suffering from physical impairments—including paralysis of the arms or legs or blindness—without any apparent physical cause. He described such cases as *hysterical conversion*, believing that the patient converted emotional conflicts into physical symptoms. The theories he developed—over a lifetime of treating many kinds of

Sigmund Freud (1856–1939)

abnormal behavior and analyzing his own personality—are the basis of psychoanalysis, announced to the world at the turn of the century.

Freud himself was rather neurotic in his youth, suffering from feelings of anxiety and deep depression. He retained some neurotic symptoms all his life; he was a compulsive smoker of as many as twenty cigars a day, was nervous about traveling, and was given to what were probably hypochondriacal complaints about poor digestion, constipation, and heart palpitation. However, he managed to overcome his early inclinations toward depression and lived a rich professional, family, and social life—an indication that in his case the physician had managed to heal himself, at least in large part.

One of Freud's great insights into the human personality was the discovery of how it is influenced by *unconscious processes*, especially motives of which we are unaware. At first his ideas were bitterly attacked; many people were repelled by his notion that human beings, far from being completely rational, are largely at the mercy of irrational unconscious thoughts. Many were shocked by his emphasis on the role of sexual motives (which were prominent among those that the society of that period preferred to deny). Over the years, however, the furor died out. There remains considerable question about the value of psychoanalytic methods in treating emotionally disturbed patients, but even those who criticize psychoanalysis as a form of psychotherapy are influenced by Freud's basic notions about personality and its formation. His theories will be discussed in detail in Chapter 10, and the methods of psychoanalysis will be discussed in Chapter 13.

The New Vistas of Psychobiology

Among psychologists today are a growing number whose emphasis is on studying how various facets of behavior are associated with events taking place in the body. You will be reading of their work throughout the book—for example, in studies of the psychological functions of various areas of the brain (Chapter 2), the influence of brain chemistry on emotions and drives (Chapter 9), the bodily changes associated with stress (Chapter 11), the use of drugs to alleviate anxiety and depression (Chapter 13), the role of the genes we inherit in shaping human development (Chapter 14), and how hormonal changes can affect the adjustment of adolescents (Chapter 15).

In one sense, all of behavior is rooted in some manner in the activity of the brain and nervous system, and, as you will read later on, new techniques allow us now to actually visualize what electrical and chemical changes the brain undergoes when we perceive an object, think, remember, or experience a hallucination. Indeed advances in brain research have led some scientists to conclude that everything we experience and do will one day be explained by the operations of the brain. Even psychologists have wondered if "psychology is in danger of losing its status as an independent body of knowledge" (Peele, 1981).

Most scientists, biologists as well as psychologists, think not. For one thing, as neuropsychologist Elliot Valenstein has pointed out, the workings of the brain are so complex as to defy complete understanding and will always remain something of a mystery. More important, no matter how complete our understanding of the brain, its structures and circuits do not work independently as if in a vacuum. The brain works instead as an instrument through which behavior is altered by experience. Neuropsychologist Roger Sperry, when he received the Nobel Prize for his research on the brain (Chapter 2), emphasized this point. We cannot depend on the brain to tell us everything about the operation of the conscious mind (Sperry, 1982).

THREE MAJOR ISSUES IN MODERN PSYCHOLOGY

As even a sketchy summary of psychology's history makes clear, the science has moved in many directions. Its practitioners have had many different interests, have conducted their studies in different ways, and have reached different conclusions. Each of psychology's forebears has in one way or another advanced our knowledge of human behavior and mental processes.

Subsequent chapters of this book will be concerned mostly with specific facts that psychologists have discovered about human behavior—from the role of brain cells to social interactions. Before beginning this kind of detailed discussion, however, it is useful to examine some of the major issues to which modern psychology is addressing itself. By and large, these issues go to the very core of human experience. Since they cut so deep, they are difficult to study or resolve. On none of them are all the facts yet in, and on many of them there is still widespread disagreement. But these are the big issues to which psychology, in the broadest sense, is now dedicated.

Biological Nature or Psychological Nurture?

While not entirely new by any means, a major issue of continuing concern to psychology is the relative impact of two forces—inborn biological factors and life experiences—on human personality and behavior.

Some believe that it is possible to explain much of our behavior by understanding the structure and growth of our brain, the function of our glands, and other elements of our physical constitution—all of them largely inherited characteristics. And indeed it is obvious that the inherited structure of the human body and brain is responsible for many aspects of our behavior. It enables us, unlike lower animals, to speak a rich language that we use to communicate with one another. It gives us a superior skill at most forms of information processing. On the other hand, it also sets limits. Because of the way our brain operates, with its messages traveling at only a tiny fraction of the speed of electricity, we cannot possibly make complex mathematical calculations as fast as a computer. Because of the way our nervous systems and glands cooperate, we cannot possibly live our lives without experiencing emotions—which, though they often exhilarate us, may also plunge us into fear or despair and make us incapable of performing with the computer's cold accuracy. Our sense organs, which are part of the nervous system, are incapable of detecting certain kinds of light waves that are visible even to a bee or high-pitched sounds that are clearly audible to a dog. The structure of our bodies makes it impossible for us to live underwater like a fish or fly like a bird. Heredity has provided us with our own kind of physical equipment, and we have to live our lives within its bounds.

Granted that our biological nature has a continuing effect on our personality and behavior, what about the role of life experiences? How do they affect this raw material and shape our behavior into its eventual form? Put another way, what is the impact of our environment, the sum total of all the varying influences exerted from the moment of birth by our families, by society as a whole, and by the physical circumstances of our lives?

The relative importance of inherited biological characteristics and experiences has long been a subject of considerable debate. William James, for example, believed that much of our behavior is regulated to a great extent by powerful human instincts present at birth—including pugnacity, rivalry, sociability, shyness, curiosity, acquisitiveness, and love. Watson, on the other hand, believed the newborn child can be turned into almost any kind of adult through conditioned reflexes established by the environment. The debate is often called the *nature-nurture* controversy. It still continues—though it has been modified greatly by modern findings in *behavior genetics*, the study of the role of inherited traits in shaping behavior.

Today we know that it is not possible to treat our biological nature and life experiences as separate, independent forces. In order to become a great basketball star, for example, a child would typically have to inherit a combination of height, speed, and endurance. But without exposure to the sport and opportunity to practice, even the best endowed child would never become skilled at this activity. Thus it is not possible, when looking at a basketball hero, to say how much of his ability is due to what he inherited and how much to his environmental opportunities. As you will see in many other examples throughout the book—whether it is in the development of language, the display of intelligence, or the onset of abnormal behavior—the two forces operate in tandem to give each of us our unique identity.

Continuity or Change?

No one would argue with the fact that you are quite different today from the human being you were at birth, or the person you will be in the closing years of your life. But how different? Is human development marked by continuity—that is, a series of gradual and cumulative changes, with the echoes of each stage of life embedded in the later ones? Or are there significant *dis*continuities—that is, changes so dramatic that some characteristics vanish and new ones emerge?

It is possible to find examples of both stability and change in studying behavior, and human development appears to be a mix of both themes. Psychologists who study memory claim that once a memory is formed, it can never be entirely lost, and studies of mentally ill individuals often suggest that early trauma, such as abuse in childhood, can leave profound effects in adult life. But on the other hand, there is evidence that the brain undergoes marked changes over time, with some circuits phasing out and new ones added—dramatically changing our repertoire of behaviors. And there is evidence that environmental changes and new experiences—a different job, marriage, a sudden

How much of what we become is inherited and how much is due to environmental influences?

Three Major Issues in Modern Psychology

trauma—can dramatically shift the course of development for good or ill. Psychology must study both continuity and change. It must strive to understand to what extent we become just different versions of our earlier selves, and to what degree we can become "a different person," difficult to recognize from our earlier identity.

Context: Does Who You Are Depend on Where You Are?

For many decades, psychology was chiefly interested in the individual. The science was content to separate the individual person from others, much like a zoologist cutting one elephant out of the herd for measurement and labeling, and to study this person's behavior as it appeared in the laboratory or in test results. Any characteristic that could be observed was generally assumed to represent a customary and consistent pattern of behavior. A person found to be helpful and generous would be helpful and generous in general under any circumstances. An aggressive person would always tend to be aggressive, an anxious person always anxiety prone, an achievement-oriented person always focused on achievement.

It is now clear, however, that human behavior is not as consistent as was once believed. Often a person's actions depend on the context—that is, on the particular situation in which the behavior occurs. A person may be generous at home but selfish at work, aggressive with a spouse but submissive with friends, anxious in an unfamiliar place but calm and relaxed in familiar surroundings. A major issue in psychology, therefore, is to understand more fully how human behavior depends on where we are—and particularly on the people around us.

The manner in which the situation and the people in it can influence behavior is the primary concern of the specialists in social psychology, which is the subject of Chapter 16. But all branches of psychology have been greatly influenced by the rise of this important issue. More and more it appears that we cannot always fully understand individuals by

This coach might behave quite differently off the basketball court.

studying them in isolation. The human personality and human behavior, far from being fixed and unchanging, seem to be in constant flux as the result of interaction between the individual and the environment—the situation of the moment, the number of people found in the situation, and the kinds of people these other people in the situation happen to be.

ETHICAL STANDARDS OF PSYCHOLOGISTS

In studying the effects of special tutoring on disadvantaged children, a psychologist may probe for details of each child's family life and then, in an experiment, provide an enriched teaching program to half the children while denying it to the others. In analyzing the dynamics of family communication, a psychologist may contrive a situation to generate family conflict and then record the interactions among husband, wife, and child. In studying the effects of sleep deprivation on the brain, a team of psychologists may deprive monkeys of sleep to the point of total collapse. As these three examples suggest—and you can think of many more—there are occasions when the work of psychologists raises moral dilemmas.

The American Psychological Association (APA) has devoted considerable effort to develop a code of ethics for guiding its members in resolving ethical dilemmas they might encounter in the course of their work. In pursuing their goals of studying behavior and the factors that influence behavior, psychologists must "make every effort to protect the welfare of those who seek their services and of the research participants that may be the subjects of study" (American Psychological Association, 1981). The APA is prepared to expel any member who clearly violates the ethical guidelines, a few of which are discussed here.

Protecting the Confidentiality and Rights of Human Subjects

In gathering information from others, psychologists are required to protect its *confidentiality*. Whether the information is gained during testing, counseling or therapy sessions, in the course of an attitude survey, or as part of an experiment on learning with college students doesn't matter. Whatever the context, to violate the confidentiality of the information provided by the psychologist's clients or subjects would be a breach of ethical principles.

An even broader principle requires that psychologists protect the *rights* of subjects participating in psychological research. No matter how sincere the psychologist's research aims, this principle is intended to ensure that psychologists must consider both the benefits to society and the dignity and welfare of the research subjects themselves. A specific requirement obliges psychologists to try to avoid concealing the aims of an experiment or deceiving subjects, if at all possible, in the course of conducting a study.

Of course, some methods of studying behavior seem clearly unacceptable. For example, no psychologist would consider urging a brain operation just for the sake of studying its effects. But in other cases, the line is more difficult to draw. When, for example, are psychologists justified in deceiving their subjects—such as by telling them they are administering electric shocks to another person, when in fact the other person is a confederate who is only pretending to be shocked? There are, of course, many borderline cases that psychologists can decide only by carefully weighing the possible harm to their subjects against the value to humanity of the knowledge they may discover. In any case, psychologists are required to obtain the consent of potential participants in research studies, and to explain the nature and purposes of the research in advance—or, if necessary, afterward.

Care in the Use of Animals for Research

Throughout this book, you will be reading about research with animals that is intended to shed light on various aspects of human behavior—on the operations of the brain, the basic elements of learning and memory, the nature of emotions and drives, the effects of stress on health, the influences of genes and environment on development, and much more. About 7 percent of psychological studies use animals as subjects (Miller, 1985a). During the past few years, there has been a great deal of discussion concerning the use of animals in behavioral research. Indeed various animal rights organizations have charged the field of psychology with outright abuse and even torture of monkeys, rats, and other animals.

Such charges have proved groundless (Coile and Miller, 1984) and, moreover, the contributions made through animal research are impressive—among them understanding and alleviating the effects of stress and pain; discovery and testing of drugs to help the mentally ill; new knowledge about the mechanisms of alcohol and drug addiction; and insights into the care and protection of the human fetus (Miller, 1985a). Such advances are possible because psychologists can vary the environments and experiences of animals in ways that would be out of the question for human subjects. Nevertheless, the APA requires that its members take special care in the use of animals in psychological research, avoiding needless harm and exploitation. Psychologists must proceed with a sure sense of ethical behavior and the humane treatment of all forms of life.

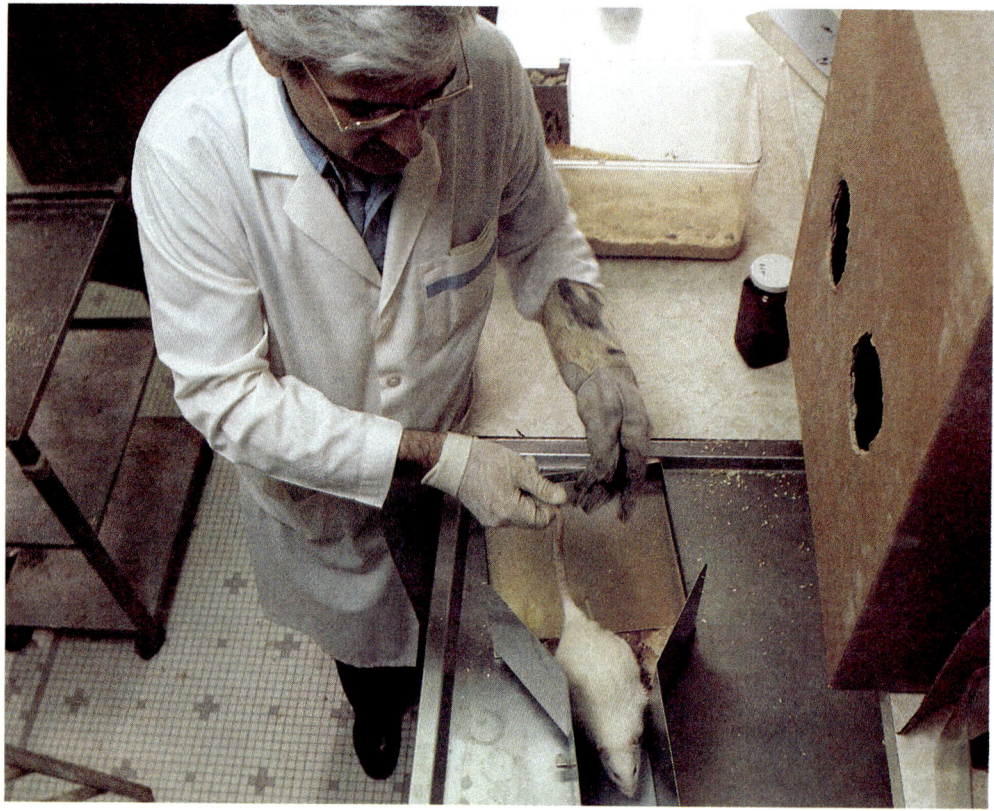

Psychological research often requires animal subjects—but they must be treated humanely.

SUMMARY

Psychology's goals and interests

1. Psychology is *the systematic study of behavior and the factors that influence behavior.*
2. The goals of psychology are *to understand behavior* and *to predict behavior.*
3. Many psychologists are concerned only with *basic science,* or knowledge for the sake of knowledge. Others are chiefly interested in *applied science,* or the use of psychological findings to help society carry on its everyday tasks, tackle its problems, and improve the quality of life.
4. Fields of applied psychology include:
    a. *School psychology,* which tests pupils, analyzes learning problems, and evaluates teaching methods.
    b. *Industrial psychology,* which includes the selection and training of employees and the study of workers' morale and cooperation.
    c. *Environmental psychology,* which deals with ecological problems like pollution and overcrowding.
    d. *Community psychology,* which deals with the social environment and how it could better serve human needs.
    e. *Health psychology,* which deals with the ways we can improve our health by altering our behavior.
    f. *Clinical psychology,* which helps diagnose deep-seated psychological problems and treat such problems through *psychotherapy.*
    g. *Counseling psychology,* which involves helping those with milder problems of social and emotional adjustment—such as school difficulties, choice of vocation, or marriage conflicts.

How psychologists study human behavior

5. The methods used by psychology to study behavior include *naturalistic observation, participant observation, interviews* and *case histories, questionnaires, tests* and *measurements,* and *experiments.*
6. The results of tests and measurements are analyzed through mathematical techniques called *psychological statistics.*
7. Psychological statistics have greatly enhanced our knowledge of *individual differences* by showing that almost all physical traits (like height) and psychological characteristics (like intelligence) follow the *normal curve of distribution*—with most measurements clustering around the average and only a few falling at the lowest or highest extremes.
8. *Correlation* is a statistical tool used to determine how much relationship, if any, exists between two different measurements—such as the IQs of parents and the IQs of their children.

The ultimate method: experimentation

9. The *experimental method,* which is the science's most powerful tool, is an attempt to discover cause and effect through a rigidly controlled examination of whether behavior changes when conditions change.

10. The experimenter controls the *independent variable*, which is set up independently of anything the subject does or does not do, and then studies the *dependent variable*, which is a change in the subject's behavior resulting from a change in the independent variable.

11. Experiments often use both an *experimental group*, whose behavior is studied under new conditions, and a *control group*, who are not placed under the new conditions.

12. In a *single-blind* experiment, the subjects do not know whether they belong to the experimental group or the control group. In a *double-blind* experiment, neither the subjects nor the experimenter knows.

Psychology yesterday, today, and tomorrow

13. Psychology was founded in 1879 when the first laboratory was opened by Wilhelm Wundt at a German university. The early psychologists, including the American William James, were chiefly interested in human consciousness, which they studied through *introspection*, looking inward at mental processes.

14. The school of *behaviorism*, a rebellion against introspective studies, was founded by John Watson, who declared that mental processes cannot be seen or measured and therefore cannot be studied scientifically. Watson believed that psychologists should study what people do, not what they think.

15. Watson held that human behavior is a series of actions in which a *stimulus*—that is, an event in the environment—produces a *response*—that is, an observable muscular movement or some physiological reaction, such as increased heart rate or glandular secretion, that can also be observed and measured with the proper instruments. He believed that through establishment of *conditioned reflexes*, a type of learning, almost any kind of stimulus could be made to produce almost any kind of response.

16. B. F. Skinner, who succeeded Watson as leader of the behaviorist school, agrees that human beings are creatures of their environment whose behavior depends on the kinds of learning to which they have been subjected—and who are therefore not to blame for their failures or deserving of credit for their achievements.

17. *Gestalt psychology*, which takes its name from a German word meaning "pattern" or "configuration," maintained that events must be considered as a whole in studying any psychological phenomenon—from a perceptual process to personality—because "the whole is greater than the sum of its parts." The Gestalt school also stressed the entire situation, or context, in which the "whole" is found.

18. Many of the Gestalt ideas survive in today's trend toward *cognitive psychology*, which is interested in all the ways we learn about our environment, store the knowledge in memory, and use it to think and act intelligently in new situations. These various forms of mental activity are often called *information processing*.

19. A core idea in cognitive psychology is that we build *mental models of reality* from information about the world provided by our sense organs, which we can then examine for meanings and guidance in behavior.

20. Today's *humanistic psychology* also stems in part from the Gestalt school. The humanists believe we are unique organisms because we have values and goals and seek to express ourselves, grow, fulfill ourselves, and find peace and happiness.

21. The opposite of humanistic psychology is Sigmund Freud's *psychoanalysis*, which is based on the idea that behavior is often influenced by *unconscious processes*, especially motives of which we are unaware.

Three major issues in modern psychology

22. A growing number of psychologists are studying how various facets of behavior are associated with events that take place in the body.

23. There is a continuing debate, often called the *nature-nurture* controversy, over the relative importance of heredity and environment in establishing behavior.

24. The nature-nurture controversy has been modified greatly by modern findings in *behavior genetics*, the study of the role of inherited traits in shaping behavior.

25. Human development is a mix of both continuities (a series of gradual and cumulative changes) and discontinuities (dramatic changes that cause some characteristics to vanish and new ones to appear).

26. Human behavior is not as consistent as was once believed; often a person's actions depend on the context in which the behavior occurs.

Ethical standards of psychologists

27. A code of ethics developed by the American Psychological Association requires its members to protect the *confidentiality* and *rights* of individuals participating in psychological research.

28. The American Psychological Association also requires that its members take special care in the use of animals in psychological research, avoiding needless harm and exploitation.

IMPORTANT TERMS

applied science
basic science
behavior genetics
behaviorism
case history
clinical psychology
cognitive psychology
community psychology
conditioned reflexes
confidentiality
control group
correlation
counseling psychology
dependent variable
double-blind
environment
environmental psychology
experiment
experimental group
experimental psychology
Gestalt psychology
health psychology
heredity

humanistic psychology
hysterical conversion
independent variable
individual differences
industrial psychology
information processing
interviews
introspection
measurements
mental models of reality
naturalistic observation
nature-nurture
normal curve of distribution
participant observation
personality psychology
physiological psychology
psychoanalysis
psychological statistics
psychotherapy
public opinion survey
questionnaire
response
rights of subjects

school psychology
single-blind
social psychology

stimulus
tests
unconscious processes

RECOMMENDED READINGS

Christensen, L. B. *Experimental methodology*, 2d ed. Boston: Allyn & Bacon, 1980.

Cohen, D. *The power of psychology and the power of psychologists.* New York: Croom Helm, 1987.

Hall, C. S., and Lindzey, G. *Theories of personality*, 3d ed. New York: Wiley, 1978.

Hearnshaw, L. S. *The shaping of modern psychology: an historical introduction.* New York: Routledge & Kegan Paul, 1987.

Meyers, L. S., and Grossen, N. E. *Behavioral research: theory, procedure, and design*, 2d ed. San Francisco: Freeman, 1978.

Pryzwansky, R. N., and Wendt, R. W. *Psychology as a profession: foundations of practice.* New York: Pergamon Press, 1987.

Rogers, C. *Freedom to learn: a view of what education might become.* Columbus, Ohio: Merrill, 1969.

Saccuzzo, D. P. *Psychology: from research to applications.* Boston: Allyn and Bacon, 1987.

Watson, R. I. *The great psychologists: from Aristotle to Freud.* Philadelphia: Lippincott, 1978.

Wertheimer, M. A. *A brief history of psychology.* New York: Holt, Rinehart & Winston, 1979.

Woods, P. J. *The psychology major: training and employment strategies.* Washington, D.C.: American Psychological Association, 1979.

PART 2

BIOLOGICAL BASES OF BEHAVIOR

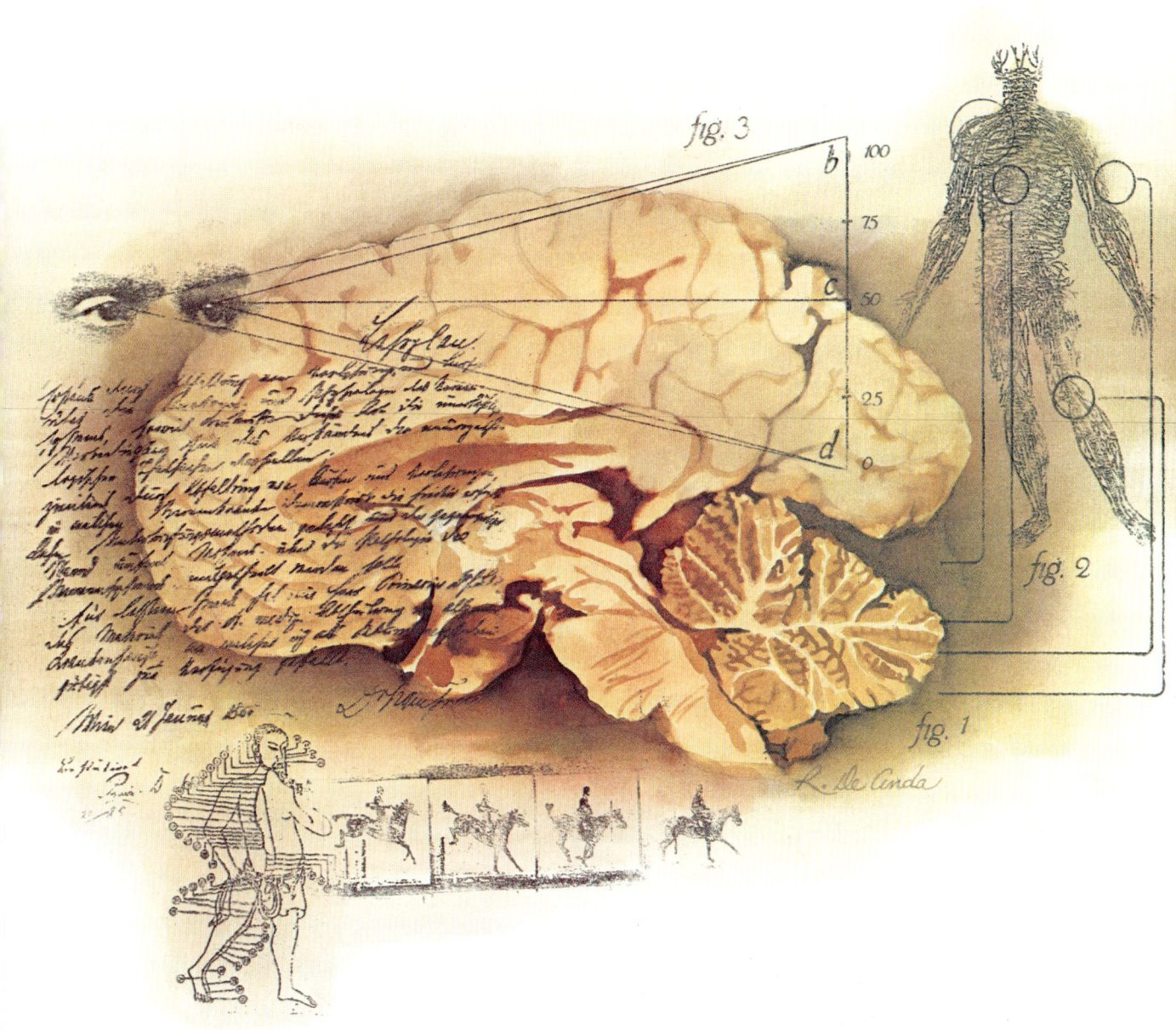

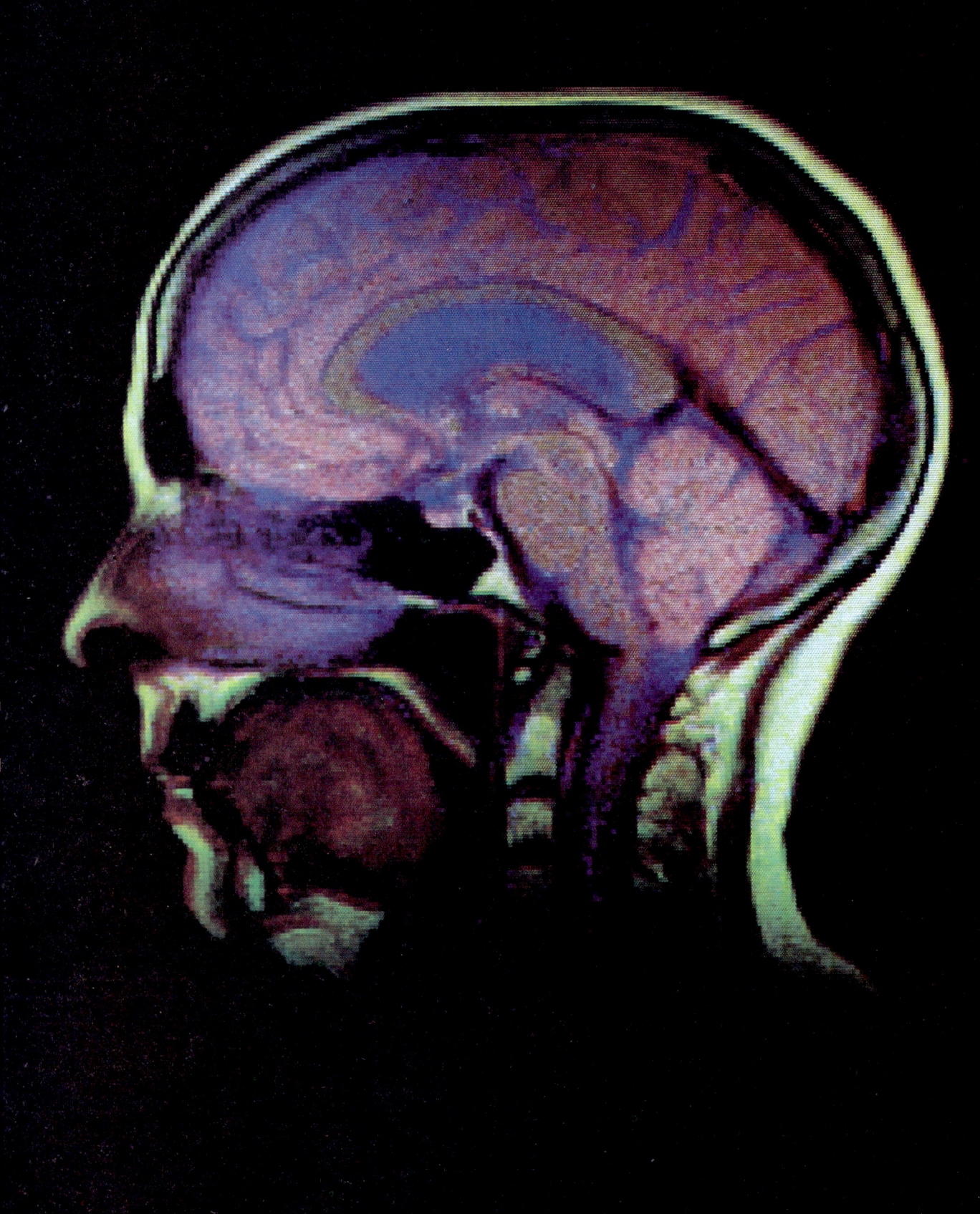

CHAPTER

2

BRAIN, BODY, AND BEHAVIOR

THE PRIVILEGED BRAIN AND ITS POWERFUL CONNECTIONS — 42

Our thinking cap: the cerebral cortex
The team of billions: the brain's nerve cells and what they do
The nervous system—linking brain, body, and behavior

THE BRAIN IN ACTION: 1. SENSING THE WORLD AND RESPONDING TO IT — 46

Taking in and interpreting what goes on around us
Processing and relaying sensory information
Getting the body to move
Fine movements and the miracle of coordination and balance

THE BRAIN IN ACTION: 2. THINKING, PLANNING, AND REMEMBERING — 52

Memory's storehouse
Intellectual development and brain growth
Left brain and right brain
Splitting the two brain halves
How specialized is each of the two brain hemispheres?

THE BRAIN IN ACTION: 3. PRODUCING EMOTIONS AND KEEPING OUR BODIES IN TUNE — 57

Generating passions and feelings
Staying alive and physiologically balanced
The brain's able assistant: the autonomic nervous system

THE BRAIN'S COMMUNICATIONS NETWORK — 64

The neuron's communications equipment: "receivers" and "senders"
How neurons send their messages to one another
Getting the message: to fire or not to fire
How neurons give their all—or nothing at all
The chemical brain
The down side of chemicals—natural and manufactured
Turning electricity and chemistry into meanings and feelings

SUMMARY — 73

IMPORTANT TERMS — 76

RECOMMENDED READINGS — 76

PSYCHOLOGY IN EVERYDAY LIFE

Are men's and women's brains different? — 58
Health psychology: the interplay between our mental and physical well-being — 65
Brain grafts: potential source of healing — 71

As you read this page, you are moving your eyes, holding and feeling this book, balancing your body, and perhaps hearing the sounds of music or conversation nearby. You are also breathing, digesting, and possibly scratching your head. All the while you are absorbing, processing, reacting to, and somehow storing the information contained on the page. None of this everyday miracle could happen without the marvelously coordinated activity of your brain.

Indeed all the human capacities you will read about in this book—to gather information, learn and remember, act intelligently, move about, develop skills, feel emotions, cope with stress, relate to others—are managed within the brain. Think of all the things you did in the last 24 hours. Whatever you did—sleep, dream, wake up, shower, get dressed, drive your car, play tennis, study, get angry, make love—you accomplished through the powers of your brain.

The marvelous instrument that reigns over your behavior hardly looks equal to the task. It perches on top of your spine, beneath your skull—three pounds of grayish-pink, soft, strangely wrinkled tissue the size of a grapefruit. How can this small mass of matter manage all its tasks?

The energy to operate the brain comes from the activity of billions of nerve cells that are in constant communication with each other and with their counterparts throughout the body. The result is a network of brain-and-body systems that is surely one of the great miracles of nature. Knowledge of how these systems work—and exactly what they accomplish—is essential to an understanding of the entire field of psychology.

THE PRIVILEGED BRAIN AND ITS POWERFUL CONNECTIONS

For good reason, the brain has been described as "a very privileged organ" (Calne, 1981). Nature has devised ways to protect it from harm and to give it preferential treatment over every other organ of the body. The brain is encased in the skull's thick bone, and it is surrounded by a fluid that helps cushion it from injury in case of sudden impact. Although it makes up only 2 percent or less of the average person's total weight, it uses 20 percent of the body's total oxygen supply. When the body is deprived of food, it is the first to get its share of whatever nutrients are coursing through the blood. Moreover, a "blood-brain barrier" keeps many potentially harmful substances in the blood from ever entering the brain.

The brain has won its supreme status for good reason. With its vast and complex responsibilities, injury to it—for example, in an auto accident or from a gunshot wound—can critically affect vital psychological and physical functions. The key to the brain's mastery is its powerful connections with other parts of the body. Without them the brain would be helpless to direct and manage our behavior.

Our Thinking Cap: The Cerebral Cortex

If the top of a person's head were transparent and you looked down from above, you would see the brain as shown in Figure 2-1: a mass of gray tissue so rich in blood vessels that it takes on a pinkish cast. It resembles a walnut, but it is soft and pulsing with life. This is the part of the brain that is chiefly responsible for remembering, thinking, and planning—the activities that make you more intelligent than other animals. It is called the cerebral cortex, and, as shown in Figure 2-2, nature has made it larger in proportion to body size in human beings than in most other species. As can be seen in Figure 2-3, it is really too large to fit comfortably into the human head. But it has been ingeniously compressed

Figure 2-1 A topside view of the brain

The photograph shows the human brain as seen from above, displaying the elaborate folds and creases described in the text. Note especially the vertical line, resembling a narrow ditch, running down the middle from the top of the photo (which is the front of the brain) to the bottom. This is a deep fissure that divides this top part of the brain into two separate halves, or **hemispheres,** *as discussed in the text.*

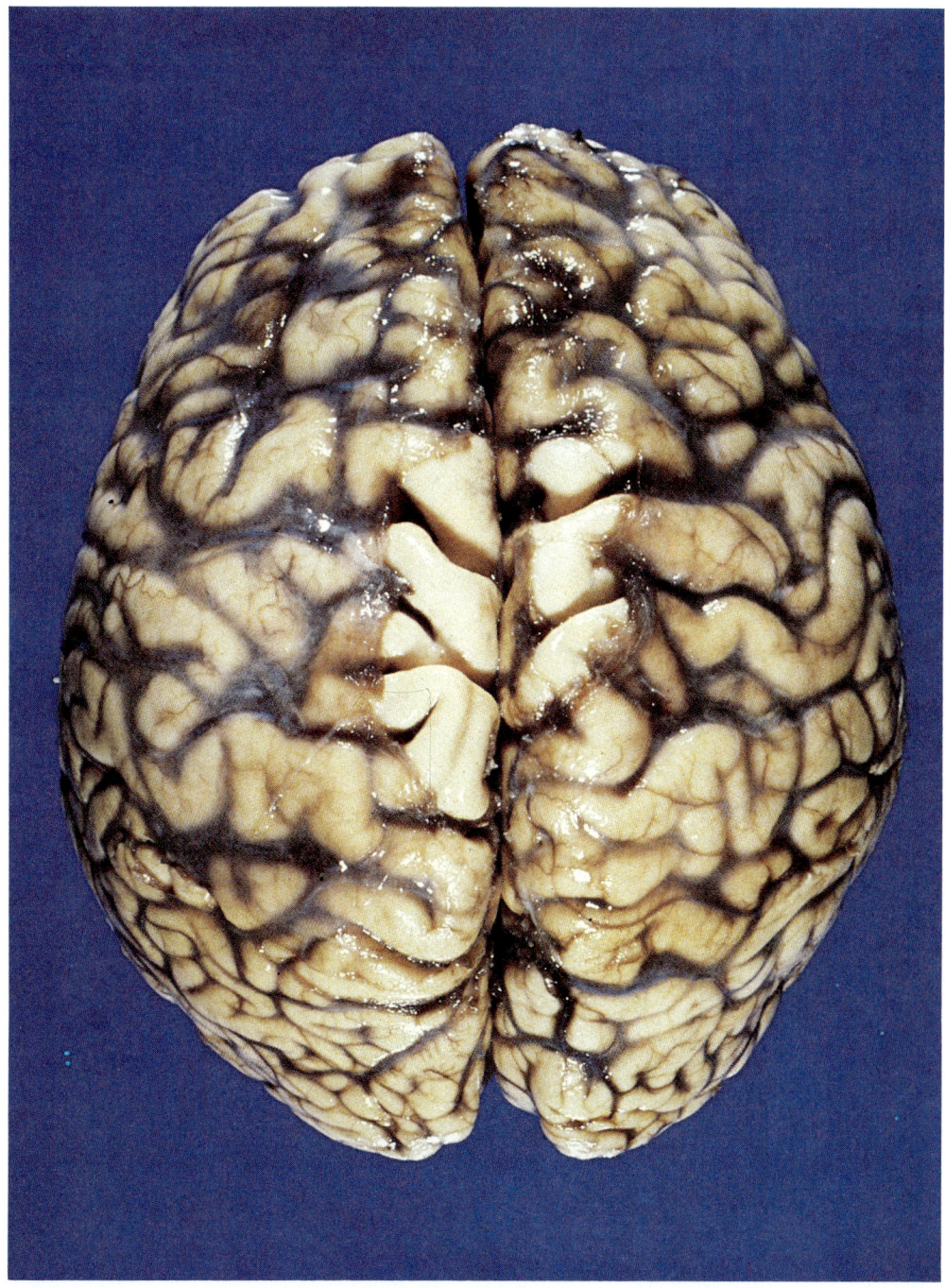

Figure 2-2 The evolution of the human brain

The size of the brain increases dramatically as we go up the evolutionary ladder—from fish to mammals.

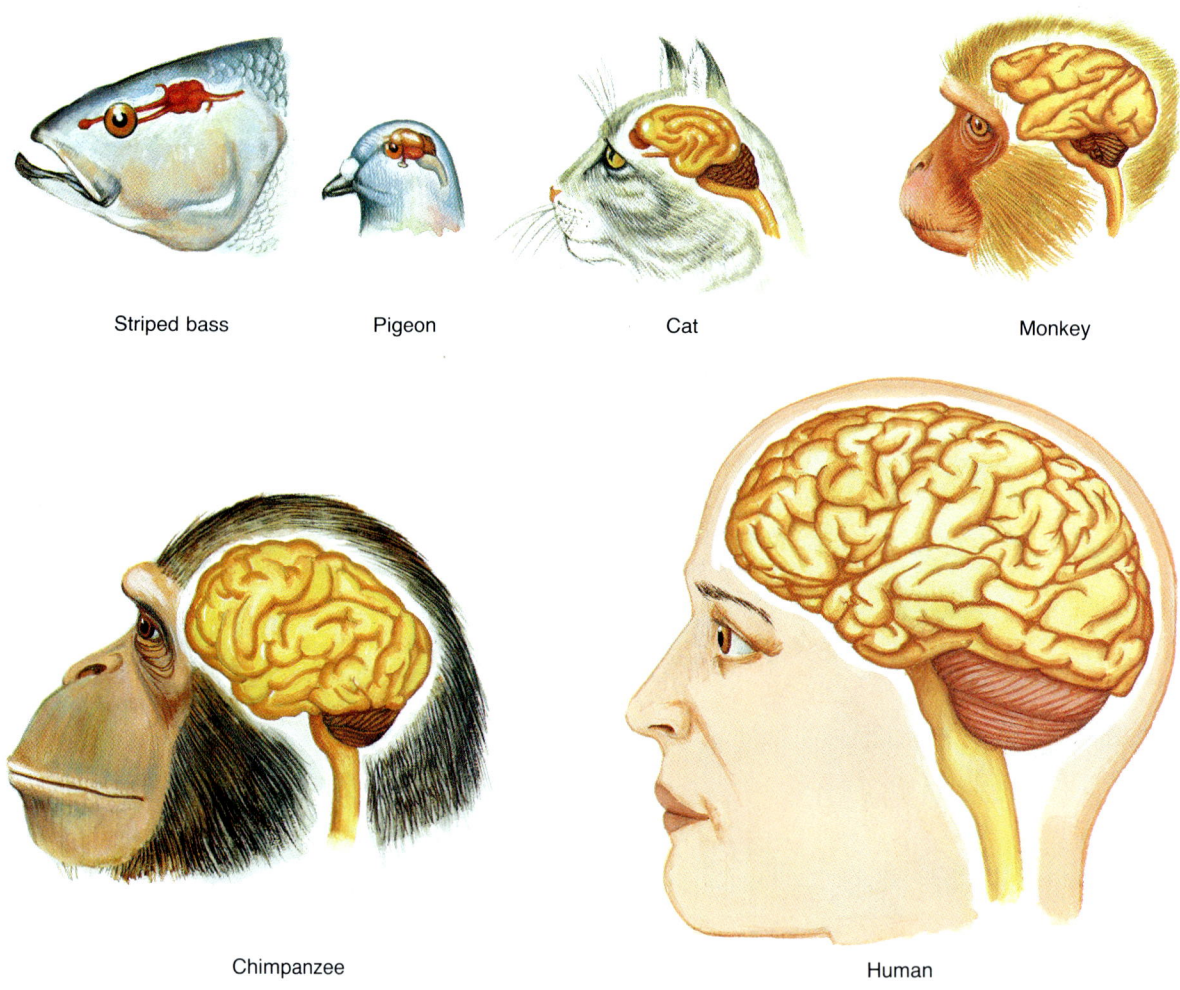

Striped bass   Pigeon   Cat   Monkey

Chimpanzee   Human

to fit into the skull by the intricate foldings and refoldings apparent in Figure 2-1. What you see in the photograph is actually only about a third of the cerebral cortex. All the rest is hidden in the creases.

The cortex is actually the surface, about one-eighth of an inch (3 mm.) thick, of the human brain's largest single structure, the *cerebrum*, which lies on top of all the other parts of the brain. As is apparent in Figure 2-1, the cerebrum is split down the middle into a left half, or *left hemisphere*, and a right half, or *right hemisphere*.

Although the two hemispheres look like mirror images, they differ slightly in form and are often engaged in different activities—almost as if we have two brains doing our thinking. This arrangement has provoked a number of fascinating questions that will be discussed later.

Beneath the cerebrum, and totally hidden by its bulk when the brain is viewed from above, lie a number of other structures with their own special roles to play in our behavior.

Figure 2-3 The surprising size of the brain's cerebral cortex

If it were laid flat, its many folds "ironed out," the cortex would measure about 1.5 square feet (.14 square meters) in area (Ornstein and Thompson, 1984).

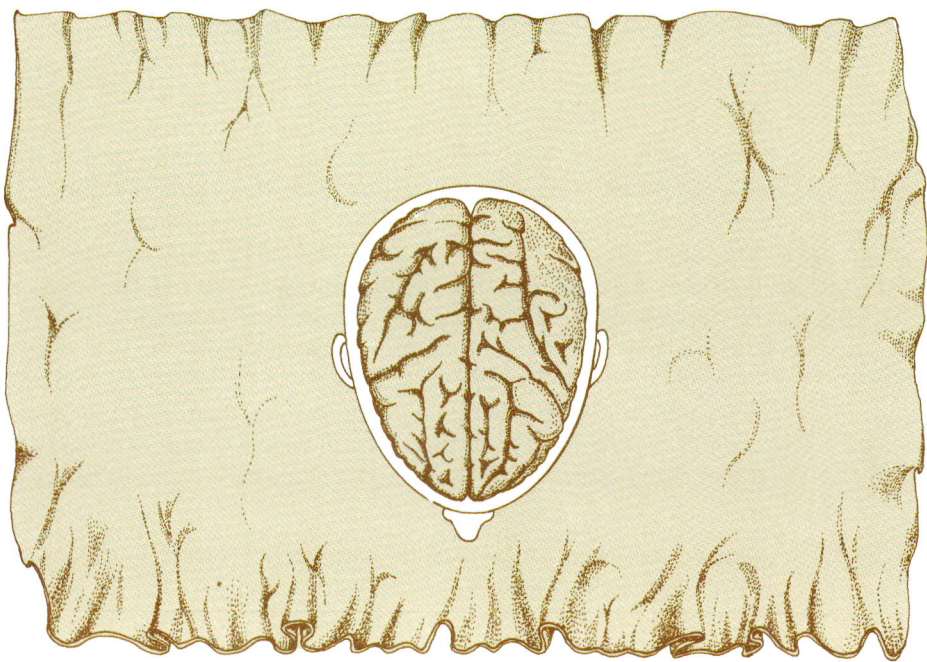

We share with other forms of animal life a number of these structures—those, for example, that generate our emotions and maintain our basic life functions. But it is the cerebrum and its cortex, comprising 80 percent of the human brain, that make us special. Without them, we humans are "almost a vegetable, speechless, sightless, senseless" (Hubel and Wiesel, 1979).

The Team of Billions: The Brain's Nerve Cells and What They Do

The brain contains a staggeringly large number of separate *neurons,* or nerve cells. Estimated to be between 50 and 200 billion, they are woven into an intricate tapestry of connections and interconnections. Each of these fiberlike cells may receive messages from thousands of other neurons, process these messages in various ways, then pass its own messages along to thousands more. The total number of possible connections is so great that it totally defies the imagination. One estimate places it at an unthinkable 50 trillion (Rosenzweig and Lieman, 1982).

No two neurons are precisely identical in form (Stevens, 1979)—and one reason the brain is so versatile is that the cells are also of many different types, with their own specialized functions. Depending on how finely the differentiations are made, there are at least 100 types and perhaps as many as 500 (Hubel, 1978), far more cell types than other organs of the body possess.

The primary job of most brain cells is transmitting messages. Others, however, perform different tasks. The brain, for example, has some cells that operate very much like

The Privileged Brain and Its Powerful Connections

sense organs—serving as its "eyes" and "ears" to observe changes in the bloodstream and thus detect when the body needs food or water. Others are sensitive to changes in the body's internal temperature. The brain also has neurons that operate like miniature glands, producing complicated chemicals called *hormones* (named after the Greek word meaning "activators" or "exciters"). These hormones are released into the bloodstream and travel through the body, stimulating many kinds of physical activity.

The Nervous System—Linking Brain, Body, and Behavior

The neurons of the brain can affect our behavior only because there are links between them and other parts of the body. These links are forged by the rest of the human nervous system, composed of neurons of various kinds that connect with the brain. The neuron fibers of the nervous system, called *axons*, extend throughout the body as shown in Figure 2-4. The axons that lie outside the brain and *spinal cord* comprise the *peripheral nervous system*, a network that extends to the fingertips and feet. All the neurons of the peripheral nervous system eventually connect to the *central nervous system*—made up of the spinal cord, which is, in part, a sort of master cable to the brain, and the brain itself.

Neurons differ in length as well as kind. Some, especially in the brain, are only the tiniest fraction of an inch in length. Others are more than three feet (about one meter) long. For example, the neurons that enable you to wiggle your toes extend all the way from the lower part of the spinal cord to the muscles of the toes. Neurons can be grouped into three classes:

1. *Afferent neurons* are neurons of the senses. The word afferent is derived from the Latin word *ad*, which means "to" or "toward," and *ferre*, which means "to bear" or "to carry." The afferent neurons of the peripheral nervous system carry messages from our eyes, ears, and other sense organs toward the central nervous system. When they reach the brain, they are translated into our experiences of vision, hearing, touch, taste, and smell.

2. *Efferent neurons* carry messages from the central nervous system in an outward direction—ordering muscles to contract and directing the activity of the body's organs and glands.

3. *Connecting neurons*, which are the most numerous, are communications neurons that carry messages between other neurons. They are stimulated only by another neuron. They do not end in muscle or gland tissue but only at junctions with other neurons, which they either stimulate or inhibit from sending their own messages. Most of these connecting neurons, though not all, are found in the brain and spinal cord.

Every moment of our lives, day and night, afferent neurons carry information to the brain, and efferent neurons dispatch the brain's decisions and directions. As the center of this ceaseless activity of the nervous system, the brain performs all the essential and wondrous functions that will be discussed in this chapter: to take in and respond to what is going on in the outside world, to manage our intellectual operations, and to regulate our emotions and ensure our very survival.

THE BRAIN IN ACTION: 1. SENSING THE WORLD AND RESPONDING TO IT

You are driving down the street, and a child darts into the path of your car. In a twinkling, the muscles of your right leg tense and your foot hits the brake, bringing

Figure 2-4 The human nervous system

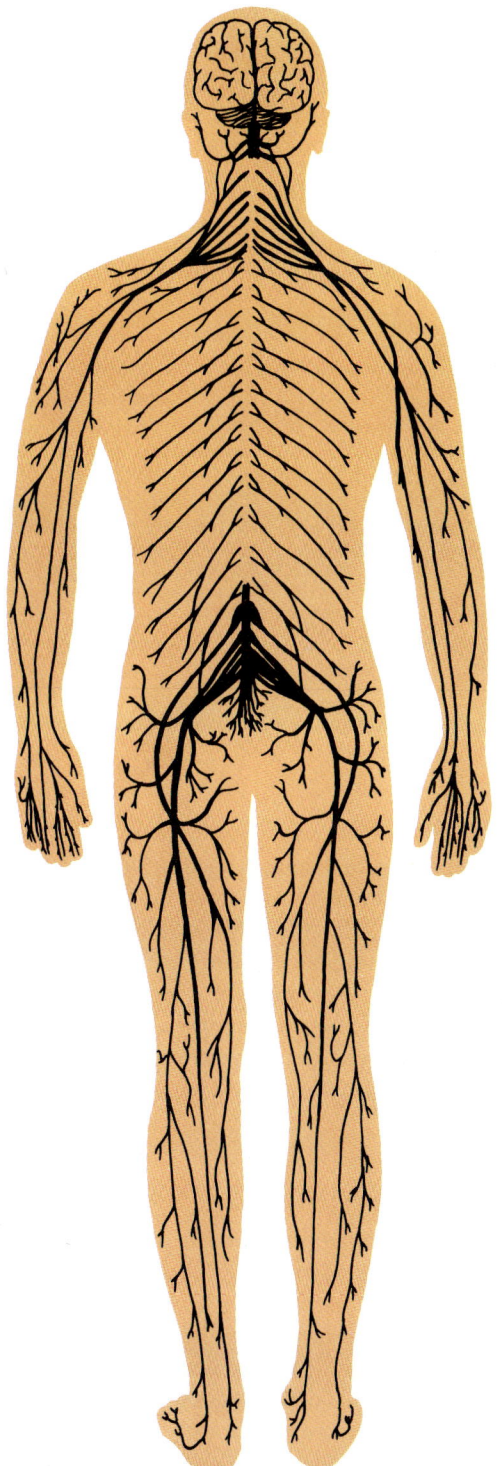

Like the tributaries that form a river, individual neuron fibers at all the far reaches of the body join together to form small nerves, which is the name for bundles of neuron fibers. The small nerves join with others to form larger nerves, at last becoming the very large ones that join with the central nervous system—the brain and the spinal cord. Twelve cranial nerves, *in pairs going to the left and right sides of the head, connect directly with the brain. There are also 31 pairs of large spinal nerves, connected with the spinal cord at the spaces between the bones of the spine.*

The driver's abilities to see the child, realize what might happen, and slam on the brakes—all in an instant—depend on the workings of the brain.

your car safely to a stop. Or you are in bed sound asleep. Suddenly there are shouts of "Fire!" You awake with a start, jump out of bed, run down the hall, pick up your child, and head out of the house to safety.

Though we tend to take our behavior in such situations for granted, it is actually quite remarkable. Such acts require the teamwork of millions of neurons, receiving and sending messages with blinding speed. Our capacities to get information from the world, process that information, and respond to it all depend on the intricate functioning of the brain—both the cerebral cortex and the related structures lying below it, as well as the brain's links to the peripheral nervous system.

Taking in and Interpreting What Goes on around Us

Most of the information picked up by our sense organs is eventually transmitted, by way of the brain's many pathways, to the cerebral cortex. As shown in Figure 2-5, the cortex has specialized areas that receive the sensory messages for vision and hearing. It also contains a long strip, known as the *somatosensory cortex*, that receives messages for touch from the feet (at the top) to the head (at the bottom). In these specialized areas, the messages are analyzed and interpreted. The brain decides which messages are important and what they mean. The sounds of speech—which are of particular importance because language plays such a large role in human behavior—have an area of their own especially concerned with understanding the meaning of words and sentences.

Figure 2-5 Some areas of the cerebral cortex with special functions

On this drawing of the cerebral cortex as it would be seen from the left side of the body, the colored portions represent areas that are known to perform some of the special jobs described in the text (Geschwind, N. The specialization of the brain. Scientific American, *1979, 186).*

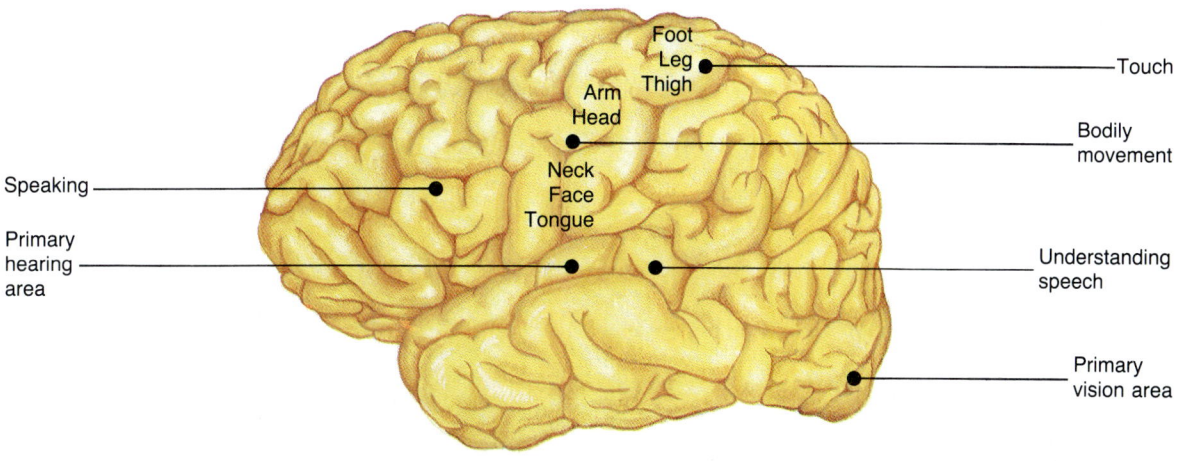

The importance of the cerebral cortex in registering and processing sensory information becomes dramatically clear in cases of harm to any of these portions of the brain (Williams, 1979). Depending on the location and extent of injury to the back part of the cortex responsible for vision, for example, an individual might suffer varying degrees of blindness, even though the eye and its own muscles and nerves remain perfectly intact. If the area for understanding speech is injured, an individual might no longer be able to interpret what is being said, even though all parts of the ear are perfectly healthy and the sounds of the words spoken are clearly heard. In such cases, the afflicted persons literally cannot get the words "through their heads."

Processing and Relaying Sensory Information

Sensory information from the outside world is processed and organized in the lower parts of the brain before it ever reaches the cortex. Serving as a relay station for sensory messages from the body to the cortex is the *thalamus,* shown in Figure 2-6. (The thalamus also acts as a relay station for some of the messages traveling in the opposite direction, especially some of the messages going out from the cortex calling for body movements described in the next section.)

Sensory information is processed as well in a network of nerve cells near the base of the brain called the *reticular activating system*. The network gets its name from the fact that it appears under a microscope as a crisscrossed (or reticulated) pattern of nerve fibers. As shown in Figure 2-6, it extends downward to the bottom part, or stem, of the brain, where brain and spinal cord join together.

Nerve pathways carrying messages from the sense organs to the cerebrum have side branches in the reticular activating system. These side branches stimulate the system to send its own nerve impulses upward to the cerebrum, arousing it to a state of alertness and activity. Animals whose reticular activating system is destroyed remain permanently un-

Figure 2-6 A sectional view of the brain

Individual parts of the human brain are shown here as they would be seen if the brain were divided down the middle from front to back. The functions of the various structures are described in the text (London, P. Beginning psychology. The Dorsey Press, 1978).

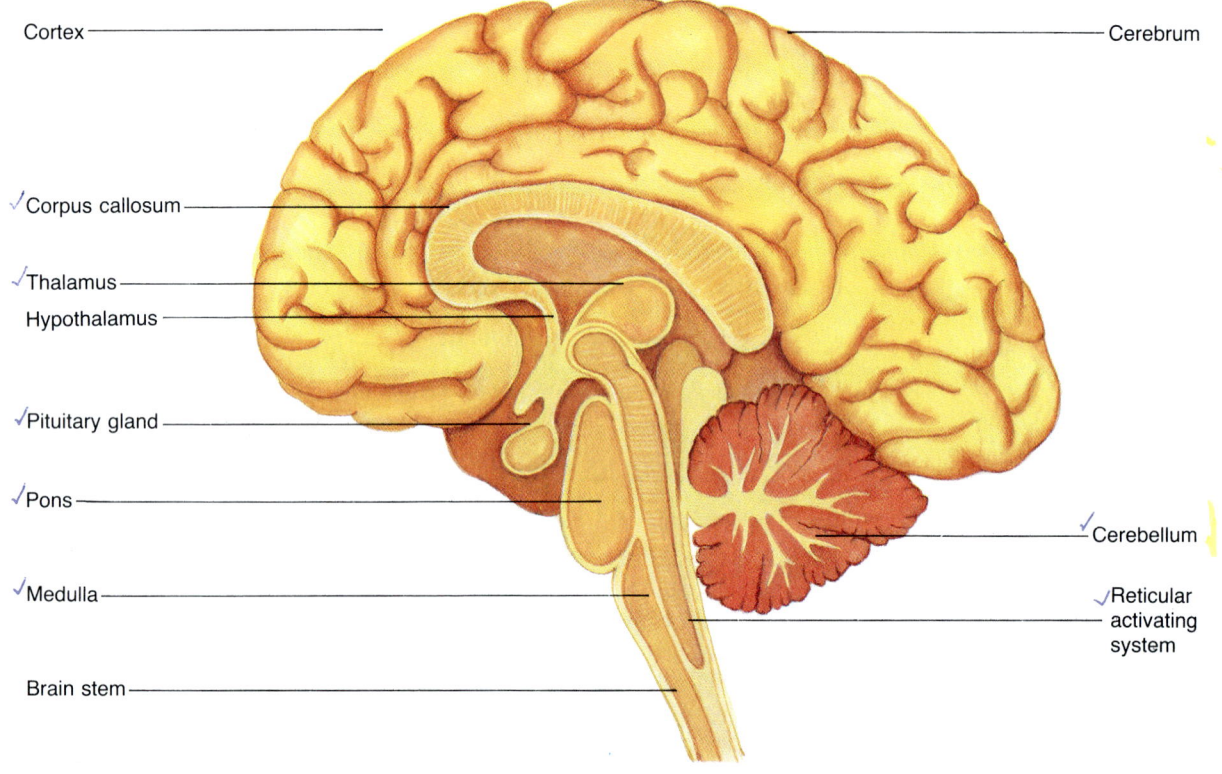

conscious for lack of such arousal. If the reticular activating system is electrically stimulated, sleeping animals will awaken immediately (Rosenzweig and Lieman, 1982).

The reticular activating system also helps us to focus selectively on those sensory signals that are the most important. For example, when you are reading a newspaper, it blocks unimportant messages—the sounds in your room or flashes of lightning outside—and prepares the cortex to receive the ones that matter.

Getting the Body to Move

Sometimes the reactions of the nervous system are immediate—as when we quickly move our hand away from a hot stove. Such responses do not require commands from the brain, but are instead the results of connections in the spinal cord. But most of the movements we make—from the gross muscular adjustments of the arms and legs when we lift things or run, to the tiny adjustments of finger muscles when we thread a needle or play the guitar—are initiated in the cortex (Evarts, 1979).

The actual sequence of events in the brain that results in voluntary movements is complex and not yet completely understood, but we do know that many parts of the brain are engaged in the process. A specialized strip on the cortex, shown in Figure 2-5, controls body movements from feet to head. Known as the *motor cortex*, it initiates body movements in response to orders from other parts of the brain. In the case of the simple act of picking up a glass, for example, you must first have an intention of performing the act before actually executing the action (Libet, 1985).

The cortex also has an area for speaking that moves the vocal cords and muscles associated with them in a way that produces meaningful sounds. When a stroke or other injury damages this area of the cortex, the result is often a loss of the incomparable human gift of speech—the ability to formulate and utter precisely the words that convey our ideas. It is from this portion of the brain also that you are able to manufacture the sounds that give voice to your feelings—a shriek of delight when you see your home team score a winning touchdown, a groan of despair when you hear about the death of a friend, or a sigh of contentment when you feel the embrace of a loved one.

Fine Movements and the Miracle of Coordination and Balance

As shown in Figure 2-6, there lies below the cerebrum and attached to the back of the brain stem a bulging structure that looks like a tree in full bloom. Called the *cerebellum*, it is essential for many aspects of movement. The cerebellum, which has been called a "magnificently patterned, orderly and fantastically complex piece of machinery" (Hubel, 1979), has many connections with parts of the cerebral cortex that initiate muscular activity.

One of the special roles of the cerebellum is to coordinate all the various finely regulated muscular movements of which we are capable, such as typing or playing the piano. If the cerebellum is damaged, movements become jerky, and great effort and concentration are required to perform even what was once such an automatic activity as walking. Victims of damage to the cerebellum also have difficulty speaking, which requires well-coordinated movements of the muscles of the vocal cords, windpipe, and mouth.

The cerebellum also controls body balance and is the part of the brain that keeps us right side up. It plays an important role in allowing us to do things that require great

Without the brain's cerebellum, such feats would be impossible.

equilibrium. An example is shooting a pistol at a target. Studies of champion marksmen in the Russian Army showed that, although many parts of their body moved, the pistol remained virtually immobile (Evarts, 1979). With millions of neurons sending their messages to and fro—from the eyes, the cerebral cortex, the arms and fingers—somehow the brain, thanks largely to the cerebellum, is able to integrate all these messages into an act of exquisite balance and precision. Like the cerebrum, the cerebellum is divided into two lobes, or hemispheres. The left and right lobes are connected by the *pons*, which gets its name from the Latin word for bridge. The neurons of the pons serve as a bridge or cable that transmits messages between the two hemispheres of the cerebellum.

THE BRAIN IN ACTION: 2. THINKING, PLANNING, AND REMEMBERING

The brain areas responsible for monitoring sensations and controlling movements make up only about a quarter of the cerebral cortex. The rest of it, all the unshaded parts in Figure 2-5 (p. 49), helps us reason, relate past experiences to present ones, and plan for the future—in other words, all the intellectual processes that raise us far above the level of other organisms.

These unspecified areas, known as the *association cortex*, also contribute to our ability to be aware of ourselves and our relationship to the world, our ability to contemplate what has been and what might yet be. No other species has so much of its cortex devoted to association areas, a clue to their importance in uniquely human capabilities. The association areas in the front portion of the brain—called the *frontal lobes*—seem to play a key role in such human capacities as solving problems, planning, and relating the past with the present. Though we take our consciousness for granted, it is a strange and wonderful thing, allowing us to examine our own lives, understand those of others, and create the ideas, arts, and technologies that are hallmarks of human society.

Memory's Storehouse

The association areas of the cortex, especially the frontal lobe, are vital in the process of storing our memories of what happened to us—and thus helps us learn from experience. If, for example, the frontal lobe is destroyed, a person has great difficulty remembering past events. But the complex task of storing and retrieving information seems to require the cooperation of other parts of the brain as well, most notably the *hippocampus* (Passingham, 1985; Murray and Mishkin, 1985).

The hippocampus lies beneath the cortex close to the area involved in processing speech shown in Figure 2-5, but it is difficult to illustrate clearly. It appears to be essential in transforming new information into long-lasting memories. Consider, for example, the much-studied case of H. M., a man of above-average intelligence, whose hippocampus was surgically destroyed in an attempt to treat his epilepsy. H. M. kept all his old memories from the time before his operation, but apparently could not establish any new ones. He could not learn the address of the new house to which his family had moved. He read the same magazines over and over again, and worked the same jigsaw puzzles, without ever realizing that he had seen them before. As H. M. described his life: ''Every day is alone in itself, whatever enjoyment I've had, and whatever sorrow I've had . . . Right now I'm wondering. Have I done or said anything amiss? You see, at this moment everything looks clear to me, but what happened just before? That's what worries me. It's like waking from a dream; I just don't remember it'' (Milner, 1970).

Intellectual Development and Brain Growth

The highly developed abilities of human beings depend in large measure on the cerebrum and its cortex. Even before birth, in the darkness of the womb, they grow so rapidly that they almost seem to explode as Figure 2-7 shows. Growth continues at a furious pace after birth—so much so that the baby's brain triples in weight in the first six months of life. By the age of two the brain reaches three-quarters of its ultimate weight (finally achieved in the late teens to early twenties), and it is precisely during these opening years that the child makes remarkable strides in motor skills, speech, and the human capacity to remember and reflect.

In monkeys at the age of two years, the cerebral cortex seems to function about as well as it ever will (Goldman, 1974). But for human babies, the cortex still has considerable growing to do, and parents watching their children in the preschool years can see the growth reflected in behavior. Young children display ever-expanding abilities to think, plan, and remember. From an infant who could see, hear, smell, and cry well enough at birth, the child in the first grade has become a person who can begin to read, understand, question, and wonder. All the various stages of children's intellectual development described later in the book are dependent on the progressive growth and maturation of the cerebral cortex (Tanner, 1978).

Figure 2-7 The brain's explosive growth before birth

During each minute in the womb, the brain of the infant-to-be gains tens of thousands of new brain cells. The folds on the brain's surface begin to appear at about the middle of pregnancy—as the cortex grows rapidly to fill the top of the tiny fetus skull (Cowan, W. M. Development of the brain. Scientific American, *1979).*

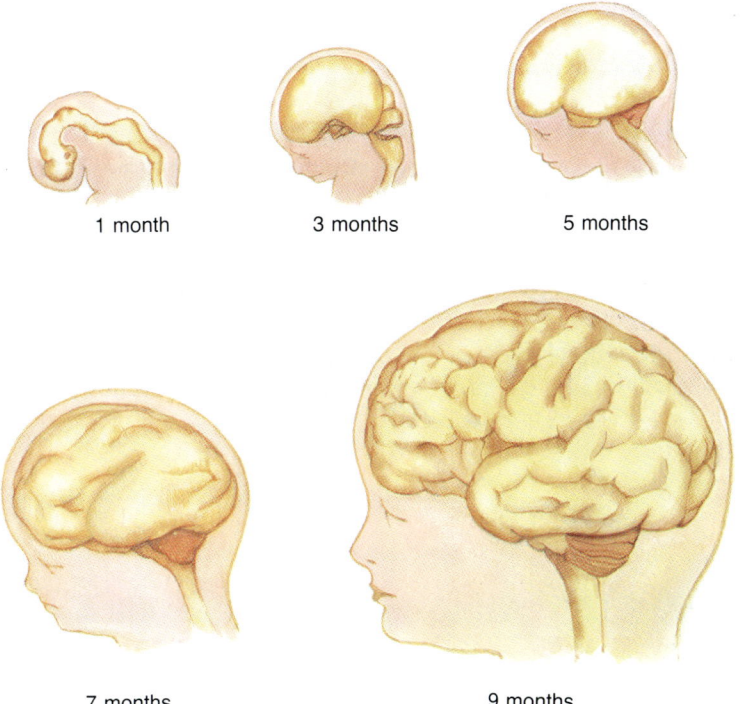

Do rich early learning experiences influence the brain's growth? This question has attracted the interest of a number of psychologists, and the answer seems to be yes. Almost all the brain's neurons are present at birth. The number increases afterwards only by a small amount, and only in certain areas (Greenough, 1982). Yet the brain quadruples in weight from birth to adulthood. Some of the added weight comes from the growth of supporting tissue. But perhaps more important is the growth of new offshoots from nerve cells—much as a young tree develops new branches. By sprouting new branches, neurons increase their interconnections with other neurons, thus providing new pathways for messages in the brain.

Experiments have shown that animals raised in an enriched environment containing numerous objects to look at and manipulate develop heavier brains than those raised in ordinary bare cages, and their brains have more interconnecting offshoots (Rosenzweig and Bennett, 1978). Further, the rats living in enriched environments are better at learning mazes and other types of complex tasks (Thompson, 1985). Similar effects are thought to occur in humans.

Left Brain and Right Brain

As was noted in Figure 2-1 (p. 43), the topmost part of the brain—the cerebrum and the cerebral cortex—is divided into two halves, or hemispheres. Each half seems to have somewhat different responsibilities for memory, reasoning, and language.

Most of the nerve fibers connecting the brain with all the various parts of the body through the spinal cord cross from one side to the other. This means that the left hemisphere ordinarily receives sensory messages from and controls movement in the right side of the body. The right hemisphere deals with the left side of the body. If like most people you write with your right hand, it is your left hemisphere that directs the movements. The left hemisphere also has greater control of the use of language—speaking and understanding the speech of others. Thus in most people the left hemisphere is the dominant one—the one we most often use and rely on.

A stimulating childhood environment may speed the rate at which the young brain grows.

The two hemispheres cooperate very closely. They have numerous interconnections, especially through a structure called the *corpus callosum* (shown in Figure 2-6, p. 50) that resembles a thick telephone cable between the two hemispheres. Thus each half of the cerebrum and cerebral cortex communicates with the other half.

Splitting the Two Brain Halves

What would happen if the corpus callosum were cut or missing and the two halves of the brain could not communicate? We know the answer because surgeons sometimes cut the connecting link as a last resort to relieve patients of crippling epileptic seizures. This "split-brain" operation produces some strange results. Patients may show little change in their intelligence, personality, or general behavior, yet careful testing reveals that in some ways they act as if they have two independently functioning brains.

This has been strikingly demonstrated by a number of experiments, such as the one illustrated in Figure 2-8. The results showed that the left brain of the split-brain patients did not seem to have much conception of form or spatial relationships. It produced only separate details of the model drawings, without putting them together into a whole. The right hemisphere seemed to have a much better idea of the total pattern of the model drawings, but it had only a shaky grasp of many of the details. Neither brain, working separately, could reproduce the model drawings with much accuracy. Try drawing the cross and cube yourself with the hand you *don't* normally use for writing. You will find that your own brain, with its corpus callosum intact, enables you to do a fairly good job even with the "wrong" hand.

How Specialized Is Each of the Two Brain Hemispheres?

Such split-brain experiments show that the two hemispheres, when separated, perform different functions. Although the hemispheres look symmetrical overall, certain areas are slightly larger on the left side, while others are slightly larger on the right. These physical

Figure 2-8   Drawings by a split-brain subject: the right brain does better

When a split-brain patient was asked to reproduce the drawings at the left, he could create only parts of the figures with his right hand, controlled by his left brain. He did better at reproducing the drawings as a whole with his left hand, controlled by the right brain—though he was still far from perfect (Bogen, 1969).

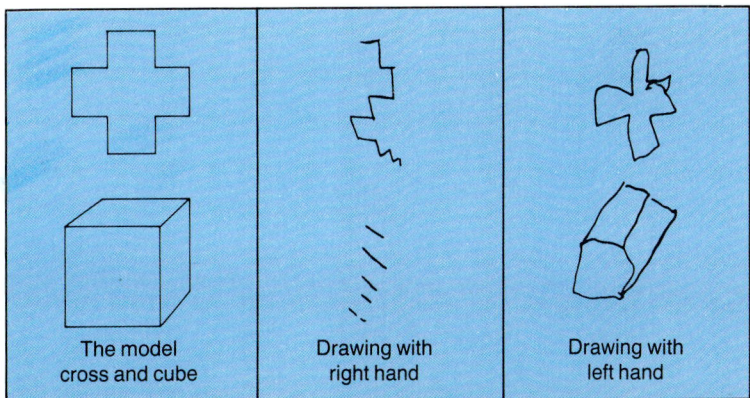

differences have been seen even in unborn fetuses, an indication that they are innate rather than acquired through experience and learning (Galaburda, 1984).

A number of psychologists have concluded that the left hemisphere is more skilled at dealing with items of symbolic information—like words and numbers—considered one by one in a logical sequence. This is the kind of mental work we call "reasoning," in which we arrive at logical conclusions in a step-by-step fashion. The left hemisphere is also particularly adept at language, in which sounds are put together in logical order into words, and words are arranged into sentences. By contrast, the right hemisphere appears to be more skilled at considering whole patterns—seeing the forest, not the trees. For example, it excels at the perception of visual information such as paintings or spatial locations and of the melodies in a song or symphony.

Roger Sperry, a neuropsychologist who received the Nobel Prize for his creative studies of split-brain animals and humans, has observed that this work has helped psychology to begin to translate "the mental forces of the conscious mind" into "objective science" (Sperry, 1982). However, our knowledge about the division of labor between the two hemispheres in normal people remains incomplete. There is evidence that the two hemispheres are both active in most things we do, although for specific tasks one may be more active than the other. For example, as shown in Figure 2-9, when a normal person was trying to master the toy shown in the photo (a spatial task), measurements of his brain's electrical activity indicated that his right hemisphere was doing most of the work. When he switched to writing a letter (a language task), there was more activity in the left hemisphere (Ornstein, 1978).

Jerre Levy, once one of Sperry's collaborators and an expert on the roles of the two hemispheres, sums up our current understanding this way: "Normal people have . . . one gloriously differentiated brain, with each hemisphere contributing its specialized abilities" (Levy, 1985). She challenges the popular notion that individuals tend to be "left-brained" or "right-brained." Levy agrees that one hemisphere is usually more active than the other,

Nobel laureate Roger Sperry pioneered in research on brain hemisphere functions.

Figure 2-9 A normal subject tackles a spatial task. What do his brain waves show?

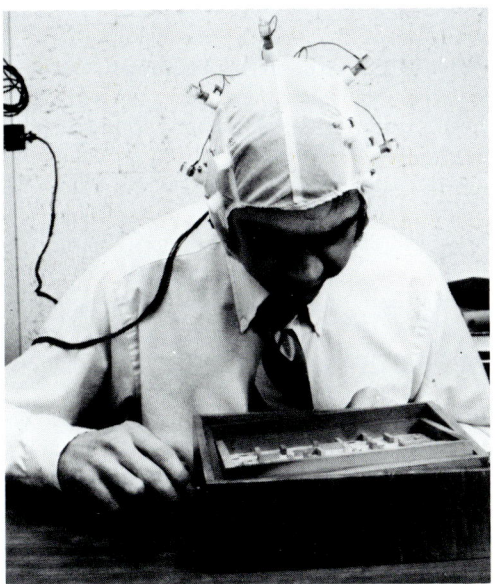

This subject, a graduate student, has been fitted with a skull cap that holds electrodes against various parts of his scalp. The electrodes are hoooked up to an electroencephalograph, *or EEG for short, that records the electrical activity (or brain waves) occurring beneath them. For what the waves showed when the subject was trying to perform a delicate feat of judging space and movement to get a steel ball through a labyrinth, see the text.*

and that people's relative strengths in verbal or spatial skills are linked somewhat to which hemisphere they favor. But, she argues, there is no evidence that people are purely "left-brained" or "right-brained," and in any case, "differences in activation of the hemispheres are but one of many factors affecting the way we think." The link between the favored hemisphere and people's mental abilities is still being explored by physiological psychologists studying human intellectual functions. One of the factors of interest is gender differences—as discussed in the box on Psychology in Everyday Life called "Are Men's and Women's Brains Different?"

THE BRAIN IN ACTION: 3. PRODUCING EMOTIONS AND KEEPING OUR BODIES IN TUNE

The remarkable feats of the brain described thus far—allowing us to make sense of our environment, move about in the world, and think as humans—are impressive in their own right. But even with them, our lives would be flat and barren were it not for the deeply moving sensations we call emotions. True, the emotions of fear and anger are often upsetting and sometimes destructive. However, they also help us cope with the world and meet its crises, motivating us to action. And there are other emotions that greatly enrich our lives, such as love and joy. These feelings, too, are produced by our brain, working in concert with our body.

The brain not only regulates our emotions; it also ensures our personal physical survival by keeping our body in healthy working order. It oversees the fundamental functions of breathing, pumping blood, and maintaining adequate blood pressure. It also tells us when we need food or drink, and keeps body chemistry in balance. The brain seems to watch out for our survival as a species, too; it is deeply involved in our sexual develop-

Psychology in Everyday Life
Are Men's and Women's Brains Different?

Men and women have obvious physical differences, and they differ intellectually as well. On average, women are better at verbal tasks, while men excel at spatial and mathematical ones (Maccoby and Jacklin, 1974). Cultural factors such as sexual stereotyping undoubtedly encourage such differences, but there may be another source as well: the nature of men's and women's brains.

The brains of boys and girls appear to develop at different rates even before birth. The left hemisphere matures more rapidly in girls and the right hemisphere in boys—thus potentially advancing verbal skills in the former and spatial skills in the latter (Levy, 1974). Moreover, the brains of men and women are slightly different in structure and organization. For example, a part of the corpus callosum, the cable of nerve fibers connecting the two hemispheres, is thicker in women's brains (deLacoste-Utamsing and Holloway, 1982), and women's two hemispheres are anatomically more symmetrical than those of men (Wada, Clark, and Hamm, 1975). These factors may aid communication between the hemispheres and provide a boost to some verbal skills.

Psychologist Doreen Kimura, a leading researcher on hemispheric function, has looked at differences in male and female brain organization not only *across* the hemispheres, but also *within* hemispheres. Based on her own studies and those of others, Kimura finds that for certain verbal tasks— for example, naming words that begin with a particular letter—the brains of men and women are organized alike. In the case of both, only the front of the left hemisphere is involved. But for the general task of producing speech, men use both the front and back of the left hemisphere, while women use mostly the front. Moreover, men may develop speech disorders if either the front or the back of the left hemisphere is injured—but in women, only injuries to the frontal area cause such disorders. Kimura interprets these findings to mean that for the task of speaking, women depend on a smaller, more localized brain area than do men.

Despite these intriguing clues, it is still too soon to say with certainty how much such differences in brain structure and organization contribute to the performance of men and women on a wide range of intellectual tasks. Furthermore, as Kimura points out, generalizations about how men and women differ as groups say little about what particular individuals can and cannot do. She concludes: "There may be no inherent characteristics unique to the brains of either sex that necessarily limit the intellectual achievements of individual men or women" (Kimura, 1985).

For now, then, the bottom line appears to be this: Yes, in general the brains of men and women are different in certain subtle ways. But much more important, each man and woman remains a unique human being.

---

ment and behavior. Our lives are finally at an end only when the brain ceases its last flicker of activity.

Generating Passions and Feelings

Of special importance in our emotional life is a network of brain structures and pathways near the brain's center known as the *limbic system*. Making up about one-fifth of our brain, it is illustrated in Figure 2-10. The limbic system has connections to another key player in our emotional lives and our physical survival: the *hypothalamus*, the brain's most direct link to the body glands that are active in fear, anger, and other emotions. The hypothalamus, attached to the master gland, the *pituitary* (see Figure 2-6, p. 50), is actually *its* master. Working in concert with portions of the limbic system, the hypothalamus delivers messages that help produce the "stirred-up" bodily processes that accompany emotion. The actual feelings we experience

Figure 2-10 The brain's limbic system

The word limbic *means "bordering," and the limbic system is so named because its parts form a border, or loop, around the deepest core of the cerebrum. The functions of the system and some of its key parts are described in the text.*

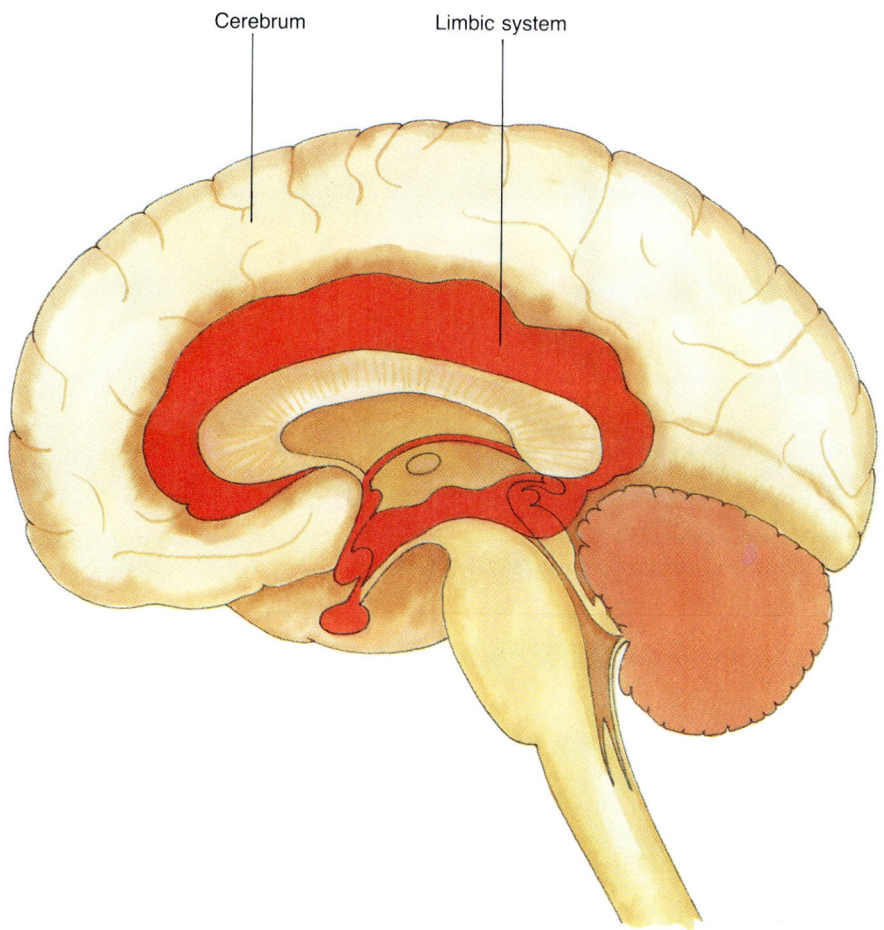

are another aspect of the human consciousness for which the cerebral cortex is responsible. In one way or another, the brain accounts for our vivid appreciation of life's pleasures and our sorrow over its tragedies.

In lower mammals, the limbic system appears to contain the programming that directs the instinctive patterns in which they feed, mate, fight, and escape from danger. There is evidence that when animals learn to anticipate that a stressful experience—such as a shock—is coming, the limbic system becomes active (Herrmann, Hurwitz, and Levine, 1984). Laboratory experiments have shown that surgery or electrical stimulation of various parts of the limbic system can cause animals to behave in ways that appear unusually docile or unusually aggressive, as illustrated in Figure 2-11. Damage to one part of the limbic system will reduce the fear and avoidance that many animals display when faced with a novel stimulus, while damage to another part will erase inhibitions on attack behavior and make many animals vicious.

The experience of joy and sadness, like other emotions, depends on the brain.

Staying Alive and Physiologically Balanced

The body's well-being depends on keeping its many functions on a reasonably even keel despite the many events and environmental changes we continually encounter. For example, we need to keep internal temperature stable in all seasons and levels of exertion, and must maintain a proper supply of oxygen, water, and various other substances that cells need to function well. The state of dynamic equilibrium achieved when these processes are working right and our physiological systems are well-balanced is called *homeostasis*.

The air we breathe, the water we drink, and the food we eat are the raw materials required to keep our cells properly supplied and working correctly. We need a central management system to order these supplies, make sure they arrive on time, distribute them where they are needed, and see that they are processed properly. The brain provides that management.

For example, the hypothalamus, besides being a center for emotional behavior, helps to maintain homeostasis by signalling when the body needs more food or water and by regulating states of wakefulness and sleep. It also acts like a highly accurate thermostat, keeping our body temperature close to 98.6 F degrees by reacting to messages from temperature sensors in the skin and from its own temperature-sensing cells.

Our continuing survival depends as well on the *medulla*, shown in Figure 2-6 (page 50), a structure in the brain stem that is responsible for coordinating such vital bodily processes as breathing, heart rate, and digestion. Infants who die suddenly without any apparent cause (victims of the so-called "sudden-infant-death" syndrome) often have a medulla that is not fully developed and, therefore, does not react quickly to loss of oxygen when there is a breathing problem that might otherwise have proved insignificant (Valdes-Dapena, 1980).

Figure 2-11 The limbic system and aggression

The photographs show the effect of electrical stimulation of the brain through electrodes planted in or around the limbic system of the cat. At left, under stimulation at one particular spot, the cat calmly ignores its traditional prey, the rat. At right, stimulation at another spot makes the cat assume a hostile posture toward a laboratory assistant with whom it is ordinarily on friendly terms.

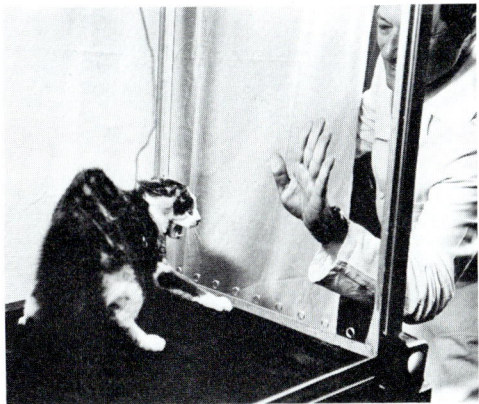

The Brain's Able Assistant: The Autonomic Nervous System

In controlling bodily processes, the brain has an effective assistant in the form of the *autonomic nervous system*, or ANS for short. The word *autonomic* means independent or self-sufficient—and in many ways the autonomic nervous system operates on its own, as its name suggests, without much if any conscious control. Even if we try we cannot ordinarily command our stomach muscles to make the movements that help digest food. We cannot order the muscles of the blood vessels to channel a strong flow of blood to the stomach to aid digestion—or to redirect the flow of blood toward the muscles of the arms or legs when we have to do physical work. We cannot make our hearts pump faster or slower. But the ANS can do all these things and does so constantly, even when we are asleep or in a deep coma caused by an anesthetic or a brain injury.

In addition, the ANS exercises considerable independent influence on important bodily structures called *endocrine glands*, or glands of internal secretion, which are also resistant to conscious control. Unlike the sweat glands that deliver perspiration to the skin, or the salivary glands that deliver fluids to the mouth, the endocrine glands discharge their products directly into the bloodstream. These substances, as mentioned earlier, are called *hormones*. They influence many bodily activities, including those associated with emotional behavior. The endocrine glands and their functions are listed in Figure 2-12.

The autonomic nervous system exerts its impact on important body processes through a number of centers called *ganglia*, as shown in Figure 2-13. These are like small brains scattered throughout the body. They consist of masses of nerve cells packed together and connected with one another—just as in the brain itself but on a much smaller scale. Some of these neurons, as you can see in Figure 2-13, have long fibers over which they send commands to the glands, the heart muscles, and the muscles of the body's organs and blood vessels. Others are connected to the brain and the spinal cord—which means that the ANS, though independent in many ways, does take some orders from above. In the case of being wakened by shouts of "Fire," your ears send a message to your brain, which

Figure 2-12 The human endocrine glands

The endocrine glands receive messages from the brain and ANS that make them spring into action or sometimes slow down. The glands influence the excitability of the brain and the rest of the nervous system, helping create emotional experiences.

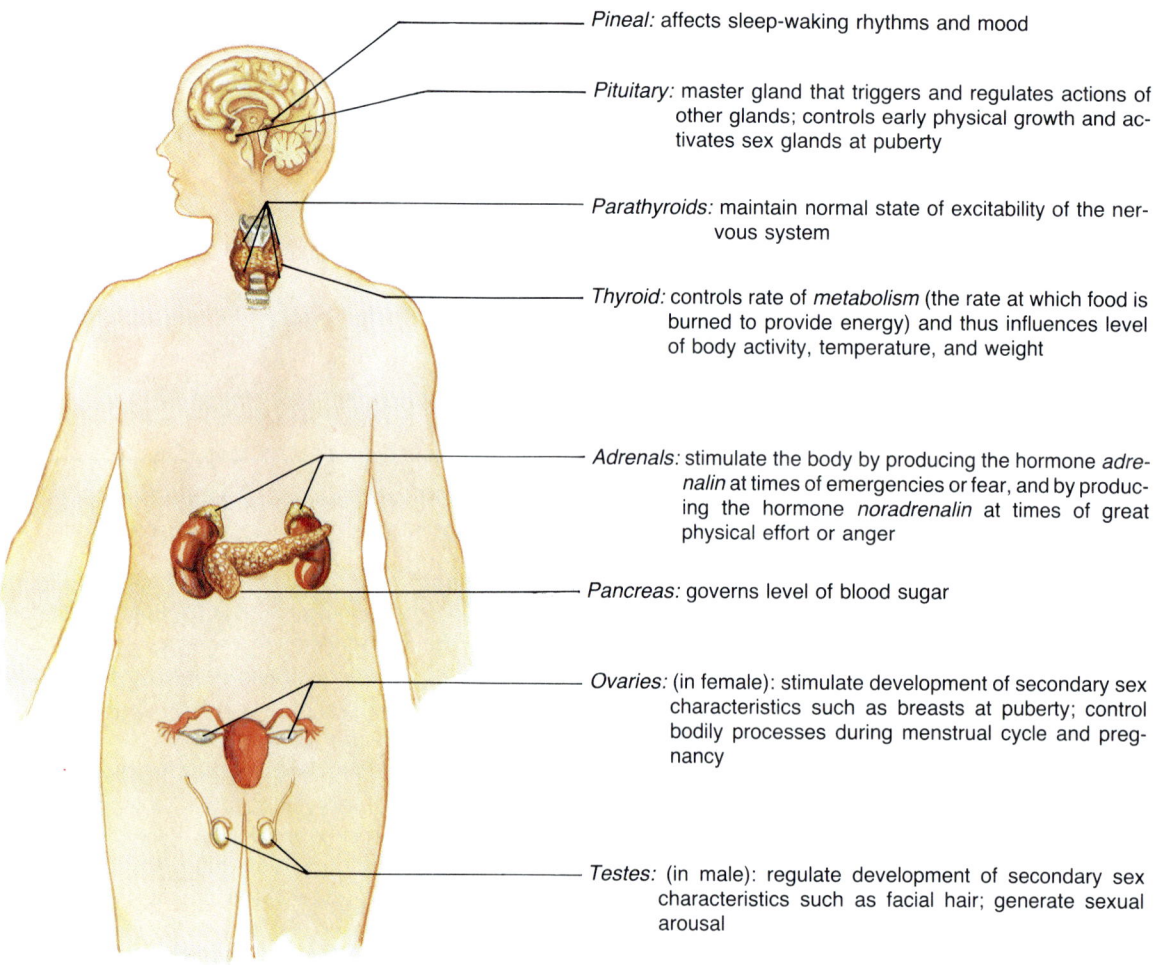

Pineal: affects sleep-waking rhythms and mood

Pituitary: master gland that triggers and regulates actions of other glands; controls early physical growth and activates sex glands at puberty

Parathyroids: maintain normal state of excitability of the nervous system

Thyroid: controls rate of *metabolism* (the rate at which food is burned to provide energy) and thus influences level of body activity, temperature, and weight

Adrenals: stimulate the body by producing the hormone *adrenalin* at times of emergencies or fear, and by producing the hormone *noradrenalin* at times of great physical effort or anger

Pancreas: governs level of blood sugar

Ovaries: (in female): stimulate development of secondary sex characteristics such as breasts at puberty; control bodily processes during menstrual cycle and pregnancy

Testes: (in male): regulate development of secondary sex characteristics such as facial hair; generate sexual arousal

then sends an emergency command to the ANS, which in turn springs into action through its various connections with the glands and muscles.

As shown in Figure 2-13, there are two divisions of the ANS, differing in structure and function.

The Parasympathetic Division: Running the Ordinary Business of Living The *parasympathetic division* connects with the stem of the brain and the lower part of the spinal cord. It is made up of a number of widely scattered ganglia, most of which lie near the glands or muscles of organs to which it delivers its messages. Because it is so loosely constructed, it tends to act in piecemeal fashion, delivering its orders to one or several parts of the body but not necessarily to all at once.

Chapter 2 Brain, Body, and Behavior

Figure 2-13 Autonomic nervous system
The long chain of ganglia of the **sympathetic division** *extends down the side of the spinal cord, to which it makes many connections. (There is a similar chain on the other side of the body.) The* **parasympathetic division** *has small ganglia near the glands and smooth muscles that both divisions help control, though in different ways (after Crosby, Humphrey, and Lauer, 1962).*

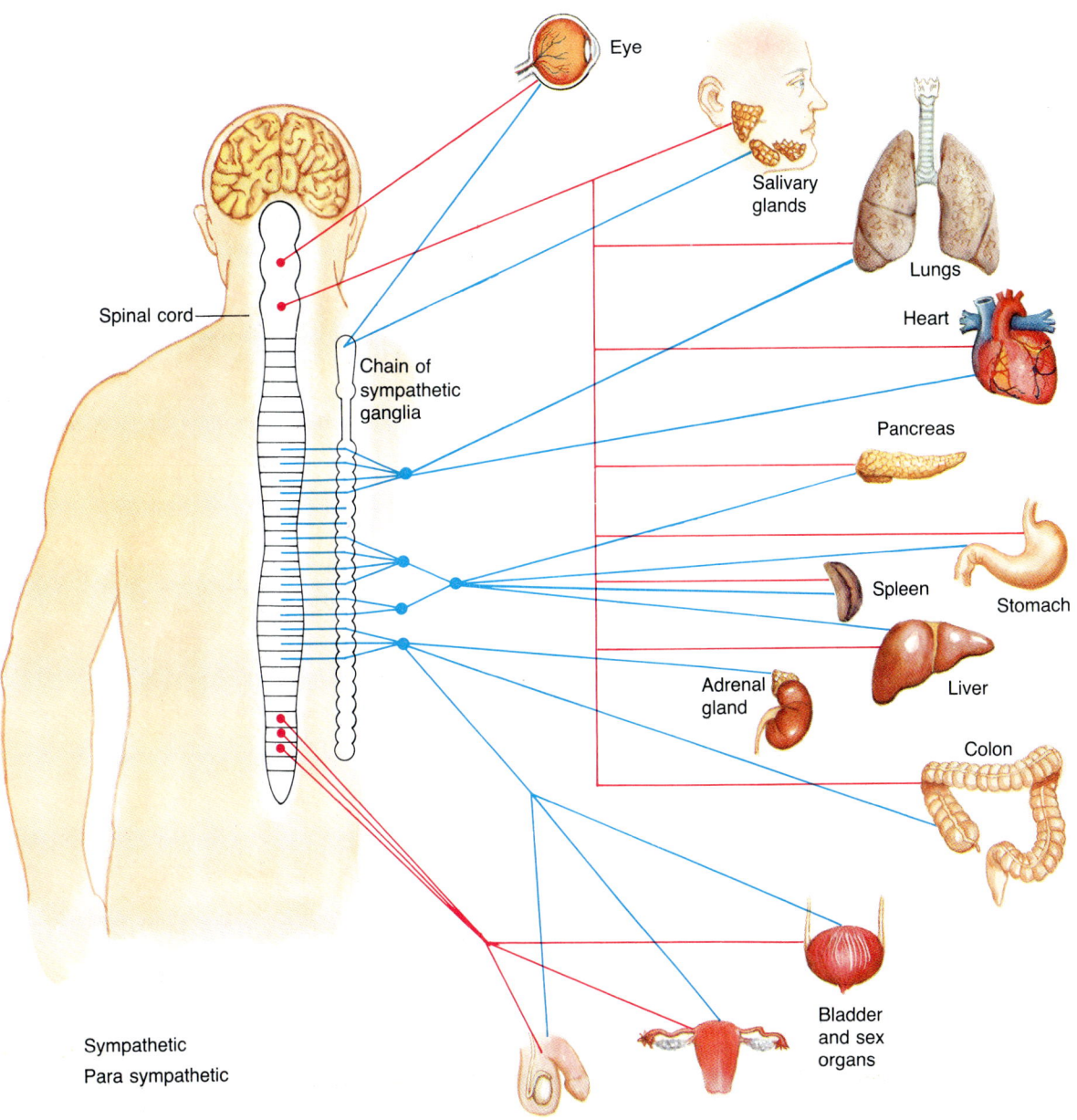

The Brain in Action: 3. Producing Emotions and Keeping Our Bodies in Tune

In general, the parasympathetic division seems to play its most important role during those frequent periods when no danger threatens and the body can relax and go about the ordinary business of living. It tends to slow down the work of the heart and lungs. It aids digestion by stimulating our salivary glands, producing wavelike motions of the muscles of the stomach and intestines, and encouraging the stomach to produce digestive acid and the liver to produce the digestive fluid called bile. It also brings about elimination of the body's waste products from the intestines and bladder. At times, however, the parasympathetic division abandons these usual tasks and helps mobilize the body for emergency action. When it does this—operating in ways that are not yet understood—it seems to assist and supplement the work of the other part of the autonomic system, the sympathetic division.

The Sympathetic Division: Meeting Emergencies The *sympathetic division* is shown in Figure 2-13 as a long chain of ganglia extending down the side of the spinal cord. There is a similar chain, not shown, on the other side of the cord. All the many ganglia of the sympathetic division are elaborately interconnected. Note that many of the nerve fibers going out from the chains of ganglia meet again in additional ganglia in other parts of the body, where they again form complicated interconnections with nerve cells that finally carry commands to the glands and smooth muscles. For this reason the sympathetic division, unlike the parasympathetic, tends to function as a unit.

When the sympathetic division springs into action, as when you experience fear or anger, it does many things all at once. Most notably, it commands the adrenal glands to spill their powerful stimulants into the blood stream. By acting on the adrenal glands, liver, and pancreas, it increases the level of blood sugar, thus raising the rate of metabolism and providing additional energy. It causes the spleen, a glandlike organ in which red corpuscles are stored, to release more of these corpuscles into the bloodstream, thus enabling the blood to carry more oxygen to the body's tissues. It changes the size of the blood vessels—enlarging those of the heart and muscles of body movement and constricting those of the muscles of the stomach and intestines. It makes us breathe harder. It enlarges the pupils of the eyes, which are controlled by muscles, and slows the activity of the salivary glands. ("Wide eyes" and a dry mouth are characteristic of a number of strong emotions such as fear.) It also activates the sweat glands and contracts the muscles at the base of the hairs of the body, causing the hair to rise on animals and producing gooseflesh in human beings. In general, the changes prepare the body for emergency action—such as fighting or running away.

Clearly there is a very close marriage between the brain and the body, linked together as they are through numerous physical and chemical connections. The implications of this link are discussed in a box on Psychology in Everyday Life called "Health Psychology: The Interplay between Our Mental and Physical Well-being."

THE BRAIN'S COMMUNICATIONS NETWORK

The brain carries out its many functions through a constant exchange of messages, speeding through its untold billions of pathways. It is hard to imagine the extraordinary hubub of activity taking place in your nervous system right now. Messages rich in information are being "flashed" back and forth to every part of your body.

The messages take the form of nervous impulses that resemble tiny electrical charges, each barely strong enough to move the needle of the most sensitive recording device. The nervous impulses are produced by the neurons, which have been aptly described as the

Psychology in Everyday Life
Health Psychology: The Interplay between Our Mental and Physical Well-being

Although the brain issues most of the orders, it relies heavily on feedback from the body to tell it how the body is doing and to guide its subsequent actions. This kind of ongoing interplay of brain and body makes it extremely difficult to disentangle what is "mental" from what is "physical."

It may also blur the distinction between mental and physical disorders. For example, as you will see in Chapter 12, many people who suffer from the mental disorder of depression may have, in addition to their unhappy thoughts, a number of physical symptoms such as lack of energy, loss of appetite and sexual desire, and sleep problems (American Psychiatric Association, 1980). Furthermore, their endocrine system often shows signs of abnormal functioning. Conversely, in many people with physical illnesses, mental symptoms may accompany or follow from their disorders. Thus, for example, after some infections or open heart surgery, people may become depressed.

Increasing recognition of the interplay of body and mind, based on the growing knowledge of how they interact, has encouraged the rise of the relatively new discipline of *health psychology*. Health psychologists study the association of psychological and physiological factors in health and illness, and attempt to help us apply their findings to improve both our mental *and* physical health. For example, a number of studies have shown that when surgical or heart-attack patients are provided with information, coping skills, and emotional support, their recovery is speeded up (Mumford, Schlesinger, and Glass, 1982). Psychologists

Some behaviors, such as this, can significantly affect health.

studying health and behavior have also identified certain behaviors—cigarette smoking, alcohol abuse, poor nutritional habits, little exercise—that increase the chances of disease and early death (Miller, 1983).

It seems clear that the field of health psychology promises not only more effective methods of treating illness when it does occur, but more efficient methods of preventing illness in the first place (Institute of Medicine, 1982).

"building blocks" of the brain (Stevens, 1979). They are the basic units in the entire nervous system. The neurons start sending their messages long before birth and continue humming with activity throughout life. If every neuron in the brain fired off its impulse at the same instant, the entire amount of electricity produced would be just about enough to power a small transistor radio. Yet these tiny impulses somehow account for all the accomplishments of the brain and the rest of the nervous system.

The Neuron's Communications Equipment: "Receivers" and "Senders"

Although neurons show many variations, they all resemble the drawing in Figure 2-14 in a general way. The *dendrites* are the "receivers." When they are properly stimulated, they set off the nervous impulse, which travels the fiberlike length of the neuron to the other end. In between is the *cell body*, which has a *nucleus*, or core, containing the genes that caused the cell to grow into a neuron in the first place. The cell body performs the process of metabolism, converting food supplied by the blood stream into energy. Moreover the surface of the cell body is dotted with numerous *receptor sites* that are also capable of responding to stimulation, like the dendrites, and setting off nervous impulses, which travel down the fiberlike *axon* to the *end branches*, which are the neuron's "senders."

The axon's *myelin sheath*, found in many but not all neurons, is a whitish coating of fatty protective tissue that increases the speed at which the nervous impulse travels. Transmission is further improved by the *nodes*, which are constrictions of the sheath acting as little booster stations that help nudge the impulse along to the end branches, the "senders" that deliver the neuron's message.

Some neurons have their end branches in glands or muslces, which their impulses stimulate into action. Most neurons, however, particularly in the brain, have end branches that connect with other neurons. Their job is communication—passing messages along to other neurons.

How Neurons Send Their Messages to One Another

The nervous impulse can only travel the length of the neuron that produces it—from dendrites or receptor sites to the end branches of the axon. There is stops. It can go no farther. It can, however, influence other neurons by delivering its message.

The key to transmission of the message is the *synapse*, the connecting point where an end branch-sender of one neuron is separated by only a microscopic distance—a millionth of an inch—from a dendrite-receiver of another neuron. At the synapse, where the two neurons almost touch, the first can influence the second in various ways. Sometimes the electrical charge arriving at the synapse is enough in itself to produce an effect. Usually,

Figure 2-14 A more or less typical neuron

A typical neuron is a fiber-shaped cell with **dendrites** *at one end, an* **axon** *at the other end, and a* **cell body** *somewhere in between. The functions of the various structures are explained in the text.*

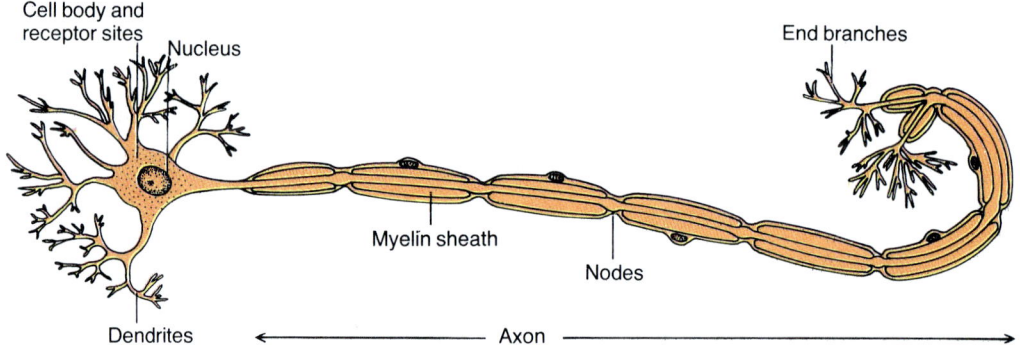

however, the action is chemical. The senders of the axon contain small amounts of chemical substances called *neurotransmitters*. When the neuron fires, a burst of these substances is released at the synapse. The chemicals flow across the tiny gap between the two neurons and act on the second neuron.

Figure 2-15 is a photograph of parts of the neuron that play an especially important role in the transmission of messages—the little swellings called *synaptic knobs* at the very tips of the branches of the axon. It is these knobs that actually form synapses with other neurons at their dendrites or cell-body receptor sites. An enlarged drawing of a synapse is shown in Figure 2-16.

In the first neuron the neurotransmitter is produced in the cell body and delivered down the length of the fiber to the *synaptic vesicles*, where it is stored until called upon. When the neuron fires, the nervous impulse reaching the synaptic knob causes the vesicles to release their transmitter chemicals. These neurotransmitters flow across the *synaptic cleft* and act on the receptors of the second neuron. Some of the neurotransmitters act as stimulants, urging the second neuron to fire off its own nervous impulse. Others, however, do the opposite, instructing the second neuron to refrain from action. They act to *inhibit* any activity in the second neuron.

Figure 2-15 The synaptic knobs

This photograph, taken at a magnification of about 2,000 times life size, was the first ever made of the synaptic knobs. It shows some of the structures in a snail (Lewis, Zeevi, and Everhart, 1969).

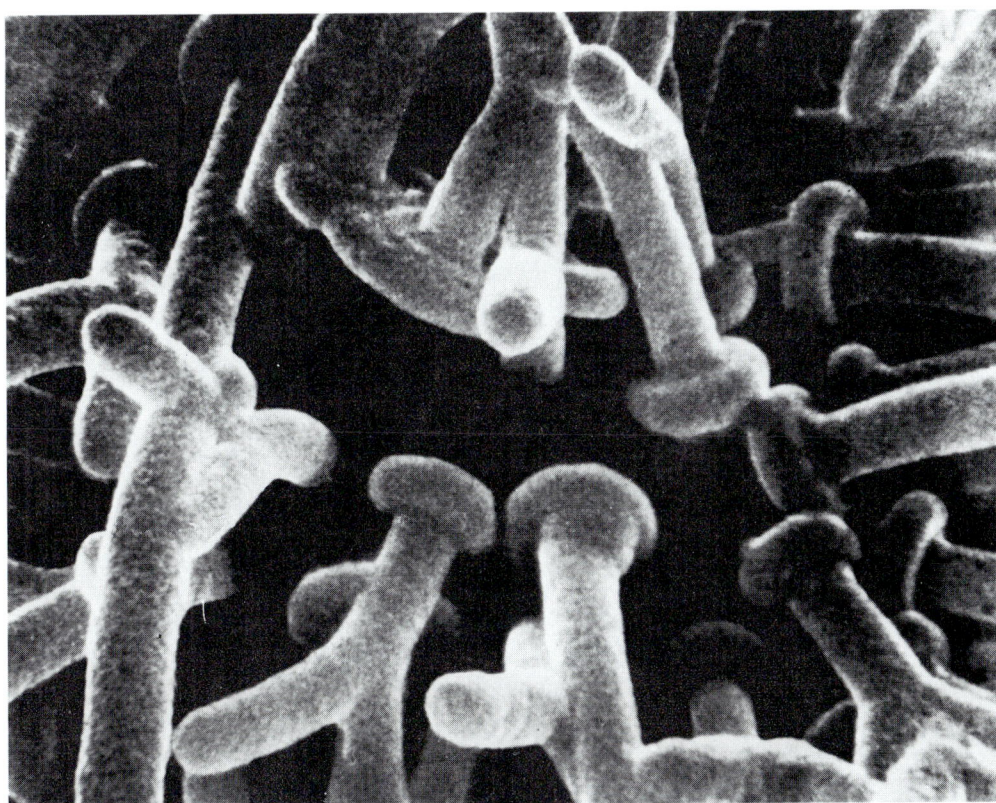

Figure 2-16 Where neuron meets neuron: the synapse

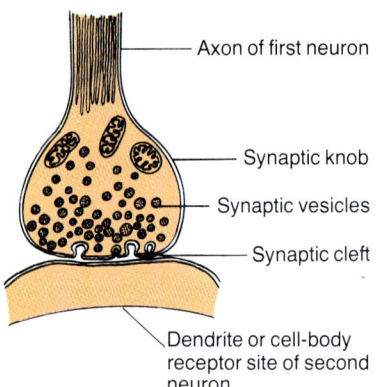

The axon of the first neuron ends in a synaptic knob, separated from the second neuron by only a tiny gap called the **synaptic cleft.** *What happens at the cleft is described in the text.*

Getting the Message: To Fire or Not to Fire

Will the second neuron fire or will it not? On this question, it must be emphasized that the neuron has synapses with as many as several thousand others whose axon end branches are in close contact with its dendrites or cell-body receptor sites. At any given instant, the neuron may be receiving messages from a few, many, or all of these axons. Some of the mesages are delivered by neurotransmitters that tell it to fire, others by neurotransmitters that do the opposite. Moreover, the neuron itself responds in different ways depending on where the message arrives. Some of its receptor sites are like switches that signal "on." Stimulation at these points tends to make the neuron fire. Other receptor sites are like "off" switches. Stimulation of these points tends to inhibit the neuron from firing.

Thus whether the neuron fires or not depends on the whole pattern of messages it receives. Ordinarily it will not fire in response to a single message arriving at one of its many dendrites or on its cell body. Instead the firing process requires multiple stimulation—a whole group of messages arriving at once or in quick succession from the other neurons with which it has synaptic contact. Moreover the messages that represent signals to fire must outweigh the messages that inhibit it from firing.

In the brain, with all its multiple interconnections, activity goes on constantly at many thousands of synapses all at the same time. Each neuron in the network is receiving messages from hundreds or thousands of other neurons. The nervous impulses it receives may have no effect at all. They may be too few in number or too far apart in time to make it fire. Or the incoming messages urging it to fire may be canceled out by messages that inhibit firing. Then the messages it receives may not get through at all. On the other hand, the messages may make it fire anywhere from just once to many times in rapid succession—and in turn influence all the many other neurons with which its own axons form connections.

At each of these new synapses, the process is repeated. The message may get through or not. It may inhibit other neurons or it may cause them to fire—again just a single time or many times in quick succession. Thus once a message gets started through the brain, its possible pathways are virtually unlimited. One neuron's impulses may stimulate a few or many other neurons into action. The new impulses may travel in any one of many directions or in a number of directions at once. They may be few or many, slow or rapid. And at each new switching point the process is repeated, introducing thousands of possible new pathways. Small wonder that the human nervous system is capable of so many accomplishments. By comparison with the brain, the nation's telephone network is just a child's toy.

Although the electrochemical messages travel in complex ways, the process is highly organized. Nerve cells are arranged in ways that permit those engaged in similar tasks to work together. The chemical receptors on the neurons are also quite specific; they will only recognize certain kinds of neurotransmitters. Neurons that send or receive the same neurotransmitters form special pathways or circuits, and these are often grouped together in particular parts of the brain to perform specific tasks as a team. For example, many parts of the cortex involved in vision and motor activity are organized in columns of cells to perform tasks in concert.

How Neurons Give Their All—or Nothing at All

The nervous impulse—the tiny charge of electricity that passes down the length of the neuron fiber—can best be compared to the glowing band of fire that travels along a lighted fuse. In the neuron, however, no combustion takes place. What actually happens is that there is an exchange of chemical particles from inside and outside the nerve fiber, creating different electrical charges between them. Once the nervous impulse created by this change of electrical charges has passed down the length of the fiber, the neuron quickly returns to its normal state and is ready to fire off another impulse.

The neuron ordinarily operates on what is called the *all or none principle*. That is to say, if it fires at all it fires as hard as it can, given its physiological condition at the moment (which, in complex ways, can be altered by the messages it is receiving from other neurons). All stimuli of sufficient power set off the same kind of impulse—as strong as the neuron is capable of producing at that moment.

After the neuron has fired, it requires a brief recovery period before it can fire again. This recovery period has two phases. During the first phase the neuron is incapable of responding at all. During the second phase it is still incapable of responding to all the stimuli that would ordinarily make it fire, but it can respond if the stimuli are powerful enough. The length of the recovery period varies. Some neurons recover slowly and can fire only a few times per second. A few recover so swiftly that they can fire as often as 1,000 times a second when sufficiently stimulated. Most are in between, with a maximum firing rate of several hundred times a second.

Figure 2-17 shows the actual sequence of nervous impulses fired off by a neuron over a period of several tenths of a second, under three different kinds of stimulation. These tracings of the neuron's activity demonstrate that stronger stimulation makes the neuron fire more often but not with greater strength.

The Chemical Brain

Those little jolts of electricity shown in Figure 2-17 represent the basic activity that goes on inside the nervous system, in humans as well as other animals. Each neuron ordinarily produces only one kind of impulse, its own little unvarying "beep." Yet somehow these monotonous beeps—by the rate at which they are produced, the patterns they form, and the way they are routed through the brain—manage to account for the miracles of human cognition and consciousness. They tell us what our eyes see and our ears hear. They enable us to learn and to think. They direct our glands and internal organs to function in harmony. They direct our muscles to perform such intricate and delicate feats as driving an automobile or playing a violin.

Figure 2-17 A neuron's messages: alike but in different patterns

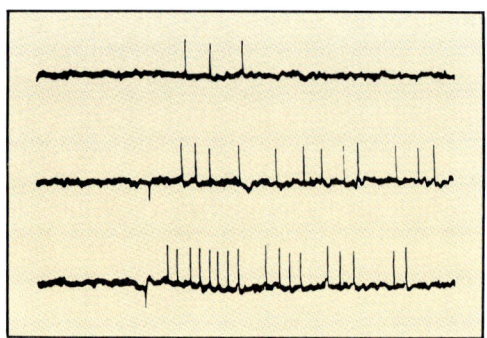

These are the tracings from an electrode that was attached to the neuron of a rat. Each upward movement of the lines shows a separate impulse. The neuron was from the rat's tongue, and the stimulus was salt solution in varying strengths. The response of the neuron to the weakest salt solution is shown in the top line. In the center line the stimulus was ten times stronger and in the bottom line a hundred times stronger. Note that the neuron's responses to these different intensities of stimulation varied only in rate and pattern, not in the strength of its individual impulses (Pfaffman, 1955).

Different neurons, in transmitting their nervous impulses, release different kinds of neurotransmitter chemicals at the synapse. These chemicals must be properly balanced if the whole enterprise is to function properly. Anything that affects the amount and effectiveness of these chemicals in the brain cells is likely to profoundly influence our thoughts, feelings, and activities.

There are nine brain chemicals generally recognized as neurotransmitters, and many more are expected to be identified (Iversen, 1982). They are necessary for normal brain functioning and behavior, but when the balance is disturbed, serious psychological problems may arise. Three of the best known neurotransmitters are *acetylcholine* (which is involved in the memory problems of patients with Alzheimer's disease); *norepinephrine* (involved, with other neurotransmitters, in major depression); and *dopamine* (involved in schizophrenia and Parkinson's disease). For a discussion of an innovative way to overcome disturbed dopamine transmission in Parkinson's disease, see the box on Psychology in Everyday Life called "Brain Grafts: Potential Source of Healing."

In addition to the neurotransmitters, there are other essential chemicals known as *peptides*. Some of these chemicals act like neurotransmitters. But most are more like hormones, because they are usually released into the bloodstream and affect both parts of the nervous system and distant organs outside it. Scientists first discovered some of these substances in locations far from the brain, such as in the intestines.

Brain peptides can be as powerful in their effects as synthetically manufactured drugs prescribed by doctors. Some seem to affect parts of the brain associated with pain and with emotion and mood (Bloom, Lazerson, and Hofstadter, 1985). Others have profound influences on behavior—including, for example, drinking, muscular movement, and memory (Iversen, 1982). More than 50 peptides have already been identified, and their number is growing (Snyder, 1984).

One group of brain peptides has been named *endorphins*—from the Greek word meaning "the morphine within"—because they are similar in structure and effect to the powerful painkiller morphine (Thompson, 1985). The endorphins may help explain the mystery of acupuncture (sticking fine needles into various parts of the body), an ancient technique widely used by Chinese physicians to reduce pain and treat physical ailments. Applying needles in this way seems to increase production of the brain's own brand of morphine—

Psychology in Everyday Life
Brain Grafts: Potential Source of Healing

Until recently, the idea of transplanting portions of the brain was approached largely by writers of science fiction. But now the possibility of actually grafting healthy tissue to replace diseased or injured portions of the brain has been demonstrated by brain scientists (Wyatt and Freed, 1983). Research has shown that the brain is usually less likely to reject newly grafted tissue than are body organs (Wyatt and Freed, 1985).

One promising area for the use of brain grafts is in relieving the symptoms of Parkinson's disease, a brain disorder that causes body movements—even walking—to become uncoordinated. The disease appears to be caused by damage to an area of the brain stem called the *substantia nigra*, or "black substance," where neurons normally secrete dopamine. When cells in this area die, cells in the *corpus striatum*—a part of the brain involved in movement—lose their required chemical inputs of dopamine and begin to function incorrectly.

To imitate Parkinson's disease in adult rats, researchers destroyed the substantia nigra, producing a movement disorder. They then removed substantia nigra tissue from healthy rat fetuses and implanted it into the brains of the injured rats. The grafts survived, grew, and functioned nine months after the surgery, sending out dopamine to the corpus striatum and largely correcting the movement disorder.

What about humans? Working with patients seriously afflicted with Parkinson's disease, scientists in Sweden removed a part of the adrenal gland—found just above the kidney—that also produces dopamine. They then transplanted this tissue near the affected portion of the patients' brains. Improvement has ranged from a few days to a few months (Wyatt and Freed, 1985).

What are the prospects for brain grafts? Right now they are strictly experimental, but some researchers predict they will be common in a decade. Others realistically point out that considerable research is still necessary before the technology can be widely applied. Yet the possibilities are there—including grafting tissue that produces the right brain chemicals to treat Alzheimer's disease, replacing diseased with healthy tissue in the hippocampus to remedy memory loss, and even grafting entire eyes to restore lost vision (Bjorkland and Steveni, 1984; Freed, de Medinaceli, and Wyatt, 1985). Perhaps we are truly on the threshold of translating research on the chemistry of the brain into enormous help for millions of brain-diseased people.

---

as if a natural pain barrier is set up when the needle is inserted (Facklam and Facklam, 1982). There are hints that substances derived from endorphins can help in treating schizophrenia (Snyder, 1982), but the therapeutic uses of these chemicals are just beginning to be explored.

Our understanding of brain peptides, and of endorphins in particular, is accelerating by leaps and bounds. However, because much of this knowledge is quite new (the first endorphins were only discovered in 1975), our picture of how many brain peptides there are and what they can do is still sketchy. It is clear, however, that they play an important part in our feelings and behavior.

The Down Side of Chemicals—Natural and Manufactured

When the complex interplay of electrical and chemical messages in our brains is working properly, we usually respond appropriately to the events and people in our lives. Despite some rocky times and temporary setbacks, we rebound, regain our psychological composure, and carry on.

But some people seem to lack such psychological resilience and seem to lose their ability to cope even under the mildest stress. Many lines of evidence suggest that some people have inborn vulnerabilities—possibly disturbances in the chemical functioning of their brains—that may at times become visible as serious mental illnesses. Although the precise nature of these vulnerabilities is still unknown, there is considerable evidence that when such people are actively mentally ill, their brain chemistry is awry; they may have too much or too little of certain neurotransmitters, or have an improper balance among several of them.

Although major mental illnesses cannot now be cured with medication, certain drugs do seem to correct aspects of disturbed neurotransmission enough to make patients' behavior more normal. For example, some antidepressant medications appear to work by increasing brain levels of the neurotransmitter norepinephrine, and the drugs used to treat schizophrenia block the receptors for the neurotransmitter dopamine. There is also evidence that antianxiety drugs such as Valium achieve their effect in part by increasing the activity and amount of a natural neurotransmitter that produces a sense of calm (Braestrup, 1982).

All the substances commonly thought of as "drugs"—from marijuana to heroin—exert their mind-altering influences by acting on the brain's neurotransmitters. So do other substances we don't normally view as "drugs," such as alcohol, nicotine, and the caffeine in coffee and soft drinks, although their effects are less dramatic. Many medications prescribed by physicians (in addition to those used to treat mental illness), such as sleeping pills and some drugs for heart patients, also affect neurotransmitters. This is why people sometimes develop some symptoms of mental illness from the medications they take for physical disorders.

Many mental problems can be treated effectively with drugs. But *psychopharmacology*—the study of how medically prescribed drugs affect the brain, body, and behavior—is still an inexact science, limited by lack of knowledge of precisely what goes wrong in the brain in various types of mental illness, and by the current inability to design drugs precise enough to correct only the brain's chemical problems without producing side effects.

Further, people are so complex that their mental problems—and the solutions to them—are rarely solved completely by medications alone, however powerful and precise. For this reason, as described in Chapter 13, those who treat mentally ill people often use combinations of approaches, giving medications when they are needed, but also helping patients understand their problems and cope with the feelings, persons, and situations that they find most troublesome.

Turning Electricity and Chemistry into Meanings and Feelings

One of the great mysteries in psychology is how the electrical and chemical activity in the brain can produce our thoughts and emotions. No one really knows, although there are hints from various kinds of research. Seymour Kety, a leading investigator of the biological foundations of behavior, acknowledges that remarkable progress has been made in understanding the structures of the brain, the relationships among its parts, and the effects of brain chemistry on behavior. But he maintains that biology is not able with its tools alone to unravel the mysteries of human personality and experience (Kety, 1982). And Nobel

Prize-winning brain scientist John Eccles has observed: "I go all the way with my fellow scientists in understanding the brain physically. But it doesn't explain me, or human choice, delight, courage, or compassion. I think we must go beyond. . . . There is something apart from all the electricity and chemistry we can measure" (Facklam and Facklam, 1982).

Psychologists work to understand human behavior at many different levels—from analyzing the most minute workings of brain cells to the broad interactions of people with one another in groups, from observing behavior in animals to plumbing the breadth and depth of human feelings. All of these approaches are needed to answer the central question: How and why do we behave as we do? Understanding how the brain works is an essential part of the picture, but it is only one part. The remaining chapters will show how other aspects of psychology also help to answer the same question.

SUMMARY

The privileged brain and its powerful connections

1. The *brain* governs all our psychological and physical functions through its connections with other parts of the body.
2. The topmost and largest part of the brain is the *cerebrum,* covered by the *cerebral cortex*. The cerebrum and its cortex are split down the middle into a *left hemisphere* and a *right hemisphere*.
3. The cerebral cortex, larger in human beings in relation to body size than in any other species, is the part of the brain responsible for remembering, thinking, and planning.
4. The human brain contains between 50 and 200 billion fiberlike nerve cells (or *neurons*) that are primarily responsible for transmitting messages. However, some neurons act as sense organs sensitive to changes in body temperature and blood chemistry (thus detecting when the body needs more food or water), while others act as glands that secrete chemicals into the bloodstream (thus stimulating many kinds of bodily activity).
5. The neurons of the brain affect behavior through the rest of the nervous system, which is made up of various kinds of neurons connected with the brain. The *peripheral nervous system* is made up of the outlying neurons throughout the body. The *central nervous system* is made up of the brain and *spinal cord*.
6. *Afferent neurons* carry impulses from the sense organs to the brain. *Efferent neurons* carry messages from the brain to the glands and muscles. *Connecting neurons* are the intermediaries between other neurons.

The brain in action: 1. Sensing the world and responding to it

7. The specialized areas of the cerebral cortex responsible for analyzing and interpreting messages from the sense organs are referred to as the *somatosensory cortex*.
8. The *thalamus* is a relay and processing center for messages from the sense organs and for motor commands from the cerebral cortex to the peripheral nervous system.

9. The *reticular activating system* helps keep the top part of the brain in a state of arousal and activity.
10. The specialized strip on the cerebral cortex that controls body movements and speech is called the *motor cortex*.
11. The *cerebellum* controls body balance and the coordination of complicated muscular movements.

The brain in action: 2. Thinking, planning and remembering

12. The *association cortex*, which makes up the unspecified areas of the cerebral cortex, is concerned with consciousness—our awareness of ourselves and our ability to think about the past and imagine the future.
13. The *hippocampus* appears to be essential in the transformation of new information into long lasting memories.
14. The rapid development of the cerebral cortex in early life is related to the growth of the child's intellectual abilities.
15. The right hemisphere of the brain deals with the left side of the body. The left hemisphere controls the right side of the body and the use of language; in most people it is the dominant hemisphere.
16. The two hemispheres are in constant communication through the *corpus callosum*, a thick cable of interconnecting neurons.
17. Experiments with patients whose corpus callosum has been cut—split-brain patients—indicate that the left hemisphere specializes in individual items of information, logic, and reasoning, while the right hemisphere specializes in information about form, space, music, and entire patterns and is the intuitive half of the brain.

The brain in action: 3. Producing emotions and keeping our bodies in tune

18. The *limbic system*, a network of brain structures and pathways, helps regulate emotional behavior.
19. A prominent part of the limbic system is the *hypothalamus*—the brain's most direct link to the body glands that are active in emotions. The master gland, the *pituitary*, is attached to the hypothalamus.
20. The hypothalamus also plays a role in maintaining the body's *homeostasis*, the state of stability in such matters as internal temperature and chemical balance.
21. The *medulla* is responsible for a number of essential bodily processes including breathing, heart rate, and digestion.
22. The *autonomic nervous system* exercises a more or less independent control over the glands, the heart muscles, and the muscles of the body's organs and blood vessels. It helps regulate breathing, heart rate, blood pressure, and digestion. In times of emergency it works in conjunction with the endocrine glands to mobilize the body's resources for drastic action.
23. The *endocrine glands*, or *ductless glands*, influence behavior by secreting *hormones* (or activators) into the bloodstream. The most important endocrine glands are:

a. The *pineal*, which affects mood and fertility.
   b. The *pituitary*, which is the master gland, producing hormones that control growth, cause sexual development at puberty, and regulate other glands.
   c. The *parathyroids*, which maintain a normal state of excitability of the nervous system.
   d. The *thyroid*, which regulates metabolism and affects levels of body activity, temperature, and weight.
   e. *Adrenals*, which secrete the powerful stimulants *adrenalin* (active in states of emergency or fear) and *noradrenalin* (active during physical effort or anger).
   f. The *pancreas*, which governs blood sugar level.
   g. The female *ovaries* and male *testes*, which regulate sexual characteristics and behavior.
24. The autonomic nervous system is composed of two parts: (1) the *parasympathetic division*, which is most active under ordinary circumstances; and (2) the *sympathetic division*, which is active in emergencies.

The brain's communications network

25. Each neuron in the nervous system is a fiberlike cell with receivers called *dendrites* at one end and senders called *end branches* at the other. Stimulation of the neuron at its dendrites—or at *receptor sites* on its cell body—sets off a nervous impulse that travels the length of the fiber, or *axon*, to the end branches, where the impulse activates other neurons, muscles, or glands.
26. The key to the transmission of nervous messages is the *synapse*, a junction point where a sender of one neuron is separated by only a microscopic distance from a receiver of another neuron.
27. The sending neuron can stimulate the receiving neuron electrically at times, but it usually releases chemical *neurotransmitters* that flow across the tiny gap of the synapse and act on the receiving neuron.
28. A neuron ordinarily fires on the *all or none principle*—if it fires at all, it fires as hard as it can. Most neurons have a maximum firing rate of several hundred times a second.
29. Since each neuron usually produces only its own little unvarying impulse, the miracles of human consciousness and cognition are determined by the rate at which the impulses are produced, the patterns they form, and the way they are routed through the brain.
30. Anything that alters the amount and effectiveness of neurotransmitters in the brain is likely to profoundly influence our thoughts, feelings, and activities.
31. Among the best known neurotransmitters are *acetylcholine* (which seems to be involved in the memory problems of patients with Alzheimer's disease), *norepinephrine* (involved, with other neurotransmitters, in major depression), and *dopamine* (involved in schizophrenia and Parkinson's disease).
32. *Peptides* are chemicals that act like neurotransmitters but are more like hormones, since they are released into the bloodstream and affect both parts of the nervous system and the distant organs outside it. One group of brain peptides, called *endorphins*, is similar in structure and effect to the powerful painkiller morphine.

33. Many mental problems can be treated effectively with drugs. But *psychopharmacology*—the study of how medically prescribed drugs affect the brain, body, and behavior—is still an inexact science.

IMPORTANT TERMS

acetylcholine
adrenalin
adrenals
afferent neuron
all or none principle
association cortex
autonomic nervous system
axon
brain
cell body
central nervous system
cerebellum
cerebral cortex
cerebrum
connecting neuron
corpus callosum
corpus striatum
dendrite
dopamine
efferent neuron
end branches
endocrine gland (ductless gland)
endorphins
frontal lobes
ganglia
hippocampus
homeostasis
hormone
hypothalamus
left hemisphere
limbic system

medulla
metabolism
motor cortex
myelin sheath
neuron
neurotransmitter
nodes
noradrenalin
norepinephrine
ovaries
pancreas
parasympathetic division
parathyroids
peptides
peripheral nervous system
pineal
pituitary
pons
psychopharmacology
receptor site
reticular activating system
right hemisphere
somatosensory cortex
spinal cord
substantia nigra
sympathetic division
synapse
synaptic cleft
synaptic knobs
synaptic vesicles
thalamus

RECOMMENDED READINGS

Brown, T. S., and Wallace, P. *Physiological psychology.* New York: Academic Press, 1980.

Bunge, M. *The mind-body problem: a psychobiological approach.* New York: Pergamon Press, 1980.

Cotman, C. W., and McGaugh, J. L. *Behavioral neuroscience: an introduction.* New York: Academic Press, 1980.

Eccles, J. C. *The understanding of the brain*, 2d ed. New York: McGraw-Hill, 1977.

Gazzaniga, M. S. *The social brain: discovering the networks of the mind.* New York: Basic Books, 1985.

Hart, L. A. *Human brain and human learning.* New York: Longman, 1983.

Restak, R. M. *The brain.* New York: Bantam Books, 1984.

Snyder, S. H. *Drugs and the brain.* New York: W. H. Freeman, 1986.

Wittrock, M. C., ed. *The brain and psychology.* New York: Academic Press, 1980.

CHAPTER

3

SENSATION: HOW WE GATHER INFORMATION

HOW THE SENSES WORK — 81

The sensory thresholds
Sensory adaptation
The secret code of the sense organs
The pattern theory of the senses

LIGHT WAVES AND VISION — 84

The physical nature of light waves
The structure of the eye
The visual receptors
Adapting to a dark—and colorless—world
Retinal coding
Visual sensitivity and acuity

THE SPECIAL WONDERS OF COLOR VISION — 91

Pathways for the experience of color
Adding and subtracting colors
Color blindness
Afterimages
Two famous and durable theories of color vision

HEARING: TURNING SOUND WAVES INTO SOUNDS — 98

The physical nature of sound
Our receptors for hearing
The hearing receptors in action
Loudness and hearing damage
How we can tell where the sound comes from

TASTE, SMELL, TOUCH—AND THE TWO FORGOTTEN SENSES — 107

Taste
Smell
The skin senses
Bodily movement and equilibrium: the two forgotten senses

SUMMARY — 114

IMPORTANT TERMS — 116

RECOMMENDED READINGS — 117

PSYCHOLOGY IN EVERYDAY LIFE

Life without sensory stimulation — 83
How noise pollution can affect the body and mind — 106

All through our waking hours—and to some extent while we sleep—we pick up from the world about us a constant flow of information essential to our survival. Suppose for a moment that there were no way for this outside information to penetrate the sheath of skin that encases the human body. Suppose we were doomed to remain unaware of the world's sights, sounds, flavors, odors, and textures. Without the input the human senses provide, all of the rest of the psychological capabilities to be described in this book—to learn, remember, create, relate to others—would be rendered useless. Small wonder that the way the senses operate to inform us about the world has always been one of psychology's prime interests.

In their own way, the information-gathering structures of the nervous system are as remarkable as the brain itself. All our awareness of the world's colors, shapes, and movements comes to us by way of just two little patches of nerve tissue inside the eyeballs. Each is only about the size of a quarter, yet they manage to inform us about an entire landscape and to distinguish about 350,000 different gradations of hue and brightness. All our awareness of the world's sounds comes to us through just two little harp-shaped collections of neurons buried in the inner part of the ear—which are versatile enough to inform us about everything from the merest rustle of a leaf to the loudest thunderclap, and from the deepest rumble of a foghorn to the highest tweet of a piccolo.

Our eyes are so sensitive that on a clear, black night they can spot a candle flame more than 30 miles away. Our noses can detect a single drop of perfume wafted through the air in a three-room apartment. Our skin senses can feel an object as small and fragile as the wing of a bee dropped gently on our cheek (McBurney and Collings, 1977). Even as newborn infants, we can tell with amazing accuracy the direction a sound is coming from (Butterworth, 1981).

True, we are not as superior to lower animals in sensory activity as in brainpower. In fact many creatures surpass us. Hawks have better distance vision. Bees can detect ultraviolet light that we cannot see at all (the reason we sometimes get painfully sunburned on what looks like a hazy and harmless day). Bloodhounds and airport police dogs that can

Using the skin sense to enjoy the gentle feel of snowflakes.

sniff out a bag of marijuana hidden in a suitcase have a far keener sense of smell than ours. So do mice, who can discriminate genetically different strains by smell alone, and use this information to select mates who have a scent different from their own (Beauchamp, Yamazaki, and Boyse, 1985). Minnows, with taste organs all over their bodies, have a far superior sense of taste.

Yet our senses are fully capable of bringing us all the information about the outer world that we need, and our information-processing abilities have enabled us to add greatly to their powers. Radio extends our range of hearing to the conversation of astronauts walking on the moon. Television enables us to see what is happening on the other side of the world. With X-ray equipment scientists can peer into the human body, and with microscopes into the structure of a human cell.

HOW THE SENSES WORK

Though our sense organs vary greatly in the sensations they generate, they all work on a few basic principles. They have to be activated by a *stimulus*—a form of energy impinging on them. They must also have a *receptor* sensitive to that particular kind of stimulus. At the moment, the stimulus is the light waves reflecting off your book. The receptors are the light-sensitive cells in your eyes. You cannot see the book in a totally blackened room because there are no light waves, nor through your ears or fingertips because they have no receptors for light. When receptor cells are activated by a stimulus, they set off bursts of nervous impulses routed to the sensory areas of the cerebral cortex, where they are translated into our conscious sensations of vision, hearing, and the other senses

The Sensory Thresholds

One principle that holds for all the senses is that they are activated only by a stimulus that is at or above their *absolute threshold*, or the minimum amount of stimulus energy to which their receptors can respond. Any weaker stimulus has no effect and therefore goes unnoticed. When a physician tests your hearing by noting how far you can follow the ticking of a watch, he is making a rough estimate of your absolute threshold of hearing. In scientific studies of the relationship between stimuli and sensations, more precise measurements are used. These show that stimuli of borderline strength are sometimes detected and sometimes missed. The absolute threshold is defined as the energy level at which a subject can detect the stimulus 50 percent of the time. However, the absolute threshold will vary some, depending on the conditions under which the stimulus is presented.

The senses also have a threshold for the ability to discriminate between two stimuli that are similar in strength but not exactly alike. For example, suppose you see a flash of light, followed immediately by a different flash. How much greater intensity would the second light require before you could notice a difference? The answer, it has been found, is 1.6 percent. This is the *difference threshold* for light, also known as the *just noticeable difference*, or j.n.d. For sound the difference threshold is about 10 percent, with slight differences for high- and low-pitched sounds.

The rule that the difference threshold is a fixed percentage of the original stimulus is called *Weber's law*, in honor of the physiologist who discovered it more than a century ago. The law holds primarily over a large part of the range of stimulation. In practical terms, it means this: The more intense the sensory stimulation to which the human organism is being subjected, the greater the increase in intensity required to produce a recognizable difference. In a room where there is no sound except the soft buzz of a mosquito, you can hear a pin drop. On a noisy city street you can hear the loud honk of an automobile horn but may be completely unaware of a friend shouting to you from down the block.

Sensory Adaptation

When you undress, you sometimes notice marks on your skin caused by a wristwatch, belt, or elastic band in your clothing. Surely those areas of skin have been subjected all day to a considerable amount of pressure. Why did you not feel it?

The answer lies in the principle of *sensory adaptation*, which means that **after a time our senses adjust to a stimulus**—they get used to it, so to speak—and the sensation produced by the stimulus tends to disappear. If you hold salt water or a bitter fluid in your mouth, the taste goes away. The strong smell that greets you in a fish market soon seems to disappear. Your eyes may strike you as an exception, because your vision never goes blank no matter how long you stare at an object, but this is only because the eyes are never really still. The muscles controlling the eyeballs constantly produce spontaneous, pendulum-like motions at the rate of as many as 100 a minute, which means that light rays never keep stimulating the same receptor cells for very long. By attaching a miniature slide projector to the eyeball, casting a continuing image on the same receptor cells despite any movements, it has been found that the image quickly fades from sight (Pritchard, 1961).

All the senses demonstrate adaptation in one way or another—though a new stimulus will immediately produce a new response. In practical terms, the principle of adaptation means that our sensory equipment is built to inform us of changes in the environment—exactly the kind of information that is most valuable.

The Secret Code of the Sense Organs

The manner in which the sense organs send their information to the brain—and the way the sensory areas of the cortex manage to understand the messages and translate them into our conscious sensations—is another of the marvels of the nervous system. When a receptor cell is stimulated, all it can do is set off bursts of nervous impulses. These impulses are all of equal strength. They vary only in number and in the pattern of firing, close together in rapid succession or farther apart.

On their way to the brain the messages from the sensory receptors pass through a number of synapses—switching points at which the messages are often combined and processed into a kind of code. Each eye, for example, has about 127 million receptor cells. Right inside the eyeball, these receptors funnel their impulses into a mere one million neurons that make up the optic nerve that carries information toward the brain. Thus, on the average, the neurons of the optic nerve monitor the activity in well over 100 receptors and respond with impulses that summarize the information they have received. These messages are again processed and refined farther along the line, until finally they reach the cerebral cortex in a kind of coded shorthand that the brain cells quickly decipher, enabling us to see, hear, smell, taste, and feel. What can happen when our sense organs are denied information to send to the brain is discussed in a box on Psychology in Everyday Life called "Life Without Sensory Stimulation."

The Pattern Theory of the Senses

When scientists first began to study the operation of the senses, many of them looked for receptors designed to detect some specific quality of a stimulus—for example, a visual receptor activated by a blue light wave or a hearing receptor activated by the tone from one particular piano string. But this search has been abandoned. Through modern techniques

Psychology in Everyday Life
Life Without Sensory Stimulation

Over three decades ago, a famous experiment showed what happens to people who are deprived of sensory stimulation. The experiment is illustrated in Figure 3-1. Volunteers remained in bed, with their senses of sight, hearing, and touch masked. Except during meal periods, they tasted and smelled nothing. In other words, activity of their senses was held almost to zero.

Soon many of them were unable to think logically. Their memories became disorganized. Sometimes they felt strangely happy. At other times they felt anxious or even panicky. Some of them began to develop symptoms associated with severe mental disturbance. They saw imaginary sights and heard imaginary sounds. The experience was so upsetting that nearly half of them had to beg off within 48 hours, even though they were being paid generously for each day that they continued. Later studies have shown that about one third of all participants drop out before the end of such an experiment (Goldberger, 1982).

Other investigators, however, using similar techniques, have found less dramatic effects. One study found that sensory deprivation may even produce some beneficial effects—for example, an increase in creative thinking, an openness to experiences, and the discovery by heavy smokers that they can do without cigarettes when the usual incentives associated with smoking are removed (Suedfeld, 1975).

The conflicting results arrived at by different experimenters suggest that the expectations of subjects may play a part in the results. If you fear adverse consequences, you are more likely to experience them. Some POWs held in isolation for years have managed through a positive approach to suffer surprisingly few symptoms (Segal, 1986). Another factor is the matter of individual differences in the need for stimulation—influenced by such variables as age, earlier experiences, biological makeup, and the extent of sensory stimulation encountered before the period of deprivation begins (Schultz, 1965).

In general, however, it is safe to conclude that most of us do have a need for at least some sensory stimulation if we are to continue functioning in a normal fashion. The findings from sensory deprivation studies have helped guide those responsible for designing more secure working environments—for workers on assembly lines, truckers driving their haul over long distances, radar operators scanning their screens, and astronauts traveling in the void of space (Rasmussen, 1973). Life without sensory stimulation can become more than just boring. It can pose threats to our safety and well-being.

Prisoners often suffer from a lack of sensory stimulation.

Figure 3-1 An experiment in sensory deprivation

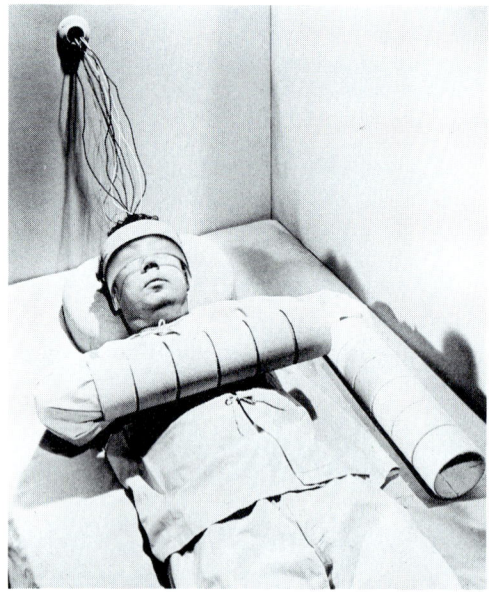

This man is taking part in an experiment designed to show what happens when activity of the human senses is reduced as near as possible to zero. The eyeshade permits him to see nothing but a dim haze. The arm casts mask the sense of touch in his hands. The room is soundproofed, and he hears nothing but the soft hum of a fan. The wires at the top of the photo recorded his brain waves (Bexton, Heron, and Scott, 1954). For what happens to him under these conditions, see the text.

it is now possible to measure the impulses in a single sensory neuron of a laboratory animal, and these measurements show that the sensory receptors are not narrowly specialized but what one investigator has termed "broadly tuned" (Uttal, 1973). The eye of a monkey—and presumably the human eye as well—contains some receptor cells that show their greatest response to a blue light wave (MacNichol, 1964). The monkey's ear contains receptors that show their greatest response to a tone of C above middle C (Rose et al., 1971).

But these receptors will also respond, to some extent and in one way or another, to a fairly wide range of light or sound waves. They are not specifically designed to detect just a single kind of stimulus, as Channel 2 on your television set is zeroed in on one station and one only.

The modern view of how the senses operate is called the *pattern theory*. This theory holds that stimuli for any of the senses affect a great many *broad-tuned receptors*. For example, the blue light from the sky will arouse receptors that can respond to shades of blue, not just the specific wavelengths of the sky's blue. Or, a particular group of receptor cells in the ear will respond to a family of similar frequencies, not just a single frequency.

Though the senses all operate on this principle, they show a considerable variety in the location of their receptors, the stimuli to which they respond, and the sensations they produce. The rest of the chapter will describe them one by one, starting with the intricacies of vision, and going on to hearing, taste, smell, touch, and finally, two senses we do not often think about—bodily movement and equilibrium.

LIGHT WAVES AND VISION

The stimulus for vision is light waves, which are pulsations of electromagnetic energy. This energy can travel over tremendous distances—as when light from a star reaches us across the vast expanses of empty space. The light waves travel at 186,000 miles (300,000 kilometers) a second, the fastest speed known and presumably the fastest possible. This is such a great velocity that a light wave, if you could manage to reflect it around the world, would make the long journey and get back to you in less than one-seventh of a second.

As can be seen in Figure 3-2, light waves are closely related to many other forms of pulsating energy, ranging from infinitesimal cosmic rays to the huge waves of household electricity, which are 100 million meters long. In this vast spectrum of electromagnetic energy, light occupies only a very small niche. The tiny band of waves we can see ranges from about 380 billionths of a meter to about 780 billionths. The shortest waves, which are seen as violet, are just a little bit longer than the invisible ultraviolet rays that cause sunburn. The longest, which are seen as red, are just a little bit shorter than the invisible infrared waves produced by a heating lamp.

The Physical Nature of Light Waves

Light has three qualities that determine the sensations it produces:

1. *Wavelength*, the distance between the peaks of the waves, determines the *hue*, the scientific term for the color we see. White light is a mixture of all the hues. When a white light such as a sunbeam is broken down into its components by passing through a prism, the wavelengths are separated to form the visible spectrum shown in Figure 3-2.
2. *Intensity*, the amount of energy in the light wave, determines the sensation of *brightness*, although not entirely. The same intensity of light ordinarily produces greater brightness at the yellow and green wavelengths in the middle of the visible spectrum.
3. *Complexity*, the degree to which the predominant wavelength is somewhat mixed with other wavelengths, determines the sensation called *saturation*. The purer the wave-

Figure 3-2 Electromagnetic energy and the visible spectrum

Various forms of electromagnetic radiation range from cosmic rays, the shortest waves, to ordinary household electricity, the longest. The visible spectrum of light, with waves ranging from about 380 to 780 billionths of a meter, occupies only a small portion of the band.

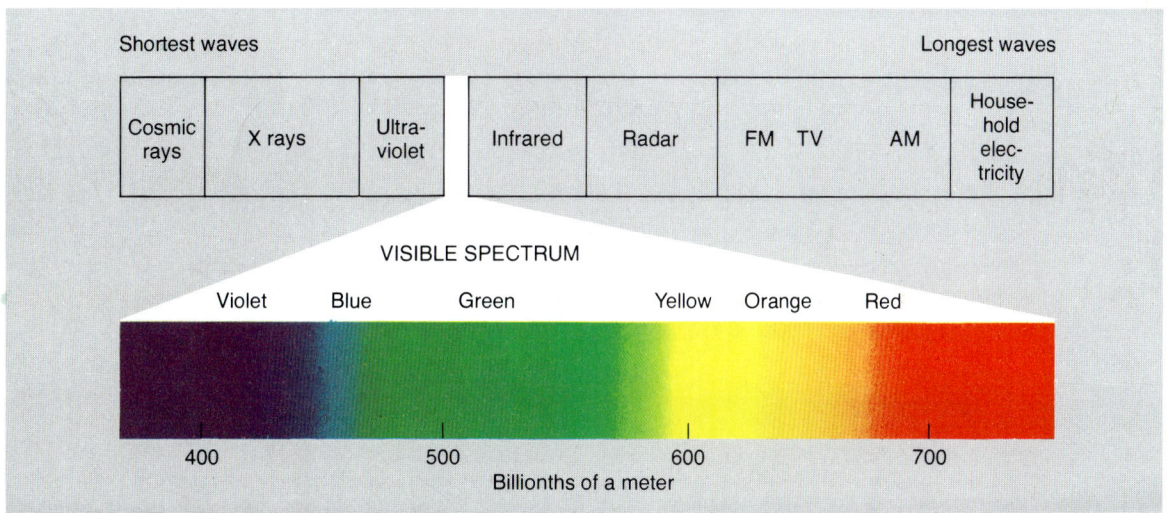

length, the greater the saturation and the more vivid the hue. When other wavelengths are mixed in, we see a hue that we often describe as duller or muddier. A pure or saturated red is strikingly colorful. If other wavelengths are added to reduce the saturation, what we see is "less red."

The Structure of the Eye

If you have ever taken photographs—especially with a camera that must be properly set and focused before the shutter is snapped—you should feel right at home with the diagram of the eyeball in Figure 3-3. The *iris* serves the same purpose as the diaphragm in a camera. When the smooth muscles of the iris open to maximum size, as they do under dim conditions, the *pupil*, which is the opening in the iris, admits about 17 times as much light as

Figure 3-3 The structure of the eye

Light waves first strike the cornea, *a transparent bulge in the outer layer of the eyeball. The cornea serves as a sort of preliminary lens, gathering light waves from a much wider field of vision than would be possible if the eyeball merely had a perfectly flat window at the front. The light waves then pass through the* pupil, *which is an opening in the* iris, *a circular arrangement of smooth muscles that contract and expand to make the pupil smaller in bright light and larger in dim light. (When you look at your eyes in a mirror, the pupil is the dark, almost black circle at the center. The iris is the larger circle around it containing the pigments that determine eye color.) Behind the pupil lies the transparent* lens, *the shape of which is controlled by the* ciliary muscles. *The lens focuses the light rays on the* retina, *which contains the light-sensitive receptors of the eye. The receptors are most tightly packed in the* fovea, *where visual acuity is greatest. Messages from the receptors are transmitted to the brain by way of the* optic nerve, *which exits from the back of the eyeball, a little off center. Attached to the eyeball are muscles that enable us to look up, down, and sideways. The space inside the eyeball is filled with a transparent substance, as is the space between the cornea and the iris (Bloom and Fawcett, 1968).*

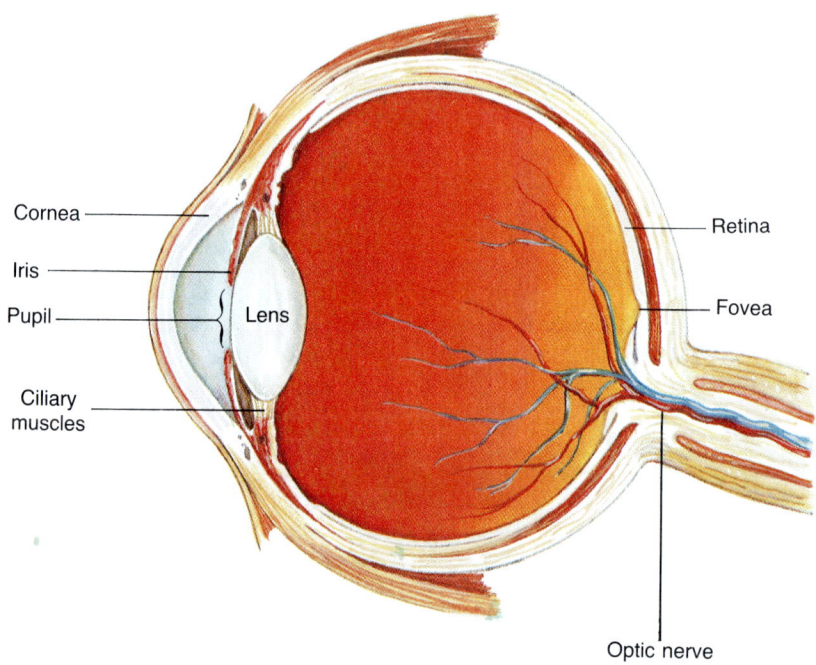

Figure 3-4 A demonstration of the blind spot

Hold the book at arm's length, close your right eye, and look at the teddy bear on the right. Now move the book slowly closer. When the image of the teddy bear at the left falls on the blind spot of your left eye, it will disappear. To demonstrate the blind spot of the right eye, repeat with the left eye closed and your gaze concentrated on the teddy bear at the left.

when it is contracted to its smallest size. The *lens* of the eye serves the same purpose as the lens of a camera but in a way that would not be possible with even the most carefully designed piece of glass. The lens of a camera has to be moved forward and backward to focus on nearby or faraway objects. The lens of the eye remains stationary but changes shape. The action of the *ciliary muscles* makes the lens thinner to bring faraway objects into focus and enables it to thicken to focus on nearby objects. Sharp images created by the lens are cast on the *retina*, the eye's equivalent of film.

Receptor cells in the retina trigger nervous impulses that leave the eyeball by way of the *optic nerve*. At the point where this cable of neurons exits, there is a small gap in the retina known as the *blind spot*, containing no receptors. We are never aware of this gap in our visual field in ordinary life, but you can discover it for yourself by examining Figure 3-4.

The Visual Receptors

Although a good camera has a sharper lens and a diaphragm with a much wider range than the iris, no photographic film can begin to compare with the efficiency of the retina. The receptors are sensitive to low intensities of light that would not register at all in a camera and can also function under high intensities that would burn out the film.

Each retina, if flattened out, would be an irregular ellipse with a total area of just about three-fourths of a square inch (slightly under five square centimeters). Packed into this small area are about 127 million receptors of the kind shown in Figure 3-5. The great majority of the receptors are long and narrow, a fact that has given them the name *rods*. The rest, numbering about 7 million, are somewhat thicker and tapered; these are called *cones*. Both rods and cones respond to different intensities of light. The rods function chiefly under conditions of low illumination and send information to the brain about movement and about whites, grays, and blacks but not about color. The cones function in strong illumination and provide sensations not only of movement and brightness from white to black but also of hue or color.

The cones are most numerous toward the middle of the retina. The area called the *fovea*, near the very center of the retina, contains only cones, packed together more tightly

Figure 3-5 The retina's receptor cells

The shapes that give the names to the eye's light-sensitive rods and cones can be seen clearly in this photograph of the retina, magnified about 45,000 times.

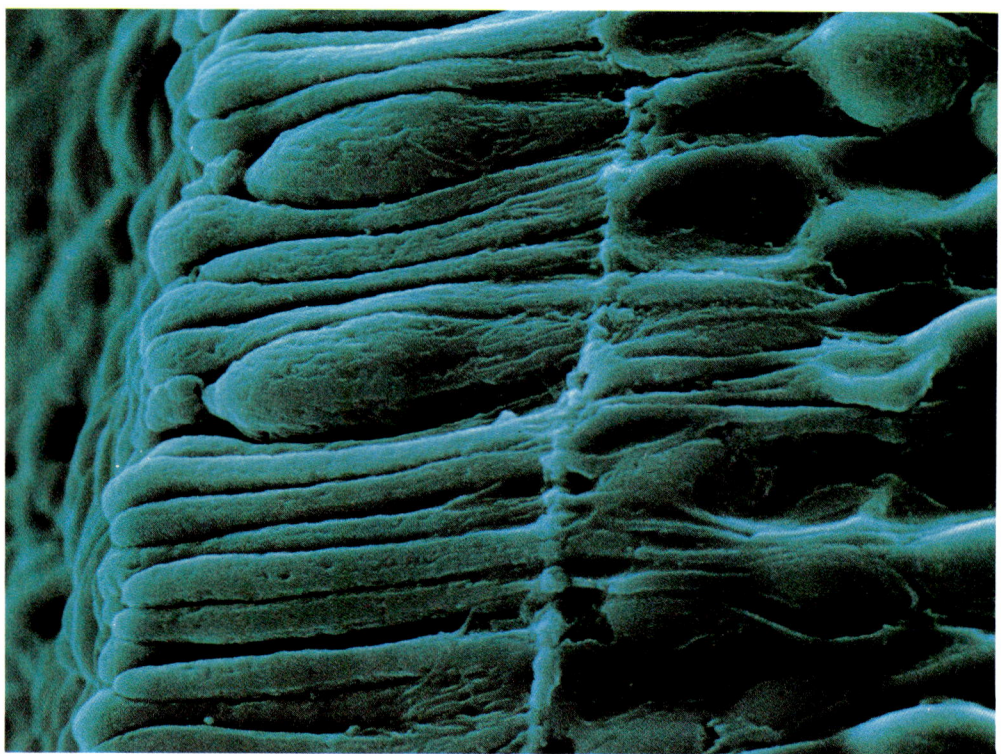

than anywhere else. This is where our vision is sharpest. When we read or do anything else that requires a very sharp image, we keep the object in the center of our field of vision so that its light waves fall on the fovea.

The manner in which light waves stimulate the receptors of the retina was discovered many years ago when physiologists managed to extract a substance called *rhodopsin* from the rods. Rhodopsin is a pigment that absorbs light, which bleaches it at a rate depending on intensity and wavelength. Thus light waves striking the retina produce chemical changes in the rhodopsin, and these changes act to stimulate the neurons next in the pathway that carries messages from receptors to brain (Wald, 1951).

The cones contain certain pigments that operate in much the same way, except that there are three different types. One is most sensitive to blue wavelengths, another to green, and the third to waves in the green-yellow portion of the spectrum. As is shown in Figure 3-6, however, all three types are broadly tuned, and their pigments respond to some degree to many wavelengths.

Adapting to a Dark—and Colorless—World

One of the most valuable aspects of our visual equipment is its ability to function under an extremely wide range of illumination. Note what happens when you walk through bright

Figure 3-6 The three types of cones and how they react

The graph lines show the sensitivity of the three cones in the retina of a monkey to different wavelengths of light. For each, the sensitivity is greatest at one particular point along the color spectrum and grows progressively weaker at lower and higher wavelengths—but there is at least some response over a wide range. The cone most sensitive to green, for example, reacts to some extent to almost the entire spectrum, all the way from blue to orange. The measure of sensitivity used here was the amount of light absorbed by the pigments in the cone (after MacNichol, 1964).

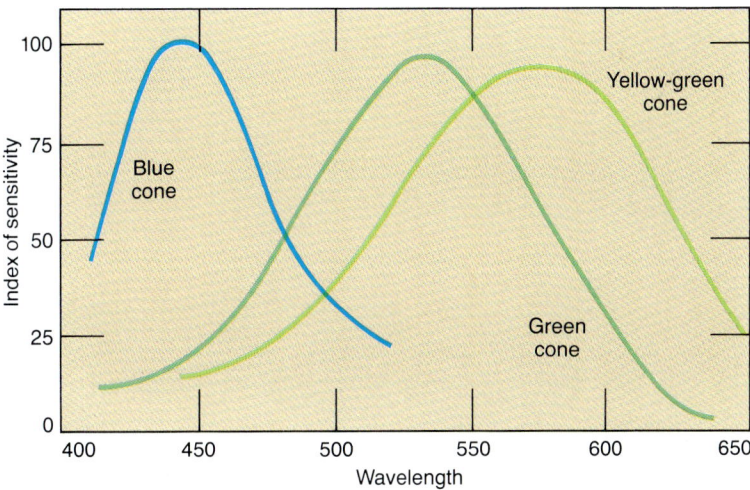

afternoon sunlight into a movie theater where there is hardly any light at all. At first the theater seems pitch-black, and you can hardly find your way down the aisle to an empty seat. But after a while your eyes undergo what is called *dark adaptation*—and you can clearly see the aisle, the seats, and the faces of the people around you.

Dark adaptation depends mostly on the rods, whose rhodopsin builds up to high levels when it goes unbleached for a time by strong light. (The production of rhodopsin, in turn, requires vitamin A—which is why people who suffer from night blindness, or inability to adapt, are advised to eat carrots.) Full adaptation to dark takes about a half hour, by which time the eyes are about 100,000 times more sensitive to light than they were in the bright sunlight. Note that you do not see colors in a dimly lighted place such as a theater—nothing but shades of gray. This is because the color-sensitive cones cannot function at low intensities of light. Only the rods respond.

Retinal Coding

The retina is much more than just a passive receiving device, responding mechanically to the presence of light waves. Besides its rods and cones, it contains many millions of neurons that are connected and interconnected into an elaborate network capable of a great deal of processing that condenses the information, and encodes it into meaningful patterns of nervous impulses that are sent to the cerebral cortex.

Some idea of how all this is accomplished within that little patch of tissue at the back of the eyeball can be gained from Figure 3-7, although the diagram is by necessity just a simplified representation of the actual complexity of the retinal network. Every rod and

Figure 3-7 The retina's processing network

This is a much simplified diagram of the complex connections and interconnections between nerve cells in the retina that process visual information and funnel it toward the brain. The direct connections run from rods and cones to bipolar cells to ganglion cells of the optic nerve. The indirect connections are made through horizontal cells and internal association cells. The way the network operates is explained in the text.

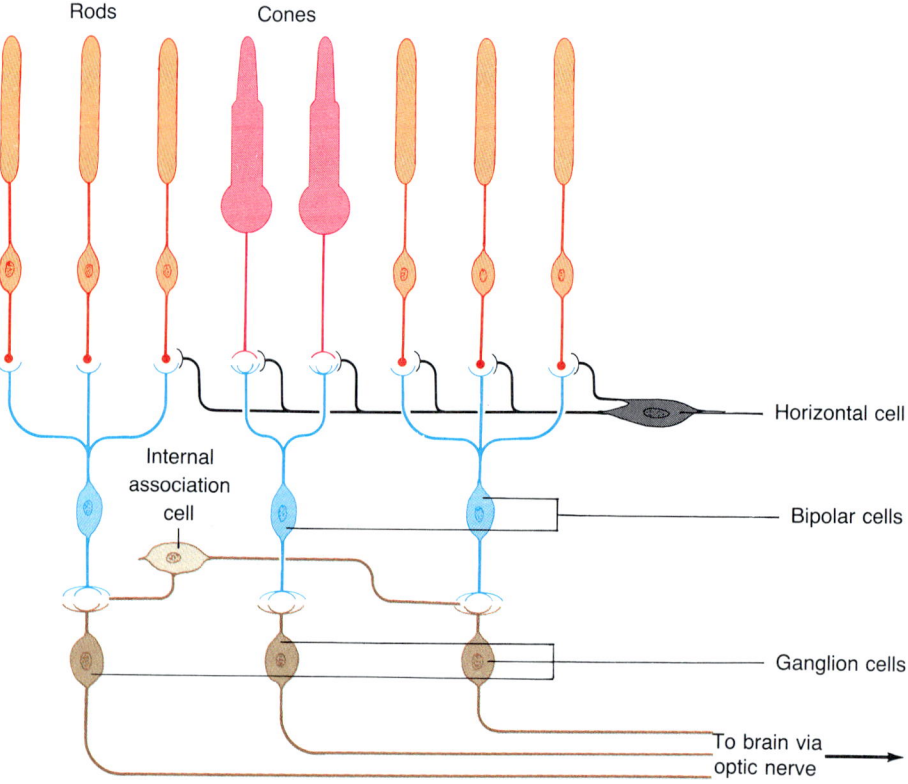

cone connects to a very short *bipolar cell* that in turn connects to a *ganglion cell* of the optic nerve. Thus the route for information can be summarized as

1. Bleaching of pigment in receptor cell
    leads to
2. Nervous impulses in bipolar cell
    leads to
3. Nervous impulses in ganglion cell

But there are many complications. At step 2 in the route a single bipolar cell may make direct contact with just one receptor cell or with many. It may also have indirect contact with some or many other receptors through a *horizontal cell*. Thus it may be stimulated to produce nervous impulses by the activity of only one receptor or in various ways by the activity of many receptors. Likewise at step 3 a ganglion cell has direct contact with just one bipolar cell or with many—and may also have indirect contact with some or many others through an *internal association cell*. It can be stimulated through any of the possible connnections. Moreover the impulses it receives often have different effects depending on what pathway has produced them. By measuring the activity of a single ganglion neuron of animals, it has been found that light striking one part of the retina may stimulate the neuron to produce a burst of impulses, while light at an adjacent part of the retina turns it off (Kuffler, 1953).

The retinal network is constructed in such a way that it permits a great amount of processing of visual information before any messages ever leave the eye. The number of possible patterns of nervous impulses created by the network—the coded messages carried by the optic nerve toward the brain—is almost beyond imagination.

Visual Sensitivity and Acuity

The retinal network, though it always bears a general resemblance to the diagram that was shown in Figure 3-7, varies in its detailed structure at different parts of the retina. At the outer part of the retina, where there are far more rods than cones and in some places no cones at all, several thousand receptors may feed into a single ganglion cell. This helps account for the far greater sensitivity of the outer part of the retina to very low intensities of light—a phenomenon you can observe for yourself by finding a very dim star in the skies at night. If you look directly at the star, so that its light waves fall at the center or fovea of the retina, it will disappear. But if you glance at it from the side, so that its waves fall on the outer part of the retina, you will see it again. One or more ganglion cells serving the outer part of the retina—and picking up messages from thousands of rods—gathered in enough stimulation to fire off a message.

The greater sensitivity to light at the outer part of the retina, however, is accompanied by a considerable loss of sharpness of vision, or *acuity*. The message sent to the brain by the ganglion cell could have originated in the stimulation of any one of the thousands of receptors it serves. Therefore the exact spot at which the retina was stimulated and the exact nature of the stimulus cannot be specified (De Valois, 1966).

At the fovea, the network takes a very different form. The ganglion cells serving the densely packed cones in this part of the retina get messages from only one or a few receptors. Thus acuity is greatest at the fovea. When you read or do anything else that requires a very sharp image, you automatically focus your eyes so that the light waves fall directly on the fovea—where there is a direct line, so to speak, from cone to optic nerve.

THE SPECIAL WONDERS OF COLOR VISION

It is a bright summer day. The sky is clear blue, the tree in the yard under which you sit is deep green, and nearby on the picnic table is a bowl of bright red apples. While we may learn to take such scenes for granted, color is a marvelous property of the objects we see. As demonstrated in Figures 3-8 and 3-10, it can be critically important in shaping our ability to make out certain aspects of the world about us (Coren, Porac, and Ward, 1984).

Despite what seems to be the case, color does not actually exist in the objects themselves. Instead it is a psychological phenomenon—an aspect of your sensory experience that is created when your brain processes the wavelengths contained in light.

Pathways for the Experience of Color

The three types of cones, each responding in its own way to different wavelengths, begin to account for our ability to distinguish all the hues of the rainbow. But the ability also depends on the coding that takes place in the complex pathway of neurons that leads from

Figure 3-8 The hidden word

Although this figure seems to be composed of a haphazard collection of gray shapes, there is actually a word hidden within it. Each letter is composed of a series of similar shapes—yet it is difficult if not impossible to detect the word despite the fact that the shape and brightness information is there. But if you turn to Figure 3-10 (page 94), where color is added to the same figure, the word virtually leaps out of the page.

the eye to the sensory areas of the cerebral cortex, through a number of switching points including a major processing and relay station in the thalamus.

The pathway begins with neurons in the retina that make contact with the receptor cells—sometimes with just one, sometimes with a number of them—and are stimulated to a greater or lesser degree by the chemical activity of the receptors. The nervous impulses in these neurons, in turn, stimulate the neurons of the optic nerve, which send their

This artist would be at a loss to capture the essence of the scene without the marvelous capacity for color vision.

impulses to the next switching point. Among the nerve cells in the pathway there appear to be four kinds responsible for color vision, each behaving in a different way in response to the messages it receives.

One type of nerve cell fires a rapid burst of impulses in response to messages indicating a blue stimulus but is turned off by a yellow stimulus, as shown in Figure 3-9. Another does just the opposite—it shows a high rate of activity in response to yellow and is turned off by blue. The third type is activated by red and slowed by green, the fourth type activated by green and slowed by red. There are also two other types of neurons that appear to be responsible for black-and-white sensations and brightness. One is turned on by white or bright stimuli and turned off by black or dark stimuli. The other works in the opposite fashion, on for dark and off for bright (De Valois and Jacobs, 1968).

This modern explanation of vision is known as the *opponent-process theory*. It is of course a pattern theory. A visual stimulus sets up a pattern of chemical response in the rods and the three kinds of cones in the retina. This pattern in turn stimulates the neurons of the visual system into their own pattern of nervous activity, with the six opponent-process cells for blue-yellow, red-green, and bright-dark all behaving in different ways. It is this pattern of nervous impulses, arriving at the visual centers of the brain, that determines what we see.

Adding and Subtracting Colors

One question that has interested researchers over the years is this: What happens to our visual sensations when various wavelengths of the spectrum are mixed together? The answer, it turns out, is not at all what everyday experiences would indicate. For example, every schoolchild who owns a paint set knows that if you have no green, you can produce it by combining blue and yellow. But every schoolchild is wrong. Mixing blue and yellow paints does not *combine* the two colors. It does something very different.

This may sound startling, but there is a simple explanation. Blue paint looks blue because it absorbs most of the wavelengths found in the white light provided by sunshine

Figure 3-9 How an opponent-processing cell works

The graph line shows the nervous impulses produced by one of the opponent-processing neurons in the visual pathway of a monkey. In the absence of any stimulation, the neuron fires at an average rate of five impulses per second. A violet-blue stimulus induces a sharp burst of activity. A yellow stimulus almost completely stops any activity (after De Valois and De Valois, 1975).

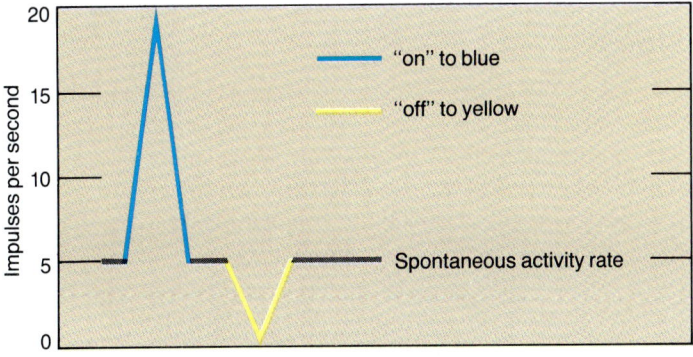

Figure 3-10 The world revealed

Note how the addition of color exposes a word buried in the jumble of colorless shapes shown in Figure 3-8.

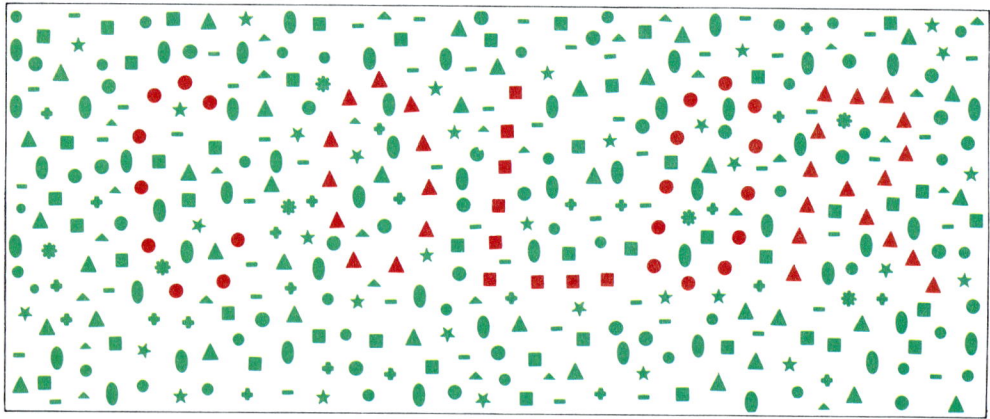

or artificial illumination. It reflects only the waves in and around the blue portion of the spectrum, including, since no paint is a pure blue, some of the green. Yellow paint absorbs most of the wavelengths of white light except those in and around the yellow part of the spectrum, again including some of the green. When you put blue and yellow paint together, you get a mixture that absorbs all the wavelengths except the ones in the green area that both paints happen to reflect. But this is not combining light waves. It is more like subtracting them.

Adding light waves together cannot be done with paint, but only with special equipment. One way is to use color filters that permit only waves of a certain length to get through, like those producing sensations of blue or yellow. When two slide projectors are equipped with different filters, two wavelengths can be thrown on the same white screen and thus actually mixed. The results are as shown in Figure 3-11. Note that the combination of blue and yellow produces not green but a neutral gray.

The laws of *color mixture*—the true blending of light waves, not the mixture of paints—are summarized in Figure 3-12. The combination of any two hues opposite each other in the circle produces gray—and such opposites are known as *complementary colors* because they cancel each other out. Two waves not opposite each other combine into the sensation of a hue somewhere between them in the circle.

Color Blindness

A few people—believed to number about 5,000 in the United States—never experience the sensation of hue at all. These people are totally *color blind* and see the world only in shades of gray, like a black-and-white photograph. Perhaps as many as another 1.5 million Americans are color blind to some extent. The most common difficulty is distinguishing reds and greens. Less common is reduced sensitivity to blues and yellows.

Most people who are color blind do not even know it. One reason is that light waves reaching the eye are seldom a fully saturated single wavelength. Both blue and yellow paints, as has been mentioned, reflect some green. Most red objects reflect some yellow waves, and most green objects some blue rays. (Traffic lights are deliberately designed this way, to help people with red-green difficulties.) Color-blind people learn to use subtle

Figure 3-11 What happens when light waves are combined

The circles show what happens when two colors are projected through filters onto the same screen. When blue and yellow are combined, the result is gray—far different from the result of mixing blue and yellow paint. Note also that the combination of red and green produces yellow. This fact greatly influenced the development of theories of color vision, as will be explained in the text. It is also the principle by which color television operates. Television tubes produce three kinds of dots on the screen—blue, red, and green—which combine to create all the hues we see.

differences in saturation—as well as brightness and other clues—to recognize and name hues they never see as the normal eye experiences them. Their deficiencies can readily be detected, however, with tests like the one shown in Figure 3-13. The tests are useful in steering people away from jobs in which color blindness would be a handicap (or, as in the case of flying an airplane, an actual hazard).

Afterimages

Another visual phenomenon is *afterimages*, which are demonstrated in Figure 3-14. (Experiment with the illustration, according to the instructions, before you go on to the next paragraph.)

What happens when you look at Figure 3-14 is this: By staring fixedly at the pattern of colors, you provide a prolonged stimulus to the receptors in the retina and the neurons that carry their messages to the brain. When the stimulus is then withdrawn (as you transfer your gaze to another part of the page) you see an afterimage that is in complementary hues to the original stimulus. If you follow the instructions carefully, this afterimage should be so vivid as to startle you—if not on the first try, at least after you have made a few practice attempts.

The Special Wonders of Color Vision

Figure 3-12 A circular guide to the hues
The laws of color mixture are summarized by this circle. To find what hue a combination of any two will produce, draw a line between them. If the line passes through the center of the circle, the result is gray. If not, the resulting hue lies in between—like a green-yellow or a blue-green.

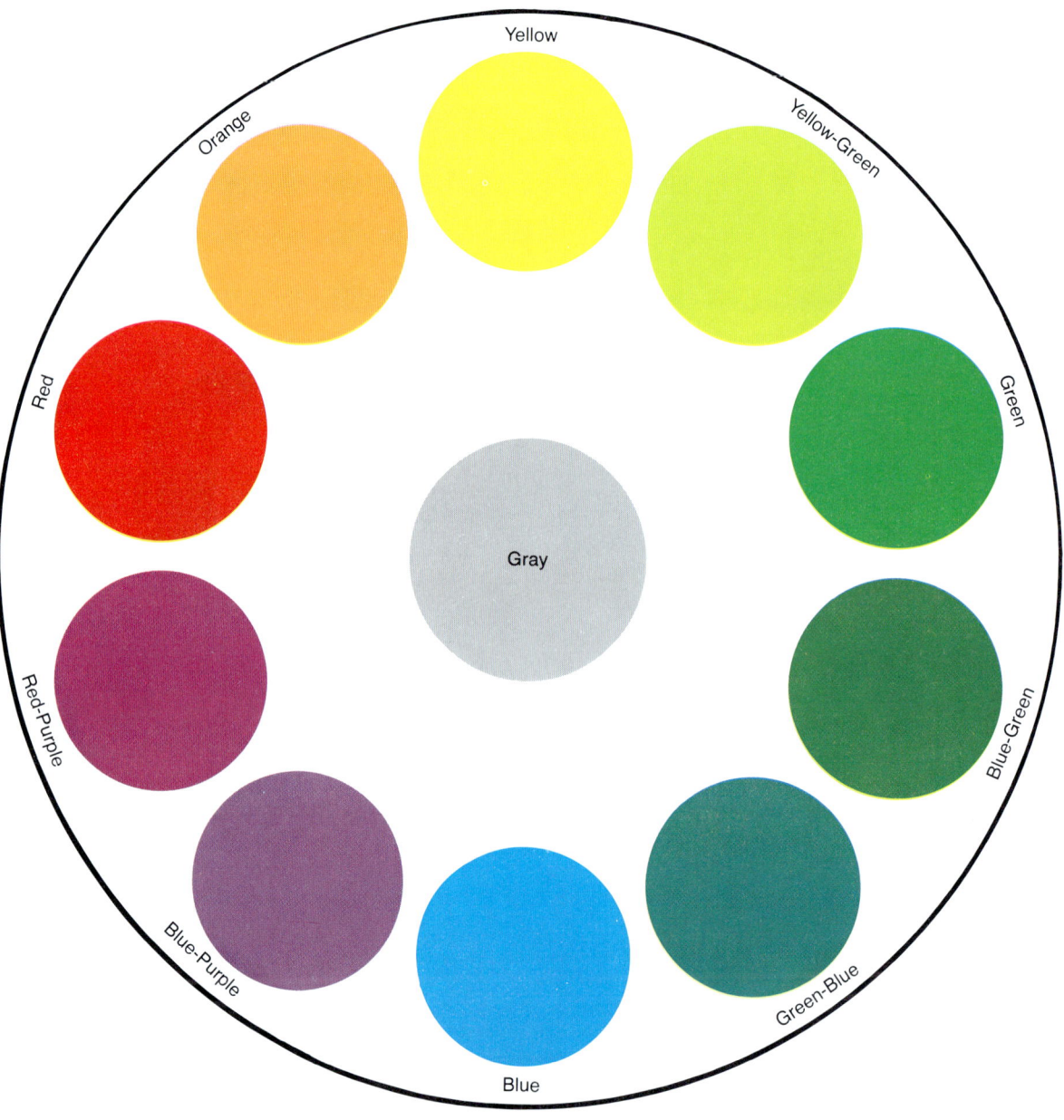

Figure 3-13   **A test of color blindness**
What numbers, if any, do you see in the circles? People with normal color vision see a 92 at the left and a 23 at the right. People with various types of color blindness see something different: only partial numbers or no numbers at all.

Figure 3-14   **A demonstration of afterimages**
Focus your eyes on the dot in the center of the circle at left and gaze steadily for a half minute or more. Then look quickly at the dot in the center of the square at right. You should see a startling change in hue.

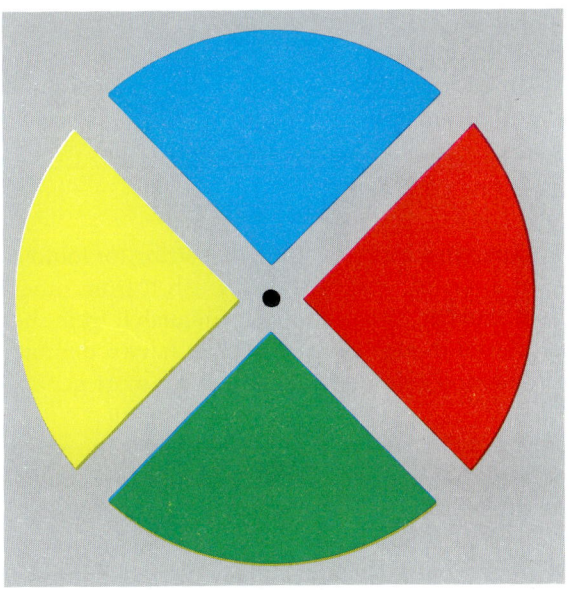

The Special Wonders of Color Vision

Actually there are two afterimages, although this is difficult to demonstrate except under laboratory conditions. Immediately after the stimulus is withdrawn you see a *positive afterimage*, in the same color as before. But this quickly vanishes and is replaced by a longer-lasting *negative afterimage*, in which the complementary colors appear.

Two Famous and Durable Theories of Color Vision

All the phenomena described earlier—afterimages, color blindness, and the laws of color mixture—have played a part in the long search for an explanation of how the sense of vision operates. The fact that a mixture of red and green waves produces yellow, as was shown in Figure 3-11, was incorporated into the famous *Young-Helmholtz theory*, which was proposed nearly two centuries ago. Young and Helmholtz, working independently, concluded that all our sensations of hue are produced by just three types of color receptors: for red, green, and blue. The sensation of yellow, with no receptor of its own, is produced by simultaneous stimulation of the red and green receptors.

The Young-Helmholtz theory, though developed long before the discovery of the retina's light-sensitive pigments, was in remarkable accord with what is now known about the receptors. It is still valid about the operation of the cones, except that what the theory held to be a red receptor has turned out to be even more sensitive to yellow, and all the cones have been found more broad tuned than Young and Helmholtz suspected. The theory was never adequate, however, to explain color blindness or afterimages.

About a century ago another famous theory was proposed as an alternative. This was the *Hering theory*, which held that the visual system must somehow operate on the basis of nervous impulses paired as black-white, red-green, and blue-yellow. This theory provided a logical explanation for all the known facts about color blindness and afterimages. For example, blue would produce its afterimages because it stimulated the blue-yellow pair in the blue direction. This nervous activity would continue for an instant after the stimulus was removed, resulting in the brief afterimage of blue. Then the complementary yellow afterimage would be produced when the blue-yellow pair acted in the opposite direction as it returned to normal.

Today's view of color vision is of course a combination of the two old theories. Modern knowledge of the retina's light-sensitive pigments and activity in individual neurons of the visual pathway has shown that Young-Helmholtz was generally correct about the receptors, Hering about the neurons. The early theories, without the help of today's laboratory techniques, made some remarkably accurate guesses.

HEARING: TURNING SOUND WAVES INTO SOUNDS

When you hit the key for middle C on a piano, a hammer strikes the string for middle C, the string vibrates, and you hear a sound. You can distinguish it from other notes, like the B just below it and the D just above it. You can also distinguish it from the middle C on any other musical instrument, even though the two sounds have a definite similarity. If you hit the key a little harder, the sound gets louder. Press the key more gently, and the sound gets softer.

Striking the piano key demonstrates some of the basic principles that govern the sense of hearing—and suggests the wide range of stimuli that our ears can detect and discriminate among. We can hear tones all the way from the deepest bass to the highest treble, and distinguish between tones that are just a tiny bit apart. We can hear anything from the merest hint of a whisper to the roar of a jet airplane, which has many millions of times more energy.

The Physical Nature of Sound

The stimulus for hearing is sound waves, traveling unseen through the atmosphere. The waves are little ripples of contraction and expansion of the air, typically produced by the vibration of a piano string or the human vocal cords or by two objects banging together. They have three qualities that determine the sensations they produce:

1. *Frequency,* or the number of waves per second, **determines the sensation of** *pitch*. The lowest sounding note on a piano measures about 27 hertz, or Hz, the scientific term for the number of cycles of contraction and expansion per second. The highest is around 4,200 Hz. Our full range of hearing extends from about 20 to 20,000 Hz.

2. *Amplitude,* or the strength of the wave, **determines the degree of loudness we hear,** although not entirely. Our sense of hearing is most sensitive to the frequencies between about 400 and 3,000 Hz, which is about the range of the human voice. Frequencies higher or lower than that do not sound as loud even when they have exactly the same amplitude. A wave of 1,000 Hz sounds louder than 10,000 Hz, which in turn sounds louder than 100 Hz, because we are least sensitive of all to low notes. The way waves vary in amplitude and frequency is illustrated in Figure 3-15.

3. *Complexity* **determines the sensation of** *timbre*, which is the quality that distinguishes a middle C on the piano from the same note on a clarinet or violin. Complexity results from the fact that virtually all sources of sound produce not just a single frequency but others as well. For example, while the middle C piano string is vibrating at 256 Hz, sections of the string also vibrate at higher frequencies though with lower amplitude. Each half vibrates at 512 Hz, twice the basic frequency, each third at 768 Hz, and so on. These additional vibrations are called overtones. All the various frequencies combine into a complex sound wave with the shape illustrated in Figure 3-16, which produces the sensation of a middle C with the timbre characteristic of its source.

Our Receptors for Hearing

What you call your ear—the flap of tissue at the side of your head—is in fact the least important part of your hearing equipment. The working parts, including the receptors, lie hidden inside the skull.

The structure is shown in Figure 3-17. The *outer ear,* or visible portion, merely collects the sound waves. The waves create vibrations of the *eardrum* that are passed along through the *middle ear,* an air-filled cavity containing three small bones that conduct the vibrations. The last of these bones, called the *stapes,* is mounted like a piston on the *cochlea*—a bony structure about the size of a pea and shaped like a snail's shell. It is the cochlea, receiving the vibrations transmitted by the stapes, which contains the *inner ear's* receptors for hearing.

The cochlea is filled with fluid. Stretched across it, dividing it more or less in half, is a piece of tissue called the *basilar membrane*. When the vibrations of sound reach the cochlea, they set up motions of the fluid inside, thus bending the basilar membrane. Lying on the membrane is the *organ of Corti,* a collection of receptors for hearing.

The Hearing Receptors in Action

With over a million essential working parts, our auditory receptor organ, the cochlea, has been described as "the most complex mechanical apparatus in the human body" (Hudspeth, 1985). Sound waves cause the entire basilar membrane to respond to wave-like, up-and-down motions that travel along its length and breadth, in turn activating the hearing

Figure 3-15 Sound waves: frequency and amplitude

The wave at the top, for the pure tone of middle C, has a frequency of 256 Hz. The wave in the middle, for the C above middle C, has twice as many cycles of contraction and expansion per second, or 512 Hz. Sounding this same note with twice the force produces the wave at the bottom, which continues at a frequency of 512 Hz but has double the amplitude, as indicated by the height of the wave. The colored portions of the wave show a single cycle of contraction and expansion.

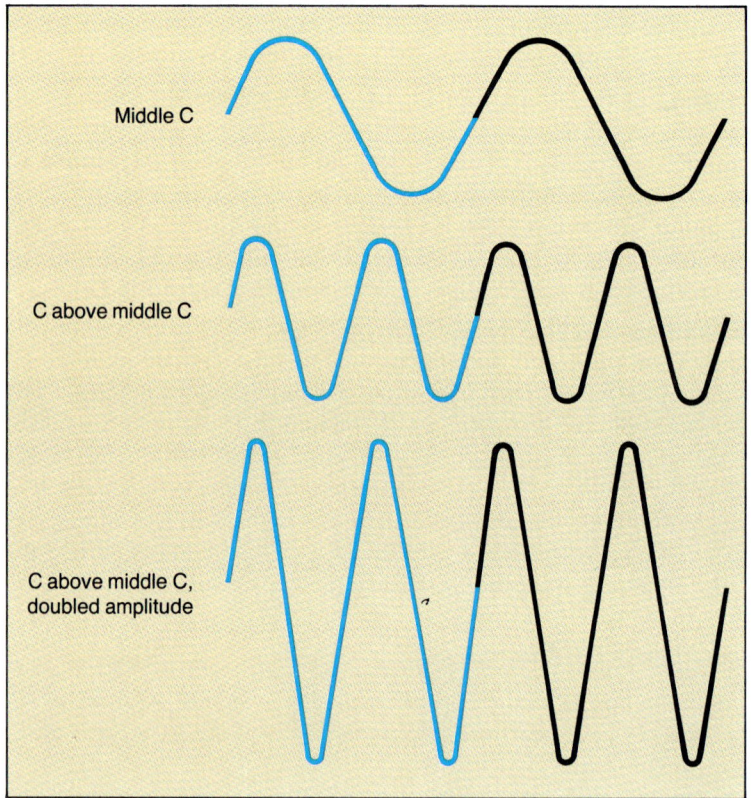

Figure 3-16 A pattern of complexity and timbre

Unlike the "pure" waves shown in Figure 3-15, the waves that usually reach our ears take this complex form. The note shown here comes from a violin. It maintains a basic frequency that produces our sensation of pitch, but each cycle of contraction and expansion is modified by overtones that change the pattern of the wave and result in our sensation of the violin's own special timbre.

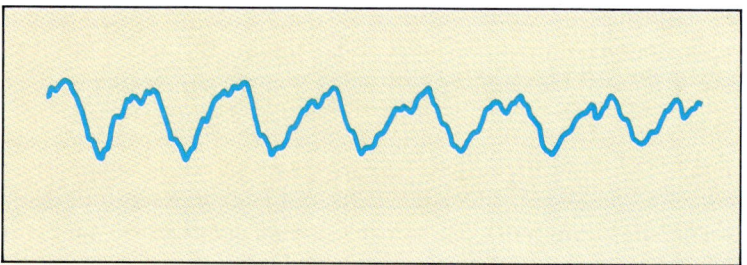

Figure 3-17 A diagram of the hearing apparatus

Sound waves enter the outer ear, *pass through the* auditory canal, *and set up vibrations of the* eardrum. *The three bones of the* middle ear *transmit the vibrations to the* cochlea *through its* oval window. *The* auditory nerve *carries messages from the hearing receptors inside the cochlea to the brain. The* Eustachian tube, *traveling from middle ear to throat, keeps the air pressure inside the middle ear at the same level as outside. (When the tube is temporarily clogged, as sometimes happens when you have a cold or ride in an airplane or elevator, you can feel a difference in pressure against the eardrum.) The* semicircular canals *play no part in hearing but are responsible for our sense of equilibrium, as discussed later.*

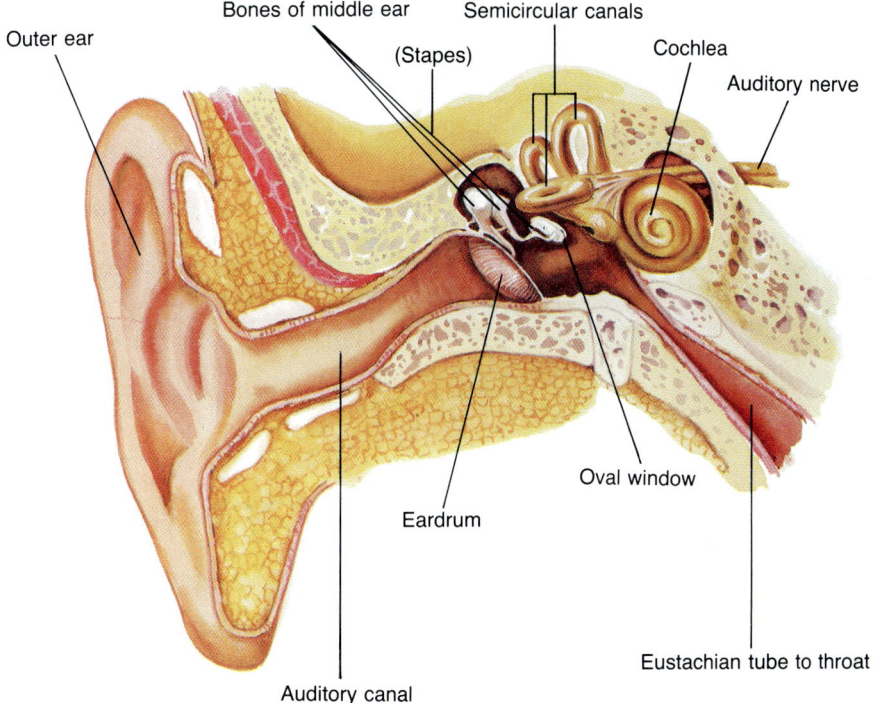

receptors resting on the membrane. The unique feature of these receptor cells is a bundle of protruding hairs as pictured in Figure 3-18. When the floor beneath the receptors moves, the hairs move and bend like tiny dancers. This stimulates the neurons of the *auditory nerve*, to which the receptors connect, to produce the nervous impulses that are routed toward the sensory areas of the cerebral cortex.

Exactly how the basilar membrane operates is described in Figure 3-19. The code of nervous impulses in which hearing messages eventually reach the cerebral cortex seems to depend in part on which receptors, at which locations along the membrane, are stimulated. This is referred to as *place theory*. The hearing receptors, however, are excellent examples of broad tuning, for they generally respond to a considerable range of frequencies. Figure 3-20 illustrates the activity of a single neuron associated with a single receptor cell. This particular neuron was stimulated to its most rapid-fire burst of impulses by a frequency of about 1,800 Hz. But it was also stimulated, though to a lesser degree, by frequencies anywhere from about as low as 300 Hz to about as high as 2,500 Hz.

Figure 3-18 The hair cell

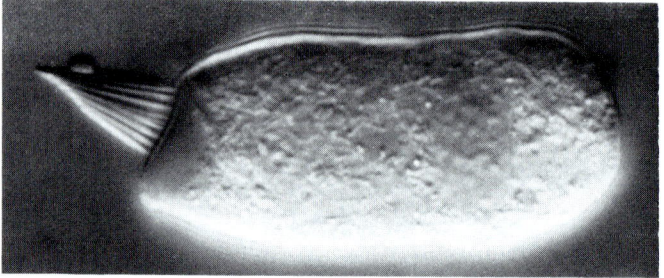

This receptor cell for hearing works in the fashion described in the text.

Figure 3-19 Waves of sound along the basilar membrane

The basilar membrane, *shown in the top part of the figure, is narrowest and stiffest along its base, where vibrations caused by the sound waves first enter the* cochlea *at its* oval window. *The membrane then becomes progressively wider and more flexible toward its other end, or* apex. *As the lower part of the figure shows, the narrower portions of the membrane—and the receptor cells at those points—move most vigorously in response to high-frequency sound waves. The wider portions and their receptors show a greater response to low frequencies.*

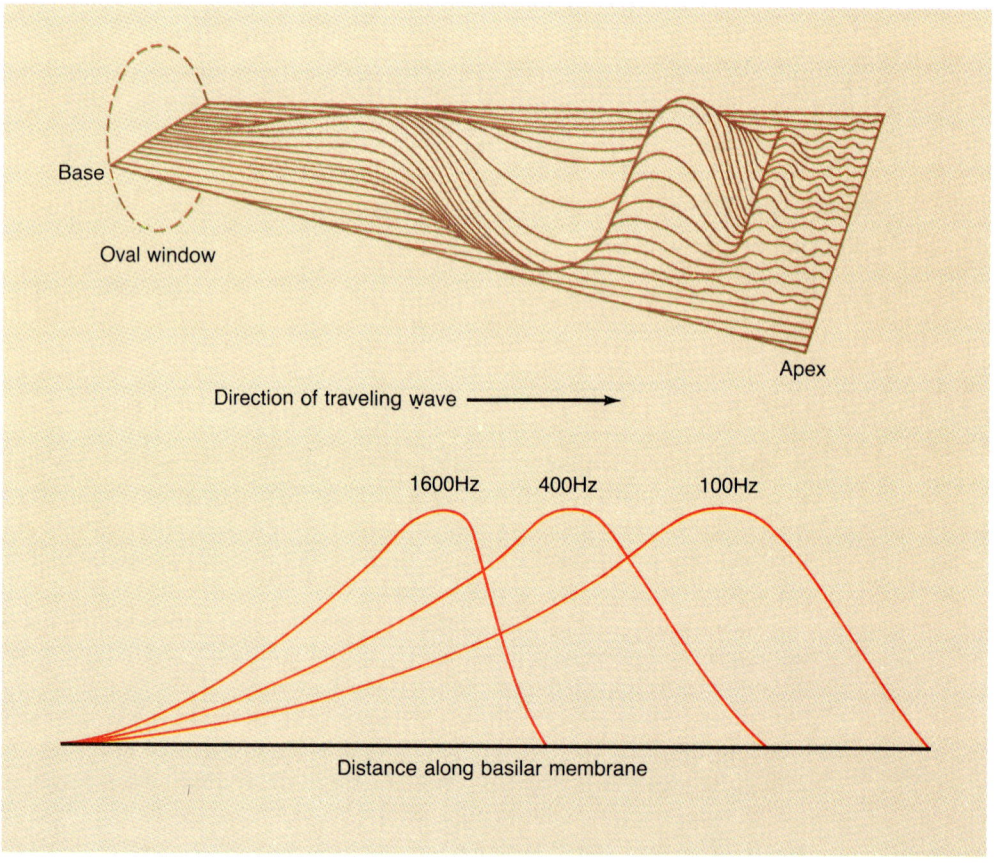

Figure 3-20 A hearing neuron and broad tuning

The graph line shows the number of nervous impulses produced by a single auditory neuron of a monkey, in response to the stimulation of a receptor cell by sound waves of different frequencies, all sounded at the same amplitude (between the level of conversation and the noise of an automobile). Note that the neuron was activated to some extent by frequencies anywhere within a range of more than 2,000 Hz. The range was even greater at higher amplitudes, smaller at lower amplitudes (after Rose et al., 1971).

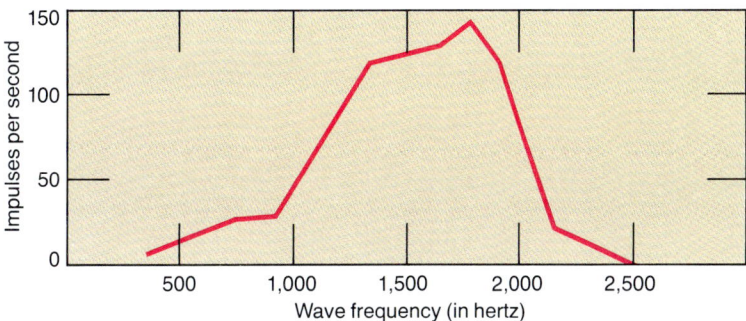

Thus the code in which hearing messages reach the cerebral cortex—and are translated into our sensations of pitch, loudness, and timbre—appears to depend not only on which particular receptors are stimulated, but also on the number of them, the rate at which each sets off nervous impulses, and especially the entire pattern of the impulses (Uttal, 1973). In fact, for the very low frequencies—those below about 400 Hz—the code does not seem to depend at all on the exact location of the receptor, because these frequencies make the basilar membrane move as a unit, to an equal degree throughout its length and breadth.

Loudness and Hearing Damage

In studying the amplitude of sound waves, researchers use what is called the *decibel scale*. Their instruments measure the amount of energy in sound waves and convert it into numerical readings on the scale shown in Figure 3-21. Such measurements are useful in many ways, particularly to ecological psychologists interested in the effects of noisy environments.

There is evidence that exposure to noise can seriously interfere with learning and thinking. One study found that children from a school near a busy airport, when tested for puzzle-solving ability, were generally less persistent and less successful than children from a quieter school (Cohen et al., 1980). Another study found that schoolchildren living on the lower floors of a high-rise apartment complex, where they received the full brunt of traffic noise from a busy highway, had generally lower reading skills than children living on the top floors (Cohen, Glass, and Singer, 1973). Noise seems to have a particularly harmful effect on information-processing abilities when it occurs at unpredictable intervals (Glass and Singer, 1973).

Prolonged exposure to sound above 85 decibels can cause hearing damage—a fact of considerable importance because the noise level in city streets often goes above that level. The damage to the cochlea is shown in Figure 3-22. Such damage is particularly likely to occur in the narrow portion of the basilar membrane to the receptor cells chiefly responsible for detecting sounds of high frequency. The way these receptors may be affected is also

Figure 3-21 Noise ratings on the decibel scale

Some frequently heard sounds register on the decibel scale of amplitude all the way from about 12 for the rustle of leaves to 120 for a thunderclap and 150 for a jet plane warming up nearby. The scale, with 0 set at the absolute threshold for a sound at 1,000 Hz, is logarithmic, with each 10 points on the scale representing a tenfold increase in energy level. Thus the noise level in a typical business office (40 decibels) represents 10 times more energy or amplitude than a whisper heard from close by (30 decibels). Note the danger zone for hearing damage, also the point at which sounds become painful to the ear.

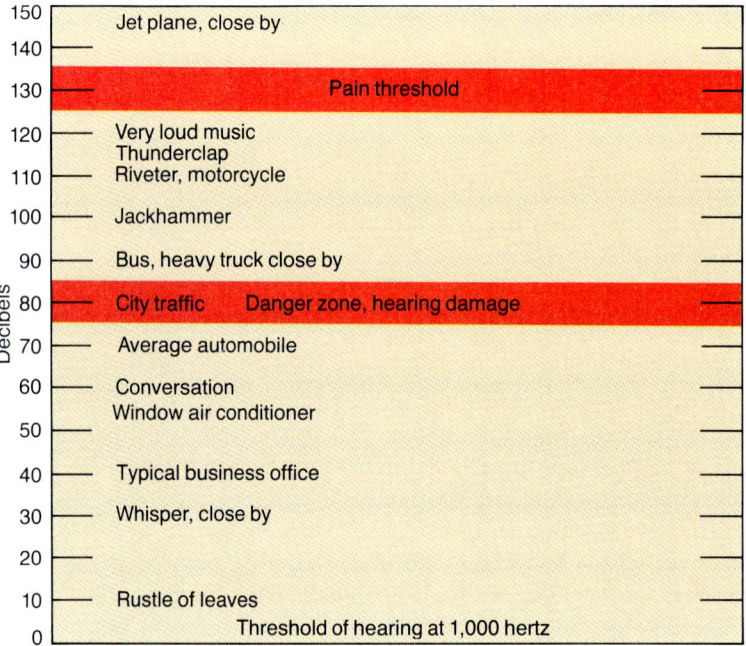

illustrated in Figure 3-22. Problems created by a noisy environment are discussed in a box on Psychology in Everyday Life titled "How Noise Pollution Can Affect the Body and Mind" (page 106).

Hearing loss caused by damage to the cochlea or to the auditory nerve is called *sensorimotor deafness*, while loss of hearing due to a ruptured eardrum or to a defect in the bones of the middle ear is called *conductive deafness*. Damage to portions of the brain critical for hearing can result in hearing loss referred to as *central deafness*.

How We Can Tell Where the Sound Comes From

If someone sitting behind you coughs, you know immediately where the sound comes from. If you hear an automobile pass by, unseen, you can tell at once in which direction it is moving. Something about the sound waves and the manner in which they stimulate your hearing receptors tells you where they come from and in what direction they are moving.

The ability to determine location seems to depend on the fact that slightly different sound waves reach the two ears. A sound wave from the left arrives at the left ear a tiny

Figure 3-22 What noise can do to the cochlea and its hearing receptors

Shown here is a normal (left) and noise-damaged (right) cochlea. Also shown are normal receptor cells on the basilar membrane of an animal and damaged cells from an animal exposed to prolonged noise.

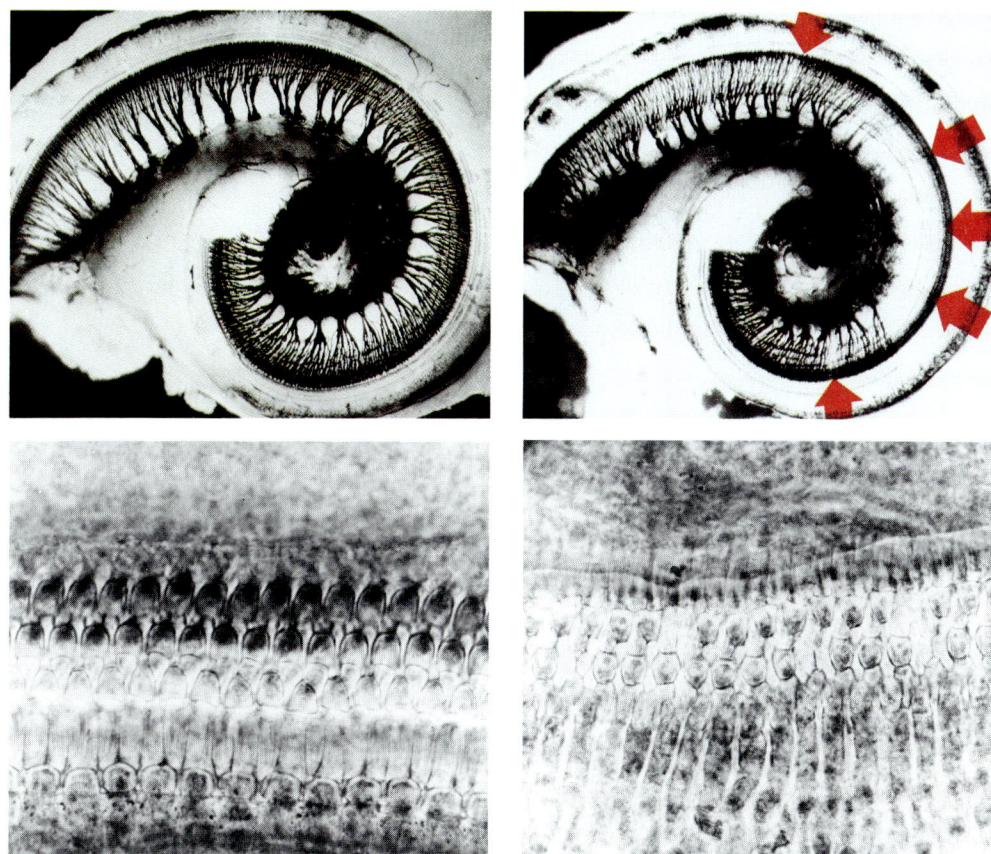

fraction of a second before it strikes the right ear, and in a slightly earlier phase of its cycle of contraction and expansion. By the time the sound wave reaches the right ear it has slightly less amplitude because it has traveled farther. And because high frequencies are more likely than low ones to be absorbed by any object that gets in the path of sound waves, the pattern of overtones has been altered by contact with the head, thus slightly changing the timbre.

The structure of the outer ear also seems to play a part, because its intricate shape bounces sound waves around much as the walls and furniture in a room affect the music from a stereo set. The two outer ears, receiving waves from different directions, reflect them toward the eardrum in different ways. Thus in a number of ways the receptors in the two ears are stimulated somewhat differently and produce slightly different patterns of nervous impulses, which the brain can usually decode into an instant judgment about the location of the sound. We are probably not so skillful at locating sounds as are animals with movable outer ears—like dogs and horses that prick their ears when curious about a noise—but we manage well enough.

Psychology in Everyday Life
How Noise Pollution Can Affect the Body and Mind

Our society may be hazardous to our ears. Millions of Americans work at jobs—in airports, construction, mining, and many other occupations—that regularly expose them to noise that can cause hearing damage. Millions more regularly encounter a dangerous noise level from heavy traffic, or bring it on themselves through their fondness for motorcycles, speedboats, power mowers, and loud music.

Noise is a subtle pollutant, with effects that are usually not immediately apparent, and most people are unaware of the risk of hearing damage. Workers in noisy jobs often reject the protection offered to them. They discard their earplugs or wear them loose for greater comfort, or poke holes in their earmuffs to provide ventilation. People willingly go to discotheques where the sound regularly hits 120 decibels or more, and listen to music through stereo earphones at more than 100 decibels. Musical tastes may be the chief villain among young people. Tests of freshmen entering college have found that as many as 61 percent of them have already suffered at least some hearing loss, and that many of them can hear no better than the average 65-year-old (Lipscomb, 1969), an age at which parts of the basilar membrane and its receptor cells normally show deterioration.

Whether caused by age or earlier in life by noise, partial deafness can create serious psychological problems. Since the loss of hearing occurs gradually, over a period of time, those who suffer from it are often unaware that they can no longer hear sounds they have always taken for granted—and especially that they have trouble understanding ordinary conversation. They may begin to suspect that other people are whispering to exclude them from the conversation, possibly even making disparaging or threatening remarks about them.

The form of abnormal behavior called *paranoia*, in which victims have delusions that other people are plotting against them and persecuting them, is often displayed by

This music lover may be inviting hearing loss from prolonged listening at high decibel levels.

elderly people suffering from deafness (Post, 1966), considerably less often by old people whose hearing is still reasonably good. Even if the result is less drastic, people with hearing difficulties often become suspicious, withdrawn, and hostile—to the point where others actually do avoid them. These problems are not necessarily related to age. Similar symptoms of confusion, agitation, irritability, and hostility have been observed in college students in whom a temporary and partial deafness was induced through hypnosis, without their realizing it (Zimbardo, Andersen, and Kabat, 1982).

Hearing loss and its possible psychological consequences are only one of the dangers of a noisy environment. A survey of available medical evidence has found that noise is linked to a number of physical ailments, including dizziness, headache, digestive disturbances, ulcers, and high blood pressure (Raloff, 1982). The rule of thumb adopted by the Environmental Protection Agency is this: Whenever you have to raise your voice to be heard above the noise in your environment, you are running a physical and psychological risk. Self-preservation dictates that you had better do something about it or get away.

TASTE, SMELL, TOUCH—AND THE TWO FORGOTTEN SENSES

It is popularly assumed that we are gifted with five senses. These are vision and hearing, already discussed, and taste, smell, and touch—with which we are about to deal.

It is true that these five senses are our sole sources of inputs from the outside world. Yet we have two other senses that we seldom even consider, but that bring us essential information about our own bodies. Without these two forgotten senses—bodily movement and equilibrium—we would find it difficult to walk or even keep from falling down, and impossible to play tennis or operate a typewriter. All the seven senses are important to the information processing we do.

Taste

Though we can recognize a great variety of foods, and either relish or reject them, taste is probably the least efficient of our senses. The flavor of food actually depends only in small part on our taste receptors. Much of the sensation is produced by other factors—warmth, cold, the consistency of the food, the mild pain caused by certain spices, and above all smell. The next time your nose is stuffed up by a cold, notice that your meals seem almost tasteless.

The taste receptors are more or less out in the open. If you examine your tongue in a mirror, you will notice that it is covered with little bumps, some tiny, others a bit larger. Inside each of the bumps, a few of which are also found at the back of the mouth and in the throat, are the *taste buds*, which contain the receptors for the sense of taste. Each bump contains about 245 taste buds, and each taste bud contains about 20 receptors sensitive to chemical stimulation by food molecules. Food dissolved in saliva spreads over the tongue, enters small pores in the surface of the bumps, and sets off reactions in the receptors. These reactions trigger activity in adjacent neurons, which fire off nervous impulses toward the brain.

The taste receptors, as the pattern theory suggests, appear to be broadly tuned to respond to many kinds of chemical stimulation. But they seem to respond most vigorously to four basic taste qualities—some to stimuli that are sweet, others to stimuli that are sour, salty, or bitter. The receptors that are especially sensitive to sweetness are concentrated near the tip of the tongue, those most sensitive to sour stimuli at the sides toward the rear.

This wine taster provides a good example of how much the sense of smell contributes to the sense of taste

Smell

The receptors for the sense of smell, as shown in Figure 3-23, lie at the very top of the nasal passages leading from the nostrils to the throat. As we breathe normally, the flow of air from nostrils to throat takes a direct path, as the figure indicates, but a certain amount rises gently to touch the smell receptors. In some little-understood manner the receptors are stimulated by gases and by the molecules of chemical substances suspended in the air. Perhaps the molecules create a chemical reaction. Perhaps the receptors respond in some way to the shape of a molecule—like locks activated by one particular key.

Many lower animals rely on the sense of smell to track down their prey or to detect the approach of an enemy—and even as a means of communicating with one another. They "speak" by secreting chemical substances called *pheromones*, whose odor has a powerful effect on others of their species. Frightened rats, for example, produce a pheromone that serves as a warning signal to other rats (Valenta and Rigby, 1968). Dogs secrete a pheromone in their urine that tells other dogs to stay away from their territory.

Many female animals, including dogs and cats, secrete pheromones that signal when they are sexually receptive. There are some indications that there may also be human pheromones that influence sexual behavior, though to a lesser extent and without our conscious awareness. Women can detect musklike odors—which are characteristic of the sex pheromones secreted by male animals—much more readily than can men or sexually immature girls. Moreover their sensitivity to these odors is greatest during the time in their menstrual cycle when the amount of the hormone estrogen in their bodies is at its peak (Vierling and Rock, 1967).

One study of dormitory residents at a women's college produced provocative results. When the college term began, the subjects reported wide differences in the dates when their menstrual periods began. Six months later, however, those who were spending a lot

Figure 3-23 The nose and its receptors

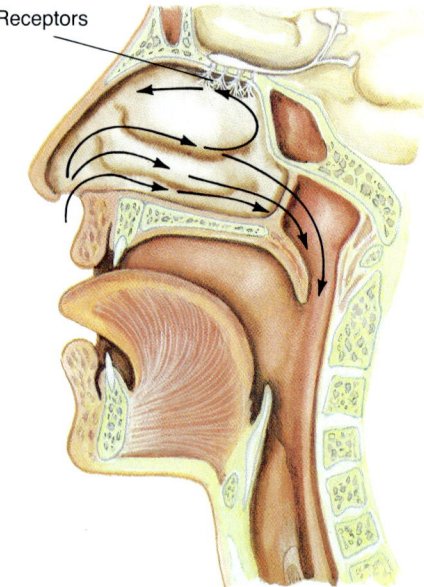

This cross section of the human head shows the position of the receptors for the sense of smell, at the very top of the nasal passages. The arrows indicate how some of the air we breathe rises to touch the receptors.

of time together as roommates or close friends reported that the dates were considerably closer together, as if there was a growing tendency for their menstrual cycles to coincide (McClintock, 1971). Perhaps pheromones secreted during the cycle had a mutual effect on the timing—a possibility that is reinforced by later experiments on the role of pheromones in synchronizing the estrous cycles of groups of rats (McClintock, 1984). And perhaps the appeal of perfumes and men's colognes—even the fact that sometimes we are strongly attracted to another person without knowing why—also indicates some mysterious language that only the nose understands.

Men's colognes are often marketed with the message that certain scents influence sexual attraction and behavior.

The Skin Senses

The receptors for the skin senses are nerve endings scattered throughout the body, just under the surface. They are sensitive to four basic types of stimulation—pressure, pain, cold, and warmth. As with the other senses, the sensation they produce appears to depend on the pattern of nervous impulses set off by a number of broad-tuned nerve endings. Indeed manipulation of the pattern can fool us into experiencing a sensation that is totally at odds with the actual stimulation. This has been demonstrated with the device illustrated in Figure 3-24. When cool water is passed through both coils, the device feels cool to the touch. When warm water is passed through both coils, it feels warm. But when one coil is warm and the other is cool, the device produces a sensation of heat—so great that anyone who grasps it immediately pulls away. Somehow the pattern of nervous impulses set up by this kind of stimulation completely fools the sense of touch.

There are variations in skin sensitivity to pain throughout the body. The nerve endings in the back of the knee and the neck region, for example, are more sensitive than those in the ball of the thumb or the tip of the nose (Coren, Porac, and Ward, 1984). Nerve endings for pain are also found in our muscles and internal organs. Indeed some of the most excruciating pains come from muscle cramps or from distention of the intestines by gas. Yet the receptors in most of the internal organs do not respond to stimuli that would cause pain if applied to the skin. The intestines, for example, can be cut or even burned without arousing any sensation of pain.

Pain sensations pose many baffling questions. Athletes in the heat of competition may suffer blows severe enough to produce deep bruises—yet feel no pain until later. People with intense and long-continued pain can sometimes be relieved through hypnosis (Goleman, 1977). Chinese surgeons often use no anesthetic, just the technique of acupuncture in which little needles are stuck in various spots of the patient's skin, shown in Figure 3-25, often far removed from the part of the body undergoing the operation. Electrical stimulation applied to the spinal cord or brain—or for that matter even a placebo, which is a mere sugar pill with no medical effect—may make severe pain disappear. Why?

The answer is not known. One theory is that many of these phenomena occur because the brain is induced in one way or another to increase its output of the morphinelike painkillers it can produce (Iversen, 1979). Another theory is based on indications that there

Figure 3-24 When you touch this harmless coil, watch out!

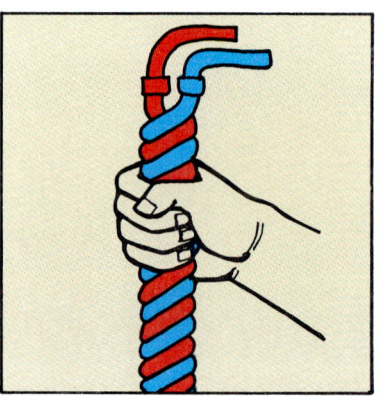

This device can fool the skin senses in startling fashion. The red and blue coils are completely separate and can be connected to different sources of water. The surprising result described in the text is obtained by running cool water through one coil and pleasantly warm water through the other.

Runners are all too familiar with the agonizing cramps experienced through the muscles' nerve endings for pain.

Figure 3-25   An acupuncture chart

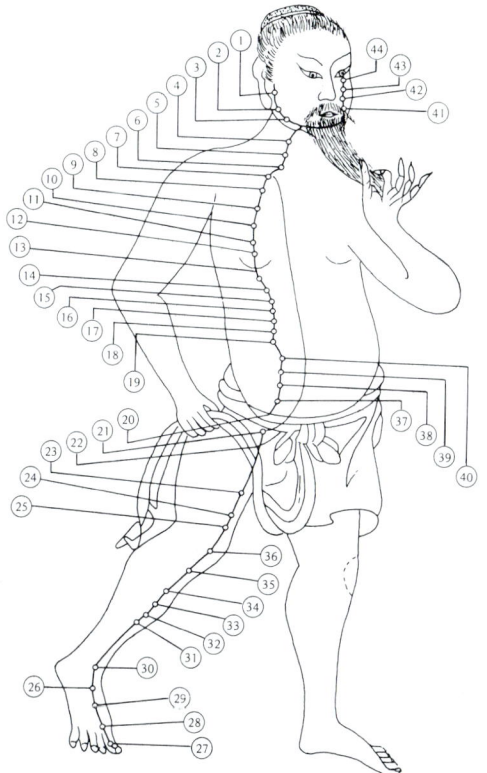

The numbers shown here indicate the spots at which needles can be inserted into the skin of a patient seeking relief from pain.

Taste, Smell, Touch—And the Two Forgotten Senses   **111**

seem to be two different pathways carrying pain messages through the spinal cord and into the brain. One is made up of "*fast*" *fibers* that signal sharp, localized pains like a pinprick. The other consists of "*slow*" *fibers* that signal duller, more generalized pains like those produced by many illnesses (Liebeskind and Paul, 1977). Some investigators believe that these two kinds of fibers interact at some kind of *gate-control mechanism* in the spinal cord, either opening it to let pain messages through or shutting it to cut off the sensations (Melzack, 1973). Such a gate might be activated by nervous impulses set up through acupuncture or electrical stimulation. In the case of hypnosis or placebos, the brain itself might send signals to the control mechanism.

Though we can only theorize about the way pain operates, we do know that it serves a purpose. Without the warning provided by pain, we might hold a hand in a flame until the tissues were destroyed, or cut off a finger while peeling an apple. Even the pain of headache, though we cannot attribute it to any specific cause, is probably a warning that we have been under too much physical or psychological strain. By forcing us to slow down or even take a day off, the headache takes us away from a situation that, if continued, might cause some serious damage to the tissues of our bodies or to our mental stability.

Bodily Movement and Equilibrium: The Two Forgotten Senses

Even in a pitch-black room, you know exactly how to move your hand to point up, down, or to either side, and to touch the top of your head or your left knee. This may not seem like much of an accomplishment—but it would be completely impossible without the generally ignored and unappreciated sense of *bodily movement*, which keeps us constantly informed of the position and motion of our muscles and bones.

This performance totally depends on the human sense of equilibrium.

The receptors for the sense of bodily movement are nerve endings found in three parts of the body. The first are in the muscles, and they are stimulated when the muscles stretch. The second are in the tendons that connect the muscles to the bones and are stimulated when the muscles contract and put pressure on the tendons. The third, and apparently most important, are in the linings of the joints between the bones and are stimulated by movements of the joints. Without the information provided by these three receptors, we would have trouble performing any of the bodily movements we now take for granted. Even to walk, we would have to concentrate on using our eyes to guide our legs and feet into the right position for each step.

The other forgotten sense is *equilibrium*, which keeps our bodies in balance and oriented to the force of gravity. Thanks to this sense, our bodies stay erect—and, if we should start to fall, we catch our balance through reflex action, without even thinking about it.

The receptors for the sense of equilibrium are hairlike cells found in fluid-filled passages that are part of the inner ear, as illustrated in Figure 3-26. The three *semicircular canals* lie at such angles to one another that any movement of the head moves the thick fluid in at least two of them, stimulating the receptors they contain. In the *vestibular sacs*, the receptors are matted together and tiny pieces of stonelike crystal are embedded in the mattings. The crystals are heavy enough to be pulled downward by the force of gravity, putting pressure on the receptors. Thus the receptors in the vestibular sacs keep us aware of being upright even when we are not moving.

Among them, the receptors for the sense of equilibrium constantly monitor the position of the head and any change in position. Besides keeping us right side up and in balance, they provide information essential to our sense of vision. By stepping toward a mirror, you can observe that your head bobs around when you walk—as it also does in

Figure 3-26 The sense organs for equilibrium

The receptors for the sense of equilibrium lie in these passages of the inner ear, next to the cochlea of the sense of hearing.

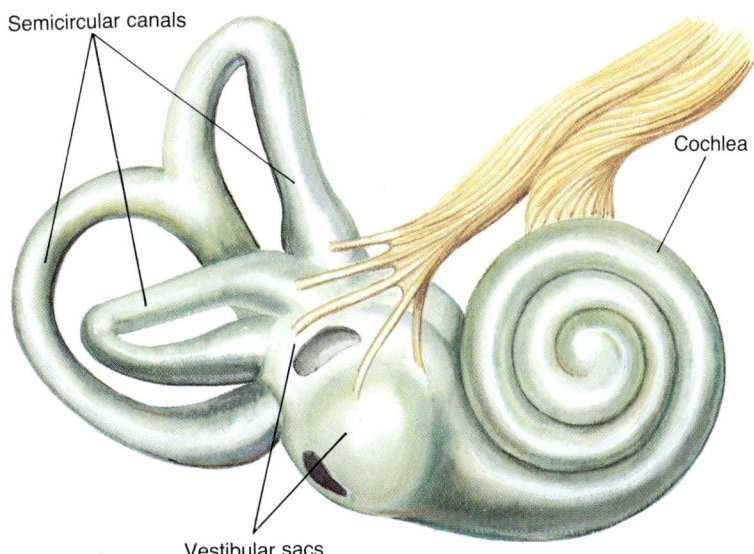

Taste, Smell, Touch—And the Two Forgotten Senses

many other circumstances. Unless the muscles controlling movement of the eyeballs made constant adjustments to hold your gaze steady, your field of vision would jiggle and blur. These adjustments are made by reflex action in response to messages from the sense of equilibrium. No matter how much you bob or shake your head, the world you see remains firmly in place.

Some people experience motion sickness when the various pathways of the sense of equilibrium become overloaded. Medicines such as Dramamine act to prevent motion sickness by inhibiting some of the nervous activity.

SUMMARY

How the senses work

1. The *senses* are the information-gathering structures of the nervous system.
2. The two requirements for sensation are (a) a *stimulus*, a form of meaningful energy impinging on the sense organs, and (b) a *receptor*, a nervous structure capable of responding to that particular stimulus.
3. To activate a sensory receptor, a stimulus must be above the *absolute threshold*, or minimum intensity required to make the receptor respond.
4. To be distinguished as different, two stimuli must vary by at least the amount of the *difference threshold*, also called *just noticeable difference*, or j.n.d. for short. *Weber's law* is that for each sense the difference threshold is a fixed percentage of the original stimulus (10 percent for sound, 1.6 percent for light).
5. All the senses display *sensory adaptation*—meaning that the sensation produced by a constant stimulus disappears after a time, though a new stimulus creates an immediate new response. Thus our senses are best equipped to provide information about change in the environment.
6. The modern view of how the senses operate is *pattern theory*. This theory holds that a stimulus affects a great many *broad-tuned receptors*, which set off nervous impulses carried to the brain by a pathway of neurons that process the information and encode it into patterns. The sensory areas of the cerebral cortex translate the patterns into our sensations.

Light waves and vision

7. The stimulus for *vision* is *light waves*, a pulsating form of electromagnetic energy. Light waves occupy a small portion of the range of electromagnetic radiation, which extends from cosmic rays (the shortest) to household electricity (the longest). Violet waves are a little longer than the invisible ultraviolet waves that cause sunburn. Red waves are slightly shorter than the invisible infrared waves produced by a heating lamp.
8. Light waves vary in *wavelength, intensity,* and *complexity*. Wavelength determines *hue*, the term for the sensation produced by a colored object. Intensity determines *brightness* (though not entirely). Complexity determines *saturation*, or the sensation of a vivid or dull hue. White light is a mixture of all the wavelengths, as can be demonstrated by passing it through a prism and obtaining a spectrum of the hues.
9. Light waves enter the eyeball through the *pupil*, which is an opening in the *iris*. They then pass through a transparent *lens*, which can change shape by the action of the *ciliary muscles* to focus the waves sharply on the *retina* at the back of the eyeball. The retina contains the receptors for vision—nerve structures called *rods* and *cones*.

10. The rods function chiefly under low illumination and send information to the brain about movements and about whites, grays, and blacks but not about color. The rods contain *rhodopsin*, a pigment that is bleached by light.

11. The cones function in strong illumination and send information to the brain about not only movement and brightness but also color. There are three kinds of cones, containing pigments that are broad tuned but most sensitive to either blue, green, or green-yellow.

12. *Dark adaptation*, which makes the eyes about 100,000 times more sensitive under low illumination than in strong light, depends mostly on the rods. At low intensities only the rods function. Because the cones do not respond, color vision is absent.

13. Processing of information picked up by the rods and cones begins in the retina, which contains an elaborate network of neurons. The direct route through the retina's network is from a receptor cell to a *bipolar cell* (which may make contact with only one or with many receptors) then to a *ganglion cell* of the optic nerve (which may make contact with one or many bipolar cells). The route may take many variations because of interconnections provided by *horizontal cells* and *internal association cells*.

14. The *fovea* provides our greatest sharpness, or *acuity*, of vision because its densely packed cones connect with only one or a few ganglion cells. The outer part of the retina is the most sensitive because as many as several thousand of its rods may feed into a single ganglion cell—and stimulation of any one of the rods may produce impulses in that ganglion cell.

The special wonders of color vision

15. The modern explanation of vision is *opponent-process theory*. This holds that nervous impulses set off by the rods and three types of cones enter a pathway to the brain containing six different types of neurons. One shows a burst of activity when the receptors respond to a red stimulus but is lowered in activity when the receptors respond to a green stimulus. Another type does exactly the opposite. It is turned on by a green stimulus but turned off by a red stimulus. Another pair of neurons responds in opposite ways to a blue or yellow stimulus. Another responds in opposite ways to white (or brightness) and black (or darkness). The total pattern of nervous impulses—activated by the response of the rods and cones to a stimulus, then carried to the visual area of the brain by the six types of neurons—accounts for our visual sensations.

16. The search for explanations of vision has always been influenced by the laws of *color mixture* and the phenomena of *color blindness* and *afterimages*. Two famous old explanations were the *Young-Helmholtz theory*, which attributed color vision to three types of cones, and the *Hering theory*, which held that vision depends on nervous impulses paired as black-white, red-green, and blue-yellow. Modern thinking is a combination of these two theories.

Hearing: turning sound waves into sounds

17. The stimulus for *hearing* is *sound waves*, which are ripples of contraction and expansion of the air. Sound waves vary in *frequency, amplitude,* and *complexity*. The frequency determines our sensation of *pitch*. Amplitude determines *loudness* (though not entirely). Complexity determines *timbre*.

18. Sound waves are collected by the *outer ear*, or visible part. The waves create vibrations of the *eardrum*, which are then passed along by the three bones of the *middle ear* to the

cochlea of the *inner ear*. In the cochlea, the vibrations set up complicated wavelike motions of the *basilar membrane*. These motions activate the hairlike receptors for hearing in the *organ of Corti*, lying on the basilar membrane. The bending of the hairlike receptors stimulates the neurons on the *auditory nerve* to produce the nervous impulses that are routed toward the sensory areas of the cerebral cortex.

19. The *place theory* holds that the code of nervous impulses in which hearing messages eventually reach the cerebral cortex seems to depend in part on which receptors, at which locations along the membrane, are stimulated.

20. The basilar membrane is narrowest and stiffest at the end where sound enters the cochlea, and the receptors at this end respond most vigorously to high-frequency waves. The membrane becomes progressively wider and more flexible toward the other end, which is most sensitive to low frequencies.

21. The amplitude of sound waves is measured on a *decibel scale* of loudness. Exposure to noise can have a harmful effect on information-processing abilities—and above 85 decibels can cause hearing damage.

22. Hearing loss caused by damage to the cochlea or to the auditory nerve is called *sensorimotor deafness*, while loss of hearing due to a ruptured eardrum or to a defect in the bones of the middle ear is called *conductive deafness*. Damage to portions of the brain critical for hearing can result in hearing loss referred to as *central deafness*.

23. Our ability to know which direction a sound comes from depends on the fact that the hearing receptors in the two ears receive a slightly different pattern of stimulation and send slightly different patterns of nervous impulses to the brain.

Taste, smell, touch—and the two forgotten senses

24. The receptors for *taste* lie mostly in the *taste buds* of the tongue. They are broadly tuned to respond to chemical stimulation—but there are four types especially sensitive to either sweet, sour, salty, or bitter.

25. The receptors for *smell* lie at the top of the nasal passages leading from the nostrils to the throat. They are sensitive to gases and to molecules of chemical substances suspended in the air.

26. The receptors for the *skin senses* are nerve endings lying just beneath the surface. They account for our sensations of pressure, pain, cold, and warmth.

27. The *sense of bodily movement* keeps us informed of the position of our muscles and bones and is essential to such complex movements as walking. The receptors are nerve endings in the muscles, tendons, and joints.

28. The *sense of equilibrium* keeps us in balance and oriented to the force of gravity. The receptors are hairlike nerve cells in the inner ear's three *semicircular canals* and *vestibular sacs*.

IMPORTANT TERMS

absolute threshold
acuity
afterimage (positive, negative)
amplitude
auditory nerve
basilar membrane

bipolar cell
blind spot
bodily movement
brightness
broad-tuned receptors
central deafness

ciliary muscles
cochlea
color blindness
color mixing
complementary colors
complexity
conductive deafness
cones
cornea
dark adaptation
decibel scale
difference threshold
eardrum
equilibrium
Eustachian tube
"fast" fibers
fovea
frequency
ganglion cell
gate-control mechanism
Hering theory
horizontal cell
hue
inner ear
intensity
internal association cell
iris
just noticeable difference
lens
middle ear
opponent-process theory
optic nerve
organ of Corti
outer ear
oval window
overtones
pattern theory
pheromone
pitch
place theory
pupil
receptor
retina
rhodopsin
rods
saturation
semicircular canals
sensorimotor deafness
sensory adaptation
"slow" fibers
stapes
stimulus
taste buds
timbre
vestibular sacs
wavelength
Weber's law
Young-Helmholtz theory

RECOMMENDED READINGS

Autrum, H., et al. *Foundations of sensory science.* New York: Springer-Verlag, 1984.
Barlow, H. H., and Mollon, J. D. *The senses.* New York: Cambridge University Press, 1982.
Goldstein, E. B. *Sensation and perception.* Belmont, Ca.: Wadsworth, 1980.
Levine, M. W., and Shefner, J. M. *Fundamentals of perception.* Reading, Mass.: Addison-Wesley, 1981.
Ludel, J. *Introduction to sensory processes.* San Francisco: Freeman, 1978.

CHAPTER

4

PERCEPTION: MAKING SENSE OUT OF OUR SENSATIONS

HOW PERCEPTION ENABLES US TO SURVIVE 120

The built-in wiring of feature detectors
Are we born with the skill of perception?
Distinguishing reality from illusion

OUR PERCEPTUAL SPECIALTIES: SELECTION AND ATTENTION 126

Detecting change, movement, and contrast
Why we select as we do
Selection and exploration

HOW WE ORGANIZE OUR PERCEPTIONS 132

Some rules of organization
Perceiving a world that is stable and consistent
Distance and depth perception
The relationship between distance and size

INTERPRETATION: DISCOVERING THE MEANING OF OUR PERCEPTIONS 141

Prototypes, feature analysis, and global processing
Expectations, mental set, and context

SUMMARY 145

IMPORTANT TERMS 147

RECOMMENDED READINGS 147

PSYCHOLOGY IN EVERYDAY LIFE

Extrasensory perception—scientific frontier or popular delusion? 125
How many inputs can you manage at the same time? 131

As you read this line, something extraordinary is happening to you. Though you are not aware of it, your central nervous system is being stimulated by an incredibly vast number of messages from the outside world. The rods and cones in your eyes are responding to a variety of light waves of many kinds and intensities. They are stimulated by the white space on the page and by a host of little black lines, curves, squiggles, and dots that make up the letters and words.

In the same fashion, when someone speaks to you, sound waves of varying frequencies and amplitudes pulsate against your eardrums. Your hearing receptors are under a rapid-fire onslaught of 600 to 720 separate sounds and pauses every minute (Hochberg, 1978). The sounds flow "in a continuous and indivisible stream," and none of them has any real identity of its own. If you chopped up a tape recording of speech into the individual sounds, you would have no idea what the sounds represented—and could never splice any of the tiny bits of tape into another meaningful recording (Levine and Shefner, 1981).

Yet somehow we humans manage automatically to make sense of the ever shifting stimulation the world provides to our sense organs. Without any conscious effort on our part, most of the time our central nervous system allows us to extract the precise information that is important to us. We know almost instantaneously what it means. The key to this remarkable accomplishment is *perception*, which can be defined as *the process through which we become aware of our environment by selecting, organizing, and interpreting the evidence from our senses*.

HOW PERCEPTION ENABLES US TO SURVIVE

Without our skills at perception, much of our learning and thinking would be laborious and perhaps even impossible. For example, how long do you suppose it would take you to read this page if you had to work at deciphering every visual stimulus that reaches your eyes? That is to say, if you had to figure out each time that a vertical line with a little horizontal dash across it is a *t*, a vertical line with a curve an *h*, a partial circle with a horizontal line across it an *e*—and that a combination of *t*, *h*, and *e* means *the*? How long would you last in big-city traffic if you had to keep asking yourself: "That patch of blue light waves out there—is it an automobile or something else? Is it moving? How fast and in what direction? Is it dangerous or can I ignore it?"

But you do not have to stop and think. You perceive a *the* or an automobile and its movement without even trying. (Even a person whose sight is restored in adulthood perceives objects clearly in only a few days.) In fact, in most cases you cannot help perceiving what you do, even if you make a deliberate effort, because perception is a process over which we have little conscious control. It enables you to move about confidently, taking for granted that you know what is going on around you and will immediately become aware of any danger. Perception is one of the remarkable psychological abilities that nature has given us—and that have enabled the human race to survive.

The Built-in Wiring of Feature Detectors

Part of our skill at perception depends on the structure of the nervous system—the way it is "wired" to extract information from the environment. The nerve pathways from the sense organs to the brain, and the sensory areas of the brain itself, contain a great number of specialized cells that are quick to detect important features of the environment. In the visual system these cells, called *feature detectors*, are especially sensitive to patterns and to movement. In the system for hearing, the feature detectors are especially sensitive to pitches and changes in pitch. Thus the cells are ideally suited to respond immediately to stimuli that represent such important information as the direction of a line, the shapes and motion of objects, and the flow of conversation.

Much of our knowledge of feature detectors comes from the research of David Hubel and Torsten Wiesel, who shared a 1981 Nobel Prize for their work. Hubel and Wiesel measured the nervous impulses in individual cells of the visual cortex of cats and monkeys, while the animals looked at a screen on which various kinds of stimuli were flashed. They found that some of the brain cells responded vigorously to a vertical bar on the screen but did not respond at all to a horizontal bar, as shown in Figure 4-1. Other cells acted in the opposite fashion, responding to a horizontal line but not to a vertical line. Others responded most vigorously to angles, and still others to movements (Hubel and Wiesel, 1965).

Similarly it has been found that the sensory areas in the brains of animals—and presumably of humans as well—contain feature detectors specialized to respond to various characteristics of sound waves. Some are activated most strongly by low-pitched sounds, others by high-pitched sounds, and still others only by a change in pitch (Whitfield and Evans, 1965).

Are We Born with the Skill of Perception?

There has been a continuing controversy over the relative contribution of the central nervous system we are born with versus experience in explaining our capacity for perception. One view is that there are inborn structures in the brain that help us interpret some phenomena as size, constancy, and color. A contrasting view is that all our perceptions come from psychological interpretations of experiences that we have over time.

Figure 4-1   How a feature-detector cell works

The spikes in the graph lines are recordings of the nervous impulses in one of the feature-detector cells of a cat's brain. In response to a horizontal bar, the cell displays only its normal amount of spontaneous activity. To an oblique bar, there is a small response. To a vertical bar—the kind of feature to which this cell is specifically sensitive—there is a sharp burst of activity (Hubel, 1963).

In the case of feature detection skills, Hubel and Wiesel studied both newborn and very young monkeys kept away from any visual stimulation since birth—and found feature detection cells in full operation. These cells were activated by the very first stimulation of the eye's receptors, responding in much the same way as the cells of older animals with visual experience (Wiesel and Hubel, 1974).

We cannot be sure, of course, that the Hubel and Wiesel findings apply to our own nervous system. Their experiments on the animal brain cannot be duplicated with humans. There is considerable indirect evidence, however, that the human nervous system is wired in the same way (McCullough, 1965). It appears that the pathways of the sensory system not only receive the inputs provided by the sense organs but begin the information processing by making an initial selection and interpretation of these inputs. It has been said that they "condense the information present in the world down to certain features that are essential to the organism" (Levine and Shefner, 1981). It is still not possible, however, to explain perception—for example, of a hand or a face—from the action of feature detectors in the brain alone. We need information gained from experience as well.

Distinguishing Reality from Illusion

The process of perception, aided by the inborn characteristics of the nervous system, is the source of our first quick impressions of what is going on around us. The process is not perfect, and our first impressions are not always in accord with the facts. For example, you may have had the experience, when riding along a highway, of being sure you saw a dead dog at the side of the road—only to discover, as you got closer, that it was just a piece of rumpled cloth. Your perceptual process, in its effort to make sense out of the visual stimulation reaching your eyes, signaled *dog* when in fact there was no dog at all. Students of

Figure 4-2 How do you perceive these drawings?

Is line a or line b longer in no. 1? In no. 2? In no. 3? Which of the two inner circles in no. 4 is larger? In no. 5, are the horizontal lines straight or curved? After you have made your judgments, you can discover with a ruler that all the lines a and b are the same size, and so are the two circles in no. 4. The lines in no. 5 are parallel.

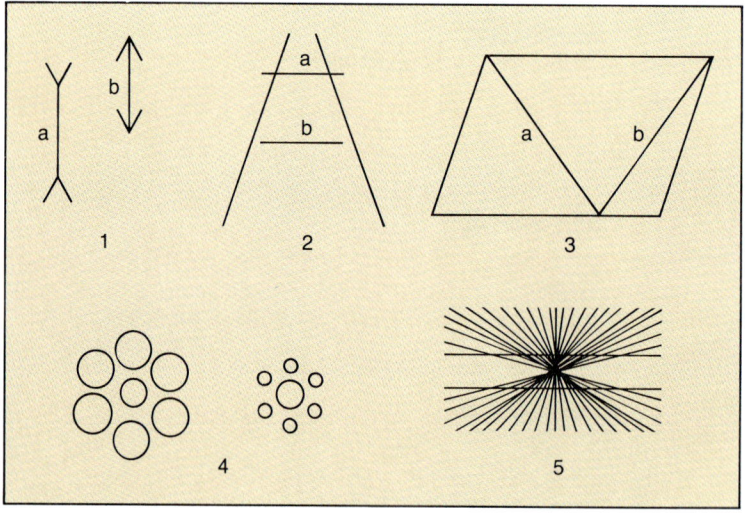

Figure 4-3 Stroboscopic motion

These are examples of the apparent motion produced by stationary objects. At top, lights 1, 2, and 3 are flashed briefly and in rapid succession. Nothing moves, and in fact there is nothing in the spaces between the lights. But the viewer perceives the light as moving smoothly from position 1 to position 3, as indicated by the shaded circles. At bottom, two slits of light shown in rapid succession appear to move as shown by the arrows. The bar at left seems to flop from vertical to horizontal. The slits at right seem to flip over and move in three dimensions, as when the page of a book is turned.

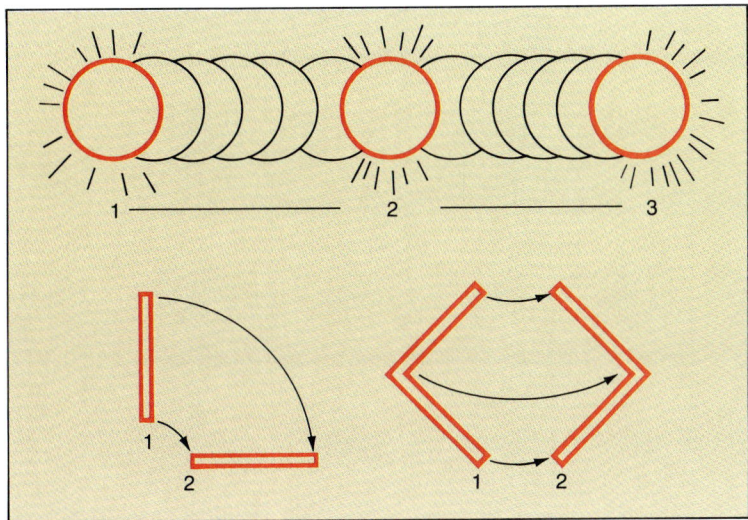

perception have shown that you can be fooled in many ways. Some of these are called *optical illusions*, a few of which are illustrated in Figure 4-2.

Sometimes we perceive motion where none exists. A stationary spot of light, viewed in darkness without any frame of reference, may seem to move of its own accord. This phenomenon is known as the *autokinetic illusion*. Another visual illusion, called *stroboscopic motion*, is illustrated in Figure 4-3. This one has been turned to advantage in motion pictures, which are actually a succession of still pictures flashed on the screen at the rate of about 24 a second, and in television, where still pictures are flashed at about 30 per second. What you actually see is a series of stationary shots similar to those in Figure 4-4. If you viewed these photos in rapid succession, as you view movies or television, your eyes would fill in the gaps and the horse would seem to jump smoothly over the hurdle.

Perceptual illusions occur in senses other than vision as well. The ancient Greek philosopher-scientist Aristotle called attention to an illusion of touch, illustrated in Figure 4-5. Perceptual illusions also take place during what are called *altered states of consciousness*—for example, during our dreams, under hypnosis, or under the influence of alcohol and mind-altering drugs, states that are described in various later chapters of this book. And some psychologists believe that there are some strange and unexplained ways we can extract information from the world without using our ordinary senses, a possibility known as ESP and discussed in a box on Psychology in Everyday Life called "Extrasensory Perception— Scientific Frontier or Popular Delusion?"

Most of the time, however, our perceptions give us an accurate view of what is going on in the world. Our first impressions, arrived at quickly and automatically, are usually correct and useful. A remarkable example is presented in Figure 4-6 (page 126).

Figure 4-4 A century-old forerunner of the motion picture industry

This famous nineteenth-century series of pictures was made by using a battery of cameras whose shutters could be tripped in rapid succession. They resemble the still photos now shown on motion picture and television screens to produce the effect of smooth motion.

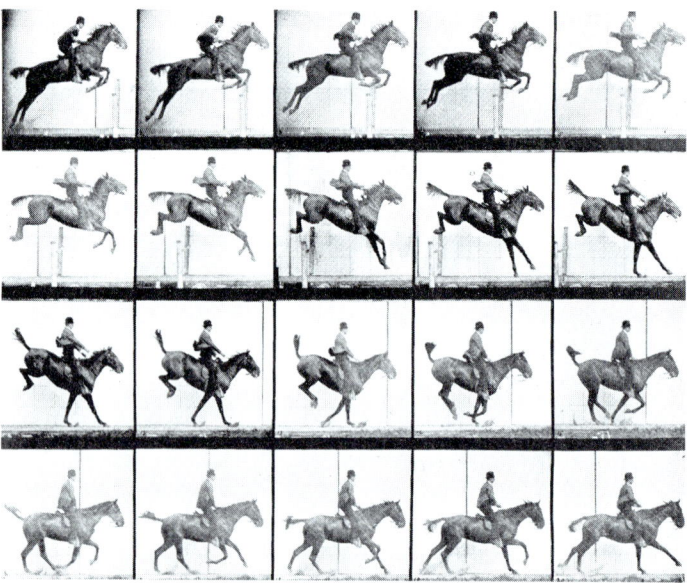

Figure 4-5 One pencil or two?

Hold your fingers as pictured in figure A and touch the point between them with a pencil. You will perceive one pencil. But if you simply cross your fingers as shown in figure B and now touch the pencil, you will perceive two distinct pencils. (If you keep your eyes closed, thus denying yourself the vision of reality, the effect may be stronger.) The best explanation of the illusion is that when the pencil is stimulating the inside of the two fingers as in figure A, the touch information is being sent to adjacent or overlapping areas of the brain cortex responsible for touch sensations. But when the pencil is stimulating the outside of the two fingers as in figure B, the information is sent to two separate areas of that part of the cortex (adapted from Coren, Porac, and Ward, 1985).

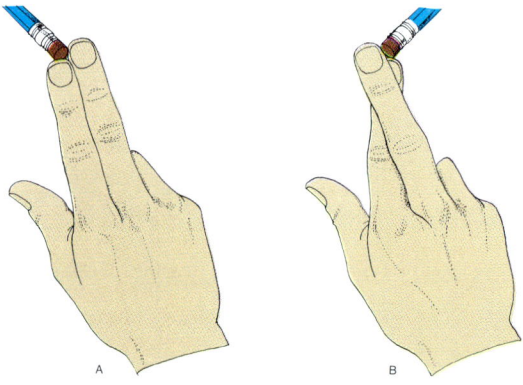

Psychology in Everyday Life
Extrasensory Perception—Scientific Frontier or Popular Delusion?

Can we humans perceive events through channels other than our eyes, ears, and the rest of the senses? In other words, do we possess ESP, short for *extrasensory perception*? Are there at least some of us who can read other people's minds, or know what an object is without looking at it, or perhaps even know in advance what is about to happen?

The idea is attractive to many people and has been found to exist in virtually all known cultures (Scheils, 1978). Nothing that science has yet discovered can explain or even allow for the existence of ESP. But every possibility is worth examining—and therefore some investigators have been engaged for many years in the field of *parapsychology*, or the study of ESP and other psychological events that seem to go beyond normal limits and defy explanation in any normal scientific way. They have done research on three kinds of ESP that have been reported from time to time:

1. *Mental telepathy*, or what is commonly known as mind reading

2. *Clairvoyance*, or the ability to perceive an object without using the ordinary senses—such as knowing what card will be turned up next from a shuffled deck

3. *Precognition*, or the ability to perceive something that has not yet happened—such as how a pair of dice will turn up on the next roll

The field of parapsychology is too complex and controversial to be covered adequately here. About all that can be said is that some researchers have reported finding subjects who seemed to display abilities at telepathy, clairvoyance, and precognition. These subjects were by no means 100 percent accurate, but they did seem to produce results that could not be explained by sheer luck (Rhine and Pratt, 1957). Other researchers have reported telepathy experiments in which the dreams of "receivers" seemed to be influenced by the thoughts of "senders" who were some distance away, in one case by 40 miles (Krippner, 1972). Many of the experiments that seem to demonstrate ESP, however, have been attacked as poorly designed and open to cheating (Hansel, 1966). Surveys find that few psychology professors and other scientists believe that the existence of ESP has been established (Wagner and Monnett, 1979; McClenon, 1982).

The controversy has some important implications for the future of society. If ESP actually exists—or is possible—then human abilities have some unexplored dimensions that may revolutionize human life and the future course of science. But if a belief in ESP is nothing more than wishful thinking and superstition, like the faith of the Greeks in their Delphic oracle, then the popular interest in it is a serious barrier to understanding human behavior. If you want to know more about the topic and judge the evidence for yourself, you can start with the books on ESP listed among the recommended readings.

Figure 4-6 Jumbled lights or a person walking?

Investigators attached small flashlight bulbs to the shoulders, elbows, wrists, hips, knees, and ankles of a person as shown in figure A. Then they made a film of the person moving around in a darkened room. Observers who watched the film saw only a pattern of light spots moving in total darkness as shown in figure B. Yet not only could they tell it was a person walking, but they could detect when the person walked with a limp or danced (Johansson, 1976). In a more recent experiment, the moving light spots were turned upside down and run backwards—but still most of the observers perceived that they were watching human movement (Sumi, 1984).

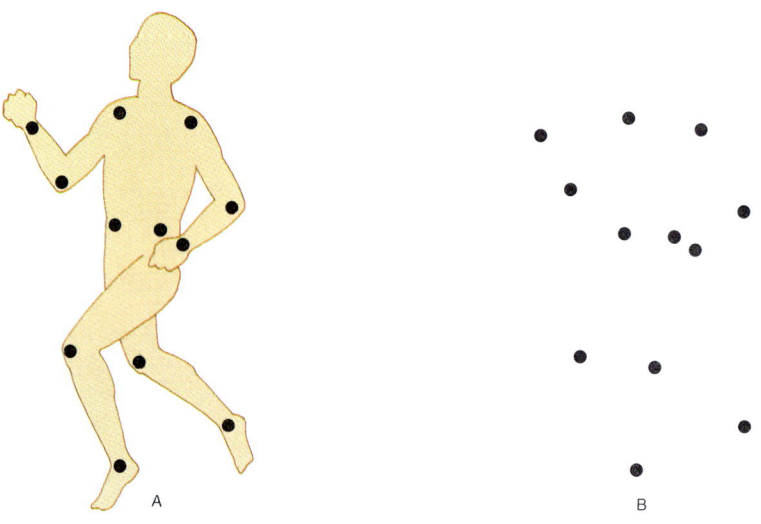

OUR PERCEPTUAL SPECIALTIES: SELECTION AND ATTENTION

Of the three functions that constitute the process of perception—selection, organization, and interpretation—*selection* heads the list. This is because we cannot possibly cope with all the varied and ever-changing stimulation that bombards our sense organs. To avoid utter confusion, we have to select and pay attention to only a small part of it. What we select depends on many factors, ranging from automatic and involuntary to conscious and deliberate.

Detecting Change, Movement, and Contrast

The newborn infant arrives with an automatic tendency to select and pay attention to visual *movement* and black-and-white *contrast*, as well as to changes in loudness and pitch. In general, change in stimulation is the most potent attraction for the attention of the baby. This makes sense, for elements of change usually contain the most useful information in the environment.

Throughout our lives our nervous system finds it impossible to ignore change. If a radio is playing softly in the background while you are reading, you may pay no attention to it—but you cannot help noticing if the sound stops. You are instantly aware of a change if the light in the room becomes brighter or dimmer. And you can recognize even extremely subtle variations in the appearance of a face, such as a narrowing of the mouth or eyes (Haig, 1984).

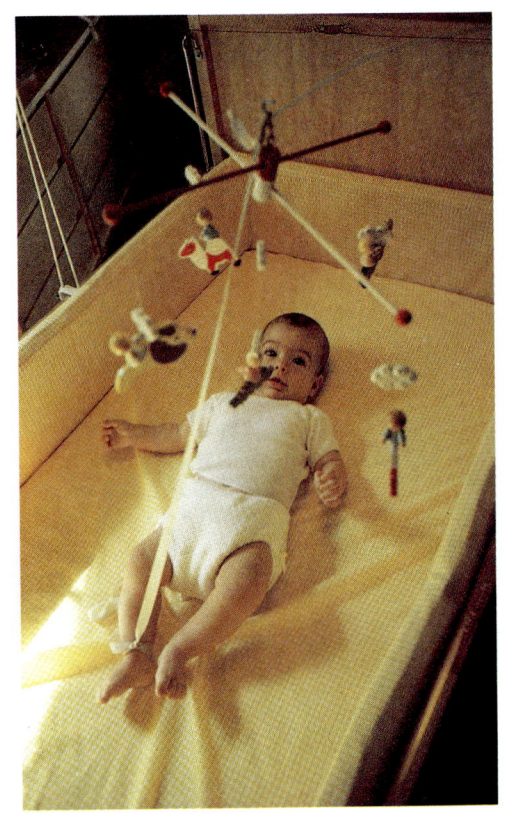

The compelling nature of movement is reflected in the attentive gaze of this infant.

    Movement, which is a form of change, is such a compelling stimulus that even very young babies try hard to follow any moving object with their eyes. When you look at a pasture full of horses, you are most aware of those that are running. An advertising sign that uses stroboscopic motion demands your attention far more than a sign that remains stationary.

    The reason movement leaps immediately to awareness probably also depends on inborn characteristics of the nervous system. It appears that the wiring of the visual system contains separate cells for motion (Sekuler and Levinson, 1977). This is a characteristic of great potential value in survival, for there are many situations in which it is more important to detect and respond quickly to the movement of an object than to know what the object may be. To our ancestors, for example, the sudden approach of a wild animal meant danger regardless of whether the animal happened to be a lion or a bear.

    Another compelling stimulus is *contrast*—like any sharp difference in the intensity of light reflected by two objects in the field of vision. Even babies are attracted by contrast (Salapatek and Kessen, 1966). In showing their early interest in the human face, what they notice particularly is the high degree of contrast between a light face and dark eyes or hairline, or between a dark face and the whites of the eyes and teeth. Our perception of the relative brightness of an object often depends on differences in the amount of light reflected from adjacent objects (Shapley, 1986). This perceptual effect, called *simultaneous brightness contrast*, is demonstrated in Figure 4-7.

    Besides change, movement, and contrast, there are two other stimulus characteristics that have a considerable effect on the process of perception. One is *size*, with large objects more compelling than small ones. When you look at the front page of a newspaper, you notice the biggest headlines first. The second is *intensity*. When you drive at night along

Figure 4-7 The same but different: a study in contrasts

The central squares in each of the four larger squares are actually the same gray. The amount of light and the wavelength reaching your eye is the same from each one. But the perceived levels of brightness of these small squares are not equal. The grays printed on dark backgrounds appear lighter than those printed on light backgrounds, as explained in the text (adapted from Coren, Porac, and Ward, 1984).

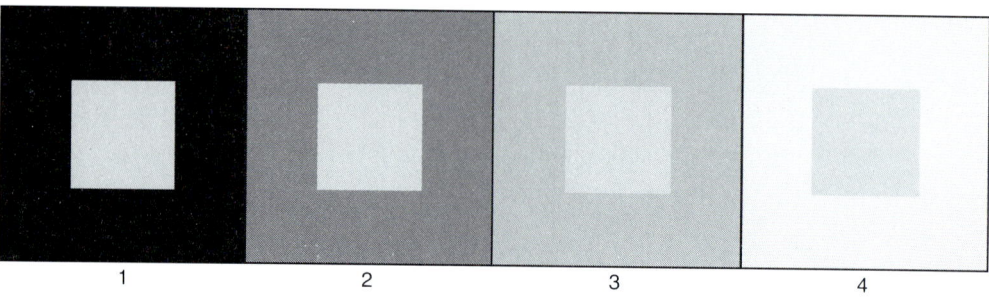

a business street where all the signs are of equal size, the brightest one is the most compelling.

Why We Select as We Do

What we select from the environment depends not only on choices dictated by the inborn tendencies of our sensory system but also on choices colored by learning and experience. As an example of the latter, consider the kinds of choices that might be made by a man

Advertisers assume we will pay more attention to large signs—and we usually do.

working as a forest ranger as he stands on a high observation tower looking out over a wide expanse of hills, valleys, open spaces, trees, and streams. Scanning the scene, he thinks he spots a plume of smoke. He raises his binoculars and focuses his eyes on this single aspect of the landscape. Only now, after selecting this one spot on which to concentrate, can he try to find some organization in the stimuli reaching his eyes (do they really represent a plume of smoke or something else?) and make an interpretation (if it is smoke is it coming from a cabin or is it the start of a forest fire?).

Between the two extremes are many gradations that are difficult to classify. The in-between choices seem to depend partly on inborn tendencies and partly on learning and experience, and often it is hard to say whether we make them consciously or unconsciously. They may reflect our entire personality or our mood of the moment. At any rate the process of perception must start in one way or another with which of all the environment's stimuli we select for further information processing.

Because so many factors can influence selection, people looking at the same event in the environment may perceive it in different ways. We are likely to pay attention to events that interest us for one reason or another. When people look at words flashed only briefly for their inspection, they are better at recognizing terms related to their own special interests than unrelated terms. Subjects interested in religion are quick to perceive words like *sacred*. Subjects interested in economics are quick to perceive *income* (Postman, Bruner, and McGinnies, 1948).

Our motives also play a part. Ambitious people are especially quick to perceive words like *strive* and *perfect* (McClelland and Liberman, 1949). In fact the way we select stimuli may be influenced by our entire personality and also by our emotional state at the moment. You can observe for yourself how mood affects selection. When you are feeling out of sorts you are likely to pay attention to anything in the environment that is potentially irritating—a noise in the next room, a watchband that feels too tight, another person's frown. When you are feeling on top of the world you may be unusually aware that the sun is shining, everybody seems to be friendly to you, and there are a great many attractive people walking around. As the old saying goes, a pessimist sees a glass that is half empty, an optimist a glass that is half full.

Selection and Exploration

What selection does, in the last analysis, is help us perceive what is likely to be important to us, ignore all the many other inputs provided by our sense organs, and concentrate on using the rest of our information-processing talents to the best possible advantage. When we notice something unusual out of the corner of the eye—usually because of movement or contrast—we move the eyeballs to bring the image to the center of the retina where our vision is sharpest. Then we make a series of scanning movements, as illustrated in Figure 4-8. These scanning movements occur even when we think we are staring fixedly at a stimulus like the Figure 4-8 photo, meaning that the eyes send the brain information about first one part of the photo, then another and still others. Somehow the brain manages to piece together this rapid succession of fragmentary bits of information into a perception of the photograph as a whole. The way this is done resembles the creation of a mosaic from tiny bits of tile—but how it is done is only dimly understood.

Though we are not aware of the eye movements, they somehow focus first on the most informative parts of the stimulus. The subject whose movements are shown in Figure 4-8 probably glanced first at the left eye, then the mouth, right eye, bright patch of hair at the top, and nose. Even these few scanning movements, taking hardly more than a single second, provided all the most essential information about the nature of the

Figure 4-8 The scanning process

The pattern of lines was made by bouncing a light beam off the white of a man's eye, thus recording his eye movements as he looked for a few minutes at the photograph of the girl. Note how many movements took place and how they provided information about all the important elements of the photo (Yarbus, 1967).

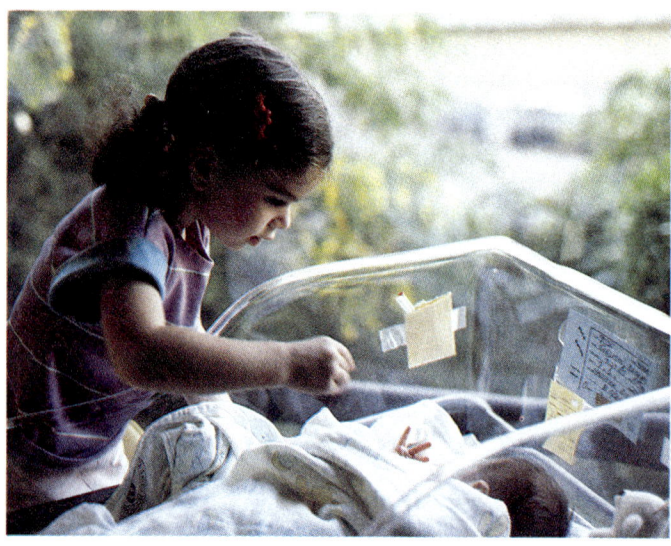

In exploring her new baby brother for the first time, this child is demonstrating what it is like to be attentive with every fiber.

photograph. The later movements served only to verify, refine, and fill in the details of the first impression.

When we direct out attention to exploring a new stimulus, many changes may take place in the body, all of such a nature that they facilitate perception and prepare for action if the stimulus calls for it. The pupils of the eye dilate and admit more light (Hess, 1965). The pattern of brain waves changes (Tecce, 1971). Heart rate and breathing speed up and the muscles of the body begin to tense. When we really pay attention, we are attentive all over. The limits of our capacities for attention are discussed in a Psychology in Everyday Life box titled "How Many Inputs Can You Manage at the Same Time?"

Psychology in Everyday Life
How Many Inputs Can You Manage at the Same Time?

As we all have noticed at one time or another, it is difficult to pay attention to more than one event in the environment at a time, and selecting one stimulus usually means losing perception of the other possible inputs. A frequent example occurs in driving an automobile. As you drive along a highway where the traffic is light, you are listening to the radio—to a football game or a news broadcast that is about to give a weather report. But now you come to a busy intersection. The traffic lights are changing. You have to slow down, veer into another lane, watch out for a car that has moved into your path. When all this activity ends, you find to your surprise that the score in the football game has changed or that the news is over and you have missed the weather report. While your attention was directed elsewhere the radio was on just as loud as before, but your perceptual processes missed it entirely.

Many laboratory experiments have shown that it is especially difficult to process two different inputs if they arrive in the same sensory channel. In studying sounds heard at the same time, experimenters have used earphones that deliver one spoken message to the right ear and a completely different one to the left ear. It has been found that subjects can pay attention to and understand either one of the two messages—but not both at once. The same applies to visual stimuli—for example, trying to take in what is happening in two films shown simultaneously, one showing a boxing match and the other a football game (Neisser and Becklen, 1975).

It is somewhat easier to pay attention to two things at once when two different senses are being stimulated. You may have noticed, for example, that you can continue to read with fairly good comprehension while listening to a radio or a telephone conversation. Apparently the mental processes required for perception can operate more efficiently on two different kinds of sensory information than on two messages in the same sensory channel.

But the theme of research on perceptual attention seems clear enough: it is not very efficient to attend to more than one input at a time no matter what the sensory channels—whether you are trying to listen to a lecture while watching a fellow student, or read this chapter while looking at a televised football game. Sometimes it is not very safe either. For example, when you are driving, it is risky to try to read billboards while looking out for other cars on the highway.

This child must block out the activity around her in order to attend to her reading.

HOW WE ORGANIZE OUR PERCEPTIONS

When we select a stimulus in the environment for further exploration, the first thing we want to know is: *What is it?* To answer this question, we have to see or hear the stimulus as something that hangs together as a unit of some kind, separate and distinguishable from all the other stimuli the environment provides. We must see light waves organized into some kind of object—an animal, an automobile, a face, something. Or we must hear a string of sound waves organized into the meaningful pattern of human speech, or a rap at the door, or an approaching car.

In vision we organize stimuli into an object largely by the perceptual principle of *figure and ground*. As you read this page, for example, your eyes are stimulated by the white space and many little black lines, curves, squiggles, and dots. Your perceptual process organizes these stimuli into black figures—letters, words, and punctuation marks—seen against a white ground. This is also the way you perceive a chair, a face, or the moon in the sky. The figure hangs together, into an organized shape. The ground is a neutral and formless setting for the figure. What separates the two and sets the figure off from the ground is a clearly perceived dividing line called a *contour*. The separation depends in part on our inborn skill at perceiving contrast, probably because of the way feature detectors operate.

Some interesting examples of how we organize visual stimuli into figure and ground are shown in Figure 4-9. In the upper drawing you can perceive a white figure—the goblet—against a red ground. Or you can perceive two red figures—the faces—against a white ground. But you cannot perceive both at once. In the bottom drawing you can perceive some strange red figures against a white ground. Or you can perceive the white figure TIE against a red ground.

Figure 4-9 The principle of figure and ground

When you first look at the top drawing you probably perceive a white goblet. In the bottom drawing you probably perceive some red figures that look a little like pieces of a jigsaw puzzle. But you can also perceive something quite different in the two drawings, as explained in the text.

Some Rules of Organization

Although the same stimuli can sometimes be grouped into very different patterns, there are a number of rules of organization that generally apply. The most important are the following:

Closure *Closure* refers to the fact that we do not need a complete and uninterrupted contour to perceive a figure. If part of the contour is missing, our perceptual processes fill in the gaps. This rule of perception is illustrated in Figure 4-10. The rule of closure also operates for sounds. A tape recording of a spoken message can be doctored so that many of the sounds are missing—consonants, vowels, syllables, or entire words. Yet if you heard the tape you would have no trouble perceiving the message.

Continuity *Continuity*, closely related to closure, is the tendency to perceive continuous lines and patterns. An example is shown in Figure 4-11. The two lines at the left, seen separated in space, have their own continuity, but when they are put together as at the right, a different kind of continuity makes us perceive them quite differently. In looking at any kind of complex visual stimulus we are likely to perceive the organization dictated by the most compelling kind of continuity.

Similarity and Proximity *Similarity and proximity* are illustrated in Figure 4-12. The checkerboard lettered *A*, with blocks all the same color and equal distances apart, has no real

Figure 4-10 Some examples of closure

Though the figures are incomplete in one way or another, we perceive them at once for what they are.

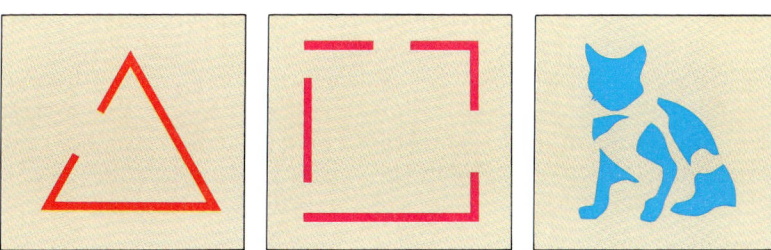

Figure 4-11 An example of continuity

At the left we clearly perceive two continuous lines that are combinations of straight and curved segments. When the two lines are put together as at the right, however, we find it difficult to perceive the original pattern. Instead we perceive a continuous wavy line running through another continuous line of straight horizontal and vertical segments.

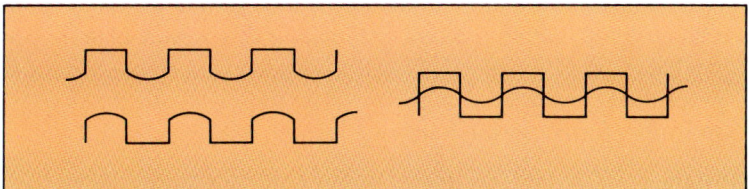

Figure 4-12 **The effects of similarity and proximity**

Drawing A has no pattern. But note what happens to your perception when some of the colored blocks are changed to white, as in B, or moved closer together, as in C.

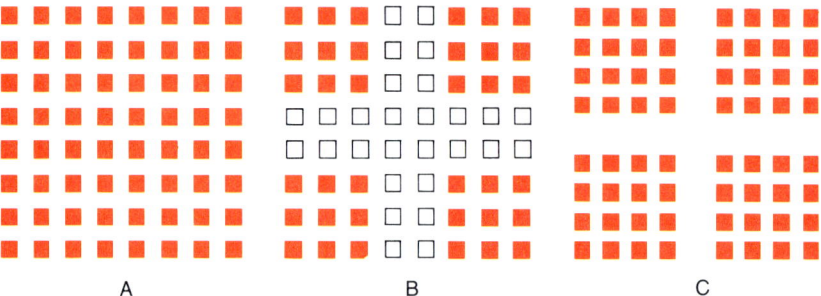

pattern inside it. If you keep looking at it and shift your eyes from one point to another, your tendency to find organization is likely to make you perceive some patterns—vertical rows, horizontal rows, or groups of squares arranged in pairs, squares, or rectangles—but these patterns are not compelling and are likely to keep shifting. In *B*, however, removing the color from some of the blocks makes a white cross fairly leap off the page. This demonstrates the rule of similarity, which is that we tend to group stimuli that are alike.

In variation *C* of the checkerboard some of the colored blocks have been moved closer together, and now you clearly perceive a pattern of four squares. This demonstrates the rule of proximity, which is that we tend to group together stimuli that are close together in space. The rule also applies to sounds. When we hear a series of sounds that are all alike, the pattern we hear depends on the timing. When we hear click-click . . . click-click . . . click-click (with the dots indicating a pause) the rule of proximity dictates that we organize the sounds into pairs. When we hear click-click-click . . . click-click-click we perceive patterns of three. Even different sounds presented this way—click-buzz-ring . . . click-buzz-ring—are perceived in groups of three.

Perceiving a World That Is Stable and Consistent

In trying to answer the question *What is it*? we have to overcome some serious handicaps. Though the objects visible in the world may have a definite and unchanging shape, the light rays they reflect to our eyes take many different patterns depending on the angle from which we view them. A dinner plate, for example, casts its true circular image only when we look straight down at it or hold it vertically in front of our eyes. From any other angle it casts different images—all sorts of ovals and ellipses. A door is a rectangle only when seen at right angles to the eyes. From other angles, as when it swings open or shut, it forms various images that are trapezoids.

This confusion seldom bothers us. Regardless of the shape of the image cast on our eyes, we know immediately that we are looking at a round plate or a rectangular door. Thanks to what is called *perceptual constancy*, we perceive a stable and consistent world. The form of perceptual constancy demonstrated by the plate and the door is called *shape constancy*. Some other forms are the following:

Size Constancy *Size constancy* refers to our tendency to recognize the actual size of an object regardless of whether the image it casts on the eye is large, as when seen close up, or small, as when seen from a distance. Figure 4-13 demonstrates how the actual size of the image creates a distorted view of the world on the film in a camera. We ourselves, viewing the same scene from the same place as the camera lens, would perceive everything in proper perspective. You can experience a perhaps even more convincing demonstration of size constancy by trying the experiment illustrated in Figure 4-14. If you follow the instructions, the images cast on your eyes by the small salad plate and the large dinner plate will

Figure 4-13 What the world would look like without size constancy

This is how two people on a beach look to a camera held at close range. If you were holding the camera, your eyes would see much the same kinds of images—hands of different sizes, exaggerated torsos, undersized heads. But you would not be aware of the distortion.

Figure 4-14 Salad plate or dinner plate?

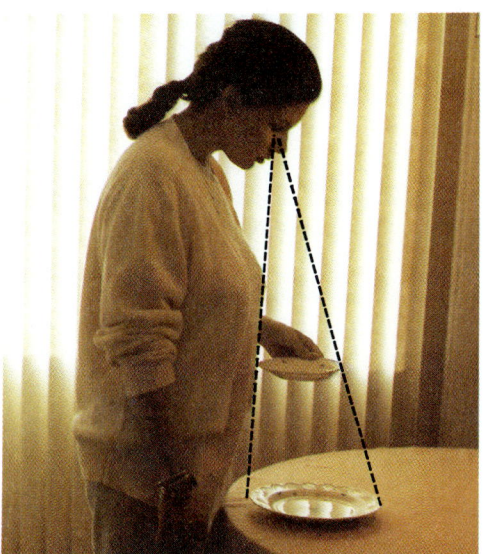

For a clear demonstration of size constancy, put a dinner plate on the table. Then move a salad plate up and down until its image exactly blots out the dinner plate. Without changing the height at which you hold the salad plate, move it to one side. The images cast on your eyes by the two plates are exactly the same size—but what do you perceive?

be exactly the same size. Yet you will find that what you perceive—and in fact cannot help perceiving—is a small plate fairly close to you and a larger plate farther away. Evidence that size constancy is present very early in life is presented in Figure 4-15.

Brightness Constancy   *Brightness constancy* can best be explained by the example of how we perceive a black shoe lying on a sidewalk in bright sunlight and the same shoe lying on a snowbank in deep shade on a cloudy winter day. In either case the shoe looks black, its

Figure 4-15   Recognizing size constancy: an inborn skill?

Six-month-old infants were shown a model of a life-size human head at a distance of 60 cm. After several exposures, they became bored and looked away. The infants were then divided into two groups. One group of babies was shown the same head model at a distance of 30 cm., while a second group was shown the head model reduced to half its size, also at a distance of 30 cm. In the first case, the actual size was the same, but the size on the retina was changed; in the second case, the actual size was changed while the retinal size remained the same. Although the retinal image had changed, the infants in the first group were still bored and looked away; those in the second group spent much more time looking at the head. Evidently a change in actual size (with retinal image the same) is a more arresting change than a change in retinal size (with actual size the same)—an indication that size constancy is already present at six months (McKenzie, Tootell, and Day, 1980).

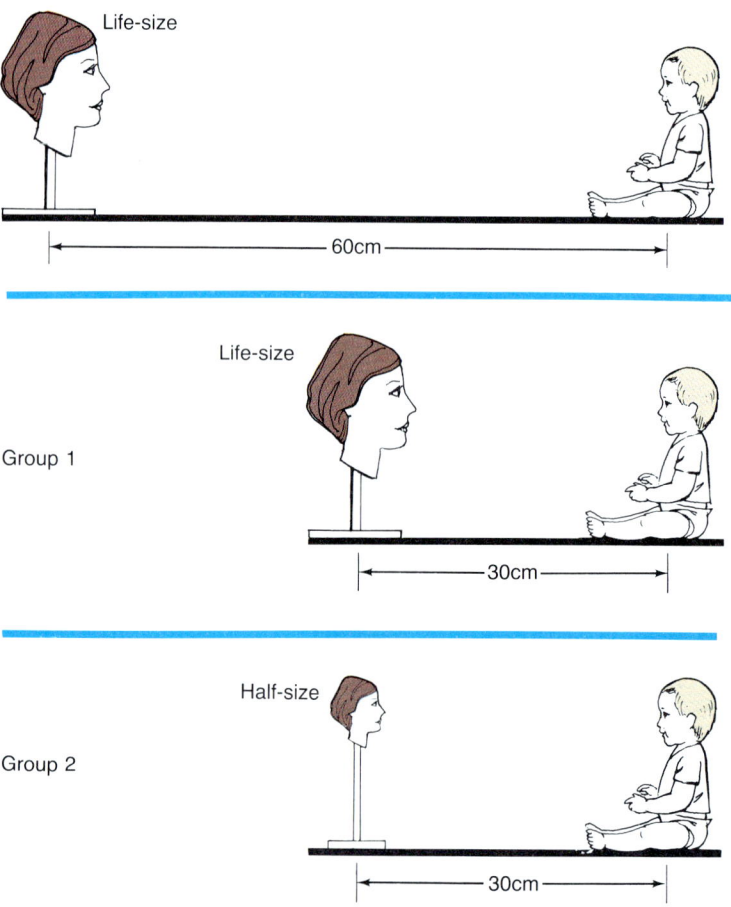

background white. But if you made some measurements with a photographer's light meter you would discover something strange. The shoe in sunlight would register just as bright on the meter as the snow in the shade—perhaps even brighter. Regardless of the actual intensity of the light waves reaching our eyes, brightness constancy gives us consistent impressions of blacks, whites, and grays and the contrasts between them. Part of the explanation seems to be the ratio of light intensity, which is about the same between sunlit shoe and sidewalk as between cloudy-day shoe and shaded snow (Hochberg, 1978).

Distance and Depth Perception

Another important question, as we explore the world, is: *Where is it?* Merely to walk around without bumping into walls and other people, we must not only perceive objects organized into patterns and shapes but also know how far away they are. Before we step off a bus we must know how deep a drop there is to the pavement. Fortunately we perceive distance and depth without even thinking.

The ability seems to depend partly on inborn wiring, as has been demonstrated with the apparatus shown in Figure 4-16. This device, known as a "visual cliff," is a piece of heavy glass suspended above the floor. Across the middle of the glass is a board covered with checkered cloth. On one side of the board the same kind of cloth is attached to the bottom of the glass, making this look like the solid, or shallow, side of the cliff. On the other side the cloth is laid on the floor, and to all appearances there is a drop on that side.

As the figure shows, a nine-month-old baby crawls without hesitation over the shallow-looking side but hesitates to crawl on the deep side. Lower animals show this tendency before any kind of learning presumably has had time to take place. Baby lambs and goats tested as soon as they are able to walk avoid the deep side. This ability seems to be the secret of how even very young animals—particularly mountain goats born into an environ-

Figure 4-16 A baby avoids a fall on the visual cliff

At left a baby fearlessly crawls toward its mother on the glass covering the shallow-looking side of the visual cliff. But at right the baby stops—seeming afraid to cross the glass that covers the apparently deep side (Gibson and Walk, 1960).

 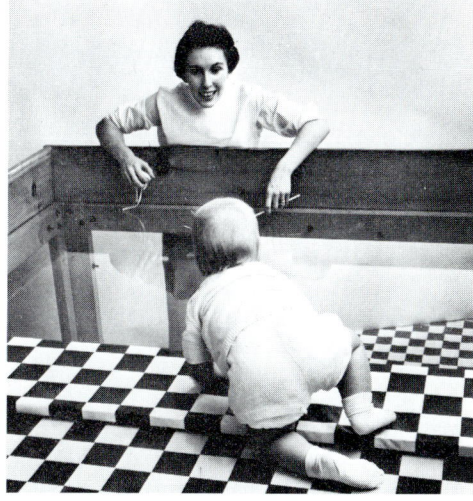

ment full of sharp and dangerous drops—manage to avoid falls. Other factors that aid the perception of depth and distance are difficult to classify as either inborn or learned. It seems that they are a combination of the two (Hochberg, 1978). Some of the most influential factors are the following:

Eye Muscles The *eye muscles* send their own messages to the brain. The muscles controlling the position of the eyeballs move to make the lines of vision from the two eyes converge on the object being viewed. At the same time, the muscles controlling the shape of the lenses operate to bring the object into the sharpest possible focus. These movements take place automatically and you are not ordinarily aware of them. But you can feel them if you deliberately shift your gaze from the farthest object within view—preferably the distant horizon—and try to look at the tip of your nose. The attempt will be unsuccessful, of course, but it will demonstrate that the muscles produce messages—which the brain somehow manages to combine with other information to help determine distance and depth.

Binocular Vision *Binocular vision* refers to the fact that the two eyes receive different images because of the distance between them, which is about 64 millimeters or 2½ inches. Like the two lenses of a three dimensional camera, the eyes view objects in the visual field from slightly different angles. The images they receive are somehow put together by the brain into a three-dimensional pattern that greatly assists the perception of depth and distance.

Interposition *Interposition* is another clue to distance perception because nearby objects block off part of our view of more distant objects. If a child is standing in front of a tree, we see all of the child's body but only part of the tree. If the tree is closer, we see the entire tree

Figure 4-17   Fooling the eye with interposition

The drawings illustrate an experiment that shows how your perception of distance can be thrown off by manipulating the clue of interposition. Two ordinary playing cards are arranged as shown in A and are the only objects visible in an otherwise dark room. You perceive clearly that the two of clubs is farther away. Now a corner is clipped from the two of diamonds, as shown in B, and the stand holding this card is moved to the right. If you now look at the cards through one eye and see them as shown in C, you perceive a small two of clubs close by and a larger two of diamonds farther away (Krech, D. and Crutchfield, R. S. Elements of psychology, 2d edition. © 1969 by Alfred A. Knopf, Inc. Reprinted by permission).

but only part of the child. Interposition is so important a clue that it can be manipulated in the laboratory to completely fool the eye, as shown in Figure 4-17.

Perspective   *Perspective* is a distance clue that has been used by artists for many centuries to create a three-dimensional impression on a flat piece of canvas. The three types of perspective are illustrated in Figure 4-18. *Linear perspective* refers to the fact that parallel lines, like the highway lanes in the photo, seem to draw closer together as they recede into the distance. *Aerial perspective* refers to the fact that distant objects, because they are seen through air that is usually somewhat hazy, appear less distinct and less brilliant in color than nearby objects. If you have lived within sighting distance of mountains or city skyscrapers you may have noticed that the mountains or buildings seem much closer on days when the air is unusually clear.

The third type of perspective is *gradient of texture*, which you can best observe by looking at a large expanse of lawn. The grass nearby can be seen so well that every blade is distinct, and therefore its texture looks quite coarse. Farther away, the individual blades seem to merge and the texture becomes much finer. It is distance also, incidentally, that causes the grass, in the words of the old aphorism, to "always look greener on the other side of the street." Only when you are close up can you see the through the blades of grass to the earth color below (Pomerantz, 1983).

Shadowing   *Shadowing*—or the pattern of light and shadow on the objects we see—also helps us perceive distance and depth. Our world is usually illuminated from above—by the sun in the daytime and overhead light fixtures at night. The top parts of three-dimensional objects receive the full force of the light waves, while the lower parts are more or less shadowed. The extent to which we use this clue is shown in Figure 4-19, where an unfamiliar pattern of shadowing creates an unusual illusion.

Figure 4-18   Perspective and distance perception

The three-dimensional effect of this photograph results from all three types of perspective—linear, aerial, and gradient of texture.

Figure 4-19 An illusion formed by shadowing

Compare what you perceive here with what you perceive when you turn the page upside down. The reason is the way distance and depth perception are affected by shadowing, as explained in the text. (The photograph is printed upside down on the page, reversing the way the shadows were actually cast.)

Figure 4-20 Size and distance

In the photograph at left, you clearly perceive a small child nearby and her mother farther away. One reason is that you know the mother is bigger. But the size of the images they cast on your eyes is almost exactly the same, as shown in the composite photo at the right, made by cutting the mother out of the original picture and pasting her next to the child (after Boring, 1964).

140 Chapter 4 Perception: Making Sense Out Of Our Sensations

Figure 4-21 **The case of the deceptive lampposts**

There is no doubt in your mind—is there?—that lamppost a is much smaller than lamppost b. Or that the wooden block x is much smaller than y? But measure them with a ruler and you will find that the two posts and the two blocks are exactly the same size. The perceived distance of the objects—with b and y seeming considerably farther away—affects your perception of their size (Beeler and Branley, 1951).

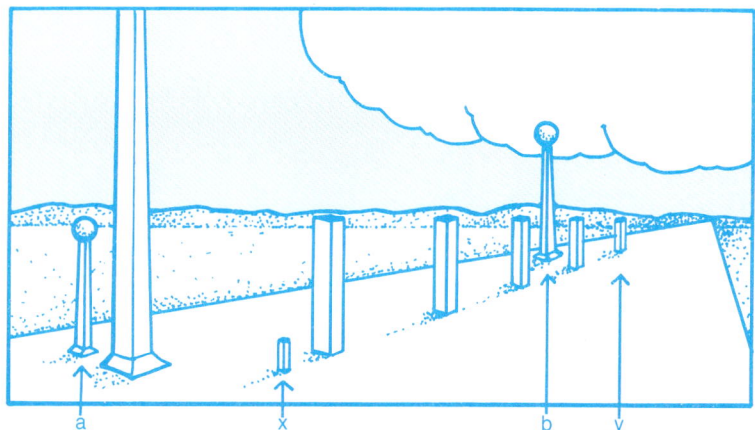

The Relationship between Distance and Size

To a very considerable extent, our perception of distance also depends on our perception of size and the principle of size constancy. We know how big a basketball is, regardless of how large or how small an image it casts on our eyes. Thus, when we see it thrown down the court, we can judge how far away it is by how large it seems in relation to the other objects in the visual field. We know roughly how big another adult is, and this helps us determine the distance between us. In the photograph in Figure 4-20—as in any similar real-life situation—we immediately perceive that we are looking at a baby close up and an adult some distance away. The relationship between perceived distance and perceived size works both ways, as is illustrated in Figure 4-21.

INTERPRETATION: DISCOVERING THE MEANING OF OUR PERCEPTIONS

Selection answers the question: Which one of all the many objects and events in the environment is worthy of attention and exploration? Organization helps decide: What is it, and where is it? But one important question remains: *What does it mean?* Finding the answer requires the third element of perception, which is *interpretation*.

Of all the elements, interpretation is the most clearly dependent on learning rather than on any inborn characteristics of the nervous system. It is ordinarily made by comparing new information provided by the senses with old information that has been acquired in the past. Note for example the symbols in Figure 4-22. You probably have never seen anything exactly like them before—but you perceive at once that all of them are the letter *E*. You have stored in memory what students of perception call a *prototype* or *schema*—a sort of generalized model of what the letter *E* looks like. You can interpret and identify the

Figure 4-22 You know what these are—but how do you know?

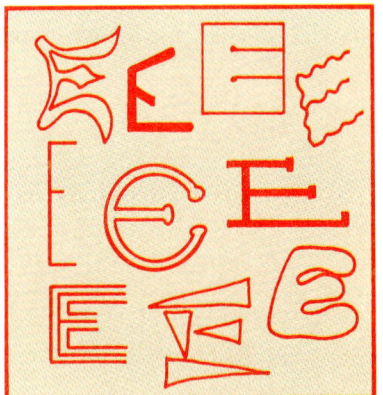

These symbols are unlike any E's you have seen before, yet you recognize them at a glance. For the explanation, see the discussion of prototypes in the text.

new symbols because they resemble this prototype. Similarly, you have prototypes that help you recognize the human face, a tree, the animal called a dog, and all the other objects and events you have become familiar with.

Prototypes, Feature Analysis, and Global Processing

The way we match a new stimulus against our prototype has been the subject of considerable study and speculation. One school of thought has been that we engage in a feature-by-feature analysis and comparison. In looking at a letter, we might note whether it has horizontal or vertical lines or both, diagonal lines moving upward to the left or right, and so on. This kind of feature analysis can be programmed into computers to enable them to recognize letters, and there is considerable evidence that it is also employed in human perception (Geyer and DeWald, 1973).

Another possibility is that we base our comparisons not on mere features but on what has been termed "global" processing—that is, the total overall pattern formed by the various individual features, viewed as a single and well-integrated unit. This suggestion was first made by Gestalt psychologists, a school of thought that has been summarized as maintaining that "the whole is greater than the sum of its parts." The Gestalt psychologists pointed out, for example, that when we look at ∷ or □ we immediately perceive a square, not four independent dots or two horizontal and two vertical lines. Similarly, the human face seems to leap into perception as a unit, without any feature-by-feature analysis of eyes, nose, and mouth. If you turn back to Figure 4-9 (page 132) and look again at the drawing that can be seen as either a goblet or two faces, you will note that you see the faces before you notice such details as nose, lips, and chin.

Many psychologists now believe that we rely at times on global processing and at other times on feature analysis, depending on the nature of the stimulus and the conditions under which we view it (Hoffman, 1980). Some stimuli lend themselves readily to global processing because their individual features just naturally seem to hang together and form an integrated whole. Others do not (Treisman and Gelade, 1980) and are therefore more suitable for feature analysis. Often it appears that we combine the two processes, taking first a global view, then attending to some of the individual features, then again considering the stimulus in its entirety (Broadbent, 1977).

Expectations, Mental Set, and Context

Experience has led us to expect certain events to happen in our world in certain familiar ways. We have a mental set toward the environment. What we perceive and how we interpret it depends to a considerable extent on our set—in other words, on our *perceptual expectations*.

Laboratory experiments have shown that manipulating people's expectations can greatly affect their perceptions. Would you believe, for example, that two people could look at exactly the same drawing—yet that one would see a man and the other would see a rat? To convince yourself, try the demonstration illustrated in Figure 4-23.

The drawing, of course, was specially designed. The final figure was deliberately made ambiguous, so that it looks both like a man's face and a rat. You can just as easily perceive one as the other. But many of the sights we encounter in real life are also ambiguous—and the way we perceive them is also likely to depend on what we expect to see.

In a similar way, interpretation also depends on the situation in which we encounter a stimulus—that is, the *context* in which it is found. For a demonstration, note Figure 4-24. There you see exactly the same unusual symbol in the middle of each of the two words. If you saw it set apart by itself, you would hardly know what it was supposed to be. You might even guess that it was a set of goal posts. In the context of the words, you immediately perceive the first of the identical symbols as an *H* and the second as an *A*.

Figure 4-23 **A little perceptual magic: now it's a man, now it's a rat**

Cover both rows of drawings, then ask a friend to watch while you uncover the faces in the top row one at a time, beginning at the left. The friend will almost surely perceive the final drawing as the face of a man. Then try the bottom row in similar fashion on another friend. This friend will almost surely perceive the final drawing as a rat. The psychologists who devised this experiment found that 85 to 95 percent of their subjects perceived the final drawing as a man if they saw the other human heads first, as a rat if they saw the animals first—though of course the final drawings are exactly alike (Bugelski and Alampay, 1961).

Interpretation: Discovering the Meaning of Our Perceptions

Figure 4-24 Same symbol, different context, different interpretation

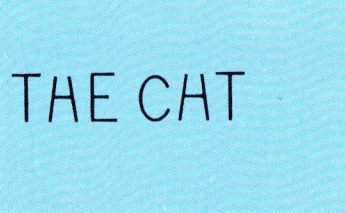

Interpretation—like all elements of perception—works in complex ways. Even simple stimuli such as the sound of various tones can activate a rich set of associations. For example, in one study subjects regarded high-pitched tones as "bright," "sharp," "small," and "fast," and low-pitched tones as "dull," "blunt," "heavy," and "sad" (Walker and Smith, 1984).

Interpretation may also be affected by our brain chemistry. Experiments have shown that introverts are better able than extroverts to detect subtle changes in an auditory stimulus (Stelmack, Achorn, and Michaud, 1977). This may be due to the fact that introverts have a higher level of activity in the brain of norepinephrine (Aston-Jones, 1985). Interpretation may also be affected by our mood or physical condition at the moment. Even small

Figure 4-25 Stimulating perception

If you look intently at the figure, you will notice that it tends to undergo a reversal. Sometimes the plane labeled A seems closer, and at other times the plane labeled B seems closer. Ask a friend to monitor you for about one minute as you look at the figure. Call out each time you perceive the figure to reverse its orientation, and have your friend count the number of reversals. Now drink a cup of coffee—which should increase the frequency of your eye movements. After 10 to 15 minutes, go through the same process again. You should find that the stimulant increases the number of the shifts you perceive (adapted from Coren, Porac, and Ward, 1984).

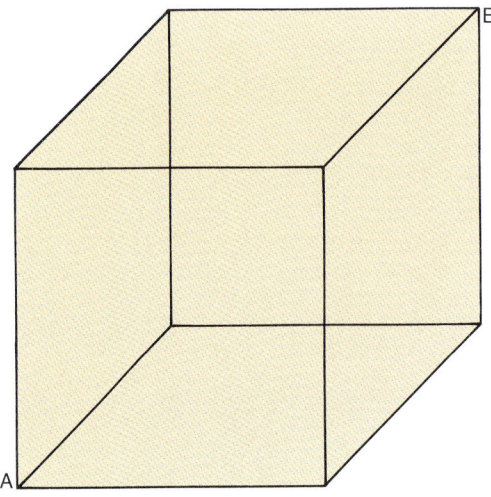

amounts of alcohol, for example, can decrease the ability to perceive when a stimulus begins to move (MacArthur and Sekuler, 1982), while stimulants such as caffeine can increase perceptual sensitivity—as demonstrated in Figure 4-25.

To show how our internal state can affect interpretation, an experimenter once asked subjects to describe pictures they were told they would see dimly on a screen. Actually there were no real pictures, only blurs and smudges. But hungry subjects, who had gone 16 hours without eating before the experiment, thought they saw all kinds of foods and food-related objects (McClelland and Atkinson, 1948). It appears that we begin our information processing by perceiving not only what we expect to see and what the situation indicates we are likely to see but also what we want to see.

Thus it is clear that our inborn perceptual skills, so important in helping us survive, are enriched and given meaning and style by the experiences we encounter throughout our lives (Rock, 1984).

SUMMARY

How perception enables us to survive

1. Perception is *the process through which we become aware of our environment by selecting, organizing, and interpreting the evidence from our senses.*

2. Our skill at perception depends in part on the inborn structure of the nervous system and its specialized nerve cells called *feature detectors*, found in the pathways from sense organs to brain and in the brain itself. In vision, some feature detectors respond sharply to patterns (such as vertical line, a horizontal line, or an angle) and others to movement. In hearing, some feature detectors are strongly activated by either low-pitched sounds, high-pitched sounds, or changes in pitch.

3. Two optical illusions are the *autokinetic illusion*, in which a stationary spot of light seen in darkness seems to move of its own accord, and *stroboscopic motion*, in which two stationary objects viewed close together in space and time seem to be moving. Moving pictures and television are based on stroboscopic motion.

4. Our perceptions of the world are usually—but not always—in accord with the facts. Among the exceptions are perceptual illusions and distortions during *altered states of consciousness* (like those produced by hypnosis or drugs).

Our perceptual specialties: selection and attention

5. *Selection* is a key element in perception because we can perceive only a few of all the many stimuli that constantly bombard our senses.

6. Selection depends on the inborn structure of the nervous system and on such learned factors as interests, motivation, emotional states, and personality; we are particularly adept at perceiving *movement, change, contrast,* and stimuli of substantial *size* and *intensity.*

7. When we select and pay attention to one event, we usually lose perception of other stimuli. It is especially difficult to process two different inputs if they arrive in the same sensory channel—for example, to pay attention to two conversations at the same time.

8. Selection helps us explore the environment, perceive what is likely to be most important, ignore the rest, and concentrate on using the rest of our information-processing talents to the best possible advantage.

How we organize our perceptions

9. *Organization* is a key element because, in order to answer the question *What is it?*, we have to see or hear a stimulus that hangs together in some kind of unit—a human face or a meaningful pattern of human speech.

10. An important factor in organization is *figure and ground*, which is the tendency to perceive an object as a meaningful unit set off from a neutral background by a dividing line called a *contour*.

11. Organization generally follows the rules of:
    a. *closure*, which refers to the fact that we do not need a complete and uninterrupted contour to perceive a figure.
    b. *continuity*, which is the tendency to perceive continuous lines and patterns.
    c. *similarity*, which is the ability to group stimuli that are alike.
    d. *proximity*, which dictates that we tend to group together stimuli that are close in space.

12. *Perceptual constancy* is the tendency to perceive a stable and consistent world even though the stimuli that reach our eyes are inconsistent and potentially confusing. Perceptual constancy includes *shape constancy, size constancy,* and *brightness constancy*.

13. In perceiving distance and depth, we rely on clues provided by movements of the *eye muscles, binocular vision, interposition, perspective,* and *shadowing*.

14. The three types of perspective are (a) *linear perspective* (parallel lines seem to draw closer together as they recede into the distance), (b) *aerial perspective* (distant objects, because they are seen through air that is hazy, appear less distinct and less brilliant in color than nearby objects), and (c) *gradient of texture* (objects seen distinctly and nearby seem to have a coarser texture, while objects farther away seem to have a finer texture).

15. Perceived distance also depends on perceived size—and this relationship works both ways.

Interpretation: discovering the meaning of our perceptions

16. *Interpretation* is a key element because it answer the question *What does it mean?* Interpretation is ordinarily made by comparing new information provided by the senses with old information acquired in the past.

17. We interpret and identify a new stimulus by matching it against generalized models that we have stored in the memory of familiar events and objects—like the letter *E* or the human face. Such a model is called a *prototype* or *schema*.

18. In matching a new stimulus to a prototype we may engage in *feature analysis* (in the case of the letter *E*, noting the three horizontal lines and the vertical line) or *global processing* (noting the overall pattern of the individual features, viewed as a single and well-integrated unit).

19. Our interpretations are influenced by *perceptual expectations*, or mental sets acquired because we have learned to expect certain events to occur in certain familiar ways. They are also influenced by the *context* in which the new stimulus is found and to some extent even by our mood, physical condition, and wishes.

IMPORTANT TERMS

aerial perspective	interpretation
altered states of consciousness	linear perspective
autokinetic illusion	mental telepathy
binocular vision	organization
brightness constancy	parapsychology
clairvoyance	perception
closure	perceptual constancy
context	perceptual expectation
continuity	perspective
contour	precognition
contrast	prototype
depth perception	proximity
distance perception	schema
extrasensory perception	selection
feature analysis	shadowing
feature detectors	shape constancy
figure and ground	similarity
global processing	simultaneous brightness contrast
gradient of texture	size constancy
interposition	stroboscopic motion
	visual cliff

RECOMMENDED READINGS

Alcock, J. E. *Parapsychology: science or magic? A psychological perspective*. Oxford: Pergamon Press, 1981.

Aslin, R. N., Alberts, J. R., and Petersen, M. R. *Development of perception: psychobiological perspectives*. New York: Academic Press, 1981.

Heil, J. *Perception and cognition*. Berkeley: University of California Press, 1983.

Hochberg, J. *Perception*, 2d ed. Englewood Cliffs, N.J.: Prentice-Hall, 1978.

Kaufman, L. *Perception: the world transformed*. New York: Oxford University Press, 1979.

Marks, D., and Kamman, R. *The psychology of the psychic*. Buffalo, N.Y.: Prometheus Books, 1980.

Michaels, C. F. *Direct perception*. Englewood Cliffs, N.J.: Prentice-Hall, 1981.

Neisser, U. *Cognition and reality*. San Francisco: Freeman, 1976.

Sekuler, R., and Randolph, B. *Perception*. New York: Knopf, 1985.

Wolman, B. B., et al., eds. *Handbook of parapsychology*. New York: Van Nostrand Reinhold, 1985.

PART 3

THE POWERS OF THE HUMAN INTELLECT

CHAPTER

5

PRINCIPLES OF LEARNING

CLASSICAL CONDITIONING 152

Pavlov and his salivating dogs
The baby who learned to fear Santa Claus
Conditioning physical symptoms and responses
The basics of classical conditioning
The timing, frequency, and predictability of reinforcement
Extinction and spontaneous recovery
Stimulus generalization and discrimination
Learning abnormal behavior
Built-in predispositions to learning

OPERANT CONDITIONING 162

The magic box of B. F. Skinner
Some principles of operant conditioning
Behavior shaping
How you learn to be superstitious
Some facts about reinforcement
Schedules of partial reinforcement
Applications of operant conditioning: behavior modification and token economies
Conditioning, biofeedback, and medicine

OPERANT ESCAPE, PUNISHMENT, AND LEARNED HELPLESSNESS 172

Escape and avoidance in human behavior
The effect of punishment on behavior
Punishment works with animals—but what about people?
Learned helplessness: the case of the passive dogs
Helplessness in human beings
How failure can lead to helplessness

THE COGNITIVE VIEW OF LEARNING 178

Chimps with ingenuity
Learning without reinforcement
Can there be learning without a response?
Cognitive maps, expectancies, and knowledge
Learning by observing

SUMMARY 184

IMPORTANT TERMS 186

RECOMMENDED READINGS 187

PSYCHOLOGY IN EVERYDAY LIFE

Scientific ethics in psychological research 156
Can behavior modification destroy human freedom? 170
Learning to feel worthy and in control 177

ll humans are far more alike than unlike at the moment of birth. All babies have much the same kinds of bones and muscles, nervous systems, glands, and sense organs. But although we are born very much alike, we turn out very different. Indeed it can be said with some confidence that no human adult, not even an identical twin, has ever been exactly like another. Each of us is unique, unlike anyone who lived before or will live again. Why?

The answer lies to a large extent in the processes of *learning*, which begin to change us almost from the moment we are born. Much of the behavior and mental activity that characterize us as adults has been learned. Because learning influences our lives in so many significant ways, it has always been a central concern of psychology.

Over the years, psychology has taken two notably different approaches to the study of learning. In the period when most psychologists preferred to study observable actions and ignore such vague and elusive matters as mental life and human consciousness, learning was generally regarded as a process that produced clear-cut and readily apparent changes in behavior. Many psychologists concentrated on lower animals and the way their behavior could be altered by experience. The science searched for laws that applied not just to humans but to all forms of animal life.

Even during this period, however, there were some psychologists who believed learning could not be fully understood without considering the subtle workings of the brain—and most especially the superior brain of the human organism. The rise of the cognitive school has popularized this view of learning as the acquisition of knowledge—one of the steps in "the human being's active interaction with information about the world" (Klatzky, 1980).

Both these approaches have been fruitful, and both are represented in what is today the generally accepted definition: *Learning is any relatively permanent change in behavior (or behavior potential) produced by experience* (Tarpy and Mayer, 1978). The words "behavior potential" refer to the knowledge we acquire and remember—like the nursery rhyme *Old Mother Hubbard*—without necessarily displaying any change in the way we act. The definition also covers the universal laws of learning that psychologists have established by observing the actual behavior of humans and lower animals.

This chapter concentrates on the laws of learning that seem to apply to all organisms. The next chapter discusses the cognitive aspects of learning—notably the way we humans manage to store all kinds of information in our memory so that we can find what we need when we need it.

CLASSICAL CONDITIONING

Suppose you suffer from a strange reluctance to be in any kind of small, enclosed place. It frightens you to step into an elevator or a closet. You breathe faster; you feel a sinking sensation in your stomach; your hands tremble. You know that this fear, which is called claustrophobia, makes no sense. But you cannot help it. You are frightened without knowing why.

Unreasonable fears of this kind trouble many people. Some are afraid of being in open spaces, as on a broad prairie or on a lake (*agoraphobia*). Some are afraid of heights (*acrophobia*), and it frightens them to look out the window of a tall building or climb to the top of a football stadium. Some are thrown into mild panic by hearing a telephone ring, or driving past a cemetery, or even getting into an automobile.

Similarly, many of us have equally unreasonable preferences for certain things, especially certain kinds of people. We may be instantly attracted to men who have mustaches or men who are bald, or to small women or women who are tall and broad shouldered. We may feel unexplained warmth toward a certain tone of voice or the way a person walks, gestures, or dresses. We know that these matters have nothing to do with what the person is really like, yet we find ourselves irresistibly drawn.

These unreasonable fears and preferences are learned responses—though often we do not know how we have learned them. In many cases they seem to be the result of *classical conditioning,* which can best be explained by discussing the work of Ivan Pavlov, a Russian scientist who performed one of the most famous experiments in the history of psychology.

Pavlov and His Salivating Dogs

Pavlov conducted his experiment in the early years of this century. His subjects were dogs, and his experimental apparatus was the simple but effective device illustrated in Figure 5-1. His concern was the type of behavior called a *reflex,* an automatic action exhibited by all organisms that possess a nervous system. One such reflex is the knee jerk. When you have your legs crossed, with one foot dangling in the air, a sharp tap just below the kneecap makes the foot jump. Another reflex makes your pupils smaller whenever a bright light strikes your eyes. The bodily changes associated with emotions are also reflex responses. For example, when a baby hears a sudden loud noise, this stimulus automatically triggers the nervous system into producing the changes in heartbeat and glandular activity that are characteristic of fear.

All reflex responses take place without conscious effort, because our nervous system is wired in such a way that the stimulus automatically produces the response. The reflexes are built in, not learned. The question that interested Pavlov was this: Can they be modified by learning?

He set about answering the question by investigating the salivary reflex, which results in secretions by the salivary glands of the mouth when food is presented. He strapped a dog into the harness shown in Figure 5-1 and then introduced a sound, such as the beat of a metronome. The dog made a few restless movements, but there was no flow of saliva. This was what Pavlov had expected. The stimulus for reflex action of the salivary glands is the presence of food in the mouth—not the sound of a metronome. When food was delivered and the dog took it into its mouth, saliva of course flowed in quantity.

Pavlov (center) in his laboratory with his assistants, his apparatus, and one of his dogs.

Figure 5-1 Pavlov's dog

A tube attached to the dog's salivary gland collects any saliva secreted by the gland, and the number of drops from the tube is recorded on a revolving drum outside the chamber. The experimenter can watch the dog through a one-way mirror and deliver food to the dog's feed pan by remote control. Thus there is nothing in the chamber to distract the dog's attention except the food, when it is delivered, and any other stimulus that the experimenter wishes to present, such as the sound of a metronome. For the discoveries Pavlov made with this apparatus, see the text (Yerkes and Morgulis, 1909).

Now Pavlov set about trying to connect the neutral stimulus of the sound with the reflex action of the salivary glands. While the metronome was clicking, he delivered food to the dog, setting off the salivary reflex. After a time he did the same thing again—sounded the metronome and delivered food. When he had done this many times, he tried something new. He sounded the metronome but did not deliver any food. Saliva flowed anyway (Pavlov, 1927). The dog had learned—through the form of learning now called classical conditioning—to exhibit the salivary reflex in response to a totally new kind of stimulus.

In the more than 60 years since Pavlov, psychologists have studied classical conditioning with a wide variety of techniques and with various species of animals—mostly domesticated rats, pigeons, and rabbits. Such learning has been shown to be possible even in the primitive sea snail (Carew, Hawkins, and Kandel, 1983). An example of one technique—for conditioning the rabbit to blink—is described in Figure 5-2. Because rabbits do not ordinarily blink their eyes, the researcher can be fairly certain that the response occurs as a result of conditioning (Gormezano, Kehoe, and Marshall, 1983).

The Baby Who Learned to Fear Santa Claus

What salivating dogs and blinking rabbits tell us about more complicated forms of human behavior was demonstrated in another famous experiment—this one performed by John Watson, the founder of behaviorism. Watson's subject was an 11-month-old boy named

Figure 5-2 Learning to blink the eye

The rabbit is placed in a plastic holder, with the head protruding from it. One end of a fine string is attached to the upper lid of one eye. The other end is attached to a small potentiometer—a device through which eyelid movements can be translated into electrical impulses and then recorded. The stimulus for the eyeblink reflex is a puff of air to the surface of the eye. In various conditioning experiments, rabbits have learned through classical conditioning to blink in response to totally new stimuli—including lights, tones, and even vibration of the animal's abdomen with a hand massager (after Domjan and Burkhard, 1986).

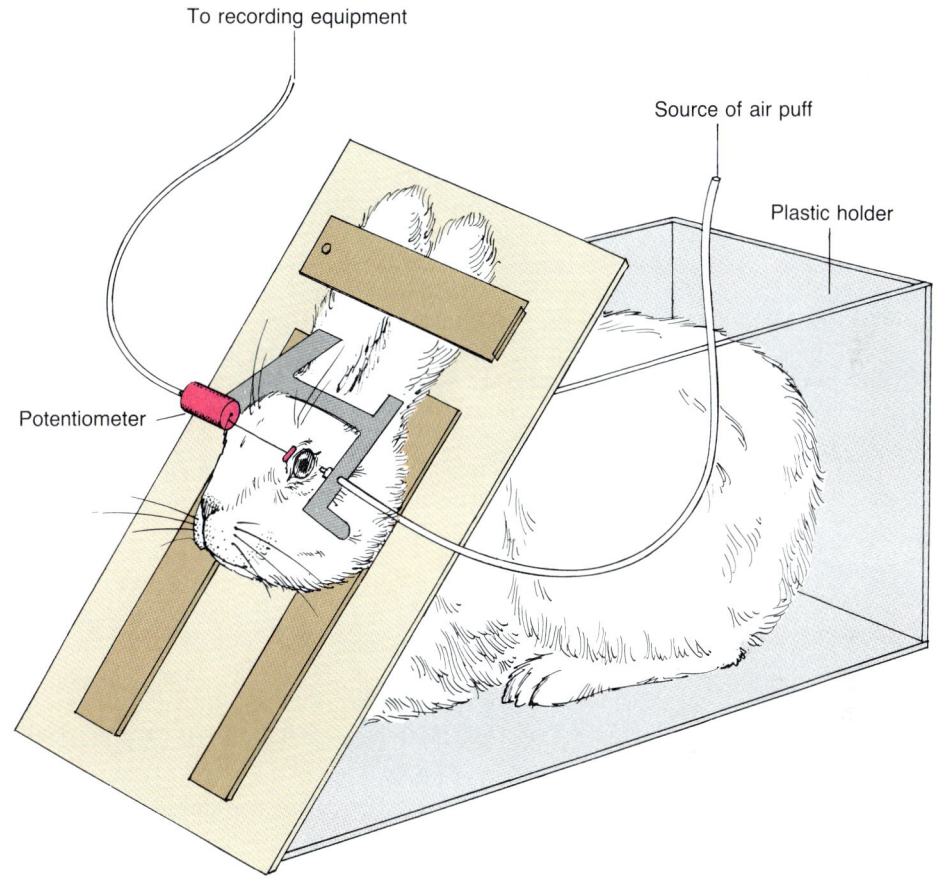

Albert. His experiment was an attempt to establish whether the reflex response of fear produced in infants by a loud noise could be conditioned to take place in response to other and previously neutral stimuli.

At the start Albert had no fear of a white rat. But every time he touched the animal, a loud noise was sounded. After a number of pairings of animal and sound, Albert began to cry when he saw the rat. He also showed strong signs of fear toward some other furry objects, including a dog and a fur coat, and a suspicious attitude toward a bearded mask of Santa Claus (Watson and Rayner, 1920). If the fear persisted, Albert may have come to be afraid of sidewalk Santa Clauses at Christmas—without ever knowing why. Unfortunately no information is available about Albert's future life because Waston lost touch with him— a fact that raises some questions of scientific ethics discussed in a Psychology in Everyday Life box called "Scientific Ethics in Psychological Research."

Psychology in Everyday Life
Scientific Ethics in Psychological Research

Put yourself for a moment in the shoes of John Watson—a psychologist with a chance to perform an experiment in conditioning a fear reaction in 11-month-old Albert. Would you do it? Or would you worry about the possibility of doing long-term harm to the child? What if the fear actually did generalize to Santa Claus, thus depriving Albert of a childhood pleasure? What if he felt uncomfortable all his life around white animals, white rugs, and white-haired people?

The Albert experiment was performed at a time when psychology, in its early excitement over obtaining the first scientific understanding of human behavior, was inclined to ignore such questions. Now the science is much more concerned about the risks to its subjects. The great majority of today's psychologists would never undertake such an experiment. Any who did would be very careful to make sure that Albert's conditioned fear was promptly eliminated through further learning—a precautionary measure that Watson omitted (Harris, 1979).

The question of ethics has been the subject of much soul-searching among psychologists (Gross and Flemming, 1982). Some methods of studying behavior seem to be clearly unacceptable. For example, no psychologist would consider urging a brain operation just for the sake of studying its effects. But in other cases, the line is difficult to draw. Are psychologists ever justified in deceiving their subjects—such as by telling them they are administering electric shocks to another person, when in fact the other person is a confederate who is only pretending to be shocked? Some psychologists defend the use of little white lies when necessary to achieve important findings (Cooper, 1976). Others consider experiments that rely on deception to be "confidence games" that the science should scorn (Forward, Canter, and Kirsch, 1976). There has been debate even over the propriety of using the technique of naturalistic observation to study people going about their usual activities—a technique that some feel may often be an invasion of privacy.

The American Psychological Association, to which most practitioners of the science belong, has drawn up a set of guidelines to ethical experimentation—and is prepared to expel any member who clearly violates them. But there are many borderline cases that psychologists can decide only by weighing any possible harm to their subjects against the value to humanity of the knowledge they may discover. This is a problem that will probably always plague a science that deals with human beings.

The Albert experiment casts considerable light on the unexplained fears we often display as adults. They are conditioned responses, learned in childhood through some long-forgotten pairing of stimuli—through an experience that may not even have impressed us very much at the time. Similarly, the experiment helps explain many of our unreasonable preferences. A liking for people of a certain type may go back to a childhood experience in which a person with that kind of face or body build or mannerisms elicited reflex responses of warmth and pleasure.

Conditioning Physical Symptoms and Responses

In one experiment, rats were put into a coma with a heavy dose of insulin, producing the drastic reaction known as insulin shock. The drug was administered with a hypodermic needle while a bright light was shining. The association of needle, light, and coma resulted in a spectacular kind of conditioning. The same kind of light was turned on, the same needle was used to inject a harmless shot of salt water—and the animals went into a coma characteristic of insulin shock (Sawrey, Conger, and Turrell, 1956).

In an experiment on asthma, people allergic to certain kinds of dust or pollen were exposed to these substances—and responded with their usual symptoms of allergy—at the same time as other neutral and harmless substances were also presented. Eventually these neutral substances alone were enough to cause asthma attacks. In some cases, even a picture of the previously neutral substance was enough to produce an attack (Dekker, Pelser, and Groen, 1957).

The experiments on coma and asthma indicate the ways in which classical conditioning can produce some of the strange physical symptoms that may bother us as adults. An asthma sufferer may have been conditioned—not in the laboratory but by some real-life experience—to have an attack when walking into a particular room or seeing a particular person or even looking at a certain kind of picture on a television screen. Events that occur in our lives, unimportant in themselves but associated with past experiences, may make us have headaches or become sick to our stomachs. We may suddenly and inexplicably show all the symptoms of having a cold, or we may experience heart palpitation, high blood pressure, dizziness, or cramps.

Recent studies show that our immune system, which produces antibodies to help us fight infection and disease, can be influenced by conditioning. Rats were conditioned to associate a novel taste with unpleasant physical reactions to a drug that suppresses the immune system. Later, when the animals were exposed only to the novel taste but not to the drug, the production of immune system antibodies was suppressed (Ader, Cohen, and Bovbjerg, 1982). This research suggests that each of us is potentially vulnerable to changes in our resistance to disease as a result of classically conditioned responses occurring without our awareness.

The conditioning process plays a role in the development of some of life's more pleasant physical responses as well. Think, for example, of the reaction of your stomach glands to the mention of a restaurant in which you have enjoyed a series of memorable dinners. Or think of the sexual response you might feel to the odor of a particular perfume or shaving lotion that you associate with a beloved friend.

The power of such conditioning was demonstrated recently in a study of male rat pups that suckled females whose nipples and vaginal odors were altered with a distinct lemon scent. The rats were then weaned and never exposed again either to females or to the lemon scent until they were sexually mature. At that point they were paired with sexually receptive females. The vaginal areas of some females were treated with lemon scent, but others were not. As shown in Figure 5-3, the contrast in sexual response was dramatic. The male rats placed with the lemon-scented females became more excited and ejaculated readily, while the other rats were considerably slower to respond (Fillion and Blass, 1986). This study suggests what powerful effects early conditioning can have on the adult.

The Basics of Classical Conditioning

With these facts in mind about the far-reaching effects that classical conditioning can have on our lives, let us now return to Pavlov's experiment and discuss this type of learning in more detail. To understand the process we must first consider its five basic elements, using the terms that Pavlov himself used to describe them.

1. The food used in the experiment was the *unconditioned stimulus*—the stimulus that naturally and automatically produces the salivary response, without any learning.

2. The sound of the metronome was the *conditioned stimulus*—neutral at the start but eventually producing a similar response.

Figure 5-3 Early conditioning of later sexual response

As explained in the text, male rat pups that suckled females treated with a lemon scent became sexually aroused by the smell after they reached puberty (Fillion and Blass, 1986).

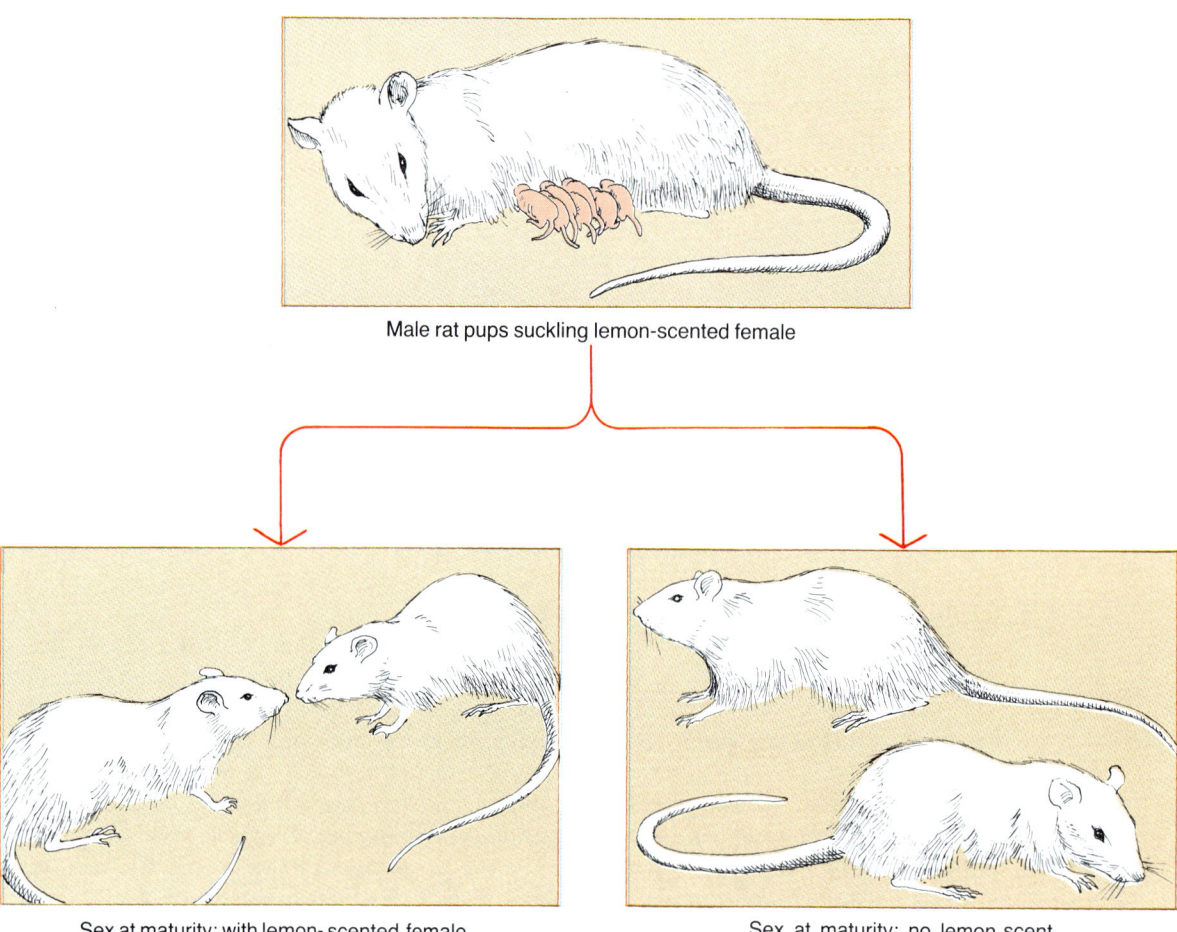

Male rat pups suckling lemon-scented female

Sex at maturity: with lemon-scented female

Sex at maturity: no lemon scent

3. Pairing the unconditioned stimulus of food with the conditioned stimulus of sound was the *reinforcement*—the key to conditioning.
4. The reflex action of the salivary glands when food was placed in the dog's mouth was the *unconditioned response*—the response that is built into the wiring of the nervous system and takes place automatically, without any kind of learning.
5. The response of the glands to the sound of the metronome was the *conditioned response*—resulting from some kind of change in the dog's nervous system produced by pairing the conditioned stimulus with the unconditioned stimulus and therefore with the salivary response.

These elements are common to all cases of classical conditioning. In Watson's Albert experiment, the unconditioned stimulus was the loud noise; the conditioned stimulus was the rat; the reinforcement was the pairing of the loud noise with the rat; the unconditioned

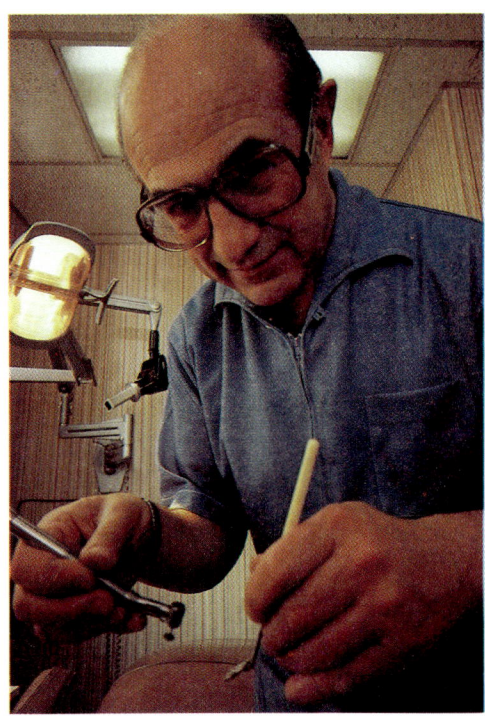

The dentist often becomes the object of conditioned fear.

response was the automatic display of fear toward the noise; and the conditioned response was the learned display of fear toward the rat.

The Timing, Frequency, and Predictability of Reinforcement

It appears that the conditioning process is most effective when the conditioned stimulus (the metronome in Pavlov's experiment) is presented just before the unconditioned stimulus (the food), as shown in Figure 5-4. The optimum interval, whether a second or half a second, has been found to vary depending on the nature of the behavior being conditioned and the reinforcement used.

The number of pairings of the conditioned and unconditioned stimulus necessary to produce a conditioned response also varies depending on the behavior being conditioned. Fear reactions in animals are readily conditioned in the laboratory. After only several presentations of a neutral conditioned stimulus with a painful conditioned stimulus such as electric shock, the conditioned stimulus will produce bodily reactions symptomatic of fear—crouching, trembling, urination, defecation—indicating that the animal has learned that the conditioned stimulus signals that a shock is coming. In real life, too, fear reactions are readily conditioned. Only one frightening experience on an airplane can create a fear reaction even to the thought of flying. Other responses—for example, the eyeblink in the rabbit—take longer to condition.

For most reactions, however, the critical factor is not the number of times that the conditioned stimulus is paired with an unconditioned stimulus, but rather the reliability with which the conditioned stimulus predicts the unconditioned stimulus (Rescorla, 1966). In one experiment, dogs were first trained to jump back and forth over a barrier in a so-called shuttle box so that they could escape an electric shock. After the dogs had learned to jump, they were divided into two groups. For one group, tones and electric shocks were presented haphazardly—so that a tone just as often came before a shock as after it. For the

Figure 5-4 The difference timing makes

Conditioning turns out to be most effective when the conditioned stimulus precedes the unconditioned stimulus by a short interval. This is called **forward pairing.** *Less effective is the presentation of both at the very same time, called* **simultaneous pairing.** *Least effective of all is the presentation of the conditioned stimulus after the unconditioned stimulus, called* **backward pairing.**

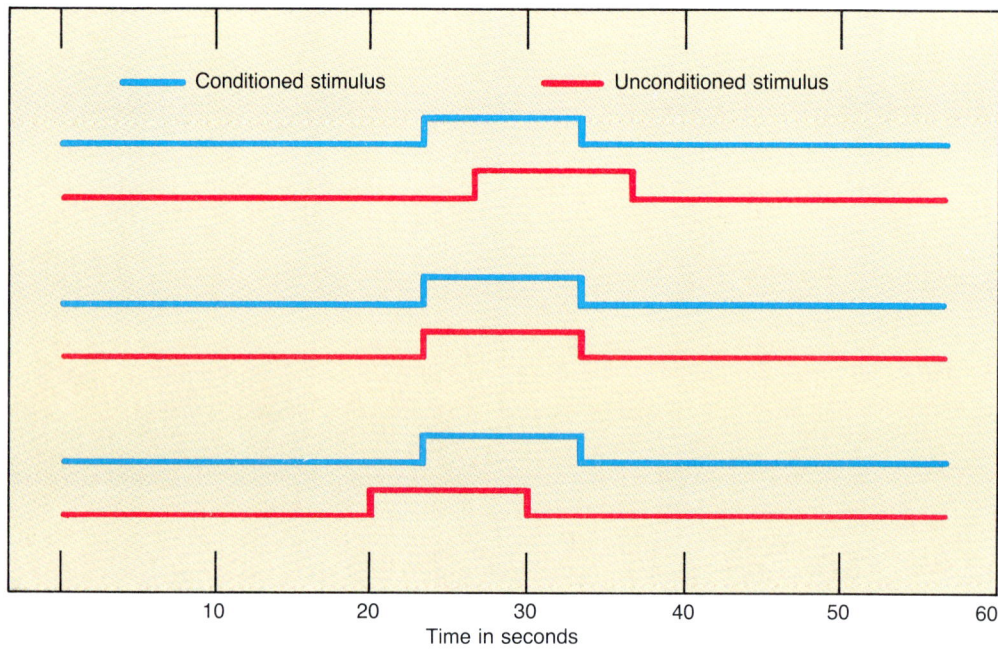

second group, the tone was usually followed by a shock. All the dogs were then presented only with tones—that is, with no shock. If learning an association between hearing a tone and feeling a shock only required that tones and shocks occur together, then the first group should have learned to jump as quickly as the second group—for both groups had experienced the same number of tones and shocks. But if learning to jump is easier when the tone *predicts* when the shock will occur, then the second group should have learned more quickly. The results showed that the dogs in the second group had the greater tendency to jump when they heard the tones.

This study suggests that we are more likely to develop a conditioned response—for example, a distaste for a particular subject—if encounters with the subject are consistently followed by unpleasant experiences. If exposure to the subject and unpleasant experiences occur together only in an unsystematic fashion, it is less likely that the conditioned response will develop.

Extinction and Spontaneous Recovery

Once Pavlov had established the conditioned salivary response, he wanted to find out how long and under what circumstances it would persist. When he merely kept sounding the metronome without ever again presenting food—in other words, when he removed the reinforcement—he found that in a very short time the flow of saliva in response to the sound began to decrease, and soon it stopped altogether, as shown in Figure 5-5. In

Figure 5-5 **The conditioned reflex: going, going, gone**

The graph shows what happened to Pavlov's dog when the conditioned stimulus of sound was no longer accompanied by the unconditioned stimulus of food. The conditioned salivary response, very strong at first, gradually grew weaker. By the seventh time the metronome was sounded, the conditioned response had disappeared. Extinction of the response was complete.

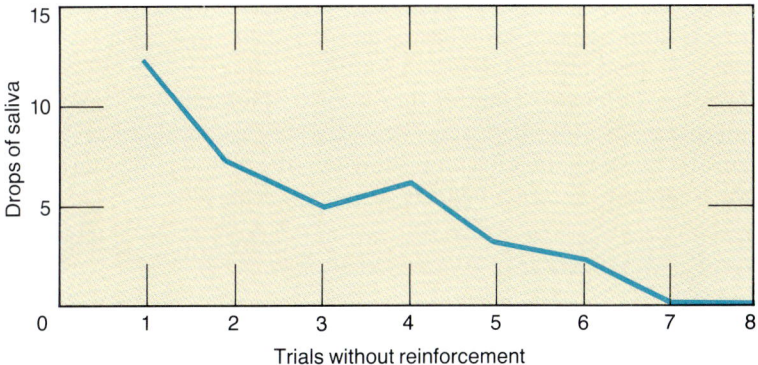

Pavlov's terminology, this disappearance of the conditioned response is called *extinction*. When he occasionally followed the sound with food—thus providing reinforcement not every time but sometimes—he found that he could make the conditioned response continue indefinitely.

Pavlov also tried another approach. He withheld reinforcement and let the conditioned response undergo extinction, then gave the dog a rest away from the experimental apparatus, and later tried again to see if there would be any response to the metronome. Under these circumstances, the conditioned response that had seemed to be extinguished reappeared. Pavlov called this *spontaneous recovery*—a phenomenon that may account for real-life situations in which unreasonable fears or preferences, learned originally through conditioning, suddenly crop up again after seeming to have vanished.

Stimulus Generalization and Discrimination

In Pavlov's experiments, it must be noted, there was nothing magic about the sound produced by the metronome. He later used many other kinds of stimuli—and found that he could just as easily condition the salivary response to the sound of a bell or to the flash of a light. He also discovered that a dog conditioned to the sound of a bell would salivate just as readily to the sound of a different bell or even a buzzer. This phenomenon is called *stimulus generalization*—meaning that once an organism has learned to make a response to a particular stimulus, it tends to display that behavior toward similar stimuli as well. Stimulus generalization explains why little Albert feared not only rats but also a bearded man.

After Pavlov had established the principle of stimulus generalization, he went on to demonstrate its opposite, *stimulus discrimination*. Here, by continuing to reinforce salivation to the bell by presenting food and omitting food when he sounded a different bell or a buzzer, Pavlov soon taught the dog to salivate only to the sound of the original bell, not to the other sounds. The dog had learned to discriminate between the stimulus of the bell and the other stimuli.

Classical Conditioning

Learning Abnormal Behavior

Pavlov also discovered that by taking advantage of the stimulus discrimination effect he could condition dogs to behave in abnormal ways. First, he projected a circle and an ellipse on a screen and conditioned dogs to discriminate between the two. Then he gradually changed the shape of the ellipse so that it looked more and more like a circle. Even when the difference in appearance was very slight, the dogs still made the discrimination successfully. But when the difference became too small for the dogs to recognize, and discrimination was impossible, the dogs acted strangely disturbed. They became restless, destructive, or apathetic and developed muscle tremors and tics (Pavlov, 1927).

Pavlov's experiments suggest that human abnormal behavior may also result from problems and difficulties that occur through classical conditioning. This possibility will be explored later in the chapter in connection with the phenomenon known as *learned helplessness*, which can have profound effects on human behavior.

Built-in Predispositions to Learning

The power of conditioning depends on the degree to which the organism is prepared by its biological nature to learn to associate a particular pairing of stimuli. One experiment demonstrated this important fact in the following fashion: A rat was permitted to drink some sweet-flavored water while a bright light was flashed and a noise was sounded. Later the rat was made sick to its stomach through X-ray irradiation. Under these circumstances, what did the rat learn? It turned out that the animal learned to avoid sweet-tasting water. It did not learn to avoid the light or the noise (Garcia and Koelling, 1966). This raises an important issue—because a rat placed in the same situation, except with an electric shock substituted for the subsequent illness, quickly learns to avoid the flashing light and the sound as well as the food.

Different species are predisposed by their heredity to learn to react to some stimuli but not to others. For example, experiments show that in contrast to rats, birds relate sickness not to taste but to visual cues. In humans, too, the pairing of conditioned stimulus with the response is stronger in some combinations than others. Studies of situations under which people learn food aversions, for example, show that they usually learn them as a result of illness—and not when eating the food is associated with accidents such as breaking a limb or getting cut. Moreover, the illness is much more likely to result in conditioned aversion to the actual foods involved rather than to related factors such as where the food was eaten (Garb and Stunkard, 1974; Logue, Ophir, and Strauss, 1981).

OPERANT CONDITIONING

Classical conditioning, as has been seen, changes reflex behavior that, in the absence of any learning, would occur only in response to specific stimuli—like salivation to the presence of food. But reflexes are not the only form of behavior. For example, if a rat is placed in a cage, it exhibits many types of behavior that seem to be spontaneous and self-generated, not mere predetermined responses to any kind of stimulus. The rat may sniff at the cage, stand up to get a better look at things, scratch itself, wash itself, and touch various parts of the cage. Similarly, babies in their cribs display many spontaneous actions. They move their arms and legs, try to turn over or grasp a blanket or the bars of the crib, turn their heads and eyes to look at various objects, and make sounds with their vocal cords.

Such actions are not reflexes set off by some outside stimulus. The actions are initiated by the rat or the baby—put in motion by the organism itself. So instead of having something in the environment produce a response, we have here just the opposite. The rat or the baby is acting on the environment. It might be said that the organism is "operating" on the world around it—and often bringing about some kind of change in the environment. Hence this type of activity is called *operant behavior.*

Like inborn reflexes, operant behavior can also be modified through learning. One way is through a form of learning that, since it resembles classical conditioning in a number of respects, is called *operant conditioning.*

The Magic Box of B. F. Skinner

The classic demonstration of operant conditioning was performed by B. F. Skinner with the special kind of cage shown in Figure 5-6. When Skinner first placed a rat in the cage, it engaged in many kinds of spontaneous operant behavior. Eventually, besides doing other things, it pressed the bar. A pellet of food automatically dropped into the feeding cup beneath the bar. Still no learning took place. In human terms, we might say that the animal did not "notice" any connection between the food and the bar, and it simply ate the food and continued its random movements as before. Eventually it pressed the bar again, causing another pellet to drop. After several such occurrences the animal "noticed" what had happened and formed an association between the act of pressing the bar and the appearance of food. The rat now began pressing the bar as fast as it could eat one pellet and get back to the bar to release another (Skinner, 1938).

To put this another way, the rat operated on the cage (now famous as the "Skinner box") in various ways. One particular kind of operant behavior, pressing the bar, had a

Figure 5-6 Learning in the Skinner box

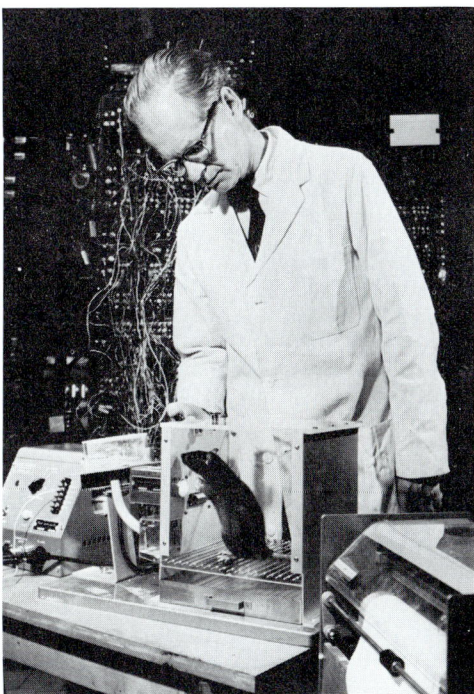

With this simple but ingenious invention, a box in which pressure on the bar automatically releases a pellet of food or a drop of water, Skinner demonstrated many of the rules of operant behavior. For what happens to a rat in the box, see the text.

rewarding result—it produced food. Therefore the rat repeated that behavior. Using the same language that is applied to classical conditioning, we say that the presentation of the food was a reinforcement of the bar-pressing behavior. The rule in operant conditioning is that operant behavior that is reinforced tends to be repeated—while operant behavior that is not reinforced tends to be abandoned.

Some Principles of Operant Conditioning

The Skinner box prompted a host of new studies of learning. It was found that operant conditioning followed many of the laws laid down by Pavlov for classical conditioning. Conditioned operant behavior, like the conditioned reflex response, was subject to *extinction*. That is, if the rat was no longer rewarded with food for pressing the bar, it eventually stopped pressing. *Spontaneous recovery* also occurred: After a rest away from the Skinner box, the rat started pressing again.

Experiments with pigeons, which are especially good subjects in their own version of the Skinner box, clearly showed *stimulus generalization*. A pigeon that had learned to obtain food by pecking at a white button would also peck at a red or green button. But if only the operant behavior toward the white button was reinforced, the pigeon displayed *stimulus discrimination*. In that case the pigeon learned to peck only at the white button and to ignore the red and green ones.

Behavior Shaping

Psychologists interested in operant conditioning have developed a method of teaching animals many complicated and unusual forms of behavior, a process called *shaping*. Figure 5-7 illustrates one way this process can be used. A pigeon is led step by step, through reinforcement by food as it gets closer and closer to performing the desired activity, to

This performance by killer whale Shamu at Sea World in San Diego is the outcome of behavior shaping.

Figure 5-7 Shaping a pigeon's behavior

How can a pigeon be taught to peck at that little black dot in the middle of the white circle on the wall of its cage? When first placed in the box, the bird merely looks about at random (A). When it faces the white circle (B), it receives the reinforcing stimulus of food in the tray below (C). Step by step, the pigeon is first rewarded for looking at the circle (D), then not until it approaches the circle (E), then not until it pecks at the circle (F). The next step, not illustrated here, is to withhold the reward until the pigeon pecks at the dot.

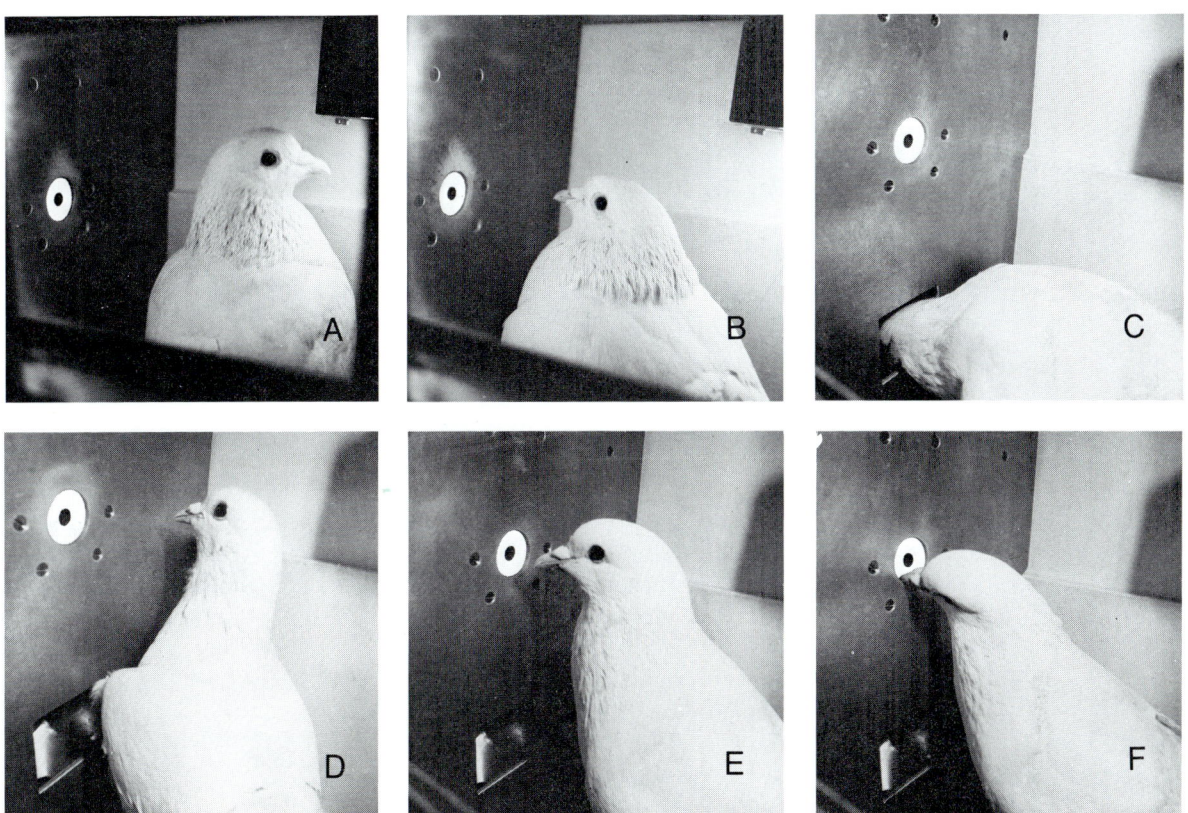

exhibit a form of behavior that it might never have hit upon spontaneously. Pigeons shaped in this manner have become excellent quality control inspectors in manufacturing plants—watching drug capsules roll by on a conveyer belt and signaling when a defective one appears (Verhave, 1966). Shaping is also the technique used to train animals to perform unusual and spectacular tricks.

How You Learn to be Superstitious

Do you have a "lucky" sweater that you always wear to exams because it helps you get good grades? Do you win more tennis matches if you wear the same pair of socks and carefully pull on the right one before the left one?

If so, you are probably exhibiting the effects of operant conditioning—and have more in common with Skinner's pigeons than you might suspect. Pigeons, too, sometimes learn to be superstitious. Skinner showed this by retooling one of his boxes so that it delivered

In the hope of overcoming a losing streak during the summer of 1986, these New York Mets began to balance baseballs on their caps as they sat in the dugout. The team won the game—and the superstition took on a life of its own.

food from time to time without any rhyme or reason, and regardless of what the pigeon in the box did or did not do. As a result, the birds developed some strange and unusual habits. A bird that happened to be flapping its wings when the food appeared might continue to flap incessantly, as if it "believed" that this produced food. Some pigeons learned to crane their necks, or to peck at a blank wall, or to keep moving in circles.

Many human superstitions, not only our own individual quirks but those common to many people, probably originated in a similar manner. One widely held superstition may have been started by a boy who walked under a ladder and promptly fell into a mud puddle. Another may have been started by a girl who found a clover with an extra leaf, then promptly found a penny.

Some Facts about Reinforcement

The term reinforcement, as you have probably noticed, keeps cropping up in these discussions of operant conditioning. It lies at the very core of the process. With animals, it is easy to provide reinforcement. Food and water constitute an obvious kind of reward, and experimenters in operant conditioning call them *primary reinforcers*. But humans seldom do any learning in order to receive food or water. Instead they usually seem to learn for less tangible rewards, such as praise or acceptance. Indeed even animal trainers often use the reward of affection rather than food. Such rewards are called *secondary reinforcers*, and it has been assumed that they have gained their value through some kind of conditioning process that linked them originally with primary reinforcers. A simple example of secondary reinforcement is illustrated in Figure 5-8.

The effects of the timing of reinforcements have been studied in great detail. In most animal experiments, it has been found, immediate reinforcement produces the most rapid learning. Any delay reduces the amount of learning, and too long a delay usually produces no learning at all, as is shown in Figure 5-9. The same thing holds true for young children. It is almost impossible to teach a 4-year-old to stay out of the street, for example, if the child is not rewarded at once for doing so, or punished for not doing so (Wickelgren, 1977).

Figure 5-8 The chimp and the poker chip

Why is the chimp dropping the chip into the slot? The reason is that the chip was used as a secondary reinforcer in a learning experiment—and now, when placed in a vending machine, it produces a primary reinforcement by making food drop into the tray.

Nevertheless, there are instances in which animals and humans will learn an association even when the delay between the conditioned stimulus and reinforcement is relatively long. For example, in the experiments in which rats learned to avoid a particular taste when it was followed by bodily discomfort, the delay between the taste and the discomfort could be several hours without impeding the learning process. And we humans can think about an event for a long time and, therefore, learn associations despite considerable intervening delays.

Figure 5-9 Oops . . . the reinforcement came too late

The steep drop in the curve shows how rapidly learning fell in an experiment in which reinforcement—food presented when rats pressed the bar in a Skinner box—was delayed for intervals ranging from a few seconds to about two minutes. Note that there was no learning at all when reinforcement was delayed for slightly more than 100 seconds (Perin, 1943).

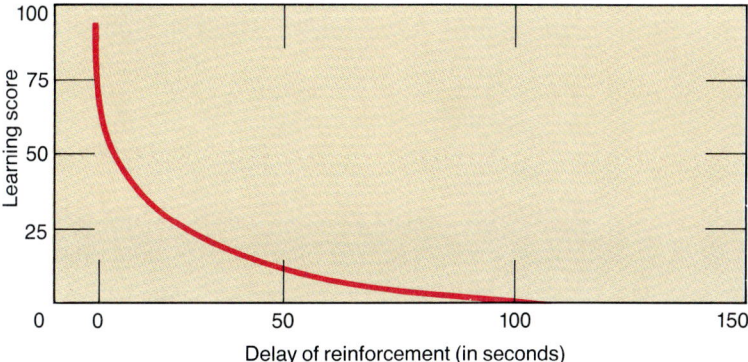

Operant Conditioning

Experimenters have also studied the effects of *constant reinforcement* (reward for each performance) as compared with *partial reinforcement* (reward on some occasions but not on others). They found that while learning generally takes place more rapidly with constant reinforcement, the behavior is more persistent (that is, more resistant to extinction) with partial reinforcement (Robbins, 1971). This finding has many applications to real-life situations. For example, parents who want their children to acquire a lasting tendency to work hard in school and get good grades will probably accomplish more with partial than with constant reinforcement. The trick is not to offer reinforcement for every good grade, but rather to bestow praise and affection (and possibly material rewards as well) a little more sparingly.

The long-lasting effects of partial reinforcement may also create problems in bringing up children. Suppose a little girl starts having temper tantrums whenever she asks for something and it is denied. Her parents try to ignore her behavior—but every once in a while, just to quiet her down, they give in and let her have what she wants. What they have done is set up a situation where the operant behavior of temper tantrums (the very thing they would like to eliminate) produces the reward of candy, or whatever it is the girl wants, on a schedule of partial reinforcement (the very thing most likely to make the behavior resist extinction and occur over and over again).

Schedules of Partial Reinforcement

Psychologists differentiate between two basic types of partial reinforcement schedules, as indicated in Figure 5-10. In the first, called *ratio schedules*, the reinforcement is delivered only after the subject responds a certain number of times. (In the case of Skinner's rats, the animal would receive a pellet of food only after pressing the bar, say, three, or four, or five times.) In the second, called *interval schedules*, the reinforcement is delivered only after a certain period has passed. (For example, the rat would receive a pellet, say, every minute, or two, or three.)

Figure 5-10 Schedules of partial reinforcement

Reinforcers for learning may be delivered in four major ways as discussed in the text.

TYPE OF REINFORCEMENT SCHEDULE	WHEN REINFORCERS ARE GIVEN	EXAMPLE
Ratio		
Fixed	After a fixed number of responses	Getting paid after every ten office files you finish
Variable	After a variable number of tries around some average	Making a sale after anywhere from one to twenty tries—but on the average, after five
Interval		
Fixed	For first response after a fixed interval of time has passed	Getting paid every week as soon as you turn in a file
Variable	For first response after a variable amount of time has passed	Making a sale after anywhere from one to seven days—but on the average, after three

For both types of schedules, another differentiation can be made. If either the ratio or interval is the same each time, the schedule is termed *fixed*. On the other hand, if the ratio or interval changes to some degree each time, the schedule is termed *variable*.

Applications of Operant Conditioning: Behavior Modification and Token Economies

Parents who want their children to stop throwing temper tantrums and animal trainers who want their dolphins to jump through hoops have something in common: both are trying to mold behavior. All of us are constantly trying to influence behavior—our own actions as well as those of the people around us (Stolz, Wienckowski, and Brown, 1975). We try to lose weight, quit smoking, get higher grades, perform better on the job, or overcome a block in writing (Boice, 1982). We try to influence other people to give us a good grade or a raise, show us more appreciation and respect, or stop doing things that annoy us. In so doing we often practice what psychologists call *behavior modification*, based largely on operant conditioning and the use of secondary reinforcement.

As psychologists use the term, behavior modification means any deliberate program designed to influence and change behavior through learning. The assumption is that behavior is controlled to a considerable degree by its consequences. If a certain type of behavior "works"—that is, if it results in reinforcement through some tangible reward or praise or even just a feeling of self-esteem—it is likely to be learned and repeated. If it does not produce satisfactory results, it will be abandoned.

Experiments in behavior modification have produced some dramatic results. One of the first attempts was made with a 3-year-old girl in a nursery school who was too shy and withdrawn to take part in any of the group activities. Instead she tried to hide by staying on the floor, either motionless or crawling. How could she be led to get up, start moving around, and join the other children? The secret turned out to be very simple. As long as she was on the floor, her teachers ignored her. As soon as she got up on her feet, they flattered her with attention. Given this reinforcement, she quickly became an active member of the group (Harris et al., 1965). The same kind of behavior modification—ignoring undesirable actions and rewarding desirable ones—has since been successful in many other situations. One special kind of behavior modification, in which the reinforcement is a sort of make-believe cash payment for desirable behavior, is called a *token economy*. It is widely used in mental hospitals, where it was originated as an attempt to improve the general atmosphere and the daily lives of patients. For dressing properly, eating in an acceptable manner, and working at useful jobs, patients are rewarded with tokens that they can use like money to "buy" such privileges as movies, rental of radios or television sets, cigarettes, candy, and opportunities for privacy. These token economies have produced some remarkable changes in behavior, as can be seen in Figure 5-11.

Token economies have also been used successfully in schools, particularly to help retarded or emotionally disturbed children and those with learning problems (O'Leary and Drabman, 1971). Token economies and behavior modification in general are not infallible, but they have been found clearly effective in many situations. They have also inspired some fears, as discussed in a Psychology in Everyday Life box called "Can Behavior Modification Destroy Human Freedom?"

Conditioning, Biofeedback, and Medicine

Another attempt to apply the principles of conditioning—in this case to the field of medicine—has added a new word to the English language. The word is *biofeedback*, which did not appear in dictionaries published even 15 years ago but is now widely used.

Figure 5-11 Behavior modification revolutionizes a hospital

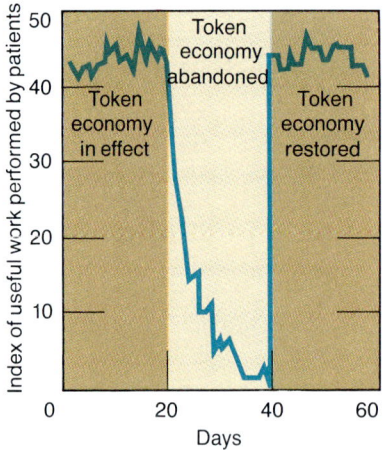

Under a token economy, patients worked actively at useful jobs and helped run the hospital (line in colored area at left). From the 20th to 40th days of the experiment, the token economy was abandoned and the patients quickly went back to their old passive ways (line in center area). As soon as the token economy was put back in effect, they again pitched in as shown by the line in the colored area at right (Ayllon and Azrin, 1968).

Psychology in Everyday Life
Can Behavior Modification Destroy Human Freedom?

To many people the term *behavior modification* conjures up visions of a totalitarian society in which the rulers, by cynically manipulating rewards and punishments, turn the citizenry into a docile flock of sheep meekly obeying their masters. One experimenter showed subjects a videotape of a teacher who was using reinforcement techniques to influence the classroom behavior of students. Subjects who saw the tape after being told it was a demonstration of behavior modification expressed a good many objections to the teacher's methods. Obviously the term had prejudiced them—because subjects who saw the tape after hearing it described as a demonstration of "humanistic education" praised the teacher for the very same actions (Woolfolk, Woolfolk, and Wilson, 1977).

Are people's fears justified? Could unscrupulous use of the laws of learning produce knee-jerk acceptance of a dictator's oppression? The answer is almost certainly no.

One indication comes from the type of behavior modification called behavior therapy, described later in the book. People who undertake behavior therapy not just willingly but in fact eagerly—hoping to learn to give up cigarettes or lose weight or free themselves from some unreasonable fear—sometimes fail completely. In other words, even the most expert application of learning principles, on an individualized basis and on people who want it to work, cannot always succeed.

Moreover, actions learned through behavior modification tend to be abandoned once the rewards stop. This happened in the token hospital economy shown in Figure 5-11, and it has also been demonstrated in other experiments. In one of them, two groups of nursery school children began a new activity—drawing for the first time with felt-tipped pens. Group A was encouraged to master the new technique with the promise of a fancy certificate of merit with a gold star and red button. Group B merely drew for the fun of drawing. Several weeks later, after Group A's quest for the certificate of merit was over, these pupils seemed to have lost much of their interest in the new pens—but the pupils in Group B were as enthusiastic as ever (Lepper, Greene, and Nisbett,

Attempts have been made to apply biofeedback to all the various bodily activities over which we ordinarily have no conscious control, including heart rate, blood pressure, and the movements of the stomach muscles. Perhaps one reason we cannot control these activities is that we are not usually aware of them. We do not know how fast our heart is beating, whether our blood pressure is high or low, or whether our alimentary canal is busy digesting food. Nor are we aware of many other bodily events—for example, tenseness in our forehead and neck muscles (which appears to be the cause of tension headaches), spasms of the blood vessels in our head (migraine headaches), or the patterns of our brain waves (which may be related to epilepsy and also, in another form, to feelings of relaxation, peace of mind, and happiness).

Biofeedback procedures attempt to give us control over these activities by providing a moment-to-moment reading of what is going on in our body. With headache patients, for example, electrodes are attached to the muscles of the forehead and neck and connected to a device that clicks rapidly when the muscles are tense, more slowly when they begin to relax. Given this knowledge of what is going on, patients may learn to control the activity of their muscles. Similarly, through devices that monitor and report the volume of blood in the forehead, migraine sufferers may learn to direct the flow of blood away from the vessels in the head that cause the problem (Tarler-Benlolo, 1978).

1973). Such findings have led some psychologists to question the long-term effectiveness of behavior modification even for the most laudable purposes. The problem is that "token rewards may lead to token learning" (Levine and Fasnacht, 1974).

Rewards can indeed backfire, as was once clearly demonstrated in a way that was as amusing as it was convincing. A monkey watched while an experimenter put a piece of banana under one of two identical containers. Then a screen was placed between the containers and the monkey. After a brief period the screen was removed and the monkey was permitted to choose between the two containers. It was not surprising that the monkey went directly for the one containing the banana. The surprising thing was the monkey's behavior when the experimenter secretly substituted a lettuce leaf for the banana while the screen hid the view. Ordinarily a monkey is happy to get a piece of lettuce, but a banana is a much greater delicacy—like a juicy steak compared with a dry hamburger for human beings. And in this case the poor monkey, having expected a banana, was outraged, refused to have anything to do with the lettuce, and screamed in anger at the experimenter (Tinklepaugh, 1928). A dictator bent on controlling the populace through behavior modification would have to be careful to keep supplying bananas instead of lettuce—and hope that the citizenry never tired of bananas.

Will these children continue to compete in track just because of the medals they won?

Operant Conditioning 171

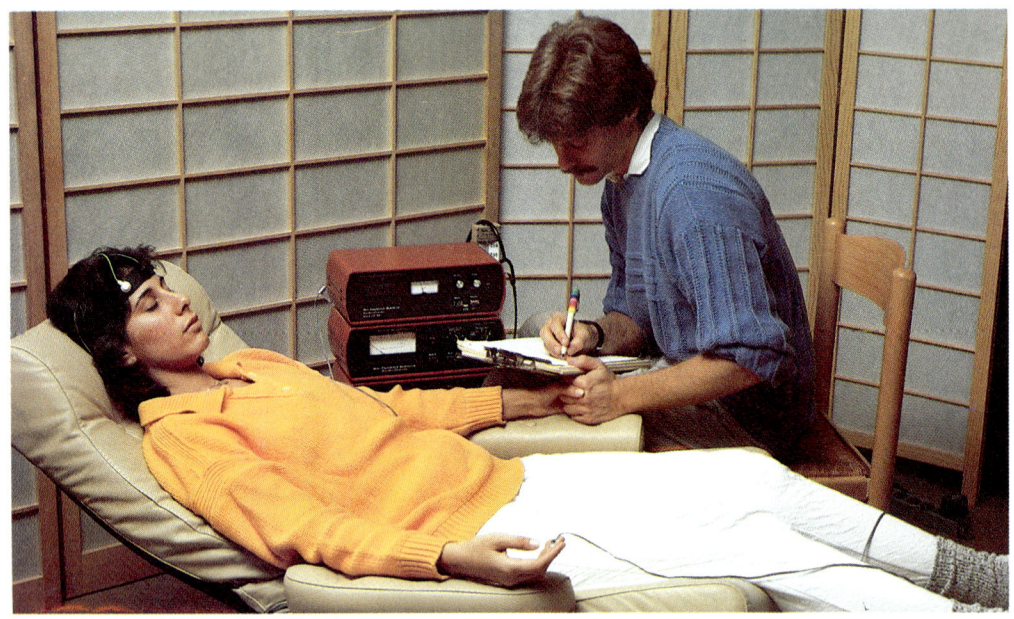

As described in the text, biofeedback can be used to treat headaches associated with tension.

Even in the treatment of headaches, where biofeedback has had its greatest successes, the results have varied from patient to patient and have not always been satisfactory. One reason may be that people show wide individual differences in the ability to learn to control their bodily activities, just as they differ in other skills. Although the technique has not yet proved nearly so spectacular as the publicity often suggests (Miller, 1985b), biofeedback is being studied further by psychologists and researchers in numerous hospitals and medical schools.

OPERANT ESCAPE, PUNISHMENT, AND LEARNED HELPLESSNESS

Another finding made in studies of operant conditioning has many implications for real-life behavior. This is the finding that operant conditioning can be established with two very different kinds of reinforcement. The first, called *positive reinforcement*, has already been described. It takes the form of such desirable rewards as food, praise, and valuable tokens. The other kind, called *negative reinforcement*, is the termination of something painful or otherwise unpleasant—for example, an electric shock.

When negative reinforcement is used in the laboratory, animals usually learn very quickly. This has best been demonstrated by placing dogs in a device called a shuttle box that has two compartments separated by a barrier. The barrier is high enough to discourage the animal but low enough to jump over when there is a real incentive. One of the compartments has a metal floor through which a shock can be administered; the other does not.

When the dog is placed in the wired compartment and the electricity turned on, the animal quickly learns to jump across the hurdle to the other side. This behavior is called *operant escape*. If some kind of warning is given, such as a light turned on or off a few seconds before the shock is administered, the animal will quickly learn to jump the hurdle when the light changes and thus miss the shock entirely. This behavior is called *operant avoidance*.

Escape and Avoidance in Human Behavior

A great deal of everyday human behavior seems to represent some form of operant escape and avoidance, learned through negative reinforcement. For example, a young boy finds the presence of a stranger in his home distasteful—and he wants to escape. He may make a series of random movements and eventually hide his head in his mother's lap, thus shutting out the sight and sound of the stranger. Having once discovered this kind of escape, he may generalize the behavior to other situations—and conceivably turn into the kind of adult who stays away from social functions and remains as inconspicuous as possible in the most inconspicuous kind of job.

Many defenses against events that arouse unpleasant anxiety appear to be forms of operant escape and avoidance. You may have noticed that many people who are made anxious by criticism become overapologetic. This may very well be a form of conditioned operant behavior that in some way served as a successful escape from anxiety in the past— perhaps with a mother who stopped criticizing and instead showed affection when her child apologized.

You may also know people who try to avoid anxiety by deliberately insulating themselves from situations that might upset them—for example, social events, travel, or difficult jobs. The price they pay for this form of operant avoidance is often a limited lifestyle with few adventures or satisfactions.

The Effect of Punishment on Behavior

Operant behavior can also be conditioned—in some cases and to some extent—through the use of *punishment*. Here the goal is not to reinforce a response, and therefore make it likely to occur again in the future, but to eliminate a response by following it with an unpleasant experience. Most people and indeed society as a whole seem to believe in the effectiveness of punishment as a form of behavior modification. Toddlers are punished by a slap on the hand if they grab at a fragile lamp or by a slap on the bottom if they whine too much. Older children are punished if they are "sassy," get into fights or into the cookie jar, or refuse to do their homework.

Researchers studying marriage have found that it is not uncommon for one or both partners to use punishment in an attempt to change the other's behavior. Note this case: A husband was annoyed because whenever his wife was in a bad mood, she had the habit of swearing at the children if they misbehaved. In an effort to change her behavior, he yelled at her, or stormed out of the house for the evening, or stopped doing household chores when she swore at the child. The wife, in turn, was annoyed because the husband always left the den in a mess—with newspapers, magazines, and books scattered over the floor and on top of the television set. In an effort to change *his* behavior, she threw out his magazines, stopped talking to him, and rejected his sexual approaches whenever he left his den in a mess (Patterson, Hops, and Weiss, 1975). Both were saying, in effect, "Yes, I'm punishing you by being as unpleasant as I can—and I'll do it until you change your ways."

The question is: Does punishment really work? In the case of the sour-tempered wife and the messy husband, it did not. They wound up taking their problems to a marriage counselor. But the question cannot always be answered with a simple yes or no. It is surrounded by many complications, all bearing on our attempts to get along in society and with our fellow human beings.

Punishment Works with Animals—but What About People?

In general, punishment often results in rapid and long-lasting learning by animals (Solomon, 1964). As might be expected from what was said earlier about delayed reinforcement, the punishment is most effective if administered as soon as possible after the behavior that the experimenter wants to eliminate (Campbell and Church, 1969).

The punishment is most effective of all when combined with reward—that is, when the "wrong" behavior is punished and the "right" behavior is rewarded. This has been shown by placing a rat in a simple **T**-shaped maze. The animal starts at the bottom of the **T** and has the choice, when it reaches the top, of turning either right or left. The rat will learn the "correct" turn very quickly if rewarded with food when it turns right and punished with shock when it turns left. A real-life demonstration of the same principle is provided by the housebreaking of a young puppy, which, as countless dog owners have discovered, is best accomplished by punishing the animal immediately by slapping it with a rolled-up newpaper when it wets the rug and showing it that the same act is praiseworthy when performed outdoors.

In at least some cases, punishment also helps babies and small children to learn. Its use is sometimes unavoidable. A slap on the hand when a child reaches toward a forbidden object may be the only way to prevent damage, as when the object is a fragile lamp, or even serious injury, if the object happens to be a sharp knife.

With older children and adults, however, the effectiveness of punishment is much less clear. One reason is that it is impossible to say how any given individual feels about any particular kind of supposedly punishing treatment. If that statement strikes you as peculiar, consider this situation: A mother and father make it a regular practice, when their children misbehave, to raise a great fuss. They yell at the children, call them to task, bawl them out, threaten them with everything from being sent to bed without supper to a thorough spanking. They believe that this punishment will make the children mend their ways. The children, however, may view the situation in an entirely different light. Let us say that their parents ordinarily ignore them, displaying very few signs of interest or affection. Thus, to the children, the intended punishment is actually a form of attention, which they desperately crave. It constitutes a positive reinforcement that they are likely to seek again and again. In these cases even a spanking may be regarded as a positive reinforcement.

Psychologists are well aware that punishment often achieves exactly the opposite of its intended effect (Feshbach, 1983). It can create a vicious circle within a family: The child misbehaves, the parent punishes, and the punishment leads to further misbehavior (Miller, 1975). Punishment may also have far-reaching side effects. Studies of children who received drastic verbal or physical punishment have shown that they tend to acquire a dislike for the people who punish them, such as their parents or teachers (Munn, Fernald, and Fernald, 1969). These children often become aggressive and punishing toward other children—and as adults frequently are cruel to their own offspring.

Learned Helplessness: The Case of the Passive Dogs

Most of the time, when we expect unpleasant experiences we do whatever we can to avoid them. A student manages to avoid taking a difficult course, or a person allergic to ragweed gets away from it in the fall of the year. But there are some conditions in which such coping responses do not occur, and instead we become apathetic and appear to be helpless.

This was first demonstrated in an experiment in which a dog was strapped into the kind of harness used by Pavlov. The dog then received a series of 64 electrical shocks, each lasting five seconds, delivered at random intervals. There was no way the dog could avoid the shocks or escape from them before the five seconds were up. The next day the dog was placed in a shuttle box. From time to time the light inside the box was dimmed, and a few seconds later a shock was administered through the floor of the compartment in which the dog had been placed. The animal could avoid the shock altogether by jumping over the

Figure 5-12 Results of an experiment in learned helplessness

The rapid rise in the solid line shows how quickly "normal" dogs learned how to cope with an electric shock delivered in a shuttle box, as explained in the text. The colored lines shows the very different behavior of animals that had acquired learned helplessness—*and therefore seemed incapable of learning how to do anything about the shock.*

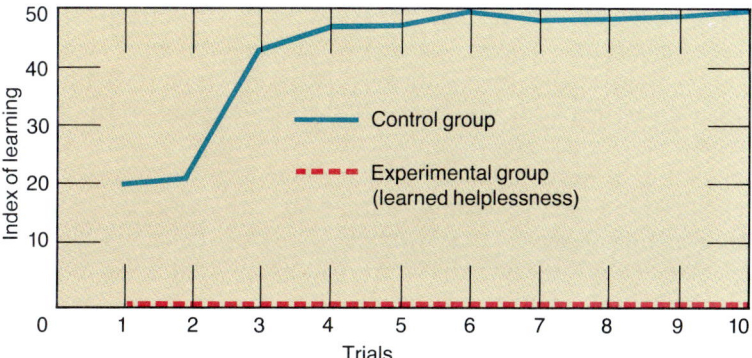

hurdle into the other compartment when the warning light was dimmed, or it could escape the shock by jumping after the electricity was turned on. If the dog did not jump into the other compartment, the shock continued—this time for a full 50 seconds.

The results of the experiment, shown in Figure 5-12, were dramatic. A number of dogs were used in the experiment. All had 10 trials in the shuttle box during which they could learn to avoid or escape the shock. But the amount of learning that took place was small. Most of the animals simply accepted the shock for the full 50 seconds, making no attempt to leap over the hurdle. They behaved in totally different fashion from a control group of dogs which had not previously received inescapable shocks. These "normal" dogs learned very quickly to leap the hurdle in time to avoid the shock or to escape in a hurry once the shock had begun.

How are we to account for the failure of the experimental dogs to learn—for their acceptance of a severe and long-lasting shock? The experimenters attribute it to what they have called *learned helplessness.* That is, while the dogs were in the Pavlov harness they learned that nothing they could do would have any effect on whether they received a shock or for how long. In human terms, they had no hope that they could do anything about the shock, even when moved to the shuttle box, and they therefore had no incentive to try to escape (Maier, Seligman, and Solomon, 1969).

Helplessness in Human Beings

Humans as well as animals can be led to acquire learned helplessness through simple laboratory procedures. In one experiment, for example, college volunteers were subjected to an earsplitting noise. They were told that they could stop the noise by learning how to manipulate some control devices—but actually these devices had no effect. Later, when placed in another situation where it would have been easy to move a control lever and turn off the noise, the subjects made no effort and simply put up with the noise until the experimenter called a halt (Hiroto, 1974).

Children who are continually yelled at or spanked no matter what they have done may very well acquire learned helplessness. They may decide that they have no control over when, how, or why they are punished. They may give up trying to learn what their parents are trying to teach them, in which case the attempts to punish them into learning the difference between good behavior and bad become self-defeating.

How Failure Can Lead to Helplessness

The original experiment on learned helplessness, performed with dogs in the late 1960s, opened up a new line of psychological investigation. Punishment, it has been found, is not the only possible cause of learned helplessness. An even more common cause is failure—at any of the tasks we face throughout life, in the classroom or in the outside world.

In laboratory experiments, many of the symptoms of a temporary kind of learned helplessness have been produced by giving students problems that they were told could be solved but that were in fact impossible (Tennen and Eller, 1977). In real-life situations, children have been found to display learned helplessness as a result of continual failure in a school assignment, such as mathematics (Dweck, Goetz, and Strauss, 1977). They may take a pessimistic attitude toward their general abilities and prospects for the future. Adults may acquire similar feelings because of failure to find or hold a job or to establish satisfactory social relationships.

These findings are of great practical importance to all of us because failure is an inevitable part of life. We cannot always succeed at everything. In college, only a few students get all A's and only one is at the top of the class. Not all would-be athletes make the team, and only one is chosen most valuable player. In the world of jobs, a dozen people may be competing for a promotion that only one of them can get. In our social relations, not all of us can be the most popular or the best looking.

Thus, all of us experience failure of one kind or another at one time or another. If failure produces learned helplessness, we may become as passive and psychologically crippled as the dogs in the Pavlov harness. We may become victims of a deep depression—a "blue funk"—that a psychiatrist would classify as abnormal (Depue and Monroe, 1978). But, though everyone experiences failure, not everybody suffers drastic consequences. One of the contributions of studies of learned helplessness has been to offer some clues as to when, how, and why this unhappy result is likely to occur—and what we might do about it. This is discussed in the box on Psychology in Everyday Life called "Learning to Feel Worthy and in Control."

The inevitable failures experienced in life can produce learned helplessness under certain conditions.

Psychology in Everyday Life
Learning to Feel Worthy and in Control

To understand any symptoms of learned helplessness ask yourself this question: When you fail, where do you place the blame?

Suppose you are in love—but the object of your affections rejects you. It makes a great deal of difference whether you blame yourself, blame her or him, or blame women or men in general. Blaming yourself usually results in a serious loss of self-esteem and is closely associated with lack of confidence in the future (Garber and Hollon, 1977). Sometimes it produces serious depression (Rizley, 1978). The particular way in which you blame yourself is also important. If you merely blame your behavior in that one particular relationship, your feelings of helplessness will probably be less severe. But if you blame yourself in general—your own worth and character, so to speak—you are much more likely to be in trouble (Peterson and Seligman, 1984). Thus it is better to think, "Well, I just did the wrong thing that time," than to decide, "That's the way I am and it seems I'm just plain unattractive to women (or men)."

If you blame the other party or the other sex in general—thereby attributing your failure to outside factors—you preserve your self-esteem. But this does not necessarily exempt you from the symptoms of helplessness. Again it appears that if you make a sweeping condemnation—of all women (or all men)—your helplessness is likely to generalize and handicap you in other situations. If you blame one particular person—"She (or he) is overly competitive and rejecting"— there is less likelihood that the incident will affect other relationships (Abramson, Seligman, and Teasdale, 1978).

Any form of learned helplessness can cause serious problems. One group of investigators has cited the example of an accountant who gets fired from his job. If his symptoms do not generalize to other situations, he may continue to be a good husband and father and to function well in social situations. But the symptoms may cripple him nonetheless. He may be unable to prepare his own income tax return or try for a new job in accounting. If the helplessness becomes generalized, his entire life may be affected. He may become sexually impotent, neglect his children, and avoid any social contacts (Abramson, Seligman, and Teasdale, 1978).

Though most of us suffer at times from learned helplessness—when failure makes us question our own abilities and call ourselves incompetent, lazy, unattractive, and generally good for nothing—our pessimistic attitudes fortunately do not usually last very long. We have trouble with math but overcome it by working a little harder—or make up for our lack of mathematical ability by doing well in another subject. Though one person of the opposite sex rejects us, we soon find someone else who likes us a great deal. After being fired, we find another job at which we are more efficient—and we end up feeling much better about ourselves and the world.

When we do this, we provide our own very effective therapy—for we are doing exactly what a therapist would try to do if our problems were so severe that we had to seek help. The best treatment for learned helplessness, it has been found, is to give people some evidence that they do have the ability to succeed (Teasdale, 1978). Sometimes they have set their goals impossibly high and have to be taught to be more realistic. Sometimes they have to work at developing their skills at performing their jobs or conducting their social relationships. But mostly therapists seek to provide situations in which people who suffer from learned helplessness can and do succeed, thereby discovering that they are more competent at more things than they thought they were. This new confidence generalizes to other situations (Bandura, Jeffery, and Gajdos, 1975), and they begin to feel a growing faith in their ability to control their own futures.

THE COGNITIVE VIEW OF LEARNING

For many years the laws of classical and operant conditioning dominated psychologists' view of learning. The behaviorist school thought of all human behavior as conditioned more or less by events in the environment. The prevailing view was that there is little difference between humans going about their daily lives and a rat negotiating its way through a simple **T** maze. The rat's behavior can be accurately predicted if we know in which arm of the **T** it has previously been rewarded with food and in which arm it has been punished by a shock. The expectation was that we could also predict people's behavior fairly well if we simply knew which of their actions had been rewarded in the past and which had been punished, and in what way and to what extent (Miller and Dollard, 1941).

Even during the heydey of this view, however, there were dissenters since some experimental results, even with rats, did not fit easily into the laws of conditioning. These results led to the rise of a cognitive view of learning. In this view, the human organism, far from being a passive product of experience, is always actively interacting with the environment.

Chimps with Ingenuity

One of the first influential experiments along cognitive lines was reported by the German psychologist Wolfgang Köhler as far back as the 1920s. Köhler worked with chimpanzees, creating situations in which they had to demonstrate considerable ingenuity to get at a banana placed tantalizingly out of reach. Sometimes the food was just a little farther than arm's length away from a chimp behind a barrier. Sometimes it was suspended overhead, too high to reach by jumping. So near and yet so far.

Could the chimpanzees learn to get the food? As it turned out, they managed in a number of clever ways. The animals behind the barrier found they could use sticks, available within arm's reach, to rake in the banana. The animals who saw the food overhead hit upon several strategies, two of which are illustrated in Figure 5-13. To Köhler, this kind of learning went far beyond any stimulus-response connections established by conditioning. He held that the animals had learned through *insight*—or what today would be called cognition. That is, they evaluated the situation, called on their past knowledge about sticks and boxes, and processed all this information in terms of cause and effect.

Learning without Reinforcement

Another influential experiment, reported in 1930 and performed with rats in a maze, produced results that cast doubt on the theory that reinforcement is essential to learning. The rats were divided into three groups. Group 1 always found food at the end of the maze—a clear-cut and immediate reinforcement. The Group 2 rats were simply placed in the maze and permitted to move around in any way they chose, never finding any food. Group 3 was treated the same way as Group 2 for the first 10 days, receiving no reinforcement. Then, after the tenth day, food was placed at the end of the maze, as it had been all along with Group 1.

How the three groups performed, as measured by how direct a route they took without entering blind alleys, is illustrated in Figure 5-14. Note that the rats in Group 1 learned rapidly, as the laws of operant conditioning would have predicted, improving every day right from the beginning. As might also have been predicted, the rats in Group 2, which were never reinforced, did not display much learning. But note the strange behavior of Group 3. For the first 10 days this group also showed little learning. Then, on the eleventh

Figure 5-13 You can't keep a good chimp down
Faced with the problem of reaching a banana suspended high overhead, the chimpanzee at left has managed by balancing a long stick beneath it and quickly climbing up. The chimpanzee at right has hit upon the "insight" of piling three boxes one atop another as a makeshift step stool (Köhler, 1925).

day, when a reward was provided at the end of the maze, the rats immediately began running the course like veterans. Even in just wandering about the maze for 10 days, without any reinforcement, they apparently had learned a great deal about the correct path. As soon as a reward was provided, they began to demonstrate this knowledge.

The experiment seemed to show that even lower animals can learn without the immediate reinforcement considered essential to classical and operant conditioning—and in fact without any reinforcement at all. In cognitive terminology, the rats moving around the maze without any reward had acquired and stored knowledge about the pathway, which they could call on as soon as it was useful in helping them get to food as rapidly as possible.

Such experiments along with others suggest that reinforcement is an event that attracts and focuses attention (Rescorla and Holland, 1982). Think, for example, of the sudden taste

The Cognitive View of Learning

Figure 5-14 A funny thing happened on the way through the maze

The graph shows the surprising behavior of three groups of rats placed in a maze under different conditions of reinforcement. For the meaning of the lines, which chart the rats' progress in learning the way through the maze, see the text (Tolman and Honzik, 1930).

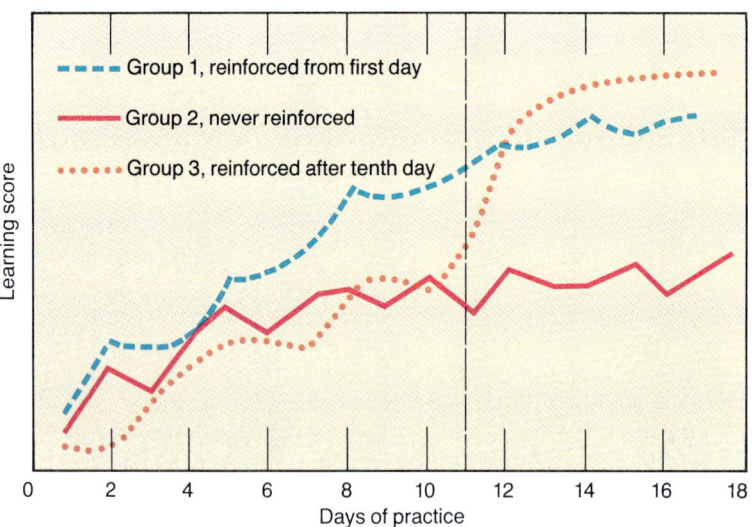

of food when an animal is hungry or an unexpected frown from a teacher when a student has given a wrong answer. Both are events that alert the organism, leading it to concentrate on the behavior just performed. The effectiveness of a reinforcing event is thus related to its capacity to evoke attention to the behavior just displayed.

Can There Be Learning without a Response?

Just as the maze experiment demonstrated that learning is possible without reinforcement, other experiments have shown that learning can take place without a response. In one of the most famous studies the subject was a dog in a Pavlov-type harness. The unconditioned stimulus was an electric shock to the paw, the unconditioned response the pulling away of the paw, and the conditioned stimulus a high tone sounded just before the shock was delivered. The animal, of course, was quickly conditioned to pull its paw away at the sound of this tone—and it also showed stimulus discrimination by ignoring a low tone that was never followed by shock. So far just a routine example of classical conditioning and stimulus discrimination.

But now the experimenter did the same thing with another dog—except that this dog's leg was paralyzed with a drug, so that it would not be pulled away. When the high tone was sounded and the shock delivered, the animal could not respond. Yet when the process was repeated later, after the drug had worn off, the dog pulled its paw away immediately at the sound of the high tone while ignoring the low tone. It had learned to avoid the shock and to discriminate between the two tones—even though the establishment of a stimulus-response connection was impossible during the conditioning trials (Solomon and Turner, 1962).

Cognitive Maps, Expectancies, and Knowledge

The various experiments just described—Köhler's chimpanzees and their "insight," the rats that acquired learning without any reinforcement, and the paralyzed dog that learned to avoid a shock—led many psychologists to seek a new definition of learning. Granted, humans as well as lower animals often establish a simple stimulus-response connection through classical and operant conditioning, with reinforcement a part of the process. But in cases where some other kind of learning occurs, in ways not accounted for by the laws of conditioning, just what is it that the organism learns—and how does the learning take place?

Edward Tolman, who collaborated on the experiment with the three groups of rats in the maze, suggested the term *cognitive map* (Tolman, 1948). From many studies of behavior in mazes, Tolman concluded that even animals learn not just mere responses that propel them to a reward but a knowledge of the spatial features of the environment—of where things are and "what leads to what." Reinforcement does not produce the learning but instead merely leads animals to use what they already know. If a reward is provided in one part of the cognitive map, they will manage to go there, in one way or another. If there is punishment, they will avoid that spot.

Subsequent experimenters, working with types of learning that did not pose the spatial problems found in mazes, enlarged Tolman's terminology into the idea of acquiring *expectancies* (Bolles, 1972). Even in classical conditioning, they suggested, Pavlov's dogs learned to salivate to the sound of the metronome because they expected the sound to be followed by food. In operant conditioning, rats in a Skinner box learn to press the bar because they expect the action to be followed by food.

Today's cognitive psychologists have expanded these suggestions into the all-embracing term *knowledge*. What is learned, according to the cognitive school, is all sorts of knowledge—the "maps" of pathways acquired by Tolman's rats, the expectancies about food acquired by Pavlov's dogs, and a human's knowledge that Main Street is one block north of Broadway, an aspirin can be expected to relieve a headache, $2 \times 4 = 8$, the past tense of *swim* is *swam*, and the earth is round.

The cognitive psychologists regard "the human organism as an active seeker of knowledge and processor of information"—with learning being the step in which we acquire information that we then modify, manipulate, store, and use in various ways (Klatzky, 1980). They view learning as one element in a closely related series of processes—notably perception, memory, and language and cognition—that are discussed in other chapters of this book.

Learning by Observing

One way of acquiring knowledge that has been widely studied is *learning through observation* (or, as some psychologists prefer, *learning through modeling* or *learning by imitation*). All three terms refer to the process through which we learn by observing the behavior of others.

It has been known for some time that even lower animals learn by observation and imitation. In one of the early experiments, a cat was taught in a Skinner box to obtain food by pressing the bar when a light went on. Another cat, which had been watching, was then placed in the box. This second cat began very quickly to press the bar when the light went on. Through observation, it had learned much faster than the first cat (John et al., 1968). Subsequent experiments have demonstrated many kinds of observation learning by many animals, from mice to dolphins.

The behavior of children is often modeled from observations of the adults around them.

With humans, one of the most dramatic examples of observation learning was recorded on film by Albert Bandura. In this experiment, children watched a movie showing an adult striking a large doll with a hammer. When the children then had an opportunity to play with the doll themselves, they showed remarkably similar behavior. The photographs of this experiment, some of which are shown in Figure 5-15, have greatly influenced psychologists' attitudes toward observation learning. (They have also raised some serious questions about the effects of the violence shown in the movies and on television.)

Cognitive theorists do not think of observation learning as merely an automatic and unthinking imitation of what one has seen. Rather they believe that we begin in early childhood, and continue throughout our lives, to observe what goes on around us and to store up the information that this observation provides. We observe what other people seem to value, how they go about getting what they value, their behavior in general, and the results of their behavior. At the same time, we make judgments. We may or may not decide to value what they value. We may imitate their behavior, adopt some but not all of it, or reject it entirely. As Bandura has stated, learning by observation is "actively judgmental and constructive rather than a mechanical copying" (Bandura, 1974).

Closely akin to observation learning, of course, is the kind of learning you are doing at this moment—and that people do in many ways in many situations. This is learning by receiving instruction from someone else, as when reading a textbook (or a recipe) or listening to a teacher in the classroom (or to a tennis pro telling you how to improve your serve). The cognitive psychologists would say that in our information processing we have the benefit not only of the knowledge stored in our own memories but, through language, of all the knowledge possessed by our fellow human beings and indeed the wisdom of the ages as recorded in our libraries.

Figure 5-15 See aggression, learn aggression

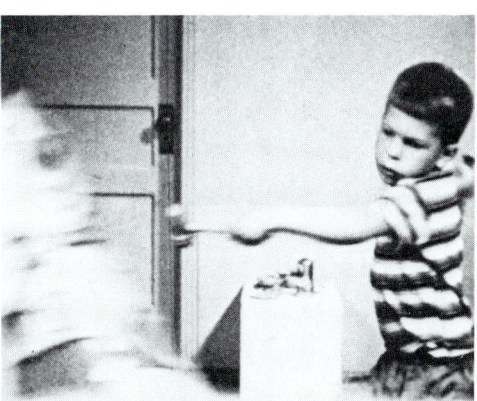

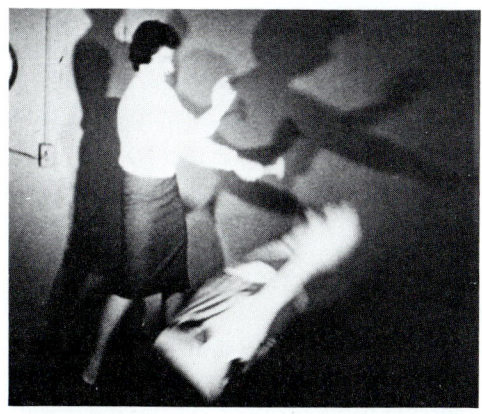

Why are the boy and girl at left acting so aggressively toward the toy? And why does their aggressive behavior take such remarkably similar form? The answer is reminiscent of the old saying "Monkey see; monkey do." The children were imitating the behavior of a model—the woman below, who had behaved in exactly this fashion in a movie they had seen.

The Cognitive View of Learning 183

SUMMARY

Classical conditioning

1. Learning is *any relatively permanent change in behavior (or behavior potential) produced by experience.*

2. One of the simplest and most universal forms of learning concerns the *reflex*, which is an inborn and built-in response to a stimulus.

3. Through learning, a reflex response can become attached to a stimulus that did not originally cause the response. The process was demonstrated when Pavlov taught a dog to respond to a sound with the salivary reflex, which originally was caused only by the presence of food in the mouth. This type of learning is called *classical conditioning*.

4. In classical conditioning, the stimulus that naturally sets off the reflex (in Pavlov's experiment, the food) is called the *unconditioned stimulus*. The previous neutral stimulus to which the reflex becomes attached (the sound) is called the *conditioned stimulus*.

5. The original reflex response (in Pavlov's experiment, salivation) is called the *unconditioned response*. The response to the conditioned stimulus is the *conditioned response*.

6. The pairing of the unconditioned stimulus and the conditioned stimulus is called *reinforcement*. Conditioning turns out to be most effective through the use of *forward pairing* (the conditioned stimulus precedes the unconditioned stimulus by a short interval). Less effective is *simultaneous pairing* (presentation of both at the very same time), and the least effective of all is *backward pairing* (presentation of the conditioned stimulus after the unconditioned stimulus).

7. When reinforcement is no longer provided (in Pavlov's experiment, if food no longer accompanies the sound), the conditioned response tends to disappear—a process called *extinction*. After a rest period, however, the conditioned response may reappear—a process called *spontaneous recovery*.

8. When a response has been conditioned to one stimulus, it is also likely to be aroused by similar stimuli—a process called *stimulus generalization*. Through further conditioning, however, the organism can learn to respond to one particular conditioned stimulus but not to other stimuli that closely resemble it—a process known as *stimulus discrimination*.

9. Classical conditioning by past events accounts for many of the unreasonable fears and preferences displayed by human adults—also for such strange physical symptoms as unexplained headaches or nausea.

10. The power of conditioning depends on the strength of the organism's native tendency to respond to the actual pairing of stimuli used. Evidently various species are prepared by nature to make stronger associations between particular stimuli and responses than to others.

Operant conditioning

11. Another type of learning, demonstrated by Skinner, concerns *operant behavior*—the random or exploratory activities in which organisms engage, not in reflex response to a stimulus but as a self-generated way of "operating" on the world around them.

12. Skinner showed that a rat in a cage containing a bar would eventually press the bar as part of its operant behavior—and would learn to keep pressing if rewarded with food. This form of learning is called *operant conditioning*.

13. In operant conditioning, the *reinforcement* is the reward (in Skinner's experiment, the food). The rule is that operant behavior that is reinforced by a reward tends to be repeated, while operant behavior that is not reinforced tends to take place only at random intervals or is abandoned.

14. Like classical conditioning, operant conditioning also displays *extinction*, *spontaneous recovery*, *stimulus generalization*, and *stimulus discrimination*.

15. Through operant conditioning, animals can be taught to perform complex tasks by rewarding them for the successful completion of each step that leads to the desired behavior. This process is called *shaping*.

16. Rewards that the organism finds basically satisfying, such as food and water, are *primary reinforcers*. The less tangible rewards for which human beings often learn, such as praise or acceptance, are *secondary reinforcers*.

17. Operant learning usually takes place fastest with *constant reinforcement*, or reward for each performance. But learning is usually more resistant to extinction with *partial reinforcement*, or rewards on some occasions and not on others.

18. The two basic types of partial reinforcement schedules are: (a) *ratio schedules*, in which the reinforcement is delivered only after the subject responds a certain number of times, and (b) *interval schedules*, in which reinforcement is delivered only after a certain period has passed. If either ratio or interval is the same each time, the schedule is termed *fixed*. On the other hand, if the ratio or interval changes to some degree each time, the schedule is termed *variable*.

19. The use of rewards to influence human activities—for example, praising a withdrawn nursery school child to encourage sociable behavior—is called *behavior modification*.

20. A special form of behavior modification, widely used in mental hospitals, provides reinforcement in the form of tokens that can be spent like money for goods and privileges. This method is called a *token economy*.

21. *Biofeedback* is an operant conditioning technique that attempts to relieve physical ailments through devices that provide the subject with moment-to-moment readings of such bodily activities as muscle tension and blood flow.

Operant escape, punishment, and learned helplessness

22. Operant conditioning can be established through either *positive reinforcement*, in the form of desirable rewards, or *negative reinforcement*, which is the termination of something painful or otherwise unpleasant, like an electric shock.

23. Experiments with negative reinforcement have shown that animals are very quick to learn *operant escape*, or how to get away from the shock, and *operant avoidance*, or how to prevent the shock by taking some kind of action before it occurs. Many human defenses against events that arouse unpleasant anxiety appear to be forms of operant escape or avoidance.

24. In *punishment*, the goal is not to reinforce a response, and therefore make it more likely to occur in the future, but to eliminate a response. Although punishment often produces rapid learning in animals, it is of questionable value in influencing human behavior.

25. One result of punishment, in both animals and human beings, may be *learned helplessness*—a tendency to believe that events cannot be controlled and to give up trying to learn.

26. Learned helplessness can be caused not only by punishment but also by failure. The effects depend partly on whether victims blame themselves or outside factors.

27. Learned helplessness may apply only to one kind of activity or situation, or it may become generalized and affect the victim's entire approach to life.

28. Therapists try to treat learned helplessness, which can result in seriously abnormal behavior, by persuading victims that they have more ability to succeed than they realize.

The cognitive view of learning

29. Cognitive psychologists regard learning as a process—with the human organism, far from being a passive product of experience, actively interacting with the environment.

30. Among the experiments that helped lead to the cognitive view are (a) Köhler's findings that chimpanzees learn through *insight*, or what is known today as cognition; (b) the discovery that rats in a maze may display a special type of learning—which takes place without reinforcement and lies dormant until there is reason to use it; and (c) the temporarily paralyzed dog that learned how to escape from a shock even though it could not make a response during the learning trials.

31. Various psychologists have suggested that what is learned is not just a simple stimulus-response connection but a *cognitive map* (of a maze, for example) or an *expectancy* (for example, that food will follow the sound of a metronome). The cognitive view now includes both these theories in the all-embracing idea that what we learn is *knowledge* of many kinds.

32. One form of acquiring knowledge is *learning through observation* (also called *learning through modeling* or *learning by imitation*). Closely akin to observation learning is the familiar process of learning through instruction, for instance by listening to a teacher or reading a book.

IMPORTANT TERMS

backward pairing
behavior modification
biofeedback
classical conditioning
cognitive map
conditioned response
conditioned stimulus
constant reinforcement
expectancy
extinction
fixed schedule
forward pairing
insight
interval schedule
knowledge

learned helplessness
learning through observation (or modeling or imitation)
negative reinforcement
operant avoidance
operant behavior
operant conditioning
operant escape
partial reinforcement
positive reinforcement
primary reinforcer
punishment
ratio schedule
reflex
reinforcement

secondary reinforcer
shaping
simultaneous pairing
spontaneous recovery
stimulus discrimination

stimulus generalization
token economy
unconditioned response
unconditioned stimulus
variable schedule

RECOMMENDED READINGS

Adams, J. A. *Learning and memory.* Homewood, Ill.: Dorsey Press, 1980.
Hall, J. F. *An invitation to learning and memory.* New York: Cambridge University Press, 1983.
Hill, W. F. *Learning: a survey of psychological interpretations.* New York: Harper & Row, 1985.
Hulse, S. H., Egeth, H. E., and Deese, J. E. *The psychology of learning*, 5th ed. New York: McGraw-Hill, 1980.
Leahey, T. H., and Harris, R. J. *Human learning.* Englewood Cliffs, N.J.: Prentice-Hall, 1985.
Pavlov, I. P. *Conditioned reflexes.* New York: Oxford University Press, 1927.
Seligman, M. E. P. *Helplessness.* San Francisco: Freeman, 1975.
Skinner, B. F. *The behavior of organisms.* New York: Appleton-Century-Crofts, 1938.
Wickelgren, W. A. *Learning and memory.* Englewood Cliffs, N.J.: Prentice-Hall, 1977.

CHAPTER

6

HOW WE REMEMBER AND WHY WE FORGET

THE RANGE OF HUMAN MEMORY — 191

Sensory memory: now you have it, now you don't
Short-term memory: how information is processed for keeping
Long-term memory: keeping information indefinitely
The process of retrieval
Solving the mystery of the memory trace

WHY DO WE FORGET? — 196

How psychologists measure remembering and forgetting
Some factors in forgetting
Factor 1: the memory trace fades
Factor 2: the retrieval process fails with changes in setting or mood
Factor 3: the retrieval process fails through interference
Factor 4: we are motivated to forget

ENCODING AND TRANSFER — 204

Chunking—putting many little facts into one neat package
The associative network theory
Creating links between new and old
What we encode, remember, and retrieve

THE ENCODING PROCESS AND LEARNING — 209

The importance of meaning and organization
Learning by rule or by rote
Using learning to build on learning

SOME STRATEGIES FOR ENCODING — 213

Using categories
Clustering—packaging information for long-term memory
Storing visual information in memory

SUMMARY — 220

IMPORTANT TERMS — 222

RECOMMENDED READINGS — 223

PSYCHOLOGY AND EVERYDAY LIFE

Should we accept limits on our capacities to remember? — 194
How much faith can we put in courtroom witnesses? — 208
A rule for learners: take your time — 212
Making up your own system for remembering — 219

On occasion most of us have watched a quiz show on television and seen an agonized contestant grope unsuccessfully to remember the name of a tune, a book, or a movie—and thus lose the chance to win a coveted prize. We ourselves have had somewhat comparable experiences. There must have been many occasions when you said, "I'm sorry, I've forgotten your name." Or, "I meant to send you a birthday card, but I just plain forgot." Or, after an exam, "I knew the answer, but I couldn't remember it."

Human memory is often blamed, apologized for, and agonized over. Yet, no matter how forgetful or absentminded you may consider yourself at times, there is an enormous amount of knowledge stored somewhere—and somehow—within your nervous system. Adult humans do not have to be prize-winning scholars to know the meanings of many thousands of English words and perhaps some foreign words as well, plus rules of mathematics, and many basic facts about geography, science, and history. Not to mention such practical matters as how to drive a car, read a map, operate a calculator, make a phone call, and shop for food and clothing. The marvel is not how much we forget but how much we remember.

To cognitive psychologists, with their emphasis on knowledge as a key part of the human experience, learning and memory are of course closely related. Learning is the way we acquire all the many forms of knowledge we possess and utilize. Memory is the storehouse in which we keep all this information—carefully sorted and saved so that we can find it quickly when we need it.

We do not always succeed, however. Sometimes we let a piece of information slip through our hands, so to speak, and we say we have forgotten—perhaps permanently, perhaps just for the time being. How well we remember information depends in large part on how well we have learned it in the first place, and how carefully we have stored it away.

At every stage of life, memory is an important element of human behavior.

THE RANGE OF HUMAN MEMORY

- You are driving to the beach and hear on the radio that the temperature is 87 degrees. But at that moment you have to swerve to avoid an oncoming car. When the crisis is over, you try to remember what the temperature is, but you find that you have completely forgotten. It seems as if the information never registered at all in your memory.

- You are in a phone booth and look up a friend's phone number. You start repeating the number as you turn from the book and drop a coin into the phone. You have successfully remembered the number. But you get a busy signal—and by the time you fish the coin out of the return slot, drop it back into the phone, and wait for the tone, you find you have forgotten the number.

- You are not very good at remembering names, but at a party you meet a man whose name is Ronald Marston. You remark on the coincidence: his first name is the same as your brother's, and his last name is the same as your best friend's. Two years later, you meet the man again. You have absolutely no trouble saying, "Hi, you're Ronald Marston, aren't you?"

As these examples suggest, memories may persist over a time span that varies over an extremely wide range: a mere fraction of a second (like the weather report heard while driving); less than a minute (like the telephone number you forget right after looking it up); or a lifetime (like the name that has a special meaning for you). For convenience, psychologists divide the range into three stages of memory, illustrated in Figure 6-1. It will be helpful to refer to the figure as you read the description of the three stages in the following pages.

Figure 6-1   The three stages of memory

This diagram offers a quick summary of how the three stages of memory operate. The sights, sounds, and other stimuli in the environment register briefly in sensory memory. *Some are promptly lost but others are transferred to* short-term memory. *There again some are lost but others are rehearsed and "kept in mind" long enough to be transferred to* long-term memory—*a more or less permanent storehouse from which they can later be retrieved (Shiffrin and Atkinson, 1969).*

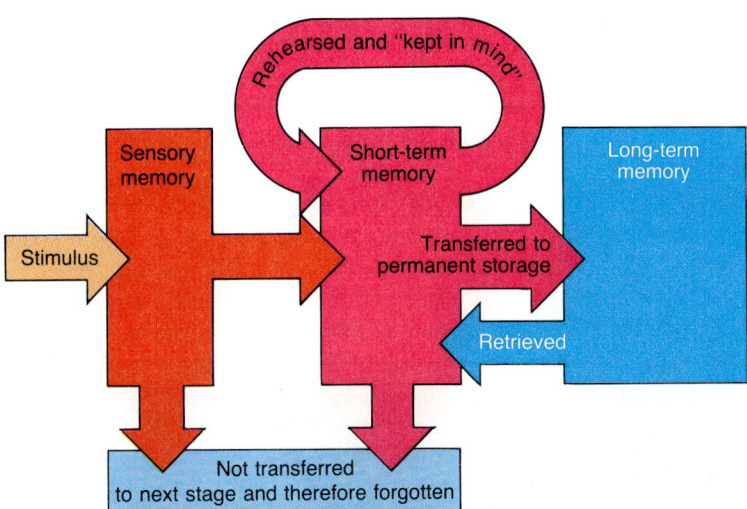

Sensory Memory: Now You Have It, Now You Don't

Everything that impinges on our sense organs seems to remain available at least a brief instant, but sometimes no longer. These very brief memories, of which we are typically unaware, are called *sensory memory*. They contain just the lingering traces of information sent to the brain by the sense organs.

There is probably a sensory memory process for each of the senses—so that, for example, we are able to remember for an instant the sight of lightning after it has flashed across the sky, or the sound of a car horn after it has passed. But these traces begin to deteriorate and vanish rapidly—usually within a half second if it is something we have seen, and within two seconds if it is something we have heard—unless they are transferred to the second of the three stages of memory.

Short-Term Memory: How Information is Processed for Keeping

The second of the three stages is *short-term memory*, into which some but not all of the information from sensory memory is transferred. Unless some processing takes place within short-term memory, however, information held there deteriorates and seems to be forgotten completely within about 30 seconds (Shiffrin and Atkinson, 1969). So much information is lost in this way that one psychologist has described short-term memory as a "leaky bucket" (Miller, 1964). However, this is not entirely a disadvantage. For example, a bank teller remembers only briefly that he is cashing a customer's paycheck for $150.89. By the time the next customer steps up to the window, the figure $150.89 has already vanished from his memory. This is just as well—for he would be totally confused by the end of the day if he recalled every transaction starting with the first one of the morning.

It appears that much of the forgetting we do from short-term memory is intentional (Bjork, 1972). We have no need to remember the information. We do not want to remember it—and it would only get in our way, for the capacity of the short-term memory is quite small in terms of amount of information as well as time span, as portrayed in Figure 6-2. On the average, in the adult, it holds seven unrelated items—exactly the number of digits in a phone number—although for some people the limit is only five and for others it is as many as nine. When short-term memory is full to capacity with its five to nine items, new information can be added only by dropping some of the old (or by grouping the items, as will be described later). We often throw out the old items deliberately. We do so by manipulating the processes that go on in short-term memory (Sperling, 1967).

First, although we remain unaware of it, there must be some kind of *scanning* of the information that is being held briefly in sensory memory. From the constant flow of sights, sounds, and other messages from the sense organs, some particular items must be *selected* as worthy of attention.

To help with the processing, the information held in short-term memory is usually transferred in some way that makes it as simple and easy to handle as possible. This process is called *encoding*, for it resembles the manner in which a computer can take complicated facts—for example, the information on your tax return—and codify them for easy processing. The encoding can take the form of a *schema*, or mental representation of the information to be remembered; the verbal meaning of the information; or its physical characteristics. For example, suppose you happened upon two dogs engaged in a fight. You could encode the event as the visual scene of the fight, verbally as "a dogfight," or as the sounds of snarling and barking. Or, of course, you could use all three forms of encoding. Some psychologists believe that verbal encoding allows information to be remembered with the greatest accuracy over a long period.

Figure 6-2   The brief lifespan of short-term memory

Even individuals with a relatively good memory span have a limited capacity to recall digits immediately after they are presented—and however good or poor the memory span, the capacity gets weaker when the digits are presented more rapidly (after Lyon, 1977).

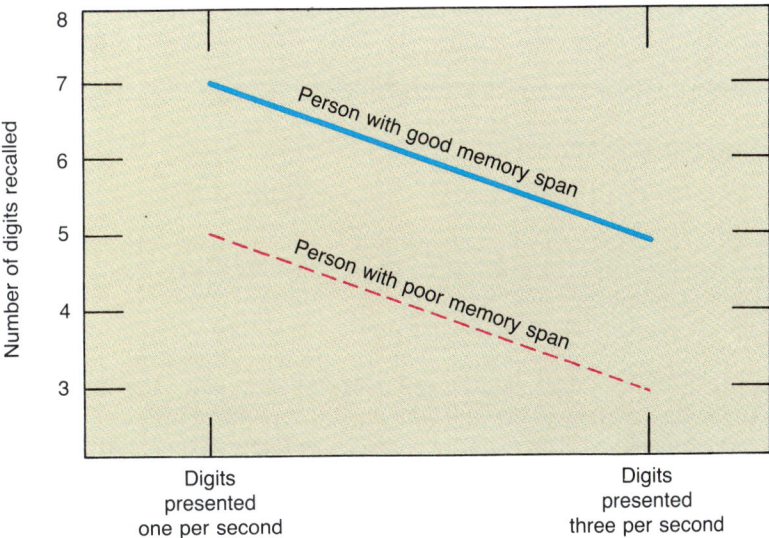

If information selected for attention and encoded is to be held for any length of time, some sort of *rehearsal system* must be set up. That is, the information must be deliberately repeated to be kept in mind and prevented from slipping out of the "leaky bucket." Through rehearsal, information can be kept in short-term memory as long as desired—though the amount of information that can be kept alive is quite small. From a list of learned items, what we are most likely to remember is governed by the *primacy effect* and the *recency effect*—meaning that we tend to remember the earlier and later portions. For instance, if you were introduced to seven or eight people at a party, you would probably remember the first two and the last two persons rather than the middle ones.

Finally, if the information is to be remembered more or less permanently, it must be passed along and stored in *long-term memory*. The process seems to take place somewhat as follows. The new information, held in short-term memory and kept alive through rehearsal, is associated with any relevant pieces of information that already exist in long-term memory. Comparisons are made and relationships sought. Further encoding and recoding take place. When this so-called *transfer process* is successful, the new information is more or less permanently fitted into long-term memory, like a new item dropped into an appropriate file.

Long-Term Memory: Keeping Information Indefinitely

How long is long-term? As you surely have discovered to your sorrow at times, it is not always as long as we would wish. But many long-term memories persist for a lifetime. An elderly person may hear a tune and remember the lyrics learned decades earlier. As for how much information we can store in long-term memory, there is really no way of knowing. Certainly the capacity is very large.

Most people have the meanings of tens of thousands of words stored in memory. Some have vocabularies that run into the hundreds of thousands. With the help of these words we accumulate all kinds of facts about the world. It has been estimated that the items of information and relationships held in memory must number in the tens of millions, and all of these pieces of information are somehow represented in the brain. It may even be that the memory storehouse has an unlimited capacity—though this is a matter of debate with some important implications for our educational system and our own life plans, as dis-

Psychology in Everyday Life
Should We Accept Limits on Our Capacities to Remember?

All psychologists agree that human memory is a remarkable storehouse with a vast capacity for words, numbers, facts, and details, as well as relationships, rules, and general principles. Most psychologists believe that we use only a fraction of our abilities—and that our storehouse remains empty and waiting, an untapped resource. The majority view is that, although we know and remember a great deal, we have the potential to accomplish much more.

A contrasting view—which raises some provocative questions for society and for the way we plan our lives—is that the human capacity to learn and remember, though very large, has definite limits. Moreover, according to this view, most of the time most of us operate fairly close to capacity. We learn and remember about as much as the workings of our nervous systems permit. We would all be happier if we recognized our limitations and took a more charitable view of our own accomplishments and those of other people. The schools would do a better job if they recognized that students cannot learn everything all at once. Thus this view questions the value of such educational practices as asking elementary school pupils to learn the names of European capitals and high school students to learn foreign languages.

Psychologist Wayne A. Wickelgren argues that *what* we learn—in school or in our life experiences—is far more important than *how much* we learn. In the educational system, "emphasis should be on the quality rather than the amount of knowledge that students are required to learn." The schools should concentrate on information that "we can *use* to achieve some important goal"—such as the general principles that provide "insight and understanding" of our universe, our society, and the workings of the human organism: "It is of far less general value to know the superficial physical characteristics of various plants and animals than to know about nutrition, disease, first aid, the anatomy and physiology of the human body, and the general principles of living systems." Wickelgren concedes that learning a foreign language may provide some personal, social, and intellectual satisfactions—but questions whether this is as valuable in the early school years as acquiring a broader understanding of human experience.

In planning your own life, Wickelgren suggests, it is wise to set priorities, concentrate on learning what is really important to you, and avoid attempting the impossible. Moreover, he suggests that there has to be a trade-off between time spent studying and time spent applying what you do know: "Some people who know more than others have accomplished less as a direct result of their learning."

Recognizing the limitations of memory, Wickelgren believes, can also help us understand and sympathize with other people: "It is unreasonable to tell a co-worker or friend in a five-minute period ten things you want that person to do and expect him or her to remember it all without mistakes. . . . One source of friction in personal relations and of inefficiency in job performance could be eliminated if we remembered that the capacity for learning and memory is limited" (Wickelgren, 1977).

cussed in a Psychology in Everyday Life box titled "Should We Accept Limits on Our Capacities to Remember?"

The Process of Retrieval

We cannot possibly be conscious at any given moment of all the millions of items of information we hold in long-term memory. Most of the information just lies there, unused. Then there comes a time when the situation we face calls for us to use a particular piece of information. Let us say that we are reading one evening by the light of a single lamp. Suddenly the light goes out—and we are left in the dark. The situation calls for action, and for the use of the knowledge we have stored in long-term memory about lamps, electricity, and alternative sources of light.

An order has arrived at memory's storage house, calling for the immediate delivery of some of the items held there. We need information, and to be able to use it we must engage in the process called *retrieval*. That is, we must find the right items, pull them out, and deliver them to short-term memory, where we can actively think about them.

Look back at Figure 6-1 (page 191) and note the two arrows showing the interaction between short-term and long-term memory. One arrow indicates the process in which new information is transferred from short-term memory into more or less permanent storage. The other arrow indicates the retrieval process, in which information that has been stored in long-term memory is called back into short-term memory, or in other words back into consciousness, where we can think about it and use it.

The human retrieval process operates in wondrous ways, more directly and efficiently than most computers. We do not have to rummage through all the items stored away to find what we need. Instead we are capable of what has been called *direct-access retrieval* (Wickelgren, 1981). Our storehouse is organized in such a way that we can ordinarily go directly to the right "place," put our hands on the items we need, and deliver them promptly to short-term memory. The way we accomplish this highly efficient organization is discussed later in the chapter.

Solving the Mystery of the Memory Trace

Every time we store a new piece of information in the long-term memory, the brain—indeed we ourselves—are somehow changed. We can do something—recall a new fact or engage in a new kind of behavior—that we could not do before. Obviously something has happened inside. But what?

Psychologists do not know for sure. They must confine themselves to saying that a *memory trace* has been established. Some psychologists believe there are several kinds of memory traces, perhaps corresponding to the three different stages of memory. Others believe that just a single type of trace, which may last anywhere from a fraction of a second to a lifetime, accounts for all forms of memory (Wickelgren, 1981).

Whatever the nature and number may be, the memory trace surely represents some kind of change in the nervous system. Most often the change takes place in the brain, especially in the highest part, or cortex, of the brain. It probably occurs at the switching points, or synapses. When we learn something, we route nervous impulses over a particular pathway, passing through a number of synapses in a particular pattern. The various kinds of nervous activity that take place along this pathway presumably have a lasting effect that makes it possible to reactivate the pattern on future occasions—thus enabling us to remember what we have learned. The most recent research on this subject suggests that the changes entail the strengthening of existing synapses rather than the addition of new ones (Rakic et al., 1986).

Riding a bicycle is an example of a behavior that may depend on memory traces established many decades earlier.

Establishment of the memory trace seems to depend at least in part on the brain's *neurotransmitters*, the chemicals that pass messages along from one neuron to another. Studies of lower animals indicate that when one neuron stimulates another neuron to fire, by releasing its neurotransmitters into the synapse between them, these chemicals produce a lasting change in the efficiency of the synapse (Kandel and Schwartz, 1982). The second neuron becomes more likely to fire again in the future, thus making it easier for nervous impulses to travel the same pathway again.

One neurotransmitter that has received attention in recent years is *acetylcholine*, which appears to be decreased in patients suffering from *Alzheimer's disease*, a disorder of the brain whose victims suffer progressive deterioration of memory and other intellectual functions (Coyle, Price, and Delong, 1983). The chemical basis of memory is far from simple, however, and undoubtedly many other neurotransmitters are involved (Squire and Davis, 1981). Certainly the process is far too complex to offer quick and easy results from any kind of "learning pill." We will just have to reconcile ourselves to the fact that laying down long-term memories usually requires the kind of work that will be described later in the chapter.

Why Do We Forget?

Memory cannot be discussed without also discussing forgetting. They are opposite sides of the same coin. We learn something—that is, we store some piece of information in our memory. Sometimes this information persists and we can call on it whenever we need it. We say that we remember. Sometimes the information seems to disappear or elude us—and we say we have forgotten. Why do we remember some things and forget others?

How Psychologists Measure Remembering and Forgetting

Attempts to investigate the twin processes of remembering and forgetting face many obstacles. There is no way psychologists can examine the nervous system to see what kinds of changes have been laid down in it by learning and how well these changes persist. They can only devise tests to determine how much is remembered and how much is forgotten. Unfortunately, these tests can never make a direct measure of memory. All they can measure is how well people *perform* on the tests—and their performance is not an entirely accurate indication of how much they remember. Memory may be adversely affected by poor motivation, anxiety, distractions, and many other factors. The tests of remembering and forgetting must always be viewed with reservations. But psychologists, in their effort to do the best they can have adopted three methods for measuring what is remembered—recognizing that one measure alone may be a misleading index of an individual's capacity to remember.

Recall One way to show you have learned the Gettysburg Address is to recite it—which demonstrates that you can *recall* it, or bring it out intact from wherever it is stored in your memory. In school, a common use of recall is in the essay type of examination. When teachers ask, "What is classical conditioning?" they are asking you to recall what you have learned.

Recognition Often we cannot recall what we have learned, at least not completely, but we can prove that we remember something about it by being able to *recognize* it. For example, you may not be able to recall the Gettysburg Address. But if someone asked you what begins with the words "Fourscore and seven years ago," you might immediately recognize the speech, thus demonstrating that you certainly remember something about it. As shown in Figure 6-3, even patients suffering from *amnesia*, or severe breakdown of

Figure 6-3   The difference the test makes

When amnesia sufferers were compared with normal subjects on various tests of memory, they did only about a third as well when the task was to recall words learned earlier. But they did just as well when the task was to complete the words after recognizing a few of the letters (after Graf, Squire, and Mandler, 1984).

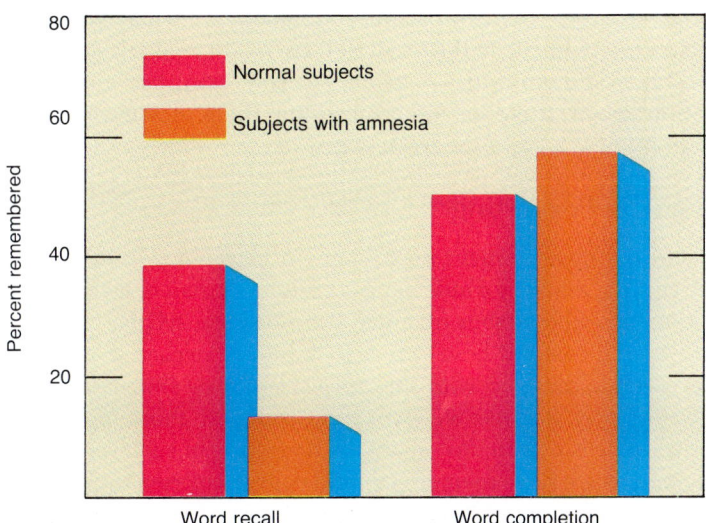

The Range of Human Memory

Figure 6-4 Recognition over time

The decay of our capacity to recognize material drops slightly after a few hours or days have passed, but more steeply as the weeks and months roll by (after Shepard, 1967).

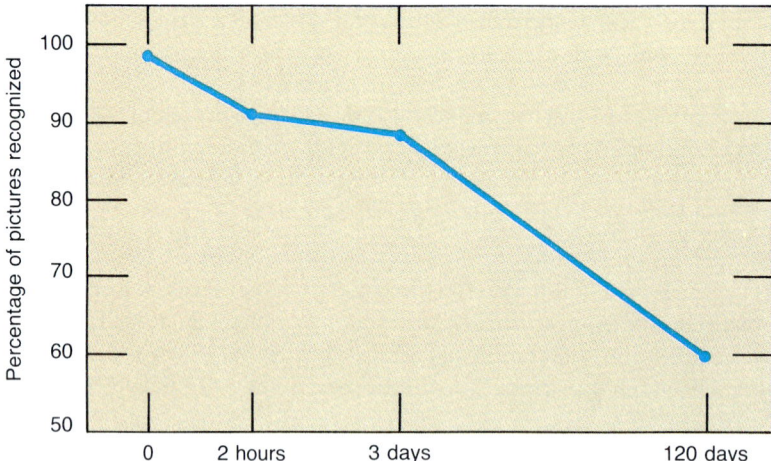

memory, can do well in recognizing words they have learned, but fail at recalling them (Graf, Squire, and Mandler, 1984).

In multiple-choice examinations you are asked to choose the right answer from among several possible answers and thus prove that you recognize it. Because recognition is easier than recall, many students would rather take a multiple-choice test than an essay examination. But, as shown in Figure 6-4, the capacity to recognize material learned earlier is diminished with the passage of time (Shepard, 1967).

Relearning The most sensitive method of measuring memory is one that is seldom used. This is the method of *relearning*, which is accurate but cumbersome. All of us once learned the Gettysburg Address, or, if not that, then some other well-known piece of writing (anything from a nursery rhyme to Hamlet's soliloquy). We may not be able to recite these pieces now; so we would fail on the recall test. We might recognize them if we saw or heard them again. This would prove that we remember something but would not be a very precise measure of how much. If we set about relearning them, however, the length of time this took us would serve as a highly accurate measure.

Some Factors in Forgetting

Relearning was the measurement used in one of psychology's earliest and most famous studies of forgetting, made by a nineteenth-century German named Hermann Ebbinghaus. For his experiments, Ebbinghaus invented the nonsense syllable. He learned lists of such syllables and then measured how long it took him to relearn the lists to perfection after various intervals. He came up with the *curve of forgetting* shown in Figure 6-5. The curve does not always apply, because we learn some things so thoroughly that we never forget them. However, it tells a great deal about the forgetting of such varied kinds of learning as motor skills, poems we have memorized, and college courses we have taken. Its message is this: *When we learn something new, often we quickly forget much of it, but we remember at least some of it for a long time.*

Figure 6-5 Ebbinghaus's famous curve of forgetting

Ebbinghaus memorized lists of 13 nonsense syllables similar to those shown here, then measured how much he could remember after various intervals. After 20 minutes, he remembered only 58 percent and after about an hour only 44 percent. After the initial sharp dip, however, the curve flattened out. After one day he remembered about 34 percent and after two days about 28 percent. Although the graph line does not extend that far, he recalled 21 percent after a month (Ebbinghaus, 1913).

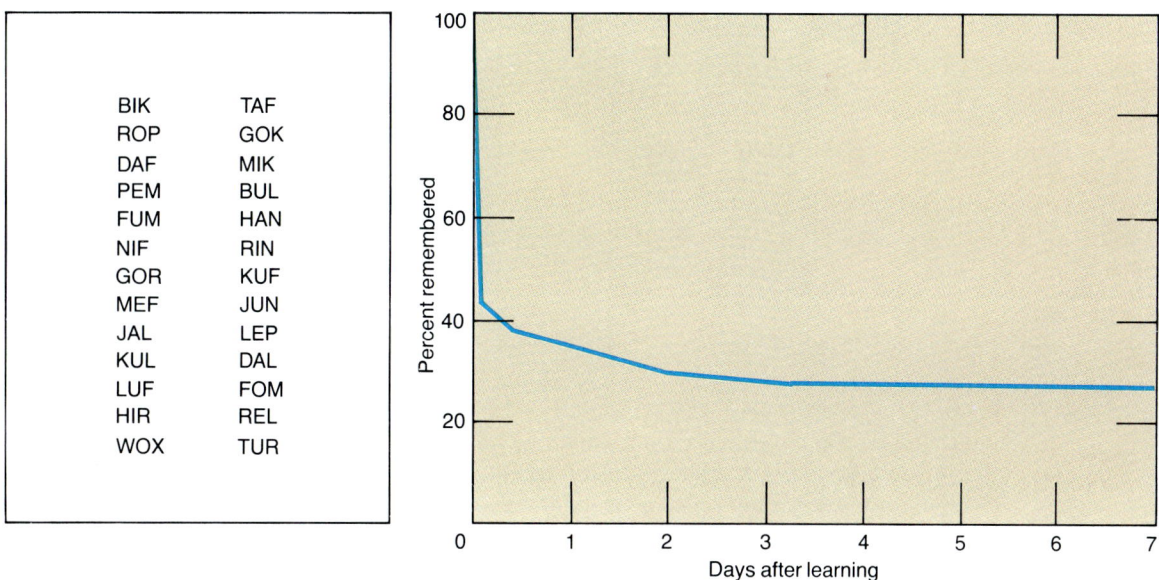

As to why we forget, the answer is not yet fully known. But there are a number of factors worth considering. All the factors may be important at least in part, for forgetting may be such a complex process that it takes place in different ways under different circumstances.

Factor 1: The Memory Trace Fades

One of the oldest ideas about forgetting assumes that the memory trace, whatever its physical nature, is subject to decay—that it begins to fade as time goes on and sometimes disappears entirely. This view regards the memory trace as resembling a path worn into a plot of grass. It can be kept functioning through use, as a pathway can be kept clear by continuing to walk over it. But without use the memory trace may vanish, as a pathway becomes overgrown when abandoned.

Many of today's memory theorists continue to believe that the memory trace has some physical quality that changes with the passage of time, often reducing the likelihood that it can be retraced or reactivated. This view is supported by findings that show changes in brain synapses with learning (Rakic et al., 1986). The trace is thought to have two qualities. The first is its *strength*—meaning how likely it is to "pop into mind." This quality, the strength of the memory trace, is at its peak immediately after learning and declines with the passage of time. The second quality is *resistance to extinction*, meaning how well the trace can manage to survive and become immune to fading or decay (Wickelgren, 1977).

Establishing a resistance to extinction takes a certain amount of time. It requires what memory theorists call *consolidation*, a period during which the trace undergoes a process

By continuously rehearsing their required body movements, these dancers are less likely to forget them with the passage of time.

that might be compared with the hardening or "setting" of a newly laid sidewalk. (During the consolidation period whatever changes are produced at the synapses by learning may become more permanent.) The consolidation process takes place most rapidly in the first minutes after learning—but it continues, though at a gradually slowing rate. Thus, though the memory trace may decrease in strength with the passage of time, it may also become more and more resistant to extinction as the years go by—especially if the person rehearses the information.

The idea that time affects both the strength and resistance of the memory trace is based in part on studies of people who have suffered amnesia because of head injuries. This type of amnesia often takes a very strange form. Patients may be unable to remember anything that happened in the past five years yet have a normal memory for events that happened earlier. As they begin to get over the effects of their injuries, their memories return on a predictable time schedule. First they recover their memory for events that are five years old, then for four-year-old events, and so on until their recovery is complete (Weiskrantz, 1966). It would appear that the older their memory traces, the more resistant the traces were to temporary disruption by injury.

Many experiments have been performed in search of factors that might affect the memory trace for better or worse. One such factor is the emotional content of a memory. In one study, when students were asked to focus on the feelings associated with an event, it led to improved recall (Nigro and Neisser, 1983). If we have a strong emotional reaction—for example, as many did to the assassination of President Kennedy, the attempted shooting of President Reagan, or the explosion of the space shuttle Challenger—it is likely that we will remember many details about the event (Pillemer, 1984). Indeed, many people are able to remember their experience of emotional events in such photographic detail—exactly what they were doing, who they were with, who said what—that the phenomenon has been given the name "flashbulb memories" (Brown and Kulik, 1982). Such vivid recollections may exist because memory is closely tied to the limbic system, the brain's seat of emotions (Mishkin, 1986). We are also more likely to recall details of events that are surprising and of considerable personal consequence (Rubin and Kozin, 1984).

For many people, the explosion of the space shuttle Challenger *will comprise a "flashbulb memory," as explained in the text.*

Factor 2: The Retrieval Process Fails with Changes in Setting or Mood

Some memory traces, once established as part of long-term memory, may persist for as long as we live. But the information may be unavailable for recall. We cannot retrieve it, and we say we have forgotten it—although the memory trace still exists. Thus, forgetting may not be due to the loss of a memory trace but rather a failure in retrieval (Kintsch, 1977).

Temporary forgetting caused by failure in retrieval is an everyday experience. There undoubtedly have been many occasions when you found yourself unable to remember some item of information, then later on recalled it perfectly, especially if something happened to "jog your memory."

It has been found that important similarity between conditions at the time of retrieval and at the time of learning and encoding may serve as a cue that stimulates the memory. The principle has been stated thus: "When the conditions of encoding and recall are most similar, then recall will be best" (Klatzky, 1980). Some kinds of information are more easily retrieved in the same physical setting in which the learning took place (for example the same classroom)—or even through visualizing the setting (Smith, 1979). This suggests that we might find it helpful, when trying to remember a name, to try to recall the physical circumstances in which we met or last saw that person. Such memory for particular events, or episodes, is referred to as *episodic memory*. This contrasts with memory for information which is independent of the specific occasion on which we learned it, referred to as *generic memory*.

Factor 3: The Retrieval Process Fails Through Interference

Another possible explanation for failure of retrieval is that our ability to remember any given piece of information is interfered with by other information stored in memory. Our memory for what we learn today is often adversely affected by what we have learned in the past and also by what we will learn in the future. The various pieces of information

The Range of Human Memory

compete for attention and survival—and not all of them can prevail. There are two major types of interference:

Proactive Interference When old information causes us to forget new information, the process is called *proactive interference*. The phenomenon of proactive interference can be demonstrated through simple laboratory procedures, such as asking subjects to try to learn and remember several lists of words. The results of one such experiment are illustrated in Figure 6-6. Note the steady decline in the subjects' ability to remember new materials caused by more and more proactive interference from prior learning.

The reason for proactive interference is a matter of debate. But it is known to be greatest when we try to learn new information that is similar to old information already stored in memory—as was the case with the word lists used in the experiment shown in Figure 6-6. Proactive interference is considered less troublesome when the new information is substantially different from the old, as is illustrated in Figure 6-7. In this experiment, one group of subjects watched four videotaped broadcasts of news items that all fell into the same general category, for example national political developments. Another group watched similar news items on the first three tapes. But the fourth tape abruptly switched the subject, for example from national politics to foreign affairs. As the figure shows, both groups remembered less and less over the first three trials. On the final tape, the first group continued to display a decline caused by proactive interference—but the second group, with proactive interference reduced because of the change to a different topic, did much better. The same phenomenon is apparent when we try to remember a number of songs we have heard in the past. We have the least difficulty remembering those that are least similar to others (Halpern, 1984).

Figure 6-6 How the old interferes with the new

In one of the classic experiments on proactive interference, *subjects learned a list of paired adjectives. Two days after learning, they were tested for their recall of list 1 and asked to learn list 2. After a similar interval they were tested on list 2 and learned list 3. Two days later they were tested on list 3 and learned list 4. Finally, after another two-day interval, they were tested on list 4 and the experiment ended. The steady decline in the height of the bars show how learning list 1 interfered with memory for list 2, how learning lists 1 and 2 interfered with memory for list 3, and so on (Underwood, 1957).*

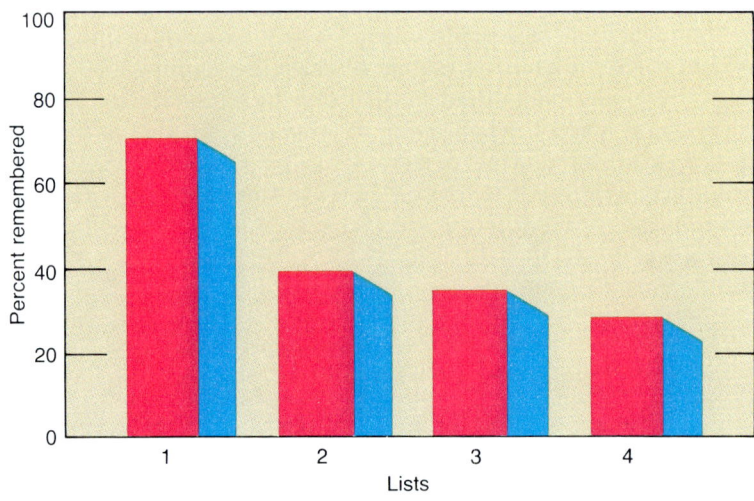

Figure 6-7 **Changing the subject as an antidote to proactive interference**

The bars show the results of an experiment in which subjects watched a series of four videotapes of old news broadcasts. After each tape they were tested on how much of it they remembered. For both groups, the recall scores began a steady decline as listening to tape 1 interfered with their ability to remember tape 2 and listening to tapes 1 and 2 interfered with their memory for tape 3. But note the discrepancy between the two groups on tape 4. Group 1 subjects continued to show a decline, but group 2 suddenly displayed a sharp improvement (Gunter, Berry, and Clifford, 1981). For the reason, see the text.

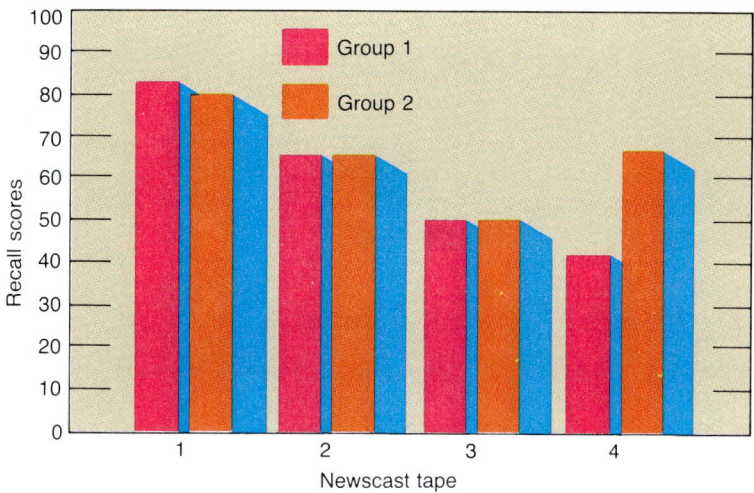

In everyday life, you experience proactive interference when you have been studying the same course material—for example, this chapter on memory—for several hours. Your ability to remember what you have read in the third hour becomes poorer. The reason is not just fatigue. If you were to turn to entirely new material—for example, history—it is likely you would remember more from your third hour of study.

Retroactive Interference In proactive interference, old information gets in the way of remembering new information. The opposite situation—when new information causes us to forget old information—is called *retroactive interference*. Again the similarity between old and new materials plays an important role in recall. When subjects learn a new list of words with the same meaning as the words in a previously learned list (synonyms), they experience more retroactive interference than when the new list contains very different materials, such as nonsense syllables.

Perhaps the most interesting—and consoling—fact about retroactive interference is that it has a greater effect on unimportant materials that are not worth remembering anyway (like lists of words learned in a laboratory) than on important and meaningful materials. Retroactive interference often makes us forget the specific details of what we have learned, especially if the details are not essential, but it is not nearly so likely to make us forget the basic theme and meaning of what we have learned (Christiaansen, 1980). Thus, you will probably forget some of the things you learn in this course because of retroactive interference from information you will learn in future courses and from your life experiences. You may not remember the exact meaning of such terms as classical conditioning and reinforcement, but you will probably always remember the general principles of learning and of how memory operates.

The Range of Human Memory

Even for world leaders, is it sometimes possible to forget details of events because they are too painful to remember?

Factor 4: We Are Motivated to Forget

The fact that we seem to forget some things deliberately was mentioned earlier in connection with the processes that take place in short-term memory. Many theorists believe that at times we also forget information stored in long-term memory because we want to forget it, whether consciously or not. It may be emotionally uncomfortable to remember the name of a person we dislike, or the painful emotional problems we had at a certain stage of life.

Motivated forgetting has been widely studied by psychoanalysts, who have found that it often plays a part in abnormal behavior. Indeed, most of us are troubled by persistent memories of embarrassing and painful events that we would gladly forget if only we could.

ENCODING AND TRANSFER

The factors that help explain why we forget offer some valuable hints on how we can avoid the handicap and embarrassment of forgetting. The motivation factor suggests that we are more likely to remember when we want to remember. The other factors indicate that we will be most efficient at remembering if we can manage to store information in such a way that the memory traces will not fade away with the passage of time and that the information can be retrieved when we want it—remaining more or less intact despite interference from previous and future learning.

All these matters depend on how we encode and transfer information to long-term memory. Thus the key to remembering lies in two related questions: What is the nature of the encoding process that creates our store of knowledge and how can we do the processing more effectively—and learn and remember to greater advantage?

Chunking—Putting Many Little Facts into One Neat Package

One of the important elements in encoding can best be explained by taking another look at short-term memory, with its capacity of about seven unrelated items. Note what happens if you look briefly at this string of letters:

tvfBIYmcasATNbcnASA

You will probably find it impossible to remember all 19 letters, or anywhere near that number. But note what happens with just a slight change:

tvFBIymcaSATnbcNASA

The 19 letters are now turned into a mere six units—each containing familiar combinations of initials—and fall well within the limits of short-term memory. You would have no trouble remembering them after a mere few seconds of study (after Bower, 1970).

This process, in which a number of individual units of information are combined into one—wrapped together securely, so to speak, in a single neat package—is called *chunking* (Miller, 1956). Chunking greatly increases the scope of short-term memory, which can hold about seven big packages of information just about as well as it can handle seven small individual items. We encode many forms of information into chunks—letters into words (as illustrated in Figure 6-8), words into phrases (*frying pan, chicken chow mein*), phrases into sentences (*Mary had a little lamb*), individual digits into memorable dates (1492, 1776), and so on.

Figure 6-8   A classroom demonstration of chunking

The instructor first shows the blackboard as in the upper photo. How many of the 49 letters can the class possibly remember after studying the board for a minute or two? Not many, because each line in the column contains seven letters—and seven is about the capacity of short-term memory. But then she shows the board in the photo below. The task becomes much easier, for each line of letters has been rearranged into a familiar word that constitutes a single chunk, and there are now just seven chunks to deal with instead of 49 individual letters.

Encoding and Transfer

Obviously chunking requires some interaction between short-term and long-term memory. We would not readily form the chunks TV and FBI, for example, unless we were already familiar with these combinations of letters. And obviously much of the information in long-term memory has been encoded and stored there in chunks. For example, as we come to understand a body of knowledge such as American history, we chunk it into periods: the Revolution, the Civil War, World War I, World War II, the Vietnam War, and so on. Now it becomes easier to remember the many specific facts associated with each period.

The Associative Network Theory

Most researchers now believe that memory can best be described and explained as a complicated network in which thousands upon thousands of words and ideas are all connected and interconnected by long and far-reaching strands of association (Anderson and Bower, 1973). As new information is encoded into the network, new linkages are formed to old information already contained there. Some of these links or associations are direct, others more roundabout. Some are strong, some weak. Some are long-lasting, resistant to forgetting, and easy to retrieve. Others are weaker and less likely to be recalled.

This view of memory, called the *associative network theory*, accounts for the extraordinary human ability at direct retrieval. Leading to every fact or chunk of information in the network are countless linkages. Through one link or another we can usually find a quick and direct route to what we need—and, once we have it, we can then also pull out any or all the other chunks with which it is connected.

We encode new information into long-term memory by noting how it relates to what we have already stored—and thus we add it to the network along with all the appropriate associations to existing information. A new fact or chunk of facts is woven into the network, attached by many far-reaching new strands through which, if they are solid and strong enough, we can reach and retrieve it when we need it.

Creating Links Between New and Old

The vital role of associations or linkages between new information and old has been demonstrated in an ingenious experiment in which subjects were asked to read a paragraph that at first glance seems so unusual that it is difficult to follow, let alone understand and remember. Try reading the paragraph yourself, as slowly as you like, then turn away from the book and see how much you can recall.

> With hocked gems financing him, our hero bravely defied all scornful laughter that tried to prevent his scheme. "Your eyes deceive," he had said. "An egg, not a table, correctly typifies this unexplored planet." Now three sturdy sisters sought proof. Forging along, sometimes through calm vastness, yet more often over turbulent peaks and valleys, days became weeks as many doubters spread fearful rumors about the edge. At last from nowhere welcome winged creatures appeared, signifying momentous success (Dooling and Lachman, 1971).

In all probability you can remember very little of the paragraph, in which all kinds of unusual details come thick, fast, and without much apparent rhyme or reason. But suppose you had been told, before reading the paragraph, that it was a fanciful description of Columbus's voyage to America in 1492. In that case you could have fitted it into what you already know about the discovery of America—and undoubtedly, like one group of subjects in the experiment, you would have been able to encode and remember much of it. This act of encoding takes effort and energy—which, according to one view, is why a negative or depressed mood interferes with the process. When we are upset, we divert the conscious attention needed to accomplish the encoding task (Ellis and Ashbrook, 1987).

What We Encode, Remember, and Retrieve

In the encoding process we add something new to the associate network. But just what is it that we add? Is it an exact copy of something we have done, seen, or heard—like a movie or a tape recording? Or is it something else?

In some cases what we encode is clearly a faithful copy. An experimenter once asked college students to recite the words to *The Star Spangled Banner,* Hamlet's soliloquy, and other familiar passages of verse and prose. Whatever they remembered at all, it turned out, was almost a word-by-word reproduction (Rubin, 1977). But this kind of verbatim encoding and retrieval is rare. In most cases we seem to engage in what is called *constructive processing*. We encode and retrieve not an exact copy of the information we receive—as from a printed page or a lecture or a conversation—but whatever meanings and associations we have found. We remember not "what was out there" but what we ourselves "*did* during encoding"—that is, the way we processed the information and related it to the knowledge already held in long-term memory (Craik and Tulving, 1975).

In most cases, therefore, we remember what we consider important—the theme or underlying meaning—and forget or distort many of the details, such as the exact wording. One study has suggested this analogy: When we read or hear something, we make mental notes—like the brief reminders you might jot down in your notebook while listening to a lecture. It is these notes, not the actual words we read or heard, that we store in some appropriate "pigeonhole in memory" until we need them. While stored in the pigeonhole, the various factors that cause forgetting may cause some of the notes to become smudged. Some of them may even get lost. Thus, when we try to retrieve the information, we find that it is incomplete—only a sketchy reminder of what we actually read or heard. All we can do is "fetch the notes from their pigeonhole and from this fragmentary information reconstruct what . . . was in the original message"—or rather what we now have come to believe was in it (Clark and Clark, 1977). The same process applies to our memory for other items such as melodies heard, scenes observed, or people encountered.

When this listener tries later on to retrieve the information she is receiving, she may add details that are different or even entirely new.

Psychology in Everyday Life
How Much Faith Can We Put in Courtroom Witnesses?

In a courtroom one witness after another takes the stand and swears under oath that the defendant was the man seen leaving the scene of a murder, a revolver still in his hand. The defendant claims he was miles away at the time. The prosecution case is strong. The defense case is weak. Verdict: guilty. Sentence: life imprisonment.

Has justice been done? Maybe. But maybe not. There have been a number of cases in which innocent people have been identified, tried, and convicted for crimes they did not commit. The fact that eye witness accounts can be grossly unreliable was observed decades ago (Stern, 1904). New studies of how memories are often the products of constructive processing, as described in the text, cast additional doubt on courtroom testimony and pose the question of how often our system of justice may go wrong—not only in criminal cases but in all kinds of lawsuits, from accident claims to anti-trust proceedings (Wells and Loftus, 1984).

A number of experiments have been performed by showing subjects videotapes or slides of such events as automobile accidents and asking them later what they saw. The results have demonstrated that "eye-witness accounts" are often wrong about important details. For example, subjects are sometimes sure they saw a stop sign at the scene of the accident, when in fact there was only a yield sign. Errors are particularly likely to occur if the experimenter talks to the subjects immediately after the pictures have been shown, before the test of recollections, and asks questions that suggest a false possibility—for example, "Did the car stop at the stop sign?" when there was no stop sign (Loftus, Miller, and Burns, 1978). The recollections of real-life eyewitnesses may be similarly distorted by any questions they answer for police at the scene of an accident, or later for their acquaintances or for the lawyers. Even the way a question is worded may influence what they think happened, though the questioner may have no intention of misleading them. And their capacity to recall accurately may be a function of their mood. As shown in Figure 6-9, when we are depressed, recall is less sharp than otherwise (Ellis et al., 1985).

One has to wonder. How many defendants have been found guilty or innocent of crimes, how many verdicts have been reached by juries in lawsuits of all kinds, on the basis of witnesses' confident descriptions of what they saw or heard—though it never really happened?

Because of unreliable eyewitness testimony, the man in the top photo was put in prison for crimes committed by the man in the bottom photo.

Figure 6-9   How mood affects memory

In one study, college students were asked to study a list of sentences. A depressed mood was induced in some of them by having them read a series of depressing statements, while the others remained in a neutral state. The results showed a significantly poorer capacity by the depressed-mood subjects to recall certain key words in the sentences (after Ellis et al., 1985).

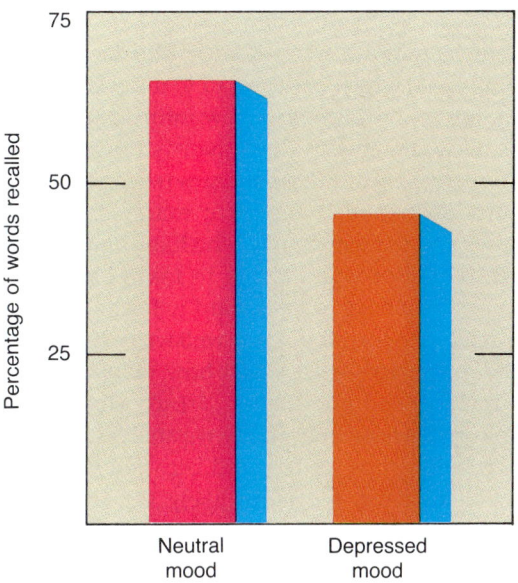

With the brief and sometimes smudged or incomplete mental notes, we do the best we can. We try to make sense out of them. We fill in the missing details—sometimes accurately and sometimes not. Thus a great deal of what we think we remember never really happened—or, if it did, it was different in many respects from the way we remember it. Memory, as one scholar has said, is often "unreliable, given to invention, and even dangerous" (Bower, 1978).

These omissions and distortions pose serious problems at times—especially in legal trials where precise details may be crucial to the outcome. This issue is discussed in a Psychology in Everyday Life box titled "How Much Faith Can We Put in Courtroom Witnesses?" Despite the problems, the associative network serves us well in most cases, particularly in remembering and retrieving the most basic and important meanings and the general principles of the information we have processed.

THE ENCODING PROCESS AND LEARNING

The associative network of long-term memory is so large and complex, and its linkages so intricately connected and interconnected, that tugging at one strand can produce far-reaching and sometimes unpredictable results. Suppose, for example, that you are asked to retrieve everything you remember about the word *angel*. You might begin by pulling out information from paintings you have seen of winged figures in white robes, with halos and playing harps. From there you might move on to describe the churches you have seen, the prayers you have learned, and the principles underlying the world's major religions. You might go on to talk about morality, then about a priest or rabbi who played a significant part in your life.

Your progression of associations may lead almost anywhere—and if you are asked to do the same thing tomorrow the pathway may take an entirely different route. Of course the associations vary from person to person. To another individual, the word *angel* may immediately suggest the California baseball team and lead to a discussion of Yankee Stadium, Babe Ruth, candy bars, and eventually some unsuccessful personal experiences with dieting.

As these examples of retrieval indicate, every item of information in long-term memory is associated with many other items, which in turn lead to innumerable other associations. How likely you are to remember and retrieve any new information depends on how well you manage to add it to this network—that is, how many strong associations you form to linkages that already exist. Effective encoding sometimes takes place without much effort. You do not have to make any deliberate attempt, for example, to remember important events in your life or the names and faces of people who have played significant parts in it. But often—and especially in school or when trying to master a new skill, like chess or repairing electronic equipment—you have to work hard to form the associations.

Thus memory is closely related to learning. How well we remember generally depends on how well we learn in the first place—that is, on how many links or associations we establish between new information and information already stored in the network. This kind of encoding depends in turn on how thoroughly we analyze and understand the new information and how many relationships we can find between the new and the old. The richer and more elaborate our analysis, the more likely we are to form a long-lasting memory that will resist forgetting and be easy to retrieve (Kintsch, 1977).

The Importance of Meaning and Organization

In studying a page like this one, it is futile just to read and re-read the words without making any attempt to understand them. The words may eventually begin to seem familiar, like old friends—but mere familiarity, without careful attention and analysis, is no guarantee of successful encoding. We sometimes learn and remember surprisingly little about familiar objects and events. What counts in learning is something quite different:

> The critical thing for most of the material you learn in school is to understand it, which means encoding it in a way that makes it distinctive from unrelated material and related to all the things it ought to be related to in order for you to use it. . . . The time you spend thinking about material you are reading and relating it to previously stored material is about the most useful thing you can do in learning any new subject matter (Wickelgren, 1977).

To put this another way, the key to successful encoding is to figure out the meaning of new information and organize it into some unified and logical pattern that can be readily associated with other information. Because meaning is so important, some things are just naturally easier to learn and encode into memory than others. If the materials themselves make sense—that is, if they are intrinsically meaningful—we have a good head start on our processing. Thus it is much easier to remember lists of actual three-letter words (such as SIT, HAT, BIN, COW) than lists of three-letter nonsense syllables. In fact it is easier to remember lists of nonsense syllables that resemble real words than syllables that are truly nonsensical. An experiment performed many years ago showed that subjects are about 50 percent better at remembering syllables like DOZ, SOF, LIF, and RUF, all of which remind most people of actual words, than totally unfamiliar syllables like ZOJ, JYQ, GIW, and VAF (McGeoch, 1930). Similarly, we are more likely to encode and remember passages of poetry than prose since poetry has not only meaning but a kind of internal logic and organization provided by the cadence and rhymes.

Learning by Rule or by Rote

Both meaning and organization help account for the fact that we usually remember longer if we learn by *rule* (that is, if we try to understand the underlying principles or logic) than if we learn by *rote* (or simply try to memorize materials by repeating them mechanically without any regard to what they mean).

Some things, of course, simply have to be learned by rote. There is no other way to learn the multiplication tables or the sequence of letters in the alphabet. And, as these examples suggest, some information learned by rote is never forgotten. But most college courses would be almost impossible to encode into lasting memory by rote—and fortunately most courses readily lend themselves to learning by rule. They have patterns of meaning and organization, built around underlying principles, and are presented by instructors and in textbooks in ways designed to help you find, understand, and analyze those patterns. They can be studied and encoded effectively through logical approaches like the SQ3R system that is described in Appendix A to this book.

Learning often depends more on the kind of cognitive processing and encoding we do than on the amount of time we spend (Craik and Tulving, 1975). Thus even a small amount of time spent finding meaning, organization, and relationships is generally more effective than a great deal of time devoted merely to rehearsing what is on a page more or less verbatim. Nevertheless, time is ordinarily an important factor—as is discussed in a Psychology in Everyday Life box called "A Rule for Learners: Take Your Time."

Using Learning to Build on Learning

Another practical implication of psychology's studies of encoding is this: The more we already know, the easier it is to learn and remember something new. As we go through school and college, we acquire a bigger vocabulary, more mathematical symbols and rules, more knowledge of the general principles of science, human behavior, and the workings of our society. All this previously stored information helps us understand the new information, relate it to past knowledge, and encode it solidly into our memory network.

The fact that learning builds on learning has never been expressed more eloquently than by William James, even though James lived and wrote many years before the discovery of most of what is now known about encoding and memory.

> *The more other facts a fact is associated with in the mind, the better possession of it our memory retains.* Each of its associates becomes a hook to which it hangs, a means to fish it up by when sunk beneath the surface. Together, they form a network of attachments by which it is woven into the entire tissue of our thought. The "secret of a good memory" is thus the secret of forming diverse and multiple associations with every fact we care to retain. . . . Most men have a good memory for facts connected with their own pursuits. The college athlete who remains a dunce at his books will astonish you by his knowledge of men's records in various feats and games, and will be a walking dictionary of sporting statistics. The reason is that he is constantly going over these things in his mind, and comparing and making series of them. They form for him not so many odd facts but a concept-system—so they stick. So the merchant remembers prices, the politician other politicians' speeches and votes, with a copiousness which amazes outsiders, but which the amount of thinking they bestow on these subjects easily explains. The great memory for facts which a Darwin and a Spencer reveal in their books is not incompatible with the possession on their part of a brain with only a middling degree of physiological retentiveness [by which James means inborn ability for remembering]. Let a man early in life set himself the task of verifying such a theory as

that of evolution, and facts will soon cluster and cling to him like grapes to their stem. Their relations to the theory will hold them fast; and the more of these the mind is able to discern, the greater the erudition will become (James, 1890).

Of course, the possession of a great deal of information increases the possibility of proactive and retroactive interference. But any tendency to forgetting that this may create

Psychology in Everyday Life
A Rule for Learners: Take Your Time

Most of the time, effective encoding requires deliberate effort—we have to work at it—and a certain amount of time. You can safely assume that the more time you spend the more you are likely to remember, provided of course that you use the time effectively. There are no short cuts in learning. For example, nothing is gained through "speed reading," which is the popular name for techniques that are supposed to enable you to read a printed page much faster while still comprehending everything the words mean. In fact, studies have shown that the faster you read the less you are likely to understand and remember (Graf, 1973).

There are certain advantages, of course, in saving time through the rapid scanning of materials that you do not need to remember, or when you are glancing through a long and complicated article or book in which there are only a few specific pieces of information that you want to seek out and concentrate on. But in general any increase in reading speed, beyond your normal rate, saves time only at the expense of remembering. The kind of encoding that results in long-lasting memory, like the weaving of a strong and far-flung net, simply cannot be rushed.

Even after new information has been encoded into memory, it usually pays to spend some more time studying it—possibly because practice and repetition somehow increase the strength and retrievability of the memory traces in the network. This fact is expressed in the *law of overlearning*, which states: After you have learned something, further study tends to increase the length of time you will remember it. The law of overlearning seems to explain why we never forget such childhood jingles as "Twinkle, twinkle little star," or the stories of Cinderella and Goldilocks and the Three Bears. Long after we knew these things by heart, we continued to recite or listen to them over and over again. We not only learned but overlearned.

The law of overlearning also explains why cramming is not a satisfactory way to learn the contents of a college course. By cramming, students may learn enough to get a passing grade on an examination, but they are soon likely to forget almost everything they learned. A little overlearning, on the other hand, is like time spent thinking about new materials and trying to understand them and relate them to previous information. It is a good investment in the ability to remember for a long time.

Extra time and a deliberate pace for study is likely to pay off on examination day.

is more than offset by the increased chances of finding more associations between new and old and thus weaving the new information more solidly into the network.

SOME STRATEGIES FOR ENCODING

The fact that learning builds on learning helps explain what would otherwise be a baffling aspect of schoolwork. Insofar as can be measured, children entering high school have matured to the point where they possess all the nervous system equipment that makes learning possible. Their innate ability to learn will not increase much, if at all. They are already about as smart, to use the popular term, as they will ever be. Yet everybody knows that high school seniors can learn things that would be beyond high school freshmen—and college students can go a long step further. People who go back to college when they are in their 40s or older, as many do nowadays, are often surprised to find how much easier the work seems than when they were younger. They are better at learning because they already know more.

The information stored in memory is not, however, the entire explanation. There is another reason all of us get better and better at encoding and remembering new information as time goes on: Our classroom work and our life experiences provide us with something that is perhaps even more valuable than facts and general principles. We learn how to learn.

One need not be a great scholar. Even the monkey shown in Figure 6-10 learned to learn. Asked to perform a long series of learning tasks that were similar in general but different in detail, the monkey showed remarkable improvement. It developed what is called a *learning set*—a successful strategy for approaching the learning task. In an experiment with humans, using a similar but more difficult series of problems, the results were

Figure 6-10 What is this monkey learning?

All the monkey seems to be learning is that it will find food under one of the two objects in front of it but not under the other. When the photo was taken, the food was always under a funnel and never under a cylinder, regardless of which was on the left or right. At other times, the food was under a circle but not a rectangle, a cube but not a sphere, a black object but not a white object, and so on. At first the monkey had trouble learning where to find the food. But after the experiment had gone on long enough—with several hundred pairs of objects—the monkey mastered the problem on the very first trial. Whether or not it found the food under the first object it examined, it went almost unerringly to the correct object the next time the pair was presented (Harlow, 1949).

Given equal ability, the older person on the left may be a better learner—for reasons explained in the text.

much the same. It was also found, as might be expected, that college students were quicker to develop effective learning sets or strategies than fifth-graders. In turn the fifth-graders were quicker than preschool children (Levinson and Reese, 1967).

Using Categories

One useful strategy that all of us adopt, in one way or another, helps us deal with materials that do not at first glance seem to hang together of their own accord. We often manage to organize and encode this type of information by breaking it down into *categories*—a method best explained by the example shown in Figure 6-11. Note that the 18 words on the list, presented at random, do not seem to have much in common. They do not fall into any kind of obvious pattern—and you might think that, if you wanted to encode them into memory, you would have to learn them by rote. This is the way the experimenter's control group went about trying to memorize them—painfully and, as will be seen in a moment, without much lasting success.

Another group of subjects, however, got some help. To these subjects, the words on the list were presented in the manner shown in the diagram of Figure 6-11. The subjects were helped to see that all the words fell into the general category of minerals, that this category could be broken down into the subcategories of metals and stones, and that these subcategories could again be divided into three different kinds of metals (rare, common, and alloys) and two different kinds of stones (precious stones and stones used in masonry).

The control group and the experimental group were both asked to try to learn several such lists, containing 112 words in all, within four trials. The difference in the amounts learned by the two groups was striking. As Figure 6-12 shows, the subjects who had been helped to organize the words into categories proved far superior. They remembered all 112

Figure 6-11 An experiment on categories as an aid to encoding

The control group saw the list of 18 words presented at random. The experimental group saw them as arranged in the diagram. For how well the two groups learned and remembered, see the text and Figure 6-12.

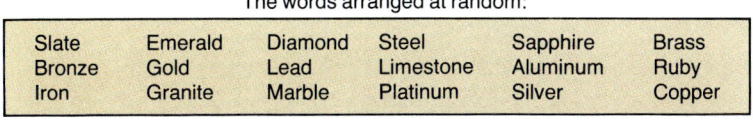

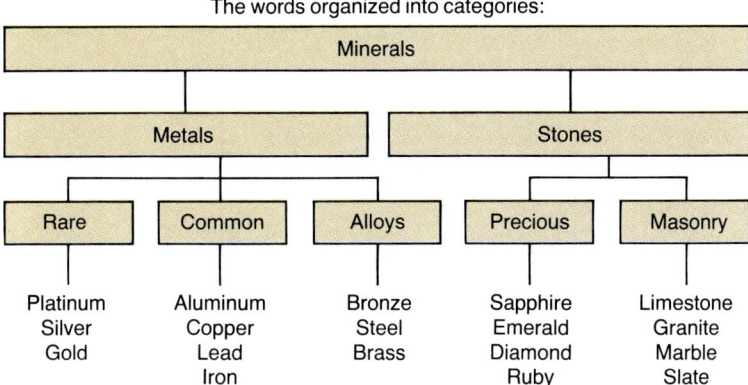

Figure 6-12 Did the categories make a difference? Yes, indeed.

The solid line shows how rapidly the experimental subjects were able to learn as a result of seeing the words in Figure 6-11 arranged in categories. Subjects who tried to memorize the words by rote (broken line) did not do nearly so well.

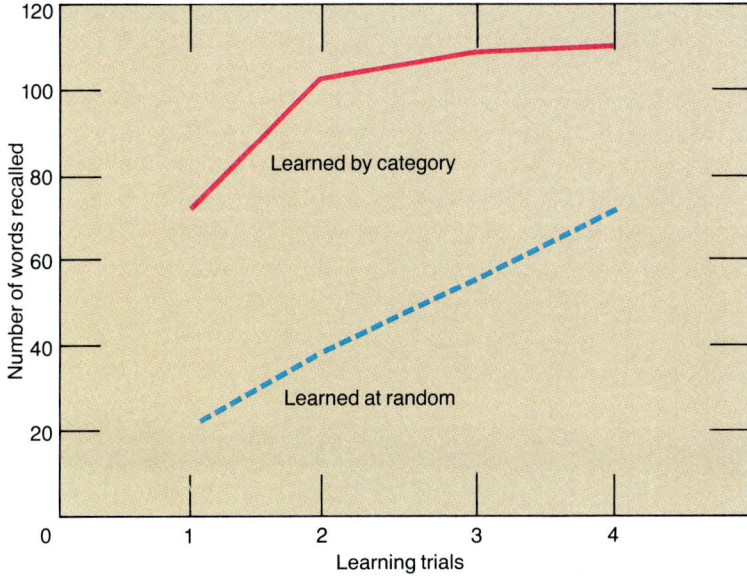

Some Strategies for Encoding   215

words perfectly on the third and fourth trials—a level never even approached by the subjects who tried to learn the words by rote (Bower et al., 1969).

Clustering—Packaging Information for Long-Term Memory

Organizing materials into categories bears considerable resemblance to the chunking process that enables us to hold seven large packages of information in short-term memory as readily as seven small individual items. In both cases a number of small units of information are lumped together into a single unit. When the process refers to short-term memory, it is called *chunking*; and when it relates to long-term memory, it is called *clustering*. Information can be organized into clusters formed by categories, by meanings, by logic, or in other ways. And information stored in some form of cluster tends to hang together in a solid unit that becomes a strong part of the associative network.

Clustering also aids retrieval. Within each tightly bound and cohesive cluster there are a number of individual items of information. In the search of memory that goes on during retrieval, we have a much better chance of finding one of many items than any single item. And when we manage to find this one item, we can pull the whole cluster of information out with it.

An example might occur on an essay examination where you are asked to define the term *stimulus generalization*. At first the meaning of the term eludes you. You seem to have forgotten it. But then, as you continue to search through your memory network, the word *stimulus* leads you to the term *conditioned stimulus*—and thus to the whole package of information that falls into the category of classical conditioning. Out pour all the facts you have clustered there, including the meaning of *stimulus generalization*.

One interesting way we encode clusters into long-term memory is demonstrated by how much we remember of the things we read, such as stories. If the story moves in a straight line, with one event leading logically to the next, we can usually remember a good deal of it. If the story jumps around, switching from one point of view to another, we are less likely to remember it (Black, Turner, and Bower, 1979).

We seem particularly adept at clustering together materials that have a cause-and-effect relationship that binds them into a logical entity. An indication comes from an experiment in which two groups of college students studied slightly different versions of the same story. Version 1 contained pairs of sentences like these:

> He lowered the flames and walked over to the refrigerator, seeing a bowl he had left on the table. Suddenly it fell off the edge and broke.
>
> While he was sitting on a huge log he found an old pocket knife. He felt sad as they took a few more pictures and headed back.

In version 2 the sentence pairs were changed to read like this:

> He lowered the flames and walked over to the refrigerator, bumping a bowl he had left on the table. Suddenly it fell off the edge and broke.
>
> While he was sitting on a huge log he lost an old pocket knife. He felt sad as they took a few more pictures and headed back.

Note that the changes, though small, create a cause-and-effect relationship in the version 2 sentence pairs that does not occur in version 1. *Bumping a bowl* (version 2) is a logical reason for the bowl to fall off the table; *seeing a bowl* (version 1) is not. Someone who *lost an old pocket knife* is likely to have felt sad, while someone who *found an old pocket knife* is not. As

Figure 6-13 If one event causes another, you are likely to remember both

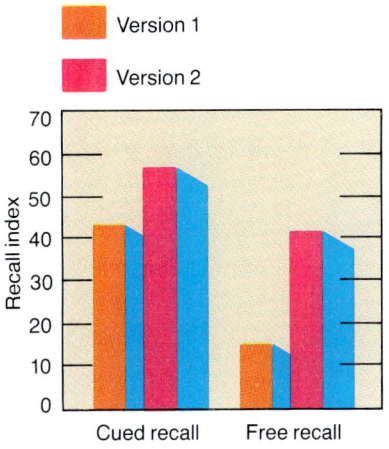

The bars show the results of the experiment, described in detail in the text, with two versions of the same story. Note how much more was remembered by subjects who read version 2 (the cause-and-effect version) than subjects who read version 1—when tested for either "free recall" (how much they remembered without prompting) or "cued recall" (how well they could remember the second of two sentences after the first was read to them).

is illustrated in Figure 6-13, establishing the cause-and-effect relationship produced a significantly better memory for the version 2 sentences (Black and Bern, 1981).

Similarly, it has been demonstrated that one good way to remember a list of unrelated items is to make up a story about them that ties them all together. Let us say, for example, that you are going to a supermarket to buy the following 10 items, listed in the order you would find them along the route you take through the aisles:

1. coffee
2. hamburger
3. charcoal
4. milk
5. paper cups
6. light bulbs
7. matches
8. facial tissues
9. broom
10. dog food

One way you can be almost sure of remembering everything in proper order is to make up a story like the one presented in Figure 6-14. Such stories have been found remarkably helpful. The experiment in Figure 6-15, for example, found an extremely large difference in recall of word lists between subjects who wove the words into stories and subjects who did not.

Storing Visual Information in Memory

Made-up stories are particularly helpful if you try to form a mental picture or image of the events, like the drawings in Figure 6-14. Studies have shown that there are many situations in which the use of *imagery* helps to encode, remember, and retrieve information (Bower, 1972). One reason seems to be that we have an extraordinary ability to remember visual information. This was demonstrated in a famous experiment in which subjects looked at a set of over 600 colored pictures—then were tested on how many they could recognize when the pictures were shown again, now paired with another picture they had not seen before. In all the subjects spotted 97 percent of the original pictures—a far better performance than could ever be attained with the same large number of words (Shepard, 1967).

Some Strategies for Encoding

Figure 6-14 Remembering a shopping list

The ten supermarket items listed in the text can be easily recalled in order by making up this story: I was sitting in my kitchen one evening drinking a cup of coffee *when my neighbor came in with her child to invite me to a Saturday cookout. She said we would grill* hamburgers *over* charcoal. *I asked her to sit down and join me for coffee, and I poured the child some* milk *in a* paper cup. *While we were talking the* light bulb *burned out, and my neighbor lit some* matches *to help me replace the bulb. In the darkness the child spilled some milk, and we wiped it up with* facial tissues. *I heard my dog at the door and went to let it in. There was another dog that wanted to enter, but I chased it away with a* broom *and fed my pet its* dog food *while my neighbor and I finished our coffee (after Bower, 1978).*

Figure 6-15 How well do made-up stories work? *Extremely* well.

The graph lines show the results of an experiment in which one group of students made up stories to help them remember a dozen lists of words, while a control group was merely asked to try to memorize the lists. When tested later, the subjects who made up stories remembered their lists almost perfectly. The other subjects had forgotten most of their words (Bower and Clark, 1969).

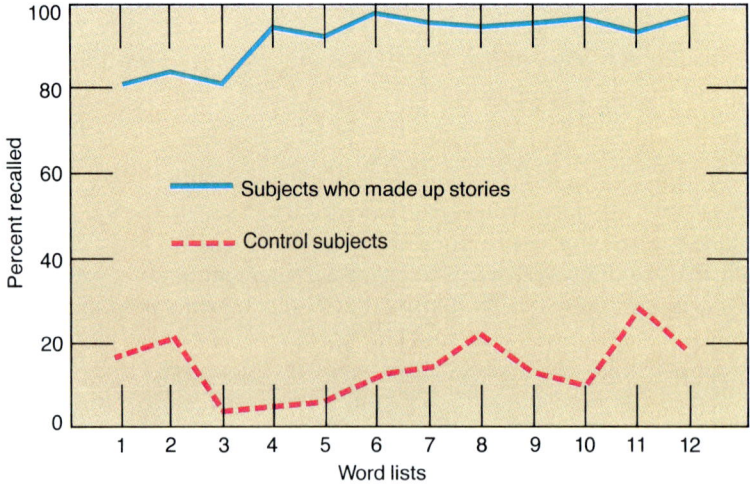

218 Chapter 6 How We Remember and Why We Forget

Psychology in Everyday Life
Making up Your Own System for Remembering

In ancient Greece, orators used to develop devices to help them remember the points they wanted to make in their long speeches. We now call such devices *mnemonic*—after the Greek word for memory. The method of the ancient orators was based on the spatial arrangement of a temple with which they were thoroughly familiar—that is, the order in which they walked past the doorways, rooms, statues, and other objects within the temple walls. For each location, they created a mental image associating the spot with a topic in their speech. For example, if they wanted to start by discussing medicine, they might visualize a famous physician of the day pushing through the temple entrance. To try this method yourself, you can base it on the layout of your home, its rooms, and its prominent pieces of furniture.

A somewhat more complicated mnemonic system, for remembering things like shopping lists or chores to be done during the day, has been used in a number of psychological experiments and found extremely helpful. You begin by memorizing this jingle:

> One is a bun; two is a shoe;
> Three is a tree; four is a door;
> Five is a hive; six is sticks;
> Seven is heaven; eight is a gate;
> Nine is wine; ten is a hen.

To use this device to help remember the supermarket shopping list mentioned earlier, the trick is to form a mental image connecting the items on the list (coffee, hamburger, and so on) with the words in the jingle that rhyme with the numbers (bun-one, shoe-two, and so on). Similar systems, more elaborate in that they can provide memory hooks for as many as 100 items, are the secret behind the seemingly incredible feats performed by the "memory experts" who quickly learn long lists of objects or people's names. For remembering things that do not hang together through any organization or logic, mnemonic devices are unquestionably useful. One reason is that they take advantage of the well-established value of imagery. Another is that they provide a ready-made framework into which the new information can be clustered.

Some simple little mnemonic devices with which you are probably familiar include the jingle that begins "Thirty days hath September" (for remembering how many days there are in each month), the sentence "Every good boy does fine" (for remembering the notes in music), and "I left port" (for remembering the difference between the port, or left side, of a ship and the starboard, or right side). Note that the value of all mnemonic aids is limited to materials that would otherwise have to be encoded and stored by rote. For most of the knowledge we acquire, there is no substitute for the kind of information processing that seeks meanings, organization, relationships, and rules.

The ability to encode visual information and imagery is the basis of most techniques called *mnemonic devices*, discussed in a Psychology in Everyday Life box, "Making up Your Own System for Remembering."

One interesting sidelight is that lower animals encode considerable amounts of information into memory without the help of language—which makes possible the search for meaning and organization that characterizes so much of human encoding. Studies show that even a monkey, an animal far lower in intellectual development than its cousin the chimpanzee, can perform much like a human being on a test of memory for pictures (Sands and Wright, 1982). Encoding visual characteristics seems to be a more fundamental skill than the human encoding of verbal information—but we do not know whether the two are different in kind or merely in degree.

SUMMARY

The range of human memory

1. Memories may last from a fraction of a second to a lifetime. The range is divided into three stages of memory: (a) *sensory*, (b) *short-term*, and (c) *long-term*.

2. *Sensory memory* is made up of the lingering traces of information sent to the brain by the senses. The information is forgotten within a second unless transferred to short-term memory.

3. *Short-term memory* has a capacity of about seven unrelated items of information, which are forgotten within about 30 seconds unless further processing takes place.

4. The information processing in short-term memory includes: (a) *scanning* of the information in sensory memory and selection of some items as worthy of attention, (b) *encoding* of information (to make it simple and easy to handle), (c) *rehearsal* (to keep information in mind for more than 30 seconds), and (d) further encoding that results in *transfer* of the information to long-term memory.

5. Encoding can take the form of a *schema*, or mental picture that represents the information to be remembered, the verbal meaning of the information, or its physical characteristics.

6. Through rehearsal, information can be kept in short-term memory as long as desired—though the amount of information that can be kept alive is quite small. From a list of learned items, we are most likely to remember the earlier and later portions rather than the middle items. This is called the *primacy effect* and the *recency effect* in short-term memory.

7. *Long-term memory* is a more or less permanent storehouse of information.

8. *Retrieval* is the process that recalls information held in long-term memory back to short-term memory, where we can actively think about it and use it.

9. Exactly what happens inside the nervous system when we store information in long-term memory is not known. Psychologists say that a *memory trace* has been established, but they can only speculate as to what this trace is, how it is formed, and why it sometimes seems to persist forever and sometimes seems to vanish.

10. Formation of the memory trace seems to depend at least in part on: (a) the brain's *neurotransmitters* and (b) the strengthening of existing synapses rather than the addition of new ones.

11. Neurotransmitters are the chemicals that pass along messages from one neuron to another. It appears that neurotransmitters increase the efficiency of the *synapse*. The neurotransmitter that has received attention in recent years is *acetylcholine*, which appears to be decreased in patients suffering from *Alzheimer's disease*, a disorder of the brain whose victims suffer progressive deterioration of the memory and other intellectual functions.

Why do we forget?

12. How well people remember and how much they forget cannot be measured directly but only by how well they *perform* on tests of memory. Three methods used by psychologists to test performance are: (a) *recall*, (b) *recognition*, and (c) *relearning*.

13. Tests of performance show that we often quickly forget much of what we have just

learned, but remember at least some of it for a long time. The fact that we forget rapidly at first but more slowly later on is shown by the *curve of forgetting*.

14. There are four theories of why we forget, all of which may be true at least in part and at times: (a) *fading of the memory trace,* (b) *failure in retrieval,* (c) *interference from other information stored in memory,* and (d) *motivated forgetting,* or forgetting because we want to forget.

15. Some kinds of information are more easily retrieved in the same physical setting in which the learning took place. Such memory for particular events, or episodes, is referred to as *episodic memory*; this is in contrast to memory for items independent of the specific occasion in which we learned them, referred to as *generic memory*.

16. When old information causes us to forget new information, the process is called *proactive interference*. The opposite, when new information causes us to forget old information, is called *retroactive interference*.

Encoding and transfer

17. The manner in which we encode and transfer information to long-term memory determines how well we will be able to remember and retrieve it.

18. In the process called *chunking*, we combine a number of individual units of information into one package—such as when we combine the seven letters UCPIRTE into the single word PICTURE.

19. Chunking increases the scope of short-term memory, which can hold around seven big packages of information about as well as it can handle seven small items. In the interaction between short-term and long-term memory, information is often transferred to storage in chunks.

20. The prevailing view is the *associative network theory,* which describes memory as a complex network in which countless items of information are connected and interconnected by long and far-reaching strands of association.

21. The theory holds that we encode new information into long-term memory by noting how it relates to what we have already stored—and thus add it to the network with all the appropriate associations of existing information.

22. Sometimes we encode and can retrieve a faithful copy of the information—as when we recite a familiar poem word for word. More frequently we engage in *constructive processing*—encoding and retrieving the theme or underlying meaning and trying to fill in the details, sometimes accurately and sometimes not. It has been said that memory is often "unreliable, given to invention, and even dangerous."

The encoding process and learning

23. How well we remember generally depends on how well we have learned in the first place—that is, on how thoroughly we understand new information and how many associations we find between new and old.

24. Finding meaning and organization is useful in forming associations. It is generally more effective to learn by *rule* (trying to understand the underlying principles) than by *rote* (simply trying to memorize materials by repeating them mechanically without any regard to what they mean).

25. The *law of overlearning* states: After you have learned something, continuing to work at learning it tends to increase the length of time you will remember it.

Some strategies for encoding

26. *Clustering* is the encoding and storing into long-term memory of information organized into packages composed of a number of small units (like chunking in short-term memory). Clusters of information can be formed by categories, meaning, logic, or in other ways.
27. *Made-up stories* are a method of clustering items of information that would not otherwise hang together. Made-up stories are particularly helpful if you try to form a mental picture or image of the event.
28. *Imagery* is helpful because we have an extraordinary ability to remember visual information—a fact that has led some psychologists to believe we have two separate ways of encoding and storing information—one for physical attributes and the other for knowledge that can be put into words.
29. *Mnemonic devices* are tricks, like the "Thirty days hath September" jingle, that help provide a memory framework for materials that otherwise would have to be learned by rote. Many mnemonic devices rely on imagery for their effectiveness.

IMPORTANT TERMS

acetylcholine	neurotransmitter
Alzheimer's disease	overlearning, law of
amnesia	primacy effect
associative network	proactive interference
categories	recall
chunking	recency effect
clustering	recognition
consolidation	rehearsal
constructive processing	relearning
curve of forgetting	retrieval
encoding	retroactive interference
episodic memory	RNA
generic memory	rote
imagery	rule
learning set	scanning
long-term memory	schema
made-up stories	sensory memory
memory trace	short-term memory
mnemonic devices	synapse
motivated forgetting	transfer

RECOMMENDED READINGS

Cohen, G., Eysenck, M. W., and Le Voi, M. E. *Memory: a cognitive approach*. Philadelphia: Open University Press, 1986.

Ellis, H., and Hunt, R. R. *Fundamentals of human memory and cognition*, 3rd ed. Dubuque, Iowa: Brown, 1983.

Estes, W. K., ed. *Handbook of learning and cognitive processes*, Vol. 6. Hillsdale, N.J.: Erlbaum, 1979.

Harris, J. E., and Morris, P. E. *Everyday memory: actions and absent-mindedness*. Orlando: Academic Press, 1984.

Kintsch, W. *Memory and cognition*. New York: Wiley, 1977.

Klatzky, R. L. *Memory and awareness: an information-processing perspective*. New York: W. H. Freeman, 1984.

Nilsson, L. G., ed. *Memory problems and processes*. Hillsdale, N.J.: Erlbaum, 1979.

Tulving, E. *Elements of episodic memory*. New York: Oxford University Press, 1983.

CHAPTER 7
LANGUAGE AND THOUGHT

THE ROLE, STRUCTURE, AND RULES OF LANGUAGE 227
The basic sounds that make up language
Units of meaning: the morphemes
From words to sentences: vocabulary and grammar
The rules of syntax

HOW WE PRODUCE AND UNDERSTAND MESSAGES 229
Problems of the speaker
Problems of the listener

THE REMARKABLE FEAT OF LEARNING LANGUAGE 231
From babbling sounds to coherent language
Human interaction and language skills
Discovering grammar
How parents help—and how children help themselves
Theories of language learning
The "language" of apes

CONCEPTS: WORDS THAT DO DOUBLE DUTY 239
Concepts without words
The enriching interplay between language and concepts
How concepts help us think: the drawing of inferences
The role of concepts in learning and memory

But the puzzle remains: precisely what is a concept?
Does language distort the way we view the world?
Or do we develop language to match the world about us?
New language through new thinking

HOW WE THINK AND SOLVE PROBLEMS 247
Rules and premises as bases for thinking
When thinking is logical—and illogical
Problem solving: algorithms and heuristics
Pitfall 1: failure to analyze the problem
Pitfall 2: thinking what we would like to think
Pitfall 3: functional fixedness
Pitfall 4: relying on what is readily available

SUMMARY 255

IMPORTANT TERMS 257

RECOMMENDED READINGS 257

PSYCHOLOGY IN EVERYDAY LIFE
A flexible language for a complex society 230
How can our schools educate kids who do not speak "standard English"? 234

The two previous chapters have shown that learning brings us information about the world we live in and that memory serves as its storehouse. The question now becomes: How do we *use* this information.

One way we use our knowledge is to *communicate* with others—and thus engage in the cooperative activities essential to carry on the basic tasks of human society. In every society ever known, we humans have developed a language that conveys messages understood by all of us, enabling us to work, play, and live together. We use language to tell each other how we feel, what we need, what we desire. We use it to amuse ourselves in conversation, to form friendships, and to help one another grow and transport food, build houses and office skyscrapers, and manufacture and distribute clothing. With language, we can express everything from a child's simple request for a glass of milk, to a lover's declaration of passion, to the most complex scientific theories.

You will quickly appreciate the importance of language if you find yourself in a foreign country, not knowing a word of the native tongue and unable to find anyone who speaks English. You cannot ask for or receive directions. You cannot order food, except by pointing. You cannot ask for a physician, except by making gestures of distress. If you do find a doctor, you cannot describe your symptoms. You might be able to communicate to some extent through facial expressions and gestures—but otherwise you are almost as helpless as a baby who has not yet learned to talk.

Language helps us acquire information by providing labels for the objects and events in the environment. It helps us encode information into memory by providing many of the linkages in the associative network of memory. It helps us think and solve problems. Indeed, much of the thinking we do would be impossible without the use of words and the ideas they represent.

Language communicates thoughts and feelings.

THE ROLE, STRUCTURE, AND RULES OF LANGUAGE

In evolutionary terms, language is a "uniquely human activity" that gives us a tremendous advantage over all other animals (Miller, 1981). In coping with the environment we need not discover everything all by ourselves. Instead we can profit from the knowledge that our fellow human beings have acquired. Written language makes available to us the recorded learning of the past—the philosophies of the ancient Greeks, the mathematical systems of the ancient Arabs, the scientific discoveries of Galileo. Thanks to language, each of us knows more than any one person, starting from scratch, could discover in a thousand lifetimes.

The origin of human language is lost in the mists of antiquity. But we can assume that its first purpose was to exchange messages of vital concern to survival—to enable people to *communicate* with one another about food supplies and how to obtain them, about danger and how to avoid it. Other animals, lower on the evolutionary scale, also manage to do this in one way or another. Bees that have found a new food supply go back to the hive and perform a dance, the nature and speed of which tell the other bees how to get to the food (Von Frisch, 1950). Chimpanzees use sounds and gestures to warn their friends of danger and to threaten their enemies. But only humans have ever developed a method of exchanging so many messages of so many varied and complex meanings.

The Basic Sounds That Make Up Language

Basically language is an agreement among those of us who speak the same language that certain sounds, put together according to rules that all of us know and use, convey meaningful messages intended by the speaker and understood by the listener. The sounds that constitute language depend on the capacity of the human brain and vocal cords to produce them—and the number is limited. This may seem hard to believe, in view of the apparent complexity and variety of all of the sentences that can be heard in the halls of the United Nations—but it is true. No language contains more than 85 basic sounds, and some contain as few as 15. English has about 40, or a few more depending on regional dialects.

The basic sounds, called *phonemes*, might be described as the building blocks of language. In English, the phonemes include such sounds as the short *a* in *pat*, the long *a* in *pate*, the consonant *p* as in either *pat* or *pate*, the *ch* in *chip*, the *th* in *the*, and the *sh* in *shop*. Thus the word *pat* contains three phonemes. By changing any of the three, you can produce many different words. Changing the first phoneme will give you *bat, cat, chat*, and so on. Changing the second creates *pate, pet, pit, pout*, and others. A new sound at the end creates *pack, pad, pal, pan*, and more. If you play around with the word *pat* in this way, changing just one of the three phonemes at a time, you will find that you can produce more than 30 different words.

Units of Meaning: The Morphemes

By themselves, the phonemes usually have no meaning. (Although some meaningful units, like the first person pronoun *I*, are made up of a single phoneme.) But they can be put together, in combinations of two or more, to form units that do have meaning. For example, we can start with the phoneme *t*, add the phoneme pronounced as *ee*, then add the phoneme *ch*, and arrive at the combination *teach*. The result is called a *morpheme*—a combination of phonemes that possesses meaning in and of itself. Like *teach*, many morphemes are words. Others are prefixes or suffixes, which can in turn be combined with other morphemes to form words. For example, we can combine the three morphemes *un* (a prefix), *teach* (a word in itself), and *able* (a suffix) to form the word *unteachable*. Or we can start with the same morpheme *teach*, add *-er* (meaning *one who*) and *-s* (to denote the plural), and form the word *teachers*. The plural *-s* is one of the most commonly used morphemes, as is *-ed* to indicate the past tense of a verb (walk*ed*, talk*ed*).

Some very long words represent a single morpheme—for example, *hippopotamus*. But most long words are combinations of morphemes and therefore of meanings. Note the following:

$$\underbrace{\text{piti}}_{1} \underbrace{\text{ful}}_{2}$$

$$\underbrace{\text{dis}}_{1} \underbrace{\text{joint}}_{2} \underbrace{\text{ed}}_{3}$$

$$\underbrace{\text{in}}_{1} \underbrace{\text{sur}}_{2} \underbrace{\text{mount}}_{3} \underbrace{\text{able}}_{4}$$

The building blocks of language, though simple, make possible a tremendous variety of expression. The 40 English phonemes (which are written using only the 26 letters of the alphabet) are combined in various ways to produce more than 100,000 morphemes. These are in turn combined with one another to produce the 600,000 or more words found in the largest dictionaries.

From Words to Sentences: Vocabulary and Grammar

Words alone, however, are not enough to make language possible. True, we must understand and agree on what is called *semantics*, or the meaning of the morphemes and words in our language. But, in addition, we must know how to string the words together into meaningful sentences. Thus every language has two essential elements: (1) a *vocabulary* of meaningful morphemes and words, and (2) a set of rules, called *grammar*, for combining the words into an almost infinite number of sentences that can be constructed to express an almost infinite variety of semantic meanings. In this book alone there are thousands of sentences that you have never before encountered, yet whose meaning you understand immediately.

Vocabularies differ from one language to another, of course, and often greatly. The English word *house* is *maison* in French and *casa* in Spanish, and in Chinese it is pronounced something like *ook*. The rules of grammar, however, though they vary in detail, share some basic similarities in all languages—including the dead languages of the past as well as those spoken today. Presumably this is because people everywhere have the same abilities and limitations in the use of language (Clark and Clark, 1977).

The Rules of Syntax

Among the most important rules of grammar are those called *syntax*, which relate to sentence structure. The rules of syntax regulate the manner in which nouns, verbs, adjectives, and adverbs are placed in proper order to form phrases—and the way the phrases are combined to form sentences that convey a meaning readily understood by anyone who speaks the language. Without these rules, language would be a jumble. For example, even very young children know the meaning of the individual names and words *Bill, quickly, who, the, down, was, street, saw, walking, John, a, sweater, his, in, yellow, friend*. But when presented in that order, the words do not convey any message. Rearranged according to the rules of syntax, they become the meaningful sentence:

John, who was walking quickly down the street, saw his friend Bill in a yellow sweater.

If that is the message you want to convey about John and Bill, you have to arrange the words in that order. Any change in the arrangement might convey an entirely different meaning, as for example:

John, who was in a yellow sweater, quickly saw his friend Bill walking down the street.

Bill saw his friend John, who was walking quickly down the street in a yellow sweater.

You will find that you can use the 16 words to express several other meaningful sentences, simply by altering the syntax.

The rules of syntax vary somewhat from language to language. Thus we place adjectives before nouns (*red house*), while the French place them after the nouns (*maison rouge*). Some languages permit the speaker to say "Ice the man slipped on" to emphasize it was ice that caused the person to fall. But the pattern has a logic: "what belongs together mentally is placed close together syntactically" (Vennemann, 1975). We may not be aware of all the rules either as children or as adults, but we follow them even if we cannot explain what they are. In combination with the agreed-on meanings of morphemes and words, rules are the magic key to human communication (Chomsky, 1965). They probably form the only kind of system that could meet the needs of our civilization—as explained in a Psychology in Everyday Life box titled "A Flexible Language for a Complex Society."

HOW WE PRODUCE AND UNDERSTAND MESSAGES

Producing language—speaking or writing new sentences created on the spot—requires thinking and planning. Understanding language also demands the most complex kind of mental activity.

Especially in the case of the spoken word, communication depends on close cooperation between speaker and listener. The speaker, having a purpose in mind, must carefully choose words and produce sentences that will "get the message across." The listener then must interpret the meaning and intention of the combination of sounds reaching the ear.

Suppose, for example, you are in a room with a friend who is sitting near a window. You want the window opened wider. How, exactly, shall you phrase the suggestion? From all the possible words and syntactic arrangements available, you decide to say, "It's hot in here." Now your friend has to do some processing—for the words "It's hot in here" can be interpreted in a number of different ways. Your friend has to decide: Were you merely stating a fact? Do you mean that you want the window opened wider—or shut? Are you perhaps suggesting that both of you move to a different room? The possibilities have to be considered and accepted or rejected. Your friend will probably get the message, but not without working at it. For both speaker and listener, the use of language "makes full contact with our full cognitive abilities" (Clark and Clark, 1977).

Problems of the Speaker

One way to get some idea of the difficulty of producing language is to make a tape recording of some of your own utterances, especially when you are trying to explain something fairly

Psychology in Everyday Life
A Flexible Language for a Complex Society

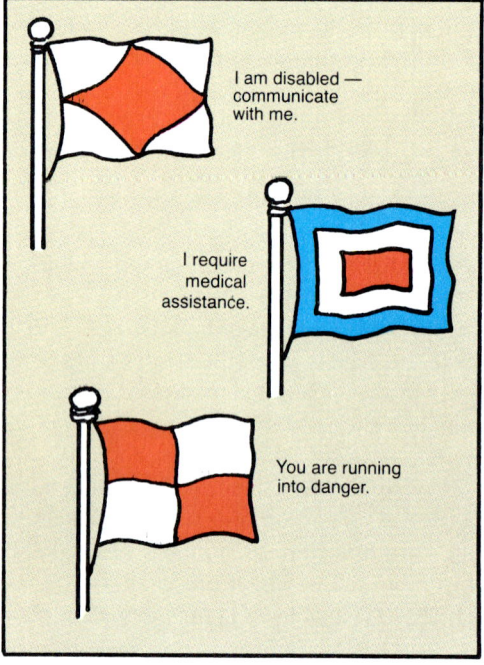

The flags shown here are three of the signals used in an international system of communication among ships at sea. Each of them conveys a single, simple message—in two cases a request for a specific kind of help, in the other a specific warning.

Suppose that your language, which is your own communications system, worked the same way. For each idea that you wanted to express—everything from "Let's eat" to "Psychology is the systematic study of behavior"—you would need a separate "flag" of some kind, in the form of a spoken or written word. How many flags or spoken words—each conveying only one simple message—would you need to convey everything that you now say in the course of an ordinary day? How long would it take just to tell a classmate that you would like to go along to a movie but have a history examination tomorrow and must study, and besides you have to do some laundry and return a book to the library—so all in all, though you appreciate the invitation and would like a rain check, you feel you must say no?

How long would it take to write a letter to a relative explaining what you have been studying in this psychology course? How many pages would the letter run, and how much postage would it cost?

The number of flags you would need, each conveying its own message, is almost beyond imagination. In fact, no matter how many flags you had, you would not be able to communicate more than a fraction of what you now do. Most of the thoughts you express in the course of an ordinary day take the form of sentences you have never used or heard before. You make the messages up on the spot. Your listeners, in most cases, have never before heard the same combination of words. If you were a ship captain, you would be constantly designing and sewing up new flags. Your listeners, never having seen the flags before, would not have the faintest idea what they meant.

Thus the flags used by ship captains, though valuable in their own specific way, lack the all-purpose flexibility of human language. Our system, combining the simple building blocks of a small number of phonemes according to the established rules of grammar, enables us to exchange an unlimited number and variety of messages. It would be difficult indeed to imagine any other system that could possibly enable us to live in the complex societies we have developed.

complicated. Hearing the tape afterward, you will probably be shocked at how tongue-tied you sound, for the spoken word is not nearly so smooth and fluent as is generally believed. As we talk, we often have to stop and think. Our speech is full of long pauses, *and-uhs* and *ers*. We make mistakes or fail to express ourselves clearly and have to amend our utterances with phrases like *I mean* or *that is to say*. Sometimes we stop in the middle of a sentence, leave it unfinished and start all over. We make "slips of the tongue" and end up saying something quite different from what we intended, often when we are preoccupied or distracted (Reason, 1984).

When we produce sentences, we must first think of the meaning we want to convey—perhaps a message that will be several sentences long. Then we have to plan each sentence and each part of a sentence. We have to find the right words to flesh out the sentence and then put the words in their proper places. Finally we have to command all the muscles we use in speech to carry out the program we have planned—even as we are mentally racing ahead to what we want to say next (Clark and Clark, 1977).

Problems of the Listener

When you listen to someone speak, and try to interpret the meaning and intent, you have to engage in what is probably an even more difficult form of information processing. The only raw data you have are the sound waves produced by the speaker's voice and transmitted through the air to your ears. Ordinarily these waves meet with considerable competition from other sounds elsewhere in the vicinity. Other people are carrying on conversations in the same room. Footsteps thud against the floor. A telephone rings. A door slams. You may think you hear every word and every syllable uttered by the speaker—but in fact you do not. Many of the sounds are blotted out.

Even if you heard all the words, your ears could not immediately identify them. Many English words sound pretty much alike—for example *writer* and *rider, wave* and *waif.* Moreover, most of us are very careless about the way we pronounce words. We say not *I'm going to* but *I'm gonna*, not *Won't you* but *Woncha?*, not *Give me* but *Gimme.* Regional accents further confuse matters. Bostonians say not *Harvard* but *Havad.* Many Southerners say not *whether* but *whethah.*

Two psychologists once made high-fidelity tape recordings of some everyday conversations, then cut up the tapes so that they could play back separate portions—anything from a single word to longer phrases. Listeners to these excerpts had a hard time recognizing what they heard. When they listened to a single word, they failed to identify it more than half the time. Even when they heard a phrase three words long, they missed it nearly 30 percent of the time (Pollack and Pickett, 1964). What this shows is that making sense out of the sound waves that strike our ears is as difficult as trying to read a page on which paint has been splattered, making it impossible to recognize many of the words.

In listening we carry out many mental processes all at the same time. We simultaneously try to recognize sounds, identify words, look for syntactic patterns, and search for semantic meaning. When sounds and words are in themselves vague or unintelligible—as so often happens in everyday speech—the processing for syntax and semantics creates order out of chaos (Clark and Clark, 1977). All this takes place so smoothly that we are not even aware of the mental work we do when listening or the handicaps we overcome.

THE REMARKABLE FEAT OF LEARNING LANGUAGE

Considering the mental work required to produce and understand language, it seems almost a miracle that children learn to use it so quickly. Yet they do—including children growing up in a home where two different languages are spoken. During the second year of life, such children are already able to understand that a certain word in English has the same meaning as another word in the second language. One mother kept a diary describing her child, who was learning both English and Estonian. By the age of

The growing capacity to use language is one of the most remarkable feats of the early years.

two, the child knew enough to use English when speaking to people outside the home, and Estonian while speaking to relatives inside (Vihman, 1985).

By the end of their second year, many children are already speaking such sentences as "Baby drink milk." By the age of 5, they understand the meaning of about 2,000 words (Smith, 1926). By about the age of 6, they have learned virtually all the basic rules of grammar. They can string words together according to the rules to create meaningful new sentences of their own. And they understand the meaning of sentences they have never heard before. By the time they are ten, children are able to produce a veritable torrent of language—about 20,000 to 30,000 words each day (Wagner, 1985).

From Babbling Sounds to Coherent Language

Everything about the use of language must be learned except how to create the sounds, which is an inborn ability common to all normal children. Early in life, all babies begin to produce many sounds that resemble the phonemes of language—presumably because of movements of the muscles of the mouth, throat, and vocal cords associated with breathing, swallowing, and hiccupping. This "*babbling*" occurs spontaneously. It is not an attempt to imitate sounds that have been heard—as was demonstrated by observations of a deaf baby whose parents were deaf and mute. This baby never heard a sound, yet did the same kind of babbling as any other child (Lenneberg, 1967).

It appears that children of all nationalities make the same sounds in their earliest babbling. It has been found, for example, that there are no differences among the babbling sounds of infants born to families that speak English, Russian, or Chinese (Atkinson, MacWhinny, and Stoel, 1970). American infants have been observed to utter sounds that are not used by English-speaking adults but only by people who speak French or German (Miller, 1951). Soon, however, babies begin to concentrate on the sounds appropriate to their own language, which they hear from their parents and others around them. The other sounds, not used in English, fade away through disuse.

Sadly for those of us who try to learn foreign languages after we have grown up, these other sounds often disappear completely. Many of us who try to learn French or German are never able to pronounce some of the phonemes properly, even though we may have done so quite naturally when we were babies. This fact has an important bearing on one of the current debates over public policy in education, as explained in a box on Psychology in Everyday Life titled "How Can Our Schools Educate Kids Who Do Not Speak 'Standard English'?"

Human Interaction and Language Skills

As for how children learn all the many other things required for the use of language, psychologists have some clues and some theories—but as yet they have found no single and totally satisfactory explanation. About all that can be said for certain is that children acquire language faster if they are spoken to frequently and distinctly as part of their social interactions.

Mere exposure without interaction does not appear to be enough. A case has been reported of a boy named Jim, the son of deaf parents who used only sign language. As deaf parents often do, they encouraged him to listen frequently to radio and television, to make up for their own inability to provide him with the sounds of speech. Although Jim had normal hearing and speech ability, he did not seem to profit much from his experiences with television. In his preschool years he knew only a few advertising jingles and some words he had probably picked up from playmates. He lagged far behind other children his age until arrangements were made for an adult from outside the home to engage him regularly in direct, two-way conversation (Sachs and Johnson, 1976). Similarly, it has been noted that children in the Netherlands who listen regularly to nearby German television stations do not ordinarily learn any German as a result (Snow et al., 1976).

In interaction between child and mother or some other intimate caretaker, the two communicate from the very beginning. In speaking to their babies, mothers and other caretakers use a special tone of voice, rhythm, and style—called "motherese"—that seems to help stimulate linguistic development since it is especially well suited to the young infant's perceptual and attentional capacities (Fernald, 1983). When mothers of infants a few days old are asked to speak in this fashion without their children present, they actually

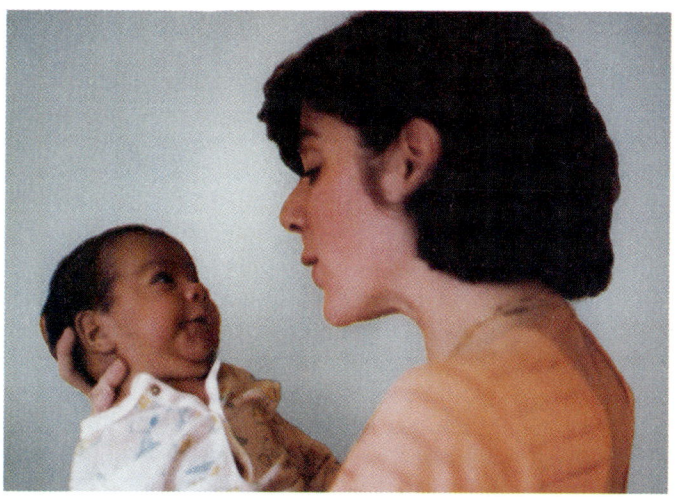

By speaking to her baby, this mother is fostering the development of language.

Psychology in Everyday Life
How Can Our Schools Educate Kids Who Do Not Speak "Standard English"?

The United States, as a melting pot for people from all over the world and with many different language backgrounds, has always faced a serious educational problem. Today the problem centers mostly on the Spanish-speaking population. We have more than 14 million citizens of Hispanic origin—including many children who have grown up in homes where only Spanish is spoken. These children—like their predecessors from homes where only Italian or German or Polish or Yiddish was spoken—often face serious difficulties in acquiring knowledge in English-speaking schools.

How can these children receive the American ideal of equal educational opportunity? One possible way—urged by many Spanish-speaking parents—is to have them taught in Spanish by Spanish-speaking teachers. It has been suggested that this should be done throughout the early grades of elementary school. Later, English would be introduced and taught as a second language (as many English-speaking American children are now taught Spanish or French). Even after the children began to learn English, they would continue to devote as much time to Spanish and Latin-American history and culture as to United States history and English literature.

The suggestion has considerable appeal. It would preserve a cultural heritage—that is, fluency in the language of origin and familiarity with the traditions and customs of the Spanish-speaking world. Especially for children in the early grades, it would avoid the dislocations and handicaps of attending schools that use an unfamiliar language—and possibly the learned helplessness caused by failure.

But to function fully and efficiently as members of our English-speaking society, all children must eventually become adept at English. And psychological findings raise some serious questions about delaying the process. There is no evidence that growing up in a two-language home poses a problem for most children. In fact, economically disadvantaged children who learn both Spanish and English have a slight advantage in intellectual skills (Diaz, 1985). Moreover, as the text states, the ability to pronounce unused phonemes decreases with age. Most people who acquire a new language after childhood never manage to speak it without an accent (Oyama, 1973). Indeed, learning a new language at all becomes more difficult, for reasons that are not entirely understood.

Thus Spanish-speaking schools represent a trade-off, with certain advantages but also some dangers that would not be apparent without psychology's studies of language. The same findings apply to children from homes where American Indian languages are spoken, and also to black children whose parents speak what is sometimes called "black English" as opposed to "standard English." Black English is almost a lan-

speak quite differently (Fernald and Simon, 1984). Somehow, partly as a result of this early interaction, and also, of course, as a result of the child's own developing cognitive capacities, the child quickly acquires an understanding of the structure of language and a mastery of the processes of producing and understanding it (Gleitman, Newport, and Gleitman, 1984).

The first accomplishment of children is to speak a few meaningful single words that name objects: *baby, mama, milk*. A few months later, they begin to string two words together by adding a verb: *baby walk, see mama*. The average length of their utterances increases as shown in Figure 7-1 (page 236). Some children learn more quickly than others—but all normal children show steady and consistent progress. After their second birthday, the tendency of babies to use speech rather than gestures to communicate becomes increas-

guage of its own, with its own rules of pronunciation and grammar. Where standard English calls for the sentence *I asked John if he played baseball*, for example, black English calls for *I asked John do he play baseball*. In the way it applies its rules, black English is just as consistent as any other language (Farb, 1974). Some linguists feel that it is more direct and expressive than standard English as spoken by many middle-class Americans. It does, however, create problems for children who, though fluent in black English, must cope with schools—and later with a society—in which a very different language is demanded. How can education be best tailored to such students?

What kind of difficulties do these Hispanic children face in their English-speaking school?

ingly strong (Shore, O'Connell, and Bates, 1984). The child's acquisition of words proceeds in concert with their efforts to solve the puzzles posed by the world around them. Thus, for example, the word *gone* appears only when the child begins to grapple with the mystery of objects that disappear—and later reappear (Gopnik, 1984). Similarly, children begin to speak words connoting success at a task ("there"), or failure ("no—oh, dear") only when they become aware of right and wrong solutions and must deal with these matters (Gopnik and Meltzoff, 1984). And they begin to use words necessary to deal with new situations.

In general, during the first two years, maturation of the brain is a major determinant of language development. No one has ever found an infant under eight months old who could speak and understand words. Once the brain's growth permits language, environmental experiences begin to assume a greater role.

Figure 7-1 Children's speech: from simple to complex

Charted here is the increasing complexity of the language spoken by three children whose utterances were carefully recorded over a period of months to determine the average number of morphemes they strung together in each burst of speech. The fastest progress was made by Eve, who was observed from the time she was 18 months old. Less quick to use longer strings of words were Adam and Sarah, both of whom were studied beginning at 27 months. Although the three children progressed at different rates, there were some remarkable similarities in their development (after Brown, Cazden, and Bellugi-Klima, 1969).

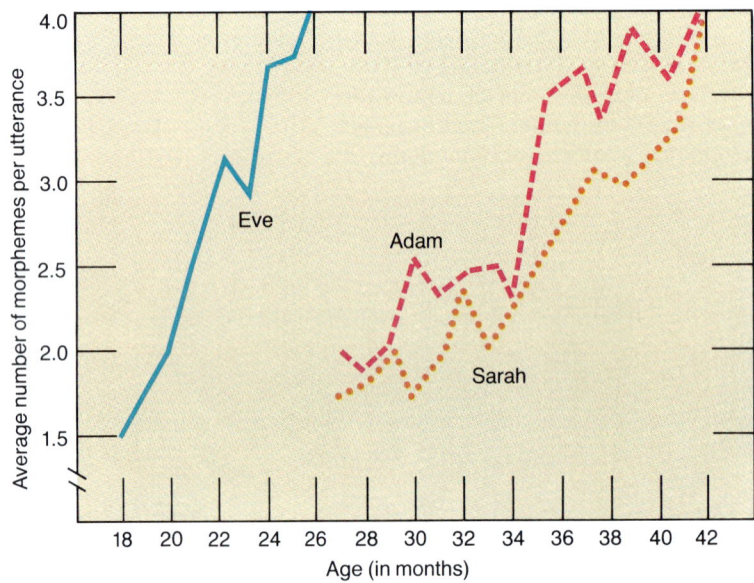

Discovering Grammar

Even at an early age, children acquire some of the rules of grammar practiced by the adults around them. At about the age of two, for example, children are likely to say such things as *gooses swimmed*. Even though the statement is not put correctly, it shows that they have learned something about the rules. They have discovered that ordinarily a noun can be made plural by adding an *-s* and a verb can be turned into the past tense by adding an *-ed*. We can hardly blame them for the fact that our language is not always consistent and decrees that the plural of *goose* is *geese* and the past tense of *swim* is *swam*.

Children learn the rules of grammar in a remarkably consistent pattern. Whether they are fast learners or slow, and regardless of the size or nature of their vocabularies, they seem to acquire their knowledge in a predictable order. In English, one of the first such morphemes is usually *ing*, added to a verb to denote an action going on at the moment. Somewhat later comes the addition of an *-s* to words to make them plural. And still later the use of an *-'s* to indicate possession. Most children learn to use some of the articles (*the, a, an*) before they add an *-ed* to a verb to convey the past tense (Brown, 1973). In other languages the order may be different, but in general, the order of learning morphemes is determined by the distinctiveness of their sounds and the regularity with which they are used. The English sounds *ing* and *-'s*, for example, satisfy both criteria, and, therefore, tend to be learned early. (Slobin, 1985).

With minor variations, the first two-word utterances of children are similar regardless of whether they are learning to speak English, Russian, or Samoan (Slobin, 1971). Children usually put nouns before verbs ("mommy eat," not "eat mommy"), and verbs before objects ("throw ball," not "ball throw"). They seem to go about learning the rules in much the same way (Slobin, 1973)—with the ultimate aim of using them to make sense.

How Parents Help—And How Children Help Themselves

Adults help children learn in a number of ways. They speak to children slowly, with many pauses (Broen, 1972). They use short sentences (Newport, 1975) and often repeat words or phrases to help the child understand. All in all, by gearing their speech to the child's level of ability to follow and comprehend the words, they provide what have been called "language lessons in miniature" (Clark and Clark, 1977)—helping the child pick up not only meaning but grammar (Vorster, 1974).

There is evidence that preschool and kindergarten children can be helped by special training to learn language (Gordon, 1984). Children who first listened to an adult act out a sentence and then imitated the adult showed improved language compared to those who did not have this training (Roth, 1984). For the most part, however, children must figure out the rules of grammar by themselves, for parents seldom provide feedback on whether their child's utterances are within the rules or not. It has been found that mothers almost never correct or punish errors in syntax. They ignore mistakes of this kind although they usually correct children for speaking in a way that gets the facts wrong. Thus when one of the children in the study illustrated in Figure 7-1 said, *Mama isn't boy; he a girl*—a statement that was factually correct though grammatically all wrong—the mother replied approvingly, *That's right*. When another of the children said of a television program, *Walt Disney comes on Tuesday*—a statement grammatically correct but factually wrong—the mother was quick to point out the error with the firm comment, *No, he does not* (Brown, 1973).

Nonetheless, even without much direct guidance, children learn the rules quickly. They are much more likely to wind up using correct syntax, on which they have received no feedback, than always telling the truth, on which they have received a great deal of feedback.

Theories of Language Learning

At one time most psychologists believed that the manner in which language is learned could be explained fully in terms of operant conditioning. They thought that some of the sounds babies make in their early babbling are reinforced by their parents' smiles, fondling, or other forms of approval. These sounds tended to be repeated. The same process of reinforcement was believed to account for the manner in which babies start to string sounds together into meaningful sentences (Skinner, 1957).

Later, some psychologists who became impressed by the importance of learning through observation proposed a different theory. They suggested that language is learned not through operant conditioning but through imitation of the way parents combine phonemes into meaningful morphemes, then string morphemes together into meaningful words and sentences.

Both these theories may account for some language learning, but neither offers a complete explanation. It is difficult to see how operant conditioning can lead children to acquire rules that will enable them to create new sentences of their own—especially since they may receive positive reinforcement in the form of approval for grammatically incorrect utterances (*Mama isn't boy; he a girl*) and disapproval when their grammar is correct (*Walt Disney comes on Tuesday*). It is also difficult to see how imitation can result in completely new and original sentences—and in fact there is evidence that children who do very little imitating learn language just as well as children who do a lot of it (de Villiers and de Villiers, 1978).

A totally different theory has been proposed by Noam Chomsky, a linguist at the Massachusetts Institute of Technology. Chomsky suggests that the human brain is wired in such a way that we are born with some kind of *"innate mechanism"* for learning and using language. This innate mechanism enables us as children to do some rapid information processing on the language we hear from our elders. We quickly develop our own notions of how adults string sounds together to convey meaning. Later we modify and expand these notions as we get more experienced at communicating with others—and soon we are using the rules of grammar in such a sophisticated fashion that we can understand or express almost anything. The Chomsky theory holds that, in a sense, we cannot help learning language and using it the way we do. This is simply the way our brains operate—a behavior for which we are prepared by our biological inheritance. Just as fish are born to swim and moles to burrow, we are born to speak and understand language.

The "Language" of Apes

Many attempts have been made in recent years to explore the question of whether any other animals, especially chimpanzees and other apes, may possibly share the human talent for language. One problem is that even the apes seem unable to use their vocal cords to make the sounds of human speech. Therefore experimenters have tried substitutes—for example, the sign language used by deaf people, which was the basis of an early study made by Beatrice and Allen Gardner with the chimpanzee named Washoe shown in Figure 7-2.

After about four years of training, Washoe had learned a vocabulary of more than 130 signs, including *you, please, cat, enough,* and *time*. Moreover, she could string the signs together into statements like *hurry gimme toothbrush* (Gardner and Gardner, 1972). She even made up a word of her own using the signs available to her—*water-bird* to describe a duck. The Gardners are convinced that Washoe learned sign language in much the same way a human child learns the spoken word—and indeed that she displayed about as much command of language as a three-year-old.

Figure 7-2 A chimpanzee "talks"

At the age of 2½, the chimpanzee named Washoe makes the sign language signal for "hat."

Another approach was taken by David Premack with a chimpanzee named Sarah, who was taught to communicate by using symbols made of plastic cut into various shapes. The pieces each represented a word, and the words could be arranged in order on a magnetized board. Sarah learned the meanings of numerous words and sentences like *Mary give apple Sarah*. Once she understood the meaning of the words *take*, *dish*, and *red*, she obeyed a command expressed in a sentence she had never seen before: *Sarah take red dish*. When her caretaker showed her two foods she liked, chocolate and a banana, she spontaneously created the sentence *Mary give Sarah banana chocolate*—which needs only an *and* between the two food names to be exactly the way a human child might ask for two things at once (Premack, 1976).

For a time many psychologists believed that the Washoe and Sarah experiments cast serious doubt on Chomsky's theory that the ability to use language is a species-specific activity confined to human beings. It is now generally accepted, however, that the experiments show only that apes are capable of understanding symbols, communicating with them, and using them in various kinds of information processing. They do not show the flexibility and creativity that even three-year-olds do. Most psychologists believe that there is a qualitative difference between human language and the communication capacities of apes.

Despite the accomplishments Premack observed in Sarah, he believes that while there are some similarities between chimp communication and human language, these two are very different (Premack, 1985). That is the conclusion also of another psychologist, Herbert Terrace, who conducted a long-term study of a chimpanzee playfully named Nim Chimpsky. Terrace began with high hopes of showing that Nim could acquire human facility with language. After five years, however, he reached the reluctant conclusion that most of Nim's communication was little more than a "subtle imitation" of his teachers, learned for the sake of obtaining rewards. There seemed to be no indication of any knowledge about syntax or of the human child's growing ability to produce longer and more complex messages. To take the most pessimistic view, Nim never greatly surpassed the performance of a dog that learns to obey the spoken commands of *sit* or *heel* (Terrace, 1979).

CONCEPTS: WORDS THAT DO DOUBLE DUTY

One feature of our language deserves special attention because it makes possible our great flexibility in the use of words for both communication and information processing in general. This is the fact that only a few of the words we use are the names of specific, one-of-a-kind objects—for example, the planets Mars and Venus. Most words, on the contrary, represent whole groups of objects, events, actions, and ideas. Even a simple word like *water* means not only the colorless fluid in the glass we hold in our hands but also any somewhat similar substances anywhere, including the salty contents of the oceans and the raindrops that fall from the sky. *Justice* represents many different abstract ideas held by people around the world at various times in history and embodied in various legal codes and practices.

Such words are called *concepts*—which can be defined roughly as mental representations of similarities between objects or events that we know are also different from one another. For example, to know the concept *water* is to know that the substances in drinking glasses, oceans, and raindrops, though they take different forms, are in fact similar in some way. Many kinds of similarities can contribute to the formation of concepts. Some concepts grow out of the physical attributes of objects as they appear to our senses—for example, similarities in the appearance of roses and tulips (*flowers*), the sound of a singing voice and a brass band (*music*), and the feel of a piece of paper and a windowpane (*smooth*). Some are based on similarities in relationships between physical attributes: *bigger* applies to such diverse pairs of objects as fly-to-gnat, adult-to-child, and Texas-to-Delaware, and *louder* applies to shout versus whisper or thunderclap versus shout. Other concepts take note of similarities in function. Dwelling, for example, embraces a one-family house, a high-rise apartment, a tepee, and an igloo. An abstract concept like *justice* lumps together events that share the idea that a person is treated fairly by an authority whether the person is a criminal and the authority is a judge, the person is a minority member and the authority is a state, or the person is a football player and the authority is a referee.

Whether or not two words or ideas are viewed as belonging to the same concept depends on the individual's knowledge and on the ability to detect an aspect of similarity (Murphy and Medin, 1985). Thus for a child, "robin" and "Paris" do not belong to a concept, but for many adults they are linked to the concept of spring.

Concepts without Words

Though words that express concepts make up a large part of our vocabulary, concepts can be formed without using any language at all. Many learning experiments have shown that animals, which have no language, can acquire concepts of triangles and other qualities. Dogs obviously have a concept of *tree*, and will behave toward a tree they have never seen before just as they behave toward more familiar trees. Pigeons display a similar skill. For example, they can detect *tree* in pictures of scenes containing a wide variety of trees (Herrnstein and de Villiers, 1980).

Human babies acquire concepts before they learn how to talk. The first similarities they note are of physical attributes like color and shape (Linn et al., 1982), and one of their first concepts is of the human face. By the time they are a year old, they already seem to lump objects together by similarities in function, creating concepts like furniture and food (Ross, 1980). Children seem almost addicted to finding concepts, and this helps account for their remarkable ability to acquire language. Presumably they must have some concept of

These three-year-olds in a Head Start program are learning letters of the alphabet while learning concepts for shape.

things like *furniture* and *food* before they can understand and use these words. There are still many puzzles to be resolved here. For example, it is not known why three-year-olds find it easier to learn concepts for shape—like square or circle—than concepts for color—like red or green (Bornstein, 1985).

The Enriching Interplay between Language and Concepts

If language is not essential for acquiring concepts, however, it is certainly a great help. Much of our communication and thinking depends on words that represent complex concepts embedded within other concepts, in a way that would be impossible without language. Note, for example, the term *human being*. What the term means to us goes far beyond any physical attributes (two legs, erect posture, and so on) or functions (being students, working at jobs). We have a far richer concept of *human being* as the highest (which is itself a concept) of mammals (another concept)—a mammal being a particular kind of organism (still another concept) that produces (another) its young (another) inside (another) the body (another) of the mother (another), which nurses (another) the baby (another) after (another) birth (still another).

Language helps us find meanings, relationships, and similarities and thus build concepts on top of concepts. Without language, it would be difficult to find much resemblance between a two-legged human being walking on the land and a whale swimming in the ocean. Our concept word *mammal*, however, includes both of them.

Just as our language enriches our concepts, so do our concepts enrich our language. It is concept words that make it possible to use the 26 letters and 40-odd phonemes of the English language to express an unlimited number of messages. Suppose we lacked the concept *people* and had to talk about each individual by a different and distinct name. Or had no concept *dwelling* and had to use a different word for each place where someone lives—and the same for every item of furniture and food. We would find ourselves as limited as the ship captains using the flags that were shown on page 230. We would even be more limited—for even the flags, as you will note if you look back at them, depend on the concept words *disabled, assistance, danger*, and others.

How Concepts Help Us Think: The Drawing of Inferences

The use of concepts lends a tremendous variety and versatility to the kind of information processing we call thinking. When we encounter a new object or experience, we do not ordinarily have to deal with it as a unique event of which we have no prior knowledge and must learn about from scratch. Instead we can fit it into some already existing concept (Bruner, Goodnow, and Austin, 1956). A dog of a species we have never seen before is instantly recognizable as a dog. A strange new sculpture by a modern artist is immediately recognizable as a piece of art. Concepts "give our world stability. They capture the notion that many objects or events are alike in some important respect, and hence can be thought about and responded to in ways we have already mastered" (Smith and Medin, 1981).

One important way concepts help us think can be demonstrated by this example: Someone says to you, "There is a bird in Brazil called a cariama. Does it have wings?" Almost immediately, you answer, "Yes." You do not know this from your own experience, but have reached your answer through the useful form of thinking called *inference*—or drawing logical conclusions from facts already known. You have been told that a cariama fits into the concept *bird*. Your concept of bird includes the fact, previously learned and stored in memory, that birds have wings. Therefore it is reasonable to infer, even though you have never seen a cariama, that it too has wings.

The process of inference enables you to think about many matters without having any direct knowledge of the situation (Collins and Quillian, 1972). At the end of a long day's drive, you feel confident that you will find a motel room if you push on another 50 miles toward Atlanta. You can make this inference because, even though you have never been there before, you know Atlanta is a big city and your concept of cities includes the presence of motels on their outskirts.

Our inferences are sometimes wrong. Suppose, for example, that the question about the Brazilian bird was, "Does a cariama fly?" Again you would probably answer yes, because your concept of birds includes flight. But there are a few birds that do not fly, and the cariama may just happen to be one of them.

Most of our inferences, however, are correct and valuable. Just as the rules of grammar enable us to generate sentences we have never spoken before and to understand sentences we have never heard before, so does the process of inference enable us to think about all kinds of matters we have never actually encountered. We can generalize about the new and unfamiliar from what we have observed about similar objects or events. Most of what we know—or think we know—is based on inference rather than on direct observation.

The Role of Concepts in Learning and Memory

While reading these pages on concepts, you may have been reminded of the topic discussed in the previous chapter on memory—that is, the way categories help us organize information and encode it into long-term memory. Concepts and categories are closely related. Many concepts represent categories, and many concept words describe them.

Concepts and categories are one of the ways language helps us learn and remember. They make possible all kinds of chunking and clustering that help us process information in short-term memory and encode it efficiently into a network of long-term memory. As we acquire more information, we change our concepts in many ways—refining or enlarging them and forming new ones. Out of our simplest concepts, like faces, food, and furniture, we build increasingly complex concepts that serve as high-level clusters of related information and ideas. Thanks to these new "and ever more complex combinations of simpler ideas," we can remember and "think about complex subject matter just about as easily and efficiently as we could previously think about simpler subject matter" (Wickelgren, 1981).

Language accounts to a great extent for the fact that learning builds on learning—or, in William James's words, that new items of information "cluster and cling like grapes to a stem." It does so both by helping us acquire concepts and giving us specific words that help us remember and think about specific details. It is difficult to imagine, for example, how a surgeon could be trained without all the words that medical science has developed over the years to describe the human body—some representing the general principles of how the body is put together and functions, others identifying specific anatomical structures. Effective surgery would probably be impossible without an "effective language" (Bross, 1973).

The relation between language and learning and memory is a two-way street. As one study stated, "Learning new words enables children to conquer new areas of knowledge, and these new areas enable them to learn new words, and so on" (Clark and Clark, 1977). This is one reason, unfortunately, that children from poorly educated families often have a difficult time in school, thus continuing a vicious circle that leads one generation after another to have trouble getting along in society. Children whose parents have very little formal education and use a limited vocabulary start school with a severe handicap. There are hundreds of words and concepts that they have never heard of but that are already familiar to children whose parents are better educated. They simply do not have the same kind of "effective language" that makes it easy to find similarities and relationships between the new information presented in school and their prior knowledge.

But the Puzzle Remains: Precisely What Is a Concept?

Though concepts play such a large and useful part in our learning and thinking, and have been studied extensively by psychologists and linguists, they continue to be something of a puzzle. The exact nature of concepts is not clear and there are a number of conflicting points of view.

One view, suggested by Eleanor Rosch, is that from our observations of events in the world we form a notion of a typical bird (or vegetable or fruit or anything else). For most Americans, the typical bird seems to be a robin—which is rather small, has two short legs and two wings, flies, sits in trees, and sings. Then we lump other living creatures into our prototype of bird, or reject them, depending on how much family resemblance they bear to our typical bird the robin. We know immediately that thrushes and song sparrows, which are very similar to robins, fit into our concept of birds. We need a little more time to decide that a chicken is a bird, because it is a good deal larger than a robin and does not fly or sit in trees (Rosch and Mervis, 1975).

Sometimes, Rosch has pointed out, the boundary lines for family resemblances are extremely "fuzzy." Therefore we may have trouble deciding whether a bat fits the concept of bird or animal and whether a tomato is a vegetable or a fruit (Rosch, 1973). The same "fuzziness" in the way we form concepts makes it difficult to classify a 16-year-old female as a girl or a woman, and rheumatism as a disease or something else. Our concepts and categories—and indeed our thinking in general—are not always so neat as we would like them to be. But perhaps this simply reflects the fact that our world is itself rather disorganized and not easy to describe in cut-and-dried terms.

Sometimes we rely on factors other than family resemblances to establish what is typical—including the degree to which the item represents an ideal, or how often we encounter it (Barsalou, 1985). The typical food to be eaten while on a diet, for example, is not determined by its physical features but by notions about the ideal diet food in that category or the frequency with which it occurs.

It appears that we are more apt to notice similar features in things that are in many ways dissimilar when we get our information verbally rather than visually. In one experiment, when subjects were asked to read pairs of sentences about Eskimos and Americans, they judged the two groups to be more similar than when they were asked to look at pictures of the two (Gati and Tversky, 1984). Because a concept contains a "bundle" of features, the specific ones we pick out and use will change with the situation—as is illustrated in Figure 7-3.

Does Language Distort the Way We View the World?

One of the interesting questions about language and thinking is this: Is it possible that language restricts our information-processing abilities? Does it perhaps serve as a pair of faulty eyeglasses through which we get only a limited and sometimes distorted view of the world?

One prominent language student, Benjamin Whorf, suggested that people who use different languages have very different ways of looking at the world and different concepts about the similarities and relationships that it displays. In studying many languages, Whorf found one group of American Indians who lump together with a single word things that fly—insects, airplanes, and even airplane pilots. He found other languages that do not have any devices for distinguishing the past, present, and future tenses of verbs (Whorf,

Figure 7-3 "Hot"—what does the concept mean?

As illustrated here, the concept "hot" contains features that vary from one context to another. For example, it can mean overheated, "cool," or on a winning streak.

1956). In Whorf's view, such differences are bound to affect the way people who speak these languages conceive the world, organize it, and think about it.

This is an intriguing theory—and it seems to receive a certain amount of support from some of the matters discussed in the last few pages. The trained surgeon, with an "effective language" of anatomy, looks at and thinks about the human body differently from the rest of us. Children who start school with impoverished vocabularies probably conceive of the world in more limited fashion than their more fortunate classmates. It would appear that information processing can be influenced not only by the use of different languages but also by differences in the vocabularies of people who speak the same language.

Or Do We Develop Language to Match the World about Us?

There is a great deal of evidence, however, that language is usually tailored to human thinking, rather than vice versa. Among all the many languages of the world, there are more basic similarities than differences. Certainly on the matter of the physical objects and everyday events found in the world, people everywhere seem to perceive them, find names for them, organize them into concepts and categories, and think about them in ways that are often very similar.

Some colors, for example, seem particularly striking—doubtless because of the way the sense organs of the eye and the process of perception operate. And, though languages differ in the number of colors for which they have names, the names usually refer to the colors that "hit the eye," like red and yellow, not to all the many other hues and shades found in nature (Kay, 1975). Similarly, most languages have terms for shapes that human perception seems to find compelling, such as squares and circles. Most languages also have terms for basic emotions like fear and anger, for dimensions of objects like height and length, and for distance and direction (Clark and Clark, 1977).

Eleanor Rosch has suggested that our concepts about the physical world are based on what is actually "out there" in nature. That is to say, they are molded by and reflect the physical realities of the environment. Objects just naturally fall into groups like birds and animals, vegetables and fruits—and our language acknowledges this fact (Rosch, 1977). Our brains are wired to notice certain attributes of the objects and events we encounter—and family resemblances in these attributes form the basis of our concepts.

New Language through New Thinking

Another indication that language is tailored to human thinking is the fact that language changes when people's thinking changes. Note, for example, all the new words that football has created while developing to its present highly technical level. There were no such terms in the English language, even a few years ago, as *cornerback, noseguard*, and *safety blitz*. All grew out of the need to find new terms for new concepts developed by inventive coaches.

When we need a new word, we coin it—or borrow it from another language. (Many everyday "English" words are borrowed—*goulash* from Hungarian, *whiskey* from Gaelic, *sabotage* from French.) And as additions to the language become more and more widely used, we often shorten them to make them more convenient (Zipf, 1949). Thus the original term *moving picture* has been condensed to *movie, gasoline* to *gas, telephone* to *phone*. Specialists in certain areas of knowledge, such as surgeons, coin or borrow their own vocabulary and often engage in their own form of shortening terms for simplicity and convenience.

Designing circuitry on a computer demands a specialized vocabulary.

All in all, though thinking may in some ways be molded and limited by language, as Whorf has pointed out, the human brain seems remarkably capable of adapting this useful tool to its own advantage. One study stated: "Apparently when people lack a word for a useful concept, they soon find one.... What this suggests is that language differences reflect the culture and not the reverse" (Clark and Clark, 1977). The moral for all of us is that we have in language a tool of virtually infinite possibilities—limited, for all practical purposes, only by how well we learn to handle it.

HOW WE THINK AND SOLVE PROBLEMS

Sometime when you are engaged in thinking—about anything at all, from your plans for the next meal to your ideas about religion and politics—stop yourself and examine what kind of process has been going on. Most likely you will find you have been talking to yourself—thinking through the use of language, and especially words that represent concepts.

Thinking is one of those terms that everybody understands but nobody quite knows how to define. It is probably best described as the *mental manipulation of information*. In the learning and memory stages of information processing, we build a store of knowledge about the objects and events we have encountered—a sort of mental representation of the world and the way it operates. In the thinking stage, we process this inner representation in various ways to add to our understanding of the world and solve the problems it presents. Our thinking is often entirely independent of physical objects and actual events. We can think about objects that are not present at the moment (like an architect planning a house that does not yet exist), about events that occurred in the past (a childhood birthday party), or about abstract concepts that have no physical reality at all (religion and politics).

Thinking does not necessarily require language. Animals obviously do some kind of thinking, and so do human babies before they have learned to speak. An artist working on

To be "lost in thought" often involves the manipulation of information stored in memory.

a painting thinks in terms of mental images—a mind's-eye picture of what the details and final results should look like. Musicians compose and orchestrate by manipulating "sounds" that they hear only inside themselves. Mathematicians manipulate their own symbols and formulas. But most of us generally think in words, and language greatly enlarges the scope of our thinking.

We think about many things in different ways. As we observe the world around us, we seek to find some kind of order in its objects and events. We look for meanings and relationships that enable us to form concepts and categories. As we accumulate more knowledge, these concepts change and become more and more refined and elaborate. The mind, it has been said, is constantly working on its knowledge (Bowerman, 1974)—trying to understand and absorb the new and revising the old in light of the new.

Rules and Premises as Bases for Thinking

Among the important pieces of information we process during our thinking are the *rules* that govern the relationships and interactions among the objects and events in the environment—in other words, the facts we have learned about the way the world operates. We have learned from experience that water, if heated enough, will boil and turn to steam. We have also discovered that an egg placed in boiling water will start to turn hard, and if left long enough will become hard-boiled. In thinking about cooking, these are some of the rules we manipulate.

Some of the rules we use come from our own observations—that is, from the kind of pragmatic, everyday experience that helps us reason and solve problems (Cheng, 1985). Others represent the pooled observations of many people—the kinds of information found in our libraries. When we think about the sky and the solar system, we utilize astronomy's rule that the moon revolves around the earth and the earth and other planets revolve around the sun. When we think about the distance around a circular lake that we know to be a half mile wide, we use the mathematician's rule that the circumference equals the diameter (here .5 mile) times π (3.1416).

We also base much of our thinking on what are called *premises*, or basic beliefs that we accept even though they cannot be proved. The line between a premise and a rule is often hazy and difficult to draw, for many generally accepted beliefs are really not probably true. Even in science, for example, such ideas as the theory of evolution and many advanced mathematical theories are still only premises, though they are in accord with the best observations currently possible and have at least a certain claim to validity.

Many premises are the result of individual experience. They are not necessarily based on objective observation, and they vary greatly from one person to another. Some of us, from what we have observed, believe that most people are honest—and much of our thinking about other people is based on this firmly held premise. Others hold just as firmly to the premise that most people are dishonest. Some think and act on the premise that it is wise to keep one's nose to the grindstone, others on the premise that all work and no play makes Jack a dull boy.

When Thinking Is Logical—and Illogical

When you express an opinion and explain why you have reached it, a friend may say, "That's logical. I agree." Or, on the contrary, "Your logic is wrong. I disagree." Logical thinking means drawing conclusions that follow inescapably from the rules we have learned and the premises we have adopted. A simple example would be in answering the question: *Does a whale nurse its young?* You have learned the rule that all mammals nurse their young. You know that a whale is a mammal. Therefore it follows that a whale must nurse its young.

Illogical thinking means drawing conclusions that are not justified by such evidence as rules, facts, and premises. For example, a young woman may decide to become a schoolteacher as a result of this line of thought: "My mother says she was extremely happy when she was teaching. Therefore I will be happy teaching." Her thinking is illogical because she may have very different tastes from her mother's and the teaching profession may have changed in the meantime. A man with a stomachache takes a pill that was once prescribed for a friend, thinking, "The pill helped him, and therefore it will help me." But his stomachache may be entirely different and may only be aggravated by the medicine.

When we accuse people of being illogical, we are often incorrect. Their logic is perfectly sound, granted their premises, and it is the premises that we disagree with. Was it illogical for Christopher Columbus's critics to believe he would fall off the earth if he kept sailing west? No, for they based their reasoning on the premise that the earth was flat—and, if so, Columbus's ships would indeed fall off like plates pushed to the edge of a table. Their logic was right but their premise was wrong, because the earth is not flat.

Many arguments and misunderstandings among statesmen and nations as well as between husbands and wives are caused not so much by fallacies in logical thinking as by starting from different premises. One economist, using flawless logic, may conclude that taxes should be raised. An equally brilliant economist, using equally faultless logic, may conclude that taxes should be lowered. One person decides, after much reasonable thought, that capital punishment is wrong. Another person, after equal consideration, decides it is essential. Which of the economists and opinions on capital punishment is right and which is wrong? We cannot really say, because we have no way of establishing the validity of the premises on which they are based.

We cannot be sure that a premise is wrong unless it clearly violates the truth, and this is seldom the case. We know for a fact, as the navigators of Columbus's time did not know, that the earth is spherical rather than flat. If a man claims to be Napoleon, we know he is unquestionably wrong and we doubt his sanity. But mostly we hold our premises more or less on faith. We can agree or disagree with another person's premises but cannot usually prove them right or wrong. Thus people whose thought processes are totally logical can reach entirely different conclusions.

Problem Solving: Algorithms and Heuristics

Much human thinking is an attempt at *problem solving*, designed to cope with the innumerable problems faced by all human beings. As a student you must solve not only the theoretical problems in your math courses but also many everyday problems. You have a certain number of dollars available for tuition, books, clothes, housing, food, and entertainment. How can you best allot the dollars to these expenses? A person starting a long automobile trip must ask: What highways will provide the best route? How can the trip best be broken up into how many days on the road? A mechanic looking at a stalled automobile must ask: What is wrong? How can I fix it?

Many studies have been made of problem solving—the pitfalls to avoid and the most effective ways to go about it. The most effective strategy, when it is available, is to use what is called an *algorithm*. The word originally was used to describe mathematical formulas and procedures—which of course guarantee a correct solution to any problem that deals with numbers, provided we understand the problem and know the proper algorithm to apply. The term has now been broadened to include any specific technique that can be followed step by step and will produce a correct solution without fail. An example would be the

"Murchison's theory is that it's dog hair in your fuel line."

Drawing by Booth, © 1984, The New Yorker Magazine, Inc.

problem of calling a friend who is not listed in the phone book. You know the number begins 445-57——but have forgotten the last two digits. You can use an algorithm by trying every possible number from 445-5700 through 445-5799. The method may keep you busy for a long time—especially if the correct number turns out to be 445-5799—but it cannot fail.

For most of the problems we face, no algorithm is available and we have to rely instead on what are called *heuristics*. These are rules of thumb—approaches that have worked for us in the past, in somewhat similar situations, and may work again though there is no guarantee. A driver who comes to a fork in an unfamiliar country road, while trying to get to a town known to be somewhere toward the west, chooses the path that seems from the position of the sun to head more westerly—though it may later curve and turn south. A chess player, who cannot possibly predict all the possible moves in the game, follows the rule of thumb of trying to control the center of the board—which does not guarantee winning but usually helps.

Pitfall 1: Failure to Analyze the Problem

Among the dangers we face in problem solving, one of the most common is a failure to analyze the situation thoroughly—and instead jump to an incorrect view of the nature of the problem and the possible solution. This pitfall is beautifully illustrated by the experiment illustrated in Figure 7-4, which you should try for yourself before going on to the next paragraph.

The problem presented in the figure is fairly simple—yet few people manage to solve it. The answer is that you must turn over cards 1 and 3. If card 1 has a blue glove on the back, or if card 3 has a blue hat on the back, then the statement you are asked to prove or disprove is false. But if card 1 has a gray glove on the back, and card 3 has a gray hat on the back, then the statement is true.

Most people insist that the cards to turn over are 1 and 4. But in fact card 4 has no bearing on the problem. Regardless of whether the hat on the back is blue or gray, this card cannot prove or disprove the statement. The reason people tend to fall into the error of

Figure 7-4 Can you solve this problem?

The four cards, which have symbols on both sides, lie on a table so that you can see them as shown here. You are told that each card has on one side a hat, which may be either blue or gray, and on the other side a glove, which also may be either blue or gray. You are asked to prove or disprove this statement: Every card that has a blue hat on one side has a gray glove on the other side. How many cards—and which ones—would you have to turn over to find out whether the statement is true or false? For the answer, see the text (after Wason, 1971).

picking this card seems to be that they take too much for granted in reading the problem. From the statement given in the experiment, *Every card that has a blue hat on one side has a gray glove on the other side*, they assume that it is also true that every card that has a gray glove on one side must have a blue hat on the other side. But this has never been stated and is not part of the problem. The psychologist who devised the experiment made many similar studies and found that most people have this tendency to jump to unwarranted assumptions about the nature of the problem (Wason, 1971). The tendency is most pronounced when the task at hand is unfamiliar, but less so when it relates to our own interests.

Pitfall 2: Thinking What We Would Like to Think

Closely allied to the error of failing to analyze the problem and making unwarranted assumptions is the fact that we sometimes tend to let our personal biases get in the way. We try hard—and sometimes against all the weight of evidence and logic—to find the answer we would like to find. The way our personality traits can affect problem solving has been demonstrated by the experiment shown in Figure 7-5, which you should try for yourself before going on to the next paragraph.

Fewer than half the students who took part in the experiment checked the correct answer, which is *D. He made $20*. But the most interesting development was that there turned out to be a significant difference between male and female students. As is shown in Figure 7-6, considerably more men than women got the correct answer, perhaps because almost twice as many women as men checked *B. He broke even*.

The experimenter concluded that a sizable proportion of women tend to favor the "broke even" answer because the female personality is less aggressive than the male—and more inclined to be "communal, selfless, and kind" (Hormuth, 1982). Many of the women

Figure 7-5 How did these horse trades turn out?

This was the question posed to around 650 students taking an introductory psychology course. Each of the five possible answers was checked by at least four students. After you have reached your own answer, see the text and Figure 7-6 for the results of the experiment and what they tell us about a pitfall in problem solving.

A man buys a horse for $60. A week later he sells it for $70. A few days later he buys it back for $80, only to sell it again for $90. What was the financial result of his transactions?

A. He lost $10.
B. He broke even.
C. He made $10.
D. He made $20.
E. He made $30.

Figure 7-6 A strange case of sex differences in solving a horse-trading problem

The bars show the percentages of men and women college students who selected the various possible answers to the horse-trading problem shown in Figure 7-5. Note how many more women than men selected "broke even" and how many more men than women selected "made $20."

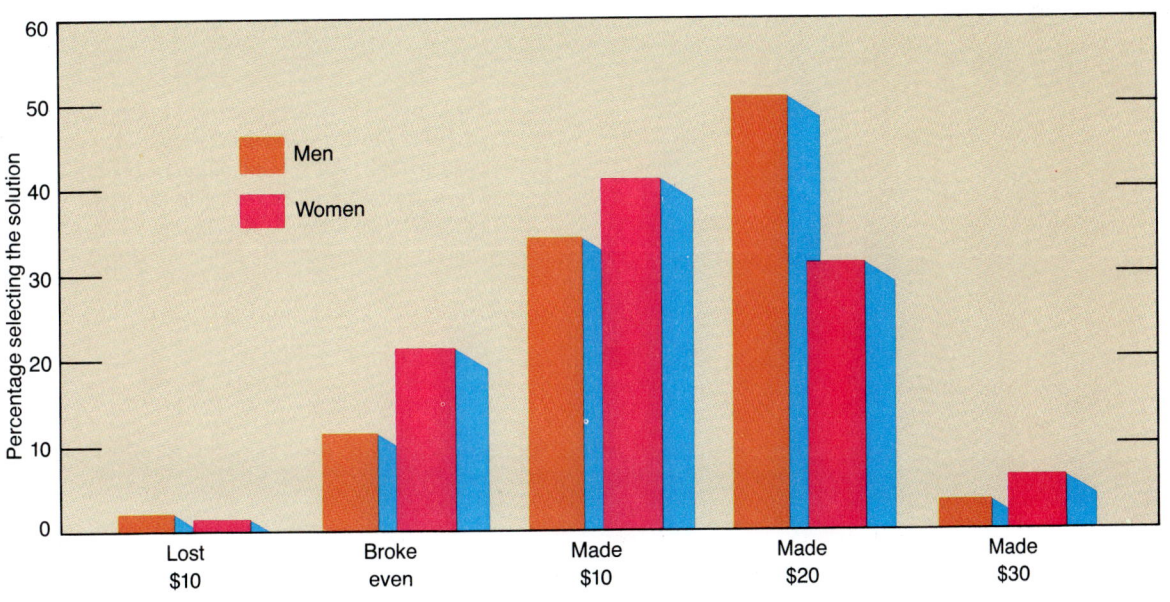

How We Think and Solve Problems

students seemed to prefer to think of people as breaking even in financial transactions rather than taking risks and winding up with a profit or loss. We all have a tendency to reach conclusions agreeable to our own personality traits and opinions. It was established many years ago that people often find logic in even the most faulty reasoning if they agree with the statement it supports—and find flaws in even the most logical reasoning if they disagree with the conclusion (Janis and Frick, 1943).

Pitfall 3: Functional Fixedness

Another tendency we all share is to get into a rut in our view of the world and the way it operates. In particular, we tend to think of an object as functioning only in one certain way—and therefore to ignore its other possible uses. This pitfall, called *functional fixedness*, was best demonstrated in the famous old experiment illustrated in Figure 7-7. Examine the figure and see if you can solve the problem before you read on to the next paragraph. The problem is especially difficult when you have only a photograph and cannot actually manipulate the objects—but, with effort and luck, you may find the answer.

The problem can be solved, as you will see when you turn to Figure 7-8 (page 254), only by forgetting about the way a box is ordinarily used. You have to empty the box of all the matches, tack it to the door, and turn it into your candle stand. Though this seems simple enough once you know it, fewer than half the subjects thought of it when the experiment was first performed (Duncker, 1945).

Functional fixedness reduces our efficiency at solving many everyday problems. A nail file is for filing nails—and we may completely overlook the possibility of using it to tighten a screw and thus repair a broken lamp. A goldfish bowl is for holding fish—and the first person who converted one into a terrarium for growing house plants had to break some powerful old associations.

Functional fixedness is one form of a more general phenomenon called *persistence of set*. Over the years we develop a mental set toward problems—that is, our own habitual

Figure 7-7 Problem: how to mount the candle on a door so it won't drip on the floor

These were the objects used in an experiment described in the text. Subjects were asked to figure out a way to turn them into an improvised candle stand. Try it yourself before turning to the next page for an illustration of how it can be done.

way of approaching them. We tend to follow the same approach even in situations where other methods would be more appropriate. One almost sure way to improve your ability to solve new problems is to work at greater flexibility by trying at the very start to think of several possible ways to define the problem and the goal, as well as a number of different strategies that might work.

Pitfall 4: Relying on What Is Readily Available

The fourth common pitfall is best explained by indulging in a bit of fantasy. Suppose your life depends on a modern-day version of one of those old mythical tests—like slaying a dragon—devised by a king seeking a worthy heir to his throne. The test is this: The king pulls a book from his library shelves. He turns at random to a page and circles the first word he finds that either begins with an *r* (like *road*) or has *r* as its third letter (like *carpenter*). You have to guess which. If you are right, the kingdom is yours. If you are wrong, off with your head.

How would you go about deciding? Most people, it has been found, start by trying to figure the odds. They see how many words they can recall that begin with an *r*, then how many they can recall with *r* as the third letter. They find it much easier to think of words starting with *r*, decide the chances are heavily weighted in that direction—and make the wrong guess. As it happens, there are more words in which *r* is the third letter rather than the first. But we pay much more attention to the first letter than any other when encoding words into memory, and therefore words like *road* and *rock* are more readily available than words like *cork* and *farm* (Tversky and Kahneman, 1973).

If you were to associate primarily with individuals who lead this young woman's lifestyle, how would your own decisions in life be influenced?

Figure 7-8 The candle stand solution

The problem posed in Figure 7-7 can be solved only by finding an unusual way of using the box that held the matches. Just use the thumbtacks to fasten it to the door—and, lo, you have a candle stand to catch the drippings.

Much of our real-life thinking and problem solving also depend on the availability of information we have stored in memory. Recent events are likely to have an especially strong influence on our thinking—sometimes unduly. A good example comes from the world of sports, where we are often influenced by what we know about the recent performance of athletes. Both basketball players and fans believe that a player's chances of making a shot are greater if he has just made one than if he has just missed. But the actual records of players on two professional teams show that this belief in a player's "hot hand" or "streak shooting" is not supported by the facts (Gilovich, Vallone, and Tversky, 1985). We are also more influenced by an event that has a personal impact than by something we read in a newspaper. (A homeowner is more likely to buy additional fire insurance after watching a neighbor's house burn down than after watching televised fires in other parts of the city.)

Our reliance on the most readily available information often serves a useful purpose, because by and large our memory operates to make the most important information the easiest to recall. But there are times when relying on the readily available prevents us from solving a problem or causes an error (Tversky and Kahneman, 1973). Note this common occurrence: If we associate with people who lean strongly toward a certain lifestyle and opinions, we may accept their judgment as the representative wisdom of all humanity—and be influenced accordingly in important decisions about career, purchases, marriage, and morals. In actual fact, their behavior and beliefs may be just a minority phenomenon that is not typical of most people—and not at all suitable for us.

As in the case of functional fixedness, the availability pitfall can be avoided by being flexible in approaching the problem. Somewhere in your memory storehouse you have many kinds of information that might help. The first information that comes to mind, as you start searching your memory may or may not help. You may do better to stop and think: What other information do I have that bears on the problem? How can I think about the problem in a way that will help me find this other information? Thinking, as has been said, is the manipulation of information—and, in problem solving, the more we manipulate the information the better.

SUMMARY

The role, structure, and rules of language

1. Language is a "uniquely human activity" made possible by the structure and dynamics of the human brain.
2. The basic function of language is *communication*. It enables us to exchange an unlimited number and variety of messages and pass knowledge along from one generation to the next.
3. Language also helps us acquire information (by providing labels for the objects and events in the environment), to encode information into memory, and to think and solve problems.
4. The building blocks of language are the basic sounds called *phonemes*. English has about 40 phonemes, and no language has more than 85.
5. Phonemes are combined into meaningful sounds called *morphemes*, which may be words, prefixes, or suffixes. English has more than 100,000 morphemes, which are combined in turn to produce more than 600,000 words.
6. *Semantics* is the meaning of a language's morphemes and words.
7. Every language has two essential elements: (a) a *vocabulary* (or set of morphemes and words with meanings dictated by semantics) and (b) a *grammar* (or set of rules for putting morphemes and words together).
8. An important part of grammar is the rules of *syntax*, which govern sentence structure.

How we produce and understand messages

9. When we produce sentences, we must: (a) think of the meaning we wish to convey, (b) plan each sentence and part of a sentence, (c) find the right words to flesh out our thoughts, and (d) put the words in their proper order.
10. In listening, we carry out many mental processes all at the same time. We simultaneously try to recognize sounds, identify words, look for syntactic patterns, and search for semantic meaning.
11. When we listen to speech, the individual sounds and words are often vague or unintelligible but our information processing makes order out of chaos—so smoothly that we are not even aware of the mental work we do or the handicaps we overcome.

The remarkable feat of learning language

12. Children display a remarkable ability to learn language. At the age of two most children speak three-word sentences; at five they understand the meaning of about 2,000 words; at six they have acquired virtually all the basic rules of grammar; and at ten they are able to produce a veritable torrent of language—about 20,000 to 30,000 words each day.
13. Everything about the use of language must be learned except the inborn ability to create sounds. In early infancy, the use of sounds that resemble the phenomes of language are called *babbling*.
14. In learning language, the crucial factor appears to be communication and interaction between child and mother, or some other intimate caretaker.

15. In general, during the first two years of development, maturation of the brain is a major determinant of language development. During the later years, environmental experiences assume a greater role.
16. Learning the rules of grammar appears to proceed in much the same fashion for babies the world over, regardless of what language they are learning to speak.
17. Some theorists have suggested that language is learned through operant conditioning, others that it is acquired through observation, learning and imitation. More recently Noam Chomsky has proposed the theory that the human brain is wired in such a way that we have an "innate mechanism" for learning and using language.
18. At one time it appeared that apes are capable of using sign language in much the same way human beings use words. More recent evidence, however, suggests that their abilities are very limited.

Concepts: words that do double duty

19. Only a few words are names of specific, one-of-a-kind objects. Most are concepts, which can be defined roughly as mental representations of similarities between objects or events that are also different from one another.
20. Some concepts are based on similarities between physical attributes. Some are based on similarities in relationships between physical attributes (*bigger, louder*), and some on similarities in function (*dwelling, furniture*). Concepts like *justice* and *religion* lump together abstract ideas that are in some way similar.
21. Young babies and animals can acquire some concepts without language—but language enables us to build concepts on top of concepts and adds tremendous variety and versatility to our thinking and communication.
22. Our knowledge of concepts enables us to make useful *inferences* by drawing logical conclusions about new and unfamiliar objects and events from what we already know.
23. Many concepts represent *categories*, or groupings that help us organize information and encode it into long-term memory.
24. A number of theories have been proposed to explain the exact nature and formation of concepts. One theory, suggested by Eleanor Rosch, is that from our observations of the world we form a notion of a typical object, for example, a robin that seems to be a typical bird—then lump other creatures into our concept of bird, or reject them, depending on how much family resemblance they show to a robin.
25. Benjamin Whorf has suggested that people who use different languages have different ways of looking at the world, organizing it, and thinking about it. There is considerable evidence, however, that we tailor our language to our thinking, adding new words whenever we need them.

How we think and solve problems

26. *Thinking*, defined as *the mental manipulation of information*, can be accomplished without language—but language is chiefly responsible for the fact that our thinking is independent of physical objects and events and can range widely in space and time.
27. Among the important pieces of information we use in our thinking are the *rules* that we have learned govern the relationships and interactions among objects and events.

28. We also base our thinking on *premises*, which are basic beliefs that we accept even though they cannot be proved.
29. The most effective strategy in problem solving is an *algorithm*—a mathematical formula or other procedure that will guarantee a correct solution if followed step by step.
30. When an algorithm is not available, we use *heuristics*, or rules of thumb that have worked in similar situations and may work again.
31. Pitfalls in problem solving include: (a) failure to analyze the problem, (b) thinking what we would like to think, (c) functional fixedness, and (d) relying on the most readily available information.
32. The pitfalls can often be avoided by greater flexibility in analyzing the problem, thinking of several possible ways to define the problem and the goal, seeking a number of different strategies that might work, and searching memory for additional information that may help (instead of concentrating solely on the most readily available information).

IMPORTANT TERMS

algorithm
babbling
communication
concept
functional fixedness
grammar
heuristics
inference
"innate mechanism"
morpheme

persistence of set
phoneme
premises
problem solving
rules
semantics
syntax
thinking
vocabulary

RECOMMENDED READINGS

Brown, R. *A first language*. Cambridge, Mass.: Harvard University Press, 1973.

Chomsky, N. *Language and mind*, enl. ed. New York: Harcourt Brace Jovanovich, 1972.

Clark, H. H., and Clark, E. V. *Psychology and language*. New York: Harcourt Brace Jovanovich, 1977.

Ellis, A., and Beattie, G. *The psychology of language and communication*. New York: Guilford Press, 1986.

Greene, J. *Language understanding: a cognitive approach*. Philadelphia: Open University Press, 1985.

Lass, N. J., et al. *Speech, language and hearing*. Philadelphia: Saunders, 1982.

Miller, G. A. *Language and speech*. San Francisco: Freeman, 1981.

Smith, E. E., and Medin, D. L. *Categories and concepts*. Cambridge, Mass.: Harvard University Press, 1981.

Wessells, M. G. *Cognitive psychology*. New York: Harper & Row, 1982.

CHAPTER

8

INTELLIGENCE: ITS MEANING AND MEASUREMENT

THE NATURE OF INTELLIGENCE: SOME DIFFERENT VIEWS   261

Is intelligence a general ability? The views of Spearman and Thurstone
What skills make up intelligence? The views of Guilford, Gardner, and Sternberg
Piaget's theory of intelligence
Piaget's four steps in mental growth:
    1. The sensorimotor stage
    2. The preoperational stage
    3. The stage of concrete operations
    4. The stage of formal operations
What Piaget's theory implies for educating children

INTELLIGENCE TESTS: WHAT CAN THEY ACTUALLY TELL US?   270

Mental age, chronological age, and IQ
Some widely used intelligence tests: individual and group
Measuring aptitude versus achievement
IQ and school success
IQ and occupational level
IQ and creativity
Artificial intelligence—the computer's "IQ" and "creativity"
Does IQ determine success in life?

IQ AND THE ISSUE OF HEREDITY VERSUS ENVIRONMENT   282

Family similarities in IQ
But is it the family genes or the family environment?
The interplay between heredity and environment
Some ways that environment can affect IQ
Dramatic shifts in IQ level: why do they occur?

THE SCIENCE OF TESTING MENTAL ABILITIES   290

The first requirement: objectivity
The second requirement: reliability
The third requirement: validity
The fourth requirement: standardization
Vocational aptitude tests
Interest tests and the matter of appraising personality

SUMMARY   293

IMPORTANT TERMS   296

RECOMMENDED READINGS   296

PSYCHOLOGY IN EVERYDAY LIFE

Capitalizing on your IQ   264
The social impact of intelligence testing   277
Why smart people fail in life   283
The issue of race and intelligence   285
Lessons about IQ for parents and teachers   290

Among the words we use most frequently are adjectives describing the human attribute that is the subject of this chapter. Note how often you hear comments like these:

That was a very *intelligent* remark.
What a *brilliant* idea.
Now there's a really *smart* child.
I just did a terribly *dumb* thing.
That was not too *bright* of you.
Don't ask such *stupid* questions.

Intelligence, or lack of it, is one of the most widely discussed of all human characteristics. But, although the word is used in conversation as if everyone understood its meaning, psychologists who have spent a lifetime trying to agree on a definition are not so sure how best to define it. Perhaps the most practical definition of intelligence was proposed by David Wechsler, who constructed a number of today's most widely used intelligence tests. He defined intelligence as *the capacity to understand the world and the resourcefulness to cope with its challenges.* That is to say, you are intelligent if you know what is going on around you, can learn from experience, and therefore act in ways that are successful in your particular circumstances. Your behavior is intelligent if it has meaning and direction and is rational and worthwhile (Wechsler, 1975). Clearly, what is rational and worthwhile will vary with where and when we live. What Wechsler's definition seems to say is, for example, that a person who was considered highly intelligent in Egypt in 500 B.C. might not be considered so in the United States in 1988.

The subject of intelligence raises many questions. Four central ones are these:

- Is intelligence best viewed as a single ability or a combination of different abilities?
- Can a person be highly skilled in some areas of mental ability but well below average in others?
- What is actually measured by intelligence tests? If, for example, one of today's intelligence tests shows that a person has an IQ of 110 (or 90 or 100 or 120), how much does that tell us about that person's chances for getting along in school—and, more important, for leading a happy and successful life?
- Granted that some people are more intelligent than others, what roles do heredity and environment play in such differences?

A great deal of psychological research has been devoted to these questions. Indeed many of them, as you will soon see, are still topics of considerable debate.

David Wechsler (1896–1981)

THE NATURE OF INTELLIGENCE: SOME DIFFERENT VIEWS

One problem plaguing all investigators is that intelligence can mean different things to different people—and has done so from time to time and place to place throughout human history. The ancient Greeks considered intelligence to mean talent for oratory. The Chinese, until the twentieth century, judged it to mean mastery of the written word, which is a different skill. Some tribes in Africa attribute intelligence to a person with hunting ability, many South Pacific islanders to a person with the ability to navigate a canoe. Even in our own nation, intelligent behavior can mean different things to colleges, corporations, rural farm areas, and inner city ghettos.

Wechsler pointed out, therefore, that the way we use the word *intelligence* represents a value judgment. That is to say, we call people intelligent when they have qualities that we ourselves—or our society as a whole, or the special part of society in which we live—consider resourceful and worthwhile. In general, our American culture admires fluency in language and talent for mathematics and science. The most intelligent people, according to the consensus, are those who can analyze facts, reason about them logically, and express their conclusions in convincing words. These are the very qualities that are associated with doing well in our schools—and, as will be seen later, our intelligence tests measure academic ability better than they measure anything else.

Is Intelligence a General Ability?
The Views of Spearman and Thurstone

One of the first influential theories of intelligence was suggested many years ago by Charles Spearman, who applied sophisticated statistical analysis to the results of test scores on many kinds of abilities from reading comprehension to visualization of spatial relationships. Spearman concluded that the score on any test depends in part on an *s factor*, meaning a specific kind of skill at that particular kind of task. But people with a high level of s factor on one task also tend to make high scores at other tasks—a fact that Spearman believed could only be explained by a pervasive kind of mental ability that he called the *g factor*, for *general intelligence* (Spearman, 1927).

Another psychologist, L. L. Thurstone, disagreed with the idea of general intelligence and set out to disprove it. He too gave dozens of different tests to schoolchildren, measuring their ability at a wide range of tasks—and he, too, despite his original aim, wound up

Every culture has its own view of what intelligent behavior consists of—hunting skills in a bushman society and teaching skills in American society.

convinced that a g factor affects many different skills. Thurstone proposed the theory that intelligence is composed of this general factor plus seven specific skills that he called *primary mental abilities*:

1. *Verbal comprehension*—indicated by size of vocabulary, ability to read, and skill at understanding mixed-up sentences and the meaning of proverbs.
2. *Word fluency*—the ability to think of words quickly, as when making rhymes or solving word puzzles.
3. *Number*—the ability to solve arithmetic problems and to manipulate numbers.
4. *Space*—the ability to visualize spatial relationships, as in recognizing a design after it has been placed in a new context.
5. *Associative memory*—the ability to memorize quickly, as in learning a list of paired words.
6. *Perceptual speed*—indicated by the ability to grasp visual details quickly and to observe similarities and differences between designs and pictures.
7. *General reasoning*—skill at the kind of logical thinking that was described in Chapter 7.

As the next section will show, studies of intelligence during the past two decades have tended to support the view of Thurstone. While individuals tend to differ in overall intellectual ability, they appear to differ much more dramatically in a hierarchy of specific abilities (Kail and Pellegrino, 1985).

What Skills Make Up Intelligence? The Views of Guilford, Gardner, and Sternberg

Today's intelligence tests usually measure performance on most of the seven primary abilities proposed by Thurstone. But people who are skillful at any one of them do not always do well on others. The correlations among them are so low that a few psychologists have questioned the existence of the g, or general, factor (Stevenson, Friedrichs, and Simpson, 1970).

One group of investigators, headed by J. P. Guilford of the University of Southern California, extended the work of Thurstone and concluded that intelligence seems to be made up of no less than 120 different kinds of ability. The 120-factor theory, illustrated in Figure 8-1, maintains that an individual may display a very high level of ability at some tasks, average ability at others, and low ability at still others. Guilford and his associates devised finely differentiated tests for many of the 120 factors—and found very little relationship between their subjects' scores on one test and their scores on many of the others (Guilford, 1967).

Among other things, Guilford found that people differ widely in their abilities to deal with different kinds of materials (or *contents*, as they are termed in Figure 8-1). For example, some people are very good at handling *semantic contents*, or language and ideas. These people might be outstanding as writers and philosophers. Others excel at working with *symbolic contents*, such as numbers. These people might be most productive as mathematicians or accountants. Others do best with *figural contents*, such as pictures or specific objects. These people would seem best suited to becoming commercial artists or master mechanics.

Recent theories also focus on specific rather than general mental abilities. Howard Gardner has described a set of seven fundamental but separate "intelligences": linguistic ability, skills in logic and mathematics, the ability to use spatial concepts, musical ability,

Figure 8-1 Guilford's 120-factor theory of intelligence

The separate kinds of ability suggested by Guilford are represented by the small individual blocks contained in the cube. The theory maintains that each factor is the ability to perform one of five different types of mental operations on one of four different kinds of material, or contents, with the aim of coming up with one of six different kinds of end results, or products. Thus the total number of abilities that make up intelligence (or blocks in the cube) is 5 × 4 × 6, or 120. Followers of the theory measure the mental operation called "divergent thinking" by asking a question such as "How many uses can you think of for a brick?"—and noting how many different answers the individual can come up with and how imaginative the answers are. One test of the mental operation called "evaluation" is to present the four words cat, cow, mule, and mare and ask whether these are best categorized as: (a) farm animals, (b) four-legged animals, or (c) domestic animals. The answer will be found at the bottom of page 264.

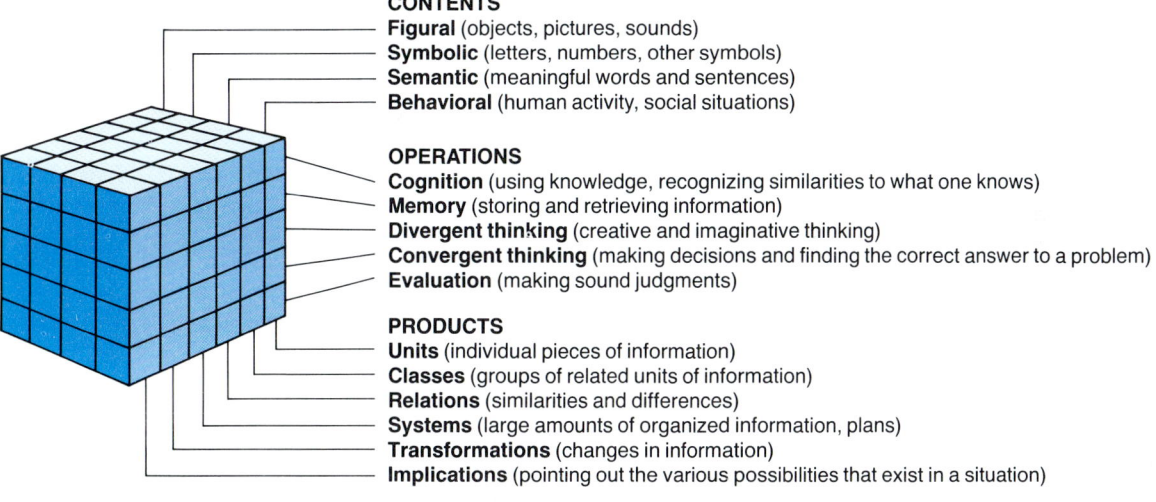

CONTENTS
- **Figural** (objects, pictures, sounds)
- **Symbolic** (letters, numbers, other symbols)
- **Semantic** (meaningful words and sentences)
- **Behavioral** (human activity, social situations)

OPERATIONS
- **Cognition** (using knowledge, recognizing similarities to what one knows)
- **Memory** (storing and retrieving information)
- **Divergent thinking** (creative and imaginative thinking)
- **Convergent thinking** (making decisions and finding the correct answer to a problem)
- **Evaluation** (making sound judgments)

PRODUCTS
- **Units** (individual pieces of information)
- **Classes** (groups of related units of information)
- **Relations** (similarities and differences)
- **Systems** (large amounts of organized information, plans)
- **Transformations** (changes in information)
- **Implications** (pointing out the various possibilities that exist in a situation)

---

skills of motor movement and coordination, interpersonal skills, and the ability to understand one's self (Gardner, 1983). Robert J. Sternberg has proposed a "triarchic" or three-part, theory of intelligence emphasizing that intelligence involves (1) specific behaviors that differ from one cultural environment to another; (2) the ability to deal with new situations; and (3) both knowledge as well as actual performance (Sternberg, 1985).

The theories of Guilford, Gardner, and Sternberg that minimize the importance of a g factor have their followers and their critics—and the search for new knowledge about the nature of intelligence continues. Meanwhile, the present theories all offer useful guidance to people who are planning their education and careers—as will be seen in a box on Psychology in Everyday Life called "Capitalizing on Your IQ."

Piaget's Theory of Intelligence

Another view of intelligence came from the Swiss psychologist Jean Piaget, who spent more than a half century studying the mental development of his own and other children as they grew from infancy through adolescence. Unlike the views we have considered thus far, which concern how people differ in a broad range of specific abilities, Piaget's theory is concerned with identifying the way mental abilities develop early in life in all of us.

Piaget's observations have greatly influenced psychology's current position on how we think, reason, solve problems, and use our intelligence to understand and adapt to our

Psychology in Everyday Life
Capitalizing on Your IQ

Whatever the exact nature of intelligence is finally discovered to be—if indeed the mystery can ever be solved—there seems to be no doubt that all of us, at any given point in our lives, are gifted with a certain amount of it. Except for the most retarded, all humans possess more information-processing ability, "capacity to understand," "resourcefulness to cope," or whatever one chooses to call it, than any of the lower animals. Within our own species we vary over a wide range. But whatever our own level may be, we can use psychology's knowledge to apply our intelligence to the best possible advantage. Our school systems, likewise, can use the findings to guide students into the most productive possible lives.

One of the most crucial decisions that everyone must make—and one that is especially urgent during the school years—is the choice of job and career. If you manage to find the right job, suited to your own particular abilities, you are likely to perform well and be successful and happy in your work. The wrong job can be a disaster. You probably know people who find life miserable because they are trying to adjust to jobs they find a constant struggle—where they have to work painfully hard, and run very fast, just to stay in place. No matter how hard they try, they never manage to get on top of the work they have chosen. They are always worried about mistakes and failure. Yet all the psychological theories about the nature of intelligence suggest that they might have found some other line of work easy, pleasant, and rewarding.

The general-factor theories suggest that two people, though the same in IQ, may perform very differently at different kinds of tasks. On test items that measure one of Thurstone's seven primary mental abilities—and on a job that utilizes that special ability—you may do as well as someone with an IQ as much as 15 points higher. At another, you may perform no better than someone with an IQ 15 points lower. Theories like Guilford's, based on specific abilities, suggest that the swing can be even greater.

Ability, of course, is not the only factor in determining your "fit" to a job. A lot depends on your own particular interests and personality traits. Of two jobs at which you are equally good, you might love one and hate the other. Other things being equal, however, you are likely to be comfortable

---

world. He has been a major figure in the rise of the cognitive school, and no introduction to modern psychology would be complete without a discussion of the essential elements of his theory.

Piaget concluded that our mental growth—which he defined as an increased ability to adapt to new situations—takes place because of two key processes that he calls *assimilation* and *accommodation*. Assimilation is the process of incorporating a new stimulus into one's existing cognitive view of the world. Accommodation is the process of changing one's cognitive view and behavior when new information dictates such a change.

As a simple example, consider a young boy who has a number of toys. To these familiar old toys we add a new one, a magnet. The boy's initial impulse will be to assimilate the new toy into his existing knowledge of other toys; he may try to bang it like a hammer,

---

Although all three of the answers to the question posed in Figure 8-1 are correct, the best answer is (c) domestic animals. This makes the finest and neatest distinction between the four animals and other kinds of animals. "Farm animals" is not the best answer because a cat is often found elsewhere. "Four-legged animals" is not the best answer because almost all animals have four legs.

and successful at a job that suits your talents. The school years—and especially college—provide an opportunity to learn your strong points and weaknesses. If you find mathematics difficult, the theories of intelligence would suggest that you quickly abandon any thought of being an engineer or accountant. Difficulty in English courses, especially composition, is a warning against attempts to find a career where fluency in language is important, such as journalism, teaching, the law, or politics. Similarly, the subjects you find easier and more interesting than others point to your best opportunities for a fruitful career. Many people, without ever having heard of a g factor or Guilford's work, have found that the best thing that happened to them in college was discovering that they were unusually good at something they had never suspected.

Happiness often means choosing a job you enjoy.

throw it like a ball, or blow it like a horn. But once he learns that the magnet has a new and unprecedented quality—the power to attract iron—he accommodates his view of toys to include this previously unfamiliar fact. He now behaves on the revised assumption that some toys are not designed to bang, throw, or make noise with but to attract metal.

There is always tension, Piaget concluded, between assimilation (which in essence represents the use of old ideas to meet new situations) and accommodation (which in essence is a change of old ideas to meet new situations). The resolution of this tension results in intellectual growth. Thus we can develop our cognitive skills only through active interaction with the objects and other people in our world. We need an environment that exposes us to new situations and new problems and thus challenges us to exercise and increase our mental skills.

Another key word in the Piaget theory is *operations*. The term is difficult to define. Roughly, an operation is a sort of dynamic mental rule for manipulating objects or ideas into new forms and back to the original, like the rule that four pieces of candy (or the mere figure 4) can be divided into two parts of two each, then put back again into the original four. The full meaning will become clearer as our discussion proceeds.

Jean Piaget (1896–1980)

Piaget's Four Steps in Mental Growth: 1. The Sensorimotor Stage

Piaget found that mental growth, beginning at birth, takes place in a series of four stages, in each of which the child thinks and behaves in quite different fashion than earlier. He maintains that the child grows intellectually not like a leaf, which simply gets larger every day, but like a caterpillar that is eventually transformed into a butterfly (Piaget, 1952).

In the first or *sensorimotor stage*, during about the first 18 months of life, children have not yet learned to use language and symbols to represent the objects and events in the environment. Infants begin to know the world in terms of their own sensory impressions of its sights, sounds, tastes, and smells. But soon they begin to discover the relationship between their actions toward the objects they perceive and the consequences that follow. By the age of four to six months, babies are aware that they can produce results through physical activity. They will repeatedly kick at toys hanging over their cribs, apparently to make them swing and thus produce a change of stimulus that they find interesting. By the age of 12 months they act as if they know that objects are permanent and do not mysteriously disappear. If a toy is shown to them and then is hidden behind two pillows side by side in the crib, they know how to find it. They look first behind one of the pillows. If the toy is not there, they look behind the other.

2. The Preoperational Stage

From about 18 months to around the seventh birthday, children are in what Piaget calls the *preoperational stage*. They have acquired language and can manipulate symbols. They may behave toward a doll as if it were a child and toward a stick as if it were a gun. They often put objects together in appropriate groups—for example, all their red blocks into one pile and the blue blocks into another. But their actions are still dictated largely by the evidence of their senses. They have not yet developed the kinds of concepts that would enable them to form meaningful categories. They are not yet capable of thinking in terms of the dynamic rules of operations.

Children of about four or five, for example, can learn to select the middle-sized of three rubber balls. They have attained what Piaget has called an *intuitive understanding* that the

This child, in Piaget's sensorimotor stage, delights in discovering the results of his own muscular movements.

middle-sized ball is bigger than the small one but smaller than the big one. But if three balls of very different size from the original three are then shown, they must learn to make the selection all over again (Stevenson and Bitterman, 1955)—because they have not yet grasped the operational rule that distinguishes all middle-sized objects, of whatever nature, from those larger or smaller.

3. The Stage of Concrete Operations

Some time between the ages of six and eight, American children enter the *stage of concrete operations*—the period at which, as the name implies, they first begin to reason about concrete events in the world. They now become capable of manipulating ideas about events mentally. One of their accomplishments is the discovery of the important concrete operational rule that Piaget calls *conservation* illustrated in Figure 8-2—that is, the fact that you can change the appearance of an object—like a ball of clay—without changing its volume, mass, number, or weight.

Children are now able to learn a variety of operational rules. They know, for example, that if object no. 1 is as heavy as object no. 2, and no. 2 is as heavy as no. 3, then nos. 1 and 3 must be equal in weight. They have also acquired considerable sophistication in the use of concepts and categories. They realize, for example, that "all the pets that are dogs" plus "all the pets that are not dogs" go to make up a category called "all pets." They also realize that objects or attributes can belong to more than one concept. They know that animals can be tame or wild, furry or feathered.

Thus children in the stage of concrete operations show an ability to reason logically and apply operational rules. But as Piaget's name for the stage implies, they reason more effectively about objects that they can see or feel than about verbal statements. Suppose, for example, that children of this age are asked: "A is the same size as B, but B is smaller than C; which is bigger, A or C?" They may not be able to answer—for the question requires thinking about an abstract idea rather than about concrete objects.

Figure 8-2 Figuring out the conservation rule

A child of five still in the preoperational stage, will say that the taller beaker has more water. In contrast, a child of seven who has entered the concrete operations stage, will say that the glasses still have the same amount of water. The ability to reverse events mentally—for example, to see that it is possible to pour the water from beaker C back to B—is a key advance in concrete operations.

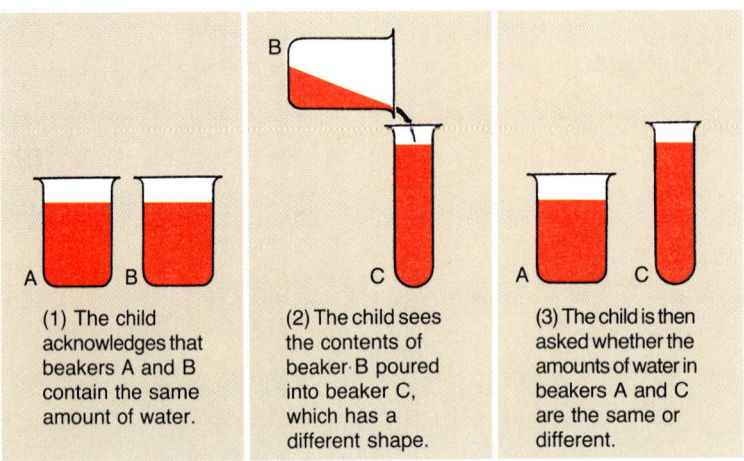

(1) The child acknowledges that beakers A and B contain the same amount of water.

(2) The child sees the contents of beaker B poured into beaker C, which has a different shape.

(3) The child is then asked whether the amounts of water in beakers A and C are the same or different.

4. The Stage of Formal Operations

The fourth and final period of mental growth—the *stage of formal operations*—begins at around the age of 12. In a giant leap toward intellectual skill, children in their adolescent years acquire the ability to reason logically not just about actual objects but about abstract ideas and possibilities. They acquire full mastery of the important rules that Piaget calls operations and can apply them to all kinds of situations, real or imagined. They can assume hypothetical conditions and make correct inferences, thus manipulating their own thoughts as readily as they once manipulated colored blocks. It is probably not a coincidence that the emergence of this stage is associated with maturation of those portions of the brain's frontal cortex that play an important role in thought processes (Stuss and Benson, 1986).

The dramatic difference between the stages of concrete and formal operations is demonstrated by children's response to a question that requires them to analyze a theoretical situation—for example, "If all unicorns have yellow feet and I have yellow feet, am I a unicorn?" Younger children, still confined to the world of actual objects, cannot answer because they are incapable of reasoning about such nonexistent matters as unicorns and having yellow feet. Older children, having reached the stage of formal operations, can examine the logic of the hypothetical problem and quickly answer, "No."

In Piaget's words, "Thought takes wings." Adolescents no longer waste time trying to answer questions or solve problems with trial and error techniques. Instead they make definite plans to apply an operational rule. They try to think systematically of all the possible solutions, then reexamine their thinking to make sure they have indeed exhausted all the possibilities.

One prominent characteristic of the stage of formal operations is preoccupation with one's own thought processes. Adolescents think about their own thoughts and are curious

These third-graders can understand math concepts more readily by manipulating concrete objects.

to learn how these thoughts are organized and where they will lead. This inquiring attitude often causes conflict with the standards of the adult world. Adolescents become keenly aware that people do not always practice what they preach, and they begin to question such ideals as democracy, honesty, self-sacrifice, and turning the other cheek. They may decide that many of the beliefs and values they have been taught are "phony"—and to search instead for a different set of moral principles and a new philosophy of life.

What Piaget's Theory Implies for Educating Children

In one way or another you have progressed through the four stages of intellectual development as charted by Piaget. Your timing may have been on the fast side or the slow side, for there are considerable individual differences in the age at which children move from one stage to the next. But the transformation from sensorimotor infant to adolescent capable of formal operations seems to take place in the same manner for most people—even for children of different nationalities, and regardless of what kind of education they receive (Goodnow and Bethon, 1966).

It appears impossible to speed up the process by trying to teach the reasoning skills appropriate to a more advanced period (Brown, 1965). Children can understand only experiences and information that match their fund of vocabulary, facts, and rules—or that are just a bit in advance of their existing information and cognitive skills. If a new experience or idea has no readily apparent connection with what they already know, they are not likely to learn much if anything about it. They may not even pay attention to it.

On the other hand, it appears that the progress of many children is retarded as the result of their unstimulating home environment or failure and criticism in the early years of school. Children from low-income homes, in particular, may become so discouraged that they never take full advantage of the abilities they develop during the stage of formal operations. They may have a good deal more intelligence than they display or even realize. One reason is that their environment may lead them to make low scores on intelligence tests, which in turn leads both them and their teachers to have lower expectations for them, which leads to a further inhibition of their ability to display the skills measured by the tests. Hence the importance of taking a realistic look at intelligence tests, which is the next topic.

INTELLIGENCE TESTS: WHAT CAN THEY ACTUALLY TELL US?

For Piaget, intelligence referred to the improved ability of all children to perform the reasoning operations that permit adaptation to the environment. He was not concerned with individual differences in the kinds of abilities measured by *intelligence tests*. Such tests began as a psychologist's solution to a problem faced by Paris schools at the beginning of the century, when compulsory education began. Many classrooms were crowded, and slow students were holding up the progress of the faster ones. One solution, it seemed, would be to identify the children who lacked the mental capacity required by the standard curriculum and put them in a separate school of their own. But how could they be recognized?

A French psychologist named Alfred Binet who went to work on the problem realized that the task of identifying the poorer students could not safely be left to the teachers. There was too much danger that teachers would show favoritism toward children who had pleasant personalities and would be too harsh on those who were troublemakers. There was also the question of whether teachers could recognize children who appeared dull but in fact could have done the work if they had tried (Cronbach, 1949).

To avoid these pitfalls, Binet developed a test designed to measure potential ability at school tasks rather than performance in school—and to produce the same scores regardless of the personalities or prejudices of those who gave or took the test. Binet's test was first published in 1905, has been revised as recently as 1985, and is still used widely today. In fact all modern intelligence tests bear a considerable resemblance to Binet's original work.

Alfred Binet (1857–1911) with his daughters

Figure 8-3 An examiner's set of materials for the newly revised (1985) Stanford-Binet test

Small children taking the Stanford-Binet Intelligence Scale are asked to perform various tasks with a paper doll and toys.

In the United States, one of the best-known current versions of the original test is the *Stanford-Binet Intelligence Scale*. With the simple kind of physical equipment shown in Figure 8-3, it can be given successfully even to children who are too young to have developed a wide range of language skills. Older children and adults are asked questions that measure such things as vocabulary, memory span for sentences and numbers, and reasoning ability. Some of the test items used at various age levels are shown in Figure 8-4.

Mental Age, Chronological Age, and IQ

The scoring method originally used by Binet was based on the concept of *mental age*, or MA for short. As children mature, they are able to pass more and more of the items on tests of this type. The testing of large numbers of children has shown exactly how many items the average child is able to pass at the age of six or seven or whatever the child's actual age happens to be. To examiners, actual age in years and months is known as *chronological age*, or CA for short.

For the average child, mental age and chronological age are equal. But children who have less intelligence than average are unable to pass all the items suitable to their age level and thus show an MA that is lower than their CA. Those who have more intelligence than average pass some of the items designed for older children and thus show an MA that is higher than their CA.

The relationship between mental age and chronological age was the original basis for that well-known term *intelligence quotient*, or IQ. The average IQ was arbitrarily set at 100, a convenient figure, and the individual child's IQ was determined by the formula

$$IQ = \frac{MA}{CA} \times 100$$

Intelligence Tests: What Can They Actually Tell Us?

Figure 8-4 Some Stanford-Binet test items

As shown by these examples, the questions asked very young children do not demand fluency in language. The questions increase in difficulty, particularly in matters of language and reasoning, at higher age levels.

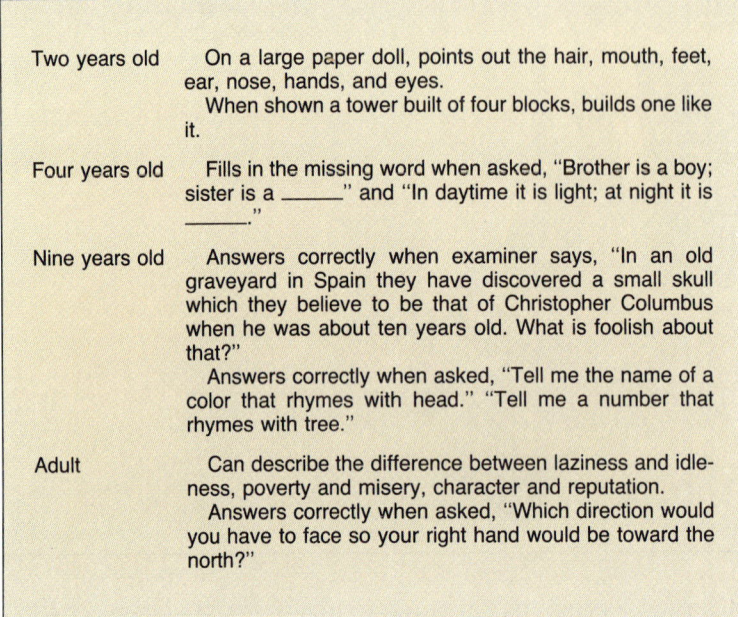

When MA and CA are equal, the formula results in an IQ score of 100. When MA exceeds CA, the score falls above 100, and when the reverse is true, the score falls below 100. The intelligence quotient can thus still be thought of in terms of its original meaning. The average IQ is 100. The ability to pass items above one's age level indicates an IQ of more than 100, and the inability to pass all the items appropriate for one's age level results in an IQ of less than 100. In actual practice, the IQ of an individual taking the Stanford-Binet or other intelligence tests is now determined from tables that translate the individual's raw score on the test and chronological age into an IQ figure. The way IQs are distributed in the population, according to the Stanford-Binet test, is shown in Figure 8-5. Keep in mind that the classifications used are arbitrary and should not be considered as rigid labels.

Some Widely Used Intelligence Tests: Individual and Group

The Stanford-Binet is only one of many tests now available. Even more widely used today are three devised by David Wechsler—the Wechsler Adult Intelligence Scale (or WAIS for short), another for children aged 7 to 16, and still another for children 4 to 6½. The distinguishing feature of the Wechsler tests is that they contain two separate kinds of items, called verbal and performance. The verbal items measure vocabulary, information, general comprehension, memory span, arithmetic reasoning, and ability to detect similarities between concepts. The performance items measure ability at completing pictures, arranging pictures, working puzzles, substituting unfamiliar symbols for digits, and making designs with blocks as shown in Figure 8-6.

Figure 8-5 Ranges of IQ and how many people are found at each level

Administering the Stanford-Binet test to thousands of people has shown that one person in a hundred comes out with an IQ over 139 and can be classified as "very superior." (In popular terminology, this person is a "genius.") Three in a hundred come out with IQs below 70 and are classified as "mentally retarded." Almost half of all people have IQs in the "average" range of 90 to 109.

IQ	Classification	Percentage of people
Over 139	Very superior	1
120-139	Superior	11
110-119	High average	18
90-109	Average	46
80-89	Low average	15
70-79	Borderline	6
Below 70	Mentally retarded	3

Figure 8-6 A performance item on a Wechsler test

With colored blocks of various patterns, the subject is asked to copy a design as one of the performance items on a Weschler Intelligence Scale. The examiner notes how long the task takes as well as how accurately it is performed.

A subject's IQ can be calculated for the test as a whole or for the verbal items and the performance items considered separately. This feature is often an advantage in testing people who lack skill in the use of the English language, for they may score much higher on the performance items than on the verbal items.

Both the Stanford-Binet and the Wechslers are *individual tests*, given to one person at a time by a trained examiner. The advantage of individual tests is that the examiner can readily detect if the results are being influenced by such factors as poor vision, temporary ill health, or lack of motivation. Their disadvantage, of course, is that they cannot conveniently be used to test large numbers of people, such as all the pupils in a big school.

Available for large-scale testing of many people at the same time are a number of *group tests*—typically taking the form of printed questions, such as those shown in Figure 8-7, which are answered by making penciled notations. Among the widely used group tests are the Scholastic Aptitude Tests, or SAT, taken each year by about a million high school juniors and seniors and used by many colleges and universities as one of the methods of judging applicants. The SAT has two parts, one for verbal ability and the other for mathematics, with the possible score on each part ranging from 200 to 800. In recent years the average scores have been around 431 on the verbal scale and 475 on the mathematical. Since the students taking the test are a selected group who have already proved their ability to get along in school, the 431 and 475 averages represent an IQ of well over 100.

It is well known that a number of colleges and universities have a cutoff point for SAT scores and will rarely admit a student who falls below that level. Therefore the SAT terrifies many high school seniors. Actually, however, the SAT affects college admissions less often than is generally supposed. A survey made around the start of this decade found that only 48 percent of American institutions of higher learning even require all applicants to take

Figure 8-7 A group intelligence test for young children

These are sample items for second- and third-graders from the Otis-Lennon School Ability Test. Sample items demonstrate how the questions should be answered and are not counted in the actual scoring. The actual items in this test range from about as difficult as the sample items shown here to much more difficult. At this age level, the person administering the test reads the instructions to the children taking it. Older children and adults taking group tests read the instructions themselves, so that the tests can be given just by handing them out.

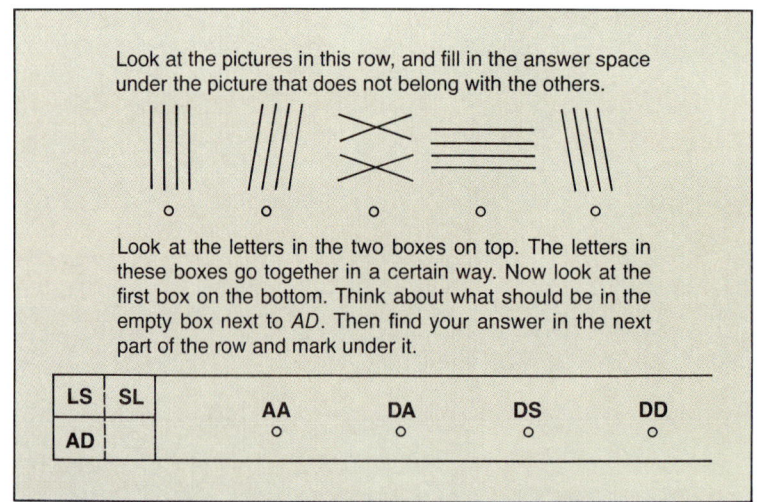

the test. Only 2 percent listed SAT scores as the "most important" factor and another 43 percent as "very important." Many more institutions were found to give greater weight to grades in high school, which 31 percent called "most important" and another 34 percent "very important" (AACRAO and the College Board, 1980). High school grades, it has been established, do just as well as SAT scores in predicting success in college (Trusheim and Crouse, 1982).

The United States has so many institutions of higher learning, with such various admissions policies, that it is "not very difficult for even the minimally academically motivated student to gain admission to some college" (Hargadon, 1981). High school seniors in other nations would envy their American counterparts. In China, for example, college applicants have to take a three-day examination covering six different subjects—and of the 3 million students who take the exam only 300,000 are accepted (Butterfield, 1980).

Measuring Aptitude versus Achievement

Since the work of Binet, all intelligence tests have been what are called *aptitude tests*, measuring a person's ability to learn a new skill or perform an unfamiliar task. Such tests are, at least in theory, far different from *achievement tests*, which measure how much learning or skill a person has actually acquired. Intelligence tests attempt to determine how well the individual will be able to perform academic work in the future. Academic achievement tests, on the other hand, show how much the individual has accomplished in the past. For example the Iowa and Stanford achievement tests, widely used in elementary and high schools, show how much pupils have learned about such classroom subjects as reading and arithmetic—and how they compare with other pupils around the nation. A final exam in college is in essence an achievement test, the purpose of which is to measure how much you have learned about the course.

In designing an aptitude test—for academic talent or anything else—one serious problem is that it is usually impossible to measure ability without any regard for past achievement. It has been said that "all tests reflect what a person has learned" (Anastasi, 1981). If you look back at the items from the Stanford-Binet test shown in Figure 8-4 (page 272), you will see that many of them require at least some kind of prior learning. To answer correctly, a two-year-old must have learned the meaning of the words *hair, mouth,* and *hands*. The nine-year-old must have acquired some fairly rich concepts of age and physical growth. The adult must have learned the points of the compass and the distinctions between such words as *laziness* and *idleness*.

Intelligence tests try to surmount this problem, insofar as possible, by measuring subjects' ability to use their existing knowledge in a novel way. Thus two-year-olds are asked to apply to a paper doll their knowledge about their own mouth and hair. Adults are asked to make a novel spatial orientation based on their knowledge of the compass. Moreover, in constructing intelligence tests an attempt is made to base all the questions on knowledge and skills that everyone has had an equal chance to obtain. It is assumed that every two-year-old has had an opportunity to learn the meaning of *hair, mouth,* and *hands,* that every four-year-old knows the meaning of *houses* and *books,* and that every adult should have been exposed to information about the points of the compass. No questions are asked that can be answered only by a child who has had nature study in summer camp, or only by an adult who has studied trigonometry or Spanish.

Nonetheless there is a certain amount of bias in intelligence tests. In a nation containing as many diverse social and ethnic groups as the United States, not all people are exposed to the same kinds of basic knowledge. The tests favor those who have acquired the knowledge and language skills typical of the middle and upper-middle classes and fostered by a school system largely staffed by middle-class teachers. Thus the tests produce some uneven results. Children from middle-class and upper-class homes make higher scores in general than children from lower-class homes (Janke and Havighurst, 1945). City children tend to make higher scores than children from rural areas (McNemar, 1942). Black children and children of ethnic groups from some other cultural backgrounds make lower average scores (Herzog and Lewis, 1970). Thus there appears to be little question that IQ test results are affected by past experience, although psychologists differ in their assessments of how much bias actually exists in such tests.

IQ and School Success

Scores on intelligence tests, besides being affected by past learning, also depend to a considerable extent on many personality factors: "Whenever one measures a child's cognitive functioning, one is also measuring cooperation, attention, persistence, ability to sit still, and social responsiveness" (Scarr, 1981). Motivation is especially important—and therefore it is not surprising that middle-class children, who are strongly encouraged to take pride in the mastery of reading, writing, spelling, and arithmetic, make higher scores on the average than lower-class children who are less motivated toward academic success. Also important is what is often called adjustment, or psychological well-being—a fact that produces higher scores among children from stable and secure family backgrounds.

Thus intelligence tests cannot hope to measure, with pinpoint accuracy, an individual's sheer, disembodied skill at information processing (or Wechsler's "capacity to understand the world"). Nonetheless the IQ, as determined by any of the standard group or individual tests, is a good indication of how well a person is likely to do in school. Many studies have been made of the relationship between IQ and grades in classes all the way from elementary school to the university level, and all have shown correlations ranging from .40 to .60 or even higher (Wing and Wallach, 1971). The correlations have long been known to be greater for some forms of school achievement such as reading comprehension than others such as reading speed. Such correlations may be affected when families and schools place heavy emphasis on certain areas of academic success. For example, Japanese schoolchildren do better in tests of math skills than American children because, in recent decades, Japanese parents and teachers have placed a greater emphasis on learning arithmetic (Stevenson et al., 1985; Stevenson, Lee, and Stigler, 1986).

The relationship between IQ and school achievement stems from Binet's basic aim in designing the original test, which was to predict how well an individual pupil could be expected to perform in the classroom. Binet tried many test items of many different kinds and kept only the items on which pupils who were successful in their classes did better than those who were failing. He deliberately avoided the use of any items, such as measures of physical dexterity or musical talent, that did not seem relevant to grades. It would perhaps be more fitting to say that his test and its modern counterparts measure an individual's AQ, or academic quotient, rather than IQ, or intelligence quotient. The fact that the tests are called measures of intelligence, rather than something more modest, is one reason they have come under attack in recent years by many psychologists as well as by outside critics and the legal system, as explained in a box on Psychology in Everyday Life called "The Social Impact of Intelligence Testing."

IQ and Occupational Level

Though the IQ is a good predictor of success in school, there is some question as to how well it predicts anything else. What about jobs, for example? Does a high IQ mean you are destined for a high-level occupation, a low IQ for a low-level job?

Psychology in Everyday Life
The Social Impact of Intelligence Testing

The history of intelligence testing has taken a curious twist. Until the 1960s it was "generally considered to be one of psychology's major success stories" (Tyler, 1976). Today it is one of the most controversial aspects of the science—passionately criticized by many "concerned citizens and parents, teacher organizations . . . psychologists . . . and consumer advocate groups" (Glaser and Bond, 1981), though also stoutly defended by many (Snyderman and Rothman, 1987).

The basic issue is as much a matter of social policy as of scientific validity. Critics question not only the accuracy of the tests and the way they are administered and scored but also the social consequences—on the ground that testing perpetuates the advantages now enjoyed by middle-class and upper-class Americans and is unfair and harmful to the lower classes and to minorities, notably blacks and Hispanics (Carroll and Horn, 1981). They point out that the lower average scores made by minority groups bar a disproportionate number of them from jobs and promotions in industry and civil service, and also cut off many educational opportunities.

In education, a particularly controversial issue is the assignment of young pupils to the special classes set up in many school systems for the "educable mentally retarded" found to have IQs of 50–70. Theoretically these classes protect the pupils from failure in the standard curriculum and provide remedial training that may enable them to resume a place in their suitable grade later on. One of Binet's purposes in creating his test was to find children whose intelligence was not developing properly and raise their IQ through special instruction. Critics maintain, however, that the instruction is often slipshod and the "retarded" label forever dooms the child to a second-rate education.

The complexities of the controversy were apparent in the conflicting views of two groups of eminent educators that were published almost simultaneously a few years ago. A panel appointed by the National Academy of Sciences, which concentrated on examining the scientific evidence for and against testing, concluded that tests have proved on the whole to be valid and useful in predicting how well an individual will do in the classroom or on a job. Although testing should not be the only criterion, said the Academy's panel, it is not in itself unfair to minorities, whose lower average scores merely reflect their disadvantaged background (National Research Council, 1982).

The opposite conclusion was reached by the Commission on the Higher Education of Minorities, which concentrated chiefly on the social consequences. The Commission found that all forms of testing as now practiced—including even classroom exams used to determine a student's grades—serve no real educational purpose and merely "pose special obstacles to the development of minority students." Instead of trying to rank students in comparison with one another, the Commission suggested, the schools should measure the progress and growth of the individual student—for the "principal function" of the educational system is to "increase the competence of students" and help them "lead more productive and fulfilling lives" (Astin, 1982).

One massive body of evidence bearing on these questions comes from a study of the many thousands of men who took the Army's group intelligence test during the Second World War. The results, some of which are illustrated in Figure 8-8, indicate that there is indeed a relation between IQ and occupation—but less than one might expect. The average IQ of such professional people as accountants and engineers was around 120, and the average for truck drivers and miners was below 100. But there was a wide range of IQs in every occupation. The IQs of accountants ranged from about 95 to over 140. The IQs of

Figure 8-8 Jobs and IQs

The bars show the range of IQs of men in various occupations. Miners, for example, were found to have IQs from under 60 to nearly 130. The average IQ for each occupation is indicated by the vertical black lines inside the bar. For miners, the average was 93. For an interpretation of the figures, see the text (Harrell and Harrell, 1945).

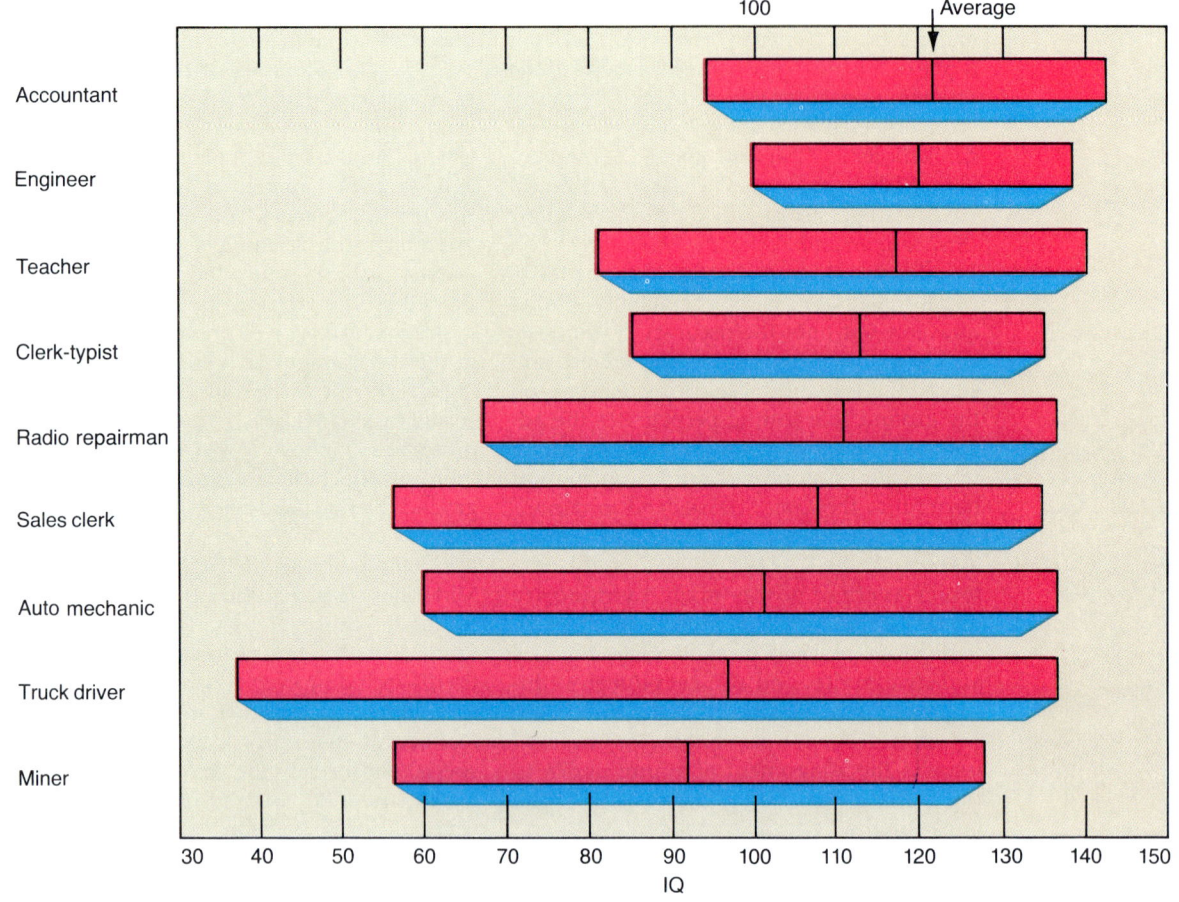

truck drivers showed a particularly wide range—all the way from under 40 to nearly 140. Some accountants had IQs lower than the average for truck drivers—and a number of truck drivers (and miners and mechanics as well) had IQs higher than the average for accountants, engineers, and teachers.

One explanation for these findings undoubtedly is the amount of education the men in the study had received. Of two people with equal IQs, the one able to go to college may become an accountant or engineer. The other, unable for one reason or another to go to college or even complete high school, may have to settle for a job of much lower prestige. In fact other studies have shown that education is the chief factor in determining occupational status (Duncan, Featherman, and Duncan, 1972). In general, college graduates have better jobs than high school graduates, who in turn have better jobs than those who have not completed high school. The relation between IQ and job status, such as it is, seems to depend chiefly on the fact that people with higher IQs generally manage to acquire more education than others, barring such circumstances as illness or family financial problems. (Various studies have found correlations ranging as high as .70 between IQ and years of school completed.)

IQ and Creativity

Since about 1 percent of subjects who take the Stanford-Binet test show IQs of 140 or more, as was shown in Figure 8-5 (page 273), there are more than two million people in the United States who qualify as what are popularly known as "geniuses." They are capable of extraordinary feats of mental skill—but obviously not many of them will ever display the kind of outstanding originality that we associate with creative genius as displayed by a Shakespeare, Michelangelo, Beethoven, Einstein, or Edison. True creativity is extremely rare, and its relation to intelligence uncertain (Barron and Harrington, 1981).

Having superior intelligence definitely "does not guarantee creativity" (MacKinnon, 1962). In some fields, for example painting and sculpture, there appears to be very little if any correlation between IQ and creative ability (Barron, 1968). Most fields seem to require what has been called a "threshold" IQ, higher in the sciences than in literature or music. Above that minimum requirement creativity depends less on intelligence than on other factors (Crockenburg, 1972).

A clue to the other factors comes from studies showing that creative people tend to have a number of traits in common that are not shared by most other people. Generally speaking, they were lone wolves in childhood. They either were spurned and rejected by other children or sought solitude themselves. If being different from other children caused them anxiety, they eventually overcame it. They grew up with no need to conform to the people and the ways of life around them. In fact creative people *want* to be different and original and to produce new things. They are not afraid of having irrational or bizarre thoughts, are willing to examine even the most foolish-seeming ideas, and are not worried about success or failure. Many of them are aggressive and hostile, not at all the kind of people who win popularity contests (MacKinnon, 1962).

Many attempts have been made to devise tests that will spot creative people so that they may receive special treatment to encourage their talents. One such test is illustrated in Figure 8-9. Other tests ask subjects to think up as many uses as possible for objects such as a brick or paper clip (Guilford, 1954), or ways to improve familiar objects like writing instruments, carpenters' tools, and children's toys (Torrance, 1966).

If potentially creative people could be spotted early and protected from pressures toward conformity—particularly in the elementary school classroom—perhaps more of them would actually flourish. But there are many difficulties in the testing and encouragement of creativity. Creativity is not a skill that can readily be taught (Mayer, 1983). For one thing, true creativity requires even more than mere originality. Sheer novelty—or what might be called "offbeat" thinking—is not necessarily creative. Besides being new and unusual, a creative idea must also be *appropriate*. A new scientific theory must be in accord with the known facts. When we look at a painting or hear music we must have some perception of aptness, of a disciplined relationship to the world as we know it, if we are to consider the work of art esthetically pleasing and thus genuinely creative.

Artificial Intelligence—The Computer's "IQ" and "Creativity"

A new approach to the study of human intelligence—and even of the nature of human creativity—is based on the way computers have managed to perform many of the accomplishments once believed to be the sole prerogative of the human brain. These electronic

Figure 8-9 A test of creativity

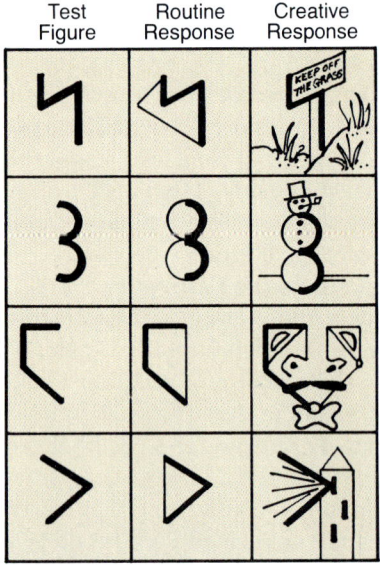

Subjects are asked to start with the simple lines in the left-hand column and turn them into any kind of drawing the lines suggest. Most subjects produce the kinds of drawings shown in the middle column. Very creative people come up with imaginative elaborations like those in the right-hand column (Barron, 1958).

machines, with circuits programmed to provide what is called *artificial intelligence*, can perform many tasks of great complexity. In the business world, they make out payrolls, write checks, keep track of immense inventories, and in some cases operate manufacturing plants with very little human help. In the medical field, they analyze a patient's symptoms and make a creditable diagnosis. They guide spaceships to Mars and Venus and pilot the space shuttle back to a perfect landing. Along lighter lines, they play creditable games of checkers and chess—well enough, indeed, to beat most of us run-of-the-mill human players.

There seem to be a number of similarities between artificial intelligence and human intelligence. When one of today's sophisticated computers is presented with a problem to solve, it does many of the things a human would do. It analyzes the problem and calls on the information stored in its memory bank to provide an appropriate solution. The first computer experts began by studying the way people report they approach a problem, then designing a program to guide the electronic brain through similar steps. Thus the way people think has contributed to the development of more intelligent computers, and in turn computer science has "contributed valuable hypotheses to cognitive psychology about human thought processes" (Simon, 1982).

Many psychologists look to the computer for further light on human thinking and intelligence, and many computer scientists regard themselves as psychologists. But just how much real resemblance there is between human and artificial intelligence is still an open question. The circuits of the computer are very different from the pathways through the multiple synapses of the brain. The electronic impulses racing through the computer at the speed of light travel at least three million times faster than nervous impulses. Many of today's computers—for example, those that play the best game of chess—are designed more to take advantage of that speed than to "think" like a human player.

George Miller of Princeton University, who devoted several years of study to a search for what computers can tell us about human thinking and creativity, is one psychologist

A robotic hand can sense the degree of firmness with which to grasp an object. But does this mean that the robot can "think" and "behave" as humans do?

who has concluded that the resemblances are not worth pursuing: "How computers work seems to have no real relevance to how the mind works, any more than a wheel shows how people walk" (Miller, 1983). It may be that the computer will eventually be classed with other machines that duplicate human behavior—but in a manner bearing no similarity to the way we ourselves perform the acts. (Like the pitching machine used by baseball teams, which delivers every possible kind of pitch without in any way duplicating the muscle movements of a human player's back, shoulders, arms, and hands.) Even so—and many psychologists remain more hopeful—computers already serve as valuable assistants to human thinking.

Does IQ Determine Success in Life?

One of the most important questions about IQ is the extent to which it relates not just to classroom grades or choice of occupation but to successful living. This is a difficult question to answer, for success is an elusive concept. It can hardly be defined in terms of income, for many people have little interest in making a lot of money. Other types of success—efficiency and pleasure in one's job, good human relations, happiness in general—are hard to measure. Thus the answer has never been definitely established and is a matter of considerable dispute among psychologists.

One study that has led many psychologists to consider a high IQ to be a great asset in achieving success of any kind was made with a group of 1,500 California schoolchildren who qualified as mentally gifted, with IQs of 140 or more, putting them in the top 1 percent of the population. The study was begun in 1921 by Lewis M. Terman and continued by him and his associates for many years, as the children grew into adulthood and middle age.

As children, Terman's subjects were superior in many respects besides IQ. They were above average in height (by about an inch), weight, and appearance. They were better adjusted than average and showed superiority in social activity and leadership.

In later life, not all the gifted children lived up to their early promise. Some of them dropped out of school and wound up in routine occupations. Some, even though they went to college, turned out to be vocational misfits and drifters. But these were the exceptions, and their records tended to show problems of emotional and social adjustment and low motivation toward achievement. On the whole the group was outstandingly successful. A large proportion went to college, achieved above-average and often brilliant records, and went on to make important contributions in fields ranging from medicine and law to literature and from business administration to government service.

They also seemed to display a high level of physical and mental health, a death rate lower than average, and a lower divorce rate. One psychologist has expressed this view of the Terman study:

> Findings such as these establish beyond a doubt that IQ tests measure characteristics that are obviously of considerable importance in our present technological society. To say that the kind of ability measured by intelligence tests is irrelevant or unimportant would be tantamount to repudiating civilization as we know it (Jensen, 1972).

There are, however, many dissenters. A number of investigators, after studying not just the mentally gifted but people in general, have reported finding little or no relationship between IQ and success outside the classroom. Grades in school, closely correlated with IQ, have been found to be unrelated to actual efficiency at such diverse jobs as bank teller, factory worker, or air traffic controller (Berg, 1970)—or even at scientific research (Taylor, Smith, and Ghiselin, 1963).

Some scholars have concluded that IQ bears on success only to the extent that an IQ in the lower ranges may make it impossible for a person to complete high school, perform successfully in college, or qualify for certain demanding jobs. For people in or above the 110–120 range, differences in IQ do not seem to have much effect on actual achievement in later life (Wallach, 1976). Certainly success as measured by income appears to depend mostly on other factors (Jencks, 1972). The issue of success in relation to IQ is discussed in a box on Psychology in Everyday Life titled "Why Smart People Fail in Life."

IQ AND THE ISSUE OF HEREDITY VERSUS ENVIRONMENT

Like many other human qualities studied by psychologists, intelligence is influenced by heredity as well as environment. Most agree the two forces work in tandem—that a child's inherited predispositions work in conjunction with environmental factors to shape the development of intelligence (Rose and Wallace, 1985). But there is disagreement on the relative contribution of each. Some maintain that heredity is more important than environment (Eysenck, 1981), while others believe the reverse (Kamin, 1981). On no other issue has the nature-nurture controversy been waged more heatedly. One reason is that the evidence on both sides can be interpreted in so many different ways (Walker and Emory, 1985). Another is that the controversy bears on a number of social problems—for example, the question of whether intelligence can be changed through preschool and other programs designed to improve the environment in which children grow up.

Psychology in Everyday Life
Why Smart People Fail in Life

Almost all of us know seemingly intelligent people who consistently fail at what they do. As psychologist Robert J. Sternberg has pointed out, many people come into the world with remarkable intellectual gifts, but because of other factors that get in their way, they find that all their native abilities are of little consequence. Here is a list of 20 such factors (Sternberg, 1986):

1. Lack of motivation
2. Lack of impulse control—for example, "shooting from the hip" with the first solution to a problem instead of giving thought to other possibilities
3. Lack of perseverance
4. Using the wrong abilities—that is, not capitalizing on strengths
5. Inability to translate thought into action
6. Unwillingness to apply oneself to produce a tangible product
7. Inability to complete tasks and to follow through
8. Failure to take the initiative—usually out of an unwillingness to make a commitment
9. Fear of failure
10. Procrastination
11. Blaming others—or oneself—for no reason
12. Excessive self-pity
13. Excessive dependency
14. Wallowing in personal difficulties
15. Distractibility and lack of concentration
16. Spreading oneself too thin or too thick
17. Inability to delay gratification
18. Inability or unwillingness to see the forest for the trees
19. Not applying the right abilities in the right situation
20. Too little self-confidence—or too much

Undoubtedly we can think of other factors to add to this list. In any case, few would argue with Sternberg's view that what really matters is not only the level of our intelligence, but also how we manage it. Our goal, he maintains, should be to realize fully whatever abilities each of us has.

Family Similarities in IQ

Many studies have indicated that the more closely related two people are—that is, the greater their similarity in genetic background—the more similar their IQs are likely to be. Correlations between the IQs of children and their parents, brothers and sisters, and even more distant relatives all seem to show that IQ tends to "run in families."

The studies are summarized in Figure 8-10. Note the top bar, which shows the relationships found between parents and children. Different investigators found different correlations, but the figures range up and down from a midpoint of about .50. The second bar from the top shows that the correlations between brothers and sisters living with their parents have also been found to cluster around .50. The third bar shows that children of the same parents, even when separated and brought up in different homes, still display a fairly high correlation, with the figures clustering around .35. Identical twins, who have inherited the same genes, show very high correlations when brought up together, and impressively high correlations even when separated and brought up apart from each other.

Much of the case for the nature side of the debate rests on those top five bars in the figure—and especially on the bar for identical twins reared in different homes. If people

Figure 8-10 **Family resemblances in IQ**

The bars show the range of correlations—and the midpoint within the range—found in various studies of comparisons in IQ between blood relatives and also between people who lived in the same home even though they were not related. The correlation between unrelated people who grew up in different homes would of course be zero. For a discussion of the correlations shown here—and how they have been interpreted—see the text (Erlenmeyer-Kimling and Jarvik, 1963; Jencks et al., 1972; Kamin, 1979; Walker and Emory, 1985).

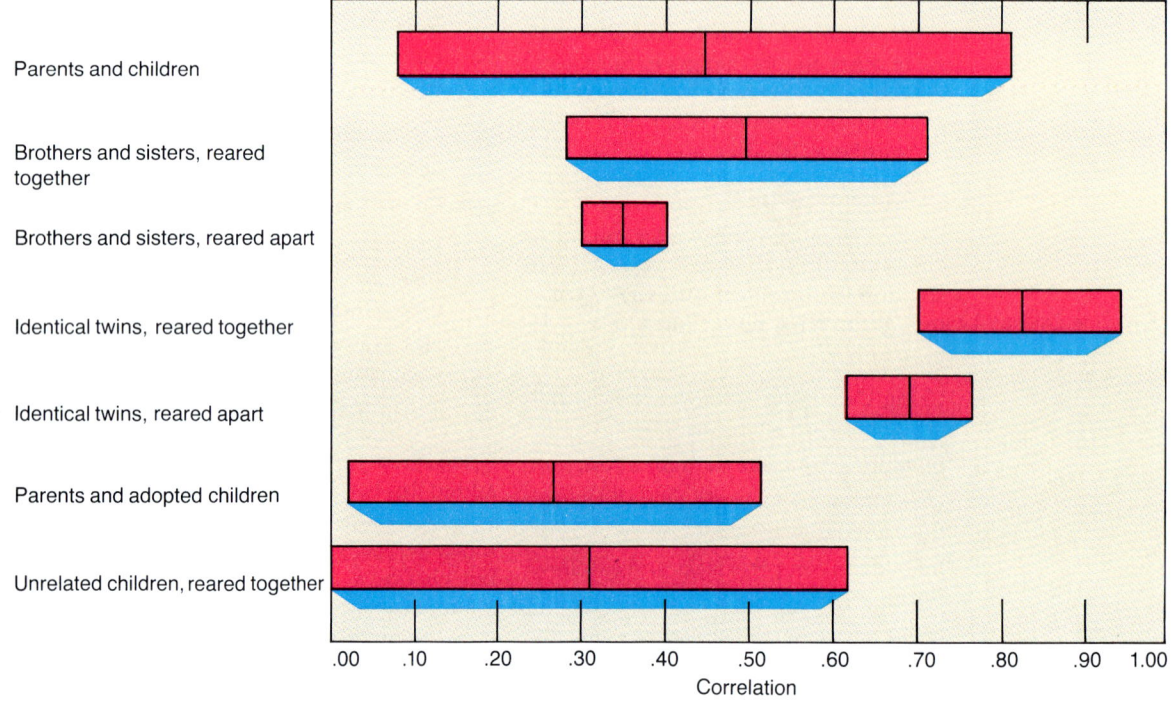

with exactly the same genes show a correlation of somewhere between .62 and .77 even when they grow up in different environments, then the influence of heredity on IQ would appear to be very strong indeed..

But Is It the Family Genes or the Family Environment?

The correlations, however, do not impress those who take the nurture side of the argument. The figures on identical twins who grew up in different homes, for example, have been challenged on a number of grounds—including the small number of subjects (such twins are difficult to find), the kinds of intelligence tests that were used, and possible bias in the way the tests were administered and scored. Leon Kamin of Princeton University, who has carefully examined the studies, has also concluded that the environments in which the twins grew up were probably much more similar than the term "reared apart" would imply. In many cases, he found, the two were brought up in families that were closely related— for example, one by the actual mother, the other by a grandmother or an aunt. Sometimes the two grew up in the same town and went to the same school, and in at least one case they actually lived next door to each other. This tendency toward similarity in environment, Kamin concluded, might be just as responsible as the identical genes for the high correlations in IQ (Kamin, 1981).

Psychology in Everyday Life
The Issue of Race and Intelligence

One of the curious aspects of the nature-nurture debate is the vast amount of attention lavished in recent years on the question of possible racial differences in intelligence. Many dozens of scholarly articles have argued the question pro and con. Countless news stories have reported the newest scraps of evidence and the latest shifts in opinion.

All this concern centers on the well-established fact that—on the average—blacks score 10 to 15 points lower on IQ tests than whites. The issue is why. Some psychologists and biologists have decided that in all probability there is an innate, genetically determined difference between the races (Jensen, 1969; Eysenck, 1981). Others have concluded that there is only a difference in the environment (Nichols, 1984).

Almost ignored in the crossfire has been the majority opinion among psychologists, which is not nearly so newsworthy as the debate. Most psychologists believe there is really no way of deciding how much of the black-white difference in average scores can be explained by heredity and how much by environment (Loehlin, Lindzey, and Spuhler, 1975) or bias in the tests. It has been pointed out that we know so little about the complex ways cultural and environmental factors affect IQ that we can "say nothing about genetic differences" (Block and Dworkin, 1976) and can "make only wild speculations about racial groups" (Scarr-Salapatek, 1971).

To any of us as individuals, the argument is unimportant. Both blacks and whites show a wide and overlapping range of individual differences in IQ, and our own score is not affected by the average for the race or ethnic group to which we belong. As for the social significance of the argument, note this comment by Leon Kamin:

> There is no way of providing a definite answer to the question of black-white differences until and unless we are able to build a society in which blacks and whites are exposed to similarly favorable—and nondiscriminatory—environments. The irony is that if we succeed in building such a society, nobody will any longer be interested in answering the question (Kamin, 1981).

The pronurture side also points to the studies summarized in the bottom two bars of Figure 8-10. Note that some fairly substantial correlations, ranging up to .50, have been found between foster parents and adopted children to whom they were totally unrelated by blood. Note also the bar for unrelated children who were brought up together, usually through adoption into the same home. One study found a zero correlation for such children—the figure that would be expected for unrelated people chosen at random—but other findings have ranged as high as around .60. Both these bars, to the psychologists on the nurture side, indicate the strong influence of environment (Walker and Emory, 1985).

So the debate goes on and sometimes grows bitter, because it spills over into the issue of whether there are racial differences in IQ, as discussed in a box on Psychology in Everyday Life titled "The Issue of Race and Intelligence." But many psychologists—perhaps a substantial majority—have concluded that there is no way of making a final judgment on whether heredity or environment, in their constant interaction, has the greater influence. One widely accepted suggestion is that the inherited genes probably set a top and bottom limit on an individual's possible IQ score—and the environment then determines where within this range the score will actually fall. Some believe that the range is around 20–25 points (Scarr-Salapatek, 1971)—in other words, that a more or less average person may wind up with an IQ of 85 if brought up in a deprived environment but 105 to

110 if brought up under ideal conditions. Some psychologists believe the range may be even greater, especially for individuals born with the possibility of superior intelligence (Gottesman, 1963).

The effect of the interaction between heredity and environment on IQ has been compared to what happens when a mixture of seeds is planted in different kinds of soil (Lewontin, 1976). Since the seeds contain various combinations of genes, they attain a fairly wide range of differences in height under any growing conditions. When planted in ideal soil, as shown in Figure 8-11, they may vary from say 2 to 4 feet tall. But in poor soil they may grow only as high as about 1 to 3 feet. Looking at any single one of the plants, without full knowledge of the genes it inherited or the soil that provided its environment, how can anybody say why it is as tall or as short as it is?

The Interplay between Heredity and Environment

We have no way of knowing how many genes play a part in helping determine an individual's IQ—or in what way these genes regulate the structure and dynamics of the human brain, the rest of the nervous system, and other traits that may also influence intelligence. Clues are being sought in a variety of studies—including those that relate early characteristics to later intelligence. For example, studies of infants who are by nature alert and adept at noting visual or auditory changes in their environment appear to have higher IQs when they reach elementary school age (Rose and Wallace, 1985; O'Conner, Cohen, and Parmelee, 1984).

There is some evidence that not all of the components of intelligence as measured by IQ tests are equally influenced by heredity. As shown in Figure 8-12, among identical twins, there is a greater similarity in verbal than in nonverbal skills (Segal, 1985), suggesting that the former are more heavily influenced by genetic factors. It is impossible to say for sure, however, in what way and to what extent the influence of any or all of an individual's genes can be enriched or stunted through interaction with the environment. One theory, of which

Figure 8-11   The analogy between IQ and plant growth

Like human IQs, the height of these plants shows a wide range of individual differences. Why? One reason is the genes they have inherited, which produce differences regardless of the growing conditions. Another is the environment, which makes the average height much larger for the plants grown in good soil than for the plants in poor soil.

Figure 8-12 Heredity: a stronger role in verbal skills?

The Wechsler Intelligence Scale for Children was given to both identical and nonidentical eight-year-old twins. The identical twins turned out to be strikingly similar in their scores on verbal tests such as vocabulary and verbal information—but less so in their scores on nonverbal tests such as picture completion and picture arrangement. In the latter, the scores for identical twins were no more similar than those for nonidentical twins (Segal, 1985).

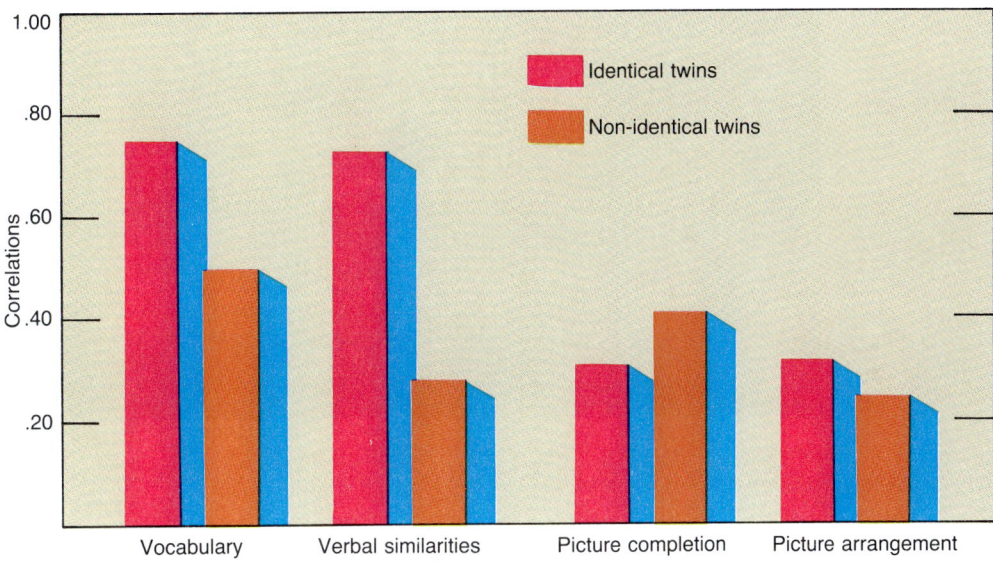

Sandra Scarr is the chief proponent, holds that many genetic traits play a part and that their interaction with the environment takes three important forms:

1. Parents who are themselves intelligent, and therefore likely to pass along to their offspring the genes associated with a high IQ, are also likely to provide a favorable environment. For example, "parents who read well and enjoy reading are likely to provide their children with books"—and in turn "their children are more likely to be skilled readers who enjoy the activity."

2. Children who have inherited favorable genes, for not only intelligence but appearance and personality, are more likely to evoke favorable responses from their environment: "Socially engaging, cheerful children get more social interaction than passive, sober children. In the intellectual arena, cooperative, attentive children receive more pleasant and instructional interactions from the adults around them than uncooperative, distractible children."

3. As children grow older, they take an active part in creating their own environments—and in choosing what aspects of the environment they will respond to and learn from. Again their inherited tendencies are related to their environment, and that environment in turn further encourages the tendencies (Scarr, 1981).

Thus some children grow up in homes that give them what Scarr calls "a double dose of advantage"—a good genetic background plus a good environment. Other children tend in general to grow up in homes that give them just the opposite—a less favorable genetic background plus an unfavorable environment.

For reasons explained in the text, these happy children are more likely to enjoy more social interaction than somber ones.

Some Ways That Environment Can Affect IQ

One way environment influences IQ is reminiscent of the analogy of the seeds growing in barren soil. Poor nutrition, it has been shown, stunts the development of a child's nervous system as well as physical growth. In a study made in South Africa, undernourished children were found to have IQs that averaged 20 points lower than children who had received an adequate diet (Stock and Smythe, 1963).

The psychological environment is also important. It plays a large part in the relation of IQ to social class and to the correlations of between .32 and .59 that have been reported between children's IQs and parents' educational level (Pearson, 1969). Middle-class mothers, it has been found, spend more time than lower-class mothers talking to their young children, playing with them, and encouraging them to learn and to solve problems on their own. A very high correlation of .76 has been found between children's IQ and parents' scores on a scale that measures how much encouragement and help they offer in using language and increasing vocabulary, how much motivation and reward they provide for intellectual accomplishment, and the opportunities for learning they provide in the home, including personal help, books and other forms of stimulation (Wolf, 1963).

The difference in average IQ between children born into lower-class homes and those born into middle-class and upper-class homes has been found to increase through early childhood (Bayley, 1970). On the other hand, children of lower-class parents, if adopted into families that are above average in education and income, wind up with higher IQs than might have been expected. A study made in France managed to compare a group of such adopted children with their blood brothers and sisters who remained in the original home with the parents. The adopted children had an average IQ of 111. Their brothers and sisters averaged only 95 (Schiff et al., 1978). Moreover, the IQs of the adopted children turned out to be virtually identical to those of the natural children with whom they were reared (Schiff et al., 1982). Another study of black and interracial children adopted into above-average homes found that they had an average IQ of 106, considerably higher than would have been expected had they remained with their mothers (Scarr and Weinberg, 1976). The earlier the adoption takes place the better, indicating that the environment is important even during the earliest months of life—and perhaps especially so.

Dramatic Shifts in IQ Level: Why Do They Occur?

Many people think of IQ as remaining stable throughout life, like the temperature inside a building controlled by a thermostat that never lets the thermometer rise or fall more than a few degrees. In truth, however, children often show substantial changes in IQ over the years. They do so even when they continue to live in what seems to be an unchanging environment—that is, in the same home with the same parents and brothers and sisters, at the same level of social class.

This puzzling fact was demonstrated in a study in which the progress of 140 girls and boys was carefully followed over a ten-year period, from the time they were 2 years old until they were 12. Intelligence tests given every year indicated that about half the children showed just about the same IQ from one year to the next and indeed from the start of the ten-year period to the end. But for the other half there were changes upward or downward that in some cases reached striking proportions. In Figure 8-13, which illustrates some of the individual records from this study, note that one child's IQ rose from about 110 to 160, and another's dropped from about 140 to 110.

Figure 8-13 IQ from year to year: it may stay the same, rise, or fall

These graphs were obtained from annual tests of children's IQs as they grew up. About half the children showed nearly straight-line results as in A, with IQ remaining almost constant. Some showed substantial increases, such as the 20-point rise in B. A few showed very striking improvement, such as the 50-point rise in C. And some showed decreases of as much as 30 points, as in D (Sontag, Baker, and Nelson, 1958).

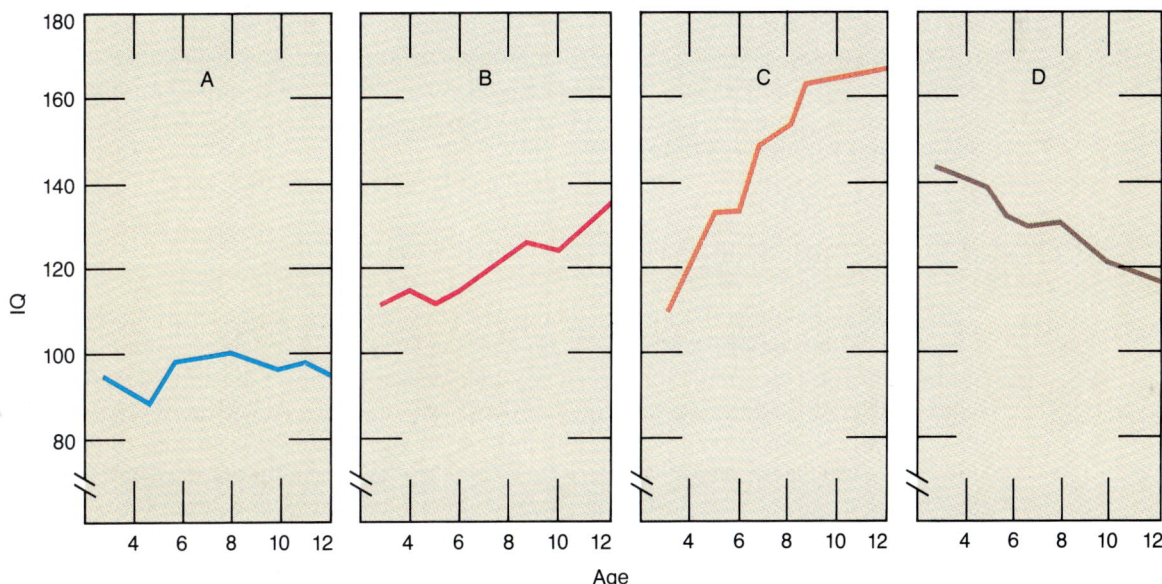

> ## Psychology in Everyday Life
> ### Lessons about IQ for Parents and Teachers
>
> As reported in the text, numerous studies indicate that the IQ is by no means a constant and unchanging trait like a person's fingerprints—and that a score made on any given day is by no means an unerring guide to the future. They constitute a warning to parents and teachers not to take the results of an intelligence test too seriously by giving up on a child who has made a low score or expecting too much from a child who has made a high score.
>
> The studies also provide further evidence that IQ scores depend on motivation and adjustment as well as on cognitive skills. It seems that children are most likely to gain in IQ over the years if the parents provide a stable emotional climate, serve as models of intellectual achievement, and emphasize and reward intellectual accomplishment and independence. Teachers and schools striving toward Binet's goal of improving intelligence are most likely to succeed if they consider the child's personality as well as IQ. Especially in the case of low-scoring children, "interventions that address the motivational and adjustment aspects of learning may well be more effective than those that primarily address the cognitive lags" (Scarr, 1981).

The study found some noteworthy personality differences between the children who showed increases and those who showed declines. The children whose IQ went up were more independent, competitive, and likely to take the lead in conversation. They showed strong motivation to master intellectual problems, worked harder in school, and persisted at even the most difficult tasks.

A similar study of children between the ages of 2 and 18 also found striking changes in IQ, with over half the subjects varying by 15 or more points at some time during a 16-year period. The investigators noted that the subjects who showed the greatest changes up or down were those "whose life experiences had also fluctuated between disturbing and satisfying periods," indicating that health and emotional adjustment help account for the shifts. One girl, for example, showed a sharp decline at a time when she was suffering from asthma and poor vision and her family was undergoing considerable strain and economic hardship (Honzik, MacFarlane, and Allen, 1948). Some important implications of such findings are discussed in a box on Psychology in Everyday Life titled "Lessons about IQ for Parents and Teachers."

THE SCIENCE OF TESTING MENTAL ABILITIES

This final section of the chapter, on the way psychologists construct tests of intelligence and various other traits, must begin with the fact that informal tests of human ability go back to the beginnings of history. Mythology and literature are full of stories about young men who had to slay a dragon to prove they were brave enough to deserve the hand of the princess—or people who had to answer riddles posed by wise men to prove that they were intelligent enough to become rulers. The ancient Chinese used tests to select people for governmental posts. The ancient Greeks made selections on the basis of tests they developed for both physical and mental skills (Doyle, 1974).

Until very recently, however, tests were based largely on guesswork, and the results doubtless left a great deal to be desired. (Slaying a dragon does not necessarily make a man a good husband. Nor does answering a riddle necessarily indicate leadership ability.) Even today, a great many of the tests in newspapers and magazines have dubious value. If you want to take one of these popular tests for the fun of it, fine. But you cannot take seriously the claim that such tests will show how good a spouse or parent you are likely to be, or whether you are suffering from depression or in danger of becoming an alcoholic, or any of the other things they claim to tell you about yourself.

Constructing a test that will actually do a good job of measuring what it is supposed to measure is a science in itself—a difficult job to which many psychologists have devoted many years of study. The difficulties can best be explained by discussing the four strict requirements that a test must meet to qualify as scientifically sound.

The First Requirement: Objectivity

A satisfactory test should be *objective*—that is, it should provide results that are not affected by the personal opinions or prejudices of the person who gives and grades it. The first intelligence test, as was mentioned earlier, was an attempt to obtain a more objective measure of a child's ability to profit from classes in school than could be provided by the opinion of the teacher, which might be colored by the child's personality, behavior in class, or family's position in the community.

Insofar as is possible, psychological tests are designed so that any qualified person can present them to the subject in the same manner and under the same testing conditions. A uniform method is provided for scoring the results. Thus the person taking the test should get the same score regardless of who administers and scores it.

The Second Requirement: Reliability

To show why a test must also be *reliable*, an analogy can be drawn between a test and an oven thermometer. If the thermometer is reliable—that is, if it gives the same reading every time for the same amount of heat—the cook can count on roasts and pies to come out of the oven in perfect shape. On the other hand, if the thermometer is damaged and unreliable, it may give a reading of 300 degrees on one occasion and 400 degrees on the next, even though the actual temperature is exactly the same. In this case the food is likely to be somewhat disappointing.

Just as a good thermometer must produce consistent temperature readings, a good test must produce consistent scores. One way of determining the reliability of a test is to compare the same person's score on all the odd-numbered items with the score on all the even-numbered items; these two scores should be similar. Or two versions of the test can be constructed and given to the same person on two different occasions. Again, the scores should be similar.

The Third Requirement: Validity

The most important requirement of all is *validity*. That is, a test must actually measure what it is intended to measure. There are a number of ways to determine this. Common sense is one of them; the items in the test must bear a meaningful relationship to the characteristic being measured. (The thought of trying to assess musical ability by asking questions on the rules of football does not make sense and must be rejected.) But common sense is not always enough. It would seem perfectly logical, for example, to assume that tests of finger dexterity would measure aptitude for dentistry—yet one scientific study found that finger dexterity actually shows a negative correlation with the income of dentists (Elton and Shevel, 1969).

A better way is to observe the behavior of people who have taken the test and determine whether they behave as their test scores predicted. Thus the validity of intelligence tests, as measures of academic ability, has been shown by the high correlations between IQ and school grades. A test of aptitude for dentistry could be proved valid or invalid by following the careers of people who took it—or, to save time, by determining the test scores of dentists who are already practicing and whose abilities and performance are already known.

The Fourth Requirement: Standardization

The final requirement of scientific testing can best be explained by imagining this situation: A psychologist has drawn up a 100-question test that can be given and scored objectively. It has proved reliable, and it seems to be a reasonable and valid measure of aptitude for working with computers. Another psychologist decides to use the test and gives it to a college student, who answers 60 of the items correctly. What does this score of 60 tell the psychologist? By itself, not very much. The psychologist cannot know, after giving the test to a single person, whether a score of 60 indicates exceptional aptitude, very low aptitude, or something in between.

As this example indicates, the results of a test are generally not very useful unless they can be compared with the scores of other people. Thus most tests, before they are considered ready for use, are themselves tested by administering them to a large and representative sample of the population. Records are kept of how many people score at all the possible levels from highest to lowest. This process, called *standardization*, makes it possible to determine whether the score made by an individual is average, low, or high. The individual's ranking can even be pinpointed precisely. We can say that the score falls (let us say) on the 71st *percentile*—that is, the individual has done better than 71 percent of all people, while 29 percent of all people make the same or a higher score.

All the accepted intelligence tests have been standardized on large samples of the population. They meet the requirements of objectivity and reliability and have proved valid for predicting academic success (although, as you have seen, their validity for doing anything else is in question). Many other kinds of tests, devised for special purposes, have also been constructed with the greatest possible regard for scientific accuracy.

Vocational Aptitude Tests

Some tests attempt to measure specific talents that would be useful at specific kinds of jobs. These are called *vocational aptitude tests* and are widely used in counseling people on choice of career.

Tests have been developed for all kinds of special skills, among them musical ability, dealing with details as required in clerical jobs, manual dexterity, and the motor coordination required to operate complicated machinery. These tests are often used by industry in selecting job applicants and by the military services in assigning people to specific tasks such as radio operator or astronaut.

Some vocational aptitude tests attempt to measure several different skills and arrive at a sort of aptitude profile that shows where the test taker is strongest and weakest. One such test measures skill at spelling and grammar, dealing with numbers, clerical speed and accuracy, mechanical problems, and several types of thinking and reasoning. Those taking the test can be advised that they will probably do best in a job requiring the skills for which they score highest.

Interest Tests and the Matter of Appraising Personality

Also used in vocational guidance are *interest tests*—which attempt to measure how the subject feels about various activities. The tests try to establish whether the subject is interested in or bored by such activities as literature, music, the outdoors, mechanical equipment, art, science, social affairs, and all kinds of specific activities ranging from butterfly collecting to repairing a clock or making a speech. Tests of this type provide an indication of the sort of work in which subjects are likely to be happiest.

A great deal of time, energy, and ingenuity has gone into the creation of *personality tests*, which are potentially the most valuable of all. A test that could accurately distinguish between normal and maladjusted personalities would enable clinical psychologists to find the people most in need of psychotherapy and perhaps lead to the development of new methods of treatment. It would make comparisons possible among people who have grown up in different environments and with different experiences and thus greatly add to the knowledge of human development. By spotting certain kinds of disturbed personalities, it could conceivably prevent such tragedies as assassination attempts.

Personality tests will be discussed in detail in Chapter 14. Suffice it to say here that they present as many difficulties as opportunities. Few psychological tests at present are entirely satisfactory. Tests of vocational aptitudes and interests, for example, usually show a much lower correlation with actual success on a job than intelligence tests show with school achievement. Nonetheless the tests often offer valuable clues about an individual's personality, patterns of skills, and preferences for certain activities. They are often a helpful guide to clinical psychologists and vocational counselors.

SUMMARY

The nature of intelligence: some different views

1. *Intelligence* is the capacity to understand the world and the resourcefulness to cope with its challenges.
2. One theory is that intelligence is composed of a pervasive mental ability called the *g factor*, for general intelligence, plus a number of *s factors*, or specific kinds of skill at a particular task.
3. Thurstone suggested that the specific skills are for verbal comprehension, word fluency, number, space, associative memory, perceptual speed, and general reasoning—which he called the seven *primary mental abilities*.
4. Several theories stress the importance of specific rather than general abilities. Guilford believes that intelligence is made up of no less than 120 kinds of ability and that a person may rank high in some of them but low in others. Gardner proposed the existence of seven fundamental but separate "intelligences." Sternberg suggests a triarchic theory of intelligence which includes the planning and executing of mental activity and the capacity to deal with novelty and to adapt to the environment.
5. Both the Thurstone and the Guilford theories suggest that two people with the same intelligence may perform differently at different kinds of tasks—and that success and happiness on a job depend largely on choosing work that suits your own particular strengths and weaknesses.
6. Piaget, whose studies of intellectual development in children made him a major figure in the rise of the cognitive school, concluded that intellectual growth is basically an increased ability to adapt to new situations. The key processes in development, he

found, are *assimilation* (incorporating a new stimulus into one's existing cognitive view of the world) and *accommodation* (changing one's cognitive view and behavior when new information dictates such a change).

7. A key word in Piaget's theory is *operation*—meaning a sort of dynamic mental rule for manipulating objects or ideas into new forms and back to the original—like the rule that four pieces of candy (or the figure 4) can be divided into two parts of two each, and then restored to the original four.

8. Piaget charted children's intellectual development through four stages: (a) the *sensorimotor stage*, birth to 18 months, in which children know the world only through their sensory impressions and the results of their motor (or muscular) movements; (b) the *preoperational stage*, 18 months to about seven years, in which they have acquired language and can manipulate symbols, but do not yet grasp the dynamic rules of operation; (c) the *stage of concrete operations*, six to eight years, when they can manipulate ideas mentally and translate them into concrete terms; and (d) the *stage of formal operations*, beginning at about 12 years, when they can apply operational rules and logical reasoning to abstract ideas and possibilities.

Intelligence tests: what can they actually tell us?

9. *Intelligence tests* provide a measure of *intelligence quotient*, or *IQ*. The intelligence quotient gets its name from the fact that it was originally determined by comparing a child's *mental age* (as shown by the ability to pass test items that can be passed by the average child of various ages) with *chronological age* (or actual age).

10. The average IQ is 100, and almost half of all people score between 90 and 109.

11. An *individual test* is given by a trained examiner to one person at a time. Two widely used individual intelligence tests are the Stanford-Binet Intelligence Scale and the Wechsler Adult Intelligence Scale.

12. A group test of intelligence can be given to many people at the same time. One well-known example is the Scholastic Aptitude Tests (SAT).

13. Intelligence tests are *aptitude tests*, which measure ability to learn a new skill or perform an unfamiliar task. In theory, aptitude tests are different from *achievement tests*, which measure how much skill or learning a person has actually acquired. However, it is usually impossible to measure ability without any regard for past achievement—and "all tests reflect what a person has learned."

14. Intelligence tests are biased to some extent in favor of people who have acquired the knowledge, language skills, and motivation typical of the middle and upper-middle classes. Such children make higher average scores than children from lower-class homes. City children make higher scores than rural children. Blacks and members of other ethnic cultures make lower average scores.

15. Scores on intelligence tests also depend on motivation, adjustment, and other personality factors.

16. Although the tests cannot hope to measure sheer, disembodied skill at information processing, they are good predictors of success in school. Studies have found correlations of .40 to .60 or even higher between IQ and grades in classes from the elementary through the college level. Correlations within subject areas may be affected by stress placed on families or schools in that particular area.

17. Psychologists disagree about the extent to which IQ is related to occupation and success in general. Any correlation may depend on the fact that a certain minimum

IQ is required to complete high school and college and to perform successfully in some of the more demanding occupations.

18. *Creativity* is extremely rare, even among people with superior IQs. Besides intelligence, it seems to depend on personality factors—for example, a disdain for conformity and success, a willingness to examine even the most foolish-seeming ideas, and a desire to be "different" and original.

19. Computer science, which has created electronic machines that perform many feats associated with the human brain, has created a new approach to the study of intelligence. Many psychologists expect the *artificial intelligence* of the machine to shed new light on human thinking. But some have decided that there are so many differences between machine and brain that "how computers work seems to have no real relevance to how the mind works."

20. Sternberg lists 20 factors which may interfere with people's use of intelligence. He suggests that management of intelligence is more important than level of intelligence.

IQ and the issue of heredity versus environment

21. Psychologists agree that intelligence is clearly influenced by both heredity and environment. But controversy exists over which factor is more important.

22. One widely accepted suggestion is that inherited genes probably set a top and bottom limit on an individual's potential IQ score and that environment then determines where within this range the score will actually fall. The possible difference between growing up in a deprived environment and an ideal environment has been estimated at around 20–25 points—and perhaps even greater for individuals born with the possibility of superior intelligence.

23. Scarr has suggested that many genetic traits play a part and that their interaction with the environment takes three forms: (a) parents likely to pass along favorable genes are also likely to provide a favorable environment; (b) children with favorable genes for intelligence, appearance, and personality are likely to evoke more favorable responses from the people around them; and (c) as children get older, they play an active part in creating their own environments.

24. Even when brought up in what seems to be an unchanging environment (same home, parents, and social class), children sometimes show changes in IQ over the years ranging as high as 50 points up or down. The shifts may be related to motivation and other personality factors, health, and emotional adjustment.

The science of testing mental abilities

25. To qualify as scientifically sound a test should be:
    a. *Objective*—meaning that the subject will receive the same score regardless of who administers and scores the test.
    b. *Reliable*—yielding similar scores when the same person is tested on different occasions.
    c. *Valid*—actually measuring what it is supposed to measure.
    d. *Standardized*—pretested on a large and representative sample so that an individual's score can be interpreted by comparison with the scores of other people.

26. *Vocational aptitude tests* measure ability to perform the special tasks required in specific jobs.

27. *Interest tests* measure how much an individual likes or dislike various activities—thus providing a clue to what sort of job might be most congenial.
28. *Personality tests* attempt to measure all the many traits that make up personality and to distinguish between normal and maladjusted patterns.

IMPORTANT TERMS

accommodation
achievement test
aptitude test
artificial intelligence
assimilation
chronological age
(stage of) concrete operations
conservation
creativity
figural contents
(stage of) formal operations
g factor
individual test
intelligence
intelligence test

interest test
IQ
mental age
objective
operational rules
personality test
preoperational stage
primary mental abilities
reliable
sensorimotor stage
standardization
symbolic contents
s factor
valid
vocational aptitude test

RECOMMENDED READINGS

Buros, O. K., ed. *The mental measurements yearbook*. Highland Park, N.J.: Gryphon, published annually.

Dean, R. *Introduction to assessing human intelligence: issues and procedures*. Springfield, Il.: Thomas, 1987.

Evans, P., and Waites, B. *IQ and mental testing: an unnatural science and its social history*. New York: Macmillan, 1981.

Eysenck, H. J., and Kamin, L. *The intelligence controversy*. New York: Wiley, 1981.

Gould, S. J. *The mismeasure of man*. New York: Norton, 1981.

Matarazzo, J. D., and Wechsler, D. *Wechsler's measurement and appraisal of adult intelligence*, 5th ed. New York: Oxford University Press, 1972.

Scarr, S. *Race, social class, and individual differences in IQ*. Hillsdale, N.J.: Erlbaum, 1981.

Terman, L. M., and Oden, M. H. *The gifted child grows up*. Stanford: Stanford University Press, 1974.

PART 4

EXPLAINING INDIVIDUAL BEHAVIOR AND PERSONALITY

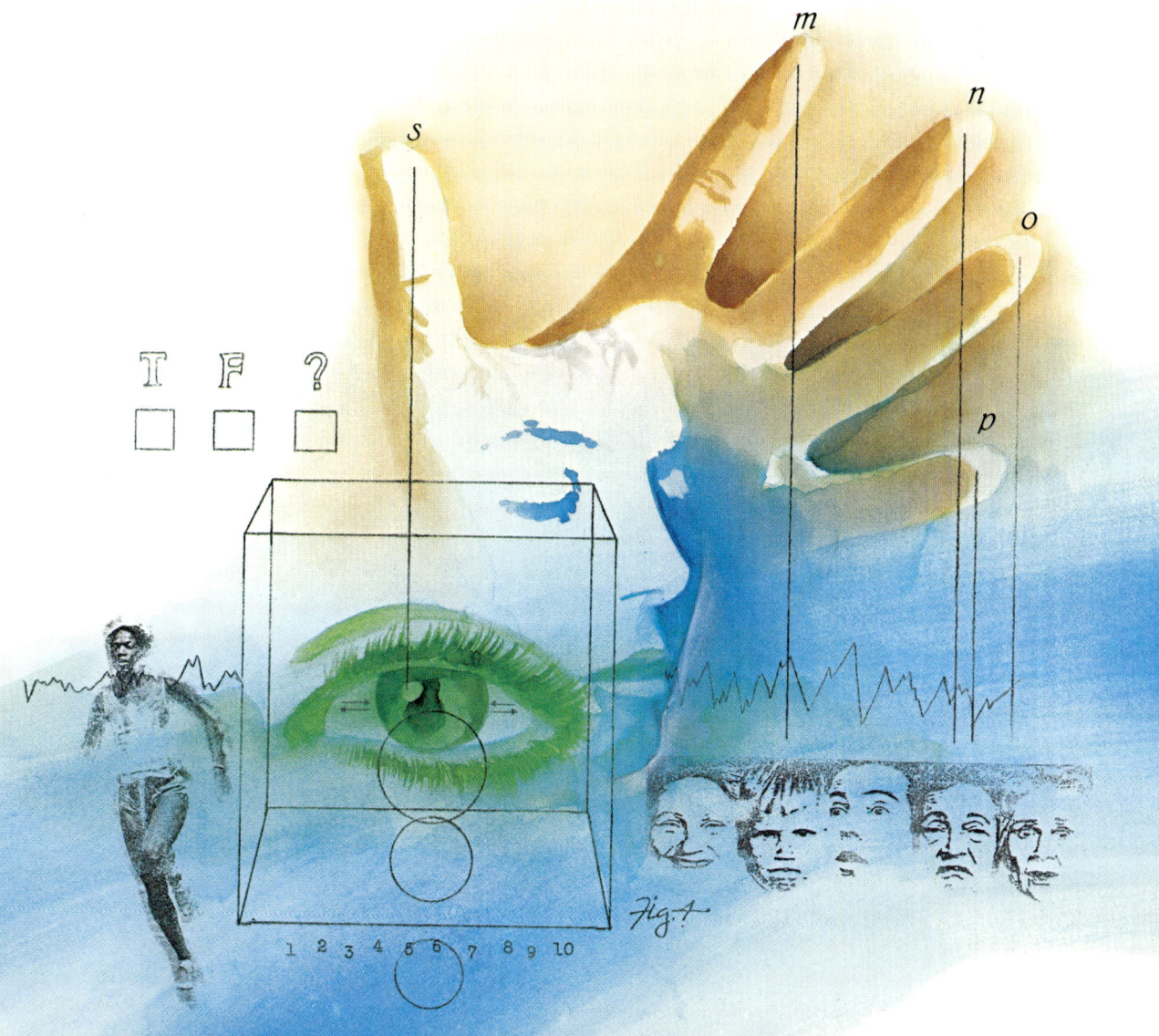

CHAPTER 9
EMOTIONS, DRIVES, AND MOTIVES

THE ROLE OF THE BODY IN EMOTIONS   301

Linking bodily changes to events and thoughts
The body's often hidden changes
The role of the autonomic nervous system and glands
Changes in the facial muscles—and what they might tell us
Facial expression and the brain hemispheres
What do your eyes reveal?
Feedback theories of emotion: the James-Lange view and others

THE BRAIN: KEY TO EMOTIONAL BEHAVIOR   310

The brain hemispheres and emotion
The Cannon-Bard theory
The role of mental processes in emotion: the cognitive position
Cannon-Bard from the cognitive view
James-Lange from the cognitive view

INDIVIDUAL DIFFERENCES IN EMOTION AND THEIR EXPRESSION   314

The role of learning
Differences that are inborn
Emotional stress—for better or worse

HOW DRIVES AFFECT BEHAVIOR: HUNGER AND THIRST   317

The body's hunger signals
Hunger and the hypothalamus
Body weight and hunger
Why some people get fat
Do fat people have too many fat cells?
Thirst

SLEEP: THE OTHER THIRD OF OUR LIVES   324

The stages of sleep
The why of sleep
How much sleep do we need?

THE POWER OF THE SEX DRIVE—AND OTHER DRIVES   327

Animal sexual behavior
Human sexual behavior
Other drives

THE NATURE OF HUMAN MOTIVATION   331

The motive to achieve
The motive to exert power
People who shun power
Needing others: motives for affiliation and dependency

OTHER MOTIVES THAT SHAPE WHO WE ARE   338

The motive for certainty
Playing by the rules: the motive to meet standards
The hostility motive

HOW MOTIVES INFLUENCE BEHAVIOR   340

Motive hierarchies and targets
The effect of incentive value
Assessing your chances of success
Expectancy of success and locus of control
Long-range plans, too much motivation, and running scared

SUMMARY   344

IMPORTANT TERMS   346

RECOMMENDED READINGS   347

PSYCHOLOGY IN EVERYDAY LIFE

The truth about lie detectors   303
Weight control through behavior control   322
Avoiding chemical warfare in the bedroom   328
Partner communication: cornerstone of good sex   331

Thus far this book has concentrated on the remarkable ability of the human organism to process information—the way we gather knowledge of our world through our sensory equipment and the process of perception, store the knowledge in memory, manipulate it, think and communicate about it, and use it to understand and deal intelligently with our environment.

But we humans are far more than mere thinking machines. Unlike the computer, we do not function with cool and automatic precision. We experience emotions—as vivid as towering rage and overwhelming joy. To understand the role of emotions in your life, imagine, if you can, living in a world without them. You would feel much the same whether you suddenly inherited a fortune or lost all your savings, whether you were watching the climax of a passionately romantic movie or being followed down a dark street in the dead of night. No matter what happened, you would never be filled with happiness, touched by sadness, swept up in excitement, or seized by fear.

Life would be unbearably dreary and boring. What would there be to make events memorable—whether a surprise party or a funeral, a weekend outing, or a Monday morning exam? Moreover, chaos would soon overwhelm us. If people never felt sorry or ashamed, why would anyone hold back from harming others? If we never felt afraid, what would prompt us to protect ourselves in the face of danger?

Although emotional experiences give a unique flavor to our lives and help regulate our existence, there is far from perfect agreement among individuals as to whether or not a particular state of feeling should be considered an emotion (Shields, 1984). The subject raises many difficult questions. Just what is an emotion? What happens when we become angry or sad, happy or ashamed? Why do some people lose control of their emotions and begin to behave in strange and irrational ways? These questions have always interested psychologists. Though all the answers are not yet in, their findings have shed considerable light on the relationships among our emotions, behavior, and what is happening inside our brain and body.

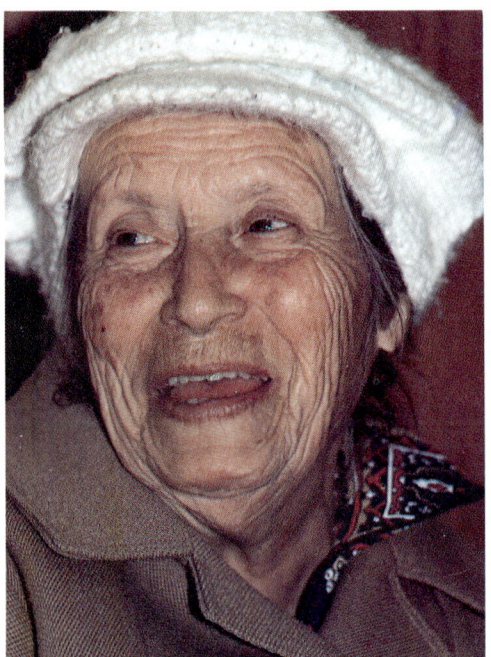

Emotions affect us throughout the lifespan.

THE ROLE OF THE BODY IN EMOTIONS

"I could hardly breathe." "My heart was in my throat." "I had butterflies in my stomach." "My face was beet red." One characteristic that differentiates *emotions* from other psychological states is that they are accompanied by bodily changes—for example, in the heart, the stomach, and the muscles, or in neurotransmitters and hormones.

Thus we naturally assume that people are emotional when their voices rise, when they blush or get pale, when their muscles grow tense or tremble. We know that we are emotional—even if we manage to conceal all outward signs—when we feel that we are inwardly shaking, or are "hot under the collar," or that our mouth is dry, our pulse racing, or our stomach "full of butterflies." There are also quieter emotions in which the body seems to be relaxed. Such are the calm, peaceful, and contented feelings we experience when we enjoy a sunbath, a beautiful piece of music, or a satisfying meal. In these cases, too, the body is affected in some manner.

Linking Bodily Changes to Events and Thoughts

The changes our body undergoes in emotion do not exist in a vacuum. They are linked to two other factors operating when we experience emotion: a specific event in the environment and thoughts triggered by the event.

Consider the emotion of anger. You are likely to experience anger when something happens that frustrates your achievement of a goal-directed activity—for example, when a cop stops you on the highway as you are headed to an important appointment. Such an event typically is accompanied by a series of bodily changes—an increase in heart rate, the production of norepinephrine in the brain, and muscular tension. And there are accompanying thoughts of hate and hostility.

Whenever a person experiences an emotion—anger, sadness, anxiety—the same trio of factors are present: a particular event (or the memory of an event), changes in the body, and thoughts generated by the episode (Shields, 1984). Suppose, for example, someone were to jostle you and step ahead of you in a restaurant line. Whether or not you experience anger would depend on whether the event were linked to changes in your bodily state and thoughts of rudeness. It is the combination of all three that spells anger—as is the case in each major human emotion.

Figure 9-1 An open display of emotion in the cat

An angry cat shows many outward bodily signs of emotion. The animal crouches and growls. Its hair stands on end, its ears are laid back, and its eyes are wide and staring (Young, 1961).

The Body's Often Hidden Changes

The fact that emotion is accompanied by changes affecting many parts of the body is most apparent in the behavior of lower animals, such as the cat pictured in Figure 9-1. It is often less obvious among human beings, for most of us have learned to hide many of the outward signs of emotion. But the changes can readily be measured with laboratory equipment, like the polygraph illustrated in Figure 9-2. This is an elaborate version of what is commonly called a lie detector, a controversial device that is discussed in a box on Psychology in Everyday Life called "The Truth about Lie Detectors." The changes can also be shown by chemical analysis of the composition of the blood.

When we experience a strong emotion, such as fear, our heartbeat may increase from the normal rate of around 72 per minute to as high as 180. Blood pressure may also rise sharply, and blood is often diverted from the digestive organs to the muscles of movement and to the surface of the body, resulting in flushed cheeks and the sensation of warmth. The composition of the blood changes. The number of red corpuscles, which carry oxygen, increases markedly. Secretion of hormones by the endocrine glands produces changes in the level of blood sugar, the acidity of the blood, and the amount of adrenalin and noradrenalin (powerful stimulants secreted by the adrenal glands) in the bloodstream.

The normal movements of the stomach and intestines, associated with the digestion and absorption of food, usually stop during anger and rage. In other emotional states they may show changes resulting in nausea or diarrhea. The body's metabolic rate tends to go

Figure 9-2 A machine that measures emotions

This device produces continuous tracings of bodily processes that often change during emotion. The bands around the man's body measure his rate and depth of breathing. The sleeve around his upper arm measures blood pressure. Electrodes attached to his hand measure what is called the galvanic skin reflex, or changes in the electrical activity of the skin caused by activity of the sweat glands.

Psychology in Everyday Life
The Truth about Lie Detectors

It has been estimated that at least a million Americans a year are asked to take a lie detector test. Some are defendants, plaintiffs, or witnesses in legal cases. Others are job applicants or workers in chain stores, banks, supermarkets, or other companies that try to spot dishonesty. Still others are executives in industrial firms or government agencies that require periodic loyalty checks.

Many people believe the polygraph is an infallible scientific instrument and place absolute confidence in its results. The test is certainly based on a sound principle—namely that people are likely to become physiologically "stirred up" when they feel so threatened by a question that they answer it untruthfully. But psychology has found that a perfectly innocent person may react emotionally to a critical question—and thus appear to be lying when actually telling the truth. And career criminals who are veteran liars can feel no anxiety or guilt about anything—and can therefore tell outrageous untruths without showing the slightest emotional ripple. As shown in the accompanying figure, this can lead to some seriously mistaken conclusions (Kleinmumtz and Szucko, 1984).

To complicate matters, scoring test results may be influenced by the purely subjective impressions of the examiners. Their interpretation of the tracings of physical reactions to test questions may be colored by personal biases about the subject's age, sex, social class, or race. All in all, the great weight of psychological evidence is that lie detector tests have no real claim to being "scientific" or infallible (Lykken, 1981), and we should never reach a final conclusion about whether a person is lying based solely on the polygraph (Ekman, 1985).

Lie detector testing has become a thriving American industry, and it is likely that a significant number of legal and administrative decisions are unfairly influenced by the results. This is a good example of psychology misapplied—how the science can be warped when its findings are used without sufficient safeguards and caution.

Note how many would be misjudged were the polygraph the sole determinant of guilt or innocence.

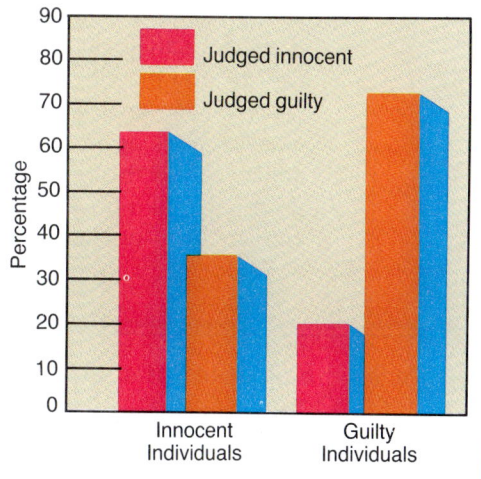

up. Both the food molecules in the bloodstream and the body tissues themselves are burned off at a faster rate, creating additional energy. We may gasp or pant. The salivary glands may stop working, causing the feeling of dryness in the mouth often associated with fear and anger. The sweat glands, on the other hand, may become overactive, as shown by the dripping forehead that may accompany embarrassment or the "cold sweat" that sometimes accompanies fear. The tiny muscles at the base of the hairs may contract and raise goose flesh. Finally the pupils of the eyes may enlarge, causing the wide-eyed look that is characteristic of rage, excitement, and pain. Of course, all of these reactions do not necessarily take place in every episode of strong emotion such as fear or anger (Campos, 1983), but they tend to form a pattern.

The Role of the Autonomic Nervous System and Glands

The bodily changes that accompany emotion are regulated by the autonomic nervous system and the endocrine glands, over which—as described in Chapter 2—we ordinarily have no conscious control. It is not surprising, therefore, that we do not seem to have much control over our emotions. They often seem to boil up of their own accord, and we feel them even if we manage to hide all outward signs. Even in situations in which we have determined in advance to remain calm, we often find ourselves unaccountably angry, frightened, or anxious.

Although a pattern of bodily changes characterizes each emotion, certain changes occur in several emotions. For example, the adrenal glands are active when we experience both anger and fear. Thus psychologists have found it difficult to match any particular bodily state with any particular emotional experience. Moreover, the same person, on two separate occasions when reporting feelings of joyousness, may show a different pattern of bodily change. And a group of people who report feeling exactly the same emotion (say of joy or distress) may show a number of different patterns. It is very hard to determine through physiological measurement alone what kind of emotion a person is experiencing. A similar physiological response may occur, for example, when we play tennis, make love, or face a crisis (Rose, 1980).

Changes in the Facial Muscles—and What They Might Tell Us

A number of other bodily changes that often accompany emotion have nothing to do with the autonomic nervous system, the glands, or the visceral organs. Instead these changes represent activity of the muscles of movement over which we do ordinarily have conscious control. You probably have been aware of some of them—for example, muscular tension (as when the teeth are clenched in anger) or trembling (which occurs when two sets of muscles work against each other). When emotionally excited, many people have a tendency to blink their eyes or make nervous movements, such as brushing back their hair or drumming their fingers. Emotions are often expressed vocally in laughter, snarls, moans, and screams—or revealed by changes in the speed, pitch, and loudness of speech as shown in Figure 9-3. They are also revealed in such facial expressions as smiles, grimaces, and

---

Figure 9-3 Examples of speech patterns that reflect emotion

Speech patterns often vary sharply depending on the emotion experienced. The patterns are so consistent that some emotional states can be identified with surprising accuracy just from the sound of a person's voice (Scherer, 1986). From the opening "hello" of a telephone conversation, for example, we can often tell whether the person on the other end is happy or sad.

	Patterns of speech		
Emotion	Tempo	Pitch	Volume
Happiness	Fast	High	Loud
Sadness	Slow	Low	Soft
Contempt	Slow	Low	Loud

Figure 9-4 An emotion-detecting device

Electrodes placed on the forehead and cheeks measure the activity of muscles responsible for facial expressions. They can detect changes in emotion not apparent to the eye.

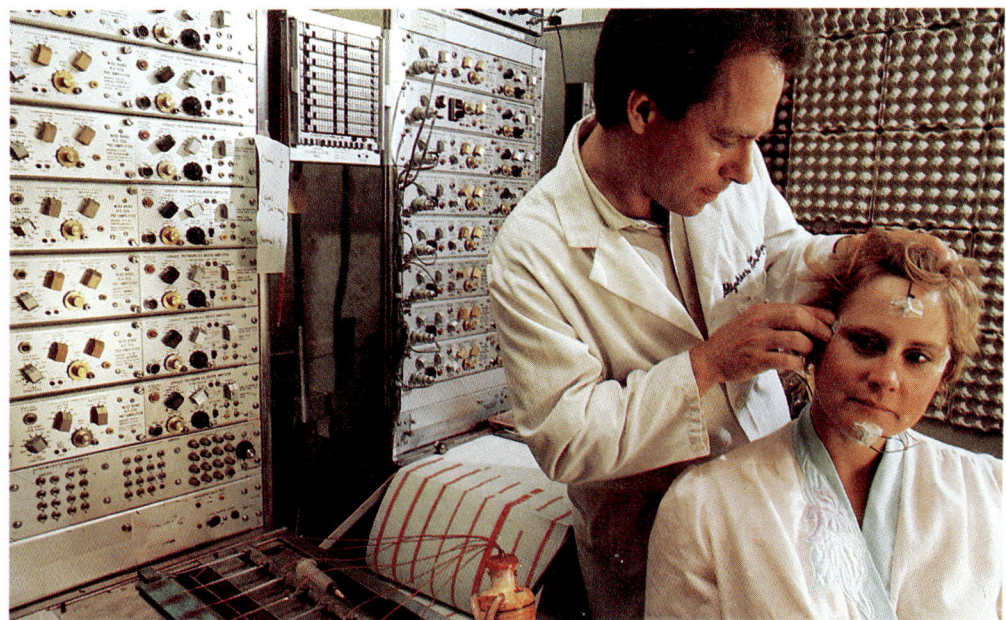

frowns. In fact even just thinking about experiences that are happy, sad, or infuriating can produce strikingly different patterns of activity in tiny muscles of the face. Though the changes are often too small to be seen, they can be detected by measuring the electrical activity of muscle cells (Schwartz, 1982), using instruments like the one shown in Figure 9-4.

One group of psychologists maintains that facial expressions are a key factor in emotional experience. They hold that every basic emotion is accompanied by a characteristic facial pattern that occurs automatically because of the manner in which our bodies and brains are programmed by heredity (Izard, 1977). The various patterns, they believe, are the product of evolution, since an ability to communicate through facial expressions has considerable survival value. Especially for animals that do not have a spoken language, it is an advantage to be able to avert hostility through facial expressions of friendliness or submission. Expressions of fear can alert other members of the group to the presence of danger. Thus the process of natural selection has favored the survival of individuals carrying genes programming their facial expressions (Andrew, 1965).

This theory is based in part on a study that used the photographs shown in Figure 9-5. These photos and several others were shown to subjects in a number of different societies, and the subjects were asked to try to identify the emotions being displayed (as you are asked in the caption accompanying the faces). There was remarkable agreement about the emotions—not only among subjects in the United States, Argentina, Brazil, China, and Japan but among members of isolated societies in New Guinea (Ekman, 1971). The study indicates that the facial expressions that accompany at least some emotions seem to be universal and unlearned, as if they were indeed genetically programmed—set by

Figure 9-5 Facial expressions of emotion: can you identify them?

Try to match these faces with the emotions of anger, disgust, fear, happiness, sadness, and surprise. The answers will be found at the bottom of the page.

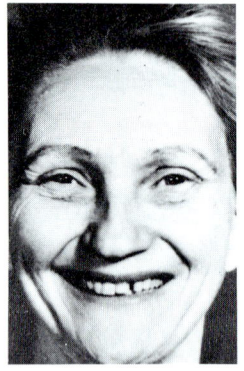

1

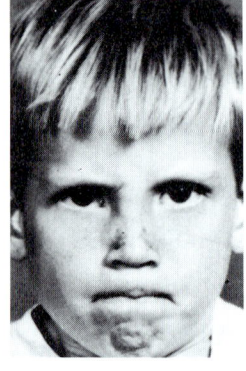

2

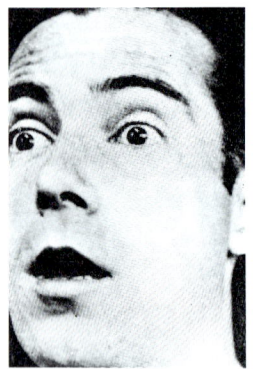

3

4

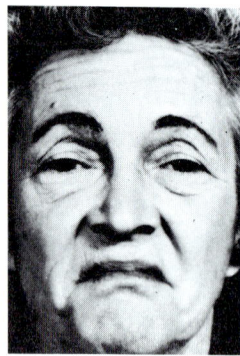

5

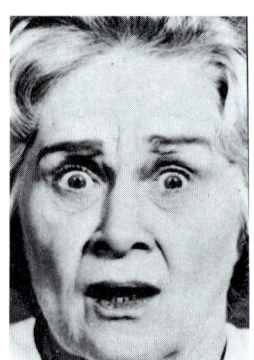

6

nature rather than nurture. More recently, similar agreement across cultures has been found in judgments of the facial expression of contempt (Ekman and Friesen, 1986). Furthermore, most adults agree on the emotion thought to be reflected by the facial expressions of very young babies (Izard and Dougherty, 1982), as shown in Figure 9-6.

There are times, of course, when the face does not reveal an individual's internal emotional state. In one experiment, 72 women experienced intense pain when they immersed their hands and arms in extremely cold water. Initially, there were the expected facial changes: cheeks raised, eyelids tight, eyes closed in a blink, and upper lips raised and the corners pulled back. But even though the subjects experienced increasing pain during the experiment, their facial changes became much less apparent as they became

---

The emotions being expressed in Figure 9-5 are: (1) happiness, (2) anger, (3) surprise, (4) sadness, (5) disgust, and (6) fear.

Figure 9-6 Emotions of infants: written all over their faces

Notice the similarity of these facial expressions to those of the happy and sad adults pictured in photos 1 and 4 of Figure 9-5. For the significance of the photographs, see the text.

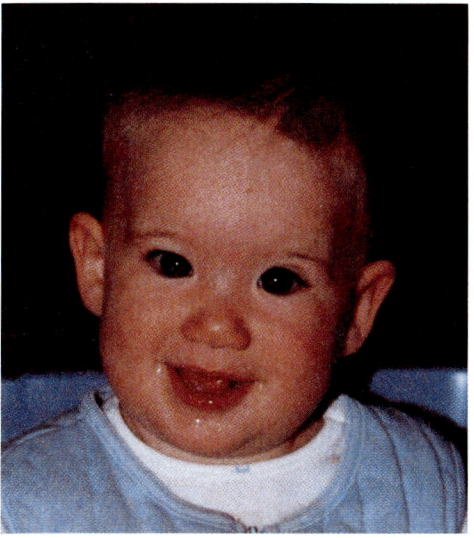
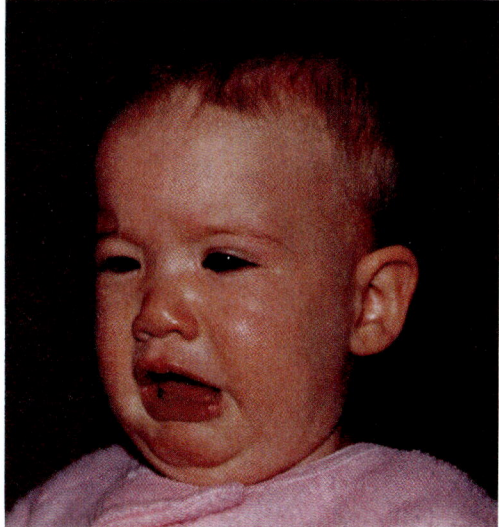

habituated to their situation (Craig and Patrick, 1985). Moreover, most people do not show a distinct facial expression when they experience certain emotions—for example, guilt, envy, or apprehension when telling a lie.

Facial Expressions and the Brain Hemispheres

A provocative finding about facial expressions was made in an experiment that used the three photographs shown in Figure 9-7. Before you read the next paragraph, look at the photos and try to determine your answer to the question posed in the caption.

If the three photos struck you as being alike yet somehow different, there is a reason. *A* is an undoctored photograph of the man. The other two are composites, made by splitting the original photo down the middle and flopping the two halves. In *B*, you see the man as he would appear if his entire face was like the right side. *C* shows the face as if it was made up of two left sides. If you found that *C* seemed to display the most intense emotion, you have considerable company. When the experimenters showed the three photographs—and similar ones of other people displaying various other emotions—they found that subjects tended to agree that the left-face composites gave the most intense impression (Sackheim, Gur, and Saucy, 1978).

The experiment is in line with what is known about the differences between the left brain and right brain. The left hemisphere of the brain seems to specialize in language, logic, and details. The right hemisphere seems to specialize in spatial relationships, form, music, and in achieving intuitive understanding of "the big picture" instead of concentrating on details. There is also some evidence that the right hemisphere plays a dominant role in activating the muscles of the face (Gatz, 1970; Peele, 1961) and in emotional reactions (Davidson and Schwartz, 1976). Thus it seems possible, as the experiment with the composite photographs suggests, that expressions on the left side of our face give the best

Figure 9-7 Three expressions of emotion: which is the strongest?

In all three photographs the man is expressing disgust. In which one, would you say, is his expression clearest and strongest? The way most people answer this question is explained in the text.

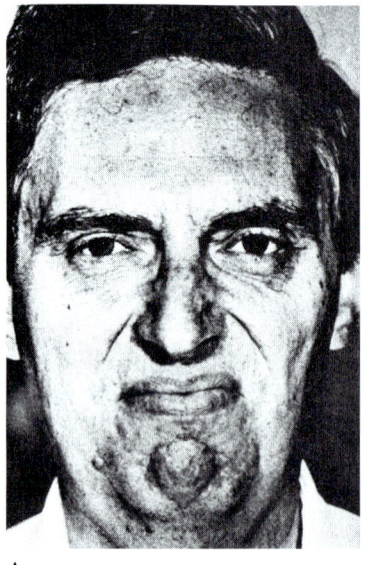
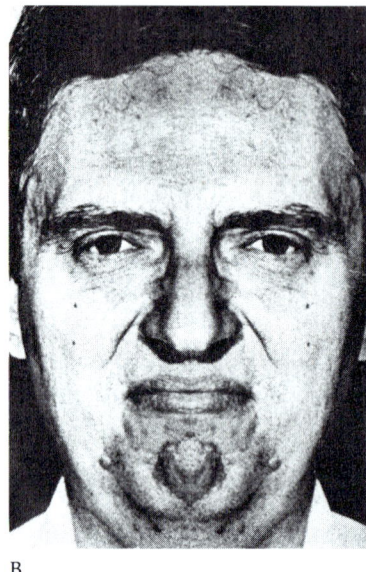
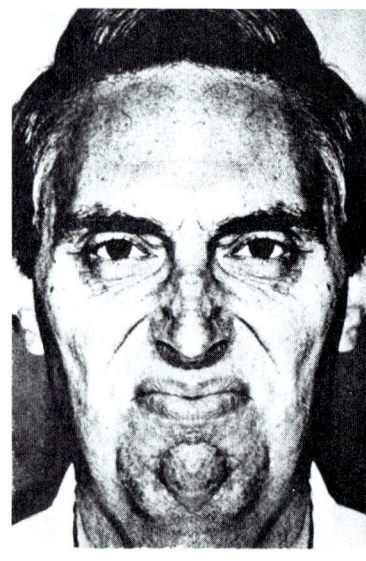

A B C

indication of the emotion we are experiencing. All this is still somewhat speculative—but it suggests that, if you want to know how other people really feel, you should concentrate on the expression on the left side of their face and ignore the right side. This is not as easy to do in the ordinary rapid flow of conversation and changes in facial expression as in a laboratory where photographs can be manipulated, but it may prove worth the effort.

What Do Your Eyes Reveal?

Back in the sixteenth century a French poet wrote that the eyes are "windows of the soul." Modern psychology testifies that these words were more than a felicitous figure of speech. Studies have shown that one very sensitive measure of some emotions is the size of the pupil of the eye.

Pupil size is a good indication of even such a mild emotion as interest. One experiment that demonstrates this fact is illustrated in Figure 9-8. In general, it was found that subjects showed significant increases in pupil size when they looked at pictures they found interesting, but no increase when they looked at something they found unpleasant (Hess, 1965). In another experiment, male subjects looked at the two photographs shown in Figure 9-9, which you should examine before reading the next paragraph.

The only difference in the two photographs in Figure 9-9 is that the one at the left has been retouched to make the woman's pupils seem larger; the one at the right to make them seem smaller. Yet this slight difference made a considerable difference in the way subjects responded—and perhaps in the way you reacted. When the subjects were asked in which photo the woman seemed to be more sympathetic (or warmer, happier, or more attractive), they tended to pick the face with the large pupils. When they were asked in which one she

Figure 9-8 A photographic record of pupil response

This series of photographs, taken over a period of four seconds, shows a man's eye as he looked at a picture of a woman's face. Note the rapid increase in pupil size from the normal, at left, to the right, where the diameter was about 30 percent greater.

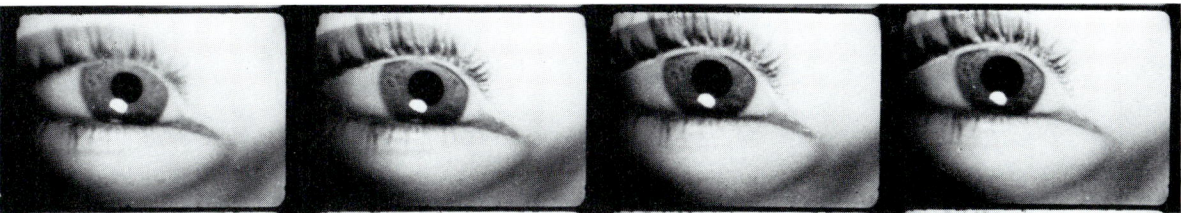

Figure 9-9 An experiment in judging facial expressions

Take a careful look at these two photographs. In which of them does the woman appear to be more sympathetic? In which does she seem to be angrier? Or do you find no difference? For the opinions of subjects who took part in an experiment using the photos, see the text.

seemed angrier (or more unfriendly or more selfish), they tended to pick the one with the small pupils (Hess, 1975). Moreover, their own pupils grew wider when they looked at the photo with the large pupils than when they looked at the other.

All in all, it appears that pupil size—which is controlled by the autonomic nervous system and the smooth muscles of the iris—not only reflects emotional states but serves as a clue that all of us use in assessing how other people feel. We may not even be conscious of the fact, but we seem to be somehow aware that large pupils indicate interest and therefore warmth and acceptance. Long before psychology began studying this matter, women used belladonna, a drug that dilates the pupils, as a standard part of their cosmetic equipment. They believed that putting drops of belladonna in their eyes made them more attractive—indeed the word *belladonna* means "beautiful lady." Perhaps they were right, though for reasons not understood at the time. Along similar lines, we speak warmly of children who are "wide-eyed" with wonder at Christmas—and we describe unfriendly and hostile people as being "sharp-eyed" or "gimlet-eyed."

Feedback Theories of Emotion: The James-Lange View and Others

The various changes that take place in the body, welling up without conscious control and often despite our determination to suppress them, have naturally commanded the attention of psychology from its earliest days. They were the basis of the first important theory of emotions—which was proposed by William James, one of the science's founding fathers, and represented a radical change in thinking about emotional behavior. Common sense says that we cry because we are sad, strike out because we are angry, tremble and run because we are afraid. James made the suggestion—startling to the scientific world of his day and even now to someone who hears it for the first time—that things are exactly the opposite.

James said that emotion occurs in this fashion: Certain stimuli in the environment set off the physiological changes. These changes in turn stimulate the various sensory nerves leading from the visceral organs and other parts of the body to the brain. It is these sensory messages from our aroused bodies that we then perceive as emotion. In other words, we do not cry because we are sad. On the contrary, we feel sad because we are crying. Similarly, we do not tremble because we are afraid, but feel afraid because we are trembling (James, 1890).

This notion that the physiological changes come first and that the perceived emotion is a feedback from the changes was also proposed at about the same time by the Danish scientist Carl Lange. It persisted more or less unchallenged for many years as the *James-Lange theory of emotion*. The weakness of the theory is that it is so difficult to match any particular kind of bodily state (and whatever kind of feedback this might produce) with any particular emotion.

A more recent theory has been proposed by psychologists impressed with the role of the facial muscles. They too believe that our feelings of emotion represent a feedback of bodily sensations—but not so much from the visceral organs as from the muscles of the face, which, as has been said, they believe are programmed by nature to respond in certain definite ways to certain stimuli in the environment (Tomkins, 1962). Again the question is one of matching. Can the feedback from specific facial expressions be matched with the experience of specific emotions? Proponents of the facial feedback theory believe that the matching exists (Izard and Dougherty, 1982), but other psychologists are skeptical (McCaul, Holmes, and Solomon, 1982).

THE BRAIN: KEY TO EMOTIONAL BEHAVIOR

Whether or not our feelings of emotion depend on feedback—either from the visceral organs, as the James-Lange theory presumed, or from the facial muscles—is just one of the many problems that continue to make emotions a topic of speculation and debate. But there is no doubt that emotions are accompanied by bodily changes of many kinds—ranging, as has been said, from pupil size to activity of the glands, digestive organs, heart muscles, and even the chemical composition of the blood. Nor is there any doubt that the activity of the brain changes—a fact that many psychologists now believe is the real key to emotional behavior.

The Brain Hemispheres and Emotion

As described in Chapter 2, psychologists have concentrated in the past on studying the differing roles of the two brain hemispheres in cognition. More recent studies point to differences between the two sides of the brain in the regulation of emotional behavior as well. In general, the right hemisphere appears to be more active in regulating negative emotions such as sadness and fear while the left hemisphere appears to be more active in regulating positive emotions such as happiness (Davidson, 1984).

Evidence comes from both clinical and experimental studies. One team focused on over 100 cases of people who experienced inexplicable outbursts of either crying or laughing. The investigators found that lesions on the left side of the brain, leaving the right side intact, were more frequently associated with crying; in contrast, lesions on the right side of the brain, leaving the left side intact, were more frequently associated with laughing (Sackheim and Gur, 1978). Moreover, depressed subjects often show greater activation of the right frontal lobe than do nondepressed subjects (Schaffer, Davidson, and Saron, 1983). One laboratory experiment demonstrating the roles of brain hemispheres in emotion is summarized in Figure 9-10. It shows that stimuli with an unhappy connotation get a faster response from the right hemisphere, while the opposite is true for stimuli with a happy connotation (Reuter-Lorenz and Davidson, 1981).

Figure 9-10 Right for sad, left for happy

When subjects were presented with pictures of sad faces to their left visual field, which connects with the right brain hemisphere, the reaction time was faster than when the same pictures were presented to the right visual field, which connects with the left hemisphere. The opposite was true for happy faces (Reuter-Lorenz and Davidson, 1981).

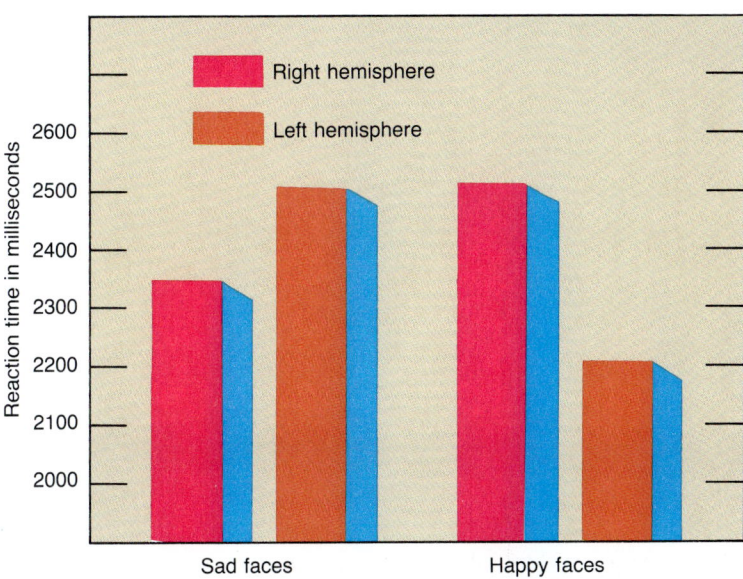

The Cannon-Bard Theory

Another famous theory of emotions, the *Cannon-Bard theory*, was the first to emphasize the fact that brain as well as bodily activity changes with emotion. The theory held that certain stimuli in the environment cause the hypothalamus* to fire off patterns of nervous activity that have two simultaneous effects. One, the hypothalamus arouses the autonomic nervous system and thus triggers the various physiological changes associated with emotion. Two, at the same time, the hypothalamus sends messages to the cerebral cortex that result in our feelings of emotion. Note that the Cannon-Bard theory attaches no importance to the feedback of bodily sensations, which is the basic element of the James-Lange theory. It considers the physiological changes to be a sort of side effect—useful in preparing the body to take appropriate action but not essential to our conscious experience of emotion.

At first glance, the Cannon-Bard and James-Lange theories seem totally at odds. It would appear that if one is right, the other must be wrong. But, as so often happens in science, each of two apparently contradictory theories may have some components that are correct.

The Role of Mental Processes in Emotion: The Cognitive Position

A number of psychologists, all leaning more or less to the cognitive school, have contributed to a new view of emotions. Their ideas are still being formulated and refined and at present differ in many respects, as you will see if you take an advanced course in emotional behavior. For our present purposes, however, their ideas can be put together into a sort of composite picture of the *cognitive theory of emotion*. The discussion that follows ignores some of the fine points that are at issue, and perhaps no single psychologist would agree with all the generalities—but it will serve as an introduction to this important area of research.

---

*Actually Cannon believed that the thalamus was the key. But it has since been found that the hypothalamus, with its close relationship to the autonomic nervous system and the pituitary gland, is the important structure.

The mental state of these two people is likely to affect their view of everything around them.

The cognitive view emphasizes the conscious experience of emotion—that is, the mental processes that account for such feelings as joy, anger, and fear (Lazarus, 1982). Many factors contribute to this experience. One is information about events in the environment, delivered to the cortex (or highest part of the brain) from the sense organs. Another is the brain's storehouse of information about similar events in the past, which aids in appraising and interpreting the new stimuli. Another is patterns of nervous impulses in the hypothalamus and the rest of the brain's limbic system—which, acting through the autonomic nervous system and probably also directly on the pituitary gland, create the physiological changes of being stirred up or toned down. Still another is feedback from these physiological changes, delivered to the cortex via sensory neurons from the visceral organs and the muscles of the body and face. All these factors interact to produce the emotions we experience—and sometimes to initiate behavior that expresses our emotions, intensifies the pleasant ones, or helps us escape from the unpleasant ones.

Some psychologists think of emotional experiences as another of the altered states of consciousness such as those produced by hypnosis or drugs. People who strike back with unaccustomed vigor in anger or panic in fear sometimes say afterward, "I wasn't myself" or "I must have been out of my mind." And certainly emotions, like other altered states, do affect perception. To a joyous person, the world appears bright and cheerful. To a person caught up in distress and disgust, the world is full of gloom and disaster (Izard, 1977).

Cannon-Bard from the Cognitive View

The cognitive psychologists, you will have noted, agree with Cannon-Bard about the importance of the hypothalamus—but not with the theory that messages sent from the hypothalamus to the cortex account for our emotions. Though the exchange of messages between hypothalamus and cortex works in both directions, the new view holds that the cortex plays the commanding role by appraising events that occur in the environment. At any given moment, the information received by the cortex from the sense organs may be neutral in terms of emotional impact, in which case we make a cognitive decision that no emotional reaction is called for. The information may set off patterns of nervous impulses, traveling from cortex to hypothalamus, that are associated with the emotion of interest. The sense organs may convey what the cognitive process decides is good information that calls for joy, or bad information calling for distress, anger, or fear. Sometimes the sensory information compels our attention and creates an emotional reaction even when we are busy with other matters (Nielsen and Sarason, 1981). For example, while absorbed in study at a library table, we may respond to a sexually attractive person who happens to walk by. Also of course we may experience more than one emotion in response to an event (Polivy, 1981). We may feel both sad and angry, for example, after being rejected by a friend, or both fearful and excited while entering an airplane.

The cognitive appraisal of the environment is often immediate and almost automatic (Arnold, 1960)—something like the rapid first impression that occurs in perception. If we find a snake in our path, for example, everything seems to happen at once. Our hearts jump. We feel afraid. We leap back. All this seems to occur without any conscious decision making. At other times our appraisal is more complex and deliberate (Lazarus and Averill, 1972). An example is the "slow burn" we sometimes experience when we hear a remark and have no immediate reaction. But then we think about it, decide it was insulting, and get angry.

On some occasions the appraisal appears to follow rather than precede physiological arousal. For some reason that we do not understand at the moment, our bodies become stirred up or toned down. Perhaps stimuli in the environment have affected the unconscious workings of our minds. Perhaps we have exhibited a conditioned reaction—as in Watson's famous experiment in which the child Albert's fear response was conditioned to furry animals and men with beards. At any rate, we experience some kind of change in the nature and level of our internal sensations, which we must then try to appraise and interpret (Schachter and Singer, 1962). For example, a student sitting alone in a room at night may become aware of unusual bodily sensations and interpret them as feelings of loneliness. A student who has a similar pattern of sensations when a difficult examination is coming up may interpret them as anxiety. Another who has put in an unusually hard day's work may decide that they simply represent fatigue. Such cases of unexplained arousal are infrequent (Maslach, 1978), but they do occur.

James-Lange from the Cognitive View

Just as the cognitive view accepts the Cannon-Bard theory in part, so does it agree with the James-Lange theory that bodily sensations are an essential aspect of emotion. It maintains that the brain and body work together in many ways during emotional experiences. For example, the student who interprets bodily sensations as representing anxiety over an examination may, as a result of this interpretation and labeling, experience additional activity of the autonomic nervous system, intensified physiological changes, and greater feedback—all of which add to the feeling of anxiety. On the other hand, attributing the feelings to fatigue may reduce the activity of the autonomic nervous system, dampen the physiological activity, and thus lessen the bodily feedback and the feelings being experienced.

The cognitive view maintains, however, that bodily states are not enough in themselves to account for all the very different emotions we experience. Once we become aware that bodily changes are taking place, what really determines our feelings is our cognitive activity—our thinking about the stimulus that has produced the changes and the entire environmental situation in which it occurred.

INDIVIDUAL DIFFERENCES IN EMOTION AND THEIR EXPRESSION

If someone asked you how many different kinds of emotions a human being can experience, how would you answer? Our language contains hundreds of words that describe emotional feelings—and your answer might depend on how many of these words you are familiar with, also how many of them you use to appraise and label your own feelings. Other cultures use different labels. People in the Caroline Islands, for example, have two different words meaning anger—one for justified anger toward someone who has acted improperly, the other for anger that cannot readily be explained by another person's behavior (Lutz, 1982).

One psychologist has suggested that there are ten basic emotions, listed in Figure 9-11. Our other emotional experiences, according to this view, are combinations of two or more of these ten. The possible ways in which ten emotions can be combined, of course, run into the thousands. If feelings of interest are considered to be emotions, as in this listing, then it appears that we experience some amount of emotion during most or all our waking hours (Izard, 1977). But the more spectacular feelings that people usually think of as emotions (joy, anger, fear, and the like) occupy less of our time—probably under 10 percent for most of us.

Figure 9-11 **One psychological view of the range of emotions**

The fundamental human emotions, according to one investigator, are those listed at the top of the table. Other emotions that we frequently experience, notably those at the bottom, are combinations of some of the fundamental feelings (after Izard, 1977).

The ten basic emotions

anger	guilt
contempt	interest-excitement
disgust	joy
distress	shame
fear	surprise

Four important complex emotions

anxiety
(fear plus anger, distress, guilt, interest, or shame)

depression
(distress plus anger, contempt, fear, guilt, or shame)

hostility
(a combination of anger, contempt, and disgust)

love
(interest plus joy)

The Role of Learning

There are of course marked individual differences in emotional experience. Some of these differences are the result of learning. Even simple classical conditioning, as was discussed in Chapter 5, can create unreasonable fears and unreasonable preferences. Because of this kind of childhood conditioning, some individuals have intense emotional reactions to objects or events in the environment that leave other people entirely unmoved. Moreover, the more complex cognitive processes that help determine emotional experience vary greatly from one person to another, mostly because of associations laid down in long-term memory through learning.

Behavior resulting from emotion also shows many individual differences. Some people have learned to suppress many of the outward signs of emotion. (Such people are often called "poker-faced.") Others are quick to display their feelings. (They are said to "wear their hearts on their sleeves.") Displays of emotion vary from culture to culture, obviously because of what these cultures have taught their members about appropriate behavior. When Navaho or Apache Indians are angry, they do not raise but lower their voices. When inhabitants of the Andaman Islands want to show joy at greeting a visiting relative, they sit down in the visitor's lap and weep (Opler, 1967).

Differences That Are Inborn

On the other hand, some differences appear to be inborn. Studies of very young children, who have not yet had the opportunity to do much learning, have shown that some are much more inclined to smile than others, while some have a pronounced tendency to be irritable and cry at the slightest provocation.

This Russian display of feeling would be rare in our own culture.

There is considerable evidence that one inborn difference affecting emotions is the sensitivity of the autonomic nervous system (ANS), which controls many of the bodily changes associated with emotion. Some of us seem to react to weaker stimulation of the ANS than others—and to react more rapidly and with greater intensity. Patterns of ANS activity also vary. In the same kind of emotional situation, one person may consistently show a rapid heartbeat, while another may show only a small change in heart rate but a pronounced increase in skin temperature (Lacey and Lacey, 1958). Differences of this kind can be observed even in children (Tennes and Mason, 1982). Two-year-olds who are chronically anxious, timid, and shy have been found to have a heart rate that is unusually high but generally stable. Two-year-olds who are less fearful usually have a heart rate that is low and subject to considerably more variation.

Certainly any abnormality of the glands or nervous system can have a drastic effect on emotional experience. One demonstration comes from a study of people who had suffered injuries to the spinal cord and had lost all bodily sensations below the point of damage. These people reported that their emotions were considerably less intense after the injury than before. The higher up the spine the damage had occurred, and thus the less feedback of bodily sensations they retained, the greater was the loss of emotional intensity (Hohmann, 1966).

Emotional Stress—for Better or Worse

Because the emotions are associated with so many physiological changes, often of a highly turbulent nature, they put the body under considerable stress. They can be physically exhausting, as is evident from the "washed-out" feeling that often follows an outburst of anger or a serious scare. Wear and tear on the body are caused by pleasant as well as unpleasant emotions. As one investigator has stated, "A painful blow and a passionate kiss can be equally stressful" (Selye, 1976).

Up to a point, *emotional stress* is an unavoidable and even desirable aspect of life. Some of our most glorious moments arise from the tension and excitement of joy and love. The milder emotion of interest adds zest and meaning to our work, our recreation, and our social relationships. Without our emotions and their accompanying stress, our lives would be drab and colorless.

Even fear is useful. It helps us avoid or escape from situations that threaten our well-being and sometimes our lives. It makes us drive more carefully and plan more constructively for the future. Unless fear becomes so intense as to create panic, it can help us perform better in many situations. When the wear and tear of emotional stress persist too intensely and for too long a time, however, they can create disastrous effects. The topic of stress—and the various ways we attempt to cope with it—will be discussed in Chapter 11.

HOW DRIVES AFFECT BEHAVIOR: HUNGER AND THIRST

Besides emotions, there is another group of psychological conditions that are accompanied by physiological changes and have a pronounced effect on behavior. For example, as you know from experience, a state of hunger can make you jumpy, jittery, and unable to concentrate. The urge to find food, when the body lacks it, can be just as strong as the tendency to run away in fear or strike back in anger.

No clear dividing line exists between emotions and such drive states as hunger. As in the case of emotions, the hunger drive encompasses three components: an event in the environment (in this case, the deprivation of food), bodily changes (for example, changes in blood sugar level), and a cognitive component (thoughts about food and the search for it). Both emotions and drives may produce strong sensations, and both may trigger behavior—sometimes of the most explosive kind.

Yet there is a difference, and even in ordinary conversation we would not think of referring to hunger—or thirst, or the sex drive—as an emotion. The drives center on the process of homeostasis, or the maintenance of bodily stability. It is one of the brain's functions, as was explained in Chapter 2, to preserve homeostasis by making sure our bodies have a constant supply of all the substances our cells require to perform efficiently. When our bodies lack any of these substances, we experience a *drive*—which can be defined as *a pattern of brain activity resulting from physiological imbalances that threaten homeostasis*. Among the drives are *hunger* (caused by the lack of food), *thirst* (lack of water, which makes up two-thirds of our bodies), and *breathing* (the need for oxygen). The breathing drive goes unnoticed most of the time, but people who are drowning or being suffocated will fight as hard for air as they would fight for food when starving.

The pattern of brain activity that constitutes a drive makes us seek whatever our bodies need to maintain homeostasis. By so doing—for example, by finding food or water—we restore the physiological balance, change the pattern of brain activity, and thus satisfy the drive.

The Body's Hunger Signals

How do we know that we are hungry?

Common sense tells us that we have hunger pangs in the stomach, which feels empty and overactive and sometimes actually growls for food. This commonsense explanation is partially true. There are nerve fibers that carry messages to the brain from the stomach (Ball, 1974), and also from the mouth, throat, and intestines. Moreover, the sustained distension of the stomach will indeed make us feel satiated and affect eating behavior (Stellar, McHugh, and Moran, 1985). But the role of the stomach is not altogether so simple. Animals stop eating even when their stomachs are far from full—when they have eaten a substance that is nutritious. If the stomach is filled with an equal amount of non-nutritious bulk, the animal will continue eating. This means that our stomach walls contain receptors that are sensitive to nutrients that are dissolved in the stomach acids. Evidently these receptors relay the message to the brain that nutritious material is on its way into the

Figure 9-12 The liver and hunger signals

The balance of glucose and glycogen affects eating behavior, as described in the text.

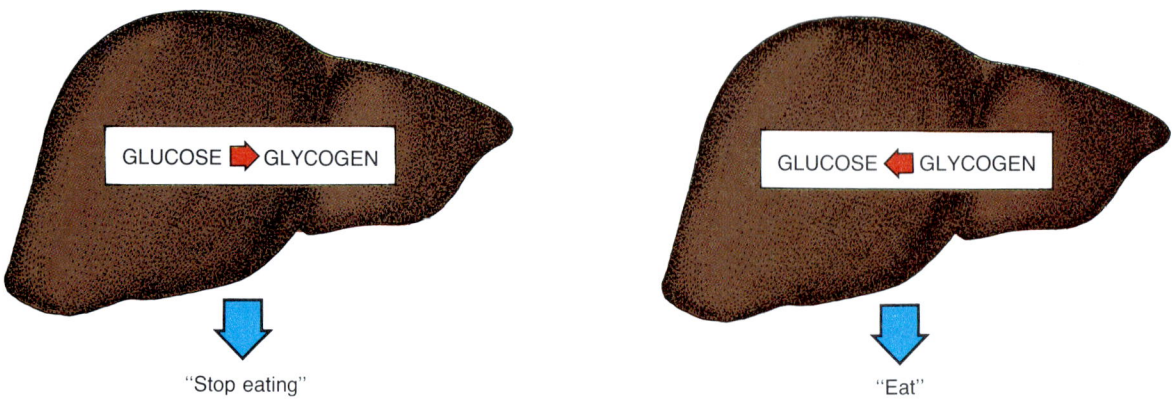

system (Deutsch, Puerto, and Wang, 1978). The message is probably facilitated through the action of an intestinal hormone (Stellar, McHugh, and Moran, 1985).

More important than sensations and messages from the stomach, it appears, are hunger messages originating in the liver, which maintains the role of manager of the body's food metabolism. After we eat, there is an overly generous supply of glucose in the blood, and the extra glucose in converted to *glycogen*, or "animal starch," in the liver. As portrayed in Figure 9-12, while the liver is actively manufacturing glycogen, we are not hungry. But when we have not eaten for a time, the liver begins to pour glucose into the blood from its store of glycogen, and this change in glucose leads to hunger and eating (Le Magnen, 1984).

Hunger and the Hypothalamus

At one time, it was believed that two areas of the hypothalamus play the key role in hunger, and in a straightforward way. It was thought that stimulation of the *lateral hypothalamus* (LH) triggers eating, while stimulation of the *ventromedial hypothalamus* (VMH) inhibits eating. And indeed, when cells in the LH are destroyed, animals refuse food or drink and will survive only if fed artificially. In contrast, as shown in Figure 9-13, damage to cells in the VMH produces overeating and obesity.

But recent studies of the LH and VMH reveal a more complicated story. For one thing, a rat stimulated in the presumed hunger area of the hypothalamus does not necessarily eat. If no food is present, the animal will do something else. It may drink water or gnaw on wood (Valenstein, Cox, and Kakolewski, 1970), as if the stimulation merely produced some kind of general arousal. Moreover, animals can be made to start eating by electrical stimulation of brain areas outside the hypothalamus (Valenstein, 1973)—or sometimes just by pinching a rat's tail (Valenstein, 1976).

It appears that the hunger drive depends on brain patterns that are far more complex than mere on and off switches. Some of the nerve cells in the hypothalamus seem to be sensitive to changes in the food supply present in the bloodstream, particularly the levels of fatty compounds and blood sugar (Le Magnen, 1984). But the hypothalamus also responds to messages carried by nerve fibers from various parts of the stomach and from the intestine. The hunger drive is also affected by outside stimuli—such *"incentive objects"* as

Figure 9-13 The hypothalamus and obesity

Surgically produced lesions in portions of the hypothalamus led this rat to so overeat that it tripled its normal weight. Similar findings have been achieved in studies of various species—including monkeys, chickens, and humans.

Window displays like this play a role in the experience of hunger.

How Drives Affect Behavior: Hunger and Thirst

the smell of food from a restaurant kitchen or the sight of pastries in a bakery window—and by our eating habits and the social relationships we have built around eating. (We tend to feel hungry around our usual dinner time regardless of our physiological condition, and we usually eat more when we are with family or friends than when we are alone.) Thus the hunger drive cannot be explained in any simple way. It appears to be the result of an intricate system of bodily and psychological states—among them the action of intestinal hormones, the level of glucose in the blood, the activity of the brain, and the presence of cues for eating in the environment.

Body Weight and Hunger

The hunger drive is closely related to the fact that the body contains a large number of cells, scattered throughout, that are especially designed for the storage of fatty compounds. In evolutionary terms, survival of the species presumably depended on the ability of these *fat cells* to store up energy that would tide the body over the prolonged periods of starvation that humans once experienced frequently (and still do in many places). Under ordinary circumstances, the hunger drive keeps these cells filled to an appropriate level with fatty compounds. But when the body lacks other sources of food and energy, the fat cells are emptied and their contents used as fuel. This raises the level of fatty compounds in the bloodstream—a change that serves as one of the triggers for the hunger drive.

Since the amount of fat stored in the body largely determines a person's weight, the hunger drive usually tends to keep our body weight at its ideal level (Stellar and Corbit, 1973). Ordinarily we eat enough to maintain our reserve stores of fat and keep our weight from falling too low (Nisbett, 1972). But we stop short of consuming an excess of food that would become fat deposits and make us too heavy (Hervey, 1969).

Even a slight change in food intake can have a drastic effect on weight. For example, adding as little as ten medium-sized potato chips a day to one's usual diet would result in a gain of about eleven pounds a year. Yet most of us stay at the same weight over long periods of time. One is reminded of the workings of a thermostat that manages, by turning a furnace on and off, to keep a building within a temperature range of one or two degrees.

Why Some People Get Fat

In the United States, it has been estimated, somewhere between a quarter and a third of all adults are at least 20 percent over their ideal weight—some by as much as 20 or 50 or even 100 pounds (Kolata, 1985). The reason is a mystery that many psychologists have spent years trying to unravel—in part because obesity can lead to severe psychological problems as well as to physical disorders such as high blood pressure, diabetes, and heart disease (Grinker, 1982).

In some cases, obesity seems to stem from metabolic disturbances. Instead of turning food into energy at the normal rate, the body stores an excessive amount of fat deposits. In most cases, however, obesity is simply the result of eating too much and exercising too little (Stunkard, 1985).

But why do people eat too much? Sometimes there seem to be emotional reasons. Clinical psychologists have found that many overweight patients overeat to relieve anxieties over competition, failure, rejection, or sexual performance. A study of both lower-class urban residents and American Indians showed that individuals who undergo a great deal of stress and have an opportunity to eat will do so—and that the process, maintained over a sufficient period of time, will lead to obesity (Pine, 1985).

Some people eat simply as a matter of habit—regardless of whether their hunger drive signals the need for food. Often they are inveterate "snackers"—a trait they share in common with those given to smoking (Green and Tapp, 1986). Others have a strong preference for such high-calorie foods as butter, cheese, ice cream, pastries, and candy. Contrary to popular belief, however, it is not so much that obese people have a "sweet tooth," but that they appear to prefer foods that have relatively high fat content (Drewnowski et al., 1985).

Studies have found that the eating patterns of fat people are unusual in several respects. For one thing, fat people tend to eat whenever they have the opportunity, even if they have already had a meal and would not normally be hungry. This was demonstrated in striking fashion in the experiment illustrated in Figure 9-14. In another experiment, in which clocks were manipulated to make the subjects think that dinner was being served later than usual, fat people ate more than their customary amount, though people of normal weight did not (Schachter and Gross, 1968). Whenever overweight people sit down to a table, they tend to eat more and eat faster (Schachter, 1971). They are particularly likely to eat a lot when the food tastes unusually good—and more likely than people of normal weight to be turned off by food that tastes bad (Nisbett, 1968).

In all these respects, the eating habits of overweight people closely resemble those of animals that have become fat after surgical destruction of part of the hypothalamus. Moreover, overweight people behave in a number of other ways very much like animals with damage to this part of the brain. They tend to be emotional and irritable (Rodin, 1972; Rodin, Elman, and Schachter, 1972), to be more lethargic and less active than average (Bullen, Reed, and Mayer, 1964), and to have less interest in sex (Nisbett and Platt, 1972).

It is possible that overweight people have some kind of brain abnormality affecting regions of the hypothalamus—something akin to the surgical destruction in experimental animals (Schachter, 1971). Or it may be that the bloodstream of overweight people carries some kind of chemical, produced by a quirk in the manner in which their alimentary canals and livers process food, that overstimulates the hypothalamus and thus creates more frequent and more intense hunger (Miller, 1975). Whatever the source of obesity, the condition is best dealt with through programs of management of eating behavior (Stunkard, 1986). One such program is described in the box on Psychology in Everyday Life titled "Weight Control through Behavior Control."

Figure 9-14 One clue to overeating

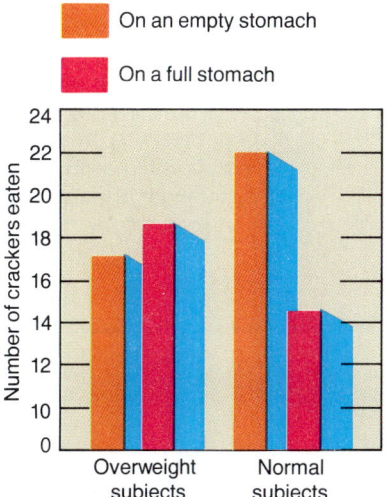

An experimenter worked with two groups of subjects, one group of normal weight and the other anywhere from 14 to 75 percent overweight. When the subjects arrived at the laboratory, having skipped the previous meal, half from each group were fed sandwiches, the other half nothing. They then took part in what they thought was an evaluation of the taste of five different kinds of cracker presented to them in separate bowls. They were told that they could eat as few or as many of the crackers as they wished in making their judgments. As the graph shows, the amount eaten by the subjects of normal weight was considerably lower if they had just eaten sandwiches. The overweight subjects, however, actually ate somewhat more on a full stomach than on an empty stomach. For a possible explanation of these results, see the text (Schachter, 1971).

Psychology in Everyday Life
Weight Control through Behavior Control

The principles of behavior therapy, to be described in Chapter 13, have been successfully applied in the management of eating behavior among people who tend to be overweight. For anyone who is battling against weight gain, here are the major steps of a tested program that focuses on changing eating habits and controlling the cues for eating (Stunkard, 1986).

1. *Monitor your eating behavior.* Keep careful records of the food you eat, how much, at what time of day, where you are, who you are with. You may be quite surprised at how much you eat, and in what varied circumstances.

2. *Control the stimuli that precede eating.* Once you identify where and when you do most of your eating, begin to control your eating (and that includes snacking) by confining it to one place. In this way you will learn to avoid eating, for example, while watching TV, reading, talking to a friend, or studying.

3. *Develop techniques to take charge of the act of eating.* For example, practice taking only smaller portions, and eat slowly. Obesity patients are often encouraged to count each mouthful of food, or each chew or swallow.

4. *Reward yourself*—not only for signs of weight loss, but even before them, for following the prescribed behavior. Give yourself points for keeping accurate records, eating in one place, pausing after each swallow, and so on. Then convert your accumulated points into rewards such as buying something you have wanted, or treating yourself to a play or movie. Additional rewards are in order when the pounds begin to come off.

5. *Restructure your thinking.* Verbalize your internal thoughts and make a conscious effort to counter negative thoughts with positive ones. For example, if you hear yourself say "It's taking so long to lose weight," counter with "But I *am* losing it, and this time I'm going to learn to keep it off."

6. *Diet.* Many of the diet books that make the best-seller lists are actually promoting dangerous courses of action (Stunkard, 1986). Moreover, *going on* a diet implies that eventually you will be *going off* it. The most effective "diet" may not be a diet at all, but rather a gradual change to foods that you can continue to eat indefinitely. This means increasing complex carbohydrates, particularly fruits, vegetables, and cereals, and decreasing the intake of fats and concentrated carbohydrates. Check with a doctor first—and then you can do your own monitoring of the foods you eat.

7. *Exercise.* Most successful weight reduction programs include an exercise component. The point is that expending more calories than you take in is going to result in losing pounds. Programmed sports activities are not necessarily the answer. Instead, practice getting off the bus stop too soon or too late, parking the car some distance from your destination, or using the stairs instead of the elevator. The effects are likely to be more than physical. "Even if exercise had no metabolic benefits, its psychological benefits would still warrant its use in the management of obesity" (Stunkard, 1986).

Do Fat People Have Too Many Fat Cells?

Another theory of obesity blames the cells designed for storage of fatty compounds. It has been found that at least some overweight people have an unusually large number of these cells in their bodies (Björntorp, 1972). In extreme cases, they may have fully three times as

If the amount of fat cells in the body is established in early childhood, this toddler may well have obesity problems all her life.

many as people of normal weight (Knittle and Hirsch, 1968). The cells may be voracious consumers of fatty compounds carried by the bloodstream.

Thus overweight people, because of their excessive number of fat cells, may be more or less constantly hungry for reasons they cannot control by any act of will power. Their hunger may become particularly intense if they try to diet. It has been suggested that many fat people, because of the social pressure against obesity, are actually underweight rather than overweight in terms of the requirements of their own bodies (Nisbett, 1972). Recent evidence suggests that the biochemical signals to overeat may come from the fat cells themselves (Kolata, 1985).

Why do some people have more fat cells than others? The answer seems to lie partly in heredity. Identical twins, who have inherited the same genes, are twice as likely to fall in the same weight range as are fraternal twins (Stunkard, Foch, and Hrubec, 1986). Additional evidence for a strong hereditary factor comes from studies of adoptive children, as illustrated in Figure 9-15.

Overeating in the period immediately after birth may also be a factor. Experiments with rats indicate that the number of fat cells in their bodies is increased by giving them excessive amounts of food in the first three weeks of life, after which overfeeding no longer has this effect. Similarly, the number of fat cells in the human body seems to be established during early childhood and to remain relatively constant from then on. Adults who go on starvation diets show a decrease in the size of these cells, as their contents are drawn on for fuel, but no decrease in the number of cells (Hirsch and Knittle, 1970). People who deliberately overeat to gain weight show an increase in the size of the cells but no increase in number (Sims et al., 1968). One approach to the obesity problem may be to urge mothers not to push babies to overeat during the early period when the number of fat cells is being established. But of course this approach comes too late for overweight people beyond the age of childhood, who continue to have their difficulties despite everything that has been learned thus far about the hunger drive.

Figure 9-15 Fat parents, fat children

Adults who had been adopted as children turned out to be thin, plump, or fat according to the size of their biological mothers rather than the size of the mothers who reared them. The pattern applies equally in the case of fathers as well (Stunkard, Foch, and Hrubec, 1986).

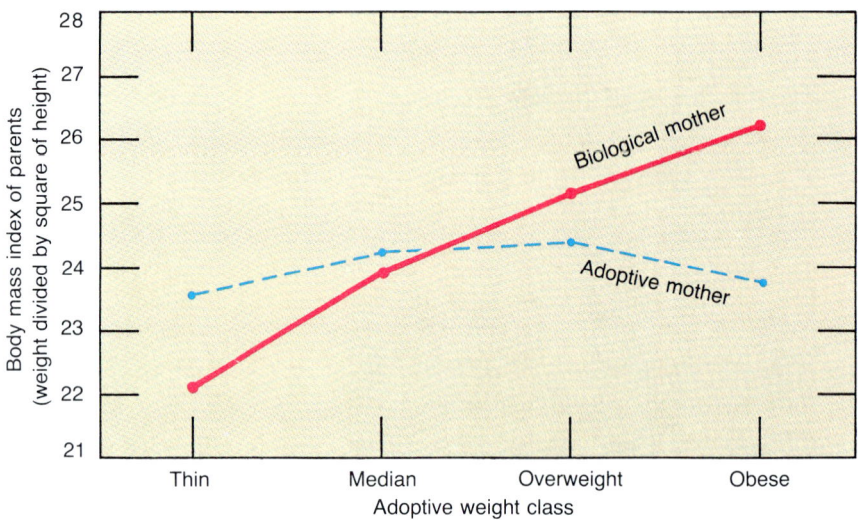

Thirst

The *thirst drive* resembles the hunger drive in many respects. The commonsense observation—that we get thirsty when our mouths are dry—again turns out to be partially true. The drive does depend in part on messages carried to the brain from the mouth—as well as from the throat, which seems to signal how much water has passed through, and from the stomach, which signals whether it is empty or full (Blass and Hall, 1976). But still this is not the full explanation. A person may feel thirsty even when nerve fibers from the mouth and throat are under anesthesia, sending out no messages at all (Cofer, 1972).

Again the hypothalamus plays an important part. A lack of water causes the cells of the body to become dehydrated, and certain nerve cells in the hypothalamus appear to be sensitive to this change (Rolls and Rolls, 1982). Moreover, when we lose water, the body immediately activates mechanisms to conserve it. A lack of water reduces the volume of blood flowing through the body, causing sensory receptors in the heart and blood vessels to send signals to the brain (Epstein, Kissileff, and Stellar, 1973). The reduced volume of blood also causes the kidneys to produce a chemical that stimulates the hypothalamus (Epstein, Fitzsimons, and Simons, 1969). Moreover, water loss results in the release of a hormone that helps prevent further loss through urination (Rolls and Rolls, 1982). Thus the thirst drive is triggered by various signs of imbalance in the body's water supply. Much as in the case of hunger, the goal of the thirst drive is water, not the mere act of drinking.

SLEEP: THE OTHER THIRD OF OUR LIVES

The *sleep drive* plays an important part in the rhythm of our daily lives. This drive appears to be triggered by imbalances in brain chemistry, and possibly body chemistry as well, that build up when we are awake and active. When we sleep, we correct the chemical imbalances and wake up ready to function again at full efficiency.

The Stages of Sleep

The way sleep differs from the waking state of consciousness has been shown by studies of brain waves and body activity, measured by electrodes attached to people sleeping through the night in laboratories. The studies have shown quite clearly that sleep is by no means a state of suspended animation in which the body and brain are shut down for a time. Sleep is not just a slowing down but a kind of activity in its own right. The brain continues to be highly active—though in a different way.

Moreover, it has been found that there are several kinds, or stages, of sleep that range from very light to very deep. These are portrayed in Figure 9-16. About a quarter of the night is spent in *paradoxical sleep*—which gets its name from the fact that the brain's activity is very similar to the waking state but the bodily muscles are almost totally relaxed. When subjects who are in paradoxical sleep are awakened, about 80 to 85 percent of them report

Figure 9-16 The stages of sleep

As you pass over the threshold of sleep, your brain waves begin to portray a shifting pattern, and you descend through a series of four levels of sleep. Then, after about 70–90 minutes, you enter still another stage, known as the REM period of vivid dreaming. After perhaps ten minutes, you turn over in your bed and begin shifting down the levels of sleep again, to return in another 90 minutes or so for a longer REM dream.

Stage	Brain Waves	Behavior/Sensations	Depth of Sleep	Physiological Changes	Dreams
1	Small and pinched; irregular and rapidly changing	Sometimes a floating sensation, drifting with idle thoughts and dreams	Can still be awakened easily, and will insist has not been asleep	Muscles relaxing, pulse growing even, breathing becoming regular, temperature falling	Images and thoughtlike fragments
2	Growing larger, quick bursts	If eyes are open, will not see	May be awakened with a modest sound	Eyes roll slowly from side to side	Some thoughtlike fragments and low intensity dreams
3	Large, slow waves - one a second	Removed from the waking world	Takes louder noise to awaken	Muscles relaxed, breathing even; heart rate slowed, temperature declining, muscles relaxed, blood pressure dropping	Rarely recalled
4	Very large, slow waves	Period of beginning sleep walking, or bed wetting	The deepest sleep, most difficult to awaken	Even breathing, heart rate, blood pressure; body temperature slowly falling	Poor recall makes this seem a dreamless oblivion most of the time. Rare nightmares.
REM	Irregular and small - resembles those of waking	Rapid eye movements (REMs) as if watching	Hard to bring to the surface and reality	Lies limp, chin muscles slack; penile erections and increased vaginal congestion; increased gastric secretions; fluctuating blood pressure; irregular pulse, respiration; twitching of fingers and toes	Very vivid dreams 85% of the time

they have been dreaming. In fact during paradoxical sleep the eyes dart quickly about as if following a series of visual images. Therefore this stage is also known as *REM sleep*—REM standing for the *rapid eye movement* that can be observed.

The Why of Sleep

As you probably have observed for yourself, a sleepless night produces unpleasant after-effects. Merely lying in bed and resting is no substitute for real sleep (Mendelson et al., 1984). In fact any lack of sleep below your natural requirements, whether from insomnia or other causes, is likely to make you feel tired, irritable, and generally below par. Although some people have been known to go without sleep entirely for a number of days without suffering any apparent damage (Webb and Cartwright, 1978), the older we get the more our performance and well-being suffer. And recent studies of animals show that the penalties can be severe indeed. One investigator, making certain that the rats he was studying did not sneak in even tiny "microsleep" periods, induced profound and lethal metabolic changes in the rats in as little as a week (Rechtschaffen, 1983).

Even when only the normal cycles of sleep and waking are disrupted, we pay a price. This can be seen whenever there is a significant shift in schedules—for example, when we travel across time zones, and jet lag makes us feel as if our normally routine functioning is terribly out of kilter. Investigators have found that shift work has the same effect, creating a reduction in efficiency, irritability, fatigue, physical symptoms, depression, and a reduction of mental acuity (Akerstedt, Torsvall, and Gillberg, 1982).

These facts raise the question: Why do we sleep at all? It has been commonly assumed that sleep allows the body and brain to recoup from the wear-and-tear of daily activity—and indeed investigators have found an increase in deep sleep and total sleep time after

Midnight in an emergency room—what effect might long and irregular hours have on the medical staff?

the expenditure of physical energy (Shapiro et al., 1981). But, as noted earlier, sleep is hardly a time of total inactivity for the brain and body, and so other factors must be at play.

One line of research suggests that the answer may lie in a sleep-producing chemical substance that has been found in the brains of animals and most recently in human urine. When even very tiny amounts of this chemical are injected into the brains of other animals, it causes about a 50 percent increase in very deep, dream-free sleep (Maugh, 1982). If the chemical factor could be produced synthetically, it might solve the problems of people who experience sleep disorders. At present, however, investigators have to process more than 4 tons of urine to obtain about a millionth of an ounce.

There are some indications that other substances produced by animals and humans may also induce sleep. Body chemistry as well as brain chemistry may play a part. Some investigators have suggested that ordinary sleep serves to restore the body's chemical balance, while REM sleep restores the brain's ability to function (Hartmann, 1973)—perhaps by somehow renewing the chemical substances that help transmit nervous impulses (Moruzzi, 1972).

How Much Sleep Do We Need?

Young adults sleep an average of 7½ hours a night (Webb and Cartwright, 1978), but there are wide individual differences. Some people prefer to sleep as long as 10 hours or more, others only a few hours. One woman was found to get along on 45 minutes of sleep a night (Meddis, Pearson, and Langford, 1973). Whatever your own sleeping habits may be, you are stuck with them. They cannot be comfortably changed. In one experiment some couples were asked to try to get along on less sleep by cutting down slowly—a half hour a week. None of them ever got below 5 hours a night and all of them eventually gave up the attempt (Johnson and MacLeod, 1973).

Whatever our sleep quota, most people are occasionally troubled by *insomnia*—the inability to fall asleep or to stay asleep—and a surprising number of people suffer from it chronically. One national survey showed that 35 percent of the American people complain of difficulties with sleep, and perhaps half of them consider it a major problem (Mellinger and Balter, 1983). Among the people most likely to experience difficulty in falling asleep are those suffering from anxiety, while those most likely to encounter problems with awakening much too early are those suffering from depression (National Institute of Mental Health, 1983). While such people have occasionally been helped over the short run with sleeping pills, prolonged use of drugs for inducing sleep can actually lead to chronic sleep disturbances (Mendelson, 1980). The same is true for anyone who tries to combat a period of sleeplessness with regular use of drugs—as discussed in a box on Psychology in Everyday Life called "Avoiding Chemical Warfare in the Bedroom."

THE POWER OF THE SEX DRIVE—AND OTHER DRIVES

One of the most powerful forces in human behavior occupies a puzzling position in psychological thinking. Should sex, which pervades so many human activities, be classified as a drive? Perhaps—for among lower animals it has all the characteristics of a drive. Should it be regarded as an emotion? Perhaps—for sexual passion is one of the most intense human feelings and closely related to the emotion called love. Yet it does not quite fit into either of these categories. Nor does it exactly fit the definition of a motive, discussed later in this chapter. The dilemma is based in part on the fact that sexual behavior differs in animals and humans.

Psychology in Everyday Life
Avoiding Chemical Warfare in the Bedroom

It is estimated that American doctors write over 20 million prescriptions a year for sleep drugs (Mendelson, 1980). In addition, millions more use over-the-counter sleep medications in the hope of getting "a good night's sleep."

The evidence is that "no drug-induced sleep is a substitute for normal sleep," and "nightly use of sleeping pills for long periods of time actually can make sleep more difficult" (U.S. Department of Health and Human Services, 1981). Most sleep drugs change the normal rhythm of brain activity, robbing us of the required cycle of sleep stages outlined in Figure 9-16. Moreover, the human body adapts to these drugs after repeated use. As a result, increasingly larger doses are required to bring on sleep, and the penalties pile up during the day. Many of the drugs adversely affect daytime mood, alertness, and performance—including driving skills (Mendelson, 1984). Eventually, chronic users show evidence of fatigue, irritability, difficulty in concentration, poor coordination, depression, and even bizarre changes in personality. And the drugs can introduce extremely disturbing nightmares (Hartmann, 1984).

Preferable by far are nondrug approaches to better sleep. For one thing, regular exercise tends to benefit sleep—but the exercise should be done during the day, not right before bedtime (U.S. Department of Health and Human Services, 1981). It helps, too, to avoid stimulants such as coffee and cigarettes. And, yes, our grandmothers were evidently right: a glass of milk before bedtime can act as a natural sedative. Milk contains the chemical substance *l-tryptophan*, which often does indeed have a soporific effect (Regestein, 1980). Avoiding chaotically irregular schedules can be important, as well. Each of us has a naturally best time for sleep, and trying to force a new time each night can produce erratic sleep.

Most important, experts agree that lying in bed and ruminating about sleeplessness is likely to generate stress and simply prolong the problem. When you have an occasional bout with insomnia, it is a good idea, therefore, to get out of bed and do something—read, write letters, watch TV—until your body tells you it is time to return to bed. In the long run, it is important to resist the easy temptation to go to the medicine cabinet and begin a dangerous course of "chemical warfare" in the hope of conquering insomnia.

Animal Sexual Behavior

If this were a text about lower animals, sex could be discussed in much simpler terms. Among nonhuman mammals sex is almost as direct a drive as hunger, though less frequently triggered. Usually the female sex drive is quiescent, and over long stretches of time the female is not sexually attractive to the male of her species. At regularly recurring periods, however, the ovaries release hormones that activate a sex control mechanism centered in the hypothalamus of the brain. During these periods, which vary in frequency and length from species to species, the female seeks sexual contacts and engages in the kind of courtship and copulation characteristic of the species. The female's readiness is apparent from such clues as odors, vocal signals (the sex "calls" of cats), or changes in the color and size of the genitals. These cues in turn prompt the male to initiate sexual behavior.

There appears to be an anatomical basis for the common observation that in animals (and humans as well), males are more readily aroused and initiate sex more often than females. In male rats, one study has identified a set of motor neurons in the spinal cord that mediate motor actions involved in sexual behavior; these neurons grow in size under the influence of androgen—a hormone lacking in females (Kurz, Sengelaub, and Arnold,

1986). In humans, investigators have found that an area of the hypothalamus related to sexual arousal is larger in males than in females (Swaab and Fliers, 1985).

Sex in many animals also resembles a drive in that the behavior that satisfies it is largely unlearned. Even when rats are raised in total isolation, with no opportunity to learn about the anatomy of the opposite sex or about the species' characteristic sexual behavior, they usually copulate like other rats at the first opportunity. Farther up the evolutionary scale, however, some learning seems necessary. Male and female monkeys raised in isolation do not ordinarily know how to behave toward each other at the first meeting (Harlow and Harlow, 1962).

Human Sexual Behavior

Among humans, sex bears only slight resemblance to a drive. True, sexual activity is most frequent during the years when the concentration of sex hormones in the bloodstream is highest, from puberty into the middle years. But men and women of all ages can have the desire and ability to engage in sexual activity. The female's desires are not significantly dependent on her monthly hormone cycles. Nor is her sexual attractiveness to the male. Some people—both men and women—seek out sexual contacts frequently, without any particular stimulation by glandular cycles or external cues. Others never engage in sexual activity, even in the most provocative situations.

Between men and women, there are more similarities than differences in sexual needs and responses (Masters, Johnson, and Kolodny, 1986). True enough, there are some contrasts: women tend to experience multiple orgasms, while men do not; women typically seek prolonged touching, caressing, and stroking before intercourse, while men are more quickly aroused and spent; as shown in Figure 9-17, men are more accepting of sex without love; and men are fertile into old age, while women are not. But many of the perceived

Figure 9-17 How people feel about sex without love

Men—both heterosexuals and gays—tend to accept sex without love more readily than do women, including lesbians (adapted from Blumstein and Schwartz, 1983).

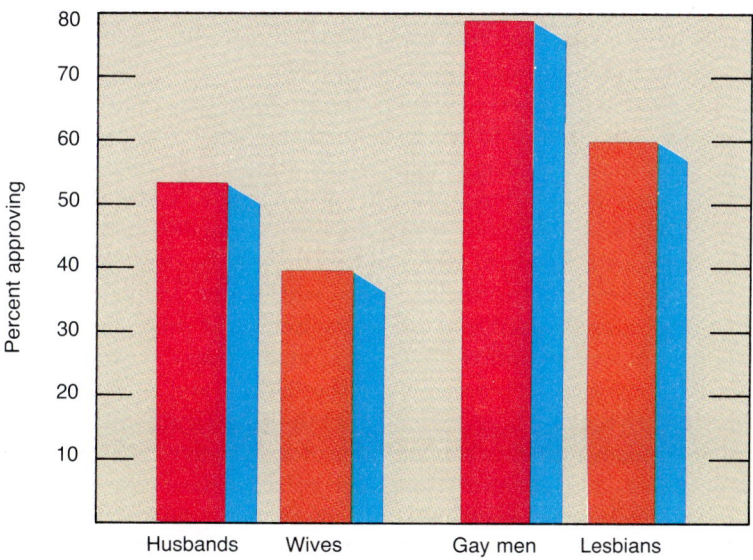

differences between the sexes are social stereotypes. Men and women enjoy sex equally and at about the same ages. Men are not more promiscuous than women. Both about equally engage in *voyeurism* (sexual gratification from watching sex scenes), use fantasy to enrich their sex lives, want variety, struggle with boredom, and like oral sex. Both become sexually impaired when self-esteem is impaired, or when burdened by anxiety about sexual performance.

Human sexual behavior clearly does not depend on some "sex center" in the brain that operates like an on-off switch. Rather, it seems to result from a combination of many nervous pathways ranging all the way from the spinal cord to the cerebral cortex (Whalen, 1976). Some of these pathways may be programmed by heredity. Some are influenced by the activity of the sex glands in complex ways that have thus far defied analysis (Beach, 1976). Others may not depend on glandular activity at all.

Sexual behavior is influenced by a whole array of desires and preferences that all of us begin to learn in childhood and may continue to revise throughout our lives. Indeed any sexual practice humans can imagine and bring off is being employed, often with greater frequency than most people would imagine (Masters, Johnson, and Kolodny, 1985). Sexual behavior is molded by our personalities, moral standards, and social relationships—the ways in which we have learned to regard our parents and brothers and sisters, establish friendships, and view marriage and some of the problems that occur in marriage. Some people value sexual experiences less for the physical gratification they provide than as acts of communication and friendship. The importance of openness in sexual relationships is discussed in a Psychology in Everyday Life box titled "Partner Communication: The Cornerstone of Good Sex."

Other Drives

The *temperature drive* is common to all warm-blooded animals. In humans its goal is to maintain the body's inner temperature at about 98.6° Fahrenheit (37° centigrade). It appears to be controlled by cells in the brain that are sensitive to temperature changes. When stimulated by increased warmth, they send off messages that cause perspiration (which cools the body through evaporation) and that also cause more blood to move toward the surface of the body, where it loses heat more quickly. When stimulated by cooling, these brain cells induce shivering (the constriction of blood vessels in the skin) and increased bodily activity and heat production (Miller, 1969).

The *elimination drive* serves to rid the body of its waste products.

The *pain drive* leads us to avoid events that would damage our bodies. It accounts for such learned behavior as keeping our hands away from flames, being careful with sharp objects, and resting or swallowing medicine to relieve a headache.

A school of scientific thought called *sociobiology* maintains that at least some forms of social behavior are also akin to drives and are dictated by inherited biological traits (Wilson, 1975). One example is altruistic behavior—such as the willingness of a father to risk his own life to save his children from a burning house. By doing this, the sociobiologists say, the father attempts to ensure the survival of others who can pass along the human genes, which are the chemical components of inheritance—and especially genes that he shares with his children because they descend from the same forebears. In other words, the theory states that altruism and other similar forms of cooperative behavior help preserve the pool of human genes—and genes dictating such behavior have been more likely to survive and be passed along through past generations. By stressing the role of the genes in determining social behavior, sociobiology takes an extreme pronature position in the nature-nurture debate. The theory is interesting but controversial, and many psychologists are skeptical.

Psychology in Everyday Life
Partner Communication: The Cornerstone of Good Sex

Most serious researchers agree that establishing a satisfactory sexual relationship is an immensely complicated task that takes time and effort. Above all else, most believe, it requires honest and unabashed communication about the partners' desires and preferences.

Masters and Johnson have termed open discussion of sexual likes and dislikes the "absolute cornerstone" of a successful relationship (Masters and Johnson, 1963). Their treatment of sexually unsuccessful couples centers on the exchange of information, through gestures as well as words (Masters, Johnson, and Kolodny, 1985). And pioneer sex-researcher Paul Gebhard says, "The chief stumbling block to sexual fulfillment is the fact that couples don't talk enough about their feelings. Even couples who have been married for 20 years—and know each other's preferences in food, reading, and music like the backs of their hands—often hesitate to tell each other what they like, dislike, or view with indifference in sexual matters" (Gebhard, 1979).

Unfortunately, open communication about sexual preferences is difficult for most people. It violates the popular belief that sexual performance is a natural gift and that everybody should automatically be "good in bed" without the need for any instruction, even without giving the matter any thought. Or the idea that techniques picked up from a sex manual are sure to be effective with any partner under any circumstances, which is also untrue. The individual differences in tastes and responses are far too great to permit any magic formula for success. Moreover, many people find that too much attention to technique turns sex from a spontaneous expression of love into a mechanical

Good communication and good sex go hand in hand.

performance that they find unsatisfactory or even distasteful. Regardless of sexual preference, the commitment made between couples that is revealed in sexual pleasure is more in the head than in the genitals (Masters, Johnson, and Kolodny, 1986).

The evidence seems to indicate that every sexual relationship is unique, bringing together two partners who are themselves unique. Most researchers believe that the partners have to learn by themselves how to make the relationship work—and that this learning process depends mostly on the give and take of communication.

THE NATURE OF HUMAN MOTIVATION

Each morning as we read the newspaper or watch the news on TV, we learn of stories that evoke a single question: Why? Why did the college basketball star, on the eve of a fabulous professional career, risk death—and die—using cocaine? Why did the powerful and wealthy executive turn his back on his career and retire to a life of public service? Why did the poor and ordinary woman risk her life chasing down an armed and dangerous mugger?

The question "why" is the focus of the study of *motivation*. The term comes from the Latin word for movement—and the subject deals with what arouses, energizes, or moves us to action—and what keeps the action going. Though motives—like emotions and drives—are difficult to pin down and study scientifically, they seem to control much human behavior and, therefore, have always been one of psychology's basic concerns.

Many of the early psychologists believed that motives could be explained by built-in patterns of behavior, or instincts. These psychologists were impressed by the instinctive behavior displayed by many animals—for example, the way a spider spins its web and salmon migrate from river to ocean and back to the river to spawn. Since we humans are also a form of animal life, why not assume that we too behave in accordance with instincts? The pioneer American psychologist William James theorized that there were no less than 17 powerful human instincts: imitation, rivalry, pugnacity, sympathy, hunting, fear, acquisitiveness, constructiveness (the urge to build), play, curiosity, sociability, shyness, secretiveness, cleanliness, jealousy, love, and mother love (James, 1890).

It is now known that humans have few if any instincts. Certainly we do not exhibit any elaborate built-in patterns of behavior, determined by the inherited wiring of the nervous system, like the web-spinning behavior of spiders or the spawning behavior of salmon. Human habitations are a great deal more varied and flexible in design. Yet there obviously are some forces within the human personality that initiate, energize, direct, and organize behavior. The drives and stimulus needs that were previously discussed in this chapter often serve as such forces—but there are also others, such as the 17 urges that James thought of as instincts. These forces are now called motives. Most psychologists define a motive as *a desire to reach a goal that has value for the individual*.

Some psychologists believe that motives are derived from the biological demands of the various drives. Attempts to attain success and power, for example, might evolve from the hunger or sex drive. Other psychologists believe that motives are cognitive processes that depend mostly on learning. Their view is based in part on the widespread individual differences that have been found in motivation. They hold that each of us, as a result of our individual life experiences and patterns of thinking, comes to value certain goals above others. Today most psychologists believe that there are probably only a small set of universal motives, but a far larger number that are typical of any given culture. Even in the same family, one brother may exhibit a strong tendency to be dependent on other people, another brother to be hostile to authority, a sister to achieve success in school and career. In contrast to emotions and drives, which are propelled by physiological factors, motives are perpetuated primarily by cognitive factors—that is, by the individual's perceptions of desired goals.

In studying motives, psychologists ask these questions: Why do certain goals—for example, success and power—have so much value that we devote vast amounts of effort and planning to reach them? And why do the strength of such goals vary so greatly from person to person?

The Motive to Achieve

All people are typically motivated to use their skills to master certain goals. Beginning in childhood, we want to improve our ability and performance at those tasks valued by society—whether it be farming, hunting, or learning to read. This urge to attain optimal levels on important tasks is called the *achievement motive*. Very few people, of course, have a uniformly high standard of achievement in all their undertakings. For some people the achievement motive is directed mostly at athletic prowess, for others at intellectual mastery, musical skills, or making money. People with a strong achievement motive tend to work hard at the things they tackle and to make the most of their talents. They engage in "competition with a standard of excellence" (McClelland, 1985). When people who score high on tests of the achievement motive are matched with people of equal ability but lower in achievement motive, they do better on the average in many ways. They not only make better grades in high school and college, but in their life work they are more likely to rise above their family origins and move upward in society (Crockett, 1962). A study of top performers in various fields—among them sculptors, Olympic swimmers, mathematicians—showed that drive and determination as much as great natural talent led to success (Bloom, 1985).

One reason people high in achievement motive are more successful in their careers appears to be that they are realistic about their abilities and the chances they are willing to

Brooke Shields and her mother—a parent's aspirations can influence the child's zeal for achievement.

The Nature of Human Motivation 333

take. They prefer jobs in which they have a reasonable chance of success and can obtain reasonable rewards. People low in achievement motive, on the other hand, are more inclined either to settle for an easier but low-paying job or to make a grandiose stab at a high-level job that is beyond their capacities (Morris, 1966).

Why do some of us develop a stronger desire for achievement than others? There are many reasons relating to our experiences in home and school, what we read and what we see on television, and the people we come to admire (and therefore try to imitate) or dislike. Our estimate of our own abilities, which may be accurate or distorted, also plays a part. So does the way we define ourselves. We tend to put extra effort into tasks that are critical to our self-concept (Tesser, 1985).

The way our parents treated us as children may be a crucial factor. In one study, a group of children was divided into those who scored high and those who scored low for achievement motive. Their mothers were then asked at what ages they had demanded that the children start to show signs of independence—that is, go to bed by themselves, entertain themselves, stay in the house alone, make their own friends, do well in school without help, and later earn their own spending money and choose their own clothes. Questions were asked about 20 such forms of independent behavior. As Figure 9-18 shows, all the mothers had made the 20 demands by the time their children were 10 years old. But the children who turned out to be high in achievement motive were urged to be independent at much earlier ages than the others. Encouraging independence in early childhood seems to strengthen the achievement motive—and parents who are overprotective seem to discourage it.

Evidence from a variety of studies begins to portray the characteristics of parents who tend to cultivate high achievement motivation in children. They leave little doubt in the

Figure 9-18 Early training and the achievement motive

Do parents who encourage young children to be independent also encourage the achievement motive? So it would appear from these results of a study, described in the text, of the ages at which mothers demanded 20 forms of independent behavior. The mothers who turned out children high in achievement motive made about as many demands at the age of 2 as the mothers of children low in achievement motive made at the age of 4—and about as many by the age of 5 as the other mothers by the age of 7 (Winterbottom, 1953).

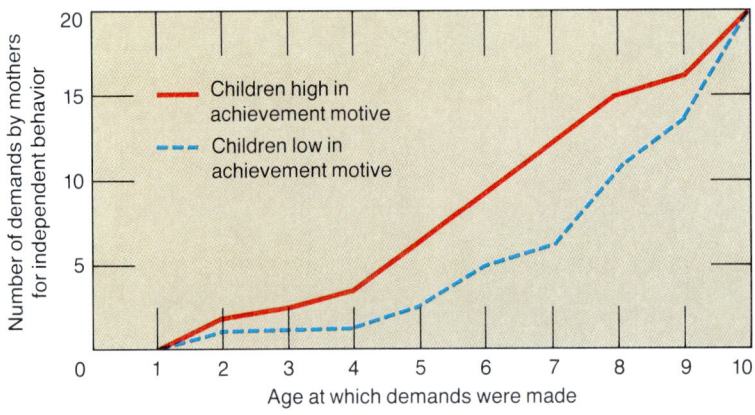

334 Chapter 9 Emotions, Drives, and Motives

child's mind about the value of achievement—rewarding their children when they perform well and admonishing them when they do not. They talk about achieving individuals as the kinds of people they admire, holding them up as models. Moreover, the parents make their own aspirations obvious. And they stimulate in their young not only self-reliance, but curiosity, and exploration (Segal and Segal, 1985).

The Motive to Exert Power

The desire to be in a position of control—to be the boss, to give orders, to command respect and obedience—is called the *power motive*. At first glance, it may seem very much like the achievement motive. But the achievement motive is directed toward performing well at whatever one chooses to undertake. The power motive, on the other hand, has less to do with good performance than with being top dog. Studies of American presidents have shown that those who had a strong power motive (as judged from their speeches) tended to take strong and decisive actions and had a great impact on our society—but were not necessarily good presidents who made important and constructive contributions (Winter and Stewart, 1978).

It has been found that college students who have a strong power motive tend to be officers in campus organizations, serve on student-faculty committees, and work for the school newspaper and radio station. They like to have nameplates, credit cards, and possessions associated with prestige, such as tape recorders, television sets, and framed pictures. They are quick to take up new fashion trends (Winter, 1973). The power motive, it would seem, is not without its internal costs, as demonstrated in Figure 9-19. When group conflict presents a threat to power, it is those whose power motive is strong who become physiologically aroused (Foder, 1985). Both on the campus and in later life, men high in power motive tend to do considerable drinking (Brown, 1975) and to be reckless when they gamble (McClelland and Teague, 1975).

Though people with a strong power motive often become leaders of their group, they do not necessarily serve the group's best interests. Evidence demonstrates that they provide the members with less information and fewer options than do leaders with a weaker urge for power. They also show less concern for moral issues raised by the group's activities and decisions (Fodor and Smith, 1982).

In men, the motive often seems to interfere with establishing satisfactory relationships with the opposite sex. A study of college students who were going together found that men who were high in power motive tended to be less satisfied than other men with their relationships, and so did their partners. Moreover, these couples were much more likely to break up (Stewart and Rubin, 1976). When men high in power motive do marry, they seem to prefer submissive wives (Winter and Stewart, 1978), and their marriages are less likely to be successful (McClelland et al., 1972).

In a complex society such as ours, the power motive doubtless serves a useful purpose. Somebody has to run the government, the corporations, and all the other organizations that are essential to the functioning of an industrial nation. Moreover, though people who aspire to positions of power may pay a price in their personal relationships, they seem to find many satisfactions. Among the United States presidents of this century, it appears that those highest in power motive were the ones who enjoyed the job the most (Barber, 1972). But the power motive probably also directs the behavior of dictators, gang leaders, and the builders of fraudulent financial empires.

Figure 9-19 **The power motive and body arousal**
Group leaders were tested for muscle tension as they led a controversy-filled discussion. Faced with conflict and a threat to their role, those high in power motive showed significantly greater tension than those for whom the power motive was low in importance (Fodor, 1985).

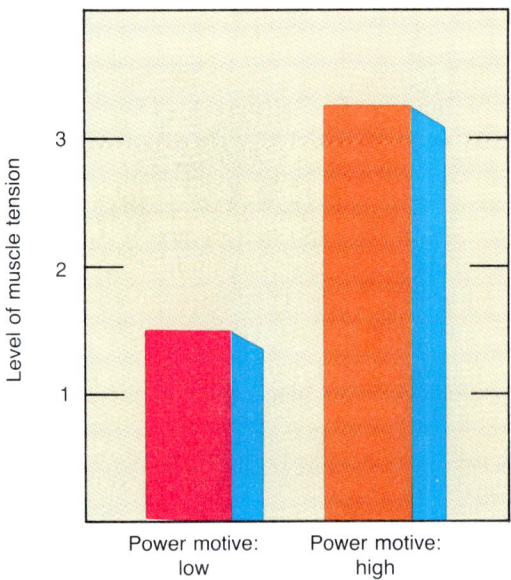

People Who Shun Power

Some people, instead of seeking power, seem strongly motivated to avoid it, as if they feared rather than admired it. They shun situations in which their actions can be controlled by other people, and they do not like to exercise control themselves. The motive to avoid power is especially likely to occur among men who were the youngest members of a large family—perhaps because of early experiences in which they felt pushed around by older and more powerful brothers and sisters.

People who are motivated to avoid power try very hard to preserve their independence from authority. In college, they dislike anything that smacks of regimentation—such as large lecture classes and required courses of study. They would rather be graded on a paper they have prepared on their own than on an examination (Winter, 1973). A study of college women who had this attitude toward power showed that they were more likely than other students to leave the campus before graduation, by either transferring to another school or sometimes dropping out altogether (Stewart, 1975).

People with a strong motive to avoid power are not very interested in such possessions as stereo sets and automobiles. When they do have material possessions, they are quick to lend to others. If they own cars, they are more likely than other people to have an accident—almost as if to show their lack of concern. They tend to be closemouthed about their own affairs, even to the point of lying, if necessary, to preserve their privacy. They shun careers in which they would have power over others and gravitate toward jobs in which they can help others, such as teaching (Winter and Stewart, 1978).

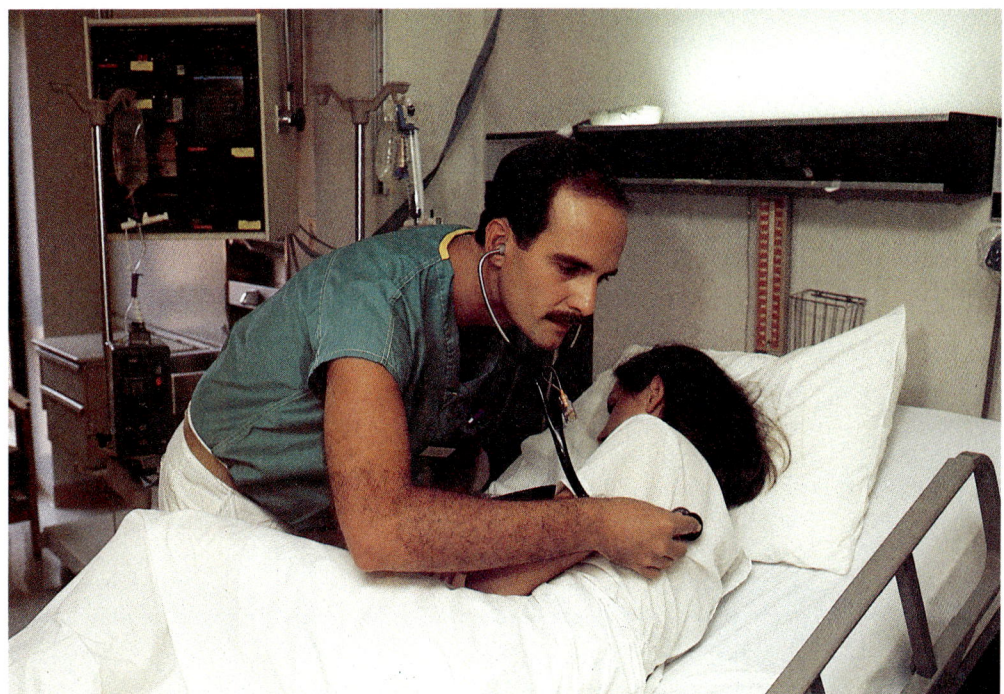

Nursing is not a likely career for those who crave power.

Needing Others: Motives for Affiliation and Dependency

As young children, all of us seek close attachments with our parents and, later, friendly relationship with others. The strength of this tendency, however, varies widely. Some people maintain close ties with their parents all their lives and are extremely sociable in general. They are "joiners" who always like to be in a group and prefer to work in jobs where they cooperate with and have the help of others. Other people prefer to spend their time alone and to be on their own in their work. Some even appear to be loners who care very little for human companionship.

The desire to be around other people and have close relations with them is the *affiliation motive*. It is particularly noticeable in people who are experiencing unpleasant emotions, for there seems to be considerable truth in the adage that "misery loves company." This fact was demonstrated by an experiment in which university women were asked to visit a psychology laboratory. When they arrived, they found a frightening piece of apparatus awaiting them and were told it was designed to deliver severe electrical shocks. After having been made anxious about the nature of the experiment, they were told that they had their choice of waiting their turn alone or in company. Fully 63 percent preferred company, with most of the rest saying they did not care one way or the other. In a control group of women who had not been made anxious about the experiment, the number who preferred company while waiting was only 33 percent (Schachter, 1959).

In jobs that call for a group effort, it has been found that people high in affiliation motive would rather be with their friends even when they could work with strangers who were more competent and could offer more help. They are more pleased by signs that their group is getting along well emotionally than by its accomplishments. There is some evidence that students with a strong affiliation motive make better grades in classes where everyone is friendly and the instructor takes a personal interest and calls students by name (Tschukitscheff, 1930), although this seems to be far more true of men than of women.

Closely allied to the desire for affiliation is the *dependency motive*, which also appears to exist in all of us. The dependency motive probably stems from our experiences as babies, when we are completely dependent on our parents. This tendency to rely on others—at least at times and for certain things—never leaves us. We continue to have a strong urge to depend on others to organize our lives, set up our schedules, help us with our work, comfort us, and give us support and pleasure. Like affiliation, the dependency motive is especially prominent in troubling situations. Hospital patients, for example, often have mixed feelings. Despite their illness and worry, they may enjoy the opportunity to be dependent on their physicians and nurses.

Behavior that stems from the dependency motive has been found to be more common among women than men. But this is because our society, at least until recently, has considered dependency to be appropriate, feminine, and rather attractive in women. The motive itself is probably equally strong in men—but they are less likely to display it because society has frowned on dependent behavior on the part of males. Often the motive is gratified by men in subtle ways. They may take their problems to the teacher or to the boss (though usually under the guise of being logical rather than emotional). Or they may tend to rely on columnists and television commentators for an interpretation of world events—and to give enthusiastic allegiance to political leaders with strong personalities.

OTHER MOTIVES THAT SHAPE WHO WE ARE

The motives that have just been discussed—achievement, power, affiliation, and dependency—are the easiest to study and have received the most attention from psychologists. Other motives, however, also seem to influence all of us, sometimes very strongly.

The Motive for Certainty

Even very young children display a strong *motive for certainty*—that is, a desire to feel at home in their world, to know where they stand, to avoid the discomfort of unfamiliar and surprising events. They clearly enjoy the certainty represented by their own bed, their own toys, the presence of familiar people and objects in their environment. As they grow a little older, they like to have rules set for their conduct; they like the certainty of knowing what they are permitted to do and what they are not permitted to do. The prospect of uncertainty—sleeping in a strange house, being taken care of by a strange baby-sitter, going to school for the first time—is likely to upset them.

Adults too tend to be motivated toward the known and away from the unknown. For some, such as explorers and astronauts, other motives prove stronger. In general, however, the desire for certainty operates strongly in most of us at most times. We like to feel that we know how our relatives and friends will act toward us, what is likely to happen tomorrow in the classroom or on the job, and where and how we will be living next year.

In some people, the motive for certainty is so strong that they seem to avoid any kind of change, even when the price of inaction is very high. You undoubtedly know people who continue to work in jobs they hate, or who persist in marriages they have long since decided are hopeless. Apparently they would rather stay with the known, no matter how unpleasant, than face the unknown. For most of us, however, the desire for certainty operates to keep our lives on an even keel.

Playing by the Rules: The Motive to Meet Standards

All of us, as we grow up, begin to set rules for our own behavior. Through learning what society values and through identification with our parents and other adults, we acquire inner standards of many kinds. We also acquire a strong *motive to live up to our standards*. Most people want to be attractive, responsible, friendly, skillful, generous, honest, and fair. Some, because of a different early environment, have standards that call for them to be domineering, tough, and rebellious.

Our standards form what is called our *ego ideal*—our notion of how we would always think and act, if we were perfect. Many of us acquire such high standards that we cannot possibly live up to all of them at all times. In fact the motive to live up to inner standards often requires us to suppress other powerful motives. Our standards may tell us that we should not take food from another person even if we are hungry, that we should be kind even to people toward whom we feel hostile, that we should play fair no matter how much we want to win. As a result, we often feel shame and guilt, over our thoughts if not our actual conduct. In popular terms, our conscience hurts. When we fail to meet our standards, the pangs of conscience can be painful indeed. This is why people who commit crimes sometimes behave in such a way that they are almost sure to be caught. Apparently they prefer punishment by imprisonment to the self-punishment that results from a serious failure to live up to inner standards.

The Hostility Motive

Though most of us do not like to admit it, all of us have a *hostility motive*. Evidence first appears in children at about two years of age. Up to then, all they seem to want from other people is their presence and the stimulation, help, and approval they provide. But at this stage, children begin to want something else from others. They want—at times—to see other people display signs of worry, fears of discomfort, actual pain. Later they may hope that misfortune will befall others and that they will have the gratification of knowing about it.

Some scientists regard hostility as a biological trait that makes aggression as inevitable for human beings as fighting over territory is for baboons and other animals (Lorenz, 1966). Others, probably a majority, believe that the hostility motive is learned and that it stems from the fact that children cannot have everything they want. They cannot always eat when they want to. They have to learn to control their drive for elimination except when they are in the bathroom. They cannot have the toy that another child owns and is playing with. Their mothers cannot always cater to their whims. Other children, bigger than they are, push them around.

Aggression resulting from hostility may take such forms as argumentativeness, sarcasm, physical and mental cruelty, and fighting. Yet, while all people are motivated at some time by hostility, not everyone displays aggression. Boys and men are more inclined to aggressive behavior than girls and women, for our society has traditionally approved of a certain amount of aggression in males, but has discouraged it in females. The social environment—especially the attitudes toward violence held by parents and by the community as a whole—seems to be a strong influence. Researchers recently studied a town in Mexico where violence was generally approved and admired. In this town violent incidents were very common. In another town public opinion disapproved of violence. Here violent incidents were rare (Paddock, O'Neill, and Haver, 1978). Researchers have also found numerous small societies, for example in isolated parts of New Guinea and the Philippine Islands, where aggressive behavior is almost unknown (Bandura, 1973).

In our society, this scene has been more typical of boys.

There is considerable evidence that aggressive behavior is most likely to occur among people who, for whatever reason, happen to be in a high state of arousal. Experiments have shown that aggression seems to be provoked by the discomfort of being exposed to loud noise (Geen and O'Neal, 1969) or working in an overheated room (Baron and Lawton, 1972)—even by the physical arousal created by brisk exercise (Zillman, Katcher, and Milavsky, 1972). Some psychologists have suggested that the high level of violence in our society can be explained at least in part by the fast pace of modern life and the noise and crowding that occur in our cities (Geen, 1976).

It has also been established that aggression is encouraged by watching other people behave aggressively—that is, through the kind of observation learning that was illustrated on page 183 with the photographs of children attacking a doll with a hammer after watching a movie of an adult doing this. Experiments on imitation of aggression raise the issue of how our society has been affected by all the violence depicted in the movies and on television.

HOW MOTIVES INFLUENCE BEHAVIOR

One reason we are not very good at analyzing the motives of other people is that motives may not necessarily result in any behavior at all. For one thing, they may be thwarted by outside events—the circumstances of our lives—over which we have no control. The key here is *opportunity*—for we cannot fulfill any of our desires unless we have a chance to try. The achievement motive is often the victim of lack of opportunity. For example, a young woman wants very badly to have a professional career, but for lack of money she cannot get the necessary education. A young man wants very badly to work in advertising, but cannot find any advertising firm that will hire him.

Lack of opportunity may also thwart the affiliation motive. Young people eager for the companionship of the opposite sex may live in a community where young men greatly outnumber young women, or vice versa. For older people, the lack of opportunity is caused by the fact that women live much longer than men. Among Americans who are 45 or older, there are almost 8 million more women than men (U.S. Bureau of the Census, 1986).

In other cases, motives are never gratified for reasons that lie within the self. Some people have a strong desire for achievement yet never show any signs of striving for success—though they do not lack opportunity. Others have strong motives for power yet merely go on their happy-go-lucky way, never trying to attain positions of power. All the many individual factors that determine whether we try to satisfy motives, how hard we try, and how we go about seeking satisfaction are the subject of the rest of this chapter.

Motive Hierarchies and Targets

All of us seem to have motives for achievement, power (or avoidance of power), affiliation, dependency, certainty, living up to standards, hostility, and (if we accept Maslow's theory) self-actualization. But there are great differences in the strengths of these desires. Each of us has built up a highly individual *hierarchy of motives* in which some have a top priority, while others are much less urgent—often depending on the intensity of the emotion associated with them. The position a motive occupies in the hierarchy plays a considerable part in determining how hard, if at all, we try to satisfy it (Atkinson, 1974). Some of us have such a strong affiliation motive that we are willing to ignore a weaker desire for achievement to avoid making our friends jealous. On the other hand, some of us are so intent on achievement or power that we are willing to sacrifice the friendships dictated by a weaker affiliation motive.

Our hierarchy of motives changes from time to time with the situation of the moment. No matter how high the affiliation motive may be in the hierarchy, none of us is invariably eager for affiliation at all times and with all people. (Indeed most of us know people with whom we would not care to affiliate under any circumstances.) Nor are we always inclined to satisfy our motives for achievement or hostility, however strong they may be in general.

To a great extent, our desires of the moment depend on what psychologists call our *motive targets*—that is, the people to whom our various motives are directed. For example, a man may have strong motives for achievement toward his business associates, for power toward the members of his political club, for affiliation towards his parents, and for dependency toward his wife. His desires will change during the course of the day as he moves from one relationship to another. The motive targets, as well as the hierarchy, help determine which motive will prevail.

The Effect of Incentive Value

As was mentioned in the last chapter, the hunger drive can be triggered by such incentive objects as the smell of food from a restaurant kitchen or the sight of pastries in a bakery window. In a somewhat similar way, motives are also triggered by incentives in the environment.

For example, a college woman goes home at the end of the day with no particular plans for the evening. A friend calls and suggests they go to an 8 p.m. tryout for parts in a school play. Going to the tryouts is a potential incentive to act on any one of a number of motives—for achievement, say, or for affiliation. Whether the student responds eagerly or turns down the suggestion will depend in large part on how much *incentive value* trying out for a play holds for her.

The incentive value of any event or object varies considerably from one person to another. Two students may have equally strong desires for achievement, but one student's motive may center on finishing school as quickly as possible and starting on a job, the other's on getting good grades. Good grades are such a strong incentive for some students that they cheat on tests, although an A obtained in this manner is a dubious form of achievement (Johnson, 1981). As incentives for the affiliation motive, one student may place great value on joining a certain campus organization, while another may not value that organization at all.

Assessing Your Chances of Success

Another factor that affects our decision to act or not to act on our motives is how much chance we have to get what we want. We are not likely to try very hard, if at all, unless we have a reasonable expectation of success. The college woman invited to try out for the campus play will probably turn down the suggestion if she believes that she has absolutely no chance—even though she places a high incentive value on getting a part. A male student may be highly motivated to call up a woman he has met in one of his classes, and he may place a high incentive value on going out with her. But if he feels shy and awkward around women and considers himself unattractive and uninteresting, he will probably take no action.

In gauging our chances of success, we try to make a realistic appraisal of the situation. We may decide not to try out for a campus play because we have never had any acting experience. We may abandon any thought of a career in accounting because we always have trouble in math courses. But often we are influenced not so much by the facts as by our self-image—our own perception of ourselves and our abilities. Some people have an exaggerated opinion of their talents and are inclined to try anything (a tendency that may bring them one disappointment after another). On the other hand, people who have acquired learned helplessness always tend to be pessimistic about their chances, whatever the situation. They may be capable of far more success—at fulfilling their motives for achievement, affiliation, and other goals—than they themselves believe. They give up without really trying.

Expectancy of Success and Locus of Control

Closely related to learned helplessness is another phenomenon that has been studied by many psychologists interested in the relationships between motives and behavior. This is the matter of whether we believe that we are in control of our own lives or at the mercy of outside events (deCharms and Muir, 1978). It has been found that some people assume their chances of success depend largely on *internal factors*—their own abilities and efforts. Others feel that success depends more on *external factors*—sheer luck and the inherent difficulty of attaining whatever goal they seek (Weiner, 1974).

The psychological term for this phenomenon is *locus of control*. (*Locus* is the Latin word for *place*.) People who assume that the locus of control is internal tend to take responsibility for their own actions and to try hard to implement their motives. They also seem to feel that other people create their own successes and failures—and they are reluctant to give money or help to those who are in trouble (Phares and Lamiell, 1975). They are not easily influenced by the opinions of other people and are careful though not timid in the risks they are willing to take (Strickland, 1977).

People who assume that the locus of control is external are less likely to strive for the goals dictated by their motives. They tend to rely on luck—and to be sympathetic to others who are in trouble, whom they regard as "down on their luck." They are readily influenced by the opinions of others (Sherman, 1973) and inclined to be reckless. When things go badly for them, the effect on their mood seems to linger for a long time (Lefcourt et al., 1981). When they do succeed—in the classroom, a job, or marriage—they are less likely to take credit for their success than to consider themselves blessed by circumstances, or to decide that whatever they did right must have been pretty easy. All of these are of course general tendencies. None of us believes totally in external control or internal control.

Long-range Plans, Too Much Motivation, and Running Scared

All the factors just mentioned help determine how hard we try to implement a motive, if we try at all. Moreover, our behavior at any given moment also depends on our long-range thinking about our goals. If the college woman invited to the tryout aspires to become a professional actress—or if she seeks a long-term affiliation with a group of theater people—she is much more likely to act than if she regards the experience as just a momentary diversion. Psychology's findings about the relationship of motives to behavior have been summarized in the theory that our actions in any situation are influenced by the following interplay of forces (Atkinson and Raynor, 1978):

1. *The strength of our motive* (as determined by our hierarchy of motives and the target to which we are directing our actions)
2. *The way we perceive our chances of success* (influenced by our attitude toward locus of control and any feelings of learned helplessness we may have acquired)
3. *The incentive value* of what we are doing or could be doing at the moment
4. *The relationship of present to future actions*—in other words our judgments about the possibilities to which our behavior may lead, especially the incentive value of these future actions and the way we perceive our chances of future success

An interesting sidelight is the finding that a very high level of motivation does not always help attain a goal. On the contrary, a motive can be so strong as to be self-defeating (Atkinson, 1976). We may be so intent on the goal, so eager to attain it, that we lose our perspective and our performance suffers. This is often true of people who have a strong affiliation motive and want very badly to be liked. You have probably known people who tried so hard to win your friendship that their constant attentions, favors, and flattery became a nuisance.

Some evidence has also been found that attempts to implement a motive are often hampered by the fear of failure. This is especially true of the achievement motive. An example might be a young woman who has long-range plans to become a lawyer. She takes a crucial examination that has great incentive value because she must meet the admission standards of the law school she wants to attend. Her fear of failure may make her "run scared" and perform far below her capabilities.

SUMMARY

The role of the body in emotions

1. *Emotions* are always accompanied by bodily changes. The body may be stirred up or relaxed.
2. The changes our body undergoes when we experience emotion are linked to two other factors: a specific event in the environment, and thoughts triggered by the event.
3. Many of the bodily changes in emotion are controlled by the autonomic nervous system and the endocrine glands. These changes include: (a) heart rate, (b) blood pressure, (c) blood circulation, (d) the composition of the blood, (e) activity of the digestive organs, (f) metabolic rate, (g) breathing, (h) salivation, (i) sweating, (j) goose flesh, and (k) pupil size.
4. Other bodily changes in emotion are controlled by the muscles of movement. These changes include: (a) muscular tension, (b) trembling, (c) eye blinking and other nervous movements, (d) vocal expressions of emotion, and (e) facial expressions.
5. One theory holds that every basic emotion represents in part a characteristic pattern of facial expression programmed by heredity.
6. Pupil size generally increases when a person experiences interest or pleasure.
7. The *James-Lange theory* held that emotions occur when a stimulus in the environment sets off physiological changes. Feedback from these changes, sent to the brain from the body's sensory nerves, is then perceived as emotion. We do not tremble because we are afraid, but feel afraid because we are trembling.

The brain: key to emotional behavior

8. There may be differences between the two sides of the brain in the regulation of emotion; the right hemisphere appears to be more active in regulating negative emotions, while the left hemisphere appears to be more active in regulating positive emotions.
9. The *Cannon-Bard theory* maintained that emotions occur when a stimulus in the environment sets off patterns of nervous activity in the hypothalamus. These patterns were considered to have two simultaneous effects: (a) they are sent to the autonomic nervous system, where they trigger the bodily changes of emotion; and (b) they are sent to the cerebral cortex, where they cause perception of emotion.
10. Today's cognitive psychologists regard emotions as composed of many complex factors. These include: (a) information about events in the environment, delivered to the cerebral cortex by the sense organs; (b) the brain's storehouse of information, which helps appraise and interpret new events; (c) patterns of nervous activity in the hypothalamus and the rest of the brain's limbic system, which trigger the autonomic nervous system into producing bodily changes; and (d) feedback from the bodily changes.
11. The cognitive view agrees with James-Lange that feedback of physiological changes is important—and with Cannon-Bard that activity of the hypothalamus plays a part. But it holds that neither theory is the full explanation. What really determines emotions is the cognitive activity resulting from the stimulus that has produced the bodily changes and the entire environmental situation in which it occurs. This cognitive activity shows wide individual differences because of prior experience and learning.

Individual differences in emotion and their expression

12. Inborn factors that help create individual differences in emotional experience include: (a) sensitivity of the autonomic nervous system, and (b) the size and activity of the endocrine glands.

13. Emotions can be physically exhausting and put the body under considerable stress. But they are also desirable and useful, adding interest to life and helping us to function more effectively.

How drives affect behavior: hunger and thirst

14. A *drive* is a pattern of brain activity resulting from physiological imbalances that threaten homeostasis. The drives include *hunger, thirst, breathing, sleep, temperature, elimination,* and *pain*.

15. The *hunger drive* depends on: (a) nerve cells in the hypothalamus—especially in the *lateral* and *ventromedial* areas—that are sensitive to changes in the food supply contained in the bloodstream, and (b) information sent to the hypothalamus from the alimentary canal to the liver. The hunger drive is also affected by incentive objects in the environment (the sight or smell of food) and by eating habits and social relationships built around eating.

16. Although the hunger drive operates to keep most people at a normal weight, more than one-fourth of American adults are at least 20 percent overweight. Possible explanations of obesity include: (a) metabolic disturbances; (b) overeating to relieve anxiety; (c) overeating simply as a matter of habit; (d) an unknown chemical in the bloodstream, caused by abnormalities in the way the alimentary canal and liver process food; and (e) an excess of the bodily cells that store fatty compounds.

17. The *thirst drive* depends on: (a) nerve cells in the hypothalamus that are sensitive to dehydration, (b) signals sent to the brain from the heart and blood vessels when the volume of blood is lowered by lack of water, and (c) stimulation of the hypothalamus by a chemical produced by the kidneys.

Sleep: the other third of our lives

18. The *sleep drive* appears to depend on imbalances in brain chemistry and possibly body chemistry.

19. In *ordinary sleep*, which occurs through most of the night, brain waves show a different pattern from that of waking hours, and the muscles of the body are more relaxed. In *paradoxical sleep*, which occurs for about a quarter of the night, the brain's activity is very similar to the waking state but the bodily muscles are almost totally relaxed. Paradoxical sleep is also known as *REM sleep*—REM standing for the rapid eye movements that accompany it. Some psychologists believe that ordinary sleep restores the body's chemical balance, while REM sleep restores the brain's ability to function.

The power of the sex drive—and other drives

20. The human sexual urge is difficult to classify as either a drive, emotion, or motive, though it has some of the characteristics of all three.

21. Among animals, sex is clearly a drive. In human beings sexual behavior depends on many nerve pathways and glandular influences, as well as on a whole array of learned preferences that people begin to learn early in childhood and may revise all their lives.

The nature of human motivation

22. A motive is *a desire to reach a goal that has value for the individual*.
23. Among important motives are desires for *achievement, power, affiliation*, and *dependency*.

Other motives that shape who we are

24. Motives for *certainty, living up to inner standards*, and *hostility* can also strongly influence behavior.

How motives influence behavior

25. Often a motive cannot be fulfilled because of lack of opportunity. In particular, we may never have the opportunity to gratify all our desires for achievement.
26. All of us seem to possess all the human motives, but to a widely varying degree. An individual pattern of motives, from strongest to weakest, is a *hierarchy of motives*.
27. The strength of a motive at any given moment depends on the presence of *motive targets*, or the people to whom the various motives are directed.
28. Our perception of our chances of success depends in part on *locus of control*—or whether we believe success depends on *internal factors* (our own abilities and efforts) or *external factors* (such as luck).
29. Factors that help determine whether we will try to fulfill a motive include: (a) the strength of the motive (determined by the motive hierarchy and motive targets), (b) the way we perceive our chances of success, (c) the *incentive value* of any action we might take, and (d) the relationship of present to future actions (our judgment of long-term consequences).

IMPORTANT TERMS

achievement motive
affiliation motive
breathing drive
Cannon-Bard theory
cognitive theory
dependency motive
drive
ego ideal
elimination drive
emotion
emotional stress
external factors
fat cells
glycogen
hierarchy of motives
hostility motive
hunger drive
incentive object
incentive value
insomnia

internal factors
James-Lange theory
l-tryptophan
lateral hypothalamus
locus of control (place)
motivation
motive for certainty
motive targets
motive to live up to our standards
opportunity
pain drive
paradoxical sleep
power motive
REM sleep
sleep drive
sociobiology
temperature drive
thirst drive
ventromedial hypothalamus
voyeurism

RECOMMENDED READINGS

Buck, R. *Human motivation and emotion*. New York: Wiley, 1976.

Carlson, N. R. *Physiology of behavior*, 2d ed. Boston: Allyn and Bacon, 1981.

Frijda, N. H. *The emotions*. New York: Cambridge University Press, 1986.

Geen, R. G., Beatty, W. W., and Arkin, R. M. *Human motivation: physiological, behavioral, and social approaches*. Boston: Allyn and Bacon, 1984.

Harr, R. *The social construction of emotions*. New York: Blackwell, 1986.

Plutchik, R., and Kellerman, H., eds. *Emotion: theory, research and experience*. New York: Academic Press, 1980.

Scherer, K. R., and Ekman, P. *Approaches to emotion*. Hillsdale, N.J.: Erlbaum, 1984.

Strongman, K. T. *The psychology of emotion*, 3rd ed. New York: Wiley, 1987.

Suedfeld, P. *Restricted environmental stimulation: research clinical applications*. New York: Wiley, 1980.

Toates, F. M., and Halliday, T. R., eds. *Analysis of motivational processes*. New York: Academic Press, 1981.

CHAPTER

10

PERSONALITY AND ITS MEASUREMENT

THEORIES OF PERSONALITY 350

Defining personality
The personality hierarchy
The four components of personality theory

THE PSYCHOANALYTIC THEORY OF SIGMUND FREUD 352

Anxiety, repression, and the unconscious mind
Id and pleasure principle
Ego and reality principle
Superego and Oedipus conflict
Superego versus ego versus id

DISSENTING DISCIPLES: OTHER SCHOOLS OF PSYCHOANALYTIC THEORY 356

Carl Jung: the role of temperament
Some ways that Jung disagreed with Freud
Alfred Adler and Karen Horney: the power of social influences
Some later trends in psychoanalysis

HUMANISTIC THEORIES OF PERSONALITY 364

Carl Rogers and the role of self-image
The roots of maladjustment
Our better selves: the quest for self-actualization

PERSONALITY FROM THE BEHAVIORAL POINT OF VIEW 367

B. F. Skinner and radical behaviorism
Social learning theory

TYPE AND TRAIT THEORIES 370

Personality and physiological characteristics
Searching for the traits that define personality types
The issue of consistency

MEASURING PERSONALITY 378

Objective tests
Situational tests
Projective tests

SUMMARY 381

IMPORTANT TERMS 384

RECOMMENDED READINGS 384

PSYCHOLOGY IN EVERYDAY LIFE

Beneath the surface: the search for unconscious motives 353
How much difference does sibling order make? 361
The riddle of multiple personality 374

Mean. Sweet. Nice. Sexy. Smart. Interesting. Marvelous. All these adjectives—and countless more—are used regularly in daily conversation to describe the human *personality*. But if you were asked to describe in detail what you actually mean by the word, you would probably run into difficulty.

The challenge we face in describing and understanding personality is obvious. What we so casually refer to as personality is such a complex phenomenon that the English language has at least 18,000 words to describe the myriad traits that comprise it. The characteristics that define personality are based on all the intricate processes covered in this book: the patterns of emotions, the intensities of drives, and the hierarchies of motives described in the previous chapter; the characteristics of temperament with which you were born; the tides of anxiety and stress that you experience and the diverse efforts you make to cope with them; and your beliefs about the people and the world about you. Small wonder that there are so many personalities in the world—and that the concept of personality is so difficult to understand and describe.

The effort to do so extends back to antiquity. The riddle of personality has been approached over the centuries by philosophers, poets, physicians, religious leaders. But only in the last century have scientists confronted the challenge of making systematic observations about the human personality and drawing conclusions from them. That is what this chapter is about.

THEORIES OF PERSONALITY

In a sense, the entire science of psychology represents an attempt to create a comprehensive theory of personality—in other words, a set of general principles that will explain why people are alike in some ways and very different in others. But some psychologists have been especially interested in seeking these general principles. They have developed a number of theories that try to explain which personality traits are most important, the likeliest patterns of relationships among traits, the manner in which these patterns become established in individuals, and (at least by implication) how they can be changed. Some of the main theories developed over the years have been accompanied by their own techniques of treating people suffering from personality disturbances, as will be seen in Chapter 13. First, however, we must define personality and explain what all personality theories try to accomplish.

Personality can best be defined as the *total pattern of characteristic ways of thinking, feeling, and behaving that constitute the individual's distinctive method of relating to the environment.* There are four key words in the definition: (1) *characteristic*, (2) *distinctive*, (3) *relating*, (4) *pattern*.

To be considered a part of personality, a way of thinking, feeling, or behaving must have some continuity over time and circumstance. It must be *characteristic* of the individual. We do not call a man bad tempered if he "blows up" only once in 10 years. We say that a bad temper is part of his personality only if he shows it often and in many different circumstances.

The way of thinking, feeling, or behaving must also be *distinctive*—that is, it must distinguish the individual from other individuals. This eliminates such common American traits as eating with a knife and fork, placing adjectives before rather than after nouns, and carrying a driver's license—all of which are more or less the same for every American and do not distinguish one person from others.

Though these first two elements are essential, they are not the whole story. For example, a woman might always wear a ring that is a family heirloom and the only one of its kind in the world. Wearing the ring is therefore both characteristic and distinctive. But this would hardly be considered part of her personality (unless perhaps she attached some deep significance to the ring, regarding it as a symbol of self-esteem and social acceptance). To be a part of personality, a trait must play a part in how a person goes about *relating* to the world, especially to other people. It is because of this element of relating that personality traits are often thought of as positive or negative. A positive trait, such as friendliness, helps the individual relate to people and events in a constructive manner. A negative characteristic, such as fear of social contacts, may produce anxiety, failure, and loneliness.

Of the multitude of possible personality traits, all of us possess some but not others. It is the particular *pattern* of characteristics we possess and display—the sum total and organization—that is the final element in the definition of personality.

The Personality Hierarchy

The various traits that make up the personality—all the characteristic and distinctive ways of relating to the environment—exist in a hierarchy from strong to weak. Some ways of thinking, feeling, and behaving are easily and frequently aroused. Others are less likely to occur. In a social situation, for example, there are many ways an individual can relate to the others in the group. The individual can be talkative or quiet, friendly or reserved, boastful or modest, bossy or acquiescent, more at ease with men or more at ease with women. One person may characteristically withdraw into the background, and we say that such a person is shy. Another may characteristically display warmth and try to put the others at their ease, and we say that such a person is outgoing. Another may be talkative, boastful, and domineering, and we say that such a person is aggressive or "pushy." In each of the three individuals, certain responses are strong in the personality hierarchy and easily aroused.

Each person's hierarchy has a certain amount of permanence. The shy person behaves shyly under many circumstances, and the aggressive person has a consistent tendency to be boastful and domineering. However, the hierarchy may change considerably depending on the circumstances. A young woman who is aggressive around people her own age may behave shyly in the presence of older people. A man who is usually shy may have one close friend with whom he is completely at ease. All of us, no matter how friendly or reserved we may be, are likely to have a strong tendency to make friends if we have been isolated for a long time, such as after an illness or a stretch at a lonely job. After a round of parties, on the other hand, we are likely to want some solitude. The businessman who is ordinarily interested in his job and eager to talk about it may shun conversation when he gets home late at night after a hard day's work.

The Four Components of Personality Theory

Many general theories of personality have been proposed over the years. They differ in many respects, but they all have four elements in common (Maddi, 1972):

1. Every theory is based on some fundamental viewpoint toward the basic quality of human nature. It assumes that there is a *core personality* composed of tendencies and traits common to all of us. Different theories take different views of this common core, as will be seen, but all of them take for granted that it exists and is a force in shaping personality.

2. Every theory maintains that the tendencies and traits that make up the common core of personality are channeled in various different directions in different individuals by the process of *development*—all the experiences we encounter, from our childhood relationships with our parents throughout the rest of our lives. Thus all theories agree that personality is the product of both nature (the common core that is part of our heritage) and nurture (the effect of individual development), though they do not necessarily agree on whether nature or nurture is more influential.

3. Every theory is concerned with what are called *peripheral traits*—that is, all the distinctive ways in which people relate to the environment. The peripheral traits are viewed as the inevitable result of the way individual development has acted on the common core of personality.

4. Finally, every theory is concerned with the task of identifying and defining the inner processes, or dynamics, by which the peripheral traits are established and maintained.

THE PSYCHOANALYTIC THEORY OF SIGMUND FREUD

The most famous of all views of personality is Sigmund Freud's *psychoanalytic theory*. Freud's writings about personality development and the treatment of psychological disorders have been widely read and debated. His views have had a profound influence on many psychologists and on society in general, especially in the United States.

A key idea in Freud's theory of personality is that all humans—children as well as adults—possess a basic energy, called *libido*, directed at maximizing pleasure. Many of the acts that bring pleasure, however, cause conflict as well—for example, revenge to relieve anger, uninhibited sexual behavior, or retaining dependent ties with parents beyond childhood. As a result, some of the motives that arise from the libido are repressed—causing the kinds of adjustment problems and abnormal symptoms discussed in Chapter 12. One of Freud's most imaginative ideas, detailed later in this section, was that the kind of symptoms a person develops depends on the stage of early development when repression occurs.

Anxiety, Repression, and the Unconscious Mind

Freud believed that anxiety is the central problem in mental disturbance—so painful an emotion that we will go to almost any length to eliminate from conscious awareness any motive or thought that threatens to cause anxiety.

The unconscious mind, composed in part of repressed motives and thoughts, was another of Freud's most influential concepts. He was the first to suggest the now widely held theory that the human mind and personality are like an iceberg, with only a small part visible and the rest submerged and concealed. All of us, he maintained, have many unconscious motives that we are never aware of but that nonetheless have powerful influences on our behavior. Some examples are discussed in a Psychology in Everyday Life box titled "Beneath the Surface: The Search for Unconscious Motives."

The details of Freudian theory are difficult to summarize. For one thing, he revised and enlarged on them throughout a prolific writing career that spanned four decades. Moreover his followers have continued to make refinements, especially of the new ideas he developed late in life. The discussion here is confined to the basic principles (especially those that have had the greatest influence on psychologists) as they are now viewed by psychoanalytic theorists who regard themselves as classical Freudians. To begin the discus-

Psychology in Everyday Life
Beneath the Surface: The Search for Unconscious Motives

If you have ever tried to guess at other people's motives, you know how futile the exercise can be. Indeed we cannot always be sure of our own motives. "I can't believe I did that" is an admission we all make at times.

One idea of Freud's that has influenced many psychologists holds that human activities are often a response to *unconscious motives*—to wishes and desires that we are not aware of, that in fact we might vehemently deny, but that influence our behavior nonetheless, sometimes to a striking degree. The idea of unconscious motives raises some thorny psychological problems, among them the question of how a desire that is unconscious can operate to produce relevant behavior. But his idea does seem to explain some aspects of human behavior that would otherwise be baffling.

One example of what appears to be an unconscious motive is the phenomenon known as posthypnotic suggestion. While subjects are under hypnosis, they may be told that after they awaken from the trance they will go and raise a window the first time the hypnotist coughs—even though they will not remember having received this instruction. Later the hypnotist coughs, and, sure enough, the subjects do open a window. If asked why, they say that the room was getting stuffy or that they felt faint. They have no suspicion that the real reason was to comply with the hypnotist's demand.

Other examples are all around us. A mother may seem to believe in all sincerity that she has the most generous, affectionate, and even self-sacrificing motives toward her daughter. Yet an unprejudiced observer might say that the mother's real motives are to dominate the daughter, keep her from marrying, and hold on to her as a servant. A man may earnestly deny that he has any hostile motives. Yet we may see that he performs many subtle acts of aggression against his wife, his children, and his business associates. A person may feel genuinely motivated to go to the dentist or to keep a date with a friend, yet conveniently "forget" the appointment.

Although the notion of unconscious motives is puzzling, many psychologists agree that it is valid, including some who reject other aspects of Freud's theories. Accepting the idea leads to a rather startling conclusion: If motives can affect behavior even though they are completely unconscious, then we will often find it as difficult to analyze our own motives as to know the motives of others.

---

sion, let it be said that Freud conceived of the human personality and mind as composed of three major parts that he called the *id, ego,* and *superego.**

Id and Pleasure Principle

The *id*, or most basic and primitive of the three parts, springs from what Freud held to be two inborn drives that all humans possess. One of these drives is the *libido*, consisting of sexual urges and such related desires as to be kept well-fed, warm, and comfortable. The other is a drive toward aggression—to attack anyone or anything that interferes with gratification.

The drives arouse the id to a state of excitement and tension. In seeking to relieve the tension, the id operates on what Freud called the *pleasure principle*, imperiously seeking

---

*The three terms have been standard since they appeared in the first translation of Freud's writings into English. For greater accuracy and help in understanding the meaning, it has been suggested that the id might better be called the *it*, the ego the *I*, and the superego the *upper-I* (Bettelheim, 1983). You may find it useful to keep these alternative terms in mind while reading the next pages.

results and tolerating no delay. To satisfy the libido, the id seeks complete possession of everything desired and loved. To satisfy the drive for aggression, it wants to destroy everything that gets in the way. As we grow up, we learn to control the demands of the id, at least after a fashion. But it remains active and powerful throughout life—a sort of beast within. Although it is unconscious and we are not aware of its workings, it continues to struggle to relieve its tensions and find instant gratification.

Freud believed that human sexual development takes place in a series of stages in which the sexual energy of the libido focuses on different parts of the body. During about the first year and a half of life, or what he called the *oral stage*, the desires and gratifications concern the mouth, tongue, and such activities as sucking and eating. This is followed by the *anal stage*, from about 1½ to 3, in which the desires and gratifications move to the other end of the alimentary canal and are concerned with the act of emptying the lower bowel or refraining from the act. This is followed by the *phallic stage*, in which the libido is principally focused on the external sex organ, male or female. At puberty the child then enters the *genital stage*, which represents the adult and final step in sexual development, characterized by love for another person.

Freud believed that if there was either excessive gratification of a motive or insufficient gratification, then a fixation would occur—meaning that the original focus of that motive persisted to an abnormal degree into adult life. Thus a fixation during the infant's oral stage might be displayed in adult life as an extreme dependence on others or an excessive concern with eating or smoking. And a fixation during the anal stage might cause either a passion for order and cleanliness or the hoarding of money.

Ego and Reality Principle

The conscious part of the mind that develops as we grow up is called the *ego*. This is the "real" us as we like to think of ourselves, including our knowledge, skills, beliefs, and conscious motives. The ego operates on the *reality principle*. It does our logical thinking and tries to help us get along in the world. Freud believed that the intellectual and social skills we use every day develop because we must learn, beginning in childhood, how to deal with the demands of the id. To the extent that these demands can be satisfied in some reasonable way, the ego permits satisfaction. But when the id's demands threaten to get us rejected by society, the ego represses them or tries to provide substitutes that are socially acceptable. Freud held that artistic creativity, for example, represents a channeling of the libido away from open sexual expression and into the production of paintings and literature. But the ego's task is even more complicated. It has to satisfy not only the id but the rules of society that we incorporate in our sense of what is acceptable human behavior.

Superego and Oedipus Conflict

The ego, in its constant struggle to meet the irrational demands of the id in some rational way, has a strong but troublesome ally in the *superego*, the third part of the mind as conceived by Freud. In a sense that is what the superego is. Every scholar who has written about human nature has recognized that, in addition to our desires and our ability to gratify them, we also possess a conscience, a sense of right and wrong. But Freud's concept of the superego is much stronger and more dynamic than the word "conscience" implies. Much like the id, the superego is mostly unconscious, exerting a far greater influence over our behavior than we realize. It is largely acquired as a result of the *Oedipus complex*, an important element in Freudian thinking.

According to psychoanalytic theory, all children between the ages of about 2½ and 6 are embroiled in a conflict of mingled affection and resentment toward their parents. The male child has learned that the outer world exists and that there are other people in it, and the id's demands for love and affection reach out insatiably toward the person he has been closest to—the mother. Although the child has only the haziest notion of sexual feelings, his libido drives him to want the total love of his mother and take the place of his father with her. But his anger against his father, the rival with whom he must share her, makes him fearful that his father will somehow retaliate. To further complicate matters, his demands for total love from his mother are of course frustrated—and he also wants to get rid of her and take her place in the affections of his father. Thus he becomes overwhelmed with strong feelings of mingled love, rage, and fear toward both parents.

This period of turmoil takes its name from the Greek legend in which Oedipus unwittingly killed his father and married his own mother and then, when he discovered what he had done, blinded himself as penance. Girls, according to Freudian theory, go through very similar torments in the years from 2½ to 6, except that their love becomes directed mostly toward their father. (This is sometimes called the Electra complex, after another Greek legend of a woman who loved her father and conspired to kill her mother—but Freud himself never used the term, because he believed the conflict took basically the same form for both sexes.)

The Oedipus complex must somehow be resolved. This is accomplished through the process of identification with the parents. That is to say, we resolve our feelings of mingled love and hate for our parents by becoming like them, by convincing ourselves that we share their strength and authority and the affection they have for each other. In this process of identification, we adopt what we believe to be the standards of our parents, behaving in ways that are likely to bring their approval. Their moral judgments, or what we conceive to be their moral judgments, become our superego. This helps us hold down the demands

According to Freud, little girls get embroiled early in a conflict-filled relationship with father.

The Psychoanalytic Theory of Sigmund Freud

of the id, which have caused us such intense discomfort during the Oedipal period. But, forever after, the superego tends to oppose the ego. As our parents once did, our superego punishes us or threatens to punish us for our transgressions.

In their own way, the demands of the superego are just as insatiable as the demands of the id. Its standards of right and wrong and its rules for punishment are far more rigid, relentless, and vengeful than anything in our conscious minds. Formed at a time when we were too young to distinguish between a bad wish and a bad deed, the superego may sternly disapprove of the merest thought of some transgression—which explains why some people who have never actually committed a bad deed still have strong feelings of guilt throughout life.

Superego versus Ego versus Id

The three parts of the mind are often in conflict, and Freud regarded conflict as the core of human personality. One result of the three-way struggle is anxiety, which is produced in the ego whenever the demands of the id threaten to create danger or when the superego threatens to impose disapproval or punishment. Anxiety arouses the ego to fight the impulses or thoughts that have created it. In one way or another—by using repression and the other defense mechanisms, by turning the mind's attention elsewhere, by gratifying some other impulse of the id—the ego defends itself against the threat posed by the id or the superego and gets rid of the anxiety.

In a sense the conscious ego is engaged in a constant struggle to satisfy the insatiable demands of the unconscious id without incurring the wrath and vengeance of the largely unconscious superego. To the extent that our behavior is controlled by the ego, it is realistic and socially acceptable. To the extent that it is governed by the passions of the id and the unrelenting disapproval of the superego, it tends to be maladjusted and neurotic.

If the ego is not strong enough to check the id's drives, a person is likely to be selfish, impulsive, and antisocial. But if the ego checks the id too severely, other problems may arise. Too much repression of the libidinal force can make a person incapable of enjoying a normal sex life or giving a normal amount of affection. Too much repression of aggression can seriously handicap a person in the give and take of competition. If the ego is not strong enough to check the superego, the result may be vague and unwarranted feelings of guilt and unworthiness, even an unconscious need for self-punishment. Thus it is the three-way conflict among ego, id, and superego, according to Freud, that often results in abnormal behavior.

DISSENTING DISCIPLES: OTHER SCHOOLS OF PSYCHOANALYTIC THEORY

Freud was an important innovator who made many contributions to understanding the human personality. He was the first to recognize the role of the unconscious and the importance of anxiety and defenses against it. He also dispelled the myth, widely accepted before his time, that children do not have sexual urges or hostile impulses. He was a pioneer in recognizing the effect of childhood experiences on personality development and in highlighting the conflict between our private impulses and the need to adapt to society.

Freud's theory, however, has had many critics, and the unwavering belief in his notions of the mind and personality has declined in recent years. To begin with, it has proven impossible to demonstrate the existence of an id, an ego, or a superego. Morever, there is no validation of the existence of the libido, nor Freud's belief that the stage at which fixation occurs serves to determine adult symptoms.

Some critics believe that Freud overemphasized the role of sexual motivation by generalizing from the conflicts of patients who had grown up during the repressive Victorian age. More to the point, society has performed a massive experiment testing Freud's emphasis on sexuality. Although we have witnessed in recent decades considerable relaxation of social restraints on sexual behavior (and presumably, therefore, much less repression of the sexual drive), there has not been an accompanying decrease in the incidence of abnormal symptoms. This fact suggests that sexual conflict is not the major cause of mental health problems.

Long before today, even in Freud's own lifetime, some of his disciples broke away from him and established competing schools of psychoanalytic thought.

Carl Jung: The Role of Temperament

One Freudian disciple who broke away was Carl Jung, who believed that Freud did not give enough emphasis to variations in personality based on culture as well as on inherited characteristics of temperament. Anticipating modern studies of brain and behavior, Jung viewed differences in temperament as related to brain activity and the ability of the brain to understand and interpret experience.

Jung invented the famous words *introvert* and *extrovert*. Introverts are people who tend to live with their own thoughts and to avoid socializing. Extroverts, Jung proposed, are people whose chief interest is in other people and the events around them. He felt that the fulfillment of the human personality requires the expression of both introversion and extroversion—but that one tends to develop at the expense of the other, making people either too concerned with their own thoughts and feelings or too preoccupied with people and external events. In typing humans in this way, Jung anticipated by decades the work of psychologists, to be described later in this chapter, who devoted themselves to identifying and measuring the basic traits that comprise the human personality.

Carl Jung (1875–1961)

Some Ways That Jung Disagreed with Freud

Jung strongly believed that Freud had overestimated the importance of sexuality. He felt that the libido was far richer than Freud assumed—an all-encompassing life force that included deep-seated attitudes toward life and death, virtue and sin, and religion. Jung's theories place more emphasis than Freud's on the intellectual and especially the spiritual qualities of the human personality, and less on the urges toward sex and aggression. Jung saw a greater difference between humans and animals than did Freud. Whereas Freud was relatively skeptical about human nature, Jung glimpsed the heroic in humanity—as well as the idealistic and romantic. In doing so, he gave early voice to the positive view of personality proposed by humanistic theories, to be described in the next section.

In contrast to Freud, who believed that many of the qualities of the human personality were the product of experience, Jung proposed that humans possess a *collective unconscious*—an inheritance from the events that have occurred in human history, and perhaps even in the days before humanity appeared, when only lower animals roamed the world. In a sense, modern studies in neuroscience have lent support to this idea. As shown in Chapter 4, for example, beginning in early childhood, the human brain does indeed allow us all to perceive and experience the world in ways that are universal. In the collective unconscious also lie traces of primitive humanity's fears and superstitions, the belief in magic, and search for gods. There also are memories of the great events in which humanity has participated—its disasters, its conquests and defeats, its happy and unhappy love

For Jung, this artistic product is an expression of the collective unconscious.
Vincent van Gogh, *The Starry Night*, 1889, oil on canvas. Collection, The Museum of Modern Art, New York. Acquired through the Lillie P. Bliss Bequest.

affairs, its moving experiences with birth and death. Because of the collective unconscious, every person embodies in a sense the entire gamut of human experience. Jung believed that each of us, of whatever sex, possesses elements of both woman and man, mother and father, hero, prophet, sage, and magician.

To Jung, the collective unconscious was a significant part of the core of personality, a universal aspect of the human condition. It influences our behavior in ways that we can understand only dimly or not at all. It finds expression in the work of the artist and accounts for the strong emotions we sometimes feel, without knowing why, when we look at a great painting or statue. It crops up in our dreams, often giving them a strange and mystical quality.

Freud viewed psychological symptoms—anxiety, depression—as the outcome of internal conflict within the individual. Jung anticipated contemporary views by being more sensitive to the role that society and the individual's life environment play in the development of such mental problems. This emphasis on the impact of social factors on personality was carried considerably further by other psychoanalytic theorists who followed Freud.

Alfred Adler and Karen Horney: The Power of Social Influences

Another early disciple who rejected Freud's focus on sexuality was Alfred Adler, whose theory of *individual psychology* placed great emphasis instead on the innate tendency of people to be cooperative and psychologically tuned-in to the lives of others. Adler believed that individuals encounter problems in life because they develop inappropriate goals and patterns of living that block the realization of their social interest. While the theory remains unproven, as shown in Figure 10-1, it does appear possible to differentiate among various

Figure 10-1 The social-mindedness of various groups

Using a Social Interest Personality Scale based on the ideas of Adler described in the text, one contemporary investigator showed that a concern for the welfare of others varies as one might expect in groups like those identified here (Crandall, 1980).

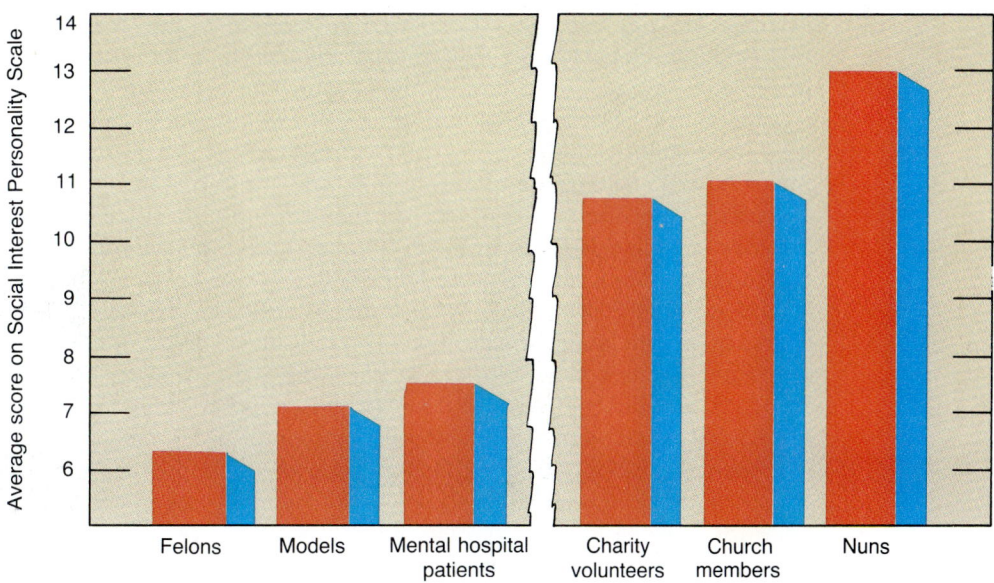

Alfred Adler (1870–1937)

groups of individuals in terms of their degree of concern for the social welfare of others (Crandall, 1980).

Adler also proposed that we are born with a tendency to strive for superiority—not necessarily in terms of influence or success in competition with others, but rather of self-perfection and self-realization. He viewed the motives for power and aggression as distortions of the more basic urge for personal fulfillment. Adler observed that many people appear to be engaged in constant efforts to overcome feelings of inferiority, based not only on physical flaws, but psychological and social ones as well. Such efforts often begin early, based, for example, on the young child's perceptions of the capacities of an older sibling. One of Adler's most insightful observations was the importance of birth order in shaping personality development—a subject of modern research described in a Psychology in Everyday Life box titled "How Much Difference Does Sibling Order Make?"

Another student of Freud who broke with him was Karen Horney, whose view of the human personality, like Adler's, was essentially optimistic. She also believed humans to be capable of growth and self-realization. The capacity is sometimes blocked, however, by a pattern of responses to life's *basic anxiety*—which is the feeling of being isolated and helpless in a potentially hostile world (Horney, 1945). Horney's views on the importance of the child's early experiences of love and security are reflected in much of the research on early attachment described in Chapter 14, and she was among the first psychoanalytic theorists to shift the view of women in society away from the male perspective that dominated earlier theories (Feshbach and Weiner, 1986). For example, she took exception to Freud's notion that penis envy is a state shared by women as a result of their biological nature, and

Psychology in Everyday Life
How Much Difference Does Sibling Order Make?

Were you the firstborn in your family—or did you come along later? This may seem like an odd question to ask in a discussion of personality, but it is more relevant than it may appear.

Firstborn children are more likely than others to have a strong motive for achievement. For example, students who are firstborns get higher grades than later-borns. They are also more competitive and have higher educational aspirations (Falbo, 1981). Their high achievement motive has led many firstborns to become outstandingly successful. They are more likely to become national merit scholars, get Ph.D.'s, and be listed in *Who's Who* (Sutton-Smith, 1982). Any list of prominent people—eminent scholars, even presidents of the United States—contains a high proportion of firstborns. The well-known people whose photos are shown in Figure 10-2 all were firstborn children.

One possible explanation is that parents treat firstborn children differently from later children. They devote more time to the firstborn, are more protective, take a greater part in the child's activities, interfere more, and expect more (Hilton, 1967; Scarr and Grajek, 1982). The firstborn child is criticized more often, and expected to conform to adult standards (Baskett, 1984). Later children receive less attention and guidance from their parents and are more influenced by their relations with other children, including their siblings.

There are other possible explanations as well. One is that firstborns may be driven to do better than the newcomers to the family because they feel cast aside—in Adler's words, "dethroned"—by their siblings' arrival (Adler, 1928). More likely, the tendency toward achievement by firstborns may be the result of the fact that they are more apt to do better in school at earlier ages and go on to college (Sutton-Smith, 1982). On the average, firstborn children score higher on standard intelligence tests—again probably because they enjoy special benefits in their family relationships. They are the ones who benefit most from enriching, one-to-one contacts with their parents. From studies of large populations of children, one investigator finds that the more children there are in families—especially without wide gaps between them—the lower their average intelligence level is likely to be (Zajonc, 1986).

In addition to achievement and intelligence patterns, psychologists have sought to identify other characteristics among firstborns as well. Firstborn children, again perhaps because of their early close interactions with their parents, have been found to be more trusting of authority than later-born children (Suedfeld, 1969). Firstborn men, though not women, have a strong tendency to conform to social pressures (Sampson and Hancock, 1967). Moreover, just as the youngest child in the family seems to fear and shun power, firstborns often rate high in the motive to attain power. There seems to be some truth in an observation made by Adler, who once described the firstborn child as a "power-hungry conservative" (Adler, 1928). There are of course many exceptions to these generalities.

she contended that Freud, her teacher, did not appreciate how society's view of women produces problems of self-confidence and self-fulfillment.

In departing from Freud's theories of personality, both Adler and Horney turned their view away from the internal struggles of the individual, and focused attention instead on the importance of the ways we relate to others in society—a modern emphasis of psychology discussed in the final chapter of this book.

Figure 10-2 Besides success, what do these people have in common?

All these people, whose careers would indicate a high level of achievement motive, share another attribute—all were firstborn children. Clockwise from top left, they are: Bill Cosby, Mikhail Gorbachev, Indira Gandhi, Jane Fonda, Martin Luther King, Jr., Margaret Mead.

Karen Horney (1885–1952)

Some Later Trends in Psychoanalysis

In recent years, new generations of psychoanalysts have added to and in some ways revised Freud's theories—as he himself was constantly doing throughout his lifetime. These *neopsychoanalysts*, or new psychoanalysts, have tended to move away from Freud's emphasis on the id and its biologically determined instincts and toward greater concern with the ego and its attempts to deal with reality. One group, led by Heinz Hartmann, has concentrated on such ego processes as perception, attention, memory, and thinking. They regard the ego as an important force in itself rather than a mere mediator between the id and the superego (Hartmann, 1951).

Another group of neopsychoanalysts have turned their attention to cultural and social influences on personality, which were largely neglected by Freud. One prominent member of this group was Erich Fromm, who suggested that personality problems are caused by conflicts between the basic human needs and the demands of society. The core of personality, according to Fromm, is the desire to fulfill oneself as a human being—that is, to achieve a kind of unity with nature in the special way that is dictated by the human ability to think. Lower animals have no need to seek such unity, for they are simply a part of nature. They are not aware of any separation between themselves and their environment, including their fellow animals. But people must seek the unity through their own efforts; they must fulfill what Fromm regarded as the five basic and unique human needs (listed in Figure 10-3).

It would be possible, Fromm believed, to create a society in which these needs could be harmoniously fulfilled. But no such society has ever existed. Therefore all of us tend to experience frustrations and personality problems. It is society, Fromm said, that is "sick"—and it will remain so until people can relate to one another "lovingly" and "in bonds of brotherliness and solidarity," can transcend nature "by creating rather than by destroying," and can gain a sense of selfhood through their own individual powers "rather than by conformity" (Fromm, 1955).

Erich Fromm (1900–1980)

Figure 10-3 Fromm's five basic human needs
The neopsychoanalytic theory of Erich Fromm holds that the core of human personality is the desire to fulfill these needs. Personality problems arise when the attempt to gratify them is frustrated. (From The sane society *by Erich Fromm. Copyright © 1955 by Erich Fromm. Reprinted by permission of Holt, Rinehart and Winston Publishers.)*

1.	Relatedness	This need stems from the fact that human beings have lost the union with nature that other animals possess. It must be satisfied by human relationships based on productive love (which implies mutual care, responsibility, respect, and understanding).
2.	Transcendence	The need to rise above one's animal nature and to become creative.
3.	Rootedness	The need for a feeling of belonging, best satisfied by feelings of affiliation with all humanity.
4.	Identity	The need to have a sense of personal identity, to be unique. It can be satisfied through creativity or through identification with another person or group.
5.	A frame of orientation	The need for a stable and consistent way of perceiving the world and understanding its events.

HUMANISTIC THEORIES OF PERSONALITY

Much closer to the theories of Adler, Horney, and Fromm than to Freud's are the humanistic theories of personality. These theories assume a core of personality almost opposite to the Freudian assumption. Freud believed that the core was conflict, springing in large part from the ruthless and pleasure-seeking demands of the id. Humanistic theories, on the contrary, hold that human nature is basically good and that the core of personality is the desire to perfect our skills and find peace and happiness, rather than to fulfill urges toward sexuality and aggression. Their belief is that all people want to grow in positive ways and will do so if only they have the chance and the proper encouragement.

Carl Rogers and the Role of Self-image

Among the prominent humanistic theorists was Carl Rogers, who stressed the importance of the self-image all of us carry around. This self-image, or *phenomenological self*, represents the way we perceive ourselves as functioning human beings. It consists of our judgments about our abilities, accomplishments, attractiveness, and relationships with other people. In part it is based on our own observations of our behavior and the reactions of other people. But it is also highly subjective, depending on our feelings about ourselves and the way we evaluate ourselves from good to bad.

Thus the phenomenological self does not necessarily correspond to reality. Many people who are considered successful and highly respected by others perceive themselves as unworthy failures. Nor does the phenomenological self necessarily resemble the kind of person we would like to be. Neurotic people, in particular, often display striking differences when asked to describe first what they consider to be their real self, then the ideal self they wish they were (Butler and Haigh, 1954).

To a considerable extent, our phenomenological self depends on the way we believe ourselves to be accepted and esteemed by other people. We need to feel approved if we are to lead meaningful lives in harmony with ourselves and with others, displaying a personality that is trusting, spontaneous, and flexible. We must grow up in a family and social environment that treat us with what Rogers called *unconditional positive regard*. That is to say, we must be valued and trusted. Our opinions and behavior must be respected. We must be accepted and loved for what we are, even when we do things of which others may disapprove.

Unfortunately, few people grow up in such a completely favorable atmosphere. Most are treated with what Rogers called *conditional positive regard*. Their families and later society at large respond warmly to only some of their thoughts and actions, disapprovingly to others. The "forbidden" thoughts and actions are likely to become a source of maladjustment.

Carl Rogers (1902–1987)

The Roots of Maladjustment

Maladjustment and abnormal behavior, in Rogers' view, are caused by people's failure to integrate all their experiences, desires, and feelings into their phenomenological image of self—a failure that often stems from conditional positive regard with its accompanying criticism and punishment. This idea can best be explained by an example. A young boy thinks of himself as being good and as being loved by his parents. However, he also feels hostility toward a younger brother, which he expresses one day by breaking his brother's toys. His parents punish him, and he now faces a crisis in integrating the experience into his image of self. He is forced to change his image in some way. What will he do?

All of us, says Rogers, try to perceive our experiences and to behave in a way that is consistent with our images of ourselves. When we are confronted with new experiences or new feelings that seem inconsistent with the image, we can take one of two courses:

1. We can recognize the new experiences or feelings, interpret them clearly, and somehow integrate them into our image of self. This is a healthy reaction. The boy just mentioned, for example, could under ideal circumstances decide that he does feel hostility toward his brother. This is something he must reckon with, but it does not make him "bad" or doom him to the scorn of his parents and society.

2. We can deny the experiences or feelings or interpret them in distorted fashion. Thus the boy may deny that he feels any hostility toward his brother and maintain that he broke the toys in retaliation for his brother's hostility (thus adopting the defense mechanism of projection). Or he may interpret the experience as proving that he is not a good boy but a bad boy, thus acquiring feelings of shame and guilt. He may decide that his parents do not love him and therefore feel rejected.

This second course of action is likely to cause trouble. Rogers believed that maladjustment represents an ever-widening gulf between phenomenological self-image and reality. Maladjusted people tend to regard any experience that is not consistent with their self-image as a threat. Their phenomenological self, as they conceive of it, does not match their true feelings and the actual nature of their experiences. Sometimes they find ways of banishing the experience from their conscious thoughts. In any case they must set up more and more defenses against the truth, and more and more tension results.

Well-adjusted people, on the other hand, are those whose self-image is consistent with what they really think, feel, do, and experience—and who are willing to accept themselves as they are. Instead of being rigid, their phenomenological self is flexible and changes constantly as new experiences occur.

Our Better Selves: The Quest for Self-actualization

A good deal of human history seems to revolve around the motive for hostility (leading to acts of violence, revenge, and war) and the motive for power (which has produced such despots as Hitler and Stalin). But should history lead us to make a pessimistic view of human nature? Among those who think otherwise are the humanistic psychologists—who believe that the most powerful motivating force in human beings is the aspiration toward benevolent and spiritual goals. The humanists' view of human personality is expressed in the *theory of self-actualization*, which holds that people will always pursue the highest and most idealistic aims unless their development is warped by a malevolent social environment.

The theory was formulated by Abraham Maslow, one of the leading humanists. Maslow believed that humans are innately inclined to seek beauty, goodness, truth, and the

Figure 10-4 **Maslow's pyramid of motives**

Maslow's theory holds that human motives take the form of this pyramid. Once the physiological motives *at the bottom have been satisfied, human beings are freed to pursue the* safety motives—*and so on up the higher levels. For the meaning of the self-actualization motive that is at the very top, see the text.*

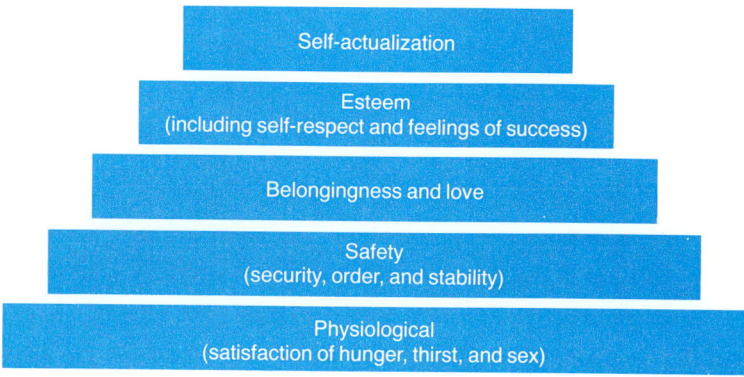

fullest possible development of their own unique potentialities for perfection and creativity. Human motives, he theorized, take the form shown in Figure 10-4. The physiological motives at the bottom of the pyramid are the most urgent. People must satisfy their hunger and thirst drives before they can undertake the search for safety, which is the next step upward. And only in a safe and stable society can they then begin to seek the higher goals to which human nature aspires.

The goal at the very top of the pyramid, self-actualization, is a sort of all-encompassing self-fulfillment. Self-actualizing people have satisfied their search for such aesthetic pleasures as order, symmetry, and beauty. They accept themselves and others and the realities of existence, and they rejoice in the experience of living. Self-actualizers are spontaneous and creative and have a keen sense of humor. They have made the most of their abilities and have become all they are capable of becoming (Maslow, 1970). All this, to Maslow, represents the goal toward which all humans by their very nature are motivated—though deprivation and social pressures may prevent some of them from ever reaching this ideal level of development. Some of the people Maslow would probably have regarded as having attained the top of his pyramid are shown in Figure 10-5.

One study indicates that people who seem to be self-actualizing are likely to be free from tendencies to be neurotic (Knapp, 1965)—in other words, that self-actualization and what is often called "mental health" go hand in hand. But in general Maslow's theory does not lend itself to experimental proof or disproof. It must be taken largely on faith. To many psychologists the theory has the intuitive ring of truth. To others it seems too optimistic.

PERSONALITY FROM THE BEHAVIORAL POINT OF VIEW

Humanistic theories hold that the core of personality is the urge to grow in a constructive way. Freud's psychoanalytic theory holds that the core is conflict. Another prominent group of theories take still another view. These are the *behavioral theories*, which reject

Figure 10-5 Some famous self-actualizers

These are some of the people whom Maslow probably would have regarded as having reached the very peak of human motivation: (A) Jonas Salk; (B) Woody Allen; (C) Mother Teresa; (D) Rudolf Nuryev.

A

B

C

D

Freud's notion of the primitive drives of the id and do not necessarily take any stand at all on the question, so vital to the humanistic approach, of whether human nature is basically good or evil. Instead, behavioral theories regard personality as largely composed of habits—that is to say, of habitual ways of responding to the situations that arise in one's life. Beginning at birth, our experiences mold us in accordance with the principles of learning that were discussed in Chapter 5. Depending on what responses we have learned to display to events in the environment, we may either cope successfully or become helpless and troubled by anxiety or depression.

One of the earliest behavioral theories of personality was developed in the 1940s by John Dollard and Neal Miller, who attempted to use learning theory to explain some of the murkier psychoanalytic concepts of Sigmund Freud. Dollard and Miller proposed that to understand an individual's behavior—whether normal or not—it was necessary to focus on four factors: *cue* (stimulus), *response, drive,* and *reinforcement* (Dollard and Miller, 1950). Consider a concrete case: Suppose a friend always becomes hostile and sarcastic whenever you beat her at tennis. The cue for her is your sharp game, and her response is aggression. The drive could be an urge for power, and the reinforcement for her behavior the look of pain on your face. Or the drive could be a need for attention, and the reinforcement the feel of your consoling arm around her shoulder. The central point for Dollard and Miller was that what we call personality is learned in the same way as any other conditioned behavior.

B. F. Skinner and Radical Behaviorism

Among the best known advocates of the behavioral approach to personality is B. F. Skinner, who, unlike Miller and Dollard, rejected the existence of internal processes such as drives altogether (Skinner, 1953). Skinner maintained that we can understand personality only by applying the operant-conditioning laws described in Chapter 5. Called *radical behaviorism* because it totally rejects the belief that humans possess a free will, Skinner's theory argues that we learn to be a particular kind of person just the way we learn anything else in life—through positive or negative reinforcement. External circumstances, not some inner motivation, is what ultimately defines personality. In effect, an individual moving through the environment resembled a complicated version of a rat moving through a T-maze. We can predict the rat's behavior if we know in which arm of the T it has been rewarded with food and in which arm it has been punished by shock. Similarly, we could predict a human's behavior if only we knew the full story of which of this person's actions had been rewarded by society and which had been punished.

Although Skinner's behavioristic view has been attacked because it regards humans as too passive, the view does in fact open up the possibilities for change. Once it is known what reinforcers maintain a certain pattern of behavior, logic dictates that withdrawing them can cause extinction of that behavior. And by the same token, new reinforcers can be used to shape alternate ways of behaving. Such processes are the basis of many forms of treatment known as *behavior therapy*, described in Chapter 13.

Social Learning Theory

When behavioral theories of personality based on learning were first formulated, most of psychology's knowledge of learning was confined to classical and operant conditioning. Thus the theories originally stressed the way unreasonable fears can be acquired through classical conditioning and the role of reinforcement in molding operant behavior. Considered especially important were the rewards and punishments provided first by the family and later by society in general.

Most learning theorists today take a more cognitive view of the manner in which experience creates habitual forms of behavior. They agree that rewards and punishments influence learning, but they believe that people learn by means other than direct reinforcement. And factors inside the person—such as inner standards—are also important.

One prominent social-learning theorist is Albert Bandura, whose concept of *reciprocal interaction* regards humans as highly active processors of information who are constantly interacting with the environment (Bandura, 1977). To be sure, the environment affects us, but as illustrated in Figure 10-6, the opposite is true as well. For example, in the case described earlier, losing at tennis may cause your friend to behave in a hostile manner—and eventually lead you to respond in kind, causing friction in the friendship. But your friend would create a far different environment if she were "a good sport" and lost gra-

Figure 10-6 Bandura's theory of reciprocal interaction
Each individual affects the environment, which, in turn, influences the individual's behavior—as explained in the text.

ciously. What this implies is that we are *not* just passive responders—we can choose how we want to affect the world around us:

> Humans [have] a capacity for self-direction. They do things that give rise to self-satisfaction and self-worth, and they refrain from behaving in ways that evoke self-punishment. . . . To ignore the influential role of covert self-reinforcement in the regulation of behavior is to disavow a uniquely human capacity (Bandura, 1974).

According to Bandura and other learning theorists, we adopt many of our responses to the environment through a process called *observational learning*. Often without even being aware of it, we take on important behavior patterns that define our personality by modeling the actions of others.

TYPE AND TRAIT THEORIES

One approach to the subject of personality sidesteps issues of personality dynamics of the kind addressed by psychoanalytic, humanistic, and social learning theorists. It focuses on the task of understanding how we differ rather than why. This is the approach of *type* and *trait theories*, whose proponents are intent not on explaining behavior, but simply on describing it—as comprehensively and meaningfully as possible.

The task of describing personality is not as easy as it might seem. As pointed out earlier, there are many thousands of words in the English language that portray the myriad aspects of the human personality. This being so, how can we classify human beings in a manner that helps us understand what they are basically like?

Personality and Physiological Characteristics

Some of the earliest theories of personality attempted to "type" people by their physical characteristics. Ancient Greek physicians believed that there were four types of personalities, each related to different fluids inside the body. *Sanguine* people had a rich flow of blood, making them happy, warm-hearted, and optimistic. *Melancholy* people had an excess of black bile, which accounted for their moodiness. *Choleric*, or bad-tempered, persons had an excess of yellow bile. And *phlegmatic* persons were slowed down and made listless by an excess of phlegm.

Melancholic

Phlegmatic

Choleric

Sanguine

A medieval portrayal of the four temperaments described in the text.

Today we know that personality differences cannot be explained so simply—although comparable theories have persisted into modern times. Early in this century, a German psychiatrist, Ernst Kretchmer argued that body types were directly related to personality and emotional disorder: People who were thin had a tendency to become schizophrenic, while those who were fat were more likely to tend toward manic-depression (Kretschmer, 1925). The best known proponent of a physiological theory of personality is William H. Sheldon, who measured the physical characteristics of many subjects and decided that three basic body builds are correlated with three basic personality types—as portrayed in Figure 10-7.

Figure 10-7 Body types and personality

Sheldon proposed that three body types are correlated with three types of temperament: the **endomorphs**, *with soft, rounded bodies and protruding bellies, are sociable, talkative, happy-go-lucky, given to the good life;* **mesomorphs**, *with hard, square-shaped bodies and well developed muscles, are physically active, energetic, and assertive; and* **ectomorphs**, *with tall, thin bodies, are solitary, high strung, intellectual, and introverted. Which type would you guess each of these people to be? (A) Andy Warhol, (B) Luciano Pavarotti, and (C) Sylvester Stallone.*

Few contemporary psychologists would subscribe to such simplistic notions. The correlation between body types and personalities are modest indeed (Hall and Lindzey, 1978). Moreover, correlations don't tell us about causes. We cannot say that being fat makes us jolly any more than we can say that being jolly makes us fat. The image of the rotund, cheerful person—or of the well-built, self-confident person—are stereotypes generated from only fragmentary evidence (Tucker, 1983).

Still, it should be pointed out that all theories of personality depend at least in part on physiology. Today there is general agreement among investigators that the structure and functioning of the brain, the glands, and the autonomic nervous system have important effects on behavior. As will be made especially clear in Chapter 12, which deals with abnormal behavior, both anatomy and physiology do indeed help shape personality—not in the simple ways proposed by Sheldon, but through complex interactions of the endocrine system, nervous system, blood chemistry, and the neuromuscular network. An example of the tie between human physiology and personality is discussed in the Psychology in Everyday Life box titled "The Riddle of Multiple Personality."

Searching for the Traits That Define Personality Types

An important approach to describing personality arises from trait theories, which focus on identifying specific underlying human characteristics. Unlike type theories, trait theories regard each individual as varying along many dimensions at the same time. "The complexity of human behavior makes it difficult to fit individuals neatly into a few simple categories. . . . For most personality characteristics, people fit at some point on a continuous distribution of that characteristic rather than into the either-or categories provided by type concepts" (Feshbach and Weiner, 1986).

In his pioneering work, Gordon Allport focused much of his career on developing a better understanding of personality by identifying and measuring a series of fundamental human traits (Allport, 1961). These were of three kinds, which he called *dispositions*. *Cardinal dispositions*—for example, the desire for money or power—color an individual's entire lifestyle. Most of us, Allport believed, are without such overriding motives. Rather, we can better be identified by our *central* dispositions, or consistent tendencies. These are the kind of qualities—for example, "serious," "kindly," "honest"—that you might recite if you were fixing up a friend with a date. Finally, Allport identified *secondary* dispositions, which may surface in specific situations but which are not usually characteristic of an individual's behavior. For example, in front of girls, a normally gregarious adolescent might become a shrinking violet.

Another psychologist who spent many years in the search for our basic personality traits is Raymond B. Cattell, who wanted to go beyond classifying traits and sought to learn how varied traits fit together to help define the human personality (Cattell, 1965, 1973). Cattell started his quest by trying to identify *surface traits*, or the most visible aspects of personality—like friendliness, rudeness, or kindness. Through records of life histories, behavioral observations, questionnaires, and objective tests of the kind described in the next section, Cattell amassed data about these traits for large numbers of individuals. He found that surface traits appeared in clusters around a single, basic trait. He referred to such underlying aspects of personality as *source traits*. As described in Figure 10-8, Cattell concluded that 16 basic source traits lie behind most of the observable differences in human behavior.

Another effort to encompass the human personality was undertaken by Hans Eysenck, a British psychologist who proposed that many variations in human behavior can be explained by two key dimensions (Eysenck, 1981). One of them—extroversion-introversion—

Psychology in Everyday Life
The Riddle of Multiple Personality

One of the most baffling forms of mental illness is called *multiple personality*, a disorder in which the person appears to be two or three distinct individuals. One investigator has described how dramatic the shifts between personalities can be:

> The various personalities alternate in their control over the behavior of the body, manifest dramatic differences in posture, speech, values, and ideas, and often claim to be of different age or sex than the actual body. The transitions among the various alternate personalities are usually very rapid, completed within a minute or two... (Putnam, 1982).

Books and movies such as *The Three Faces of Eve* have helped popularize the condition, but only recently have researchers begun to understand more fully the nature and causes of multiple personality.

For many years, multiple personality was understood only in terms of psychological dynamics, especially exposure to early psychological trauma. Today's clinical evidence does support the importance of such experiences. One repeated finding is the high incidence among people with multiple personality of severe abuse—physical and sexual—in childhood (Putnam et al., 1986). The splitting off of personalities appears to be a way of coping with the severe stress. "The alternate personalities, with their separate memories and feelings, serve to compartmentalize the trauma suffered by the individual" (Putnam, 1982).

Today, however, the underlying physiology of the disorder is being studied as well. One major finding is that brain-wave activity of each of the personalities shown by an individual is distinct. In effect, the different personalities seem to be using different brain circuits. When control subjects, including skilled actors, were asked to *pretend* to be someone else, no such changes in brain wave patterns were evident. This would mean that alternate personalities "are not merely an elaborate act, but are actual shifts in personality accompanied by significant changes in brain activity" (Putnam, 1982).

Research on personality has come a long way since the early emphasis on body fluids or physical build. But we know now that no understanding of personality development and behavior is complete without an appreciation of how personality factors influence bodily processes—and the reverse as well.

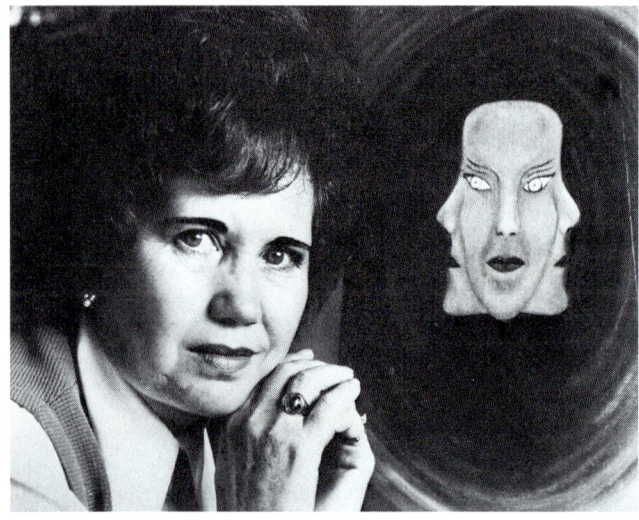

Chris Sizemore is shown here with her self-portrait, Three Faces in One. *The most famous example of multiple personality, she is Eve of the film* The Three Faces of Eve.

Figure 10-8 Sixteen traits that help define personality

Identified here are the extremes of 16 personality traits proposed by Raymond Cattell to describe the human personality. These became the basis of a well-known test—the Sixteen Personality Factor Questionnaire—*that produces a personality "profile" for any person taking it.*

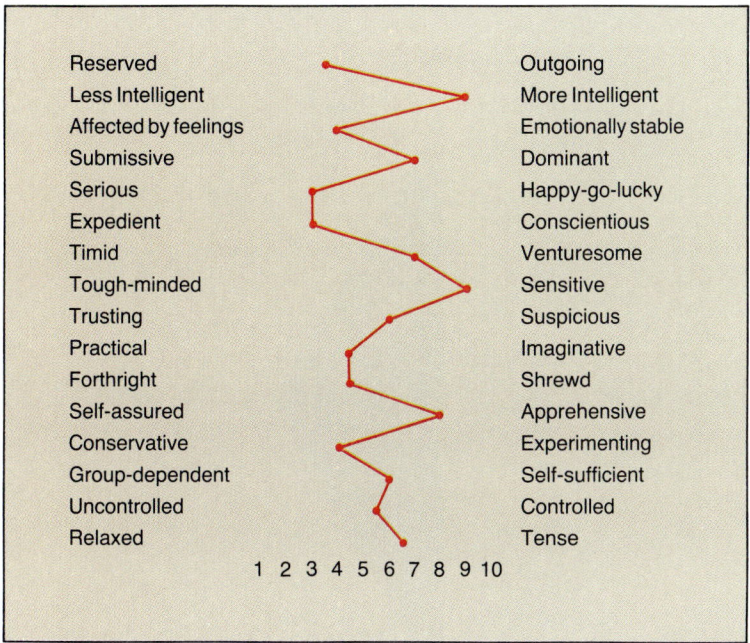

echoes the typology proposed by Jung. The second is stability-instability. As shown in Figure 10-9, these two dimensions are defined by a variety of specific personality traits.

However logical and neat they seem, all trait theories are beset by a nagging question: How consistent are our personality characteristics over time and across different life situations?

The Issue of Consistency

Evidence from a number of studies suggests that some personality traits tend to remain consistent over long periods of time (Moss and Sussman, 1980). In one long-range study, the investigator assessed 100 men and women over a span of 25 years and found that they did not vary much in such qualities as dependability, emotional control, and aesthetic interests (Block, 1971). We seem not to change a great deal as the years go by in our emotional style and the way we interact with others (Block, 1981; Conley, 1984).

It is true enough, of course, that we do not always behave consistently in widely different situations (Mischel, 1968, 1984). As pointed out in the closing chapter of this book on social psychology, you may be quite a different person in different social contexts—for example, at home and on a date. But while your sociability, say, or your mood might vary from situation to situation, your *average* over many situations is more stable and predictable (Epstein, 1983). This fact allows individuals who know you intimately to show surprising consistency when rating you on such traits as shyness or aggressiveness (Kenrick and

Figure 10-9 Eysenck's two personality dimensions

Shown here are various traits that make up the two major personality dimensions proposed by Eysenck. Note that the four combinations that emerge bear a startling resemblance to the basic personality types described by the early Greeks.

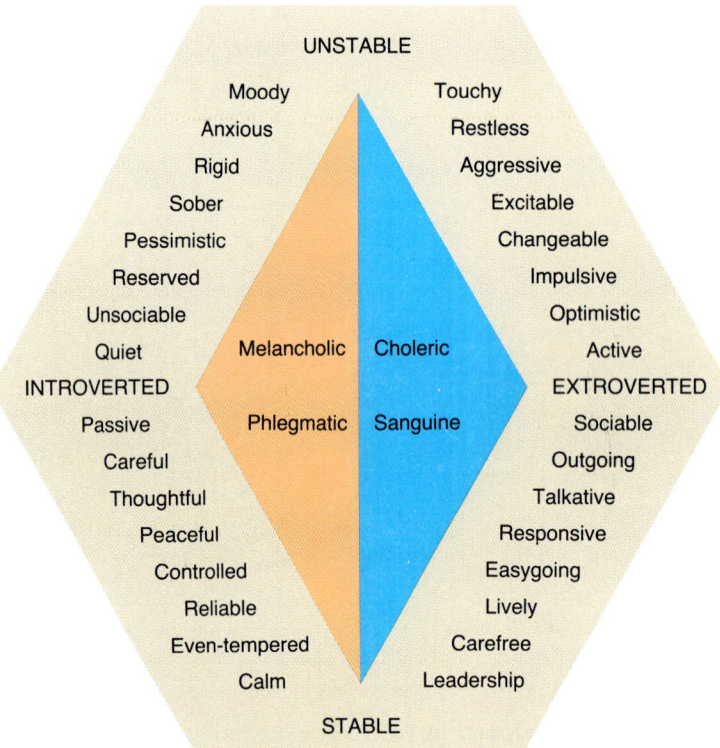

Stringfield, 1980). In one study, several hundred adults were rated by their marriage partners and acquaintances, after having been rated twice before—in both 1935 and 1954. The results suggest that even across the varied experiences of decades of life, there are certain personality traits—including the extrovert and introvert qualities first described by Jung—that appear to remain stable and recognizable throughout adulthood (Conley, 1985).

In general, most psychologists conclude that although our traits change in accord with the situations in which we find ourselves (Loevinger and Knoll, 1983), there is a kernel of consistency that comes through nevertheless. In a recent study, a group of extroverted and introverted individuals were asked to describe how they would feel in a competitive game situation. As you might expect, the introverts viewed such games to be less friendly and less enjoyable (Graziano, Feldesman, and Rahe, 1985)—an attitude consistent with their underlying personality.

Try to project what you might be like if you shifted from a funeral, to a classroom, to a basketball game. As you moved from one situation to another, you would undoubtedly become more talkative and boisterous. But some traits would probably be apparent in all situations. If you are a more-than-usually-quiet individual, you would probably

One woman, three roles—as volunteer, mother, and office manager. Does any basic personality trait come through in all of them?

Type and Trait Theories

appear more quiet than most, whatever the setting (Rorer and Widiger, 1983). Such an assumption—that there are basic constants that make up the human personality despite variations in behavior in different situations—is what underlies the important field of personality testing.

MEASURING PERSONALITY

If psychologists had a test that measured personality accurately and reliably, it would be one of their most valuable tools. Clinical psychologists could quickly analyze their clients' strengths and weaknesses, pinpoint sources of stress and anxiety, and determine the most effective way of helping in the struggle to cope. Guidance counselors would have a surefire guide to jobs and careers, for personality is a major factor in determining whether a person will be happy and successful as a salesperson, teacher, police officer, or accountant. Marriage counselors could quickly discover sources of friction and ways to relieve them—or spot couples so incompatible that the situation is hopeless. Research psychologists would have an invaluable aid in studying the conditions that foster or inhibit the flowering of personality.

Thus psychologists have spent a great deal of time, effort, and ingenuity on the creation of personality tests. Their goal, unfortunately, has been elusive. They have devised several hundred tests that are useful in many ways, but they have yet to find the perfect test. Perhaps they never will. Personality is such a complex matter—the product of a tangled and endless weaving together of experiences beginning at birth, continuing throughout life, and unique for each individual—that the difficulties in measuring it are staggering.

All the personality tests now in use have some virtues but also many limitations. The tests fall into three major classes: (1) *objective tests*, (2) *situational tests*, and (3) *projective tests*.

Objective Tests

Many people have attempted to devise a measure of personality that meets the standard of objectivity considered ideal in any psychological test. They have come up with some *objective tests* whose scores are not seriously affected by the opinions or prejudices of the examiner. Since these tests are administered according to a standard procedure, the results should be the same regardless of who gives or scores them.

The most widely used objective test is the *Minnesota Multiphasic Personality Inventory*, or MMPI for short. The test (now being revised to reflect changes in the American culture in the half century since it was developed) is made up of nearly 600 statements like those shown in Figure 10-10. For each statement, subjects are asked to check whether or not it is true of their own behavior or to mark "cannot say." The method of scoring compares the individual subject's responses with those made in the past by large numbers of other people—especially with the scores made by people known to have such personality traits as tendencies to pessimism and depression, anxiety over health, emotional excitability, delinquency, or tendencies toward schizophrenia and paranoia.

The MMPI has served as the basis for the development of other widely used objective tests of personality. One example is the *California Personality Inventory*, or CPI for short. This test contains nearly 500 items, yielding scores that measure such dimensions of personality as dominance, sociability, self-acceptance, self-control, and responsibility. Various combinations of scores on the scales of the CPI have been found to be typical of persons who succeed in school and various fields of work (Anastasi, 1982).

Figure 10-10 Some items from a personality test

The Minnesota Multiphasic Personality Inventory *is made up of statements like these, which subjects are asked to mark true, false, or cannot say of their own behavior. (Source:* Minnesota Multiphasic Personality Inventory. *Copyright 1943, renewed 1970 by the University of Minnesota. Published by the University of Minnesota Press, Minneapolis. All rights reserved.)*

T	F	Can't say	
☐	☐	☐	I have certainly had more than my share of things to worry about.
☐	☐	☐	I think that I feel more intensely than other people do.
☐	☐	☐	I have never done anything dangerous for the thrill of it.
☐	☐	☐	I think nearly everyone would tell a lie to keep out of trouble.
☐	☐	☐	I am happy most of the time.
☐	☐	☐	I tend to be on my guard with people who are somewhat more friendly than I had expected.
☐	☐	☐	My mother or father often made me obey even when I thought that it was unreasonable.
☐	☐	☐	I feel uneasy indoors.
☐	☐	☐	I refuse to play some games because I am not good at them.
☐	☐	☐	I find it hard to keep my mind on a task or job.

Situational Tests

In a *situational test*, the examiner observes the behavior of the subject in a situation deliberately created to bring out certain aspects of personality. For example, in a situational stress test, subjects might be asked to carry out some difficult mechanical task with the assistance of "helpers" who are in fact stooges and who behave in an uncooperative and insulting fashion (U.S. Office of Strategic Services, 1948). Or subjects might be put through what is called a stress interview, in which the people asking the questions are deliberately hostile and pretend to disbelieve the answers (MacKinnon, 1967).

Situational tests have been widely applied in efforts to select people with personality traits that are appropriate for particular jobs—for example, as police officers or spies. One weakness of these tests is that it is difficult to know whether the situation actually seems real to the subjects and whether their motivation and behavior are the same as in real life. Moreover, two different examiners watching a subject's behavior may reach different conclusions about it. Thus situational tests, though they may give valuable clues to personality traits, must be used and interpreted with caution.

Projective Tests

The term *projection* was mentioned in the preceding chapter as a defense mechanism in which people attribute to others some of their own anxiety-causing motives. *Projective tests of personality assume that a similar mental process can be observed and measured, even in people who are not using it as a defense mechanism, by providing conditions that encourage it.* In the *Thematic Apperception Test*, or TAT for short, these conditions are created by asking the subject to make up stories about pictures like the one in Figure 10-11, which you should examine before reading on.

Measuring Personality

Figure 10-11 A projective test: what is happening here?

What story does this picture tell? What led up to the situation? What is happening? How will events turn out? These are the questions asked in the Thematic Apperception Test, which uses drawings similar to this one. Try making up your own story before reading the discussion of the TAT in the text. (© Murray, 1971. Reprinted by permission of the Harvard University Press.)

The picture in Figure 10-11 is deliberately ambiguous. It could mean almost anything. Thus, in responding to it, you are likely to project some of your own personality traits. The story you make up may very well reveal something about your own motives, feelings, anxieties, and attitudes. Sometimes the amount of self-revelation is clear and dramatic, as in this story made up by one subject:

The older woman represents evil and she is trying to persuade the younger one to leave her husband and run off and lead a life of fun and gaiety. The younger one is afraid to do it—afraid of what others will think, afraid she will regret the action. But the older one knows that she wants to leave and so she insists over and over again. I am not sure how it ends. Perhaps the younger woman turns and walks away and ignores the older woman.

The TAT technique has found extensive and successful use in measuring the strength of the achievement motive (McClelland, Clark, and Lowell, 1953). A tendency to invent stories that contain frequent, intense elements of striving and ambition—or that on the contrary show little concern with success—appears to be a better measure of the achievement motive than the judgment of people who know the subjects well (French, 1959) or even the subjects' own assessment of their desire to achieve (deCharms et al., 1955).

The *Rorschach Test* uses inkblots like the one shown in Figure 10-12. When subjects are asked what they see in the blots, they ordinarily mention 20 to 40 things of which they are reminded. Their responses are scored for various characteristics that seem to reveal personality. For example, a tendency to respond to the blot as a whole may indicate that the subject thinks in terms of abstractions and generalities, while a tendency to pick out many minor details that most people ignore may indicate an overconcern for detail.

A number of other less formal projective techniques have been developed (Anastasi, 1982). In a *word association test*, the examiner calls out a word, such as "mother" or "bad"

Figure 10-12   Another projective test: what do you see?

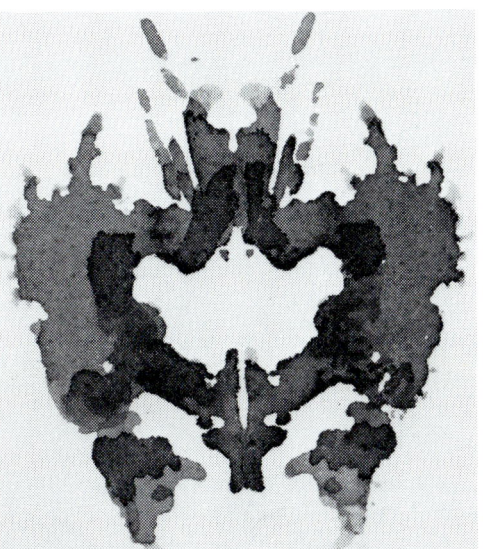

This is an inkblot like those used in the Rorschach Test. *Subjects are asked to examine it and report everything they see in it (Klopfer and Davidson, 1962).*

or "money," and the subject is asked to respond as quickly as possible with the first word that comes to mind. The examiner notes the nature of the associations that the test words suggest and also the speed with which the subject responds. Any unusual delay in responding is taken to indicate that the test word arouses some kind of conflict. In a *draw-a-person test*, the subject is simply asked to draw a picture of a person on a blank sheet of paper. The sex of the drawing, its size, the facial expression, and other characteristics may contain personality clues. In a *sentence completion test*, the examiner gives the subject a series of partially completed sentences such as the following:

> I sometimes feel. . . .
> When by myself. . . .
> When I was young. . . .

The subject is asked to complete the sentences with the first thoughts that come to mind. The responses, like the TAT stories, may suggest motives and conflicts.

SUMMARY

Theories of personality

1. *Personality* is the total pattern of characteristic ways of thinking, feeling, and behaving that constitute the individual's distinctive method of relating to the environment. The various traits that make up the personality exist in a hierarchy from strong to weak.

2. Personality theories are concerned with four aspects of human behavior. They assume (a) that there is some *core of personality* common to all human beings, (b) that these common tendencies and characteristics of human beings are channeled in various directions by the process *of development*, (c) that the core of personality as modified by development makes each person a unique individual displaying a unique pattern of

the *peripheral traits* that are generally known as personality, and (d) that identifying and defining inner human qualities help to explain the peripheral traits.

The psychoanalytic theory of Sigmund Freud

3. Freud's *psychoanalytic theory* assumes that the core of personality is conflict—springing from a basic, pleasure-seeking energy called the *libido*.

4. Psychoanalytic theory holds that the human mind has three parts or forces: (a) the unconscious *id*, (b) the largely conscious *ego*, and (c) the largely unconscious *superego*.

5. The primitive id contains the person's instinctive drives toward sexuality and aggression. The drives arouse the id to a state of excitement and tension. In seeking to relieve the tension, the id operates on what Freud called the *pleasure principle*.

6. In regard to the libido, Freud believed that human sexual development takes place in four stages: (a) oral, (b) anal, (c) phallic, and (d) genital.

7. The ego is the conscious part of the mind that operates on the *reality principle*—it does our logical thinking and tries to help us get along in the world.

8. The superego is acquired largely as a result of the *Oedipus complex*, a conflict of mingled love and hate toward the parents that all children are assumed to undergo between the ages of 2½ and 6. Children resolve the conflict by identifying with their parents and adopting what they consider to be their parents' moral judgments, which form the superego.

9. The central problem in mental disturbances, according to psychoanalytic theory, is anxiety—produced in the ego when the demands of the id threaten to create danger or when the superego threatens to impose disapproval or punishment.

Dissenting disciples: other schools of psychoanalytic theory

10. Among the successors of Freud who have proposed variations in his theory are:
    a. Jung, who introduced the concepts of *introvert* and *extrovert* and of a *collective unconscious*.
    b. Adler, who rejected Freud's focus of sexuality and developed the theory of *individual psychology*—placing greater emphasis on the innate tendency of people to be cooperative and to strive for self-perfection.
    c. Horney, who believed human beings are capable of self-realization if they are not blocked by *basic anxiety*—the feeling of being isolated and helpless in a potentially hostile world.
    d. Hartmann, who emphasized the role of such ego processes as perception, attention, and thinking in dealing with reality.
    e. Fromm, who stressed the importance of social and cultural influences on personality.

Humanistic theories of personality

11. *Humanistic theories* hold that human nature is basically good and that the core of personality is the desire to perfect our skills and find peace and happiness.

12. Rogers's humanistic theory stresses the self-image, or *phenomenological self*, which represents the way we see ourselves, our abilities, and our relationships with other people. Maladjustments occur when people fail to integrate all of their experiences, desires, and feelings into the phenomenological self, which is therefore at odds with reality.

13. Humanistic theorist Abraham Maslow formulated the theory of *self-actualization*. It maintains that people will always pursue the highest and most idealistic aims unless their development is warped by a malevolent social environment.

Personality from the behavioral view

14. *Behavioral theories* regard personality as largely composed of habits—that is to say, of habitual ways of responding to the situations that arise in one's life.

15. Dollard and Miller's behavioral theory of personality proposed that in order to understand an individual's behavior, it is necessary to focus on four factors: (a) *cue (stimulus)*, (b) *response*, (c) *drive*, and (d) *reinforcement*.

16. The *radical behaviorism* of B. F. Skinner rejects the existence of internal processes and maintains that we can understand personality only by applying the laws of *operant conditioning*.

17. *Social learning theories* hold that the core of personality is the habitual ways we have learned to respond to events in the environment. The theories originally stressed classical and operant conditioning and reinforcement through rewards or punishments. Many of today's social learning theorists take a more cognitive view and emphasize inner standards, self-reinforcement, and self-punishment.

18. A prominent social learning theorist is Albert Bandura, whose concept of *reciprocal interaction* regards human beings as highly active processors of information who are constantly interacting with the environment.

Type and trait theories

19. *Type* and *trait* theories focus on the task of understanding how we differ. Its proponents are intent not on explaining behavior, but simply describing it—as comprehensively and meaningfully as possible.

20. Ancient Greek physicians described four personality types: (a) *sanguine*, (b) *melancholy*, (c) *choleric*, and (d) *phlegmatic*.

21. In attempting to identify a series of basic and limited human traits, Gordon Allport proposed the concept of *dispositions*. *Central dispositions* are consistent tendencies; *secondary dispositions* surface in specific situations.

22. Another psychologist, Raymond Cattell, sought to learn how traits fit together and help define the human personality. He identified *surface traits*—the most visible aspects of personality—and *source traits*—the underlying aspects of personality.

23. Personality traits tend to remain consistent over long periods of time.

Measuring personality

24. There are three types of *personality tests*:
    a. *Objective tests*, such as the Minnesota Multiphasic Personality Inventory (MMPI) and the California Personality Inventory (CPI).
    b. *Situational tests*, in which the examiner observes the behavior of the subject in a situation deliberately created to reveal some aspect of the subject's personality.
    c. *Projective tests*, such as the Thematic Apperception Test and the Rorschach Test, in which subjects supposedly insert or project aspects of their own personality into the stories they make up about ambiguous pictures or into the kinds of objects they see in inkblots. Other more informal types of projective techniques include *word association*, *draw-a-person*, and *sentence completion tests*.

IMPORTANT TERMS

anal stage
basic anxiety
behavior therapy
behavioral theory
cardinal dispositions
central dispositions
choleric
collective unconscious
conditional positive regard
core of personality
CPI
cue (stimulus)
development
draw-a-person test
drive
ectomorphs
ego
endomorphs
extrovert
genital stage
id
individual psychology
introvert
libido
melancholy
mesomorphs
MMPI
multiple personality
neopsychoanalysts
objective tests
observational learning
Oedipus complex
oral stage
peripheral traits
personality
phallic stage
phenomenological self
phlegmatic
pleasure principle
projective test
psychoanalytic theory
radical behaviorism
reality principle
reciprocal interaction
reinforcement
response
Rorschach test
sanguine
secondary dispositions
self-actualization theory
sentence completion test
situational test
source traits
superego
surface traits
TAT
trait theory
type theory
unconditional positive regard
word association test

RECOMMENDED READINGS

Arnoff, J., and Wilson, J. P. *Personality in the social process*. Hillsdale, N.J.: Erlbaum Associates, 1985.
Bandura, A. *Social learning theory*. Englewood Cliffs, N.J.: Prentice-Hall, 1976.
Campbell, J., ed. *Portable Jung*. New York: Penguin Books, 1976.
Drapela, V. J. *A review of personality theories*. Springfield, Il.: Thomas, 1987.
Hall, C. S., et al. *Introduction to the theories of personality*. New York: Wiley, 1985.
Loevinger, J. *Paradigms of personality*. New York: Freeman, 1987.
Ross, A. O. *Personality*. New York: Holt, Rinehart, and Winston, 1987.
Rychlak, J. F. *Introduction to personality and psychotherapy: a theory-construction approach*, 2d ed. Boston: Houghton Mifflin, 1981.

PART 5

PERSONAL ADJUSTMENT AND MENTAL HEALTH

CHAPTER
11
COPING WITH LIFE'S ANXIETIES AND STRESS

HOW ANXIETY AFFECTS BEHAVIOR 389

Situations that provoke anxiety
Frustration and conflict as sources of anxiety
Uncertainty and doubt as sources of anxiety
General and specific anxiety
The impact of anxiety on social behavior
The impact of anxiety on learning and grades
Anxiety and the willingness to take risks

STRESS AND ITS REPERCUSSIONS IN THE BODY AND MIND 399

Physical and mental inputs to stress
Stress and the general adaptation syndrome
Psychosomatic illnesses: psychological causes, physical effects
Differences in stressful experiences—who gets sick and who doesn't?
Differences in stress resistance—who gets sick and who doesn't?
Stress and the immune system
High blood pressure, the power motive, and anger
The psychological effects of stressful events

SUCCESSFUL COPING AND MENTAL HEALTH 411

Assertive coping: from flat tires to captivity
Three approaches for dealing with stressful situations
Mental health, adjustment, and the normal personality

DEFENSE MECHANISMS AND OTHER PROBLEMATIC FORMS OF COPING 416

Rationalization
Repression
Sublimation
Identification
Reaction formation
Projection
The pro and con of defense mechanisms
Aggression in response to anxiety and stress
Withdrawal and apathy
Regression

SUMMARY 422

IMPORTANT TERMS 424

RECOMMENDED READING 424

PSYCHOLOGY IN EVERYDAY LIFE

Understanding the nature of life's conflicts 392
Attitudes that heal as much as medicine 404
Wouldn't it be nice never to suffer stress? (Or would it?) 405
Increasing our natural stress resistance levels 409
What does being normal mean? 416

The time has come to make a decision. Tomorrow morning you have an appointment to tell your faculty advisor whether you will continue in your college's business school for the coming year or take off for New York's theater scene to work at becoming a set designer. For weeks you've been mulling over the decision, and for days you've thought hard about the pros and cons of the different courses of action. A business degree promises excellent financial rewards, something you've always wanted. But a life in the arts means excitement, colorful companions, and fame—your fondest dream come true. You have shown talent for both career possibilities, and your parents will support either decision. Now you must decide—and you feel terrible. Worse yet, there are no plausible reasons for your feelings—worried, wound up, tense, "jumpy." All these terms are attempts to label what psychologists call *anxiety,* an emotion that has far-reaching effects on human behavior and personality.

Anxiety is likely to arise whenever a person is torn between conflicting desires. You may experience it when your friends urge you to join their card game just as you are setting off for the guest lecture you had planned to attend, or when a waiter's rudeness brings a sharp reprimand to your lips but speaking out would shatter your self-image of unflappable poise. Although everyone does not use the same words to describe anxiety, all of us know firsthand what it feels like and that it can affect the way we function.

All of us have also encountered periods when the minor irritations and major problems of living pile up and seem almost unbearable. A law school student described such a situation. "I have three exams next week, and I'm told my whole career can depend on the grades I get. But I have to spend precious time hunting for a summer job or else I'll never be able to pay my debts. Meanwhile I'm struggling with a big decision. My girlfriend wants us to get married now, but I think we should wait until I finish law school. Life seems almost too much for me." The familiar result for this student was distressing physical symptoms—a racing heart, shortness of breath, trembling hands, queasy stomach, and headaches. When this happens, we are experiencing what psychologists call stress, the body's reactions to outside pressures. When the strains of life become too severe or overwhelming, the stress they cause may take the form of physical illness and even death.

The psychological experience of anxiety and the physiological states of stress are two powerful influences on human behavior. Life being what it is, we cannot avoid them. We are bound to encounter them many times in the natural course of events. If we seriously fail to cope with them, we may get physically sick or lapse into the kinds of abnormal behavior described in the next chapter. Most of us, however, learn to cope—and thus not

Intense stress, if prolonged, can affect our health.

only keep our bodily well-being and our behavior within normal bounds, but even face life with reasonable optimism and zest. Our ability to do so is evidence of the surprising strength and resilience of the human personality.

HOW ANXIETY AFFECTS BEHAVIOR

Anxiety can be defined as *an unpleasant feeling accompanied by a premonition that something undesirable is about to happen.* As described in Figure 11-1, the feeling is closely related to the emotion of fear. Indeed it is very difficult to draw a sharp dividing line between them. The main difference is that usually fear is a reaction to a specific stimulus and has a "right now" quality about it. (We see a snake, know exactly what we are afraid of, and recognize that we are afraid right here and now.) Anxiety ordinarily does not have an obvious cause and is not so much concerned with the here and now as with some future unpleasantness. (When we arrive on a new job, we have no idea what lies in store for us or why we should worry about it.)

The imaginary or unrecognized source of anxiety makes it particularly difficult to handle. We usually cannot explain why we feel as we do or what it is that we fear may happen. Yet, for some unexplained reason, we find ourselves in the grip of the most uncomfortable of emotions. Our feelings can be intensely painful or can become chronic like a dull toothache, interfering over long periods with our sleep, appetite, and moods. The word *jumpy*, often applied to the feelings, is especially apt—for people plagued by anxiety are likely to have a lower threshold for other kinds of emotional response. They may be irritable and quickly moved to anger, and they may also overreact to pleasurable stimuli. They tend to have wide swings of mood and their behavior is often unpredictable.

Figure 11-1   The many faces of anxiety and fear

The similar emotional states of anxiety and fear can vary considerably in intensity, and they are given many different labels—some of which are displayed here (adapted from Horowitz, 1985).

EMOTIONAL STATE	DESCRIPTION
Distraught panic	Weak knees, lump in throat, dry mouth, sweatiness, heart palpitations, tingles, faintness, sense of impending harm to self and others, feelings of terror and dread.
Excited and disorganized	Feeling worried about having made or being about to make wrong decisions, trouble concentrating, restless body.
Apprehensive and vigilant	Racing thoughts, tense, overly alert to outside stimuli, unable to relax, tics or twitches, sense of urgency or impatience.
Worried	Preoccupation with possible misfortunes, inability to put aside cares, fretting, nervous, pressured, tense muscles, "butterflies" in the stomach.
Irritable	Tense, feeling others are unsympathetic, feeling unsympathetic to others, brusque, prone to be sarcastic, whiney, or rude, easily hurt by others.
Queasy	Pallor or greening of complexion, slowing of heart rate, feeling nauseous and weak.

Situations That Provoke Anxiety

Although the causes of anxiety are difficult to pinpoint, there appear to be five situations in which it is most likely to occur:

1. We have conflicting motives. (Such as wanting to dedicate our lives to helping others, yet at the same time wanting the solitude to write great novels.)
2. We experience a conflict between our behavior and an inner standard. (As when we do something we believe to be wrong.)
3. We encounter some unusual event that we cannot immediately understand and adjust to. (For example, when arriving on a new campus, not knowing what kind of behavior is expected.)
4. We are faced with events whose outcome is unpredictable. (For example, the score we will make on an important test.)
5. We confront the loss of a beloved person. (For example, when a close friend or parent becomes desperately ill.)

In all these cases, the emotion of anxiety is clearly related to motives. In situations 1 and 2, it is produced by a conflict between motives or between a motive and an inner standard. In situations 3 and 4 it is produced by frustration of the motive for certainty. And in situation 5, it is produced by frustration of the affiliation motive.

Frustration and Conflict as Sources of Anxiety

Psychologists define *frustration* as *the blocking of motive satisfaction by some kind of obstacle*. The obstacle may be physical: Our motive to get somewhere on time may be blocked—therefore frustrated—by a traffic jam. Obstacles may also arise from social circumstances or personal shortcomings or, most commonly, from conflicting motives. Thus any one of a number of different types of obstacles may frustrate our motives to feel secure, or to become musicians or athletes, or successful in our relations with people we like. Frustration is a universal experience. Our environment is full of situations that often seem tailor-made to keep us from fulfilling our wishes. Even the nature of our own body and personality makes frustration inevitable.

It is virtually certain, given the nature of human aspirations and human society, that we will never gratify all our motives. We are almost bound, therefore, to encounter frustration. This is one of life's most unpleasant experiences and can have extremely unfortunate results—for frustration is a frequent cause of anxiety and the abnormal behavior that will be discussed in the next chapter.

In popular usage, the term frustration refers to the unpleasant feelings that result from the blocking of motive satisfaction—that is, the feelings we experience when something interferes with our wishes, hopes, plans, and expectations. But these feelings, which are really emotional responses to frustration, take so many forms—often occurring together—that they cannot be described scientifically. They may range from mild anxiety to murderous rage, from confusion to disappointment to anger to depression to apathy.

There are wide individual differences in the ability to tolerate frustration. This has been found true even among young children (Rutter, 1983). Among adults, the evidence is all around us. You doubtless know men and women who carry on in normal fashion and even appear relatively calm and cheerful despite serious physical handicaps or tragic disappointments. You probably know others who are reduced to panic or temper tantrums if the breakfast bacon is too crisp.

The most common source of frustration and its accompanying anxiety is *conflict*—which psychologists define as *the simultaneous arousal of two or more incompatible motives, resulting in unpleasant emotions such as anxiety or anger*. The phrase "unpleasant emotions" is an essential part of the definition. A person whose motives are in genuine conflict experiences anxiety, uncertainty, and the feeling of being torn and distressed. This is why conflict is a potential threat to normal behavior.

One type of conflict occurs between the motive to live up to inner standards and some other motive. For example, most children acquire a desire to live up to a standard that calls for them to be obedient and respectful to their parents. Yet at times they may be motivated by hostility and want to strike out against their parents. Even though they do not actually commit any hostile act, the desire itself may produce anxiety or guilt. Adolescents and adults often experience similar conflict over what would happen to their self-respect and their image in society if they struck out angrily against a teacher or boss. Some are troubled by a conflict between an inner standard calling for independence and toughness and the motive to show signs of dependency or affection.

Another type of conflict occurs when two motives for different and incompatible goals are aroused at the same time. The achievement and affiliation motives are especially likely to pull in opposite directions (Reisman, 1981). An example that you may have experienced is this: It is the night before an examination. The achievement motive, in the form of a desire for a good grade, pulls you in the direction of locking yourself in your room and studying. But friends call and suggest going to a party. The affiliation motive now pulls strongly in the opposite direction. Only one of the two motives can be satisfied. An agonizing decision must be made.

To complicate the problem, the decision is likely to cause anxiety no matter which way you turn. If you decide to study, you risk anxiety over losing the goal of being with your friends—and perhaps over the possibility that their regard for you may suffer. If you decide instead to go out with your friends, you risk anxiety over your grade—and perhaps also over the possibility of rejection by your teachers or parents. The variety of such dilemmas are described in a box on Psychology in Everyday Life called "Understanding the Nature of Life's Conflicts."

Uncertainty and Doubt as Sources of Anxiety

Circumstances that provoke anxiety vary among individuals. But anxiety is likely to arise whenever the future is shrouded in uncertainty and doubt. You may experience it when you come to class to take an important exam, sit in the doctor's office waiting to learn what your X rays and lab tests show, or drive on the highway and suddenly see the flashing light of a police car looming behind you. Even astronauts, trained for years to face their task, show evidence of anxiety as they sit at their controls, knowing that in a few seconds they will blast off into the void of space.

The most striking demonstration of the built-in potential of uncertainty for creating anxiety comes from an experiment that had totally unexpected and at first glance mysterious results. The subjects, all college men, were asked to listen to a voice counting to 15. At the count of 10, they were told, they might receive an electric shock. Whether or not this would happen depended on the draw of 1 card from a pack of 20, which was shown to them. For one group, the deck contained only 1 shock card and 19 no-shock cards—so that these subjects knew their chances of shock were only 1 in 20, or 5 percent. For the second group, the chances were 50 percent. For the third group, the chances were 95 percent.

As the counting began, measurements were made of the subjects' physiological arousal, which presumably indicated the amount of anxiety they experienced. Common

Psychology in Everyday Life
Understanding the Nature of Life's Conflicts

Life is full of conflicts over pairs of goals that cannot be attained. Our conflicts are often so complex that coping with them becomes terribly difficult. To help recognize the complexity, it is useful to note that some of our motives incline us to *approach* a desirable goal (as does the motive for achievement), while others make us seek to *avoid* something unpleasant (like the anxiety and guilt that result from failure to live up to our standards). Psychologists noted many years ago that these two desires to approach the good and avoid the bad can result in a truly bewildering array of conflicts (Lewin, 1935), all falling in general into the four following classes:

1. An *approach-approach conflict* takes place between two motives that both make us want to approach desirable goals. However, we cannot reach both goals, for attaining one of them means giving up the other. We cannot simultaneously satisfy the motive to watch the late movie on television and the motive to get a good night's sleep. We cannot simultaneously roam around the world and settle down in a career. Thus we are often torn between alternatives—each of which would be thoroughly pleasant except for our regret over losing the other.

2. An *avoidance-avoidance conflict* occurs between two motives that make us want to avoid two alternatives that are both unpleasant. For example, you are too keyed up over tomorrow's examination to get to sleep. You would like to avoid the unpleasantness of tossing and turning in bed, and you could do so by taking a sleeping pill. But you would also like to avoid the grogginess you will suffer tomorrow if you do take the sleeping pill.

3. An *approach-avoidance conflict* occurs when fulfilling a motive will have both pleasant and unpleasant consequences. For young people, the thought of getting married often creates an approach-avoidance conflict. Being married has many attractions—but it also means added responsibilities and loss of freedom.

4. A *double approach-avoidance conflict*, the most complex and unfortunately the most common type of all, takes place when we are torn between two goals that will both have pleasant and unpleasant consequences. A college woman from a small community wants to become a certified public accountant. But she knows that the best opportunities in this field exist in large cities, and she is worried about the crowded and impersonal aspects of big-city life. Now she falls in love with a classmate who plans to go into business with his father, who runs a small-town automobile agency. She wants very much to marry this man and she likes the idea of living with him in a small community. But she knows that this community will give her very little opportunity for her chosen career as an accountant. Which way shall she turn?

Often there is no fully satisfactory solution to the conflicts we face in everyday life. But understanding their nature can help us cope—and arrive at sensible resolutions.

---

sense suggested that the group with the 50 percent chance of shock would show the most anxiety. The 5 percent group would feel relatively safe, and the 95 percent group would consider themselves almost certain to receive a shock and would be reconciled to it. Even the experimenters expected this result. To their amazement, however, the 5 percent group showed by far the most anxiety, as illustrated in Figure 11-2.

Why should this have happened? The answer lies in the comments of the 50 percent group. These subjects said they decided that their chances of getting a shock were high enough to lead them to expect it—thus reducing the uncertainty—and merely to hope they would be spared. Thus they felt very much like the subjects in the 95 percent group, who were almost sure to get a shock. The subjects in the 5 percent group, on the other hand, experienced much more uncertainty. They felt that their chances of getting a shock were so low that they could not expect and reconcile themselves to it. Yet neither could they dismiss the possibility. It was this greater uncertainty that made them experience the greatest anxiety of all.

Another example of anxiety caused by uncertainty may occur in a noisy environment. Noise in itself does not usually create problems. We may find it distracting at first but usually adapt to it quickly. For most people, even exposure to frequent noise such as airplanes flying low overhead does not lead to serious difficulties (Tarnopolsky, Watkins, and Hand, 1980). But when we are working at a difficult task such as studying for an exam, noise can produce anxiety if it occurs at unpredictable intervals. We become vigilant and edgy—waiting, so to speak, for the other shoe to drop.

In general, the more information people have as they prepare to face an anxiety-provoking experience, the better they feel. But the result appears to depend to some degree on how apprehensive they are to begin with. For those who are very anxious, information about what lies in store may actually increase the problem. In one study, a group of women,

Figure 11-2 An experiment with surprising results

Subjects who had only a 5 percent chance of receiving a shock at the count of 10 showed more physiological arousal—hence presumably more anxiety—than subjects who had a 50 percent chance or a 95 percent chance. The measure of physiological arousal shown here is electrical conductivity of the skin, affected by activity of the sweat glands (Epstein and Roupenian, 1970). For an explanation of this unexpected result, see the text.

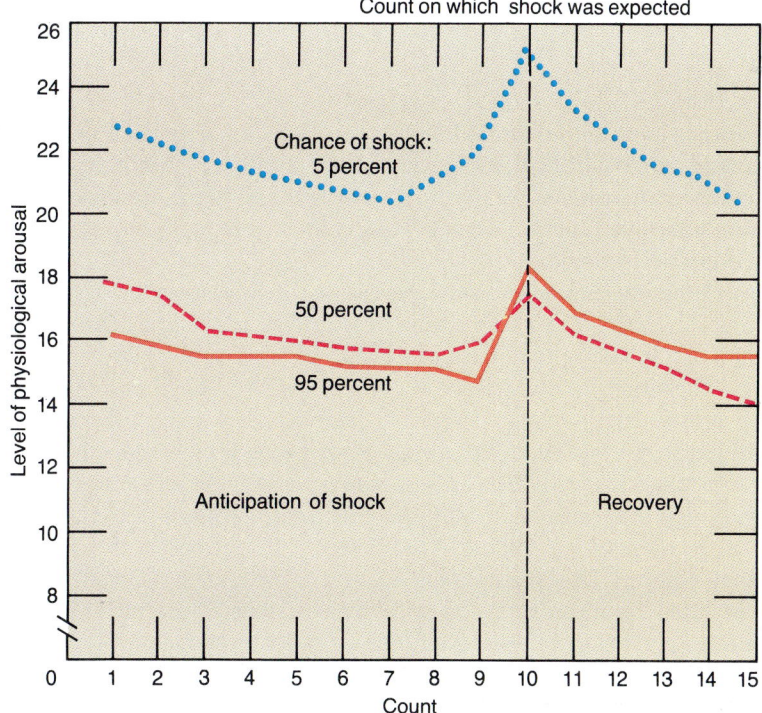

Anxiety can be bred by uncertainty.

about to have their hands immersed in painfully cold water, received detailed information about what to expect. The information helped reduce the anxiety of those who were not overconcerned about the experience—but it compounded the anxiety of women who approached the experiment with extreme foreboding (McCaul, 1980).

Anxiety is also relieved by alcohol and by such tranquilizers as Valium and Librium, presumably because these drugs reduce the activity of the brain's neurotransmitter noradrenaline. However, researchers point out that the relief is obtained at a price. Any antianxiety drug reduces the ability to cope realistically with the environment by meeting changes and challenges (Gray, 1978).

General and Specific Anxiety

Many studies have demonstrated the universality of feelings of anxiety (Tuma and Maser, 1985), and research with various species—from goldfish to chimpanzees—has led scientists to conclude that such feelings and the biological changes accompanying them serve an important adaptive function. Anxiety alerts us to threats to our survival and spurs us to initiate appropriate action.

Unfortunately, however, some people seem to display anxiety in too many of the situations they face. They feel anxious regardless of whether they are working in their classroom or job, taking part in a social event, picking up the telephone, shopping, or even starting a vacation. They worry about many things and have a vague uneasiness about all future events. Such people are victims of *general anxiety*. Others display only *specific anxiety* in some particular situation but not at other times (Spielberger, 1971). One well-known example is stage fright, which strikes many people who are otherwise generally free of anxiety. A type of specific anxiety often found among college students has to do with taking tests. *Test anxiety*, as it is called, is so common that it has been one of the most widely studied of all forms. Investigators have found that it can be relieved—and performance on tests can often be improved—by such measures as relaxation training and practice at concentrating on the test itself rather than on one's inner feelings (Wine, 1971).

Both general and specific anxiety seem to feed on themselves. The victim, having become anxious, is painfully aware of the signs of emotional arousal (increased heart rate, sweaty palms, butterflies in the stomach)—and the very awareness increases the amount of anxiety. Relaxation training presumably counteracts this vicious circle. So do biofeedback techniques, which can be used to recognize and control internal bodily changes associated with anxiety (Rice and Blanchard, 1982). One experiment showed that even such a simple device as deliberately controlling one's breathing, to half the normal rate, can significantly lower some of the physiological signs of anxiety and the feelings of anxiety as well (McCaul, Solomon, and Holmes, 1979).

The Impact of Anxiety on Social Behavior

Some people manage to hide any outward signs of anxiety, but it is such a powerful emotion that it often affects social behavior—at times to a significant extent. One timely study measured the way anxiety over crime influenced the everyday lives of people in Chicago, San Francisco, and Philadelphia. It was found that well over twice as many women as men were concerned about being harmed by criminals. (Fear of rape probably explains much of the difference.) Moreover, as is shown in Figure 11-3, women were twice as likely as men to isolate themselves from others and to take unusual measures to protect themselves when they were outside their home. Thus it appeared that fear of crime severely limited the women's social behavior, narrowing their choices of where to go and what to do in order to feel safe.

Behavior resulting from anxiety, of course, is not always logical or sensible. The precautions the women in this study were found to take did not necessarily guarantee their safety—for attacks often occur in the home (McDermott, 1979). Similarly, everyone knows people who suffer anxiety on social occasions such as mixers and dances. Socially anxious people become distressed at being looked at or talked about. Worry over being evaluated—and possibly found wanting—is the most important feature of social anxiety (Smith, Ingram, and Brehm, 1983). To prevent the unpleasant feelings from arising, they may avoid most or even all social gatherings. Indeed anxiety can lead to behavior so far removed from reality that it must be considered abnormal, as will be explained in the next chapter.

Figure 11-3 Anxiety: the difference it can make in everyday activities

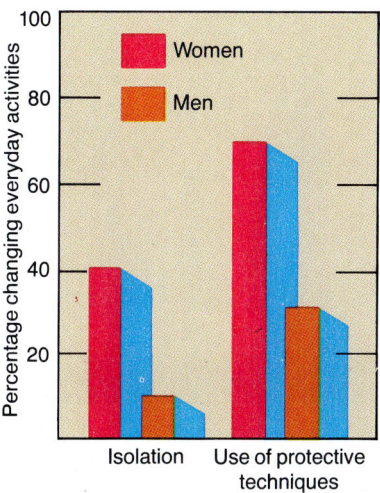

The bars show that women—because they are more fearful of crime than men—are much more likely to alter their social behavior. They are four times more likely to isolate themselves—to avoid public transportation and parks and to stay home after dark. They are well over twice as likely to adopt unusual protective tactics such as wearing shoes that make it easier to run, or choosing their bus seat to avoid passengers who look dangerous (Riger and Gordon, 1981).

The Impact of Anxiety on Learning and Grades

Of particular interest to college students is the influence of anxiety on the ability to learn and on grades. Does it promote learning by increasing the desire to learn? Or does it interfere with learning?

Insofar as the facts can be determined, it appears that people high in anxiety do better than others at simple learning tasks but more poorly than others at difficult learning tasks (O'Neil, Spielberger, and Hansen, 1969). Presumably their anxiety impairs the intense concentration required for the learning of complicated materials. They seem distracted, as if their anxiety forces them to focus on the way they feel rather than on the tasks at hand (Holyrod et al., 1978). People high in anxiety seem to do particularly badly at reasoning when they are put under pressure, such as being told they have a short time to answer test questions (Leon and Revelle, 1985).

How does anxiety affect actual performance in college? This question was explored by an investigator who selected one group of male students who appeared to be relatively high in anxiety and another group relatively low in anxiety. He examined their college board scores, as an indication of their ability, and their actual grades in college. He found that students with the lowest levels of scholastic ability made approximately the same grades regardless of whether they were high or low in anxiety. So did students with the highest levels of scholastic ability. But at the in-between levels of ability—where, of course, most students fall—the students who were low in anxiety made significantly better grades than did the anxious students. Full results of the study appear in Figure 11-4.

Figure 11-4 Anxiety and performance in college

The bars show the average grades made by high-anxiety and low-anxiety students of different levels of scholastic ability as indicated by their college board scores. Note the pronounced differences found between the two groups at the middle ranges of scholastic ability (Spielberger, 1962).

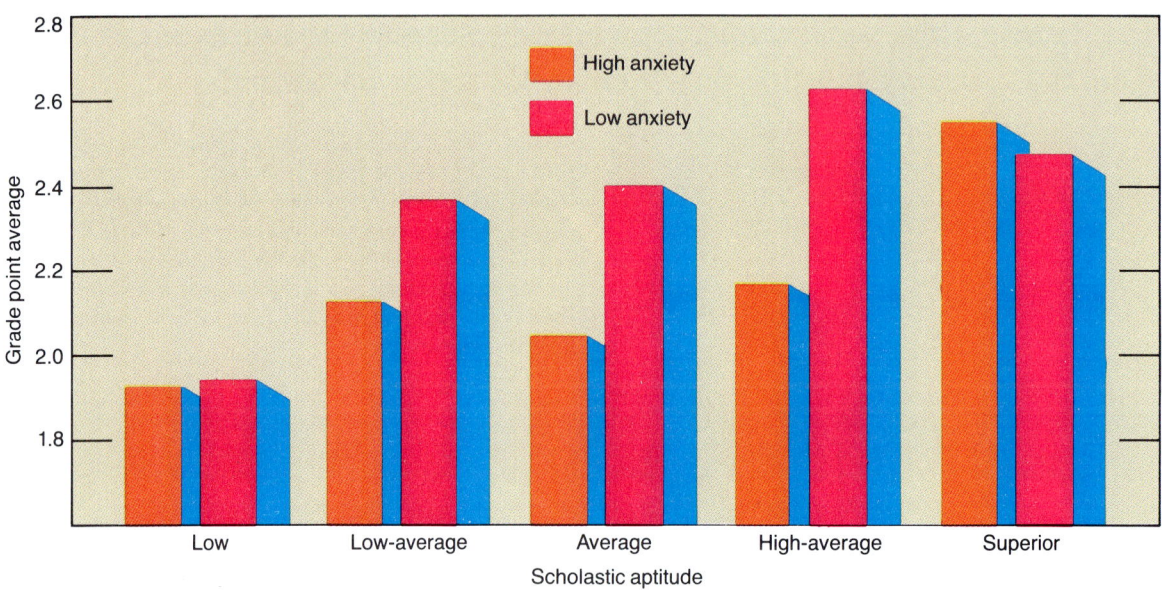

A follow-up study was made with anxious freshmen who were making such low grades that they were in danger of flunking out of college. One group of these freshmen took an active part in a counseling program in which they received advice about their problems in college, methods of study, campus life in general, and their relations with professors—advice that presumably would reduce their anxiety about the college situation. Another group, matched as closely as possible for college board scores, type of high school attended, and other factors that influence performance in college, did not receive counseling. From midterm to the end of the first semester the counseling group made an average improvement of more than half a grade point. The group that was not counseled improved by less than a tenth of a grade point (Spielberger, Denny, and Weitz, 1962). Anxiety about the college situation appears to be a frequent—though perhaps correctable—cause of failure in college. Anxiety about a particularly difficult subject such as mathematics can also be reduced with treatment, leading to improved performance (Bander, Russell, and Zamostny, 1982).

Another recent study suggests that the relationship between anxiety and learning can work in reverse as well—that we can become anxious because we are having trouble learning rather than the other way around. This study found that students in an advanced psychology course who were very anxious about tests did well enough on multiple-choice questions but had difficulty on short-answer questions, essay questions, and take-home exams—all of which require a more comprehensive recall of what has been learned. The students also reported problems in learning new material and picking out important points in reading assignments. The researchers concluded that the anxiety resulted from an inadequate grasp of the subject matter and suggested that the students might be helped as much by acquiring new learning strategies as by practicing anxiety-reducing techniques (Benjamin et al., 1981).

Anxiety and the Willingness to Take Risks

One characteristic that influences the way people live their lives is the amount of risk they are willing to take. Some people are very conservative and hate to go out on a limb. Others seem to be born gamblers who take all kinds of chances. There appears to be a strong relationship between this refusal or readiness to take risks and anxiety.

An experiment that demonstrates this fact is illustrated in Figure 11-5. Note that subjects who appeared to be relatively free from anxiety tended to scorn the "sure thing" in the game that was used in the experiment. They made very few throws from the close distances where they were almost certain to succeed but would receive only a low score. They also tended to avoid the high risk of gambling that they could score from the longest distances, where they would have received the highest scores. Subjects who appeared to be relatively high in test anxiety made many more shots from the short distances and also "went for broke" more often by trying from the longest distances.

The experiment suggests that people who are highly anxious about success and failure tend to adopt either a very conservative or a very risky strategy in life situations. They are inclined to settle for the sure thing and thus avoid failure that would add to their anxiety, or else they tend to take the chances at which success is so unlikely that they can readily excuse their failure. You have probably observed people who take few chances in life, settle for jobs that seem beneath their abilities, and yet take an occasional flier in a gambling casino or a risky investment. Less anxious people, on the other hand, seem to have enough confidence to take the middle-range risks that are most likely to lead to success in the long run.

Figure 11-5 Anxiety, conservatism, and "going for broke"

Two groups of subjects played an experimental game in which they tossed rings at a peg, trying from any distance they chose. They were told that for ringing the peg from close distances they would receive low scores, from middle distances middle scores, and from far distances very high scores. Note that subjects who had been found low in anxiety chose a strategy of intermediate risks. Those who had been found high in anxiety tended to be either very conservative or to go for broke (Atkinson et al., 1960).

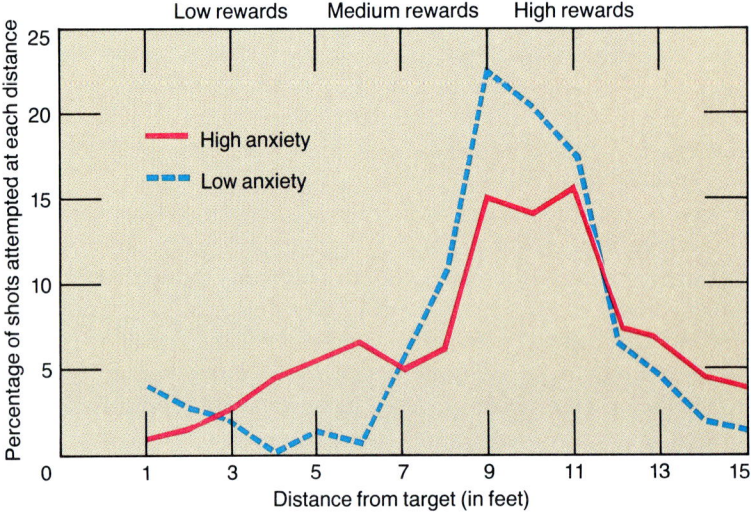

High anxiety can lead to high risks.

STRESS AND ITS REPERCUSSIONS IN THE BODY AND MIND

To psychologists, as has been said, the term *stress* applies to the body's reactions to outside pressures—in other words, to the physiological wear and tear caused by attempting to adjust to events that cause emotional and other forms of arousal. In everyday language, of course, the word is also applied to the events themselves. Psychologists often refer to such events as *stressors*. The fact that many situations place a serious burden on the human organism has gained popular recognition in all the references made today to the "stress and strain" of modern life. Even people who have never taken a psychology course acknowledge that our society puts all of us under severe and often painful pressure caused by competition (for acceptance to college, grades, jobs, and promotions) and by social demands, worries about economic security and the possibility of war, crowded streets, and many similar concerns. People disillusioned with modern life often use the contemptuous term "rat race"—implying that existence has become a constant, mindless struggle for a prize of dubious value.

There is no question that modern life is filled with stressors of various sorts. Many events that are commonplace in our daily lives have been found to produce signs of stress even in lower animals. Exposure to noise—a standard feature of city life—raises the blood pressure of rats. Dogs that are raised in isolation and then suddenly introduced into a normal environment exhibit a long-lasting fear that makes them incapable of appropriate behavior (Fuller, 1967). The human counterpart would be the abrupt shift of environment we experience when changing schools, jobs, or places of residence—or even the more general kinds of rapid change that have been occurring in technology, politics, and family life.

Whether life is more difficult today than in the past is questionable. Some psychological counselors believe that stress is more severe than ever before for college students. They note that today's students are under pressure from the high cost of education, an uncertain job outlook, and stiff competition from their peers for everything from seats at a varsity basketball game to slots in a graduate program. As a result, serious stress-related illnesses such as depression, migraine headache, and eating and sleeping disorders are seen as a new *syndrome*, or pattern of processes and symptoms that characterize a disease. Called "student shock," the syndrome is emerging not only among young people with long-time problems but even among those who were formerly well adjusted (Gottschalk, 1983). However, human beings have always been subject to conditions that cause stress. Once upon a time the pressures came from fighting the elements and dangerous animals and constant scrambling for the next meal. Throughout history our ancestors were beset by pain, illness, and the danger of violent death. Today's sources of stress, though different, may be no more burdensome than those of the past—and indeed may actually be less so for many people. There is no way of knowing for sure.

Physical and Mental Inputs to Stress

Psychologists define stress as *the body's reaction to anything that threatens to damage the organism*. Stress can be caused by a disease germ, air or noise pollution, the physical danger faced by a football player or a firefighter, or the psychological danger posed by the impending death of an intimate person. It can arise in any situation that produces prolonged severe anxiety and the accompanying physical wear and tear of intense emotion. Stress thus depends not only on outside events but on our feelings about them.

One person may experience severe stress over an occurrence that leaves another person relatively calm. The difference between them may lie not only in their physical re-

How much stress do you think this family is under?

sponse to the event but also in their cognitive interpretation of it. What we think of a potential stressor can make us feel stressed even if our body does not react. This was demonstrated in a study using an experimental stressor called a "sonic confusor" that increases heart rate and blood pressure and produces psychological arousal. Subjects were patients with severed spinal cords, resulting in their having no sympathetic-nervous-system feedback to the brain from organs such as the heart or stomach. Their reaction to the experimental stressor was compared to that of healthy control subjects. The results showed that the patients' subjective feelings of stress were similar to those of control subjects even though the patients—unlike the control subjects—had no physical reactions to the stressor (Heidbreder et al., 1984). Evidently the subjective experience of stress does not necessarily require feedback from the body.

Stress and the General Adaptation Syndrome

The damaging potential of stress, whatever its origin, was dramatically demonstrated by Hans Selye, who experimented with animals and exposed them to stressful physical conditions, such as the injection of poison in doses not quite strong enough to kill. The results, however, seem to be much the same as those produced in humans by any form of external or internal pressure, including prolonged anxiety or other emotional tension.

Selye found that when an animal was injected with poison, its body automatically tried to defend itself. Most notably, its endocrine glands immediately sprang into action (as they also do in human emotional arousal). The adrenal glands in particular showed striking changes. They became enlarged and produced more adrenalin. They also discharged their stored-up supply of the hormones known as steroids, which make many contributions to the body's well-being. Because of this high level of activity of the adrenal glands, numerous physical changes occurred in the animals. For example, tissue was broken down into sugar to provide energy. The amount of salt normally found in the bloodstream was sharply reduced.

After a few days of continued exposure to stress-producing conditions, the animals seemed to adapt. The adrenal glands returned to normal size and began to renew their supply of steroids. The salt level in the blood rose to normal or even higher. Apparently the animals had adjusted to the situation and were perfectly normal.

Their recovery, however, was only temporary. After several weeks of continued pressure, the adrenal glands again became enlarged and lost their store of steroids. The level of salt in the blood fell drastically. The kidneys, as a result of receiving an excess of hormones, underwent some complicated and damaging changes. Eventually the animals died, as if from exhaustion. They had been killed, so to speak, by an excess of the hormones they had produced in their own defense.

Another of Selye's important findings was that even during the period of apparent recovery, the animals were not so normal as they seemed. If a second source of stress was introduced during this period, the animals quickly died. In attempting to adapt to the original source of stress, apparently they had used their defenses to the maximum and were helpless against a new form of pressure (Selye, 1956).

To describe the sequence of events that takes place during prolonged stress—the initial shock or alarm, the recovery or resistance period, and at last exhaustion and death—Selye coined the phrase *general adaptation syndrome*.

Psychosomatic Illnesses: Psychological Causes, Physical Effects

There are many indications that the damaging effects of stress found in animals also occurs in humans. For example, people who did not move away after the accident that damaged the Three Mile Island nuclear power plant were living in a situation of prolonged emotional tension. As long as 17 months after the incident, they were secreting higher levels of stress-related hormones, reporting more symptoms of depression and anxiety, and performing more poorly on behavioral tasks than control subjects (Schaeffer and Baum, 1984).

Stress caused by frustration, conflict, or any sort of prolonged emotional upset can be just as drastic as the kind Selye produced by injecting poison. The physical results often

Some jobs invite stress—and its consequences.

take the form of *psychosomatic illnesses*, meaning bodily ailments that stem at least in part from mental and emotional causes. Diseases that frequently seem to be psychosomatic include high blood pressure, heart attacks, stomach ulcers, diabetes, tuberculosis, multiple sclerosis, and possibly some forms of cancer (Miller, 1975)—as well as a host of minor illnesses including the common cold. Thus, for example, air traffic controllers, especially in high-traffic airports, have a greater incidence than other workers of high blood pressure, stomach ulcers, and diabetes (Rose, Jenkins, and Hurst, 1978).

One study has suggested that perhaps all illnesses, not only those regarded as psychosomatic, usually are triggered by stress-producing situations. The study was made by compiling case histories of a group of patients suffering from a wide variety of physical ailments. It was found that all the patients had undergone some experience, shortly before the onset of the disease, that was psychologically distressing. The experiences most frequently reported are listed in Figure 11-6. The study indicates that under ordinary conditions our bodies are able to resist such external causes of illness as viruses and bacteria. When our usual defenses are weakened by stress, we are likely to get sick. The time factor involved was analyzed in a study of men enrolled in a Navy submarine school. The subjects completed a survey of life experience covering the past year, dating each experience and rating its desirability and impact. Analysis of this information in relation to the subjects' medical records revealed a strong positive correlation between stressful life events occurring 7 to 12 months in the past and illnesses occurring in the subsequent half-year (Antoni, 1985).

Can stress keep those who are sick from getting well? One team of researchers studied children with puzzling cases of diabetes, a metabolic disorder that can usually be kept in check with injections of the drug insulin. For these children, however, the medicine was totally ineffective. No matter how high a dose they received, their diabetic attacks could

Figure 11-6 The emotional background of illness

Case histories of patients suffering from physical illnesses showed that all of them had recently experienced some type of stressful situation. The most common trigger for the illnesses was feelings of resentment or hostility (Luborsky, Docherty, and Penick, 1973).

Emotional state believed to have triggered illness	Percentage of cases
Resentment or hostility	17
Frustration or rejection	13
Depression, hopelessness	13
Anxiety	13
Feelings of helplessness	12
Separation from a loved one	9
Stressful changes in life situation or threatening situation	9
Difficulties in relationship with therapist or experimenter	4
Miscellaneous	10

not be controlled. All these children, it turned out, were living in homes torn by conflict and tension and were constantly enmeshed in the quarrels of their parents. Eventually, they suffered near-fatal blood disturbances that required hospitalization. Once in the hospital, however, they could be treated successfully. As soon as they were removed from their stressful environment, even routine doses of insulin proved effective (Minuchin et al., 1975).

Can stress actually kill, as it killed Selye's animals? Some evidence that it can comes from a study of middle-aged men who died suddenly of heart attacks. Their backgrounds showed that four out of every five had been feeling depressed for periods ranging from a week to several months. (Depression, as will be seen later, is often a result of prolonged stress.) Just before the fatal attack, at least half of them had been in a situation likely to produce sudden and intense emotional arousal—in some cases an unusually heavy work load or other bustle of activity, in other circumstances a high level of anxiety or anger (Greene, Goldstein, and Moss, 1972). It seems likely that stress was at least a contributing factor in their deaths.

Differences in Stressful Experiences—Who Gets Sick and Who Doesn't?

Everybody undergoes stressful experiences—yet not everybody comes down with a psychosomatic illness. Why? One reason seems to be that no two people have the same experiences and that each experience has a sort of built-in potential for creating a certain level of stress, high or low. After studying the life experiences and medical records of large numbers of people, one group of investigators developed the Life Stress Scale shown in Figure 11-7, which assigns a numeric value to the amount of stress that adjusting to various new events seems to create. Note that these events include not only misfortunes but pleasurable happenings—such as getting married, achieving something outstanding, and even going on vacation or celebrating Christmas. Indeed getting married, assigned a figure of 50, was found fully half as stressful as the death of a husband or wife, which tops the list with 100.

The likelihood of psychosomatic illness, the investigators concluded, is determined by the total number of stress units that occur within a single 12-month period. When the number exceeded 200, more than half the people in the study developed health problems. Thus the scale indicates that a person is more likely than not to become sick if a single year's experiences include divorce (73 units), losing a job (47), a change in finances (38), the death of a close friend (37), and a change to a new kind of work (36). When the total exceeded 300, nearly 80 percent of the subjects became ill.

Several researchers have found more recently that major life events, though consistently related to health, are not always strong predictors of future illness. More potent than major life events may be the repeated strains of daily life—hassles—such as losing your wallet, getting stuck in traffic, or bickering with your parents. One research team investigated the relationship of health to both major life events and daily hassles occurring over a year-long period in a group of adults. The results showed "hassle scores" to be more strongly associated with physical health than life-events scores (deLongis et al., 1982). The findings point to the truth of the saying that it is the "last straw" that breaks the camel's back.

If an accumulation of even mildly stressful experiences can result in illness, can psychological tactics aimed at reducing stress help a person who is ill to recover? The answer appears to be yes—as discussed in a box on Psychology in Everyday Life titled "Attitudes That Heal as Much as Medicine."

Figure 11-7 A scale of stress produced by various events

These are some of the figures in the Life Stress Scale, discussed in the text (Holmes and Rahe, 1967).

Experience	Stress units	Experience	Stress Units
Death of spouse	100	Change to new kind of work	36
Divorce	73	Change in work responsibilities	29
Separation	65	Trouble with in-laws	29
Jail term	63	An outstanding achievement	28
Death of close family member	63	Wife starts job or stops	26
Getting married	50	Begin or end school	26
Being fired	47	Trouble with boss	23
Reconciliation in marriage	45	Change in work conditions	20
Retiring	45	Move to new residence	20
Getting pregnant	40	Changing schools	20
Sex problems	39	Changing social activities	18
New member in family	39	Vacation	13
Change in finances	38	Christmas holidays	12
Death of close friend	37	Minor law violation	11

Psychology in Everyday Life
Attitudes That Heal as Much as Medicine

The relationships that have been found between stress and physical ailments shed considerable light on what was previously a medical mystery. Part of the puzzle centered on the fact that until recently only a few medicines or medical techniques were physically effective in combating disease. Some of the methods used in the past—such as drawing blood from an already weak patient by applying leeches—were actually harmful. Yet patients treated by the old methods often made spectacular recoveries. Even today, witch doctors in primitive societies cure many ailments as if by magic, as do faith healers in our own society.

Another part of the puzzle concerned that famous medical device called the placebo—a mere sugar pill, with no remedial value at all. Physicians have known for a long time that the number of people whose physical symptoms vanish after they take a placebo may be just as high as if real medicine had been prescribed. This phenomenon, called the *placebo effect*, causes great confusion in attempts to study the effectiveness of new drugs.

The key to the mystery now appears to be that any form of treatment comforts the patient, relieves stress, and thus helps the body mobilize its own defenses and throw off disease. The famous "bedside manner" of doctors in our great-grandparents' day may have been just as effective, in its own way, as today's techniques. Perhaps it would help today with the many people who complain that physicians—for all their blood tests, X rays, and wonder drugs—often take an impersonal approach to illness that makes patients feel more like case histories than like suffering human beings. Compassion and caring can be healing medicines.

Differences in Stress Resistance—Who Gets Sick and Who Doesn't?

Although the Life Stress Scale continues to serve as a guide to the potentially stressful effects of various experiences, critics regard it as too arbitrary to apply to all people under all circumstances (Rabkin and Struening, 1976). For one thing, any attempt to generalize ignores individual differences in our basic level of physical fitness. One investigation showed that the level of life stress is associated with poorer health for people who are not very fit to begin with, but it has less impact on the health of those who are in good shape (Roth and Holmes, 1985). Another important source of difference is an individual's attitude toward life's events. Some people take a much calmer view than others of divorce, loss of a job, or the other matters listed in the stress scale. Even the death of a spouse may produce more relief than stress for someone it releases from an intolerable relationship (Rutter, 1983). In fact some people seem unmoved by anything at all that happens to them—a peculiar phenomenon discussed in a box on Psychology in Everyday Life titled "Wouldn't It Be Nice Never to Suffer Stress (Or Would It?)"

People also differ widely in how they interpret a given stressful event. As Figure 11-8 shows, some people are quick to conclude that the crises they face are entirely of their own

---

Psychology in Everyday Life
Wouldn't It Be Nice Never to Suffer Stress (Or Would It?)

Some people sail blithely through life with hardly a hint of stress. No matter what happens to them, no matter what kind of crisis they face, they rarely seem to suffer any pressure or tension. On our own more jittery days we may consider them the most fortunate of people—and even envy them their composure. But are they really so lucky? Would we really like to be in their shoes?

A clue to the answer comes from a study of a number of people who were in the midst of unusually stressful experiences, including some who had been torn away from their families and uprooted from their native country (Hinkle, 1974). Among these people there were some who seemed unshaken by the loss of home, community, friends, and in some cases even marriage partner. But these stress-free individuals seemed to be a breed apart, with attitudes and feelings foreign to most of us.

For one thing, they seemed totally unconcerned about other people—and in no way responsible for anyone else. If a family member was in trouble, they refused to worry because "nothing can be done about it." Some declined to help a sick parent—or relative—because "it would be too much for me."

One might say they acted as if interested only in their own well-being—except that even their own welfare did not seem to concern them very much. No matter how difficult their circumstances, they saw no reason to be upset or bitter. If their lot in life turned out to be poverty-stricken and lonely, so be it. Such matters, they felt, were beyond their control. Some of them turned down a chance to increase their income by working overtime because it might be too tiring, or a promising transfer to another job because it was too much trouble, or a promotion because it would mean too much responsibility.

They seemed to have made a trade-off. They avoided the wear and tear of stress by never letting themselves care much about anything. They avoided any attempt to extend themselves—in their own behalf or to help anyone else. They were content to avoid stress by ignoring life's exciting challenges, its precious opportunities, and what most of us would consider its obligations.

If we could all be like them, would we be happier? Would the human community be better off?

Figure 11-8   Contrasting attributions for stressful events

In interpreting stressful events, some of us show a pessimistic perspective, while others of us are decidedly more upbeat. This style of reacting makes a difference in our resistance to stress when crises occur (Peterson and Seligman, 1984).

	Pessimist	*Optimist*
	Internal: "I can't do these math problems. I'm just naturally stupid."	*External:* "These problems were rigged."
	Stable: "Math has always been a difficult subject and always will be."	*Unstable:* "With a different teacher, things would be a lot better."
	Global: "Doing poorly in math is going to undermine everything I do."	*Specific:* "One test score doesn't make a career."

doing, that their reaction will last, and that it will undermine everything they do. These are essentially pessimists. In contrast, there are others who view the crises they face as arising from external circumstances, as transient, and as unrelated to the rest of their lives.

How we interpret the stresses we face can significantly affect our well-being—and perhaps even our longevity. This is suggested by a study of the causal explanations of events on the ball field given by members of the Baseball Hall of Fame. Explanations of the outcome of games were gathered from sports pages of *The New York Times* and *The Philadelphia Inquirer*. Interviewed by reporters after the game, some players displayed an optimistic, explanatory style—for example, "We lost because our top hitter had a sore finger, but he'll be OK in a day or two," or "We picked off the runner because my catcher and I have perfected our signals." Other players gave neutral or pessimistic explanations of events on the ball field—for example, "My aim is still good but I don't have the stuff I used to." It turns out that those players who interpreted the game results optimistically lived considerably longer than the others (Seligman, 1986).

There are widespread individual differences in physical as well as psychological reactions to outside pressures—another reason some people get sick while others do not. One study, for example, compared two groups of subjects, all of whom had been exposed to what appeared to be equal amounts of outside pressure (such as job difficulties, loss of a loved one, or financial problems). The group that developed illnesses of one kind or another turned out to have two characteristics: (1) a strong tendency to prolonged anxiety and worry, and (2) a past history of some kind of bodily weakness, such as a vulnerable stomach or heart. The group that did not get sick showed neither of these traits (Hinkle, 1974). Another researcher refined this "vulnerability" model of serious stress-related illness. He reviewed the literature on heart disease and sudden death, then tested his ideas in studies with animals. He concluded that an acute stressor does not usually provoke a potentially deadly illness—for example, heart attack—in healthy people, but it does do so in the person who is vulnerable because of some flaw in the body system involved in the stress response—such as the arteries of the heart (Natelson, 1983).

Are there certain personality "types" who are more or less vulnerable to stress? A study was made of executives of a midwestern utility company, all of whom had experienced various stressful situations, including transfer to a new job in a new city. An attempt was made to compare the personality traits of those who became ill and those who did not. Those who escaped illness turned out to have much more of what the researcher termed "hardiness." For one thing, they were more committed to themselves, their work, their families, and their social roles than were the illness-prone executives. They tended to have an internal locus of control (see Chapter 9) and a sense of being responsible for their own destiny. They made vigorous attempts to face and solve their problems, in contrast to the more passive approach of the illness-prone (Maddi and Kobasa, 1984). Another study—of spouses of families in an urban community—suggests that stress-resistant individuals are more self-confident, energetic, and ambitious. They are also less inclined to keep their feelings of strain bottled up, and enjoy more support from their families (Holahan and Moos, 1985).

Although such studies indicate that active efforts to cope with stressful situations reduce the likelihood of illness, there is also evidence that too intense an effort can be harmful. In assessing the chances of suffering a heart attack, some investigators have found that the greatest risk is among people whose behavior they have termed Type A, people who are typically hard-driving and successful, including numerous corporation executives (National Institutes of Health, 1981). These people have an extremely high achievement motive and believe they can overcome any obstacle if only they try hard enough. They are ambitious and competitive and have a sense of urgency about getting tasks done on time. They usually work to the limit of their endurance and sometimes beyond it. When thwarted, they react with hostility or unexpressed anger—characteristics which appear also to reduce the chances of recovering after a heart attack (Case et al., 1985). The probability of suffering a heart attack, some investigators find, is considerably less among Type B people—who are more easygoing and place less value on success (Friedman and Rosenman, 1981).

Stress and the Immune System

What are the pathways through which stress exerts its potentially harmful effects on health? This is a question of intense practical interest to both psychologists and physicians. Uncovering the hidden links in the chain that begins with stress and ends in illness could reveal new approaches to prevention as well as treatment. The search for these covert connections centers on the *immune system—the body's intricate defense network of organs and tissues that produce protective cells such as lymphocytes (white blood cells)*. The immune response springs into action against various intruders that threaten the organism, from bacteria, viruses, and new growths (such as tumors) to ragweed pollen and bee venom. The immune response is extraordinarily complex and researchers have only begun to penetrate its secrets.

Studies of the impact of stress on the human immune system suggest that the net effect is a suppression of immunity, and, therefore, a vulnerability to becoming ill. One research team, noting that the death of a spouse is associated with increases in illnesses and death among surviving spouses, made a study of men whose wives were dying of cancer. They found that the ability of the men's immune systems to produce protective white blood cells was significantly decreased for two months following the wives' deaths. Even a year later, white blood cell production had not returned to normal levels (Schleifer et al., 1983).

Milder forms of stress may also reduce immune response. A study of medical students showed that the activity of white blood cells that help fend off viral infections such as flu was significantly decreased at final examination time as compared to one month earlier. As shown in Figure 11-9, there was even greater suppression of these protective cells among

Figure 11-9 The body's immune response to stress

Immune system protection (measured by the percentage of intruder cells killed) declined for students as they approached examination time. Protection was especially weak among students high on a scale of stressful life changes as well as on a scale of loneliness (adapted from Kiecolt-Glaser, 1984).

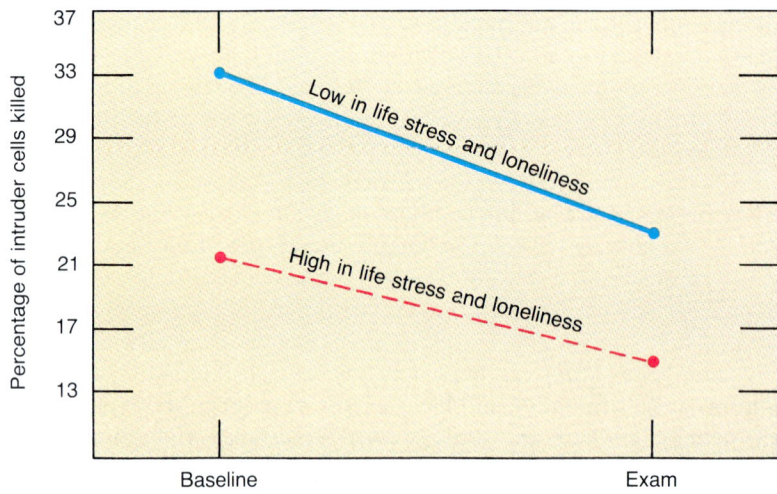

students who were experiencing especially stressful life events and who were also especially lonely. The results suggest that there may be some truth to the popular belief that we are more likely to suffer a bout of flu or the common cold in the wake of a stressful period (Kiecolt-Glaser et al., 1984).

Not all bereaved spouses become ill, of course, nor do all students experiencing examination stress develop colds. Researchers are finding evidence indicating that it is not so much stress itself that influences susceptibility to illness but rather how a person responds to being stressed—in other words, how well or poorly a person copes. For example, another study of protective cell activity was made with subjects who reported experiencing considerable life stress in the previous year. Those reporting many symptoms of anxiety and depression had only one-third the immune level of those reporting few such symptoms. Put another way, "poor coping" was associated with immune suppression, while "good coping" accompanied healthy functioning of the immune system (Locke et al., 1984). As shown in the next section, each of us has a favorite style of coping. But it appears that we can always learn new coping skills that might improve our ability to manage stress. This possibility is discussed in a box on Psychology in Everyday Life titled "Increasing Our Natural Stress Resistance Levels."

Prolonged exposure to an environmental stressor appears to be a significant factor in the development of high blood pressure—a life-threatening illness often considered to be psychosomatic. In one study, researchers examined the effects of living in an Israeli community that had long been a terrorist target, as well as the effects of war, on the blood pressure of pregnant women. Hospital records of blood pressure measured immediately before women gave birth to their babies were gathered for women living in the high-stress, terrorist-target community and for women living in medium- and low-stress Israeli com-

Psychology in Everyday Life
Increasing Our Natural Stress Resistance Levels

Selye believed that we all have our own individual pattern of resistance to damage by stress. The limits to what we can withstand are set by two factors. One is our general ability to adjust to stressful situations, or what Selye called our "supply of adaptation energy." The other is the amount of wear and tear that the weakest part of the body can tolerate without succumbing to psychosomatic illness. (Some people have weak stomachs and are inclined to get ulcers. Some have heart structures that are susceptible to damage.)

Selye believed that both the limiting factors in withstanding damage from stress—adaptation energy and the tolerance level of the weakest part of the body—are the result of heredity, determined by our genes. But this viewpoint may have been colored by his background in biology. Many psychologists hold that tolerance of distress also depends on nurture. They believe that we can learn to cope with anxiety and stress in a constructive way rather than letting them overwhelm and damage us (Miller, 1976).

A recent study offered an impressive example of how learning new coping skills may protect health. The subjects were men with Type A behavior who had already suffered a heart attack. One group received psychological counseling aimed at helping them curb their competitiveness, easily aroused hostility, and sense of urgency. A second group was given the standard advice to heart patients about diet and exercise. Three years later, the group that received standard advice (and presumably continued to cope in their habitual style) had suffered twice as many heart attacks as the group that was encouraged to learn different, more easygoing ways of coping (Friedman and Ulmer, 1985).

There is some evidence, too, that many people can learn to increase their capacity to manage stress by practicing stress-reduction techniques. Biofeedback, described in Chapter 5, helps some individuals control the physical symptoms of stress (Miller, 1983). So does the practice of relaxation exercises, including periods of meditation, which has long been a part of philosophies and religions in Oriental civilizations (Benson et al., 1977; Benson and Proctor, 1984). Even regular exercise can sometimes help reduce the corrosive effects of stress—for example, by strengthening the capacity of the heart and lowering blood pressure (Roviaro, Holmes, and Holmsten, 1984).

Evidently each of us can improve—at least to some degree—the capacity to resist stress that nature has willed us.

Exercise is one avenue for stress reduction.

munities. The results showed that the women living in the high-stress environment had significantly higher blood pressure than those who lived in the low-stress environment, with women living in the medium-stress environment in between. An outbreak of war increased the women's blood pressure in all three places, but the increase was greater in the high- and medium-stress locations than in the low-stress location (Rofé and Goldberg, 1983).

High blood pressure may also arise from an internal "stressor" such as the motive for power, described in Chapter 9. In a remarkable study, men in their early thirties were measured for motivation and for tendencies to gratify or inhibit their motives. Twenty years later, their patterns of blood pressure were measured. The study found that the early tests of motivation were remarkably accurate in predicting which of the subjects would have high blood pressure in later life. By far the greatest number of cases occurred among men who had been found, when in their thirties, to have a strong power motive that they tried to inhibit (McClelland, 1979). Presumably the strong motivation, kept bottled up, produced frequent anger and thus chronic stress. There is evidence that people whose power motive is frustrated are vulnerable to other psychosomatic illnesses as well (McClelland et al., 1980).

Many people with high blood pressure tend to conceal strong feelings of anger and resentment with submissive behavior—and thus avoid open confrontations with others (Weiner, 1982). It has been suggested that this may be one reason high blood pressure is twice as prevalent among blacks—many of whom have resented their status in society but have kept their anger in check—as among whites (Krantz et al., 1981).

The Psychological Effects of Stressful Events

Along with the physical wear and tear of stress, notably psychosomatic illness, go many psychological effects. One study, for example, showed that the most important direct determinants of daily mood—a person's overall sense of feeling well or poorly—were daily stressors and their physical symptoms (Eckenrode, 1984). Indeed the difference between normal behavior and abnormal behavior, which will be the topic of the next chapter, seems to depend in large part on the amount of anxiety and stress that people experience. The amount, in turn, depends on the type of event.

As in the case of physical illness, stressful life changes that are pleasurable—becoming engaged, getting married, being promoted at work—are not as damaging as unpleasant ones. One investigator, reviewing various studies, has identified three kinds of events that have been found to be especially harmful (Rutter, 1983): (1) events that mean the loss of an important relationship—for example, divorce (Paykel, 1978); (2) events that cannot be controlled and therefore produce a feeling of helplessness—for example, a tragic accident; and (3) events that pose a long-term threat because they have lasting consequences—for example, a lingering illness or the loss of a job (Brown and Harris, 1978).

The physical and psychological effects are sometimes difficult to separate. This is especially true in the case of *depression*, a common emotional disturbance that can range in severity from mild to crippling. One investigator has estimated that as many as 30 million Americans can expect to suffer from depression at some time in their lives (Kline, 1974). They may not even know what is wrong—for the milder form of depression does not necessarily cause them to feel unhappy or "blue." Nor do they necessarily appear depressed to their friends. Mild states of depression typically result in feelings of unexplained fatigue and lack of enthusiasm. These victims may have trouble getting any work done and may lose interest in activities that once gave them pleasure. Often they think they must be suffering from some disease, such as mononucleosis, that causes a lack of energy. Yet physical tests show nothing wrong.

There is considerable evidence that depression is related to brain chemistry. In particular, it seems to be associated with low levels of the neurotransmitter noradrenalin or with reduced effectiveness in the way this neurotransmitter operates at the brain's synapses (Schildkraut, 1969). Animal experiments have shown that the amount of noradrenalin in the brain may decline substantially during stress (Weiss, Glazer, and Pohorecky, 1976).

A tendency toward depression, especially in its more extreme forms, appears to be at least partly the result of heredity (Winokur, 1981). Apparently some people are born with a type of brain chemistry that is prone to low levels of noradrenalin and thus depression, just as other people are born with weak stomachs or weak hearts that are vulnerable to damage by stress. At any rate, depression is an emotional disturbance in which the physical and psychological aspects of stress appear closely intermingled. Many other psychological disturbances also seem to represent some form of failure to cope successfully with stressful experiences and their physical and emotional effect (Lazarus, 1978). If we have learned to handle stress and anxiety, our behavior remains within normal bounds. If not, we may slip across the line into abnormal behavior.

SUCCESSFUL COPING AND MENTAL HEALTH

The photographs in Figure 11-10 show that even small children display different reactions to stressful situations. One child makes a strenuous effort to cope. Another quickly gives up.

Adults display an even wider range of differences. They may try to fight off the cause of the stress or throw up their hands. They may succeed in surmounting the stressful situation or they may fail. When they fail, as is sometimes inevitable, they may find a way of reconciling themselves to the situation—or, on the other hand, they may develop physical ailments or a crippling amount of anxiety, anger, or learned helplessness. To a considerable extent, all abnormal behavior is the result of unsuccessful coping. Some sort of maladjustment occurs between the individual and the environment (especially the social environment: family, friends, fellow workers, bosses, teachers). The individual experiences anxiety and stress and wants to relieve them—but does not know how (Lazarus, 1978).

In experiments with animals, successful coping has been found to be an effective defense against stress. In one study, two groups of rats were subjected to the stress of electric shocks. One group was permitted to learn a warning signal. In human terms, they figured out when the shock was coming and could brace for it, and thus in the meantime they had less to fear. The other group received no warning at all. Although both groups were exposed to the same number and intensity of shocks, the animals that had no way of preparing for the shock had decreased brain levels of noradrenalin, which, as noted earlier, is characteristic of people suffering serious depression. But the animals that could cope better—because they knew when to expect a shock and could relax in the meantime—showed an increase in brain noradrenalin (Weiss et al., 1975). It has been suggested that such studies indicate "there may even be some psychological advantage from meeting and successfully coping with a manageable source of stress" (Miller, 1976). A similar experiment studied the effects of controllable and uncontrollable stressors on the immune system. The results showed that the immune functioning of animals able to escape from shock was no different from that of unstressed animals. But the animals subjected to stress they could not control by escaping had depressed immune responses (Laudenslager and Ryan, 1983).

Assertive Coping: From Flat Tires to Captivity

To constructive attempts to deal with anxiety and stress, some psychologists have applied the term *assertive coping*. Often this response takes the form of direct attempts to change the stressful situation. Whether the stressor is as mundane as a flat tire that will make us late for an appointment, as challenging as school difficulties, or as harrowing as captivity by cruel enemies, there is often some way we can take steps to prevail over our predica-

Figure 11-10 To cope or not to cope?

These two 13-month-olds, photographed in a psychology laboratory, react in very different ways to a fence that separates them from mother and toys. The child above makes an active effort to cope with the situation by first trying to climb the fence, then struggling to squeeze around it. The child below sees no possible solution and bursts into tears.

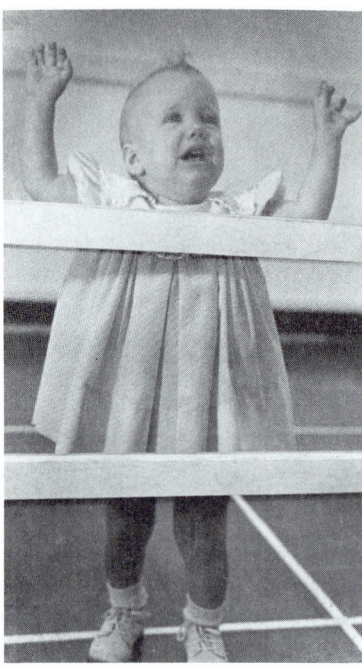

ment. A motorist frustrated by a flat tire can get busy changing it or find a phone to seek help. A student who wants to be an engineer but is weak in certain areas of mathematics can find a tutor to help master them. Even prisoners of war and civilians seized as hostages—brutally stripped of every physical and psychological means of defending themselves—have found ways to change their dire situation.

Americans taken prisoner during the war in Vietnam coped assertively for years with a situation more stress-laden than most of us can imagine. Though their captors ordered them not to talk to each other, and punished them for violations, they developed a secret communications system—a kind of mutual support network—in which taps on the wall, floor, or ceiling stood for letters of the alphabet. Even in solitary confinement, they developed some effective methods of assertive coping. Some adopted a program of physical exercise. Others passed the time by inventing new games, or by memorizing stories. A few kept busy by keeping a careful census of the insects in their cells. Without toothbrushes to preserve their teeth they made picks of bamboo sticks and wire and dental floss out of threads of their clothing or blankets. Similarly bold coping techniques were used by the 52 American hostages held for 14 months in Iran (Segal, 1986). As one of them, Ambassador Bruce Laingen, said after his release: "We're like tea bags. We don't know our own strength until we get into hot water."

Three Approaches for Dealing with Stressful Situations

Most of the time, most of us confront only the stressors of everyday life. For example, let us say that we are experiencing frustration. One of our motives has been blocked. We feel bad about the situation. We may even suffer anger so intense that it amounts to rage and sets the stomach churning. Yet, if we can keep our wits about us, perhaps we can somehow manage to overcome the obstacle. We can face up to the difficulty and try to find some way through or around it. We can regard the situation as an exercise in problem solving and get busy seeking the answer, which may take one of the following three forms:

1. Changing the Environment   Even a hungry animal, barred from getting food by a closed door, often tries to outwit its environment by gnawing through the barrier. A motorist frustrated by a flat tire can get busy changing it or try to find a phone and seek help. A student who wants to be an accountant but is weak in certain areas of mathematics can tackle these subjects and try to master them. Couples frustrated by a bad marriage can engage in assertive coping by going to a marriage counselor—or, if necessary, by ending the marriage.

Assertive coping with the environment consists in a meaningful attempt to change the situation in a constructive way that has a reasonable chance of success. Even though the attempt may fail, the effort itself seems to combat the damaging effects of stress. One study analyzed the effect on pilots and crews of the stressors of routine military flight. Preflight measurements of cortisol, a stress hormone, were found to be the same for both groups. However, postflight levels were higher in crew members whose activities only indirectly affected the safety of the flight (radio operators, navigators) than they were in pilots—those with their hands literally on the controls of the aircraft. It is likely that the pilots experienced less stress than the crew because they, unlike the crew, were in a position to cope directly with the psychologically threatening environment of flight (Leedy and Wilson, 1985).

2. Changing Our Own Behavior   In many cases, the stress we suffer comes not so much from the environment as from our own behavior. Failure in college can result from inattention in class or insufficient study. Social unpopularity may reflect a grumpy, timid, or over-

Being a passenger is often more stressful than being the pilot—who is in control.

aggressive approach to other people. (The way people's behavior toward us is largely determined by our own actions is one of the concerns of Chapter 16.)

Thus at times the only effective way to reduce stress is to change our own behavior. For example, people with financial problems often can escape only by setting up a strict budget and resisting their urge to spend (Ilfeld, 1980). The couple who undertake marriage counseling will probably find that both partners have to make adjustments in the ways they act toward each other. Indeed people who seek counseling or therapy of any kind are in effect asking for help in changing their own behavior and attitudes.

Numerous investigators have found that seeking the psychological support of others—for example, friends, relatives, associates—is one of the most effective ways for people to relieve stress and escape its damaging consequences (Greenblatt, Becerra, and Serafetinides, 1982). Confiding in others does not come easily to every person, of course, and men in particular may have to change habitual behavior in this regard in order to gain the advantage it brings. Under extreme duress, the support gained through friendships can mean survival itself. This was true, for example, even for some who survived the incredibly hideous conditions of Nazi concentration camps during the Second World War (Schmolling, 1984).

3. Managing the Internal Wear and Tear   Sometimes a stressful situation persists no matter how hard we try to change the environment or our own behavior. During severe economic recessions many people continue to suffer the strains of unemployment and lack of money no matter how hard they try or how far they travel in search of a job. Efforts to cope with the situation by changing their own behavior—such as training themselves for a new line of work—may fail. A person may also be helpless to do anything about such sources of stress as the illness of a family member, the lack of talent for a chosen career, or immovable social, sexual, or racial prejudice.

In situations of genuine helplessness—not learned helplessness—there is just no escape from the source of stress. The only form assertive coping can take is an effort to control the effects. We must somehow keep the physical and emotional wear and tear within bounds, so that they do not destroy us physically or psychologically. There is no magic formula for this kind of coping, but many people have succeeded at it—even those enduring major personal tragedies, or the hundreds of thousands of people who somehow kept their sanity and spirit in the horror of concentration camp captivity. One characteristic of those who keep from being overwhelmed is that they avoid blaming themselves for their misfortune. Constant self-recrimination can lead to helplessness, limiting our capacity to prevail over stress (Segal, 1986). For example, crime victims who somehow feel partly responsible for their fate do not cope as well as those who are free of self-blame (Bard and Sangrey, 1986). The same seems to be true of those enduring racial prejudice (Neff, 1985).

As the three points discussed above indicate, a person's ability to deal constructively with stressful events is not a unitary trait. "The essence of stress, coping, and adaptation is change," according to two researchers who have explored the issue (Folkman and Lazarus, 1985). The impact of the event itself, they point out, usually takes place in stages: anticipation, occurrence, and aftermath. Moreover, emotional reactions as well as efforts to cope as the stressful event unfolds are parts of a complex, dynamic process.

Consider, for example, the case of students informed of the date of an examination. They may experience seemingly contradictory emotions—first anxiety, then anger, then frustration, then exhilaration. In a similarly dynamic fashion, they may at first deny the importance of the event, then strive to meet the problem head-on. As the process unfolds, the students may use different and changing combinations of assertive coping tactics. For example, they may turn from seeking the support of others to diligent study. At any given stage of the process, some will be more successful than others, of course—reflecting both individual differences in cognitive appraisal of the stressful episode and in coping ability (Folkman and Lazarus, 1985).

Mental Health, Adjustment, and the Normal Personality

In talking about managing the internal effects, we are really discussing what is often called *mental health*. It is difficult even to define mental health, much less offer suggestions for attaining it. Perhaps it consists, as one psychologist has suggested, in harmony among physical well-being, effective functioning as a member of society, and a high level of personal morale (or sense of self-worth and self-reliance). Preserving mental health is possible even in the most difficult situations because the anxiety and stress we experience depend not so much on what the environment does to us as on the way we view ourselves and our relations to the environment (Lazarus, 1978). In exactly the same situation, a person with low self-esteem and an external locus of control suffers far more than a person with a positive self-image and an internal locus of control.

Equally difficult to arrive at is a definition of normal personality and normal behavior. In attempting to do so, psychologists for many years emphasized the word *adjustment*. Normal personality traits, it was generally believed, are those that help people adjust to the environment and to other people—in other words, to accept the realities of the physical world and of society and to behave in harmony with them. This description of the normal personality still persists to some extent. Many colleges even offer a course called the psychology of adjustment.

In recent years, however, many psychologists have come to believe that adjustment is too passive and negative a term, implying a self-effacing conformity to what other people are thinking and doing. Some have decided that adjustment, if taken to mean a more or less unquestioning acceptance of some aspects of society—such as mass killings in warfare and the spending of human resources on military equipment rather than on education—is itself abnormal (Laing, 1960).

Thus the emphasis has shifted. Growing numbers of psychologists now regard normal behavior not as mere adjustment but as an active effort to cope with the problems of life and achieve some kind of honest self-awareness, independence, and fulfillment. As was mentioned in Chapter 10, Maslow has suggested the term self-actualization. Other psy-

Psychology in Everyday Life
What Does Being Normal Mean?

Adding the term mental health to the English language—and its equivalent to languages around the world—has produced some unfortunate side effects. The term has often been misinterpreted and exaggerated, as have been the goals of Sigmund Freud and the newer schools of psychotherapy. Many people are intimidated by the concepts of mental health and the normal personality, which they see as demanding perfection beyond the reach of most ordinary mortals. They are vaguely dissatisfied because they worry that they—and life itself—should be far better than they are.

Actually, psychology's message to society is reassuring rather than frightening. Asked to describe the normal personality, most psychologists would probably agree on the following six points. Note especially the first of them.

1. Being normal does not mean being perfect. Everybody gets angry, has hostile thoughts, gets greedy at times, and does foolish things. Everybody encounters frustrations and conflicts and experiences anxiety and stress. Nobody can cope in a completely successful manner at all times. We can only do our best—which probably means to function more or less satisfactorily despite the inevitable problems of the human condition.

2. Normal people are realistic. They have learned not to expect perfection, either in themselves or in others. They are aware of their own limitations and accept the fact that other people also have limitations. Since they do not have unduly grandiose expectations, they are not surprised or overly ashamed or angry when they themselves fail or when others fail them.

3. Normal people can "roll with the punches." They may be unhappy at times over the state of the world or over personal disappointments, but they manage to live with these situations. They are confident of their ability to cope with whatever situations may arise—not necessarily as well as they would like, but at least after a fashion. They are flexible and can change their plans. Indeed according to Selye, the secret of a healthy

chologists have defined normal people as those who maintain a stable sense of identity (Erikson, 1968)—or who possess the inner freedom to make their own decisions rather than yielding to pressures from the environment and from other people (Bühler, 1968). Some of the current thinking about being normal is summarized in a box on Psychology in Everyday Life titled "What Does Being Normal Mean?"

DEFENSE MECHANISMS AND OTHER PROBLEMATIC FORMS OF COPING

Besides assertive coping, people devise many other ways of trying to handle anxiety and stress. These other ways, by and large, are not nearly so effective. They may serve as stopgaps in an emergency. They may even be practiced over long periods, as a sort of life strategy, with some success and without serious damage. But they are questionable at best—and, when carried to extremes, they carry a serious risk. They lie in a sort of gray area between successful coping and downright failure to cope—or, in other words, between normal and abnormal behavior.

life is to live to the full extent of our capabilities, but not to put undue strain on ourselves. The trick, he says, is to "determine our optimum speed of living, by trying various speeds and finding out which one is most agreeable" (Selye, 1976). If we find the pace damaging, we can pull back. If we thrive on it, we can venture a little further.

4. Normal people possess a certain amount of enthusiasm and spontaneity. They find things to do that give them pleasure, whether working productively or watching a sunset.

5. Normal people have a good deal of independence. They do not shift, like a weather vane, with every change in the wind, either in society as a whole or among their associates. They do not mind being alone. Indeed they enjoy a certain amount of privacy.

6. Normal people are capable of feeling and showing affection and of establishing close relationships with others—not necessarily many others, but a chosen few. They can love and be loved.

Living with a sense of fulfillment.

Prominent among them are certain devices, first described by Sigmund Freud, called *defense mechanisms*. Freud regarded these mechanisms as unconscious psychological processes, mental or symbolic, that people develop to relieve anxiety. Unlike assertive coping, they are not deliberate efforts to change the environment or one's own behavior or to deal realistically with anxiety and stress. All defense mechanisms are based to some degree on self-deception and distortion of reality. Yet everybody adopts some of them at one time or another. They are not necessarily harmful. But psychotic people often display them in exaggerated form.

Rationalization

One defense mechanism has been recognized ever since Aesop started the phrase sour grapes with his fable about the fox. (The fox, unable to reach an inviting cluster of grapes, consoled itself by deciding they would have been sour anyway.) Freud's name for this defense mechanism is *rationalization*—an attempt to deal with stressful situations by claiming that they never really occurred.

People often resort to rationalization to explain away their frustrations. A man, rejected by a woman, convinces himself that she was not nearly so attractive or interesting as he had supposed. A woman, turned down when applying for employment, convinces herself that the job was not really worth having.

People also use rationalization to reduce the anxiety caused by conflicts between motives and inner standards. A mother's real reason for keeping her daughter from dating may be jealousy, a motive of which her conscience disapproves. She rationalizes by claiming she is acting for the daughter's own good. A student cheats on an examination and rationalizes by claiming that everybody cheats.

Repression

Some people who suffer anxiety and stress over their motives simply try to banish the motives from their conscious thoughts—to the point where they seem to be totally unaware of their desires. This defense mechanism is called *repression*. People who at one time suffered severe anxiety and stress over sexual motives may repress these motives so thoroughly that they no longer seem to be aware of any sexual feelings or desires at all. Other people seem oblivious to the fact that they have any desires for dependency or hostility. Some cases of *amnesia*, or loss of memory, appear to be exaggerated forms of repression.

Sublimation

A motive that causes anxiety may also be transformed unconsciously into a different but related motive that is more acceptable to society and to oneself. This defense mechanism is known as *sublimation*, a process that enables a "shameful" motive to find expression in a more noble form. Freud believed that works of art are often the result of sublimation—that the Shakespeares and Michelangelos of the world may very well have channeled forbidden sexual urges into artistic creativity. Similarly, Freud believed that people may sublimate their urges toward cruelty into a socially approved desire to become surgeons, prosecuting attorneys, or even teachers with the authority to discipline the young.

Identification

Another mechanism for relieving anxiety is to take on the virtues of some admired person or group that seems free of such anxiety. This process is called *identification*. An example would be a man, anxious about his own lack of courage, who identifies with a brave movie hero or a group of mountain climbers so that he can believe he too possesses their daring. A woman anxious about her lack of social acceptance may identify with a popular roommate.

In a more complex form, identification may be established with a figure of authority who is resented and feared. Thus a young man may defend himself against the anxiety aroused by hostile feelings toward his boss by identifying with the boss. He may imitate the boss's mannerisms and express the same opinions, thus persuading himself that he possesses the same power. This type of identification may also be made with a group. Young people, anxious about their feelings of envy and hostility toward an exclusive clique, may identify with the group and adopt its standards. A study of prisoners in German concentration camps during the Second World War showed that some of them imitated the characteristics of the very guards from whose brutality they were suffering (Bettelheim, 1943).

Reaction Formation

People who display a trait to excess—that is, in an exaggerated form that hardly seems called for by the circumstances—may be using the defense mechanism called *reaction*

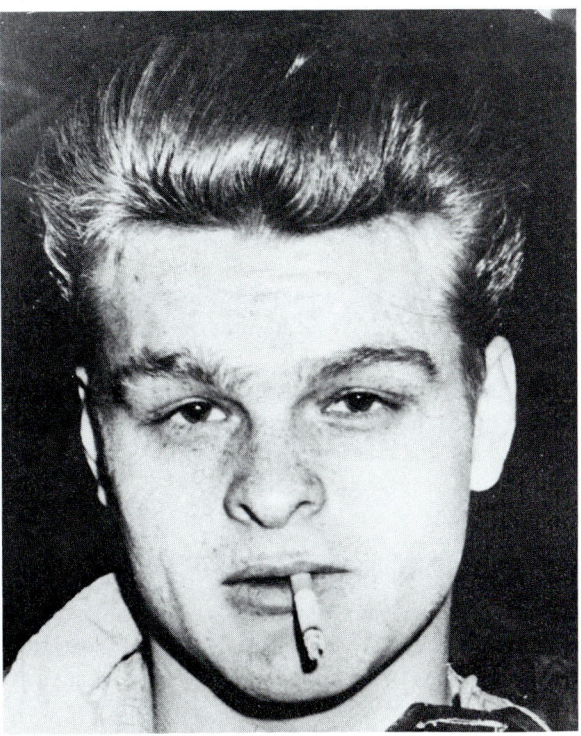

Mass murderer Charles Starkweather in a James Dean pose.

James Dean, the rebellious movie star with whom Charles Starkweather so completely identified.

formation. They are pretending to possess motives that are the exact opposite of the real motives that are causing their anxiety. For example, a man appears to be the soul of politeness. He is constantly holding doors for other people, saying "Yes, sir," and "Yes, ma'am," always smiling, agreeable, and apologetic for his mistakes. This exaggerated politeness and concern for others may simply be a defense mechanism he has adopted to conceal the fact that he has hostile motives and that his hostility is making him anxious. A woman who dresses in a provocative manner and is constantly flirting and telling risqué stories may be concealing her sexual inhibitions and fear of being unattractive.

Projection

The woman who claims that everybody is dishonest and the man who is convinced of the immorality of the younger generation may have reached their conclusions through honest examination of the evidence. On the other hand, they may be exhibiting another defense mechanism called *projection*, in which people foist off or project onto other people motives or thoughts of their own that cause them anxiety. The woman who talks too much about dishonesty may be concealing her own strong tendencies toward dishonesty. The man who talks too much about the immorality of young people may be concealing his own promiscuity.

Projection often plays a part in disagreements between the sexes. Many women complain that their men are distant and remote, although a disinterested observer may clearly see that it is the women who are withdrawn and inaccessible. Men who are torn by sexual conflicts and urges toward infidelity may falsely accuse their partners of being unfaithful. A marriage counselor who hears accusations by one partner of unacceptable behavior or improper motives always looks for the possibility that the complaints represent projection rather than truth. Projection is one of the most powerful and dangerous of the defense mechanisms. It works very effectively to reduce anxiety, but it does so at the risk of a completely distorted view of the truth about oneself and others.

The Pro and Con of Defense Mechanisms

The six defense mechanisms just discussed are the most common and easily recognizable. There are others—among them *denial*, in which a person refuses altogether to accept reality in order to dispel anxiety. (How many cigarette smokers, for example, successfully block out the fact that their habit can cause serious disease?) We humans are remarkably ingenious at finding new ways to delude ourselves. In one way or another, we persuade ourselves that we did not really want the goals we cannot achieve, that our motives are completely admirable, that we are living up to our own and society's standards, that our disappointments are somehow bearable, and that a threatening situation is really no threat at all.

Because anxiety and stress are so common, all of us use defense mechanisms from time to time—either those that have been mentioned or others of our own invention. Though these defense mechanisms are usually irrational, they often serve a useful purpose. They may help us through crises that would otherwise overwhelm and disable us. If nothing else, they may gain us time in which we can gather the strength, maturity, and knowledge needed to cope more realistically and constructively with our anxiety and stress. This is often true, for example, of cancer patients who practice denial until they are emotionally ready to face up to their bleak prognosis (Breznitz, 1983). Only in extreme cases does the use of defense mechanisms slip over into the realm of abnormal psychology.

Aggression in Response to Anxiety and Stress

Other reactions to anxiety and stress also lie near the borderline between normal and abnormal behavior. One of the most common is *aggression*, which is often produced by frustration. Children frustrated by other children who take their toys often get angry and strike out with their fists. Frustrated adults may kick at a tire that has gone flat, break an offending golf club, hit a tennis ball into the next county, or shout insults to a driver who has cut them off. This kind of behavior, aimed specifically at the source of the frustration, is called *direct aggression*.

When a direct attack on the source of frustration is impossible, people may demonstrate *displaced aggression* and vent their emotions on an innocent bystander. A man angry at a powerful and overdemanding boss goes home and behaves aggressively toward his wife and children. (In everyday language, he uses them as scapegoats.) A little girl angry at her parents takes out her aggression on a smaller child or on a pet. Scapegoating accounts for a great deal of the prejudice displayed against minority groups and foreigners. The prime example occurred when Hitler made the Jews scapegoats, blaming them for all the frustrations and conflicts that Germany was suffering in a time of economic and political tension.

Withdrawal and Apathy

Some individuals react to difficult situations by *withdrawal*. To avoid further anxiety and stress, they shun close contacts with other people or any attempt to gratify their motives. We say of such people that they have "retreated into a shell" or that they have "quit trying."

"Well, you can just rebuild the fort later, Harold . . . Phyllis and Shirley are coming over and I'll need the cushions."

The Far Side © 1986 Universal Press Syndicate. Reprinted with permission. All rights reserved.

Rather than trying to cope assertively with their difficulties, they choose to escape by narrowing the horizons of their lives—often in drastic and self-limiting ways.

In similar fashion, some people display *apathy*. They are sad and listless, seem to lose all interest in what happens to them, and have a difficult time finding energy for the ordinary chores of life.

Regression

Many parents have described how their children, faced with frustration, begin to behave in a manner more appropriate to younger levels of development. The arrival of a new and competing sibling can be the occasion for a child already in the first grade to begin wetting the bed, for example, or sucking the thumb. This type of behavior—retreating toward activities that usually characterize a lower level of maturity—is called *regression*.

Displays of regression as a reaction to frustration and stress are common. Frustrated adults may regress to such childish behavior as weeping or throwing temper tantrums. People who are victims of extreme emotional disturbance sometimes display striking degrees of regression, as illustrated in Figure 11-11. They are among the types of people discussed in the next chapter—which describes in detail what happens when efforts to cope fail, and the human personality falls apart.

Defense Mechanisms and Other Problematic Forms of Coping

Figure 11-11 A case of regression.
The girl at the left, a 17-year-old psychiatric patient, found the old photograph of herself in the center, taken when she was 5. She then cut her hair and made every attempt to look as she had at 5, as at the right (Masserman, 1961).

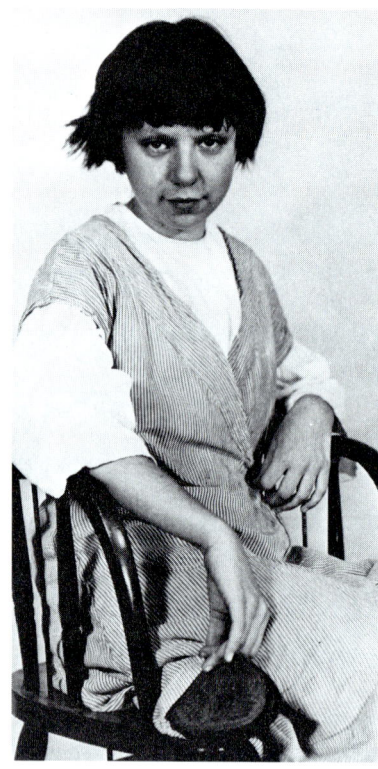

SUMMARY

How anxiety affects behavior

1. *Anxiety* is a vague, unpleasant feeling accompanied by a premonition that something undesirable is about to happen.
2. Anxiety is closely related to motives, especially conflicts between motives and frustration of the motive for certainty.
3. *Frustration* is the blocking of motive satisfaction by some kind of obstacle. The obstacles may be: (a) physical obstacles, (b) social circumstances, (c) personal shortcomings, or (d) conflict.
4. A *conflict* is the simultaneous arousal of two or more incompatible motives, resulting in unpleasant emotions.
5. Types of conflict are: (a) *approach-approach* (seeking two desirable goals), (b) *avoidance-avoidance* (seeking to prevent two undesirable alternatives), (c) *approach-avoidance* (over

a goal that will have both pleasant and unpleasant aspects), and (d) *double approach-avoidance* (when we are torn between two goals that both have some desirable and some undesirable aspects).

6. Any situation clouded with uncertainty has a built-in potential for creating anxiety.

7. People who display anxiety in many different situations are victims of *general anxiety*. Those who display it in some particular situation but not at other times have *specific anxiety*. A specific type common among college students is *test anxiety*. Some anxieties—for example about crime—can substantially affect social behavior.

8. People high in anxiety do better than others at simple learning tasks but more poorly at difficult learning tasks. In college, anxiety does not seem to affect the grades of students of either highest or lowest learning ability. Among students of in-between ability, those with high anxiety make significantly lower grades than those with low anxiety.

9. In their approach to life, people high in anxiety tend either to be very conservative and avoid risks or to "go for broke." People low in anxiety tend toward the middle-range risks that are most likely to lead to success in the long run.

Stress and its repercussions in the body and mind

10. *Stress* is the body's reaction to anything that threatens to damage the organism—from a disease germ to intense and prolonged emotion.

11. The damaging potential of stress was demonstrated by Hans Selye in experiments with animals subjected to small doses of poison. Selye found that the body automatically tries to defend itself in ways that include striking changes in activity of the endocrine glands, especially the adrenals. After a time the body seems to adapt and the glands return to normal. If the stressful conditions continue, however, the recovery proves to be only temporary and the animal dies—killed by an excess of hormones the body produced in its own defense. This sequence of events is called the *general adaptation syndrome*.

12. The bodily changes described by Selye also seem to occur in human beings, often as part of the stress caused by frustration, conflict, or any prolonged emotional upset. They often take the form of *psychosomatic illnesses*, meaning bodily ailments that stem at least in part from mental and emotional causes.

13. A potent predictor of future illness is the repeated strains of everyday life. Other reasons why some people get sick and some do not can be attributed to differences in: (a) physical health, (b) attitudes toward life events, and (c) interpretations of any given stressful event.

14. The *immune system* is the body's intricate defense network of organs and tissues that produce cells such as lymphocytes (white blood cells). Studies of the impact of stress on the human immune system suggest that the net effect is a depression of immunity, and, therefore, a vulnerability to becoming ill.

15. Three kinds of stressful events are especially damaging psychologically: (a) the loss of an important relationship, (b) uncontrollable events, and (c) events that pose long-term threats.

16. The psychological effects of stress include *depression*. This appears to be associated with low levels or reduced effectiveness of the brain's supply of the neurotransmitter noradrenalin, which apparently can occur during stress.

Successful coping and mental health

17. *Assertive coping* is an effective defense against stress. It may take three forms: (a) an attempt to change the environment and relieve the stressful situation, (b) changing one's own behavior, or (c) keeping the emotional and physical wear and tear within bounds.
18. Assertive coping is one key to *normal behavior*, which many psychologists define in terms of honest self-awareness, independence, fulfillment, a stable sense of identity, and inner freedom.

Defense mechanisms and other problematic forms of coping

19. Among questionable forms of coping are the *defense mechanisms* described by Freud. These are unconscious psychological processes, mental or symbolic. They include: (a) rationalization, (b) repression, (c) sublimation, (d) identification, (e) reaction formation, (f) projection, and (g) denial.
20. Other questionable reactions to anxiety and stress include: (a) direct aggression, (b) displaced aggression, (c) withdrawal or apathy, and (d) regression.

IMPORTANT TERMS

adjustment
aggression
amnesia
anxiety
apathy
approach-approach conflict
approach-avoidance conflict
avoidance-avoidance conflict
assertive coping
conflict
coping
defense mechanism
denial
depression
direct aggression
displaced aggression
double approach-avoidance conflict
frustration
general adaptation syndrome

general anxiety
identification
immune system
mental health
normal behavior
placebo effect
projection
psychosomatic illness
rationalization
reaction formation
regression
repression
specific anxiety
stress
stressor
sublimation
syndrome
test anxiety
withdrawal

RECOMMENDED READING

Christie, M., and Mellett, P. *Foundations of psychosomatics*. New York: Wiley, 1981.
Elliot, G. R., and Eisdorfer, C., eds. *Stress and human health*. New York: Springer Verlag, 1982.

Krohne, H. W., and Laux, L., eds. *Achievement, stress, and anxiety.* Washington, D.C.: Hemisphere, 1982.
Levine, S., and Ursin, H. *Coping and health.* New York: Plenum, 1980.
Neufeld, R. W. J., ed. *Psychological stress and psychopathology.* New York: McGraw-Hill, 1982.
Sarason, I. G., Spielberger, C. D., and Milgram, N. A., eds. *Stress and anxiety,* Vol. 8. Washington, D.C.: Hemisphere, 1982.
Steptoe, A. *Psychological factors in cardiovascular disorders.* New York: Academic Press, 1981.
Tuma, A. H., and Maser, J. D. *Anxiety and the anxiety disorders.* Hillsdale, N.J.: Erlbaum Associates, 1985.

CHAPTER

12

ABNORMAL PERSONALITY AND BEHAVIOR

THE NATURE AND SCOPE OF ABNORMAL BEHAVIOR   428

What characterizes the abnormal personality?
How many people have a mental disorder?
The cost—economic and emotional

THE ROOTS AND VARIETIES OF ABNORMAL BEHAVIOR   431

Biological factors
Psychological factors
Environmental factors
Forms and shades of abnormality

SCHIZOPHRENIA: RARE BUT DEVASTATING   435

Symptoms of schizophrenia
Searching for schizophrenia's roots

AFFECTIVE DISORDERS: DISTURBANCES OF MOOD   438

Major depression: the darkest shade of blue
Suicide and the death of hope
Manic-depressive illness: too high, too low
Biological roots of affective disorders
Why are women more often depressed than men?

ANXIETY DISORDERS   441

Generalized anxiety disorder
Panic disorder
Obsessive-compulsive disorder

PERSONALITY DISORDERS: MORE DISTURBING THAN DISTURBED   446

Antisocial personality: reckless and ruthless
Paranoid personality: always suspicious, always threatened
Narcissistic personality: loving the face in the mirror

SUBSTANCE ABUSE: THE PERILOUS PLEASURES OF ALCOHOL AND DRUGS   450

Becoming dependent
Portrait of an alcoholic
From cooling out to blacking out
Men, women, and drinking
Causes of alcoholism
Using drugs to alter how we feel
How drug users become drug abusers
Portrait of a heroin addict

SUMMARY   459

IMPORTANT TERMS   460

RECOMMENDED READINGS   461

PSYCHOLOGY IN EVERYDAY LIFE

Is it always just in the mind?   433
Depression in childhood: how vulnerable are the young?   442
Emotional scars that linger   444
Heavy drinking, heavy price   453

Not long ago, a psychology student immersed in a chapter like this one approached her professor anxiously. "I honestly think I'm mentally ill," she said in a panic. "I'm beginning to see myself on almost every page."

The student's reaction was hardly unique. You may also find this chapter disturbing. You may feel that some of the descriptions of emotional problems are distressingly familiar, and by the time you finish reading the chapter, you, too, might conclude that you are the victim of a full-blown mental disorder. Why might this occur?

There are two reasons. First, as you study the causes of mental disorders, you will probably find at least some of them in your own background. Most people, if you asked them to search their past for experiences that could have led to a psychological collapse, would have little trouble doing so. Second, you probably have in fact experienced to some degree a number of the symptoms you will be reading about. So have most of us. It is a rare person indeed who has not discovered how it feels to become anxious or depressed, how easy it is to feel physically ill when we are in conflict, or how we can become so frustrated and angry that the whole world seems to be against us.

Yet, while all of us may have had some of the same experiences and symptoms as persons clearly identified as abnormal, most of us go through life without ever suffering an actual breakdown in psychological functioning. The task of identifying that breaking point—where the human personality goes significantly awry—is among the most challenging in the field of psychology.

THE NATURE AND SCOPE OF ABNORMAL BEHAVIOR

The wild-eyed, unkempt man on the street corner who constantly mumbles to himself and insists he is Jesus is clearly acting strange. So, too, is the woman who is so deeply depressed that she has withdrawn from the world and no longer even leaves her bed in the morning to get dressed or eat. Psychologists would not hesitate to describe their behavior as abnormal. Nor would psychologists hesitate to describe as distinctly normal people who are functioning at the peak of their powers and feeling good about themselves and others. Most people, however, fall well between these two extremes—in the gray area between what is clearly normal and what is not. It is virtually impossible, therefore, to arrive at an absolute definition of *abnormal behavior.*

Nevertheless, a working definition needs to be established. It would be impossible to study abnormal psychology without setting at least some standards for abnormal behavior—and for differentiating it from the normal.

What Characterizes the Abnormal Personality?

Is it abnormal to believe in witches? It was not considered so by the American colonists. Is it abnormal for a young woman to faint from the excitement of attending a dance or the embarrassment of hearing profanity? It was not considered so in Victorian England. Is it abnormal to turn angry and suspicious every time you encounter disappointment and frustration? Among a group of New Guinea natives called the Kaluli, such responses are the accepted norm (Schieffelin, 1985). Is suicide abnormal? To most Americans, it may seem the ultimate in abnormality. Yet in East Asia a Buddhist priest who commits suicide as a form of political protest is regarded as exhibiting strength of character rather than abnormality.

In some hunter-gatherer societies, people spend as little as ten hours per week earning a livelihood. In our society would such behavior seem normal?

From a statistical viewpoint, behavior can be called abnormal if it is uncommon and unusual—as popular terminology recognizes by referring to it as "odd." But this is not the whole story, for even unusual forms of behavior are not generally called abnormal unless they are regarded as undesirable by the particular society in which they occur. In our own society, the habit of working 18 hours a day is probably rarer than heroin addiction. Yet an 18-hour workday is generally considered admirable or at least acceptable and is therefore called normal. Heroin addiction is considered undesirable and therefore called abnormal.

Since personal happiness is highly valued in the United States, people who are happy are generally regarded as being free of any abnormality. Though this criterion is widely accepted, there are some notable exceptions. Many people who commit vicious acts that could hardly be considered normal—such as wartime atrocities and mass murders in peacetime—seem to be perfectly happy.

In general, however, a useful working definition of abnormal behavior embraces the three points that have been mentioned. An abnormal personality trait or type of behavior is: (1) statistically unusual, (2) considered undesirable by most people, and (3) a source of unhappiness to the person who possesses or displays it. It must be admitted that the definition is not very satisfactory from a scientific point of view and would not be accepted enthusiastically by many psychologists—chiefly on the ground that it sets up rigid standards that enable our society to label as abnormal anybody whose behavior is disliked or considered disruptive, whether or not that behavior can be judged abnormal by any scientific measure.

Most mental disorders are now characterized by the pattern, severity, and duration of clusters of behavioral symptoms and by the levels of impairment they produce in people's lives. But, as described later in this chapter, efforts are under way also to develop additional criteria—such as tests of blood or brain activity—that can aid in determining when someone is mentally ill (Feinberg and Carroll, 1984).

How Many People Have a Mental Disorder?

One way of estimating the extent of abnormal behavior is to identify how many people are actually diagnosed as having a mental disorder. The task is not easy. Mental disorders affect people of all ages, races, and walks of life. Moreover, there are many people who are not easily recognized as having a mental disorder. They may appear to get along in school, hold jobs, and conduct more or less successful family and social relationships. But their chronic feelings of anxiety or depression significantly interfere with their well-being and effectiveness. Others are charming and even popular, but they deeply distrust others, constantly manipulate them, and are even sadistic and abusive in private. Still others, despite their apparent normality, have secret lives that desperately depend on drugs or alcohol.

A recent national survey attempted to overcome many such problems of estimating prevalence. It was based on sampling many households in selected locations around the country, using carefully constructed interviews that permitted rough diagnoses to be made. The results, shown in Figure 12-1, showed that about 20 percent of the U.S. population suffers from a diagnosable mental disorder during a six-month period (Myers et al., 1984). The highest rates of most disorders appear to occur in the prime of life—between 25 and 44 years of age (Freedman, 1984).

Figure 12-1 The scope of mental disorder

As shown here, a mental disorder of some kind appears to be the fate of one out of every five Americans (Myers et al., 1984).

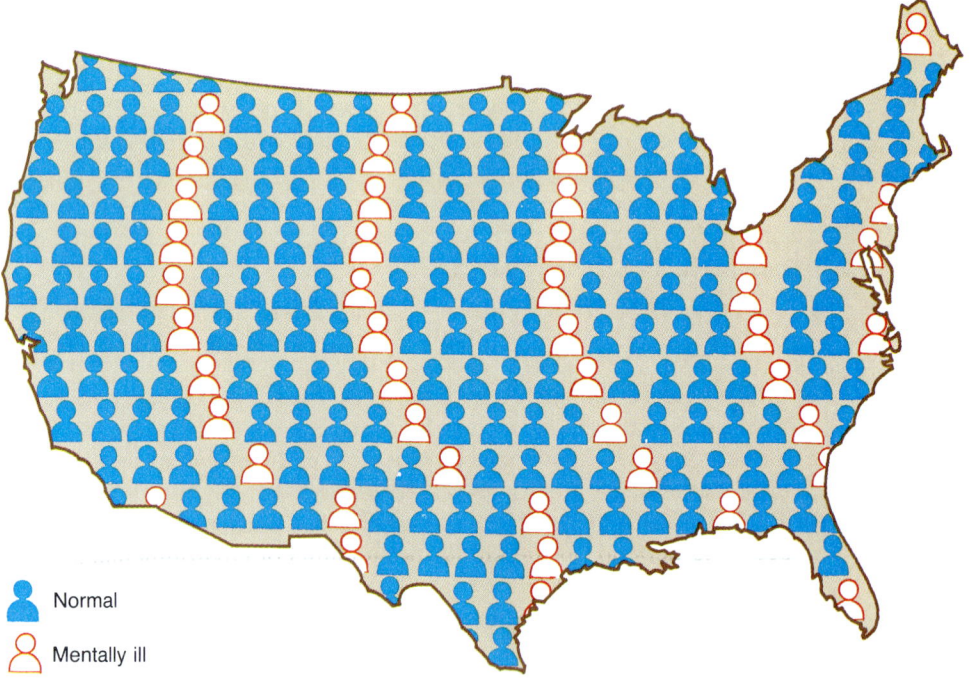

A large portion of our homeless population is composed of former mental patients.

The Cost—Economic and Emotional

The direct economic cost of caring for the mentally ill has been estimated at close to $20 billion a year (Frank and Kamlet, 1985). The cost in lost income and productivity is at least 1.5 times more. These figures portray the enormous financial toll exacted on society by emotional disorders.

No statistical data, however, can portray the full impact of mental disorders in human terms. Anyone who has actually experienced periods of intense anxiety or depression knows how disabling they can be and how much agony they can cause. Patients in the throes of terminal-cancer pain who also had a history of severe depression were asked to compare the two. Most reported that the physical pain was more bearable—and far preferable to the psychological pain of their mental illness (Jamison, 1982).

THE ROOTS AND VARIETIES OF ABNORMAL BEHAVIOR

The origins of abnormal behavior vary to some degree from one type of disorder to another. But in general, people seem to have a "breaking point" at which they lose their psychological balance. That fragile point varies enormously from person to person. It seems to depend on the kinds and amounts of environmental stressors people face and their abilities to handle them. These abilities, in turn, depend on their biological makeup, their personalities, the kinds of support they get from other people, and their learned styles of coping.

Some people seem to have biological vulnerabilities so great that they develop mental disorders seemingly without any pressure from external stressors. Others, as described in the previous chapter, seem practically invulnerable, able to endure and triumph over conditions that would break the minds and spirits of most people. Still others, for reasons not yet clear, seem to develop personalities that are enduringly abnormal.

Biological Factors

Wide individual differences exist in glandular activity and sensitivity of the autonomic nervous system—perhaps also in the activity of the brain centers concerned with emotion. These individual differences may incline one person to be much more easily aroused and more intensely emotional than another. Thus some people, because of their inherited biological makeup, probably experience a great deal more emotional and physical wear and tear than others.

Certainly there is considerable evidence that heredity can contribute to tendencies toward the most severe forms of abnormal behavior. Schizophrenia, for example, is more common among the close relatives of schizophrenics than among people whose family background shows no other cases. Studies also indicate that hereditary factors may produce tendencies toward disabling forms of depression and perhaps toward other less extreme forms of abnormal behavior as well (Tsuang and Vandermey, 1980).

Biological factors that contribute to psychological breakdown may also include medical conditions—and even some drugs used to treat them. These are discussed in a box on Psychology in Everyday Life titled "Is It Always Just in the Mind?"

Psychological Factors

Whatever our biological heritage, our acquired psychological traits also play a key role in determining how much anxiety and stress we are likely to experience, and how much we can tolerate without succumbing to mental illness. For example, people who have—but cannot fulfill—high needs for power, achievement, or approval may become extremely vulnerable.

Particularly significant are our inner standards. An event—such as receiving a barely passing grade on a final exam—may produce little or no anxiety in a person with relatively low standards of mastery and competence. But it may produce almost unbearable anxiety in a person with higher standards. Clinical psychologists often see people who are crippled by anxiety over violations of norms for sexual behavior, honesty, hostility, or dependency that would seem trivial to most of us.

Environmental Factors

One extremely influential element common to many mental disorders appears to be environmental stressors. The role of stressors in precipitating abnormal behavior has been studied since the early part of this century. As described in Chapter 5, Pavlov's experiments in the 1920s showed how it is possible to make dogs restless, hostile, destructive, or apathetic by having them perform increasingly difficult—and ultimately impossible—discriminations among shapes. More recent studies of learned helplessness, also described in Chapter 5, show how the condition is the product of stressful situations which the victim regards as inescapable. The importance of environmental factors is underscored by the evidence that mental disorders disproportionately affect people living in poverty (Shapiro et al., 1985). Perhaps an even clearer example is the breakdown suffered by soldiers enduring the stress and trauma of combat, most recently in Vietnam (Hendin and Haas, 1985).

Although stressful events in a person's current social environment can powerfully affect vulnerability to mental disorder, the stage may be set by the character of earlier

Psychology in Everyday Life
Is It Always Just in the Mind?

Doctors and psychiatrists have long recognized that stress and conflict can affect our physical well-being. Now it is clear that the reverse is equally true. Psychological symptoms, sometimes quite severe, can arise from ailments of the body rather than from disturbing life experiences. About 10 percent of patients treated in psychiatric clinics are found to suffer from hidden medical conditions that gave rise to their psychological complaints (Hall, 1980a). With appropriate medical treatment, their symptoms usually clear up rapidly.

Even those of us who never feel the need for psychotherapy may at times suffer what appears to be emotional distress but actually stems from physical problems. For example, a brilliant college sophomore became constantly anxious and downcast, stayed in bed instead of attending classes, dropped her social life, slept poorly, and became belligerent toward her family and suspicious of her friends. A perceptive physician ordered blood tests, which showed the patient was suffering the emotional distress typical in severe cases of mononucleosis, popularly known as "mono." This is a blood infection that responds quickly to medication—and six months later the student was back on top of her work and filled with a sense of well-being.

Such cases are not unusual. People suffering from anemia, a deficiency in red blood cells, often complain of being depressed, unmotivated, and unable to concentrate. So do many patients who have hepatitis, an inflammation of the liver (Schwab, 1980). A diseased thyroid gland can cause rapid swings of mood, uncontrollable restlessness and agitation, disturbed sleep, and anxiety to the point of panic and even hallucinations (Hall, 1980b). Hypoglycemia, an abnormally low level of blood sugar, has been known to produce similarly severe personality disturbances in children as well as adults.

Psychological complaints can even arise from physical conditions that are quite routine. Periods of deep melancholy often accompany cases of the flu, and in many women the metabolic changes produced by the menstrual cycle. Many medicines for common ailments can cause psychological disturbances as a side effect (Hall, Stickney, and Gardner, 1980). Two such medicines are cortisone, often used to treat "tennis elbow," and sedatives prescribed for insomnia. Both can trigger depression far more devastating than the original complaints.

For anyone who experiences emotional problems, an important first step is to have a doctor look carefully for possible physical causes, which are sometimes well concealed and difficult to uncover. More often than is generally supposed, appropriate medical treatment—without the need for psychotherapy—is the key to restoring mental health.

environments. Children who grow up in broken families, or are physically or sexually abused, or who live with a severely mentally ill parent may be vulnerable to mental illness in later life (Rutter, 1986). Growing up in poverty may also contribute to later vulnerability—perhaps because of the psychologically stressful existence of deprivation, or perhaps because deprived conditions often contribute to poorer physical health before and after birth, and to impaired biological capacity to cope with anxiety and stress.

Forms and Shades of Abnormality

Abnormal behavior takes many forms. Some deviations from the normal are so slight that they are popularly termed mere quirks—strange little habits like eccentricities in dress or speech. People who have somehow picked up such habits may seem a bit odd at times, but

A traumatic combat environment can leave emotional scars.

they are not seriously discomforted or prevented from functioning effectively. At the other extreme are the serious forms of mental disturbance that render their victims out of touch with reality and incapable of conducting the ordinary affairs of life. These drastic forms of abnormal behavior are relatively rare. In a sort of twilight zone between normal behavior and extreme abnormality are long-lasting emotional disturbances characterized by high levels of stress and anxiety. Their victims usually function day-to-day, but below par and without feelings of contentment. They are the people who are most likely to seek relief through psychotherapy.

In a sense, every case of abnormal behavior is unique. Each person experiences an individual pattern of stressful situations and responds to them in individual ways dictated by an individual set of biological, psychological, and environmental factors. Thus any attempt to classify the symptoms has to be somewhat arbitrary. But some kind of classification is essential. Researchers everywhere must speak a common language in their studies of the causes of various types of abnormal behavior. A common terminology is also necessary for reliable diagnoses and appropriate treatments (Williams and Spitzer, 1981).

The roster of behavior patterns our society regards as evidence of mental disorder has evolved over time—based on a combination of social attitudes and values, experiences of people who treat patients, and research on the underlying causes and patterns of abnormal behavior. The classification scheme now used by most psychologists and other mental health professionals was established in 1987 by the American Psychiatric Association in its *Diagnostic and Statistical Manual of Mental Disorders (Revised)*—or *DSM III (R)*. The manual presents detailed descriptions of patterns of abnormal behavior. The patterns cover a broad spectrum ranging from those popularly known as neurotic to more devastating ones often referred to as psychotic.

The current classification scheme may change, of course. As our knowledge and our views of mental illness change, disorders are included, excluded, regrouped, and relabeled. (For example, homosexual behavior, once considered to be a mental disorder, is no

434   Chapter 12 Abnormal Personality and Behavior

longer regarded as such.) The sections that follow deal with the major groupings of seriously abnormal personality and behavior patterns.

SCHIZOPHRENIA: RARE BUT DEVASTATING

The symptoms began to appear when Ralph was 19 years old. He became suspicious of his classmates, insisting that they were developing a special language so that they could carry out their secret plans to destroy him. His dress became slovenly, and sometimes, even in the heat of summer, he would wear three sweaters to protect him from "the poisonous rays that will appear at noon." His few friends would often find him in a corner of the library, mumbling to himself. Once Ralph refused to eat for an entire week. He was convinced that the food was poisoned to punish him for his grandmother's death. He imagined that she had died as a result of a magic word he had secretly thought of in his own mind.

As time passed, Ralph's behavior became even more bizarre. He would stand at the window for hours on end, staring at passers-by and mumbling nonsensical phrases like "gloop-in-the-soup" or "brangle my strangle." He complained that the neighbors were spying on him, and he would scream obscenities at them. He believed he had enormous powers and wrote letters to the President to offer solutions for all the world's problems. He was chosen, he said, to act as peacemaker not only between nations but also between the United States government and the creatures who were about to arrive from outer space.

By the time he was hospitalized, nothing Ralph said or did made any sense. Once he tried to climb into the toilet and have a nurse flush him away. He ordered his doctors to leave the room because, as he explained it "I am attending a conference with God, George Washington, and IBM."

Ralph is one of the estimated two million people in the United States suffering from *schizophrenia,* a devastating mental disorder that is often chronic. About 40 percent of the beds in American mental hospitals are now occupied by patients with schizophrenia. The disorder is particularly common among young adults in their twenties and occurs more often among men than among women. Overall the chances that a person will develop the disease are roughly 1 in 100 (Myers et al., 1984).

Symptoms of Schizophrenia

Individuals are generally considered to be suffering from schizophrenia when they display the following disturbed behavior (Rosenhan and Seligman, 1984):

1. *Perceptual difficulties*—for example, the inability to understand others' speech, to identify people, to gauge the passage of time, or to know what is real and what is not. Often there are *hallucinations,* or false sensory experiences—seeing things, hearing things—that have a compelling sense of reality.

2. *Thought disorders*—including incoherent speech, quick shifts of ideas from one topic to a totally unrelated one. Often there are *delusions,* or false and bizarre beliefs such as the conviction that other people can hear their thoughts, that they no longer exist, or that their heads and arms are missing.

3. *Emotional disturbances*—including the absence of any feeling, remoteness, and inappropriate reactions such as laughing in the face of a sad episode

In schizophrenia, many of the normal processes described in this book—from the ability to perceive the world to the capacity to relate to other people—go completely hay-

An immobile schizophrenia patient.

wire. People with the disorder lose touch with the real world. They hear voices that are not there, speak a language that does not exist, laugh for no reason, or sit motionless for hours on end (American Psychiatric Association, 1987). What could possibly cause the human personality to become so completely disorganized?

Searching for Schizophrenia's Roots

Most investigators have concluded that schizophrenia is not just a single disturbance but that it is made up of many types that have been grouped together merely because they exhibit certain resemblances. Moreover, an increasing number of studies suggest that these different types have different causes, manifestations, and responses to treatment.

Heredity does seem to set the stage for many types of schizophrenia, although the specific vulnerability is not yet known. Schizophrenia is associated in many patients with increased levels of the neurotransmitter dopamine in the brain. Virtually all drugs that are effective in treating schizophrenic symptoms interfere with the action of dopamine. At the same time, certain drugs that intensify the symptoms release dopamine. As shown in Figure 12-2, recently developed techniques for observing the brain in action offer further indications that schizophrenics differ from normal people in brain metabolism (Buchsbaum and Haier, 1987). Furthermore, in schizophrenics the brain ventricles—which are the fluid-filled cavities of the brain—are often enlarged (Meltzer, 1987).

It has also been found that schizophrenics show abnormal patterns of eye movements when they try to track a moving object, such as a swinging pendulum. Many of their close relatives, though not themselves victims of schizophrenia, display the same unusual tracking pattern, as if there were a family tendency to do so (Holzman, 1987). The unusual patterns might indicate some defect in parts of the nervous system responsible for perception—which might in turn account for the fact that schizophrenics seem out of touch with reality as perceived by normal people.

Evidence for the genetic origin of schizophrenia is strong, as indicated in Figure 12-3. Even if some inherited defect is the basis for the disorder, however, the fact that not all people from the same family become schizophrenic points to the influence of other factors in determining whether the inborn tendency will affect behavior. Environmental stresses may play a role, as might prenatal experiences. It is intriguing that the season of gestation, or birth, may affect a person's vulnerability to schizophrenia; there is an excess of winter births among schizophrenics (Watson et al., 1984).

Figure 12-2 The schizophrenic and normal brain: a difference in metabolic activity

The photos were produced by the brain-scan technique known as positron emission tomography, *or* PET. *The technique produces an image of the brain containing various colors that reflect the level at which glucose—the brain's main fuel—is being metabolized. The more active a particular part of the brain, the more glucose is being burned up. The most active areas are indicated by the darker colors. In the schizophrenic patient (left), the level of glucose metabolism appears highest in the rear portions of the brain that contain the visual centers, suggesting that a hallucination may be under way. But the brain of the normal subject (right) is burning up the most glucose in the frontal area, where higher level thought processes are organized. When the PET scans were made, neither the patient nor the normal subject was being stimulated in any way. They were unmedicated and resting with their eyes closed in a dark, acoustically insulated room.*

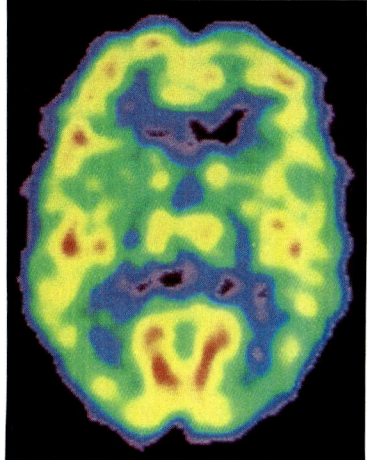 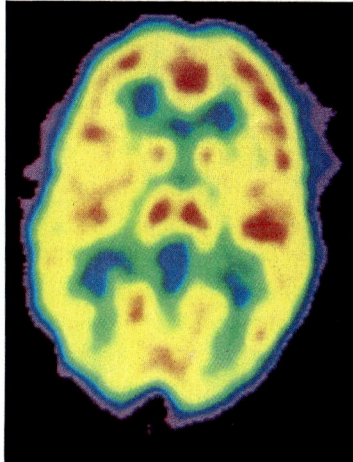

Figure 12-3 Vulnerability to schizophrenia: the difference heredity makes

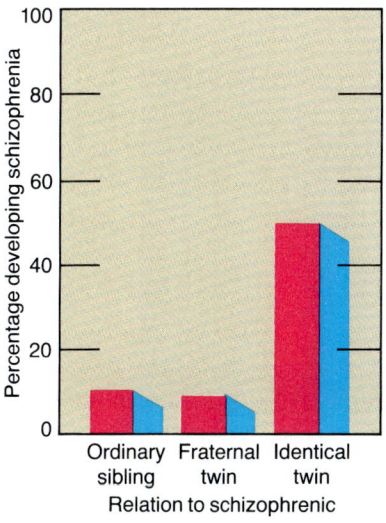

The fraternal twin of a schizophrenic has about the same chance of developing the disease as an ordinary sibling—about one in ten. But for an identical twin of a schizophrenic, who has inherited exactly the same genes, the chances increase to fifty-fifty (Gottesman and Shields, 1982).

AFFECTIVE DISORDERS: DISTURBANCES OF MOOD

All of us know from personal experience that events—both major and minor—can affect our mood, or what psychologists call our *affect*. There are times when life is marred by grief—when a friend dies, a treasured relationship breaks up, or the job you worked so hard to get is given instead to someone else.

For most people, the feelings usually mirror the significance of the event. The loss of a favorite book and the loss of a child normally are not expected to evoke the same dip in mood. Moreover, however painful the stress or loss, we can expect after a reasonable period to bounce back and feel like our "old self" again. Many people, however, experience a clinical, or major, *depression*—a plunge in mood so severe and prolonged that it can ultimately overwhelm the entire personality and cause many of life's functions to grind to a halt.

Major Depression: The Darkest Shade of Blue

For Susan, a bright college sophomore, episodes of disabling depression occurred whenever she felt she was being rejected. Her most recent signs of the disorder were evident soon after she failed to win a place on the school newspaper. Susan's friends noticed that her voice became flat and lifeless, her face gray and strained, her eyes clouded and always on the verge of tears. She lacked energy for even the most routine tasks—getting up for school, shopping, going to the library. Though she had always been a fan of the movies, she completely lost interest in them. She began withdrawing from friends—even her boyfriend. She had trouble sleeping, she barely ate, and she could no longer concentrate. When a close friend questioned her, concerned about her changed behavior, she admitted that she felt like a failure and would always probably be one.

Susan's case demonstrates many of the ways that depression differs from the passing feelings of dejection we often call "the blues." Severely depressed people are quite different from those who can best be described as "unhappy" (Gotlib, 1984). They experience not only unrelenting sadness but intense helplessness and hopelessness as well. They lose all semblance of self-esteem and are filled instead with grinding self-recriminations and guilt. They have no zest for either work or play. They may find that even routine acts of thinking and speaking are slowed and take enormous effort. In the most severe cases they may suffer delusions and hallucinations. Depression causes physical problems as well. Sleep is

The pain-filled face of depression.

Figure 12-4 A brief test for depression

The items are from a test called the Self Rating Depression Scale. The checks in the boxes would be made by a person who is depressed in the most extreme way. Note that such a person would feel that all the positive emotions and experiences mentioned in the test apply "none or a little of the time," while all the negative ones apply "most or all of the time." (Copyright William W. K. Zung, 1965. All rights reserved. Reproduced with author's permission.)

	None or a Little of the Time	Some of the Time	Good Part of the Time	Most or All of the Time
1. I feel down-hearted, blue, and sad				✔
2. Morning is when I feel the best	✔			
3. I have crying spells or feel like it				✔
4. I have trouble sleeping through the night				✔
5. I eat as much as I used to	✔			
6. I enjoy looking at, talking to, and being with attractive women/men	✔			
7. I notice that I am losing weight				✔
8. I have trouble with constipation				✔
9. My heart beats faster than normal				✔
10. I get tired for no reason				✔
11. My mind is as clear as it used to be	✔			
12. I find it easy to do the things I used to	✔			
13. I am restless and can't keep still				✔
14. I feel hopeful about the future	✔			
15. I am more irritable than usual				✔
16. I find it easy to make decisions	✔			
17. I feel that I am useful and needed	✔			
18. My life is pretty full	✔			
19. I feel that others would be better off if I were dead				✔
20. I still enjoy the things I used to do	✔			

disturbed—especially by early morning awakenings—and the appetite for food and sex tends to diminish or disappear. Depressed people may also complain of poor digestion, heart palpitations, headache, visual disturbances, or dizziness. Other indicators of depression are identified in Figure 12-4.

Suicide and the Death of Hope

Although the most prominent signs of depression may differ from one person to another, all severely depressed people share an inability to experience any pleasure whatsoever—or to imagine that they ever will again. As one depressed person put it:

> Everything I see, say, or do seems extraordinarily flat and pointless; there is no color, there is no point to anything. Things drag on and on, interminably. I am exhausted, dead inside. I

Affective Disorders: Disturbances of Mood

want to sleep, to escape somehow, but there is always the thought that if I really could sleep, I must always and again awake to the dullness and apathy of it all (Goldstein, Baker, and Jamison, 1980).

It would be difficult to convince this individual that depression is actually a self-limiting disorder, meaning that most people eventually recover from an episode of depression even without treatment. Those in the grip of a depressive episode feel hopeless about virtually everything, and with the outlook so dark, about 15 percent of depressed people eventually choose self-destruction as a way out of their misery. Of all the symptoms of depression, it is hopelessness that appears most likely to awaken suicidal thoughts (Beck et al., 1985).

Manic-depressive Illness: Too High, Too Low

When people have recurrent episodes of depression like the one just described, the disorder is called *unipolar depression*. But there is another severe affective disorder—known as *bipolar depression* or *manic-depressive illness*—in which the lows alternate with exaggerated highs. For those suffering from this disorder, the emotional pendulum swings wildly from intense excitement to deep melancholy, at first with long time intervals in between, but later with frequent and abrupt shifts from high to low.

In the manic phase, people with manic-depressive illness tend to be talkative, restless, aggressive, boastful, and often destructive. They develop a feeling of intense well-being and even ecstacy. Sexual and moral inhibitions disappear and life is one uninterrupted "high." The manic person needs little sleep and is filled with abundant energy and grandiose notions. A professional golfer in one of his manic episodes believed he was a messiah handpicked by God to save the world from evil, put an end to racial prejudice, and discover a cure for cancer. He was thrilled by the assignment and intended to complete it (Kindred, 1978).

Like this man, people in the grip of mania feel capable of any undertaking, ignoring any harmful consequences. On the spur of the moment they may suddenly give away all their possessions, or embark on outlandish trips. In extreme cases, their thoughts become disconnected, jumping from one idea to another without any apparent logic. Sometimes the condition resembles schizophrenia, and some manic-depressives are mistakenly diagnosed as schizophrenics (Carpenter and Stephens, 1980). Soon, however, most manic individuals plummet back to the depressed phase, becoming so gloomy and hopeless that they are virtually immobilized.

Biological Roots of Affective Disorders

As with schizophrenia, some evidence suggests that mood disorders have a genetic basis. The risk of developing manic-depressive illness is less than 1 percent in the population at large. But it rises to around 15 percent among the close relatives—parents, siblings, and children—of manic-depressives. One study of adopted individuals who had a mood disorder found that similar problems were three times more prevalent among their blood relatives than among their adopted relatives (Nurnberger and Gershon, 1982).

There is evidence also that mood disorders are related to disturbances in the chemistry of the brain—to such an extent that the symptoms sometimes appear without any provocation. The levels of a number of neurotransmitters appear to be disturbed in depression, and various drugs used to treat the disorder—to be described in the next chapter—work by altering the balance of these neurotransmitters. Among depressed individuals, there also appears to be a disturbance in the functioning of hormones regulated by the pituitary and adrenal glands. For example, many people suffering from severe depression have an excess amount of *cortisol*, a hormone secreted by the adrenal gland under stress or emotional upset (Carroll et al., 1981). Additional evidence of the biological basis of depression comes from observations of the abnormal brain waves of victims of the disorder while they are asleep (Kupfer et al., 1985).

It is not yet clear whether mood disorders are caused by these various biochemical factors or whether the disorder causes the biochemical changes. The most widely held theory is that some people are genetically vulnerable to biochemical imbalances, which are likely to occur in response to levels of stress that other people would not find disrupting.

Why Are Women More Often Depressed Than Men?

Mood disorders occur twice as often among women than men, and twice as many women as men take antidepressant drugs (Mellinger and Balter, 1981). The reason is not entirely clear. Women may be more vulnerable due to their biological makeup. Or, they may be the victims of their social role, which creates a kind of learned helplessness that contributes to depression (Nolen-Hoeksema, 1987).

Some investigators feel that the sex difference may reflect women's greater readiness to express feelings of depression and to seek help. Others suggest that men may be just as prone to depression, but that they express their dark moods through alcoholism (Bucher et al., 1981). For both sexes, the chances of experiencing depressive episodes increase with age. But this does not mean that young people are free of the disorder—as is discussed in a box on Psychology in Everyday Life titled "Depression in Childhood: How Vulnerable Are the Young?"

ANXIETY DISORDERS

The poet W. H. Auden described our era as the Age of Anxiety. And so it seems to be. Perfectly normal people have many anxious moments—as is clear from the previous chapter. Anxiety also gnaws at many with mental illness of all sorts. But in some people, anxiety is the preeminent symptom; it dominates their lives. These are people who suffer from one or another form of *anxiety disorder*. They outnumber all other groups of mentally ill individuals—some 13 million people, or more than 8 percent of the U.S. population, according to the latest estimate (Myers et al., 1984).

Anxiety disorders can take a number of forms, all of them arising when situations that produce conflict and frustration remain unresolved. In some cases, anxiety itself is clearly the most prominent symptom. In other cases, individuals develop disabling patterns of behavior—such as staying home to avoid crowds or washing their hands every half hour—as a way of keeping their underlying anxiety under control.

Many victims of anxiety disorders function well enough so that even their close friends may not become aware of their symptoms. Moreover, unlike schizophrenics and manic-depressives, they stay in touch with reality and can admit that their feelings and behavior are illogical. However, certain types of anxiety disorders can be crippling and may prevent people from functioning in their social relationships or at work. There are four common forms of anxiety disorders: generalized anxiety disorder and panic, phobic, and obsessive-compulsive disorders. Discussions of each follows.

Psychology in Everyday Life
Depression in Childhood: How Vulnerable Are the Young?

The aggressive child can be seriously depressed.

Numerous studies have found that the risk of serious depression increases in the later years of life. But does this mean that children are free of the disorder?

For many years the answer was assumed to be yes. Until the early 1960s, the term "childhood depression" did not appear in American textbooks on child psychiatry (Cytryn, McKnew, and Bunney, 1980). Now, however, it has become clear that children as well as adults can suffer from depression. Yet the ailment still goes unrecognized—and untreated—in too many cases.

The major reason is that by far the most common form of depression in children does not appear to be depression at all. Three types of problems often hide an underlying decay of mood in children:

1. Conduct disorders including hyperactivity, delinquency, irritability, and aggressiveness.
2. Physical complaints such as headaches, stomachaches, and bed-wetting.
3. School problems including school phobia, truancy, and poor scholastic performance.

Most parents and pediatricians are likely to

Generalized Anxiety Disorder

As the name implies, victims of *generalized anxiety* feel anxious, but with no specific focus. Freud described the condition as "free-floating anxiety." Each day is filled with a general feeling of tension, uneasiness, and vague fear. People displaying such anxiety feel irritable and jumpy, and they are uncomfortable with other people. They are constantly "on edge," unable to concentrate and filled with doubts about their ability to work or study. Their level of anxiety is likely to shoot up as a result of minor events that would not affect a normal person (Hamilton, 1982).

Many anxious people are constantly concerned about their health—often needlessly, although they may actually develop physical symptoms. Their autonomic nervous system is overactive, producing heart palpitations, shortness of breath, hot flashes, cold sweats, nausea, diarrhea, and frequent urination. Because they find it difficult to "turn off" at night, they wake up feeling as tired as when they went to bed. Friends may point out that it makes no sense to live continuously as if the world were about to cave in, but victims cannot seem to control the apprehension that hovers menacingly over them and clouds virtually every aspect of their lives.

overlook the possibility that such conditions may actually be masking a pervasive mood of depression. But careful observation of children by informed child psychiatrists and psychologists can often strip away the mask (Petti, 1981).

Even when the signs of depression are more obvious, the disorder is still easy to overlook in children. Because children are unaware of the meaning of depression, they do not complain of it openly in the same way that adults do. Moreover, many children can still be active and show some interest in their environment even while quite depressed. Closer attention, however, shows that depression produces symptoms in them comparable to those found among severely depressed adults.

Childhood depression, as in the case of adults, is likely to occur as a result of both genetic vulnerability and a stressful environment. Some cases are of long standing, arising when children are subjected to continuous stress. Their lives are filled, for example, with repeated separations from loved ones, abuse, family strife and violence, or the day-in and day-out trauma of being reared by an emotionally disturbed parent. Other cases last for a much briefer time, usually triggered by an identifiable, immediate cause. It could be the sudden death of a parent, an unexpected and uprooting move to a new city, or the arrival of a new sibling who seems to capture all of mother's love and attention.

In cases of either type, children suffer sharp downswings in mood like those endured by adults. They look sad and feel even sadder, are moody, cry easily, and sleep and eat poorly. They are burdened with a sense of worthlessness, hopelessness, and guilt. Finding no pleasure in life, some entertain thoughts of suicide, and a small but increasing number actually commit the act (Frederick, 1978).

The line between abnormal depression and everyday cases of "the blues" is as difficult to draw among children as among adults. But this much is certain: Youth is no shield against the ravages of depression, long regarded to be a painful consequence only of adult stress. More pediatricians, teachers, and parents need to learn to recognize the condition. A more widespread awareness of the signs of childhood depression would bring children the appropriate medical treatment they need—and restore to them their lost well-being and productivity.

Panic Disorder

Some people living in a state of anxiety experience periodic episodes when their undercurrent of tension turns into a flood of terror. They are then said to be suffering from a *panic disorder*. Often for no apparent reason, they are suddenly overwhelmed with a sense of disaster and imminent death. They also may have feelings of unreality, or believe that they are about to lose control and "go crazy." One man has described his transition from anxiety to panic this way:

> I feel anxious and fearful most of the time; I keep expecting something to happen but I don't know what. It's not the same all the time. Sometimes I only feel bad—then suddenly for no reason it happens. My heart begins to pound so fast that I feel it's going to pop out. My hands get icy and I get a cold sweat all over my body. My forehead feels like it is covered with sharp needles. I feel like I won't be able to breathe and I begin panting and choking. It's terrible—so terrible. I can go along for a while without too much difficulty and then suddenly without any warning it happens (Denike and Tiber, 1968).

Many generally anxious people have their lives pretty much under control until a panic attack erupts. One perplexed college senior is a case in point. She describes her attacks as coming "out of the blue" and making her feel suddenly as if a rapist had a knife at her throat or she was being buried alive. "But," she admits, "there's absolutely no reason in sight. I might be driving the car to school feeling pretty good and wham—all I can think about is racing home and ducking under the covers until the crisis passes."

Unlike victims of panic attacks who face no real threat to explain their terror, some people do experience shocking events that are frightfully stressful. These can result in anxiety problems that have been grouped under a special category called *post-traumatic stress disorder*—described in a box on Psychology in Everyday Life titled "Emotional Scars That Linger."

Phobic Disorder

States of anxiety sometimes become attached to a specific object, situation, or activity. The victim is then regarded as suffering from a *phobic disorder*—in other words, displaying an unreasonable fear. ("Phobia" is the Greek word for fear.) Many of us refer to ourselves casually as having one sort of phobia or another. "I have a phobia about spiders," you might hear some people say as they scrupulously survey the back yard before a picnic.

Psychology in Everyday Life
Emotional Scars That Linger

Some people are unlucky enough to endure traumatic stresses that lie far outside the range of usual human experience. They include victims not only of natural disasters such as floods and earthquakes, but also of shockingly stressful experiences that human beings themselves devise—among them rape, assault, and kidnapping. Victims of human-induced stress on a large scale can be found among survivors of military combat and of captivity and torture in prisoner-of-war and concentration camps. Indeed most people who suffer psychological trauma do so at the hands of one another rather than from events totally outside human control.

Survivors of extremely traumatic experiences are sometimes left with special anxiety problems. Some act as if they have been numbed by the shock of their ordeal. Their interest in life is diminished, and they feel alienated from the people around them (Walker, 1981). Others develop a tendency to remain constantly on the alert—as if disaster is sure to strike again at any moment. They tend also to startle easily. People who have lived through auto crashes may panic at the sound of cars in the night. Those who have endured a mugging or rape may respond with a start whenever they hear strange sounds, and some former POWs and hostages report similar reactions whenever they hear approaching footsteps. Survivors of psychological trauma are likely also to keep reliving their experience. They suffer from nightmares in which the shattering episode is reenacted in all its terrifying detail, and by day they find themselves suddenly overwhelmed by harrowing memories whenever they are exposed to situations that even remotely resemble the original event.

Post-traumatic stress reactions can occur at any age. In 1976, 26 California children were kidnapped at gunpoint by three masked men who took over the bus on which they were returning from school. The victims, ranging from 5 to 14 years of age, were first driven around in totally darkened vans for 11 hours. Then they were buried in a "hole," which was actually a truck-trailer placed underground and covered with a layer of earth. After 16 hours, the kidnappers finally left and the terrorized children dug themselves out.

Follow-up studies of 23 of the children showed that each of them was still painfully affected by the trauma as long as a year later.

Others will tell you that they cannot stand thunderstorms, and so they carefully check and recheck the weather forecast before starting out on a trip. Most of us manage to function quite well despite such fears. Victims of a phobic disorder, in contrast, find that their morbid fears recur so frequently and are so intense that they interfere with day-to-day activities and even become the controlling factors in their lives. Among the anxiety disorders, phobic disorder is the most common, affecting an estimated 11 million people in the United States in a six-month period (Myers et al., 1984).

Two common phobias are *claustrophobia* (fear of confinement in small places, which makes some people unable to ride in elevators) and *acrophobia* (fear of high places, which affects some people when they have to climb to the top of a theater balcony). Phobias can be acquired through simple conditioning in childhood, as the child Albert acquired his fear of furry animals. But they can also develop in more complex ways—for example, as a means for displacing basic anxieties about sex or social interactions onto something more tangible.

The most crippling of all phobias is *agoraphobia*, or fear of public places that can include streets, stores, buses, trains, or virtually anywhere outside the house. In fact, victims often become imprisoned in their own homes, which they perceive as the only safe place to be.

They all lived in fear that something terrible would happen to them again. A number of them were sure that the kidnappers, although long since arrested, would be back—and they found themselves being kidnapped repeatedly in their dreams. All the children now listened and watched in fear for signs of danger—in the dark, when alone, near strangers or cars, or when they felt confined. Eight of them, although perfectly safe, suffered attacks of such overwhelming anxiety that they screamed and ran for help. An 11-year-old boy refused to sleep in his bedroom for nights on end because he believed the ceiling was about to collapse, and an 8-year-old girl who now depended on a nightlight for security jumped out of bed in panic every time the heater in her room turned on (Terr, 1981).

Some people get over a traumatic experience soon enough, but others are troubled by symptoms for years on end. One team of investigators studied 27 women who had been raped as long ago as 16 years. The victims continued to suffer from episodes of depression, tension, and fatigue. They experienced not only sexual problems, but difficulties in developing any close personal relationships. Two of the women eventually became so disturbed that they had to be hospitalized, and four reported that they subsequently returned to long-abandoned patterns of alcohol and drug abuse (Ellis, Atkeson, and Calhoun, 1981). A number of elderly concentration camp survivors broke down completely decades after their ordeal was over when they had to be hospitalized for medical reasons. The experience was sufficiently similar to imprisonment to reopen fully the old psychological wounds (Edelstein, 1982).

There is some evidence that traumatic episodes inflicted by others leave worse scars than those occurring by accident or as a result of a natural catastrophe (American Psychiatric Association, 1980). Crime victims, hostages, and combat veterans are examples of those likely to suffer especially from their ordeals. Whether or not this is actually so in every case, it seems clear enough that untold psychological pain could be prevented if somehow human beings were able to learn one day to avoid making victims of each other.

Agoraphobia typically takes hold after a number of severe panic attacks. The person then begins to avoid situations in which the attacks happened, but soon this avoidance response spreads to other situations. Eventually it becomes impossible to go anywhere at all—certainly not alone. In many ways the individual with agoraphobia behaves very much like the young child suffering from *school phobia* who desperately clutches mother's hand and screams in terror at the thought of venturing out into the world.

Phobias are more likely to be found among adolescents and young people than older people. Like panic attacks, they are—at least in their milder forms—also more common among females than males (Costello, 1982). One possible explanation of this sex difference is that fearfulness has long been more acceptable among women than men.

Obsessive-compulsive Disorder

Obsessions are thoughts that keep cropping up in a persistent and disturbing fashion. Some anxiety-ridden people are obsessed with the idea that they have heart trouble or that they are going to die by a certain age. A common and mild form of obsession is the feeling of people starting out on a trip that they have left the door unlocked or the stove turned on.

Compulsions are irresistible urges to perform some act over and over again, such as washing one's hands dozens of times a day. The hostess who cannot bear to see a knife or fork out of line at the table and keeps emptying her guests' ashtrays is exhibiting mild forms of compulsion. So is the student who cannot get any work done unless his papers are arranged in neat piles on his desk and he has a half-dozen freshly sharpened pencils waiting all in a line.

Obsessive-compulsive reactions sometimes serve the purpose of covering up underlying feelings of hostility. This was the case for one woman whose marriage was on the rocks, but who could never express her intense feelings of anger toward her husband. Instead she developed compulsions that made her home life a shambles. She continually scrubbed, cleaned, and washed, and she developed a long and rigid set of procedures for ordering groceries, making list after list until the stores were already closed. Her preparations for dinner were so elaborate that the meal was fixed—if at all—only long after bedtime. Victims of obsessive-compulsive disorder tend to use up energy in repetitious thoughts or acts instead of spontaneous expressions of feeling. As a result, many appear to be cold and remote individuals.

PERSONALITY DISORDERS: MORE DISTURBING THAN DISTURBED

People suffering from schizophrenia, depression, or anxiety may have isolated or recurrent episodes of abnormal behavior, but return to their "normal selves" the rest of the time. In contrast, some forms of abnormal behavior are integral parts of the entire personality. These forms of behavior, known as *personality disorders*, may arise out of some underlying and deep-seated conflict, but the people who have them may not feel any particular discomfort such as depression or panic. Instead they behave in ways that are often painful to others. They seem to lack any desire—or perhaps ability—to act in ways that are socially acceptable, and they rarely seek to change by getting help. Their patterns of behavior often surface at an early age and become so deeply ingrained that even friends or family members may find it difficult to distinguish the disorder from the person.

Although personality disorders are not easy to classify, it is possible to differentiate over a dozen different types (American Psychiatric Association, 1987). Discussions of three of them follow, and a half dozen others are described in Figure 12-5.

Figure 12-5 Characteristics of people with personality disorders

We all know people who have traits somewhat like the ones listed. But for people with personality disorders, the patterns are so pervasive that it becomes virtually impossible for them to adapt to the demands of the real world. As a result, their social relationships and their work are likely to suffer significantly.

Type of personality disorder	What the person is like
Histrionic	Highly excitable, often reacting to tiny events with gigantic displays of emotion; shallow and not very genuine; quick to form friendships—but soon becomes demanding and inconsiderate; seductive and tries to dominate the opposite sex; egocentric and needs to control others, sometimes even by threatening or actually attempting suicide
Passive-aggressive	Aggressive and resentful toward others—but only indirectly through such annoying techniques as procrastination, stubbornness, and intentional inefficiency; lacks self-confidence and has a pessimistic attitude
Dependent	Lacks self-confidence and initiative; manages to let other people take responsibility for everything in life—even for major decisions about job or career; cannot stand the idea of being self-reliant; needs to depend on others at all costs—even if the other person is mean and abusive; sees self as dumb and helpless
Compulsive	Perfectionistic and so absorbed in trivial details as to be unable to see "the big picture"; overly serious and stingy and rarely does anything spontaneously; intent on having others conform to "my way of doing things"; indecisive, afraid of making a mistake, and unable to establish priorities; puts even routine work ahead of friends
Schizoid	Unable to build close social relationships or even to feel any warmth toward others; indifferent to almost everything, including the feelings of people; reserved and withdrawn—a true "loner"; humorless, dull, and aloof; vague and indecisive; absentminded and given to daydreaming; sometimes seems removed from the real world—but without the seriously abnormal symptoms of schizophrenia
Borderline	Impulsive, unpredictable, and easily upset; gets uncontrollably angry for little reason; quickly shifts mood—from depression to irritability to anxiety; feels empty and bored inside and is unable to establish a firm sense of identity; lives on the border of reality, slipping beyond it during periods of heavy pressure and stress

Antisocial Personality: Reckless and Ruthless

An extreme form of personalty disorder is *antisocial personality*. People with this type of personality seem to lack any normal conscience or sense of social responsibility and to have no feeling for other people. Some of these sociopaths, as they are called, may seem on the surface to be quite charming, candid, and generous—but in truth they are selfish, ruthless, and addicted to lying. They have no affection for anyone but themselves and take advantage of others without a shred of guilt. The apparent absence of anxiety of any kind is one of the outstanding characteristics of the sociopath—and of course a factor that makes antisocial personality completely different from most other disorders.

Charles Manson, born fatherless to a teenage prostitute, beaten as a child, in trouble all his life—and eventually a murderer.

Sociopaths are likely to be in and out of trouble all their lives; they rarely learn from experience and appear to have no desire to help themselves. Instead of becoming independent, self-supporting adults, they are impulsive and reckless—unable to keep a job, maintain an enduring marital or sexual relationship, or act as a responsible parent. Lacking respect for the law, they often end up spending periods of their lives in prison. Such a person is sometimes also referred to as a "psychopath," a word that comes up frequently in court cases to describe criminals who appear to experience no remorse for even the most cruel deeds. They are good examples of the antisocial personality in its most extreme form.

The causes remain a mystery, but antisocial behavior patterns usually begin in childhood. It is rare for people to be diagnosed as having an antisocial personality unless they displayed similar problems before they reached 18 years of age. One study followed up over 500 adults seen in a child guidance clinic 30 years earlier. Most of those with antisocial personality had already been in trouble as children—with their parents, teachers, and often the law. They had a history of school truancy, stealing, lying, irresponsibility about money, heavy involvement in sex, staying out late, or running away from home. The more antisocial symptoms children displayed, the more likely they were to grow up as antisocial adults (Robins, 1978).

There is some evidence that sociopaths tend to have autonomic nervous systems that are especially insensitive and difficult to arouse (Hare, 1978). This biological characteristic might lead them to seek emotional excitement and at the same time to be oblivious to danger (such as the consequences of committing a serious crime). They also seem to respond less to punishment than other people. But as in most other forms of abnormal behavior, it is unlikely that biological factors alone account for an antisocial personality. The social environment appears to weigh heavily in the development of the disorder. The chances of developing an antisocial personality disorder are high for those raised by a parent who has the disorder. Growing up with antisocial companions and in high-crime neighborhoods are also factors—but these carry much less weight if the parents themselves are free of antisocial behavior (Robins, 1978). The backgrounds of those sociopaths who end up as criminals reveal the same combination of biological traits and environmental circumstances (Wilson and Herrnstein, 1985).

Paranoid Personality: Always Suspicious, Always Threatened

All of us feel suspicious at times—and it is a good thing that we do. You would be ignoring your own best interests if you were not wary when hearing strange sounds in your basement at night, or on discovering that a classmate's essay bears an uncanny resemblance to your own. But the basement prowler may turn out to be a cat, and the apparent case of plagiarism a coincidence. For normal people, once there is evidence that such suspicions are not warranted, they are dispelled. Wariness wanes and trust is established.

In contrast, people with a *paranoid personality* are unable to give up their constant suspicions and mistrust of other people—even when the facts clearly point the other way. Worse yet, they may even become suspicious of anyone who tries to reason with them. They expect at any moment to be tricked, and they are always on guard and worried about the hidden motives of others. Paranoid individuals often seem to be devious and scheming. They also appear hostile and defensive—and so stubborn and rigid that they are unable to compromise.

It is extremely hard to build satisfying relationships with paranoid individuals. At work such people tend to be intensely concerned with rank, always needing to know who is in control. Moreover, everything is taken personally. For example, if a company established a new regulation that required all employees to sign in and out of work, paranoid individuals would feel that the rule was specifically devised only to get at them. In marriage they can become insanely jealous for no reason, yet they are incapable of intimacy because they can trust no one. It is impossible for a person to be suspicious all the time and still have the capacity to be yielding, tender, or sentimental.

People with a paranoid personality disorder are often quite bright. In their own distorted way, they display highly prized capacities such as sensitivity, quickness of thought, and great consistency. Yet underneath, paranoid persons feel grossly inferior. Because they are always fighting off feelings of inadequacy, they tend to blame everything on others. In extreme cases, this process results in delusions of persecution. Some paranoid individuals manage to compensate for their feelings of inferiority by developing delusions of power and grandeur. Among them are extremely disturbed paranoid persons who end up actually believing that they are the Pope or the President.

Narcissistic Personality: Loving the Face in the Mirror

In an ancient Greek legend, Narcissus was a beautiful young man who fell in love with his own reflection in a pool—so much so that he remained glued there until he died. His name is the basis for a trait known as narcissism—or self-love—which in extreme form dominates the personality of those with a *narcissistic personality*.

People with this disorder are often quite charming and attractive, but once you get to know them, they are easy to dislike. They seem to have an inflated sense of their own importance, acting as if they were God's gift to humanity. Unlike obsessive-compulsive individuals who constantly seek perfection, narcissistic people claim it (Akhtar and Thomson, 1982). They feel entitled to everything and end up using people for their own purposes, including sex. Often they give the impression that they really like you when all they actually want is to get you to do something for them. They offer little in return, and worse

"Is there someone else, Narcissus?"

Drawing by Charles Addams; © 1974 The New Yorker Magazine, Inc.

still, can excuse nothing of others. For example, if you chance to have an accident and as a result miss an appointment with such a person, it is not likely that you will be forgiven. Narcissists can rarely manage to put themselves in another's place.

Narcissistic individuals crave constant attention and admiration because they are trying desperately to compensate for painful feelings of emptiness and worthlessness lurking beneath the surface. That is also why they tend to daydream of incredible successes in their work or their love affairs. They are extremely superficial, totally preoccupied with appearances. They would rather be seen with the "right people" than enjoy the company of close friends. They also fake the feelings they think are appropriate in any situation to impress others. How they look is so important to them that they can easily spend hours grooming themselves. The narcissist of today stands transfixed at the mirror instead of the reflecting pool.

Some might claim that this disorder is becoming more common because there is a greater acceptance in our culture of selfish behavior (Wallach and Wallach, 1983). For example, books intended to teach us how to look out for ourselves first—or how to get everything we want out of life at any cost—tend to become best-sellers. But there is no evidence from research that narcissistic behavior is any more prevalent today than in the days of Narcissus.

SUBSTANCE ABUSE: THE PERILOUS PLEASURES OF ALCOHOL AND DRUGS

The use of alcohol or drugs cannot itself be viewed as a psychological disorder. Otherwise countless people would be considered abnormal for sipping a cocktail to relax before dinner or taking a sedative to get to sleep when upset. The use of substances that affect the central nervous system is considered abnormal when it becomes so frequent and

Richard Pryor, a famous victim of substance abuse.

heavy that users can no longer function normally—whether in the family, at school, or at work. Moreover such people continue to seek alcohol and drugs despite damage to their health and the threat to life itself.

Becoming Dependent

An indication that alcohol or drug use is departing from normal is the development of psychological dependence. When this happens, users no longer view the substance as an incidental feature of life or as a way to promote pleasure and well-being. Instead they believe it to be essential in order to handle the day-to-day stresses of life. An executive might come to believe that he could not possibly endure the daily grind of corporate life without gulping a few swallows of the gin hidden in the desk drawer for "emergencies." Or a student might be convinced that without marijuana there would be no way to survive the tensions of school.

Many people who are psychologically dependent on alcohol and certain drugs become physically dependent—or *addicted*—as well. Their bodies develop a *tolerance* for the substance, meaning that they now require increasingly large doses to produce anything like the desired effect. Moreover they will now suffer from *withdrawal symptoms*—painful physical and psychological reactions—when they stop using the substance. Withdrawal from alcohol results in *delirium tremens*, popularly known as the "DTs," which are a state of intense panic that includes agitation, tremors, confusion, horrible nightmares, and even hallucinations. It is not unusual for alcoholics in the throes of the DTs to be convinced that bugs are crawling all over their bodies. Withdrawal from stimulants such as cocaine produces depression, disorientation, and irritability.

The suffering produced by withdrawal is usually so great that addicts will go to any lengths to return to using the substance. Many do so despite a strong wish to "kick the habit" and return to a more normal existence.

Portrait of an Alcoholic

At age 24, Cathy reluctantly entered an alcoholism treatment center under a judge's orders after she was caught driving while drunk. But she did not admit that she was at fault. "The cops only stopped me because they have a thing about young people," Cathy said. "I wasn't weaving across the highway at all. Besides, I've driven home in much worse shape and nothing ever happened." She would not acknowledge how blurred her vision was that night, how clouded her judgment, how slowed her reflexes—and how close she came to having a tragic traffic accident.

Cathy did not admit either that it was her alcohol problem that caused her to lose her job as a waitress. "My boss was just too picky," she said. "He wouldn't give me a break. Everyone drops a tray once in a while or yells at customers when they're giving you a hard time. And sometimes things come up and you just can't call in to say that you'll be late for work." She would not concede that her morning gulps of Scotch would leave her so shaky she could not possibly hold a tray straight, or that some days she awoke with such a deadly hangover that she felt too sick to reach for the phone and call her supervisor.

As Cathy talked to her counselor, she revealed many of the telltale signs of alcoholism. At parties she would mix especially strong drinks for herself so that her friends would not know how much she was drinking. She sometimes turned down invitations to social events where she knew there would be no liquor served. She would angrily move on to another bar if a bartender refused to serve her another drink. And she abandoned friends who did not drink heavily because, in her view, they were "no fun."

After a few weeks of treatment, Cathy relaxed her defenses and admitted that she had a problem. She owned up to the fact that she often did feel guilty about her drinking, and that when sober, she regretted the things she said or did while drunk. From time to time she had promised herself to cut down, but she could never follow through. There were also many times when she felt so depressed that she wondered whether life was worth living. But always after a few drinks, nothing mattered any more except having still another.

Cathy had all the classical symptoms of alcoholism: dependence on alcohol; loss of control over drinking; continuing to drink despite physical, psychological, and social ill effects; and refusing to admit there is a problem.

First Lady Betty Ford—apparent normality in the midst of addiction.

From "Cooling Out" to Blackouts

Cathy had her first drink when she was 15 years old, and like many alcoholics, she began to drink often because she found that it helped her get rid of that "uptight" feeling and gave her a better self-image. Under the influence of a drink or two, many people find they can socialize more easily, be less on guard about what they might say, and worry less about what others might think. That is because alcohol actually does suppress nerve impulses in areas of the brain that control our social behavior.

Heavier drinking, however, can transform a pleasantly "high" state into intoxication. After a number of drinks, speech becomes slurred, and memory and motor coordination deteriorate. Heavy drinkers begin to shed their inhibitions altogether, and their moods tend to swing to one extreme or the other. Past a certain point, they may enter periods of *blackout*. During such periods, they behave as if they are conscious of their actions, yet later they have no recollection whatsoever of the events that took place. For example, an alcoholic may awaken the morning after a drinking binge to find the car smashed, but remember nothing about hitting a tree on the way home. Cathy's friends once told her that on a previous night, she had undressed and danced on a bar table—but she could recall nothing of the episode. Alcohol had begun to affect the normal functions of her brain. The long-term penalties of alcoholism are discussed in a Psychology in Everyday Life box titled "Heavy Drinking, Heavy Price."

Men, Women, and Drinking

Among Americans who drink, roughly 10 percent suffer problems associated with the habit or are actually alcoholics. Surveys consistently indicate that males are heavier drinkers than

---

Psychology in Everyday Life
Heavy Drinking, Heavy Price

The road from an occasional drink to dependence on alcohol is strewn with heavy physical penalties. Over the long haul, alcoholics run into a variety of serious health problems. Alcohol itself has little food value, and because heavy drinkers also usually eat poorly, they often suffer severe malnutrition. *Cirrhosis* of the liver—meaning that the liver has become scarred and hardened—may result from this poor nutrition as well as from the irritating effects of alcohol. Alcoholics run a greater than normal risk also of suffering heart problems, high blood pressure, anemia, impotence, gastrointestinal disorders, and cancers of the tongue, mouth, larynx, esophagus, and liver (Eckardt et al., 1981).

Heavy drinking for long periods leads to cognitive and emotional problems as well. Alcohol destroys brain cells—which is why studies of alcoholics show that their perceptual skills and problem-solving abilities are weakened (Silberstein and Parsons, 1981). Although alcohol at first gives users the idea that their feelings of depression are lighter, it actually deepens them—as it did in Cathy's case (Aneshensel and Huba, 1983). An unusually large number of people with drinking problems commit suicide, and more than a third of all suicides involve alcohol. A significant number of industrial accidents, drownings, burns, and falls have also been attributed to drinking. So, too, have many cases of assault, rape, child abuse and neglect, and family violence.

Measured in both physical and psychological consequences, the price of heavy drinking is heavy indeed.

females. The percentage of adult drinkers who consume 120 or more drinks per month is five times higher for men than for women (Clark and Midanik, 1982). As shown in Figure 12-6, problems associated with the use of alcohol are much more prevalent among men.

One reason may be that heavy drinking by women is seen as less acceptable. One study has found that more women than men regard alcoholics to be socially inadequate (Furnham and Lowick, 1984). Women may be less prone than men to try to fight off their feelings of depression and anxiety by drinking. To handle the same complaints, they are more likely instead to receive prescription drugs from their physicians—as shown in Figure 12-7. Some researchers believe that the actual number of female alcoholics is greater than the statistics show. Because drinking by women is less acceptable, many cases are kept from the attention of doctors and the staffs of clinics treating alcoholics (Sandmaier, 1980). However, the courage of public figures such as former First Lady Betty Ford to admit publicly to their alcohol problems and treatment may encourage more alcoholic women to seek help.

Causes of Alcoholism

People from all walks of life can fall victim to alcoholism, as any meeting of the self-help organization known as Alcoholics Anonymous demonstrates. What is the common denominator? While alcoholism has no single cause, heredity apparently plays some role. As in the case of schizophrenia, the chances that twins will both become alcoholics is much greater for identical twins than for fraternal twins. One study focused on children who were adopted in the first few weeks of life. Those who had been fathered by alcoholics were four times more likely to develop the disorder later in life than were similar adoptees born to fathers who were not alcoholics. Factors in the children's upbringing—including being raised by an alcoholic or living in a home broken by death or divorce—did not affect the results (Goodwin et al., 1973).

Researchers have not identified an "alcoholic personality," although there is some evidence that individuals who experience a greater-than-usual reduction in autonomic stress reactions with the help of alcohol are at higher risk for the disorder (Sher and

Figure 12-6   Sex differences in the extent of alcohol-related behavioral problems

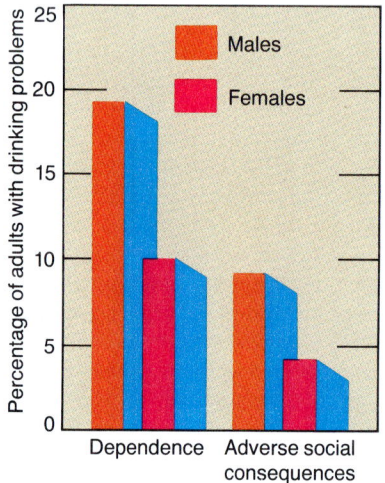

Males are twice as likely as females to show signs of dependence on alcohol. Among such signs are skipping meals when drinking, sneaking drinks, drinking in the morning, drinking before a party to make sure to get enough, gulping drinks, hands shaking after drinking, morning drinking to get rid of a hangover, and blackouts. Males are also twice as likely to suffer adverse consequences from alcohol such as problems in family and social relationships, encounters with police, and auto accidents (Clark and Midanik, 1982).

Figure 12-7 Sex differences in the number of patients taking medicine for psychological complaints

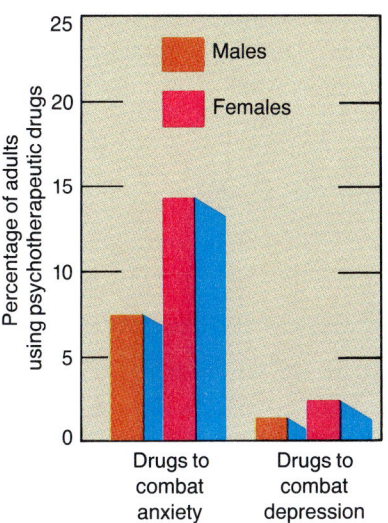

Over 11 percent of the adult population in the United States takes medicines prescribed by their doctors to relieve anxiety. The proportion of women who do so, however, is nearly double that of men. The same pattern applies to drugs prescribed for the relief of depression—although the overall percentages are smaller (Mellinger and Balter, 1981).

Levenson, 1982). Many alcoholics also tend to be immature, dependent, and lacking in self-esteem, but such traits are by no means common to most alcoholics. Similarly, many alcoholics come from broken and unhappy homes, but there is no consistent pattern (National Institute on Alcohol Abuse and Alcoholism, 1980). Nor does the popular image of the alcoholic as a "skid row drunk" hold up in real life. It is estimated that only 5 percent of all alcoholics fit this stereotype. People from all walks of life can fall victim, including hard-driving politicians, high-strung performers, harried waitresses, and anxious college students.

Using Drugs to Alter How We Feel

The use of drugs goes far back in history. It would appear that humanity has always been interested in finding substances that relieve anxiety, produce feelings of contentment and happiness, and sometimes result in strange experiences that make the user perceive the world in a distorted fashion, have hallucinations of imaginary sights and sounds, and perhaps attain a mystical, religious sense of oneness with the universe. Such states are referred to as *altered states of consciousness*.

Some of the mind-altering substances used today are so routine a part of our social scene that they are seldom even thought of as drugs. Alcohol, of course, is probably the best example. Nicotine, whose effects constitute the chief appeal of smoking, is a chemical that acts in several different ways—sometimes as a stimulant, sometimes as a sort of tranquilizer relieving feelings of anxiety. And caffeine, found in coffee and tea, is a powerful stimulant.

The substances ordinarily thought of as drugs include a number of substances whose use is illegal, ranging from marijuana to heroin and cocaine, as well as prescription drugs like sleeping pills and stimulants taken for "kicks" rather than on a physician's orders. All the mind-altering drugs create their effects by temporarily changing the activity of the brain—certainly by assisting or hindering the transmission of messages at the brain's innumerable switching points, perhaps also by changing the circuits over which messages ordinarily flow.

Almost invariably, the effect depends not only on the drug itself and the amount used but also on the user's frame of mind, the circumstances in which the drug is used, and the behavior of companions. Certainly the user's expectations play an important part. It has been found that cocaine users, who expect to get "high" from sniffing the powder, may not know the difference when another substance that produces the same sensation in the nose is substituted for the real thing (Van Dyke and Byck, 1982).

How Drug Users Become Drug Abusers

The use of drugs increased rapidly in the United States during the 1960s and 1970s. The increase was especially pronounced among young people, who began experimenting with

Figure 12-8 Commonly used drugs and their possible effects

Many of the drugs listed may be therapeutic when prescribed in appropriate doses by a physician—but lethal when they are taken in larger quantities without medical supervision. Individuals vary considerably in their responses to drugs. How quickly a person becomes addicted depends on the availability of the drug, how often and in what doses it is used, and the user's physical condition and psychological makeup (Vaillant, 1978).

Type of drug	Examples	Effects of use	Effects of overdose	Effects of withdrawal
Hallucinogens	LSD Phencyclidine (PCP)	Hallucinations, paranoid behavior, distorted body image, anxiety, tremors, nausea, chills, increased pulse and heart rates, amnesia	Loss of contact with reality, seizures, coma	None
Inhalants	Nitrous oxide (whippets, laughing gas) Hydrocarbons (glue)	Feelings of euphoria, giddiness excitement, loss of inhibitions, aggressiveness, delusions, headache, depression, nausea, drowsiness	Weak memory, confusion, unsteady walk, erratic pulse and heart beat, death	Insomnia, loss of appetite, depression, headache, irritability
Narcotics	Heroin Morphine	Feelings of euphoria, drowsiness, slowed breathing, nausea	Slow and shallow breathing, clammy skin, convulsions, coma, death	Watery eyes, runny nose, loss of appetite, irritability, panic, tremors, chills, sweating, cramps, nausea

drugs at earlier and earlier ages (Johnston, Bachman, and O'Malley, 1982). More recently, there is evidence that the use of illicit drugs—with the exception of cocaine—has either remained stable or declined. Nevertheless, nearly 37 million Americans—about one in five people 12 years of age or older—use one or more illicit drugs in the course of a year (National Institute on Drug Abuse, 1986).

Some people have a much greater need than others for the gratifying experiences that drugs can produce. Among such people are those who become victims of *drug abuse*—the repeated use of drugs for other than medical purposes in ways that result in physical and psychological disturbances. The most commonly abused drugs and some of their abnormal effects are listed in Figure 12-8.

There are many theories as to why some people get "hooked" on drugs. According to one theory, it all depends on the view they have of themselves (Gold, 1980). After experimenting with drugs, some people develop a belief that they are unable to cope without

Type of drug	Examples	Effects of use	Effects of overdose	Effects of withdrawal
Cannabis	Marijuana Hashish	Feelings of euphoria, relaxed inhibitions, increased appetite, disoriented behavior, increased heart and pulse rates, dizziness	Anxiety, paranoid behavior, loss of concentration, slowed movements, distorted sense of time, hallucinations	Insomnia, hyperactivity
Depressants	Barbiturates Tranquilizers	Slurred speech, drowsiness, disorientation, drunken behavior	Shallow breathing, cold and clammy skin, weak and rapid pulse, coma, death	Anxiety, insomnia, tremors, delirium, convulsions, death
Stimulants	Cocaine Amphetamines	Hyperactivity, euphoria, increased pulse rate and blood pressure, insomnia, loss of appetite, irritability, aimless behavior	Agitation, increased body temperature, panic, convulsions, hallucinations, tremors, death	Apathy, long spells of sleep, irritability, depression

them. Continued use sets up a vicious circle. As these users rely more and more on drugs to feel in control, they repeatedly confirm their belief that they are powerless to cope on their own. Each failure to function without drugs strengthens that belief until they become addicted and are in actual fact unable to face life without chemical assistance.

Another theory is that people who slip across the line from occasional experimentation with drugs to abuse have difficulty handling their anxieties about achievement (Misra, 1980). According to this theory, such individuals turn to drugs in the first place to find temporary relief from the pressure to achieve and the fear of failure. Once the effects of the drug wear off, their anxieties return and they again seek the relief they know the drug will bring. Soon they begin to depend on the drug to block out their anxieties. The process continues to spiral until the effect of the drug becomes an end in itself. The goal now is no longer only freedom from tension but a state of uninterrupted contentment. In effect, the drug abuser seems to be saying: "I may not amount to as much as my friends, but I have something they do not have—an existence without pressures or responsibilities."

One view of the road to drug abuse is based on a more general principle called the *opponent-process theory of emotion* (Solomon, 1980). According to this theory, the human nervous system seeks to balance out any deviation from normal equilibrium in emotional experience. Thus, every emotion triggers an opposing emotion that lingers after the first one is "switched off." For example, after fearful flyers endure a frightening trip, they begin to feel ecstatic. Or, as a sequel to the misery of childbirth labor, many women tend to feel euphoric. In the same way, the discomfort, or "low," that a drug user feels when the effects of the drug wear off leads to the motivation for repeated use of the drug as a means for establishing the opposing "high." Ultimately, the result is the onset of tolerance—and addiction. In effect, the drug user becomes an abuser through the frequently repeated experience of contrasting unpleasant and pleasant emotional states (Solomon, 1986).

Portrait of the Heroin Addict

In the case of heroin, which poses perhaps the most serious drug abuse problem, one investigator found six characteristics prominent among addicts (Nurco, 1979): Inability to cope with intense feelings of anger, usually generated by frustration; need for immediate gratification; inability to establish adequate sexual identity; rejection of society's goals and the means typically used to achieve them; proneness to take risks as a way of proving personal adequacy; and constant need to deal with boredom.

In some ways heroin addicts resemble people with antisocial personalities. They generally have trouble conforming to society's rules, and live without attachments to work, family, or religion (Robins, 1980). It is sometimes hard to tell whether the complications of addiction—such as marital problems, unemployment, and crime—are the result of drugs or the sources of psychological stress leading to drug use in the first place. Since only a small percentage of those who experiment with drugs ever become addicted despite the stress in their lives, some investigators assume that a specific biochemical abnormality may exist among those who suffer addiction.

As in the case of all mental disorders, by understanding what drug abuse is and how it develops, we may be less fearful of it and more compassionate toward its victims. One of the great challenges for psychology is to learn how to spare more people the pain of mental disorders, lighten the burdens of those who do succumb, and—as described in the next chapter—help our society respond more appropriately to their needs.

SUMMARY

The nature and scope of abnormal behavior

1. *Abnormal behavior*, though difficult to define, is generally considered to be behavior that is: (a) statistically unusual, (b) considered undesirable by most people, and (c) a source of unhappiness to the person who displays it.
2. It is estimated that at least 20 percent of the U.S. population suffers from a diagnosable mental disorder during a six-month period. The economic cost of caring for the mentally ill has been estimated at close to $20 billion a year.

The roots and varieties of abnormal behavior

3. Abnormal behavior hinges on two factors: (a) the amount of stress and anxiety a person experiences and (b) the person's ability to handle this amount.
4. The ability to handle stress and anxiety appears to be determined by (a) biological factors (such as glandular activity and sensitivity of the autonomic nervous system), (b) psychological factors (such as motives and anxiety over failure to fulfill them), and (c) environmental influences.

Schizophrenia: rare but devastating

5. *Schizophrenia* is characterized by extreme disorganization of personality. Schizophrenics typically display: (a) perceptual difficulties (*hallucinations*), (b) thought disorders (*delusions*), and (c) emotional disturbances.
6. In many patients, schizophrenia is associated with increased levels of the neurotransmitter dopamine in the brain. It has also been found that schizophrenics appear to have defects in brain metabolism and in parts of the nervous system responsible for perception. Evidence for the genetic origin of the disorder is strong.

Affective disorders: disturbances in mood

7. Abnormal *depression* is marked by a severe and prolonged mood of sadness, helplessness, and hopelessness. Depressed individuals suffer from lowered self-esteem and motivation, guilt, sleep difficulties, physical complaints, and disturbances of perception and thought. The risk of suicide is especially high in depression.
8. When episodes of depression recur without other abnormalities of mood, the disorder is called *unipolar depression*. Exaggerated mood fluctuations from intense excitement to deep melancholy are characteristic of *bipolar depression*, or *manic-depressive illness*. Evidence exists that genetic and biochemical factors are involved in the development of these disorders.
9. Mood disorders occur twice as often among women than men. For both sexes, the chance of experiencing depressive episodes increases with age.

Anxiety disorders

10. *Anxiety disorders* arise when situations that produce conflict and frustration remain unresolved. Four common types of anxiety disorders are *generalized anxiety disorder, panic disorder, phobic disorder,* and *obsessive-compulsive disorder*.

Personality disorders: more disturbing than disturbed

11. Some forms of abnormal behavior, difficult to classify, are called *personality disorders*. Unlike other forms, they are not expressed in specific symptoms or clearly related to anxiety and stress. People with these disorders seem to lack the desire or ability to act in socially acceptable ways. Three major types are *antisocial personality, paranoid personality*, and *narcissistic personality*.

Substance abuse: the perilous pleasures of alcohol and drugs

12. Indications that alcohol or drug use is departing from normal are the development of *psychological dependence* and *physical dependence*, or *addiction*. Addiction victims develop *tolerance* for the substance (meaning that they require increasingly large doses to produce the desired effect), and they suffer *withdrawal symptoms* (painful physical and psychological reactions when they stop using the drug).

13. Persons who suffer from *alcoholism* become strongly dependent on alcohol and lose control over the act of drinking. They continue to drink despite the serious physical and psychological problems alcohol produces, including brain and liver damage, malnutrition, impaired problem-solving abilities, and disruption of family life. Alcoholism has no single cause, but heredity apparently plays some role.

14. *Altered states of consciousness*, in which the brain activity and perception do not operate in the usual fashion, can be produced by a variety of drugs ranging from *nicotine* (in tobacco) and *caffeine* (in coffee and tea) to heroin and cocaine.

15. *Drug abuse* is the repeated use of drugs for other than medical purposes resulting in severe physical and psychological disturbances. Abusers of multiple drugs are likely to have especially serious medical, personal, and social problems.

16. A modern explanation of drug abuse is the *opponent-process theory of emotion*. It holds that the human nervous system seeks to balance out any deviation from normal equilibrium in emotional experiences. Thus, every emotion triggers an opposing emotion that lingers after the first one is "switched off." Ultimately, for the drug abuser, the result is the onset of tolerance and addiction.

IMPORTANT TERMS

abnormal behavior
acrophobia
addiction
affective disorder
agoraphobia
alcoholism
altered states of consciousness
antisocial personality
anxiety disorder
bipolar depression
blackout
caffeine
cirrhosis

claustrophobia
compulsion
cortisol
delirium tremens
delusion
depression
drug abuse
DSM-III (R)
generalized anxiety disorder
hallucination
manic-depressive illness
narcissistic personality
nicotine

obsession	psychological dependence
obsessive-compulsive disorder	schizophrenia
opponent-process theory of emotion	school phobia
panic disorder	stress
paranoid personality	substance abuse
personality disorder	suicide
phobic disorder	tolerance
physical dependence	unipolar depression
post-traumatic stress disorder	withdrawal symptoms

RECOMMENDED READINGS

Altrocchi, J. *Abnormal behavior.* New York: Harcourt Brace Jovanovich, 1980.

Berger, G. *Mental illness.* New York: Watts, Franklin, 1981.

Blane, H. T., and Leonard, K. E. *Psychological theories of drinking and alcoholism.* New York: Guilford Press, 1987.

Cutting, J. *The psychology of schizophrenia.* New York: Churchill Livingstone, 1985.

Eisdorfer, C., et al. *Models for clinical psychopathology.* Jamaica, N.Y.: Spectrum Publications, 1981.

Hamburg, D. A., Elliott, G. R., and Parron, D. L., eds. *Health and behavior: frontiers of research in the biobehavioral sciences.* Washington, D.C.: National Academy Press, 1982.

Klein, D. F., and Rabkin, J. G., eds. *Anxiety: new research and changing concepts.* New York: Raven Press, 1981.

Leavitt, F. *Drugs and behavior,* 2d ed. New York: John Wiley & Sons, 1982.

Rachman, S. J., and Hodgson, R. J. *Obsessions and compulsions.* Englewood Cliffs, N.J.: Prentice-Hall, 1980.

Sarason, I. G., and Sarason, B. R. *Abnormal psychology: the problem of maladaptive behavior,* 5th ed. Englewood Cliffs, N.J.: Prentice-Hall, 1987.

Sartorius, N., and Ban, T. A. *Assessment of depression.* New York: Springer-Verlag, 1986.

CHAPTER 13
PSYCHOTHERAPY AND OTHER TREATMENT APPROACHES

DYNAMIC THERAPY — 465
Classical Freudian psychoanalysis
Dynamic therapies today

HUMANISTIC THERAPY — 468
Client-centered therapy
Other humanistic approaches

BEHAVIOR THERAPY — 470
The process of relearning
Newer trends in behavior therapy: encouraging assertive coping
Learning to cope through observation and guided participation

THERAPY IN GROUPS — 477
Traditional group therapy
Encounter groups
Large group awareness training
Other group approaches: treating real-life situations

BIOLOGICAL THERAPIES — 480
Drug therapy
Electroconvulsive therapy
Psychosurgery

COMMUNITY MENTAL HEALTH — 484
Community mental health centers
Crisis intervention
Self-help groups

ATTITUDES TOWARD PEOPLE WHO NEED PSYCHOLOGICAL HELP: HOW THEY CAN HURT OR HEAL — 487
The importance of family supports
The importance of community supports

SUMMARY — 490

IMPORTANT TERMS — 491

RECOMMENDED READINGS — 492

PSYCHOLOGY IN EVERYDAY LIFE
Choosing a psychotherapist — 469
How well—and for whom—does psychotherapy work? — 471
How useful is hypnotherapy? — 474
Is self-therapy possible? — 488

Beth, age 26, is an attractive, intelligent schoolteacher. After a string of romantic disappointments, she has become abnormally depressed and anxious. She has spells of weeping, often without provocation; begins wandering through the house before dawn, moaning and wringing her hands in agitation; and is plagued by feelings of guilt so punishing she is sure that God is about to take her life. On many days she feels totally panicked, refusing to leave her apartment. Not long ago, she told her mother she felt that the entire world had turned against her.

Disturbed and frightened, Beth—accompanied by a devoted friend—sits now in the waiting room of a local mental health clinic. Soon a clinical psychologist will emerge from her office and ask her to come in. For nearly an hour, these two—one a calm helper and the other desperately needing help—will talk and react to one another. Thus begins a course of treatment—eventually including both psychotherapy and the prescription by a physician of mood-lifting drugs—designed to help Beth both understand and overcome the abnormal feelings and thoughts that plague her.

That scenario, so common today, would have been played out quite differently in the past. In ancient times, people who displayed abnormal personality patterns were often flogged, starved to death, or burned and stoned (Valenstein, 1986). In the Middle Ages, "insane asylums" were created to imprison those who became mentally ill. There inmates were punished for their behavior—chained in dark, filthy cells and treated like beasts rather than human beings. As recently as in early American colonial times, patients were still locked up like animals and even exhibited to Sunday afternoon sightseers who paid an admission fee to taunt and ridicule them.

Punishment and incarceration as means for treating mental illness were not invented out of the blue. They were based on theories of the day about what causes abnormal behavior and how best to deal with it. When the ancients chipped holes in the skulls of the

This sixteenth century painting depicts the treatment of a mental disorder through the removal of a piece of the skull—thus allowing "madness" to escape.

Chapter 13 Psychotherapy and Other Treatment Approaches

mentally ill or burned them with hot irons, it was because they believed that demons had possessed the victims, and that such treatment would speed the demons' escape. And when Benjamin Rush, often called "the father of American psychiatry," sanctioned those cruel Sunday afternoon exhibitions, it was because he believed that "terror acts powerfully on the body through the medium of the mind, and should be employed in the cure of madness" (Deutsch, 1949).

Today, of course, approaches to treatment are much more benign and humane. But many of them are also based on major views of human personality—such as those described in Chapter 10—and on views about why the personality goes awry. For example, psychologists who believe that abnormal behavior originates in the emotional experiences of early life will focus on helping the individual understand and overcome these childhood events. On the other hand, those who are convinced that abnormal behavior results from the use of self-defeating responses to people and situations will attempt to teach more appropriate responses—and ignore probing into the patient's past.

Although the exact number of persons seeking treatment for psychological problems is not known for certain, estimates suggest the total exceeds 15 million persons over 18 years of age (Shapiro et al., 1984). They receive help from a variety of practitioners—primarily psychologists, psychiatrists (who are medically trained), social workers, and marriage and family counselors. In hospital settings, psychiatric nurses are engaged in treatment as well. The variety of therapeutic techniques used numbers over 350 (Herink, 1980). This chapter will describe major psychological approaches to treatment and a few important medical interventions as well.

DYNAMIC THERAPY

Psychotherapists who employ a *dynamic* approach to therapy believe that effective treatment must focus on the underlying mental and emotional forces that, they believe, generated the individual's problems. They view these forces as beginning to influence behavior and personality in early childhood.

While it is true enough that all psychotherapy is intended to alter behavior, therapists with a dynamic orientation probe deeply into the individual's makeup in the hope of changing basic attitudes and responses. As will be shown subsequently, other psychotherapists see their mission simply to alter behavior and thus rid their patients of painful symptoms—without worrying about the underlying dynamics. For dynamic therapists, however, the crucial element is *insight*—an uncovering and awareness of the potent and far-reaching forces, including motives, emotions, and conflicts operating in the individual's unconscious. The hoped-for result is a major change in the individual's personality.

Classical Freudian Psychoanalysis

Known as *psychoanalysis*, the method of treatment developed by Freud was designed to bring into awareness the unconscious desires and conflicts that he considered the source of abnormal anxiety and guilt. The chief tool in psychoanalysis is *free association*, which often produces insights into hidden psychological processes. If you were to undertake psychoanalysis, you would be asked to lie on a couch, as relaxed as possible, and speak out every thought that occurred to you—no matter how foolish it might seem, how obscene, or how insulting to the analyst. In this situation, as when drifting off to sleep, conscious control of mental processes is reduced to a minimum and unconscious forces become more apparent. The analyst would pay particular attention to occasions when your thoughts encounter what is called *resistance*—that is, when your train of thought seems to be blocked by anxiety and repressions indicating unconscious conflicts. The analyst would also study your fantasies and slips of the tongue in a search for clues to unconscious desires and conflicts.

Another psychoanalytic technique used to uncover unconscious motives and conflicts is *dream analysis*. Freud believed that dreams often reveal deeply hidden conflicts, though in disguised ways that require painstaking interpretation. Forbidden sexual desires, in particular, he thought, are likely to crop up—often in hidden form in which the male genital organ is symbolized by a snake, a tower, or an airplane, and the female genital organ by a basket or flower. Freud identified over two dozen symbols for the male genitals and over twenty for the female (Rycroft, 1986). Freud labeled the unconscious sexual and aggressive material found in dreams as its *latent content*; in contrast, he identified the conscious material—that is, the actual images of the dream—as its *manifest content*. During therapy, the analyst interprets the manifest content of a dream in a way that exposes its latent content—and thereby helps identify and ultimately resolve conflicts deeply rooted in the patient's unconscious. Freud regarded the dream as "the royal road to the unconscious."

Another clue to the unconscious is what analysts call *transference*. Freud believed that in a sense none of us ever completely grows up. Neurotic people in particular tend to retain their childhood emotional attitudes toward such well-loved and much hated persons as their parents and their brothers and sisters, and they often display or transfer many such attitudes to the analyst. Psychoanalysts deliberately remain passive, neutral listeners most of the time, trying to be a blank screen onto which patients can "project" their feelings about key people in their lives. At times they might try desperately to please the analyst, as they once tried to please their parents. At other times they might resent and hate the analyst, who actually had done nothing to provoke these feelings.

Through transferences, free associations, dreams, and reports of everyday behavior, a pattern would gradually emerge of the unconscious problems that the analyst would say represented the patient's real-life difficulties. The analyst would then interpret the problems and help the patient acquire insights into the unconscious processes and gain control over them. The goal in analysis is to strengthen the ego and provide what one analyst called "freedom from the tyranny of the unconscious" (Kubie, 1950).

Dynamic Therapies Today

Classical psychoanalysis has never attracted a large following. The American Psychoanalytic Association, to which most practitioners of psychoanalysis belong, has recently numbered only about 3,000 members (Newman, 1986). Moreover, new generations of psychoanalysts have added to and in some ways revised Freud's theories and techniques.

Practitioners of classical psychoanalytic therapy approach their patients guided by Freud's views of the origins of abnormal personality development, as described in Chapter 10. For these traditional Freudians, unconscious sexual and aggressive drives—and how they are handled—are paramount. Following Freud, however, a number of psychoanalytic therapists—taking their cues from the theories of analysts such as Adler, Horney, and Fromm (also described in Chapter 10)—began to place greater emphasis on the importance of social and cultural forces in their patients' lives. Today, many therapists, while still using a dynamic approach, feel also that it is as important for their patients to gain insight into what is happening in their environment—their work, marriage, friendships—as into what may have gone wrong in childhood.

Dynamic therapy today diverges from classical psychoanalysis in matters of technique as well as theory. In its classic form, psychoanalysis is a long process, requiring three to five visits a week for two to five years or more, and is, therefore, very expensive. In recent

Figure 13-1 The major features of brief psychotherapy

For practical reasons, including financial, brief psychotherapy is currently the treatment of choice for many people seeking help (Koss, Butcher, and Strupp, 1986).

Feature	Role of therapist
Prompt intervention	Offers timely treatment to wide range of patients
Limited time	Estimates the number of sessions required—usually not more than 25—after assessing patient's problems
Limited goals	Helps patient achieve rapid improvement of symptoms, and provides insight into source of problems and future coping strategies
Maintenance of focus	Selects specific area to work on, such as problematic family relationships
High therapist activity	Talks as much as required to make interpretations and offer support and guidance

years, however, many dynamically oriented therapists have attempted to shorten the treatment period (Strupp and Binder, 1984). As indicated in Figure 13-1, they have adopted new and faster techniques for helping people achieve, if not full "freedom from the tyranny of the unconscious," at least enough insight to cope with their more serious problems. There is no intention to effect character change—although such changes sometimes do take hold. During therapy sessions, the therapist takes a more active, directive role in helping patients focus on and solve specific problems such as their ways of relating to others, rather than on reliving childhood memories. Moreover, the traditional psychoanalytic couch is often no longer in evidence; in its stead there is face-to-face discussion between patient and therapist. And there is less emphasis on free association and more on a focused analysis of specific conflicts and anxieties. Evidence suggests that such psychotherapy has about the same success rate as longer-term treatment programs (Johnson and Gelso, 1980).

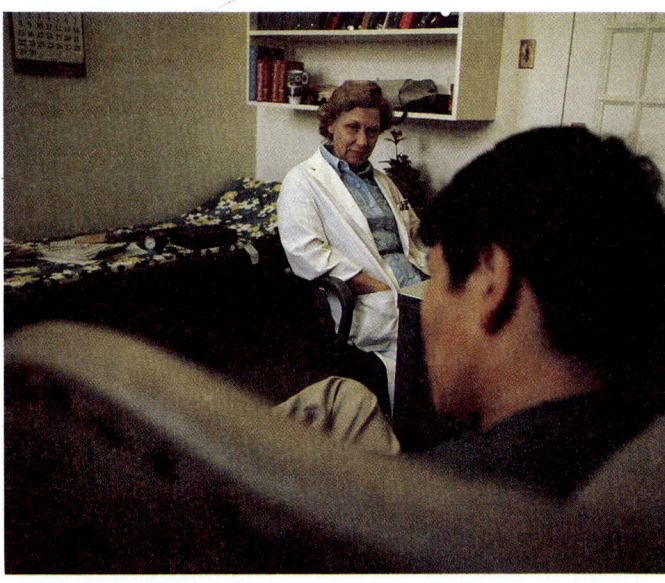

A therapist and hospital patient meet in face-to-face interaction.

HUMANISTIC THERAPY

Humanistic theories of personality—with their emphasis on self-actualization and the perfecting of personal strengths—are reflected in humanistic approaches to psychotherapy. Unlike psychoanalysis, they do not demand a rigid set of procedures. For example, the humanistic therapist participates in the treatment as much as necessary to facilitate self-awareness and self-acceptance. All matters of technique are secondary to the goals of treatment: to explore the client's inner experience solely from the client's own perspective; and to encourage personal responsibility, freedom, and will, both with regard to the changes taking place in therapy and the more general ways that individuals choose to conduct their lives (Rosenhan and Seligman, 1984).

Client-centered Therapy

Client-centered therapy, developed by Carl Rogers, is one of the most prominent examples of the humanistic approach. Unlike psychoanalytic therapists who see themselves as the force behind behavior change, client-centered therapists give this responsibility to the client. As Rogers saw it, the task of the therapist is to facilitate—in a nondirective manner—the process of helping individuals understand and control their own lives.

Of central importance to client-centered therapy is the great warmth and acceptance the therapist displays toward the client. An understanding therapist creates a nonthreatening situation in which the clients are free to explore all their thoughts and feelings, including those they have been unable to deal with for fear of condemnation by other people or by their own consciences. Likewise, in the safety of this relationship with an accepting therapist, clients are expected to acquire gradually the ability to resolve their conflicts. The process, Rogers said, takes three steps: (1) clients begin to experience, understand, and accept feelings and desires (such as sexuality and hostility) that they had previously denied to consciousness; (2) they begin to understand the reasons behind their behavior; and (3) they begin to see how they can undertake more positive forms of behavior. In a word, they learn to be themselves.

Originally, Rogers refrained from expressing any reactions he had toward the conduct of the client. Later, however, he identified three important qualities necessary for an effective client-centered therapist: unconditional positive regard, empathy, and genuineness. As described in Chapter 10, *unconditional positive regard* means the acceptance of individuals for what they are and trust in their ability to grow. Such acceptance, free from value judgments and criticism, promotes a trusting relationship between client and therapist. Empathy, according to Rogers, is the ability of the therapist to understand the feelings of the client and to communicate this understanding. Finally, therapists should always be "genuine"—that is, they should frankly describe their own feelings, including disapproval of some of the client's actions. But humanistic therapists in general are very careful to distinguish between criticism of an action and criticism of the person. An important key of humanistic treatment is for the therapist to be viewed as genuinely warm and sincere at all times. Thus the match between therapist and client becomes an important factor—as indeed it is in all forms of therapy. The matter is discussed in a box on Psychology in Everyday Life titled "Choosing a Psychotherapist."

Many of us who hear about humanistic therapy for the first time ask: If all people were encouraged to be completely themselves, would the world not suddenly be filled with aggressive, brawling, murderous, sexually unrestrained, self-seeking egoists? Rogers answered with an unqualified no. He found that when people accept themselves, they tend to be more accepting of others.

Psychology in Everyday Life
Choosing a Psychotherapist

Given the number and variety of therapists, the selection of one by a prospective client is by no means an easy task. Following are some practical steps that can help in the decision:

1. *Ask for referrals.* General practitioners, as well as many medical specialists, often refer patients to psychotherapists and are likely to know who is available and reputable in the community. Others in the service professions may also be of help: lawyers, teachers, school counselors, often stymied by the personality problems of their clients, end up suggesting therapy, and thereby accumulate a knowledge of the professionals in their area. Another good source is the local Mental Health Association.

2. *Talk to former patients.* It is better to interview those who have already completed therapy than those who are still in it. Psychotherapy patients can be emotionally swayed by what happened in their therapy session yesterday, and it might be difficult to correct for their momentary feeling of enthusiasm or disappointment.

3. *Ask for expert consultation.* An appointment with a prominent psychologist or psychiatrist in the community—for example, the head of a university or hospital department—can be used for a "diagnostic consultation." Such a widely experienced person can help narrow down the number of choices—in part by helping match therapists available with the particular problem at hand.

4. *Interview the prospective therapist.* With a few referrals in hand, the most direct way of learning how a particular therapist works is by spending an hour in a "feeling out" interview. In arranging an appointment, it is wise to make clear that the intent is to explore the possibilities, not to actually begin treatment. Many psychotherapists believe this "courtship" is so important that they do not charge for preliminary visits from prospective clients, unless therapy is actually begun (Parloff, 1987).

The match between patient and "healer" remains a distinctly personal matter. The therapist's personality and how it meshes with the patient's can be even more important than the therapist's theoretical orientation and specific approach. Today, about half of all therapists no longer limit themselves to any single method (Smith, 1982). Instead they take what is called an *eclectic* approach, selecting from the various tools of treatment available those that seem most beneficial, and "integrating them into a treatment package believed to be most effective regardless of their theoretical orientation" (Parloff, London, and Wolfe, 1986).

Other Humanistic Approaches

The techniques of psychotherapy used by humanistic psychologists are based on the belief that people will grow in constructive ways if they can be helped to explore and use their current hidden potential. Thus, for example, while *Gestalt* therapists help their patients explore the past, they do so only as a means of encouraging them to understand and control the present. Individuals treated by Gestalt therapists are sometimes urged to relive early emotional experiences as vividly as they can. They are even helped to act out these feelings—to swear, kick, and scream—but all in the interest of teaching them that they now can understand their feelings and be responsible for controlling them (Rosenhan and Seligman, 1984). In confronting their emotions, they are taking a major step in gaining strength to take charge of them.

Practitioners of *existential psychotherapy* also emphasize the strength of the human spirit. In direct contrast to Skinner, they believe strongly in the importance of free will. They maintain that the events in our lives do not control our destinies—for what really counts is our own attitude toward these events, which we are free to choose for ourselves. We are all responsible for our own behavior. We can make our own decisions and thus control our own attitudes and thoughts—and thus rise above even the most adverse events in our environment.

One existential approach, known as *logotherapy* ("meaning" therapy), was developed by Victor Frankl while he was an inmate of a Nazi concentration camp. Logotherapy stresses the importance of finding a meaning in life—and each individual's capacity to create such a meaning. It was during his own incarceration that Frankl concluded that life can be made purposeful even in the most atrocious circumstances. Except for his sister, his entire family perished. He lost every possession and everything he valued was destroyed. Hungry, cold, always expecting death, how could he still want to live? Frankl found meaning in his efforts to aid others instead of focusing on his own personal circumstances. He continues to teach that, by reappraising our lives, we are free to find a guiding rationale for our existence.

Frankl urges therapists to divert patients from spending precious time endlessly searching for the sources of their anxiety and depression. Instead he believes patients should be urged to pay attention to the healthier parts of their personalities and encouraged to dwell on the meaningful things they can do and the contributions they can make (Yalom, 1980).

BEHAVIOR THERAPY

Therapists who practice *behavior therapy* use techniques based on the principle of learning and conditioning described in Chapter 5. The goal of behavior therapy, also referred to as behavior modification, is unlike that of dynamic or humanistic therapy in that it makes no attempt at a dramatic restructuring of the individual's underlying personality or approaches to life. Instead the goal is simply to get rid of the troubling symptom—whether depression, phobias, compulsions, or sexual malfunctions. What has been learned, behavior therapists assume, can be unlearned. The purpose is not to unearth the reasons for the problem but simply to alter the self-defeating and painful behavior.

If, for example, a patient has divorced two husbands and is considering a third marriage, an analyst would argue that she needs to analyze and understand her feelings about men—perhaps her early attitudes towards her father—before making another commitment. A behavior therapist, on the other hand, would not focus on past history. Instead the goal would be to alter behavior in the present, to help the patient learn practical new ways of relating to men, and to help her overcome the self-defeating interpersonal habits that got her into trouble in the past. In other words, insight does not matter; behavior does. Because behavior therapists attack behavior and attitudes directly, this approach is especially useful when trying to ameliorate problems that can be readily identified—for example, fears and phobias. It is useful also when dealing with specific problems such as overdrinking, shyness, aggressiveness, or sexual "hang-ups." The effectiveness of therapy is easier to measure when the problems attacked are so specific, but the issue of evaluating therapy remains a thorny one. It is discussed in a box on Psychology in Everyday Life titled "How Well—and for Whom—Does Psychotherapy Work?"

Psychology in Everyday Life
How Well—and for Whom—Does Psychotherapy Work?

Especially in the United States, where psychotherapy has flourished more vigorously than anywhere else, it represents a large investment by society. It is impossible to estimate how many millions of hours have gone into the training of psychotherapists, the practice of various treatment methods, and research into new and better methods. Certainly people who undertake psychotherapy spend millions of dollars every year. Are the time and money a good investment? How much does psychotherapy contribute to society?

Except in the case of clearly defined problems such as specific phobias, the results of therapy, unfortunately, are very difficult to assess. It is hard to determine whether a client has improved at all, much less to exactly what extent. Often different opinions are held by the therapist, the client, and outside observers such as the client's family and friends. Moreover many people who experience troublesome symptoms—for example, mild anxiety or depression—get over them eventually without any treatment at all.

One severe critic of psychotherapy is the British psychologist H. J. Eysenck, who became famous in the 1950s for a series of studies that led him to conclude therapy is no more helpful than the passage of time. But subsequent investigations have swayed more psychologists—including those who do not themselves practice therapy—to a very different conclusion. A recent survey of the best available evidence gathered over the years indicates that there can no longer be much doubt about the overall value of psychotherapy. Data from 475 controlled studies of about 25,000 clients who had undergone therapy showed that on the average they were better off at the end of the treatment than about 80 percent of those with comparable complaints who went without help (Smith, Glass, and Miller, 1980). Moreover, it appears that psychotherapy reduces by about a third the extent to which clients feel the need to seek care for medical complaints (Mumford et al., 1984).

Is one method of therapy better than another? There is no real evidence that the type of treatment makes a difference. Therapists are about equally helpful regardless of their theoretical background or the techniques they use (Stiles, Shapiro, and Elliot, 1986). Their personal qualities seem to be more important than their methods. They are most effective if they themselves are well adjusted, if they are experienced, and if they establish a warm and close relationship with the client. Both men and women appear to be equally successful as therapists (Strupp and Binder, 1984).

Do some clients have a better chance for improvement than others? It does not seem to matter whether the client is young or old, male or female. But the nature of the problem makes considerable difference. The less serious the disturbance, the greater the likelihood of improvement. Thus people with minor maladjustments of recent origin usually do better than people with severe and long-standing maladjustments. Those who are troubled only by reactions of anxiety or depression are much more likely to benefit than victims of schizophrenia. Cases of sociopathic personality are extremely resistant to treatment—perhaps because sociopaths do not experience the intense anxiety that most other disturbed people are eager to escape.

A desire to get rid of the psychological problem is one of the most important of all factors increasing the likelihood of success. Just as strong motivation for change is highly favorable, so is a willingness to work hard at eliminating the difficulties and a belief that the treatment will help. Clients do best when they trust and like their therapist and are convinced that the therapist understands their predicament, sympathizes with them, and is going about the treatment in a way that promises relief (Strupp, 1986).

A behavior therapist works with a patient suffering from acrophobia.

The Process of Relearning

Behavior therapy, as first practiced by learning theorists, tried to eliminate whatever conditioned reflex or conditioned response was causing trouble—for example, an unreasonable fear produced by heights or confined spaces, or the habit of responding to certain situations with anxiety or anger. The behavior therapist made a direct attack on such symptoms of abnormal behavior by trying to break the old stimulus-response connection and substituting a more effective response. Among the techniques they developed and still use in many cases are the following:

Desensitization A method often used to eliminate phobias is *desensitization*, which originally consisted of attempts to associate the fear-causing stimulus with relaxation rather than with panic. If you sought relief from an unreasonable fear of snakes, for example, the therapist would ask you to relax as much as possible, then to imagine you were looking at a snake in a mildly fear-producing situation, such as from a distance. If you could do this without losing your feeling of relaxation, you would then be asked to imagine a slightly more threatening sight of a snake—and so on until you could remain relaxed while imagining that you held a snake.

Actual relaxation, it has been found, is not essential. Phobias can be desensitized and eliminated simply by visualizing yourself in situations that have caused fear, while in the presence of a therapist who encourages the visualization process and praises improvement in the ability to respond calmly (Wilkins, 1971). Apparently, just thinking about the feared stimulus, in an atmosphere that offers support and promises relief, is often enough to produce results.

Extinction The method of extinction is a direct attempt to break a troublesome stimulus-response connection. In one case, it produced spectacular results with a nine-month-old boy who had somehow acquired the habit of vomiting shortly after every meal, weighed only twelve pounds, and was in danger of starving to death. An electrode was attached to his leg and shocks were administered whenever he began to vomit, continuing until he stopped. After a few experiences, the boy learned to stop vomiting as soon as the shock occurred, then soon quit altogether. After a few weeks he weighed 16 pounds, was released from the hospital, and continued to gain weight at home, showing no signs of going back to the habit (Lang and Melamed, 1969).

The extinction of a response by pairing undesirable behavior with a disagreeable stimulus, such as shock, is called *aversive conditioning*. The person under treatment learns to abandon the undesirable action in order to avoid the unpleasant consequences with which the therapist causes it to be associated. Aversive conditioning is always used with caution—or when nothing else seems possible, as in the case of the starving boy—but has proved effective in a number of situations, such as treating men who were sexually incapacitated by sadistic fantasies (Davison, 1968), or by transvestism (Marks, 1968), which is the desire to dress in the clothing of the other sex.

Reinforcement Behavior therapists also use a technique that is the direct opposite of aversive conditioning. Often they employ *reinforcement* of a positive kind as a reward for more effective and more desirable behavior. For example, one group of behavior therapists, dealing with a retarded adolescent boy who engaged in self-injurious and disruptive

This effort to give up smoking by making it a "shocking" experience is an example of adverse conditioning.

Behavior Therapy

behavior at school, rewarded him with a glass of orange juice and verbal praise any time he showed signs of calm, sitting behavior. Given this kind of push toward acceptable behavior—with juice and praise as the reinforcers—the adolescent's self-destructive behavior significantly declined in both frequency and intensity (Tierney, 1986). The technique of reinforcement has also been used in the form of a *token economy* (see Chapter 5), which has produced dramatic improvement in the behavior of mental hospital patients rewarded with tokens good for movies and other privileges.

Newer Trends in Behavior Therapy: Encouraging Assertive Coping

Some of the original practitioners of behavior therapy continue to believe that classical or operant conditioning produces the ineffective responses characteristic of most people whose adjustment is poor (Wolpe, 1976). Accordingly, they rely on such techniques as desensitization, extinction, and reinforcement to change the responses. But many of today's behavior therapists have moved in a more cognitive direction. They now seek to change their clients' basic thought patterns. In treating depression, for example, therapists who practice *cognitive behavior therapy* try to bring to light the unrealistically negative views that depressed people tend to develop about their own capacities, the world about them, and the future. They attempt to help their clients by entirely altering such self-defeating habits of thinking (Rush and Beck, 1978).

The difference between normal and abnormal behavior, according to the current view of behavior therapy, often lies in a person's own convictions about ability or lack of ability to cope successfully with anxiety-producing or stressful situations. These convictions about "self-efficacy," as Bandura terms it, determine whether people will make any effort at all to cope, how hard they will try, and how long they will persist. Thus the key to therapy and behavior change is regarded as an enhanced regard for one's own self-efficacy. The key to

---

Psychology in Everyday Life
How Useful Is Hypnotherapy?

The use of hypnosis to alter an individual's state of consciousness and to bring about changes in behavior is called *hypnotherapy*. The nature of the hypnotic state is unknown. Psychologists know only how to produce it, not what it is. The hypnotist may ask the subject to sit as relaxed as possible and stare fixedly at some small object, such as a key, the tip of a pencil, or a point of light. Meanwhile the hypnotist speaks in a quiet and repetitious monotone, suggesting that the subject is growing more and more relaxed, that the subject's eyes are tiring, and that the subject is becoming sleepy. Soon the subject seems to respond to the suggestions: The eyelids flutter and close. The body becomes limp. The head droops, and apparently the subject is sound asleep.

There is no similarity, however, between the hypnotic state and real sleep. The brain waves show a different pattern. So do many measures of bodily activity. Moreover the subject remains fully conscious of the hypnotist's voice and responds to the hypnotist's suggestions. One characteristic of the hypnotic state is an intense and sharply focused attention on the hypnotist's words and the perceptions and events that are suggested (Hilgard and Hilgard, 1975). Therapists employing hypnosis frequently use techniques of *posthypnotic suggestion*, intended to produce desired behaviors after the subject is no longer hypnotized.

Hypnotherapy has been used in the treatment of stress-related eating disorders by helping patients learn to relax during the

this better feeling about oneself, in turn, is successful performance in situations that have previously caused anxiety or stress (Bandura, 1986). The behavior therapist makes every effort to foster success, using any method that seems promising. Some therapists, in their attempts to modify self-defeating perceptions and behavior and improve coping, use the technique of hypnosis (Frankel and Zamansky, 1978). This is discussed in a Psychology in Everyday Life box titled "How Useful Is Hypnotherapy?"

Learning to Cope through Observation and Guided Participation

One method now used by behavior therapists is based on observation learning. Subjects with a phobia for snakes, for example, have been asked to watch a movie of other people approaching and eventually playing with a snake (see Figure 13-2). The subjects can stop the movie and turn it back at any time they begin to feel fearful. By eventually seeing the movie through to the end, they can observe that all people shown, though perhaps frightened at first, were finally able to pick up a snake and even drape it around their neck—all without suffering any harm. If others could do this, why not the subjects?

The observation learning provided by the movie helps considerably to relieve the snake phobia, as can be seen in Figure 13-3. Even more effective, however, is the further step of watching a live model handle a snake, then joining the model—who again suffers no harm and indeed actually enjoys the experience—in playing with the snake. This _guided participation_ in a previously anxiety-producing activity is another method used by behavior therapists.

In most attempts to enhance feelings of self-efficacy, therapists try to arrange real-life situations in which the client can practice assertive coping with successful results. People suffering from intense stage fright have been treated effectively by guiding them step by step through the delivery of a make-believe speech (with the therapist being the only

---

periods of anxiety that frequently trigger an eating binge. The technique has also helped some people overcome specific fears—of animals, flying, or public speaking. Its greatest effectiveness has been in alleviating pain associated with burns, injuries, or psychosomatic conditions such as ulcerative colitis and migraine headaches. However, attempts to use hypnotherapy to alter addictive behavior, including drinking and smoking, have not met with great success (Wadden and Anderson, 1982).

Because people under hypnosis may give detailed accounts of events they could not recall under ordinary circumstances, therapists sometimes use hypnosis to dredge up forgotten experiences that may have caused psychological problems. There is considerable question, however, about the accuracy of such recollections. One psychiatrist has found that recollections of childhood experiences obtained under hypnosis often prove to be inaccurate (Orne, 1982). There is an analogy here between hypnosis and another altered state of consciousness we all know as dreams. Most of us have had the experience of not being quite sure whether something actually happened to us or occurred only in a dream.

The verdict on hypnotherapy applies to one degree or another to other techniques of therapy: It may work, but not with everyone, and certainly not with all types of psychological problems.

Figure 13-2 Scenes from a movie that cures the fear of snakes

The photographs are stills from a motion picture that has successfully applied observation learning to the treatment of snake phobia, as described in the text.

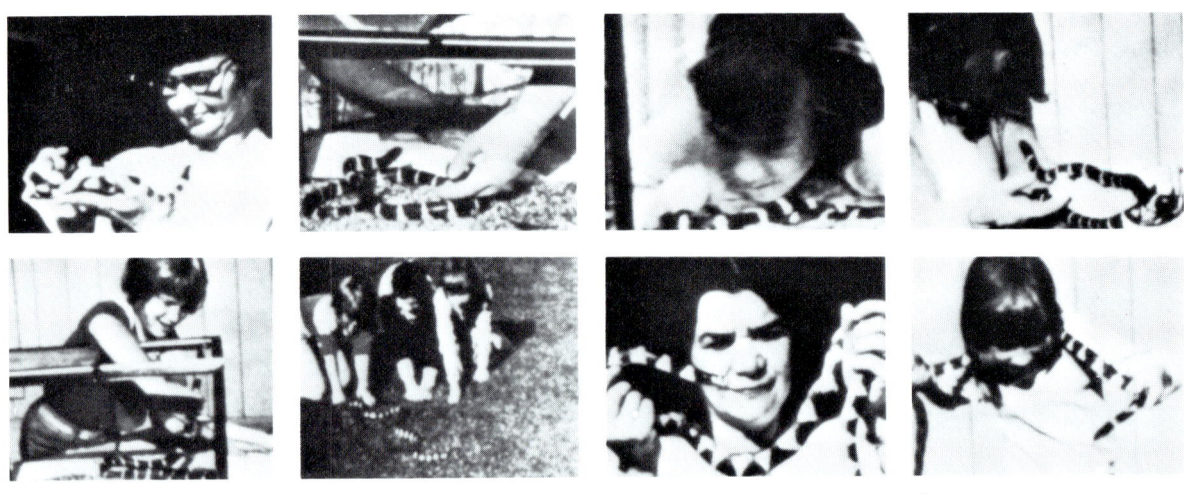

Figure 13-3 Snake phobia: different treatments, different results

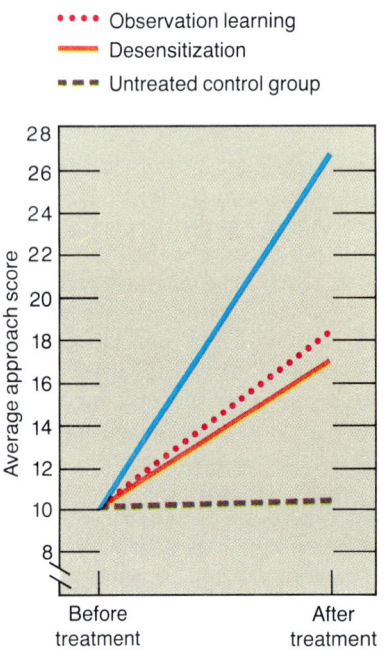

Three groups of subjects suffering from snake phobia were treated through different techniques of behavior therapy: desensitization, observation learning (watching the movie illustrated in Figure 13-2), and guided participation in handling a snake. All three methods produced improvement, but in varying degrees (Bandura, Blanchard, and Ritter, 1969). A score of zero meant that a subject could not even enter a room in which there was a snake. To achieve a perfect score of 29, subjects had to let a snake crawl over their lap while holding their hands passively at their sides.

audience), to brief comments made before just a few listeners (with the therapist again present to provide support and encouragement), to a full-scale address delivered in a large auditorium. People afraid to fly in airplanes have been taken by the therapist on inspection tours of a plane motionless on the ground during servicing, then on brief flights with the therapist alongside, then on longer flights—which finally they managed alone. One study evaluated the progress of people treated in this manner for severe phobias about public speaking, travel, shopping trips, heights, crowds, and other such matters. It was found that 80 percent got over their fears within a few days, though about half required some additional guidance and practice to make the cure permanent (Hardy, 1969). Moreover enhanced feelings of self-efficacy created by successful performance in one situation tend to improve the ability to cope with other situations as well (Bandura, Jeffery, and Gajdos, 1975).

THERAPY IN GROUPS

Therapists of quite different orientations have adapted their approaches for use in *group therapy*, or the treatment of several patients at the same time. The method is in part the child of necessity, for there are not enough trained therapists to treat all prospective clients individually. But it also seems to have genuine advantages with some clients. Joining a group may relieve the individual's anxieties by demonstrating that other people have the same problems. It also creates an interactional or social give-and-take that is impossible in a face-to-face session with a therapist. Some psychologists believe many clients show the greatest progress when treated through a combination of group and individual psychotherapy.

Traditional Group Therapy

In the traditional therapy group, the therapist meets with a small number of individuals, usually from six to nine. The therapist typically determines the composition of the group, selecting participants on the basis of what is known of their problems and how each member can be anticipated to engage in the give-and-take of the group situation. Over time, however, each group usually develops its own style, its own way of dealing with explosive subjects such as love and hate, guilt and anger, sex and suspicion. The quality of

A group therapy session for cocaine users.

the leader is important. It takes a well-trained therapist to track the complex interactions among group members and to explain what is happening as the interactions unfold.

For many people, group therapy turns out to be an effective vehicle for growth and change. For them, learning new ways to deal with the world is often best accomplished not in a one-to-one relationship with a therapist, but in a setting where human interactions typically take place and where they can be analyzed and changed. Therapy in a group gives each participant a circle of people who will learn to share their feelings with each other and to understand and deal with them. In a group setting interpersonal difficulties can be exposed from behind a facade of "put-ons." Group therapy has been described as a "living laboratory" where therapists can zero in on their patients' usual ways of dealing with people and help them try out new ones.

Encounter Groups

About 25 years ago, the *encounter group* emerged as an outgrowth of the humanistic approach stressing openness and honesty in interpersonal relationships. In an encounter group, a number of people meet with the goal of shedding the masks they usually wear in public and presenting their true feelings. Encounters are usually led by a trained therapist, though sometimes they meet without a leader. The emphasis is on activities, games, and conversations that encourage members to interact with open displays of emotion, approval, criticism, affection, and hostility. The goal is to throw off the ordinary social restraints and explore what are often called "gut feelings." The assumption is much the same as in humanistic therapy—namely, that people will grow in a positive direction if freed of artificial barriers against perceiving their true self and interacting with others honestly and openly. The humanistic psychologist Carl Rogers was himself a leader in the encounter group movement.

The effectiveness of encounter groups is controversial. At one time, Rogers considered them superior in some ways to his humanistic therapy as practiced on a one-to-one basis (Rogers, 1969). Abraham Maslow, who devised the humanistic concept of self-actualization, concluded that encounter groups are highly useful in encouraging self-awareness and self-expression but can help relieve only minor difficulties, not serious neurotic problems (Maslow, 1969). One study of the effects on some 200 college students who had taken part in encounter groups found that about a third changed for the better, a third were unchanged, and a third changed for the worse (Lieberman, Yalom, and Miles, 1973). The possibility of harm rather than improvement, it has been suggested, is especially great for people who have low self-esteem and cannot cope with group criticism (Kirsch and Glass, 1977).

Large Group Awareness Training

In recent years, as the popularity of encounter groups has waned, a growing number of individuals have begun to participate in *large group awareness training* programs, which incorporate processes as diverse as education, spiritual enlightenment, encounter, and traditional group psychotherapy (Finkelstein, Wenegrat, and Yalom, 1982). Groups as large as 200 or more are led by a "trainer" through a variety of psychological "exercises," among them aggressive confrontations, relaxation exercises, and situations designed to induce mutual trust. Known under such names as "Lifespring" and "Actualizations," these are essentially self-improvement programs as much as actual therapy groups. Some, like the program known as "est," are popular for a time and are then replaced by newer ones.

It is estimated that nearly a half million people have participated in these group experiences, and the pace appears to be accelerating. Although many participants are pleased with the outcome, there is still no evidence that such large group programs have a significant therapeutic effect (Finkelstein, Wenegrat, and Yalom, 1982).

Other Group Approaches: Treating Real-life Situations

A number of forms of group therapy have been specially devised for the purpose of allowing the therapist to observe and analyze real-life problems in the group setting. One such form that has survived over many years is *psychodrama*, first developed in the 1930s by the Viennese psychiatrist J. L. Moreno. In psychodrama, the therapist helps participants gain insight into their conflicts and problems by dramatizing them as if in a play. In effect, the therapist serves as "stage director," and each member of the group acts out a problem situation in turn. Other members play supporting roles, and then everyone discusses the episode.

The observation by the therapist of real-life situations can be useful as well in group therapy designed to address a very specific problem area. One example is *assertiveness training*, in which the goal is to teach people to stand up for their rights without violating the rights of others. In addition to providing counseling and teaching assertive behavior through modeling, an essential element of the group experience is for participants to role-play real-life interactions. This allows the leader to provide feedback not only on what the client says in situations calling for assertiveness, but also the voice quality and "body language" used to say it.

The analysis of relationships as they are actually played out in life is essential also for therapists practicing *family therapy*, an approach based on the belief that the family plays a

Family therapy often pinpoints critical problems in relationships.

Therapy in Groups

key role in producing maladaptive behavior. Underlying this belief is the view that interactions among family members are often the cause of an individual's problems—that the disordered behavior of an individual is merely a symptom of a much larger problem rooted in the family's dynamics. Family therapy sessions typically include mother, father, and children as participants, although extended family members may at times be included as well. Under the therapist's guidance, they work as a unit, and the goal of the therapist is to help resolve any one individual's problems by changing the behavior patterns of the entire family. In this sense, the family—its structure and organization—becomes the therapist's client (Epstein and Vlok, 1981). Thus the therapist may play back video recordings of sessions to allow participants to see how they actually interact, or even visit the home at times to observe the family in its natural setting.

BIOLOGICAL THERAPIES

The therapies described to this point have been based on interpersonal communication between patient and therapist—on that "specialized human relationship designed to facilitate changes in the patient's cognitions, feelings, and actions" (Strupp, 1986). As described in the previous chapter, however, biological factors can play an important role in the development of abnormal behavior. Changes in glandular activity and in brain chemistry are often associated with profound changes in personality and behavior. *Biological therapies* are intended to help the patient by changing these underlying physiological mechanisms. Such therapies are based on the belief that psychological conditions can be influenced by nonpsychological methods—by chemical, hormonal, or physical interventions that can affect the brain either directly or indirectly—and thus produce or inhibit certain behaviors and alter mood. Often, of course, biological therapies are used in conjunction with other therapies described in this chapter.

Drug Therapy

The most widely and successfully used form of biological treatment is *drug therapy*—also called *chemotherapy*—which is the prescription of drugs intended to produce specific changes in mood or behavior. During the early 1950s, the development of drugs that controlled the symptoms of schizophrenia was a major landmark in the treatment of severely disturbed individuals. Patients who were agitated and unmanageable became calm and cooperative. Furthermore, these drugs greatly improved the atmosphere of mental hospitals, making it possible to discharge patients more quickly than ever before. As shown in Figure 13-4, the introduction of drug treatment drastically reduced the number of patients cared for in institutions for the mentally ill.

Since the early 1950s, a variety of drugs have been shown to be helpful not only in combating the disoriented behavior and hallucinations of schizophrenia, but anxiety states and depression as well. Figure 13-5 identifies the three major classes of drugs used in the treatment of psychological disorders. A more detailed description of them follows:

Drugs for Schizophrenia (Major Tranquilizers) Used successfully to control the most disruptive symptoms of schizophrenia, *major tranquilizers* (also referred to as *antipsychotic drugs*) have permitted many individuals to be treated in the community rather than in the hospital. Such drugs have proven especially effective in reducing hallucinations, delusions, and the disordered thinking typically displayed by schizophrenic individuals (National Institute of Health, 1985). They have enabled some patients, though by no means all, to return to a more or less normal life. Moreover, tranquilizing drugs have greatly improved the atmosphere of mental hospitals by calming patients who were previously unmanageable.

Figure 13-4 The drop in mental hospital population

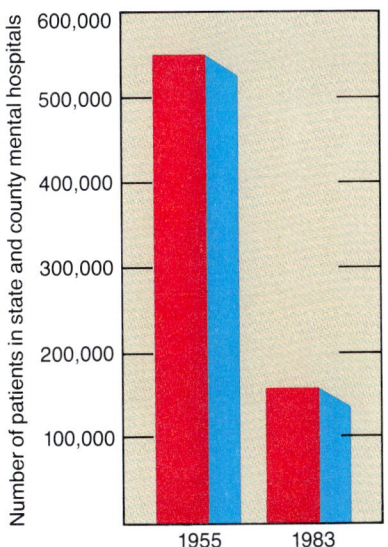

In 1955, there were over a half million people in U.S. state and county mental hospitals. By 1983, the total was reduced to one-fourth that number. The sharp decline is due primarily to the development of medicines that eliminate the most disabling symptoms of mental disorder as well as the introduction of mental health treatment centers in communities across the nation (U.S. Department of Health and Human Services, 1986).

Figure 13-5 Examples of drugs used for mental disorders

The use of various drugs has reduced some of the most powerful symptoms suffered by emotionally disturbed individuals.

THREE MAJOR DRUG GROUPS	TRADE NAMES	EFFECTS
Drugs for Schizophrenia		
Phenothiazines	Thorazine Stelazine Mellaril	Fewer hallucinations and delusions; less disordered thinking, and better emotional expression
Drugs for Depression		
MAO Inhibitors	Nardil Parnate	Improved mood, sleep, and appetite; fewer negative thoughts
Tricyclics	Elavil Trofanil	
Lithium	Eskalith Lithobid	Control of mood swings
Drugs for Anxiety		
Benzodiazepines	Valium Librium	Sedation, muscle relaxation, less anxiety

The therapeutic effect of drugs used to treat schizophrenia patients is thought to be related to their impact on the neurotransmitter dopamine. As described in Chapter 12, schizophrenia patients often have unusually high dopamine levels in the brain. By blocking dopamine receptors at the nerve synapses, these drugs reduce the actual amount of dopamine in the brain. The process is illustrated in Figure 13-6.

Biological Therapies

Figure 13-6 How drugs may act to help in schizophrenia

As described in the text, in many patients with schizophrenia there is an increased level of the neurotransmitter dopamine in the brain. A number of the major tranquilizer drugs—which reduce the most extreme symptoms typical of schizophrenia—prevent dopamine from crossing the synaptic cleft, or gap, between one neuron and the next.

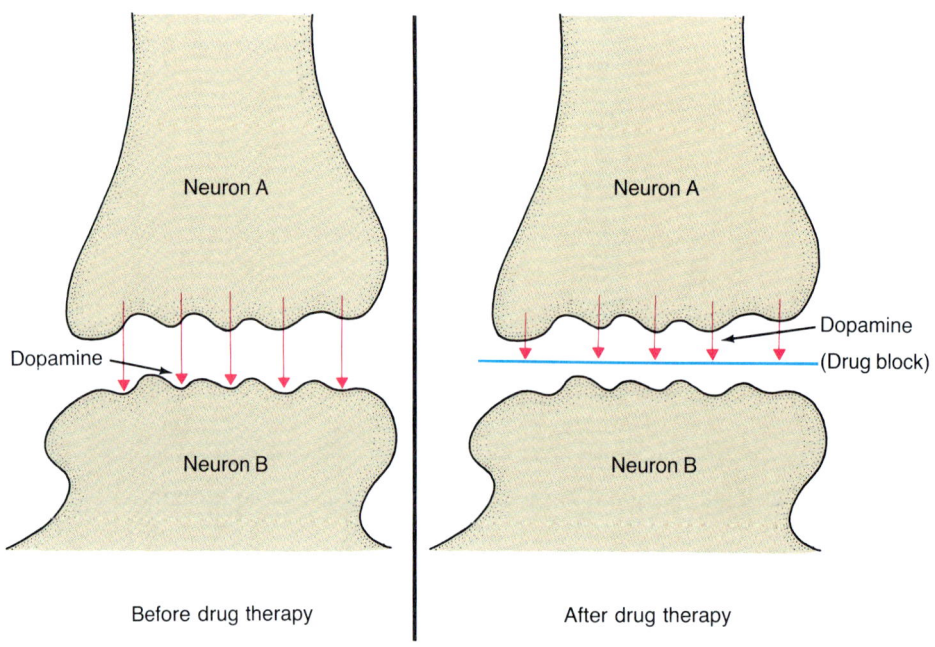

Although the benefits of antipsychotic drugs are well established, there is growing concern about the risks involved in long-term treatment. Some patients who have undergone treatment for many years develop *tardive dyskinesia,* a serious motor disorder characterized by involuntary movements, primarily of the face, mouth, lips, and tongue. Others may develop tremors or jerking fits, which in turn must be treated with another drug. Although the reduction of dosage may decrease the incidence of such side effects (Kane, 1983), it is clear that the continuous use of drugs in the treatment of disorders such as schizophrenia must be carefully monitored by knowledgeable physicians (Falloon and Liberman, 1983).

Drugs for Depression   Persons who experience major depression are often treated with *antidepressant drugs.* All of them act as "psychic energizers." After a period of two to four weeks, individuals treated with these drugs often show significant signs of improvement, including relief from insomnia, a return of appetite for food, and an improvement in mood.

Antidepressants are believed to work by increasing the brain's supply of two neurotransmitters—*norepinephrine* and *serotonin*—often found to be deficient in depressed patients. The *monoamine oxidase (MAO) inhibitors,* as the name suggests, prevents the brain enzyme *monoamine oxidase* from breaking down norepinephrine and serotonin at the nerve synapse. The result is an increased concentration of these two neurotransmitters in the brain. The *tricyclic antidepressants* prolong the level of functioning of norepinephrine and serotonin in the brain (Mcgeer and Mcgeer, 1980). Because the tricyclic drugs produce fewer side effects than the MAO inhibitors, they are used more widely in the treatment of depression. Recent studies show them to be as effective as various forms of psychotherapy in helping patients overcome depressive symptoms (Elkin et al., 1986). Although used mainly for depression, tricyclics are also regarded as the most effective treatment for blocking repeated panic attacks of agoraphobia patients (Tuma and Maser, 1985).

Also sometimes used in treating depression, but especially when it is accompanied by swings toward manic states, are the salts of the metallic element *lithium*. This medication, taken regularly, often helps prevent the extreme ups and downs of mood typical of manic-depressive individuals (National Institute of Health, 1984). As in the case of all medications affecting the central nervous system, however, the dosage and possible side effects must be carefully monitored (Baastrup, 1980).

Drugs for Anxiety (Minor Tranquilizers)   These drugs, which include such well-known trade names as Valium and Librium, are among the most widely used antianxiety medications. They are often prescribed by doctors to alleviate the symptoms associated with stress and tension. Their effects are believed to arise through an inhibition of activity of the central nervous system.

Because of concerns about the chronic use of tranquilizing drugs and subsequent addiction, prescriptions for them have declined notably within the past decade. It is recognized, too, that dependence on a pill to dissipate painful anxiety may reduce a person's motivation to get at the underlying cause—and to adopt better ways of coping with stress.

Like all biological therapies, drug therapy is an attempt to remedy the first of the factors mentioned in the preceding chapter as working together to produce abnormal behavior—biological, psychological, and environmental. Since the search for medications is still in its infancy, it seems likely that the future will bring many new drugs that relieve the biological causes of personality problems. It may even turn out that some disorders are primarily biological, in which case new medications may prove to be a specific cure. However, it is generally believed that abnormal symptoms and behavior typically spring from psychological as well as biological causes and, therefore, that psychotherapy should accompany treatment with drugs.

Electroconvulsive Therapy

Electroconvulsive therapy (ECT), known in the past as "electroshock therapy," has been used since the 1930s, but it continues to be a controversial treatment (Runk, 1985). People treated in this manner are first sedated and then receive a brief electric current or shock through electrodes attached to the skull. The result is a convulsion lasting about a minute, after which the patient is unconscious for a short time.

ECT has been found to be very effective in treating cases of depression that have not responded to drugs or other treatments. According to a panel of experts recently assembled to evaluate ECT, "not a single controlled study has shown another form of treatment to be superior to ECT in the short-term management of severe depressions" (National Institute of Health, 1985). Nonetheless, many clinicians and researchers believe that ECT can cause long-lasting memory impairment and possibly brain damage, and therefore are opposed to its use. The general consensus, however, is that used with the proper medical safeguards, it can work effectively for patients unresponsive to other approaches and can be a life-saving technique for those on the brink of suicide.

How does ECT actually work to relieve depression? The answer is not known for certain, but it probably increases the brain's supply of norepinephrine and other neuro-

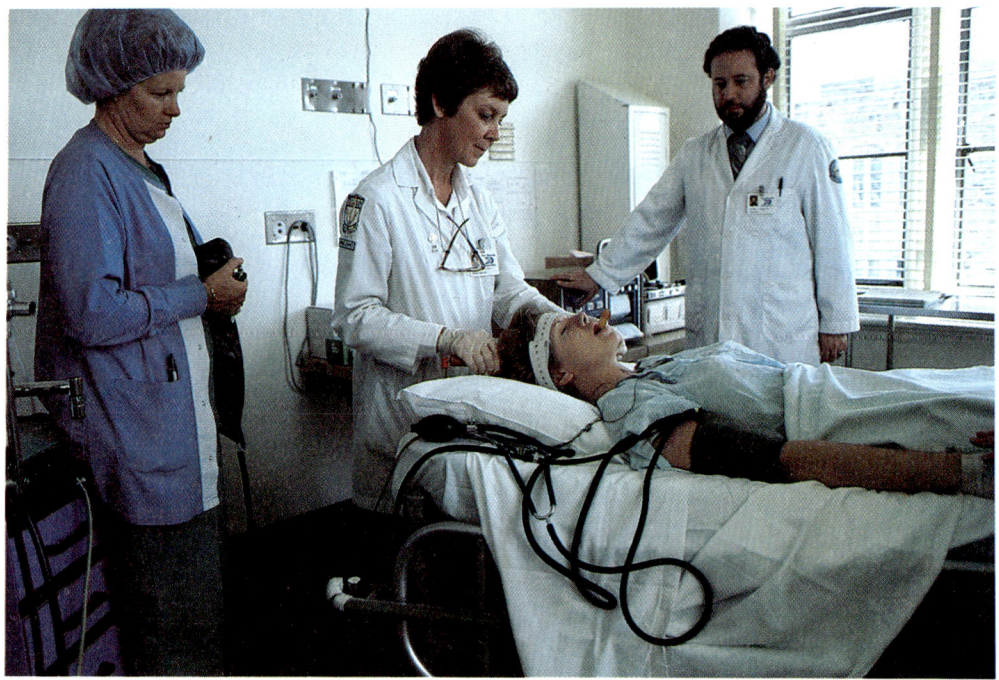

A patient receives electroconvulsive therapy.

transmitters. Since the electric current actually shocks the entire brain, identifying the one effective ingredient of ECT is very difficult (Rosenhan and Seligman, 1984).

Psychosurgery

One very radical and highly controversial biological treatment is *psychosurgery*, in which parts of the brain are severed, removed, or destroyed. The surgery typically results in a cutting of the neural connections between the frontal lobes and the limbic system or certain portions of the hypothalamus—both believed to play a part in the expression of emotions. In the late 1940s and early 1950s, psychiatric practitioners utilized psychosurgery extensively. They regarded it as the quickest and most effective solution for many severe disorders, including uncontrollable urges toward violence. But follow-up studies showed that many patients, though improved in some ways, lapsed into a vegetable-like existence, unable to function effectively. As a result, the use of psychosurgery has been significantly reduced within the past few decades, especially since drug therapy has proven to be an effective alternative (Valenstein, 1986).

Although newer surgical techniques appear to result in less intellectual and emotional impairment, psychosurgery is seldom used today except as a last resort for patients who are hopelessly suicidal, suffer from crippling forms of epilepsy, or are victims of severe, continuous, and otherwise unrelievable pain.

COMMUNITY MENTAL HEALTH

In the early 1960s, spurred especially by a message on mental health to Congress by President Kennedy, the United States undertook what Kennedy described as a "bold new approach" for dealing with mental health problems. The major outcome was the construction and staffing of hundreds of community mental health centers across the country. These centers were intended to meet the needs of millions of citizens—including former mental hospital patients, the poor, and members of minority groups—who needed psychological help but were not receiving it.

It was in part to meet this need that *community psychology* emerged as a special branch of psychology. Community psychologists are oriented to action. Rather than working as therapists to whom clients come for help, they provide "outreach" services to the community. For example, they work on the staff of community mental health centers, organize and run programs designed to intervene in crises, and provide services to high-risk groups such as drug addicts. Community psychology is based in part on the premise that conditions in society can either cause or worsen mental health problems, and thus the field is devoted also to building needed changes into places where people spend so much of their lives, including schools and the work place. For example, community psychologists might attempt to set up new forms of interaction to replace existing patterns that are causing trouble between school administrators and students, employers and workers, or public officials and citizens (Gibbs, Lachenmeyer, and Sigal, 1980). The goal is to strengthen the mental health of individuals as much by preventing problems as by providing therapy after the problems have begun taking their toll.

Community Mental Health Centers

A law passed by Congress in 1963 proposed the development of one community mental health center for every 50,000 people in the United States. Although funding for such centers waned in the intervening years, over 600 came to fruition, providing a new and comprehensive approach to helping people with mental health problems.

"Storefront" programs such as this one can be precious to individuals in psychological pain.

To begin with, community mental health centers were designed to treat mentally disturbed individuals in their home communities rather than sending them to hospitals where they are cut off from family and society. The centers provide not only inpatient care, but also partial hospitalization through which individuals might receive therapy at the center during the day but return home in the evening. Or they can work during the day—a therapeutic force in itself—and stay overnight at the center.

Psychologists and other mental health professionals working in community treatment centers also provide outpatient care in clinics through which individuals are treated on an intermittent basis without becoming totally divorced from their families, jobs, or schools. Many centers operate so-called "storefront clinics" where staff are available day and night to respond to emergencies such as episodes of abuse in the family, suicide threats, or panic attacks. An important role for psychologists in the array of community services is to offer consultation and education to individuals in the community who are often on the front lines of providing psychological help without actually being trained to do so. For the most part, people do not bring their personal problems and crises to mental health professionals, but prefer to talk instead to members of the clergy, lawyers, teachers, physicians, police, or welfare workers (Cowan, 1982). These "natural caregivers," not trained in therapy, profit from the advice and consultation of psychologists who offer them knowledge about the basic concepts and techniques of therapy.

Crisis Intervention

Some psychologists and other mental health professionals provide an important service in *crisis intervention* programs designed to deal with immediate, stress-filled situations that beg for quick attention. The crisis may be an accident, a fire, a runaway child, the loss of a job, a rape—any episode where direct and immediate emotional support is likely to be therapeutic. The goal is to use any therapeutic maneuver or intervention that appears helpful. It can entail home visits to the family, repeated and prolonged telephone contacts, or seeing to it that an abused wife is given shelter. The point is to focus on the immediate circumstances and reduce the troublesome effects of traumatic events.

For many people, the nearest source of help in a crisis is the telephone. Thus the "hotline" has emerged as an important therapeutic resource for people in crisis. While the telephone lacks the intimacy and power of face-to-face contact, the delivery of advice,

A "hotline" counselor responds to a distraught caller.

sympathy, and comfort via telephone can be critical in seeing a stressed person through a traumatic episode and preventing breakdown. The hotline also allows callers to be referred to appropriate individuals and agencies for help. While psychologists themselves do not typically work at the telephone, they can provide an important service by advising and consulting with those volunteers who do so.

Self-help Groups

Self-help groups, also referred to as *mutual support groups*, are based on the belief that when we come together with individuals facing comparable problems, we help ourselves as well as others. Some groups use professional advisers but most do not. They are diverse in size and the structure and frequency of meetings, for the help given does not have the constraints of time, place, or format (Riessman, 1984). Group meetings can take place in a basement, apartment, mental health center, church, school rap room—virtually anywhere in the community.

Probably no group more clearly reflects the healing effects of mutual support than Alcoholics Anonymous, or A.A. Each chapter is a fellowship of individuals who share their experiences, strengths, and hopes with one another in order to help themselves—and others—recover from the misuse and abuse of alcohol. It is estimated that some 15 million Americans belong to self-help groups, assisting them through a broad spectrum of life crises (Riessman, 1985). Included are groups in which the jobless organize to help one another find work; burned-out professionals sustain one another; parents of young children with cancer see one another through their ordeal; and widows and widowers attempt to pick up the pieces of their lives. There are groups for couples who are infertile, parents whose children use drugs, divorced persons, isolated older people, the handicapped, suicide-prone individuals, and former mental hospital patients.

Self-help groups are effective for at least three reasons. To begin with, simply to put feelings into words is a healing experience. People find that expressing even their most morbid concerns helps them build a bond with others who are equally troubled. There is nothing that cannot be discussed and understood by the members of the group. Second, communication helps people recognize that others who face similar problems manage to survive. It helps them discover models with whom they can identify. Third, people learn in self-help groups that reactions to stress are not unnatural. Being unduly anxious, sad, or upset is generally not approved of in our society, and many people struggling with problems are uncomfortable because they see themselves as being more upset than they should be. The company of others gives them the assurance that they are really not so atypical in their reactions (Segal, 1986). The ability of lay persons to help each other raises the question whether ordinary individuals acting alone can also help themselves simply by reading about and applying mental health programs. This is discussed in a box on Psychology in Everyday Life titled "Is Self-therapy Possible?"

ATTITUDES TOWARD PEOPLE WHO NEED PSYCHOLOGICAL HELP: HOW THEY CAN HURT OR HEAL

Attitudes displayed toward individuals who require therapy have improved over time. But such individuals—especially those who require hospital care—are still far from universally accepted either within the family, at work, or in the community. How people receiving treatment are viewed by others can be critical. It can help determine whether they

Psychology in Everyday Life
Is Self-therapy Possible?

Can we serve as our own psychotherapists—solving our own problems and correcting any tendencies toward abnormal behavior? How helpful are all the popular books that suggest ways to better mental health and greater self-fulfillment?

These questions are not easy to answer. For one thing, advice on self-help techniques varies widely—from articles written by untrained people to carefully documented books in which serious therapists explain their theories and methods. The former are worthless and potentially harmful. The latter seem to help some readers but not others.

All psychologists agree that sound knowledge about psychological processes encourages the development of normal, healthy, and effective personality. Thus everything in this course is potentially helpful. Some topics of particular value as signposts toward mental health are psychology's knowledge about the way unreasonable fears can be acquired through conditioning, learned helplessness and how it can be counteracted, emotions, motives, anxiety, stress, assertive coping with anxiety and stress, and the wellsprings of abnormal behavior, as well as the personality theories and methods of therapy described in this chapter. Also highly pertinent are many of the topics still to come—especially the manner in which personality develops and changes throughout life (Chapters 14 and 15) and the ways in which behavior is molded for better or for worse by relationships with other people (Chapter 16).

One difficulty with all attempts at self-therapy, however, is that they lack the support of a warm and encouraging relationship with others—either in a mutual support group or with an understanding therapist. Without these, real change and healing are difficult to accomplish.

---

will continue to be overwhelmed by their symptoms and even get worse, or become well and function productively in society (National Institute of Mental Health, 1980).

The Importance of Family Supports

Many studies have shown that those who are attempting to overcome disabling psychological disorders can benefit from the support of people in their immediate environment—especially their families. An international study showed that people in underdeveloped countries who suffer from serious mental disorders tend to recover more quickly and suffer fewer recurrences than do those in industrially advanced countries (World Health Organization, 1979). A major reason given for the difference is that family members in underdeveloped countries are more likely to take responsibility for caring for victims. With few mental health professionals available, they are more prone to stay close to those relatives who become psychologically disabled and offer them the kind of support and encouragement they need to increase their chances of recovery.

Family support appears to be especially important for victims of serious disorders such as schizophrenia and severe depression. One study shows that the risk of suicide is considerably less for deeply depressed persons who have close ties with relatives (Slater and Depue, 1981). Other studies reveal that recovered schizophrenics are less likely to suffer a relapse if family members play down any anxiety they might have and instead exert a calming influence (Hooley, 1985). It appears critical also that relatives not blame the victim for succumbing to schizophrenia, but rather indicate their belief that schizophrenia is a legitimate and acceptable condition (Vaughn and Leff, 1976).

The Importance of Community Supports

One of the ironies of life for many people who have been treated for an emotional disorder is that when they finally get themselves and their lives together and have overcome their private pain, the world often greets them with distrust and outright prejudice. Particularly for those who are hospitalized—however briefly and for whatever reason—the fact that they were hospitalized at all erroneously suggests to many people that they are "crazy" or "psycho," and therefore untrustworthy, unemployable, or perhaps even dangerous. Just when recovering patients need a helping hand and a boost, they experience rejection. Small wonder that some relapse.

The stigmatization of people who have sought psychological help can have an especially negative impact on their careers. Even those who are fully recovered may face discrimination in the workplace. Senator Thomas Eagleton lost a vice-presidential nomination in 1972 when his earlier treatment for depression was revealed. Individuals identified as having had a psychological problem are often caught in a vicious cycle. At work they may be unfairly perceived as incompetent and their performance rated as poor for no tangible reason. Feeling alienated and unappreciated, their anxieties may begin to rise and their performance may actually deteriorate (Farina, 1982).

A positive response by the community to people who require psychological help can assist even those with serious disturbances to regain full functioning. Therapists work hard with their patients to help them overcome their symptoms, realize their potential, and take their rightful place in society—but full recovery requires society's willingness to accept them as fully capable members of the community. Although it has no name, this itself is a powerful therapy.

The 1972 national Democratic ticket—almost. As described in the text, Senator Thomas Eagleton (second from left) became a victim of the stigma of emotional disorder.

SUMMARY

Dynamic therapy

1. *Dynamic therapy* is based on the assumption that an individual's problems are generated by underlying mental and emotional forces.

2. The most prominent example of dynamic therapy is Sigmund Freud's *classical psychoanalysis*. Freud's method is designed to dredge up into awareness the unconscious desires and conflicts that he considered the source of anxiety and guilt. It uses the techniques of *free association* and examines *transference*, dreams, and slips of the tongue to provide insights and thus achieve "freedom from the tyranny of the unconscious."

3. Modern dynamic therapies diverge from classical psychoanalysis by placing less emphasis on unconscious sexual and aggressive drives and placing greater emphasis on the importance of social and cultural factors.

Humanistic therapy

4. *Humanistic therapy*—with its emphasis on self-actualization and the perfecting of personal strength—attempts to: (a) explore the client's inner experience solely from the client's own perspective, and (b) encourage personal responsibility, freedom, and will.

5. Carl Roger's humanistic approach, or *client-centered therapy*, provides an atmosphere of *unconditional positive regard* in which clients are free to explore all their thoughts and feelings, including those they have been unable to perceive clearly for fear of condemnation by others or by their own consciences. Other humanistic approaches include *Gestalt therapy, existential psychotherapy*, and *logotherapy*.

Behavior therapy

6. *Behavior therapy* regards personality disturbances as learned responses that can be changed through relearning. Its techniques include *desensitization, extinction* of undesired behavior (sometimes through *aversive conditioning*), *reinforcement* of more desirable behavior, *cognitive behavior therapy, observation learning*, and *guided participation* to help encourage assertive coping.

Therapy in groups

7. *Group therapy* is the treatment of several patients at the same time. Among the group approaches are: (a) *traditional group therapy*, which allows the participants to share their feelings with each other; (b) *encounter groups*, which encourage members to interact with open displays of emotion; and (c) *large group awareness training*, which comprise elements as diverse as education, spiritual enlightenment, encounter, and traditional group therapy.

8. Other group approaches include *psychodrama, assertiveness training*, and *family therapy*.

Biological therapies

9. *Biological therapies* hold that psychological conditions can be influenced by nonpsychological methods—by chemical, hormonal, or physical interventions that affect the brain either directly or indirectly—and thus produce or inhibit certain behaviors that alter mood.

10. The most widely and successfully used form of biological treatment is *drug therapy* (*chemotherapy*), which is the prescription of drugs intended to produce specific changes in mood or behavior.

11. The three major classes of drugs are: (a) drugs for schizophrenia (*major tranquilizers*), (b) drugs for depression, and (c) drugs for anxiety (*minor tranquilizers*).

12. *Electroconvulsive therapy* (*ECT*), a highly controversial biological treatment, has been found to be very effective in treating cases of depression that have not responded to other treatments. Persons who are treated in this manner are first sedated, and then receive a brief electrical current through electrodes attached to the skull. The result is a convulsion lasting about a minute.

13. Another highly controversial biological treatment is *psychosurgery*, in which parts of the brain are severed, removed, or destroyed. Psychosurgery is seldom used today except as a last resort for patients who are hopelessly suicidal, suffer from crippling forms of epilepsy, or are victims of unrelievable pain.

Community mental health

14. *Community psychology* is based in part on the premise that the conditions in society can either cause or worsen mental health problems, and thus the field is devoted to providing "outreach" services to society.

15. Community mental health centers are designed to: (a) treat mentally disturbed individuals in their home communities rather than in a hospital setting, and (b) provide outpatient care in clinics through which individuals are treated on an intermittent basis.

16. *Crisis intervention* programs are designed to deal with immediate, stress-filled situations that beg for quick attention. The "hotline" is one example.

17. *Self-help groups* are effective for three primary reasons: (a) it is a healing experience to simply put feelings into words; (b) communication allows individuals to recognize that others who face similar problems manage to survive; and (c) individuals learn that reactions to stress are not unnatural.

Attitudes toward people who need psychological help: how they can hurt or heal

18. Attitudes toward people with mental disorders can be critical in determining whether or not such individuals will recover sufficiently to function in society. Family support is particularly important.

19. A positive response by the community to people who require psychological help can assist even those with serious disturbances to regain full functioning.

IMPORTANT TERMS

antidepressant drug
antipsychotic drugs
assertiveness training
aversive conditioning
behavior therapy
biological therapy
chemotherapy

client-centered therapy
community psychology
cognitive behavior therapy
crisis intervention
desensitization
dream analysis
drug therapy

dynamic therapy
electroconvulsive therapy (ECT)
encounter group
existential psychotherapy
extinction
family therapy
free association
Gestalt therapy
group therapy
guided participation
humanistic therapy
hypnotherapy
insight
large group awareness training
latent content
lithium
logotherapy
major tranquilizer
manifest content
minor tranquilizer
monoamine oxidase (MAO)
monoamine oxidase inhibitor
mutual support group
norepinephrine
posthypnotic suggestion
psychoanalysis
psychodrama
psychosurgery
reinforcement
resistance
self-help group
serotonin
tardive dyskinesia
token economy
transference
tricyclic antidepressant
unconditional positive regard

RECOMMENDED READINGS

Belkin, G. S. *Contemporary Psychotherapies*, 2nd ed. Monterey, CA.: Brooks/Cole Publishing, 1987.

Bloch, S. *An introduction to the psychotherapies*, 2nd ed. New York: Oxford University Press, 1986.

Erdelyi, M. H. *Psychoanalysis: Freud's cognitive psychology*. New York: W. H. Freeman, 1985.

Freud, S. *New introductory lectures on psychoanalysis*. Edited by Stachey, J. New York: Norton, 1965.

Garfield, S. L. *Psychotherapy: an eclectic approach*. New York: Wiley, 1980.

Norcross, J. C. *Casebook of eclectic psychotherapy*. New York: Brunner/Mazel, 1987.

Rogers, C. *On becoming a person: a therapist's view of psychotherapy*. Boston: Houghton Mifflin, 1970.

Whitaker, C. A., and Malone, T. P. *The roots of psychotherapy*. New York: Brunner-Mazel, 1981.

PART 6

HOW WE DEVELOP AND RELATE TO SOCIETY

CHAPTER

14

THE WORLD OF CHILDHOOD

LIFE'S OVERTURE: FROM CONCEPTION TO BIRTH 496

Chromosomes, genes, and the stamp of heredity
How sex and other characteristics are determined
Life in the womb
The process of birth

NEWBORN BABIES: SIMILAR BUT DIFFERENT 502

Differences in sensitivity and adaptation
Differences in irritability and response to stress
Easy, slow-to-warm-up, and difficult babies
How lasting are early traits?
Effects of early neglect and trauma

THE DEVELOPMENT OF BODY AND MIND 510

Physical maturation
Intellectual development

THE FLOWERING PERSONALITY: BIRTH TO EIGHTEEN MONTHS 515

The power of early attachment
Attachment and exploration
The dawn of anxiety

LEARNING LIFE'S SOCIAL REQUIREMENTS: EIGHTEEN MONTHS THROUGH THREE YEARS 520

Social demands, inner standards, and the emergence of self
The role of rewards and punishments

THE PRESCHOOL YEARS: FOUR AND FIVE 523

The process of identification
Sex typing: learning to be a girl or a boy

THE INFLUENCE OF TEACHERS AND PEERS: SIX TO TEN 527

The new world of the classroom
Finding a place among peers
The road to being dominant or submissive
New emphasis on inner standards
The threshold of adolescence

SUMMARY 531

IMPORTANT TERMS 533

RECOMMENDED READINGS 533

PSYCHOLOGY IN EVERYDAY LIFE

Protecting the development of the unborn child 501
Is there a foolproof formula for bringing up children? 507
Psychology's optimistic message to parents 509
How day-care programs affect the young child 518
Do we value our teachers enough? 528

I t's all a matter of the body's fluids. The baby's personality is in those juices right from the start."

"Totally blank, that's what they are. It's the environment that takes over from the first breath."

"They're all born in the grasp of Satan. Some will shake loose, some won't."

"It's Mom—she's the real key to the child's personality."

Those views of child development were voiced over the centuries by figures as diverse as the ancient Greek physician Hippocrates, the seventeenth-century philosopher John Locke, the eighteenth-century religious leader John Calvin, and Sigmund Freud. They are only four of a parade of philosophers, physicians, clergymen, and everyday armchair experts who have claimed answers to the puzzles of human development.

Only in the twentieth century, however, has there been a concentrated scientific effort to understand how children develop as they do. Researchers have turned to studies of children themselves in an attempt to build a science of childhood, with painstaking observations of their subjects—at birth, in the cradle, on the playground, at the school, in the community.

The fabric of childhood personality and behavior is a many-stranded thing, and psychology has taken important steps toward sorting out these strands. The influences that will mold the child's psychological traits are the domain of developmental psychologists, chiefly devoted to the study of the ways in which children gradually acquire all of the patterns of behavior described in this book. Their work has taught us a great deal about the way our mental and physical abilities blossom in childhood, and the way both inner traits and outside influences shape and reshape our personalities from the instant life begins in the womb.

LIFE'S OVERTURE: FROM CONCEPTION TO BIRTH

T he overture to human development, played out in the mother's womb, is brief but awesome. In only nine months, two microscopic cells become transformed into a fully formed human infant. Developmental psychologists recognize that the future of each of us is shaped to a degree during this period.

To begin with, the impact of heredity is exerted once and for all at the moment of union between mother's egg cell and father's sperm cell. Then, from the instant of conception, the impact of the environment begins to leave its mark. When babies give up their home in the womb, they have already undergone experiences that can influence how the characteristics they inherit will actually unfold in the outside world.

Chromosomes, Genes, and the Stamp of Heredity

We now have considerable knowledge about the mechanics of heredity, which explain how life is passed on from one generation to the next. A new life begins, of course, when the egg cell produced by the mother is penetrated and fertilized by the sperm cell of the father, as shown in Figure 14-1. The two join into a single cell—and this cell eventually grows into a human baby. It does so by a process of division. The single cell splits and becomes two living cells, then each of these in turn splits to make four, and so on.

Thus the original fertilized egg must somehow contain the whole key of life. Something inside it must direct the entire development from single cell to baby at birth (whose body contains about 200 billion cells organized into the various specialized parts of the body) and beyond that from infant to fully matured adult. Something in it must also

Figure 14-1 The moment of conception

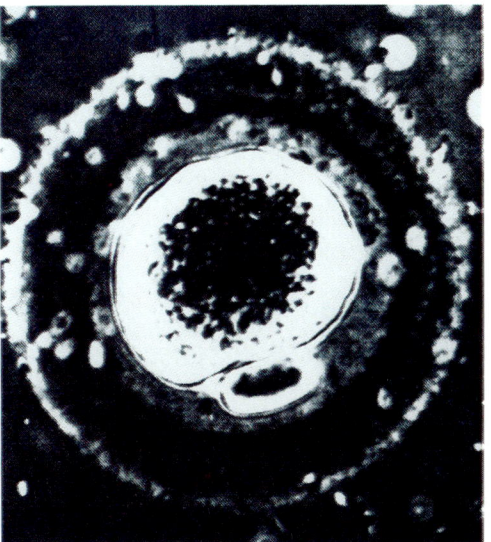

The large round object is a human egg cell. At this moment it is being fertilized by a male sperm cell that has worked its way deep inside and can no longer be seen. Other sperm cells, with small heads and long tails, are also attempting to pierce the egg but have arrived too late.

determine the inherited characteristics of the individual to be born—the color of the eyes and hair, the facial features, the potential size, and psychological characteristics such as potential intelligence and patterns of behavior.

This "something" is the *chromosomes*—the tiny structures shown in Figure 14-2 as seen under a powerful microscope. The original fertilized cell contains 46 chromosomes. When the cell splits, the chromosomes also divide. Thus each cell of the newborn baby as well as of the fully grown human body contains exactly the same 46 chromosomes that were present in the fertilized egg with which life began. The chromosomes hold the key to the development of the human being and are the carriers of heredity.

Figure 14-2 The human chromosomes

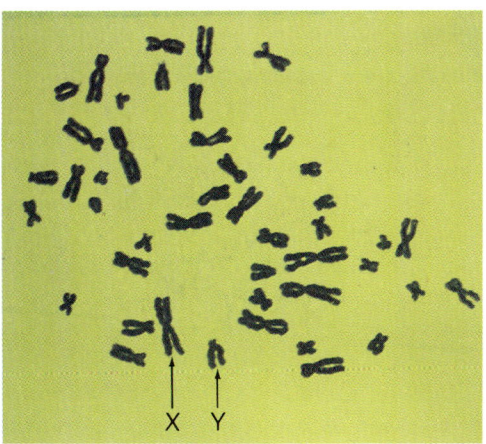

When enlarged 750 times, human chromosomes look like this. These are from a man's skin cell, broken down and spread out into a single layer under the microscope. The labels point out the X and Y chromosomes, which determine sex as will be explained later in the chapter.

Life's Overture: From Conception to Birth   497

Figure 14-3   A single gene

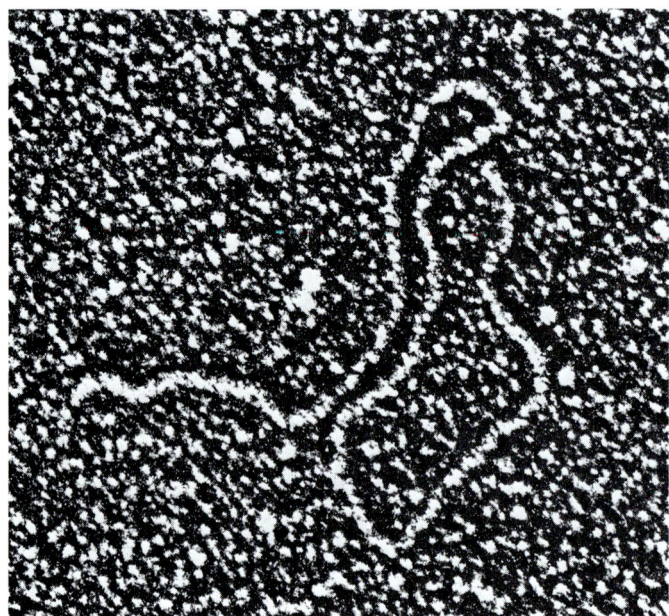

The first gene ever isolated and photographed under high magnification was this twisted strand taken from one of the bacteria frequently found in the human intestinal tract. It is 55 millionths of an inch long (Shapiro et al., 1969).

Each chromosome, though tiny in itself, is composed of hundreds of even smaller structures called *genes*, each of which is a molecule of a complex chemical called DNA (deoxyribonucleic acid). Scientists have managed to extract a single gene from a chromosome of one of the lower organisms and, through a microscope, take the photograph of it shown in Figure 14-3. Human genes have not yet been isolated, examined, or counted. But it is believed that there are at least 20,000 of them in each human cell and perhaps as many as 125,000. Each gene is believed to be responsible—sometimes by itself but more often in combination with other genes—for some particular phase of development. It is the particular kinds of genes we possess that make us develop into human beings and into the individual human being that each of us is.

How Sex and Other Characteristics Are Determined

In the living cell, the 46 chromosomes are not arranged as they were shown in Figure 14-2, where they were deliberately separated and spread out to pose for their microscopic portrait. Instead they are arranged in 23 pairs. In each pair the two chromosomes are similar in structure and function and are composed of genes of similar structure and function.

To form the cells of reproduction—the female egg and the male sperm—the chromosome pairs split apart. One set goes into one egg or sperm cell, and the other half into another cell. Thus each reproductive cell has only 23 chromosomes, not 23 pairs. Fertilization of an egg by a sperm, as shown in Figure 14-1, rejoins the chromosomes into the 23 pairs needed for normal growth.

One of the pairs in the fertilized egg cell plays a particularly significant role in development. It determines whether the fertilized egg will be a girl or boy. If you look back at Figure 14-2 you will note that two chromosomes are pointed out by arrows. One of them, as the caption states, is called an *X chromosome*, the other a *Y chromosome*. Despite their different appearances, they constitute a pair—the only exception to the rule that paired chromosomes are similar in structure. You will also note that the chromosomes in Figure 14-2 are from a cell taken from a male. The X-Y pairing always produces a male. When there is an X-X pair, the result is always a female.

This, then, is how the critical factor of sex is determined. When the mother's X-X pair of chromosomes splits to form an egg cell, the result is always a cell containing an X chromosome. When the father's X-Y pair splits to form two sperm cells, however, the X chromosome goes to one of the cells, the Y chromosome to the other. If the sperm cell with the X chromosome fertilizes the egg, the result is an X-X pairing and a girl. If the sperm cell with the Y chromosome fertilizes the egg, the result is an X-Y pairing and a boy. The sex of the baby is a matter of chance, depending on which sperm meets the egg.

Chance also determines many other characteristics, for there are many billions of combinations of the chromosomes and genes carried by the parents. In the formation of two reproductive cells, the two halves of a chromosome pair travel at random, some to one cell and some to the other cell. Moreover, in the splitting process they often leave some of their own genes behind and pull others away with them. The resulting baby is a unique individual. It is assumed that every human being—except for identical twins—has a unique combination of genes. Never before, unless by remote chance, did the same combination exist; never again is it likely to be repeated.

Life in the Womb

Most people think of environmental forces as operating only after the child is born—at home, at school, in the community—anywhere that the child interacts with people and things in the world. All these are important, of course, as we shall soon see. But the environment, like heredity, begins to exert its influence earlier, at the very start of life's journey, when the speck of matter that will one day become a child is just beginning to unfurl in the womb.

Over the approximately 280 days of prenatal development, the initial squirming bit of flesh undergoes a remarkable series of changes. During the first eight weeks—between the instant of fertilization and the moment that a recognizable embryonic human being is formed—the infant-to-be increases nearly 2 million percent in size. Alterations in the size, shape, and type of body cells take place with remarkable speed. The number of body cells increases from 1 to 26 billion during the first nine months of life as body structures increase in size and complexity.

All the while, the central nervous system—the machine that will ultimately form the foundation for the child's mental and physical capacities—is taking root. During each minute in the womb, the brain of the infant-to-be gains tens of thousands of new cells. As early as seven weeks after conception, some sections of the developing brain can already be discerned, and the nerves that feed electrical impulses from the brain to various parts of the body are in place and beginning to work. The budding arms of the fetus will now move in response to tapping on the sac that protects it. By the time the fetus is 20 weeks old, the nervous system is mature enough to make the developing baby sensitive to touch, pain, and changes in temperature. Surprisingly, the brain waves of a 30-week-old fetus look just the same prior to being born as they do in the real world. The brain is clearly "turned on" long before normal delivery.

The findings from studies of prenatal life show clearly that starting at the very instant of conception, the development of a child can be affected dramatically by the quality of the environment in the womb. The implications of these findings are discussed in a box on Psychology in Everyday Life titled "Protecting the Development of the Unborn Child."

The human embryo at seven weeks, with the spine already clearly evident.

The Process of Birth

The vast majority of babies wriggle and squirm into the world—or are pulled into it by forceps—as healthy and normal human beings. Nevertheless, events surrounding the birth process can affect the child's later development.

The ease or difficulty with which a baby is born and how quickly the baby begins to breathe can affect the baby's well-being. From the time the first contractions of labor begin and the new baby's head starts to squeeze its way into the world, the tiny brain is vulnerable. If there is very strong pressure on the head of the fetus, the blood vessels in the brain may rupture, leading to *anoxia*, or a loss of oxygen supply to the nerve cells. If the baby fails to begin to breathe soon after being separated from the mother's source of oxygen, the resulting anoxia may affect the brain's metabolism and result in motor paralysis (Rosen, 1985).

Psychology in Everyday Life
Protecting the Development of the Unborn Child

From follow-up studies, we now know about many factors that can affect the future well-being of children while they are still taking shape in mother's womb.

If the mother's diet during pregnancy lacks proper nutritional values and vitamins, the baby may have difficulty attaining the IQ level that its genes might otherwise have made possible. Mothers who eat contaminated foods may give birth to children who are less responsive and more easily upset (Jacobson, 1984). Mothers who experience prolonged anxiety or anger during pregnancy may have babies who are of less than average size, overactive, and inclined to have digestive problems—as if they, too, had been subjected to damaging stress.

Mothers who smoke constantly may pollute the unborn baby's blood supply with carbon monoxide and thus deprive the baby of oxygen and nutrients essential for healthy development. In one study, maternal cigarette use during pregnancy was associated with poorer attention in four-year-old preschool children (Streissguth et al., 1984). There is now evidence that pregnant women who are heavy smokers actually store potentially dangerous chemical products in their placenta—the organ that carries oxygen and nourishment to the baby—thus putting the baby at risk (Everson et al., 1986).

Some babies, born to mothers who use sedatives and tranquilizers, appear sluggish and withdrawn. Others, born to women who use narcotics, are themselves full-fledged addicts at birth. And heavy drinking of alcohol by the pregnant mother may damage the baby's central nervous system, producing a pattern of physical and psychological abnormalities that limit at the very start the infant's chances for reaching its potential (Freeman, 1985).

Does all this mean that most unborn babies are at risk in the womb?

Not at all. The great majority of babies are born healthy, even those of mothers who have smoked some, used liquor in moderation, eaten a less-than-perfect diet, received medication, or experienced some emotional upsets during pregnancy. Moreover, newborns have a surprising capacity to recover from all but the most severe prenatal stress. The effects of many early complications can eventually be reversed if the baby's later experiences are good ones (Werner and Smith, 1982).

Despite the hopeful outlook, however, caring parents-to-be cannot ignore the many factors known to pose a threat to a child's healthy development in the womb. Expectant mothers and fathers need to take every reasonable precaution they can to make sure that their babies get off to the best possible start (Mussen et al., 1984).

Even when complications in the birth process occur, however, most babies eventually show no damage. A lot can depend on what happens later. A group of Hawaiian children who suffered stresses at birth were studied over a period of 18 years. Their early impairments were linked to later problems in physical and psychological development only when combined with persistently poor environmental circumstances such as chronic poverty, family instability, or maternal health problems. Those children who were raised in more affluent homes, with an intact family and a well-educated mother, showed few, if any, negative effects of the stresses endured at birth—unless, of course, there was severe damage to the central nervous system (Werner and Smith, 1982).

Prematurity may also affect the course of the baby's development (Ross, 1985). The more premature and underweight the newborn is, the greater the likelihood of physical and mental impairment. But once again, the eventual outcome is likely to be influenced by later environment. Those prematurely born infants receiving excellent care usually show

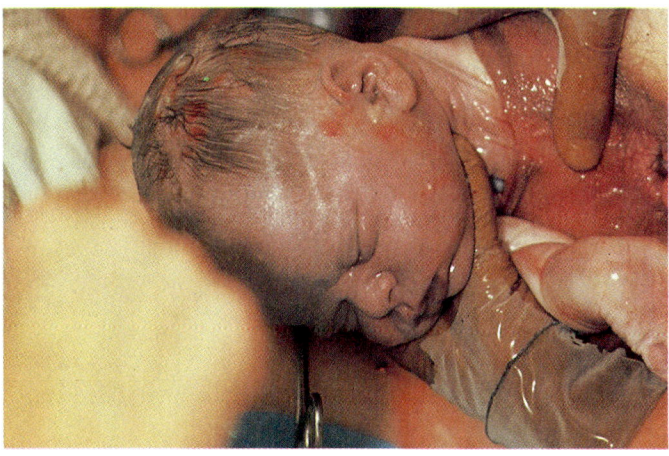

Significant complications at birth can affect later development.

little long-range handicap, while those with poor care are much more prone than full-term children to encounter developmental difficulties later on in childhood.

NEWBORN BABIES: SIMILAR BUT DIFFERENT

The human baby, though more helpless at birth than most other newborn organisms, is nonetheless a miraculous creation—ready to experience most, if not all, of the sensations given our species. From the moment the first breath is drawn, all normal babies are sensitive to stimuli in their environment. They can learn to distinguish between musical tones as close as C and C-sharp, vertical and horizontal lines, and the taste of plain and sugar water. Babies only a few hours old can follow a moving object with their eyes, and can soon distinguish two designs as subtly different as those shown in Figure 14-4. After only a week, newborns can differentiate between the smell of their own mother's milk and the smell of milk from another mother (Werner and Lispsitt, 1981), and by two weeks they can make a similar discrimination between underarm odors (Crenoch and Porter, 1985).

All babies also respond to stimuli with a wide range of inborn reflex behavior that allows them to escape pain, avoid harsh stimuli, and seek food. For example, if the sole of

Figure 14-4 The visual skills of newborns

Infants as young as five months are capable of detecting the differences between the pattern shown in circle 1, and variations of that pattern such as those shown in circles 2 and 3 (adapted from Linn et al., 1982).

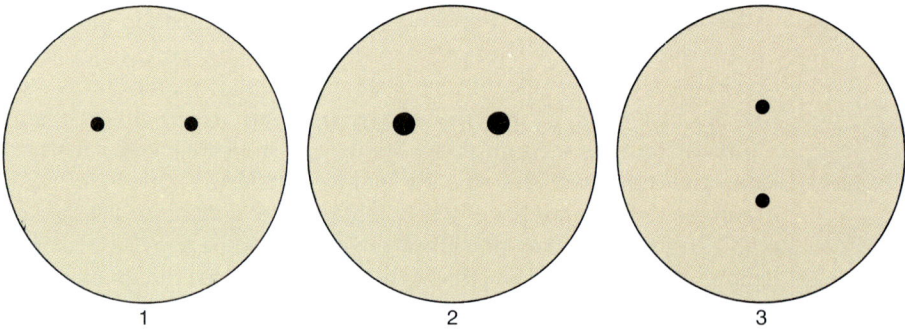

Figure 14-5 The newborn's rooting response
When the side of an infant's mouth is touched (A), the reflex response is to turn the head toward the stimulus (B) and then try to suck the finger (C), as if it were a source of food.

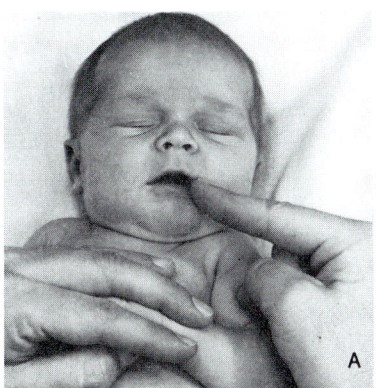 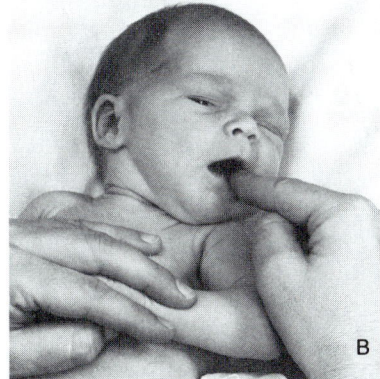 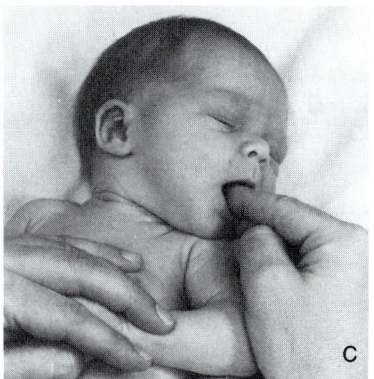

the foot is gently pricked with a pin, infants quickly draw the foot away—a reflex that enables them to escape pain. If a bright light is flashed, they protect themselves by closing their eyelids. And if the side of the mouth is touched, they display the so-called *rooting reflex*, as explained in Figure 14-5. Some of the infant's reflexes are permanent while others disappear within a few months. The major reflexes of the newborn—and the kinds of stimuli that release them—are listed in Figure 14-6.

Though all normal babies are aware of their environment and can react to the stimuli it presents, they differ in their degree of sensitivity and style of response. They differ also in level of activity, mood, friendliness, and other ways that parents are quick to recognize and describe as their babies' "nature." These characteristic styles of behavior are displayed so early that they almost surely represent biologically determined qualities present at birth.

Figure 14-6 The reflexes of healthy newborns
At birth, the baby's reflexes are so universal that they are used as a standard test to establish that the new arrival has a healthy nervous system.

STIMULUS	REFLEX
Tap upper lips	Lips protrude
Tap bridge of nose	Eyes close tightly
Shine bright light	Eyelids close
Clap hands	Eyelids close
Put fingers in hand	Hand closes
Press the ball of foot	Toes flex
Scratch sole from toe to heel	Big toe bends up, small toes spread
Prick sole with pin	Knee flexes
Touch side of mouth	Turns head, opens mouth, and sucks
Hold baby up, stomach down	Head lifts, legs extend

Newborn Babies: Similar but Different

To what extent are such traits likely to persist and to what extent are they modified by environment and experience?

Differences in Sensitivity and Adaptation

Studies have shown wide individual differences in sensory threshold. With some babies, even the most gentle stroking of the skin produces a muscular reflex. Other babies do not respond unless the stroking is fairly firm. Some babies cry when exposed to sounds or light flashes of low intensity, others only when the intensity is much higher.

There are also differences in how rapidly babies display sensory adaptation and quit responding. Some babies, for example, get used to loud sounds very quickly; others cry or appear upset even after long repetition. Some babies appear to become bored with a stimulus more quickly than others. If a series of pictures of the human face is projected on a screen above the crib, some infants pay close attention for a long time. Others soon stop looking, as if they had rapidly tired of the repetitive stimulus. Similarly, some babies are more attentive and alert than others. They differ, for example, in the degree to which their heart rate is affected by novel sounds of varying intensity. Such early powers of perceptual discrimination, when combined with a stimulating environment, may portend well developed intellectual capacities later on. In one study, researchers found that among four-month-old babies, those who were physiologically most responsive to sounds have higher IQ scores at age five (O'Connor, Cohen, and Parmelee, 1984).

Differences in Irritability and Response to Stress

One important difference among infants is their degree of irritability. Some babies begin to fret, whine, or cry at the slightest provocation. Once they begin to fret, they often work themselves up into what looks like a temper tantrum and soon are bellowing at the top of their lungs. Other babies do not fret unless their discomfort and pain is intense or lasts a long time. Even then they may fret only for a half minute or so and then stop, as if possessing some mechanism that inhibits the buildup of extreme upset.

Some notable differences have been found as well among babies of different ethnic backgrounds in their response to situations that are challenging or difficult. If placed face down in their cribs, Caucasian infants immediately turn their heads to one side, whereas Chinese babies leave their faces placidly buried in the sheets. An even more striking difference has been demonstrated by pressing a cloth briefly against the baby's nose. Caucasian and black babies try to fight off the cloth by turning away or trying to dislodge it with their hands. Chinese babies simply accept the situation and start breathing through their mouths. Such differences in response may reflect a tendency of Chinese babies to be less active and less easily distracted than their Caucasian counterparts (Hsu et al., 1981). A notable difference between Americans of Caucasian and Indian descent is illustrated in Figure 14-7.

Evidence from animal research suggests that the genetic constitution of the species is associated with varying degrees of vulnerability to stress. In one dramatic study, the experience of being raised in isolation for six months resulted in different consequences for monkeys coming from different but closely related species. One species showed extremely deviant social behavior, while another showed relatively normal behavior (Sackett et al., 1981).

Easy, Slow-to-warm-up, and Difficult Babies

One group of investigators, after studying more than a hundred children from birth through elementary school, came to the conclusion that most newborn Americans fall into

Figure 14-7 Happy Indian baby, unhappy Caucasian

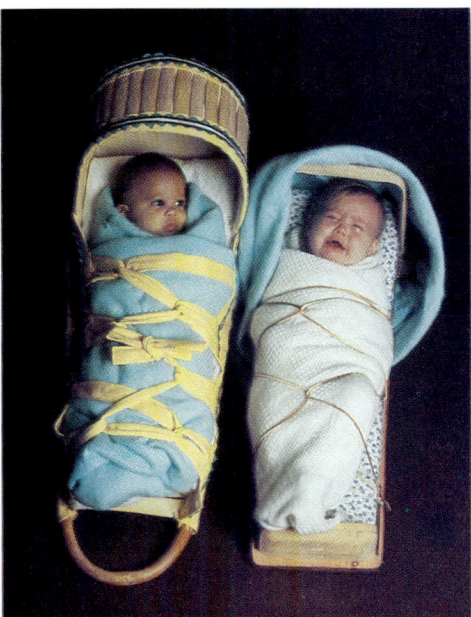

These two infants have been placed on a cradle board, which Navaho Indian mothers have used for generations to carry their young. The Navaho baby is perfectly content. The Caucasian baby lodges a vigorous protest.

three distinct classes of temperament:

1. *Easy* children are generally cheerful. Their reactions to stimuli show a low to moderate intensity. They establish regular habits of eating and sleeping and are quick to adapt to new schedules, foods, and people.

2. *Slow-to-warm-up* children are less cheerful; indeed their mood seems slightly negative. Their responses are low in intensity. Their eating and sleeping habits vary and they tend to withdraw from their first exposure to a new experience. They take time to adjust to change.

3. *Difficult* children seem unfriendly and hard to please. They are given to unusually intense reactions, such as loud laughter, frequent loud crying, and temper tantrums. They show little regularity in eating and sleeping and are easily upset by new experiences.

A striking example of the difference between an easy and a difficult baby is shown in Figure 14-8. The photographs, which were taken several years apart, are of an older sister and a younger brother—an indication that early differences in temperament do not necessarily reflect the parents' personalities or child-rearing methods. Regardless of the parents' behavior or the general atmosphere of the home, about 40 percent of the children in the study were easy, 15 percent slow-to-warm-up, and 10 percent difficult. The remaining 35 percent showed a mixture of the three different kinds of temperament (Thomas, Chess, and Birch, 1970).

The investigators concluded that the three types require very different treatment during infancy and in the early years of school. Easy children thrive under almost any kind of treatment in early childhood—but, having adapted so well to the home environment, they may have trouble when their teacher and schoolmates make different demands. Slow-to-

Figure 14-8 A contrast in infant temperament

Both these babies are three months old and are being offered a new kind of cereal for the first time. The girl at the top, an easy baby, eagerly accepts the new experience. The boy at the bottom, a difficult baby, fights it.

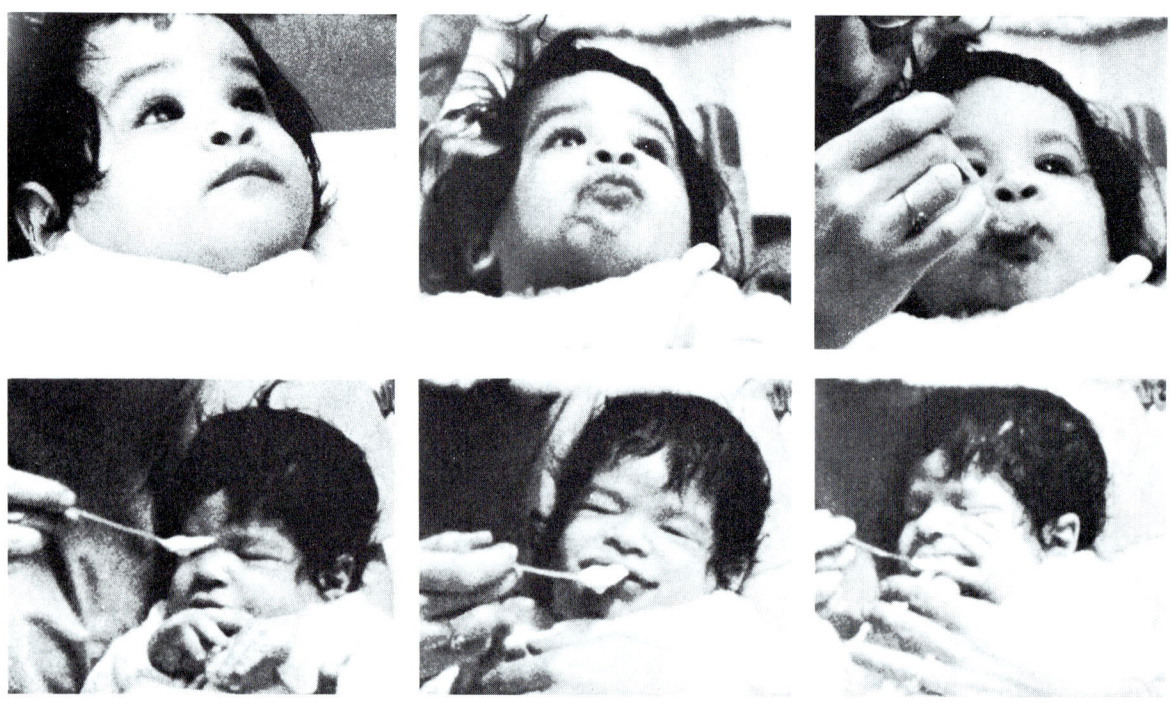

warm-up children require considerable patience. They do their best when encouraged to try new experiences but allowed to adapt at their own pace. Too much pressure heightens their natural inclination to withdraw.

Difficult children present a special problem. Because of their irregular habits, their resistance to adjustment, and their negative attitude, they are hard to live with—a trial to their parents and later their teachers. There is even evidence that mothers of difficult and irritable one-year-old boys tend to back off from their natural attempts to teach and train (Maccoby, Snow, and Jacklin, 1984). Attempts to force such babies to behave like other children may only make them more negative and difficult. Their parents must exercise exceptional understanding and tolerance to bring them around—slowly and gradually—to getting along with other individuals.

These findings about inborn differences in temperament, together with the other new knowledge about variations in sensitivity, activity, and irritability, are of great potential value to parents, the staffs of day-care centers, and teachers, especially in the early grades. The findings disprove the popular assumption that all young children are more or less alike and should behave as if cut from the same pattern. Developmental psychology has established that infants are individuals who require individual treatment if they are to develop to their maximum capability. The search by many parents for all-purpose techniques to use in rearing their children is discussed in the box on Psychology in Everyday Life titled ''Is There a Foolproof Formula for Raising Children?''

Psychology in Everyday Life
Is There a Foolproof Formula for Raising Children?

As you know if you have been a parent—or will discover if you become one—our society does not lack for advice about bringing up children. Grandparents, in-laws, neighbors, and friends all have firm opinions. Bookstores are full of volumes of counsel, many claiming to present the only surefire formula for success. You can hear or read that babies have to be pampered or should not be pampered, that they need or do not need a firm schedule of eating and sleeping, that they require a constant diet of hugging and kissing or of firm discipline, that spanking will doom them to lifelong mental health problems or is the only way to turn them into upright and responsible adults. How can a conscientious parent, eager to give the child the best possible start in life, know which views are right and which are wrong?

One clue comes from studies of child-rearing practices around the world—which, it turns out, show a remarkable diversity. Do babies need to be held a lot? Among some of the Indian people in Guatemala, they are held by an adult for more than six hours a day. But in parts of the Netherlands, they are held only while feeding and spend the rest of the day tightly bound in bassinets, alone in a little room of their own (Rebelsky, 1967). In some places children are encouraged to stand up for their rights—but among some of the Eskimos any display of aggression is immediately squelched (Briggs, 1970). In the United States parents are usually urged to communicate with their children and explain their actions to avoid any hint of rejection—but in rural sections of Norway a mother who finds her four-year-old son blocking her way simply picks him up and moves him, without saying a word (Baldwin, 1975). There are parts of the world where parents generally assume that the child's personality will thrive on sympathy and affection, others where the child is regarded as an untamed creature whose natural instincts must be curbed, and still others where it is believed that the child's nature is determined at birth and that parents should stand aside and let nature take its course.

There are all kinds of theories and methods—yet it appears that the outcome, by and large, is very much the same. By any tests or standards of emotional well-being or intelligence, no significant differences have been found among the children of various countries by the time they reach later childhood. The oft-held babies of Guatemala grow up no more secure than the seldom-held babies of the Netherlands. The Eskimo and Norwegian children turn out to be similar to each other and to children everywhere.

The worldwide studies show that no foolproof formula exists. Developmental psychologists know of no specific actions a parent can take—holding, cuddling, kissing, spanking, other forms of discipline—that will guarantee a happy and productive future. Children thrive on acceptance—but there are many different ways to demonstrate acceptance. Children wither under rejection—but what seems like rejection to an outside observer, or by the rules set out in a manual, may not be considered rejection by the child or the parents.

Guatemalan mothers holding their babies.

How Lasting Are Early Traits?

The traits displayed by babies in the early weeks and months of life endure for varying periods of time. One trait that appears to be relatively persistent is timidity. When faced with an unfamiliar event—a new face or a new toy—some babies show signs of considerable anxiety. They stop playing, turn quiet, and look wary. Their heart rate is also different from that of other babies in similar situations. It goes up slightly and remains stable—a sign that these babies may be trying unsuccessfully to understand a strange and troubling event. Timid babies go on to display signs of the trait for several years when they find themselves in novel predicaments (Kagan et al., 1984).

Many early traits, however, show little staying power as the environment begins to exert its influence. A follow-up of the easy, slow-to-warm-up, and difficult babies described earlier showed that the pattern no longer held up by the time they were 6 to 12 (Thomas and Chess, 1972).

Various comparable studies have shown how rapidly change can occur in early childhood. One study explored such traits as irritability, readiness to smile, attentiveness, activity level, and vocal excitability. No significant relationship was found between the way babies scored on these psychological attributes before they were a year old and the way they scored at 27 months. There were even some spectacular reversals of behavior. One boy, as an infant, worried the investigators because he kept rocking his body and sucking on his forearm. By the time he was just a few months over 2 years old, his behavior was perfectly normal. A follow-up of the children, moreover, found no meaningful relationship between their 27-month-old behavior (in regard to irritability, attentiveness, activity level, and vocal excitability) and the scores they made at age 10 on reading and intelligence tests. What such studies have to say to mothers and fathers concerned about the development of their children is discussed in the box on Psychology in Everyday Life titled "Psychology's Optimistic Message to Parents."

Effects of Early Neglect and Trauma

One topic that has always interested developmental psychologists is the effect of an extremely unfavorable early environment. Many of the first studies produced pessimistic results. It was found that monkeys raised in isolation—a form of total neglect—grew up with many symptoms of maladjustment. They were unfriendly, aggressive, and sexually incompetent (Harlow and Harlow, 1966). Among human babies with a severely deprived childhood, many lasting effects of deprivation were observed (Spitz, 1946). One investigator made a study of children who had spent the first three years of their lives in the impersonal atmosphere of an orphanage, then had gone on to foster homes. Later these children were compared with a control group of children of the same age and sex who had been brought up from the very start in foster homes, where presumably they received more care and encouragement than is possible in an institution. Even after some years had passed, the orphanage children were found to be notably more aggressive, with strong tendencies to have temper tantrums, to kick and hit other children, and to lie, steal, and destroy property. They tended to be emotionally cold, isolated, and incapable of affectionate relationships (Goldfarb, 1944).

There seems to be no doubt that deprivation can seriously affect development. However, other studies have indicated that the ill effects are often reversible. In one experiment, monkeys were isolated inside black boxes from birth until they were six months old. When they were permitted to leave the boxes, their behavior was decidedly abnormal. But they were then permitted to associate with other infant monkeys who had a normal social

Psychology in Everyday Life
Psychology's Optimistic Message to Parents

What conclusion can parents and prospective parents draw from the findings of developmental psychologists about the individual differences displayed by babies and the way these differences persist or vanish as years go by? What do the facts tell us about rearing our children?

The studies described in the text point to one message above all: It is very difficult to predict, from the way children behave in the early months or years, how they will behave even in the elementary school years, much less as adolescents or adults. This is hardly surprising, for development depends on many complex interactions between children and the people and events in their environment. We cannot know, at any given moment, what form these interactions will take in the months and years to come (Rutter, 1986). Moreover, we do not yet fully understand how different experiences mold development along different lines. The child's future, like life itself, defies attempts at prediction. All we can be sure of is that the years between infancy and adulthood will be full of unforeseen events—and that these events will often bring striking changes in the patterns of temperament and behavior seen in the cradle.

Yet there is a natural tendency for parents to be wrapped up in the events of the moment, and to become discouraged and pessimistic if a child is difficult, irritable, overactive, or seemingly unable to pay attention. The findings of developmental psychology suggest not pessimism but optimism about children and their potentialities. Difficult babies—boisterous, stubborn, and headstrong—often quiet down as they get older. Babies who seem restless and inattentive in the cradle often learn to concentrate and become star pupils in school. Even babies who seem anxious may turn out to be perfectly normal. If parents can remember that babies show a wide range of individual differences, need individual treatment, and thrive on warmth and love—and if they can tolerate behavior that at the moment may hardly be ideal—their patience will usually be rewarded.

background. Within a few months the black-box monkeys began to improve and after six months they seemed almost completely normal in their social behavior (Suomi and Harlow, 1972).

Human subjects have also been found to display a remarkable ability to bounce back from the numbing effects of an unstimulating early environment. One study was made in an isolated Indian village in Guatemala, where babies are kept inside the family's windowless hut for most of the first year of life. (The tribe members believe that sunlight, air, and the stares of certain people cause illness in the young.) It was found that the babies, when they emerge from the hut, appear severely retarded by the standards of other societies. But they soon catch up in the development of physical skills, and by adolescence they do as well as most children on some tests of perception and memory (Kagan and Klein, 1973).

There is considerable evidence also that early traumatic stresses—separations, illnesses, hospitalizations—especially if sufficiently frequent and prolonged can hamper later development (Rutter, 1983). But there is evidence as well that, under the proper conditions for growth, such early potential handicaps can be overcome (Garmezy, 1983).

Much remains to be learned about the effects of early neglect, deprivation, and trauma. The evidence to date, however, suggests these tentative conclusions: Human infants are extremely impressionable, and their environment has a profound effect on their development from the moment they are born. A highly unfavorable environment can produce drastic damage. But infants often prove to be resilient and malleable—that is, capable of changing when circumstances change. Under the proper conditions for growth, early handicaps can sometimes be overcome.

THE DEVELOPMENT OF BODY AND MIND

Most new parents are quick to recognize the outward physical growth of the infant. The baby's birth weight doubles in the first three months and triples in one year. By the end of the first year, the baby's height typically increases by almost 50 percent. But there are inward changes as well. The fibers of the nervous system grow and form additional connections to other fibers, and they become faster and more efficient messengers of information to and from the brain. The brain itself grows in size and weight. Its growth spurt during the first three months will never again be matched in life. Neuroscientists suspect that before the first year of life is over, the number of synapses—those critical connections between nerve cells in the brain—reaches a peak never again matched in our lifetime.

The results of all this are some of nature's most spectacular events: the growth of the newborn baby into eager toddler (sometime after the first birthday), experimenter with language (starting near the end of the second year), and eventually six-year-old schoolchild, about to solve the mysteries of reading and writing. How many and varied are the accomplishments of those early years. How many new worlds are faced and conquered.

Part of this rapid early development is the result of *maturation*—the physical changes, taking place after birth, that continue the biological growth of the organism from fertilized egg cell to adult. Almost day by day, simply as the result of getting older, babies become capable of new feats of physical, perceptual, and mental skill.

Physical Maturation

Even before birth, babies begin to use their muscles. Their movements can usually be felt in the womb in about the twentieth week of pregnancy. Newborn babies have all the muscle fibers they will ever possess, but the fibers still have a lot of growing to do. Eventually, at full maturity, the muscles will weigh about 40 times as much as they weighed at birth. The muscles of posture, creeping, and standing must mature as shown in Figure 14-9 before the baby can walk alone, at around the age of 15 months. The muscles of the hands and arms, as they mature, produce increased skill at reaching and grasping, as shown in Figure 14-10.

The skeleton at birth is largely composed of cartilage, which is softer and more pliable than bone but gradually hardens. The fibers of the nervous system grow and form additional synaptic connections to other fibers, and some of them develop protective sheaths that make them faster and more efficient conductors of nervous impulses. The brain, in particular, grows in size and weight—very rapidly during the first two years, then more slowly until growth is complete.

Much of the baby's remarkable progress in the early months of life reflects maturation of the body and the nervous system. Thus children all over the world, regardless of child-rearing practices, tend to display various skills at about the same age. They begin to smile at the sight of a human face at about 4 months, show vocal excitement to a new voice at 9 months, and search for a hidden object that they saw being covered by a piece of cloth at about 12 months. They begin to utter some of the basic sounds of language in the first few days of life—but they cannot really use speech until around 18 months. Evidence suggests that their brains may be mature enough earlier, but their voice boxes are not yet ready (Bonvillian, Orlansky, and Novack, 1983).

Figure 14-9   How the muscles of movement mature

As is explained in the text, the process of maturation accounts for the increasing ability of babies to move around. Shown here are the progress from birth to walking alone and the average age at which each stage of development occurs.

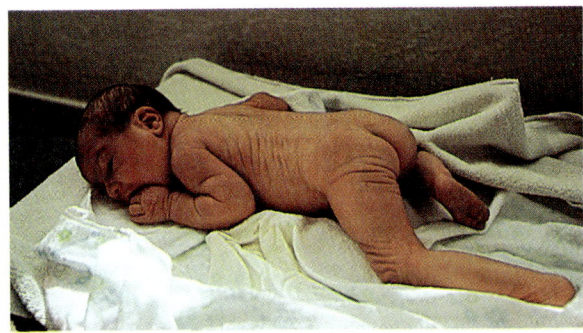

newborn

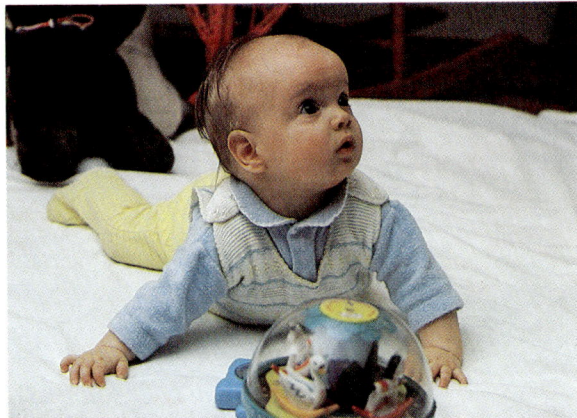

chin up: 2 months

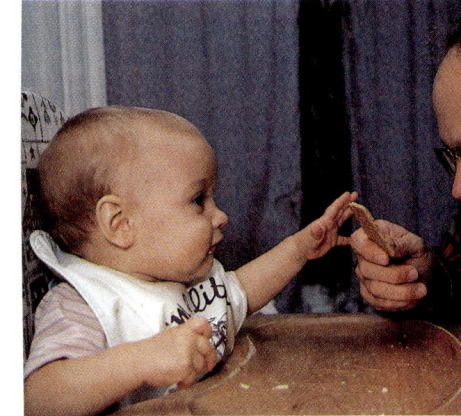

sit in high chair, grasp: 6 months

stand: 9 months

climb: 13 months

walk alone: 15 months

The Development of Body and Mind

Figure 14-10 First attempts at reaching

Maturation produces rapid changes in what happens when a bright toy is held over a baby's crib. Very young babies (A), typically lying with head to one side, pay only slight attention. Later (B) they occasionally watch the hand that is extended in the same direction the head is turned. At about 3½ months (C) they no longer hold the head to the side and may clasp their hands together beneath the toy. Soon they begin to raise their clasped hands toward the object (D). This is the final stage before they actually reach for the object with an open hand and try to grasp it (White, Castle, and Held, 1964).

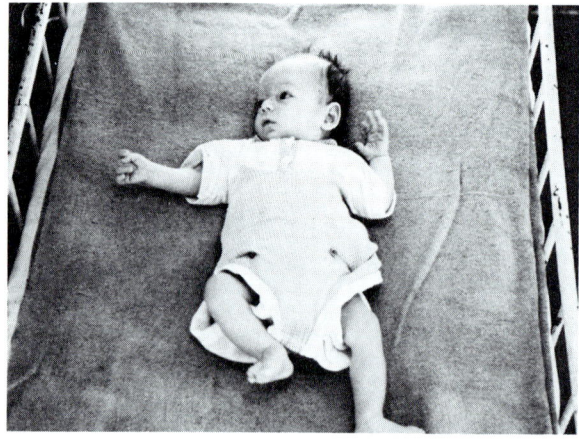

A

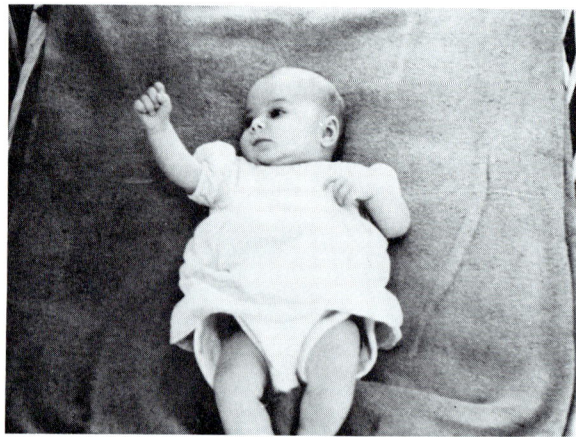

B

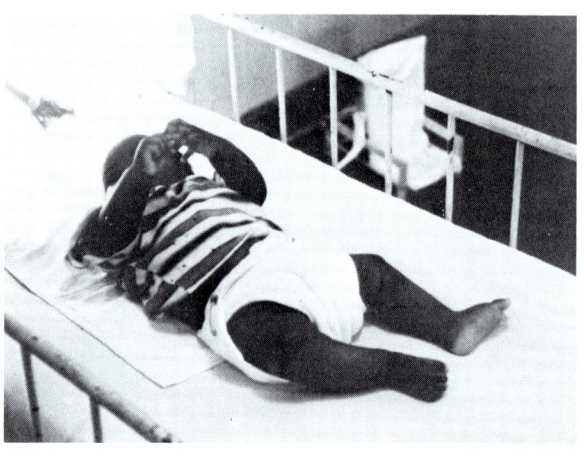

C

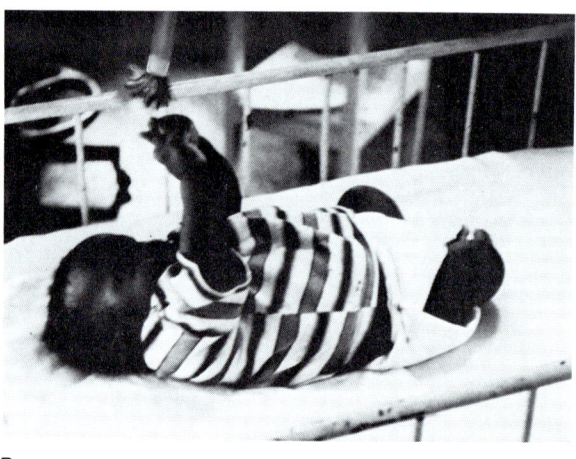

D

The process of maturation cannot be speeded up to any great extent. Indeed attempts to push children far beyond their level of maturation may be harmful (McGraw, 1943). Their environment does have some effect, however. Encouraging infants to perform skills—though without forcing them—is likely to produce the appearance of these skills at a somewhat earlier age. Infants whose parents talk to them a great deal may themselves begin speaking as early as the first birthday or shortly thereafter. Infants with less encouragement may not start until the age of two or even later. Skill at such cognitive tasks as remembering long lists of objects develops much earlier in societies that consider such activities important for young children than in societies that consider them unimportant.

Intellectual Development

During the opening years of life, children reveal a dazzling succession of intellectual capacities, each more intricate and advanced than the one that preceded it. Some of the most important of them are listed in Figure 14-11. While we take such skills for granted in adults, they are remarkable in infants who have only just begun to function in the world. Equally remarkable is the rapid and steady pace at which a given skill develops. The ability to recognize a familiar stimulus, for example, gets stronger with the passage of only a brief time. One-month-old infants who have learned to recognize a frequently repeated word lose the ability if a day passes without their hearing that word spoken. Only three months later, however, they can recognize a familiar word after interruptions of as long as a week or two. The ability of babies to recall past events also becomes more solidly entrenched over the space of only a few months as is shown in Figure 14-12. Such changes appear to be correlated with the maturation of the frontal lobe of the brain, as indicated in Figure 14-13.

Many factors contribute to intellectual development. One is improvement in the process of perception. As children grow older, they begin to know what to search for in the environment and how to go about it. They develop strategies for seeking important information and ignoring irrelevant information. Their attention becomes more selective and they are able to maintain it over a longer time span. Their scanning of the environment becomes more systematic and orderly.

Progress in perceptual efficiency has been charted by recording children's eye movements, as shown in Figure 14-14. When one-month-olds are shown a design, they are likely

Figure 14-11 Some intellectual skills that emerge early in life

The appearance and growth of these skills reflect a progressive maturation of the young child's central nervous system as described in the text (Kagan, 1981).

SKILL	AGE AT WHICH IT EMERGES	WHAT THE BABY SEEMS TO BE THINKING
Recognition	First 6 months	I recognize that the rattle I am looking at is different from the one I just saw a second or two ago.
Retrieval of past events	8–12 months	I recall that a little while ago you hid my rattle under that blanket.
Juggling the present with memories of the past	8–18 months	I am aware of that bright, round thing across the room, but I also remember that dad can reach it and bounce it to me.
Imitation	9–24 months	I am going to dial a number on that phone just as mom did yesterday.
Use of symbols	12–24 months	I think I'll use this sand to feed my doll.
Language	18–24 months	I don't have to point and cry anymore to get a drink. I can just say "milk" and get the same result.
Self-awareness	18–24 months	I just saw mom put that puzzle together, and I'm getting terribly upset because I think she wants me to do the same thing—but I can't.

Figure 14-12   The baby's progress in short-term memory

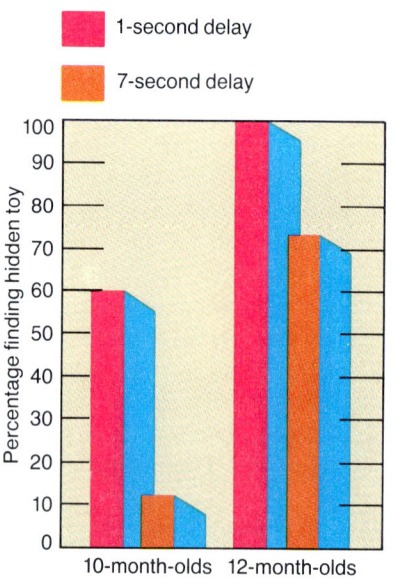

The bars show the percentages of 10- and 12-month-old babies who could recall where a toy was hidden after brief delays. The babies watched a toy being placed under one of two cloths, and a screen was then lowered to block their view for 1 second or 7 seconds. The task of finding the toy gets harder, of course, as the delay gets longer. But more important, no matter how long the delay, note how sharply the ability to find the toy improves with the passage of only two months (Kagan, Kearsley, and Zelazo, 1978).

Figure 14-13   Changes in brain function in the first year

In the opening months of life, the sensory and motor areas of the brain's cortex are more active than the frontal lobe, which does not become significantly active until the babies reach about the eighth month (adapted from Chugani and Phelps, 1986).

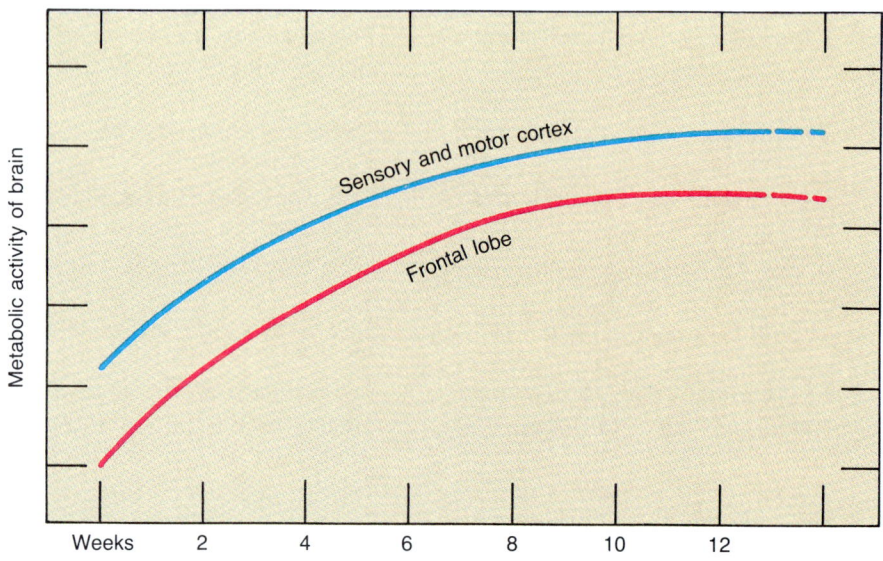

Figure 14-14 Early advances in eye movements and scanning

When babies were shown the design at the left, a typical 1-month-old scanned only one part of the outer border. A typical 2-month-old quickly arrived at the "heart of the matter" with the scanning pattern shown at the right (Salapatek, 1975).

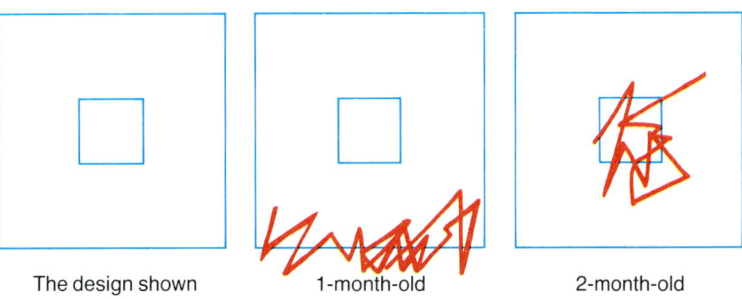

to scan whatever feature their eyes first encounter—usually part of the external border. Only one month later, they scan the essential elements of the design. As children get older, they become increasingly efficient in using visual perception to search for information. They also become more adept at perceiving details (Gibson, 1969) and organizing them into meaningful patterns and entities.

Another important factor in intellectual development is the baby's growing skill in understanding and using language. There is some evidence that parents can help advance this skill by talking to their babies, especially one-to-one (Olson, Bates, and Bayles, 1984). In turn, adeptness with language facilitates the formation of concepts—which helps organize information into categories and facilitates the mental processing that creates long-lasting memories.

THE FLOWERING PERSONALITY: BIRTH TO EIGHTEEN MONTHS

As with intellectual progress, the development of the personality also seems to proceed in an orderly way, through a series of stages merging one into another. All the aspects of personality—emotions, motives, and ways of coping with conflicts—begin to appear and undergo change. As children grow and move into the world, they enter new and widening circles of influence. Their changing social experiences mold their personalities in many different ways, for better or for worse. So do their developing intellectual skills, which allow them to become increasingly aware of themselves and the meaning of events around them—often with strong emotional impact.

The first stage of personality development lasts from birth to about the age of 18 months. During this period the infant has only limited social experiences, usually centering on one person who constitutes the greatest influence. Usually this person is the mother. It can, however, be someone else—the father, a grandparent, a baby-sitter, or a day-care teacher who takes care of the baby's first needs. Personality development is affected by the establishment of *attachment* to the person who constitutes the main source of interaction, comfort, and care.

The Power of Early Attachment

Much psychological thinking about the very earliest development of attachment stems from a famous series of experiments by Harry F. Harlow, who took baby monkeys from their own mothers and placed them with doll-like objects that he called "*surrogate mothers.*" As is shown in Figure 14-15, Harlow gave his baby monkeys two such surrogate mothers. One was made of wire, with a bottle and nipple from which the monkey received milk. The other was made of sponge rubber and terry cloth; it was an object to which the baby monkey could cling.

As the photographs show, the baby monkeys strongly preferred the terry-cloth doll to the wire doll. They clung to the terry-cloth mother even when feeding from the other. When a new object was placed in the cage, they clung to the terry-cloth mother while making their first hesitant and tentative attempts to discover what this strange and at first frightening object might be (Harlow, 1961). Obviously something about the terry-cloth surrogate provided the baby monkey with what humans could call comfort, protection, and a secure base from which it could explore new aspects of the environment.

In human infants during the first two years of life, attachment takes the form of a strong tendency to approach particular people, to be receptive to care and consolation from them, and to be secure and unafraid in their presence. Human babies, like monkeys, seem to be born with an innate tendency to become attached to the adults who care for them. They show a strong preference for those who have served as continuous caretakers—especially when they are bored, frightened, or distressed by the unfamiliar or unexpected.

One study has shown that young children, separated from their mothers during the birth of another child, became more agitated, depressed, and withdrawn; they also cried more and experienced increased heart rate and awakenings from sleep. As illustrated in Figure 14-16, when mother returned, the symptoms abated (Field and Reite, 1984).

Figure 14-15 Baby monkey and surrogate mothers

The baby monkey has been taken from its own mother and placed with two surrogate mothers. Note how it clings to the terry-cloth mother, even when feeding from the wire mother and especially when exploring a new and unfamiliar object that has been placed in the cage.

Figure 14-16 Baby's response to mother's absence

During play sessions, the average heart rate for babies rose sharply while mother was hospitalized and then dropped back when she was home once again.

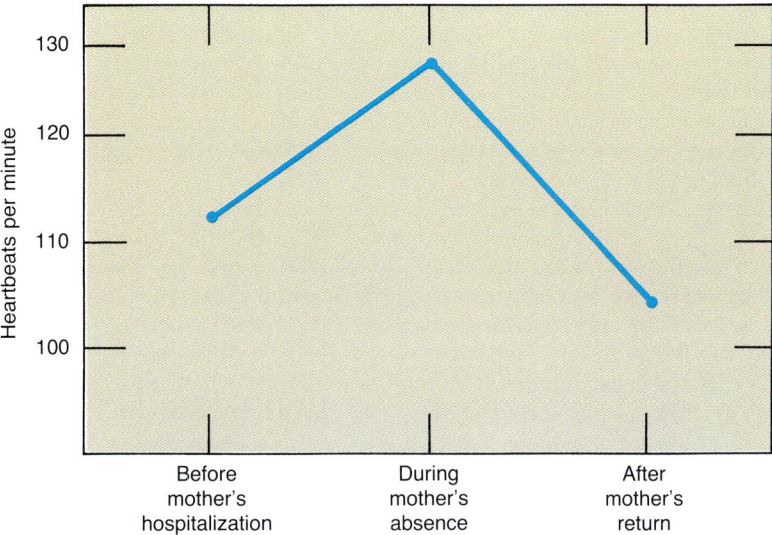

Such findings have raised many questions in the minds of parents about the advisability of day-care programs—an issue discussed in the box on Psychology in Everyday Life called "How Day-care Programs Affect the Young Child."

Attachment and Exploration

The inborn tendency to attachment is a valuable asset in survival. It helps infants find nurturance and protection from distress and dangers, real or imagined. It also seems to make them more receptive to parental standards. For example, one study found that strongly attached one-year-olds were more likely than others to obey the requests and commands of their mothers nearly a year later (Londerville and Main, 1981). But if the tendency to remain closely attached to a parent persisted, children would never outgrow their dependence on their caretakers. To become self-sufficient, they must explore the environment, encounter new objects and new experiences, and learn how to cope with them.

Oddly, though attachment and exploration seem to be conflicting tendencies, they actually work hand in hand. Note in Figure 14-15 how the baby monkey engages in both activities at once—cautiously exploring a new object while clinging to its terry-cloth surrogate mother. Human babies also seem to gather courage for exploration from their attachment to their mothers. In one experiment, babies just under a year old were placed in a strange room that contained a chair piled high with and surrounded by toys. When baby and mother were in the room together, the baby actively looked at the toys, approached them, and touched them. All this exploratory behavior dropped off, however, if a stranger was present or if the mother left the room (Ainsworth and Bell, 1970).

Psychology in Everyday Life
How Day-care Programs Affect the Young Child

In recent years, especially with both parents frequently working outside the home, day-care programs for young children have grown in popularity. What are the effects on the children?

Some authorities have warned that the consequences are likely to be dangerous for the child's emotional development (Dreskin and Dreskin, 1983). But the evidence points to a more qualified conclusion: The consequences depend on the quality of the day-care program itself—on what goes on inside the program. Day-care programs are not universally good or bad.

One of the most important things for parents to look for is the ratio of staff to children. In well-run, adequate centers, one caretaker is not responsible for more than three to four infants or five to six toddlers. It is important also to look carefully at the choice of playthings and learning materials that the children have available—whether infants, for example, are exposed to a variety of stimulation and have opportunities to practice new abilities as they mature. One recent study focused on nine day-care centers which differed in the degree of stimulation they offered for language development. Children from those centers where the caregivers talked a lot performed best on tests of language development (McCartney, 1984).

Another issue is: Do the children have enough time for their own individual pursuits—to move around with some freedom? Or are they regimented in an endless and sometimes taxing day of structured activities?

Under the right conditions, early group care need not have hidden dangers. Children tend to develop—socially, emotionally, intellectually—as they would if they had remained at home. Indeed they appear to become "attached" to the new environment as they would to a home caretaker. When preschool children are transferred to another setting and separated from their usual teachers and playmates, they display psychological and physiological symptoms—for example, agitation and sleeplessness—similar to those they might have displayed earlier in life at home when mother was absent (Field and Reite, 1984).

However, if day-care conditions are poor—if the program is understaffed, provides little variety and few pleasures, and restricts the child's explorations—then the child's development can indeed be affected adversely (Segal and Segal, 1985).

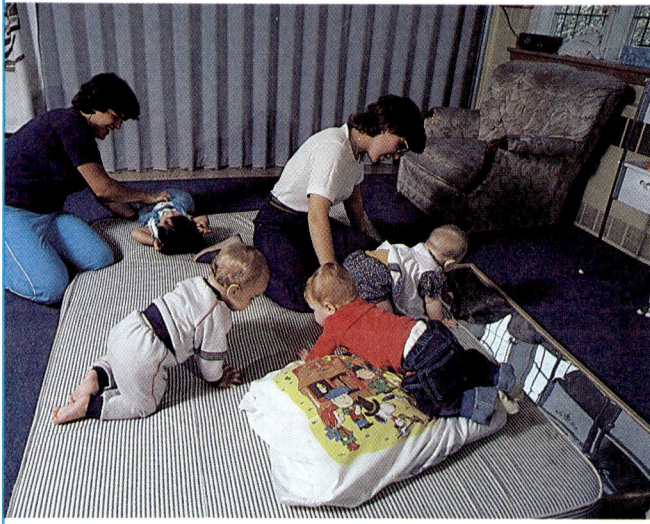

A high quality day-care program in action.

The Dawn of Anxiety

The experiment just described also produced results that point to another phase of development in the first 18 months—namely, the first appearance of signs of anxiety. When the babies were left alone in the room, many of them very quickly began to cry, made what appeared to be a rather frantic search for the mother, or did both. They were exhibiting *separation anxiety*, which rarely appears among American babies until around the age of 8 months.

Separation anxiety seems to emerge as an outgrowth of some of the child's newly developed intellectual skills. At 8 months, most babies are able for the first time not only to call to mind past events, but also to compare them with the here and now. When mother departs, they can now recall her former presence—and at the same time realize that she is no longer there. Not being able to understand the inconsistency, they become anxious and cry. Later, when babies can also anticipate that mother will return, the inconsistency is more easily resolved, and separation anxiety begins to fade.

It might seem simpler to regard separation anxiety as reflecting the child's attachment to the caretaker, but this does not seem to be the case. Babies brought up at home, with their mothers almost always around and with opportunities for attachment at a maximum, are no more likely to show separation anxiety than children who spend much of their time at day-care centers (Kearsley et al., 1975). As is shown in Figure 14-17, separation anxiety appears to be a universal experience regardless of child-rearing practices.

Figure 14-17   The emergence of separation anxiety: a universal pattern

In widely different cultures, babies younger than 7 months rarely cry when their mothers leave them. Between 12 and 15 months, however, the experience is almost sure to bring distress and tears—and then the impact begins to weaken. The pattern shown here applies equally everywhere children have been studied, including isolated villages in the Guatemalan highlands and remote areas of the African Kalahari Desert (Kagan, Kearsley, and Zelazo, 1978).

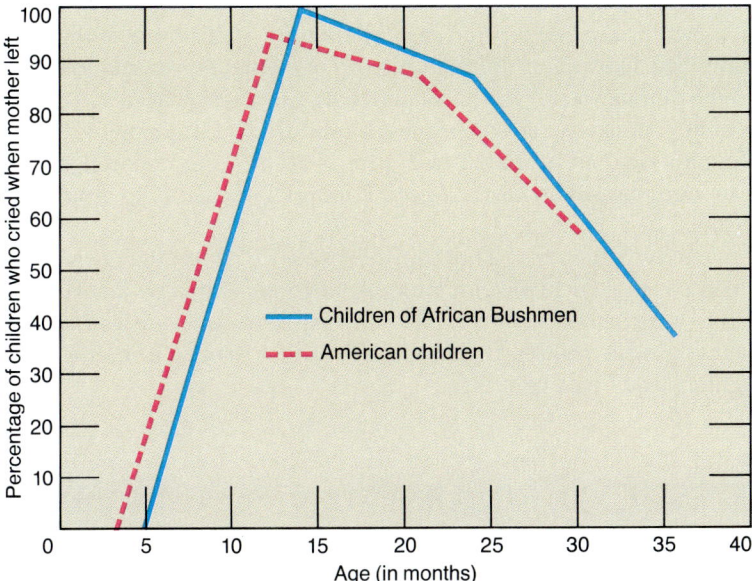

The Flowering Personality: Birth to Eighteen Months

Figure 14-18 A weird "stranger" and infant anxiety

The baby is reacting to the sight of the distorted mask—perhaps because it violates perceptual expectancies. At an earlier age, before learning what the human face is supposed to look like, the baby might have smiled instead of showing anxiety.

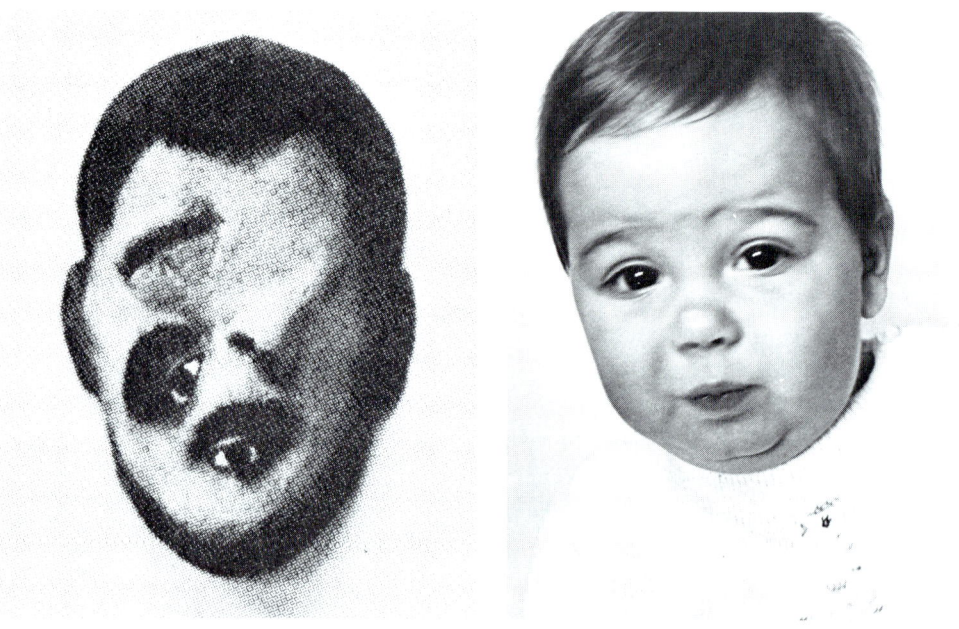

Even before separation anxiety becomes apparent, babies show what is called *stranger anxiety*. They will usually smile if the mother shows her face above the crib. But if a stranger's face appears, they often show anxiety by turning away and perhaps breaking into tears. Again, the explanation may be that the appearance of the strange face creates uncertainty. The baby has acquired some sort of mental representation or perceptual expectation of the familiar face, which is violated by the unfamiliar face. Behavior that seems to indicate stranger anxiety can sometimes be produced by showing the baby a distorted mask of the human face, as is shown in Figure 14-18. Among children everywhere, stranger anxiety first appears at about the age of 7 months, increases to around the first birthday, then declines.

The anxiety babies may show in the presence of strangers reflects a more general principle in psychological development: Anxiety generated by an event is less likely if the event can be anticipated. For example, one-year-old infants are less frightened by mechanical toys that produce noises on a predictable rather than an unpredictable schedule (Gunnar, Leighton, and Peleaux, 1984).

LEARNING LIFE'S SOCIAL REQUIREMENTS: EIGHTEEN MONTHS THROUGH THREE YEARS

The second important period in personality development, roughly from 18 months through the third year, is dominated by children's first important experiences with the demands of society. When they leave the crib and begin walking about the house, they find innumerable objects that look like toys provided for their own special delight but that in fact are expensive and fragile pieces of household equipment—or, like knives and electric light cords, are dangerous. They discover that they can no longer do whatever they please. The rules of the home say that they must not destroy valuable property and must not get into dangerous situations. At the same time they encounter a rule of society holding that the elimination drive must be relieved only in the bathroom. They undergo that much-discussed process called toilet training. In one situation after another, they find that life is filled with prohibitions and regulations.

The horizons of children at this age widen greatly. They leave the self-centered environment of the crib and begin to take their place in a world where people and their property rights must be respected. When the attachment to parent or other caretaker is strong and the relationship between them is good, children seem to want to comply (Maccoby, 1979). Others must learn the hard way to control the aggressive feelings sometimes ignited by the imposition of new limits on their behavior. Whether smoothly or with stormy difficulty, children begin to become disciplined members of society.

Social Demands, Inner Standards, and the Emergence of Self

In toilet training, children must learn *not* to do something—not to respond immediately to the bodily sensations that call for relief of the elimination drive. They must also learn *not* to respond to such external stimuli as the cupboard full of dishes that they would like to explore or the lamp that they would like to smash to the floor. In other words, they begin in this period to control and forgo forms of behavior that would ordinarily be their natural responses to internal or external stimuli.

The process through which parents impose discipline—and teach children to live by the rules of society—is helped along considerably by a dramatic change from within as

Learning one of life's early rules.

well. Around the age of two, children first develop a sense of right and wrong—inner standards and the desire to live up to them, one of the most powerful motives. In one study, two-year-olds watched someone play in a complicated manner—such as pretending to use toy kitchenware to cook a meal for a family—and then were told that it was their turn to play with the toys. Just a few months earlier, the process passed without incident. Now, however, many of them broke into tears or ran to their mother. Apparently they felt obligated to play with the toys in an equally sophisticated manner, yet they were unsure of their ability. This newly developed uncertainty over living up to a standard that was entirely self-imposed—since nobody taking part in the experiment suggested that they imitate the cooking—created anxiety and distress (Kagan, 1981). Even subtle violations of standards appear to be disturbing. Children will now point to a cracked toy, dirty hands, torn clothing, or a missing button and show their concern. They can discern—even from changes in the sound of father's voice or the shape of mother's eyes—that their own behavior elicits judgmental responses from others.

Children in the second year, along with developing inner standards, also are gaining a clearer definition of themselves as individuals. In the company of peers, the two-year-old begins making sharp distinctions between "I" and "mine" versus "you" and "yours." One investigator, studying peer interactions at this age, has shown how this emerging sense of self leads children to seize toys—not as evidence of selfishness, but as a kind of proclamation of self-awareness (Levine, 1983).

The Role of Rewards and Punishments

In learning to meet the social demands, rewards and punishments probably also play a part. Children are usually rewarded with praise and fondling when they are successful at toilet training or refrain from playing with a lamp after being told "No." And they may be punished, with disapproval if not physically, when they soil themselves, break something, or get into forbidden places. But the desire to live up to inner standards of proper conduct seems to appear even before children have learned to become anxious over possible punishment—and to have a stronger influence on behavior.

Punishment can actually upset the delicate balance between children's natural, constructive urge to explore the environment and the requirement of social discipline. This early period of life holds exciting possibilities for children and their self-image as active, competent, and increasingly self-sufficient human beings. By moving about in the world

Some early explorations need limits.

for the first time, they acquire all kinds of fascinating information about the environment. By handling objects—and sometimes, unfortunately, destroying them—they learn that they have some power over the environment. They discover that they can roam about the world and perhaps rearrange it to their liking. They learn that they can satisfy many of their own desires. By reaching into the cookie jar, they can relieve hunger. By crawling under the coat a visitor has thrown on the sofa, they can find warmth. One of the responsibilities of parents is to aid children in their explorations and discoveries while at the same time setting appropriate limits on their behavior.

THE PRESCHOOL YEARS: FOUR AND FIVE

By the time children are four, they begin to venture outside the home and play with other children. They may go to nursery school or kindergarten. This increasing social experience appears to be essential to normal development. Even monkeys, if raised solely in the company of the mother, with no opportunity to interact with other young monkeys, often turn out to be overfearful or overaggressive (Suomi, 1977). As children move into broader social circles, they learn among other things that the world is made up of males and females, for whom society decrees different kinds of behavior. Boys begin to take on the characteristics that society considers appropriate to males, and girls to take on the characteristics considered appropriate to females.

Children of four and five become adept at using language and concepts. They continue to acquire inner standards and the urge to live up to them—and this process gives them their first feelings of guilt, representing that mysterious mechanism called conscience. Moreover a new factor begins to influence their personalities. This is the period in which children begin to identify with their parents.

The Process of Identification

Exactly what identification means and how it takes place are matters of debate. To psychoanalysts, it is a complex process involving the Oedipus complex and the superego, as was explained in Chapter 10. To many psychologists it means that children come to feel that they and their parents share a vital bond of similarity. Children bear the family name. They are often told that they look like their parents. Thus they consider themselves in many significant ways to be similar to their parents. Consequently they feel more secure, for they view their parents as stronger and more competent than themselves. They begin to imitate their parents' behavior to increase this similarity—and to share vicariously in the parents' strengths, virtues, skills, and triumphs.

Children with intelligent parents often come to think of themselves as intelligent. A boy whose father holds a job requiring physical strength usually begins to think of himself as being strong, and a girl with an attractive mother thinks of herself as being attractive. One study has shown that mother's clearly stated attitudes about the importance of learning during the child's preschool years is reflected in a higher level of school achievement six years later (Hess et al., 1984).

Unfortunately, children identify with their parents' faults as well as their virtues, and it is not unusual for children to become aware of their parents' defects. They may see that their father is unable to hold a job and is the object of ridicule in the community or that mother drinks too much and is unwelcome in the neighbor's house. They may hear relatives criticize their parents. Or they may hear warring parents criticize each other's conduct.

Under such circumstances many children begin to believe that they too are unworthy, unlovable, hateful, stupid, lazy, or mean.

The identification with undesirable qualities can be a burden to children from economically disadvantaged homes or from minority groups beset by prejudice. Children may identify with what they come to believe are undesirable qualities of their social class or ethnic group, and as a result they experience the anxiety that arises from such a belief.

When Parents Die or Divorce

Children may also be affected adversely by the death of a parent. While it is not clear what the most vulnerable age may be (Garmezy, 1983), it would appear that the loss is often especially painful when it happens during the preschool years. As Figure 14-19 shows, a substantial number of delinquent boys come from homes in which a parent died or was absent for other reasons, with the percentage of delinquency greatest among the boys who were the youngest when the absence began. Of the many ways in which the death of a parent can hamper a child's development, one is interference with the normal workings of the identification process. But what happens subsequently matters. One study showed that the effects of early loss may be ameliorated if the quality of the child's relationship with the mother replacement is a good one, and if a new marriage brings stability to the life of the child (Birtchnell, 1980).

The fate of children of divorce also depends on what happens after the breakup. True enough, many children treated for psychological problems have experienced the distress of parental discord and divorce (Hetherington and Camara, 1984), and the impact on school achievement and emotional well-being may reverberate even in late adolescence and the early adult years (Wallerstein, 1985). The results may depend, however, on other factors. One study found that among girls who were in preschool when their parents separated, school achievement depended on a continuing strong identification with a competent mother and a solid relationship between mother and child. For boys, the key factor was father's continuing interest or the presence of an involved and committed stepfather (Wall-

Figure 14-19 Delinquency and loss of a parent

A study of the home backgrounds of delinquent boys, as compared with a matched control group of nondelinquent boys, found that considerably more of the delinquents had lost a parent through death, divorce, or other causes—particularly when they were very young (Bowlby, 1961).

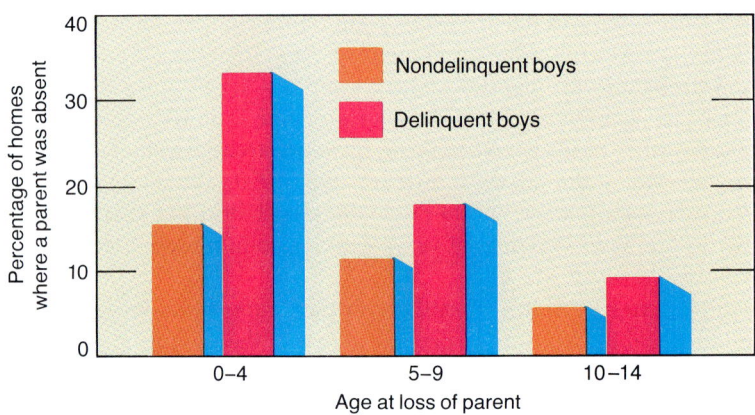

A father's commitment can blunt the effects of divorce.

erstein and Kelly, 1980). In another study of college students, investigators showed that the potentially negative consequences of divorce were diminished for those students whose parents continued to relate to one another in a positive way after their divorce (Fine, Moreland, and Schwebel, 1983).

Sex Typing: Learning To Be a Girl or Boy

Look in on any nursery school or kindergarten, and you are likely to notice some striking differences in the play activities of girls and boys. Chances are you will find girls playing with dolls or pretending to keep house, while boys are competing in a car racing contest or building a skyscraper. And if a fight happens to break out among the children, the odds are good that it will be boys rather than girls who are in the thick of things. Our society has traditionally defined males as being aggressive, independent, and dominant, females as being unaggressive, dependent, and submissive. The matter of masculinity versus femininity boils down to still another aspect of the relationship between internal physiology and the effects of experience.

To start with, differences in behavior between the two sexes may depend in part on the effects of the different hormones produced by the sex glands. The male sex glands produce large amounts of hormones called *androgens*, the female glands large amounts of a hormone called *estrogen*. Many scientists believe that the two hormones may affect the developing brain. Androgen may program the circuits of the brain to operate in ways distinctively masculine, estrogen in ways typically feminine. One study, for example, shows striking anatomical differences between male and female monkeys in an area of the hypothalamus that influences sexual behavior. In this area the male's neurons contain more numerous and more varied synapses than the female's—probably because of the "masculinizing influence" of the male hormone before birth (Ayoub, Greenough, and Juraska, 1983).

But despite any inborn tendencies, experiences in the environment remain the crucial factor. Children learn to act masculine or feminine through a process called *sex typing*. Parents treat their offspring in different ways depending on the sex. When cooing to a baby

How will society's pressure for sex typing affect the way each of these girls is viewed by others?

in a crib they use one tone of voice toward a girl, a different one toward a boy (Weitzman, 1975). They dress the two sexes differently—even in the case of twins of opposite sex (Brooks and Lewis, 1974).

Even parents who say they believe in treating the two sexes in the same way make distinctions. Some convincing evidence comes from an experiment with young and theoretically liberated mothers. All these women claimed that boys and girls were alike and should be treated alike. Almost all of them said that they encouraged their girls to be rough-and-tumble and their boys to play with dolls. But their conduct showed otherwise (Will, Self, and Datan, 1974). From infancy onward, fathers exhibit sex-typing behavior as well. They typically offer more attention to sons, and encourage achievement in them while stimulating dependency in their daughters (Sheperd-Look, 1982).

Pressures for sex-typing also emerge from television. TV shows designed for children proclaim the message that males are the world's movers and shakers, females the weak subordinates. A study of children's programs and the accompanying commercials showed that about three-fourths of all the characters on the screen were male, only about a fourth female. Little boys usually went camping, played football, and played with toy cars and construction sets. Little girls usually play at cooking and keeping house (O'Kelly, 1974). Children, especially girls, who watch more television, develop more sexually stereotyped attitudes (Morgan, 1982).

Similar sex typing pressure comes from books and schools as well. In children's picture books girls are generally portrayed as passive and doll-like, winning attention and praise only for their attractiveness, working mostly at tasks designed to help and please their brothers and fathers. Boys, on the other hand, are mostly shown as adventuresome, admired for their skill and achievements, and engaging in acts requiring independence and self-reliance (Weitzman et al., 1972). Teachers in nursery schools have been found to follow a similar pattern. In one way or another, often through praise, they encourage boys to be independent and aggressive, but they praise girls mostly for their appearance (Joffe, 1971). Girls are viewed as considerably more altruistic and helpful than boys—despite the fact that their actual classroom behavior shows no marked differences (Shigetomi, Hartmann, and Gelfand, 1981).

The message sinks in very early. When offered a choice, girls as young as three or four display their femininity in the kinds of toys they select—the customary dolls, toy stoves, and dish sets. Boys shun such toys and prefer guns, trucks, and cowboy suits (Maccoby and Jacklin, 1974). When the opportunities arise, boys are more likely than girls to take risks (Ginsburg and Miller, 1982).

Thus from the beginning society has worked to switch children's development onto one track if they are female, and a different track if they are male. The results are likely to affect their entire cognitive style—the way they perceive the world and process information (Bem, 1981). The collisions to which this can lead later on—especially today when the old masculine-feminine traditions are being questioned—will be described in the next chapter.

THE INFLUENCE OF TEACHERS AND PEERS: SIX TO TEN

The social influences that begin in the preschool years expand dramatically when children enter elementary school. Suddenly they spend much of their time with new teachers. They come into close contact with large numbers of their peers—boys and girls of the same age with whom they share work and play. They have to prove their competence at school tasks and at skills admired by fellow pupils. Although the home continues to be important in development, outside factors begin to play an increasingly influential role.

The New World of the Classroom

In the world that children enter at six there is a new adult—the teacher—whose discipline they must conform to and whose acceptance they must court. Ordinarily the teacher is a woman, like the mother, and children's behavior toward their mother can be generalized toward her. But boys who are identifying with their father and rebelling against their mother often have trouble in the early grades. They may be less fearful of rejection by the teacher and therefore more reluctant to accept her influence. They typically get lower marks and cause more disciplinary problems than do girls.

The teacher usually plays a dual role in pupils' development. First, she teaches the intellectual skills appropriate to our society. Second, and perhaps even more important to personality development, she tries to encourage a motive for intellectual mastery. It is in the early years of school that children crystallize their inner standards of intellectual mastery and begin to feel anxiety if they do not live up to the standards. By the age of ten, some children have developed an expectancy of success that is likely to bolster their self-confidence throughout life. Others have developed expectations and fears of failure—even the signs of learned helplessness. Many children who are actually very competent academically develop disparaging self-perceptions and illusions of incompetence (Phillips, 1984). Such outcomes depend largely on the school experience, the impact of which is discussed in a box on Psychology in Everyday Life called "Do We Value Our Teachers Enough?"

Finding a Place among Peers

Besides adjusting to teachers and schoolwork, children must also learn to live with their schoolmates. During the years from six to ten these peers have a particularly strong influence. For one thing, children in school can now evaluate themselves in relation to their classmates (Marsh and Parker, 1984). They can determine their rank on such attributes as intelligence, strength, and skills of various kinds. For another thing, they can freely express

Psychology in Everyday Life
Do We Value Our Teachers Enough?

Many of us remember from our own childhood how much difference a teacher could make in our motivation and school performance. Some teachers never seemed to communicate or inspire, while others seemed to care a great deal and bring out the best in us. Dramatic cases even exist of children who were once given up as failures—but who were later transformed into competent and achieving individuals by a charismatic teacher who was able to give them self-confidence and a sense of purpose (Segal, 1986).

An extensive study of schools in London found that physical factors—the size of the school, the age of the buildings, or the space available—do not seem to matter very much. What does matter is the way pupils are dealt with in the school. They accomplish more and display fewer behavior problems when they are given positions of responsibility and opportunities to help run the school, when they are rewarded and praised for their work, and when staff members are available for consultation and help. They also do better when teachers emphasize their successes and good potential rather than focus on their shortcomings (Rutter, 1983).

It would seem logical for the teaching profession to be held in high esteem. But this does not seem to be the case. A study by the National Institute for Education concluded that the relative status of teaching among American occupations has declined over the past 30 years, and that its standing as a white-collar job is even more marginal than in the past. While an unusually large number of young people who want to be community leaders and are concerned with social justice train to become teachers, it is precisely those who have such aspirations and con-

The teacher's powerful impact.

cerns who are most likely to abandon the profession. Most of those who stay on as teachers are looking only for job security and favorable working hours (Vance and Schlechty, 1982).

How motivated are today's teachers, how committed to their work? Two surveys, made 20 years apart, provide a disappointing answer. In 1961, 50 percent of teachers said they would certainly become teachers again if they could start all over. In 1981, only 21 percent gave the same positive response. The National Institute for Education study reaches a somber conclusion: The quality of those entering teaching is falling fast and will continue to fall unless somehow the teaching profession is accorded a status comparable to other human service occupations. Could we be ignoring one of society's most precious assets?

---

among their peers the rebelliousness and hostility they so commonly feel toward the adult world. At the same time, it is in the company of their peers that they can best satisfy their need for unqualified acceptance. Even when young children acknowledge each other's faults, they manage to do so without conveying rejection. They typically grant each other sufficient "idiosyncracy credits" to permit them to behave inappropriately at times without losing face (Fine, 1981).

A sign of later problems?

Peers often serve effectively to advance each other's development. They can provide models for learning such positive traits as generosity, empathy, and helpfulness. They can teach other academic skills with surprising effectiveness, and sometimes do a better job than parents of relieving the anxieties and agitation encountered in growing up (Furman, Rahe, and Hartup, 1981). Indeed those young children who remain socially isolated—or whose peer relationships are constantly turbulent and unsatisfactory—appear more likely than others to have a rocky road ahead. They report a pervasive sense of loneliness (Asher, Hymel, and Renshaw, 1984), and later on, they are more prone to drop out of school, to become delinquents, or to suffer psychological problems requiring professional help (Asher, Oden, and Gottman, 1981).

Becoming Dominant or Submissive

One personality trait that is partially set by the end of the early school years is the tendency to be dominant or submissive in relations with other people. Children of ten who actively make suggestions to the group, try to influence and persuade others, and resist pressure from others often tend to remain dominant in their social relations. Children who are quiet and like to follow the lead of others often remain passive and submissive.

The tendency to be dominant or submissive is in part a function of group acceptance. Children who believe that they are admired by the group are likely to develop enhanced self-confidence and dominance over others. Children who do not consider themselves admired by the group are likely to develop feelings of inferiority and to be submissive. Physical attributes play an important part. The large, strong boy and the attractive girl are more likely to be dominant. The small, frail boy and the unattractive girl are likely to be submissive. Other factors are identification with a dominant or submissive parent and the kind of control exercised by the parents. Permissive parents tend to influence their children in the direction of dominance, while parents who restrict their children's activities tend to influence them in the direction of submissiveness.

New Emphasis on Inner Standards

Although the motive to live up to inner standards appears by about the age of two, it plays a relatively minor part in behavior for some years. A preschool girl, for example, does not think of a kiss from her mother in terms of inner standards. She values the kiss for its own sake, because it satisfies the motive for affiliation and affection. By the time she is about eight, however, she takes a different view. She is likely to have developed an inner standard that says in effect, "I should be valued by my parents"—and she values a kiss as evidence that she is living up to this standard.

In general, in the early school years the desire to live up to inner standards begins to take a top position in the hierarchy of motives. Three standards that become especially important at this time are these:

Being valued by parents, teachers, and peers.

Mastering physical and mental skills.

Achieving harmony between thoughts and behavior. (Children develop a standard that calls for them to behave rationally and sensibly—and in a way that confirms their self-concept and their identification with their parents and their other heroes.)

The Threshold of Adolescence

By the age of ten, children have made spectacular progress from their helpless days in the crib. Their bodies and nervous systems have grown to near maturity. They are capable of many physical skills. Intellectually, they are well along in Piaget's stage of concrete operations and about to embark on the final stage of formal operations. Their personality has changed and blossomed. They now display many individual differences in personality—like those apparent in Figure 14-20.

Figure 14-20   Two sisters, two different personalities

These twins exhibit very different reactions to the photographer, who is a stranger to them. The girl at the right is wary and tentative while her sister is warm and cooperative.

Figure 14-21 Some relationships between childhood traits and adult personality

The correlations were obtained by rating the behavior of children aged 6 to 14, then making ratings of the same subjects after they had become young adults. For males, note that dependence in childhood shows almost no correlation with dependence as an adult—but striving for achievement shows a high correlation. For females, disorganized behavior in childhood shows little correlation with displays of anger in adulthood—but striving for achievement shows a fairly high correlation (Kagan and Moss, 1962).

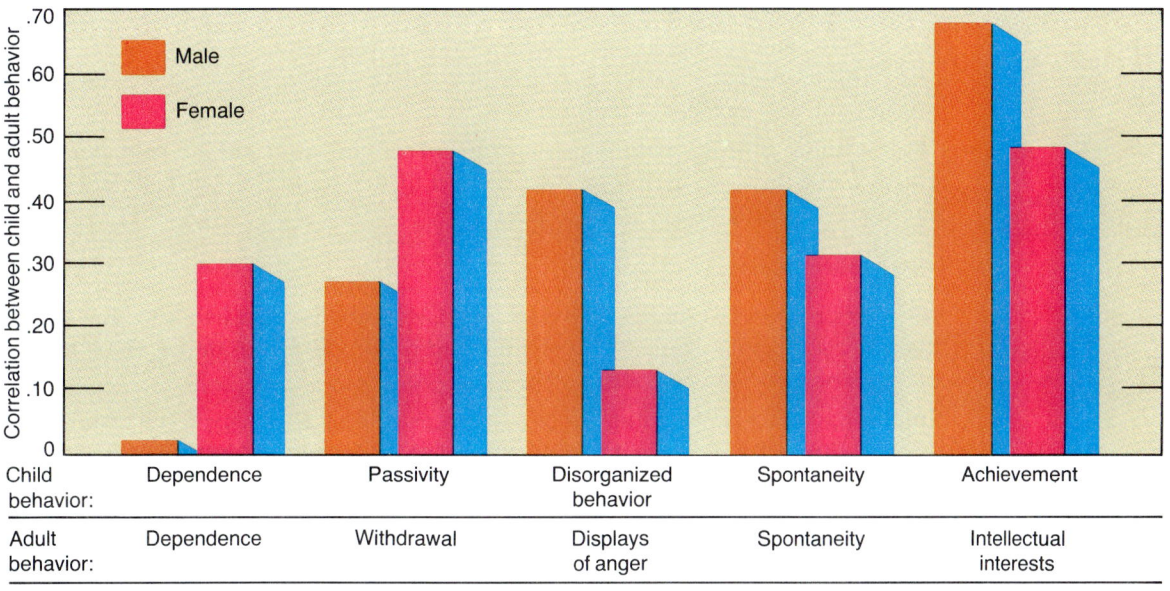

In some ways, the ten-year-old child offers a reasonably accurate preview of the future adult. The trend of physical development and the pattern of mental processes have been established. Personality traits have emerged and may persist through adolescence and into adulthood, as indicated by the correlations shown in Figure 14-21. But note that the correlations are by no means perfect. Some are indeed very low. The child's personality is still subject to change—for development, though it proceeds rapidly and dramatically through the first ten years, does not end at that point. Adolescence and adulthood, as will now be seen, may switch development into entirely new channels.

SUMMARY

Life's overture: from conception to birth

1. *Developmental psychology* studies the ways in which children gradually acquire their patterns of thinking, emotions, motives, and other aspects of personality—and the ways in which these patterns may change in later life.

2. The mechanisms of human heredity are the 23 pairs of *chromosomes*, 46 in all, found in the fertilized egg cell and repeated through the process of division in every cell of the body that grows from the egg.

3. Each chromosome is made up of a large number of *genes*, which are composed of a

chemical called DNA. The genes direct the growth of cells into parts of the body and also account for the individual differences we inherit.

4. Being female or male is determined by the *X chromosome* and the *Y chromosome*. An X-X pairing in the fertilized egg cell creates a female. An X-Y pairing creates a male.

5. The development of a child can be affected dramatically by the quality of the environment in the womb.

6. Over approximately 280 days of prenatal development, the developing baby undergoes a remarkable series of changes. During the first eight weeks, an infant increases nearly two million percent in size; as early as seven weeks, the nervous system, brain, and parts of the body can be discerned; by twenty weeks, the child is sensitive to touch, pain, and changes in temperature.

7. The ease and difficulty with which a baby is born, how quickly the baby begins to breathe, and the term of pregnancy can affect the baby's well-being. Loss of oxygen supply to the nerve cells is called *anoxia*.

Newborn babies: similar but different

8. All babies respond to stimuli with a wide range of inborn reflex behavior that allows them to escape pain, avoid harsh stimuli, and seek food. For example, if the side of the mouth is touched, they display the *rooting reflex*.

9. Studies have shown wide individual differences among infants in (a) the response of sensory threshold, (b) how rapidly babies display sensory adaptation and quit responding, (c) the child's degree of irritability, and (d) the child's vulnerability to stress.

10. Babies at birth differ in (a) sensory thresholds and adaptation, (b) activity and irritability, and (c) temperament. Most appear to be *easy children*, some *slow-to-warm-up*, and some *difficult*.

11. Traits displayed in infancy endure for varying periods of time. Most early traits are altered by childhood environment.

12. Human infants are extremely impressionable. An unfavorable environment may produce drastic and sometimes long-lasting abnormalities. But infants are also resilient and malleable—capable of changing when circumstances change.

The development of body and mind

13. Physical development, including the acquisition of such skills as walking and talking, depends largely on the process of *maturation*—the physical changes, taking place after birth, that continue biological growth from fertilized egg cell to adult.

14. Factors contributing to intellectual development include improvement in the process of perception and growing skill at understanding and using language.

The flowering personality: birth to eighteen months

15. Personality development from birth to 18 months is characterized by *attachment* to the mother or other caretaker. This period is marked by the appearance of *separation anxiety* and *stranger anxiety*.

Learning life's social requirements: eighteen months through three years

16. The second important period in personality development, roughly from 18 months through the third year, is dominated by children's first important experiences with the demands of society.

17. Children in the second year (a) develop inner standards and desire to live up to them, and (b) begin making sharp distinctions between "I" and "mine" and "you" and "yours." In learning to meet social demands, rewards and punishment play a part in influencing behavior.

The preschool years: four and five

18. The preschool years, 4 and 5, are characterized by (a) *identification* with the parents, (b) the first notions of *sex typing* and conduct appropriate to males and females, and (c) the first feelings of guilt and conscience.

The influence of teachers and peers

19. From 6 to 10, children come under the strong influence of their peers—that is, other children. Peers provide (a) evaluation, (b) a social role, and (c) an opportunity for rebellion against the adult world. During this period children acquire a tendency to be dominant or submissive and strong inner standards calling for (a) being valued by parents, teachers, and peers; (b) mastering physical and mental skills; and (c) achieving harmony between thoughts and behavior.

20. By age 10, a child offers a reasonably accurate preview of the future adult.

IMPORTANT TERMS

androgens
anoxia
attachment
chromosomes
difficult children
easy children
estrogen
genes
maturation

rooting reflex
separation anxiety
sex typing
slow-to-warm-up children
stranger anxiety
surrogate mother
X chromosome
Y chromosome

RECOMMENDED READINGS

Biehler, R. F. *Child development: an introduction*, 2d ed. Boston: Houghton Mifflin, 1981.

Clarke-Stewart, A., and Friedman, S. *Child development: infancy through adolescence*. New York: Wiley, 1987.

Eisenberg, N. *Contemporary topics in developmental psychology.* New York: Wiley, 1987.

Fogel, A., and Melson, G. *Child development: individual, family, and society*. St. Paul: West Publishing, 1987.

Gallagher, J. J., and Ramey, C. T. *The malleability of children*. Baltimore: P.H. Brookes Publishing, 1987.

Illingworth, R. S. *The development of the infant and young child: normal and abnormal*, 9th ed. New York: Churchill Livingstone, 1987.

Osofsky, J. D. *Handbook of infant development*, 2nd ed. New York: Wiley, 1987.

CHAPTER
15
ADOLESCENCE, ADULT LIFE, AND OLD AGE

ADOLESCENCE: JOY OR MISERY? 536

Physical growth in adolescence
Physical changes, body image, and eating disorders
The world of teenage sex
Moral development
The quest for identity: adolescents at home and at work

DEVELOPMENT IN ADULTHOOD 544

Some surprising turnabouts in adulthood
Dealing with crises: Erikson's theory of psychosocial development
Choosing and pursuing a career
Adult sex roles—and the conflicts they can create
Love—and usually marriage
The adventure of parenthood
Middle age—its tensions and satisfactions

GROWING OLD: THE CHALLENGES AND THE TRIUMPHS 554

The aging body
The intellectual capacities of older people
Mental health in the later years

THE PSYCHOLOGY OF DYING 559

Attitudes toward death
When a mate dies
The stages of dying
The experience of death

SUMMARY 564

IMPORTANT TERMS 566

RECOMMENDED READINGS 566

PSYCHOLOGY IN EVERYDAY LIFE

Teenagers on the home front 543
Why adolescents destroy themselves 544
The male's sex role problems 550
Paths to a long and happy life 561

Not too long ago, many psychologists believed that the period of childhood set the course for the rest of life. After the first few years, they were convinced, we simply acted out a script written earlier. As a result, the study of development was confined to the growing child.

Today, however, psychologists view development as a process that continues throughout our existence. Studies have shown that we humans continue to profit from new experiences, learn, and change—sometimes in spectacular ways—for as long as we live. As this chapter will convey, adolescence, adulthood, and even the later years may channel development into entirely new patterns. Thus developmental psychology has expanded to the study not only of infancy and childhood, but of the full spectrum of human development.

ADOLESCENCE: JOY OR MISERY?

In adolescence, we are suspended between the childhood years just past and the adult years still to come. Most Americans remain in school at least until they are around 18. Many go to college until their early twenties. Some people who train for professions—for example, physicians—may not be able to earn a living until they are 30. It is difficult to determine, therefore, exactly at what point in this extended preparation for full participation in society the child becomes the adolescent and the adolescent becomes an adult. Moreover, although adolescence is regarded as spanning roughly the period between 10 and 20 years, its beginning and ending can vary considerably from one individual to another. A number of criteria for defining the boundaries of adolescence are identified in Figure 15-1. All of them suggest that the period is one of dynamic and often dramatic change.

Figure 15-1 The definition of adolescence

One problem encountered in studying adolescence is deciding what the boundaries of the period actually are. Presented in the table are a number of markers used by various psychologists to distinguish this period from childhood and adulthood (Steinberg, 1985). Keep in mind, however, that there is no strict, one-for-all definition. Moreover, the period itself is actually an invention of modern industrial society. In simpler societies, even today in many parts of the world, the transition from childhood to full membership in the community is so smooth and imperceptible that it does not even have a name.

AREA OF DEVELOPMENT	WHEN ADOLESCENCE BEGINS	WHEN ADOLESCENCE ENDS
Biological	Beginning of growth spurt	End of growth spurt
Emotional	Beginning of detachment from parents	Reaching separate sense of identity
Interpersonal	Shifting interest from parents to peers	Development of intimacy with peers
Cognitive	Start of more advanced reasoning abilities	Full development of advanced reasoning
Educational	Entry into junior high school	Completion of schooling
Moral	Becoming tuned in to others' expectations	Beginning to behave by the dictates of personal conscience

The question of whether such changes bring joy or misery has been pondered by many psychologists—and by many adolescents as well. The first American psychologist to become concerned with the problem of growing up concluded that adolescence was all in all a difficult time of life—a period of "storm and stress" (Hall, 1904). Many other psychologists agree. One study found that substantial numbers of people, looking back on their lives when they had reached the age of 30, felt that their adolescent years were the time when they were most confused and their morale was at its lowest ebb. They mentioned such difficulties as striving for recognition from peers of their own and the opposite sex, being under anxiety-producing pressures from their parents for scholastic and social achievement, and trying to establish their independence while still financially dependent on their parents (Macfarlane, 1964).

Other psychologists, however, have reached different conclusions. Some studies have found that most adolescents, far from being in bitter rebellion, have a warm and mutually respectful relationship with their parents (Sorenson, 1973). Some investigators have even concluded that most adolescents, far from being hopelessly confused and demoralized, are actually well adjusted (Offer, Ostrov, and Howard, 1982). The conflicting evidence may reflect the vast range of individual differences that mark a period when all of us undergo rapid and intense growth and change—both physical and psychological.

Physical Growth in Adolescence

In physical terms, adolescence is usually defined as beginning with the onset of puberty—marked by menstruation in the female and production of sperm in the male. This typically occurs sometime between the ages of 11 and 18, usually a year or two earlier in girls than in boys. The onset of puberty is almost invariably accompanied by rapid physical growth. A girl may suddenly grow 3 to 5 inches in height in a single year, a boy 4 to 6 inches. Along with growth comes a change in physical proportions and strength. The girl begins to look like a woman, the boy like a man. All these changes are set into motion by increased activity of the pituitary gland, which stimulates the sex glands to produce large quantities of the hormones estrogen in the female and androgens in the male.

The first menstrual period, known as *menarche*, is the benchmark of physical maturity in girls—although fertility often arrives only after the first few cycles. In our culture in the past, many girls entered adolescence with ambivalent feelings—a mixture of excitement and fear. Recent studies, however, suggest that the attitudes of adolescent girls toward menarche are less negative now than was the case a couple of decades ago. The change is probably due to the more open and undefensive presentation of information about menstruation in homes, schools, and the media than was true in the past (Grief and Ulman, 1982).

The timing of puberty appears to be important psychologically. Early puberty can be a mixed blessing. On the one hand, it can have a positive effect because accelerated physical development tends to increase popularity with peers, particularly among boys who become stronger and better athletes. On the other hand, it can also have detrimental effects because it reduces the time children need to prepare for dramatic changes and their new status and responsibilities. Early puberty, for example, can make a girl seem sexually provocative at a time when she is still unable psychologically to cope with such reactions (Clausen, 1975). Reaching the stage at about the same time as peers and classmates, at least for girls, would appear to permit the smoothest transition (Petersen, 1981).

Later maturation can be a mixed blessing as well. Although it provides added time to prepare emotionally for changes in social status, it means a continued childlike appearance and short stature—which tend to be disadvantages in the peer culture. Boys especially are at a special disadvantage. If they are slow to show the growth spurt, they continue to be treated as "little boys," while their bigger and more mature classmates are gaining new respect.

Most studies of this subject have focused on the outward physical changes adolescents undergo at puberty. Recently, however, one research team used hormone levels as a criterion. The researchers found that when hormone levels associated with puberty are high for a given age, the result is an increase in emotional difficulties, especially for boys (Susman et al., 1985). But it is not clear whether the biological changes cause the stress reactions—or the other way around.

Physical Changes, Body Image, and Eating Disorders

Because adolescence brings dramatic changes in physical appearance, it is a time when self-image is very much dependent on body image. Adolescents who see themselves as deviating from the "ideal" physique can quickly lose their self-esteem. Being overweight can be particularly devastating to teenagers concerned about how they appear to others (Steinberg, 1985).

This concern is regarded as one of the factors that lead some adolescents—particularly adolescent girls—to embark on abnormal and, ultimately, life-threatening steps to remain thin. The result in some cases is a disorder known as *anorexia nervosa*, in which the already emaciated individual continues on a starvation diet in an effort to keep weight down. Young women with this disorder continue to be terrified about gaining weight even when they have already lost as much as a fourth to a half of their normal body weight. Even more common is *bulimia*, a disorder in which the individual engages in eating binges, and then induces vomiting or takes laxatives in order to avoid gaining weight.

Both disorders—which in many cases occur together—undoubtedly have complex causes. For example, there may be a biological predisposition such as a hormone imbalance; often the individual is chronically anxious and depressed; and in many cases, the disorder seems to run in families (National Institute of Mental Health, 1987). But underlying the abnormal behavior is usually an adolescent's extremely disturbed body image (Steinberg, 1985).

The World of Teenage Sex

One adolescent activity of overriding importance revolves around the first serious attempts to establish relationships with the opposite sex. Sexuality is a prominent concern during the adolescent years not only because of the physical changes that puberty brings, but because adolescents must try to establish their sexual identities at the same time that they are coping with all the other difficulties of becoming adults.

Society's attitudes towards sex are more permissive today than in the past. As shown in Figure 15-2, half of today's young people have experienced sexual intercourse by the time of high school graduation. The percentage of girls with sexual experience in the 15–19 age group increased from 27 percent in 1971 to 43 percent in 1982 (Pratt, 1984). The figures for teenage boys have not increased nearly so much—from about 72 to 78 percent—but in recent years far fewer male adolescents have had their experience exclusively with prostitutes or "bad" girls, far more with friends or classmates.

Although many adolescents have come to view premarital intercourse as the norm, they have not become advocates of promiscuity or casual sex. Being emotionally involved has become an important benchmark for accepting sexual relationships (Steinberg, 1985). A number of sex counselors in colleges have noted, along with a decline in promiscuity, a growing concern for commitment, marriage, and children (Stern, 1983).

Figure 15-2 Sexual experience among young people

Although intercourse is generally rare before the ninth grade, it rises to about 50 percent by the end of high school—with a higher rate for boys than for girls (after Dreyer, 1982).

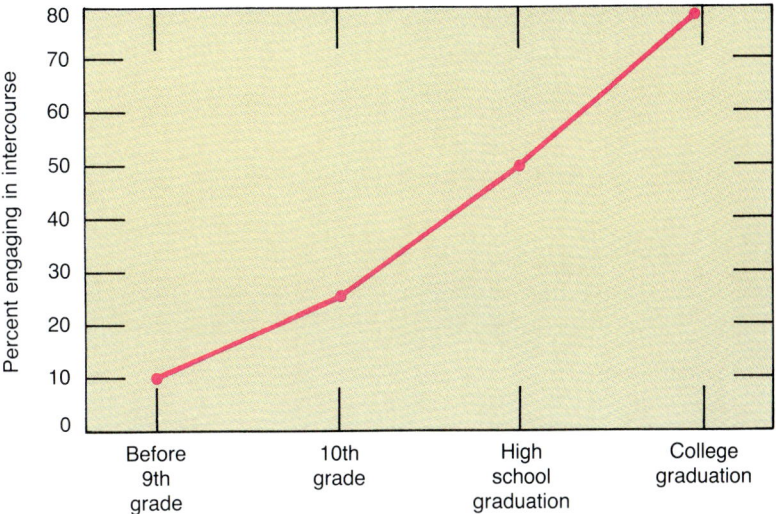

Adolescents continue, however, to face many self-doubts and confusions in the area of sex. Recent surveys of college students show that the drift toward increasingly liberal attitudes, which began in the mid-1960s, started to level off and even reverse itself somewhat during the early 1980s. But although relatively fewer students say that they believe premarital sex to be right today than ten years ago, the actual practice of premarital sex is still increasing (Robinson and Jedlicka, 1982).

Moreover, the new pattern of sexual activity has been accompanied by a sharp rise in teenage pregnancies. A survey at the start of the 1980s showed that, among women between the ages of 15 and 19 living in metropolitan areas, about 16 percent had become pregnant (Zelnick, Kantner, and Ford, 1981). The pregnancy rate is higher for black girls than for white, a difference that reflects the fact that black adolescents more often engage in sex without planning safeguards against conception (Smith and Udry, 1985).

Indeed the majority of American teenagers enter the world of sex without using any form of contraception. Many first sexual encounters are largely spontaneous, and so there is no planning ahead. One recent study suggests that sexual anxiety influences the use of contraceptives; those who are in conflict about sex fail to prepare adequately for their sexual encounters (Geis and Gerrard, 1984). Many teenagers feel that being "carried away" is morally acceptable, but having planned-for sex is not (Byrne and Fisher, 1983). In addition, when adolescents do try to prevent conception, they tend to use male-controlled methods—the condom or withdrawal—instead of more effective ones such as diaphragms, birth control pills, or intrauterine devices (IUDs).

Because the increased rate of premarital sex among young adolescents has outpaced teenagers' use of birth control, most experts on adolescence conclude that a strong need exists for more effective sex education and counseling for young people. Becoming a parent in adolescence is not, of course, always followed by dire consequences (Chilman, 1982). Still, it is "for many young people an extremely disruptive event, which often curtails educational, occupational, and economic opportunities" (Steinberg, 1985).

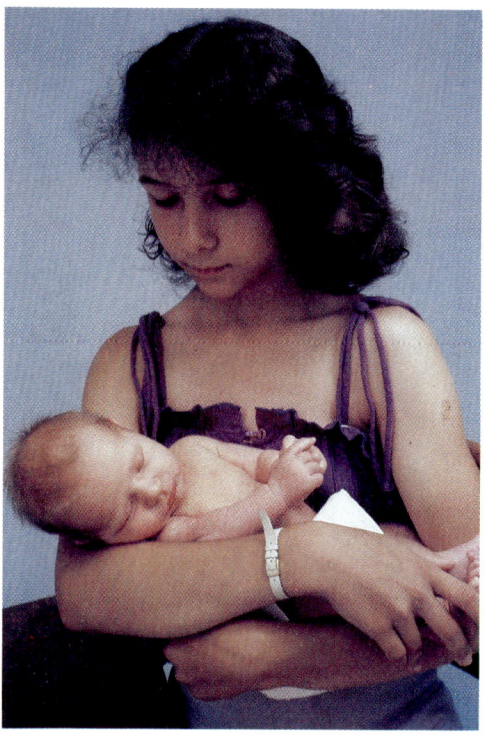

How ready is this teenager for the role of parent?

Moral Development

Moral standards in general—not only of sexual but of other types of behavior as well—usually undergo rapid and often lasting change during adolescence. Though such standards appear much earlier, they are originally based mostly on a desire to obtain approval and avoid criticism. In adolescence, the standards take a new form—dictated not by mere self-interest but by principles.

The manner in which moral judgments develop was studied extensively by Lawrence Kohlberg, who questioned boys seven years old through adolescence. Kohlberg presented his subjects with a number of hypothetical situations involving moral questions like these: If a man's wife is dying for lack of an expensive drug that he cannot afford, should he steal the drug? If a patient who is fatally ill and in great pain begs for a mercy killing, should the physician agree? By analyzing the answers and particularly the reasoning by which his subjects reached their answers, Kohlberg determined that moral judgments develop through a series of six stages, as shown in Figure 15-3. Children in the two stages of what he calls the preconventional level base their ideas of right and wrong largely on self-interest. They are concerned chiefly with avoiding punishment and gaining rewards. Later, in the two stages of what he calls the conventional level, they become concerned about the approval of other people. Finally, in the two stages of the postconventional level, they become concerned with abstract moral values and the dictates of their own consciences.

Thus children's reasons for good behavior progress from sheer self-interest to a desire for the approval of others, and finally to a concern for their own moral values and the approval of their own consciences. This stage-by-stage development takes place as children begin to understand—and prefer—increasingly complex patterns of moral reasoning. As the process unfolds, they tend to reject as invalid the bases for moral judgments that they used in earlier stages (Walker, de Vries, and Bichard, 1984).

Figure 15-3 Kohlberg's stage theory of moral development

Summarized in the table are the six stages in moral development *found by Kohlberg. Among seven-year-olds, almost all moral judgments are made at the preconventional level. By 16, only a few are made at this level, and judgments made at the postconventional level become important (Kohlberg, 1963, 1967).*

PRECONVENTIONAL LEVEL

Seven-year-old children are oriented to the consequences of their behavior.	Stage 1. Defer to the power of adults and obey rules to avoid trouble and punishment.
	Stage 2. Seek to satisfy their own needs by behaving in a manner that will gain rewards and the return of favors.

CONVENTIONAL LEVEL

At around ten, children begin to become oriented to the expectations of others and to behave in a conventional fashion.	Stage 3. Want to be "good" in order to please and help others and thus receive approval.
	Stage 4. Want to "do their duty" by respecting authority (parents, teachers, God) and maintaining the social order for its own sake.

POSTCONVENTIONAL LEVEL

Adolescents become oriented to more abstract moral values and their own consciences.	Stage 5. Think in terms of the rights of others, the general welfare of the community, and a duty to conform to the laws and standards established by the will of the majority. Behave in ways they believe would be respected by an impartial observer.
	Stage 6. Consider not only the actual laws and rules of society but also their own self-chosen standards of justice and respect for human dignity. Behave in a way that will avoid condemnation by their own consciences.

The Quest for Identity: Adolescents at Home and at Work

Adolescents typically want to feel grown-up, and they crave independence. They seek to establish a sense of *identity*—that is, to think of themselves as possessing a distinct and unique character, of being people in their own right—distinct from their parents and siblings. But the search is surrounded by troublesome questions: *Who am I? What am I? What do I want to do with my life?*

The cognitive development of adolescents has advanced to a stage in which they can think in abstractions, form theories about what life is all about, and contemplate what society might be rather than what it seems to be. Often their thinking makes them critical of the values held by society and by their parents. Indeed the relationship between adoles-

A job can often bolster the adolescent's self-esteem.

cents and parents is often fraught with difficulties. These difficulties—and avenues for overcoming them—are discussed in the box on Psychology in Everyday Life called "Teenagers on the Home Front."

Often the question of identity comes down to the practical matter of choosing a career—a task complicated by the fact that today's society seems to offer a bewildering number of possibilities. Proportionately more American teenagers are now employed in part-time jobs than at any other time in recent decades (U.S. Department of Labor, 1987). By the time they graduate from high school, around 80 percent of adolescents will have had formal work experience (Steinberg and Greenberger, 1980).

But the results can be a mixed blessing, and the advantages—in terms of education, social development, and occupational opportunities—do not always appear to be as great as many would assume (Greenberger and Steinberg, 1985). One study of high school students assessed the benefits and costs of part-time employment. Working did encourage a sense of personal responsibility—punctuality, dependability, and self-reliance. But at the same time it diminished a sense of social responsibility—that is, concern for others. Working also reduced commitment to school, family, and friends; led to cynical attitudes toward work and the acceptance of unethical work practices; and paved the way to an increased use of cigarettes and marijuana (Steinberg et al., 1982). Another disappointing finding: There is no evidence that those high school students who work are destined to earn higher incomes later in life than those who do not (Steinberg, 1982).

In their struggle for identity, adolescents tend to emphasize such values as love, friendship, privacy, tolerance, self-expression and self-fulfillment. Although perhaps less so than in recent decades, many are skeptical of the ethics and efficiency of government, business, and other social institutions. Some feel altogether alienated from society—a fact that may help explain why delinquency, adolescent pregnancies, and suicide have increased in the last few decades (Education Commission of the States, 1985). The growing problem of teenage suicide is discussed in detail in a Psychology in Everyday Life box called "Why Adolescents Destroy Themselves."

Psychology in Everyday Life
Teenagers on the Home Front

Adolescents often complain that parents are impossible to live with. Parents complain that their children are impossible. Are they both right? Is this an inescapable fact of life?

Clashes are inevitable. Adolescents, in the midst of their struggle to establish identity, tend to be wrapped up in their own thoughts—preoccupied with their emerging view of the world, their behavior, and their appearance. They sometimes seem oblivious to anything else, including clocks, chores, and social amenities. Parents, as it happens, are often going through an identity crisis of their own. At the time their children are in adolescence, parents are at an age when they encounter heavy financial obligations and career demands. Some must even simultaneously fill the role of parent-in-law to a new young adult, grandparents to a new baby, and protectors of aging and dependent parents (Shanas, 1980).

The adolescent search for independence often takes the form of a struggle against authority and discipline. To parents, surrendering authority often comes hard. After regarding daughters and sons as children for so many years, it is difficult to start treating them as adults. How can the problems be made more bearable?

A great deal, it turns out, depends on the parents. Studies have shown that two kinds of parents aggravate the difficulties. The first insist that their word is law and that adolescents have no right to make any decisions. The second take a totally hands-off position—either because they do not really care or because they have exaggerated notions about the wisdom of letting children "do their own thing." In the first case, adolescents frequently display continued dependency, lack of confidence, and low self-esteem (Kandel and Lesser, 1972). In the second case, they may fail to develop a sense of responsibility for their own actions. Adolescents whose parents do not monitor their children's behavior and provide discipline are more likely to be classified as juvenile delinquents (Patterson and Stouthamer-Loeber, 1984).

It appears that the best antidote to adolescent aches and pains is the opportunity to identify with and imitate parents who are neither too strict nor too permissive. Such parents are warm but firm, and while they are eager for their children to develop autonomy and self-direction, they still leave no doubt that they are responsible for their children's behavior (Biller, 1981; Hill, 1980). There is strong evidence that such parents—reasonable, fair, respectful, and eager for their children's advance to maturity—are most likely to show the road to adult responsibility and happiness.

An adolescent who operated without a sense of limits.

Psychology in Everyday Life
Why Adolescents Destroy Themselves

Depression—the breeding ground for suicidal thoughts.

Suicide rates among teenagers and young adults have tripled in the past three decades. During the same period there has been relatively little change in the suicide rate for the overall population (Eisenberg, 1984). Suicide is the second leading cause of death among young people—after accidents and homicides.

Why?

There is no single answer. Among the reasons are the following:

- Society may be changing in ways that have made adolescence a more difficult time—with increased demands and decreased sources of support. Adolescent stresses include the pressure to assume adult roles faster, an increasing rate of family breakup, high rates of mobility, and uncertain career opportunities (Steinberg, 1985).

- In contemporary society, with its ready access to alcohol, drugs, cars, and other potentially lethal instruments, the opportunity to act on suicidal impulses is more readily at hand than in the past. Nearly two-thirds of all adolescents who commit suicide use available firearms (Boyd, 1983).

Despite the problems and the casualties, research strongly indicates that "the great majority of teenagers share a common core of values with their parents, retain harmonious family relationships, and respect the need for discipline" (Graham and Rutter, 1985). Most are at least reasonably well adjusted, confident about their future, and resilient enough to work through the stresses they encounter in the transition to adulthood.

DEVELOPMENT IN ADULTHOOD

Though adolescence is in a sense the last step in the transformation of the infant into the adult, development does not end when we become old enough to vote, earn our own living, and marry if we wish. At 18, we have lived less than a quarter of today's average lifetime. We will still face new crises and either solve or fail at them. We may still change spectacularly in many respects.

The beginning and end of any one stage of adult life is even more difficult to assign than is the case in childhood and adolescence. Individuals move at a different pace—and sometimes imperceptibly—from one period to another as they choose careers, marry and

- Often there is an immediate precipitating cause such as feeling rejected and running away from home; being the victim of abuse; experiencing a humiliation before parents and friends; being stuck in a family where there is parental discord, disruption, violence, and divorce; interpersonal problems with parents or peers; and the breakup of a romantic relationship (Frazier, 1985). Recent evidence suggests, too, that adolescents predisposed to suicide may be moved to actually commit the act as a result of watching portrayals of teenage suicides in movies on television (Gould and Shaffer, 1986), or in television news stories (Phillips and Carstensen, 1986).

- Certain personality and behavior patterns seem to place adolescents at higher risk for suicide, among them withdrawal and isolation, anger, resentment, and impulsive behavior (Silver, 1984).

- There may be complex predisposing factors at work early in life. Researchers have recently found that children whose mothers were chronically ill during pregnancy and who experienced significant respiratory problems at birth appear more vulnerable to suicide years later. Such children, because they are at greater-than-usual risk for developmental problems, may be more likely to experience chronically poor relationships with their parents during childhood (Salk et al., 1985).

In spite of the statistics, keep in mind that most adolescents, however unhappy they may be for a time, never even consider suicide. Moreover, most of those who do are seriously depressed. Like depressed adults, they are likely to conclude that there is just never going to be a solution to a serious life problem—and thus view suicide as their only way out.

For suicidal adolescents, the most effective preventive approach is to get them help early. A variety of mental health services available in the community can readily be identified by calling the state or county mental health department. Many communities also have a 24-hour suicide prevention hot line listed in the telephone directory. Threats of suicide do not, of course, always result in the act—but they always deserve to be taken seriously by concerned family and friends.

From youth to late adulthood—a portrait of change.

build a family, and engage in the world of work. The adult years bring on slow physical alterations as well. We may continue to look the same to ourselves, but not to our acquaintances. (Indeed people who attend a fortieth college reunion often have difficulty recognizing old classmates.) At the same time we change on the inside. Personality patterns may become as unrecognizable as faces.

Some Surprising Turnabouts in Adulthood

Threads of our lives as children and adolescents are often visible over the years, but sometimes the personality and behavior of young adults seem to bear little relation to those of adolescent life.

Some of the most startling about-faces have been observed among people who were seriously maladjusted as adolescents. It has been found that even the most troubled adolescent—a failure in school, unsuccessful in social contacts, unpopular and despondent—may turn into a successful, happy, well-liked, and highly respected adult. In one study, 166 boys and girls were observed from shortly after birth until they were 18 years old, then observed again at the age of 30. As an example of the kind of change that some of them displayed between adolescence and adulthood note this finding:

> [One subject]—a large, awkward, early-maturing girl who labored under the weight of her size and shyness, feeling that she was a great disappointment to her mother—worked hard for her B average to win approval and was a pedestrian, uninteresting child and adolescent. She had periods of depression, when she could see no point of living. Then, as a junior in college, she got excited over what she was learning (not just in grades to please her mother) and went on to get an advanced degree and to teach in college. Now she has taken time out to have and raise her children. . . . [She is] full of zest for living, married to an interesting, merry, and intelligent man she met in graduate school.

Similarly, a girl who was expelled from school at 16 and a boy expelled at 15—for failing grades and misbehavior—were found to have developed into "wise, steady, understanding parents who appreciate the complexities of life and have both humor and compassion for the human race." An adolescent boy who could only be described as a "listless oddball" had turned into a successful architect and excellent husband and parent who called his adult life "exciting and satisfying." All told, just about half the subjects were living richer and more productive lives as adults than could have been predicted from their adolescent personalities (Macfarlane, 1963).

What causes such marked changes between adolescence and the age of 30? One possibility is that some people are just naturally "late bloomers." It takes them a long time—and often a change of environment that gets them away from their parents and even to a new community—to find themselves. Taking on a meaningful job may help. So may marriage, with all its responsibilities, and its opportunities for forming an abiding, supportive relationship. In one recent study, researchers reconstructed the lives of a group of young women who had been born into abusive and broken families, placed in foster care, and encountered mostly trouble as adolescents. As young adults, however, a sizable number of them were found to be contented, productive, and free of the grinding problems of their earlier years. In many cases, it turned out, they were lucky enough to find supportive and caring husbands, and as a result, they were now enjoying stable family lives far removed from the miserable ones they had known in their younger years (Quinton and Rutter, 1983).

Sometimes the problems of a troubled adolescence prove a blessing in disguise as the years go by. If adolescents go through a period of "painful, strain-producing, and confusing experiences" but manage to survive them, these experiences may in the long run produce greater insight and stability (Macfarlane, 1964).

Dealing with Crises: Erikson's Theory of Psychosocial Development

The idea that personality growth depends on facing and meeting crises is the basis of an influential theory proposed by Erik Erikson, a psychoanalyst who bases his conclusions on observations of people he has treated at all ages, some in childhood and others at various stages of adulthood. Erikson speaks in terms of *psychosocial development*. That is to say, he holds that development is a twofold process in which the psychological development of individuals (their personalities and view of themselves) proceeds hand in hand with the social relations they establish as they go through life. He has suggested that this development can be divided into eight stages, in each of which individuals face new social situations and encounter new problems (or "psychosocial crises"). They may emerge from the new experiences with greater maturity and richer personalities—or they may fail to cope successfully with the problems and their development may be warped or arrested.

Erikson's eight stages are shown in Figure 15-4. They begin with the child in the first year of life. At this stage the child's social relations are confined to the caretaker. Out of this relationship, Erikson believes, the child learns either to trust the social environment and what it will bring in the future or to be suspicious and fearful of others. In later stages the social environment widens and new psychosocial crises occur, again with outcomes that may be favorable or unfavorable.

Choosing and Pursuing a Career

Early adulthood demands many new adjustments. One entails job and career and often intense preoccupation with efforts to start up the vocational ladder. Many young people believe that, while they are still in their early twenties, they must pick an occupation and begin a well-defined path of work. In reality, however, the process is much more complicated. The course of a career is usually based on the ebb and flow of decisions made over time.

There are at least six factors that can influence an individual's choice of occupation (Kimmel, 1980). These include background factors—for example, socioeconomic level, intelligence, sex, education—that may set boundaries on the range of occupational choice; role models such as an older sibling with whom individuals identify and whom they wish

Working for pay produces psychic as well as dollar income.

Development in Adulthood

Figure 15-4 Erikson's stage theory of "psychosocial crises"

Erikson views the life cycle of development, from cradle to grave, as passing through eight stages. Each stage brings new social experiences and new crises—which, if surmounted successfully, lead to constant growth and a steadily enriched personality (Erikson, 1963).

STAGE	CRISIS	FAVORABLE OUTCOME	UNFAVORABLE OUTCOME
CHILDHOOD			
First year of life	Trust versus mistrust	Faith in the environment and future events	Suspicion, fear of future events
Second year	Autonomy versus doubt	A sense of self-control and adequacy	Feelings of shame and self-doubt
Third through fifth years	Initiative versus guilt	Ability to be a "self-starter," to initiate one's own activities	A sense of guilt and inadequacy to be on one's own
Sixth year to puberty	Industry versus inferiority	Ability to learn how things work, to understand and organize	A sense of inferiority at understanding and organizing
TRANSITION YEARS			
Adolescence	Identity versus confusion	Seeing oneself as a unique and integrated person	Confusion over who and what one really is
ADULTHOOD			
Early adulthood	Intimacy versus isolation	Ability to make commitments to others, to love	Inability to form affectionate relationships
Middle age	Generativity versus self-absorption	Concern for family and society in general	Concern only for self—one's own well-being and prosperity
Aging years	Integrity versus despair	A sense of integrity and fulfillment; willingness to face death	Dissatisfaction with life; despair over prospect of death

to emulate; life experiences—for example, deciding to become a doctor because of the early death of a parent from cancer; interests and personality traits that can be realized and expressed in a particular occupation; and rational assessments of the job market and areas of opportunity.

Work often deeply affects an individual's sense of well-being. Success on the job can have a potent impact on self-esteem, marital satisfaction, and physical health. There is evidence that job satisfaction increases over the years—at least for the middle class (Staines and Quinn, 1979)—and that it is dependent on such factors as the willingness to accept challenges and exercise independence (Gruenberg, 1980). The opportunity to do the best job possible, even more than pay, also appears to be important (Yankelovich, 1982).

Until recently, psychologists focused their studies of work primarily on its role in a man's life, but now there is increased attention to the role of work in the lives of women as well. However slowly, the sex role of women in society is changing. This factor, combined with an increase in life expectancy and length of marriages, the lower birth rate, and the decline in value of the family's dollars, have occasioned a remarkable increase in the number of married women—over 50 percent—who are paid employees in jobs outside the home (U.S. Public Health Service, 1985).

A great majority of working wives hold their jobs mostly because they need or want the money. But a public opinion poll has also found a fair number—nearly 15 percent—who say they work chiefly to have something interesting to do (Roper, 1980). Work can profoundly affect a woman's feeling of well-being. An in-depth study of about three hundred 35- to 55-year-old women in the Boston area revealed a strong relationship between working for pay and a woman's sense of pride and mastery (Baruch, Barnett, and Rivers, 1983). But because of the persistence of sex-role stereotypes, the path for women in the world of work is still not always a smooth one.

Adult Sex Roles—and the Conflict They Can Create

History tells us that women have never shared equally in society's esteem, praise, privileges, and rewards. In one way or another, they were treated as the inferior sex in ancient Egypt, Greece, and Rome—and, on our own continent, by the Indians (Tavris and Offir, 1977). In fact sexual discrimination may have been the first form of social inequality (Robertson, 1977), practiced before people ever thought of discriminating against one another on the basis of race and social class. The division of labor between the sexes has varied from society to society—but no matter how they were split up, those assigned to men have always been considered more important (Goode, 1965).

Although the pattern may be changing somewhat, it still continues. Even today, despite affirmative action programs, relatively few women pursue careers in scientific and technical fields (U.S. Department of Labor, 1987). Although girls do as well as boys in mathematics in the early grades, fewer females take advanced high school or college math courses and become physicists, engineers, or computer scientists (Meece et al., 1982). Note which sex dominates the following pairs of people likely to work together on a daily basis: physician and nurse, dentist and dental hygienist, bank officer and teller, airplane pilot and flight attendant, store manager and sales clerk (England, 1979).

Overall, women have lower rates of employment, more intermittent employment, and lower earning power than men. While 45 percent of men earn more than $25,000 per year, only 13 percent of women do so (U.S. Bureau of the Census, 1986b). Women are also still at a disadvantage with regard to both private pension plans and social security benefits. Through the year 2055, these benefits are expected to be only two-thirds those for men (U.S. Public Health Service, 1985).

Psychological studies suggest why such differences continue to exist. In many particulars, sex role stereotypes have changed surprisingly little in the past two decades. Both sexes continue to view men as more forceful, independent, stubborn, and reckless than women; and women continue to be viewed as more well mannered, kind, emotional, and submissive than men (Werner and LaRussa, 1985). In their day-to-day behavior, many men seem to reinforce the stereotype. They tend more than women to display a concern with external prestige and power (Gaeddert, 1985). More so than women, they continue also to associate sex with power (Hendrick et al., 1985) and, perhaps because of their higher status, to take prerogatives at work that women do not. For example, they are much more likely to behave in a dominating fashion toward their female co-workers and to use intimate gestures and sexual innuendos on the job (Radecki and Jennings, 1980).

Perhaps the greatest problem of all for women results from the fact that they feel impelled to give full expression to their motives for affiliation and dependency, but are under pressure to suppress their motive for achievement in the world of work. In the past it was common for women, even the most capable ones, to conceal their intelligence, abandon interest in such masculine subjects as mathematics and science, and shun either a career or settle for such traditionally feminine jobs as nursing. Many people still do not consider it feminine to be too successful—especially at tasks that have been regarded as for men only. Nor is it feminine to be competitive and aggressive, especially when these conflict with a desire to help and support others (Gilligan, 1982). And here is where many women find themselves in a bind.

Society tends to reinforce the stereotype of women as desirable for the their looks, but not useful for their minds. Consider this finding: When photographers of newspapers and magazines take pictures of individuals, they tend to emphasize the faces of men and the bodies of women. The implication drawn by the investigators is that the man's identity rests on relatively durable mental qualities, while the woman's identity has to do with more ephemeral—and exploitable—qualities of physical attractiveness (Archer at al., 1983).

Sex typing clearly creates conflicts for women in our society. Less well publicized is the fact that sex typing also creates conflicts for men, a subject discussed in the box on Psychology in Everyday Life called "The Male's Sex Role Problems."

Psychology in Everyday Life
The Male's Sex Role Problems

It is not always easy to be as masculine as society has urged men to be. Nor is it easy to rebel against the masculine role—which for most men is as deeply ingrained an inner standard as femininity is for most women.

The male conflict is exactly the opposite of the female conflict. Boys and men are encouraged—often overencouraged—to express their motives for power, achievement, and hostility. They are expected to welcome every opportunity to leap into competition and assert their status and position so that they do not appear weak. But they are expected to muffle their motives for affiliation and dependency and to suppress or at least conceal their emotions of sympathy, tenderness, and vulnerability. They have to keep a stiff upper lip—avoiding any show of fear or grief—even in the face of serious disappointment and tragedy.

The struggle to play the masculine role can be fraught with anxieties. The motives for affiliation and dependency, discussed in Chapter 9, are universal. So are the emotions that accompany them. One recent study showed that men, although they are quite ready to have close social interactions with other men when the situation warrants, actually enjoy fewer such interactions than women do with their women friends (Reis, Senchak, and Solomon, 1985). Society's demands to suppress the motives for affiliation and dependency in effect add up to a demand to transcend human nature, and efforts to do so can never completely succeed (Stevens, 1974).

It is perhaps as difficult to be automatically typed as superior as to be automatically typed as inferior. Men as well as women suffer anxieties over the way they are sex-typed to perform—which may be totally at odds with their own motives and emotions, not to mention their physical strength and other capabilities. It seems clear enough that as long as traditional sex role standards continue to influence human behavior, they will cause inner conflicts—for men as well as women.

Love—and Usually Marriage

Erikson believes that the really critical event of early adulthood centers on moving into a relationship marked by love, intimacy, and commitment. For most of us, this means marriage. Statistics show that about 95 percent of Americans get married sooner or later (U.S. Bureau of the Census, 1984).

Most of us have wondered what it is that determines the actual selection of a mate. Aristotle was among the first to point out that "we like those who resemble us and are engaged in the same pursuits," and indeed we are more likely to fall in love with and choose as mates someone who shares our beliefs and attitudes. Most of us pick spouses of the same religion and race, and similar to us in intelligence, age, educational level, and economic status—although, as the number of interreligious and interracial marriages climbs, there are, of course, a growing number of exceptions to the pattern (Murstein, 1982).

As shown in Figure 15-5, marriage seems to protect our mental health. But unfortunately, the number of unsuccessful marriages continues to be high. Among all adolescent and adult Americans, 13.6 million are divorced (U.S. Bureau of the Census, 1986a). For most people, "unlucky in love" means the tendency to select the wrong partner, and it is just such a faulty selection process that is often given as the reason for the high rate of divorce. One team of researchers suggests, however, that the divorce rate is high not because people make foolish choices, but because they are drawn together for reasons that matter less as time goes on. As indicated in Figure 15-6, what brings a couple together at the start appears to become less important as the years go by, and those qualities that matter most later on are rarely the ones that figure heavily in the early stages of the

Figure 15-5 Marital status and mental health

Many studies reveal that married people are less lonely, less depressed, and less likely to feel emotionally disturbed than those who remain single. Worst off emotionally, however, are those who have been divorced (adapted from Cargan and Melko, 1982).

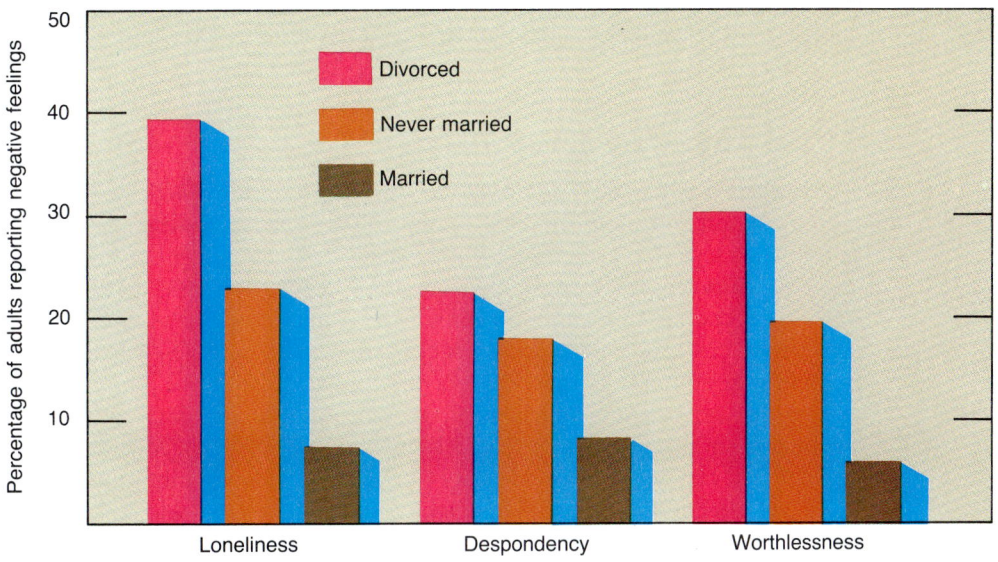

Figure 15-6 **How the focus of a marital relationship changes over time**

As most adults recognize, passion is the quickest to develop and the quickest to fade. Feelings of intimacy develop more slowly, and a sense of commitment even more gradually.

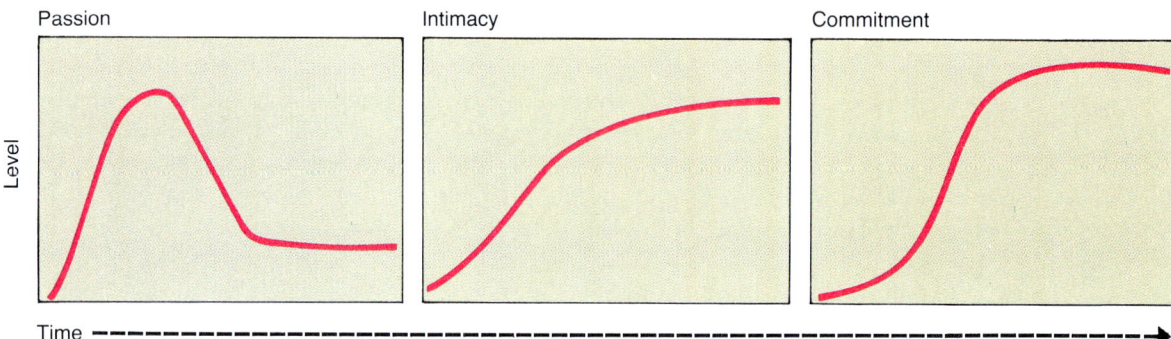

relationship. No relationship is stable over time—but the basic, underlying ingredient of a loving and enduring marriage appears to be the ability to communicate and to satisfy the needs of the partner (Sternberg and Grajek, 1984; Sternberg, 1986).

Cohabitation, an arrangement in which men and women live together in a sexual relationship, has been advocated before marriage by many as a way to prolong the courtship period, allowing the participants to learn more about their partners and themselves, and thus strengthen a future marriage (Simenauer and Carroll, 1982). The prevalence of such an arrangement has increased. There were about 2 million cohabiting heterosexual couples in 1984—well over three times the number there were in 1970 (U.S. Bureau of the Census, 1985). There has been no thorough study, however, to indicate how many couples who live together eventually marry, or how such marriages turn out. One study does suggest that cohabiting couples, who are usually younger and poorer than married couples, may indeed be waiting to determine whether their marriage would be emotionally and financially sound before actually taking the step (Glick and Spanier, 1980). But there is really no good evidence that living together first leads to more satisfying marriages (De Maris and Leslie, 1984).

The Adventure of Parenthood

Couples today have more freedom of choice in deciding whether to become parents than ever before in history. While there are still many couples who decide not to have children, most choose to do so. One estimate is that 75 to 80 percent of today's young women will eventually have at least one child (Bloom and Trussell, 1983).

Of course, there are problems. Having a child, perhaps more than any other of life's events, creates complex and sweeping changes in the roles wife and husband play in the marriage and in their lifestyles. As one study has described it, parenthood is hard work; it requires a sense of responsibility; it is often stressful; and once you have begun, you cannot quit when you feel like it (LeMasters and DeFrain, 1983). Most of all, parenting requires skills of various kinds: sensitivity to children's cues and their needs at various stages of development; being able to help them cope with stresses and adversities; knowing how to talk and play with them and to use appropriate disciplinary techniques (Rutter, Quinton, and Liddell, 1983).

The nature of the parenting experience naturally varies in different situations. It matters whether one child or several are in the household (Schaffer and Liddell, 1984), whether the parents get along (Hauser, 1985), and whether or not there are social supports available to the family (Belsky, 1984). One study found that those couples who coped best with the demands of parenthood were able to communicate their feelings to each other, showed adaptability to the baby's needs, viewed parenthood as a responsibility to be shared, continued to pursue their own adult interests, found some time to spend away from baby, and depended on friends and relatives for information, advice, and for help in caring for the child (Miller and Sollie, 1980). All of this is easier, of course, for the affluent than for the poor.

Most young adults who embark on the adventure of parenthood find it a significant and rewarding experience, offering incomparable satisfactions (Veroff, Douvan, and Kulka, 1981). Contentment in marriage does not deteriorate if the children are planned for and if the parents are psychologically prepared for their responsibilities (Feldman, Biringen, and Nash, 1981).

For many adults, according to Erikson, raising children represents their most important achievement. The crisis of middle age, Erikson taught, lies in whether we have achieved *generativity*, which is largely "the concern in establishing and guiding the next generation," or whether instead we are mired in narrow concentration on our own interests—especially in matters of getting ahead in life, making money, and enjoying material comforts.

Middle Age—Its Tensions and Satisfactions

Many people report feeling that, as we pass our childhood, the years seem to slip by more quickly. Early youth gives way to a sort of transition period during the thirties and early forties, in which people are neither still very young nor yet middle-aged. At 45, by Census Bureau definition, we officially enter our middle age—though some still feel youthful on that birthday and others have thought of themselves as starting to get old long before then. Many begin to feel some anxiety about the encroachment of the sixties—and the spectre of joining the ranks of the elderly in our society.

During the so-called midlife transition period, people may feel adrift for a period as they attempt to make the transition to the later stages of life. Ideally, Erikson believes, the crisis of middle age produces a wider outlook on the meaning of life—a sense of kinship with one's fellow human beings, with the ebb and flow of history, with nature itself. Old goals, especially selfish ones, may be abandoned. New satisfactions of the spirit may be found. People sometimes make radical changes in their lifestyles. Men may switch careers—moving from a job they have held because of accident or habit, or for financial reasons, into something they have always wanted to do. Women who have spent their early years working as homemakers and mothers may take an outside job for the first time, thus encountering new problems but also finding new satisfactions. For those who have structured a satisfying existence, middle age has been described as often being "the fullest and most creative season in the life cycle," in which we are less overwhelmed by the ambitions, passions and illusions of youth (Levinson, 1978).

One dramatic shift in middle life is often the inclination to begin expressing elements of personality that remained suppressed earlier (Cytrynbaum et al., 1980). With most career goals met and mastered, marital adjustments made, and children reared and grown, many men and women begin to move out of the stereotyped sex roles they maintained during the earlier decades. Women become less dependent and submissive and begin to display many masculine traits; they become more independent, assertive, and competitive. Men,

Is this middle-aged man reluctant to leave his youth behind?

at the same time, tend in mid-life to become less aggressive and competitive and take on some of the characteristics of the feminine role (Zube, 1982).

While such shifts can create conflicts and stress, they often reflect increased mellowing and self-assurance that middle age brings. Many adults at middle age are able often by virtue of their experience to cope more successfully than are younger people (Pruett, 1980). When the crisis of middle age is met successfully—and a quieter and deeper attitude toward the rhythm of life is established—people are prepared to grow old with grace and contentment. The process of development, from its seeds in the newborn baby, has come to full flower.

GROWING OLD: THE CHALLENGES AND THE TRIUMPHS

Until recently, the average life expectancy in the United States was about 50 years. This is still true in parts of the world that have not caught up with today's advanced techniques of sanitation, nutrition, and medical science. But thanks to modern knowledge and technology, the average life expectancy for Americans is up to 75 years (National Center for Health Statistics, 1985), and further strides in curing disease are soon expected to add still more.

When our country declared its independence, only 2 percent of the population was 65 or over, and as recently as a century ago, people over 65 were still a rarity. Except for a small minority, the psychology of aging was not a matter of concern in the past. As shown in Figure 15-7, however, the percentage of people who have passed what is generally considered to be the retirement age of 65 has virtually tripled since the turn of the century. Moreover, those who are 65 can expect to live nearly another 17 years (National Center for Health Statistics, 1987). The population aged 85 and over is expected to rise from 2.3 million

Figure 15-7 The increasing U.S. population over 65

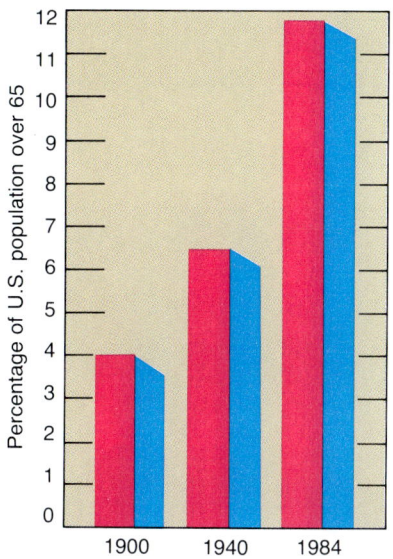

In 1900, the number of Americans over 65—3.1 million persons—made up only 4 percent of the population. In the next 84 years, their number swelled to 28 million, or nearly 12 percent of the population—and this percentage is expected to rise further before the end of the century (Brotman, 1981; U.S. Bureau of the Census, 1984).

in 1980 to 4.9 million by the year 2000 (Rosenwaike, 1985). Small wonder that the problems and pleasures of the retirement years have become very much a part of psychological investigation.

The Aging Body

The later years, like earlier periods of life, bring physical changes. *Senescence*, or the weakening and decline of the body, actually begins almost as soon as we stop growing during young adulthood. Although the changes are not visible, the body reaches its greatest strength in late adolescence, and then grows weaker throughout our adult years. But the declines—in the output of the heart, in reaction time, in frequency of sexual intercourse—are so gradual that they are of little significance in our day-to-day living.

While there is no specific age at which these changes become obvious, many of them become apparent as we approach the seventh decade of life. Changes in the spinal column may result in a stooped posture. Acuity in vision and hearing deteriorates. Sensitivity to odor and taste diminishes, as shown in Figure 15-8. Blood arteries and vessels harden. The body's capacity to fight disease weakens, and changes in the central nervous system lead to a slowdown in behavior in general.

There are a number of theories to explain the aging process. Some suggest that aging is caused by the damage that occurs in various body systems throughout life—damage caused by normal "wear and tear," or harmful substances that we breathe or eat. Another theory says that aging results from a slow buildup of damage to the chemical DNA that directs the machinery of every body cell. Others ascribe aging to changes in body hormones, and still others to the breakdown of the immune system, the body's weapon for fighting disease. There are no simple answers to the mystery of aging, and most scientists believe that it is a complex process involving many body systems, with the crucial factor being a growing inability of the body's cells to function properly (National Institute on Aging, 1984).

Growing Old: The Challenges and the Triumphs

Figure 15-8 Loss of sense of taste with aging

The percentage of elderly who can correctly identify some common foods, presented in pureed form, is significantly lower than is the case for 20-year-olds (Schiffman, 1977).

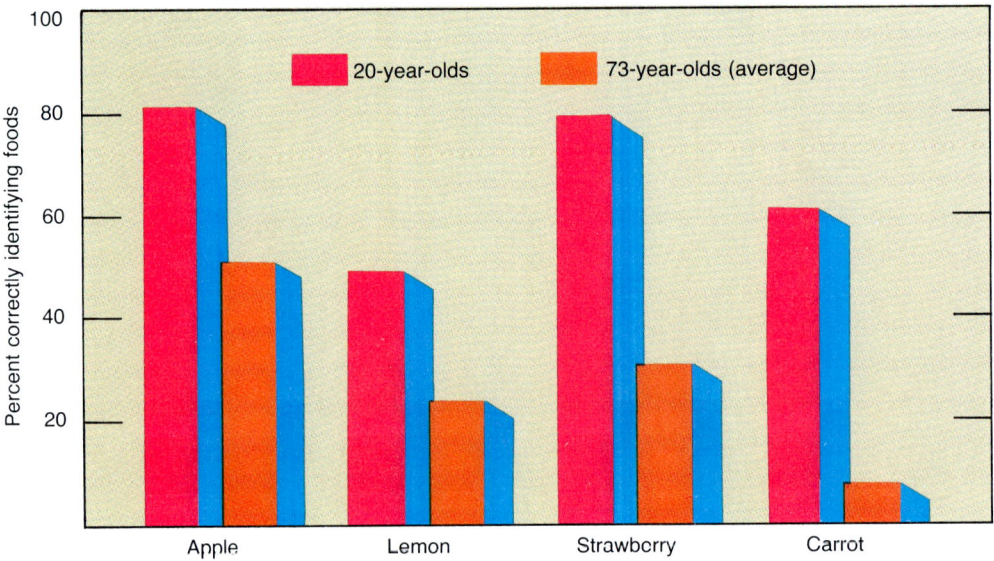

The facts of aging have led to a stereotype of the older person as "over the hill"—a portrait that is essentially inaccurate. True enough, in some cases, especially in extreme old age, damage to the brain's cells causes *senile dementia*, or senility, with symptoms such as disorientation, poor attention, loss of memory, and inability to store new information. But senility, contrary to popular assumption, is not an inevitable result of aging. Rather, it is a disease that afflicts a small proportion—from 5 to 8 percent—of old people (Kay and Bergmann, 1980).

One neurological illness, *Alzheimer's disease*, is an especially cruel, progressive form of dementia that is now recognized as the most common cause of severe intellectual and emotional impairment in older individuals (National Institute of Mental Health, 1984). It usually leads to death in seven to ten years (Heston and White, 1983). Recent research with aged primates suggests the possibility of a drug—clonidine—that may one day help improve the memory capacities of elderly people afflicted with this disorder (Arnsten and Goldman-Rakic, 1985).

Despite the realities of the aging body, getting old doesn't necessarily mean getting weak and sick. The vast majority of older people report that they are in reasonably good health, with no major limitations on their activity for health reasons (National Center for Health Statistics, 1985). This fact is reflected in the often surprisingly high level of intellectual and emotional functioning of the aged.

The Intellectual Capacities of Older People

It is commonly believed that intellectual capacities decline as people grow older—and indeed many studies in the past have pointed in this direction (Willis and Baltes, 1980). One of the problems with these studies, however, is that they are based on averages of the

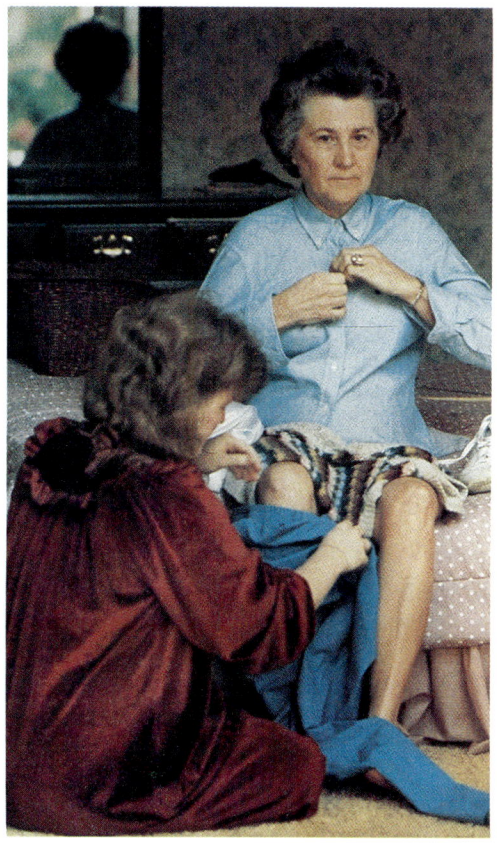

Caring for a victim of Alzheimer's disease.

scores made on tests by many individuals of a given age (Schaie and Hertzog, 1983). In any cross section of older people, researchers are bound to find a number suffering from undiagnosed physical ailments, and the atypically low scores they make on the tests given them are likely to pull down the overall averages.

More revealing, therefore, are studies that follow a sample of the same people over many years. Such studies tend to present a more optimistic view of the intellectual capacities of older people. In one study, for example, researchers tracked the mental abilities of individuals from age 22 to 67. They found evidence of only slight decline in intellectual functioning before age 60, and while more significant changes showed up later, even then there was a wide range of individual differences (Schaie and Hertzog, 1983). Moreover, a recent study shows that the loss of certain mental skills such as inductive reasoning and spatial perception can be reversed with surprising ease with the use of simple mental exercises (Schaie and Willis, 1986).

Another problem with past studies of the intellectual capacities of older people is that they gave too much weight to speed of response. True enough, older people are slower in their response time (Cerella, 1985), but it seems unfair to conclude that cognitive ability drops in late adulthood because it takes 70-year-olds longer than 17-year-olds to complete a task such as reassembling a puzzle (Berger, 1983). Our perceptual capacities also slow down as we grow old, and, with it, our capacities to remember. In the later years, just as in early childhood, we tend to remember information more effectively if it is presented to us at a slower pace (Pezdek and Miceli, 1982). But again, speed itself may indicate very little about the nature and quality of thought in late adulthood.

Nearly two decades ago, psychologist Raymond Cattell proposed that intelligence can be divided into two major kinds of abilities—*fluid intelligence* and *crystallized intelligence* (Cattell, 1971). Today it is generally agreed that, as we grow older, we experience a decline in the first, but not the second.

Fluid intellectual abilities are dependent on neurological development and relatively independent of education and cultural influences. Among these are perceptual skills and memory span—for example, grouping letters or numbers with common elements, or remembering a series of six digits. Older people are usually not as efficient at such tasks. Crystallized abilities, in contrast, require the capacity to use an accumulated body of general information in order to make judgments and solve problems. Here it is not speed that is demanded, but the capacity to deal insightfully with issues and options. As indicated in Figure 15-9, such functions actually seem to improve with the passing years—as long as individuals remain active in their environment.

Mental Health in the Later Years

How many people find happiness in their aging years, and how many fail? Psychology's findings are, by and large, contrary to what is generally assumed.

Our society has been described as youth-oriented—and old age is often thought of as a period of decrepitude and dissatisfaction. Younger people—with their emphasis on growth, progress, and strength—assume that life will become less and less zestful with the passage of time. Therefore, they give the aging years the lowest rating of all for happiness and quality of life, and they view any signs of "going downhill" with fear and prejudice (Butler and Lewis, 1977). In fact, however, the vast majority of elderly persons in the community are free of emotional problems, and have the psychological resources necessary to manage an effective and independent life (Romaniuk, McAuley, and Arling, 1983).

Figure 15-9 Intellectual capacities of the aged

Portrayed here are changes taking place in two types of intellectual capacities over the life span as described in the text. The upshot appears to be that older people may not be as "sharp," but they are often even more perceptive and wise than in the earlier decades.

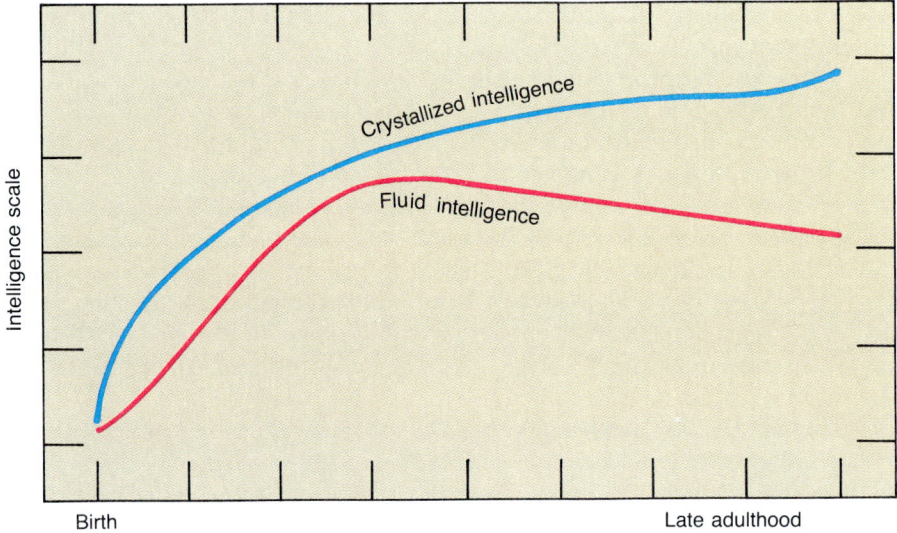

To be sure, there are problems. Some people, after retiring, are plagued by financial difficulties. Some suffer from chronic illnesses. Among people 65 and over are about 1.5 million widowers and 8.1 million widows (U.S. Bureau of the Census, 1986a), and the stresses they encounter in adjusting to their loneliness are reflected in their own subsequent mortality rates. Men especially seem to have a difficult time. One study showed that the mortality rate was 61 percent higher for widowers between the ages of 55 and 64 than for those in the same age range who were married. Among both men and women who lost their mates, the death rate was higher for those who lived alone than for those who shared a household with someone else (Helsing, Szklo, and Comstock, 1981).

Even in late adulthood, patterns of psychological and social adjustment are as varied as in earlier periods of life (Bornstein and Smircina, 1982). Some psychologists who study aging believe that diversity increases with age and that, in the later years, patterns of personality and behavior are more pronounced than at any earlier age (Schaie, 1981). Some examples of extraordinary productivity in the later years are given in Figure 15-10.

For many people, retirement is threatening because it formally ushers in the period of old age (Glick, 1980). But most studies show that when retirees maintain their health and have an adequate income, they find this a rewarding stage of life (Barfield and Morgan, 1978). The concept of retirement often no longer means the end of employment, but rather the initiation of self-chosen and self-directed activity (Atchley, 1982). Most people seem to find that the retirement years are not nearly so bad as they were led to expect—surprisingly full of pleasures that may differ in kind and intensity but are nevertheless as fulfilling as the joys of youth. A key factor appears to be the presence of a network of friends, at least some of whom are viewed as intimates (Heller and Mansbach, 1984).

Even among those who are 85 and older, researchers find diversity not only in physical well-being but in emotional, behavioral, and social characteristics as well. While many people at this stage in life are infirm and dependent, many others are still active and work (Suzman and Riley, 1985). Some insights on this subject are presented in the Psychology in Everyday Life box on "Pathways to a Long and Happy Life" (see page 561).

To Erikson, the aging years represent a fork in the road that can lead either to a heartwarming sense of integrity or to feelings of despair. People who succeed in negotiating this crisis live out the final years of their lives with a sense of self-fulfillment and wisdom. They face the inevitability of death without fear or regret. Those who fail—often because they have not surmounted life's earlier crises—wind up embittered. They are dissatisfied with the way they have lived their lives. They regret what might have been. The prospect of dying fills them with despair.

THE PSYCHOLOGY OF DYING

The chief reason for today's increased life expectancy is that science has conquered diseases such as pneumonia that formerly killed people in the prime of life. Most deaths today result from chronic, long-lasting conditions—for example, cancer and ailments of the heart and circulatory system (Manton and Soldo, 1985). Thus people are more likely to be aware that they are approaching the end of life—and must somehow reconcile themselves.

Attitudes toward Death

Death is a reality virtually throughout our lives. When children are between five and seven years old, they already understand the concept that death is universal—and that it is irreversible (Speece and Sandor, 1984). But the challenge of facing death emerges more

Figure 15-10 Some great achievers in the "sunset" years

A. *Pablo Picasso completed magnificent portraits at 73, married for the second time at 77, then went on creating artistic marvels until age 90.*
B. *Jomo Kenyatta becomes Kenya's first president at 70 and led his country for 14 years.*
C. *"Grandma" Moses, who won international fame as an artist, took up painting as a hobby at 76.*
D. *Golda Meir was named prime minister of Israel at 71 and held the job for five years.*
E. *Frank Lloyd Wright completed New York's Guggenheim Museum at 89 and continued teaching until his death a year later.*

A

B

C

D

E

Psychology in Everyday Life
Pathways to a Long and Happy Life

The twinkle of youth in the eyes of an "old" man in Soviet Georgia.

Can anything be done to slow aging or extend life? The question has been with us since the beginning of time, and there is still no simple answer. But there are some hints—from both medicine and psychology.

According to the U.S. government's National Institute on Aging, "there are no known 'antiaging treatments,' drugs, or nutritional supplements that slow aging or extend life." But your chances of staying healthy and living a long time improve if you don't smoke, eat a balanced diet and maintain your appropriate weight, exercise regularly, have regular health checkups, allow time for rest and relaxation, drink alcoholic beverages in moderation, and avoid overexposure to the sun and cold (National Institute on Aging, 1984).

There are psychological factors to consider as well. Among those who reach age 60 with no serious medical problems, an individual's attitudes and program of life activities may be more important in determining longevity than genetic or purely physiological factors (Segerberg, 1982).

A factor that seems critical is the opportunity to stay in control of your life. One study focused on men and women over 62 who were hospitalized and who subsequently, on discharge, were scheduled to enter a nursing home. Half of them were given an opportunity to participate actively in the decision, and half of them were not. Initially, the health of people in both groups was the same. After one year, however, those in the group given some say about entering a nursing home were healthier, and fewer had died than in the group given no choice (Rodin, 1980).

For those already in nursing homes, the investigator was struck by the impact of such seemingly trivial changes as allowing older people to decide when to go see a movie or how to arrange their rooms. As a result of just such choices, their health and emotional well-being improved, and the death rate dropped. By providing options, evidently it is possible to change the aged individual's approach to life from passivity and helplessness to activity and efficacy.

The factors that seem to make for a long life appear to be present in certain remote regions of the world—in Abkhasia of the Georgian Soviet Socialist Republic, in Pakistan, and in Peru. There you will find unusually large populations over 80 who remain active, alert, witty—and respected. In all these communities, daily life requires exercise; even breathing demands work since the elevations are over 3,000 feet. Diet is low in fat, alcohol consumption is moderate, and cultural traditions of respecting the aged are strong. Indeed among the Abkhasia there is no word for aged, and no word for retirement (Berger, 1983).

Do these people know something we should?

insistently with the passing years, when the reality of leaving this world is more closely upon us.

Contrary to popular assumption, fear of death is not pervasive among the elderly. Indeed a number of studies show that, with increasing age, earlier anxieties about death become muted. The nature of beliefs about dying appear to be less important in reducing anxiety than the certainty with which these beliefs are held (Smith, Nehemkis, and Charter, 1983–84), and earlier experience with death—of a close friend or family member—tends to reduce anxiety about death (Cole, 1978–79).

Death becomes more acceptable if, as older people review their lives, they experience a sense of what Erikson described as integrity and fulfillment—a feeling that they have lived a whole and satisfying life. The capacity to face death with equanimity is diminished among those who have a distinct and pervasive sense of having lived a life that was not fully realized, with tasks or goals that yet remain to be completed, as well as among those who feel that their control over what remains of life has slipped away (Silverberg, 1985). Old people tend to fear a slow and lonely death more than they do death itself (Rogers, 1980). Those who accept death with equanimity view it as part of the continuity of life—"as a point in a journey down an endless road full of travelers who have gone before and will follow. During the journey all leave their own unique mark along the way, enriching those they have encountered and accompanied" (Wyatt, 1985).

When a Mate Dies

Among Americans 65 and over, about 14 million are married and living with their spouses (U.S. Bureau of the Census, 1985). In general these are the most fortunate of the elderly. Studies have shown that older people typically consider their marriage to be just as happy as when they were younger or even more so (Foster, 1982).

Unfortunately the marriage that prospers into old age, surmounting the problems of retirement and achieving greater happiness than ever before, must inevitably end in sadness when one of the partners dies. Since women, on the average, live about seven years longer than men, usually it is the wife who survives and faces the new crisis of widowhood. There are about 11 million widows in our nation, most of them elderly. Indeed over half of all women over 65 are widows (U.S. Bureau of the Census, 1985). There are, of course, widowers as well, but not nearly so many—not quite 2 million. And since there are about six times as many widows as widowers of 65 and over, the widowers have a far better chance of remarrying, and many of them do.

Some people recover from grief over the death of a partner relatively unscathed, while for others bereavement is associated with extremely debilitating mental and physical effects that may persist for years (Osterweis, Solomon, and Green, 1984). Evidence from a number of studies suggests that men suffer more. The death rate for widows is only slightly higher than for other women, but the rate for widowers is over 60 percent greater than for married men (Helsing, Szklo, and Comstock, 1981). The reason probably lies in a combination of factors, including the fact that, without their mates, men are likely to find fewer sources of social support, and that men are, by and large, biologically more vulnerable to stress (Stroebe and Stroebe, 1983).

The Stages of Dying

Based on intensive work with several hundred patients facing death, Elisabeth Kübler-Ross concluded that most people experience predictable stages in the process (Kübler-Ross,

1969). First comes denial—"I don't believe this is happening to me"; next comes anger—"Why does this have to happen to me?"; then bargaining—"If you let me survive just a few more years, dear God, I'll never get angry again"; then depression—"I'll never see my grandchildren grow up"; and finally acceptance—"I guess my number is up, and that's the way it has to be."

At least some of these stages are probably experienced by most people facing death, but they are hardly predictable for everyone. Moreover, many people, living in the knowledge that the end is near, manage to find new and transforming meanings in what remains of their lives. One investigator, who has worked with terminally ill cancer patients, is struck by "how many of them use their crisis and their danger as an opportunity for change." Many of them rearranged their priorities and began to live fully in the present. They were able to communicate more deeply with loved ones than before they were stricken. And they enjoyed a vivid appreciation of nature and of their relationships with family and friends (Yalom, 1980).

The Experience of Death

Some individuals prefer to face death in a hospital setting so that everything possible can be done to postpone the ultimate moment. But the advent of modern medicine has brought with it the capacity to sustain life in ways that many people view as a curse rather than a

Finishing life at home with caring family.

blessing. Many people die in intense physical pain and anxiety, attached to a series of life-support tubes, machines, and intravenous drips (Smyser, 1982).

One alternative is the *hospice*, a European term meaning a sheltered place for weary travelers, but which now refers to a facility where terminally ill patients are helped to die with a minimum of pain and a maximum of dignity. There are now over 1,500 hospice programs in the United States designed to help dying patients maintain a decent quality of life and overcome the emotional trauma of the death experience (National Hospice Organization, 1986). Hospices provide physician-directed medical services—but also psychological, social, and religious assistance as well as sufficient pain-killing drugs to diminish suffering (Wyatt, 1985). Family members are invited to participate as much as they can and at any time. Many hospices have programs of out-patient as well as in-patient care, so that if the patient wishes to die in the familiar surroundings of home, in the midst of family, the required medical and psychological support is available.

Some critics find fault with the hospice concept. For example, they fear that it may cause patients to give in to death too readily, and that, if the concept is widely accepted, there may not be enough medical and pyschological specialists available to staff high-quality programs (Aiken and Marx, 1982). But for now, the hospice programs appear to provide an alternative arrangement of care that reduces the anguish of death, and fills the needs of dying patients and their families.

Psychologists have only recently begun to study the cognitive and emotional processes that occur with the knowledge that death is imminent. The findings are sparse and inconclusive. But the search goes on for information that may help ease this final episode and surround dying with a grace and dignity befitting the human spirit and the remarkable flow of events from the cradle to the grave.

SUMMARY

Adolescence: joy or misery?

1. A number of criteria are used to determine the boundaries of adolescence. Although the period is seen roughly to lie between ages 10 and 20, adolescence has a variety of beginnings and endings for each individual.

2. Psychologically, adolescence may be a period of "storm and stress"—with much confusion over establishing independence, striving for recognition, and being under anxiety-producing scholastic and social pressure. However, some studies have shown that adolescents are well adjusted.

3. In physical terms, adolescence is usually defined as beginning with the onset of puberty—marked by menstruation in females and production of sperm in males. The onset of puberty is almost invariably accompanied by rapid physical growth. Concern about body image and being overweight can lead to eating disorders such as *anorexia nervosa* and *bulimia*.

4. Sexuality is a prominent concern during the adolescent years not only because of the physical changes puberty brings, but because sexual activity assumes a new social meaning during this period in the life cycle.

5. Although society's attitudes toward sex are more permissive today than in the past, adolescents still feel that emotional involvement is important for accepting a sexual relationship.

6. Moral standards—of sexual and other types of behavior—usually undergo rapid change during adolescence. Kohlberg has suggested that *moral development* occurs in six stages, in which children's reasons for good behavior progress from sheer self-interest to a desire for the approval of others and finally to a concern for their own values and approval of their own consciences.

7. Adolescents seek to establish a sense of *identity*—that is, to think of themselves as possessing a distinct and unique character, of being people in their own right.

Development in adulthood

8. Continuing development in the years after adolescence often produces striking changes. Some of the most troubled and despondent adolescents turn out to lead happy and fulfilling lives as adults, while some untroubled and self-confident adolescents do not live up to their early promise.

9. One of the prominent proponents of the idea that development is a lifelong process is Erikson, who holds that *psychosocial development* (psychological changes occurring with changes in the social environment) proceeds in eight stages extending from infancy to old age.

10. Work often deeply affects an individual's well-being. Success on the job can have a potent impact on self-esteem, marital satisfaction, and physical health.

11. Conflicts for women in our society can be created by *sex role stereotyping*—where women are encouraged and often expected to act in traditional feminine roles. Similar conflicts are experienced by men.

12. According to Erikson, the critical event in early adulthood is moving into a relationship (usually marriage) marked by intimacy, commitment, and love.

13. *Cohabitation*, or intersexual living together, has been advocated before marriage to allow participants to learn more about their partners and themselves, and thus strengthen a future marriage. However, there is really no evidence that living together first draws a couple closer together.

14. Having a child creates complex and sweeping changes in the roles husband and wife play in their marriage. If the children are planned for and the parents are psychologically prepared for their responsibilities, contentment in marriage does not deteriorate.

15. Middle adulthood is marked by a transition period where people attempt to make the shift to the later stages in life. While such shifts can create conflicts and stress, they often reflect the increased mellowing and self-assurance that middle age brings.

Growing old: the challenges and the triumphs

16. With the dramatic increase in the number of people age 65 and over, the problems and pleasures of the retirement years have become very much a part of psychological investigation.

17. The later years, like the earlier periods of life, bring physical changes. *Senescence*, or the weakening and decline of the body, often becomes obvious during the seventh decade of life.

18. *Senile dementia*, or senility, with symptoms such as disorientation, poor attention, loss of memory, and inability to store new information, is a disease that significantly afflicts a small proportion of old people. A neurological illness, called *Alzheimer's disease*, is a form of dementia that is now recognized as the most common cause of intellectual impairment in older people.
19. Intelligence can be divided into two major kinds of abilities: (a) *fluid intelligence* and (b) *crystallized intelligence*.
20. Fluid abilities are dependent on neurological development and are relatively independent of the impact of education and cultural influences. Crystallized intelligence, in contrast, requires the capacity to use an accumulated body of general information in order to make judgments and solve problems. Today it is generally agreed that, as we grow older, we experience a decline in the first, but not in the second.
21. Most people seem to cope with the problems of the retirement years and find them fulfilling. A key factor appears to be the presence of a network of friends, at least some of whom are viewed as intimates.

The psychology of dying

22. Fear of death is not pervasive among the elderly. Death becomes more acceptable if older people experience a sense of what Erikson described as integrity and fulfillment—a feeling that they have lived a whole and satisfying life.
23. The stages most people experience in the process of facing death are: (a) denial, (b) anger, (c) bargaining, (d) depression, and (e) acceptance. The *hospice* is a facility designed to help dying patients maintain a decent quality of life and deal with the emotional trauma of the death experience.

IMPORTANT TERMS

Alzheimer's disease
anorexia nervosa
bulimia
cohabitation
crystallized intelligence
fluid intelligence
generativity
hospice

identity
menarche
moral development
psychosocial development
senescence
senile dementia
sex role stereotyping

RECOMMENDED READINGS

Birren, J. E., et al. *Developmental psychology: a life-span approach.* Boston: Houghton Mifflin, 1981.

Conger, J. J., and Peterson, A. C. *Adolescence and youth: psychological development in a changing world*, 3d ed. New York: Harper & Row, 1984.

Csikszentmihalyi, M. C., and Larson, R. *Being adolescent: conflict and growth in the teenage years.* New York: Basic Books, 1984.

Erikson, E. H. *Identity and the life cycle.* New York: Norton, 1980.

Henig, R. M. *The myth of senility: the truth about the brain and aging.* Glenview, Ill.: Scott Foresman, 1985.

Hughes, F. P., and Noppe, L. D. *Human development across the lifespan.* St. Paul: West Publishing, 1985.

Schaie, K. W., and Geiwitz, J. *Adult development and aging.* Boston: Little, Brown, 1982.

Wolman, B., ed. *Handbook of developmental psychology.* Englewood Cliffs, N.J.: Prentice-Hall, 1982.

CHAPTER 16
SOCIAL PSYCHOLOGY: HOW WE RELATE TO EACH OTHER

LEARNING SOCIETY'S WAYS—AND CONFORMING TO THEM 570

The process of socialization
Our tendency to obey and conform
Conformity in daily life
The Asch experiment: would you agree that a wrong answer is right?
The Milgram experiment: could you turn into a torturer?
Why we conform
Social comparison: how you form your opinion of yourself

HOW WE ACQUIRE—AND SOMETIMES CHANGE—OUR ATTITUDES TOWARD LIFE 580

Why your attitudes are not always consistent
Prejudices and stereotypes
How life experiences can create new attitudes
Attitude change and the theory of cognitive dissonance
Behavior change as a key to attitude change
How "persuasive communications" can alter our attitudes

TRYING TO FIGURE OUT WHY PEOPLE BEHAVE AS THEY DO: ATTRIBUTION THEORIES 586

Is it the person or the situation?
Guessing what people are like by guessing how they feel
Your influence on other people's actions
How self-fulfilling prophecies can cause damage
Self-perception theory—or "Why did I do that?"

FORMING SOCIAL RELATIONSHIPS: HOW WE BECOME ATTRACTED TO ONE ANOTHER 591

Propinquity and familiarity: "I like you because I know you"
Similarity: "I like you because we seem so alike"
Reciprocity: "I like you because you like me"
Physical attractiveness: "I like you because of your looks"
Why looks count: the strength and persistence of first impressions

AGGRESSION AND ALTRUISM 597

Is aggression bred into our genes—or learned?
The nature of caring: studies of altruism
Bystander apathy: neglecting the needs of others

SUMMARY 601

IMPORTANT TERMS 604

RECOMMENDED READINGS 604

PSYCHOLOGY IN EVERYDAY LIFE

How much do you think people can change? 586
You get what you expect—so expect the best 589
Guidance from attribution theories 591

Undoubtedly you know some people who are so anxious to please others that they continually change their behavior, depending on whom they are with. These people, driven to make the best impression, are always monitoring what they say and do in an attempt to be the right person in the right place at the right time (Snyder, 1983).

While such cases are extreme, most of us react somewhat differently in different situations. For example, whether we are with friends or strangers can affect how well we cope with pain (Spanos et al., 1984), or whether we will "choke" under the pressure of performing a difficult task (Baumeister, 1984). A person may be scrupulously honest in dealing with business associates yet cheat while playing cards with friends, generous toward some people but stingy toward others, domineering around close relatives but meekly submissive around in-laws. Children, too, are profoundly influenced by the social setting. They may be aggressive and disruptive at home, yet docile and cooperative in school (Segal and Segal, 1985).

Because the human personality is not consistent in all situations, it cannot be entirely understood by studying the individual in isolation. Hence the importance of social psychology, which studies how "a person's thoughts, feelings, and actions are affected by others" (Feldman, 1985)—a definition that covers cognitive processes and emotions as well as actions. The relationship between social situation and individual, it should be added, is a two-way street. Other people influence us and we influence them. That is to say, how we feel and what we do is determined at least in part—and often to a great extent—by what other people are doing or what we think they expect us to do. At the same time, what we do or seem to expect helps determine what they do.

LEARNING SOCIETY'S WAYS—AND CONFORMING TO THEM

Other people are important to us and influence us because we humans are social animals. We do not prowl the world alone or in the company of only a mate, as some other organisms do. Indeed we do not seem capable of existing in isolation. We need the company and help of other humans to acquire even such necessities as food, clothing, shelter, and protection against enemies. We can survive only by establishing some kind of *society*—which is the term applied to any group of people who occupy a given geographical area and cooperate in a pattern of living that is accepted by its members. Big or little, simple or complex, the society is a universal way of life—suggesting that the establishment of relations with others and susceptibility to their influence is a basic human characteristic.

The Process of Socialization

The society into which we are born begins to influence us almost from the moment of birth. We develop from child to adult in close interaction with our parents, family, teachers, and schoolmates. From these people, we learn the ways of our own society. We learn the English language. We learn how people in our society behave toward one another and express or conceal their emotions. Later we learn what they believe and what they value. We learn the customs and laws that dictate a whole host of activities, from finding a mate to conducting a business deal. This process is called *socialization*—the way children are integrated into the society through exposure to the actions and opinions of other members of the society. In many ways, children become creatures of their society (Benedict, 1959), molded by the customs and rules that make up its *culture*, or established way of life.

The term "culture" embraces all the physical objects the society produces as part of its lifestyle—its clothing, shelter, tools, and artistic creations. The term also includes the

These students are being socialized by the rules of a particular culture.

society's language, beliefs, political structure, family relationships, rules, and customary patterns of behavior. All these aspects of culture vary greatly around the world. There are societies in which the women do all the work and the men devote themselves to ceremony and self-adornment (Mead, 1935), in which two friends would never dream of competing against each other in games or athletic contests (McGrath, 1964), and even in which young boys practice oral sex on older adolescent boys for a number of years so that they might successfully grow into manhood (Herdt, 1981).

In a society as complex as ours, not every child is socialized to follow the same customs and rules. Within our society there exist many *subcultures*, or ways of life that differ from one another in many important respects. Some of these subcultures exist partly because the nation has been settled over the years by people from many different parts of the world, bringing with them their own particular customs and values. Other subcultures have a religious basis. Still others depend on occupation and social class. All in all the United States is a nation of many subcultures holding very different views on religion, politics, militarism, sexual behavior, and lifestyles in general.

Our Tendency to Obey and Conform

Whatever the customs and rules may be, every culture and every subculture encourages its children to conform to them. Socialization is a universal process. In one way or another, it gives all of us a lifelong tendency to think and act like the people with whom we have grown up.

There are always rebels, of course, who resist the influence of socialization and break the rules or even fail to conform to them most of the time. Despite the exceptions, however, most people follow the customs and rules they have learned and behave as they believe they are expected to behave. Social psychologists have found that most humans everywhere display strong tendencies toward (1) *obedience*, or submission to authority, and (2) *conformity*, which is defined as the yielding by individuals to pressures from the group in which they find themselves. The group applying the pressure may be the society as a whole or any part of it, such as our family, friends, classmates, or business associates. It may even be made up of total strangers, such as the people sitting around us on a bus or in a theater. Of course, on many occasions, we tend to believe that there is group pressure on us to conform when, in reality, there is none.

Conformity in Daily Life

The tendencies toward obedience and conformity—and the difference between them—were demonstrated decades ago in a simple little experiment built around a campus doorway that was in frequent use. On the doorway an urgent sign suddenly appeared:

ABSOLUTELY NO ADMITTANCE
USE ANOTHER ENTRANCE

The sign, of course, was put up by a psychologist, who then sat by to see what happened. One person after another, even those who had been walking through the doorway every day, turned back—thus exhibiting obedience to society's rules. But then the experimenter arranged for confederates to appear, ignore the sign, and march right in. Given this example, others walked in too (Freed et al., 1955). They were now exhibiting conformity to the behavior of the confederates.

If you make a point of looking for similar examples, you will see them all around you. If a traffic light sticks, showing red to motorists approaching from all four directions, the drivers all come to a halt and wait patiently for a change. But when at last one or two venture across the intersection, others follow. When a pedestrian on a crowded city sidewalk stops to stare at the upper floor of a tall building, others are likely to stop and stare too, even if they find nothing worth watching. (If you and some companions want to try it, you may soon find quite a crowd of imitators.) People even manage to resemble one another in appearance. As the street scenes in Figure 16-1 show, styles change over the years—but at any given moment in history, everybody looks pretty much like everybody else.

It is amusing but not very significant that all of us tend to gawk at a building when others are doing it—or that we follow the dictates of fashion in clothing, hair styles, and growing or not growing beards. Often, however, obedience and conformity have a much more profound effect on behavior.

The Asch Experiment: Would You Agree That a Wrong Answer Is Right?

One of the classic experiments on conformity was performed in the 1950s at Swarthmore College by Solomon Asch. It used the method illustrated in Figure 16-2, in which one real subject, who thought he was taking part in a study of perceptual discrimination, sat at a table with a group of confederates of the experimenter. The experimenter showed pairs of white cards with black lines of varying length, such as the lines shown in their relative sizes in Figures 16-3 and 16-4, and asked the group which of the lines in Figure 16-4 matched the test line.

The real subject was always seated where he would hear the judgments of several confederates before making his own. Sometimes the confederates gave the right answer,

Figure 16-1 Styles change over the years—but people remain look-alikes

These street scenes photographed over a span of three-quarters of a century show how the way Americans look has shifted since 1910. Yet, no matter when the camera records them, they all look more or less like their contemporaries.

1910

late 1930s

late 1980s

Learning Society's Ways—And Conforming to Them

Figure 16-2   Asch's famous study: will student 6 conform to the group?

Of these seven students in the Asch experiment, student 6 is the only real subject. All the others are in league with the experimenter. Student 6 believes the experiment is about discrimination among lines like those shown in Figures 16-3 and 16-4—but in fact it is designed to find out how far he and other subjects will go in conforming to the group.

Figure 16-3   A test line in the Asch experiment

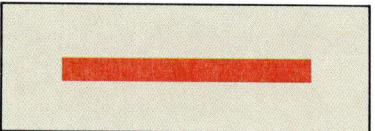

This is a scaled-down version of one of the lines Asch showed to the group. Which of the lines in Figure 16-4, he asked, matches it?

Figure 16-4   Which line matches?

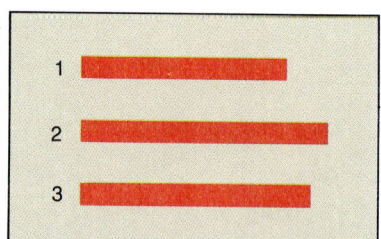

The group was asked to judge which of these lines was the same as the line in Figure 16-3. The correct answer is 2. But the experimenter's six confederates at the table insisted unanimously that it was line 1—which is in fact the least like the test line.

but on some trials they deliberately called out the wrong answer. On these trials 37 percent of the answers given by the real subjects who took part in the experiment were also incorrect. In other words, the subjects conformed with the group's wrong judgment much of the time.

Only one subject out of four remained completely independent and did not conform at any time. Even the subjects who showed independence, however, experienced various kinds of conflict and anxiety, as is readily apparent from the photographs of the subject in Figure 16-5. Some of their comments later were: "At times I had the feeling, to heck with it, I'll go along with the rest." "I felt disturbed, puzzled, separated, like an outcast from the rest." Thus the urge to conform—to go along with the group—was strong even among the most independent subjects (Asch, 1956).

Figure 16-5 **An "independent" subject—shaken but unyielding**

In the top photo, student 6 is making his first independent judgment, disagreeing with the group's otherwise unanimous but incorrect verdict. In the other photos his puzzlement and concern seem to increase until, preserving his independence despite the pressure from the group, he announces (bottom), "I have to call them as I see them."

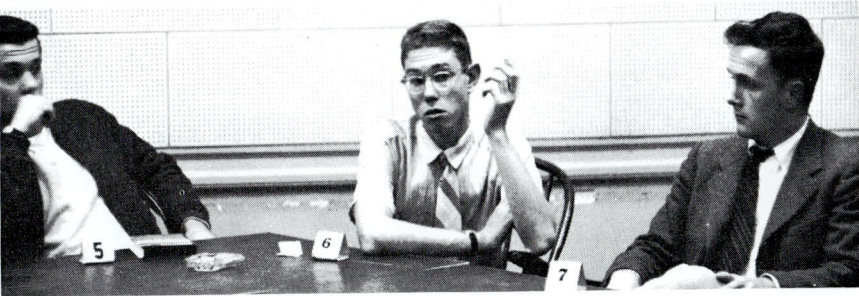

The Milgram Experiment: Could You Turn into a Torturer?

Another experiment that produced even more dramatic results—and in this case frightening ones—was performed by Stanley Milgram in a laboratory at Yale. Milgram selected 80 men of various ages and occupational backgrounds and asked them to take part in what he said was an important experiment in learning. Each subject was assigned to a group of four people—the other three of whom, unknown to the subject, were Milgram's assistants. One of the assistants was the "learner" in the make-believe experiment. The other two assistants and the subject were the "teachers," and their job was to instruct the "learner" by punishing him with an electric shock when he made an error. The subject was put at the controls that regulated the amount of shock (see Figure 16-6). Actually, no electricity was hooked up to the controls and no learning took place. The "learner" deliberately made errors and only pretended to feel pain when punished.

Of the 80 subjects, half were placed in a control group. These subjects were not subjected to any pressure to raise the shock levels and did not raise them very high. Thirty-four of these 40 control subjects stopped at shock levels listed as "slight" or "moderate." Only six went above 120 volts. But it was a far different story with the other 40 subjects.

Figure 16-6   The Milgram experiment

In these scenes from a film on the Milgram experiment, A shows the panel, which subjects believed to control the level of shock. In B, electrodes are attached to the wrists of a "learner." In C, a subject who will be at the control panel receives a sample shock of the kind he believes he will administer. In D, a subject breaks off the experiment after reaching as high a shock level as he is willing to administer.

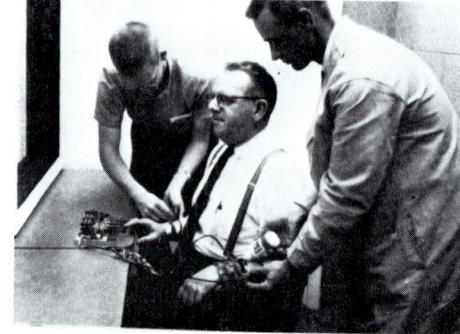
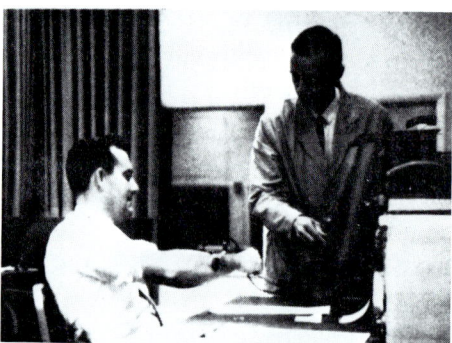

These 40 were strongly urged by their fellow "teachers" to raise the amount of electricity higher and higher—and they did. Only six of them refused to go above 120 volts. The other 34 went right on, even though the "learner" at first shouted that the shocks were becoming painful and later began to groan and finally scream in pain. Seven of the subjects went up to what they thought was the maximum they could deliver—a "highly dangerous" shock of 450 volts. Many of the experimental subjects showed signs of doubt and distress about engaging in such a cruel act, yet they went along with the group anyway (Milgram, 1964).

The obedience displayed in Milgram's experiment does not mean, of course, that adults will inevitably behave in a similar fashion. Nearly two decades later, a group of scientists conducted a somewhat similar experiment, but with different results. The subjects, living in a working-class town in the Midwest, were persuaded to be videotaped as they discussed the merits of a legal case concerning a service station manager whose license had been revoked because of allegedly immoral behavior. After the coordinator of the experiment had asked a few members of the group to argue as if they were offended by the service station manager's behavior, he requested that all of the subjects sign an affidavit giving the service station the right to introduce the tapes of the group discussion as evidence in court. The result was anger and rebellion on the part of a number of participants (Gamson, Fireman, and Rytina, 1982). The contrast with Milgram's earlier results are probably due to at least two factors: recent changes in our post-Watergate society that have encouraged a more distrustful attitude toward authority than was the case when the Milgram experiment was run, and the fact that there was ample opportunity in this case for group discussion about whether or not the request being made was fair.

Why We Conform

The question, nevertheless, remains: Why do we have a tendency to conform? Why is it so powerful that it can sometimes make us behave in unexpected ways?

(1) Our Dependence on Approval   One reason seems to be that we depend on the people around us for many of our psychological satisfactions. It is pleasant to win approval as an accepted, well-liked member of the group. It is highly unpleasant to be rejected by the group and perhaps even subjected to ridicule (Aronson, 1984). Thus it is generally easier and more rewarding to conform. It can be very difficult to stand alone as a single dissenter in virtually any culture. In Japan, for example, the tendency to conform is even stronger than in the United States. It is more painful for a Japanese adult to rebel against peer values and to experience the rejection of the group than it is for an American (Azuma, 1982).

Studies have shown that if we are in a group that expresses unanimous agreement, we are under much stronger pressure to conform than if even one person disagrees. This was demonstrated in a variation of the Asch experiment in which one of the confederates sitting around the table was a black and some of the actual subjects were known to be prejudiced against blacks. When the confederates were unanimous in the incorrect answers they gave, all the subjects showed the usual tendency to conform. But when the black confederate broke the unanimity of the group by giving the correct answer, the subjects were much less likely to conform (Malof and Lott, 1962). Even those who might have been expected to reject the black confederate's opinion seemed to welcome the excuse he gave them for breaking away from the others.

(2) Our Respect for Authority and Its Symbols   Another reason for conformity and obedience is the tendency we have as members of a group to accede to the requests or demands of those who appear to be in legitimate control. In the Milgram study, the experimenter was not a brutish looking man, and he spoke calmly and softly. But he was constantly

Mass suicides in The People's Temple, Guyana, November 1978. The urge to conform can be exploited to a gruesome extreme.

present and in charge of the situation; he was wearing the scientist's white coat and doing "scientific research." It is noteworthy that when the experimenter left the room and delivered his directions by telephone, the degree of conformity was reduced (Milgram, 1974).

(3) Our Need for Guidance Still another reason for conformity is that we need the help of other people in developing an accurate view of our physical and social environment. We cannot get through life successfully, and may not even survive, unless we understand ourselves and our world—and often other people are the only guide we have. To cite some extreme examples, you can get killed if you venture out in a boat at a time when a more experienced mariner would know a storm is about to churn up waves that may swamp you, of if you eat a mushroom that an expert would immediately recognize as poisonous. On a more commonplace level, you are not likely to get past a job interview if you misjudge the interviewer's concern for promptness and neat appearance—or hold a job very long if you have a false notion of its requirements or your talent for it.

The need for guidance to successful behavior is the basis of an important psychological concept called the *theory of social comparison*. The theory holds that we usually have no objective and scientific way to evaluate our abilities, opinions, or the propriety of our actions (Festinger, 1954). Therefore we can only judge ourselves by comparing ourselves with other people—usually our friends or other people we believe to be similar to ourselves, but sometimes strangers whom we happen to be around. The more uncertain we are of where we stand and how we should act, the more likely we are to make and rely on the comparisons (Radloff, 1959). For example, if you go to a party where you are the only stranger, how can you fit in without seeing how the others act? On a new campus, how are you expected to dress, behave in the classroom, and get along with your fellow students?

The result of the Milgram experiment can be readily explained by the theory of social comparison. The subjects were in a highly uncertain situation. They had no way of knowing what to think or how to behave—so they looked to others for information. They compared their own opinions with the opinions of the others in the group. When the others proved to be so positive about raising the shock levels, who were they to argue otherwise?

Social Comparison: How You Form Your Opinion of Yourself

The theory of social comparison also holds that our search for guidance strongly influences our self-esteem—indeed our entire self-image. We judge our abilities and our worth, the theory maintains, mostly by comparing ourselves with other people. Otherwise we cannot know if we are good students, good teachers, or good athletes, unless we compare our ability with another person's. Even children feel impelled to try to determine how they rank in comparison with their peers (Marsh and Parker, 1984). We must also ask ourselves, "What do other people think of me?"

The opinions of other people play a far greater part in self-esteem than could ever be imagined by a person who has never been exposed to social psychology and its emphasis on social influences. For dramatic evidence, note this experiment and its surprising results:

The subjects were women attending high school or college. They were asked to try their hand at a problem-solving task containing 25 items. After they had finished, the experimenters pretended to grade their attempts and then told them how they had scored. Actually, no grading was ever done. The experimenters simply decided arbitrarily to tell half the subjects that they had done badly, the other half that they had done very well.

This false information about performance was allowed to "sink in" for a time. Then the experimenters flatly admitted their deception. The women were told that their scores had never actually been compiled and that there was no truth at all in the information that they had done badly or well. Once the truth was out, the women were asked to rate their own ability at that kind of problem solving, estimate how many problems they had in fact solved correctly, and also predict how many they would solve correctly on a future trial.

As is shown in Figure 16-7, the results were startling. Apparently the women who had been told they did badly were never quite able to get over the loss of self-esteem they

Figure 16-7 **It is not true—but I believe it!**

The graph illustrates the results of the experiment with high school and college women discussed in the text. Subjects who were told they failed at a problem-solving task had a significantly lower opinion of their ability than subjects who were told they succeeded—even though they knew that the information about their performance had no relation to the facts (Ross, Lepper, and Hubbard, 1975).

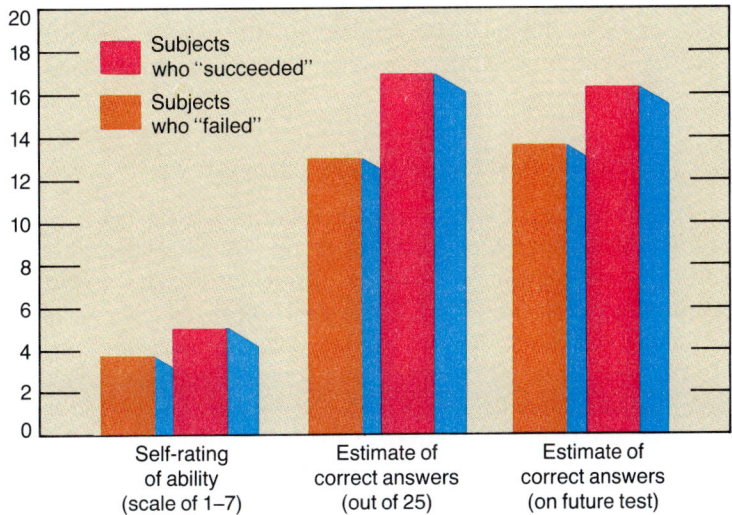

suffered—even though they knew that the unfavorable rating bore no relation to facts and meant absolutely nothing. The women who had been told they did well, on the other hand, were much more confident—even though they too knew that the information was meaningless. There could hardly be a more convincing demonstration of the way other people's opinions shape our own views—even of ourselves.

HOW WE ACQUIRE—AND SOMETIMES CHANGE—OUR ATTITUDES TOWARD LIFE

All of us, as we grow up, acquire many strong beliefs and feelings, or what social psychologists call *attitudes*, toward people and situations. We have favorable or unfavorable attitudes toward members of various ethnic groups, foreigners, rich people, poor people, males, females, homosexuals, children, teenagers, and old people. We have strong attitudes toward the nation's political parties, national defense, taxation, welfare, crime, unions, religion, and all the other issues and institutions in society.

Attitudes are not just mere off-the-cuff judgments that we make casually and can easily change. Instead they are deeply ingrained—as if constituting a basic part of our personality. We acquire many of them as part of the socialization process, and they tend to influence us throughout life. We are very much in favor of things toward which we have a positive attitude—and very much against things toward which we have a negative attitude.

It is chiefly this "for" or "against" quaility that distinguishes attitudes from more superficial and less influential opinions. Our belief that the earth is round is an example of a mere opinion, not an attitude. We are neither for nor against roundness—and in the unlikely event science suddenly discovered that the earth is in fact shaped like a football, we would not hesitate to change our opinion. An attitude, because it concerns something that really matters to us, is far more resistant to change. A congresswoman with a strongly disapproving attitude toward abortion is not easily persuaded, even by her most influential colleagues, to vote for federal funding of abortion clinics. (If you want to know what some of your own strongly held attitudes are, ask yourself what it is you believe in so devoutly that, if you were proved wrong, it would cause you to feel upset. Perhaps it is a belief about the nature of individual freedom, marital fidelity, or personal independence.)

Investigators have devoted considerable study to how people acquire attitudes, cling to them, but sometimes change them—and when, under what circumstances, and to what extent the attitudes predict what the individual will actually do (Brigham and Wrightsman, 1982).

Why Your Attitudes Are Not Always Consistent

Attitudes are not necessarily based on evidence. Some of them simply represent the effects of socialization and conformity to the social group. We have taken them over lock, stock, and barrel from the people around us—without ever looking at the evidence at all. Nor are they necessarily logical or consistent. Some psychologists have concluded that the most remarkable thing about our attitudes is the amount of inconsistency we manage to tolerate (Bem, 1970). We are surprisingly adept at reconciling widely dissimilar attributes in a given individual (Asch and Zukier, 1984).

For example, Mayor Smith is running for reelection. Mr. and Mrs. Jones, like their friends and neighbors, have a strongly favorable attitude toward Mayor Smith and the mayor's political party. But one day something rather upsetting occurs. The local newspaper publishes a strong and extremely persuasive editorial that describes in detail how

Mayor Smith has failed to solve a number of urgent city problems. In fact the mayor has accepted graft as an inducement to permit gambling and to tolerate inferior performance on building contracts.

Will Mr. and Mrs. Jones change their attitude toward Mayor Smith? Not necessarily. Instead, they may do any one of several things. They may convince themselves that the newspaper is simply biased against the mayor. They may engage in a mental debate with the editorial and disprove its allegations, at least to their own satisfaction. Or they may put the whole editorial right out of their mind and simply refuse to think about it. Our ingenuity at finding ways of maintaining our attitudes despite strong opposing arguments seems almost boundless. Consider, also, the fact that citizens in Boston once elected as their mayor a man who was in jail for a crime.

Prejudices and Stereotypes

Two kinds of attitudes that often fly in the face of fact are so common that social psychologists have given them special names:

1. A *prejudice* is an attitude that an individual maintains so stubbornly as to be virtually immune to any information or experiences that would disprove it. In our society, one of the most common prejudices is held by some whites against blacks and by some blacks against whites.
2. A *stereotype* is an attitude, shared by large numbers of people, that disregards individual differences and holds that all members of a certain group behave in the same manner. People are making judgments on the basis of stereotypes when they claim that all women are flighty or that all men are male chauvinists.

We tend to cling to our prejudices and stereotypes—so much so that when we find a member of a group who runs counter to our preconceptions of the group as a whole, we are likely to dismiss the case as atypical, or a "fluke" (Lord, Lepper, and Mackie, 1984). In our personal relationships, we may judge new acquaintances on the basis of stereotypes and thereby become suspicious of certain kinds of people who might actually prove highly congenial if we were only to give them a chance.

How would you judge this woman on the left on first impression? (She is actually Margaret Thatcher, British Prime Minister.)

How Life Experiences Can Create New Attitudes

We tend to cling to our attitudes in general like a child to a security blanket—and perhaps for some of the same reasons. Yet attitudes are not entirely permanent and unyielding. Sometimes the dyed-in-the-wool Republican switches to the Democratic party. Or a confirmed atheist joins a church—and a devout churchgoer drops out. Public opinion polls taken at intervals over recent decades have shown sharp changes in prevailing attitudes toward many institutions and issues.

One reason attitudes change is that the socialization process continues throughout life. In our early years, our parents are the chief instruments of socialization and we tend to adopt their attitudes as our own. But as we grow older and are exposed to other socializing influences, the early influence of our parents begins to weaken. Although about 80 percent of elementary school children prefer the same political party as their parents, one study found that the number drops to only about 55 percent among college students (Goldsen et al., 1960). The freshman year in college is particularly likely to produce attitude change (Freedman, Carlsmith, and Sears, 1970).

When we take a job, we undergo a new kind of socialization. Each time we change jobs or get a promotion, each time we move to a new neighborhood or a new community, we come under new influences. We can also be swayed by what we read and by what we see on television. The world changes and we change with it. Our attitudes can be compared to a house that undergoes frequent remodeling, expansion, and repainting over the years. In some ways the house never changes, yet is never really the same.

Attitude Change and the Theory of Cognitive Dissonance

What kinds of new experiences and new information are most likely to produce attitude changes? One answer comes from proponents of what is called the *theory of cognitive dissonance*. This theory maintains that we have a strong urge to be consistent and rational in our thinking and to preserve agreement and harmony among our beliefs, feelings, and behavior—and therefore our attitudes. When consistency and harmony are broken, we experience cognitive dissonance. We may manage to tolerate the inconsistency, as the Joneses did in the case of Mayor Smith. But cognitive dissonance tends to be highly uncomfortable, and we may be strongly motivated to restore harmony by making some kind of adjustment.

In some cases, new factual information is enough to create cognitive dissonance and bring about a change in attitude. For example, many people who were once strongly opposed to birth control have been greatly influenced by all the factual information that has appeared in recent years about the population explosion and the danger of worldwide overcrowding. They once had the cognitive belief that a growing population was a good thing. This cognitive belief has now changed, and their attitude toward birth control has changed with it.

Events that have a strong emotional impact may also create an inconsistency that calls for change. For an example, imagine what would happen if a man who had always regarded women as second-class citizens found himself in love with a woman who was an ardent feminist. Or consider an actual laboratory experiment in which college women underwent a deeply emotional experience related to cigarette smoking. The women, all heavy smokers, were asked to act out a scene in which the experimenter pretended to be a physician and they his patients. Each subject, visiting the "doctor," got bad news about a persistent cough from which she had been suffering; her X ray had shown lung cancer; immediate surgery was required; before the operation she and the doctor would have to discuss the difficulty, pain, and risk. The experimenter tried to keep the scene as realistic as possible and to involve each subject emotionally to the greatest possible degree. As a result, almost all the women quit or drastically cut down on smoking. A follow-up 18 months later found that they continued to show a significant change in their smoking habits (Mann and Janis, 1968).

Behavior Change as a Key to Attitude Change

It seems logical that a change in an attitude, caused by new beliefs or new emotional responses, should cause a change in behavior. Yet, strangely enough, the sequence of events is often exactly the opposite. In many cases, the change in behavior comes first, and this new behavior creates the change in attitude.

Many studies have shown that experimental manipulation of behavior can produce remarkable results. One such experiment concerned the highly controversial action of President Gerald Ford in extending a blanket pardon to his predecessor, Richard Nixon, for any crimes committed during the Watergate incident. College students who strongly opposed the pardon were asked to write essays taking the opposite view and justifying Ford's action. This simple act of writing an essay tended to create a more favorable attitude toward the pardon (Cooper, Zanna, and Taves, 1978). A similar experiment was conducted with students who favored the legalization of marijuana. After they were asked to write an essay opposing legalization, their attitudes tended to show considerable change (Fazio, Zanna, and Cooper, 1977).

In our everyday lives, new social situations often push us in the direction of changes in behavior, and these in turn often lead to changes in attitudes. This has been especially noticeable in recent years in the attitudes of whites toward blacks and of blacks toward whites. In general, it has been found that people who have attended school or worked with members of the other race hold more favorable attitudes, while those who have had no interracial contacts tend to feel less favorably (Pettigrew, 1969). Undoubtedly the explanation is that new forms of behavior—that is, dealing with members of the other race, studying or working with them, and treating them as friendly companions—have produced attitude changes. The theory of cognitive dissonance maintains that the friendly behavior produced an imbalance that was remedied by abandoning the disapproving attitude.

How "Persuasive Communication" Can Change Our Attitudes

All of us are under constant pressure to adopt new attitudes. Politicians bombard us with speeches and press releases intended to foster favorable attitudes toward them and their party. Advertisers spend millions of dollars every year to try to create favorable attitudes toward their products. Many organizations work hard to win support for such causes as conservation, kindness to animals, and pollution control. To social psychologists, all such attempts to change attitudes by transmitting information and making emotional appeals are known as *persuasive communications*. Because persuasive communications potentially have a great effect on society, they have been studied in considerable depth.

Attempts to influence the attitudes of large numbers of people face many handicaps. For one thing, persuasive communications do not ordinarily reach many people. A politician may make the most impassioned and convincing plea for support—yet his speech will be heard in person by only a few thousand people at most. Even if part of the speech is shown on television, it will reach only a small proportion of Americans. Newspaper accounts of a political speech reach and impress an even smaller audience, and editorials

In July of 1987, Colonel Oliver North became an overnight hero to many Americans. Why do you think his televised communications were so persuasive?

have a smaller readership still. It has also been found that the audience likely to watch or read any appeal for attitude change—and to pay attention to it—is determined largely by a factor called *selective exposure*. This means that, by and large, persuasive communications reach only people who are already persuaded. Since we tend to associate with people we like and to read or listen to communications we find interesting, we are exposed mostly to people and communications we already agree with.

But let us assume that a persuasive communication does succeed in reaching us, despite the handicaps, and that it argues for a viewpoint to which we are opposed. To adopt it, we will have to change an attitude. Several factors help determine whether we will be persuaded to do so.

(1) The Credibility of the Source Some sources are likely to have considerable influence. Others are less likely to convince us and may in fact only make us more opposed to what they are proposing. If the communication comes from someone whose knowledge or motives are suspect—in other words, from a source of low credibility—we tend to disregard it. If it comes from people who clearly know what they are talking about—in other words, from a source of high credibility—we are much more likely to accept it. The effectiveness is enhanced if the source seems to be fair, objective, and not particularly interested in wielding influence.

(2) The Nature of the Communication What kind of arguments does the source present, and how and when are they presented? In general, appeals to the emotions tend to be especially effective—particularly appeals to fear (Sears, Freedman, and Peplau, 1985). As illustrated in Figure 16-8, such appeals can change not only attitudes but behavior as well.

Figure 16-8 **Getting scared into taking a tetanus shot**

The graph illustrates the results of a study in which college students were urged to get inoculations for tetanus. The disease was described in detail—how serious it was and that it was easy to contract—but to different degrees for each of three groups. For one group, the descriptions were extremely vivid, and the disease was made to seem as highly fearsome as possible; for a second group, a moderate amount of fear was aroused; and for a third, only very little. The greater the fear aroused, the more students not only said they intended to take shots, but actually reported to the university health service to be inoculated (Dabbs and Leventhal, 1966). In this case, although the communication aroused strong fear, the person could easily act and do something effective.

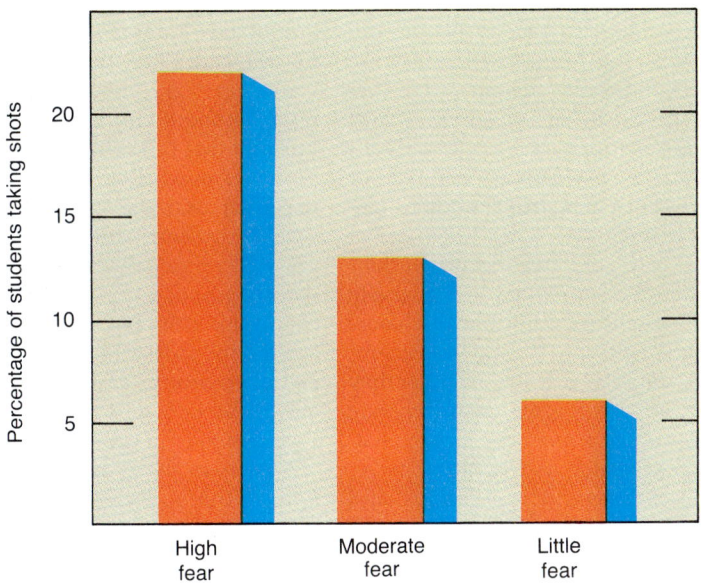

But the arousal of too much fear will backfire if the person cannot do anything to deal with the danger. See Figure 16-8 for an example. Presumably the listener becomes upset and tries to forget the whole matter (Janis, 1967). The effectiveness of a communication appears to be increased if it seems to present a fair rather than a one-sided argument, especially if it is addressed to an intelligent, well-educated audience (Hovland, Lumsdaine, and Sheffield, 1949). With a less intelligent audience, a one-sided argument is likely to be more effective, perhaps because the listeners would be confused by hearing both sides (Aronson, 1984).

(3) The Audience   Who is listening may be just as important as what is said and the source of the communication. For example, some people are more easily persuaded than others. The crucial factor seems to be one's own opinion of oneself. People who are low in self-esteem tend to be much more easily persuaded than people who are high in self-esteem (Cohen, 1959). Similarly, people who are anxious about social acceptance are more easily persuaded than those who have little anxiety (Sears, 1967). In an odd way, the possibility that listeners will change their arguments is also affected by their beliefs about the nature-nurture argument. This fact is so significant—especially as an influence that can discourage change for the better—that its implications are discussed in a box on Psychology in Everyday Life called "How Much Do You Think People Can Change?"

Psychology in Everyday Life
How Much Do You Think People Can Change?

One of the great barriers to progress—for both individuals and society as a whole—is the fact that many people take a pessimistic view of the nature-nurture argument. Although there is strong evidence that most human behavior is influenced just as much by environment and learning as by heredity—and often more so—many people still cling to the belief that human nature is determined at birth and resists any attempt to alter or improve it. This belief is evident in such familiar expressions as "People don't change," "That's just human nature," or "That kid was born to be bad." About themselves, people often say, "I can't help it; I'm just built that way," or "I was born unlucky."

The belief that human nature is largely inherited is a powerful deterrent to change in attitudes and behavior. In one experiment, university students were asked whether they thought the next five years might change their attitudes about some of their personality characteristics (such as whether they regarded themselves as trusting, curious, and so on) and toward various social issues (such as capital punishment and legalization of marijuana). It turned out that their answers depended largely on whether they thought their present attitudes were the result of nature or nurture (Festinger, 1954). If they considered an attitude to be largely a matter of learning (as a majority did for being trusted or for favoring legalization of marijuana) they were significantly more likely to foresee possible change than if they regarded the attitude as something innate (as a majority did for the trait of curiosity).

Unfortunately our society has a way of implying that personality traits—and especially any undesirable ones—are inborn and immutable. Many people become convinced that they are just naturally "dumb," or "awkward," or "bad." Accepting these labels as representing their inherited nature makes it unlikely that they will even consider change possible, much less try to achieve it. Suppose, for example, that an adolescent boy who is in constant trouble feels he was "born" to be a delinquent. He is likely to be totally unresponsive to any appeals to change his attitudes and behavior. If he could be convinced that his delinquency is the result of environmental influences, as it probably is, he would be much more receptive to the possibility of change.

Perhaps the greatest potential contribution of the social psychologists to human happiness and progress is the evidence they have accumulated about the influence of nurture in the form of the social environment. The findings indicate that personality, attitudes, and behavior are more elastic than is generally realized and that change for the better—in both human happiness and the way society functions—is always possible.

TRYING TO FIGURE OUT WHY PEOPLE BEHAVE AS THEY DO: ATTRIBUTION THEORIES

You have probably heard this old joke: A psychoanalyst runs into a woman acquaintance who greets him with a cheery "Good morning"—and he walks away asking himself, "I wonder what she meant by that?" Like many jokes, it contains a glimmer of wisdom. All of us spend a good deal of our time trying to anlayze why other people acted as they did, because only if we know their reasons can we respond appropriately.

A friend pays you a compliment. If you decide the words were sincere, you respond with pleasure. If you decide that the compliment was merely a hypocritical prelude to a request for a favor, you are turned off. At a family reunion an elderly uncle slumps into a chair and grasps at his chest, complaining of severe pain. You may rush him to a hospital emergency room—or, if you suspect he is merely bidding for attention and sympathy, do nothing.

The search for the causes of behavior is the basis of what are called *attribution theories*, which attempt to explain why and how we go about making the search. The various theories all assume that we want to know why people act as they do because we want our social interactions to have the most favorable possible outcome (Heider, 1944)—that is, we hope to avoid embarrassing and possibly costly mistakes and maximize the satisfactions and rewards. If we can attribute behavior to some underlying motive or other cause, we have a valuable clue to where we stand, what is likely to happen next, and how we can best deal with the situation. Thus we all perform a good deal of amateur psychoanalysis, seeking in various ways and as best we can to interpret the meanings and future implications of behavior.

Is It the Person or the Situation?

For almost any action, there are a number of possible explanations. Note these simple examples: One morning a waitress smiles at us and says she hopes we enjoy our meal. On the other hand the man at the filling station scowls as he takes our money. One possibility is that the waitress is a basically warm and friendly person, and the man at the filling station is hostile and bad tempered. In that event their behavior was due to what are called *dispositional factors*, or deep-seated and consistent personality traits. There is also the possibility, however, that the waitress acted as she did only because her boss had just warned her against being her natural surly self around customers—and the man at the filling station, though ordinarily good-humored, had a bad headache. In these events their behavior was caused by *situational factors*, or circumstances that forced them in that direction.

We usually attribute other people's actions to dispositional factors, thus ignoring social psychology's evidence that people are not nearly so consistent as generally assumed, and that their behavior so often depends on the circumstances. This tendency to favor dispositional factors—rather than aspects of the situation that may provide a far better explanation—is so powerful and widespread that it has been called the *attribution error* (Ross, 1977).

Why we should fall into this mistake in judging others is difficult to explain. Perhaps it is built into our culture. In fact, one investigator recently found that the tendency to attribute an individual's behavior to enduring personality traits is not nearly so great among Hindus as it is among Americans (Miller, 1984).

Drawing inferences about the personalities of other people from their behavior—regardless of how much the situation might have affected that behavior—leads to many unwarranted assumptions by teachers about their students, by family members about other members of the family, probably even by psychotherapists and counselors about their clients (Jones, 1979). It helps explain why "con artists," who are often psychopaths adept at exuding a false charm, find so many willing victims.

Guessing What People Are Like by Guessing How They Feel

The attribution error sometimes gets compounded because we reach our mistaken conclusions on the basis of mistaken impressions. An example occurred in an experiment in which psychologists made a videotape, without a sound track, of a college woman being interviewed. They then showed the videotape to two groups of male subjects. One group was told that the topic of the interview was sex, the other that it was politics. Afterward the subjects were asked to rate the woman on a scale of how nervous and anxious she seemed to be. Their ratings turned out to depend on what they had been told about the interview. If they thought the topic was sex, they found that the woman showed considerable anxiety. They assumed that the woman would be made anxious by a discussion of sexual behavior. If they thought the topic was politics, they found that she showed less anxiety. Thus exactly the same behavior—the same videotape of the same woman—created two very different impressions.

Next the two groups of subjects were asked to rate the woman's general tendency to be calm or flustered—in other words, her basic disposition. The results followed the same pattern. Subjects who believed that the interview was about sex, and that it had flustered her, decided she was just naturally inclined to be apprehensive, nervous, and anxious. The others did not (Snyder and Frankel, 1976).

The subjects jumped to the erroneous conclusion that acting flustered during a sex interview—a situation that might produce a certain amount of anxiety in almost everyone—indicated a disposition to be easily flustered in general. But the mistake was compounded by the fact that they only *thought* the woman acted flustered.

Why did this happen? We can assume that the subjects took the situation into account in judging the woman's behavior. They felt that a sex interview would naturally produce anxiety. Therefore they interpreted her behavior during the interview as showing anxiety. But in judging her general disposition, they fell into the attribution error and ignored situational factors. Thus they made a double error. They inferred her basic disposition from behavior that was itself only inferred. They made two guesses—either or both of which may have been totally wrong.

All of us are probably guilty at times of this compounded error. We watch person A being treated by person B in what we consider an abusive manner. Such treatment would make us angry—so we assume that A is angry. Then, on the basis of this assumption, we further assume that A tends to be hot-tempered in general. We watch person C making a fuss over person D. Such attention from C, whom we like very much, would greatly please us—so we assume that D is pleased. Then, on the basis of this assumption, we further assume that D is friendly and easily pleased in general. We could be dead wrong in thinking that A is angry or that D is pleased—and how they happen to feel in this particular situation does not necessarily reflect their basic disposition anyway.

Your Own Influence on Other People's Actions

One situational factor we often ignore, in committing the attribution error, is the effect of our own behavior on the actions of others. A team of social psychologists has described the cases of two women, Jane and Mary, each of whom has marital problems. Jane spends the afternoon telling her hairdresser about her new wardrobe. Mary, meanwhile, spends her afternoon telling a casual acquaintance all about her troubles. Why has Jane revealed so little information about herself whereas Mary has disclosed so much?

You might conclude that the difference is due solely to the contrasting personalities of Jane and Mary—one a self-contained, private person, the other more open and self-revealing. But in fact the difference may be due largely to the people they find themselves with—Jane with a hairdresser who herself is silent and withdrawn, Mary with an acquaintance who is just dying to "tell all." People tend to disclose a great deal about themselves—something they might not usually do—when they are with others who open up about their own personal lives. And we tend to disclose less about ourselves when we are with others who do not open up (Miller, Berg, and Archer, 1983).

It is important to recognize that we ourselves, by the way we act, may produce the very actions that we incorrectly interpret as indicating another person's deep-seated per-

Psychology in Everyday Life
You Get What You Expect—So Expect the Best

Over a decade ago, a team of psychologists conducted an experiment that was simple in design but that had some surprising and significant results. The subjects were college men. Each of them was merely asked to become acquainted, over the telephone, in a ten-minute conversation, with a college woman he had never met. Before the call was made, the subject saw what he was told was a photograph of the woman. Actually the photograph was of someone else. Half the subjects saw the picture of a woman who had been judged particularly attractive by an independent panel. The other subjects saw the picture of a woman who had been judged physically unattractive.

The phone calls were made and recorded on tape. In analyzing the tapes, the experimenters found something that seems utterly baffling. There seemed to be two completely different types of women on the phone. One type—those believed by the male students to be the person in the attractive photo—sounded warm, charming, and humorous. The other type—those believed by the men to be the person in the unattractive photo—sounded cold, clumsy, and humorless. How could this be?

The answer is simple. There also seemed to be two very different types of men on the tapes. If the male subjects thought their telephone partner was attractive, they expected her to be warm and charming—and they themselves were friendly, eager, and easy to respond to. If they thought she was unattractive, they expected her to be cold and humorless—and they themselves cast a pall over the phone call, inviting a chilly and stilted response. By thus setting the tone of the conversation, they pushed their partner into the very kind of behavior they expected (Snyder, Tanke, and Berscheid, 1977).

The gloomy prophecy made by half the male subjects was that their telephone partner would be unsociable—and since they acted accordingly, their prophecy was fulfilled. The other half of the men did exactly the opposite—and made their optimistic predictions come true.

This experiment makes a point worth remembering in social relationships: In everyday dealings with other people, it pays to be an optimist. When you have high hopes that the other person will be likable, your own friendly and accepting actions go a long way toward guaranteeing that the person will indeed behave in a likable manner. But if you expect to dislike someone, your own pessimistic and sour actions almost guarantee a cold and unsympathetic response. It is probably equally true that expecting other people to like us also tends to be a self-fulfilling prophecy. If we expect to be liked, we behave in a likable fashion. If we fear rejection, we tend to act tense, guarded, and not likable at all—and thus bring about the very thing we dreaded. By and large, people treat us not only as we treat them but also as we expect to be treated.

---

sonality traits. This tendency can lead to a *self-fulfilling prophecy*—that is, a prediction that comes true not because it was right but simply because it was made in the first place. Self-fulfilling prophecies based on false attributions and mistaken impressions are commonplace, with implications discussed in a box on Psychology in Everyday Life called "You Get What You Expect—So Expect the Best."

How Self-fulfilling Prophecies Can Cause Damage

One place where the self-fulfilling prophecy flourishes—often with harmful effects—is the classroom. Teachers frequently decide very early in the school year that some students can be expected to do well, while others are not worth much attention. In the elementary schoolroom, for example, they may make this decision on the basis of personal appearance and social class (Rist, 1970). Or they may have taught a pupil's older brother or sister and expect the younger child to be cut from the same cloth (Seaver, 1973). Once teachers have made their prophecy, for whatever reason, they tend to ignore their "dull" pupils and provide much more attention and help to the "bright" ones (Cooper, 1979). This behavior has a considerable effect on the pupils' actual progress in the classroom (Crano and Mellon, 1978). The ones tagged as "dull," possibly through no fault of their own, have little opportunity or encouragement to change that reputation.

Compounding the problem is the fact that a prophecy about another person's behavior may seem to come true, in the eyes of the prophecy maker, regardless of how the other person actually does behave. Once we have decided that people are likely to be "bright" or "dull" (or friendly, hostile, charming, humorless, or anything else) we are likely to interpret whatever they do as evidence of that trait. Many actions do not in themselves tell very much about the person who performs them—and an observer who starts with a bias is free to assign whatever meaning the bias dictates (Darley and Fazio, 1980). Teachers may find the very same action to be a sign of stupidity in a "dull" pupil but of intelligence in a "bright" pupil.

Self-fulfilling prophecies and other aspects of attribution theories, along with the power of first impressions, influence our society in many ways. All of us are inclined to judge behavior—and sometimes create it—on the basis of what we expect others to do. Our expectations can be created by a stereotype claiming that certain types of behavior are characteristic of members of racial or ethnic groups, or of social classes or the two sexes. Or the expectation can represent a hasty first impression—or even what we have heard, true or not, of the other person's reputation. Unfortunately, such an expectation can have far-reaching and drastic results, especially when it is held by a person with the power of a teacher, employer, police officer, or psychiatrist. As one study of the matter has concluded, an expectation about another person can "significantly affect the life" of that person—"perhaps for the better, but as many who do this research fear, often for the worse" (Darley and Fazio, 1980). Some lessons to guide us are contained in a box on Psychology in Everyday Life titled "Guidance from Attribution Theories."

Self-perception Theory—or "Why Did I Do That?"

Besides seeking the reasons for other people's behavior, we also make frequent attempts to analyze our own actions—especially on occasions when we find ourselves doing something we cannot quite understand. We try to gain some perception of what it was about ourselves or the situation that made us act as we did (Bem, 1972). The way we make the search is the basis of a special kind of attribution theory called *self-perception theory*.

Some examples you may have experienced are these: You are playing a friendly game of tennis, lose your temper, and throw your racket into the net—even though the outcome of the game means very little to you. Watching a charity telethon, you impulsively call the number shown on the screen and pledge a contribution much larger than you can really afford. You are puzzled. You are likely to ask yourself, "Why did I do that?"

Again, as in the case of other people's behavior, we can decide that we were pushed into our behavior by situational factors: We lost our temper because our tennis opponent or the spectators did something that was bound to provoke us. We pledged too much to the charity because the people on the telethon were so attractive and persuasive. Or we can decide on dispositional factors: We lost our temper because we hate to lose and are sometimes easily angered. We were overgenerous to the charity because we are generous at heart and do not always stop to think before we act.

Psychology in Everyday Life
Guidance from Attribution Theories

Attribution theories suggest some lessons to guide us in our day-to-day social relationships. They tell us that we had best be cautious and tentative when we act as amateur analysts looking for the reasons behind other people's actions. Yet the attempt at analysis, it must be added, is often useful and not necessarily doomed to failure. Despite the difficulties, we can manage to make a careful enough study to judge people more or less correctly:

- Take account, when you can, of situational factors. If, for example, a person seems withdrawn or confused, try to determine whether that is his or her usual frame of mind or simply the result of anxiety about next Monday's test.

- Search for any information that would indicate whether an act is typical or just an uncharacteristic incident. For example, do not decide that a person is hot-tempered because of a single display of anger.

- When possible, seek and consider the opinions of other observers. These can help you determine whether your attributions are on the mark or way off.

Other people are so important to us that we simply must try to understand them. We have to make attributions of some kind—and we do the best we can. It is safe to assume that most of the time, a person's behavior is based on a combination of both internal disposition and the particular situation at hand.

Strangely, when we look for the causes of our own behavior we tend to look for situational rather than dispositional factors—just the opposite of what we do when analyzing other people. If we do badly in school, for example, our faculty advisor is likely to attribute our failure to laziness or lack of ability. We ourselves are likely to attribute it to too heavy a course load, emotional strain over personal problems, or some other situational factor (Jones and Nisbett, 1972). Even if we do something rather praiseworthy, such as stopping on a highway to help an elderly couple change a tire, the same thing is likely to happen. An outsider watching our behavior would probably attribute it to a consistent disposition to be friendly and helpful. We ourselves would be inclined to emphasize the situational factors. We would say that the couple seemed very nice, unable to cope with their problem, and badly in need of help. In short, we tend to attribute causality to whatever forces we perceive to be paramount (Brown, 1986).

Attribution theorists believe that our self-perceptions have an important bearing on changes in attitude. When we manage to find situational factors, as we usually try to do, we have no reason to question or change our attitudes. When we are forced to decide that dispositional factors caused our behavior, however, we may be forced to reexamine and revise our attitudes (Nisbett and Valins, 1972). For example, if we have to admit that our poor grades were indeed caused by our lackadaisical attitude toward study, rather than by circumstances that were beyond our control, we may very well find ourselves jolted into making a change.

FORMING SOCIAL RELATIONSHIPS: HOW WE BECOME ATTRACTED TO ONE ANOTHER

Much of the chapter has stressed how other people influence our behavior—sometimes through persuasive communications, more often simply because of the example they set and our tendency to conform to the group in which we find ourselves. The question now arises: What determines the kinds of people who influence us most? In particular, in this diverse society, why do we become members of one group and not another?

It is of course the people around us—those with whom we have our closest and most frequent social relationships—who have the greatest impact on our attitudes and our behavior. Therefore, social psychology has extensively studied the forces that attract us to others and make us like them and associate with them (Kelley et al., 1983). The key finding has been aptly summarized in a single sentence: "We like those who reward us, and the more they reward us the better we like them" (Berscheid and Walster, 1974). But fully understanding that sentence requires an examination of what it is that we find rewarding about other people—and why.

Propinquity and Familiarity: "I Like You Because I Know You"

To a considerable extent, social relationships are dictated by sheer chance. The family you happen to be born into determines the culture and subculture into which you are socialized, which in turn helps shape your attitudes. The neighborhood you happen to grow up in provides the playmates, classmates, and teachers who influence your childhood. Even in later life, you do not have full freedom of choice. Going to college because it is close to your home or offers you a scholarship can place you in a group of students and instructors very different from those you might find on another campus. Taking a job puts you into a group of co-workers who already happen to be there. Once you have your own home, the people next door move in or out without your permission.

These children are growing up with the opportunity to become familiar with others from different ethnic and racial groups.

Some social psychologists have concluded that *propinquity*—or nearness—is the most powerful factor of all determining our associates. Obviously we cannot become part of a group whose members we never even see. Moreover it has been found that just being around other people—knowing them and getting used to them—inclines us to consider them attractive and likable. One experiment on the effect of such *familiarity* brought together pairs of subjects who did not know each other. They did not speak but merely sat across from each other in the laboratory. Some pairs saw each other on only a few occasions, others as many as a dozen times. Afterward they were asked how much they liked each other. The more often they had been together—even in this casual fashion—the greater was the mutual attraction (Freedman, Carlsmith, and Sears, 1970). Similar results have been obtained merely by exposing subjects to a photograph of another person, as is shown in Figure 16-9. Other studies show that people are likely to be most friendly with those who are familiar because they live next door in a college dormitory, an apartment building, or a row of houses (Festinger, Schachter, and Back, 1950). On some occasions even the mere prospect of becoming familiar seems to make other people more attractive.

Similarity: "I Like You Because We Seem So Alike"

Even among the people with whom you have frequent contacts, you manage to pick and choose. You spend a great deal of your time with companions of your own selection and deliberately create your closest friendships. You join groups you like and stay away from groups you find uncongenial.

One important factor in this picking and choosing is *similarity*. Given the opportunity, and all other things being equal, we tend to be attracted to people who are very much like us—or at least whom we perceive to be similar. The best demonstration was an experiment performed by a psychologist who arranged to operate a men's dormitory at a large university. The assignment of roommates was based on questionnaires and interviews about attitudes, interests, and tastes. Some roommates were put together because their replies showed them to be very similar, others because they were sharply different in many respects. As the term went on, it developed that roommates who were much alike usually got along well and became good friends. Those who were dissimilar were less likely to develop a very close relationship (Newcomb, 1961).

Figure 16-9 Even a photograph looks better the more familiar it becomes

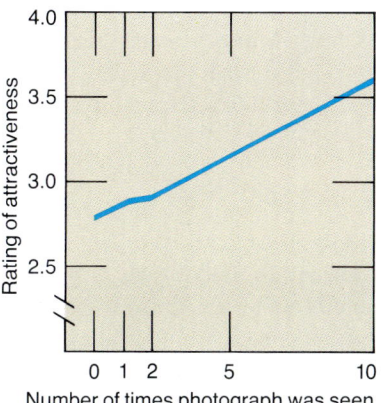

The ratings of attractiveness were made by subjects asked to look at the photograph of another person. The lowest ratings were made by subjects who had never seen the photo before, the highest by subjects who had seen it most often (Zajonc, 1968).

What similarities may have drawn these roommates together?

Indeed one reason propinquity and familiarity breed attraction is that most of the people we happen to know are usually similar to us to at least some extent. If nothing else, we have a mutual interest in the course that we and our college classmates are taking or in the job we share with co-workers. Usually we find ourselves thrown together with people of roughly the same age, education, and socioeconomic class. Often, therefore, we have many attitudes in common—and it has been found that the degree to which we find another person attractive shows a high correlation with the number of similar attitudes we share or think we share. Note the almost straight-line relationship shown in Figure 16-10.

Reciprocity: "I Like You Because You Like Me"

Many studies have shown that we tend to be attracted to people who seem to be attracted to us (Tagiuri, 1958) or who hold a high opinion of us (Worchel, 1961). We also tend to like people in whose company we have achieved satisfactions, as can be observed in the camaraderie that usually flourishes among members of a winning athletic team.

We seem to be especially attracted to people who at first do not seem to like us or hold us in high regard, then later change their mind (Aronson and Linder, 1965). Apparently there is a special reward—and thus a strong tendency toward attraction—in winning over

Figure 16-10 The more similar the attitudes, the greater the attraction

The graph shows the results of an experiment in which college students were asked to rate a stranger on a scale of attractiveness. Their only information about the stranger came from reading a set of replies supposedly given to a questionnaire about attitudes toward politics and other issues. When the experimenter rigged the stranger's answers to indicate attitudes different from those of the subjects, the attractiveness rating was low. But it went up steadily as the percentage of shared attitudes seemed to increase, forming an almost perfect correlation (Byrne, 1969).

The New York Mets winning the World Series in 1986. Experiences like this can breed an enduring camaraderie.

Forming Social Relationships: How We Become Attracted to One Another

a person who was originally critical. In general, we also have a tendency to be attracted to competent people—those who are good at what they do, whether it is singing, solving mathematical problems, playing basketball, or driving a car. We seem, however, to like very competent people to display a few obvious human frailties (Bales and Slater, 1955), so that they do not put us to shame.

Physical Attractiveness: "I Like You Because of Your Looks"

Most of us like to deny that physical appearance has anything to do with our feelings toward other people. Beauty, we have been told, is only skin deep. Some of the greatest men and women in history have been physically unprepossessing or downright ugly. It seems unfair to like or dislike someone just because of facial features resulting from an accident of heredity. For more than a half-century psychologists have been asking college students what they value most in a person of the opposite sex, and *physical attractiveness* has always wound up near the bottom of the list (Tesser and Brodie, 1971).

In actual fact, however, physical attractiveness is more influential than most people care to admit. We tend to be "turned off" by people whose appearance—especially the face—we find unattractive (Mueser et al., 1984). Even children judge one another on the basis of appearance. As early as the nursery school years, the attractive boys are the most popular, the unattractive boys the least popular (Dion and Berscheid, 1972). And later, as university students, attractive young men continue to enjoy more social interactions (Reis et al., 1982).

Why Looks Count: The Strength and Persistence of First Impressions

Why is physical attractiveness so influential? One reason seems to be that it is immediately and obviously apparent. When we meet someone for the first time, we can only guess whether this person is similar to us in attitudes, interests, and tastes. We have no clear

Was the outcome of the first televised presidential debates and ultimately the 1960 election influenced by the attractiveness of John Kennedy?

clues about competence. We can see at a glance, however, how well the person meets our own standards of attractiveness—and thus move toward acceptance or rejection.

First impressions, it has been found, have a strong and lasting influence. If we like people from the start, even merely because of their physical appearance, we tend to keep on liking them—no matter if some of their subsequent behavior is objectionable. If we dislike them at the start, we are likely to continue to dislike them—even if their subsequent behavior is above reproach.

In one recent study, subjects were 48 pairs of roommates at a university, all of whom were previously unacquainted. At the end of the year, some of the students decided not to live together any more, while others remained roommates. Whatever the decision, however, it turned out to have been made early in the relationship (Berg, 1984). Evidently the effect of bad first impressions outweighed familiarity.

Why are first impressions of people so strong and long lasting? Social psychologists say the reason is that we carry around a sort of working theory about people and their personalities. We have concluded that certain personality traits generally go together. If something convinces us at the start that a new acquaintance is "cold," for example, we automatically assume that this person is also likely to be irritable, humorless, unsociable, and self-centered. But if we perceive the new acquaintance as "warm," we expect this warmth to be accompanied by a good disposition, a sense of humor, friendliness, and generosity. This belief that personality traits come in clusters is called an *implicit personality theory.* All of us seem to hold such a theory, without being aware of it (Schneider, 1973).

Most of us believe, as part of our implicit personality theory, that physically attractive people also have many other attractive qualities. In one study in which subjects were asked to judge the personality characteristics of people shown in photographs, the subjects read all kinds of virtues into photos of attractive people. They judged the attractive people, as compared with the unattractive ones, to be considerably more interesting, strong, sensitive, sociable, poised, modest, outgoing, and sexually responsible. This was true of both male or female judges (Dion, Berscheid, and Walster, 1972).

Not all physically attractive people, of course, are admirable in every other respect—and the theory that desirable traits always come in clusters can lead us into error in other ways as well. For one thing, it inclines us to think of people as more consistent than they really are. But our theory has been developed through experience and is probably right a good deal more often than it is wrong. Right or wrong, it is one of the tools we use in conducting the social relationships that—as everything in this chapter has emphasized—are such an important part of our lives.

AGGRESSION AND ALTRUISM

Many questions about social behavior continue to puzzle scientists. One of them has to do with the basic quality of human nature. Are people essentially selfish and mean, as newspapers and television stories so often suggest? Or are they basically nurturant and loving, as the humanistic psychologists have maintained? Are humans naturally aggressive and cruel, as crime statistics, episodes of terrorism, and warfare might indicate? Or are they basically kind and helpful, as countless stories of self-sacrifice might seem to say?

Such questions may lend themselves to resolution through philosophical speculation rather than scientific evidence. But science is learning more all the time about how people sometimes treat each other with great kindness and generosity, and sometimes with thoughtless disregard for the other person's well-being and even survival.

Is Aggression Bred into Our Genes—or Learned?

Some scientists, especially biologists, have concluded that *aggression* is part of our inheritance—indeed, as one of them describes it, "an essential part of the life-preserving organization of instincts" (Lorenz, 1966). They point out that humans are just another form of animal life, and the "law of the jungle" dictates that animals must often kill to survive.

But many psychologists—perhaps a majority—believe otherwise. They have concluded that human aggression, though it may have some basis in biological inheritance, is largely the result of learning and can be controlled. Many experimental findings point in this direction. You may recall the photographs on page 183 showing how children tend to imitate an adult who attacks a life-size doll—an indication that learning through observation can produce aggressive behavior. Similarly, it has been found that adults tend to behave more aggressively after watching a film showing acts of aggression (Hartmann, 1969)—or even after watching a football game with its violent bodily contact (Goldstein and Arms, 1971).

It has also been found that many aggressive people come from aggressive families and were punished severely for childhood misconduct. They may be imitating the behavior of their parents, even though it was once painful to them. Others seem somehow to have decided, from experience, that aggression serves in some way to bring social rewards. Having used it successfully on one occasion, they may adopt it as a way of life.

There seems to be no way, at this stage of psychology's development, to say for sure whether violence is learned or is programed by heredity—or both. Whatever its origin, many scientists agree that it once had undoubted value in helping the human race survive but has become obsolete and counterproductive in our present civilization.

Is such behavior due more to nature or to nurture?

The Nature of Caring: Studies of Altruism

Social scientists use the word *altruism* to describe behavior that is kind, generous, and helpful to others. You are not very often likely to read about cases of altruism in the newspapers, but they take place with great frequency. People go to considerable trouble to help a sick neighbor, take in a family left homeless by a fire, and serve as volunteer firemen and hospital attendants. The amount of money donated each year to charities is staggering.

As in the case of aggression, some scientists see in the behavior of animals indications of a hereditary basis for altruism. Chimpanzees, for example, have been observed to share their food with another hungry chimpanzee in an adjoining cage—though they do so somewhat grudgingly (Nissen and Crawford, 1936). Many other animal studies have also produced evidence of an altruistic concern for others (Hebb and Thompson, 1968).

Some scientists maintain that altruism is an innate trait that has been passed along through the process of evolution. They point out that humans have always had a better chance of survival when living with other people than when trying to make it alone. So it seems likely that those who were willing to cooperate with others had a better chance of surviving and passing along their characteristics to future generations (Campbell, 1965). Again, as in the case of aggression, it is impossible either to prove or disprove the theory. The belief that altruism is an innate trait is somewhat strengthened by recent studies showing that many children show strong tendencies to perform altruistic acts as early as in the second year of life. Researchers have observed even 18-month-olds giving up food when someone around them is hungry; trying to come to the rescue of victims; consoling adults in distress; and expressing genuine anguish over another child's sorrow (Zahn-Waxler, Radke-Yarrow, and King, 1983).

The instinct for caring flourishes earlier in life than many have thought.

Other psychologists believe the explanation lies not in heredity but in learning. They point out that there are wide individual differences in tendencies toward altruism. Studies have shown that the people most likely to be altruistic are those who have somehow come to feel a personal responsibility for others (Schwartz, 1970) and have learned to *empathize* (Aronfreed, 1970)—that is, to feel the joys and pains of other people as if these emotions were their own. Having altruistic parents to imitate and identify with also plays a part. One study of boys who were regarded as generous found that they usually had fathers whom they perceived to be warm and helpful (Rutherford and Mussen, 1968). Another study, looking into the backgrounds of a group devoted to promoting civil rights, found that the members were characterized by a close relationship with an altruistic parent—at least one and sometimes both (Rosenhan, 1970). Whether altruism is or is not a basic and innate human trait, there seems to be no doubt that it can at least be encouraged or discouraged by learning and social influences (Mussen and Eisenberg-Berg, 1977).

Bystander Apathy: Neglecting the Needs of Others

At about 9:00 P.M. on the night of March 21, 1983, a young woman walked into a bar in New Bedford, Massachusetts. When she tried to leave, a group of men seized her, dragged her across the barroom floor, and hoisted her onto a pool table. Holding her down, they pulled off her jeans, stripped her, and forced her to perform oral sex. The victim screamed for help, but no one made a move to rescue her. In the words of the police, "She asked for help, she cried for help, she begged for help—but no one helped her."

Closely related to altruism and aggression is a question stimulated by such episodes. Why do people sometimes help others who are in trouble but sometimes completely ignore them, thus showing a remarkable degree of what social psychologists term *bystander apathy*?

Experiments show a close relationship between the number of people who witness an incident—such as a murder, a theft, or a fire—and the likelihood that anyone will offer assistance. The woman in the bar may have been a victim of the fact that, contrary to popular belief, there is no safety in numbers. Repeated experiments show that a person who needs assistance is more likely to receive it if there is only one person around than if there are many (Latané and Nida, 1981). Several reasons have been suggested. First, the presence of others may relieve any single member of the group from feelings of personal responsibility. Second, apparent indifference on the part of other spectators may cause the individual bystander to downgrade the seriousness of the situation. In some cases, bystander apathy may even represent a type of conformity. If a group of people seems to be ignoring the plight of a person in need, individual members may feel strong pressure to behave as the group is behaving.

Studies also show that people who need help are more likely to receive it in a small town than in a big city (Amato, 1981). As Figure 16-11 portrays, the likelihood of getting such help appears to be twice as good in a small town than in a large metropolis. In a large city, people can walk for blocks without meeting anyone they know. They are mere faces in the crowd. They do not have the intimate contact with friends and neighbors that might lead to offers of help.

Any increase in the degree of intimacy serves to reduce bystander apathy. Indeed the size of the group makes little difference when its members know each other and have a sense of group cohesiveness (Rutkowski, Gruder, and Romer, 1983). The same is true even when the group members simply anticipate having to interact with each other in the future (Gottlieb and Carver, 1980). This anticipation of face-to-face interaction with other bystanders may increase the possibility of being blamed in the future for inaction. Or, perhaps the

Figure 16-11 Helping behavior in communities of different size

This graph line shows the percentage of passersby who offered to help the investigator after he dropped in the street, pretending to be in pain. His leg was bandaged and smeared with realistic-looking "blood." Note that the percentage of helpers drops sharply as the community size increases beyond 20,000. The same pattern emerged when the investigator asked for other kinds of help—for example, a charitable donation, or finding directions when "lost" (Amato, 1983).

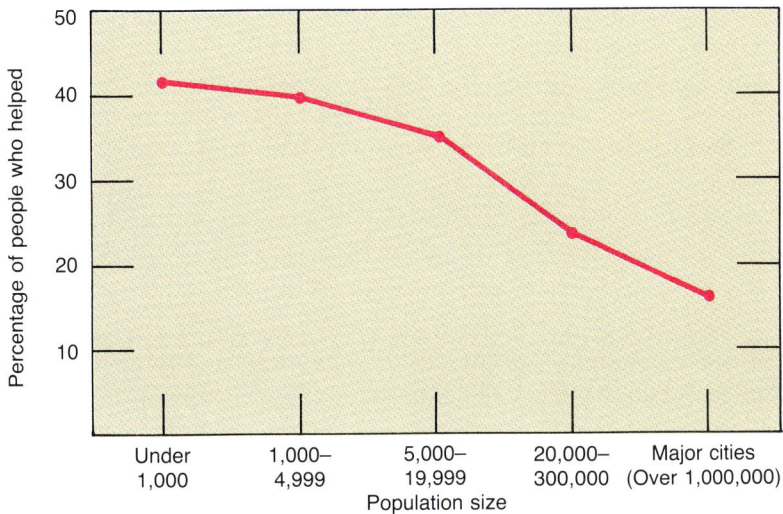

expectation of future interaction induces some degree of group cohesiveness in the group members, thus enhancing their compliance with social norms.

Even physical closeness reduces the tendency toward bystander apathy. Thus a person who collapses in the close confines of a subway car is much more likely to receive help than someone who collapses in the open spaces of a city street. This was demonstrated by investigators who fell to the floor of a New York subway car, as if suddenly stricken. When they were carrying a cane, as if they had a physical ailment, someone tried to help them in 95 percent of the cases. Even if they smelled of alcohol and carried a whisky bottle in a paper bag, indicating that they might merely have been drunk, someone went to their assistance half the time (Piliavin, Rodin, and Piliavin, 1969). The results were doubtless due to the fact that the bystanders were in a face-to-face situation with the victims and in a confined space where they could not just ignore the incident and walk right past.

SUMMARY

Learning society's ways—and conforming to them

1. Social psychology is the study of how a "person's thoughts, feelings, and actions are affected by others"—or, in broader terms, the study of how people influence and are influenced by other people.

2. *Socialization* is the process through which children are integrated into the *society* through exposure to the actions and opinions of other members of the society.

3. Children are socialized into the society's *culture*, or way of life—including its language, beliefs, political structure, rules, patterns of behavior, and the physical objects it produces and uses as part of its lifestyle.

4. A complex society like ours also has many *subcultures*, or ways of life dictated by different national and ethnic backgrounds, religions, occupations, and social classes.

5. Most people follow the customs they have learned and behave as they believe they are expected to behave. They display strong tendencies toward (a) *obedience*, or submission to authority, and (b) *conformity*, or the yielding by individuals to pressures from the group in which they find themselves.

6. One reason for conformity is that we depend on the people around us for many of our psychological satisfactions. It is pleasant to win approval as an accepted member of the group—and highly unpleasant to be rejected.

7. Another reason for conformity is the tendency we have as members of a group to accede to the requests or demands of those we regard as being in control.

8. Still another reason for conformity is that we need guidance from other people in developing an accurate view of our physical and social environment.

9. The need for guidance is the basis for the *theory of social comparison*, which holds that to live successfully we must evaluate our own conduct, abilities, and opinions—and often can do so only by comparing ourselves with other people.

How we acquire—and sometimes change—our attitudes toward life

10. *Attitudes* are strong, deeply ingrained opinions and feelings that we think of as principles that shape our conduct. We are very much "for" things toward which we have a positive attitude, and very much "against" things toward which we have a negative attitude.

11. Attitudes, though powerful, are not necessarily consistent or based on evidence. Two kinds of attitudes that often fly in the face of fact are (a) *prejudices* (for example, against other ethnic groups or religions) and (b) *stereotypes*, which assume that all members of a certain group behave in the same manner.

12. Though attitudes tend to persist, they sometimes change. One explanation for change is the *theory of cognitive dissonance*, which maintains that we have a strong desire to preserve agreement and harmony among our beliefs, feelings, and behavior. When there is a conflict—caused by factual information, the arousal of emotions, or the fact that circumstances push us into different behavior—we experience cognitive dissonance and may relieve it by changing our attitude.

13. Attempts by other people to change our attitudes—by transmitting information or making emotional appeals—are called *persuasive communications*.

14. The effectiveness of persuasive communications is affected by *selective exposure*—the fact that most such communications reach only people who are already persuaded. It also depends on (a) the credibility of the source, (b) the nature of the communication, and (c) the audience or listener. Listeners who are low in self-esteem or anxious about social acceptance are more easily persuaded.

Trying to figure out why people behave as they do: attribution theories

15. All of us spend considerable time seeking the reasons other people acted as they did. Why and how we make the search is the subject of various *attribution theories*.

16. Attribution theories all assume that we want to know the reasons behind other people's behavior because we want our social interactions to have the most favorable possible outcome; therefore we seek clues to where we stand, what is likely to happen next, and how best to handle the situation.

17. We have a strong tendency to attribute other people's behavior to *dispositional factors* rather than to *situational factors* that may provide a far better explanation. Because this tendency is so common—and ignores social psychology's finding that people's behavior is not necessarily consistent and often depends on circumstances—it is called *attribution error*.

18. One situational factor we often ignore is the influence of our own behavior on the behavior of others. So strong is this influence that often, because we expect another person to act in a certain way (for example, be friendly or unfriendly), we push the person into exactly the kind of behavior we expected—thus turning our expectations into a *self-fulfilling prophecy*.

19. In seeking the reasons for our own behavior—the subject of *self-perception theory*—we tend to look for situational rather than dispositional factors. When we are forced to accept a dispositional cause, we may change our attitudes accordingly.

Forming social relationsips: how we become attracted to one another

20. The forces that attract us to other people—and make us like them and associate with them—are important in social psychology because it is our closest associates who have the greatest effect on our attitudes and behavior. It is a general principle that "we like those who reward us, and the more they reward us the better we like them."

21. The most powerful factor may be *propinquity*, or nearness, which occurs by chance because of the family into which we are born, neighborhood, school companions, and co-workers. Propinquity is influential because of the effect of *familiarity*—for, in general, the better we know people the better we like them.

22. We are also attracted to people because of (a) *similarity*, especially in attitudes; (b) an indication that they like us; (c) their competence; and (d) *physical attractiveness*.

23. *First impressions* of other people have a strong and lasting effect. The reason is that we seem to hold an *implicit personality theory* that personality traits come in clusters—for example, that physically attractive people are also likely to be warm, sociable, poised, and interesting.

Aggression and altruism

24. The question of whether human beings have an inborn tendency to display *aggression*—or whether aggression is the result of learning—is one of the unresolved issues in psychology.

25. The people most likely to display *altruism* (a tendency to be kind, generous, and helpful to others) are those who feel a personal responsibility for others and have learned to *empathize* (feel the joys and pains of others as if these emotions were their own).

26. *Bystander apathy* is a failure to assist another person who appears in need of help. Bystander apathy tends to be greatest when there are large numbers of other people around. It is encouraged by the anonymity, lack of intimacy, and the rush of big-city life.

IMPORTANT TERMS

aggression
altruism
attitude
attribution error
attribution theory
bystander apathy
cognitive dissonance
conformity
credibility of the source
culture
dispositional factors
empathy
familiarity
first impressions
implicit personality theory
obedience

persuasive communications
physical attractiveness
prejudice
propinquity
selective exposure
self-fulfilling prophecy
self-perception theory
similarity
situational factors
social comparison theory
socialization
society
source of the communication
stereotype
subculture

RECOMMENDED READINGS

Bandura, A. *Social learning theory.* Englewood Cliffs, N.J.: Prentice-Hall, 1976.

Bem, D. J. *Beliefs, attitudes, and human affairs.* Belmont, Calif.: Brooks/Cole, 1970.

Berscheid, E., and Walster, E. C. *Interpersonal attraction*, 2d ed. Reading, Mass.: Addison-Wesley, 1978.

Crano, W. D., and Mess, L. A. *Social psychology: principles and themes of interpersonal behavior.* Homewood, Ill.: Dorsey Press, 1982.

Eiser, R. *Social psychology: attitudes, cognition, and social behavior.* New York: Cambridge University Press, 1986.

Gergen, K. J., and Gergen, M. M. *Social psychology.* New York: Harcourt Brace Jovanovich, 1981.

Hewitt, J. P. *Self and society: a symbolic interactionist social psychology*, 3rd ed. Boston: Allyn and Bacon, 1984.

Milgram, S. *Obedience to authority.* New York: Harper & Row, 1974.

Penrod, S. *Social psychology.* Englewood Cliffs, N.J.: Prentice-Hall, 1983.

APPENDIX A:
HOW TO STUDY THIS BOOK (AND OTHERS)

THE SQ3R SYSTEM OF STUDY: A
METHOD THAT WORKS   606

1. Survey
2. Question
3. Read
4. Recite
5. Review

SUMMARY   610

or students, some of psychology's most useful findings have been in the field of learning, particularly on the most effective ways to study and remember what is in a textbook. Learning and memory are such important aspects of information processing that they require two chapters of full discussion. But many of the practical implications can be summarized for your guidance in using this book to the best possible advantage.

To begin, let us say that you have six hours to devote to learning a chapter and that reading through the chapter carefully takes two hours. What should you do? Read the chapter three times?

To spend the six hours reading sounds logical, but actually it is the worst possible way to approach the task. You will learn and remember much better if you cut down the amount of reading and spend the rest of the time reciting what you have learned. Indeed you might find it best to spend *most* of your time in recitation. This fact was established many years ago in the experiment that was illustrated in part in Figure 1-8 on page 21. The full results are illustrated here in Figure A-1. They demonstrate clearly that in at least some forms of learning the most efficient method is to spend as much as 80 percent of study time in recitation.

There are many reasons for the value of recitation. For one thing it helps motivate you—for just knowing that you will try to recite what you read stimulates the desire to learn what is on the printed page. It also provides immediate feedback, telling you how much you remember. And it is good practice in recall, the ability to bring out the knowledge you have stored in memory when you need it.

THE SQ3R SYSTEM OF STUDY: A METHOD THAT WORKS

Recitation is a key point in a well-known method of studying that has produced excellent results and improved grades for students who have applied it. This is the SQ3R system (Robinson, 1962), an abbreviation for the five steps it suggests: survey, question, read, recite, and review. Since there are many individual differences in the ways students find it most convenient and effective to approach a textbook, you may want to experiment with them and adapt them to your own particular style. But you will almost surely find it useful to follow them in one way or another, going about them in your own way and devoting as much time to each of them as you prefer.

The steps as applied to this book, which is designed for maximum convenience in using SQ3R, are described in the following pages.* The system can also be used, with any necessary variations, in studying most other textbooks—although the task, as you will see, is more difficult with books that lack chapter outlines and do not organize the materials into sections and subsections identified by distinctive and meaningful headings.

1. Survey

Before starting to read a chapter, you should have a general notion of what it contains and the key points it makes. The survey need not take long. Note the title (for Chapter 1, *The Aims and Methods of Psychology*), which is in itself a very brief description of what is to come. Then look at the outline that precedes each chapter (as on page 3 for Chapter 1). The section headings, found there in colored type, list the approximately five main points

---

*If you have the Study Guide that accompanies the book, you will find instructions there for using it as a further help in the SQ3R steps.

Figure A-1 **Recitation: it beats reading hands down**

The bars show the results of an experiment in which students of various ages studied nonsense syllables for the same amount of time but in different ways. Some subjects spent the entire time reading the syllables, while others spent 20 to 80 percent of the time reciting. Tests made immediately afterward and again 4 hours later showed that their ability to remember the syllables went up in direct proportion to how much time they had spent in recitation (Gates, 1917).

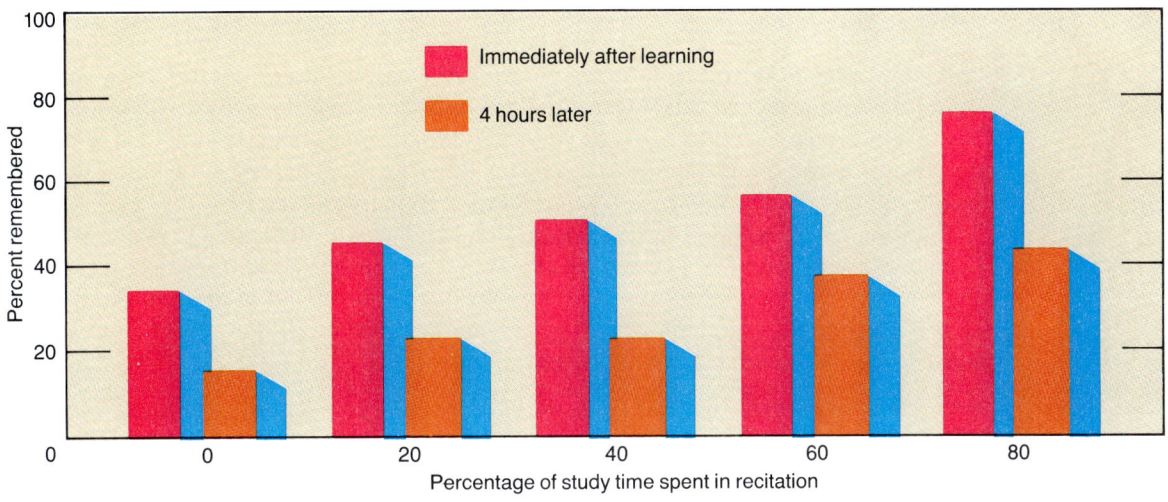

covered in each chapter. (In Chapter 1, the first two are *Psychology's Interests* and *How Psychologists Study Human Behavior.*)

This may be enough of a survey, for it will tell you that you can expect to be studying (1) psychology's goals and interests; (2) the methods it uses to study behavior, with special emphasis on (3) the experiments psychologists perform; (4) the history, present status, and future prospects of the science; and (5) the part played in behavior by heredity and environment. Or you may want to take a little more time and thumb through the chapter, noting how much space is devoted to each of the main sections, some of the secondary headings found under each, and the illustrations (which help illuminate some of the points). You might also want to look at the list of important terms at the end of the chapter. You will not yet know the meaning of many of these terms, but just being aware of them is another clue to what to expect. The whole purpose of the survey is to provide a framework that will help you organize the chapter's facts and ideas as you encounter them.

Make a similar survey at the start of each major section of the chapter, which you will find identified by a heading in this type style:

PSYCHOLOGY'S GOALS AND INTERESTS (p. 5)

HOW PSYCHOLOGISTS STUDY HUMAN BEHAVIOR (p. 11)

Thumb through the section and examine the words printed in italics for emphasis and the points that are made in the illustrations. Note especially the secondary headings, marking subsections of the discussion, which are in this type style:

Psychology Defined (p. 6)

The Objectives of Psychology (p. 7)

In other words, take a few moments to get a general idea of what this particular section of the book is going to tell you.

2. Question

This step applies to the secondary headings in the book. Each time you come to a new subsection and before you start reading it, turn its heading into a question that will pique your curiosity and orient you toward finding the answer. For the secondary heading *The Objectives of Psychology* you might ask yourself: "What is this science trying to accomplish, and why?" Or you can put the question in any other way that makes you wonder why the book is going to discuss the matter and eager to learn more about it.

The wording is not important, and you should not spend much time or effort. The idea is just to ask yourself what you will be looking for as you start to read, which in turn will help you find the gist of the subsection and organize your thoughts about it. Stopping to ask the question also reminds you to pay attention to the headings—which are valuable guides to the discussion but are ignored by many readers.

3. Read

How much to read in one chunk is largely a matter of individual preference. Some students find it best to study the entire chapter as a whole, a technique they find helpful in understanding the pattern of the materials and the way the individual topics and facts relate to one another. Some study one major section at a time (usually about five to ten pages), others only a subsection (seldom more than a single page). You may want to experiment with what works best for you—and vary the size of the chunk for various parts of the book. Some parts are more or less familiar and can be taken in fairly easily. In others new ideas may tend to crowd together and get confusing if taken in too large a dose.

Whatever you decide, read with the idea that you will make an active search for the answer to the question you have asked for each secondary heading, and that you want to comprehend and remember it. As the author of the SQ3R system has pointed out, "Reading textbooks is work"—and readers must know what they are looking for, find it, and then organize their thoughts about it.

4. Recite

You can recite what you have read by talking, either out loud or in your mind—which is what the term means to most people. But a much better way is to jot down notes summarizing what you have read. The notes should be brief—just a single word or a very few at most—and in your own language. They should be written *after* you have finished reading, not while you are in the process. (Many students make the mistake of taking notes as they go along, often in the same words used in the book and without really comprehending their meaning.)

Regardless of the size of chunk you prefer to handle, the best method is to stop at the end of each subsection, look away from the book, and try to recite the gist of what you have just read—the answer to the question you asked at the beginning and any other important information you have learned. Then jot down a brief note that summarizes the subsection. For the subsection headed *The Objectives of Psychology*, your notes might be:

A. Objectives
   1. understand behavior
   2. predict   ″
   3. question of control?

In taking notes for the subsections, you will find one small complication. Each chapter and each major section begin with some preliminary paragraphs before you come to the heading that marks the first of the subsections. Sometimes these paragraphs are merely a general introduction to what will follow. At other times—and Chapter 1 is an example—they serve not only to set the stage but also to present some important information. When this occurs, you can regard the paragraphs as a sort of subsection for recital and note-taking purposes. For these paragraphs in Chapter 1, your notes might be:

A. Psychology
   1. studies human behavior
   2. every person different
   3. why the differences?

A possible alternative to taking notes is to go back and underline the key words and key points in the subsection. This works for some students but is generally less helpful, in part because it does not force you to put the point into your own words. Moreover it may lead to reading just for the sake of finding important sentences and marking them without any real attention to the meaning. Some students fall into the mistake of making so many underlines, before they finish the subsection, of words and sentences that seem important at the time but later prove otherwise, that the page becomes a jumble of repetitions and sometimes even contradictions. You can, of course, use both techniques—first make notes, then underline the words in the book that relate to your notes, as well as details that you want to remember.

5. Review

When you get to the end of a major section of the book—for example when the heading *How Psychologists Study Human Behavior* signals the start of a new major section on page 11—look over the notes you have jotted down on the subsections and find how the various points are organized and related to one another. Or, if you have used underlines instead of notes, go back through the section and examine the points you have marked. Then, since this step is closely related to the previous one, cover up your notes or look away from the book and recite the points. If you have trouble recalling any of them, or what any of them means, take another look at your notes or the book and try again.

Turn also to the summary at the end of the chapter, where the most important points are presented briefly. For convenience in applying the SQ3R system, the summary is divided into the major sections of the chapter, with each identified by the same heading used in the text. Read the summary for the section you have been studying and make sure you are aware of all the ideas it contains, understand them, and can explain them. If not, go back to the chapter and do some more reading of what you have missed. Your review will probably take no more than five minutes in all—but it will be of tremendous value in making sure you have grasped all the points made in the section and fixing them in your memory.

When you have completed the chapter and your review of the final major section, make another review of the chapter as a whole. Here the list of important ideas will help. Go through the list and make sure you know and can explain all the terms it contains. If you can—and can also recall the points made in the summary—you have such a deep understanding of the overall meaning of the chapter that many of its details (like the kind of work done by the early psychologists Wundt, Galton, and James) should stay with you almost automatically.

SUMMARY

The SQ3R system of study: a method that works

1. *Recitation* is of great value in studying. It is better to spend as much as 80 percent of study time in an active attempt to recite than to devote the entire time to reading and rereading.

2. A study method that emphasizes recitation—and has proved effective—is the *SQ3R System*.

3. The first step in SQ3R is to *survey* the entire chapter to get a general idea of what it contains—and to do the same for each major section as you come to it.

4. The second step, performed as you start each subsection, is to turn the heading into a *question* that will pique your curiosity and orient you toward finding the answer.

5. Next *read* as big a chunk of the chapter as you find best suited to your own individual preferences—with the idea of making an active search for the answer to the question or questions you have asked, comprehending the answer, and remembering it.

6. Next, stop at the end of each subsection to *recite* the gist of what you have just read. The best method is to jot down notes—in your own words and as brief as possible—that summarize the subsection.

7. When you come to the end of a major section, *review* what is in it. Look over the notes you have taken on the subsections and find how the various points are organized and related to one another. Then cover up your notes and recite the points. Examine the chapter summary for that section to make sure you know all the key ideas, understand them, and can explain them. If not, go back to the chapter to study what you have missed.

8. After you have completed the five steps for each major section, make another review of the chapter as a whole. The summary will again help, as will the list of important terms you should know and be able to explain.

APPENDIX B: STATISTICAL METHODS

PROBABILITY AND NORMAL DISTRIBUTION 612

Dreams and prophecies: why they often come true
What happens when you toss coins: a normal curve of distribution

DESCRIPTIVE STATISTICS 614

Number in group
The statistical average (or mean)
Variability and standard deviation
Percentiles

INFERENTIAL STATISTICS: THE SCIENCE OF MAKING GENERALIZATIONS 618

Population and sample
Choosing valid control groups
Comparing two groups
Standard error of the mean
Probability and significance

THE TECHNIQUE AND SIGNIFICANCE OF CORRELATION 622

Scatter plots
Correlation coefficients
Correlation and prediction
Correlation, cause, and effect

THE MATHETICAL COMPUTATIONS 624

The mean
The standard deviation
The standard error of the mean
Differences between groups
Correlation coefficients
Contingency

SUMMARY 631

The use of statistics as a tool in psychology began with Sir Francis Galton, an Englishman who did his most important work in the 1880s. Sir Francis was interested in individual differences—how people vary in height, weight, and such characteristics as color vision, sense of smell, hearing, and ability to judge weights. He was also interested in the workings of heredity. One of the questions that fascinated him was whether taller-than-average people tend to have taller-than-average children. Another was whether successful people tend to have successful children.

Since Galton's time, many investigators have pursued similar questions, such as: Do parents of above-average intelligence tend to have children of above-average intelligence? Do strict parents tend to produce children who are more or less aggressive than the children of lenient parents? Do people of high intelligence tend to be more or less neurotic than people of low intelligence?

To answer these questions, as Galton discovered, one must first make some accurate measurements. Galton himself devised a number of tests for such abilities as vision and hearing. Newer generations of psychologists have tried to perfect tests for intelligence and personality traits. But the results of the tests are meaningless unless they can be analyzed and compared in accordance with sound statistical practices.

Psychological statistics is the application of mathematical principles to the interpretation of the results obtained in psychological studies. It has been aptly called a "way of thinking" (Hebb, 1958)—a problem-solving tool that enables us to summarize our knowledge of psychological events and make legitimate inferences from what we discover.

PROBABILITY AND NORMAL DISTRIBUTION

As an example of how we can profit from thinking in terms of statistical methods, suppose someone shows you two possible bridge hands. One is the bridge player's dream—13 spades. The other is a run-of-the-mill hand containing one ace, a few face cards, and many cards of no special value. The person who has put the hands together asks: "If you play bridge tonight, which of these hands are you less likely to pick up?"

Your first impulse would surely be to say, "The 13 spades." When a bridge player gets such a hand, the newspapers report it as a great rarity. The player is likely to talk about it forever afterward. And, in all truth, a hand of 13 spades is extremely rare. It occurs, as a statistician can quickly calculate, on an average of only once in about 159 billion deals.

But the other hand, whatever it is, is equally rare. The rules of statistical probability say that the chance of getting any particular combination of thirteen cards is only one in about 159 billion deals. The reason a hand of 13 spades seems rarer than any other is that bridge players pay attention to it, while lumping all their mediocre hands together as if they were one and the same.

Think about the hand of 13 spades in another way. Since it occurs only once in 159 billion deals, is it not a miracle that it should ever occur at all? No, it is not. It has been estimated that there are about 25 million bridge players in the United States. If each of them deals 20 times a week, that makes 26 billion deals a year. The statistical method tells us that we should expect a hand of 113 spades to be dealt on the average of about once every six years.

Dreams and Prophecies: Why They Often Come True

The fact that we can expect a hand of 13 spades to occur with some regularity explains some events in life that seem baffling to people who do not understand statistics. For example, every once in a while the newspapers report that someone shooting dice in Las Vegas has made 28 passes (or winning throws) in a row. This seems almost impossible, and in fact the mathematical odds are more than 268,000,000 to 1 that it will not happen to anyone who picks up the dice. These are very high odds indeed. Yet, considering the large number of people who step up to all the dice tables in Las Vegas, it is very likely that sooner or later someone will throw the 28 passes.

The laws of probability also explain many of the coincidences that seem—to people unfamiliar with the laws—to represent the working of supernatural powers. A woman in Illinois dreams that her brother in California has died and the next morning gets a telephone call that he was killed in an accident. This may sound like an incredible case of mental telepathy, but the laws of probability offer a much simpler explanation. Most people dream frequently. Dreams of death are by no means rare. In the course of a year millions of people dream of the death of someone in the family. Sooner or later, one of the dreams is almost sure to coincide with an actual death.

Astrologers and other seers also profit from the rules of probability. If an astrologer keeps predicting that a catastrophe will occur, the forecast is bound to be right sooner or later, because the world is almost sure to have some kind of tragedy, from airplane accident to tornado, in any given period. And a prophet who makes a reputation by predicting the death of a world leader knows that there are many world leaders and that many of them are so advanced in age that their death would not be unusual.

In a world as big as ours, all kinds of coincidences are likely to occur. The rules of statistics say that we should expect and not be surprised by them. Statistical analysis lets us view these coincidences for what they are and helps us recognize that they have no real significance.

What Happens When You Toss Coins: A Normal Curve of Distribution

One of the principles of probability, as Galton was the first to notice, has to do with the manner in which many things, including psychological traits, are distributed in the normal course of natural events. The principle can best be demonstrated by a simple experiment. Drop 10 coins into a cup, shake them, throw them on a table, and count the number of heads. Do this a number of times, say 100. Your tally will almost surely turn out to be very much like the one shown in Figure B-1.

What you have come up with is a simple illustration of normal distribution. When you toss 10 coins 100 times—a total of 1,000 tosses—you can expect 500 heads to come up, an average of five heads per toss. As the tally shows, this number came up most frequently. The two numbers on either side, four and six, were close seconds. The numbers farther away from five were increasingly infrequent. Ten came up only once, and zero did not come up at all. (Over a long period, both 10 and zero would be expected to come up on an average of once in every 1,024 tosses.)

The tally shown in Figure B-1 can be converted into the bar graph shown in Figure B-2, which provides a more easily interpreted picture of what happened in the coin tossing. Note its shape—highest in the middle, then tapering off toward the extreme left and the extreme right. If a curve is drawn to connect the tops of the bars, we have a good example of the *normal curve of distribution*—which, as was explained in Chapter 1, is typical of the results generally found in all tests and measurements, of both physical and psychological traits. The curve for distribution of IQs, which was presented in Chapter 1, is repeated in Figure B-3. Note again that most people fall around the average of 100 and that only a few are found at the far extremes below 40 or above 160. The message of the curve is that in IQ (or height or weight or almost anything else) the people who are about average are in the majority—while some are as rare as those 28 passes in a dice game.

DESCRIPTIVE STATISTICS

As a quick and convenient method of summarizing the characteristics of any group under study—as well as the distribution of these characteristics—psychologists use a technique called *descriptive statistics*. For example, suppose we draw up a new intelligence test and administer it to 10,000 college students. We wind up with 10,000 raw scores. To pass along what we have learned about the test, however, we need not quote every one of the 10,000 scores. Through the use of descriptive statistics we can summarize and condense. With just a few well-chosen numbers, we can tell other people what they need to know in order to understand our results. Among the most commonly used forms of descriptive statistics are the following.

Number in Group

Number in group is simply the total number of subjects we have studied. It is important because the chances of obtaining accurate results are greater if we study a large group than if we study only a small group. If we test only three people on our new intelligence test, we may happen to select three geniuses or three morons. A large sample is likely to be more representative of the population as a whole.

The Statistical Average (or Mean)

Another useful piece of information is what in everyday language is called the *average*. For example, six students take an examination containing 100 true-false questions and get test scores of 70, 74, 74, 76, 80, and 82. The average score—or in technical language, the *mean*—is the sum of the scores divided by the number of subjects who took the test. In other

Figure B-1 A tally of coin tosses

Ten coins were shaken in a cup and tossed on a table 100 times. This is a tally of the number of heads that appeared on each toss.

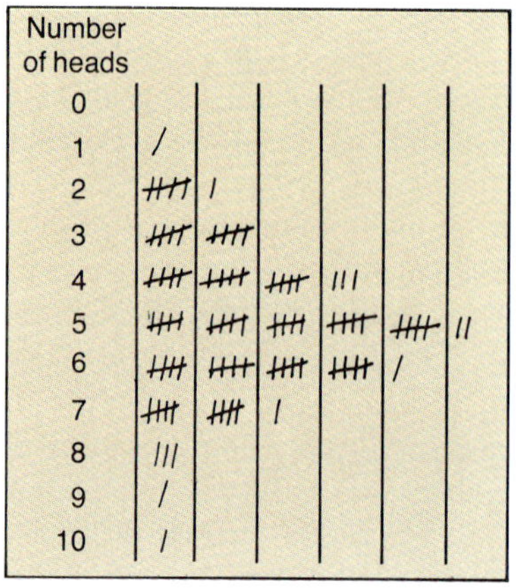

Number of heads	Tally
0	
1	/
2	⊬⊬⊬ /
3	⊬⊬⊬ ⊬⊬⊬
4	⊬⊬⊬ ⊬⊬⊬ ⊬⊬⊬ ///
5	⊬⊬⊬ ⊬⊬⊬ ⊬⊬⊬ ⊬⊬⊬ ⊬⊬⊬ //
6	⊬⊬⊬ ⊬⊬⊬ ⊬⊬⊬ ⊬⊬⊬ /
7	⊬⊬⊬ ⊬⊬⊬ /
8	///
9	/
10	/

Figure B-2 The tally in bar form

Here the tally of the coin-tossing experiment has been converted into a bar graph. Note the peak at the center and the rapid falling off toward each extreme.

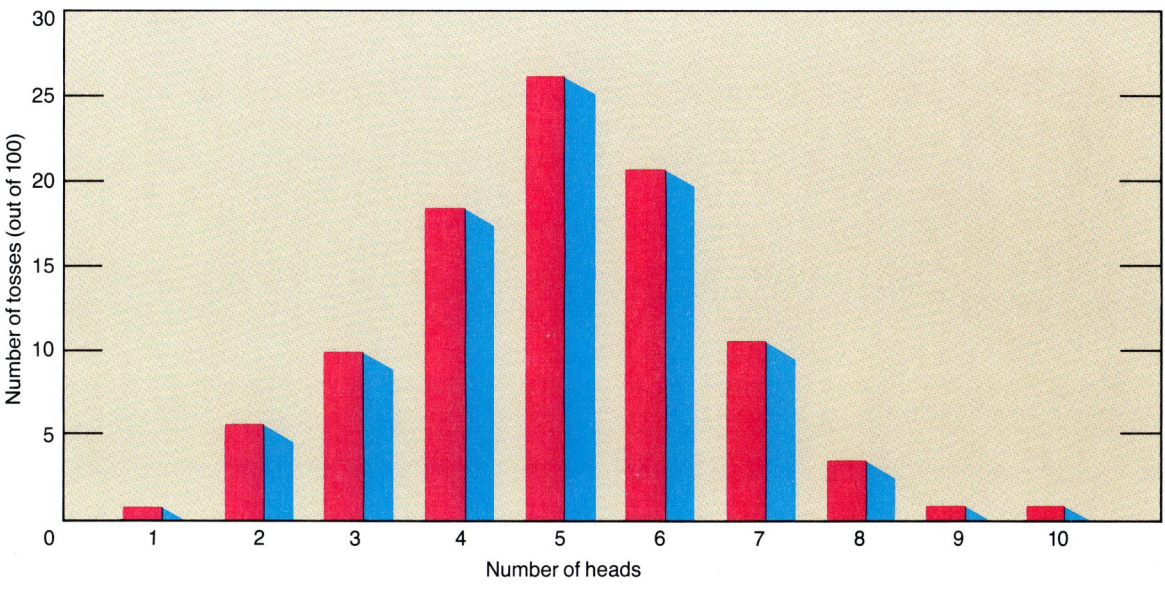

Figure B-3 The normal curve of IQ distribution

The graph was constructed from IQs found in large-scale testing (Terman and Merrill, 1937). Note that it looks very much like a line connecting the peaks of the bars in Figure B-2.

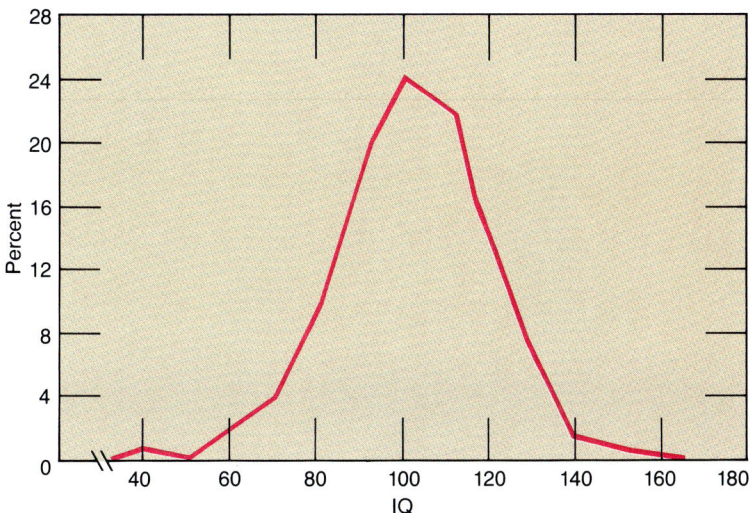

words, it is 456 divided by 6—or 76. Knowing that the mean is 76 tells us a great deal about the curve of distribution that could be drawn up from the scores. We know that the curve would center on a figure of about 76—and that the majority of scores would be somewhere in this neighborhood.

Another measure of central tendency, or the point around which the scores tend to cluster, is the *median*. This is the halfway point that separates the lower 50 percent of scores from the higher 50 percent. In the example just given, the median would be 75, because half the scores fall below 75 and the other half fall above. The median is an especially useful figure when the data include a small number of exceptionally low or exceptionally high measurements. Let us say, for example, that the six scores on the true-false examination were 70, 74, 74, 76, 80, and 100. The one student who scores 100 brings up the mean score quite sharply to 79. But note that 79 is hardly an "average" score, because only two of the six students scored that high. The median score, which remains at 75, is a better description of the data.

A third measure of central tendency is the *mode*—the measurement or score that applies to the greatest number of subjects. In the case of the true-false examination it would be 74, the only score made by as many as two of the students. The mode tells us where the highest point of the curve of distribution will be found. In a perfectly symmetrical normal

Figure B-4 Using the *SD* to analyze data

In a normal curve of distribution, the standard deviation indicates how many measurements of scores will be found at various distances from the mean. As shown here, 34.13 percent of all measurements lie between the mean and 1 SD above the mean. Measurements that are between 1 SD and 2 SDs above the mean make up 13.59 percent of the total. Measurements between 2 SDs and 3 SDs above the mean make up 2.14 percent. The same percentages are found below the mean. Note that the figures do not quite add up to 100 percent. This is because 0.14 percent of measurements are found more than 3 SDs above the mean and another 0.14 percent are found more than 3 SDs below the mean. These various percentages hold for any normal distribution, although the size of the SD differs from one curve to another.

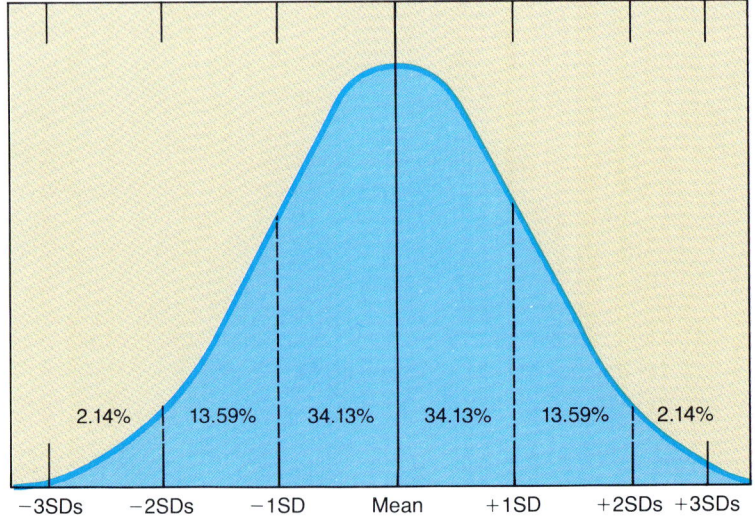

curve the mode, the median, and the mean are the same. If the distribution is not symmetrical, but on the contrary tails off more sharply on the below-average side than on the above-average side, or vice versa (as often happens), it is useful to know all three of these figures.

Variability and Standard Deviation

Even when the normal curve is perfectly symmetrical, it may take different forms. Sometimes it is high and narrow. At other times it is shorter and wider. This depends on the *variability* of the measurements, which means the extent to which they differ from one another.

A crude way to describe the variability of scores made on a psychological test is simply to give the *range* of the scores—the highest minus the lowest. A much more sensitive description is provided by what is called the *standard deviation*, often abbreviated to *SD*. The standard deviation, which is computed from the data by a formula that will be explained later, is an especially useful tool because it indicates the proportion of scores or measurements that will found under any part of the curve. As Figure B-4 shows, the rule is that 34.13 percent of all the scores lie between the mean and a point 1 *SD* above the mean; 13.59 percent lie between 1 *SD* and 2 *SD*s above the mean; and 2.14 percent lie between 2 *SD* and 3 *SD*s above the mean. Thus the *SD* gives a clear description of the variability of the measurements.

With intelligence quotients, for example, the mean is 100 and the *SD* is approximately 15. That is to say, an IQ one *SD* above the mean is 115. Armed with this knowledge alone, plus the general statistical rule illustrated in Figure B-4, we know that human intelligence tends to be distributed according to the figures in the following table:

IQ	PERCENTAGE OF PEOPLE
over 144	0.14
130–144	2.14
115–129	13.59
100–114	34.13
85–99	34.13
70–84	13.59
55–69	2.14
under 55	0.14

The *SD* is also used to compute what are called *standard scores*, or *z-scores*, which are often more meaningful than the raw scores made on a test. The z-score tells how many *SD*s a score is above or below the mean. It is obtained very simply by noting how many points a score is above or below the mean and then dividing by the *SD*. A z-score of 1 is one *SD* above the mean. A z-score of −1.5 is one-and-a-half *SD*s below the mean.

Percentiles

The meaning of *percentile* can best be explained by an example. A college man, a senior who wants to go on to graduate school, is asked to take the Graduate Record Examinations, which are nationally administered aptitude tests often used to screen applicants. He makes a score of 460 on the verbal test and 540 in mathematics. By themselves, these scores do not mean much either to him or to the faculty of the school he wants to attend. But records of other people's results on the test provide a means of comparing his scores with those of other college seniors. A score of 460 on the verbal test, the records show, lies on the 40th percentile for men. This means that 40 percent of all senior men who take the test make a lower score and 60 percent make higher score. The 540 score in math lies on the 66th percentile for men. In other words, 66 percent of senior men make a lower score, and only 34 percent make higher scores. These percentile figures show the student and the school he hopes to attend how his ability compares with that of other prospective graduate students: He is well above average in mathematical ability (only a third of male college seniors make better scores) but below average in verbal aptitude.

Percentile ratings can be made for any kind of measurement, whether or not it falls into a normal pattern of distribution. A percentile rating of 99—or, to be more exact, 99.99—means that no one had a higher score. A percentile rating of 1—or, to be more exact, 0.01—is the lowest in the group.

INFERENTIAL STATISTICS: THE SCIENCE OF MAKING GENERALIZATIONS

Descriptive statistics permits psychologists to summarize the findings of their studies and determine how one individual compares with the others. But psychologists need another tool to help them interpret and make generalizations from their studies. When psychologists study the behavior of a rat in a Skinner box, for example, they are not especially interested in how rapidly that particular animal demonstrates learning. Rather, their primary concern is to discover a general principle of behavior that says something about the learning processes of all rats—and, by implication, perhaps about the learning process in general. Psychologists studying the performance of a group of human subjects who memorize nonsense syllables—or who take part in an experiment on physical attractiveness—are not especially interested in those particular people. Their ultimate goal is to learn something about the behavior of people in general.

The mathematical tool they use is called *inferential statistics*—a set of techniques that enable them to make valid generalizations from their measurements of behavior.

Population and Sample

Inferential statistics is important because science is interested in what is called the *population*, or sometimes the *universe*—that is to say, all people or all events in a particular category. But we cannot study or measure the entire population. We cannot give an intelligence test, for example, to every human being on the face of the earth. Even if we could, we still would not have reached the entire population, because many people would have died and many new people would have been born while we were conducting our test. We must settle for a *sample*, a group of convenient size taken from the population as a whole.

The rules of inferential statistics hold that we can make valid generalizations only if the sample we use is *representative* of the population we want to study. If we are seeking some general conclusions about the intelligence of the American population, we cannot use a sample made up entirely of college students or a sample made up of high-school dropouts. If we want to learn about political attitudes, we cannot poll only Republicans or people who live in big cities or people who belong to one church or one social class. Our sample must be representative of all kinds of Americans.

One way to ensure a representative sample is to choose it entirely at *random*. If each member of the total population has an absolutely equal chance of being studied—and if our sample is large enough—then it is very likely that the sample will represent all segments of the population. For example, the experimenter who wants to study the emotional behavior of rats in a laboratory cannot just reach into a cage and pull out the first dozen animals that are closest at hand. The very fact that they are close at hand may mean that they are tamer than the others and have a different emotional temperament. To achieve a more valid sampling, the experimenter might take the first rat, reject the second, take the third, reject the fourth, and so on. An investigator interested in student attitudes toward marijuana on a particular campus might draw up an alphabetical list of all students, then interview every tenth person on the list.

In the Gallup election polls, the random sampling starts with a list of the approximately 200,000 election districts and precincts in the nation. From this master list, about 300 districts are chosen at random. Then a map of each of the 300 districts is drawn up. On the map, one house is chosen as a starting point—again at random. Beginning at that point and proceeding along a path drawn through the district, the pollsters collect interviews at each third residence or sometimes each fifth or twelfth residence, depending on the size of the sample they want (Gallup, 1972).

Choosing Valid Control Groups

The random technique of obtaining a representative sample is also standard procedure in selecting experimental and control groups. Ideally, every individual in the control group should be identical with a member of the experimental group. But this is of course impossible, because not even identical twins (who are too scarce anyway) are alike in every respect. To ensure as much similarity as possible between the experimental and control groups, subjects are usually assigned to one group or the other at random. Each individual who arrives at the laboratory has a 50-50 chance of being assigned to the experimental group and a 50-50 chance of being assigned to the control group.

Comparing Two Groups

For an example of how inferential statistics is used to compare two groups, such as an experimental group and a control group, let us imagine an experiment in which we try to determine whether physical health affects the learning ability of high school students. We select an experimental group of 16 representative, randomly chosen students who agree to take part in a rigorous health program. We arrange a supervised diet and exercise schedule, give them regular physical examinations, and promptly treat any illnesses or defects such as impaired vision or hearing. We also select a control group of 16 similar students who do not receive any special treatment. At the end of a year, we find that the experimental group has a grade-point mean of 89, with a standard deviation of 3. The control group has a grade-point mean of 85, with a standard deviation of 4. Question: Is this difference of four points between the mean of the experimental group and the mean of the control group just a statistical accident? Or does it really mean that good health produces better grades?

Although four points may sound like a lot, the question is not easy to answer. The reason is that *any* two samples of 16 people each, taken from the high-school population or any other population, are likely to have somewhat different means. Suppose we write the names of all the students in the high school (or in the city) on slips of paper and draw the slips from a hat. The grade-point mean for the first 16 names we draw may be 85, for the next 16 names 88, for the next 16 names 87. If we pull 20 different samples of 16 students each from the hat, we will find that the means vary from sample to sample, perhaps by as much as several points. So the question now becomes: Is the difference between the mean score of 89 for the experimental group and the mean score of 85 for the control group just an accidental result such as we might get by pulling samples from a hat? Or is it *statistically significant*—that is, does it indicate a real difference between our two groups?

Standard Error of the Mean

Helping answer the question is the fact that the means of randomly chosen samples, like raw measurements or scores themselves, tend to fall into a pattern of normal distribution. From our control group of 16 with a grade-point mean of 85 and a standard deviation of 4, we can figure out the distribution of all the means we would be likely to get if we continued to pick samples of 16 students at random, and we find that the curve looks like the one shown on the left in Figure B-5. We get the curve by using the formula (shown later) for the *standard error of the mean*. For the control group, the standard error of the mean turns out to

Figure B-5 How means are distributed

These graphs show how the standard error of the mean of a sample is used to infer the true mean that would be found if the entire population could be measured. In the control group of high school students, at left, the mean is 85 and the standard error of the mean is 1.0. Thus we know that the chances are 68.26 percent that the true mean for the population lies between 84 and 86 (1 standard error above or below the mean of our sample), 95.44 pecent that the true mean lies between 83 and 87 (2 standard errors above or below), and 99.72 percent that the true mean lies between 82 and 83 (3 standard errors above or below). In the experimental group, at right, the mean is 89 and the standard error of the mean is 0.75. Therefore the chances are 68.26 percent that the true mean of the experimental population would fall between 88.25 and 89.75; the chances are 95.44 percent that the mean would fall between 87.50 and 90.50; and they are 99.72 percent that the mean would fall between 86.75 and 91.25.

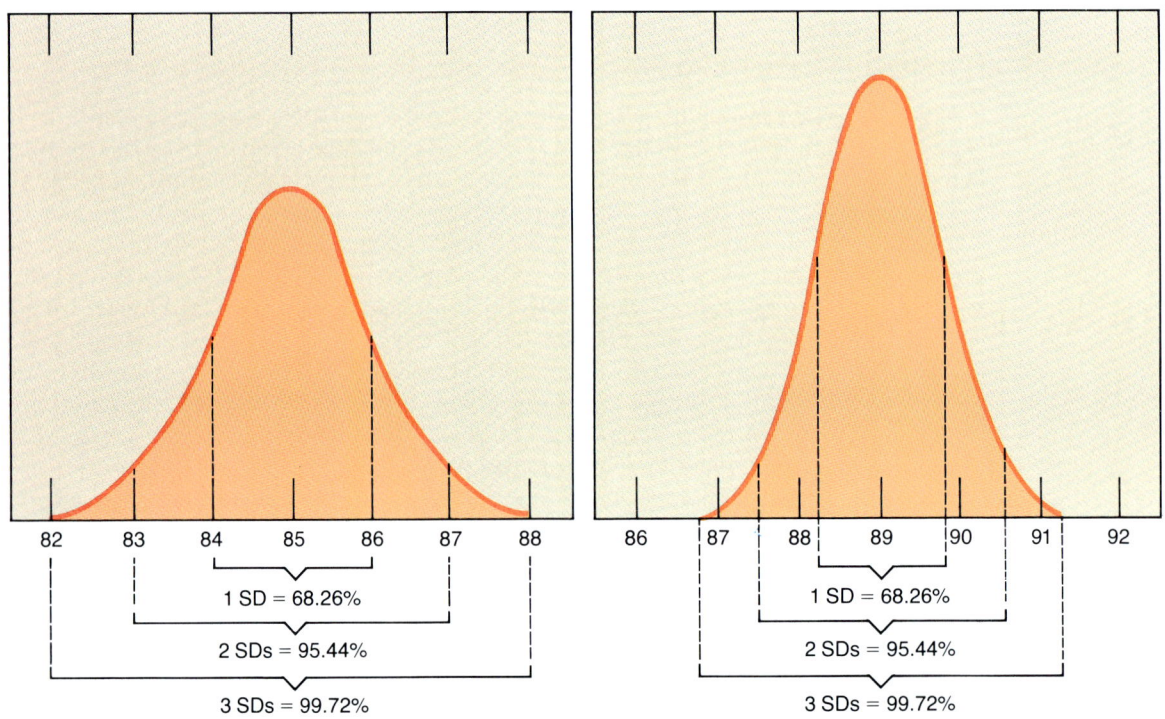

be 1.0. For the experimental group, we get the curve shown at the right in Figure B-5. For this group the standard error of the mean turns out to be .75.

Having found the two curves, we can put them together as in Figure B-6, which shows a very high probability that there is a true difference between the grades of students who receive special medical care and the grades of students who do not. The possibility that the difference we found is merely a matter of chance is represented by the small area that lies beneath the extreme right-hand end of the control curve and the extreme left-hand of the curve for the experimental group.

Probability and Significance

In actual statistical calculation the curves shown in Figures B-5 and B-6 need not be constructed. We can use the two means and the standard error of each mean to work out what is called *the standard error of the difference between two means*. We can then use this figure to work out the probability that the difference we found was due merely to chance. In the case of the hypothetical experiment we have been describing, the probability comes to less than .01.

It is an arbitrary rule of thumb in experimental work that a difference is considered *statistically significant* only when the probability that it might have been obtained by chance is .05 (5 chances in 100, or 1 chance in 20) or less than .05.

In reports on experiments that can be analyzed with this kind of inferential statistics, the probability figure is always given. You will frequently find the note

$$p \leq .05$$

This means that the difference would be found by chance only 5 times or less out of 100 and is therefore statistically significant. In virtually all the experiments cited in this book, p was .05 or less.

Figure B-6   Is the difference between the means significant?

When we superimpose the curves shown in Figure B-5, we find that they have only the small white area in common. This area represents the probability that the difference between the two means was due solely to chance. The probability that the difference is a real one is represented by the colored areas.

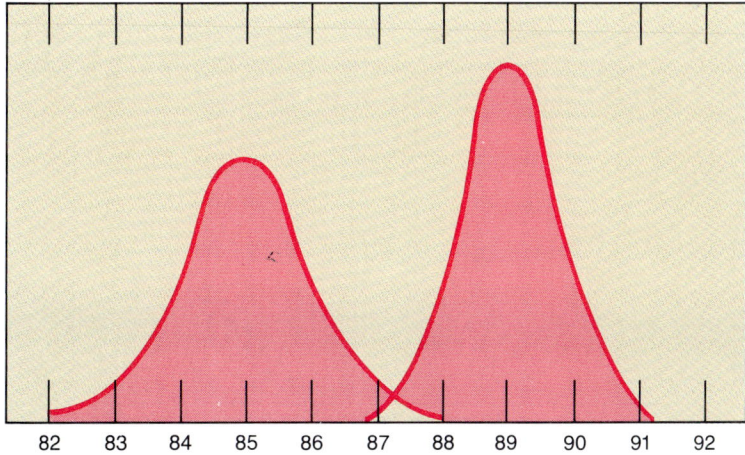

Inferential Statistics: The Science of Making Generalizations

THE TECHNIQUE AND SIGNIFICANCE OF CORRELATION

As was said in Chapter 1, *correlation* is a statistical tool used to examine two different measurements (such as the IQs of parents and the IQs of their children)—and to determine, from what would otherwise seem hopelessly jumbled numbers, what relationship if any exists between the two measurements.

Some correlations are *positive*. This means that the higher a person measures on scale X (for example, IQ) the higher that person is likely to measure on scale Y (for example, grades). Other correlations are *negative*. This means that a high score on scale X is likely to be accompanied by a low score on scale Y. For example, the frequency of premature births has been found to be less prematurity among upper-income families than lower-income families. Negative correlations also exist between aggressive behavior in children and social class and between test anxiety and grades made in schools.

Scatter Plots

A rough idea of the degree of correlation between two traits can be obtained by plotting each subject's score on scale X against the subject's score on scale Y. For each person, a dot is entered at a point corresponding to the scores on both scales, as shown in Figure B-7. The result is what is called a *scatter plot*. If the dots are scattered completely at random, we can see that the correlation is 0. If we should happen on one of those extremely rare cases where the dots form a perfectly straight line, running diagonally up or diagonally down, we know that we are dealing with a perfect correlation, either positive or negative. Most scatter diagrams fall somewhere in between. If a fairly narrow diagonal oval would enclose most of the dots, the correlation is rather high. If the oval must be fatter, the correlation is lower.

Correlation Coefficients

A more precise measure of the relationship between scores on the X-scale and scores on the Y-scale can be obtained—without the need for constructing a scatter plot—by using

Figure B-7   Scatter plots of correlations

For each subject, a dot has been placed at the point indicating both score on scale X and score on scale Y (Ferguson, G. A. Statistical analysis in psychology and education. New York: McGraw-Hill, 1959. Copyright © 1959 by McGraw-Hill Book Co.)

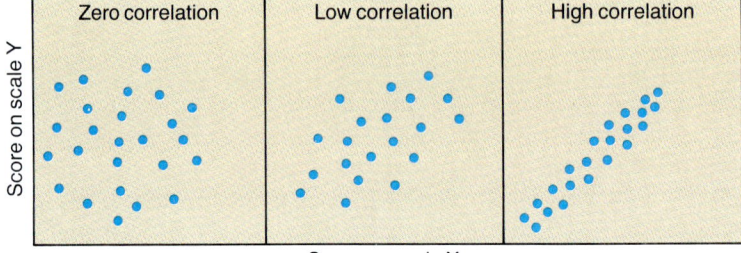

various statistical formulas for calculating a *correlation coefficient*. (The formulas are presented later.) A correlation coefficient can range from 0 (no correlation at all) to +1 (a perfect positive correlation) or −1 (a perfect negative correlation). But correlations of +1 or −1 are very rare. Even such physical traits as height and weight, which would seem to go together in almost perfect proportion, do not reach a correlation of +1. Some typical correlations that have been found in various studies are the following:

Between IQ and college grades	.50
Between parents' IQ and child's IQ	.49
Between IQ and ability at pitch discrimination	.00
Between boys' height at age 2 and height at age 18	.60
Between boys' height at age 10 and height at age 18	.88

Correlation and Prediction

The correlation coefficients in the above table show that there is a considerable relationship between boys' height at age 2 and at age 18—and an even geater relationship between height at age 10 and at age 18. Knowing that these relationships exist, we can make some predictions. We can say that a boy who is taller than average at 2—or especially at 10—has a pretty good chance of also being taller than average at 18. Because of the .50 correlation coefficient between IQ and college grades, we can suggest that high-school seniors who make high scores on intelligence tests have a good chance of getting high grades in college, and that students with very low scores run the risk of failure.

It must always be kept in mind, however, that a coefficient of correlation is less accurate in making predictions than it sounds. Only when the correlation is very close to 1, as in the scatter plot that is shown in Figure B-7, does every subject tend to show a close relationship between score on scale *X* and score on scale *Y*. Even in a correlation of .75, which sounds high, there is a considerable amount of scatter, representing subjects who scored relatively low on scale *X* but relatively high on scale *Y*, or vice versa. Since most correlations found in psychological studies are lower than .75, we must be quite tentative in making predictions.

Correlation, Cause, and Effect

Just knowing the degree of relationship implied by a correlation coefficient is often of value to psychologists. For example, it has been found that there is a positive correlation between strict discipline on the part of parents and the amount of aggressive behavior displayed by children.

Again, however, it is important not to exaggerate the degree of relationship expressed by a correlation coefficient. We cannot say that strict discipline always—or even usually—is accompanied by aggressive behavior. Moreover we must avoid jumping to conclusions about cause and effect. Did the children become aggressive because the parents were strict, or were the parents strict because the children were aggressive? Is it possible that some third factor caused both the parents' strictness and the children's aggression? (For example, it may be that parents who are generally cold and rejecting of their children tend to be strict and that it is the coldness and rejection, rather than the strictness, that make the children aggressive.)

To avoid the danger of jumping to false conclusions on the basis of correlations, keep in mind that there is a very high correlation between the number of permanent teeth that have erupted through the school-child's gums and the child's raw scores for questions answered correctly on any kind of intelligence or aptitude test. But it would be foolish to conclude that more teeth make the child smarter or that better scores make more teeth appear. Increased maturity produces both the teeth and the higher scores.

THE MATHEMATICAL COMPUTATIONS

The use of correlations and other descriptive and inferential statistics is not nearly so difficult as might be assumed. The mathematical knowledge required for these kinds of analysis is really not complicated at all. One need only be able to manipulate mathematical symbols, the most frequently used of which are explained in Figure B-8, and to apply the few basic formulas presented in Figure B-9.

The symbols and formulas are given at the start of this section on computations so that they can be found all in one place for future reference. They may seem rather difficult when

Figure B-8 Some useful mathematical symbols

These are the symbols used in the statistical formulas discussed in this appendix.

N	Number of subjects from whom a measurement or score has been obtained
X	The numerical value of an individual score
Y	If each subject is measured on two scales, the numerical value of an individual score on the second scale
Σ	The Greek capital letter sigma, standing for "sum of"
ΣX	The sum of all the individual scores on scale X
M	The mean, which is the sum of the scores divided by the number of subjects
x	A deviation score; that is, the difference between an individual score and the mean for the group of which the individual is a member
y	A deviation score on the second scale, or Y-scale
SD	The standard deviation of the scores
SE_M	The standard error of the mean; also called the standard deviation of the mean
D_M	The difference between two means; for example, the difference between the mean (M) of scale X and the mean of scale Y
SE_{D_M}	The standard error of the difference between two means, used as a measure of whether the difference is significant
p	Probability, expressed in decimals ranging from .00 (no chance) through .50 (50-50 chance) to 1.00 (100 percent chance). A result is considered statistically significant when $p \leq .05$, meaning that there are only 5 chances in 100 (or fewer) that it was obtained by chance
r	Correlation coefficient obtained by the product-moment method
ρ	Correlation coefficient obtained by the rank-difference method
z	A standard score, expressed in numbers of SDs above or below the mean
C	Coefficient of contingency; type of correlation used to find relationships between events on a nominal scale

shown all together in this fashion, but their application should be apparent from the examples that will be presented as we go along.

The kind of measurement that an investigator often wants to analyze is illustrated in Figure B-10. Here 17 students have taken a psychological test and have made scores ranging from 60 to 97. The raw scores are a jumble of figures, from which we now want to determine the mean, the standard deviation, and the standard error of the mean.

Figure B-9 Some statistical formulas

These are some of the formulas most frequently used in psychological statistics. Their use is explained in the text and in the following figures.

1. For determining the mean:
$$M = \frac{\Sigma X}{N}$$

2. For determining a deviation score:
$$x = X - M$$

3. For determining the standard deviation:
$$SD = \sqrt{\frac{\Sigma x^2}{N - 1}}$$

4. For determining a z-score:
$$z = \frac{x}{SD}$$

5. For determining the standard error of the mean:
$$SE_M = \frac{SD}{\sqrt{N}}$$

6. For determining the difference between two means:
$$D_M = M_1 - M_2$$

7. For determining the standard error of the difference between two means:
$$SE_{D_M} = \sqrt{(SE_{M1})^2 + (SE_{M2})^2}$$

8. For determining the critical ratio:
$$\text{Critical ratio} = \frac{D_M}{SE_{D_M}}$$

9. For determining the coefficient of correlation by the product-moment method:
$$r = \frac{\Sigma xy}{(N - 1)SD_x SD_y}$$

10. For determining the coefficient of correlation by the rank-difference method:
$$\rho = 1 - \frac{6(\Sigma D)^2}{N(N^2 - 1)}$$

The Mathematical Computations

Figure B-10 The raw material of statistical analysis: test scores of 17 students

These raw scores, obtained by students on a psychological test, are analyzed in the text.

1. 78	4. 74	7. 92	10. 74	13. 70	16. 82
2. 97	5. 80	8. 72	11. 85	14. 84	17. 78
3. 60	6. 77	9. 79	12. 68	15. 76	

The Mean

The formula for computing the mean, as shown in Figure B-9, is

$$M = \frac{\Sigma X}{N}$$

These symbols denote, as Figure B-8 shows, that the mean equals the sum of the individual scores divided by the number of subjects.

The way the formula is applied is illustrated in Figure B-11. The sum of the individual scores, which are shown in column one, is 1,326. The number of subjects is 17. Thus the mean is 1,326 divided by 17, or 78.

The Standard Deviation

The method of finding the standard deviation is also illustrated in Figure B-11. The formula for the standard deviation is

$$SD = \sqrt{\frac{\Sigma x^2}{N-1}}$$

This means that we square each of the deviation scores, add up the total, and divide the total by the number of subjects minus 1. The square root of the figure thus obtained is the standard deviation.

The deviation scores shown in column two have been obtained by the formula $x = X - M$ —that is, by subtracting the mean, which is 78, from each individual score. These figures in column two have then been squared to give the figures in column three. The sum of the x^2 figures is 1,224, and this figure divided by 16 (our $N = 1$) comes to 76.5. The standard deviation is the square root of 76.5 or 8.75.

The Standard Error of the Mean

Finding the standard error of the mean for our group is extremely simple. The formula is

$$SE_M = \frac{SD}{\sqrt{N}}$$

We have found that the SD of our sample is 8.75 and our $N = 17$. The formula yields

$$SE_M = \frac{8.75}{\sqrt{17}} = \frac{8.75}{4.12} = 2.12$$

Differences between Groups

For an example of how to apply the formulas for analyzing differences between groups, let us return to the hypothetical experiment mentioned earlier. We had the school grades, you

Figure B-11 **Computing the mean and *SD* of the 17 scores**

Using the formulas in Figure B-9, we first compute the mean score (M) for the 17 students, which comes out to 78. Once we have the mean, we can work out the standard deviation (SD). We start by obtaining the deviation scores (x = X − M), then squaring these deviation scores to get x².

Test scores (X)	Deviation scores (x)	Deviation scores squared (x^2)
78	0	0
97	+19	361
60	−18	324
74	−4	16
80	+2	4
77	−1	1
92	+14	196
72	−6	36
79	+1	1
74	−4	16
85	+7	49
68	−10	100
70	−8	64
84	+6	36
76	−2	4
82	+4	16
78	0	0
$\Sigma X = 1{,}326$		$\Sigma x^2 = 1{,}224$

$$M = \frac{\Sigma X}{N} = \frac{1{,}326}{17} = 78$$

$$SD = \sqrt{\frac{\Sigma x^2}{N-1}} = \sqrt{\frac{1{,}224}{16}} = \sqrt{76.5} = 8.75$$

---

will recall, of an experimental group of 16 students who took part in a health program; the mean was 89 and the standard deviation was 3. We also had the grades of a control group of 16 students; the mean for this group was 85 and the standard deviation was 4.

The difference between the two means is easily computed from the formula

$$D_M = M_1 - M_2$$

which means that the difference between the means is the mean of the first group minus the mean of the second group—in this case, 89 minus 85, or 4. To know whether this difference is statistically significant, however, we must calculate the standard error of the difference between the two means. To do so, as Figure B-9 shows, we must use the fairly complex formula

$$SE_{D_M} = \sqrt{(SE_{M1})^2 + (SE_{M2})^2}$$

Our first step is to compute SE_{M1}, the standard error of the mean of our first or experimental group. We do so as shown earlier, this time with 3 as our standard deviation and 16 as our number of subjects.

$$SE_{M1} = \frac{SD}{\sqrt{N}} = \frac{3}{\sqrt{16}} = \frac{3}{4} = 0.75$$

We also compute SE_{M2}, the standard error of the mean of our second or control group, where the standard deviation is 4 and the number of subjects is 16.

$$SE_{M2} = \frac{SD}{\sqrt{N}} = \frac{4}{\sqrt{16}} = \frac{4}{4} = 1.00$$

The SE_{M1} is 0.75 and SE_{M2} is 1.00, and the standard error of the difference between the two means is computed as follows:

$$\begin{aligned} SE_{DM} &= \sqrt{(SE_{M1})^2 + (SE_{M2})^2} \\ &= \sqrt{(0.75)^2 + (1)^2} \\ &= \sqrt{.5625 + 1} \\ &= \sqrt{1.5625} \\ &= 1.25 \end{aligned}$$

To complete our analysis of the difference between the two groups, we need one more statistical tool—the *critical ratio*. This is given by the formula

$$\text{Critical ratio} = \frac{D_M}{SE_{DM}}$$

In the case of our hypothetical experiment we have found that D_M is 4 and the SE_{DM} is 1.25. Thus

$$\text{Critical ratio} = \frac{4}{1.25} = 3.2$$

This critical ratio gives us a measure of the probability that our difference was due merely to chance. For reasons that mathematically minded students may be able to work out for themselves but that need not concern the rest of us, the magic numbers for the critical ratio are 1.96 and 2.57. If the critical ratio is as high as 1.96, then $p \leq .05$, and the difference is considered statistically significant. If the critical ration is as high as 2.57, then $p \leq .01$, and the difference is considered highly significant. The critical ratio we found for our two groups, 3.2, is well over 2.57; thus we can have some confidence that the difference was not the result of chance.

Correlation Coefficients

There are a number of ways of computing correlation coefficients, depending on the type of data that are being studied. The most frequently used is the *product-moment method*, which obtains a coefficient of correlation designated by the letter r for the relationship between two different measurements. The formula is

$$r = \frac{\Sigma xy}{(N-1)SD_x SD_y}$$

To use the formula we have to determine the amount by which each subject's score on scale X differs from the mean for all scores on scale X—in other words the value for x, the

Figure B-12 A product-moment correlation

Shown here are the calculations required to determine the product-moment correlation between the scores made by 10 subjects on two different tests, X and Y. First we compute the mean and SD for scales X and Y as was described in Figure A-11. Then we calculate each subject's deviation scores (x and y) for each scale and multiply them together to produce the product of the deviation scores (xy). Note that four subjects who scored above the mean on scale X also scored above the mean on scale Y (subjects, 2, 5, 6, and 10). Four students who scored below the mean on scale X also scored below the mean on scale Y (subjects 3, 4, 7, and 9). Only two subjects (1 and 8) scored above the mean on one test and below the mean on the other. Thus multiplying the x deviations times the y deviations gives us eight positive products and two negative products. Σxy, the total of the positive products minus the negative products, comes to 600. The correlation coefficient works out to .78.

	Test scores		Deviation scores		Product of deviation scores
Subject	X	Y	x	y	(xy)
1	60	81	−12	+ 1	− 12
2	80	92	+ 8	+12	+ 96
3	70	76	− 2	− 4	+ 8
4	65	69	− 7	−11	+ 77
5	75	88	+ 3	+ 8	+ 24
6	85	96	+13	+16	+208
7	60	64	−12	−16	+192
8	75	75	+ 3	− 5	− 15
9	70	77	− 2	− 3	+ 6
10	80	82	+ 8	+ 2	+ 16
					$\Sigma xy = 600$

$N = 10$
For scale X, $M = 72$, and $SD_x = 8.56$
For scale Y, $M = 80$, and $SD_y = 9.98$
Thus

$$r = \frac{\Sigma xy}{(N-1)SD_x SD_y} = \frac{600}{(10-1) \times 8.56 \times 9.98}$$

$$= \frac{600}{768.9} = .78$$

---

deviation score, which may be plus or minus. We must also determine the amount by which the subject's score on the second test, or scale Y, differs from the mean for all scores on scale Y—in other words, the value for y, which also may be plus or minus. We then multiply x by y for each subject and add the xy products for all the subjects in the sample. This gives us the top line, or numerator, of the formula. The bottom line, or denominator, is found by multiplying the number of subjects minus 1 $(N - 1)$ by the standard deviation of the scores on the X-scale (SD_x) and then multiplying the product by the standard deviation of the scores on the Y-scale (SD_y). An example is shown in Figure B-12.

Figure B-13 Computing a rank-difference correlation

Here the same scores that were shown in Figure B-12 have been used to find the rank-difference correlation, which comes to .76—very close to the .78 found in Figure B-12 for the product-moment correlation. Note that here we disregard the individual scores on scale X and scale Y and use merely the rank of each score as compared with the others on the X scale. Subjects 2 and 10 are tied for second place on the scale. Their rank is therefore considered to be 2.5, halfway between second and third place.

Subject	Test scores X	Test scores Y	Rank X	Rank Y	Difference in rank (D)	Difference squared (D^2)
1	60	81	9.5	5	−4.5	20.25
2	80	92	2.5	2	−0.5	0.25
3	70	76	6.5	7	+0.5	0.25
4	65	69	8.0	9	+1.0	1.00
5	75	88	4.5	3	−1.5	2.25
6	85	96	1.0	1	0.0	0.00
7	60	64	9.5	10	−0.5	0.25
8	75	75	4.5	8	−3.5	12.25
9	70	77	6.5	6	−0.5	0.25
10	80	82	2.5	4	+1.5	2.25

$\Sigma D^2 = 39.00$

$N = 10$

Thus

$$\rho = 1 - \frac{6(\Sigma D^2)}{N(N^2 - 1)} = 1 - \frac{6(39)}{10(10^2 - 1)}$$

$$= 1 - \frac{234}{990} = 1 - .24 = .76$$

In some cases it is convenient to use the *rank-difference method*, which produces a different coefficient of correlation called ρ (the Greek letter *rho*), which is similar to but not exactly the same as r. The formula is

$$\rho = 1 - \frac{6(\Sigma D^2)}{N(N^2 - 1)}$$

The method of applying the formula is demonstrated in Figure B-13. Note that the D in the formula refers to the difference between a subject's rank on scale X—that is, whether first, second, third, or so on among all the subjects—and the subject's rank on scale Y. ΣD^2 is found by squaring each subject's difference in rank and adding to get the total for all subjects.

Contingency

One other frequently used type of correlation is known as the *coefficient of contingency*, symbolized by the letter C. This is used to find relationships between events that can be measured only on what is called a *nominal scale*—where all we can say about them is that they belong to certain groups. For example, we can set up a nominal scale on which all college students taking a humanities course are grouped in class 1, all taking engineering are grouped in class 2, and all taking a preparatory course for one of the professional schools such as law or medicine are grouped in class 3. We might set up another nominal scale on which we designate the students as males or females. If we then want to determine whether there is any relationship between a student's sex and the kind of college course the student is likely to take, we use the coefficient of contingency. Its meaning is roughly the same as that of any other coefficient of correlation.

SUMMARY

Probability and normal distribution

1. *Psychological statistics* is the application of mathematical principles to the interpretation of results obtained in psychological studies.
2. The statistical method is of special importance as a *way of thinking*—reminding us that many events take place in accordance with the laws of probability and that remarkable coincidences can often be explained as occurring by mere chance.
3. Many events in nature, including many human traits, fall into the pattern of the *normal curve of distribution*. In this curve, most such events or traits cluster around the average measurement, and the number then gets smaller toward the lower and upper extremes.

Descriptive statistics

4. *Descriptive statistics* provides a convenient method of summarizing scores and other psychological measurements. Important types of descriptive statistics are
   a. The *number of subjects*, or N.
   b. Measures of central tendency, including the arithmetic average, or *mean* (total of all scores divided by N), *median* (point separating the lower half of scores from the upper half), and *mode* (most frequent score in the group).
   c. Index of *variability*, including *range* (obtained by subtracting the lowest score from the highest) and *standard deviation*, symbolized by SD. In a normal distribution, 34.13 percent of the scores lie between the mean and 1 SD above the mean, 13.59 percent between 1 SD and 2 SDs above the mean, and 2.14 percent beween 2 SDs and 3 SDs above the mean, while 0.14 percent lie more than 3 SDs above the mean. The same pattern of distribution exists below the mean.
5. *Percentiles* are used to describe the position of an individual score in the total group. A measurement on the 75th percentile is larger than 75 percent of the measurements, or, to put it another way, 25 percent of measurements lie on or above the 75th percentile.

Inferential statistics: the science of making generalizations

6. *Inferential statistics* is made up of procedures that allow us to make generalizations from measurements. It enables us to infer conclusions about a *population* or *universe*, which is the total of all possible cases in a particular category, by measuring a relatively small *sample*. To permit valid generalization, however, the sample must be *representative*. One way to ensure that the sample is representative is to choose it entirely at *random*, with each member of the population having an equal chance of being selected.

7. A set of findings is considered *statistically significant* when the probability that the findings might have been obtained by chance is only 5 in 100 or less. The figure is expressed mathematically as $p \leq .05$.

The technique and significance of correlation

8. *Correlations* between two measurements—such as scores on two different tests—range from 0 (no relationship) to $+1$ (perfect positive relationship) or -1 (perfect negative relationship).

The mathematical computations

9. The symbols and formulas for the statistical analyses are shown in Figures B-8 and B-9.

Glossary

A

abnormal behavior Behavior that is statistically unusual, considered strange or undesirable by most people, and a source of unhappiness to the person who displays it.

abnormal psychology The study of mental and emotional disturbances, their origins, and treatment.

absolute threshold The minimum amount of stimulus energy to which a receptor will respond 50 percent of the time.

accommodation The process of changing one's cognitive view when new information dictates such a change; one of the processes emphasized in Piaget's theory of intellectual development.

achievement motive The desire for success.

achievement test A test that measures the individual's present level of either skill or knowledge.

acrophobia An abnormal fear of heights.

active processing The mental work performed by a listener in interpreting speech. The listener tries to recognize sounds, identify words, look for syntactic patterns, and search for semantic meaning.

acuity A scientific term for sharpness of vision.

adaptation The tendency of the sensory apparatus to adjust to any steady and continued level of stimulation and to stop responding.

addiction See **physical dependence**.

adjustment Living in harmony with oneself and outside events.

adrenal glands A pair of endocrine glands, lying atop the kidneys.

adrenalin (*also called* **epinephrine**) A hormone secreted by the adrenal glands, associated with the bodily states of fear or "flight" situations.

aerial perspective A clue to distance perception; refers to the fact that distant objects appear less distinct and less brilliant in color than nearby objects.

affective disorder A form of mental disorder characterized by abnormalities of mood, including severe depression and swings of mood from one extreme to the other.

afferent neuron A neuron that carries impulses from the sense organs toward the central nervous system.

affiliation motive The desire to be closely associated with other people.

afterimage The visual phenomenon produced by withdrawal of a stimulus. Withdrawal is followed briefly by a positive afterimage, then by a negative afterimage.

aggression A type of behavior arising from hostile motives; it takes such forms as argumentativeness and fighting.

agoraphobia Abnormal fear of public places or of being virtually anywhere outside the home.

alcoholism The abnormal use of alcohol characterized by a strong dependence on alcohol and loss of control over the act of drinking. Usually results in serious physical, psychological, and social problems.

algorithm A problem-solving technique, for example a mathematical formula, that will produce a correct solution without fail.

all or none principle The fact that a neuron, if it fires at all, fires as intense an impulse as it can.

alpha waves A pattern of regular waves of seven to ten cycles per second characteristically found when the brain is at rest.

altered states of consciousness States of consciousness different from normal waking experience, such as those produced by sleep, hypnosis, or drugs.

altruism Behavior that is kind, generous, and helpful to others.

amnesia Loss of memory. It may be caused by physical injury or it may be a defense mechanism—an exaggerated form of repression.

amphetamine Any of a group of drugs that excite the central nervous system.

amplitude The characteristic of a sound wave that determines the loudness we hear.

anal stage The second stage of Freudian psychosexual development in which desires and gratifications are concerned with the act of emptying the lower bowel or refraining from the act.

androgens The male hormones, secreted by the testes.

androgynous Behaving in some ways society considers appropriate for females and in other ways considered appropriate for males.

antisocial personality An extreme form of personality disorder characterized by the absence of any conscience or sense of social responsibility or feeling for other people; also by selfishness, ruthlessness, and lying. People with this disorder are sometimes referred to as sociopaths or psychopaths.

anxiety An emotion characterized by a vague fear or premonition that something undesirable is going to happen.

anxiety disorder A form of abnormal behavior in which anxiety is the most obvious and outstanding symptom, or in which abnormal patterns of behavior such as obsessions and compulsions are developed to keep underlying anxiety under control.

apathy A state of indifference in which people lose all interest in what happens to them.

apparent motion The perception of motion in stimuli that do not actually move, as in *stroboscopic motion* or the *phi phenomenon*.

applied psychology The application of psychological knowledge and principles to practical situations in school, industry, social situations, and treatment of abnormal behavior.

approach-approach conflict A conflict in which the aroused motives have two incompatible goals, both of which are desirable.

approach-avoidance conflict A conflict in which the individual has a single goal with both desirable and undesirable aspects, causing mixed feelings.

aptitude A capacity to learn or to perform, such as mechanical or musical aptitude; an inborn ability that exists and can be measured even though the individual has had no special training to develop the skills (such as at mechanical or musical tasks).

aptitude test A test that measures the individual's *capacity* to perform, not the present level of skill or knowledge.

artificial intelligence The information-processing ability of electronic computers.

assertive coping A constructive attempt to get rid of anxiety and stress in a meaningful way that has some chance of success.

assertiveness training A type of therapy in which assertive responses are reinforced in an effort to reduce passive behavior in interpersonal relationships.

assimilation The process of incorporating a new stimulus into one's existing cognitive view; one of the processes emphasized in Piaget's theory of intellectual development.

association cortex Areas of the cerebral cortex that are not directly involved in consciousness but instead are concerned with our awareness of ourselves and our ability to think about the past and imagine the future.

associative network The manner in which knowledge is believed to be stored in memory in a complex network in which words and ideas are connected and interconnected by strands of associations that make them easy to retrieve.

attachment The inborn tendency of babies to approach caretakers, to be receptive to their help and to be least afraid when in their presence.

attention The process of focusing perception on a single stimulus or limited range of stimuli.

attitude An organized and enduring set of beliefs and feelings toward some object or situation and a predisposition to behave toward it in a particular way.

attribution theory The theory that social behavior is often influenced by our attempts to attribute behavior to a motive or other cause.

autokinetic illusion The illusion of self-generated movement that a stationary object, such as a point of light seen in an otherwise dark room, sometimes creates.

autonomic nervous system A complicated nerve network that connects the central nervous system with the glands and the smooth muscles of the body.

aversive conditioning A type of behavior therapy that attempts to associate a behavioral symptom with punishment rather than with pleasure and reward.

avoidance-avoidance conflict A conflict in which there is simultaneous arousal of motives to avoid alternatives, both of which are undesirable.

axon The fiber of the neuron that carries the nervous impulses to the end branches or "senders."

B

backward pairing A classical conditioning technique in which the conditioned stimulus is presented after the unconditioned stimulus.

basilar membrane A piece of tissue dividing the cochlea more or less in half for its entire length. The organ of Corti, containing the hearing receptors, lies on this membrane.

behavior The activities of an organism, both overt, or observable (such as motor behavior), and covert, or hidden (such as thinking).

behavior genetics The study of how human beings and other organisms inherit characteristics that affect behavior.

behavior modification The technique of changing the behavior, especially of disturbed people, by manipulating rewards and punishments.

behavior therapy A type of psychotherapy that concentrates on eliminating abnormal behavior, which is regarded as learned, through new forms of learning.

behaviorism A school of thought maintaining that psychologists should concentrate on the study of overt behavior rather than on "mental life" or consciousness.

binocular vision A clue to distance perception; refers to the fact that the two eyes, being about two and a half inches apart, receive slightly different images of any seen object.

biofeedback A method of achieving control of bodily and brain functions through the feedback of information about these functions.

biological therapy Therapies based on the belief that psychological conditions can be influenced by chemical, hormonal, or physical interventions and thus produce or inhibit certain behaviors and alter mood.

bipolar depression *See* **manic-depressive illness.**

blind spot The point at which the optic nerve exits from the eyeball, creating a small and mostly insensitive gap in the retina.

bodily movement The sense that keeps us informed of the position of our muscles and bones.

brain control A term for control of behavior through drugs or electrical stimulation of the brain.

breathing drive A biological drive aroused by physiological requirements for oxygen.

brightness One dimension of the visual sensation; dependent on intensity.

brightness constancy The tendency to perceive objects to be of consistent brightness regardless of the amount of light they actually reflect under different conditions of illumination.

broad-tuned receptors The receptor cells of the sense organs, sensitive to a wide range of stimuli.

bystander apathy The tendency of people, especially under crowded conditions, to ignore others who need help or situations that call for action.

C

Cannon-Bard theory A neurological theory of emotion holding that stimuli in the environment set off patterns of activity in the hypothalamus and thalamus; these patterns are then relayed both to the autonomic nervous system, where they trigger the bodily changes of emotion, and to the cerebral cortex, where they result in the feelings of emotion.

caretaker period The first eighteen months of life, during which babies' personality development depends chiefly on a close relationship with the mother or other caretaker.

case history An attempt to reconstruct a person's life to show how patterns of behavior have developed.

categories Logical groups into which materials can be lumped together; an aid to long-term memory.

cell body (of a neuron) The portion of a neuron containing its genes, as opposed to the fiber portion of the neuron.

central nervous system The spinal cord and the brain.

cerebellum The brain structure that controls body balance and helps coordinate bodily movements.

cerebral cortex The highest part of the brain, the surface of the cerebrum; a dense and highly interconnected mass of neurons.

cerebrum The large brain mass of which the cerebral cortex is the surface. It is divided into two separate halves called the left hemisphere and the right hemisphere.

certainty motive The desire to know where one stands and to be able to predict the course of events.

character disorder See **personality disorder.**

chemotherapy The prescription of drugs intended to produce specific changes in mood or behavior.

chromosome The mechanism of human heredity. There are 23 pairs of these tiny structures, 46 in all, found in the fertilized egg cell and repeated through the process of division in every cell of the body.

chronological age A person's actual age in years and months; compared with mental age to produce IQ.

ciliary muscles The muscles that control the shape of the lens of the eye.

cirrhosis The hardening and scarring of an organ—in the case of the liver, often as a result of heavy and prolonged use of alcohol.

clairvoyance The supposed ability to perceive something that is not apparent to the sense organs; a form of extrasensory perception.

classical conditioning A type of learning process through which a response becomes attached to a conditioned (or previously neutral) stimulus.

claustrophobia Abnormal fear of being in enclosed places, such as elevators.

client A term used, in preference to "patient," by clinical psychologists to refer to the people they treat.

client-centered therapy A form of therapy, developed by Carl Rogers, based on the humanistic approach designed to allow individuals to understand and control their own behavior through interactions with a non-directive therapist.

clinical psychology The branch of applied psychology concerned with the application of psychological knowledge to the treatment of personality problems and mental disorders.

closure The tendency to perceive an object in its entirety even when some details are missing.

clustering The organization of materials into groups, such as categories; an aid to long-term memory and retrieval.

cochlea A bony structure of the inner ear shaped like a snail's shell; contains the receptors for hearing.

codeine A narcotic drug derived from the poppy plant.

cognition All the mental processes entailed in thinking.

cognitive consonance Consistency and agreement among one's beliefs, feelings, and behavior.

cognitive dissonance Lack of consistency among beliefs, feelings, and behavior. The theory of cognitive dissonance maintains that people are stongly motivated to relieve such dissonance, often by changing attitudes.

cognitive map Tolman's term for one type of "model of reality"; knowledge of the spatial features of the environment acquired, for example, by rats running a maze.

cognitive psychology A school of thought maintaining that the mind does not merely react to stimuli but actively processes the information it receives into new forms and categories.

collective unconscious In Jung's theory, a repository for the events of human history, superstitions, fears, and so on, which influence all people.

color blindness A visual defect involving deficiency in color discrimination.

color constancy The tendency to perceive a familiar object as being of constant color, regardless of changes in illumination that alter its actual stimulus properties.

communication A general term for exchanges of information and feelings between two (or more) people. For its special meaning in social psychology, see **persuasive communications.**

community therapy A type of interactional therapy in which the therapist attempts to change conflicts and patterns of behavior through alteration of behavior in the community.

complementary hues Two hues that, when added one to the other, yield gray.

complex cell A feature detector cell that receives messages from a number of simple cells and can therefore respond to several kinds of stimuli.

complexity The characteristic of a sound wave that determines the timbre we hear; caused by the number and strength of the overtones.

compulsion An irresistible urge to perform some act over an over again.

concept A mental grouping of objects or ideas on the basis of similarity.

conceptual intelligence The term used by Piaget to describe the developmental process after 2 years of age, in which the child increasingly uses concepts to organize the evidence of the senses and to engage in ever more complex thinking and problem solving.

concrete operations The term applied by Piaget to the stage of intellectual development (7–11 years of age) when children can reason logically about objects they see but have yet to learn to deal with rules in the abstract.

conditional positive regard In Rogers' personality theory, the cause of maladjustments; approval of some but not all aspects of an individual's behavior.

conditioned operant Behavior learned through operant conditioning; a type of behavior with which the organism "operates" on its environment to obtain a desired result.

Glossary 635

conditioned response A response that has become attached through learning to a conditioned (or previously neutral) stimulus; an example is the salivation by Pavlov's dog to the sound of the metronome.

conditioned stimulus In classical conditioning, a previously neutral stimulus (such as a sound) that through pairing with an unconditioned stimulus (such as food) acquires the ability to set off a response (such as salivation).

cones One of two types of receptors for vision located in the retina. The cones are receptors for color and are also sensitive to differences in light intensity resulting in sensations of black, white, and gray.

conflict The simultaneous arousal of two or more incompatible motives, resulting in unpleasant emotions.

conformity The yielding by an individual to pressures from another person or, more usually, from a group.

connecting neuron A neuron that is stimulated by another neuron and passes its message along to a third neuron.

conservation The principle that such qualities as mass, weight, and volume remain constant regardless of changes in appearance; learned by the child during Piaget's stage of concrete operations.

consolidation A process, requiring time, during which the memory trace becomes more resistant to extinction.

constant reinforcement Provision of reinforcement for every desired response.

constructive processing The manner in which information is encoded into memory in the form of meanings and associations rather than as an exact copy.

continuity The tendency to perceive continuous lines and patterns.

contour In perception, the dividing line between figure and ground.

control group A group used for comparison with an experimental group. The two groups must be alike in composition and must be observed under the same circumstances except for the one variable that is manipulated in the case of the experimental group.

coping An attempt, constructive or destructive, to relieve anxiety and stress.

core of personality To personality theorists, the tendencies and characteristics common to all people.

cornea The transparent bulge in the outer layer of the eyeball through which light waves enter.

corpus callosum A large nerve tract that connects the left and right hemispheres of the cerebrum and enables the two hemispheres to cooperate and share in duties.

correlation The degree of relationship between two different factors; measured statistically by the correlation coefficient.

correlation coefficient A statistic that describes in numbers ranging from -1 to $+1$ the degree of relationship between two different factors.

cortisol A hormone secreted by the pituitary gland under stress or during emotional upset. Many people suffering from depression have excessive amounts of the hormone, which seems to persist in them for an unusually long time.

counseling psychology The branch of psychology that concentrates on vocational guidance, assistance with marital problems, and advice in other situations regarded as less serious or deepseated than the behavioral problems usually treated by clinical psychologists.

creative thinking A highly imaginative and rare form of thinking in which the individual discovers new relationships and solutions to problems and may produce an invention or an artistic creation.

credibility of the source A factor in the effectiveness of a persuasive communication.

crisis intervention Community based programs designed to deal with immediate, stress-filled situations that beg for quick attention.

critical ratio A measure of the degree of difference between two groups.

crystallized intelligence The ability—thought to increase in the later years—to use an accumulated body of general information in order to make judgments and solve problems.

culture The ways of a given society, including its customs, beliefs, values, and ideals.

curve of forgetting A graph plotting the course of forgetting.

D

decibel A measure of the amplitude of sound.

defense mechanism A process, generally believed to be unconscious, in which the individual maintains that a frustration or conflict and the resulting anxiety do not exist or have no importance.

delirium tremens A condition popularly known as the "DTs" that occurs when an alcoholic suddenly withdraws from drinking; a state of intense panic characterized by agitation, tremors, confusion, horrible nightmares, and hallucinations.

delusion A false belief, such as imagining that one is already dead.

dendrite The part of the neuron, usually branched, that has the special function of being sensitive to stimuli and firing off a nervous impulse; the "receiving" portion of the neuron.

dendritic spines Outgrowths of a dendrite, capable of being stimulated by the axon of another neuron.

denial A defense mechanism, closely related to repression, in which the individual simply denies the existence of the events that have aroused anxiety.

dependency motive The desire to rely on others.

dependent variable A change in behavior that results from changes in the conditions that affect the organism—that is, from changes in an *independent variable*.

depressant A drug that reduces activity of the central nervous system.

depression A feeling of severe and prolonged sadness, sometimes accompanied by total apathy, that occurs as a reaction to stress; possibly influenced by chemical imbalances in the brain.

descriptive statistics A quick and convenient method of summarizing measurements. Important figures in descriptive statistics are the number of subjects; measures of central tendency, including the mean, median, and mode; and measurements of variability, including range and standard deviation.

desensitization An attempt to eliminate phobias by associating the stimulus that has caused the fear with relaxation rather than with fearful behavior; a technique used in behavior therapy.

development In personality theory, the way the common core of human personality is channeled into individual patterns by learning and experience.

developmental psychology The study of changes that take place, physically and psychologically, beginning at birth and continuing throughout life.

difference threshold (*also called* **just noticeable difference** *or* **j.n.d.**) The smallest difference in intensity or quality of stimulation to which a sensory receptor will respond 50 percent of the time.

difficult children Those who seem to display an inborn tendency to negative and stubborn behavior.

direct aggression Aggressive behavior focused directly on the obstacle that has caused frustration.

displaced aggression Aggressive behavior directed against an "innocent bystander" because the cause of frustration or conflict cannot itself be attacked.

dispositional factors Behavior-producing factors that represent lasting and consistent personality traits.

dissonance theory A theory maintaining that inconsistencies among one's beliefs, feelings, and behavior create a state of cognitive dissonance that the individual then tries to relieve, often by changing an attitude.

DNA (deoxyribonucleic acid) The complex chemical of which genes are composed.

dopamine A neurotransmitter thought to play a role in schizophrenia.

double approach-avoidance conflict A conflict aroused by motives toward two goals that both have their good and bad points.

double blind An experimental technique in which neither the subjects nor the experimenter knows which subjects are in the control group and which are in the experimental group.

drive A psychological urge created by the body's demands for homeostasis.

drug abuse The repeated and excessive use of drugs, resulting in physical and psychological disturbances.

DSM-III An abbreviation for the *Diagnostic and Statistical Manual of Mental Disorders* established by the American Psychiatric Association in 1980 for the classification of various forms of abnormal behavior. The manual provides detailed descriptions of the symptoms of more than 230 mental disorders.

ductless gland *See* **endocrine gland.**

dynamic therapy Therapy based on the belief that effective treatment must focus on the underlying mental and emotional forces that generate an individual's problems.

E

eardrum A membrane between the outer part of the auditory canal and the middle ear.

easy children Those who display an inborn tendency to be cheerful and adapt quickly.

eclectic therapy Treatment in which the therapist selects various techniques from those available that seem most beneficial without concern about their theoretical orientation.

ectomorph A body type characterized by William Sheldon as tall and thin, and related by him to a personality tendency to be solitary, high strung, intellectual, and introverted.

EEG *See* **electroencephalograph.**

efferent neuron A neuron that carries impulses from the central nervous system toward the muscles or glands.

ego According to psychoanalytical theory of personality, the conscious, logical part of the mind that develops as we grow up and that is our operational contact with reality.

ego ideal Our notion of how we would always think and behave if we were as perfect as we would like to be.

electroencephalograph (EEG) A delicate instrument that measures the electrical activity of the brain.

electroshock A medical method of treating behavior disorders, especially depression, by passing an electric current through the patient's brain.

elimination drive A drive aroused by physiological requirements to get rid of the body's waste products.

emotion A feeling created by brain patterns accompanied by stirred-up or toned-down bodily changes.

emotional stress Wear and tear on the body created by the physical changes during emotional states.

empathy Understanding other people by putting yourself in their place and sharing their thoughts and feelings.

encoding The process through which information is transformed in a way that makes it simple and easy to handle and is then transferred to and stored in long-term memory.

encounter group A group of people who meet, usually under the leadership of a psychotherapist, with the goal of throwing off the masks they usually present in public and airing their true feelings.

end branches The part of the neuron that acts as the "sender" of messages to other neurons or to muscles and glands.

endocrine gland (*also called* **ductless gland**) A gland that discharges chemical substances known as *hormones* directly into the bloodstream, which then carries them to all parts of the body, resulting in many kinds of physiological changes.

endomorph A body type characterized by William Sheldon as soft and rounded with a protruding belly, and related by him to a personality tendency to be talkative, happy-go-lucky, and given to the good life.

endorphins A group of brain chemicals, similar in structure and effect to the painkiller morphine, that seem to affect parts of the brain associated with pain and with emotion and mood.

environmental psychology Study of the effects of the physical environment on physical and psychological well-being.

epinephrine *See* **adrenalin.**

episodic memory Memory for particular events or episodes.

equilibrium The sense that gives us the information needed to keep us in balance and oriented to the force of gravity.

ESP *See* **extrasensory perception.**

estrogen The chief female hormone, secreted by the ovaries.

Eustachian tube A passage between the middle ear and the air chambers of the mouth and nose; it keeps the pressure on both sides of the eardrum constant.

existential psychology A school holding that our own attitudes toward events in our life are more important than the events themselves.

expectancy One type of knowledge acquired through learning; the awareness that one event in the environment will be followed by another—in other words, "what leads to what."

expedient conformity Mere lip service to the opinion of the group.

experiment A scientific method in which the experimenter makes a careful and rigidly controlled study of cause and effect, by manipulating an independent variable (or condition affecting the subject) and observing its effect on a dependent variable (or the subject's behavior in response to changes in the independent variable).

experimental group A group of subjects whose behavior is observed while the experimenter manipulates an independent variable.

experimental psychology A branch of psychology devoted to the study of psychological phenomena as manifested by the behavior of lower organisms.

exploration The baby's early attempts to examine new aspects of the environment.

extinction The disappearance of a conditioned response (or other learned behavior) when reinforcement is withdrawn.

extrasensory perception (ESP) Any of several forms of supposed ability to perceive stimuli through some means other than the sense organs.

extrovert An individual who dislikes solitude and prefers the company of other people.

F

family therapy A type of interactional therapy that attempts to change the patterns of behavior that various members of a family display toward one another.

fantasy Images; daydreams.

"fast" fibers Neurons that carry sensory messages signaling sharp, localized pains.

fat cells Cells scattered throughout the body that are designed for the storage of fatty compounds. An excess of such cells is believed to be a common cause of obesity.

feature analysis Perceptual interpretation through examination of the individual features of an object.

feature detector A nerve cell that responds to special features of a stimulus reaching the sense organs—for example, to a horizontal line but not to a vertical line.

feedback In learning, information about how much progress is being made.

feminine The type of behavior society considers appropriate for females.

figure-ground In perception, the tendency to see an object as a figure set off from a neutral ground.

fluid intelligence The ability—thought to decline in the later years—to perform tasks based on perceptual skills and memory.

forward pairing A classical conditioning technique in which the conditioned stimulus precedes the unconditioned stimulus by a short interval.

formal operations The term applied by Piaget to the stage of intellectual development (beginning at about 11 or 12 years of age) at which the child becomes capable of thinking in the abstract.

fovea The most sensitive part of the retina; contains only cones, which are packed together more tightly than anywhere else in the retina.

free association A tool of psychoanalysis in which patients, lying as relaxed as possible on a couch, are encouraged to let their mind wander where it will and to speak out every thought that occurs to them.

frequency The characteristic of a sound wave determining the tone or pitch that we hear; measured in number of cycles per second.

frontal lobes A portion of the cerebral hemisphere in the front portion of the brain that seems to play a key role in such human capacities as problem solving and planning.

frustration The blocking of motive satisfaction by some kind of obstacle. (In popular usage, also the unpleasant feelings caused by the blocking of motive satisfaction.)

functional autonomy A principle holding that an activity that is originally a means to an end frequently acquires an independent function of its own and becomes an end in itself.

functional fixedness The tendency to think of an object in terms of its usual functions, not other possible functions; a common barrier to problem solving.

fundamental attribution error The common tendency to attribute the behavior of others to dispositional rather than situational factors.

G

galvanic skin reflex (GSR) A change in the electrical conductivity of the skin caused by activity of the sweat glands.

ganglion (*plural:* **ganglia**) A mass of nerve cells and synapses forming complex and multiple connections.

gate control mechanism A theoretical part of the spinal cord that lets pain messages through or shuts them off.

gene A tiny substance that is a molecule of *DNA*. The genes, grouped together into chromosomes, direct the growth of cells into specific parts of the body and account for inherited individual differences.

general adaptation syndrome A phrase coined by Selye for the sequence of events involved in prolonged stress; the initial shock or alarm, the recovery or resistance period, and at last exhaustion and death.

general anxiety The tendency to be anxious in many different kinds of situations.

general factor An intellectual ability posited by Thurstone as common to all the seven primary mental abilities.

generalized anxiety disorder A type of anxiety disorder marked by unfocused feelings of tension, uneasiness, and vague fear.

generic memory Memory for items independent of the specific occasion on which we learned them.

genital stage The final stage in Freudian psychosexual development characterized by sexual love for another person.

Gestalt psychology A school of thought holding that all psychological phenomena must be studied as a whole (rather than broken down into parts) and in the context in which they occur.

global processing Perceptual interpretation made by viewing the total pattern formed by the various individual features of an object.

gradient of texture A clue to distance perception; refers to the fact that nearby objects are seen more sharply and therefore appear grainier in texture than more distant objects.

grammar The rules of language for combining words into meaningful sentences.

group test A psychological test that can be given to many individuals at the same time.

group therapy A type of psychotherapy in which several patients are treated simultaneously.

GSR *See* **galvanic skin reflex.**

guided participation A technique used by behavior therapists for the practice of assertive coping.

H

hallucination An imaginary sensation, such as seeing nonexistent animals in the room or feeling bugs crawling under the skin.

health psychology A branch of psychology concerned with the relationship between psychological and physical functioning in health and illness.

hemispheres The two halves of the cerebrum and cerebral cortex. The left hemisphere appears to control language and logical thinking about details, the right hemisphere to be concerned with forms, patterns, and the "big picture."

Hering theory An early theory of color vision, holding that nervous messages must be paired as black-white, red-green, and blue-yellow; now believed to be generally true of the neurons from eye to cerebral cortex.

heroin A narcotic drug derived from the poppy plant.

heterosexuality Sexual attraction to members of the opposite sex.

heuristics A problem-solving technique; applying rules of thumb that have worked in similar situations and may—or may not—succeed again.

hierarchy of motives An individual pattern of motives, from strongest to weakest.

hippocampus A part of the brain that appears essential to the transfer of information from short-term memory to long-term memory.

homeostasis An internal environment in which such bodily states as blood circulation, blood chemistry, breathing, digestion, temperature, and so on, are kept at optimal levels for survival of the living organism.

homosexuality Sexual attraction to members of the same sex.

hormones Substances produced by the endocrine glands and secreted into the bloodstream; complicated chemicals that trigger and control many kinds of bodily activities and behavior.

hospice A facility providing both inpatient and outpatient care to help dying patients maintain a decent quality of life and deal with the trauma of the death experience.

hostility motive The desire to cause physical or psychological discomfort in others.

hue The sensation of color, determined by the length of the light wave.

human engineering A branch of applied psychology concerned with the design of equipment and machinery to fit the size, strength, and capabilities of the people who will use it.

humanistic therapy A form of psychotherapy based on the assumption that people will grow in a positive direction if only they have the chance.

hunger drive A biological drive caused by deprivation of food.

hypercomplex cell The highest type of feature detector cell, capable of making fine distinctions among stimuli.

hypnosis The act of inducing the hypnotic state, in which the subject is in a sort of dreamlike trance and highly susceptible to suggestions from the hypnotist; sometimes used in psychotherapy.

hypomania A rare form of manic-depressive illness in which the individual remains primarily in a state of manic excitement, and the depressed phase of the illness never becomes very pronounced.

hypothalamus The portion of the brain that serves as a mediator between the brain and the body, helping control metabolism, sleep, hunger, thirst, body temperature, and sexual behavior, and that is also concerned with emotions.

hysterical conversion A disorder in which psychological conflicts and stress are converted into physical symptons, typically the loss of functioning of some part of the body.

I

id According to psychoanalytical theory, the unconscious part of the human mind comprising the individual's primitive instinctive forces toward sexuality (the *libido*) and aggression.

identification (a) A process in which children try to imitate the behavior of their parents or other "heroes." (b) In psychoanalytical theory, the process through which children resolve the Oedipus complex by absorbing their parents' characteristics into themselves. (c) As a defense mechanism, an attempt to relieve anxiety by becoming like another person or group.

identity A sense of oneself as having a distinct and unique character and of being a person in one's own right.

illusion A perception that is a false interpretation of the actual stimuli.

illusory motion The perception of motion in an unchanging stimulus, such as in the *autokinetic illusion.*

imagery Forming a mental picture of events; an aid to long-term memory.

imitation *See* **learning through observation.**

implicit personality theory The assumption, held by most people, that certain personality traits are correlated with others—for example, that "warmth" of personality is accompanied by sociability and a good sense of humor.

incentive object A stimulus that arouses a drive or motive.

incentive value The particular desirability of any object or event that arouses a motive.

independence As used in social psychology, the tendency to make up one's own mind and decide on one's own behavior and thinking regardless of society's pressures.

independent variable A condition, affecting an experimental subject, that is controlled and varied by the experimenter, thus producing changes in the subject's behavior, called the *dependent variable.*

individual difference Any difference —as in physical size or strength, intelligence, sensory threshold, perceptions, emotions, personality, and so on—between the individual organism and other members of the species.

individual test A psychological test that is given by a trained examiner to one person at a time.

industrial psychology A branch of applied psychology, embracing the use of psychological knowledge in setting working hours and rest periods, improving relations between employer and employees, and so on.

inference A form of thinking; drawing logical conclusions from facts already known.

inferential statistics Statistics that are used to make generalizations from measurements.

inferiority complex A concept introduced by Adler to describe the condition of a person who for some reason has been unable to develop feelings of adequacy, independence, courage, and wholesome ambition.

information processing A description used by cognitive psychologists for the mental processes entailed in perception, learning, and thinking.

inhibition (a) The action of a neuron whose messages tend to stop another neuron from firing. (b) The suppression of behavior or emotional barriers to action, such as an inhibition against competitive or sexual activity.

"innate mechanism" Chomsky's term for a species-specific quality of the brain that enables us to learn and use language.

inner ear The portion of the ear inward from the oval window; contains the cochlea, vestibule, and semicircular canals.

inner standards The principles we develop—and are motivated to live up to—of how we are supposed to behave.

insight (a) In problem solving, the sudden "flash of inspiration" that results in a successful solution (*compare* trial and error learning). (b) In psychotherapy, the discovery by the patient of psychological processes that have caused difficulties.

instinct An elaborate and inborn pattern of activity, occurring automatically and without prior learning in response to certain stimuli in the environment.

insulin A hormone, secreted by the pancreas, that burns up blood sugar to provide energy.

intellectualization A defense mechanism in which the individual tries to explain away anxiety by intellectually analyzing the situations that produce the unpleasant feelings and making them a matter of theory rather than of action.

intelligence The ability to profit from experience, to learn new pieces of information, and to adjust to new situations.

intelligence quotient (IQ) A numerical value assigned to an individual as a result of intelligence testing. The average intelligence quotient is set at 100.

intelligence test A test measuring the various factors that make up the capacity called intelligence. It measures chiefly the individual's ability to use acquired knowledge in a novel way.

intensity The strength of light waves, accounting for sensations of brightness.

interactional therapies Types of psychotherapy that concentrate on changing the individual's behavior toward other people.

interest test A test measuring the individual's interest or lack of interest in various kinds of amusements, literature, music, art, science, school subjects, social activities, kinds of people, and so on.

interference Failures of memory caused by the effect of old learning on new or new learning on old.

intermittent reinforcement *See* **partial reinforcement.**

interpersonal attraction A person's tendencies to like other people, largely determined by such factors as similarities in attitudes, interests, and personality.

interpersonal therapies Types of psychotherapy that concentrate on changing the individual's behavior toward other people.

interposition A clue to distance perception; refers to the fact that nearby objects interpose themselves between our eyes and more distance objects.

interpretation In perception, the meaning we attach to stimuli affecting the sense organs.

interval schedule A reinforcement schedule used in operant conditioning in which reinforcement is delivered only after a certain period of time has passed.

interview A scientific method in which the investigator obtains information through careful and objective questioning of the subject.

introspection Inward examination of a "mental life" or mental process that nobody but its possessor can see in operation.

introvert A term for people who tend to be preoccupied with their own thoughts and activities and to avoid social contact.

intuitive thought The term applied by Piaget to the stage of intellectual development (4–6 years of age) when the child is developing concepts that become more and more elaborate but are still based largely on the evidence of the senses.

IQ *See* **intelligence quotient.**

iris A circular arrangement of smooth muscles that contract and expand to make the pupil of the eye smaller in bright light and larger in dim light.

J

James-Lange theory of emotion A physiological theory holding that stimuli in the environment set off physiological changes in the individual, that the changes in turn stimulate sensory nerves inside the body, and that the messages of these sensory nerves are then perceived as emotion.

just noticeable difference (j.n.d.) *See* **difference threshold.**

L

latent content In psychoanalysis, the unconscious sexual and aggressive material found in dreams.

latent learning Learning that takes place without reinforcement, almost as if by accident, then lies latent until reinforcement is provided.

lateral hypothalamus An area of the hypothalamus which is sensitive to changes in the food supply contained in the bloodstream and which, when stimulated, will cause an experimental animal to start eating.

learned helplessness A condition in which the organism has been subjected to punishment over which it has no control, leading to an impairment of the ability to learn or use old habits.

learning The process by which behavior becomes altered or attached to new stimuli.

learning by imitation *See* **learning through observation**.

learning through modeling *See* **learning through observation**.

learning through observation (*also called* **learning through modeling, learning by imitation**) A type of learning in which the behavior of another organism is observed and imitated.

lens A transparent structure of the eye that changes shape to focus images sharply on the retina.

libido According to psychoanalytic theory, a basic instinctual force in the individual, embracing sexual urges and such related desires as to be kept warm, well-fed, and happy.

lie detector A device designed to reveal whether a subject is telling the truth by measuring physiological changes, usually in heart rate, blood pressure, breathing, and galvanic skin reflex.

limbic system A set of interconnected pathways in the brain, including the hypothalamus, some primitive parts of the cerebrum that have to do with the sense of smell, eating and emotion, and other structures.

linear perspective A clue to distance perception; refers to the fact that parallel lines seem to draw closer together as they recede into the distance.

lithium A drug that is effective in treating the wide mood swings of manic-depression. It appears to work by reducing the amount of the neurotransmitter noradrenalin in the brain.

location constancy The tendency to perceive objects as being in their rightful and accustomed place and remaining there even when we move and their images therefore move across our eyes.

locus of control The belief that we are in control of our own life (inner locus) or at the mercy of outside events (external locus).

logical thinking An objective and disciplined form of thinking in which facts are carefully examined and conclusions consistent with the facts are reached.

long-term memory The permanent storehouse from which information can be retrieved under the proper circumstances.

loudness The hearing sensation determined by the amplitude of the sound wave.

LSD (lysergic acid diethylamide) A psychedelic drug.

M

made-up stories The organization of new materials by weaving them into narratives; an aid to long-term memory.

major tranquilizer A group of drugs used to control the most disruptive symptoms of schizophrenia.

manic-depressive illness (*also called* **bipolar depression**) A type of mood disorder in which the person's mood swings from deep melancholy to wild excitement.

manifest content In psychoanalysis, the conscious material comprising the actual images of a dream.

marijuana The dried leaves and flowers of the hemp plant; a drug that affects different users in different ways, often interfering with short-term memory and concentration and producing feelings of elation.

masculine The type of behavior society considers appropriate for males.

maturation The physical changes, taking place after birth, that continue the biological development of the organism from fertilized egg cell to complete adult.

mean A measure of central tendency obtained by dividing the sum of all the measurements by the number of subjects measured.

measurement The assignment of numbers to traits, events, or subjects according to an orderly system.

median A measure of central tendency; the point separating the lower half of measurements from the upper half.

meditation A technique for producing an altered state of consciousness.

medulla The connection between the spinal cord and the brain; an important connecting link that is vital to life because it helps regulate heartbeat, blood pressure, and breathing.

memory trace The basis of a theory of remembering, maintaining that learning left some kind of trace in the nervous system that could be kept active through use but tended to fade away or become distorted through lack of practice.

menarche The first menstrual period.

mental age A person's age as measured by performance on an intelligence test; a person who scores as well as the average 10-year-old has a mental age of 10 regardless of chronological age.

mental health A state of psychological well-being.

mentally gifted Having an IQ over 130.

mentally retarded Having an IQ below 70.

"mental models of reality" A key idea in cognitive psychology: the patterns of knowledge about the world that the brain builds through its information processing, stores, and uses as a guide to intelligent behavior.

mental telepathy The supposed ability of one person to know what is going on in another person's mind; a form of extrasensory perception.

mesomorph A body type characterized by William Sheldon as hard and square-shaped with well-developed muscles, and related by him to a personality tendency to be physically active, energetic, and assertive.

metabolism The bodily process that maintains life by turning food and oxygen into living tissue and energy.

middle ear The portion of the ear between the eardrum and the oval window of the inner ear; contains three bones that aid transmission of sound waves.

minor tranquilizer A group of drugs used to control anxiety, stress, and tension.

mnemonic device A form of memory aid in which memorized symbols provide organization for otherwise unrelated material.

mode A measure of central tendency; the measurement at which the greatest number of subjects fall.

modeling *See* **learning through observation**.

moral development The child's acquisition of standards of right and wrong, extensively studied by Kohlberg.

morpheme The smallest meaningful unit of language, made by combining *phonemes* into a prefix, word, or suffix.

morphine A narcotic drug derived from the poppy plant.

motion parallax A term describing the fact that when we move our heads, near objects move across our field of vision more rapidly than objects that are farther away.

motivated forgetting Forgetting because we want to forget.

motivation A general term referring to the forces regulating behavior that is undertaken because of drives, needs, or desires and is directed toward goals.

motive A desire for a goal or incentive object that has acquired value for the individual.

motive hierarchy The pattern of motive strength, from strongest to weakest.

motive targets The people to whom motives are directed. People may exhibit strong motives of affiliation toward a "target" such as their parents and of hostility toward other "targets."

motor cortex A specialized strip on the cerebral cortex that controls body movements and speech.

multiple personality A personality disorder in which the individual appears to exist alternately as two or more distinct individuals.

muscle tension Contractions of a muscle; one of the bodily changes often observed in emotion.

myelin sheath A fatty sheath, white in appearance, that covers many neuron fibers and speeds the transmission of nervous impulses.

N

narcissistic personality A personality disorder characterized by extreme narcissism, or self-love. Narcissistic individuals crave constant attention and admiration, and they use people for their own purposes.

narcotic A term applied to a group of drugs that produce repose or sleep.

naturalistic observation A scientific method in which the investigator does not manipulate the situation and cannot control all the variables; the investigator tries to remain unseen or as inconspicuous as possible.

nature-nurture The argument over the relative importance of heredity and environment.

negative reinforcement Rewarding learning through the termination of an unpleasant stimulus, for example, an electric shock.

negative transfer A process in which learning is made more difficult by interference from previous learning.

neopsychoanalysts The recent psychoanalytical theorists who have changed Freud's original ideas in various ways; "neo" means new.

nerve A group of neurons, small or very large in number, traveling together to or from the central nervous system; in appearance, a single large fiber that is in fact made up of many fibers.

nervous impulse A tiny charge of electricity passing from the dendrite end of the neuron to the end of the axon.

neuron The individual nerve cell; basic unit of the nervous system.

neurotransmitter A chemical released by one neuron that stimulates another neuron to fire; also sometimes inhibits the second neuron from firing.

nodes Booster stations along the axon of a neuron, helping speed transmission of the nervous impulse.

nonsense syllable A meaningless syllable, such as XYL or GEF, used in the study of learning.

noradrenalin One of the neurotransmitters. Also a hormone, secreted by the adrenal gland, that produces bodily changes associated with anger or "fight" situations.

norepinephrine *See* **noradrenalin.**

normal behavior Behavior that is relatively well adjusted, successful, and productive of happiness.

normal curve of distribution A bell-shaped curve that describes many events in nature; most cases cluster around the average, and the number declines approaching either the lower or the upper extreme.

O

obedience In social psychology, conformity to a figure of authority.

object constancy The tendency to perceive objects as constant and unchanging, even under varying conditions of illumination, distance, and position.

objective personality test A paper-and-pencil test administered and scored according to a standard procedure, giving results that are not affected by the opinions or prejudices of the examiner.

obsession A thought that keeps cropping up in a persistent and disturbing fashion.

obsessive-compulsive disorder A type of anxiety disorder marked by repetitious thoughts (obsessions) or acts (compulsions).

Oedipus complex According to Freud, the conflict of mingled love and hate toward the parents that every child undergoes between 2½–6 years of age.

operant avoidance Behavior, learned through operant conditioning, by which the organism attempts to avoid something unpleasant.

operant behavior Behavior that is not initially associated with or normally elicited by a specific stimulus.

operant conditioning The process by which, through learning, free operant behavior becomes attached to a specific stimulus.

operant escape Behavior, learned through operant conditioning, by which the organism seeks to escape something unpleasant.

operational rules A key concept in Piaget's theory of intelligence; a mental formula for manipulating ideas or objects into new forms and back to the original.

opium A drug derived from the poppy plant, most commonly used in the United States in the form of heroin.

opponent-process theory (of color vision) A type of pattern theory maintaining that our visual sensation of color results from three types of cones plus nerve cells. Messages they pick up from the eye are sent along as signals paired as red-or-green, blue-or-yellow, and black-or-white.

oral stage The first stage of Freudian human sexual development in which desires and gratifications focus on the mouth, tongue, and such activities as sucking and eating.

ordinary sleep A state of the organism in which brain activity is different from that in the waking state and the muscles of the body are quite relaxed.

organ of Corti The collection of hair cells, lying on the basilar membrane, that are the receptors for hearing.

organism An individual animal, either human or subhuman.

organization In learning, a form of processing; an aid to long-term memory. In perception, the tendency to find a pattern in stimuli reaching the sense organs.

outer ear The visible portion of the ear; collects sound waves and directs them toward the hearing receptors.

oval window The membrane through which sound waves are transmitted from the bones of the middle ear to the cochlea.

ovaries Glands that, in addition to producing the female egg cells, secrete hormones that bring about bodily changes known as secondary female sex characteristics.

overlearning The process of continuing to practice at learning after bare mastery has been attained.

overlearning, law of The principle that overlearning increases the length of time the material will be remembered.

overt behavior Observable behavior, such as motor movements, speech, and signs of emotion such as laughing or weeping.

overtones The additional vibrations of a source of sound, at frequencies higher than the fundamental tone it produces; the overtones account for the complexity and timbre of the sound.

P

pain drive A biological drive aroused by unpleasant or noxious stimulation, usually resulting in behavior designed to escape the stimulus.

pancreas The endocrine gland that secretes insulin.

panic disorder A type of anxiety disorder characterized by eposides of extreme terror during which the person suddenly feels overwhelmed with a sense of impending disaster and imminent death.

paradoxical sleep A state of the organism in which the brain's activity is similar to that in the waking state but the muscles are extremely relaxed; also known as REM sleep because it is accompanied by the rapid eye movements that characterize dreaming.

paranoid personality A type of personality disorder marked by constant and unwarranted suspicions and mistrust of other people.

parapsychology The study of psychological phenomena that cannot be explained in ordinary ways.

parasympathetic nervous system A division of the autonomic nervous system, composed of scattered ganglia that lie near the glands and muscles they affect. The parasympathetic system is most active in helping maintain heartbeat and digestion under normal circumstances.

parathyroids A pair of endocrine glands, lying atop the larger thyroid gland, that regulate the balance of calcium and phosphorus in the body, an important factor in maintaining a normal state of excitability of the nervous system.

partial reinforcement Reinforcement provided on some but not all occasions.

participant observation A scientific method in which the investigator takes part in a social situation, encounter group, or the like in order to study the behavior of others.

pattern theory A theory of the operation of the sense organs; it holds that our sensations are the result of the entire pattern of nervous impulses sent to the brain by many "broadly tuned" sensory receptors that respond in different ways to different stimuli.

peers For any individual, other people of about the same age and standing in the community; equals.

peptides Hormone-like chemicals affecting parts of the nervous system as well as distant organs outside it.

percentile A statistical term used to describe the position of an individual score in the total group.

perception The process through which we become aware of our environment by organizing and interpreting the evidence of our senses.

perceptual constancy The tendency to perceive a stable and consistent world even though the stimuli that reach the senses are inconsistent and potentially confusing.

perceptual expectation A form of mental set that influences interpretation.

performance Overt behavior; used as a measure of learning.

performance test An intelligence test or part of an intelligence test that measures the individual's ability to perform such tasks as completing pictures, making designs, and assembling objects.

peripheral nervous system The outlying nerves of the body and the individual neurons that make up these nerves.

peripheral traits To personality theorists, the observable traits that spring from the core of personality as channeled by individual development.

persistence of set In problem solving, the tendency to continue to apply a certain hypothesis because it has worked in other situations, often at the expense of trying different and much more efficient hypotheses.

personality The total pattern of characteristic ways of thinking, feeling, and behaving that constitute the individual's distinctive method of relating to the environment.

personality disorder A form of abnormal behavior characterized by failure to acquire mature and socially acceptable ways of coping with the problems of adult life; appears as part of the entire personality rather than being expressed in specific symptoms.

personality psychology A branch of psychology concerned with the study of how people differ in their enduring inner characteristics and traits.

personality test A test designed to measure the various characteristics that make up the individual's personality.

perspective A clue to distance perception; refers to the fact that three-dimensional objects can be delineated on a flat surface, such as the retina of the eye.

persuasive communications The transmission of information and appeals to emotion in an attempt to change another person's attitudes.

phallic stage The third stage in Freudian psychosexual development in which the libido is focused on the external sex organ, male or female.

phenomenological self A concept proposed by Rogers in his theory of personality; one's uniquely perceived self-image, based on the evidence of one's senses but not necessarily corresponding to reality.

pheromone Bodily secretions whose odor affects the behavior of other members of the species.

phi phenomenon Motion produced by a rapid succession of images that are actually stationary; the simplest form of *stroboscopic motion.*

phobic disorder A type of anxiety disorder in which the person's anxiety becomes attached to a specific object, situation, or activity resulting in an unreasonable fear, or phobia.

phonemes The building blocks of language; basic sounds that are combined into *morphemes* and words.

physical attractiveness A stronger influence than generally supposed on interpersonal attraction.

physical dependence (*also called* **addiction**) A term used to describe the condition reached by heavy users of alcohol and drugs when they require increasingly large doses to produce the desired effect, and suffer painful psychological and physical symptoms if they stop using the substance.

physiological psychology A branch of psychology focusing on the interaction between physiological functions and behavior.

pitch The property of being high or low in tone, determined by the frequency (number of cycles per second) of the sound wave.

pituitary gland The master endocrine gland that secretes hormones controlling growth, causing sexual development at puberty, and also regulating other endocrine glands.

placebo A "sugar pill" that relieves illness through psychological suggestion, although it has no medical value.

place theory A theory of hearing which proposes that tones of different pitch cause different areas of the basilar membrane to vibrate.

pleasure principle According to psychoanalytic theory, the demand of the unconscious id for immediate and total satisfaction of all its demands.

pons A structure of neurons connecting the opposite sides of the cerebellum; it helps control breathing and is apparently the origin of the nervous impulses that cause rapid eye movements during dreaming.

population In statistics, the term for all people or all events in a particular category—such as all male college students in the United States.

positive reinforcement Encouraging desired behavior through reward.

positive transfer A process in which learning is made easier by something learned previously.

posthypnotic suggestion A suggestion made during hypnosis, urging the subject to undertake some kind of activity after the hypnotic trance ends.

post-traumatic stress syndrome A special category of anxiety disorder suffered as a result of extremely shocking and stressful events—with symptoms that include loss of interest in life, insomnia and nightmares, and a tendency to keep reliving the experience.

power motive The desire to be in charge and control other people.

precognition The supposed ability to forecast events; a form of *extrasensory perception.*

preconceptual thought The term applied by Piaget to the stage of intellectual development (2–3 years of age) at which the child begins to use language to attach new meanings to stimuli in the environment and to use one stimulus as a symbol for another.

prejudice A deep-seated attitude that an individual maintains so stubbornly as to be uninfluenced by any information or experiences that might disprove it.

premise A basic belief that we use in thinking although it cannot be proved.

preoperational stage The term applied by Piaget to the period (2–7 years of age) when the child's ability to use language begins to dominate intellectual development.

primacy effect The superiority of recall of items in the first part of a list compared to those in the middle.

primary mental abilities According to Thurstone, the seven basic abilities that make up intelligence. They are verbal comprehension, word fluency, number, space, associative memory, perceptual speed, and general reasoning.

primary reinforcement Reinforcement provided by a stimulus that the organism finds inherently rewarding—usually stimuli that satisfy biological drives such as hunger or thirst.

proactive interference Interference by something learned in the past with the ability to remember new materials.

problem solving Thinking that is directed toward the solution of a problem.

programed learning A system of instruction in which the subject matter is broken down into very short steps, mastered one at a time before going on to the next.

projection A defense mechanism in which the individual hides anxiety-producing motives by accusing other people of having them.

projective personality test A test in which subjects are expected to project aspects of their own personality into ambiguous pictures or inkblots.

propinquity Physical nearness to other people, often dictated by chance; a factor in attraction.

protoplasm The basic structure of living tissue, the "stuff of life."

prototype Another term for *schema.* Also the model on which a concept is based; the ideal example of a category, to which other items included in the category bear a family relationship.

proximity In perception, one of the factors affecting organization.

psychedelic drugs Drugs, such as LSD, that often produce hallucinations and a sense of detachment from one's body.

psychiatrist A physican who has had special training in treating behavior disturbances.

psychic energizer Any of a number of drugs used to relieve depression by increasing brain activity.

psychoanalysis A type of psychotherapy developed by Freud, in which the chief tools are free association, study of dreams and slips of the tongue, and transference. Psychoanalysis attempts to give the patient insight into unconscious conflicts.

psychoanalyst A person, usually a physician, who practices psychoanalysis.

psychoanalytical theory of personality A theory originally formulated by Freud that emphasizes three parts of the personality (a) the unconscious *id,* (b) the conscious *ego,* and (c) the largely unconscious *superego.*

psychodrama A form of group psychotherapy in which the participants gain insight into their problems by dramatizing them as if in a play.

psychokinesis (PK) The supposed ability of some people to influence physical events through exercise of the mind—for example, to make dice turn up as they wish.

psychological dependence The feeling that the use of alcohol or drugs is no longer an incidental feature of life, but instead is absolutely essential in order to handle day-to-day stress.

psychological statistics The application of mathematical principles to the description and analysis of psychological measurements.

psychology The science that systematically studies and attempts to explain observable behavior and its relationship to the unseen mental processes that go on inside the organism and to external events in the environment.

psychopharmacology The study of how medically prescribed drugs affect the brain, body, and behavior.

psychophysical methods Techniques of measuring how changes in the intensity or quality of a stimulus affect sensation.

psychosexual development The Freudian theory that psychological development goes through oral, anal, phallic, and genital stages.

psychosocial development A term used by Erikson in his theory that psychological development goes hand in hand with changing social relations.

psychosomatic illness An illness in which the physical symptoms seem to have mental and emotional causes.

psychosurgery A controversial treatment for mental disturbance; cutting or destroying parts of the brain.

psychotherapy A technique used by clinical psychologists, psychiatrists, and psychoanalysts in which a person suffering from personality disorder or mental disturbance is treated by the application of psychological knowledge.

public opinion survey A scientific sampling of attitudes (for example, the Gallup poll).

punishment An attempt to eliminate undesired behavior by providing unpleasant or painful consequences.

pupil The opening in the iris that admits light waves into the eyeball.

pure science The seeking of knowledge for the sake of knowledge.

Q

questionnaire A scientific method similar to the interview but in which information is obtained through written questions.

R

random sample A statistical sample that has been obtained by chance methods that avoid any bias.

range A measurement of variability obtained by subtracting the lowest measurement from the highest.

rapid eye movement (REM) Small movements of a sleeper's eyes that occur during paradoxical sleep and dreaming.

rationalization A defense mechanism in which people maintain that a goal they were unable to attain was not desirable or that they acted out of "good" motives rather than "bad."

ratio schedule A reinforcement schedule used in operant conditioning in which reinforcement is delivered only after the subject responds a certain number of times.

reaction formation A defense mechanism in which people behave as if their motives were the opposite of their real motives; often characterized by excessive display of a "good" trait such as politeness.

reality principle According to psychoanalytic theory, the principle on which the conscious ego operates as it tries to mediate between the demands of the unconscious id and the realities of the environment.

recall A way of measuring learning. Subjects are asked to repeat as much of what they have learned as they can.

recency effect The superiority of recall of items at the end of a list compared to those in the middle.

receptor A specialized nerve ending of the senses, capable of responding to an environmental stimulus.

receptor site A spot on the cell body of a neuron that can be stimulated by the axon of another neuron.

recognition A way of measuring learning. Subjects are asked to recognize what they have learned—for example, by picking out the right answer in a multiple-choice test.

reflex An automatic and unthinking reaction to a stimulus by the organism. A reflex is inborn, not learned, and depends on inherited characteristics of the nervous system.

regression A retreat toward types of activity appropriate to a lower level of maturity; a result of anxiety and stress.

rehearsal Repeating information to keep it alive in short-term memory.

reinforcement In classical conditioning, the pairing of an unconditioned stimulus (such as food) with a conditioned stimulus (such as sound). (Here, the food is the reinforcement.) In general, the process of assisting learning by pairing desired behavior with something the organism finds rewarding.

relearning A sensitive method of measuring learning. Subjects are asked to relearn to perfection something they have learned and partially forgotten, and the time this takes is noted.

reliable test A test that gives consistent scores when the same individual is tested on different occasions.

REM See **rapid eye movement, paradoxical sleep.**

replicate To repeat an experiment at a different time with a different experimenter and different subjects but with the same results.

representative sample A statistical sample in which all parts of the population are represented.

repression A defense mechanism in which people suffering anxiety over motives seem to banish the motives from conscious thought, pushing them into the unconscious.

resistance In psychoanalysis, a blocking of the patient's thoughts by anxiety and repressions.

response A general term used to describe any kind of behavior produced by a stimulus.

reticular activating system A network of nerves in the brain stem and hypothalamus, serving as a way station for messages from the sense organs.

retina A small patch of tissue at the back of the eyeball; contains the nerve endings called rods and cones that are the receptors for vision.

retrieval The process of extracting information from long-term memory.

retroactive interference Partial or complete blacking out of old memories by new learning.

rhodopsin A light-sensitive substance associated with the rods of the retina.

rods One of the two types of receptors for vision located in the retina. The rods are receptors for light intensity, resulting in sensations of black, white, and gray.

rooting response One of the infant's inborn reflexes; an aid to finding food.

S

sample A relatively small group whose measurements are used to infer facts about the population or universe. To permit valid generalization the sample must be representative and random.

saturation The amount of pure hue present in a color as compared to the amount of other light wave lengths mixed in; thus the complexity of the mixture of waves determines saturation.

scanning A process that takes place in short-term memory; the study of information that has arrived in sensory memory from the sense organs. Also the controlled movement of the eyes when the person is studying a stimulus.

scapegoating Blaming other people, often members of minority groups, for feelings of frustration or conflict of which they are not the cause.

schema A generalized model, stored in memory, of the qualities of objects and events in the environment; also called *prototype*.

schizophrenia The most devastating of all mental disorders, in which the victim loses touch with reality and personality functioning breaks down and becomes completely disorganized.

schizophrenia spectrum According to one theory, a group of symptoms ranging from very mild to extreme, to which people may have tendencies because of an inherited defect.

school phobia An abnormal fear of leaving home to go to school experienced by children who are terrorized at the thought of venturing out into the world.

school psychology The application of psychological findings to methods of education.

secondary reinforcement Reinforcement provided by a stimulus that has acquired reward value through association with a primary reinforcing stimulus.

sedative A drug that reduces activity of the central nervous system.

selection In perception, the tendency to pay attention to only some of the stimuli that reach our senses.

selective exposure A term used by social psychologists to describe the fact that persuasive communications usually reach mostly people who already agree with them.

self-actualization Maslow's name for the human desire for self-fulfillment and harmony.

self-fulfilling prophecy An expectation about another person's behavior, leading to actions that cause the person to behave that way.

self-help group A form of community therapy based on the belief that when individuals facing comparable problems come together, they help themselves as well as others.

self-perception theory The theory that we often take the role of an outside observer trying to find the reasons for our own behavior.

semantics The meaning of the morphemes and words in language.

semicircular canals Three liquid-filled canals in the inner ear, containing receptors for the sense of equilibrium.

sense of identity The feeling sought by adolescents that they possess a distinct and unique character and are persons in their own right.

sensorimotor stage The term applied by Piaget to the period of intellectual development during the first two years of life, when the child knows the world only in terms of sensory impressions and motor activities.

sensory adaptation The tendency of sensory receptors to adjust to a stimulus and stop responding after a time.

sensory memory A memory system of very brief duration, composed of lingering traces of information sent to the brain by the senses.

sensory-motor area A part of the brain's cortex serving as a control point for sensory impressions and motor movements of the body.

sensory register *See* sensory memory.

separation anxiety Fear of being separated from the caretaker; a form of anxiety that develops in the infant of about 10 to 18 months.

set A tendency to respond in a certain way; to be prepared or "set" so to respond.

sex drive A biological drive aroused by physiological requirements for sexual satisfaction.

sex typing The process through which society molds its members into its traditional patterns of femininity or masculinity.

shadowing The pattern of light and shadow on a object; often a clue to perception of three-dimensional quality.

shape constancy The tendency to perceive objects as retaining their shape regardless of the true nature of the image that reaches the eyes because of the viewing angle.

shaping The learning of complicated tasks through operant conditioning, in which complex actions are built up from simpler ones.

short-term memory A memory system in which information is held briefly, then either transferred to long-term memory or forgotten.

similarity In perception, one of the factors affecting organization.

simple cell A feature detector cell at the lowest level.

simultaneous pairing A classical conditioning technique in which the conditioned and unconditioned stimulus are presented simultaneously.

single blind An experimental technique that keeps subjects in the dark as to whether they are in the control group or the experimental group.

situational factors Behavior-producing factors that depend on the situation of the moment, particularly the other people who are in the situation.

situational personality test A test in which the examiner observes the behavior of the subject in a situation deliberately created to reveal aspects of personality.

size constancy The tendency to perceive objects in their correct size regardless of the size of the actual image they cast on the eyes when near or far away.

sleep drive A biological drive aroused by the physiological requirements for sleep.

sleepwalking A form of dissociative reaction.

"slow" fibers Neurons that carry sensory messages signaling dull, unlocalized pain.

slow-to-warm-up children Those with an inborn tendency to need time to adjust to new situations.

smooth muscle A muscle of the internal organs, such as the stomach and intestines, or of the pupil of the eye, over which the individual ordinarily has no conscious control.

social behavior Actions taken in relation to another person or persons.

social class A subdivision of society characterized by the access it has or believes it has to power, determined in Western society largely by income and education.

social comparison theory The theory that often we can only evaluate our own abilities, opinions, and behavior by comparing ourselves with other people.

social learning theories of personality Theories maintaining that personality is made up of learned, habitual ways of responding to the environment.

social psychology The study of our behavior as members of society and the influence that the actions and attitudes of other people have on our behavior and thinking.

socialization The training of the young in the ways of the society.

society Any organized group of people, large or small.

somatosensory cortex A specialized area of the cerebral cortex responsible for analyzing and interpreting messages from the sense organs.

species-specific behavior A type of behavior toward which members of a species have an inborn tendency.

specific anxiety Being anxious in one particular situation although not in others.

spinal cord The thick cable of neurons connecting with the brain; a part of the central nervous system.

spontaneous recovery The tendency of a conditioned response that has undergone extinction to occur again after a rest period.

SQ3R system An efficient five-step study method (survey, question, read, recite, review).

standard deviation (SD) A statistical device for describing the variability of measurements.

standardized test A test that has been pretested on a large and representative sample so that one person's score can be compared with the scores of the population as a whole.

stereotype An attitude that disregards individual differences and holds that all people of a certain group behave in the same manner.

stereotyped behavior A tendency to repeat some action over and over again, almost as a ritual; a result of frustration.

stimulant A drug that increases activity of the central nervous system.

stimulus Any form of energy capable of exciting the nervous system.

stimulus complexity The relative level of simplicity or complexity possessed by a sensory stimulus. The organism apparently has stimulus needs for stimuli of a particular level of complexity found the most "comfortable."

stimulus discrimination The ability, acquired through learning, to make distinctions between stimuli that are similar but not exactly alike.

stimulus generalization The tendency of an organism that has learned to associate a stimulus with a certain kind of behavior to display this behavior toward stimuli that are similar though not exactly identical to the original stimulus.

stimulus need The tendency of an organism to seek certain kinds of stimulation. The tendency does not have the life-and-death urgency of a drive, nor is its goal as specific and clearcut. Examples are the needs for stimulation, stimulus variability, and physical contact (or tactual comfort).

stimulus variability Change and variety in stimulation; believed to be one of the organism's inborn stimulus needs.

stranger anxiety Fear of unfamiliar faces, one of the first forms of anxiety, that develops in the child at about 8 months of age.

stress The bodily wear and tear caused by physical or psychological arousal by outside events.

stress interview A form of situational personality test in which the subject is asked deliberately hostile questions and the interviewers pretend to disbelieve the answers.

stroboscopic motion Motion produced by a rapid succession of images that are actually stationary, as in motion pictures.

subculture A culture within a culture—that is, the ways of life followed by a group in a society that does not adhere to all the practices of the society as a whole.

sublimation A defense mechanism in which a forbidden motive is channeled toward a more acceptable goal, as when an artist directs sexual urges into the creation of paintings.

substance abuse The heavy and frequent use of alcohol and drugs to the point that the user can no longer function normally and continues to seek the substance despite damage to health and threat to life.

superego According to psychoanalytical theory, a largely unconscious part of the mind that threatens punishment for transgressions.

sympathetic nervous system A division of the autonomic nervous system, composed of long chains of ganglia lying along both sides of the spinal column. It activates the glands and smooth muscles of the body and helps prepare the organism for "fight" or "flight."

synapse A junction point between the axon of one neuron and the dendrite or cell body receptor site of another neuron.

synaptic cleft The tiny space between the axon of one neuron and the dendrite or receptor site of another neuron.

synaptic knob A swelling at the end of a dendrite; an important structure in the transmission of messages across the synapse.

synaptic vesicles Tiny sacs in the synaptic knob, containing neurotransmitters.

syndrome A medical term meaning the entire pattern of symptoms and events that characterize the course of a disease.

syntax The rules of language for sentence structure.

T

tabula rasa A "blank tablet"; a phrase used to describe the theory that the mind of a human baby is a "blank tablet" on which anything can be written through learning and experience.

tactual comfort Physical contact; one of the stimulus needs.

taste buds The receptors for the sense of taste; found on the tongue, at the back of the mouth, and in the throat.

teaching machine A device used in programed learning; the machine presents the program one step at a time and asks a question that the learner answers before going on to the next step.

temperature drive A biological drive aroused by physiological requirements that the body temperature be kept at a constant level (in human beings, around 98.6° Fahrenheit).

test A measurement of a sample of individual behavior. Ideally, a scientific test should be: (a) objective, (b) standardized, (c) reliable, and (d) valid.

test anxiety A form of specific anxiety common among students, centering on taking exams.

testes Glands that, in addition to producing the male sperm cells, secrete hormones that bring about secondary male sex characteristics, such as the growth of facial hair and change of voice.

thalamus The brain's major relay station, connecting the cerebrum with the lower structures of the brain and the spinal cord.

theory A statement of general principles that explains events observed in the past and predicts what will happen under a given set of circumstances in the future.

thinking The covert manipulation of images, symbols, and other mediational units, especially language, concepts, premises, and rules.

thirst drive A biological drive aroused by deprivaton of water.

threshold The minimum amount of stimulation or difference in stimulation to which a sensory receptor will respond 50 percent of the time.

thyroid gland An endocrine gland that regulates the rate of metabolism and affects the body's activity level.

tic The involuntary twitching of a muscle.

timbre The quality of a sound, determined by the number and strength of the overtones that contribute to the complexity of the sound wave.

tip of the tongue phenomenon A partially successful attempt at retrieval in which we cannot quite remember a word (for example) but seem to have it almost available or "on the tip of the tongue."

token economy An arbitrary economic system, often used in mental hospitals, in which patients are rewarded for good behavior with tokens that they can exchange like money for various privileges.

tolerance A sign of addiction to alcohol or drugs when the user begins to require increasingly large doses to produce anything like the desired effect.

trait theory A personality theory proposing that humans can be characterized by specific individual traits that can be measured on personality scales.

tranquilizer A drug that reduces anxiety and often eliminates the hallucinations and delusions of schizophrenics, apparently by slowing down the activity of the brain.

transfer of learning The effect of prior learning on new learning.

transference A psychoanalytic term for the tendency of the patient to transfer to other people (including the psychoanalyst) the emotional attitudes felt as a child toward such much loved and hated persons as parents and siblings.

tremor A shaking produced when two sets of muscles work against each other; one of the bodily changes observed in emotion.

trial and error learning A form of learning in which one response after another is tried and rejected as unsuitable, until at last a successful response is made.

true conformity Changing one's true beliefs to agree with the group.

type theory A personality theory suggesting that humans can be grouped into a small number of classes, each one having characteristics in common that set its members apart from other classes or types.

U

unconditional positive regard The basis of Rogers' humanistic therapy; total acceptance of clients as people if not all their behavior.

unconditioned response An automatic, unlearned reaction to a stimulus—such as the salivation of Pavlov's dog to food.

unconditioned stimulus A stimulus that is innately capable of causing a reflex action—such as the food that originally caused Pavlov's dog to respond with salivation.

unconscious mind In psychoanalytical theory, the bulk of the human mind, though we are not usually aware of it.

unconscious motives Desires of which we are unaware but which nonetheless influence our behavior.

unipolar depression A type of mood disorder that recurs without the swings in mood experienced in bipolar depression.

V

valid test A test found to actually measure the characteristic that it is designed to measure.

variability In statistics, the amount of variation found in a group of measurements, described by the range and standard deviation.

variable A condition that is subject to change, especially in an experiment.

ventromedial hypothalamus An area of the hypothalamus which is sensitive to changes in the food supply contained in the bloodsteam and which, when stimulated, will cause an experimental animal to stop eating.

verbal test An intelligence test or part of an intelligence test that measures the individual's ability to deal with verbal symbols; it may include items measuring vocabulary, general comprehension, mathematical reasoning, ability to find similarities, and so on.

vestibule A chamber in the inner ear containing receptors for the sense of equilibrium

visceral organs The internal organs, such as the stomach, intestines, liver, kidneys, and so on.

vocational aptitude test A test that measures the ability to perform specialized skills required in various kinds of jobs.

vocational guidance The technique of helping a person select the right life-

W

wavelength The characteristic of light waves that determines hue.

Weber's Law The rule that the difference threshold, or just noticeable difference, is a fixed percentage of the original stimulus.

withdrawal In the process of coping, a reaction in which people try to relieve feelings of frustration by withdrawing from the attempt to attain their goals. In alcoholism and drug abuse, the painful physical and psychological reactions experienced by individuals after they stop using the substance to which they are physically addicted.

X

X-chromosome One of the two chromosomes that determine sex; an X-X pairing produces a female; an X-Y pairing, a male.

Y

Y-chromosome One of the two chromosomes that determine sex.

Young-Helmholtz theory A theory stating that, since the entire range of hues can be produced by combining red, green, and blue, there must be three kinds of cones differentially sensitive to these wave lengths.

REFERENCES AND CREDITS

AACRAO (American Association of Collegiate Registrars and Admissions Officers) and the College Board. *Undergraduate admissions, 1980.* New York: College Entrance Examination Board, 1980.

Abramson, L. Y., Seligman, M. E. P., and **Teasdale, J. D.** Learned helplessness in humans. *Journal of abnormal psychology,* 1978, *87,* 49–74.

Ader, J., Cohen, N., and **Bovbjerg, P.** Conditioned suppression of humoral immunity in the rat. *Journal of comparative and psysiological psychology,* 1982, *96,* 517–21.

Adler, A. Characteristics of the first, second, and third child. *Children,* 1928, *3,* 14–52.

Aiken, L. H., and **Marx, M. M.** Hospices: Perspectives on the public policy debate. *American psychologist,* 1982, *37,* 1271–79.

Ainsworth, M. D. S., and **Bell, S. M.** Attachment, exploration, and separation. *Child development,* 1970, *41,* 49–68.

Akerstedt, T., Torsvall, L., and **Gillberg, M.** Sleepiness and shift work: Field studies. *Sleep,* 1982, *5,* 95–106.

Akhtar, S., and **Thomson, J. A., Jr.** Overview: narcissistic personality disorder. *American journal of psychiatry,* 1982, *139,* 12–20.

Allport, G. W. *Pattern and growth in personality.* New York: Holt, 1961.

Amato, P. R. Urban-rural differences in helping: Behavior in Australia and the United States. *Journal of social psychology,* 1981, *114,* 289–90.

Amato, P. R. Helping behavior in urban and rural environments: Field studies based on a taxonomic organization of helping episodes. *Journal of personality and social psychology,* 1983, *45,* 571–86.

American Psychiatric Association. *Diagnostic and statistical manual of mental disorders,* 3rd ed. Washington, DC, 1980.

American Psychiatric Association. *Diagnostic and statistical manual of mental disorders,* 3rd ed. (revised). Washington, DC, 1987.

American Psychological Association. Ethical principles of psychologists. *American psychologist,* 1981, *36,* 633–38.

American Psychological Association. *The changing face of American psychology.* Publication of the Committee on Employment and Human Resources. Dec. 1985.

Anastasi, A. Coaching, test sophistication, and developed abilities. *American psychologist,* 1981, *36,* 1086–93.

Anastasi, A. *Psychological testing,* 5th ed. New York: Macmillan, 1982.

Anderson, J. R., and **Bower, G. H.** *Human associative memory.* Washington, DC: Winston, 1973.

Andrew, R. J. The origins of facial expressions. *Scientific American,* 1965, *213,* 88–94.

Aneshensel, C. S., and **Huba, G. J.** Depression, alcohol use, and smoking over one year: A four-wave longitudinal case model. *Journal of abnormal psychology,* 1983, *92,* 134–50.

Antoni, M. H. Temporal relationship between life events and two illness measures: A cross-lagged panel analysis. *Journal of human stress,* 1985, *11,* 21–26.

Archer, D., et al. Face-ism: Five studies of sex differences in facial prominence. *Journal of personality and social psychology,* 1983, *45,* 725–35.

Arnold, M. B. *Emotion and personality,* Vol. 1. New York: Columbia Univ. Press, 1960.

Arnsten, A. F. T., and **Goldman-Rakic, P. S.** a, -adrenergic mechanisms in prefrontal cortex associated with cognitive decline in aged nonhuman primates. *Science,* 1985, *230,* 1273–76.

Aronfreed, J. The socialization of altruistic and sympathetic behavior. In J. Macauley and L. Berkowitz, eds. *Altruism and helping behavior.* New York: Academic Press, 1970.

Aronson, E. *The social animal,* 4th ed. San Francisco: Freeman, 1984.

Aronson, E., and **Linder, D.** Gain and loss of esteem as determinants of interpersonal attractiveness. *Journal of experimental social psychology,* 1965, *1,* 156–71.

Asch, S. E. Studies of independence and submission to group pressure.
    I. A minority of one against a unanimous majority. *Psychological monographs,* 1956, *70* (No. 416), Fig. 2, p. 7.

Asch, S. E., and Zukier, H. Thinking about persons. *Journal of personality and social psychology.* 1984, *46,* 1230–40.

Asher, S. R., Hymel, S., and Renshaw, P. D. Loneliness in children *Child development,* 1984, *55,* 1456–64.

Asher, S. R., Oden, S. L., and Gottman, J. M. Children's friendships in school settings. In E. M. Hetherington and R. D. Parke, eds. *Contemporary readings in child psychology,* 2d ed. New York: McGraw-Hill, 1981.

Astin, A. W. *Minorities in American higher education.* San Francisco: Jossey-Bass, 1982.

Aston-Jones, G. Behavioral functions of locus coeruleus derived from cellular attributes. *Physiological psychology,* 1985, *13,* 118–26.

Atchley, R. C. Retirement as a social institution. *Annual review of sociology,* 1982, *8,* 263–87.

Atkinson, J. W. The mainsprings of achievement-oriented activity. In J. W. Atkinson and J. O. Raynor, eds. *Personality, motivation, and achievement.* Washington, DC: Winston, 1974.

Atkinson, J. W. Resistance and over-motivation in achievement-oriented activity. In G. Serban, ed. *Psychopathology of human adaptation. Proceedings of the Third International Symposium of the Kittay Scientific Foundation.* New York: Plenum, 1976.

Atkinson, J. W., and Raynor, J. O. *Personality, motivation, and achievement.* New York: Wiley, 1978.

Atkinson, J. W., et al. The achievement motive, goal setting, and probability preferences. *Journal of abnormal and social psychology,* 1960, *60,* 27–37.

Atkinson, K., MacWhinny, B., and Stoel, C. An experiment on recognition of babbling. In *Papers and reports on child language development.* Stanford, CA: Stanford Univ. Pres, 1970.

Ayllon, T., and Azrin, N. H. *The token economy.* New York: Appleton-Century-Crofts, 1968.

Ayoub, D. M., Greenough, W. T., and Juraska, J. M. Sex differences in dendritic structure in the preoptic area of the juvenile macaque monkey brain. *Science,* 1983, *219,* 197–98.

Azuma, H. Current trends in the study of behavioral development in Japan. *International journal of human development,* 1982, *5,* 163–69.

Baastrup, P. C. Lithium in the treatment of recurrent affective disorders. In F. N. Johnson, ed. *Handbook of lithium therapy.* Baltimore: Univ. Park Press, 1980.

Baddeley, A. The cognitive psychology of everyday life. *British journal of psychology,* 1981, *72,* 257–69.

Baldwin, A. L. Personal communication, 1975.

Bales, R., and Slater, P. Role differentiation in small decision-making groups. In T. Parsons and R. Bales, eds. *The family, socialization, and interaction process.* Glencoe, IL: Free Press, 1955.

Ball, G. G. Vagotomy. *Science,* 1974, *184,* 484–85.

Bander, R. S., Russell, R. K., and Zamostny, K. P. A comparison of cue-controlled relaxation and study-skills counseling in the treatment of mathematics anxiety. *Journal of educational psychology,* 1982, *74,* 96–103.

Bandura, A. *Aggression.* Englewood Cliffs, NJ: Prentice-Hall, 1973.

Bandura, A. Behavior theory and the models of man. *American psychologist,* 1974, *29,* 859–69.

Bandura, A. *Social foundations of thought and action.* Englewood Cliffs, NJ: Prentice-Hall, 1986.

Bandura, A. *Social learning theory.* Englewood Cliffs, NJ: Prentice-Hall, 1977.

Bandura, A., Blanchard, E. B., and Ritter, B. Relative efficacy of desensitization and modeling approaches for inducing behavioral, affective, and attitudinal changes. *Journal of personality and social psychology,* 1969, *13,* 173–99.

Bandura, A., Jeffery, R. W., and Gajdos, E. Generalizing change through self-directed performance. *Behavior research and therapy,* 1975, *13,* 141–52.

Barber, J. D. *The presidential character.* Englewood Cliffs, NJ: Prentice-Hall, 1972.

Bard, M., and Sangrey, D. *The crime victim's book,* 2d ed. New York: Basic Books, 1986.

Barfield, R. E., and Morgan, J. N. Trends in satisfaction with retirement. *The gerontologist,* 1978, *18,* 19–23.

Baron, R. A., and Lawton, S. F. Environmental influences on aggression. *Psychonomic science.* 1972, *26,* 80–82.

Barron, F. The psychology of imagination. *Scientific American,* 1958, *199,* 150–56.

Barron, F., and Harrington, C. L. Creativity, intelligence, and personality. *Annual review of psychology,* 1981, *32,* 439–76.

Barron, F. *Creativity and personal freedom.* New York: Van Nostrand Reinhold, 1968.

Barsalou, L. W. Ideals, central tendency, and frequency of instantiation as determinants of graded structure in categories. *Journal of experimental psychology: Learning, memory, and cognition,* 1985, *11,* 629–54.

Baruch, G., Barnett, R., and Rivers, C. *Lifeprints.* New York: McGraw-Hill, 1983.

Baskett, L. M. Ordinal position differences in children's family interactions. *Developmental psychology,* 1984, *20,* 1026–31.

Baumeister, R. F. Choking under pressure: self-consciousness and paradoxical effects of incentives on skillful performance. *Journal of personality and social psychology,* 1984, *46,* 610–20.

Bayley, N. Development of mental abilities. In P. Mussen, ed. *Carmichael's manual of child development.* New York: Wiley, 1970.

Beach, F. A. Hormonal control of sex-related behavior. In F. A. Beach, ed. *Human sexuality in four perspectives.* Baltimore: Johns Hopkins Univ. Press, 1976.

Beauchamp, G. K., Yamazaki, K., and **Boyse, E. A.** The chemosensory recognition of genetic individuality. *Scientific American,* 1985, *253,* 86–92.

Beck, A. T., et al. Hopelessness and eventual suicide: A 10-year prospective study of patients hospitalized with suicidal ideation. *American journal of psychiatry,* 1985, *142,* 559–63.

Beeler, N. F., and **Branley, F. M.** *Experiments in optical illusion.* New York: Crowell, 1951.

Belsky, J. The determinants of parenting: A process model. *Child development,* 1984, *55,* 83–96.

Bem, D. J. *Beliefs, attitudes, and human affairs.* Belmont, CA: Brooks/Cole, 1970.

Bem, D. J. Self-perception theory. In L. Berkowitz, ed. *Advances in experimental social psychology,* Vol. 6. New York: Academic Press, 1972.

Bem, S. L. Gender schema theory: A cognitive account of sex typing. *Psychological review,* 1981, *88,* 354–64.

Benedict, R. *Patterns of culture,* 2d ed. Boston: Houghton Mifflin, 1959.

Benjamin, M., et al. Test anxiety: Deficits in information processing. *Journal of educational psychology,* 1981, *73,* 816–24.

Benson, H., et al. Historical and clinical considerations of the relaxation response. *American scientist,* 1977, *65,* 441–43.

Benson, H., and **Proctor, W.** *Beyond the relaxation response: how to harness the healing power of your personal beliefs.* New York: Time Books, 1984.

Berg, I. *Education and jobs.* New York: Praeger, 1970.

Berg, J. H. Development of friendship between roommates. *Journal of personality and social psychology.* 1984, *46,* 346–56.

Berger, K. S. *The developing person through the life span.* New York: Worth, 1983.

Berscheid, E., and **Walster, E.** Physical attractiveness. In L. Berkowitz, ed. *Advances in experimental social psychology,* Vol. 7. New York: Academic Press, 1974.

Bettelheim, B. Individual and mass behavior in extreme situations. *Journal of abnormal and social psychology,* 1943, *38,* 417–52.

Bettelheim, B. *Freud and man's soul.* New York: Knopf, 1983.

Bexton, W. H., Heron, W., and **Scott, T. H.** Effects of decreased variation in the sensory environment. *Canadian journal of psychology,* 1954, *8,* 70–76.

Biller, H. Father absence, divorce, and personality development. In M. Lamb, ed. *The role of the father in child development,* 2d ed. New York: Wiley, 1981.

Birtchnell, J. Women whose mothers died in childhood: An outcome study. *Psychological medicine,* 1980, *136,* 317–25.

Bjork, R. A. Theoretical implications of directed forgetting. In A. W. Melton and E. Martin, eds. *Coding processes in human memory.* Washington, DC: Winston, 1972.

Bjorkland, A., and **Steveni, A.** Intracerebral neural implants: neuronal replacement and reconstruction of damaged circuits. *Annual review of neuroscience,* 1984, *7,* 279–308.

Björntorp, P. Disturbances in the regulation of food intake. *Advances in psychosomatic medicine,* 1972, *7,* 116–47.

Black, J. B., and **Bern, H.** Causal coherence and memory for events in narratives. *Journal of verbal learning and verbal behavior,* 1981, *20,* 267–75.

Black, J. B., Turner, T. J., and **Bower, G. H.** Point of view in narrative comprehension, memory, and production. *Journal of verbal learning and verbal behavior,* 1979, *18,* 187–98.

Blass, E. M., and **Hall, W. G.** Drinking termination. *Psychological review,* 1976, *83,* 856–74.

Block, J. *Lives through time.* Berkeley: Bancroft Books, 1971.

Block, J. Some enduring and consequential structures of personality. In A. I. Rabin, ed. *Further explorations in personality.* New York: Wiley, 1981.

Block, N. J., and **Dworkin, G.,** eds. *The IQ controversy.* New York: Pantheon, 1976.

Bloom, B. *Developing talent in young people.* New York: Ballantine, 1985.

Bloom, L. M., Lazerson, A., and **Hofstadter, L.** *Brain, mind, and behavior.* New York: Freeman, 1985.

Bloom, W., and **Fawcett, D. W.** *A textbook of histology,* 9th ed. Philadelphia: Saunders, 1968.

Bloom, D. E., and **Trussell, J.** What are the determinants of delayed child-bearing on voluntary childlessness in the United States? National Bureau of Economic Research, working paper no. 1140, 1983.

Blumstein, P., and **Schwartz, P.** *American couples.* New York: William Morrow, 1983.

Bogen, J. Drawings by a patient. *Bulletin of the Los Angeles Neurological Society,* 1969, *34,* 73–105.

Boice, R. Increasing the writing activity of "blocked" academicians. *Behavioral research and therapy,* 1982, *20,* 197–207.

Bolles, R. C. Reinforcement, expectancy, and learning. *Psychological review,* 1972, *79,* 394–409.

Bond, E. A. *Tenth-grade abilities and achievements.* New York: Columbia University Teachers College, 1940.

Bonvillian, J. D., Orlansky, M. D., and Novack, L. L. Early sign language acquisition and its relation to cognitive and motor development. In J. G. Kyle and B. Woll. *Language in sign: An international perspective on sign language.* London: Croom Helm, 1983.

Boring, E. G. Size constancy in a picture *American journal of psychology,* 1964, *77,* 494–98.

Bornstein, M. H. Colour-name versus shape-name learning in young children. *Journal of child language,* 1985, *12,* 387–93.

Bornstein, R., and Smircina, M. T. The status of the empirical support for the hypothesis of increased variability in aging populations. *The gerontologist,* 1982, *22,* 24–243.

Bower, G. H. Organizational factors in memory. *Cognitive psychology,* 1970, *1,* 18–46.

Bower, G. H. Mental imagery and associative learning. In L. Gregg, ed. *Cognition in learning and memory.* New York: Wiley, 1972.

Bower, G. H. Improving memory. *Human nature,* 1978, *1,* 64–72.

Bower, G. H., and Clark, M. C. Narrative stories as mediators for serial learning. *Psychonomic science,* 1969, *14,* 181–82.

Bower, G. H., et al. Hierarchical retrieval schemes in recall of categorized word lists. *Journal of verbal learning and verbal behavior,* 1969, *8,* 323–43.

Bowerman, M. Learning the structure of causative verbs. *Papers and reports on child language development,* Stanford Univ., 1974, *8,* 142–78.

Bowlby, J. Childhood mourning and its implications for psychiatry. *American journal of psychiatry,* 1961, *118,* 481–98.

Boyd, J. H. The increasing rate of suicide by firearms. *The New England journal of medicine,* 1983, *308,* 872–4.

Braestrup, C. Neurotransmitters and CNS disease: Anxiety. *Lancet,* 1982, *11,* 8306, 1030–34.

Breznitz, S. *The denial of stress.* Independence, MO: The International Univ. Press, 1983.

Briggs, J. *Never in anger.* Cambridge, MA: Harvard Univ. Press, 1970.

Brigham, J. C., and Wrightsman, L. S. *Contemporary issues in social psychology.* Monterey, CA: Brooks/Cole, 1982.

Broadbent, D. E. The hidden pre-attentive process. *American psychologist,* 1977, *32,* 109–18.

Broen, P. The verbal environment of the language-learning child. *Monographs of the American Speech and Hearing Association,* 1972, p. 17.

Brooks, J., and Lewis, M. Attachment behavior in thirteen-month-old, opposite-sex twins. *Child development,* 1974, *45,* 243–47.

Bross, I. D. J. Language in cancer research. In G. P. Murphy, D. Pressman, and E. S. Mirand, eds. *Perspectives in cancer research and treatment.* New York: Liss, 1973.

Brotman, H. B. Supplement to chartbook on aging in America. The White House Conference on Aging, 1981.

Brown, G. W., and Harris T. *Social origins of depression: A study of psychiatric disorder in women.* London: Tavistock, 1978.

Brown, M. D. *The effectiveness of the personality dimensions of dependency, power, and internal-external locus of control in differentiating among unremitted and remitted alcoholics and non-alcoholic controls.* Unpublished doctoral dissertation. Univ. of Windsor, 1975.

Brown, R. *A first language.* Cambridge, MA: Harvard Univ. Press, 1973.

Brown, R., Cazden, C., and Bellugi-Klima, U. The child's grammar from I to III. In J. P. Hill, ed. *Minnesota symposia on child psychology,* Vol. 2. Minneapolis: Univ. of Minnesota Press, 1969.

Brown, R., and Kulik, J. Flashbulb memories. In U. Neisser, ed. *Memory observed.* San Francisco: Freeman, 1982.

Brown, R. W. *Social psychology.* New York: Free Press, 1965.

Bruner, J. S., Goodnow, J. J., and Austin, G. A. *A study of thinking* New York: Wiley, 1956.

Bucher, K. D., et al. The transmission of manic depressive illness. II. Segregation analysis of three sets of family data. *Journal of psychiatric research,* 1981, *16,* 65–78.

Buchsbaum, M. S., and Haier, R. J. Functional and anatomical brain imaging: Impact on schizophrenia research. *Schizophrenia bulletin,* National Institute of Mental Health, 1987, *13,* 115–32.

Bugelski, B. R., and Alampay, D. A. The role of frequency in developinig perceptual sets. *Canadian journal of psychology,* 1961, *15,* 205–11.

Bühler, C. Psychotherapy and the image of man. *Psychotherapy,* 1968, *5,* 89–94.

Bullen, B. A., Reed, R. B., and Maver, J. Physical activity of obese and nonobese girls appraised by motion picture sampling. *American journal of clinical nutrition,* 1964, *14,* 211–23.

Butler, J. M., and Haigh, G. V. Changes in the relation between self-concepts and ideal concepts consequent upon client-centered counseling. In C. R. Rogers and R. F. Dymond, eds. *Psychotherapy and personality change.* Chicago: Univ. of Chicago Press, 1954.

Butler, R. N., and Lewis, M. I. *Aging and mental health.* St. Louis: Mosby, 1977.

Butterfield, F. University exams exalt or banish 3 million in China. *New York Times,* July 19, 1980, p. 3.

Butterworth, G. The origins of auditory-visual perception and visual proprioception in human development. In R. D. Walk and H. L. Pick, Jr., eds. *Sensory perception and sensory integration.* New York: Plenum, 1981.

Byrne, D. Attitudes and attraction. In L. Berkowitz, ed. *Advances in experimental social psychology,* Vol. 4. New York: Academic Press, 1969.

Byrne, D., and Fisher, W., eds. *Adolescents, sex, and contraception.* New York: Erlbaum, 1983.

Calne, D. B. *The brain.* Publication no. 81–1813, National Institutes of Health, Rockville, MD, 1981.

Campbell, B. A., and Church, R. M., eds. *Punishment and aversive behavior.* New York: Appleton-Century-Crofts, 1969.

Campbell, D. Ethnocentrism and other altruistic motives. In D. Levine, ed. *Nebraska symposium on motivation, 1965.* Lincoln: Univ of Nebraska Press, 1965.

Campos, J. J. The current zeitgeist in emotional development: Implications for new research directions. In *Behavioral sciences research in mental health,* Vol. II, National Institute of Mental Health, Department of Health and Human Services, Feb. 1983.

Carew, T. J., Hawkins, R. D., and Kandel, E. R. Differential classical conditioning of a defensive withdrawal reflex in *Aplysia californica. Science,* 1983, Jan. 28, *219,* 397–400.

Cargan, L., and Melko, M. *Singles: Myths and realities.* Beverly Hills, CA: Sage, 1982.

Carpenter, W. T., Jr., and Stephens, J. H. The diagnosis of mania. In R. H. Belmaker and H. M. van Praag, eds. *Mania: An evolving concept.* Jamaica, New York: Spectrum Pub., 1980.

Carroll, J. B., and Horn, J. L. On the scientific basis of ability testing. *American psychologist,* 1981, *36,* 1112–19.

Carroll, J. B., et al. A specific laboratory test for the diagnosis of melancholia. Standardization, validation, and clinical utility. *Archives of general psychiatry,* 1981, *38,* 15–22.

Case, R. B., et al. Type A behavior and survival after acute myocardial infarction. *New England journal of medicine,* 1985, *312,* 737–41.

Cattell, R. B. *The scientific study of personality.* Baltimore: Penguin, 1965.

Cattell, R. B. *Abilities: Their structure, growth and action.* Boston: Houghton Mifflin, 1971.

Cattell, R. B. Personality pinned down. *Psychology today,* July 1973, 40–46.

Cerella, J. Information processing rates in the elderly. *Psychological bulletin,* 1985, *98,* 67–83.

Cheng, P. W. Pragmatic reasoning schemas. *Cognitive psychology,* 1985, *17,* 391–416.

Chilman, C. S. Adolescent childbearing in the United States: Apparent causes and consequences. In T. M. Fields et al., eds. *Review of human development.* New York: Wiley, 1982.

Chomsky, N. *Aspects of the theory of syntax.* Cambridge, MA: MIT Press, 1965.

Christiaansen, R. E. Prose memory: Forgetting rates for memory codes. *Journal of experimental psychology: Human learning and memory,* 1980, *6,* 611–19.

Chugani, H. T., and Phelps, M. E. Maturational changes in cerebral function in infants determined by ^{18}FDG positron emission tomography. *Science,* 21 Feb. 1986, *231,* 840–42.

Clark, H. H., and Clark, E. V. *Psychology and language.* New York: Harcourt, 1977.

Clark, W. B., and Midanik, L. *Report of the 1979 national survey.* National Technical Information Service, Port Royal, VA, PB No. 82–156514, 1982.

Clausen, J. A. The social meaning of differential physical and sexual maturation. In S. E. Dragastin and G. H. Elder, Jr., eds. *Life cycle.* New York: Wiley, 1975.

Cofer, C. N. *Motivation and emotion.* Glenview, IL: Scott, Foresman, 1972.

Cohen, A. R. Some implications of self-esteem for social influence. In C. I. Hovland and I. L. Janis, eds. *Personality and persuasibility.* New Haven, CT: Yale Univ. Press, 1959.

Cohen S., Glass, D. C., and Singer, J. E. Apartment noise, auditory discrimination, and reading ability in children. *Journal of experimental social psychology,* 1973, *9,* 407–22.

Cohen, S., et al. Physiological, motivational, and cognitive effects of aircraft noise on children. *American psychologist,* 1980, *35,* 231–43.

Coile, D. C., and **Miller, N. E.** How radical animal activists try to mislead humane people. *American psychologist,* 1984, *39,* 700–01.

Cole, M. A. Sex and marital status differences in death anxiety. *Omega,* 1978–1979, *9,* 139–47.

Collins, A. M., and **Quillian, M. R.** How to make a language user. In E. Tulving and W. Donaldson, eds. *Organization of memory,* New York: Academic Press, 1972.

Conley, J. J. Longitudinal consistency of adult personality.: Self-reported psychological characteristics across 45 years. *Journal of personality and social psychology,* 1985, *47,* 1325–33.

Cooper, H. Pygmalion grows up: A model for teacher expectation communication and performance influence. *Review of educational research,* 1979, *49,* 389–410.

Cooper, J. Deception and role-playing. *American psychologist,* 1976, *31,* 605–10.

Cooper, M., Zanna, M. P., and **Taves, P. A.** Arousal as a necessary condition for attitude change following induced compliance. *Journal of personality and social psychology,* 1978, *36,* 1101–06.

Coren, S., Porac, C., and **Ward, L. M.** *Sensation and perception,* 2d ed. New York: Academic Press, 1984.

Costello, C. G. Fears and phobias in women: A community study. *Journal of abnormal psychology,* 1982, *91,* 280–86.

Cowan, E. Help is where you find it. *American psychologist,* 1982, *37,* 385–95.

Coyle, J. T., Price, D. L., and **DeLong, M. H.** Alzheimer's disease: A disorder of central cholinergic innervation. *Science,* 1983, *219,* 1184–89.

Craik, F. I. M., and **Tulving, E.** Depth of processing and the retention of words in episodic memory. *Journal of experimental psychology: general,* 1975, *104,* 268–94.

Craik, K. *The nature of explanation.* Cambridge, England: Cambridge Univ. Press, 1952.

Craig, K. D., and **Patrick, C. J.** Facial expression during induced pain. *Journal of personality and social psychology,* 1985, *48,* 1080–91.

Crandall, J. E. Adler's concept of social-interest: Theory, measurement, and implications for adjustment. *Journal of personality and social psychology,* 1980, *39,* 481–98.

Crano, W. D., and **Mellon, P. M.** Causal influence of teachers' expectations on children's academic performance. *Journal of educational psychology,* 1978, *70,* 39–49.

Crenoch, J. M., and **Porter, R. H.** Recognition of maternal maxillary odor by infants. *Child development,* 1985, *56,* 1593–98.

Crockenburg, S. B. Creativity tests: A boon or boodoogle for education? *Review of educational research,* 1972, *42,* 27–45.

Crockett, H. J. The achievement motive and differential occupational mobility in the United States. *American sociological review,* 1962, *27,* 191–204.

Cronbach, L. J. *Essentials of psychological testing.* New York: Harper, 1949.

Cytrynbaum, S., et al. Midlife development: A personality and social systems perspective. In L. Poon, ed. *Aging in the 1980s: Psychological issues.* Washington, DC: American Psychological Association, 1980.

Cytryn, L., McKnew, D. H., and **Bunney, W. E.** Diagnosis of depression in children: a reassessment. *American journal of psychiatry,* 1980, *137,* 22–25.

Dabbs, J. M., Jr., and **Leventhal, H.** Effects of varying the recommendations in a fear-arousing communication. *Journal of personality and social psychology,* 1966, *4,* 525–31.

Darley, J. M., and **Fazio, R. H.** Expectancy confirmation processes arising in the social interaction sequence. *American psychologist,* 1980, *35,* 867–81.

Davidson, R. J. Affect, cognition, and hemispheric specialization. In C. E. Izard, J. Kagan, and R. B. Zajonc, eds. *Emotions, cognition, and behavior,* Cambridge, England: Cambridge Univ. Press, 1984, 320–65.

Davidson, R. J., and **Schwartz, G. E.** Patterns of cerebral lateralization during cardiac biofeedback versus the self-regulation of emotion. *Psychophysiology,* 1976, *13,* 62–68.

Davison, G. C. Elimination of a sadistic fantasy by a client-controlled counterconditioning technique. *Journal of abnormal psychology,* 1968, *73,* 84–90.

deCharms, R., and **Muir, M. S.** Motivation. *Annual review of psychology,* 1978, *29,* 91–113.

deCharms, R., et al. Behavioral correlates of directly measured achievement motivation. In D. C. McClelland, ed. *Studies in motivation.* New York: Appleton-Century-Crofts, 1955.

Dekker, E., Pelser, H. E., and **Groen, J.** Conditioning as a cause of asthmatic attacks. *Journal of psychiatric research,* 1957, *2,* 97–108.

DeLacoste-Utamsing, C., and **Holloway, R.** Sexual dimorphism in the human corpus callosum. *Science,* 1982, *216,* 1431–32.

DeLongois, A., et al. Relationship of daily hassles, uplifts, and major life events to health status. *Health psychology,* 1982, *1,* 119–36.

DeMaris A., and **Leslie, G. R.** Cohabitation with the future spouse: Its influence upon marital satisfaction and communication. *Journal of marriage and the family,* 1984, *46,* 77–84.

Denike, L. D., and **Tiber, H.** Neurotic behavior. In P. London and D. Rosenhan, eds. *Foundations of abnormal psychology.* New York: Holt, 1968.

Depue, R. A., and **Monroe, S. M.** Learned helplessness in the perspective of the depressive disorders. *Journals of abnormal psychology,* 1978, *87,* 3–20.

Deutsch, A., *The mentally ill in America.* New York: Columbia Press, 1949.

Deutsch, J. A., Puerto, A., and **Wang, M. L.** The stomach signals satiety. *Science,* 1978, *201,* 165–67.

De Valois, R. L. Neural processing of visual information. In R. W. Russell, ed. *Frontiers in physiological psychology.* New York: Academic Press, 1966.

De Valois, R. L., and **De Valois, K. K.** Neural coding of color. In E. C. Carterette and M. P. Friedman, eds. *Handbook of perception,* Vol. 5. New York: Academic Press, 1975.

De Valois, R. L., and **Jacobs, G. H.** Primate color vision. *Science,* 1968, *162,* 533–40.

de Villiers, J. G., and **de Villiers, P. A.** *Language acquisition.* Cambridge, MA: Harvard Univ. Press, 1978.

Diaz, R. M. Bilingual cognitive development: Addressing three gaps in current research. *Child development,* 1985, *56,* 1376–88.

Dion, K. K., and **Berscheid, E.** *Physical attractiveness and social perception of peers in preschool children.* Unpublished research report, 1972.

Dion, K. K., Berscheid, E., and **Walster E.** What is beautiful is good. *Journal of personality and social psychology,* 1972, *24,* 285–90.

Dollard, J., and **Miller, N. E.** *Personality and psychotherapy.* New York: McGraw-Hill, 1950.

Domjan, M., and **Burkhard, B.** *The principles of learning and behavior,* 2d ed. Monterey, CA: Brooks Cole, 1986.

Doob, A. N., and **Gross, A. E.** Status of frustrator as an inhibitor of horn-honking responses. *Journal of social psychology,* 1968, *76,* 213–18.

Dooling, D. J., and **Lachman, R.** Effects of comprehension on retention of prose. *Journal of experimental psychology,* 1971, *88,* 216–22.

Doyle, K. O. Theory and practice of ability testing in ancient Greece. *Journal of the history of the behavioral sciences,* 1974, *10,* 202–12.

Dreskin, W., and **Dreskin, W.** *The day care decision: What's best for you and your child.* New York: M. Evans, 1983.

Drewnowski, A., et al. Sweet tooth reconsidered: Taste responsiveness in human obesity. *Physiology and behavior,* 1985, *35,* 617–22.

Dreyer, P. Sexuality during adolescence. In B. Wolman, ed. *Handbook of developmental psychology.* Englewood Cliffs, NJ: Prentice-Hall, 1982.

Duncan, O. D., Featherman, D. L., and **Duncan, B.** *Socioeconomic background and achievement.* New York: Seminar Press, 1972.

Duncker, K. On problem solving. *Psychological monographs,* 1945, *58,* 1–113.

Dweck, C. S., Goetz, T., and **Strauss, N.** *Sex differences in learned helplessness.* Unpublished manuscrpt, University of Illinois, 1977.

Ebbinghaus, H. *Memory.* New York: Columbia University Teachers College, 1913.

Eckenrode, J. Impact of chronic and acute stressors on daily reports of mood. *Journal of personality and social psychology,* 1984, *46,* 907–14.

Eckhardt, M. J., et al. Health hazards associated with alcohol consumption. *Journal of the American Medical Association,* 1981, *246,* 648–66.

Edelstein, E. L. Reactivation of concentration camp experiences as a result of hospitalization. In C. D. Spielberger, I. G. Sarason, and N. A. Milgram, eds. *Stress and anxiety,* Vol. 8. Washington, DC: Hemisphere Publishing, 1982.

Education Commission of the States. *Reconnecting youth: The next stage of reform,* Denver, CO: Oct. 1985.

Eisenberg, L. The epidemiology of suicide in adolescents. *Pediatric annals,* 1984, *13,* 47–54.

Ekman, P. Universals and cultural differences in facial expressions of emotion. In J. K. Cole, ed. *Nebraska symposium on motivation,* Vol. 19. Lincoln: University of Nebraska Press, 1971.

Ekman, P. *Telling lies: Clues to deceit in the marketplace, politics, and marriage.* New York: W. W. Norton, 1985.

Ekman, P., and **Friesen, W. V.** A new pan-cultural facial expression of emotion. *Motivation and emotion,* 1986, *10,* 159–67.

Elkin, I., et al. *NIMH treatment of depression collaborative research program: initial outcome findings.* Paper read at the American Association for the Advancement of Science, May, 1986.

Ellis, E. M., Atkeson, B. M., and Calhoun, K. S. An assessment of longterm reaction to rape. *Journal of abnormal psychology,* 1981, *90,* 263–66.

Ellis, H. C., and Ashbrook, P. W. Resource allocation model of the effects of depressed mood states on memory. In K. Fiedler and J. Forgas, eds. *Affect, cognition, and social behavior.* Toronto: Hogrefe, 1987.

Ellis, H. C., et al. Emotional mood states and retrieval in episodic memory. *Journal of experimental psychology: learning, memory, and cognition,* 1985, *11,* 363–70.

Elton, C. F., and Shevel, L. R. *Who is talented? An analysis of achievement.* Iowa City: American College Testing Program, 1969.

England, P. Women and occupational prestige: A case of vacuous sex equality. *Journal of women in culture and society,* 1979, *5,* 252–65.

Epstein, A. N., Fitzsimons, J. T., and Simons, B. Drinking caused by the intercranial injection of angiotensin into the rat. *Journal of physiology* (London), 1969, *200,* 98–100.

Epstein, A. N., Kissileff, H. R., and Stellar, E., eds. *The neuropsychology of thirst.* Washington, DC: Winston, 1973.

Epstein, N. B., and Vlok, L. A. Research on the results of psychotherapy: A summary of evidence. *American journal of psychiatry,* 1981, *138,* 1027–35.

Epstein, S. The stability of behavior across time and situations. In R. Zucker, J. Aronoff, and A. I. Rabin, eds. *Personality and the prediction of behavior.* San Diego: Academic Press, 1983.

Epstein, S., and Roupenian, A. Heart rate and skin conductance during experimentally induced anxiety. *Journal of personality and social psychology,* 1970, *16,* 20–28.

Erikson, E. H. *Childhood and society,* 2d ed. New York: Norton, 1963.

Erikson, E. H. *Identity, youth, and crisis.* New York: Norton, 1968.

Erlenmeyer-Kimling, L., and Jarvik, L. F. Genetics and intelligence. *Science,* 1963, *142,* 1477–79.

Evarts, E. V. Brain mechanisms of movement. In Scientific American's *The brain.* San Francisco: Freeman, 1979.

Everson, R. B., et al. Detection of smoking-related covalent DNA adducts in human placenta. *Science,* 1986, *231,* 54–57.

Eysenck, H. J. (with Kamin, L.). *The intelligence controversy.* New York: Wiley, 1981.

Facklam, M., and Facklam, H. *The brain: Magnificent mind machine.* New York: Harcourt, 1982.

Falbo, T. Relationships between birth category, achievement, and interpersonal orientation. *Journal of personality and social psychology,* 1981, *41,* 121–31.

Falloon, I., and Liberman, R. P. Interactions between drug and psychosocial therapy in schizophrenia. *Schizophrenia bulletin,* 1983, *9,* 543–54.

Farb, P. *Word play.* New York: Knopf, 1974.

Farina, A. The stigma of mental disorders. In A. G. Miller. *In the eye of the beholder: Contemporary issues in stereotyping.* New York: Praeger, 1982.

Fazio, R. H., Zanna, M. P., and Cooper, J. Dissonance and self-perception. *Journal of experimental social psychology,* 1977, *13,* 464–79.

Feinberg, M., and Carroll, B. J. Biological "markers" for endogenous depression. *Archives of general psychiatry,* 1984, *41,* 1080–85.

Feldman, R. S. *Social psychology: Theories, research, and applications.* New York: McGraw-Hill, 1985.

Feldman, S. S., Biringen, Z. C., and Nash, S. C. Fluctuations of sex-related self-attributions as a function of stage of family life cycle. *Developmental psychology,* 1981, *17,* 24–35.

Fernald, A. The perceptual and affective salience of mother's speech to infants. In L. Feagans, ed. *The origins and growth of communication,* New Brunswick, NJ: Ablex, 1983, 5–29.

Fernald, A., and Simon, T. Expanded intonation contours in mother's speech to newborns. *Developmental psychology,* 1984, *20,* 104–13.

Feshbach, N. D. Learning to care: A positive approach to child training and discipline. *Journal of clinical child psychology,* 1983, *12,* 266–71.

Feshbach, S., and Weiner, B. *Personality,* 2d ed. Lexington, MA: Health, 1986.

Festinger, L. A. A theory of social comparison processes. *Human relations,* 1954, *7,* 117–40.

Festinger, L., Schachter, S., and Back, K. *Social pressures in informal groups.* New York: Harper, 1950.

Field, T., and Reite, M. Children's responses to separation from mother during the birth of another child. *Child development,* 1984, *55,* 1308–16.

Fillion, T. J., and Blass, E. M. Infantile experiences with suckling odors determines adult sexual behavior in rats. *Science,* Feb. 1986, *231,* 729–31.

Fine, G. A. Friends, impression management, and preadolescent behavior. In S. R. Asher and J. M. Gottman. *The development of children's friendships.* London: Cambridge Univ. Press, 1981.

Fine, M. A., Moreland, J. R., and Schwebel, A. I. Long-term effects of divorce on parent-child relationships. *Developmental psychology,* 1983, *19,* 703–13.

Finkelstein, P., Wenegrat, B., and Yalom, I. Large group awareness training. *Annual review of psychology,* 1982, *33,* 515–39.

Fodor, E. M. The power motive, group conflict, and physiological arousal. *Journal of personality and social psychology,* 1985, *49,* 1408–15.

Fodor, E. M., and Smith, T. The power motive as an influence on group decision making. *Journal of personality and social psychology,* 1982, *42,* 178–85.

Folkman, S., and Lazarus, R. S. If it changes it must be a process: Study of emotion and coping during three stages of a college examination. *Journal of personality and social psychology,* 1985, *48,* 150–70.

Forward, J., Canter, R., and Kirsch, N. Role-enactment and deception methodologies. *American psychologist,* 1976, *31,* 595–604.

Foster, B. G. Self-disclosure and intimacy in long-term marriages. In N. Stinnett et al., eds. *Family strengths 4: Positive support systems.* Lincoln: Univ. of Nebraska Press, 1982.

Frank, R. G., and Kamlet, M. S. Direct costs and expenditures for mental health in the United States, 1980. In C. A. Taube and S. A. Barrett, eds. *Mental Health, United States, 1985.* National Institute of Mental Health. DHHS Pub. No. (ADM) 85–1378. Washington, DC, 1985, 95–99.

Frankel, F. H., and Zamansky, H., eds. *Hypnosis at its bicentennial.* New York: Plenum, 1978.

Frazier, S. H. *Preventing youth suicide: A collaborative effort.* Paper presented at the National Conference on Youth Suicide, Washington, DC, June 19, 1985.

Frederick, C. Current trends in suicidal behavior in the United States. *American journal of psychotherapy,* 1978, *32,* 172–200.

Freed, A., et al. Stimulus and background factors in sign violation. *Journal of personality,* 1955, *23,* 499.

Freed, W. J., deMedinaceli, L., and Wyatt, R. J. Promoting functional plasticity in the nervous system. *Science,* 1985, *227,* 1544–52.

Freedman, D. X. Psychiatric epidemiology counts. *Archives of general psychiatry,* 1984, *41,* 931–33.

Freedman, J. L., Carlsmith, J. M., and Sears, D. O. *Social psychology.* Englewood Cliffs, NJ: Prentice-Hall, 1970.

Freeman, J. M., ed. *Prenatal and perinatal factors associated with brain disorders.* National Institute of Child Health and Human Development, NIH Publication No. 85-1149, April 1985.

French, E. G. Development of a measure of complex motivation. In J. W. Atkinson, ed. *Motives in fantasy, action, and society,* Princeton, NJ: Van Nostrand, 1959.

Friedman, M., and Rosenman, R. H. *Type A behavior and your heart.* New York: Fawcett, 1981.

Friedman M., and Ulmer, D. *Type A behavior—your heart.* New York: Fawcett, 1985.

Fromm, E. *The sane society.* New York: Holt, 1955.

Fuller, J. L. Experimental deprivation and later behavior. *Science,* 1967, *158,* 1645–52.

Furman, W., Rahe, D. F., and Hartup, W. W. Rehabilitation of socially-withdrawn preschool children through mixed-age and same-age socialization. In E. M. Hetherington and R. D. Parke, eds. *Contemporary readings in child psychology,* 2d ed. New York: McGraw-Hill, 1981.

Furnham, A., and Lowick, V., Lay theories of the causes of alcoholism. *British journal of medical psychology,* 1984, *57,* 319–32.

Gaeddert, W. P. Sex and sex-role effects on achievement strivings: Dimensions of similarity and difference. *Journal of personality,* 1985, *53,* 286–305.

Galaburda, A. M. Anatomical asymmetries. In N. Geschwind and A. M. Galaburda, eds. *Cerebral dominance: The biological foundations.* Cambridge, MA: Harvard Univ. Press, 1984.

Gamson, W. A., Fireman, B., and Rytina, S. *Encounters with unjust authority.* Homewood, IL: Dorsey, 1982.

Garb, J. J., and Stunkard, A. J. Taste aversion in man. *American journal of psychiatry,* 1974, *131,* 1204–07.

Garber, J., and Hollon, S. *Depression and the expectancy of success for self and for others.* Unpublished manuscript, Univ. of Minnesota, 1977.

Garcia, J., and Koelling, R. Relation of cue to consequence in avoidance learning. *Psychonomic science,* 1966, *4,* 123–24.

Gardner, H. *Frames of mind: The theory of multiple intelligence.* New York: Basic Books, 1983.

Gardner, R. A., and Gardner, B. T. Communication with a young chimpanzee. In R. Chauvin, ed. *Edition du centre national de la recherche scientific.* Paris:, 1972.

Garmezy, N. Stressors of childhood. In N. Garmezy and M. Rutter, eds. *Stress, coping, and child development.* New York: McGraw-Hill, 1983, 43–84.

Gates, A. L. Recitation as a factor in memorizing. *Archives of psychology,* No. 40. New York: Columbia Univ., 1917.

Gati, I., and Tversky, A. Weighing common and distinctive features in perceptual and conceptual judgments. *Cognitive psychology,* 1984, *16,* 341–70.

Gatz, A. J. *Manter's essentials of clinical neuroanatomy and neurophysiology.* Philadelphia: Davis, 1970.

Gebhard, P. H. Personal communication, 1979.

Geen, R. G. *Personality.* St. Louis: Mosby, 1976.

Geen, R. G., and O'Neil, E. C. Activation of cue-elicited aggression by general arousal. *Journal of personality and social psychology,* 1969, *ii,* 289–92.

Geis, B. D., and Gerrard, M. Predicting male and female contraceptive behavior: A discriminant analysis of groups high, moderate, and low in contraceptive effectiveness. *Journal of personality and social psychology,* 1984, *46,* 669–80.

Geyer, L. H., and DeWald, C. G. Feature lists and confusion matrices. *Perception and psychophysics,* 1973, *14,* 471–82.

Gibbs, M. S., Lachenmeyer, J. R., and Sigal, J., eds. *Community psychology.* New York: Gardner Press, 1980.

Gibson, E. J. *Principles of perceptual learning and development.* New York: Appleton-Century-Crofts, 1969.

Gibson, E. J., and Walk, R. D. The "visual cliff." *Scientific American,* 1960, *202,* 64–71.

Gilligan, C. *In a different voice.* Cambridge, MA: Harvard Univ. Press, 1982.

Gilovich, T., Vallone, R., and Tversky, A. The hot hand in basketball: On the misperception of random sequences. *Cognitive psychology,* 1985, *17,* 295–314.

Ginsburg, H. J., and Miller, S. M. Sex differences in children's risk-taking behavior. *Child development,* 1982, *53,* 426–28.

Glaser, R., and Bond, L. Introduction to a special issue on testing: Concepts, policy, practice, and research. *American psychologist,* 1981, *36,* 997–1000.

Glass, D. C., and Singer, J. E. Experimental studies of controllable and uncontrollable noises. *Representative research in social psychology,* 1973, *4,* 165–83.

Gleitman, L. R., Newport, E. L., and Gleitman, H. The current status of the motherese hypothesis. *Journal of child language,* 1984, *11,* 43–79.

Glick, P. C., and Spanier, G. B. Married and unmarried cohabitation in the United States. *Journal of marriage and the family,* 1980, *42,* 19–30.

Glick, R. Promoting competence and coping through retirement planning. In L. A. Bond and J. C. Rosen, eds. *Competence and coping during adulthood.* Hanover, NH: Univ. Press of New England, 1980.

Gold, S. R. The CAP control theory of drug abuse. In D. J. Lettieri, M. Sayers, and H. W. Pearson, eds. *Theories on drug abuse: Selected contemporary perspectives.* National Institute on Drug Abuse, DHHS Publication No. (ADM) 80–967, 1980, pp. 8–11.

Goldberger, L. Sensory deprivation and overload. In L. Goldberger and S. Breznitz, eds. *Handbook of stress: Theoretical and clinical aspects.* New York: Free Press, 1982.

Goldfarb, W. Effects of early institutional care on adolescent personality. *American journal of orthopsychiatry,* 1944, *14,* 441–47.

Goldman, P. An alternative to developmental plasticity: Heterology of CNS structures in infants and adults. In D. G. Stein, J. J. Rosen, and N. Butters, eds. *Plasticity and recovery of function in the central nervous system.* New York: Academic Press, 1974.

Goldsen, R., et al. *What college students think.* Princeton, NJ: Van Nostrand, 1960.

Goldstein, J. H., and Arms, R. L. Effects of observing athletic contests on hostility. *Sociometry,* 1971, *234,* 83–90.

Goldstein, M. J., Baker, B. L., and Jamison, K. R. *Abnormal psychology: Experiences, origins, interventions.* Boston: Little, Brown, 1980.

Goleman, D. Hypnosis comes of age. *Psychology today,* July 1977, *11,* 54–56 +.

Goode, W. J. *The family.* Englewood Cliffs, NJ: Prentice-Hall, 1965.

Goodnow, J. J., and Bethon, G. Piaget's tasks. *Child development,* 1966, *37,* 573–82.

Goodwin, D. W., et al. Alcohol problems in adoptees raised apart from biological parents. *Archives of general psychiatry,* 1973, *28,* 238–43.

Gopnik, A. The acquisition of *gone* and the development of the object concept. *Journal of child language,* 1984, *11,* 273–92.

Gopnik, A., and Meltzoff, A. N. Semantic and cognitive development in 15- to 21-month-old children. *Journal of child language,* 1984, *11,* 495–513.

Gordon, A. M. Adequacy of responses given by low-income and middle-income kindergarten children in structured adult-child conversations. *Developmental psychology,* 1984, *20,* 881–92.

Gormezano, I., Kehoe, E. J., and Marshall, B. S. Twenty years of classical conditioning research with the rabbit. In J. M. Sprague and A. N. Epstein, eds. *Progress in psychobiological and physiological research,* Vol. 10. New York: Academic Press, 1983.

Gotlib, I. H. Depression and general psychopathology in university students. *Journal of abnormal psychology,* 1984, *93,* 19–30.

Gottesman, I. I. Biogenetics of race and class. In M. Deutsch, I. Katz, and A. B. Jensen, eds. *Social class, race, and psychological development.* New York: Holt, 1963.

Gottesman, I. I., and **Shields, J.** *Schizophrenia: The epigenetic puzzle.* New York: Cambridge Univ. Press, 1982.

Gottlieb, J. and **Carver, C. S.** Anticipation of future interaction and the bystander effect. *Journal of experimental social psychology,* 1980, *16,* 253–60.

Gottschalk, E. C. "Student shock. Stress is more severe for collegians today; counselors keep busy." *The wall street journal,* June 1, 1983.

Gould, M. S., and **Shaffer, D.** The impact of suicide in television movies: Evidence of imitation. *New England journal of medicine,* Sept. 11, 1986, *315,* 690–94.

Graf, P., Squire, L. R., and **Mandler, G.** The information that amnesic patients do not forget. *Journal of experimental psychology: Learning, memory, and cognition,* 1984, *10,* 164–78.

Graf, R. C. Speed reading. *Psychology today,* Dec. 1973, pp. 112–13.

Graham, P., and **Rutter, M.** Adolescent disorders. In M. Rutter and L. Hersov, eds. *Child and adolescent psychiatry: Modern approaches.* London: Blackwell, 1985.

Gray, J. A. Anxiety. *Human nature,* 1978, *1,* 38–45.

Graziano, W. G., Feldesman, A. B., and **Rahe, D. F.** Extraversion, social cognition, and the salience of aversiveness in social encounters. *Journal of personality and social psychology.* 1985, *49,* 971–80.

Green, J., and **Tapp, W. N.** Feeding cycles in smokers, ex-smokers, and non-smokers. *Physiology and behavior,* 1986, *36,* 1059–63.

Greenberger, E., and **Steinberg, L.** *Work in teenage America.* Cambridge, MA: Harvard Univ. Press, 1985.

Greenblatt, M., Becerra, R. M., and **Serafetinides, E. A.** Social networks in mental health: An overview. *The American journal of psychiatry,* 139, Aug. 1982, 977–84.

Greene, W. A., Goldstein, S., and **Moss, A. J.** Psychosocial aspects of sudden death. *Archives of internal medicine,* 1972, *129,* 725–31.

Greenough, W. T. Lecture to the developmental Psychology Research Group, Estes Park, Colo.: June, 1982.

Grief, E., and **Ulman, K.** The psychological impact of menarche on early adolescent females: A review of the literature. *Child development,* 1982, *53,* 1413–30.

Grinker, J. A. Physiological and behavioral basis of human obesity. In D. W. Pfaff, ed. *The physiological mechanisms of motivation.* New York: Springer-Verlag, 1982.

Gross, A. E. and **Fleming, I.** Twenty years of deception in social psychology. *Personality and social psychology,* 1982, *8,* 402–08.

Gruenberg, B. The happy worker: An analysis of educational and occupational differences in determinants of job satisfaction. *American journal of sociology,* 1980, *86,* 247–71.

Guilford, J. P. A factor analytic study across the domains of reasoning, creativity, and evaluation. *Reports from the psychology laboratory,* Univ. of Southern California, 1954.

Guilford, J. P. *The nature of human intelligence.* New York: McGraw-Hill, 1967.

Gunnar, M. R., Leighton, K., and **Peleaux, R.** Effects of temporal predictability on the reactions of 1-year-olds to potentially frightening toys. *Developmental psychology,* 1984, *20,* 449–58.

Gunter, B., Berry, C., and **Clifford, B. R.** Proactive interference effects with television news items: Further evidence. *Journal of experimental psychology: human learning and memory,* 1981, *7,* 480–87.

Haig, N. D. The effect of feature displacement on face recognition. *Perception,* 1984, *13,* 505–12.

Hall, C. S., and **Lindzey, G.** *Theories of personality,* 3d ed. New York: Wiley, 1978.

Hall, G. S. *Adolescence,* Vol. 1. New York: Appleton, 1904.

Hall, R. C. W. Anxiety. In R. C. W. Hall, ed. *Psychiatric presentations of medical illness: Somatopsychic disorders.* New York: Spectrum, 1980a.

Hall, R. C. W. Medically induced psychiatric disease–an overview. In R. C. W. Hall, ed. *Psychiatric presentations of medical illness: Somatopsychic disorders.* New York: Spectrum, 1980b.

Hall, R. C. W., Stickney, S. K., and **Gardner, E. R.** Behavioral toxicity of nonpsychiatric drugs. In R. C. W. Hall. *Psychiatric presentations in medical illness: Somatopsychic disorders.* New York: Spectrum, 1980.

Halpern, A. R. Organization and memory for familiar songs. *Journal of experimental psychology: Learning, memory, and cognition,* 1984, *10,* 496–512.

Hamilton, M. Diagnosis of anxiety states. In R. J. Mathew, ed. *The biology of anxiety.* New York: Bruner/Mazel, 1982.

Hansel, C. E. M. *ESP.* New York: Scribners, 1966.

Hardy, A. B. *Exposure therapy as a treatment for agoraphobia and anxiety.* Unpublished manuscript, Palo Alto, CA, 1969.

Hare, R. Electrodermal and cardiovascular correlates of sociopathy. In R. Hare and D. Schalling, eds. *Psychopathic behavior: Approaches to research.* New York: Wiley, 1978.

Hargadon, F. Tests and college admissions. *American psychologist,* 1981, *36,* 1112–19.

Harlow, H. F. The formation of learning sets. *Psychological review,* 1949, *56,* 51–65.

Harlow, H. F. The development of affectional patterns in infant monkeys. In B. M. Foss, ed. *Determinants of infant behaviour.* London: Methuen, 1961.

Harlow, H. F., and **Harlow, M. K.** Social deprivation in monkeys. *Scientific American,* 1962, *207,* 136–46.

Harlow, H. F., and **Harlow, M. K.** Learning to love. *American scientist,* 1966, *54,* 244–72.

Harrell, T. W., and **Harrell, M. S.** Army general classification test scores for civilian occupations. *Educational and psychological measurement,* 1945, *5,* 229–39.

Harris, B. Whatever happened to little Albert? *American psychologist,* 1979, *34,* 151–60.

Harris, F. R., et al. Effects of positive social reinforcement on regressed crawling of a nursery school child. In L. Ullmann and L. Krasner, eds. *Case studies in behavior modification.* New York: Holt, 1965.

Hartmann, D. P. Influence of symbolically modeled instrumental aggression and pain cues on aggressive behavior. *Journal of personality and social psychology,* 1969, *11,* 280–88.

Hartmann, E. *The functions of sleep.* New Haven, CT: Yale Univ. Press, 1973.

Hartmann, E. *The nightmare.* New York: Basic Books, 1984.

Hartmann, H. Ego psychology and the problem of adaptation. In D. Rapaport, ed. *Organization and pathology of thought.* New York: Columbia Univ. Press, 1951.

Hauser, B. B. Custody in dispute: Legal and psychological profiles of contesting families. *Journal of the academy of child psychiatry,* 1985, *24,* 575–82.

Hebb, D. O., and **Thompson, W.** The social significance of animal studies. In G. Lindzey and E. Aronson, eds. *The handbook of social psychology,* 2d ed., Vol. 2 (Research methods). Reading, MA: Addison-Wesley, 1968.

Heidbreder, E., et al. Psychomental stress in tetraplegic man: Dissociation in autonomic variables and emotional responsiveness. *Journal of human stress,* 1984, *10,* 157–65.

Heider, F. Social perception and phenomenal causality. *Psychological review,* 1944, *51,* 358–74.

Heller, K. and **Mansbach, W. E.** The multifaceted nature of social support in a community sample of older women. *Journal of social issues,* 1984, *40,* 99–112.

Helsing, K. L., Szklo, M., and **Comstock, G. W.** Factors associated with mortality after widowhood. *American journal of public health,* 1981, *71,* 802–09.

Hendin, H., and **Haas, A. P.** *Wounds of war: The psychological aftermath of combat in Vietnam.* New York: Basic Books, 1985.

Hendrick, S., et al. Gender differences in sexual attitudes. *Journal of personality and social psychology,* 1985, *48,* 1630–42.

Herdt, G. H. *Guardian of the flutes.* New York: McGraw-Hill, 1981.

Herink, R., ed. *The psychotherapy handbook.* New York: New American Library, 1980.

Herrmann, T. F., Hurwitz, H. M. B., and **Levine, S.** Behavioral control, aversive stimulus frequency, and pituitary-adrenal response. *Behavioral neuroscience,* 1984, *98,* 1094–99.

Herrnstein, R. J., and **de Villiers, P. A.** Fish as a natural category for people and pigeons. In G. H. Bower, ed. *Psychology of learning and motivation,* Vol. 14. New York: Academic Press, 1980.

Hervey, G. R. Regulation of energy balance. *Nature,* 1969, *222,* 629–31.

Herzog, E., and **Lewis, H.** Children in poor families. *American journal of orthopsychiatry,* 1970, *40,* 375–87.

Hess, E. H. Attitude and pupil size. *Scientific American,* 1965, *212,* 46–54.

Hess, E. H. The role of pupil size in communication. *Scientific American,* 1975, *233,* 110–19.

Hess, R. D., et al. Maternal variables as predictors of children's school readiness and later achievement in vocabulary and mathematics in the sixth grade. *Child development,* 1984, *55,* 1902–12.

Heston, L. H., and **White, J. A.** *Dementia: A practical guide to Alzheimer's disease and related illness.* San Francisco: Freeman, 1983.

Hetherington, E. M., and **Camara, K. A.** Families in transition: The process of dissolution and reconstitution. In R. D. Parke, ed. *Review of child development research: The family,* Vol 7. Chicago: Univ. of Chicago Press, 1984.

Hilgard, E. R., and **Hilgard, J. R.** *Hypnosis in the relief of pain.* Los Altos, CA: William Kaufmann, 1975.

Hill, J. The family. In M. Johnson, ed. *Toward adolescence: The middle school years.* Chicago: Univ. of Chicago Press, 1980.

Hilton, I. Differences in the behavior of mothers toward first- and later-born children. *Journal of personality and social psychology,* 1967, *7,* 282–90.

Hinkle, L. E. The effect of exposure to cultural change, social change, and change in interpersonal relationships on health. In B. S. Dohrenwend and B. P. Dohrenwend. *Stressful life events: Their nature and effects.* New York: Wiley, 1974.

Hiroto, D. S. Locus of control and learned helplessness. *Journal of experimental psychology,* 1974, *102,* 187–93.

Hirsch, J., and **Knittle, J. L.** Cellularity of obese and nonobese human adipose tissue. *Federal proceedings,* 1970, *29,* 1516–21.

Hochberg, J. *Perception.* 2d ed. Englewood Cliffs, NJ: Prentice-Hall, 1978.

Hoffman, J. E. Interaction between global and local levels of a form. *Journal of experimental psychology: Human perception and performance,* 1980, *6,* 222–34.

Hohmann, G. W. Some effects of spinal cord lesions on experienced emotional feelings. *Psychophysiology,* 1966, *3,* 143–56.

Holahan, C. J., and **Moos, R. H.** Life stress and health: Personality, coping, and family support in stress resistance. *Journal of personality and social psychology,* 1985, *49,* 739–47.

Holmes, T. H., and **Rahe, R. H.** The social readjustment rating scale. *Journal of psychosomatic research,* 1967, *11,* 213–18.

Holzman, P. S. Recent studies of psychophysiology in schizophrenia. *Schizophrenia bulletin,* National Institute of Mental Health, 1987, *13,* 49–75.

Holyrod, K. A., et al. Performance, cognition, and physiological responding in test anxiety. *Journal of abnormal psychology,* 1978, *87,* 442–51.

Honzik, M. P., Macfarlane, J. W., and **Allen, L.** The stability of mental test performance between two and eighteen years. *Journal of experimental education,* 1948, *17,* 454–55.

Hooley, J. M. Expressed emotion: A review of the critical literature. *Clinical psychology review,* 1985, *5,* 119–39.

Hormuth, S. Sex differences in horse trading: a replication of Maier and Burke. *Replications in social psychology,* 1982, *2,* 24–26.

Horney, K. *Our inner conflicts.* New York: Norton, 1945.

Horowitz, M. J. Anxious states of mind induced by stress. In A. H. Tuma and J. D. Maser, eds. *Anxiety and the anxiety disorders.* Hillsdale, NJ: Erlbaum, 1985.

Hovland, C. I., Lumsdaine, A. A., and **Sheffield, F. C.** *Experiments on mass communication,.* Princeton, NJ: Princeton Univ. Press, 1949.

Hsu, C., et al. The temperamental characteristics of Chinese babies. *Child development,* 1981, *52,* 1337–40.

Hubel, D. H. The visual cortex of the brain. *Scientific American,* 1963, *209,* 54–62.

Hubel, D.H. Vision and the brain. *Bulletin of the American Academy of Arts and Sciences,* 1978, *31,* 17–28.

Hubel, D. H. The brain. In Scientific American's *The brain.* San Francisco: Freeman, 1979.

Hubel, D. H., and **Wiesel, T. N.** Receptive fields and functional architecture in two non-striate visual areas (18 and 19) of the cat. *Journal of neurophysiology,* 1965, *28,* 229–89.

Hubel, D. H., and **Wiesel, T. N.** Brain mechanisms of vision. In Scientific American's *The brain.* San Francisco: Freeman, 1979.

Hudspeth, A. J. The cellular basis of hearing: The biophysics of hair cells. *Science,* 15 Nov. 1985, *230,* 745–52.

Ilfeld, F. W. Coping styles of Chicago adults: Description. *Journal of human stress.* 1980, *6,* 2–10.

Institute of Medicine, *Health and behavior: Frontiers of research in the biobehavioral sciences.* Washington, DC: National Academy Press, 1982.

Iversen, L. L. The chemistry of the brain. *Scientific American,* 1979, *241,* 14+, 134–35+.

Iversen, L. L. Neurotransmitters and CNS disease: Introduction. *Lancet,* 1982, II, 8304, 914–16.

Izard, C. E. *Human emotions.* New York: Plenum, 1977.

Izard, C. E., and **Dougherty, L. M.** Two complementary systems for measuring facial expressions in infants and children. In C. E. Izard, ed. *Measuring emotions in infants and children.* Cambridge, England: Cambridge Univ. Press, 1982.

Jacobson, J. L., et al. Prenatal exposure to an environmental toxin: A test of the multiple effects model. *Developmental psychology,* 1984, *20,* 523–32.

James, W. *Principles of psychology.* New York: Holt, 1890.

Jamison, K. R. Personal communication, 1982.

Janis, I. L. Effects of fear arousal on attitude change: recent developments in theory and experimental research. In L. Berkowitz, ed. *Advances in experimental social psychology,* Vol. 3. New York: Academic Press, 1967.

Janis, I. L., and **Frick, F.** The relationship between attitudes toward conclusions and errors in judging logical validity. *Journal of experimental psychology,* 1943, *33,* 73–77.

Janke, L. L., and **Havighurst, R. J.** Relation between ability and social-status in a midwestern community. II. Sixteen-year-old boys and girls. *Journal of educational psychology,* 1945, *36,* 499–509.

Jencks, C., et al. *Inequality.* New York: Basic Books, 1972.

Jensen, A. R. How much can we boost IQ and school achievement? *Harvard educational review,* 1969, *39,* 1–123.

Jensen, A. R. The heritability of intelligence. *Saturday evening post,* 1972, *244,* 9.

Joffe, C. Sex role socialization and the nursery school. *Journal of marriage and the family,* 1971, *33,* 467–75.

Johansson, G. Visual motion perception. In R. Held and W. Richards, eds. *Recent progress in perception: Readings from Scientific American.* San Francisco: Freeman, 1976, 67–75.

John, E. R., et al. Observation learning in cats. *Science,* 1968, *159,* 1489–91.

Johnson, D. H. and **Gelso, C. J.** The effectiveness of time limits on counseling and psychotherapy. *The counseling psychologist,* 1980, *9,* 70–83.

Johnson, L. C., and **MacLeod, W. L.** Sleep and wake behavior during gradual sleep reduction. *Perceptual motor skills,* 1973, *36,* 87–97.

Johnson, P. B. Achievement motivation and success: Does the end justify the means? *Journal of personality and social psychology,* 1981, *40,* 374–75.

Johnston, L. D., Bachman, J. G., and **O'Malley, P. M.** *Student drug use in America, 1975–1981.* Rockville, MD: National Institute on Drug Abuse, 1982.

Jones, E. E. The rocky road from acts to dispositions. *American psychologist,* 1979, *34,* 107–17.

Jones, E. E., and **Nisbett, R. E.** The actor and the observer. In E. E. Jones, et al., eds. *Attribution.* Morristown, NJ: General Learning Press, 1972.

Kagan, J. *The second year: The emergence of self-awareness.* Cambridge, Harvard Univ. Press, 1981.

Kagan, J., Kearsley, R. B., and **Zelazo, P. R.** *Infancy: Its place in human development.* Cambridge, MA: Harvard Univ. Press, 1978.

Kagan, J., and **Klein, R. E.** Cross-cultural perspectives on early development. *American psychologist,* 1973, *28,* 947–61.

Kagan, J., and **Moss, H. A.** *Birth to maturity.* New York: Wiley, 1962.

Kagan, J., et al. Behavioral inhibition to the unfamiliar. *Child development,* 1984, *55,* 2212–25.

Kail, R., and **Pellegrino, J. W.** *Human intelligence.* New York: Freeman, 1985.

Kamin, L. Presidential address, Eastern Psychological Association, 1979.

Kamin, L. (with **Eysenck, H. J.**). *The intelligence controversy.* New York: Wiley, 1981.

Kandel, D. B., and **Lesser, G. S.** *Youth in two worlds.* San Francisco: Jossey-Bass, 1972.

Kandel, E. R., and **Schwartz, J. H.** Molecular-biology of learning-modulation of transmitter release. *Science,* 1982, *218,* 433–43.

Kane, J. M. Low dose medication strategies in the maintenance treatment of schizophrenia. *Schizophrenia bulletin,* 1983, *9,* 528–32.

Kay, D., and **Bergmann, K.** Epidemiology of mental disorders among the aged in the community. In J. Birren and R. Sloan, eds. *Handbook of mental health and aging.* Englewood Cliffs, NJ: Prentice-Hall, 1980.

Kay, P. Synchronic variability and diachronic changes in basic color terms. *Language in society,* 1975, *4,* 257–70.

Kearsley, R. B., et al. Differences in separation protest between day care and home reared infants. *Pediatrics,* 1975, *55,* 171–75.

Kelley, H., et al. *Close relationships.* San Francisco: Freeman, 1983.

Kenrick, D. T., and **Stringfield, D. O.** Personality traits and the eye of the beholder: Crossing some traditional philosophical boundaries in the search for consistency in all of the people. *Psychological review,* 1980, *87,* 88–104.

Kety, S. S. The impact of neurobiology in the concept of the mind. Paper presented at European Neuroscience Congress, Malaga, Spain, Sept. 1982.

Kiecolt-Glaser, J. K., et al. Psychosocial modifiers of immunocompetence in medical students. *Psychosomatic medicine,* 1984, *46,* 7–14.

Kimmel, D. C. *Adulthood and aging: An interdisciplinary developmental view,* 2d ed. New York: Wiley, 1980.

Kimura, D. Male brain, female brain: The hidden difference. *Psychology today,* Nov. 1985, 50–58.

Kindred, D. Yancey: Fall into darkness. *The Washington Post.* March 24, 1978.

Kintsch, W. *Memory and cognition,* 2d ed. New York: Wiley, 1977.

Kirsch, M. A., and **Glass, L. L.** Psychiatric disturbances associated with Erhard Seminars Training. *American journal of psychiatry,* 1977, *134,* 1254–58.

Klatzky, R. L. *Human memory: Structures and processes,* 2d ed. San Francisco: Freeman, 1980.
Kleinmuntz, B., and Szucko, J. J. A field study of the fallibility of polygraph lie detection. *Nature,* 1984, *308,* 449–50.
Kline, N. S. *From sad to glad.* New York: Ballantine, 1974.
Klopfer, B., and Davidson, H. H. *The Rorschach technique.* New York: Harcourt, 1962.
Knapp, R. R. Relationship of a measure of self-actualization to neuroticism and extraversion. *Journal of consulting psychology,* 1965, *29,* 168–72.
Knittle, J. L., and Hirsch, J. Effect of early nutrition on the development of rat epididymal fat pads. *Journal of clinical investigations,* 1968, *47,* 2091.
Kohlberg, L. The development of children's orientations toward a moral order. I. Sequence in the development of moral thought. *Vita humana,* 1963, *6,* 11–33.
Kohlberg, L. Moral and religious education and the public schools. In T. Sizer, ed. *Religion and public education.* Boston: Houghton Mifflin, 1967.
Kohler, W. *The mentality of apes.* Harcourt, 1925.
Kolata, G. Why do people get fat? *Science,* March 15, 1985, *227,* 1327–28.
Koss, M. P., Butcher, J. N., and Strupp, H. H. Brief psychotherapy methods in clinical research. *Journal of Consulting and Clinical Psychology,* 1986, *54,* 60–67.
Krantz, D., et al. *Behavior and health.* Paper commissioned by NRC/ABASS Committee on Basic Research in Behavioral and Social Sciences and Social Science Research Council, 1981.
Kretschmer, E. *Physique and character.* New York: Harcourt, 1925.
Krippner, S. *Experimentally induced effects in dreams and other altered conscious states.* 20th International Congress of Psychology, Tokyo, Aug. 1972.
Kubie, L. S. *Practical and theoretical aspects of psychoanalysis.* New York: International Univ. Press, 1950.
Kübler-Ross, E. *On death and dying.* New York: Macmillan, 1969.
Kuffler, S. W. Discharge pattern and functional organization of mammalian retina. *Journal of neurophysiology,* 1953, *16,* 37–68.
Kupfer, D. J., et al. Electroencephalographic sleep of younger depressives: Comparison with normals. *Archives of general psychiatry,* 1985, *42,* 806–10.
Kurz, E. M., Sengelaub, D. R., and Arnold, A. P. Androgens regulate the denndritic length of mammalian motoneurons in adulthood. *Science,* 1986, *232,* 395–98.

Lacey, J. I., and Lacey, B. C. Verification and extension of the principle of autonomic response-stereotypy. *American journal of psychology,* 1958, *71,* 50–73.
Laing, R. D. *The divided self.* Baltimore: Penguin, 1960.
Lang, P. J. and Melamed, B. G. Avoidance conditioning therapy of an infant with chronic ruminative vomiting. *Journal of abnormal psychology,* 1969, *74,* 1–8.
Latane, B., and Nida, S. Ten years of research on group size and helping. *Psychological bulletin,* 1981, *89,* 308–24.
Laudenslager, M. L., and Ryan, S. M. Coping and immunosuppression: inescapable but not escapable shock suppresses lymphocyte proliferation. *Science,* 1983, *221,* 568–70.
Lazarus, R. S. *The stress and coping paradigm.* Paper delivered at the University of Washington conference on the critical evaluation of behavioral paradigms for psychiatric science, 1978.
Lazarus, R. S. Thoughts on the relations between emotion and cognition. *American psychologist,* 1982, *37,* 1019–24.
Lazarus, R. S., and Averill, J. R. Emotion and cognition. In C. D. Spielberger, ed. *Anxiety.* New York: Academic Press, 1972.
Leedy, M. G., and Wilson, M. S. Testosterone and cortisol levels in crewmen of U.S. Air Force fighter and cargo planes. *Psychosomatic medicine,* 1985, *47,* 333–38.
Lefcourt, H. M., et al. Locus of control as a modifier of the relationship between stressors and moods. *Journal of personality and social psychology,* 1981, *41,* 357–69.
Le Magnen, J. Is regulation of body weight elucidated? *Neuroscience and biobehavior reviews,* 1984, *8,* 515–22.
LeMasters, E. E., and DeFrain, J. *Parents in contemporary America.* Homewood, IL: Dorsey, 1983.
Lenneberg, E. H. *Biological foundations of language.* New York: Wiley, 1967.
Leon, M. R., and Revelle, W. Effects of anxiety on analogical reasoning: A test of three theoretical models. *Journal of personality and social psychology,* 1985, *49,* 1302–15.
Lepper, M. R., Greene, D., and Nisbett, R. E. Undermining children's interest with extrinsic awards. *Journal of personality and social psychology,* 1973, *28,* 129–37.
Levine, F. M., and Fasnacht, G. Token rewards may lead to token learning. *American psychologist,* 1974, *29,* 816–20.

Levine, L. E. Mine: Self-definition in 2-year-old boys. *Developmental psychology,* 1983, *19,* 544–49.

Levine, M. W., and **Shefner, J. M.** *Fundamentals of sensation and perception.* Reading, MA: Addison-Wesley, 1981.

Levinson, B., and **Reese, H. W.** Patterns of discrimination learning set in preschool children, fifth-graders, college freshmen, and the aged. *Monographs of the society for research in child development,* 1967, *32* (No. 7), 1–92.

Levinson, D. J. *The seasons of a man's life.* New York: Knopf, 1978.

Levy, J. Psychobiological implications of bilateral asymmetry. In Dimond, S. J., and Beaumont, J. G., eds. *Hemispheric function in the human brain.* New York: Wiley, 1974, 121–84.

Levy, J. Right brain, left brain: Fact and fiction. *Psychology today,* May 1985, 38–44.

Lewin, K. *A dynamic theory of personality.* New York: McGraw-Hill, 1935.

Lewis, E. R., **Zeevi, Y. Y.**, and **Everhart, T. E.** Studying neural organization in *Aplysia* with scanning electron microscope. *Science,* 1969, *165,* 1140–42.

Lewontin, R. C. Race and intelligence. In N. J. Block and G. Dworkin, eds. *The IQ controversy.* New York: Pantheon, 1976.

Libet, B. Unconscious cerebral initiative and the role of conscious will in voluntary action. *The behavioral and brain sciences,* 1985, *8,* 529–39.

Lieberman, M. A., **Yalom, I. D.**, and **Miles, M. B.** *Encounter groups.* New York: Basic Books, 1973.

Liebeskind, J. C., and **Paul, L. A.** Psychological and physiological mechanisms of pain. *Annual review of psychology,* 1977, *28,* 41–60.

Linn, S., et al. Salience of visual patterns in the human infant. *Developmental psychology,* 1982, *18,* 651–57.

Lipscomb, D. M. High intensity sounds in the recreational environment: Hazard to young ears. *Clinical pediatrics,* 1969, *8,* 63–68.

Locke, S. E., et al. Life change stress, psychiatric symptoms, and natural killer cell activity. *Psychosomatic medicine,* 1984, *46,* 441–53.

Loehlin, J. C., **Lindzey, G.**, and **Spuhler, J. N.** *Race differences in intelligence.* San Francisco: Freeman, 1975.

Loevinger, J., and **Knoll, E.** Personality: Stages, traits, and the self. *Annual review of psychology,* 1983, *34,* 195–222.

Loftus, E. F., **Miller, D. G.**, and **Burns, H. J.** Semantic integration of verbal information into a visual memory. *Journal of experimental psychology,* 1978, *4,* 19–31.

Logue, A. W., **Ophir, I.**, and **Strauss, K. E.** The acquisition of taste aversion in humans. *Behavior research and therapy,* 1981, *19,* 319–33.

Londerville, S., and **Main, M.** Security of attachment, compliance, and maternal training methods in the second year of life. *Developmental psychology,* 1981, *17,* 289–99.

Lord, C. G., **Lepper, M. R.**, and **Mackie, D.** Atitude prototypes as determinants of attitude-behavior consistency. *Journal of personality and social psychology,* 1984, *46,* 1254–66.

Lorenz, K. *On aggression.* New York: Harcourt, 1966.

Luborsky, L., **Docherty, J. P.**, and **Penick, S.** Onset conditions for psychosomatic symptoms. *Psychosomatic medicine,* 1973, *35,* 187–201.

Lutz, C. The domain of emotion words on Ifaluk. *American ethologist,* 1982, *9,* 113–28.

Lykken, D. T. *A tremor in the blood: Uses and abuses of the lie detector.* New York: McGraw-Hill, 1981.

Lyon, D. R. Individual differences in immediate serial recall: A matter of mnemonics. *Cognitive psychology,* 1977, *9,* 403–11.

MacArthur R. D., and **Sekuler R.** Alcohol and motion perception. *Perception and psychophysics,* 1982, *31,* 502–05.

Maccoby, E. E. Personal communication, 1979.

Maccoby, E. E., and **Jacklin, C. N.** *The psychology of sex differences.* Stanford, CA: Stanford Univ. Press, 1974.

Maccoby, E. E., **Snow, M. E.**, and **Jacklin, C. N.** Children's dispositions and mother-child interaction at 12 and 18 months: A short-term longitudinal study. *Developmental psychology,* 1984, *20,* 459–72.

Macfarlane, J. W. From infancy to adulthood. *Child education,* 1963, *39,* 336–42.

Macfarlane, J. W. Perspectives on personality consistency and change from the guidance study. *Vita humana,* 1964, *7,* 115–26.

MacKinnon, D. W. The nature and nurture of creative talent. *American psychologist,* 1962, *17,* 484–95.

MacKinnon, D. W. *The personality of correlates of creativity.* In G. S. Neilson, ed. *Proceedings of the XIV international congress of applied psychology,* Copenhagen, 1961. Copenhagen: Munksgaard, 1962.

MacKinnon, D. W. Stress interview. In D. N. Jackson and S. Messick, eds. *Problems in human assessment.* New York: McGraw-Hill, 1967.

MacNichol, E. F., Jr. Three-pigment color vision. *Scientific American,* 1964, *211,* 48–56.

Maddi, S. R. *Personality theories,* rev. ed. Homewood, IL: Dorsey, 1972.

Maddi, S. R., and **Kobasa, S.C.** *The hardy executive: Health under stress.* Homewood, IL: Dow Jones-Irwin, 1984.

Maier, S. F., Seligman, M. E. P., and **Solomon, R. L.** Pavlovian fear conditioning and learned helplessness. In B. A. Campbell and R. M. Church, eds. *Punishment and aversive behavior.* New York: Appleton-Century-Crofts, 1969.

Malof, M., and **Lott, A. J.** Ethnocentrism and the acceptance of Negro support in a group pressure situation. *Journal of abnormal and social psychology,* 1962, *65,* 254–58.

Mann, L., and **Janis, I. L.** A followup study on the long-term effects of emotional role playing. *Journal of personality and social psychology,* 1968, *8,* 338–42.

Manton, K. G., and **Soldo, B. J.** Dynamics of health changes in the oldest old: New perspectives and evidence. *Milbank memorial fund quarterly,* 1985, *63,* 206–85.

Marks, I. M. Aversion therapy. *British journal of medical psychology,* 1968, *41,* 47–52.

Marsh, H. W., and **Parker, J. W.** Determinants of student self-concept: Is it better to be a relatively large fish in a small pond even if you don't learn to swim as well? *Journal of personality and social psychology,* 1984, *47,* 213–31.

Maslach, C. The emotional consequences of arousal without reason. In C. E. Izard, ed. *Emotion, conflict, and defense.* New York: Plenum, 1978.

Maslow, A. H. Personal communication, 1969.

Maslow, A. H. *Motivation and personality,* 2d ed. New York: Harper, 1970.

Masserman, J. H. *Principles of dynamic psychiatry,* 2d ed. Philadelphia: Saunders, 1961.

Masters, W. H., and **Johnson, V. E.** Personal communication, 1963.

Masters, W. H., Johnson, V. E., and **Kolodny, R. C.** *Human sexuality,* 2d ed. Boston: Little, Brown, 1985.

Masters, W. H., Johnson, V. E., and **Kolodny, R. C.** *Masters and Johnson on sex and human loving.* Boston: Little, Brown, 1986.

Matson, F. W. Humanistic theory: The third revolution in psychology. *The humanist,* March/April 1971, 7–11.

Maugh, T. M., II. Sleep-promoting factor isolated. *Science,* 1982, *216,* 1400.

Mayer, R. E. *Thinking, problem solving, and cognition.* San Francisco: Freeman, 1983.

McBurney, D., and **Collings, V.** *Introduction to sensation/perception.* Englewood Cliffs, NJ: Prentice-Hall, 1977.

McCartney, K. Effect of quality of day care environment on children's language development. *Developmental psychology,* 1984, *20,* 244–60.

McCaul, K. D. Sensory information, fear level, and reactions to pain. *Journal of personality,* 1980, *48,* 494–504.

McCaul, K. D., Holmes, D. S., and **Solomon, S.** Voluntary expressive changes in emotion. *Journal of personality and social psychology,* 1982, *42,* 145–52.

McCaul, K. D., Solomon, S., and **Holmes, D. S.** Effects of paced respiration and expectations on physiological and psychological responses to threat. *Journal of personality and social psychology,* 1979, *37,* 564–71.

McClelland, D. C. Inhibited power motive and high blood pressure in men. *Journal of abnormal psychology,* 1979, *88,* 182–90.

McClelland, D. C. *Achievement motive.* New York: Irvington, 1985.

McClelland, D. C., and **Atkinson, J. W.** The projective expression of needs. I. The effect of different intensities of the hunger drive on perception. *Journal of psychology,* 1948, *25,* 205–22.

McClelland, D. C., Clark, R. A., and **Lowell, E. L.** *The achievement motive.* New York: Appleton-Century-Crofts, 1953.

McClelland, D. C., and **Liberman, A. M.** The effect of need for achievement on recognition of need-related words. *Journal of personality,* 1949, *18,* 236–51.

McClelland, D. C., and **Teague, G.** Predicting risk preferences among power-related acts. *Journal of personality,* 1975, *43,* 266–85.

McClelland, D. C., et al. *The drinking man.* New York: Free Press, 1972.

McClelland, D. C., et al. Stressed power motivation, sympathetic activation, immune function, and illness. *Journal of human stress,* 1980, *6,* 11–19.

McClenon, J. A survey of elite scientists: Their attitudes toward ESP and parapsychology. *Journal of parapsychology,* 1982, *46,* 127–52.

McClintock, M. K. Menstrual synchrony and suppression. *Nature,* 1971, *229,* 224–45.

McClintock, M. K. Estrous synchrony: Modulation of ovarian cycle length by female pheromones. *Physiology and behavior,* 1984, *32,* 701–05.

McCullough, C. Color adaptation of edge-detectors in the human visual system. *Science,* 1965, *149,* 1115–16.

McDermott, M. J. *Rape victimization in 26 American cities.* Washington, DC: U.S. Department of Justice, 1979.

Mcgeer, G. L., and Mcgeer, E. G. Chemistry of mood and emotion. *Annual review of psychology,* 1980, *31,* 273–307.

McGeoch, J. A. The influence of associative value upon the difficulty of nonsense-syllable lists. *Journal of genetic psychology,* 1930, *37,* 421–26.

McGrath, J. W. *Social psychology.* New York: Holt, 1964.

McGraw, M. B. *The neuromuscular maturation of the human infant.* New York: Columbia Univ. Press, 1943.

McKenzie, B. E., Tootell, H. E., and Day, R. H. Development of visual size constancy during the 1st year of human infancy. *Developmental psychology,* 1980, *16, 3,* 163–74.

McNemar, Q. *The revision of the Stanford-Binet scale.* Boston: Houghton Mifflin, 1942.

Mead, M. *Sex and temperament.* New York: Morrow, 1935.

Meddis, R., Pearson, A. J. D., and Langford, G. An extreme case of healthy insomnia. *EEG clinical neurophysiology,* 1973, *35,* 213–24.

Mellinger, G. D., and Balter, M. B. Prevalence and patterns of use of psychotherapeutic drugs. Results from a 1979 national survey of American adults. In G. Tognoni, C. Bellantuono, and M. Lader, eds. *Epidemiological impact of psychotropic drugs.* Amsterdam: Elsevier/North Holland Biomedical Press, 1981.

Mellinger, G. D., and Balter, M. B. Prevalence of insomnia and drug treatment. Abstract at NIMH Concensus Development Conference on Drugs and Insomnia, Bethesda, MD, Nov. 15–17, 1983.

Meltzer, H. Y. Biological studies in schizophrenia. *Schizophrenia bulletin,* National Institute of Mental Health, 1987, *13,* 77–111.

Melzack, R. *The puzzle of pain.* New York: Basic Books, 1973.

Mendelson, W. B., *The use and misuse of sleeping pills,* New York: Plenum, 1980.

Mendelson, W. B., et al. The experience of insomnia and daytime and nighttime functioning. *Psychiatry research,* 1984, *12,* 235–50.

Milgram, S. Group pressure and action against a person. *Journal of abnormal and social psychology,* 1964, *69,* 137–43.

Milgram, S. *Obedience to authority.* New York: Harper, 1974.

Miller, B. C., and Sollie, D. L. Normal stress during the transition to parenthood. *Family relations,* 1980, *29,* 459–65.

Miller, G. A. *Language and communication.* New York: McGraw-Hill, 1951.

Miller, G. A. The magical number seven, plus or minus two: Some limits on our capacity for processing information. *Psychological review,* 1956, *63,* 81–97.

Miller, G. A. Language and psychology. In E. H. Lenneberg, ed. *New directions in the study of language.* Cambridge, MA: M.I.T. Press, 1964.

Miller, G. A. *Language and speech.* San Francisco: Freeman, 1981.

Miller, G. A. Personal communication, 1983.

Miller, J. G. Culture and the development of everyday social explanation. *Journal of personality and social psychology,* 1984, *46,* 961–78.

Miller, L. C., Berg, J. H., and Archer, R. L. Openers: Individuals who elicit intimate self-disclosure. *Journal of personality and social psychology,* 1983, *44,* 1234–44.

Miller, N. E. *From the brain to behavior.* Invited lecture at XII Interamerican Congress of Psychology, Montevideo, Uruguay, March 30 to April 6, 1969.

Miller, N. E. *Behavioral sciences report for the overview cluster of the President's biomedical research panel,* 1975.

Miller, N. E. The role of learning in physiological response to stress. In G. Serban, ed. *Psychopathology of human adaptation.* New York: Plenum, 1976.

Miller, N. E. Behavioral medicine: Symbiosis between laboratory and clinic. *Annual review of psychology,* 1983, *34,* 1–31.

Miller, N. E. The value of behavioral research on animals. *American psychologist,* 1985a, *40,* 423–40.

Miller, N. E. Rx: Biofeedback. *Psychology today.* Feb. 1985b, 54–59.

Miller, N. E., and Dollard, J. *Social learning and imitation.* New Haven, CT: Yale Univ. Press, 1941.

Milner, B. Memory and the medial temporal regions of the brain. In K. K. Pribram and D. E. Broadbent, eds. *Biology of memory.* New York: Academic Press, 1970, 29–50.

Minuchin, S., et al. A conceptual model of psychosomatic illness in children: Family organization and family therapy. *Archives of general psychiatry,* 1975, *32,* 1032–38.

Mischel, W. *Personality and assessment.* New York: Wiley, 1968.

Mischel, W. Convergences and challenges in the search for consistency. *American psychologist,* 1984, *39,* 351–64.

Mishkin, M. Personal communication, 1986.

Misra, R. K. Achievement, anxiety, and addiction. In D. J. Lettieri, M. Sayers, and H. W. Pearson, eds.

Theories on drug abuse: Selected contemporary perspectives. National Institute on Drug Abuse, DHHS Publication No. (ADM) 80–967, 1980, 212–14.

Morgan, M. Television and adolescents' sex role stereotypes: a longitudinal study. *Journal of personality and social psychology,* 1982, *43,* 947–55.

Morris, J. L. Propensity for risk taking as a determinant of vocational choice. *Journal of personality and social psychology,* 1966, *3,* 328.

Moruzzi, G. The sleep-waking cycle. In R. H. Adrian, et al., eds. *Reviews of psychology 64.* Berlin: Springer-Verlag, 1972.

Moss, H. A., and Susman, E. J. Longitudinal study of personality development. *Constancy and change in human development.* Cambridge, MA: Harvard Univ. Press, 1980.

Mueser, K. T. et al. You're only as pretty as you feel: Facial expression as a determinant of physical attractiveness. *Journal of personality and social psychology,* 1984, *46,* 469–78.

Mumford, E., Schlesinger, H. J., and Glass, G. V. The effects of psychological intervention on recovery from surgery and heart attacks: An analysis of the literature. *American journal of public health,* 1982, *72,* 141–51.

Mumford, J., et al. A new look at evidence about reduced cost of medical utilization following mental health treatment. *American journal of psychiatry,* 1984, *141,* 1145–58.

Munn, N. L., Fernald, L. D., Jr., and Fernald, P. S. *Introduction to psychology,* 2d ed. Boston: Houghton Mifflin, 1969.

Murphy, G. L., and Medin, D. L. The role of theories in conceptual coherence. *Psychological review,* 1985, *92,* 289–316.

Murray, E. A., and Mishkin, M. Amygdalectomy impairs crossmodal association in monkeys. *Science,* 1985, *228,* 3 May 1985, 604–06.

Mussen, P. H., and Eisenberg-Berg, N. *Roots of caring, sharing, and helping: The development of pro-social behavior in children.* San Francisco: Freeman, 1977.

Mussen, P. H., et al. *Child development and personality,* 6th ed. New York: Harper, 1984.

Myers, J. K., et al. Six-month prevalence of psychiatric disorders in three communities. *Archives of general psychiatry,* 1984, *41,* 959–67.

Natelson, B. H. Stress, predisposition, and the onset of serious disease: Implications about psychosomatic etiology. *Neuroscience and biobehavioral reviews,* 1983, *7,* 511–27.

National Center for Health Statistics. *Advanced report of final mortality statistics.* 1984.

National Center for Health Statistics. *Health, United States, 1985.* DHHS Pub. No. (PHS) 85–1232, Dec. 1984.

National Center for Health Statistics. *Vital statistics of the United States,* 2, 1987.

National Hospice Organization. *Guide to the nation's hospice.* Arlington, VA: 1986.

National Institute on Aging. *Age page: Can life be extended?* DHHS, National Institutes of Health, June 1984.

National Institute on Alcohol Abuse and Alcoholism. *Facts about alcohol and alcoholism.* DHHS Publication No. (ADM) 80–31, 1980.

National Institute on Drug Abuse, *Overview of the 1985 National Household Survey on Drug Abuse,* 1986.

National Institute of Health. Coronary-prone behavior and coronary heart disease: A critical review. *Circulation,* 1981, *63,* 1199–1215.

National Institutes of Health. Mood disorders: Pharmacologic prevention of recurrences. *Consensus Development Conference,* Vol. 4 No. 5, 1984.

National Institutes of Health. *Electroconvulsive therapy: Consensus development* (Consensus Statement). Bethesda, MD: June 1985, (5).

National Institutes of Health. Unpublished Report: *Research highlights,* 1985.

National Institute of Mental Health. *Attitudes toward the mentally ill: Research perspectives.* DHHS Publication No. (ADM) 80–1031, 1980.

National Institute of Mental Health. Consensus Development Conference on Drugs and Insomnia, Bethesda, MD, Nov. 15–17, 1983.

National Institute of Mental Health. *Alzheimer's disease.* DHHS Publication No. (ADM) 84–1323, Sept. 1984.

National Institute of Mental Health. *Useful information on anorexia nervosa and bulimia.* DHHS Publication No. (ADM) 87–1514, 1987.

National Research Council. *Ability testing: Uses, consequences and controversies.* Washington, DC: National Academy Press, 1982.

Neff, J. A. Race and vulnerability to stress: An examination of differential vulnerability. *Journal of personality and social psychology,* 1985, *49,* 481–91.

Neisser, U., and Becklen, R. Selective looking. *Cognitive psychology,* 1975, *7,* 480–94.

Newcomb, T. M. *The acquaintance process.* New York: Holt, 1961.
Newman, A. Personal communication, 1986.
Newport, E. L. Motherese. *Technical report no. 52. Center for Human Information Processing.* San Diego, CA: Univ. of California, 1975.
Nichols, P. L. Familial mental retardation. *Behavior genetics,* 1984, *14,* 161–70.
Nielsen, S. L., and Sarason, I. G. Emotion, personality, and selective attention. *Journal of personality and social psychology,* 1981, *41,* 945–60.
Nigro, G., and Neisser, U. *Cognitive psychology,* 1983, *15,* 467–82.
Nisbett, R. E. Taste, deprivation, and weight determinants of eating behavior. *Journal of personality and social psychology,* 1968, *10,* 107–16.
Nisbett, R. E. Hunger, obesity, and the ventromedial hypothalamus. *Psychological review,* 1972, *79,* 433–53.
Nisbett, R. E., and Platt, J. Unpublished data referred to in R. E. Nisbett. Hunger, obesity, and the ventromedial hypothalamus. *Psychological review,* 1972, *79,* 433–53.
Nisbett, R. E., and Valins, S. Perceiving the causes of one's own behavior. In E. E. Jones, et al., eds. *Attribution.* Morristown, NJ: General Learning Press, 1972.
Nissen, H., and Crawford, M. A preliminary study of food-sharing behavior in young chimpanzees. *Journal of comparative psychology,* 1936, *22,* 283–419.
Nolen-Hoeksema, S. Sex differences in unipolar depression: Evidence and theory. *Psychological bulletin,* 1987, *101,* 259–82.
Nurco, D. N. Etiological aspects of drug abuse. In R. I. Dupont, A. Goldstein, and J. O'Donnell, eds. *Handbook on drug abuse.* Washington, DC: U.S. Government Printing Office, January 1979, 315–34.
Nurnberger, J. I., and Gershon, E. S. Genetics. In E. S. Paykel, ed. *Handbook of affective disorders.* London: Churchill Livingston, 1982.

O'Connor, M. J., Cohen, S., and Parmelee, A. H. Infant auditory discrimination in preterm and full-term infant as a predictor of 5-year intelligence. *Developmental psychology,* 1984, *20,* 159–65.
Offer, D., Ostrov, E., and Howard, K. I. *The adolescent: A psychological self-portrait.* New York: Basic Books, 1982.
O'Kelly, C. G. Sexism in children's television, *Journalism quarterly,* 1974, *51,* 722–24.
O'Leary, K. D., and Drabman, R. Token reinforcement programs in the classroom. *Psychological bulletin,* 1971, *75,* 379–98.
Olson, S. L., Bates, J. E., and Bayles, K. Mother-infant interaction and the development of individual differences in children's cognitive competence. *Developmental psychology,* 1984, *20,* 166–79.
O'Neil, H. F., Jr., Spielberger, C. D., and Hansen, D. N. Effects of state anxiety and task difficulty on computer-assisted learning. *Journal of educational psychology,* 1969, *60,* 343–50.
Opler, M. K. Cultural induction of stress. In M. H. Appley and R. Trumbull, eds. *Psychological stress.* New York: Appleton-Century-Crofts, 1967.
Orne, M. Lecture to American Association for the Advancement of Science. Washington, DC, 1982.
Ornstein, R. The split and the whole brain. *Human nature,* 1978, *1,* 76–83.
Ornstein, R., and Thompson, R. F. *The amazing brain.* Boston: Houghton Mifflin, 1984.
Osterweis, M., Solomon, F., and Green, M. *Bereavement: Reactions, consequences, and care.* Washington, DC: National Academy of Sciences, 1984.
Oyama, S. *A sensitive period for the acquisition of a second language.* Unpublished doctoral dissertation, Harvard Univ., 1973.

Paddock, J., O'Neill, C. W., and Haver, W. *Faces of anti-violence.* International Society for Research on Aggression, Washington, DC, Sept. 1978.
Parloff, M. B. Personal communication, 1987.
Parloff, M. B., London, P., and Wolfe, B. Individual psychotherapy and behavior change. *Annual review of psychology,* 1986, *37,* 321–49.
Passingham, R. E. Memory of monkeys (Macaca mulatta) with lesions in prefrontal cortex. *Behavioral neurosciences,* 1985, *99,* 3–21.
Patterson, G. R., Hops, H., and Weiss, R. L. Interpersonal skills training for couples in early stages of conflict. *Journal of marriage and the family,* 1975, *37,* 295–303.
Patterson, G. R., and Stouthamer-Loeber, M. The correlation of family management practices and delinquency. *Child development,* 1984, *55,* 1299–307.
Pavlov, I. P. *Conditioned reflexes.* London: Oxford Univ. Press, 1927 (reprinted by Dover, New York, 1960).

Paykel, E. S. Contribution of life events to causation of psychiatric illness *Psychological medicine,* 1978, *8,* 245–53.

Pearson, C. Intelligence of Honolulu preschool children in relation to parents' education. *Child development,* 1969, *40,* 647–50.

Peele, S. Reductionism in the psychology of the eighties: Can biochemistry eliminate addiction, mental illness, and pain? *American psychologist,* 1981, *36,* 807–18.

Peele, T. L. *The neuroanatomic basis for clinical neurology.* New York: McGraw-Hill, 1961.

Perin C. T. A quantitative investigation of the delay of reinforcement gradient. *Journal of experimental psychology,* 1943, *32,* 37–51.

Petersen, A. C. *Menarche: Meaning of measures and measuring meaning.* Presented at meeting of Society for Menstrual Cycle Research, New Rochelle, NY, June, 1981.

Peterson, C., and **Seligman, M. E. P.** Causal explanations as a risk factor in depression. *Psychological review,* 1984, *91,* 347–74.

Petti, T. A. Depression in children: A significant disorder. *Psychosomatics,* 1981, *22,* 444–47.

Pettigrew, T. F. Racially separate or together? *Journal of social issues,* 1969, *25,* 43–69.

Pezdek, K., and **Miceli, L.** Life-span differences in memory integration as a function of processing time. *Developmental psychology,* 1982, *18,* 485–90.

Pfaffman, C. Gustatory nerve impulses in rat, cat, and rabbit. *Journal of neurophysiology,* 1955, *18,* 429–40.

Phares, E. J., and **Lamiell, J. T.** Internal-external control, interpersonal judgments of others in need, and attribution of responsibility. *Journal of personality,* 1975, *43,* 23–38.

Phillips, D. The illusion of incompetence among academically competent children. *Child development,* 1984, *55,* 2000–16.

Phillips, D. P., and **Carstensen, L. L.** Clustering of teenage suicides after television news stories about suicide. *New England journal of medicine,* Sept. 11, 1986, *315,* 685–89.

Piaget, J. *The origins of intelligence in children.* New York: International Univ. Press, 1952.

Piliavin, I. M., Rodin, J., and **Piliavin, J. A.** Good Samaritanism: An underground phenomenon? *Journal of personality and social psychology,* 1969, *13,* 289–99.

Pillemer, D. H. Flashbulb memories of the assassination attempt of President Reagan. *Cognition,* 1984, *16,* 63–80.

Pine, C. J. Anxiety and eating behavior in obese and nonobese American Indians and white Americans. *Journal of personality and social psychology,* 1985, *49,* 774–80.

Polivy, J. On the induction of emotion in the laboratory: Discrete moods or multiple affect states? *Journal of personality and social psychology,* 1981, *41,* 803–17.

Pollack, I., and **Pickett, J. M.** Intelligibility of excerpts from fluent speech. *Journal of verbal learning and verbal behavior,* 1964, *3,* 79–84.

Pomerantz, J. R. The grass is always greener: An ecological analysis of an old aphorism. *Perception,* 1983, *12,* 501–02.

Post, F. *Persistent prosecutory states of the elderly.* London: Pergamon, 1966.

Postman, L., Bruner, B., and **McGinnies, E.** Personal values as selective factors in perception. *Journal of abnormal and social psychology,* 1948, *43,* 142–54.

Pratt, W. F. Understanding U. S. fertility: Findings from the national survey of population growth. *Population bulletin,* Population Reference Bureau, 1984, *39,* 1–42.

Premack, D. *Intelligence in ape and man.* Hillsdale, NJ: Erlbaum, 1976.

Premack, D. "Gavagai!" or the future history of the animal language controversy,. *Cognition,* 1985, *19,* 207–96.

Pritchard, R. M. Stabilized images on the retina. *Scientific American,* 1961, *204,* 72–78.

Pruett, H. L. Stressors in middle adulthood. *Family and community health,* 1980, *2,* 53–60.

Putnam, F. W. Traces of Eve's faces. *Psychology today,* Oct. 1982, 88.

Putnam, F. W., et al. The clinical phenomenology of multiple personality disorder: Review of 100 recent cases. *Journal of clinical psychiatry,* June 1986, *47,* 285–93.

Quinton, D., and **Rutter, M.** Parenting behavior of mothers raised "in care." In A. R. Nicol, ed. *Practical lessons from longitudinal studies.* Chichester, England: Wiley, 1983.

Rabkin, J. G., and **Struening, E. L.** Life events, stress, and illness. *Science,* 1976, *194,* 1013–20.

Radecki, C., and **Jennings, J.** Sex as a status variable in work settings: Female and male reports of dominance behavior. *Journal of applied social psychology,* 1980, *10,* 71–85.

Radloff, R. *Opinion and affiliation.* Unpublished doctoral dissertation, Univ. of Minnesota, 1959.

Radtke, R. C., and **Grove, E. K.** Pro-active inhibition in short-term memory: Availability or accessibility? *Journal of experimental psychology: Human learning and memory,* 1977, *3,* 78–91.

Rakic, P. et al. Concurrent overproduction of synapses in diverse regions of the primate cortex. *Science,* 1986, *232,* 232–35.

Raloff, J. Occupational noise—the subtle pollutant. *Science news,* 1982, *121,* 347–50 and 377–81.

Rasmussen, J., ed. *Man in isolation and confinement.* Hawthorne, NY: Aldine, 1973.

Reason, J. The psychopathology of everday slips. *The sciences,* Sept./Oct. 1984, 45–49.

Rebelsky, F. Infancy in two cultures. *Nederlands tijdschrift voor de psychologie,* 1967, *22,* 379–85.

Rechtschaffen, A. Physiological correlates of prolonged sleep deprivation in rats. *Science,* July 1983, *8,* 182–84.

Regestein, Q. R. *Sound sleep.* New York: Simon and Schuster, 1980.

Reis, H. T., et al. Physical attractiveness in social interaction: II. Why does appearance affect social experience? *Journal of personality and social psychology,* 1982, *43,* 979–96.

Reis, H. T., Senchak, M., and **Solomon, B.** Sex differences in the intimacy of social interaction: Further examination of potential explanations. *Journal of personality and social psychology,* 1985, *48,* 1204–17.

Reisman, B. Conflict in an Israeli collective community. *Journal of conflict resolution,* 1981, *25,* 237–58.

Rescorla, R. A. Predictability and number of pairings in Pavlovian fear conditioning. *Psychonomic science,* 1966, *4,* 383–84.

Rescorla, R. A., and **Holland, P. C.** Behavioral studies of associative learning in animals. In M. R. Rosenzweig and L. W. Porter, eds. *Annual review of psychology,* 1982, *33,* 265–308.

Reuter-Lorenz, P., and **Davidson, R. J.** Differential contributions of the two cerebral hemispheres to the perception of happy and sad faces. *Neuropsychologia,* 1981, *19,* 609–13.

Rhine, J. B., and **Pratt, J. G.** *Parapsychology.* Springfield, IL: Thomas, 1957.

Rice, K. M., and **Blanchard, E. B.** Biofeedback in the treatment of anxiety disorders. In R. J. Mathew, ed. *The biology of anxiety.* New York: Brunner/Mazel, 1982.

Riessman, F. *Support groups as preventive intervention.* Paper presented to Vermont Conference on Primary Prevention of Psychology. June 29, 1984, Burlington, VT.

Riessman, F. Personal communication, 1985.

Riger, S., and **Gordon, M. T.** The fear of rape: a study in social control. *Journal of social issues,* 1981, *37,* 71–92.

Rist, R. C. Student social class and teacher expectations: The self-fulfilling prophecy in ghetto education. *Harvard educational review,* 1970, *40,* 411–51.

Rizley, R. Depression and distortion in the attribution of causality. *Journal of abnormal psychology,* 1978, *87,* 32–48.

Robbins, D. Partial reinforcement. *Psychological bulletin,* 1971, *76,* 415–31.

Robins, L. N. Sturdy childhood predictors of adult outcomes: Replications from longitudinal studies. *Psychological medicine,* 1978, *8,* 611–22.

Robins, L. N. The natural history of drug abuse. In D. J. Lettieri, M. Sayers, and H. W. Pearson, eds. *Theories on drug abuse: selected contemporary perspectives.* National Institute on Drug Abuse, DHHS Publication No. (ADM) 80–967, 1980, 215–24.

Robinson, I. and **Jedlicka, D.** Change in sexual attitudes and behavior of college students from 1965 to 1980: A research note. *Journal of marriage and the family,* Feb. 1982, 237–40.

Rock, I. *Perception,* Washington, DC: Scientific American Library, 1984.

Rodin, J. *Shock avoidance behavior in obese and normal subjects.* Unpublished manuscript, Yale Univ., 1972.

Rodin, J. Managing the stress of aging: The role of control and coping. In S. Levine and H. Ursin, eds. *Coping and health.* New York: Plenum, 1980.

Rodin, J., Elman, D., and **Schachter, S.** *Emotionality and obesity.* Unpublished manuscript, Yale Univ., 1972.

Rofé, Y., and **Goldberg, J.** Prolonged exposure to a war environment and its effects on the blood pressure of pregnant women. *British journal of medical psychology,* 1983, *56,* 305–11.

Rogers, C. Personal communication, 1969.

Rogers, C. R. *A way of being.* Boston: Houghton-Mifflin, 1980.

Rolls, B. J., and **Rolls, E. T.** *Thirst.* New York: Cambridge Univ. Press, 1982.

Romaniuk, M., McAuley, W. J., and **Arling, G.** An examination of the prevalance of mental disorders among the elderly in the community. *Journal of abnormal psychology,* 1983, *92,* 458–67.

Roper Organization. *Virginia Slims American women's opinion poll,* 1980.

Rorer, L. G. and **Widiger, J. A.** Personality structure and assessment. *Annual review of psychology,* 1983, *34,* 431–63.

Rosch, E. H. Natural categories. *Cognitive psychology,* 1973, *4,* 328–50.

Rosch, E. H. Human categorization. In E. Warren, ed. *Advances in cross-cultural psychology,* Vol. 1. London: Academic Press, 1977.

Rosch, E. H., and **Mervis, C. B.** Family resemblances: studies in the internal structure of categories. *Cognitive psychology,* 1975, *7,* 573–605.

Rose, J. E., et al. Some effects of stimulus intensity on response of auditory nerve fibers in the squirrel monkey. *Journal of neurophysiology,* 1971, *34,* 685–99.

Rose, R. M. Endocrine responses to stressful psychological events. *Psychiatric clinics of North America,* 1980, *3,* 251–76.

Rose, R. M., Jenkins, C. D., and **Hurst, M. W.** Air traffic controller health change study. Boston: Boston Univ. School of Medicine, 1978.

Rose, S. A., and **Wallace, I. F.** Visual recognition memory: A predictor of later cognitive functioning in preterms. *Child development,* 1985, *56,* 843–52.

Rosen, M. G. Factors during labor and delivery that influence brain disorders. In J. M. Freeman, ed. *Prenatal and perinatal factors associated with brain disorders.* National Institute of Child Health and Human Development, NIH Publication No. 85–1149, April 1985.

Rosenhan, D. L. The natural socialization of altruistic autonomy. In J. Macauley and L. Berkowitz, eds. *Altruism and helping behavior.* New York: Academic Press, 1970.

Rosenhan, D. L, and **Seligman, M. E. P.** *Abnormal psychology.* New York: Norton, 1984.

Rosenwaike, I. A demographic portrait of the oldest old. *Milbank memorial fund quarterly,* 1985, *63,* 187–205.

Rosenzweig, M. R., and **Bennett, E. L.** Experimental influences of brain anatomy and brain chemistry in rodents. In G. Gottlieb, ed. *Studies on the development of behavior and the nervous system, Vol. 4: Early influences.* New York: Academic Press, 1978, 289–327.

Rosenzweig, M. R., and **Lieman, A. L.** *Physiological psychology.* Lexington, MA: Heath, 1982.

Ross, G. Concept categorization in one to two-year-olds. *Developmental psychology,* 1980, *16,* 391–96.

Ross, G. Use of the Bayley Scales to characterize abilities of premature infants. *Child development,* 1985, *56,* 835–42.

Ross, L. The intuitive psychologist and his shortcomings. In L. Berkowitz, ed. *Advances in experimental social psychology,* Vol. 10. New York: Academic Press, 1977.

Ross, L., Lepper, M. R., and **Hubbard, M.** Perseverance in self-perception and social perception. Stanford, CA: Stanford Univ. *Journal of personality and social psychology,* 1975, *32,* 880–92.

Roth, D. L., and **Holmes, D. S.** Influence of physical fitness in determining the impact of stressful life events on physical and psychological health. *Psychosomatic medicine,* 1985, *47,* 164–73.

Roth, F. P. Accelerating language learning in young children. *Journal of child language,* 1984, *11,* 89–107.

Roviaro, S., Holmes, D. S., and **Holmsten, R. D.** Influence of a cardiac rehabilitiation program on the cardiovascular, psychological, and social functioning of cardiac patients. *Journal of behavioral medicine,* 1984, *7,* 61–68.

Rubin, D. C. Very long-term memory for prose and verse. *Journal of verbal learning and verbal behavior,* 1977, *16,* 611–21.

Rubin, D. C., and **Kozin, M.** Vivid memories. *Cognition,* 1984, *16,* 81–95.

Runk, B. Consensus panel backs cautious use of ECT for severe disorders. *Hospital and community psychiatry,* 1985, *36,* 943–46.

Rush, A. J., and **Beck, A. T.** Adults with affective disorders. In M. Hersen and A. S. Bellack, eds. *Behavior therapy in the psychiatric setting.* Baltimore: Williams and Wilkins, 1978.

Rutherford, E., and **Mussen, P.** Generosity in nursery school boys. *Child development,* 1968, *39,* 755–65.

Rutkowski, G. K., Gruder, C. L., and **Romer, D.** Group cohesiveness, social norms, and bystander intervention. *Journal of personality and social psychology,* 1983, *44,* 545–52.

Rutter, M. School effects on pupil progress: Research findings and policy implications. *Child development,* 1983, *54,* 1–29.

Rutter, M. Stress, coping, and development: Some issues and some questions. In N. Garmezy and M. Rutter, eds. *Stress, coping, and development in children.* New York: McGraw-Hill, 1983.

Rutter, M. Meyerian psychobiology, personality development and the role of life experiences. *American journal of psychiatry,* 1986, *143,* 1077–87.

Rutter, M., Quinton, D., and **Liddell, C.** Parenting in two generations: Looking backwards and looking forwards. In N. Madge, ed. *Families at risk.* London: Heinemann Educational, 1983, 60–98.

Rycroft, C. *Psychoanalysis and beyond.* Chicago: Univ. of Chicago Press, 1986.

Sachs, J. S., and **Johnson, M.** Language development in a hearing child of deaf parents. In W. von Raffler Engel and Y. LeBrun, eds. *Baby talk and infant speech* (neolinguistics 5). Amsterdam: Swets and Zeitlinger, 1976.

Sackett, G. P., et al. Social isolation rearing effects in monkeys vary with genotype. *Developmental psychology,* 1981, *17,* 313–18.

Sackheim, H. A., and **Gur, R. C.** Lateral asymmetry on intensity of emotional expression. *Neuropsychologia,* 1978, *16,* 473–81.

Sackheim, H. A., **Gur, R. C.,** and **Saucy, M. C.** Emotions are expressed more intensely on the left side of the face. *Science,* 1978, *202,* 434–36.

Salapatek, P. Pattern perception in early infancy. In L. Cohen and P. Salapatek, eds. *Infant perception: From sensation to cognition, Vol I: Basic visual processes.* New York: Academic Press, 1975.

Salapatek, P., and **Kessen, W.** Visual scanning of triangles of the human newborn. *Journal of experimental child psychology,* 1966, *3,* 155–67.

Salk, L., et al. Relationship of maternal and perinatal conditions to eventual adolescent suicide. *Lancet,* March 16, 1985, Vol. I, *8429,* 624–27.

Sampson, E. A., and **Hancock, F. T.** An examination of the relationship between ordinal position, personality, and conformity. *Journal of personality and social psychology,* 1967, *5,* 398–407.

Sandmaier, M. *The invisible alcoholics: Women and alcohol abuse in America.* New York: McGraw-Hill, 1980.

Sands, S. F., and **Wright, A. A.** Monkey and human pictorial memory scanning. *Science,* 1982, *216,* 1333–34.

Sawrey, W. L., **Conger, J. J.,** and **Turrell, E. S.** An experimental investigation of the role of psychological factors in the production of gastric ulcers of rats. *Journal of comparative and physiological psychology,* 1956, *49,* 457–61.

Scarr, S. Testing for children. *American psychologist,* 1981, *36,* 1159–66.

Scarr, S., and **Grajek, S.** Similarities and differences among siblings. In M. E. Lamb and B. Sutton Smith, eds. *Sibling relationships: Their nature and significance across the lifespan.* Hillsdale, NJ: Erlbaum, 1982.

Scarr, S., and **Weinberg, R. A.** IQ test performance of black children adopted by white families. *American psychologist,* 1976, *31,* 726–39.

Scarr-Salapatek, S. Race, social class, and IQ. *Science,* 1971, *174,* 1286–95.

Scarr-Salapatek, S. Unknowns in the IQ equation. *Science,* 1971, *174,* 1223–28.

Schachter, S. *Psychology of affiliation.* Stanford, CA: Stanford Univ. Press, 1959.

Schachter, S. Some extraordinary facts about obese humans and rats. *American psychologist,* 1971, *26,* 129–44.

Schachter, S., and **Gross, L. P.** Manipulated time and eating behavior. *Journal of personality and social psychology,* 1968, *10,* 98–106.

Schachter, S., and **Singer, J. E.** Cognitive, social and physiological determinants of emotional state. *Psychological review,* 1962, *69,* 379–99.

Schaeffer, M. A., and **Baum, A.** Adrenal cortical response to stress at Three Mile Island. *Psychosomatic medicine,* 1984, *46,* 227–37.

Schaffer, C. E., **Davidson, R. J.,** and **Saron, C.** Frontal and parietal EEG asymmetry in depressed and nondepressed subjects. *Biological psychiatry,* 1983, *18,* 753–62.

Schaffer, H. R., and **Liddell, C.** Adult-child interaction under dyadic and polyadic conditions. *British journal of developmental psychology,* 1984, *2,* 33–42.

Schaie, K. W. Psychological changes from midlife to early old age: Implications for the maintenance of mental health. *American journal of orthopsychiatry,* 1981, *51,* 199–218.

Schaie, K. W., and **Hertzog, C.** Fourteen-year cohort-sequential analyses of adult intellectual development. *Developmental psychology,* 1983, *19,* 531–43.

Schaie, K. W., and **Willis, S. L.** Can decline in adult intellectual functioning be reversed? *Developmental psychology,* 1986, *22,* 223–232.

Scheils, D. A cross-cultural study of beliefs in out-of-the-body experiences, waking and sleeping. *Journal of the society for psychical research,* 1978, *49,* 697–741.

Scherer, K. R. Vocal affect expression: A review and a model for future research. *Psychological bulletin,* 1986, *99,* 143–65.

Schieffelin, E. L. The cultural analysis of depressive affect: An example from New Guinea. In A. Kleinman and B. Good, *Culture and depression.* Berkeley: Univ. of California Press, 1985.

Schiff, M., et al. Intellectual status of working-class children adopted early into upper middle-class families. *Science,* 1978, *200,* 1503–04.

Schiff, M., et al. How much could we boost scholastic achievement and IQ scores: A direct answer from a French adoption study. *Cognition,* 1982, *12,* 165–96.

Schiffman, S. S. Food recognition by the elder. *Journal of gerontology,* 1977, *32,* 586–92.

Schildkraut, J. J. *Neuropsychopharmacology and the affective disorders.* Boston: Little, Brown, 1969.

Schleifer, S. J., et al. Suppression of lymphocyte stimulation following bereavement. *Journal of the American Medical Association,* 1983, *250,* 374–77.

Schmolling, P. Human reactions to the nazi concentration camps: A summing up. *Journal of human stress,* 1984, *10,* 108–20.

Schneider, D. J., Implicit personality theory: A review. *Psychological bulletin,* 1973, 79, 294–309.

Schultz, D. P. *Sensory restriction: Effects on behavior.* New York: Academic Press, 1965.

Schwab, J. J. Psychiatric manifestations of infectious diseases. In R. C. W. Hall, ed. *Psychiatric presentations of medical illness: Somatopsychic disorders.* New York: Spectrum, 1980.

Schwartz, G. E. Psychophysiological patterning and emotion revisited: A system perspective. In C. E. Izard, ed. *Measuring emotions in infants and children.* Cambridge, England: Cambridge Univ. Press, 1982, 67–93.

Schwartz, S. Moral decision making and behavior. In J. Macauley and L. Berkowitz, eds. *Altruism and helping behavior.* New York: Academic Press, 1970.

Sears, D. O. Social anxiety, opinion structure, and opinion change. *Journal of personality and social psychology,* 1967, 7, 142–51.

Sears, D. O., Freedman, J. L., and **Peplau, L. A.** *Social psychology,* 5th ed. Englewood Cliffs, NJ: Prentice-Hall, 1985.

Seaver, W. B. Effects of naturally induced teacher expectancies. *Journal of personality and social psychology,* 1973, 28, 333–42.

Segal, J. *Winning life's toughest battles: Roots of human resilience.* New York: McGraw-Hill, 1986.

Segal, J., and **Segal, Z.** *Growing up smart and happy.* New York: McGraw-Hill, 1985.

Segal, N. L. Monozygotic and dizygotic twins: A comparative analysis of mental ability profiles. *Child development,* 1985, 56, 1051–58.

Segerberg, O. *Living to be 100: 1,200 who did and how they did it.* New York: Scribners, 1982.

Sekuler, R., and **Levinson, E.** The perception of moving targets. *Scientific American,* 1977, 236, 60–73.

Selfridge, O. G., and **Neisser, U.** Pattern recognition by machine. *Scientific American,* 1960, 203, 60–68.

Seligman, M. E. P. Explanatory style: Depression, Lyndon Baines Johnson, and the Baseball Hall of Fame. Paper presented at meeting of the American Psychological Association, Washington, DC, 1986.

Selye, H. *The stress of life.* New York: McGraw-Hill, 1956.

Selye, H. Stress without distress. In G. Serban, ed. *Psychopathology of human adaptation.* New York: Plenum, 1976.

Shanas, E. Older people and their families: The new pioneers. *Journal of marriage and the family,* 1980, 42, 9–15.

Shapiro, C. M., et al. Slow-wave sleep: A recovery period after exercise. *Science,* 1981, 214, 1253–54.

Shapiro, J., et al. Isolation of pure *lac* operon DNA. *Nature* (London), 1969, 224, 768–74.

Shapiro, S., et al. Utilization of health and mental health services. *Archives of general psychiatry,* 1984, 41, 971–78.

Shapiro, S., et al. Measuring need for mental health services in a general population. *Medical care,* 1985, 23, 1033.

Shapley, R., Personal communication, 1986.

Sheperd-Look, D. L. Sex differentiation and the development of sex roles. In B. B. Wolman, ed. *Handbook of developmental psychology.* Englewood Cliffs, NJ: Prentice-Hall, 1982.

Shephard, R. N. Recognition memory for words, sentences, and pictures. *Journal of verbal learning and verbal behavior,* 1967, 6, 156–63.

Sher, K. J., and **Levenson, R. W.** Risk for alcoholism and individual differences in the stress-response dampening effect of alcohol. *Journal of abnormal psychology,* 1982, 91, 350–67.

Sherman, S. J. Internal-external control and its relationship to attitude change under different social influence techniques. *Journal of personality and social psychology,* 1973, 26, 23–29.

Shields, S. A. Distinguishing between emotion and nonemotion: Judgments about experience. *Motivation and emotion,* 1984, 8, 355–69.

Shields, S. A. Reports of bodily change in anxiety, sadness, and anger. *Motivation and emotion,* 1984, 8, 1–21.

Shiffrin, R. M., and **Atkinson, R. C.** Storage and retrieval processes in long-term memory. *Psychological review,* 1969, 76, 179–93.

Shigetomi, C. C., Hartmann, D. P., and **Gelfand, D. M.** Sex differences in children's altruistic behavior and reputations for helpfulness. *Developmental psychology,* 1981, 17, 434–37.

Shore, C., O'Connell, B., and **Bates, E.** First sentences in language and symbolic play. *Developmental psychology,* 1984, 20, 872–80.

Silberstein, J. A., and **Parsons, O. A.** Neuropsychological impairment in female alcoholics: Replication and extension. *Journal of abnormal psychology,* 1981, 90, 179–82.

Silver, L. B. *Adolescent suicide.* Unpublished paper, National Institute of Mental Health, April 19, 1984.

Silver, L. B., and **Segal, J.** Psychology and mental health: An enduring partnership. *American psychologist,* 1984, 39, 804–09.

Silverberg, R. A. Men confronting death: Management versus self-determination. *Clinical social work journal,* 1985, *13,* 157–69.

Simenauer, J., and **Carroll, D.** *Singles: The new Americans.* New York: Simon and Schuster, 1982.

Simon, H. A. Unity of the arts and sciences: The psychology of thought and discovery. *Bulletin of the American Academy of Arts and Sciences,* March 1982, *35,* 26–53.

Sims, E. A., et al. Experimental obesity in man. *Exerpta medica monograph,* 1968.

Skinner, B. F. *The behavior of organisms.* New York: Appleton-Century-Crofts, 1938.

Skinner, B. F. *Science and human behavior.* New York: Macmillan, 1953.

Skinner, B. F. *Verbal behavior.* Englewood Cliffs, NJ: Prentice-Hall, 1957.

Skinner, B. F. *Beyond freedom and dignity.* New York: Knopf, 1971.

Slater, J., and **Depue, R. A.** The contribution of environmental events and social support to serious suicide attempts in primary depressive disorder. *Journal of abnormal psychology,* 1981, *90,* 275–85.

Slobin, D. I. *Psycholinguistics.* Glenview IL: Scott,, Foresman, 1971.

Slobin, D. I. Cognitive prerequisites for the acquisition of grammar. In C. A. Ferguson and D. I. Slobin, eds. *Studies of child language development.* New York: Holt, 1973.

Slobin, D. I. *Cross-cultural study of language acquisition.* Hillsdale, NJ: Erlbaum, 1985.

Smith, D. Trends in counseling and psychotherapy. *American psychologist,* 1982, *37,* 802–09.

Smith, D. K., Nehemkis, A. M., and **Charter, R. A.** Fear of death, death attitudes, and religious conviction in the terminally ill. *International journal of psychiatry and medicine,* 1983–1984, *13,* 221–32.

Smith, E. A., and **Udry, J. R.** Coital and non-coital sexual behaviors of white and black adolescents. *American journal of public health,* Oct. 1985, *75,* 1200–03.

Smith, E. E., and **Medin, D. L.** *Categories and concepts.* Cambridge, MA: Harvard Univ. Press, 1981.

Smith, M. E. An investigation of the development of the sentence and the extent of vocabulary in young children. *Univ. of Iowa studies in child welfare,* 1926, 3(5).

Smith, M. L., Glass, G. V., and **Miller, T. I.** *The benefits of psychotherapy.* Baltimore: Johns Hopkins Univ. Press, 1980.

Smith, S. M. Remembering in and out of context. *Journal of experimental psychology,* 1979, *5,* 460–71.

Smith, T., Ingram, R. E., and **Brehm, S. S.** Social anxiety, anxious self-preoccupation, and recall of self-relevant information. *Journal of personality and social psychology,* 1983, *44,* 1276–83.

Smyser, A. A. Hospices: Their humanistic and economic value. *American psychologist,* 1982, *37,* 1260–62.

Snow, C. E., et al. Mothers' speech in three social classes. *Journal of psycholinguistic research,* 1976, *5,* 1–20.

Snyder, M. *The self in action.* Paper delivered at the meetings of the Midwestern Psychological Association, Chicago, 1983.

Snyder, M., Tanke, E. D., and **Berscheid, E.** Social perception and interpersonal behavior. *Journal of personality and social psychology,* 1977, *35,* 656–66.

Snyder, M. L., and **Frankel, A.** Observer bias. *Journal of personality and social psychology,* 1976, *34,* 857–64.

Snyder, S. H. Neurotransmitters and CNS disease: Schizophrenia. *Lancet,* 1982, II, 8305, 970–73.

Snyder, S. H. Neurosciences: An integrative discipline. *Science,* 21 Dec. 1984, *225,* 1255–57.

Snyderman, M., and **Rothman, S.** Survey of expert opinion on intelligence and aptitude testing. *American psychologist,* 1987, *42,* 137–44.

Solomon, R. L. Punishment. *American psychologist,* 1964, *19,* 239–53.

Solomon, R. L. The opponent-process theory of acquired motivation: The costs of pleasure and the benefits of pain. *American psychologist,* 1980, *35,* 691–712.

Solomon, R. L. The costs of pleasure and the benefits of pain. Paper presented at the meetings of the American Association for the Advancement of Science, Philadelphia, 1986.

Solomon, R. L., and **Turner, C. H.** Discriminative classical conditioning in dogs paralyzed by curare can later control discriminative avoidance response in the normal state. *Psychological review,* 1962, *69,* 202–19.

Sommers, R. *Personal space: The behavioral analysis of design.* Englewood Cliffs, NJ: Prentice-Hall, 1969.

Sontag, L. W., Baker, C. T., and **Nelson, V. L.** Mental growth and personality development. *Monographs of the society for research in child development,* 1958, *23,* (No. 2).

Sorenson, R. C. *Adolescent sexuality in contemporary America.* New York: World, 1973.

Spanos, N. P., et al. Suffering for science: The effects of implicit social demands on response to experimentally induced pain. *Journal of personality and social psychology,* 1984, *46,* 1162–72.

Spearman, C. *The abilities of man.* London: Macmillan, 1927.

Speece, M. W., and **Sandor, B. B.** Children's understanding of death: A review of three components of a death concept. *Child development,* Oct. 1984, *55,* 1671–86.

Sperling, G. Successive approximations to a model for short-term memory. *Acta psychologica,* 1967, *27,* 285–92.

Sperry, R. Some effects of disconnecting the cerebral hemispheres. *Science,* 1982, *217,* 1223–26.

Spielberger, C. D. The effects of manifest anxiety on the academic achievement of college students. *Mental hygiene*, 1962, *46*, 420–26.

Spielberger, C. D. Anxiety as an emotional state. In C. D. Spielberger, ed. *Anxiety.* New York: Academic Press, 1971.

Spielberger, C. D., Denny, J. P., and Weitz, H. The effects of group counseling on the academic performance of anxious college freshmen. *Journal of counseling psychology*, 1962, *9*, 195–204.

Spitz, R. A. Hospitalism. In R. S. Eissler, et al., eds. *Psychoanalytic study of the child, Vol. 2.* New York: International Univ. Press, 1946.

Squire, L. R., and Davis, H. P. The pharmacology of memory: A neurobiological perspective. *Annual review of pharmacology and toxicology*, 1981, *21*, 323–56.

Staines, G. L., and Quinn, R. P. American workers evaluate the quality of their jobs. *Monthly labor review*, Jan. 1979, *13*, 3–12.

Stapp, J., Tucker, A. M., and VandenBos, G. R. Census of psychological personnel: 1983. *American psychologist*, 1985, *40*, 1317–51.

Steinberg, L. Jumping off the work experience bandwagon. *Journal of youth and adolescence*, 1982, *11*, 183–206.

Steinberg, L. *Adolescence.* New York: Knopf, 1985.

Steinberg, L., and Greenberger, E. The part-time employment of high-school students: A research agenda. *Children and youth services review*, 1980, *2*, 161–85.

Steinberg, L., et al. Effects of working on adolescent development. *Developmental psychology*, 1982, *18*, 3, 385–95.

Stellar, E., and Corbit, J. B., eds. Neural control of motivated behavior. *Neuroscience research program bulletin*, *11* (No. 4), Sept. 1973.

Stellar, E., McHugh, P. R., and Moran, T. H. The stomach: A conception of its dynamic role in satiety. *Progress in psychobiology and physiological psychology*, Vol. 11. New York: Academic Press, 1985, 197–232.

Stelmack, R. M., Achorn, E., and Michaud, A. Extraversion and individual differences in auditory evoked response. *Psychophysiology*, 1977, *14*, 368–74.

Stern, M. Personal communication, 1983.

Stern, W. Wirklichkeitsversuche. *Beitrage zur psychologie der aussage*, 1904, *2*, 1–31.

Sternberg, R. J. A triangular theory of love. *Psychological review*, 1986, *93*, 119–35.

Sternberg, R. J. *Beyond IQ.* New York: Cambridge Univ. Press, 1985.

Sternberg, R. J. *Intelligence applied: Understanding and increasing your intellectual skills.* San Diego, CA: Harcourt, 1986.

Sternberg, R. J., and Grajek, S. The nature of love. *Journal of personality and social psychology*, 1984, *47*, 312–29.

Stevens, B. The sexually oppressed male. *Psychotherapy*, 1974, *11*, 16–21.

Stevens, C. F. *The neuron.* In Scientific American's *The brain.* San Francisco: Freeman, 1979.

Stevenson, H. W., and Bitterman, M. E. The distance effect in the transposition of intermediate size by children. *American journal of psychology*, 1955, *68*, 274–79.

Stevenson, H. W., Friedrichs, A. G., and Simpson, W. E. Interrelations and correlates over time in children's learning. *Child development*, 1970, *41*, 625–37.

Stevenson, H. W., Lee, S., and Stingler, J. W. Mathematics achievement of Chinese, Japanese, and American children. *Science*, 14 Feb. 1986, 693–99.

Stevenson, H. W., et al. Cognitive performance and academic achievement of Japanese, Chinese, and American children. *Child development*, 1985, *56*, 718–34.

Stewart, A. J. *Longitudinal prediction from personality to life outcomes among college-educated women.* Unpublished doctoral dissertation, Harvard Univ., 1975.

Stewart, A. J., and Rubin, Z. Power motivation in the dating couple. *Journal of personality and social psychology*, 1976, *34*, 305–09.

Stiles, W. B., Shapiro, D. A., and Elliot, R. Are all psychotherapies equivalent? *American psychologist*, 1986, *41*, 165–80.

Stock, M. B., and Smythe, P. M. Does undernutrition during infancy inhibit brain growth and subsequent intellectual development? *Archives of disorders in children*, 1963, *38*, 546–52.

Stolz, S. B., Wienckowski, L. A., and Brown, B. S. Behavior modification. *American psychologist*, 1975, *30*, 1027–48.

Streissguth, A. P., et al. Intrauterine alcohol and nicotine exposure: Attention and reaction time in 4-year-old children. *Developmental psychology*, 1984, *20*, 533–41.

Strickland, B. R. Internal-external control of reinforcement. In T. Blass, ed. *Personality variables in social behavior.* Hillsdale, NJ: Erlbaum, 1977.

Stroebe, M. S., and Stroebe, W. Who suffers more? Sex differences in health risks of the widowed. *Psychological bulletin,* 1983, *93,* 279–301.

Strupp, H. H. Psychotherapy: Research, practice, and public policy (how to avoid dead ends). *American psychologist,* 1986, *41,* 120–30.

Strupp, H. H., and Binder, J. L. *A guide to time-limited dynamic psychotherapy.* New York: Basic Books, 1984.

Stunkard, A. J. Behavioral management of obesity. *Medical journal of Australia,* 1985, *142,* (7 supplement), 513–20.

Stunkard, A. J. Personal communication, 1986.

Stunkard, A. J., Foch, T. T., and Hrubec, H. A twin study of human obesity. *Journal of the American Medical Association,* 1986, *256,* 51–54.

Stunkard, A. J., et al. An adoption study of human obesity. *New England journal of medicine,* Jan. 23, 1986, *314,* 193–98.

Stuss, D. T., and Benson, D. F. *The frontal lobes.* New York: Raven Press, 1986.

Suedfeld, P. Sensory deprivation stress. *Journal of personality and social psychology,* 1969, *11,* 70–74.

Suedfeld, P. The benefits of boredom. *American scientist,* 1975, *63,* 60–69.

Sumi, S. Upside-down presentation of the Johansson moving light-spot pattern. *Perception,* 1984, *13,* 283–86.

Suomi, S. J. Peers, play, and primary prevention in primates. *Proceedings of the Third Vermont Conference on the Primary Prevention of Psychopathology: Promoting Social Competence and Coping in Children.* Hanover, NH: Univ. Press of New England, 1977.

Suomi, S. J., and Harlow, H. F. Social rehabilitation of isolate-reared monkeys. *Developmental psychology,* 1972, *6,* 487–96.

Susman, E. J., et al. The relation of relative hormonal levels and physical development and social-emotional behavior in young adolescents. *Journal of youth and adolescence,* 1985, *14,* 245–64.

Sutton-Smith, B. Birth order and sibling status effects. *Sibling relationships: Their nature and significance across the lifespan.* Hillsdale, NJ: Erlbaum, 1982.

Suzman, R., and Riley, M. W. Introducing the "oldest old." *Milbank memorial fund quarterly,* 1985, *63,* 177–205.

Swaab, D. F., and Fliers, E. A sexually dimorphic nucleus in the human brain. *Science,* 1985, *228,* 1112–14.

Tagiuri, R. Social preference and its perception In R. Tagiuri and L. Petrullo, eds. *Person perception and interpersonal behavior.* Stanford, CA: Stanford Univ. Press, 1958.

Tanner, J. M. *Foetus into man.* Cambridge, MA: Harvard Univ. Press, 1978.

Tarler-Benlolo, L. The role of relaxation in biofeedback training. *Psychological bulletin,* 1978, *85,* 727–55.

Tarnopolsky, A., Watkins, G., and Hand, D. J. Aircraft noise and mental health. I. Prevalence of individual symptoms. *Psychological medicine,* 1980, *10,* 683–98.

Tarpy, R. M., and Mayer, R. E. *Foundations of learning and memory.* Glenview, IL: Scott, Foresman, 1978.

Tavris, C., and Offir, C. *The longest war.* New York: Harcourt, 1977.

Taylor, C., Smith, W. R., and Ghiselin, B. The creative and other contributions of one sample of research scientists. In C. Taylor and F. Barron, eds. *Scientific creativity.* New York: Wiley, 1963.

Teasdale, J. D. Effects of real and recalled success on learned helplessness and depression. *Journal of abnormal psychology,* 1978, *87,* 155–64.

Tecce, J. J. Contingent negative variation and individual differences. *Archives of general psychiatry,* 1971, *24,* 1–16.

Tennen, H., and Eller, S. J. Attributional components of learned helplessness and facilitation. *Journal of personality and social psychology,* 1977, *35,* 265–71.

Tennes, K. H., and Mason, J. W. Developmental psychoendocrinology: An approach to the study of emotions. In C. E. Izard, ed. *Measuring emotions in infants and children.* Cambridge, England: Cambridge Univ. Press, 1982.

Terman, L. M., and Merrill, M. A. *Stanford-Binet intelligence scale: Manual for the third revision, form L-M,* 1937.

Terr, L. C. Psychiatric trauma in children: Observations following the Chowchilla school bus-kidnapping. *American journal of psychiatry,* 1981, *138,* 14–19.

Terrace, H. S. *Nim: A chimpanzee who learned sign language.* New York: Knopf, 1979.

Tesser, A. Some effects of self-evaluation maintenance on cognition and action. In R. M. Sorrentino and E. T. Higgins, eds. *The handbook of motivation and cognition: Foundations of social behavor.* New York: Guilford Press, 1985.

Tesser, A., and Brodie, M. A note on the evaluation of a "computer date." *Psychonomic science,* 1971, *23,* 300.

Thomas, A., and Chess, S. Development in middle childhood. *Seminars in psychiatry,* 1972, *4,* 331–41.

Thomas, A., Chess, S., and Birch, H. G. The origin of personality. *Scientific American,* 1970, *223,* 106–07.

Thompson, R. F. *The brain: An introduction to neuroscience.* New York: Freeman, 1985.
Tierney, D. W. The reinforcement of calm sitting behavior: A method used to reduce self-injurious behavior of a profoundly retarded boy. *Journal of behavior therapy and experimental psychology,* March 1986, *17,* 47–50.
Tinklepaugh, O. L. An experimental study of representative factors in monkeys. *Journal of comparative psychology,* 1928, *8,* 197–236.
Tolman, E. C. Cognitive maps in rats and men. *Psychological review,* 1948, *55,* 189–208.
Tolman, E. C., and Honzik, C. H. Introduction and removal of reward and maze performance in rats. *University of California publications in psychology,* 1930, *4,* 257–75.
Tomkins, S. S. *Affect, imagery, consciousness, Vol. 1. The positive affects.* New York: Springer, 1962.
Torrance, E. P. *Torrance tests of creative thinking.* Princeton, NJ: Personnel Press, 1966.
Treisman, A. M. and Gelade, C. A feature-integration theory of attention. *Cognitive psychology,* 1980, *12,* 97–136.
Trusheim, D., and Crouse, J. The DTS admissions formula: Does the SAT add useful information? *Phi Delta Kappa,* Sept. 1982, 59–61.
Tschukitscheff, I. P. Über den Mechanismus der Hungerbewegungen des Magens. I. Einfluss des "satten" und "Hunger" -Blutes auf die periodische Tatigkeit des Magens. *Archiv für die gesamte psychologie,* 1930, *233,* 251–64.
Tsuang, M. T., and Vandermey, R. *Genes and the mind: Inheritance of mental illness.* New York: Oxford Univ. Press, 1980.
Tucker, L. A. Muscular strength and mental health. *Journal of personality and social psychology,* 1983, *45,* 1355–60.
Tuma, A. H., and Maser, J. D., eds. *Anxiety and the anxiety disorders.* Hillsdale, NJ: Erlbaum, 1985.
Tversky, A., and Kahneman, D. Availability: A heuristic for judging frequency and probability. *Cognitive psychology,* 1973, *5,* 207–32.
Tyler, L. E. The intelligence we test—An evolving concept. In L. B. Resnick, ed. *The nature of intelligence.* New York: Erlbaum, 1976.

Underwood, B. J. Interference and forgetting. *Psychological review,* 1957, *64,* Fig. 1, p. 61.
U.S. Bureau of the Census. Marital status and living arrangements. *Current population reports,* Series P20, No. 410, 1985.
U.S. Bureau of the Census. *Current population reports,* Series P20, No. 410, 1986a.
U.S. Bureau of the Census. *Current population reports,* Series P23, No. 146, 1986b.
U.S. Department of Health and Human Services. *Myths and facts about sleep.* DHHS Publication No. (ADM) 81-1108, 1981.
U.S. Department of Health and Human Services. *Use of mental health services.* ADMAHA update, No. 6, July 1986.
U.S. Department of Labor. *Employment and earnings.* Bureau of Labor Statistics, *34,* Jan. 1987.
U.S. Office of Strategic Services, Assessment Staff. *Assessment of men.* New York: Holt, 1948.
U.S. Public Health Service. Women's health: Report of the Public Health Service Task Force on women's health issues. *Public health reports,* Jan.-Feb. 1985, *100,* 73–106.
Uttal, W. R. *The psychobiology of sensory coding.* New York: Harper, 1973.

Vaillant, G. E. Alcoholism and drug dependence. In A. M. Nicholi, Jr., ed. *The Harvard guide to modern psychiatry.* Cambridge, MA: Harvard Univ. Press, 1978.
Valdes-Dapena, M. A. Sudden infant death syndrome: A review of the medical literature, 1974–1979. *Pediatrics,* 1980, *66,* 597–614.
Valenstein, E. S. *Brain control.* New York: Wiley, 1973.
Valenstein, E. S. Stereotyped behavior and stress. In G. Serban, ed. *The psychopathology of human adaptation.* New York: Plenum, 1976.
Valenstein, E. S. *Great and desperate cures.* New York: Basic Books, 1986.
Valenstein, E. S., Cox, V. C., and Kakolewski, J. W. Re-examination of the role of the hypothalamus in emotion. *Psychological review,* 1970, *77,* 16–31.
Valenta, J. G., and Rigby, M. K. Discrimination of the odor of distressed rats. *Science,* 1968, *161,* 599–601.
Vance, V. S., and Schlechty, P. C. *The structure of the teaching occupation and the characteristics of teachers.* Report prepared for the National Institute of Education, Contract No. NIE-81-0100. 1982.
Van Dyke, C., and Byck, R. Cocaine. *Scientific American,* 1982, *246,* 3, 128–41.

Vaughn, C. E., and **Leff, J. P.** The influence of family and social factors on the course of psychiatric illness: A comparison of schizophrenic and depressed neurotic patients. *British journal of psychiatry,* 1976, *129,* 125–37.

Vennemann, T. An explanation of drift. In C. N. Li, ed. *Word order and word order change.* Austin: Univ. of Texas Press, 1975.

Verhave, T. The pigeon as a quality-control inspector. *American psychologist,* 1966, *21,* 109–15.

Veroff, J., Douvan, E., and **Kulka, R.** *The inner American.* New York: Basic Books, 1981.

Vierling, J. S., and **Rock, J.** Variations of olfactory sensitivity to exaltolide during the menstrual cycle. *Journal of applied physiology,* 1967, *22,* 311–15.

Vihman, M. M. Language differentiation by a bilingual infant. *Journal of child language,* 1985, *12,* 297–324.

Von Frisch, W. *Bees.* Ithaca, NY: Cornell University Press, 1950.

Vorster, J. Mothers' speech to children. *Publications of the Institute for General Linguistics,* No. 8. Amsterdam: Univ. of Amsterdam, 1974.

Wada, J. A., Clark, R., and **Hamm, A.** Cerebral hemispheric asymmetry in humans. *Archives of neurology,* 1975, *32,* 239–46.

Wadden, T. A., and **Anderson, C. H.** The clinical use of hypnosis. *Psychological bulletin,* 91, 215–43.

Wagner, K. R. How much do children say in a day? *Journal of child language,* 1985, *12,* 475–87.

Wagner, M. W., and **Monnett, M.** Attitudes of college professors toward extrasensory perception. *Zetetic scholar,* 1979, *5,* 7–16.

Wald, G. The photochemical basis of rod vision. *Journal of the Optical Society of America,* 1951, *41,* 949–56.

Walker, E., and **Emory, E.** Commentary: Interpretive bias and behavioral genetic research. *Child development,* 1985, *56,* 775–78.

Walker, J. I. The psychological problems of Vietnam veterans. *Journal of the American Medical Association,* 1981, *246,* 781–82.

Walker, L. J., de Vries, B., and **Bichard, S. L.** The hierarchical nature of the stages of moral development. *Developmental psychology,* 1984, *20,* 960–66.

Walker, P., and **Smith, S.** Stroop interference based on the synaesthetic qualities of auditory pitch. *Perception,* 1984, *13,* 75–81.

Wallach, M. A. Tests tell us little about talent. *American scientist,* 1976, *64,* 57–63.

Wallach, M. A., and **Wallach, L.** *Psychology's sanction of selfishness.* New York: Freeman, 1983.

Wallerstein, J., and **Kelley, J.** *Surviving the breakup: how children and parents cope with divorce.* New York: Basic Books, 1980.

Wallerstein, J. S. Children of divorce: Preliminary report of a ten-year follow-up of older children and adolescents. *Journal of the Academy of Child Psychiatry,* 1985, *24,* 545–53.

Wason, P. C. Problem solving and reasoning. *Cognitive psychology,* British Medical Bulletin, 1971, *27.*

Watson, C. G., et al. Schizophrenic birth seasonality in relation to the incidence of infectious diseases and temperature extremes. *Archives of general psychiatry,* 1984, *41,* 85–90.

Watson, J. B., and **Rayner, R.** Conditioned emotional reactions. *Journal of experimental psychology,* 1920, *3,* 1–14.

Webb, W. B., and **Cartwright, R. D.** Sleep and dreams. *Annual review of psychology,* 1978, *29,* 223–52.

Wechsler, D. Intelligence defined and undefined. *American psychologist,* 1975, *30,* 135–59.

Weiner, B. *Achievement motivation and attribution theory.* Morristown, NJ: General Learning Press, 1974.

Weiner, H. Psychobiology of essential hypertension. In R. J. Mathew, ed. *The biology of anxiety.* New York: Brunner/Mazel, 1982.

Weiskrantz, L. Experimental studies of amnesia. In C. W. M. Whitty and O. L. Zangwill, eds. *Amnesia.* London: Butterworths, 1966.

Weiss, J. M., Glazer, H. I., and **Pohorecky, L. A.** Coping behavior and neurochemical changes. In G. Serban and A. Kling, eds. *Animal models in human psychobiology.* New York: Plenum, 1976.

Weiss, J. M., et al. Effects of acute and chronic exposure to stressors on avoidance behavior and brain norepinephrine. *Psychosomatic medicine,* 1975, *37,* 522–34.

Weitzman, L. J. Sex-role socialization. In J. Freeman, ed. *Women.* Palo Alto, CA: Mayfield, 1975.

Weitzman, L. J., et al. Sex role socialization in picture books for pre-school children. *American journal of sociology,* 1972, *77,* 1125–50.

Wells, G. L., and **Loftus, E. F.,** eds. *Eyewitness testimony: psychological perspectives.* Cambridge, England: Cambridge Univ. Press, 1984.

Werner, E. E., and **Smith, R. S.** *Vulnerable but invincible.* New York: McGraw-Hill, 1982.

Werner, J. S., and **Lipsitt, L. P.** The infancy of human sensory systems. In E. S. Gollin, ed. *Developmental plasticity.* New York: Academic Press, 1981.

Werner, P. D., and LaRussa, G. W. Persistence and change in sex-role stereotypes. *Sex Roles,* 1985, *12,* 1089–100.

Whalen, R. E. Brain mechanisms controlling sexual behavior. In F. A. Beach, ed. *Human sexuality in four perspectives.* Baltimore: Johns Hopkins, Univ. Press, 1976.

White, B. L., Castle, P., and Held, R. Observations on the development of visually directed reaching. *Child development,* 1964, *35,* 349–64.

Whitfield, I. C., and Evans, E. F. Responses of auditory cortical neurons to stimuli of changing frequency. *Journal of neurophysiology,* 1965, *28,* 655–72.

Whorf, B. L. Science and linguistics. In J. B. Carroll, ed. *Language, thought, and reality.* Cambridge, MA: M.I.T. Press, 1956.

Wickelgren, W. A. *Learning and memory.* Englewood Cliffs. NJ: Prentice-Hall, 1977.

Wickelgren, W. A. Human learning and memory. *Annual review of psychology,* 1981, *32,* 21–52.

Wiesel, T. N., and Hubel, D. H. Ordered arrangement of orientation columns in monkeys lacking visual experience. *Journal of comparative neurology,* 1974, *158,* 307–18.

Wilkins, W. Desensitization. *Psychological bulletin,* 1971, *76,* 311–17.

Will, J., Self, P., and Datan, N. Paper presented to the American Psychological Association, 1974.

Williams, J., and Spitzer, R. The reliability of the diagnostic criteria of DSM-III. In J. Wing, P. Bebbington, and L. Robins, eds. *What is a case? The problem of definition in psychiatric community surveys.* London: Grant-McIntyre, Ltd., 1981.

Williams, M. *Brain damage, behaviour, and the mind.* New York: Wiley, 1979.

Willis, S. L., and Baltes, P. B. Intelligence in adulthood and aging: Contemporary issues. In L. W. Poon, ed. *Aging in the 80's: Psychological issues.* Washington, DC: American Psychological Association, 1980.

Wilson, E. O. *Sociobiology: The new synthesis.* Cambridge, MA: Harvard Univ. Press, 1975.

Wilson, J. Q., and Herrnstein, R. J. *Crime and human nature.* New York: Simon and Schuster, 1985.

Wine, J. *Investigations of attentional interpretation of test anxiety.* Unpublished doctoral dissertation, University of Waterloo, Ont., 1971.

Wing, C. W., Jr., and Wallach, M. A. *College admissions and the psychology of talent.* New York: Holt, 1971.

Winokur, G. *Depression: The facts.* New York: Oxford Univ. Press, 1981.

Winter, D. G. *The power motive.* New York: Free Press, 1973.

Winter, D. G., and Stewart, A. J. The power motive. In H. London and J. E. Exner, eds. *Dimensions of personality.* New York: Wiley, 1978.

Winterbottom, M. R. *The relation of childhood training in independence to achievement motivation.* Unpublished doctoral dissertation, University of Michigan, 1953. Summarized in D. C. McClelland, et al. *The achievement motive.* New York: Irvington Pub., 1953.

Wolf, R. M. *The identification and measurement of environmental process variables related to intelligence.* Unpublished Ph.D. dissertation, Univ. of Chicago, 1963.

Wolpe, J. *Theme and variations.* Elmsford, NY: Pergamon, 1976.

Woolfolk, A. E., Woolfolk, R. L., and Wilson, G. T. A rose by any other name. . . . Labeling bias and attitudes toward behavior modification. *Journal of consulting and clinical psychology,* 1977, *45,* 184–91.

Worchel, P. *Self-enhancement and interpersonal attraction.* Paper read at the American Psychological Association, Aug. 1961.

World Health Organization. *Schizophrenia: An international follow-up study.* New York: Wiley, 1979.

Wyatt, R. J. *After middle age.* New York: McGraw-Hill, 1985.

Wyatt, R. J., and Freed, W. J. Progress in neurografting as a treatment for degenerative brain disease: The Parkinson's model. In W. Regelson, ed. *Intervention in the aging process.* New York: Alan R. Liff, 1983.

Wyatt, R. J., and Freed, W. J. Central nervous system grafting. In R. H. Wilkins and S. S. Rengachary, eds. *Neurosurgery,* Vol. 3. New York: McGraw-Hill, 1985.

Yalom, I. *Existential psychotherapy.* New York: Basic Books, 1980.

Yankelovich, D. The work ethic is underemployed. *Psychology today,* May 1982, *16,* 5–8.

Yarbus, A. L. *Eye movements and vision.* Translated by L. A. Riggs. New York: Plenum, 1967.

Yerkes, R. M., and Morgulis, S. The methods of Pavlov in animal psychology. *Psychological bulletin,* 1909, *6,* 257–73.

Young, P. T. *Motivation and emotion.* New York: Wiley, 1961.

Zahn-Waxler, C., Radke-Yarrow, M., and King, R. Early altruism and guilt. *Academic psychology bulletin,* 1983, *5,* 247–59.

Zajonc, R. B. Attitudinal effects of mere exposure. *Journal of personality and social psychology,* 1968, *8,* 18.

Zajonc, R. B. The decline and rise of scholastic aptitude scores: A prediction derived from the confluence model. *American psychologist,* Aug. 1986, *41,* 862–67.
Zelnick, M., Kantner, J., and **Ford, K.** *Sex and pregnancy in adolescence.* Beverly Hills, CA: Sage, 1981.
Zillman, D., Katcher, A. H., and **Milavsky, B.** Excitation transfer from physical exercise to subsequent aggressive behavior. *Journal of experimental social psychology,* 1972, *8,* 247–59.
Zimbardo, P. G., Andersen, S. M., and **Kabat, L. G.** Induced hearing deficit generates experimental paranoia. *Science,* 1982, *212,* 1529–31.
Zipf, G. K. *Human behavior and the principle of least effort.* Cambridge, MA: Addison-Wesley, 1949.
Zube, M. Changing behavior and outlook of aging men and women. *Family relations,* 1982, *31,* 147–56.

PICTURE CREDITS

Page 2 © Crosby/Photophile. 4 © Michael Yada/Zephyr Pictures. 8 (top) © Van Bucher 1984 Photo Researchers; (bottom) © Richard Pasley/Stock, Boston. 9 © Jim Pickerell 1985/FPG International. 10 Photo by Edmund Engelman, © Edmund Engelman, New York. 11 © D.C. Lowe/FPG International. 13 © Marcia Weinstein. 14 © Billy E. Barnes/Stock, Boston. 15 © Mark Antman/The Image Works. 17 Reproduced by permission of the Riverside Publishing Company, Chicago, IL. 19 © Susan Holtz. 22 The Bettmann Archive. 23 Culver Pictures. 29 Culver Pictures. 31 (top) © Tim Carlson/Stock, Boston; (bottom) Zephyr Pictures. 32 © Duomo Photography, Inc./Dan Helms 1984. 34 © Jeff Albertson/The Picture Cube. 40 © Dan McCoy/Rainbow. 43 © Martin Rotker/Taurus Photos. 48 © T. Campbell/FPG International. 51 © Tim Carlson/Stock, Boston. 54 © Miro Vintoniv/Stock, Boston. 56 Courtesy California Institute of Technology. 57 Erik Arneson. 60 © Brian Drake 1984–85/EKM Nepenthe. 61 Arthur Leipzig. 65 © L.L.T. Rhodes/Taurus Photos. 67 Courtesy of the American Association for the Advancement of Science. 78 © Kurt Thorson/EKM Nepenthe. 80 © Marion Bernstein. 83 © Jeff Albertson/Stock, Boston. 84 Courtesy Bell Labs, Short Hills, NJ. 88 Lennart Nilsson. *Behold Man*, Little, Brown & Co., Boston; Photo courtesy Bonnier Fakta, Stockholm. 92 © Gary Jochim/FPG International. 97 (top) Reichert Ophthalmic Instruments, a Cambridge Instruments Company. 102 (top) Photo courtesy Dr. A.J. Hudspeth. 105 Photos courtesy Dr. David Lipscomb and G. Bredberg, Stockholm. 106 © J. Berndt/The Picture Cube. 107 © Jean-Claude Lejeune/Stock, Boston. 109 Courtesy Pierre Cardin International. 111 © Smiley/TexaStock. 112 © Robert McElroy/Woodfin Camp & Assoc. 118 © Sullivan/TexaStock. 124 (top) American Museum of Natural History. 127 Courtesy Professor Carolyn K. Rovee-Collier/Rutgers University. 129 (bottom) © 1987 Alan Carey/The Image Works. 130 (top) A.L. Yarbus; (bottom) © Elizabeth Crews. 131 © Elizabeth Crews. 135 (top) David Moskowitz; (bottom) © Nathan Holtz. 137 William Vandivert. 139 © Susan Holtz. 140 (top) Courtesy United Nations; (bottom) © Susan Holtz. 148 © Melanie Kaestner/Zephyr Pictures. 153 Culver Pictures. 159 © Louis Goldman/Photo Researchers. 163 Nina Leen, Life Magazine © Time Inc. 164 © Sea World. 165 Reproduced by permission of H.S. Terrace, Columbia University. 166 UPI/Bettmann Newsphotos. 167 (top) Yerkes Regional Primate Research Center of Emory University. 171 © Ellis Herwig/The Picture Cube. 172 © Joel Gordon, 1985. 176 © Dagmar Fabricius/Stock, Boston. 182 © Ellis Herwig/Stock, Boston. 183 Albert Bandura. 188 © Richard Pasley/Stock, Boston. 190 © Charles Gupton/Stock, Boston. 196 © Michael Yada/Zephyr Pictures. 200 © Sisse Brimberg 1982/Woodfin Camp & Assoc. 201 © AP/Wide World. 204 Dirck Halstead/Time Magazine. 205 © Melanie Kaestner. 207 © David S. Strickler/The Picture Cube. 208 © AP/Wide World. 212 © Susan Holtz. 213 Courtesy University of Wisconsin Harlow Primate Laboratory. 214 © Michael Hayman/Stock, Boston. 224 © 1987 Alan Carey/The Image Works. 226 Taurus Photos. 232 © Ellis Herwig/The Picture Cube. 233 Courtesy Dr. Julius Segal. 235 © David E. Kennedy/TexaStock. 238 B.T. Gardner. 240 © Elizabeth Crews. 245 Courtesy FMC Corporation. 246 © Smiley/TexaStock. 252 © Susan Holtz. 253 © Dan Walsh/The Picture Cube. 254 © Susan Holtz. 258 © Gregg Mancuso/Stock, Boston. 260 Courtesy Ruth Wechsler. 261 (left) Anthro-Photo; (right) © Owen Franken/Stock, Boston. 265 © Martin Rogers 1985/Stock, Boston. 266 Bettmann Archive. 267 © Cary Wolinsky/Stock, Boston. 269 © Elizabeth Crews. 270 Courtesy Georgette and Geraldine Binet. 271 The Riverside Publishing Company, Chicago, IL, © 1986. 273 (bottom) © Lew Merrim/Monkmeyer Press. 281 Courtesy Hitachi. 288 © Joe Sohm/The Image Works. 296 © Kennedy/TexaStock. 300 (left) © Pam Hasegawa/Taurus Photos; (right) © Sullivan/TexaStock. 301 Walter Chandoha. 302 © Paul Conklin. 305 Michael K. Nichols/Magnum. 306 © Susan Holtz. 307 Andrea McCarrick. 308 Sackheim, H.A., Gur, R.C. and Saucy, M.C., *Science*, 1978, 202, 434–36 with the permission of the American Association for the Advancement of Science. 309 (top) Eckehard H. Hess; (bottom) © Sandy Roessler 1986/FPG International. 313 © B. Byers/FPG International. 317 Regis Bossu/Sygma. 319 (top) Courtesy Neal E. Miller; (bottom) The Image Works. 323 © Sharon Fox/The Picture Cube. 326 © David Burnett 1984/Woodfin Camp & Assoc. 331 © Ellis Herwig/The Picture Cube. 333 © Jeff Slocomb/Picture Group. 337 © Paul Conklin. 340 © Frank Siteman 1980/The Picture Cube. 348 © Jon L. Barkan/The Picture Cube. 355 © Dennis Hallinan/FPG International. 357 George Geister/Black Star. 358 Collection, Museum of Modern Art, New York (bequest of Lillie P. Bliss). 360 Bettmann Archive. 362 (top left) © AP/Wide World; (top right) © A. Nogues/Sygma; (middle left) © AP/Wide World; (middle right) © J.T. Atlan/Sygma; (bottom left) © AP/Wide World; (bottom right) © Steve Schapiro/Sygma. 363 HBJ Collection. 364 © AP/Wide World. 365 © Douglas A. Land. 368 (top left) © AP/Wide World; (top right) © AP/Wide World; (bottom left) © J.P. Laffont/Sygma; (bottom right) © L. Orban/Sygma. 371 Bettmann Archive. 372 (top) © Dana Fineman/Sygma; (bottom left) © Eva Sereny/Sygma; (bottom right) © AP/Wide World. 374 © Gerald Martineau/The Washington Post. 377 (top left) © Michael D. Sullivan/TexaStock; (top right) © Michael D. Sullivan/TexaStock; (bottom) © Michael D. Sullivan/TexaStock. 380 © 1943 by the President and Fellows of Harvard College; © 1971 by Henry A. Murray. 386 © Michael D. Sullivan/TexaStock. 388 © Michael D. Sullivan/TexaStock. 394 © Ellis Herwig/The Picture Cube. 398 © Topham/The Image Works. 400 © Chris Brown/Stock, Boston. 401 © Mike Maple 1986/Woodfin Camp & Assoc. 409 © Mike Vintoniv/The Picture Cube. 412 Michael Lewis. 414 © 1986 Andrew Popper/Picture Group. 417 © Herve Donnezan/Photo Researchers. 419 (left) © AP/Wide World; (right) © AP/Wide World. 422 Courtesy Jules H. Masserman, MD. 426 © Paul Conklin. 429 Anthro-Photo. 431 © David Kennedy/TexaStock. 434 © Larry Kolvoord/TexaStock. 436 © Eric A. Roth/The Picture Cube. 437 (top) Monte S. Buchsbaum, MD, UC Irvine. 438 © Joel Gordon 1984. 442 © Kevin

Horan/Picture Group. 448 © AP/Wide World. 450 Drawing by Charles Addams, © 1974 The New Yorker Magazine, Inc. 451 Steve Schapiro/Sygma. 452 Jacques Tiziou/Sygma. 462 © Lester Sloan/Woodfin Camp & Assoc. 464 Museo del Prado. 467 (bottom) © Michael D. Sullivan/TexaStock. 472 © Jacques M. Chenet/Woodfin Camp & Assoc. 473 © Lester Sloan 1985/ Woodfin Camp & Assoc. 476 (top) Albert Bandura. 477 © James Cook/Picture Group. 479 © Louis Fernandez 1982/Black Star. 484 © 1982 Will McIntyre/Photo Researchers, Inc. 485 © Philip Jon Bailey/The Picture Cube. 486 Mario Ruiz/Picture Group. 489 © Fred Ward/Black Star. 494 © Ellis Herwig/The Picture Cube. 497 (top) Dr. Landrum B. Shettles; (bottom) Taurus Photos. 498 Lorne MacHattie. 500 Lennart Nilsson, *A Child Is Born*, Dell Publishing Company, New York; Photo courtesy Bonnier Fakta, Stockholm. 502 © Peter Byron 1981/Black Star. 503 (top) Heinz Prechtl. 505 © Doris Pinney. 506 Photos courtesy Edwin Robbins and Lillian Robbins. 507 © P. Pet/FPG International. 511 (top) © Robert V. Eckert, Jr./EKM Nepenthe; (center left) © Gabor Demjen/Stock, Boston; (center right) © 1982 Dave Schaefer/The Picture Cube; (bottom left) © Peter Vandermark/Stock, Boston; (bottom center) © Robert V. Eckert, Jr./EKM Nepenthe; (bottom right) Andrea McCarrick. 512 Dr. Burton White. 516 Fred Sponholz. 518 © Joseph Schuyler/Stock, Boston. 520 Courtesy Dr. Jerome Kagan. 521 © Jeffrey W. Myers/FPG International. 522 © Miro Vintoniv/The Picture Cube. 525 © Barbara Alper/Stock, Boston. 526 (left) © Edward Lettau/FPG International; (right) © 1979 Ron Tunison. 528 © 1985 Anthony Suau/Black Star. 529 © Frank Siteman 1979/The Picture Cube. 530 © Michael D. Sullivan/TexaStock. 534 © Jocelyn Boutin/The Picture Cube. 540 © Jeff Albertson/Stock, Boston. 542 © Philip Jon Bailey/The Picture Cube. 543 © Paul Conklin. 557 © 1986 Lynn Johnson/Black Star. 560 (top left) © Mark Shaw/Photo Researchers; (top center) © Villiers/Sygma; (top right) © Werner Wolff/Black Star; (bottom left) © AP/Wide World; (bottom right) © 1983 Silvia Koner/Black Star. 561 © John Launois/Black Star. 563 © 1985 Lynn Johnson/Black Star. 568 © Susan Holtz. 571 © J. Maher/EKM Nepenthe. 573 (top) Bettmann Archive; (center) Bettman Archive; (bottom) © R. Laird/FPG International. 574 William Vandivert. 575 William Vandivert. 576 Copyright 1965 by Stanley Milgram. From the film *Obedience*, distributed by the New York University Film Division and the Pennsylvania State University, PCR. 578 © AP/Wide World. 581 RDR Productions. 584 © Lewis Atlan/Sygma. 592 © Barrera/TexaStock. 594 © Chip Henderson 1985/Woodfin Camp & Assoc. 595 © AP/Wide World. 597 © Philip Drell/Black Star. 598 © Erik Anderson/Stock, Boston. 599 © Patsy Davidson/The Image Works.

Part opening illustrations by Ruben De Anza.

NAME INDEX

(This index lists all the names cited in the text. Page numbers in *italics* refer to illustrations.)

A

AACRAO and the College Board, 275
Abramson, L. Y., 177
Achorn, E., 144
Addams, C., *450*
Ader, J., 157
Adler, A., 359–61, *359*, *360*, 466
Aiken, L. H., 564
Ainsworth, M. D. S., 517
Akerstedt, T., 326
Akhtar, S., 449
Alampay, D. A., 143
Allen, L., 290
Allport, G., 373
Amato, P. R., 600, 601
American Psychiatric Association, 65, 436, 445, 446
American Psychological Association (APA), 5, 9, 33, 34
Anastasi, A., 275, 378, 380
Anderson, C. H., 475
Anderson, J. R., 205
Andrew, R. J., 305
Aneshensel, C. H., 453
Antoni, M. H., 402
Archer, D., 550
Archer, R. L., 588
Aristotle, 123, 551
Arling, G., 558
Arms, R. L., 598
Arnold, A. P., 328
Arnold, M. B., 313
Arnsten, A. F. T., 556
Aronfreed, J., 600
Aronson, E., 577, 585, 594
Asch, S. E., 572, *574*, 575, *575*, 580
Asher, S. R., 529
Astin, A. W., 277
Aston-Jones, G., 144
Atchley, R. C., 559
Atkeson, B. M., 445
Atkinson, J. W., 145, 341, 343, 398
Atkinson, K., 232
Atkinson, R. C., 191, 192
Auden, W. H., 441
Austin, G. A., 241
Averill, J. R., 313
Ayllon, T., 170
Ayoub, D. M., 525
Azrin, N. H., 170
Azuma, H., 577

B

Baastrup, P. C., 483
Bachman, J. G., 457
Back, K., 593
Baddeley, A., 18
Baker, B. L., 440
Baker, C. T., 289
Baldwin, A. L., 507
Bales, R., 596
Ball, G. G., 317
Balter, M. B., 327, 441, 455
Baltes, P. B., 556
Bander, R. S., 397
Bandura, A., 177, 182, 339, 369–70, *370*, 474–75, 476, 477
Barber, J. D., 335
Bard, M., 415
Barnett, R., 549
Baron, R. A., 340
Barron, F., 279, 280
Barsalou, L. W., 243
Baruch, G., 549
Baskett, L. M., 361
Bates, E., 235
Bates, J. E., 515
Baum, A., 401
Baumeister, R. F., 570
Bayles, K., 515
Bayley, N., 288
Beach, F. A., 330
Beauchamp, G. K., 81
Becerra, R. M., 414
Beck, A. T., 440, 474
Becklen, R., 131
Beeler, N. F., 141
Bell, S. M., 517
Bellugi-Klima, W., 236
Belsky, J., 553
Bem, D. J., 580, 590
Bem, S. L., 527
Benedict, R., 570
Benjamin, M., 397
Bennet, E. L., 54
Benson, D. F., 268
Benson, H., 409
Berg, I., 282
Berg, J. H., 588, 597
Berger, K. S., 557, 561
Bergmann, K., 556
Bern, H., 217
Berry, C., 203

Berscheid, E., 589, 592, 596, 597
Bethon, G., 269
Bettelheim, B., 353*n*, 418
Bexton, W. H., 84
Bichard, S. L., 540
Biller, H., 543
Binder, J. L., 467, 471
Binet, A., 270–71, *270*, 276, 277
Birch, H. G., 505
Biringen, Z. C., 553
Birtchnell, J., 524
Bitterman, M. E., 267
Bjork, R. A., 192
Bjorkland, A., 71
Björntorp, P., 322
Black, J. B., 216, 217
Blanchard, E. B., 395, 476
Blass, E. M., 157, 158, 324
Block, J., 375
Block, N. J., 285
Blom, B., 333
Bloom, D. E., 552
Bloom, L. M., 70
Bloom, W., 86
Blumstein, P., 329
Bogen, J., 55
Boice, R., 169
Bolles, R. C., 181
Bond, L., 277
Bonvillian, J. D., 510
Boring, E. G., 140
Bornstein, M. H., 241
Bornstein, R., 559
Bovbjerg, P., 157
Bower, G. H., 205, 209, 216, 217, 218
Bowerman, M., 247
Bowlby, J., 524
Boyd, J. H., 544
Boyse, E. A., 81
Braestrup, C., 72
Branley, F. M., 141
Brehm, S. S., 395
Breznitz, S., 420
Briggs, J., 507
Brigham, J. C., 580
Broadbent, D. E., 143
Brodie, M., 596
Broen, P., 237
Brooks, J., 526
Bross, I. D. J., 242
Brotman, H. B., 555
Brown, B. S., 169

685

Brown, G. W., 410
Brown, M. D., 335
Brown, R., 200, 236, 237
Brown, R. W., 269, 591
Bruner, B., 129
Bruner, J. S., 241
Bucher, K. D., 441
Buchsbaum, M. S., 436
Bugelski, B. R., 143
Bühler, C., 416
Bullen, B. A., 321
Bunney, W. E., 442
Burkhard, B., 155
Burns, H. J., 208
Butcher, J. N., 467
Butler, J. M., 365
Butler, R. N., 558
Butterfield, F., 275
Butterworth, G., 80
Byck, R., 456
Byrne, D., 539, 595

C

Calhoun, K. S., 445
Calne, D. B., 42
Camara, K. A., 524
Campbell, B. A., 174
Campbell, D., 599
Campos, J. J., 303
Canter, R., 156
Carew, T. J., 154
Cargan, L., 551
Carlsmith, J. M., 582, 593
Carpenter, W. T., Jr., 440
Carroll, B. J., 429, 441
Carroll, D., 552
Carroll, J. B., 277
Carstensen, L. L., 545
Cartwright, R. D., 326, 327
Carver, C. S., 600
Case, R. B., 407
Castle, P., 512
Cattell, R. B., 373, 558
Cazden, C., 236
Census Bureau, 553
Cerella, J., 557
Charter, R. A., 562
Cheng, P. W., 247
Chess, S., 505, 508
Chilman, C. S., 539
Chomsky, N., 229, 238, 239
Christiaansen, R. E., 203
Chugani, H. T., 514
Church, R. M., 174
Clark, E. V., 207, 228, 229, 231, 237, 242, 245, 246
Clark, H. H., 207, 228, 229, 231, 237, 242, 245, 246
Clark, M. C., 218
Clark, R. A., 380
Clark, W. B., 454
Clausen, J. A., 537
Clifford, B. R., 203
Cofer, C. N., 324

Cohen, A. R., 585
Cohen, N., 157
Cohen, S., 103, 286, 504
Coile, D. C., 34
Cole, M. A., 562
Collings, V., 80
Collins, A. M., 242
Comstock, G. W., 559, 562
Conger, J. J., 157
Conley, J. J., 375, 376
Cooper, H., 590
Cooper, J., 156, 583
Cooper, M., 583
Corbit, J. B., 320
Coren, S., 91, 110, 124, 128, 144
Costello, C. G., 446
Cowan, E., 486
Cox, V. C., 318
Coyle, J. T., 196
Craig, K. D., 307
Craik, F. I. M., 207, 211
Craik, K., 27
Crandall, J. E., 359, 360
Crano, W. D., 590
Crawford, M., 599
Crenoch, J. M., 502
Crockenburg, S. B., 279
Crockett, H. J., 333
Cronbach, L. J., 270
Crosby, E., 63
Crouse, J., 275
Crutchfield, R. S., 138
Cytryn, L., 442
Cytrynbaum, S., 553

D

Dabbs, J. M., 585
Darley, J. M., 590
Datan, N., 526
Davidson, H. H., 381
Davidson, R. J., 307, 311
Davis, H. P., 196
Davison, G. C., 473
Day, R. H., 136
deCharms, R., 342
DeFrain, J., 552
Dekker, E., 157
DeLong, M. H., 196
DeLongois, A., 403
De Maris, A., 552
de Medinaceli, L., 71
Denike, L. D., 443
Denny, J. P., 397
Depue, R. A., 176, 488
Deutsch, A., 465
Deutsch, J. A., 318
De Valois, K. K., 93
De Valois, R. L., 91, 93
de Villiers, J. G., 237
de Villiers, P. A., 237, 240
de Vries, B., 540
DeWald, C. G., 142
Diaz, R. M., 234
Dion, K. K., 596, 597

Docherty, J. P., 402
Dollard, J., 178, 368–69
Domjan, M., 155
Doob, A. N., 12
Dooling, D. J., 205
Dougherty, L. M., 306, 310
Douvan, E., 553
Doyle, K. O., 290
Drabman, R., 169
Drenowski, A., 321
Dreskin, W., 518
Dreyer, P., 539
Duncan, B., 278
Duncan, O. D., 278
Duncker, K., 252
Dweck, C. S., 176
Dworkin, G., 285

E

Eagleton, T., 489, *489*
Ebbinghaus, H., 198, *199*
Eccles, J., 73
Eckardt, M. J., 453
Eckenrode, J., 410
Edelstein, E. L., 445
Education Commission of the States, 542
Eisenberg, L., 544
Eisenberg-Berg, N., 600
Ekman, P., 303, 305, 306
Elkin, I., 483
Eller, S. J., 176
Elliot, R., 471
Ellis, E. M., 445
Ellis, H. C., 206, 208, 209
Elman, D., 321
Elton, C. F., 291
Emory, E., 282, 284, 285
England, P., 549
Epstein, A. N., 324
Epstein, N. B., 480
Epstein, S., 375, 393
Erikson, E. H., 416, 547, *548*, 551, 553, 559, 562
Erlenmeyer-Kimling, L., 284
Evans, E. F., 121, 122
Evarts, E. V., 50, 52
Everhart, T. E., 67
Everson, R. B., 501
Eysenck, H. J., 282, 285, 373, 471

F

Facklam, H., 71, 73
Facklam, M., 71, 73
Falbo, T., 361
Falloon, I., 482
Farb, P., 235
Farina, A., 489
Fasnacht, G., 171
Fawcett, D. W., 86
Fazio, R. H., 583, 590
Featherman, D. L., 278
Feinberg, M., 429
Feldesman, A. B., 376
Feldman, R. S., 570

Feldman, S. S., 553
Fernald, A., 233, 234
Fernald, L. D., Jr., 174
Fernald, P. S., 174
Feshbach, N. D., 174
Feshbach, S., 360, 373
Festinger, L. A., 578, 586
Festinger-Schacter, S., 593
Field, T., 516, 518
Fillion, T. J., 157, 158
Fine, G. A., 528
Fine, M. A., 525
Finkelstein, P., 478
Fireman, B., 577
Fisher, W., 539
Fitzsimmons, J. T., 324
Flemming, I., 156
Fliers, E., 329
Foch, T. T., 323, 324
Fodor, E. M., 335, 336
Folkman, S., 415
Ford, G., 583
Ford, K., 539
Forward, J., 156
Foster, B. G., 562
Frank, R. G., 429
Frankel, A., 588
Frankel, F. H., 475
Frankl, V., 470
Frazier, S. H., 545
Frederick, C., 443
Freed, A., 572
Freed, W. J., 71
Freedman, D. X., 429
Freedman, J. L., 582, 584, 593
Freeman, J. M., 501
French, E. G., 380
Freud, Sigmund, 10, 27–28, *28*, 352–64, 368, 416, 417, 418, 442, 465–66
Frick, F., 252
Friedman, M., 407, 409
Friedrichs, A. G., 262
Friesen, W. V., 306
Fromm, E., 363–64, *364*, 466
Fuller, J. L., 399
Furman, W., 529
Furnham, A., 454

G

Gaeddert, W. P., 549
Gajdos, E., 177, 477
Galaburda, A. M., 56
Galton, Sir Francis, 21
Gamson, W. A., 577
Garb, J. J., 162
Garber, J., 177
Garcia, J., 162
Gardner, A., 238
Gardner, B., 238
Gardner, E. R., 433
Gardner, H., 262–63
Garmezy, N., 509, 524
Gates, A. L., 21
Gati, I., 243

Gatz, A. J., 307
Gebhard, P. H., 331
Geen, R. G., 340
Geis, B. D., 539
Gelade, C. A., 142
Gelfand, D. M., 527
Gelso, C. J., 467
Gerrard, M., 539
Gershon, E. S., 440
Geyer, L. H., 142
Ghiselin, B., 282
Gibbs, M. S., 485
Gibson, E. J., 137, 515
Gillberg, M., 326
Gilligan, C., 550
Gilovich, T., 254
Ginsburg, H. J., 527
Glaser, R., 277
Glass, D. C., 103
Glass, G. V., 65, 471
Glass, L. L., 478
Glazer, H. I., 410
Gleitman, H., 234
Gleitman, L. R., 234
Glick, P. C., 552
Glick, R., 559
Goetz, T., 176
Gold, S. R., 457
Goldberg, J., 409
Goldberger, L., 83
Goldfarb, W., 508
Goldman, P., 53
Goldman-Rakic, P. S., 556
Goldsen, R., 582
Goldstein, J. H., 598
Goldstein, M. J., 440
Goldstein, S., 403
Goleman, D., 110
Goode, W. J., 549
Goodnow, J. J., 241, 269
Goodwin, D. W., 454
Gopnik, A., 235
Gordon, M. T., 395
Gormezano, I., 154
Gorss, A. E., 12
Gotlib, I. H., 437
Gottesman, I. I., 286, 437
Gottlieb, J., 600
Gottman, J. M., 529
Gottschalk, E. C., 399
Gould, M. S., 545
Graf, P., 197
Graf, R. C., 212
Graham, P., 544
Grajek, S., 361, 552
Gray, J. A., 394
Graziano, W. G., 376
Green, J., 321
Green, M., 562
Greenberger, E., 542
Greenblatt, M., 414
Greene, D., 170
Greene, W. A., 403
Greenough, W. T., 54, 525
Grief, E., 537
Grinker, J. A., 320

Groen, J., 157
Gross, A. E., 156
Gross, L. P., 321
Gruder, C. L., 600
Gruenberg, B., 548
Guilford, J. P., 262–65, 279
Gunnar, M. R., 520
Gunter, B., 203
Gur, R. C., 307, 311

H

Haas, A. P., 432
Haier, R. J., 436
Haig, N. D., 126
Haigh, G. V., 365
Hall, C. S., 373
Hall, G. S., 537
Hall, R. C. W., 433
Hall, W. G., 324
Halpern, A. R., 202
Hamilton, M., 442
Hancock, F. T., 361
Hand, D. J., 393
Hansel, C. E. M., 125
Hansen, D. N., 396
Hardy, A. B., 477
Hare, R., 448
Hargadon, F., 275
Harlow, H. F., 213, 329, 508, 509, 516
Harlow, M. K., 329, 508
Harrell, M. S., 278
Harrell, T. W., 278
Harrington, C. L., 279
Harris, B., 156
Harris, F. R., 169
Harris, T., 410
Hartmann, D. P., 527, 598
Hartmann, E., 327, 328
Hartmann, H., 363
Hartup, W. W., 529
Hauser, B. B., 553
Haver, W., 339
Havighurst, R. J., 276
Hawkins, J. B., 154
Hebb, D., 599
Heidbreder, E., 400
Heider, F., 587
Held, R., 512
Heller, K., 559
Helsing, K. L., 559, 562
Hendin, H., 432
Hendrick, S., 549
Herdt, G. H., 571
Herink, R., 465
Heron, W., 84
Herrmann, T. F., 59
Herrnstein, R. J., 240, 449
Hertzog, C., 557
Hervey, G. R., 320
Herzog, E., 276
Hess, E. H., 131, 308, 309
Hess, R. D., 523
Heston, L. H., 556
Hetherington, E. M., 524

Hilgard, E. R., 474
Hilgard, J. R., 474
Hill, J., 543
Hilton, I., 361
Hinkle, L. E., 405, 406
Hiroto, D. S., 175
Hirsch, J., 323
Hochberg, J., 120, 137, 138
Hoffman, J. E., 142
Hofstadter, L., 70
Hohmann, G. W., 316
Holahan, C. J., 407
Holland, P. C., 179
Hollon, S., 177
Holmes, D. S., 310, 395, 405, 409
Holmes, T. H., 404
Holmsten, R. D., 409
Holyrod, K. A., 396
Holzman, P. S., 436
Honzik, C. H., 180
Honzik, M. P., 290
Hooley, J. M., 488
Hops, H., 173
Hormuth, S., 250
Horn, J. L., 277
Horney, K., 360–61, *363*, 466
Horowitz, M. J., 389
Hovland, C. I., 585
Howard, K. I., 537
Hrubec, H., 323, 324
Hsu, C., 504
Huba, G. J., 453
Hubbard, M., 579
Hubel, D. H., 45, 51, 121, 122
Hudspeth, A. J., 99
Humphrey, T., 63
Hurst, M. W., 402
Hurwitz, H. M. B., 59
Hymel, S., 529

I

Ilfield, F. W., 414
Ingram, R. E., 395
Institute of Medicine, 65
Iversen, L. L., 70, 110
Izard, C. E., 305, 306, 310, 313, 314, 315

J

Jacklin, C. N., 506, 527
Jacobs, G. H., 93
Jacobson, J. L., 501
James, William, 22–23, 30, 211–12, 242, 310, 332
Jamison, K. R., 429, 440
Janis, I. L., 252, 583, 585
Janke, L. L., 276
Jarvik, L. F., 284
Jedlicka, D., 539
Jeffery, R. W., 177, 477
Jencks, C., 284
Jenkins, C. D., 402
Jennings, J., 550
Jensen, A. R., 282, 285
Joffe, C., 526

Johansson, G., 126
John, E. R., 181
Johnson, D. H., 467
Johnson, L. C., 327
Johnson, M., 233
Johnson, P. B., 342
Johnson, V. E., 12, 329, 330, 331
Johnston, L. D., 457
Jones, E. E., 587, 591
Jung, Carl, 357–59, *357*, 376
Juraska, J. M., 525

K

Kabat, L. G., 106
Kagan, J., 508, 509, 513, 514, 519, 522, 531
Kahneman, D., 253, 254
Kail, R., 262
Kakolewski, J. W., 318
Kamin, L., 282, 284, 285
Kamlet, M. S., 429
Kandel, D. B., 543
Kandel, E. R., 154, 196
Kane, J. M., 482
Kantner, J., 539
Katcher, A. H., 340
Kay, D., 556
Kay, P., 245
Kearsley, R. B., 514, 519
Kehoe, E. J., 154
Kelley, H., 592
Kelly, J., 525
Kencks, C., 282
Kennedy, J. F., 484
Kenrick, D. T., 375
Kessen, W., 127
Kety, S., 72
Kiecolt-Glaser, J. K., 408
Kimmel, D. C., 547
Kimura, D., 58
Kindred, D. Y., 440
King, R., 599
Kintsch, W., 201, 210
Kirsch, M. A., 478
Kirsch, N., 156
Kissileff, H. R., 324
Klatzky, R. L., 152, 181, 201
Klein, R. E., 509
Kline, N. S., 410
Klopfer, B., 381
Knapp, R. R., 367
Knittle, J. L., 323
Knoll, E., 376
Kobasa, S. C., 407
Koelling, R., 162
Kohlberg, L., 540
Köhler, W., 178, *179*, 181
Kolata, G., 320, 323
Kolodny, R. C., 329, 330, 331
Koss, M. P., 467
Kozin, M., 200
Krantz, D., 410
Krech, D., 138
Kretchmer, E., 372
Krippner, S., 125
Kubie, L. S., 466

Kübler-Ross, E., 562–63
Kuffler, S. W., 91
Kulik, J., 200
Kulka, R., 553
Kupfer, D. J., 441
Kurz, E. M., 328

L

Lacey, B. C., 316
Lacey, J. I., 316
Lachenmeyer, J. R., 485
Lachman, R., 205
Laing, R. D., 415
Laingen, B., 413
Lamiell, J. T., 343
Lang, P. J., 473
Lange, C., 310
Langford, G., 327
LaRussa, G. W., 549
Latané, B., 600
Laudenslager, M. L., 411
Lauer, E. W., 63
Lawton, S. F., 340
Lazarus, R. S., 313, 411, 415
Lazerson, A., 70
Lee, S., 276
Leedy, M. G., 413
Lefcourt, H. M., 343
Leff, J. P., 488
Leighton, K., 520
Le Magnen, J., 318
LeMasters, E. E., 552
Lenneberg, E. H., 232
Leon, M. R., 396
Lepper, M. R., 170, 579, 581
Leslie, G. R., 552
Lesser, G. S., 543
Levenson, R. W., 455
Leventhal, H., 585
Levine, F. M., 171
Levine, L. E., 522
Levine, M. W., 120, 122
Levine, S., 59
Levinson, B., 214
Levinson, D. J., 553
Levinson, E., 127
Levy, J., 56–57, *56*
Lewin, K., 392
Lewis, E. R., 67
Lewis, H., 276
Lewis, M., 526
Lewis, M. I., 558
Lewontin, R. C., 286
Liberman, A. M., 129
Liberman, R. P., 482
Libet, B., 51
Liddell, C., 552, 553
Lieberman, M. A., 478
Liebeskind, J. C., 112
Lieman, A. L., 45, 50
Linder, D., 594
Lindzey, G., 285, 373
Linn, S., 240, 502
Lipscomb, D. M., 106
Lispsitt, L. P., 502

Locke, S. E., 408
Loehlin, J. C., 285
Loevinger, J., 376
Loftus, E. F., 208
Logue, A. W., 162
Londerville, S., 517
London, P., 469
Lord, C. G., 581
Lorenz, K., 339, 598
Lott, A. J., 577
Lowell, E. L., 380
Lowick, V., 454
Luborsky, L., 402
Lumsdaine, A. A., 585
Lutz, C., 314
Lykken, D. T., 303
Lyon, D. R., 192

M

MacArthur, R. D., 145
McAuley, W. J., 558
McBurney, D., 80
McCartney, K., 518
McCaul, K. D., 394, 395
McClelland, D. C., 129, 145, 333, 335, 380, 410
McClintock, M. K., 109
Maccoby, E. E., 506, 521, 527
McCullough, C., 122
McDermott, M. J., 395
Macfarlane, J. W., 290, 537, 546
Mcgeer, E. G., 482
Mcgeer, G. L., 482
McGeoch, J. A., 210
McGinnies, E., 129
McGrath, J. W., 571
McGraw, M. B., 512
McHugh, P. R., 317, 318
McKenzie, B. E., 136
Mackie, D., 581
MacKinnon, D. W., 279, 379
McKnew, D. H., 442
MacLeod, W. L., 327
McNemar, Q., 276
MacNichol, D. F., Jr., 89
MacNichol, E. F., 84
MacWhinny, B., 232
Maddi, S. R., 351, 407
Maier, S. F., 175
Main, M., 517
Malof, M., 577
Mandler, G., 197
Mann, L., 583
Mansbach, W. E., 559
Manton, K. G., 559
Marks, I. M., 473
Marsh, H. W., 527, 579
Marshall, B. S., 154
Marx, M. M., 564
Maser, J. D., 394, 483
Maslach, C., 314
Maslow, A. H., 341, 366–67, *367*, *368*, 415, 478
Mason, J. W., 316
Masserman, J. H., 422
Masters, W. H., 12, 329, 330, 331
Matson, F. W., 27
Maugh, T. M., II, 327

Mayer, J., 321
Mayer, R. E., 152, 279
Mead, M., 571
Meddis, R., 327
Medin, D. L., 240, 241
Meece, J. L., 549*n*
Melamed, B. G., 473
Melko, M., 551
Mellinger, G. D., 327, 441, 455
Mellon, P. M., 590
Meltzer, H. Y., 436
Meltzoff, A. N., 235
Melzack, R., 112
Mendelson, W. B., 326, 327, 328
Merrill, M. A., 17
Mervis, C. B., 243
Miceli, L., 557
Michaud, A., 144
Midanik, L., 454
Milavsky, B., 340
Miles, M. B., 478
Milgram, S., 576–78
Miller, B. C., 553
Miller, D. G., 208
Miller, G., 280–81
Miller, G. A., 192, 205, 227, 232
Miller, J. G., 587
Miller, L. C., 588
Miller, N., 368–69
Miller, N. E., 34, 65, 172, 174, 178, 321, 330, 402, 409, 411
Miller, S. M., 527
Miller, T. I., 471
Milner, B., 52
Minuchin, S., 403
Mischel, W., 375
Mishkin, M., 52, 200
Misra, R. K., 458
Monnett, M., 125
Monroe, S. M., 176
Moos, R. H., 407
Moran, T. H., 317, 318
Moreland, J. R., 525
Moreno, J. L., 479
Morgan, M., 526
Morgulis, S., 154
Morris, J. L., 334
Moruzzi, G., 327
Moss, A. J., 403
Moss, H. A., 375, 531
Mueser, K. T., 596
Muir, M. S., 342
Mumford, E., 65
Mumford, J., 471
Munn, N. L., 174
Murphy, G. L., 240
Murray, H. A., 380
Murray, E. A., 52
Murstein, 551
Mussen, P. H., 501, 600
Myers, J. K., 429, 435, 441, 445

N

Nash, S. C., 553
Natelson, B. H., 406
National Center for Health Statistics, 554, 556

National Hospice Organization, 564
National Institute of Mental Health, 327, 488, 538, 556
National Institute on Aging, 555, 561
National Institute on Alcohol Abuse and Alcoholism, 455
National Institute on Drug Abuse, 457
National Institutes of Health, 407, 480, 483
National Research Council, 277
Neff, J. A., 415
Nehemkis, A. M., 562
Neisser, U., 200
Neisser, W., 131
Nelson, V. L., 289
Newcomb, T. M., 593
Newman, A., 466
Newport, E. L., 234, 237
Nichols, P. L., 285
Nida, S., 600
Nielsen, S. L., 313
Nigro, G., 200
Nisbett, R. E., 170, 320, 321, 323, 591
Nissen, H., 599
Nixon, R., 583
Nolen-Hoeksema, S., 441
Novack, L. L., 510
Nurco, D. N., 458
Nurnberger, J. L., 440

O

O'Connell, B., 235
O'Connor, M. J., 286, 504
Oden, S. L., 529
Offer, D., 537
Offir, C., 549
O'Kelly, C. G., 526
O'Leary, K. D., 169
Olson, S. L., 515
O'Malley, P. M., 457
O'Neal, E. C., 340
O'Neil, H. F., Jr., 396
O'Neill, C. W., 339
Ophir, I., 162
Opler, M. K., 315
Orlansky, M. D., 510
Orne, M., 475
Ornstein, R., 45, 56
Osterweis, F., 562
Ostrov, E., 537
Oyama, S., 234

P

Paddock, J., 339
Parker, J. W., 527, 579
Parloff, M. B., 469
Parmelee, A. H., 286, 504
Parsons, O. A., 453
Passingham, R. E., 52
Patrick, C. J., 307
Patterson, G. R., 173, 543
Paul, L. A., 112
Pavlov, I. P., 153, 159–62, *161*, 174, 432
Paykel, E. S., 410
Pearson, A. J. D., 327

Pearson, C., 288
Peele, S., 29
Peele, T. L., 307
Peleaux, R., 520
Pellegrino, J. W., 262
Pelser, H. E., 157
Penick, S., 402
Peplau, L. A., 584
Perin, C. T., 167
Petersen, A. C., 537
Peterson, C., 177, 406
Petti, T. A., 443
Pettigrew, T. F., 583
Pezdek, K., 557
Pfaffman, C., 70
Phares, E. J., 343
Phelps, M. E., 514
Phillips, D. P., 545
Piaget, Jean, 263–70, *266*, 530
Pickett, J. M., 231
Piliavin, I. M., 601
Piliavin, J. A., 601
Pillemer, D. H., 200
Pine, C. J., 320
Platt, J., 321
Pohorecky, L. A., 410
Polivy, J., 313
Pollack, I., 231
Pomerantz, J. R., 139
Porac, C., 91, 110, 124, 128, 144
Porter, R. H., 502
Post, F., 106
Postman, L., 129
Pratt, J. G., 125
Pratt, W. F., 538
Premack, D., 239
Price, D. L., 196
Pritchard, R. M., 82
Proctor, W., 409
Puerto, A., 318
Putnam, F. W., 374

Q

Quillian, M. R., 242
Quinn, R. P., 548
Quinton, D., 546, 552

R

Rabkin, J. G., 405
Radecki, C., 550
Radke-Yarrow, M., 599
Radloff, R., 578
Rahe, D. F., 376, 529
Rahe, R. H., 404
Rakic, P., 195, 199
Raloff, J., 106
Rasmussen, J., 83
Rayner, R., 155
Raynor, J. O., 343
Reason, J., 231
Rebelsky, F., 507

Rechtschaffen, A., 326
Reed, R. B., 321
Reese, H. W., 214
Regestein, Q. R., 328
Reis, H. T., 550, 596
Reisman, B., 391
Reite, M., 516, 518
Renshaw, P. D., 529
Rescorla, R. A., 159, 179
Reuter-Lorenz, P., 311, *311*
Revelle, W., 396
Rhine, J. B., 125
Rice, K. M., 395
Riessman, F., 487
Rigby, M. K., 108
Riger, S., 395
Riley, M. W., 559
Rist, R. C., 590
Ritter, B., 476
Rivers, C., 549
Rizley, R., 177
Robbins, D., 168
Robertson, I., 549*n*
Robins, L. N., 448, 449, 458
Robinson, I., 539
Rock, I., 145
Rock, J., 108
Rodin, J., 321, 561, 601
Rofé, Y., 409
Rogers, C. R., 365–66, *365*, 468, 478, 562
Rolls, B. J., 324
Rolls, E. T., 324
Romaniuk, M., 558
Romer, D., 600
Roper Organization, 549
Rorer, L. G., 378
Rosch, E., 243
Rosch, E. H., 243
Rose, J. E., 84, 103
Rose, R. M., 304, 402
Rose, S. A., 282, 286
Rosen, M. G., 500
Rosenhan, D. L., 435, 468, 469, 484, 600
Rosenman, R. H., 407
Rosenwaike, I., 555
Rosenzweig, M. R., 45, 50, 54
Ross, G., 240, 501
Ross, L., 579, 587
Roth, D. L., 405
Roth, F. P., 237
Rothman, S., 277
Roupenian, A., 393
Roviaro, S., 409
Rubin, D. C., 200, 207
Rubin, Z., 335
Runk, B., 483
Rush, A. J., 474
Rush, B., 465
Russell, R. K., 397
Rutherford, E., 600
Rutkowski, G. K., 600
Rutter, M., 390, 405, 410, 433, 509, 528, 544, 546, 552
Ryan, S. M., 411
Rycroft, C., 466
Rytina, S., 577

S

Sachs, J. S., 233
Sackett, G. P., 504
Sackheim, H. A., 307, 311
Salapatek, P., 127, 515
Salk, L., 545
Sampson, E. A., 361
Sandmaier, M., 454
Sandor, B. B., 559
Sands, S. F., 219
Sangrey, D., 415
Sarason, I. G., 313
Saron, C., 311
Saucy, M. C., 307
Sawrey, W. L., 156
Scarr, S., 276, 287, 289, 290, 361
Scarr-Salapatek, S., 285
Schachter, S., 314, 321, 337
Schaeffer, M. A., 401
Schaffer, C. E., 311
Schaffer, H. R., 553
Schaie, K. W., 557, 559
Scheils, D., 125
Scherer, K. R., 304
Schieffelin, E. L., 428
Schiff, M., 288, 289
Schiffman, S. S., 556
Schildkraut, J. J., 410
Schlechty, P. C., 528
Schlesinger, H. J., 65
Schliefer, S. J., 407
Schmolling, P., 414
Schneider, D. J., 597
Schultz, D. P., 83
Schwab, J. J., 433
Schwartz, G. E., 305, 307
Schwartz, J. H., 196
Schwartz, P., 329
Schwartz, S., 600
Schwebel, A. I., 525
Scott, T. H., 84
Sears, D. O., 582, 584, 585, 593
Seaver, W. B., 590
Segal, J., 9, 83, 335, 413, 415, 487, 518, 528, 570
Segal, N. L., 286, 287
Segal, Z., 335, 518, 570
Segerber, O., 561
Sekuler, R., 127, 145
Self, P., 526
Seligman, M. E. P., 175, 177, 406, 435, 468, 469, 484
Selye, H., 316, 400–401, 409, 416–17
Senchak, M., 550
Sengelaub, D. R., 328
Serafitidenes, E. A., 414
Shaffer, D., 545
Shanas, E., 543
Shapiro, C. M., 327
Shapiro, D. A., 471
Shapiro, J., 498
Shapiro, S., 432, 465
Shapley, R., 127
Sheffield, F. C., 585
Shefner, J. M., 120, 122
Sheldon, W. H., 372, *372*, 373

Shepard, R. N., 198, 217
Sheperd-Look, D. L., 526
Sher, K. J., 454
Sherman, S. J., 343
Shevel, L. R., 291
Shields, J., 437
Shields, S. A., 300, 301
Shiffrin, R. M., 191, 192
Shigetomi, C. C., 527
Shore, C., 235
Sigal, J., 485
Silberstein, J. A., 453
Silver, L. B., 9, 545
Silverberg, R. A., 562
Simenauer, J., 552
Simon, H. A. 280
Simon, T., 234
Simons, B., 324
Simpson, W. E., 262
Sims, E. A., 323
Singer, J. E., 103, 314
Sizemore, C., 374
Skinner, B. F., 7, 24, 26, 163–66, 237, 369
Slater, J., 488
Slater, P., 596
Slobin, D. I., 236, 237
Smircina, M. T., 559
Smith, D. K., 562
Smith, E. A., 539
Smith, E. E., 241
Smith, M. L., 471
Smith, R. S., 501
Smith, S., 144
Smith, S. M., 201
Smith, T., 335, 395
Smith, W. R., 282
Smyser, A. A., 564
Smythe, P. M., 288
Snow, C. E., 233
Snow, M. E., 506
Snyder, M., 570, 589
Snyder, M. L., 588
Snyder, S. H., 71
Snyderman, M., 277
Soldo, B. J., 559
Sollie, D. L., 553
Solomon, B., 550
Solomon, F., 562
Solomon, R. L., 173, 175, 180, 458
Solomon, S., 310, 395
Sommers, R., 20
Sontag, L. W., 289
Sorenson, R. C., 537
Spanier, G. B., 552
Spanos, N. P., 570
Spearman, C., 261
Speece, M. W., 559
Sperling, G., 192
Sperry, Roger, 29, 56
Spielberger, C. D., 394, 396, 397
Spitz, R. A., 508
Spitzer, R., 434
Spuhler, J. N., 285
Squire, L. R., 196, 197
Staines, G. L., 548
Stapp, J., 5

Steinberg, L., 536, 538, 539, 542, 544
Stellar, E., 317, 318, 320, 324
Stelmack, R. M., 144
Stephens, J. H., 440
Stern, M., 538
Stern, W., 208
Sternberg, R. J., 263, 282, 552
Steveni, A., 71
Stevens, B., 550
Stevens, C. F., 45, 65
Stevenson, H. W., 262, 267, 276
Stewart, A. J., 335, 336
Stickney, S. K., 433
Stigler, J. W., 276
Stiles, W. B., 471
Stock, M. B., 288
Stoel, C., 232
Stol, S. B., 169
Stouthamer-Loeber, M., 543
Strauss, K. E., 162
Strauss, N., 176
Streissguth, A. P., 501
Strickland, B. R., 343
Stringfield, D. O., 376
Stroebe, M. S., 562
Stroebe, W., 562
Struening, E. L., 405
Strupp, H. H., 467, 471, 480
Stunkard, A. J., 162, 320, 321, 322, 323, 324
Stuss, D. T., 268
Suedfeld, P., 83, 361
Sumi, S., 126
Suomi, S. J., 509, 523
Susman, E. J., 375, 538
Sutton-Smith, B., 361
Suzman, R., 559
Swaab, D. F., 329
Szklo, M., 559, 562

T

Tagiuri, R., 594
Tanke, E. D., 589
Tanner, J. M., 53
Tapp, W. N., 321
Tarler-Benlolo, L., 171
Tarnopolsky, A., 393
Tarpy, R. M., 152
Taves, P. A., 583
Tavris, C., 549
Taylor, C., 282
Teague, G., 335
Teasdale, J. D., 177
Tecce, J. J., 131
Tennen, H., 176
Tennes, K. H., 316
Terman, L. M., 17, 282
Terr, L. C., 445
Terrace, H., 239
Tesser, A., 334, 596
Thomas, A., 505, 508
Thompson, R. F., 45, 54, 70
Thompson, W., 599
Thomson, J. A., 449
Thrustone, L. L., 261–62, 264

Tiber, H., 443
Tierney, D. W., 474
Tinklepaugh, O. L., 171
Tolman, E. C., 180, 181
Tomkins, S. S., 310
Tootell, H. E., 136
Torrance, E. P., 279
Torsvall, L., 326
Treisman, A. M., 142
Trusheim, D., 275
Trussell, J., 552
Tschukitscheff, I. P., 338
Tsuang, M. T., 432
Tucker, A. M., 5
Tucker, L. A., 373
Tulving, E., 207, 211
Tuma, A. H., 394, 483
Turner, C. H., 180
Turner, T. J., 216
Turrell, E. S., 157
Tversky, A., 243, 253, 254
Tyler, L. E., 277

U

Udry, J. R., 539
Ulman, K., 537
Ulmer, D., 409
Underwood, B. J., 202
U.S. Bureau of the Census, 341, 549, 551, 552, 555, 559, 562
U.S. Office of Strategic Services, 379
U.S. Public Health Service, 549
U.S. Department of Health and Human Services, 328, 481
U.S. Department of Labor, 542
Uttal, W. R., 103

V

Vaillant, G. E., 456
Valdes-Dapena, M. A., 60
Valenstein, E. S., 29, 318, 464, 484
Valenta, J. G., 108
Valins, S., 591
Vallone, R., 254
Vance, V. S., 528
VandenBos, G. R., 5
Vandermey, R., 432
Van Dyke, C., 456
Vaughn, C. E., 488
Venneman, T., 229
Verhave, T., 165
Veroff, J., 553
Vierling, J. S., 108
Vihman, M. M., 232
Vlok, L. A., 480
Von Frisch, W., 227
Vorster, J., 237

W

Wadden, T. A., 475
Wagner, K. R., 232

Wagner, M. W., 125
Wald, G., 88
Walk, R. D., 137
Walker, E., 282, 284, 285
Walker, J. I., 444
Walker, L. J., 540
Walker, P., 144
Wallace, I. F., 282, 286
Wallach, L., 450
Wallach, M. A., 276, 282, 450
Wallerstein, J., 525
Wallerstein, J. S., 524
Walster, E., 592, 597
Wang, M. L., 318
Ward, L. C., 144
Ward, L. M., 91, 110, 124, 128
Watkins, G., 393
Watson, C. G., 436
Watson, J. B., 154–55, 158–59
Watson, P. C., 250
Webb, W. B., 326, 327
Wechsler, D., 260, *260*, 261, 272, 276
Weinberg, R. A., 289
Weiner, B., 342, 360, 373
Weiner, H., 410
Weiskrantz, L., 200
Weiss, J. M., 410, 411
Weiss, R. L., 173
Weitz, H., 397
Weitzman, L. J., 526
Wells, G. L., 208
Wenegrat, B., 478

Werner, E. E., 501
Werner, J. S., 502
Wernver, P. D., 549
Whalen, R. E., 330
White, B. L., 512
White, J. A., 556
Whitfield, I. C., 121, 122
Whorf, B., 243–44
Wickelgren, W. A., 166, 194, 195, 199, 210, 242
Widiger, J. A., 378
Wienckowski, L. A., 169
Wiesel, T. N., 45, 121, 122
Wilkins, W., 472
Will, J., 526
Williams, J., 434
Williams, M., 49
Willis, S. L., 556, 557
Wilson, E. O., 330
Wilson, G. T., 170
Wilson, J. Q., 449
Wilson, M. S., 413
Wine, J., 394
Wing, W. W., Jr., 276
Winokur, G., 411
Winter, D. G., 335, 336
Winterbottom, M. R., 334
Wolf, R. M., 288
Wolfe, B., 469
Wolpe, J., 474
Woolfolk, A. E., 170
Woolfolk, R. L., 170
Worchel, P., 594

World Health Organization, 488
Wright, A. A., 219
Wrightsman, L. S., 580
Wundt, Wilhelm, 21–22, *22*
Wyatt, R. J., 71, 562, 564

Y

Yalom, I., 470, 478, 563
Yamazaki, K., 81
Yankelovich, D., 548
Yarbus, A. L., 130
Yerkes, R. M., 154
Young, P. T., 301

Z

Zahn-Waxler, M., 599
Zajonc, R. B., 361, 593
Zamostny, K. P., 397
Zanna, M. P., 583
Zeevi, Y. Y., 67
Zelazo, P. R., 514, 519
Zelnick, M., 539
Zillman, D., 340
Zimbardo, P. G., 106
Zipf, G. K., 245
Zube, M., 554
Zukier, H., 580
Zung, W. W. K., 439

SUBJECT INDEX

(Page numbers in *italics* refer to illustrations.)

A

Abnormal psychology (abnormal behavior), 9, 428–61, *429*, *431*
   adjustment and, 415
   affective disorders, 438–43, *438*, *439*, *442*
   anxiety and, 388, 395
   anxiety disorders, 441–46
   breaking point and, 431
   characteristics of, 428–29
   cost of, 431
   culture and, 428–29
   definition of, 428
   Freudian view of, 354, 356
   Jungian view of, 357
   learning, 162
   nature and scope of, 428–31
   personality disorders, 446–50, *448*, *450*
   roots and varieties of, 431–35, *434*
   schizophrenia and, 435–37, *436*, 480–82, *481*
   scope of, 430, *430*
   stress and, 388, 411, 431–33
   substance abuse, 450–58, *451*
   tests for, 429
Absolute threshold of senses, 81
Accommodation, 264–65
Acetylcholine, 70, 196
Achievement
   aging and, 559, *560*
   divorce and, 524–25
Achievement motive, 332–35, *333*, *334*, 343, 391, 392, 407
   firstborn children and, 361, *362*
Achievement tests, 275–76
Acrophobia, 152, 445, *472*
Acuity, visual, 91
Acupuncture, 110, *111*
Adaptation
   dark, 89
   sensory, 82, 504
Addiction, 451
   heroin, 429, 458
   See also Alcoholism; Drugs
Adjustment, 415
Adolescence, 530–31, *530*, *531*, 536–45
   body image in, 538
   definition of, 536, *536*
   eating disorders in, 538
   identity in, 541–44, *542*, *543*
   joy vs. misery in, 536–37
   moral development in, 540, *541*
   physical growth in, 537–38
   sex in, 538–39
   suicide in, 544–45, *544*
Adrenal glands, 302, 304, 400–401, 441
Adrenalin, 400
Adulthood, 544–54, *545*
   careers and, 547–49, *547*
   love and marriage in, 551–52
   middle age of, 553–54, *554*
   parenthood and, 552–53
   sex roles in, 549–50
   surprising turnabouts, 546
   See also Old age
Aerial perspective, 139, *139*
Affective disorders, 438–43
   biological roots of, 440–41
   in children, 442–43, *442*
   depression, 438–41, *438*, *439*
   manic-depressive illness, 440
   suicide, 439–40
   in women vs. men, 441
Afferent neurons, 46
Affiliation motive, 337–38, 343, 391, 550
Afterimages, 95, *97*, 98
Aggression, 339–40, *340*, 369, 508, 597–99
   direct, 420
   displaced, 420
   inherited vs. learned, 598, *598*
   learning and, *183*, 598, *598*
   limbic system and, 59, *61*
   psychoanalytic view of, 353–54
   in response to anxiety and stress, 420
Aging. *See* Old age
Agoraphobia, 152, 445–46
Alcohol, anxiety and, 394
"Alcoholic personality," 454–55
Alcoholics Anonymous (A.A.), 487
Alcoholism, 441, 450–55
   blackouts and, 453
   causes of, 454–55
   in men vs. women, 453–54, *454*
Algorithms, 248–49
All or none principle, 69
Altered states of consciousness, 123, 455
Altruism, 597, 599–601, *599*
   bystander apathy vs., 600–601, *601*
Alzheimer's disease, 196, 556, *557*
American Psychiatric Association, 434
American Psychoanalytic Association, 466
American Psychological Association (APA), 156
Amnesia, 197–98, *197*
Amplitude of sound waves, 99, *100*, 103
Anal stage, of human sexual development, 354, 356
Androgens, 328, 525, 537
Anemia, 433
Anger, 301–304, 309
Animals
   communication in, 227, 238–39, *238*
   emotion in, *301*, 302, 305
   for research, 34, *34*
   sexual behavior of, 328–29
   stress in, 410, 411
   surrogate mothers and, 516, *516*
Anorexia nervosa, 538
Anoxia, 500
ANS. *See* Autonomic nervous system
Antidepressants, 481, 482–83
Antipsychotic drugs (major tranquilizers), 480–82, *482*
Antisocial personality, 447–49, *448*
Anxiety, 173, 327, 388–98, 401, 408, 432
   basic, 360
   behavior and, 389–98
   causes of, 390–94, *393*, *394*
   coping with, 393–94
   defense mechanisms and, 416–22, *421*
   drugs for (minor tranquilizers), *481*, 483
   fear and, 389, *389*
   general and specific, 394–95
   hypnosis and, 474–75
   learning and grades and, 396–97, *396*
   psychoanalytic view of, 352, 356
   risks and, 397, *398*
   separation, 519–20, *519*
   social behavior and, 395, *395*
   stranger, 520, *520*
Anxiety disorders, 441–46
   generalized (free-floating), 442
   obsessive-compulsive reactions, 446
   panic, 443–44
   phobia, 444–47
APA. *See* American Psychological Association
Apathy, 421
   bystander, 600–601, *601*
Apex of basilar membrane, 102
Applied science, 7, *8*, 9

693

Approach-approach conflict, 392
Approach-avoidance conflict, 392
Aptitude tests, 14, 275–76
  vocational, 292
Army, U.S., group intelligence test of, 277–78, *278*
Artificial intelligence, 279–81, *281*
Asch experiments, 572, *574*, 575, *575*
Assertive coping, 411, *412*, 413, 417, 474–75
Assertiveness training, 479
Assimilation, 264–65
Association cortex, 52
Associative memory, 262
Associative network theory, 206
Attachment, 515–18, *516*, *517*
Attention, 126–31. *See also* Selection in perception
Attitudes, 580–86
  behavior change and, 583
  cognitive dissonance theory and, 582–83
  toward death, 559, 562
  definition of, 580
  inconsistent, 580–81
  life experiences and, 582
  toward people who need psychological help, 487–89, *489*
  persuasive communications and, 583–86, *584*, *585*
  prejudices and stereotypes, 581, *581*
  stress and, 403–405
Attractiveness, physical, 596–97, *596*
Attribution error, 587–88
Attribution theories, 586–91
  guidance from, 590, *591*
  person vs. situation and, 587
  self-fulfilling prophecy and, 589–90
  self-perception theory and, 590–91
  influence on others, 588–89
Audience, persuasive communications and, 585
Auditory canal, *101*
Auditory nerve, 101, *101*, 104
Authority, respect for, 577–78. *See also* Conformity; Obedience
Autokinetic illusion, 123
Autonomic nervous system (ANS), 61–64, *63*, 373, 448
  emotion and, 304, 309
  endocrine glands and, 61, *62*
  parasympathetic division of, 62, *63*, 64
  sympathetic division of, *63*, 64
Aversive conditioning, 473, *473*
Avoidance-avoidance conflict, 392
Axons, 46, 66–68, *66*

B

Babbling, 232
Balance, 51–52
Basic anxiety, 360
Basic science, 7, 9
Basilar membrane, 99, 101–105, *102*, *105*
Behavior. *See also specific topics*
  abnormal. *See* Abnormal psychology

anxiety and, 389–98
attitude change and, 583
changing, 413–14
context and, 32–33, *33*
continuity vs. change in, 30, 32
motives as influence on, 340–43
operant, 163
predicting, 7
shaping of, 164–65, *164*, *165*
understanding, as goal of psychology, 6, 7
Behavioral theories of personality, 367–70
Behaviorism, 23–24, 154
  radical, 369
Behavior therapy (behavior modification), 169–71, *170*, 369, 470, 472–77
  cognitive, 474
  relearning and, 472–74, *473*
Belladonna, 310
Beyond Freedom and Dignity (Skinner), 24
Binocular vision, 138
Biofeedback, 169, 171–72, *172*
  stress and, 409
Biological factors
  in abnormal behavior, 432, 433, 440–41
  See also Heredity; Nature-nurture controversy
Biological therapies, 480–84
Bipolar cells, 90, *90*
Bipolar depression (manic-depressive illness), 372, 440
Birth control, 539
Birth process, 500–502, *502*
Black English, 234–35
Blackouts, alcoholic, 453
Blindness
  color, 94–95, *97*, 98
  night, 89
Blind spot, 87, *87*
Blood pressure, high, 408–10
Body
  aging of, 555
  emotion and, 301–10, *304–309*
  movement, 50–52, 54, 107, 112–13
Body image, 538
Body types, personality and, 372, *372*
Borderline personality, 447
Brain, 42–77, 373
  cerebellum, 51–52, *51*
  cerebral cortex, 42, 44–45, *44*, 48, 49, 50–52, 82, 101, 103
  cerebrum, 44, 49
  changes in, 30
  chemical, 69–73
  collective unconscious and, 358
  communications network of, 64–73
  complexity of, 6
  cortex of, 313
  depression and, 410–11, 440–41
  electrical activity of, 56, *57*
  electroconvulsive therapy (ECT) and, 483–84, *484*
  emotion and, 57–62, *60*, 64, 307–308, *308*, 310–14, 312
  evolution of, *44*
  gender differences and, 57, 58
  growth of, 53–54, *53*, *54*

hemispheres of, *43*, 44, 52, 54–57, 307–308, *308*, 311, *311*
hippocampus, 52
homeostasis and, 317
hormones produced by, 46
hunger and, 317–21, *319*
hypothalamus of, 312, 318, *319*, 320, 321, 329
information processing and, 48–50
intellectual development and, 53–54, *53*, 513, *514*
language and, 54
limbic system of, 58–59, *59*, 61
memory and, 52
memory trace and, 195–96
movement and, 50–52, 54
multiple personality and, 374
neurons of, 45–46, 52, 54, 64–70
perception and, 121
physical well-being and, 60, 64, 65
as privileged organ, 42
reticular activating system of, 49–50
schizophrenia and, 436, *437*
sectional view of, *50*
senile dementia, 556
sense organs and, 82, 88
speech and, 510
thalamus of, 49
topside view of, 42, *43*
Brain grafts, 70, 71
Brain stem, 60, 71
Breathing, 317
Brightness, 85
Brightness constancy, 136–37
Broad-tuned receptors, 84
Broad tuning, 101, *103*
Bulimia, 538
Bystander apathy, 600–601, *601*

C

CA (Chronological age), 271–72
Caffeine, 455
California Personality Inventory (CPI), 378
Cannabis, 457
Cannon-Bard theory of emotion, 312–14
  cognitive view of, 313–14
Cardinal dispositions, 373
Career counseling, 10–11
Careers
  choosing and pursuing, 547–49, *547*
  See also Employment
Case histories, 12
Categories, encoding and, 214, *215*, 216
Cell body, 66, *66*, 67
Central deafness, 104
Central dispositions, 373
Central nervous system, 46, *47*, 450, 483, 499
  aging and, 555
Cerebellum, 51–52, *51*
Cerebral cortex, 42, 44–45, *44*, 48, 82
  association, 52
  hearing and, 101, 103
  movement and, 50–51
  size of, 42, 44, 45

somatosensory cortex of, 48
special functions of, 48–49, *49*
Cerebrum, 44, 49
Certainty, motive for, 338
Challenger (space shuttle), 200, *201*
Chemotherapy. *See* Drug therapy
Children, 496–533
   brain of, 53–54, *54*, 510, 513, *514*
   conception and birth of, 496–502, *497*, *498*, *500*, *502*
   concrete operations, stage of, 267–68, *268*, *269*
   day-care programs for, 517, 518, *518*
   depression and, 442–43, *442*
   development of body and mind in, 510–15, *511–15*
   eye movements of, 513, 515, *515*
   firstborn, 361, *362*
   formal operations, stage of, 268–69
   intelligence of, 263–70
   language learning by, 232–38, *232*, *233*, *235*, *236*
   newborns, 502–10, *502–503*, *505–506*
   personality development in, 515–20, *516*, *517*, *519*, *520*
   post-traumatic stress reactions in, 444–45
   preoperational stage of, 266–67
   preschool, 523–27, *524*, *525*
   punishment of, 522–23, *522*
   rearing of, 505, 506, 507, *507*, 509
   sensorimotor, stage of, 266, *267*
   social development of, 520–23
   stress and, 411, *412*
   teacher and peer influence, 527–31, *529*, *530*, 531
   toilet training, 521, *521*
Choleric people, 371, *371*
Chromosomes, 497–99, *497*
Chronological age (CA), 271–72
Chunking, 204–206, *205*, 216
Ciliary muscles, *86*, 87
Cirrhosis, 453
Class differences, IQ and, 288
Classical conditioning, 152–62, *159*
   abnormal behavior and, 162
   basics of, 157–59
   extinction and spontaneous recovery in, 160–61, *161*
   Pavlov and, 153–54, *153*, *154*, 157, 160–61
   physical symptoms and responses and, 156–57
   stimulus generalization and discrimination in, 161–62
   timing, frequency, and predictability of reinforcement in, 159–60, *160*
   Watson and, 154–56, 158–59
Claustrophobia, 152, 445
Client-centered therapy, 468
Clinical psychologists, 378
Clinical psychology (clinical psychologists), 9–11, *9*, *10*, 378. *See also* Abnormal psychology; Psychoanalysis; Psychotherapy
Closure, perception of, 133, *133*
Clustering, 216–17, *217*, *218*
Cocaine, 457
Cochlea, 99, 101–105, *101*, *102*, 113

damage to, 103–104, *105*
Coefficient of correlation, 17
Cognitive behavior therapy, 474
Cognitive dissonance theory, attitude change and, 582–83
Cognitive map, 181
Cognitive psychology, 25–27
   mental models of reality and, 26–27
   rise of, 25–26
Cognitive theory of emotion, 312–14
   Cannon-Bard, 313–14
   James-Lange, 314
Cognitive view of learning, 178–83
   chimpanzees and, 178, *179*
   cognitive maps, expectancies, knowledge and, 181
   observation and, 181–83, *182*, *183*
   without reinforcement, 178–80, *180*
   without response, 180
Cohabitation, 552
Cold, sensation of, 110
Collective unconscious, 358–59, *358*
Color (color vision), 85, 87–89, *89*, 91–98, *92*, *94*
   adding and subtracting, 93–94, *95*
   afterimages and, 95, *97*, 98
   complementary, 94
   mixture of, 94, *96*
   pathways for the experience of, 91–93
   theories of, 98
Color blindness, 94–95, 98
   test of, 95, *97*
Commission on the Higher Education of Minorities, 277
Communication, 226, *226*, *227*
   in animals, 227, 238–39, *238*
   brain and 64–73
   persuasive, attitude change and, 583–86, *584*, *585*
   sex and, 330, 331, *331*
   See also Language
Community mental health, 484–87, *485*
   crisis intervention and, 486–87, *486*
   self-help groups and, 487
Community mental health centers, 485–86
Community mental health specialists (community psychologists), 9, 485
Community support, therapy and, 489, *489*
Complementary colors, 94
Complexity
   of light waves, 85–86
   of sound waves, 99, *100*
Compulsions, 446
Compulsive personality, 447
Computers, artificial intelligence and, 279–81
Conception, 496–97, *497*
Concepts, 239
   enrichment and, 241
   inference and, 241–42
   language and, 239–46
   problems with definition of, 243, *244*
   without words, 240–41, *240*
Concrete operations, 267–68, *268*, 269, 530
Conditional positive regard, 365
Conditioned reflex, 23–24
Conditioned response, 158, 160–61, *161*

Conditioned stimulus, 157
Conditioning
   aversive, 473, *473*
   classical. *See* Classical conditioning
   operant. *See* Operant conditioning
Conductive deafness, 104
Cones, 87–88, *88*, *90*, 98
Confidentiality, 33
Conflict, 391
   motives and, 390–92
   types of, 392
Conformity
   Asch experiment and, 572, 574, 575, *575*
   in daily life, 572, *573*
   Milgram experiment and, 576–78, *576*
   reasons for, 577–78
   tendency to, 571–72
Connecting neurons, 46
Consciousness, 23
   altered states of, 123, 455
Conservation, 267, *268*
Constant reinforcement, 168
Contents, intelligence and, 262
Context
   behavior and, 32–33, *32*
   perceptual, 143, *144*
Continuity
   of behavior, 30, 32
   perception of, 133, *133*
Contraception, 539
Contrast, perception of, 126, 127, *128*
Control, locus of, 342–43
Control groups, 18, 20–21, *21*
Conventional level of moral development, 540, *541*
Coordination, 51–52
Coping
   assertive, 411, *412*, 413, 417, 474–75
   attitudes and, 403, 404
   behavioral changes and, 413–14
   defense mechanisms and, 416–22, *419*, *421*, *422*
   drugs and, 457–58
   with the environment, 413
   managing internal wear and tear and, 414–15
   mental health and, 411–16, *412*, *414*
   stress and, 403, 404, 409, *409*, 411–22
Core personality, 351
   development and, 352
Cornea, *86*
Corpus callosum, 50, 55
Corpus striatum, 71
Correlation method, 16–17
Cortex, 313
Cortisol, 441
Cortisone, 433
Counseling psychology, 9–11, *11*
CPI (California Personality Inventory), 378
Creativity, artificial intelligence and, 279–81
Credibility of the source, communications and, 584
Crime
   anxiety and, 395, *395*
   juvenile delinquency and, 524, *524*, 542, 543, *543*

Crisis intervention, 486–87, *486*
Crystallized intelligence, 558, *558*
Culture, 570–71
 abnormal behavior and, 428–29
 childrearing and, 507, *507*, 509
 newborn differences and, 504, *505*
 personality and, 357
 separation anxiety and, 519, *519*
 socialization process and, 570–71, *571*
 subcultures and, 571

D

Dark adaptation, 89
Day-care programs, 517, 518, *518*
Deafness, types of, 104
Death, 559–62
 attitudes toward, 559, 562
 experience of, 563–64, *563*
 marriage and, 562
 stages of, 562–63
Decibel scale, 103, *104*
Defense mechanisms, 416–22, *421*
 aggression, 420
 denial, 420
 identification, 418, *419*
 pro and con of, 420
 projection, 419–20
 rationalization, 417–18
 reaction formation, 418–19
 regression, 421, *422*
 repression, 418
 sublimation, 418
 withdrawal and apathy, 420–21
Delinquency, 542, 543, *543*
 death of parent and, 524, *524*
Delirium tremens (DTs), 451
Delusions, 435
Dendrites, 66, *66*, 68
Denial, 420
Deoxyribonucleic acid (DNA), 498
Dependency
 alcohol or drug, 451
 conformity and, 577
Dependency motive, 338, 550
Dependent personality, 447
Dependent variables, 18
Depressants, 457
Depression, 176, 177, 327, 438–43, *438*
 bipolar (manic-depressive illness), 372, 440
 brain and, 410–11, 440–41
 in childhood, 442–43, *442*
 definition of, 438
 drugs for, 440, *481*, 482–83
 electroconvulsive therapy (ECT), 483–84, *484*
 heredity and, 411
 hopelessness and, 439–40
 memory and, 208, *209*
 stress and, 401, 402, 408, 410–11
 suicide and, 439–40, 544–45, *544*
 test for, 439, *439*
 unipolar, 440
Depth, perception of, 137–39, *137*, *140*
Desensitization, in behavior therapy, 472

Development
 changing views on, 536
 intellectual. *See* Intellectual development; Thinking
 moral, 540, *541*
 personality and, 352
 physical, 499, *500*, 501, 510–12, *511*, *512*, 537–38
 psychosocial, 547, *548*
 social. *See* Social development
 See also Adolescence; Adulthood; Children; Newborns
Developmental psychologists, 7
Diabetes, stress and, 402–403
Diagnostic and Statistical Manual of Mental Disorders (Revised) DSM III (R), 434
Diet, 322
Difference threshold of senses, 81–82
Difficult children, 504–506, *506*
Direct-access retrieval, 195
Displaced aggression, 420
Dispositional factors, 587
Dispositions, 373
Distance, perception of, 137–41, *137–41*
 perspective and, 139, *139*
 size and, 140, 141, *141*
Divorce, 524–25, *525*
DNA (deoxyribonucleic acid), 498
Dominance, in school years, 529
Dopamine, 70, 71, 436, 481, 482
Double approach-avoidance conflict, 392
Double-blind technique, 20–21
Doubt, anxiety and, 390–94
Dramamine, 114
Draw-a-person test, 381
Dreams, 359
 analysis of, 466
Drives, 317–31
 breathing, 317
 definition of, 317
 elimination, 330
 hunger, 317–24, *318*, *319*, *321*, *323*, *324*
 pain, 330
 sex, 327–31
 sleep, 324–28, *325*, *326*
 sociobiology and, 330
 thirst, 317, 324
Drugs, 310
 abuse of, 450–51, 455–58
 addiction to, 429
 antianxiety, 72, 394
 antidepressants, *481*, 482–83
 antipsychotic (major tranquilizers), 480–82, *482*
 depression and, 440, *481*, 482–83
 neurotransmitters and, 72
 sex differences in use of, 454, *455*
 side effects of, 433, 456–57
 sleep and, 327, 328
 See also specific drugs
Drug therapy (chemotherapy), 480–83, *481*
 for anxiety, *481*, 483
 for depression, *481*, 482–83
 schizophrenia and, 480–82, *481*
DTs (*delirium tremens*), 451
Dynamic therapy, 465–67
 classical psychoanalysis, 465–66

 contemporary, 466–67, *467*

E

Ear
 cochlea, 99, 101–105, *101*, *102*, *105*, 113
 inner, 99, 113, *113*
 outer, 99, *101*, 105
 structure of, 99 *101*
 See also Hearing; Sound
Eardrum, 99, *101*
Easy children, 504–506, *506*
Eating disorders, 538
Eclectic therapy, 469
ECT (electroconvulsive therapy), 483–84, *484*
Ectomorphs, 372
Education
 intelligence tests and. *See* Intelligence tests
 language and, 234–35, *235*
 Piaget's theory and, 269–70
 school success and, 276
 sex, 539
EEG (electroencephalograph), 57, *57*
Efferent neurons, 46
Egg cells, 496, *497*, 498–99
Ego, 353, 354, 356
Ego ideal, 339
Electra complex, 355, *355*
Electroconvulsive therapy (ECT), 483–84, *484*
Electrodes, emotion measured with, 305, *305*
Electroencephalograph (EEG), 57, *57*
Electromagnetic energy, visible spectrum and, 85, *85*
Elimination drive, 330
Embryo, *500*
Emotion, 15, 300–17, *300*, 316, *316*. *See also* Anxiety
 in animals, *301*, 302, 305
 body's role in, 301–10, *304–309*
 brain and, 57–62, *60*, 64, 307–308, *308*, 310–14, *312*
 Cannon-Bard theory of, 312–14
 cognitive theory of, 312–14
 feedback theory of, 310, 312
 individual differences, 314–17, *318*
 of infants, 306, *307*
 James-Lange theory of emotion, 310, 312
 measuring, 302, *302*, 303, 305, *305*
 range of, 314, *315*
 schizophrenia and, 435
 speech patterns and, 304, *304*
Empathy, 600
Employment
 in adolescence, 542
 IQ and, 264–65, *265*
 retirement and, 559
 stress and, 401
 of women, 549, 550
 See also Careers
Encoding, 192, 204–19
 associative network theory and, 206
 chunking and, 204–206, *205*
 language, 226, 229
 learning and, 209–13
 strategies for, 213–19, *213*, *214*, *215*, *217*, *218*

696   Subject Index

Encounter groups, 478
End branches, 66, 68
Endocrine glands, 61, *62*, 65, 373, 400
   emotion and, 302, 304
Endomorphs, 372
Endorphins, 70–71
Energy
   adaptation, supply of, 409
   electromagnetic, visible spectrum and, 85, *85*
   stress and, 409, 410
Environment, 6
   abnormal behavior and, 432–33, *434*
   antisocial personality and, 448–49
   anxiety and, 393
   brain growth and, 54, *54*
   coping with, 413
   early traits and, 508
   effects of neglect and trauma in, 508–10
   intelligence and, 269–70, 289–90
   newborns and, 502–503
   prenatal development and, 499, 501
   psychoanalytic theory and, 357, 359
   sex typing and, 525–26, *526*
   stress and, 408–409, 413
   See also Nature-nurture controversy
Environmental Protection Agency, 106
Environmental psychologists, 9
Episodic memory, 201
Equilibrium, sense of, 107, *112*, 113–14, *113*
ESP (Extrasensory perception), 123, 125
Estrogen, 108, 525, 537
Ethics, 33–34
   in psychological research, 155, *156*
Eustachian tube, *101*
Evolution
   altruism and, 599
   of brain, *44*
   facial expressions and, 305
Exercise, 322
   stress and, 409, *409*
Existential psychotherapy, 470
Expectancies, 181
Expectations, perceptual, 143, *143*
Experimental groups, 18, 20, *21*
Experimental psychologists, 7
Experiments, 17–21
   Asch, 572, *574*, 575, *575*
   experimental and control groups in, 18, 20–21, *21*
   Milgram, 576–78, *576*
   sensory deprivation, 84
   single-blind and double-blind, 20–21
   split-brain, 55, *55*
   variables in, 18, *19*
Exploration, 517–18
   limits and, 522–23, *522*
Extinction
   in behavior therapy, 473
   in classical conditioning, 160–61, *161*
   in operant conditioning, 164
Extrasensory perception (ESP), 123, 125
Extroversion-introversion, 373, 375, *376*
Extroverts, 357
Eye
   blinking of, 154, *155*
   of children, 513, 515, *515*

   emotion and, 303, 308–10, *309*
   muscles of, 138
   structure of, 86–87, *86*
   See also Vision

F

Facial expressions, 308–10
   brain hemispheres and, 307–308, *308*
   eyes, 308–10, *309*
Failure
   fear of, 343
   learned helplessness and, 176, *176*
Familiarity, 592–93, *592*, *593*
Family
   heredity vs. environment in, 284–86, *286*
   IQ similarities in, 283–84, *284*
   therapy support and, 488
   See also Mothers; Parents
Family therapy, 479–80, *479*
Fat cells, 320, 322–23, *323*, *324*
Fear, 302–304
   anxiety and, 389, *389*
   of failure, 343
Feature analysis, 142–43
Feature detectors, 120–22, *121*
Feedback theories of emotion, 310, 312
Feelings. *See* Emotion
Figural contents, 262
Figure and ground principle, 132, *132*
Firstborn children, 361, *362*
First impression, 596–97
"Flashbulb" memories, 200, *201*
Fluid intelligence, 558, *558*
Forgetting, 196–97
   amnesia and, 197–98, *197*
   Ebbinghaus's curve of, 198, *199*
   factors in, 198–204, *200*, *201*, *204*
   measuring, 197–98, *197*, *198*
   retrieval process fails, 201–203, *202*, *203*
Formal operations, 268–69, 530
Fovea, *86*, 87–88, *91*
Free association, 465
Freedom, behavior modification and, 170–71
Free-floating (generalized) anxiety, 442
Free will, 23
Frequency of sound waves, 99, *100*, 101, *102*
Frontal lobes, 52
Frustration
   anxiety and, 390–92
   definition of, 390
   rationalization and, 417–18
Functional fixedness, 252–53, *252*, *254*

G

Ganglia, 61, *63*, 64
Ganglion cells, 90–91, *90*
Gate-control mechanism, 112
Gender differences in brain, 57, 58. *See also* Sex differences
General adaptation syndrome, stress and, 400–401
General anxiety, 394–95
General intelligence (g-factor), 261–62

Generalized anxiety disorder (free-floating anxiety), 442
General reasoning, 262
Generativity, 553
Generic memory, 201
Genes, 498, *498*
Genital stage, of human sexual development, 354, 356
Gestalt psychology (Gestalt psychologists), 24–25, *25*, *26*, 142
Gestalt therapy, 469
Glands, 373
   adrenal, 302, 304, 400–401, 441
   emotion and, 302–304, 316
   endocrine, 61, *62*, 65, 302, 304, 373
   pituitary, 58, 537
   salivary, 303
   sex, 330
   thyroid, 433
Global processing, 142–43
Glucose, 318, *318*, 437
Glycogen, 318, *318*
Gradient of texture, 139, *139*
Grammar, 228 236–37
   syntax and, 228–29
Group tests, 274–75, *274*, 277–78, *278*
Group therapy, 477–80, *477*
   assertiveness training, 479
   encounter, 478
   family therapy, 479–80, *479*
   large group awareness training, 478–79
   psychodrama, 479
   traditional, 477–78
Growth
   of brain, 53–54, *53*, *54*
   physical, 537–38
Guidance
   from attribution theories, 590, *591*
   need for, 578
Guidance counselors, 378
Guided participation, coping and, 475, 477

H

Hallucinations, 435, *437*, 455
Hallucinogens, 456
Headaches, 112
   biofeedback and, 171–72, *172*
Health
   stress and, 388, *388*, 401–10
   See also Illness; Mental health
Health psychology (health psychologists), 9, 65
Hearing, 98–106
   damage of, 103–104, *105*, 106, *106*
   ear structure and, 99, *101*
   loudness and, 103–104
   place theory and, 101
   sensory receptors, 99, 101, *102*, 103–104, *105*
   See also Ear; Sound
Heart attack, stress and, 406, *407*, 409
Helplessness
   genuine, 414–15
   learned, 162, 174–77, *175*, *176*
Heredity, 6, 496–98
   abnormal behavior and, 432

Heredity (continued)
  aggression and, 598
  altruism and, 599
  chromosomes and, 497, *497*
  conception and, 496–97, *497*
  depression and, 411
  emotions and, 315–16
  facial expressions and, 305–306
  genes and, 498, *498*
  IQ and, 289–90
  learning and, 162
  newborns and, 503–504
  schizophrenia and, 436, *437*
  sociopaths and, 448
  See also Nature-nurture controversy
Hering theory of color vision, 98
Heroin addiction, 429, 458
Hierarchy of motives, 341
High blood pressure, stress and, 408–10
Hippocampus, 52
Histrionic personality, 447
Homeless population, 431
Homeostasis, 60, 317
Homosexuality, 434–35
Hopelessness, depression and, 439–40
Horizontal cells, 90
Hormones, 46, 61, 108
  adolescence and, 537, *538*
  androgen, 328, *525*, *537*
  cortisol, 441
  depression and, 441
  emotion and, 302
  estrogen, 108, *525*, *537*
  sex differences and, 525
  steroids, 400
  stress and, 400–401
Hostility motive, 339–40, *340*
Hue, 85. *See also* Color
Humanistic psychology, 27
Humanistic theories of personality, 358, 364–67
  of Maslow, 366–67, *367*, *368*
  of Rogers, 365–66, *365*
Humanistic therapy, 468–70
  client-centered, 468
  other approaches, 469–70
Hunger, 317–24
  brain and, 317–21, *319*
  incentive objectives and, 318, *319*, 320
  signals of, 317–18, *318*
  See also Obesity
Hunter-gatherer societies, 429
Hypnotherapy, 474–75
Hypoglycemia, 433
Hypothalamus, 58, 60, 312
  hunger and, 318, *319*, 320, 321
  lateral (LH), 318
  sex and, 329
  ventromedial (VMH), 318
Hysterical conversion, 27

I

Id, 353–54, 356, 368
Identification, 418, *419*
  with parents, 355–56
  process of, 523–24
Identity, 364
  adolescent, 541–44, *542*, *543*
  definition of, 541
  of men vs. women, 550
  in middle age, 553–54, *554*
  of parents, 543
Illness
  aging and, 556, *557*
  emotional background of, 402, *402*
  psychosomatic, 401–403
  stress and, 401–408, *402*
Illogical thinking, 248
Illusions, perceptual, 122–23, 125
  touch and, 123, *124*
  visual, 122–23, *122–24*
Imagery, encoding and, 217, 219
Imitation, learning by, 181–83, *182*, *183*
Immune system
  conditioning of, 157
  stress and, 407–408, *408*, 411
Incentive objects, hunger and, 318, *319*, 320
Incentive value, 343
  motives and, 341–42
Independence, 417
  in adolescence, 543
Independent variables, 18
Individual differences, 6
  in emotion, 314–17
  in IQ, *17*
  in personality, 530, *530*
  tests and measurements of, 15–17, *17*
Individual psychology, 359–60
Individual tests, 274
Industrial psychologists, 9
Infants
  emotions of, 306, *307*;
  See also Newborns
Inferences, 241–42
Information, anxiety and, 393–94
Information processing, 26, 48–50
  retinal coding and, 89–91, *90*
Inhalants, 456
Inner ear, 99, 113, *113*
Inner standards, 521–22
  in school years, 530
Insight, 178, *179*. *See also* Cognitive view of learning
Insomnia, 327, 328, 433
Instincts, 332
Insulin, 402–403
Insulin shock, 156–57
Intellectual development
  brain and, 53–54, *53*, 513, *514*
  in children, 513–15, *513–15*
  See also Thinking
Intelligence, 259–96
  artificial, 279–81, *281*
  crystallized, 558, *558*
  definition of, 260
  environment and, 269–70, 289–90
  fluid, 558, *558*
  Gardner's theory of, 262–63
  general (g-factor), 261–62, 264
  Guilford's 120-factor theory of, 262–65, *263*
  nature of, 261–70, *261*
  old age and, 556–58, *558*
  Piaget's theory of, 263–70, *267*
  primary mental abilities and, 262
  Spearman's view of, 261
  Sternberg's theory of, 263
  Thurstone's view of, 261–62, 264
  See also Intelligence quotient; Intelligence tests
Intelligence quotient (IQ), 16–17, 271–72, 276–90, 504. *See also* Intelligence tests
  class differences and, 288
  creativity and, 279–81, *280*
  heredity vs. environment and, 282–90, *284*, *289*
  jobs and, 264–65, *265*
  occupational level and, 276–79, *278*
  plant growth and, 286, *286*
  racial differences in, 285
  ranges of, *273*
  school success and, 276
  success in life and, 281–83
Intelligence tests, 14–17, *17*, 270–82, *272*, *273*, *274*
  as aptitude tests, 275–76
  bias in, 275–76
  group, 274–75, *274*, 277–78, *278*
  individual, 274
  Scholastic Aptitude Tests, 274–75
  social impact of, 276, *277*
  Stanford-Binet, 271, *271*, 272, 274–76, 279
  Wechsler, 287
  See also Intelligence quotient (IQ)
Intensity
  of light, 85, 88
  perception and, 127–28
Interaction, reciprocal, 369–70, *370*
Interest tests, 293
Interference, 201–203
  proactive, 202–203, *202*, *203*
  retroactive, 203
Internal association cells, 90, *90*
Interposition, 138–39, *138*
Interpretation, 141–45, *142*
  expectation, mental set, and context in, 143, *143*, *144*
  prototypes, feature analysis, global processing and, 142–43, *142*
Interval schedules, 168–69, *168*
Interviews, 12
Introspection, 22–24
Introverts, 357
Intuitive understanding, 266–67
Iowa achievement test, 275
IQ (Intelligence quotient), 16–17, 271–72, 276–90, 504
Iris, 86, *86*
Irritability, in newborns, 504, *505*
Isolation, children and, 508

J

James-Lange theory of emotion, 310, 312
  cognitive view of, 314, *314*
Japan, conformity in, 577
Jobs. *See* Careers; Employment
Just noticeable difference, 81
Juvenile delinquents, 524, *524*, 542, 543, *543*

K

Kaluli, 428
Knowledge, in cognitive learning, 181

L

Language, 225–46
  brain and, 54
  concepts and, 239–46, *240*, *244*
  distortion and, 243–44
  flexibility of, 230
  foreign, 232–33
  functions of, 226, *226*, *227*
  importance of, 226
  learning of, 231–39, *232*, *236*
  listener problems and, 231
  memory and, 242–43
  producing and understanding, 229–31
  sign, 233
  speaker problems and, 229–31
  structure of, 227–29
  thinking and, 226, 229, 241–46, *245*
Large group awareness training, 478–79
Latent content, 466
Lateral hypothalamus, 318
Learned helplessness, 162, 174–77, *175*
  failure and, 176, *176*
  in human beings, 175–76
Learning, 152–87, 226
  abnormal behavior and, 162
  achievement tests and, 275
  aggression and, 183, 598, *598*
  altruism and, 600
  anxiety and, 396–97, *396*
  built-in predispositions to, 162
  cognitive view of, 178–83, *179*, *180*, *182*, *183*
  concepts and, 242–43
  conditioned, 23–24
  definition of, 152
  encoding process and, 209–13
  intelligence tests and, 276–77
  language and, 231–39, *232*, *233*, *235*, *236*, *238*, 242–43
  observation, 181–83, *182*, *183*, 370, 475, *476*
  social theory of, 369–70, *370*
  time and, 211, 212
  See also Behavior therapy; Classical conditioning; Operant conditioning
Learning set, 213–14
Lens, of the eye, *86*, *87*
Libido, 352–55, 357
  Jung's view of, 358
  Oedipus complex and, 355
Librium, 394, 483
Lie detector (polygraph), 302, *302*, 303
Life expectancy, 554, *555*, 559
Life experiences, new attitudes and, 582
Life Stress Scale, 403, *404*
Light waves, 84–91
  adding and subtracting, 93–94, *95*
  physical nature of, 85–86
Limbic system of brain, 58–59, *59*, *61*
Linear perspective, 139, *139*
Lithium, 483
Liver
  cirrhosis of, 453
  hunger and, 318, *318*
Locus of control, 342–43
Logical thinking, 247–48, 262
Logotherapy, 470
Long-term memory, *191*, 193–96
  clustering and, 216–17, *217*, *218*
  memory trace and, 195–96
  retrieval process and, 195
Loudness, 103–104, 126
Love, 551–52
  sex and, 327, 329, *329*
L-tryptophan, 328

M

MA (mental age), 271–72
Major tranquilizers (antipsychotic drugs), 480–82, *482*
Maladjustment, 366. *See also* Abnormal psychology
Manic-depressive illness (bipolar depression), 372, 440
Manifest content, 466
MAO (monoamine oxidase inhibitors), 482–83
Marriage, 551–52, *551*, *552*
  changes over time in, 551–52, *552*
  death and, 562
  mental health and, 551, *551*
  punishment and, 173
Marriage counselors, 11, 378
Maturation, 510, *511*, *512*, *512*
Meaning, language and, 227–28
Medicine, biofeedback and, 169, 171–72, *172*
Medulla, 60
Melancholy people, 371, *371*
Memory, 30, 189–223, *190*
  associative, 262
  brain and, 52
  chemical basis of, 196
  concepts and, 242–43
  depression and, 208, *209*
  encoding and, 192, 204–19, *205*, *213*, *215*, *217*, *218*
  episodic, 201
  "flashbulb," 200, *201*
  generic, 201
  intellectual development and, 513, *514*
  language and, 226, 229, 242–43
  limits of, 194
  long-term, *191*, 193–96, 216–17, *217*, *218*
  measuring, 197–98, *197*, *198*
  mood and, 208, 209
  primacy effect and, 193
  range of, 191–96, *191*
  recall and, 197
  recency effect and, 193
  recognition and, 197–98, *198*
  rehearsal system and, 193
  relearning and, 198
  retrieval and, *191*, 195, 201–203, *202*, *203*
  scanning and, 192
  schema and, 192
  selection and, 192
  sensory, *191*, 192
  short-term, 191–93, *193*, 204–206, *205*, *514*
  transfer process and, 193, 204–209
  See also Forgetting
Memory trace, 195–96
  fading of, 199–200, *200*, *201*
Men
  affective disorders in, 441
  alcoholism in, 453–54, *454*
  in middle age, 553–54
  old age and, 559
  sex roles of, 549–50
  See also Gender differences; Sex differences
Menarche, 537
Menstruation, 537
  pheromones and, 108–109
Mental abilities, 262. *See also* Intelligence; Intelligence quotient; Intelligence tests; Thinking
Mental age (MA), 271–72
Mental disorder. *See* Abnormal psychology
Mental health
  adjustment, normal personality and, 415–17
  aging and, 558–59, 561, *561*
  community, 484–87, *485*, *486*
  coping and, 411–16, *412*, *414*
  definition of, 415
  drugs and, 72
  marital status and, 551, *551*
Mental Health Association, 469
Mental hospital population, 480, *481*
Mental life, 22–23
Mental models of reality, 26–27
Mental set, 143
Mental telepathy (mind reading), 125
Mesomorphs, 372
Metabolism, 500
  emotion and, 302–303
  hunger and, 318
  obesity and, 320
Middle age, 553–54, *554*
Middle Ages, 464
Middle ear, 99, *101*
Milgram experiment, 576–78, *576*
Mind reading (mental telepathy), 125
Minnesota Multiphasic Personality Inventory (MMPI), 378, *379*
Mnemonic devices, 219
Modeling, learning through, 181–83, *182*, *183*
Monoamine oxidase (MAO) inhibitors, 482–83
Mononucleosis, 433
Mood, memory and, 208, *209*
Mood disorders. *See* Affective disorders; Depression
Moral development, in adolescence, 540, *541*
Morphemes, 227–28
Motherese, 233
Mothers
  absence of, 516–20, *517*
  separation anxiety, 519–20, *519*
  surrogate, 516, *516*
Motion, stroboscopic, 123, *123*, *124*
Motion sickness, 114
Motivation, 331–43
  achievement, 332–35, *333*, *334*, 343, 361, *362*, 391, *392*, 407
  affiliation, 337–38, 343, 391, 550
  anxiety and, 390–91
  behavior influenced by, 340–43

Subject Index 699

Motivation (*continued*)
  for certainty, 338
  conflicting, 390–92
  dependency, 338, 550
  forgetting and, 204, *204*
  hierarchy of, 341
  hostility, 339–40, *340*
  intelligence tests and, 276, 290
  male sex role problems and, 550
  to meet standards, 339
  nature of, 331–38
  power, 335, *336*, 410
  to shun power, 336, *337*
  stress and, 407, 410
  sublimation and, 418
  teachers and, 527
  unconscious, 352, 353
Motive targets, 341
Motor cortex, 51
Movement
  brain and, 50–52, 54
  as forgotten sense, 107, 112–13
  perception of, 126–27, *127*
Multiple personality, 374
Muscles
  ciliary, *86*, 87
  eye, *86*, 87, 138
  facial, emotion and, 304–307, *304–307*
  maturation of, 510, *511*
Mutual support groups, 487
Myelin sheath, 66

N

Narcissistic personality, 449–50, *450*
Narcotics, 456
National Academy of Sciences, 277
National Institute for Education, 528
Naturalistic observation, 12, *13*
Natural selection, 305
Nature-nurture controversy, 20–30, *31*
  aggression and, 598, *598*
  altruism and, 599–600
  attitude changes and, 586
  IQ and, 282–90, *284*, *286*
  sociobiology and, 330
Needs, basic human, 363–64, *364*
Negative afterimage, 98
Negative reinforcement, 172
Neglect, children and, 508–10
Neopsychoanalysts, 363–64, *364*
Nerve cells. *See* Neurons (nerve cells)
Nervous system, 46, *47*, 122, 510
  emotion and, 304, 309, 316
  peripheral, 46, *48*
  reflex responses and, 153
  See also Autonomic nervous system; Brain; Central nervous system; Neurons
Neurons (nerve cells), 82
  afferent, 46
  all or none principle and, 69
  brain, 45–46, 52, 64–70
  connecting, 46
  efferent, 46
  ganglia, 61, *63*, 64
  hearing, 101, *103*

  of pons, 52
  structure of, 66, *66*
  transmission of messages by, 66–69, *70*
Neurotransmitters, 67–72, 196, 394, 410, 440, 484–85
  dopamine, 70, 71, 436, 481, *482*
  drugs and, 72
  schizophrenia and, 436
Newborns, 502–10
  duration of early traits of, 508, *509*
  easy, slow-to-warm-up, and difficult, 504–506, *506*
  irritability and stress differences of, 504, *505*
  neglect and trauma effects and, 508–10
  reflexes of, 502–503, *503*
  sensitivity and adaptation of, 504
  visual skills of, 502, *502*
Nicotine, 455
Night blindness, 89
Nodes, 66
Noise, 103–104, *104*, 106
  anxiety and, 393
Noradrenaline, 394, 410, 411
Norepinephrine, 70, 482, 483
Normal curve of distribution, 16
Normal personality, 415–17, *417*
Nose, structure of, 108
Nucleus, of neuron, 66
Number, as primary mental ability, 262

O

Obedience
  in Milgram experiment, 576–78, *576*
  tendency to, 571–72
Obesity, 318–24
  causes of, 320–21, *321*
  fat cells and, 322–23, *323*, *324*
  hypothalamus and, 318, *319*
  weight control and, 321, 322
Objectivity, tests and, 291, 378, *379*
Observation, 12, *13*
  coping and, 475, *476*
  learning by, 181–83, *182*, *183*, 370, 475, 476
Obsessions, 446
Obsessive-compulsive disorder, 446
Occupational level, IQ and, 276–79, *278*
Occupations. *See* Careers; Employment
Oedipus complex, 353–56
Old age
  achievement and, 559, *560*
  body and, 555–56, *556*
  control and, 561
  delaying, 561
  intellectual capacities in, 556–58
  life expectancy and, 554, *555*, 559
  mental health in, 558–59, 561, *561*
  theories of, 555
  See also Death
120-factor theory of intelligence (Guilford), 262–65, *263*
Operant avoidance, 172–73
Operant behavior, 163
Operant conditioning, 162–77
  applications of, 169
  behavior modification and, 169–71, *171*

  behavior shaping and, 164–65, *164*, *165*
  biofeedback and, 169, 171–72, *172*
  extinction and, 164
  learned helplessness and, 174–77, *175*
  learning to feel worthy and, 177
  operant avoidance and, 172–73
  operant escape and, 172–73
  principles of, 164
  punishment and, 173–74
  reinforcement in, 166–69, *167*, 172
  Skinner and, 163–66, *163*
  spontaneous recovery and, 164
  stimulus discrimination and, 164
  stimulus recovery and, 164
  superstitions and, 165–66, *166*
  token economies and, 169, *170*
Operant escape, 172–73
Operations, 265
  concrete, 267–68, *268*, *269*
  formal 268–69
Opinion surveys, 13–14
Opponent-process theory
  of emotion, 458
  of vision, 93, *93*
Optical illusions, 122, 123
Optic nerve, 82, *86*, 87, 90, 92–93
Oral stage, of human sexual development, 354, 356
Organism, 7
Organization
  encoding and, 210–11
  perceptual, 132–41, *133–41*
Organ of Corti, 99
Orientation, frame of, 364
Outer ear, 99, *101*, 105
Oval window, *101*, 102
Overeating, 320–23, *321*
Overlearning, law of, 212

P

Pain
  as drive, 330
  sensation of, 110, *111*, 112
Panic disorder, 443–44
Paradoxical sleep, 325–26
Paranoia, 106
Paranoid personality, 449
Parapsychology, 125
Parasympathetic division, of autonomic nervous system, 62, *63*, 64
  nervous system, 62, *63*, 64
Parents, 552–53
  adolescent, 539, *540*
  adolescents' relations with, 541–43
  death or divorce of, 524–25, *524*, *525*
  identity of, 543
  See also Mothers
Parkinson's disease, 70, 71
Partial reinforcement, 168–69, *168*
Participant observation, 12
Passive-aggressive personality, 447
Pattern theory of the senses, 82, 84
Peers, influence of, 527–29, *529*
Penis envy, 360
Peptides, 70, 71
Percentile, 292

Perception, 26, 120–47
  altered states of consciousness and, 123
  drugs and, 123
  extrasensory (ESP), 123, 125
  feature detectors and, 120–22, *121*
  as inborn skill, 121–22
  intellectual development and, 513, 515, *515*
  intensity and, 127–28
  interpretation and, 141–45, *142–43*
  in newborns, 502, *502*, 504
  organization in, 132–41, *133–41*
  scanning movements and, 129, *130*, 131
  schizophrenia and, 435, 436
  selection and, 126–31, *127–28*
  size and, 127, *128*
  stimulating *144*, 145
  survival and, 120–26
  touch illusions and, 123, *124*
  visual illusions and, 122–23, *122–24*
Perceptual constancy, 134
Perceptual speed, 262
Peripheral nervous system, 46, 48
Peripheral traits, 352
Persistence of set, 252–53
Personality, 349–84
  abnormal. *See* Abnormal psychology
  behavioral view of, 367–70, *370*
  childhood vs. adult, 531, *531*
  core, 351
  culture and, 357
  development of, 515–20, *516*, *517*, *519*, *520*
  hierarchy of, 351
  humanistic theories of, 358, 364–67, *365*, *367*, *368*
  intelligence tests and, 276
  measuring, 378–81, *379–81*
  multiple, 374
  normal, 415–17, *417*
  physiological characteristics and, 371–73, *371*, *372*
  problem solving and, 250, *251*, 252
  psychoanalytic theory of. *See* Psychoanalysis
  theories of, 350–52
  type and trait theories of, 370–78, *371*, *372*, *375–77*
Personality disorders, 446–50
  antisocial, 447–49, *448*
  characteristics of, 447
  definition of, 446
  narcissistic, 449–50, *450*
  paranoid, 449
Personality tests, 293
Perspective, 139, *139*
Persuasive communications, 583–86, *584*, *585*
PET (positron emission tomography), 437
Phallic stage, 354, 356
Phenomenological self, 365–66
Pheromones, 108–109
Phlegmatic people, 371, *371*
Phobias, 444–47
  behavior therapy and, 475, *476*, 477
Phonemes, 227
Physical attractiveness, 596–97, *596*
Physical development
  in adolescence, 537–38
  of children, 510, *511*, 512, *512*

Physical symptoms and responses, conditioning of, 156–57
Physiological characteristics, personality and, 371–73, *371*, *372*
Physiological measures, 15
Physiological psychologists, 7
Pitch, 99, 126
Pituitary gland, 58, 537
Placebo effect, 404
Place theory, 101
Pleasure principle, 353–54
Polygraph (lie detector), 302, *302*, 303
Pons, 52
Positive afterimage, 98
Positive reinforcement, 172
Positron emission tomography (PET), 437
Postconventional level of moral development, 540, *541*
Posthypnotic suggestion, 353, 474
Post-traumatic stress disorder, 444–45
Power
  motive for, 335, *336*, 410
  shunning of, 336, *337*
Precognition, 125
Preconventional level of moral development, 540, *541*
Pregnancy, 501, 539
Prejudices, 581
Premarital sex, 538–39, *539*
Prematurity, 501–502
Premises, thinking and, 247
Prenatal development, 499, *500*, 501
Preoperational stage, 266–67
Preschool years, 523–27
  identification process in, 523–24
  parental death or divorce in, 524–25, *524*, *525*
  sex typing in, 525–27, *526*
Pressure, sensation of, 110
Primacy effect, 193
Primary mental abilities, 262
Primary reinforcers, 166, *167*
Prisoners, sensory deprivation of, 83, *83*
Proactive interference, 202–203, *202*, *203*
Problem solving, 248–54, *249*, *253*
  algorithms and, 248–49
  heuristics and, 249
  pitfalls of, 249–54, *250–52*, *254*
Projection, 419–20
Projective tests, 379–81, *380*, *381*
Propinquity, 592–93
Prototype (schema), 141–43, *142*
Proximity, perception of, 133–34, *134*
Psychiatrists, 10
Psychoanalysis (psychoanalytic theory), 10, 27–28, 368, 465–67
  of Adler, 359–60, *359*, *360*
  dream analysis in, 466
  free association in, 465
  of Freud, 352–56
  of Horney, 360–61, *363*
  of Jung, 357–59, *357*
  later trends in, 363–64, *364*
  resistance and, 466
  See also Psychotherapy
Psychobiology, 28–29
Psychodrama, 479

Psychological disorders, 9. *See also* Abnormal psychology
Psychological statistics. *See* Statistics
Psychological tests. *See* Tests
Psychology (psychologists), 6–7
  abnormal. *See* Abnormal psychology
  as applied science, 7, *8*, 9
  as basic science, 7, *8*, 9
  ethical standards in, 33–34
  history of, 21–29
  increase in, 5, *5*
  major issues in, 29–30, *31*, 32–33, *32*
  methods of, 11–21, *13–15*, *17*, *19–21*
  objectives of, 7
  social. *See* Social psychology
  types of, 7, 9–11, 22–29
Psychopharmacology, 72
Psychosocial development, 547, *548*
Psychosomatic illnesses, 401–403
Psychosurgery, 484
Psychotherapy (psychotherapists), 10, *10*, 464–71
  brief, major features of, 467, *467*
  dynamic, 465–66
  eclectic, 469
  existential, 470
  Gestalt, 469
  humanistic, 468–70
  logotherapy, 470
  results of, 471
  selection of, 468, 469
  See also Psychoanalysis (psychoanalytic theory)
Puberty, 537–38
Public opinion surveys, 13–14, *14*
Punishment
  in operant conditioning, 173–74
  social development and, 522–23, *522*
Pupil, 86–87, *86*
  emotion and, 308–10, *309*

Q

Questionnaires, 12–13

R

Race, IQ and, 285
Radical behaviorism, 369
Rapid eye movement (REM) sleep, *325*, 326–27
Rationalization, 417–18
Ratio schedules, 168–69, *168*
Reaching, first attempts at, 510, *512*
Reaction formation, 418–19
Realism, 416
Reality principle, 354
Reasoning, 56
Recall, 197
Recency effect, 193
Receptors, sensory, 81, 82, 84
  broad-tuned, 84
  hearing, 99, 101–105, *102*, *105*
  smell, 108, *108*
  taste, 107
  visual, 87–88, 90, 92, 98

Receptor sites, 66–68
Reciprocal interaction, 369–70, *370*
Reciprocity, 594, 596
Recognition, 197–98, *198*
Reflex, 153
   conditioned, 23–24
   of newborns, 502–503, *503*
   rooting, 503, *503*
   salivary, 153–54, *154*
Regression, 421, *422*
Rehearsal system, 193
Reinforcement, 158
   in behavior therapy, 473–74
   constant, 168
   learning without, 178–80, *180*
   negative, 172
   in operant conditioning, 166–69, *167*, 172
   partial, 168–69, *168*
   positive, 172
   primary, 166, *167*
   secondary, 166
   timing, frequency, and predictability of, 159–60, *160*
Relatedness, 364
Relationships, social, 591–97
   physical attractiveness and, 596–97, *596*
   propinquity and familiarity, 592–93, *592*, *593*
   reciprocity and, 594, 596
   similarity and, 593–94, *594*, *595*
Relearning, 198
Reliability, of tests, 291
REM (rapid eye movement) sleep, *325*, 326–27
Repression, 352, 356, 418
Research
   with animals, 34, *34*
   ethics and, 155, 156
Resistance, 466
Response, 23
   conditioned, 158, 160–61, *161*
   learning without, 180
   unconditioned, 158
Reticular activating system, 49–50
Retina, *86*, 87
   coding of, 89–91, *90*
   receptor cells of, 87–88, *88*
Retirement, 559
Retrieval, *191*, 195
   clustering as aid to, 216
   failure of, 201–203, *202*, *203*
Retroactive interference, 203
Rewards, social development and, 522–23, *522*
Rhodopsin, 88, 89
Rights of human subjects, 33
Risk taking, anxiety and, 397, *398*
Rods, 87, *88*, 89, *90*
Rootedness, 364
Rooting reflex, 503, *503*
Rorschach Test, 380, *381*
Rote, learning by, 211
Rules
   language learning and, 236–37
   learning by, 211
   of syntax, 228–29
   thinking and, 247

S

Salivary glands, 303
Salivary reflex, 153–54, *154*
Sanguine people, 371, *371*
SAT (Scholastic Aptitude Test), 14, 274–75
Saturation, of light, 85–86
Scanning movements
   memory and, 192
   perception and, 129, *130*, 131
Scapegoating, 420
Schema (prototype), 141–43, *142*
   memory and, 192
Schizophrenia, 372, 435–37, *436*, 447
   causes of, 436, *437*
   drug therapy for, 480–82, *481*
   symptoms of, 435–36
Scholastic Aptitude Test (SAT), 14, 274–75
School phobia, 446
School psychologists, 9
Scientific method, 6, 21. *See also* Experiments
Secondary dispositions, 373
Secondary reinforcers, 166
Sedatives, 433
Selection
   memory and, 192
   in perception, 126–31, *127*, *128*, *130*
Selective exposure, 584
Self
   emergence of, 521–22
   phenomenological 365–66
Self-actualization, 415
   theory of, 366–67, *367*, 368
Self-efficacy, 474–75
Self-esteem
   adolescents and, 538, 542
   social comparison and, 579–80, *579*
Self-fulfilling prophecy, 589–90
Self-help groups, 487
Self-image, 365–66, 538
Self-perception theory, 590–91
Self Rating Depression Scale, 439
Self-therapy, 488
Semantic contents, 262
Semantics, 228
Semicircular canals, *101*, 113, *113*
Senescence, 555
Senile dementia, 556
Senses (sensation), 6, 80–117
   absolute threshold of, 81
   adaptation of, 82
   aging and, 555, 556
   bodily movement, 107, 112–13
   difference threshold of, 81–82
   equilibrium, 107, *112*, 113–14, *113*
   pattern theory of, 82, 84
   secret code of, 82
   skin, 80, 110, *110*, *111*, 112
   smell, 108–109, *108*, *109*
   taste, 107, *107*
   workings of, 81–84
   See also Hearing; Sound; Vision
Sensitivity of newborns, 504
Sensorimotor deafness, 104
Sensorimotor stage, 266, *267*
Sensory adaptation, 82

of newborns, 504
Sensory deprivation, 82, 83, *83*, *84*
Sensory memory, *191*, 192
Sensory thresholds, 81–82
Sentence completion test, 381
Separation anxiety, 519–20, *519*
Serotonin, 482
Sex (sexuality), 327–31
   adolescent, 538–39, *539*
   in animals, 328–29
   determining, 498–99
   homosexuality, 434–35
   love and, 327, 329, *329*
   openness and, 330, 331, *331*
   psychoanalytic view of, 353–56, 358
Sex differences, 525
   in alcoholism, 453–54, *454*
   depression and, 441
   in drug use, 454, *455*
   pheromones and, 108
Sex education, 539
Sex glands, 330, 537
Sex roles, adult, 549–50
Sex typing, 525–27, *526*
Sexual response, conditioning of, 157, *158*
Shadowing, 139, *140*
Shape constancy, 134
Shaping, of behavior, 164–65, *164*, *165*
Shopping lists, remembering, 217, *218*
Short-term memory, 191–193, *193*
   chunking and, 204–206, *205*
Sight, sense of. *See* Eye; Vision
Sign language, 233
Similarity, 593–94, *595*
   perception of, 133–34, *134*
Simultaneous brightness contrast, *127*, *128*
Single-blind technique, 20
Situational factors, 587
Situational tests, 379
Sixteen Personality Factor Questionnaire, 375
Size, perception and, *127*, *128*
Size constancy, 134–36, *135*, *136*
Skinner box, 163–64, *163*, *167*
Skin senses, 80, 110, *110–11*, 112
Sleep, 324–28, *326*
   amount of, 327
   depression and, 438–39
   paradoxical, 325–26
   reasons for, 326–27
   REM, *325*, 326–27
   stages of, 325–26, *325*
Sleeping pills, 327, 328
Slow-to-warm-up children, 504–506, *506*
Smell, sense of, 108–109, *108*, *109*
Social behavior, anxiety and, 395, *395*
Social comparison, theory of, 578–80, *579*
Social development, 520–23
   role of rewards and punishment in, 522–23, *522*
   social demands, inner standards, the emergence of self and, 521–22
   toilet training and, 521, *521*
Social Interest Personality Scale, 359
Socialization, 570, 582
   process of, 570–71, *571*
Social learning theory, 369–70, *370*

Social psychology (social psychologists), 7, 32, 570–604
  aggression and altruism and, 597–601, *598, 599, 601*
  attitudes and, 580–86, *581, 584, 585*
  attribution theories and, 586–91
  conformity and, 571–78, *573–76*
  obedience and, 571–72, 576–78, *576*
  relationships and, 591–97, *592, 593, 595, 596*
  social comparison theory and, 578–80, *579*
  socialization process and, 570–71, *571*
Social relationships. *See* Relationships, social
Sociobiology, drives and, 330
Sociopath, 447–49, *448*
Somatosensory cortex, 48
Sonic confusor, as stressor, 400
Sound
  amplitude of, 99, *100*, 103
  basilar membrane and, 102
  feature detectors and, 121
  frequency of, 99, *100*, 101, *102*
  language and, 227
  physical nature of, 99, *100*
  source and direction of, 104–105
  See also Ear; Hearing
Source traits, 373
Space, as primary mental ability, 262
Specific anxiety, 394–95
Spectrum, visible, 85, *85*
Speech patterns, emotion and, 304, *304*
Sperm (sperm cells), 496, *497*, 498–99, 537
Spinal cord, 46, 54, 61, 328
Split-brain experiments, 55, *55*
Spontaneous recovery
  in classical conditioning, 160–61, *161*
  in operant conditioning, 164
Stability-instability, 375, *376*
Stage theory of moral development, 540, *541*
Standardization, of tests, 292
Standards, motive to meet, 339
Stanford achievement test, 275
Stanford-Binet Intelligence Scale, 271, *271*, 272, 274–76, 279
Stapes, 99, *101*
Statistics, 15–17
  correlation method and, 16–17
Stereotypes, 581
  aging and, 556
  sex role, 549–50
Steroids, 400
Stimulants, 457
  perception and, *144*, 145
Stimulus, 23, 81
  afterimages and, 95
  conditioned, 157
  unconditioned, 157
Stimulus discrimination
  in classical conditioning, 161–62
  in operant conditioning, 164
Stimulus generalization
  in classical conditioning, 161
  in operant conditioning, 164
"Storefront" programs, *485*, 486
Stories, encoding and, 217, *218*
Stranger anxiety, 520, *520*
Stress (stressors), 388, 399–415, *400*

abnormal behavior and, 388, 411, 431–33
absence of, 405
in animals, 410, 411
attributions for, 405–406, *406*
biofeedback and, 409
coping with, 409, *409*, 411–22, *412*
depression and, 401, 402, 408, 410–11
differences in experience of, 403–404, *404*
differences in resistance to, 405–407
emotional, 316–17
environmental, 408–409, 413
general adaptation syndrome and, 400–401
health and, 388, 401–10
hypnosis and, 474–75
immune system and, 407–409, 411
jobs and, 401
physical and mental inputs to, 399–400
preschool children and, 411, *412*
psychological effects of, 410–11
psychosomatic illnesses and, 401–402
scale of, 403, *404*
sonic confusor, 400
traumatic, 444–45
Stroboscopic motion, 123, *123*, 124
Student shock syndrome, 399
Subcultures, 571
Sublimation, 418
Submissiveness, in school years, 529
Substantia nigra ("black substance"), 71
Success, 342–43
  firstborn children and, 361, *362*
  IQ and, 276, 281–83
Sudden-infant-death syndrome, 60
Suicide, 439–40
  in adolescence, 544–45, *544*
  mass, 578, *578*
Superstitions, 165–66, *166*
Surface traits, 373
Surgery, 484
Surrogate mothers, 516, *516*
Surveys, public opinion, 13–14, *14*
Sweat glands, 303
Symbolic contents, 262
Sympathetic division, of autonomic nervous system, 63, 64
Synapses, 66–68, *68*, 82
Synaptic cleft, 67
Synaptic knobs, 67, *67*, 68
Synaptic vesicles, 67
Syndrome, 399
Syntax, 228–29

T

Taste, sense of, 107, *107*
  aging and, 555, *556*
Taste buds, 107
TAT (Thematic Apperception Test), 379–80, *380*
Teachers, 527–28
Teenagers. *See* Adolescence
Temperament
  inborn differences in, 504–506, *506*
  personality and, 357
Temperature drive, 330

Test anxiety, 394
Tests (testing), 14–17, *15*, 290–93
  for abnormal behavior, 429
  achievement, 275–76
  aptitude, 14, 275–76, 292
  of color blindness, 95, *97*
  for depression, 439, *439*
  intelligence. *See* Intelligence tests
  interest, 293
  normal curve of distribution, 16
  objectivity of, 291
  percentile and, 292
  personality, 293, 375, 378–81, *379–81*
  reliability of, 291
  of remembering and forgetting, 197–98, *197*
  standardization, 292
  validity of, 291–92
  vocational aptitude, 292
Thalamus, 49
Thematic Apperception Test (TAT), 379–80, *380*
Therapy, 464–92, *464*
  attitudes toward, 487–89, *489*
  behavior, 369, 470, 472–77, *476*
  biological, 480–84, *481, 482*
  community mental health and, 484–87, *485, 486*
  group, 477–80, *477*
  hypnosis and, 474–75
  in Middle Ages, 464
  self-, 488
  See also Psychotherapy
Thinking, 246
  in adolescence, 541–42
  aging and, 556–58, *558*
  emotion and, 301
  language and, 226, 229, 241–46, *246*
  without language, 246–47
  logical vs. illogical, 247–48
  problem solving and, 248–54, *249, 250–52*, 253, *254*
  rules and premises as bases for, 247
  schizophrenia and, 435
  weight control and, 322
Thirst, 317, 324
Three Faces of Eve, The (movie), 374, *374*
Three Faces in One (Sizemore), 374
Thyroid gland, 433
Timbre, 99, *100*
Time, learning and, 211, 212
Toilet training, 521, *521*
Token economy, 169, *170*, 474
Tolerance, 451
Touch, 80, 110, *110–11*, 112
  illusion of, 123, *124*
Traits
  differences in, 6
  in newborns, duration of, 508
  peripheral, 352
  source, 373
  surface, 373
  tests and measurements for, 14–17
Tranquilizers
  anxiety and, 394
  major (antipsychotic drugs), 480–82, *482*
Transcendence, 364

Transference, 466
Transfer process, 193
 encoding and, 204–209
Trauma
 children and, 508–10
 stress and, 444–45
Tricyclic antidepressants, 482–83
Twins
 alcoholism and, 454
 IQ and, 286, *287*
 schizophrenia and, 437
 weight of, 323
Type A behavior, 407, 409
Type B behavior, 407

U

Uncertainty, anxiety and, 390–94, *393*, *394*
Unconditional positive regard, 365, 468
Unconditioned response, 158
Unconditioned stimulus, 157
Unconscious mind, 352, 353, 466
 collective, 358–59, *358*
Unconscious processes, 28
Unipolar depression, 440

V

Validity of tests, 291–92
Valium, 72, 394, 483
Values, in adolescence, 540–42

Variables, 18, *19*
Variable schedules, 169
Ventromedial hypothalamus, 318
Verbal comprehension, 262
Verbal skills, heredity and, 286, *287*
Vestibular sacs, 113, *113*
Vision, 84–98
 binocular, 138
 color, 85, 87–89, *89*, 91–98, *92*, *94–95*, *97*
 dark adaptation and, 89
 eye structure and, 86–87, *86*
 light waves and, 84–91
 opponent-process, theory of, 93, *93*
 perceptual illusions and, 122–23, *122–24*
 retinal coding and, 89–91, *90*
 sensitivity and acuity of, 91
 sensory receptors, 87–88, 90, 92, 98
Visual cliff, 137–38, *137*
Vitamin A, 89
Vocabulary 228
Vocational aptitude tests, 292
Voyeurism, 330
Vulnerability model of stress-related illness, 406–407

W

WAIS (Wechsler Adult Intelligence Scale), 272, *273*, 274
Warmth, sensation of, 110
Wavelength, 85, 88, *89*, 93–94

Weber's law, 81–82
Wechsler Adult Intelligence Scale (WAIS), 272, *273*, 274
Wechsler Intelligence Scale for Children, 287
Weight
 control of, 321, 322
 hunger and, 320. *See also* Obesity
 of twins, 323
Withdrawal, 420–21, 451
Witnesses and memory, 208, 209
Women
 affective disorders in, 441
 alcoholism in, 453–54, *454*
 employment of, 549, 550
 middle-aged, 553
 sex roles of, 549–50
 See also Gender differences; Mothers; Sex differences
Word association test, 380–81
Word fluency, 262
Work. *See* Careers; Employment
Worthy, learning to feel, 177

X

X chromosome, 498–99

Y

Y chromosome, 498–99
Young-Helmholtz theory of color vision, 98